BUSINESS ANALYSIS AND VALUATION

IFRS EDITION

KRISHNA G. PALEPU

PAUL M. HEALY

ERIK PEEK

D1315680

CENGAGE
Learning®

Australia • Brazil • Japan • Korea • Mexico • Singapore • Spain • United Kingdom • United States

CENGAGE
Learning®

**Business Analysis and Valuation:
IFRS edition, Third Edition**

Krishna G. Palepu, Paul M. Healy &
Erik Peek

Publishing Director: Linden Harris

Publisher: Andrew Ashwin

Commissioning Editor:
Annabel Ainscow

Production Editor: Beverley Copland

Production Controller: Eyvett Davis

Marketing Manager: Amanda Cheung

Typesetter: CENVEO Publisher Services

Cover design: Adam Renvoize

For product information and technology assistance,
contact **emea.info@cengage.com**.

For permission to use material from this text or product,
and for permission queries,
email **emea.permissions@cengage.com**.

British Library Cataloguing-in-Publication Data
A catalogue record for this book is available from the British
Library.

ISBN: 978-1-4080-5642-4

Cengage Learning EMEA
Cheriton House, North Way, Andover, Hampshire, SP10 5BE
United Kingdom

Cengage Learning products are represented in Canada by
Nelson Education Ltd.

For your lifelong learning solutions, visit
www.cengage.co.uk

Purchase your next print book, e-book or e-chapter at
www.cengagebrain.com

Printed in China by RR Donnelley
2 3 4 5 6 7 8 9 10 – 15 14 13

BRIEF CONTENTS

iii

CONTENTS

PART 1

FRAME WORK   1

PART 2

BUSINESS ANALYSIS
AND VALUATION TOOLS   45

PART

4

ADDITIONAL CASES

491

PREFACE

Financial statements are the basis for a wide range of business analyses. Managers use them to monitor and judge their firms' performance relative to competitors, to communicate with external investors, to help judge what financial policies they should pursue, and to evaluate potential new businesses to acquire as part of their investment strategy. Securities analysts use financial statements to rate and value companies they recommend to clients. Bankers use them in deciding whether to extend a loan to a client and to determine the loan's terms. Investment bankers use them as a basis for valuing and analyzing prospective buyouts, mergers, and acquisitions. And consultants use them as a basis for competitive analysis for their clients. Not surprisingly, therefore, there is a strong demand among business students for a course that provides a framework for using financial statement data in a variety of business analysis and valuation contexts. The purpose of this book is to provide such a framework for business students and practitioners. This IFRS edition is the European adaptation of the authoritative US edition – authored by Krishna G. Palepu and Paul M. Healy – that has been used in Accounting and Finance departments in universities around the world. In 2007 we decided to write the first IFRS edition because of the European business environment's unique character and the introduction of mandatory IFRS reporting for public corporations in the European Union. This third IFRS edition is a thorough update of the successful second edition, incorporating new examples, cases, problems and exercises, and regulatory updates.

THIS IFRS EDITION

Particular features of the IFRS edition are the following:

- A large number of examples support the discussion of business analysis and valuation throughout the chapters. The examples are from European companies that students will generally be familiar with, such as AstraZeneca, Audi, British American Tobacco, BP, Burberry, Carlsberg, easyGroup, Finnair, GlaxoSmithKline, Hennes and Mauritz, Lufthansa, Marks and Spencer, and Royal Dutch Shell.

- The chapters dealing with accounting analysis (Chapters 3 and 4) prepare European students for the task of analyzing IFRS-based financial statements. All numerical examples of accounting adjustments in Chapter 4 describe adjustments to IFRS-based financial statements. Further, throughout the book we discuss various topics that are particularly relevant to understanding IFRS-based European financial reports, such as: the classification of expenses by nature and by function; a principles-based approach versus a rules-based approach to standard setting; the first-time adoption of IFRS; cross-country differences and similarities in external auditing and public enforcement, and cross-country differences in financing structures.

- The terminology that we use throughout the chapters is consistent with the terminology that is used in the IFRS.

- Throughout the chapters, we describe the average performance and growth ratios, the average time-series behavior of these ratios, and average financing policies of a sample of close to 7,000 firms that have been listed on European public exchanges between 1992 and 2011.

- This IFRS edition includes 17 cases about European companies. Thirteen of these cases make use of IFRS-based financial statements. However, we have also included several popular cases from the US edition because they have proved to be very effective for many instructors.

  Colleagues and reviewers have made suggestions and comments that led us to incorporate the following changes in the second IFRS edition:

- Data, analyses, problems, and examples have been thoroughly updated in the third edition.

- We have increased conciseness by incorporating key elements of the chapter in the second IFRS edition on corporate governance into this edition's Chapter 1 and by slightly changing the structure of Chapters 1 and 3.

■ The financial analysis and valuation chapters (Chapters 5–8) have been updated with a focus on firms in the apparel retail sector, primarily Hennes & Mauritz and Inditex. Throughout these chapters, we explicitly differentiate between analyzing and valuing operations and analyzing and valuing non-operating investments.

■ Chapter 6 on forecasting has been enhanced with an expanded discussion of how to produce forecasts. In addition, we have expanded the discussions on (1) cost of capital estimation and (2) asset-based valuation in Chapter 8.

■ Chapter 10 now includes a discussion of how credit ratings and default probability estimates can be used in debt valuation. Chapter 11 has been enhanced with a discussion on how to perform a purchase price allocation using the tools and techniques from Chapters 5 through 8.

■ We have updated some of the second IFRS edition's cases and have included eight new cases: Accounting for the iPhone at Apple Inc.; Air Berlin's IPO; Enforcing Financial Reporting Standards: The Case of White Pharmaceuticals AG; Measuring Impairment at Dofasco; Oddo Securities – ESG Integration; PPR-Puma: A Successful Acquisition?; TomTom's Initial Public Offering: Dud or Nugget? and Vizio, Inc.

KEY FEATURES

This book differs from other texts in business and financial analysis in a number of important ways. We introduce and develop a framework for business analysis and valuation using financial statement data. We then show how this framework can be applied to a variety of decision contexts.

Framework for analysis

We begin the book with a discussion of the role of accounting information and intermediaries in the economy, and how financial analysis can create value in well-functioning markets (Chapter 1). We identify four key components, or steps, of effective financial statement analysis:

■ Business strategy analysis
■ Accounting analysis
■ Financial analysis
■ Prospective analysis

The first step, business strategy analysis (Chapter 2), involves developing an understanding of the business and competitive strategy of the firm being analyzed. Incorporating business strategy into financial statement analysis is one of the distinctive features of this book. Traditionally, this step has been ignored by other financial statement analysis books. However, we believe that it is critical to begin financial statement analysis with a company's strategy because it provides an important foundation for the subsequent analysis. The strategy analysis section discusses contemporary tools for analyzing a company's industry, its competitive position and sustainability within an industry, and the company's corporate strategy.

Accounting analysis (Chapters 3 and 4) involves examining how accounting rules and conventions represent a firm's business economics and strategy in its financial statements, and, if necessary, developing adjusted accounting measures of performance. In the accounting analysis section, we do not emphasize accounting rules. Instead we develop general approaches to analyzing assets, liabilities, entities, revenues, and expenses. We believe that such an approach enables students to effectively evaluate a company's accounting choices and accrual estimates, even if students have only a basic knowledge of accounting rules and standards. The material is also designed to allow students to make accounting adjustments rather than merely identify questionable accounting practices.

Financial analysis (Chapter 5) involves analyzing financial ratio and cash flow measures of the operating, financing, and investing performance of a company relative to either key competitors or historical performance. Our distinctive approach focuses on using financial analysis to evaluate the effectiveness of a company's strategy and to make sound financial forecasts.

Finally, under prospective analysis (Chapters 6–8) we show how to develop forecasted financial statements and how to use these to make estimates of a firm's value. Our discussion of valuation includes traditional discounted cash flow models as well as techniques that link value directly to accounting numbers. In discussing accounting-based valuation models, we integrate the latest academic research with traditional approaches such as earnings and book value multiples that are widely used in practice.

While we cover all four steps of business analysis and valuation in the book, we recognize that the extent of their use depends on the user's decision context. For example, bankers are likely to use business strategy analysis, accounting analysis, financial analysis, and the forecasting portion of prospective analysis. They are less likely to be interested in formally valuing a prospective client.

Application of the framework to decision contexts

The next section of the book shows how our business analysis and valuation framework can be applied to a variety of decision contexts:

- Securities analysis (Chapter 9)
- Credit analysis and distress prediction (Chapter 10)
- Merger and acquisition analysis (Chapter 11)

For each of these topics we present an overview to provide a foundation for the class discussions. Where possible we discuss relevant institutional details and the results of academic research that are useful in applying the analysis concepts developed earlier in the book. For example, the chapter on credit analysis shows how banks and rating agencies use financial statement data to develop analysis for lending decisions and to rate public debt issues. This chapter also presents academic research on how to determine whether a company is financially distressed.

USING THE BOOK

We designed the book so that it is flexible for courses in financial statement analysis for a variety of student audiences – MBA students, Masters in Accounting students, Executive Program participants, and undergraduates in accounting or finance. Depending upon the audience, the instructor can vary the manner in which the conceptual materials in the chapters, end-of-chapter questions, and case examples are used. To get the most out of the book, students should have completed basic courses in financial accounting, finance, and either business strategy or business economics. The text provides a concise overview of some of these topics, primarily as background for preparing the cases. But it would probably be difficult for students with no prior knowledge in these fields to use the chapters as stand-alone coverage of them.

If the book is used for students with prior working experience or for executives, the instructor can use almost a pure case approach, adding relevant lecture sections as needed. When teaching students with little work experience, a lecture class can be presented first, followed by an appropriate case or other assignment material. It is also possible to use the book primarily for a lecture course and include some of the short or long cases as in-class illustrations of the concepts discussed in the book. Alternatively, lectures can be used as a follow-up to cases to more clearly lay out the conceptual issues raised in the case discussions. This may be appropriate when the book is used in undergraduate capstone courses. In such a context, cases can be used in course projects that can be assigned to student teams.

COMPANION WEBSITE

A companion website accompanies this book. This website contains the following valuable material for instructors and students:

- Instructions for how to easily produce standardized financial statements in Excel.
- Spreadsheets containing: (1) the reported and standardized financial statements of Hennes & Mauritz (H&M) and Inditex; (2) calculations of H&M's and Inditex's ratios (presented in Chapter 5); (3) H&M's forecasted financial statements (presented in Chapter 6); and (4) valuations of H&M's shares (presented in Chapter 8). Using these spreadsheets students can easily replicate the analyses presented in Chapters 5 through 8 and

perform ''what-if'' analyses – i.e., to find out how the reported numbers change as a result of changes to the standardized statements or forecasting assumptions.

■ Spreadsheets containing case material.

■ Answers to the discussion questions and case instructions (for instructors only).

■ A complete set of lecture slides (for instructors only).

Accompanying teaching notes to some of the case studies can be found at www.harvardbusiness.org. Lecturers are able to register to access the teaching notes and other relevant information.

ACKNOWLEDGEMENTS

We thank the following colleagues who gave us feedback as we wrote this and the previous IFRS edition:

- Constantinos Adamides, Lecturer, University of Nicosia
- Tony Appleyard, Professor of Accounting and Finance, Newcastle University
- Professor Chelley-Steeley, Professor of Finance, Aston Business School
- Rick Cuijpers, Assistant Professor, Maastricht University School of Business and Economics
- Christina Dargenidou, Professor, University of Exeter
- Karl-Hermann Fischer, Lecturer and Associate Researcher, Goethe University Frankfurt
- Zhan Gao, Lecturer in Accounting, Lancaster University
- Stefano Gatti, Associate Professor of Finance, Bocconi University Milan
- Frøystein Gjesdal, Professor, Norwegian School of Economics
- Igor Goncharov, Professor, WHU Business School
- Aditi Gupta, Lecturer, King's College London
- Shahed Imam, Associate Professor, Warwick Business School
- Otto Janschek, Assistant Professor, WU Vienna
- Marcus Kliaras, Banking and Finance Lecturer, University of Applied Sciences, BFI, Vienna
- Gianluca Meloni, Clinical Professor — Accounting Department, Bocconi University
- Sascha Moells, Professsor in Financial Accounting and Corporate Valuation, Philipps-University of Marburg, Germany
- Jon Mugabi, Lecturer in Finance and Accounting, The Hague University
- Cornelia Neff, Professor of Finance and Management Accounting, University of Applied Sciences Ravensburg-Weingarten, Germany
- Bartlomiej Nita, Associate Professor, Wroclaw University of Economics
- Nikola Petrovic, Lecturer in Accounting, University of Bristol
- Roswitha Prassl, Teaching and Research Associate, Vienna University for Economics and Business Administration
- Bill Rees, Professor of Financial Analysis, Edinburgh University
- Matthias Schmidt, Professor for Business Administration, Leipzig University
- Harri Seppänen, Assistant Professor, Aalto University School of Economics
- Yun Shen, Lecturer in Accounting, University of Bath
- Radha Shiwakoti, Lecturer, University of Kent
- Ana Simpson, Lecturer, London School of Economics
- Nicos Sykianakis, Assistant Professor, TEI of Piraeus
- Isaac Tabner, Lecturer in Finance, University of Stirling
- Jon Tucker, Professor and Centre Director, Centre for Global Finance, University of the West of England
- Birgit Wolf, Professor of Managerial Economics, Touro College Berlin
- Jessica Yang, Senior Lecturer in Accounting, University of East London

We are also very grateful to the publishing team at Cengage Learning for their help and assistance throughout the production of this edition.

AUTHORS

KRISHNA G. PALEPU is the Ross Graham Walker Professor of Business Administration and Senior Associate Dean for International Development at the Harvard Business School. During the past 20 years, Professor Palepu's research has focused on corporate strategy, governance, and disclosure. Professor Palepu is the winner of the American Accounting Association's Notable Contributions to Accounting Literature Award (in 1999) and the Wildman Award (in 1997).

PAUL M. HEALY is the James R. Williston Professor of Business Administration and Head of the Accounting and Management Unit at the Harvard Business School. Professor Healy's research has focused on corporate governance and disclosure, mergers and acquisitions, earnings management, and management compensation. He has previously worked at the MIT Sloan School of Management, ICI Ltd, and Arthur Young in New Zealand. Professor Healy has won the Notable Contributions to Accounting Literature Award (in 1990 and 1999) and the Wildman Award (in 1997) for contributions to practice.

ERIK PEEK is the Duff & Phelps Professor of Business Analysis and Valuation at the Rotterdam School of Management, Erasmus University, the Netherlands. Prior to joining RSM Erasmus University he has been an Associate Professor at Maastricht University and a Visiting Associate Professor at the Wharton School of the University of Pennsylvania. Professor Peek is a CFA charterholder and holds a PhD from the VU University Amsterdam. His research has focused on international accounting, financial analysis and valuation, and earnings management.

WALK THROUGH TOUR

Figures and Tables Numbered figures and tables are clearly set out on the page, to aid the reader with quick conceptualization.

Summary The end of each chapter has a summary designed to give an overview of the key areas that have been discussed, and to provide a snapshot of the main points.

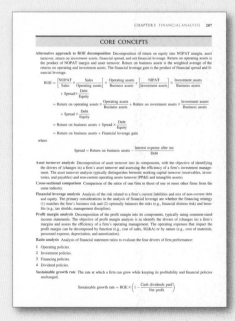

Core Concepts Core concepts are helpfully listed at the end of each chapter.

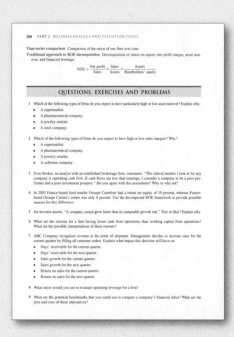

Questions/Exercises/Problems Included at the end of every chapter, a selection of questions, exercises and problems cover the major elements of each chapter's subject matter and aid knowledge and understanding.

End of Chapter Cases In-depth real-life cases are provided at the end of each chapter to offer real-life application directly to the core theory.

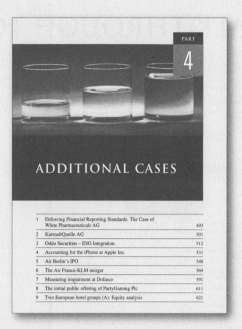

Part Four – Additional Cases Part Four contains 11 additional in-depth case studies focused on real-life companies to further enhance the learning process.

Digital Support Resources

All of our Higher Education textbooks are accompanied by a range of digital support resources. Each title's resources are carefully tailored to the specific needs of the particular book's readers. Examples of the kind of resources provided include:

- A password protected area for instructors with, for example, PowerPoint slides, an instructor's solutions manual and teaching notes for case studies included in the book
- An area for students including, for example, useful spreadsheets to accompany case studies in the book, multiple choice questions, discussion questions spreadsheets and useful weblinks

Lecturers: to discover the dedicated lecturer digital support resources accompanying this textbook please register here for access: **http://login.cengage.com**.

Students: to discover the dedicated student digital support resources accompanying this textbook, please search for the third edition of *Business Analysis and Valuation IFRS edition* on: **www.cengagebrain.com**

FRAMEWORK

A Framework for Business Analysis and Valuation Using Financial Statements

This chapter outlines a comprehensive framework for financial statement analysis. Because financial statements provide the most widely available data on public corporations' economic activities, investors and other stakeholders rely on financial reports to assess the plans and performance of firms and corporate managers.

A variety of questions can be addressed by business analysis using financial statements, as shown in the following examples:

- A security analyst may be interested in asking: "How well is the firm I am following performing? Did the firm meet my performance expectations? If not, why not? What is the value of the firm's stock given my assessment of the firm's current and future performance?"

- A loan officer may need to ask: "What is the credit risk involved in lending a certain amount of money to this firm? How well is the firm managing its liquidity and solvency? What is the firm's business risk? What is the additional risk created by the firm's financing and dividend policies?"

- A management consultant might ask: "What is the structure of the industry in which the firm is operating? What are the strategies pursued by various players in the industry? What is the relative performance of different firms in the industry?"

- A corporate manager may ask: "Is my firm properly valued by investors? Is our investor communication program adequate to facilitate this process?"

- A corporate manager could ask: "Is this firm a potential takeover target? How much value can be added if we acquire this firm? How can we finance the acquisition?"

- An independent auditor would want to ask: "Are the accounting policies and accrual estimates in this company's financial statements consistent with my understanding of this business and its recent performance? Do these financial reports communicate the current status and significant risks of the business?"

The industrial age has been dominated by two distinct and broad ideologies for channeling savings into business investments – capitalism and central planning. The capitalist market model broadly relies on the market mechanism to govern economic activity, and decisions regarding investments are made privately. Centrally planned economies have used central planning and government agencies to pool national savings and to direct investments in business enterprises. The failure of this model is evident from the fact that most of these economies have abandoned it in favor of the second model – the market model. In almost all countries in the world today, **capital markets** play an important role in channeling financial resources from savers to business enterprises that need capital.

Financial statement analysis is a valuable activity when managers have complete information on a firm's strategies, and a variety of institutional factors make it unlikely that they fully disclose this information. In this setting outside analysts attempt to create "inside information" from analyzing financial statement data, thereby gaining valuable insights about the firm's current performance and future prospects.

To understand the contribution that financial statement analysis can make, it is important to understand the role of financial reporting in the functioning of capital markets and the institutional forces that shape financial statements. Therefore we present first a brief description of these forces; then we discuss the steps that an analyst must perform to extract information from financial statements and provide valuable forecasts.

THE ROLE OF FINANCIAL REPORTING IN CAPITAL MARKETS

A critical challenge for any economy is the allocation of savings to investment opportunities. Economies that do this well can exploit new business ideas to spur innovation and create jobs and wealth at a rapid pace. In contrast, economies that manage this process poorly dissipate their wealth and fail to support business opportunities.

Figure 1.1 provides a schematic representation of how capital markets typically work. Savings in any economy are widely distributed among households. There are usually many new entrepreneurs and existing companies that would like to attract these savings to fund their business ideas. While both savers and entrepreneurs would like to do business with each other, matching savings to business investment opportunities is complicated for at least three reasons:

- Information asymmetry. Entrepreneurs typically have better information than savers on the value of business investment opportunities.

- Potentially conflicting interests – credibility problems. Communication by entrepreneurs to investors is not completely credible because investors know entrepreneurs have an incentive to inflate the value of their ideas.

- Expertise asymmetry. Savers generally lack the financial sophistication needed to analyze and differentiate between the various business opportunities.

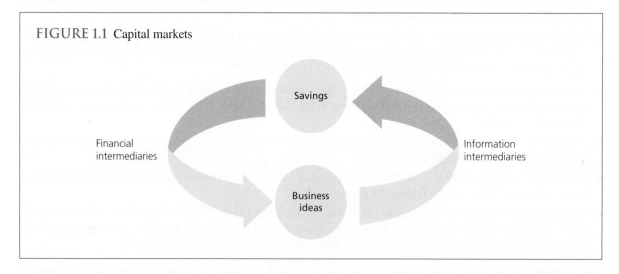

FIGURE 1.1 Capital markets

The information and incentive issues lead to what economists call the **lemons problem,** which can potentially break down the functioning of the capital market.[1] It works like this. Consider a situation where half the business ideas are "good" and the other half are "bad." If investors cannot distinguish between the two types of business ideas, entrepreneurs with "bad" ideas will try to claim that their ideas are as valuable as the "good" ideas. Realizing this possibility, investors value both good and bad ideas at an average level. Unfortunately, this penalizes good ideas, and entrepreneurs with good ideas find the terms on which they can get financing to be unattractive. As these entrepreneurs leave the capital market, the proportion of bad ideas in the market increases. Over time, bad ideas "crowd out" good ideas, and investors lose confidence in this market.

The emergence of intermediaries can prevent such a market breakdown. Intermediaries are like a car mechanic who provides an independent certification of a used car's quality to help a buyer and seller agree on a price. There are two types of intermediaries in the capital markets. **Financial intermediaries**, such as venture capital firms, banks, collective investment funds, pension funds, and insurance companies, focus on aggregating funds from individual investors and analyzing different investment alternatives to make investment decisions. **Information intermediaries**, such as auditors, financial analysts, credit-rating agencies, and the financial press, focus on providing information to investors (and to financial intermediaries who represent them) on the quality of various business investment opportunities. Both these types of intermediaries add value by helping investors distinguish "good" investment opportunities from the "bad" ones.

The relative importance of financial intermediaries and information intermediaries varies from country to country for historical reasons. In countries where individual investors traditionally have had strong legal rights to discipline entrepreneurs who invest in "bad" business ideas, such as in the UK, individual investors have been more inclined to make their own investment decisions. In these countries, the funds that entrepreneurs attract may come from a widely dispersed group of individual investors and be channeled through public stock exchanges. Information intermediaries consequently play an important role in supplying individual investors with the information that they need to distinguish between "good" and "bad" business ideas. In contrast, in countries where individual investors traditionally have had weak legal rights to discipline entrepreneurs, such as in many Continental European countries, individual investors have been more inclined to rely on the help of financial intermediaries. In these countries, financial intermediaries, such as banks, tend to supply most of the funds to entrepreneurs and can get privileged access to entrepreneurs' private information.

Over the past decade, many countries in Europe have been moving towards a model of strong **legal protection of investors' rights** to discipline entrepreneurs and well-developed stock exchanges. In this model, financial reporting plays a critical role in the functioning of both the information intermediaries and financial intermediaries. Information intermediaries add value by either enhancing the credibility of financial reports (as auditors do), or by analyzing the information in the financial statements (as analysts and the rating agencies do). Financial intermediaries rely on the information in the financial statements to analyze investment opportunities, and supplement this information with other sources of information.

Ideally, the different intermediaries serve as a system of checks and balances to ensure the efficient functioning of the capital markets system. However, this is not always the case as on occasion the intermediaries tend to mutually reinforce rather than counterbalance each other. A number of problems can arise as a result of incentive issues, governance issues within the intermediary organizations themselves, and conflicts of interest, as evidenced by the spectacular failures of companies such as Enron and Parmalat. However, in general this market mechanism functions efficiently and prices reflect all available information on a particular investment. Despite this overall market efficiency, individual securities may still be mispriced, thereby justifying the need for financial statement analysis.

In the following section, we discuss key aspects of the financial reporting system design that enable it to play effectively this vital role in the functioning of the capital markets.

FROM BUSINESS ACTIVITIES TO FINANCIAL STATEMENTS

Corporate managers are responsible for acquiring physical and financial resources from the firm's environment and using them to create value for the firm's investors. Value is created when the firm earns a return on its investment in excess of the return required by its capital suppliers. Managers formulate business strategies to achieve this goal, and they implement them through business activities. A firm's business activities are influenced by its economic environment and its own business strategy. The economic environment includes the firm's industry, its input and output markets, and the regulations under which the firm operates. The firm's business strategy determines how the firm positions itself in its environment to achieve a competitive advantage.

As shown in Figure 1.2, a firm's **financial statements** summarize the economic consequences of its business activities. The firm's business activities in any time period are too numerous to be reported individually to outsiders. Further, some of the activities undertaken by the firm are proprietary in nature, and disclosing these activities in detail could be a detriment to the firm's competitive position. The firm's accounting system provides a mechanism through which business activities are selected, measured, and aggregated into financial statement data.

On a periodic basis, firms typically produce four financial reports:

1 An income statement that describes the operating performance during a time period.

2 A balance sheet that states the firm's assets and how they are financed.

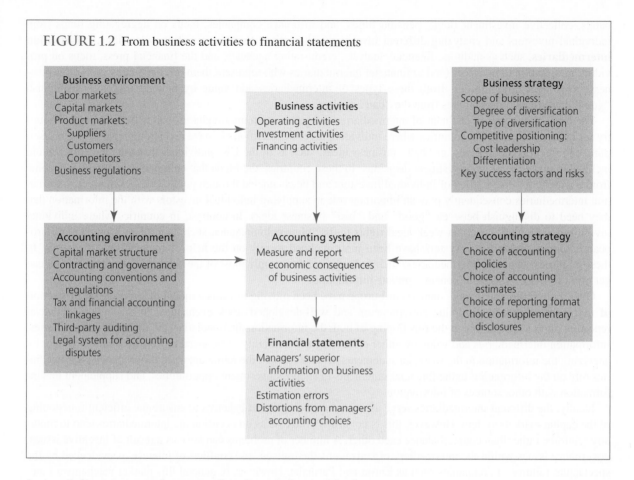

FIGURE 1.2 From business activities to financial statements

3 A cash flow statement that summarizes the cash flows of the firm.

4 A statement of comprehensive income that outlines the sources of non-owner changes in equity during the period between two consecutive balance sheets.[2]

These statements are accompanied by notes that provide additional details on the financial statement line items, as well as by management's narrative discussion of the firm's activities, performance, and risks in the Management Commentary section.[3]

INFLUENCES OF THE ACCOUNTING SYSTEM ON INFORMATION QUALITY

Intermediaries using financial statement data to do business analysis have to be aware that financial reports are influenced both by the firm's business activities and by its accounting system. A key aspect of financial statement analysis, therefore, involves understanding the influence of the accounting system on the quality of the financial statement data being used in the analysis. The institutional features of accounting systems discussed next determine the extent of that influence.

Feature 1: Accrual accounting

One of the fundamental features of corporate financial reports is that they are prepared using accrual rather than cash accounting. Unlike cash accounting, **accrual accounting** distinguishes between the recording of costs and benefits associated with economic activities and the actual payment and receipt of cash. Net profit is the primary periodic performance index under accrual accounting. To compute net profit, the effects of economic transactions are recorded on the basis of *expected*, not necessarily *actual*, cash receipts and payments. Expected cash receipts from the delivery of products or services are recognized as revenues, and expected cash outflows associated with these revenues are recognized as expenses.

While there are many rules and conventions that govern a firm's preparation of financial statements, there are only a few conceptual building blocks that form the foundation of accrual accounting. The following definitions are critical to the income statement, which summarizes a firm's revenues and expenses:[4]

- Revenues are economic resources earned during a time period. Revenue recognition is governed by the realization principle, which proposes that revenues should be recognized when (a) the firm has provided all, or substantially all, the goods or services to be delivered to the customer and (b) the customer has paid cash or is expected to pay cash with a reasonable degree of certainty.

- Expenses are economic resources used up in a time period. Expense recognition is governed by the matching and the conservatism principles. Under these principles, expenses are (a) costs directly associated with revenues recognized in the same period, or (b) costs associated with benefits that are consumed in this time period, or (c) resources whose future benefits are not reasonably certain.

- Profit/loss is the difference between a firm's revenues and expenses in a time period.[5] The following fundamental relationship is therefore reflected in a firm's income statement:

$$\text{Profit} = \text{Revenues} - \text{Expenses}$$

In contrast, the balance sheet is a summary at one point in time. The principles that define a firm's **assets**, **liabilities**, equities, **revenues**, and **expenses** are as follows:

- Assets are economic resources owned by a firm that are (a) likely to produce future economic benefits and (b) measurable with a reasonable degree of certainty.

- Liabilities are economic obligations of a firm arising from benefits received in the past that (a) are required to be met with a reasonable degree of certainty and (b) whose timing is reasonably well defined.

- Equity is the difference between a firm's assets and its liabilities.

The definitions of assets, liabilities, and equity lead to the fundamental relationship that governs a firm's balance sheet:

$$\text{Assets} = \text{Liabilities} + \text{Equity}$$

The need for accrual accounting arises from investors' demand for financial reports on a periodic basis. Because firms undertake economic transactions on a continual basis, the arbitrary closing of accounting books at the end of a reporting period leads to a fundamental measurement problem. Because cash accounting does not report the full economic consequence of the transactions undertaken in a given period, accrual accounting is designed to provide more complete information on a firm's periodic performance.

Feature 2: Accounting conventions and standards

The use of accrual accounting lies at the center of many important complexities in corporate financial reporting. For example, how should revenues be recognized when a firm sells land to customers and also provides customer financing? If revenue is recognized before cash is collected, how should potential defaults be estimated? Are the outlays associated with research and development activities, whose payoffs are uncertain, assets or expenses when incurred? Are contractual commitments under lease arrangements or post-employment plans liabilities? If so, how should they be valued? Because accrual accounting deals with expectations of future cash consequences of current events, it is subjective and relies on a variety of assumptions. Who should be charged with the primary responsibility of making these assumptions? In the current system, a firm's managers are entrusted with the task of making the appropriate estimates and assumptions to prepare the financial statements because they have intimate knowledge of their firm's business.

The accounting discretion granted to managers is potentially valuable because it allows them to reflect inside information in reported financial statements. However, because investors view profits as a measure of managers' performance, managers have incentives to use their accounting discretion to distort reported profits by making biased assumptions. Further, the use of accounting numbers in contracts between the firm and outsiders provides another motivation for management manipulation of accounting numbers. Income management distorts financial accounting data, making them less valuable to external users of financial statements. Therefore, the delegation of financial reporting decisions to corporate managers has both costs and benefits.

A number of accounting conventions have evolved to ensure that managers use their accounting flexibility to summarize their knowledge of the firm's business activities, and not to disguise reality for self-serving purposes. For example, in most countries financial statements are prepared using the concept of prudence, where caution is taken to ensure that assets are not recorded at values above their fair values and liabilities are not recorded at values below their fair values. This reduces managers' ability to overstate the value of the net assets that they have acquired or developed. Of course, the prudence concept also limits the information that is available to investors about the potential of the firm's assets, because many firms record their assets at historical exchange prices below the assets' fair values or values in use.

Accounting standards and rules also limit management's ability to misuse accounting judgment by regulating how particular types of transactions are recorded. For example, accounting standards for leases stipulate how firms are to record contractual arrangements to lease resources. Similarly, post-employment benefit standards describe how firms are to record commitments to provide pensions and other post-employment benefits for employees. These accounting standards, which are designed to convey quantitative information on a firm's performance, are complemented by a set of disclosure principles. The disclosure principles guide the amount and kinds of information that is disclosed and require a firm to provide qualitative information related to assumptions, policies, and uncertainties that underlie the quantitative data presented.

More than 90 countries have delegated the task of setting accounting standards to the International Accounting Standards Board (IASB). For example,

- Since 2005 EU companies that have their shares traded on a public exchange must prepare their consolidated financial statements in accordance with International Financial Reporting Standards (IFRS) as promulgated by the IASB and endorsed by the European Union. Most EU countries, however, also have their own national accounting standard-setting bodies. These bodies may, for example, set accounting standards for private companies and for single entity financial statements of public companies or comment on the IASB's drafts of new or modified standards.[6]

- Since 2005 and 2007, respectively, Australian and New Zealand public companies must comply with locally adopted IFRS, labeled A-IFRS and NZ-IFRS. These sets of standards include all IFRS requirements as well as some additional disclosure requirements.

- South African public companies prepare financial statements that comply with IFRS, as published by the IASB, since 2005.

- Some other countries with major stock exchanges requiring (most) publicly listed companies to prepare IFRS compliant financial statements are Brazil (since 2010) Canada (2011), and Korea (2011).

In the US the Securities and Exchange Commission (SEC) has the legal authority to set accounting standards. Since 1973 the SEC has relied on the Financial Accounting Standards Board (FASB), a private sector accounting body, to undertake this task.

Uniform accounting standards attempt to reduce managers' ability to record similar economic transactions in dissimilar ways either over time or across firms. Thus, they create a uniform accounting language and increase the credibility of financial statements by limiting a firm's ability to distort them. Increased uniformity from accounting standards, however, comes at the expense of reduced flexibility for managers to reflect genuine business differences in a firm's accounting decisions. Rigid accounting standards work best for economic transactions whose accounting treatment is not predicated on managers' proprietary information. However, when there is significant business judgment involved in assessing a transaction's economic consequences, rigid standards are likely to be dysfunctional for some companies because they prevent managers from using their superior business knowledge to determine how best to report the economics of key business events. Further, if accounting standards are too rigid, they may induce managers to expend economic resources to restructure business transactions to achieve a desired accounting result or forego transactions that may be difficult to report on.

Feature 3: Managers' reporting strategy

Because the mechanisms that limit managers' ability to distort accounting data add noise, it is not optimal to use accounting regulation to eliminate managerial flexibility completely. Therefore real-world accounting systems leave considerable room for managers to influence financial statement data. A firm's **reporting strategy** – that is, the manner in which managers use their accounting discretion – has an important influence on the firm's financial statements.

Corporate managers can choose accounting and disclosure policies that make it more or less difficult for external users of financial reports to understand the true economic picture of their businesses. Accounting rules often provide a broad set of alternatives from which managers can choose. Further, managers are entrusted with making a range of estimates in implementing these accounting policies. Accounting regulations usually prescribe minimum disclosure requirements, but they do not restrict managers from *voluntarily* providing additional disclosures.

A superior disclosure strategy will enable managers to communicate the underlying business reality to outside investors. One important constraint on a firm's disclosure strategy is the competitive dynamics in product markets. Disclosure of proprietary information about business strategies and their expected economic consequences may hurt the firm's competitive position. Subject to this constraint, managers can use financial statements to provide information useful to investors in assessing their firm's true economic performance.

Managers can also use financial reporting strategies to manipulate investors' perceptions. Using the discretion granted to them, managers can make it difficult for investors to identify poor performance on a timely basis. For example, managers can choose accounting policies and estimates to provide an optimistic assessment of the firm's true performance. They can also make it costly for investors to understand the true performance by controlling the extent of information that is disclosed voluntarily.

The extent to which financial statements are informative about the underlying business reality varies across firms and across time for a given firm. This variation in accounting quality provides both an important opportunity and a challenge in doing business analysis. The process through which analysts can separate noise from information in financial statements, and gain valuable business insights from financial statement analysis, is discussed in the following section.

Feature 4: Auditing, legal liability, and enforcement

Auditing Broadly defined as a verification of the integrity of the reported financial statements by someone other than the preparer, **auditing** ensures that managers use accounting rules and conventions consistently over time, and that their accounting estimates are reasonable. Therefore auditing improves the quality of accounting data. In Europe, the US, and most other countries, all listed companies are required to have their financial statements audited by an independent public accountant. The standards and procedures to be followed by independent auditors are set by various institutions. By means of the Eighth Company Law Directive, the EU has set minimum standards for public audits that are performed on companies from its member countries. These standards prescribe, for example, that the external auditor does not provide any nonaudit services to the audited company that may compromise his independence. To maintain independence, the auditor (the person, not the firm) must also not audit the same company for more than seven consecutive years. Further, all audits must be carried out in accordance with the International Auditing Standards (ISA), as promulgated by the International Auditing and Assurance Standards Board (IAASB) and endorsed by the EU.

In the US, independent auditors must follow Generally Accepted Auditing Standards (GAAS), a set of standards comparable to the ISA. All US public accounting firms are also required to register with the Public Company Accounting Oversight Board (PCAOB), a regulatory body that has the power to inspect and investigate audit work, and if needed discipline auditors. Like the Eighth Company Law Directive in the EU, the US Sarbanes–Oxley Act specifies the relationship between a company and its external auditor, for example, requiring auditors to report to, and be overseen by, a company's audit committee rather than its management.

While auditors issue an opinion on published financial statements, it is important to remember that the primary responsibility for the statements still rests with corporate managers. Auditing improves the quality and credibility of accounting data by limiting a firm's ability to distort financial statements to suit its own purposes. However, as audit failures at companies such as Ahold, Enron, and Parmalat show, auditing is imperfect. Audits cannot review all of a firm's transactions. They can also fail because of lapses in quality, or because of lapses in judgment by auditors who fail to challenge management for fear of losing future business.

Third-party auditing may also reduce the quality of financial reporting because it constrains the kind of accounting rules and conventions that evolve over time. For example, the IASB considers the views of auditors – in addition to other interest groups – in the process of setting IFRS. To illustrate, at least one-third of the IASB board members have a background as practicing auditor. Further, the IASB is advised by the Standards Advisory

Committee, which contains several practicing auditors. Finally, the IASB invites auditors to comment on its policies and proposed standards. Auditors are likely to argue against accounting standards that produce numbers that are difficult to audit, even if the proposed rules produce relevant information for investors.

Legal liability The legal environment in which accounting disputes between managers, auditors, and investors are adjudicated can also have a significant effect on the quality of reported numbers. The threat of lawsuits and resulting penalties have the beneficial effect of improving the accuracy of disclosure. In the EU, the Transparency Directive requires that every member state has established a statutory civil liability regime for misstatements that managers make in their periodic disclosures to investors. However, legal liability regimes vary in strictness across countries, both within and outside Europe. Under strict regimes, such as that found in the US, investors can hold managers liable for their investment losses if they prove that the firm's disclosures were misleading, that they relied on the misleading disclosures, and that their losses were caused by the misleading disclosures. Under less strict regimes, such as those found in Germany and the UK, investors must additionally prove that managers were (grossly) negligent in their reporting or even had the intent to harm investors (i.e., committed fraud).[7] Further, in some countries only misstatements in annual and interim financial reports are subject to liability, whereas in other countries investors can hold managers liable also for misleading *ad hoc* disclosures.

The potential for significant legal liability might also discourage managers and auditors from supporting accounting proposals requiring risky forecasts – for example, forward-looking disclosures. This type of concern has motivated several European countries to adopt a less strict liability regime.[8]

Public enforcement Several countries adhere to the idea that strong accounting standards, external auditing, and the threat of legal liability do not suffice to ensure that financial statements provide a truthful picture of economic reality. As a final guarantee on reporting quality, these countries have public enforcement bodies that either proactively or on a complaint basis initiate reviews of companies' compliance with accounting standards and take actions to correct noncompliance. In the US, the Securities and Exchange Commission (SEC) performs such reviews and frequently disciplines companies for violations of US GAAP. In recent years, several European countries have also set up proactive enforcement agencies that should enforce listed companies' compliance with IFRS. Examples of such agencies are the French AMF (Autorité des Marchés Financiers), the German DPR (Deutsche Prüfstelle für Rechnungslegung), the Italian CONSOB (Commissione Nazionale per le Società e la Borsa), and the UK Financial Reporting Review Panel. Because each European country maintains control of domestic enforcement, there is a risk that the enforcement of IFRS exhibits differences in strictness and focus across Europe. To coordinate enforcement activities, however, most European enforcement agencies cooperate in the Committee of European Securities Regulators (CESR). One of the CESR's tasks is to develop mechanisms that lead to consistent enforcement across Europe. For example, the Committee promotes that national enforcement agencies have access to and take notice of each other's enforcement decisions. The coming years will show whether a decentralized system of enforcement can consistently assure that European companies comply with IFRS.

Public enforcement bodies cannot ensure full compliance of all listed companies. In fact, most proactive enforcement bodies conduct their investigations on a sampling basis. For example, the UK Financial Reporting Review Panel periodically selects industry sectors on which it focuses its enforcement activities. Within these sectors, the Review Panel then selects individual companies either at random or on the basis of company characteristics such as poor governance. The set of variables that European enforcers most commonly use to select companies includes market capitalization or trading volume (both measuring the company's economic relevance), share price volatility, the likelihood of new equity issues and the inclusion of the company in an index.[9]

Strict public enforcement can also reduce the quality of financial reporting because, in their attempt to avoid an accounting credibility crisis on public capital markets, enforcement bodies may pressure companies to exercise excessive prudence in their accounting choices.

PUBLIC ENFORCEMENT PRACTICES

The fact that most countries have a public enforcement agency does not, of course, imply that all countries have equally developed and effective enforcement systems. One measure of the development of public enforcement is how much a country spends on enforcement. A recent study has shown that there still is significant variation worldwide in enforcement agencies' staff and budget size. For example, in 2006 agencies in Italy, the Netherlands, the UK, and the US spent more than twice as much as their peers in France, Germany, Spain, and Sweden.[10] Although public enforcement has important preventive effects – it deters violations of accounting rules just through its presence – another measure of its development is an enforcement agency's activity, potentially measured by the number of investigations held and the number of actions taken against public companies. Most agencies disclose annual reports summarizing their activities. So far, these reports illustrate that most actions taken by (non-US) enforcement agencies are recommendations to firms on how to improve their reporting and better comply with IFRS in the future. In a few cases the agencies took corrective actions. Following are two examples of such actions:

■ In the year ending in March 2011, the UK Financial Reporting Review Panel reviewed 268 annual reports, 236 on its own initiative and 32 in response to complaints or referrals. In only a few cases a firm had to either restate its current financial statements or adjust the prior period figures in its next financial statements. For example, in its 2008/2009 financial statements, Hot Tuna plc charged an impairment loss of £1.5 billion to a merger reserve rather than to profit or loss, as prescribed by IAS 36. As a consequence, Hot Tuna's net profit was overstated and the firm was asked to make a prior period adjustment in its 2009/2010 financial statements.

■ In March 2008 the Finnish Financial Supervisory Authority issued a public warning – an administrative sanction – to Cencorp Corporation. The Authority disclosed that Cencorp should not have recognized a deferred tax asset for the carryforward of tax losses in its 2005 and 2006 financial statements because the company lacked convincing evidence that it could utilize the carryforward in future years. In its 2007 financial statement Cencorp restated its comparative figures for 2005 and 2006.

ALTERNATIVE FORMS OF COMMUNICATION WITH INVESTORS

Given the limitations of accounting standards, auditing, and enforcement, as well as the reporting credibility problems faced by management, firms that wish to communicate effectively with external investors are often forced to use alternative media. Below we discuss two alternative ways that managers can communicate with external investors and analysts: meetings with analysts to publicize the firm and expanded voluntary disclosure. These forms of communication are typically not mutually exclusive.

Analyst meetings

One popular way for managers to help mitigate information problems is to meet regularly with financial analysts that follow the firm. At these meetings management will field questions about the firm's current financial performance and discuss its future business plans. In addition to holding analyst meetings, many firms appoint a director of public relations, who provides further regular contact with analysts seeking more information on the firm.

In the last 15 years, conference calls have become a popular forum for management to communicate with financial analysts. Recent research finds that firms are more likely to host calls if they are in industries where financial statement data fail to capture key business fundamentals on a timely basis.[11] In addition, conference calls themselves appear to provide new information to analysts about a firm's performance and future prospects.[12] Smaller and less heavily traded firms in particular benefit from initiating investor conference calls.[13]

While firms continue to meet with analysts, rules such as the EU Market Abuse Directive, affect the nature of these interactions. Under these rules, which became effective in 2004, all EU countries must have regulations and institutions in place that prevent unfair disclosure. Specifically, countries must ensure that exchange-listed companies disclose nonpublic private information promptly and simultaneously to all investors. This can reduce the information that managers are willing to disclose in conference calls and private meetings, making these less effective forums for resolving information problems.

Voluntary disclosure

Another way for managers to improve the credibility of their financial reporting is through voluntary disclosure. Accounting rules usually prescribe minimum disclosure requirements, but they do not restrict managers from voluntarily providing additional information. These could include an articulation of the company's long-term strategy, specification of nonfinancial leading indicators that are useful in judging the effectiveness of the strategy implementation, explanation of the relationship between the leading indicators and future profits, and forecasts of future performance. Voluntary disclosures can be reported in the firm's annual report, in brochures created to describe the firm to investors, in management meetings with analysts, or in investor relations responses to information requests.[14]

One constraint on expanded disclosure is the competitive dynamics in product markets. Disclosure of proprietary information on strategies and their expected economic consequences may hurt the firm's competitive position. Managers then face a trade-off between providing information that is useful to investors in assessing the firm's economic performance, and withholding information to maximize the firm's product market advantage.

A second constraint in providing voluntary disclosure is management's legal liability. Forecasts and voluntary disclosures can potentially be used by dissatisfied shareholders to bring civil actions against management for providing misleading information. This seems ironic, since voluntary disclosures should provide investors with additional information. Unfortunately, it can be difficult for courts to decide whether managers' disclosures were good-faith estimates of uncertain future events which later did not materialize, or whether management manipulated the market. Consequently, many corporate legal departments recommend against management providing much in the way of voluntary disclosure. One aspect of corporate governance, earnings guidance, has been particularly controversial. There is growing evidence that the guidance provided by management plays an important role in leading analysts' expectations towards achievable earnings targets, and that management guidance is more likely when analysts' initial forecasts are overly optimistic.[15]

Finally, management credibility can limit a firm's incentives to provide voluntary disclosures. If management faces a credibility problem in financial reporting, any voluntary disclosures it provides are also likely to be viewed skeptically. In particular, investors may be concerned about what management is not telling them, particularly since such disclosures are not audited.

THE IMPACT OF EU DIRECTIVES ON FINANCIAL REPORTING AND AUDITING IN EUROPE

During the past decade, the European Commission has issued or revised a few Directives that significantly affect financial reporting and auditing practices in the European Union. The Revised Eighth Directive (8thD; effective since 2008) regulates the audit of financial statements. In addition, the Transparency Directive (TD; 2007) and Market Abuse Directives (MAD; 2004) regulate firms' periodic and *ad hoc* disclosures, with the objective to improve the quality and timeliness of information provided to investors. Some of the highlights of these Directives include:

- Prescribing that firms issuing public debt or equity securities (public firms) publish their annual report no more than four months after the financial year-end. The annual report must contain the audited financial statements, a management report, and management's responsibility statement certifying that the financial statements give a true and fair view of the firm's performance and financial position (TD).

- Requiring that public firms publish semiannual financial reports, including condensed financial statements, an interim management report and a responsibility statement, within two months of the end of the first half of the fiscal year. The firms must also indicate whether the interim financial statements have been audited or reviewed by an auditor (TD).

- Enhancing interim reporting by requiring that public firms publish two interim management statements, describing the firms' financial position, material events and transactions (TD).

- Ensuring that each EU member state has a central filing and storage system for public financial reports (TD).

- Requiring that public firms immediately disclose any information that may have a material impact on their security price and prohibiting that insiders to the firm trade on such information before its disclosure (TD, MAD).

- Prohibiting that the external auditor provides any nonaudit services to the audited firm that may compromise his independence (8thD).

- Enhancing auditor independence by prescribing that the external auditor (the audit partner, not the audit firm) does not audit the same firm for more than seven consecutive years (8thD).

- Requiring that all audits are carried out in accordance with International Standards of Auditing (8thD).

- Requiring that all audit firms are subject to a system of external quality assurance and public oversight (8thD).

- Mandating that each public firm has an audit committee, which monitors the firm's financial reporting process, internal control system and statutory audit (8thD).

- Ensuring that each EU member state designates a competent authority responsible for supervising firms' compliance with the provisions of the Directives (8thD, TD, MAD).

Each EU member state must implement the Directives by introducing new or changing existing national legislation. Because the member states have some freedom in deciding how to comply with the Directives, some differences in financial reporting, disclosure, and auditing regulation remain to exist. To illustrate, whereas public firms in most countries are required to publish their financial statements on a quarterly basis, public firms in, for example, the Netherlands and the UK comply with local interim reporting rules if they publish a semiannual financial statement and two interim management statements. The interim management statements typically do not include financial statements.

FROM FINANCIAL STATEMENTS TO BUSINESS ANALYSIS

Because managers' insider knowledge is a source both of value and distortion in accounting data, it is difficult for outside users of financial statements to separate true information from distortion and noise. Not being able to undo accounting distortions completely, investors "discount" a firm's reported accounting performance. In doing so, they make a probabilistic assessment of the extent to which a firm's reported numbers reflect economic reality. As a result, investors can have only an imprecise assessment of an individual firm's performance. **Financial and information intermediaries** can add value by improving investors' understanding of a firm's current performance and its future prospects.

Effective financial statement analysis is valuable because it attempts to get at managers' inside information from public financial statement data. Because intermediaries do not have direct or complete access to this information, they rely on their knowledge of the firm's industry and its competitive strategies to interpret financial statements. Successful intermediaries have at least as good an understanding of the industry economics as do the firm's managers, as well as a reasonably good understanding of the firm's competitive strategy. Although outside analysts have an information disadvantage relative to the firm's managers, they are more objective in evaluating the economic consequences of the firm's investment and operating decisions. Figure 1.3 provides a schematic overview of how business intermediaries use financial statements to accomplish four key steps:

1 Business strategy analysis.
2 Accounting analysis.
3 Financial analysis.
4 Prospective analysis.

Analysis step 1: Business strategy analysis

The purpose of **business strategy analysis** is to identify key profit drivers and business risks, and to assess the company's profit potential at a qualitative level. Business strategy analysis involves analyzing a firm's industry and its strategy to create a sustainable competitive advantage. This qualitative analysis is an essential first step because it enables the analyst to frame the subsequent accounting and financial analysis better. For example,

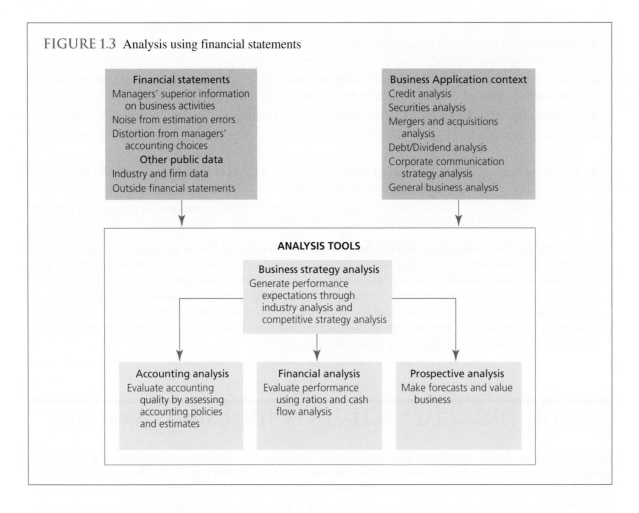

FIGURE 1.3 Analysis using financial statements

identifying the key success factors and key business risks allows the identification of key accounting policies. Assessment of a firm's competitive strategy facilitates evaluating whether current profitability is sustainable. Finally, business analysis enables the analyst to make sound assumptions in forecasting a firm's future performance. We discuss business strategy analysis in further detail in Chapter 2.

Analysis step 2: Accounting analysis

The purpose of **accounting analysis** is to evaluate the degree to which a firm's accounting captures the underlying business reality. By identifying places where there is accounting flexibility, and by evaluating the appropriateness of the firm's accounting policies and estimates, analysts can assess the degree of distortion in a firm's accounting numbers. Another important step in accounting analysis is to "undo" any accounting distortions by recasting a firm's accounting numbers to create unbiased accounting data. Sound accounting analysis improves the reliability of conclusions from financial analysis, the next step in financial statement analysis. Accounting analysis is the topic in Chapters 3 and 4.

Analysis step 3: Financial analysis

The goal of **financial analysis** is to use financial data to evaluate the current and past performance of a firm and to assess its sustainability. There are two important skills related to financial analysis. First, the analysis should be systematic and efficient. Second, the analysis should allow the analyst to use financial data to explore business issues. Ratio analysis and cash flow analysis are the two most commonly used financial tools. Ratio analysis focuses on evaluating a firm's product market performance and financial policies; cash flow analysis focuses on a firm's liquidity and financial flexibility. Financial analysis is discussed in Chapter 5.

Analysis step 4: Prospective analysis

Prospective analysis, which focuses on forecasting a firm's future, is the final step in business analysis. (This step is explained in Chapters 6, 7, and 8.) Two commonly used techniques in prospective analysis are financial statement forecasting and valuation. Both these tools allow the synthesis of the insights from business analysis, accounting analysis, and financial analysis in order to make predictions about a firm's future.

While the intrinsic value of a firm is a function of its future cash flow performance, it is also possible to assess a firm's value based on the firm's current book value of equity, and its future return on equity (ROE) and growth. Strategy analysis, accounting analysis, and financial analysis, the first three steps in the framework discussed here, provide an excellent foundation for estimating a firm's intrinsic value. Strategy analysis, in addition to enabling sound accounting and financial analysis, also helps in assessing potential changes in a firm's competitive advantage and their implications for the firm's future ROE and growth. Accounting analysis provides an unbiased estimate of a firm's current book value and ROE. Financial analysis facilitates an in-depth understanding of what drives the firm's current ROE.

The predictions from a sound business analysis are useful to a variety of parties and can be applied in various contexts. The exact nature of the analysis will depend on the context. The contexts that we will examine include securities analysis, credit evaluation, mergers and acquisitions, evaluation of debt and dividend policies, and assessing corporate communication strategies. The four analytical steps described above are useful in each of these contexts. Appropriate use of these tools, however, requires a familiarity with the economic theories and institutional factors relevant to the context.

There are several ways in which financial statement analysis can add value, even when capital markets are reasonably efficient. First, there are many applications of financial statement analysis whose focus is outside the capital market context – credit analysis, competitive benchmarking, analysis of mergers and acquisitions, to name a few. Second, markets become efficient precisely because some market participants rely on analytical tools such as the ones we discuss in this book to analyze information and make investment decisions.

PUBLIC VERSUS PRIVATE CORPORATIONS

This book focuses primarily on public corporations. In some countries, financial statements of (unlisted) private corporations are also widely available. For example, the member states of the European Union (EU) require that privately held corporations prepare their financial statements under a common set of rules and make their financial statements publicly available. All corporations must prepare at least single company financial statements, while parent corporations of large groups must also prepare consolidated financial statements.[16] Consolidated financial statements are typically more appropriate for use in business analysis and valuation because these statements report the combined assets, liabilities, revenues, and expenses of the parent company and its subsidiaries. Single company financial statements report the assets, liabilities, revenues, and expenses of the parent company only and therefore provide little insight into the activities of subsidiaries.

EU law also requires that private corporations' financial statements be audited by an external auditor, although member states may exempt small corporations from this requirement.[17] The way in which private corporations in the EU make their financial statements available to the public is typically by filing these with a local public register that is maintained by agencies such as the companies register, the chamber of commerce, or the national bank.[18]

Private corporations' financial statements can be, and are being, used for business analysis and valuation. For example, venture capitalists, which provide equity funds to mostly private start-up companies, can use financial statements to evaluate potential investments. Nevertheless, although private corporations' financial statements are also subject to accounting standards, their usefulness in business analysis and valuation is less than that of public corporations' financial statements for the following reasons.[19] First, information and incentive problems are smaller in private corporations than in public corporations. Investors and managers of private corporations maintain close relationships and communicate their information through other means than public financial reports, such as personal communication or *ad hoc* reports. Because public reporting plays only a small role in communication, managers of private corporations have little incentive to make their public financial statements informative about the underlying business reality. Second, private corporations often produce one set of financial statements that meets the requirements of both tax rules and accounting rules. Tax rules grant managers less discretion in their assumptions than, for example, IFRS. Under tax rules, the recording of costs and benefits is also typically more associated with the payment and receipt of cash than with the underlying economic activities. Consequently, when private corporations' financial statements also comply with tax rules, they are less useful in assessing the corporations' true economic performance.[20]

SUMMARY

Financial statements provide the most widely available data on public corporations' economic activities; investors and other stakeholders rely on them to assess the plans and performance of firms and corporate managers. Accrual accounting data in financial statements are noisy, and unsophisticated investors can assess firms' performance only imprecisely. Financial analysts who understand managers' disclosure strategies have an opportunity to create inside information from public data, and they play a valuable role in enabling outside parties to evaluate a firm's current and prospective performance.

This chapter has outlined the framework for business analysis with financial statements, using the four key steps: business strategy analysis, accounting analysis, financial analysis, and prospective analysis. The remaining chapters in this book describe these steps in greater detail and discuss how they can be used in a variety of business contexts.

CORE CONCEPTS

Accounting analysis Second step of financial statement analysis, aimed at scrutinizing a firm's accounting policies and estimates and undoing the firm's financial statements from any accounting distortions.

Accounting standards Set of rules governing the determination of a company's revenues, profit and (change in) financial position under a system of accrual accounting.

Accrual accounting A system of accounting under which current net profit is derived from past and current as well as expected future cash flows arising from business transactions completed in the current period.

Assets Economic resources owned by a firm that are (a) likely to produce future economic benefits and (b) measurable with a reasonable degree of uncertainty. Examples of economic resources are inventories and property, plan and equipment.

Auditing Certification of financial statements by an independent public accounting firm, aimed at improving the statements' credibility.

Business strategy analysis First step of financial statement analysis, aimed at identifying a firm's key profit drivers and business risks and qualitatively assessing the firm's profit potential.

Capital markets Markets where entrepreneurs raise funds to finance their business ideas in exchange for equity or debt securities.

Expenses Economic resources (e.g., finished goods inventories) used up in a time period.

Financial analysis Third step of financial statement analysis, which goal is to evaluate (the sustainability of) a firm's current and past financial performance using ratio and cash flow analysis.

Financial and information intermediaries Capital market participants who help to resolve problems of information asymmetry between entrepreneurs and investors and, consequently, prevent markets from breaking down. Information intermediaries such as auditors or financial analysts improve the (credibility of) information provided by the entrepreneur. Financial intermediaries such as banks and collective investment funds specialize in collecting, aggregating, and investing funds from dispersed investors.

Financial statements Periodically disclosed set of statements showing a company's financial performance and change in financial position during a prespecified period. The statements typically include a balance sheet (financial position), an income statement and a cash flow statement (financial performance). One of the primary purposes of the financial statements is to inform current or potential investors about management's use of their funds, such that they can evaluate management's actions and value their current or potential claim on the firm.

Institutional framework for financial reporting Institutions that govern public corporations' financial reporting. These institutions include:

a Accounting standards set by public or private sector accounting standard-setting bodies, which limit management's accounting flexibility. In the EU, public corporations report under International Financial Reporting Standards, set by the International Accounting Standards Board.

b Mandatory external auditing of the financial statements by public accountants. In the EU, the Eighth Company Law Directive has set minimum standards for external audits.

c Legal liability of management for misleading disclosures. The Transparency Directive requires that each EU member state has a statutory civil liability regime.

d Public enforcement of accounting standards. Enforcement activities of individual European public enforcement bodies are coordinated by the Committee of European Securities Regulators.

Legal protection of investors' rights Laws and regulations aiming at providing investors the rights and mechanisms to discipline managers who control their funds. Examples of such rights and mechanisms are transparent disclosure requirements, the right to vote (by proxy) on important decisions or the right to appoint supervisory directors. In countries where small, minority investors lack such rights or mechanisms, financial intermediaries play an important role in channeling investments to entrepreneurs.

Lemons problem The problem that arises if entrepreneurs have better information about the quality of their business ideas than investors but are not able to credibly communicate this information. If this problem becomes severe enough, investors may no longer be willing to provide funds and capital markets could break down.

Liabilities Economic obligations of a firm arising from benefits received in the past that (a) are required to be met with a reasonable degree of certainty and (b) whose timing is reasonably well defined. Examples of economic obligations are bank loans and product warranties.

Prospective analysis Fourth and final step of financial statement analysis, which focuses on forecasting a firm's future financial performance and position. The forecasts can be used for various purposes, such as estimating firm value or assessing creditworthiness.

Reporting strategy Set of choices made by managers in using their reporting discretion, shaping the quality of their financial reports.

Revenues Economic resources (e.g., cash and receivables) earned during a time period.

QUESTIONS, EXERCISES, AND PROBLEMS

1 Matti, who has just completed his first finance course, is unsure whether he should take a course in business analysis and valuation using financial statements since he believes that financial analysis adds little value, given the efficiency of capital markets. Explain to Matti when financial analysis can add value, even if capital markets are efficient.

2 Accounting statements rarely report financial performance without error. List three types of errors that can arise in financial reporting.

3 A finance student states, "I don't understand why anyone pays any attention to accounting earnings numbers, given that a 'clean' number like cash from operations is readily available." Do you agree? Why or why not?

4 Fred argues, "The standards that I like most are the ones that eliminate all management discretion in reporting – that way I get uniform numbers across all companies and don't have to worry about doing accounting analysis." Do you agree? Why or why not?

5 Bill Simon says, "We should get rid of the IASB, IFRS, and EU Company Law Directives, since free market forces will make sure that companies report reliable information." Do you agree? Why or why not?

6   Juan Perez argues that "learning how to do business analysis and valuation using financial statements is not very useful, unless you are interested in becoming a financial analyst." Comment.

7   Four steps for business analysis are discussed in the chapter (strategy analysis, accounting analysis, financial analysis, and prospective analysis). As a financial analyst, explain why each of these steps is a critical part of your job and how they relate to one another.

Problem 1 *The Neuer Markt*

Many economists believe that innovation is one of the main building blocks of economic growth and job creation. Not all economic infrastructures, however, are equally supportive of innovation. In 1995 venture capital investments in Europe amounted up to 4 percent of total Gross Domestic Product (GDP), compared to 6 percent of GDP in the US. During the second half of the 1990s European and US venture capital investments experienced an explosive but distinctively different level of growth. In fact, in 2000 venture capitalists invested an amount equal to 17 percent of European GDP in European companies, while investing 78 percent of US GDP in US companies.[21] The availability of venture capital can be crucial in the development of innovation. Venture capitalists serve an important role as intermediaries in capital markets because they separate good business ideas from bad ones and bestow their reputation on the start-ups that they finance. In addition to providing capital, venture capitalists offer their expertise in management and finance and let start-up companies benefit from their network of contacts. Their close involvement with start-ups' day-to-day operations and their ability to give finance in installments, conditional on start-ups' success, allows venture capitalists to invest in risky business ideas that public capital markets typically ignore.

To improve young, innovative, and fast-growing companies' access to external finance, several European stock exchanges founded separate trading segments for this group of companies at the end of the 1990s. Examples of such trading segments were the Nuovo Mercato in Italy, the Nouveau Marché in France, the NMAX in the Netherlands, and the Neuer Markt in Germany. These new markets coordinated some of their activities under the EuroNM umbrella. For example, starting in 1999 the markets facilitated cross-border electronic trading to create a pan-European exchange. Another important way of cooperation was to harmonize the admission requirements for new listings.[22] These requirements were not easier to comply with than the admission requirements of the traditional, established trading segments of the European stock exchanges. On the contrary, the common idea was that a separate trading segment for innovative fast-growing companies needed stricter regulation than the established segments that targeted matured companies with proven track records. If this was true, having (some) common listing requirements across European new markets helped to prevent a race to the bottom in which companies would flee to markets with lenient listing requirements and markets start to compete with each other on the basis of their leniency.

The European new markets had also harmonized some of their disclosure requirements. All new markets required that companies produced quarterly reports of, at least, sales figures. Further, most of the new markets required that companies prepared their financial reports in accordance with either US GAAP or International Accounting Standards. Given the opportunities for electronic cross-border trading, strict disclosure requirements could help in broadening companies' investor base as well as improve investors' opportunities for diversifying their risky investments. However, because the new markets experienced difficulties in further harmonizing their admission and listing requirements and eventually came to realize that the small cap companies appealed primarily to local investors, their cooperative venture was dissolved in December 2000.

One of the European new markets was the Neuer Markt, a trading segment of the 'Deutsche Börse', the German stock exchange. The Neuer Markt's target companies were innovative companies that opened up new markets, used new processes in development, production, or marketing and sales, offered new products or services and were likely to achieve above-average growth in revenue and profit. On March 10, 1997, the initial public offering of Mobilcom AG started the existence of the exchange. The offering of Mobilcom's 640 thousand shares for an issue price of €31.95 was heavily oversubscribed, as €20 million additional shares could have been sold. Mobilcom's closing price at the end of the first trading day equaled €50.10, yielding an initial return of 56.8 percent. Other success stories followed. For example, on October 30, 1997, Entertainment München, better known as EM.TV, went public on the German Neuer Markt. The Munich-based producer and distributor of children's programs was able to place 600,000 of its common shares at a price set at the upper end of the bookbuilding range, collecting approximately €5.3 million in total. There was a strong demand for the company's shares. At the end of the first trading day, the share price closed at €9.72, up by 9.4 percent. At its peak, in February 2000, EM.TV's share price had increased from € 0.35 (split-adjusted) to slightly more than €120.

At the end of February 2000, being close to its three-year anniversary, the Neuer Markt comprised 229 companies with a total market capitalization of approximately €234 billion. However, in March 2000, the downfall began, in line with the plunge of the NASDAQ exchange. In September 2000, Gigabell AG, was the first company to file for insolvency. The total market capitalization of the growth segment of the Deutsche Börse declined further from €121 billion (339 firms) at the end of 2000 to €50 billion (327 firms) at the end of 2001. Because both the "going public" and the "being public" requirements were very strict compared to other segments and markets, several companies left the Neuer Markt, changing to the less regulated Geregelter Markt. During the first years of the 2000s, several Neuer Markt firms were found to have manipulated their financial statements. For example, in September 2000, EM.TV announced that it had overstated the sales and profit figures of its most recently acquired subsidiaries, the Jim Henson Company and Speed Investments, in the company's semiannual financial statements. Following this announcement, EM.TV's market capitalization declined by more than 30 percent. Other examples include computer games developer Phenomedia and Comroad, a provider of traffic information systems that was found to have falsified more than 90 percent of its 1998–2001 revenues.

On September 26, 2002, the Deutsche Börse announced that it would close its Neuer Markt trading segment in 2003. The remaining Neuer Markt companies could join the exchange's Prime Standard segment, which would adopt the Neuer Markt's strict listing requirements (i.e., quarterly reporting; IAS or US GAAP; at least one analyst conference per year; *ad hoc* and ongoing disclosures in English), or its General Standard segment, with legal minimum transparency requirements. Approximately two-thirds of the remaining Neuer Markt firms decided to join the Prime Standard segment.

1   Do you think that exchange market segments such as the EuroNM markets can be a good alternative to venture capital? If not, what should be their function?

2   This chapter described four institutional features of accounting systems that affect the quality of financial statements. Which of these features may have been particularly important in reducing the quality of Neuer Markt companies' financial statements?

3   The decline of the Neuer Markt could be viewed as the result of a lemons problem. Can you think of some mechanisms that might have prevented the market's collapse?

4   What could have been the Deutsche Börse's objective of introducing two new segments and letting Neuer Markt firms choose and apply for admission to one of these segments? When is this strategy most likely to be effective?

Problem 2 *Fair value accounting for financial instruments*

One of the key accounting policies of banks and other financial institutions is how they recognize (changes in) the fair value of the securities that they hold in the balance sheet and income statement. The international rules on the recognition and measurement of financial instruments require a firm to recognize financial securities (other than loans and receivables) at their fair values if the firm does not intend to hold these assets to their maturities (labeled held-for-trading instruments). Changes in the securities' fair values must be recognized as gains or losses in the income statement. Financial securities that a firm initially intended to hold to their maturities but that are currently available for sale must also be recognized at their fair values. However, changes in the fair value of these available-for-sale securities are temporarily recorded in equity and recognized in the income statement once the securities get sold. If the firm intends to hold the financial instruments to their maturities (held-to-maturity instruments), they must be recognized at (amortized) historical cost.

How should the fair values of financial instruments be determined? The rules require that they be derived from quoted market prices if an active market for the assets exists (typically referred to as marking to market). If quoted market prices are not available, firms can use their own valuation technique to determine the assets' fair values (referred to as marking to model); however, their valuation should be based on assumptions that outside market participants would reasonably make, not management's own assumptions.

Complications may arise if quoted market prices are available but, at least in the eyes of some, unreliable. For example, the credit crisis of 2008 led to a substantial increase in the uncertainty about the quality and value of asset-backed securities, such as mortgage-backed loans. As a result of the heightened uncertainty, investors fled asset-backed securities and the market for such securities became highly illiquid. Observable prices from infrequent transactions remained available; however, managers of financial institutions owning asset-backed securities claimed that these prices did not properly reflect the values of the securities if one had the option to hold on to the securities until the crisis was over or the securities matured. In response to these claims, the IASB provided additional guidance and reemphasized that in declining, illiquid markets, managers had the option to use their own valuations to determine fair values. Consequently, many financial institutions choose to move away from marking to market towards adjusting market prices or marking to model.

Prior to the credit market crisis of 2008, an important detail of the international accounting rules for financial instruments was that instruments could not be reclassified between categories (with the exception, of course, of reclassifications from held-to-maturity to avail-able-for-sale). The crisis, however, led some bank managers to change their minds about which securities were actually held for trading purposes and which securities were better held to their maturities. Under great political pressure of the EU the IASB amended this rule in October 2008.[23] The amendment allowed firms to reclassify securities out of the held-for-trading category in rare circumstances, such as those created by the crisis, if management decided not to sell the securities in the foreseeable future. A survey carried out by the CESR revealed that 48 out of 100 European financial institutions reclassified one or more financial instruments in their financial statements for the third quarter of 2008.

1   Discuss how the changes in the reclassification rules affect the balance between noise introduced in accounting data by rigidity in accounting rules and bias introduced in accounting data by managers' systematic accounting choices.

2   The move from marking to market to marking to model during the credit crisis increased managers' accounting flexibility. Managers of financial institutions may have incentives to bias their valuations of financial instruments. Summarize the main incentives that may affect these managers' accounting choices.

3   Some politicians argued that fair value accounting needed to be suspended and replaced by historical cost accounting. What is the risk of allowing financial institutions to report their financial securities such as asset-backed securities at historical cost?

NOTES

1. G. Akerlof, "The Market for 'Lemons': Quality Uncertainty and the Market Mechanism," *Quarterly Journal of Economics* (August 1970): 488–500. Akerlof recognized that the seller of a used car knew more about the car's value than the buyer. This meant that the buyer was likely to end up overpaying, since the seller would accept any offer that exceeded the car's true value and reject any lower offer. Car buyers recognized this problem and would respond by only making low-ball offers for used cars, leaving sellers with high quality cars to exit the market. As a result, only the lowest quality cars (the "lemons") would remain in the market. Akerlof pointed out that qualified independent mechanics could correct this market breakdown by providing buyers with reliable information on a used car's true value.

2. Firms are allowed to combine the income statement, which describes the composition of net profit, and the statement of comprehensive income, which describes net profit and all other non-owner changes in equity, into one statement. Further, since 2009 the IFRSs refer to the balance sheet as a "statement of financial position," to the cash flow statement as a "statement of cash flows," and to the statement of comprehensive income as a "statement of total recognized income and expense." However, firms are free to choose other titles. Throughout this book we will refer to these statements as the balance sheet, the cash flow statement, and the statement of comprehensive income, which is how they traditionally have been – and still are – titled by most firms.

3. At the time of writing there is no globally accepted name for management's narrative discussion of the firm's performance. In 2010 the IASB issued a (non-binding) Practice Statement Management Commentary, advising on what firms should report in this section. Throughout this book we will refer to this section as the Management Commentary section, consistent with the IASB's labeling, and assume that it typically contains at least a Letter to the Shareholders and a review of the firm's financial performance during the fiscal year and its financial position at the end of the year.

4. These definitions paraphrase those of the IASB, "Framework for the Preparation and Presentation of Financial Statements" (also referred to as the "Conceptual Framework"). Our intent is to present the definitions at a conceptual, not technical, level. For more complete discussion of these and related concepts, see the IASB's Conceptual Framework.

5. Strictly speaking, the comprehensive net income of a firm also includes gains and losses from increases and decreases in equity from nonoperating activities or exceptional items.

6. The EU has given its individual member states the option to permit or require private companies to use IFRS for the preparation of their single entity and/or consolidated financial statements. Similarly, member states may permit or require public companies to prepare their single entity financial statements in accordance with IFRS.

7. For a description of international differences in managers' legal liability for the information that they provide in prospectuses, see R. La Porta, F. Lopez-de-Silanes, and A. Shleifer, "What Works in Securities Laws?" *The Journal of Finance* 61 (2006): 1–32.

8. See, for example, the UK HM Treasury's report (July 2008) on the "Extension of the Statutory Regime for Issuer Liability," describing motivations for making managers subject to civil liability for fraudulent misstatements only.

9. For a description of how European agencies enforced IFRS in 2006, see the results of a CESR survey described in "CESR's review of the implementation and enforcement of IFRS in the EU" (November 2007).

10. See H.E. Jackson and M.J. Roe, "Public and Private Enforcement of Securities Laws: Resource-Based Evidence," *Journal of Financial Economics* 93(2) (2009): 207–238.

11. See Sarah Tasker, "Bridging the Information Gap: Quarterly Conference Calls as a Medium for Voluntary Disclosure," *Review of Accounting Studies* 3(1–2) (1998): 137–167.

12. See Richard Frankel, Marilyn Johnson, and Douglas Skinner, "An Empirical Examination of Conference Calls as a Voluntary Disclosure Medium," *Journal of Accounting Research* 37(1) (Spring 1999): 133–150.

13. See M. Kimbrough, "The Effect of Conference Calls on Analyst and Market Underreaction to Earnings Announcements," *The Accounting Review* 80(1) (January 2005): 189–219.

14. Recent research on voluntary disclosure includes Mark Lang and Russell Lundholm, "Cross-Sectional Determinants of Analysts' Ratings of Corporate Disclosures," *Journal of Accounting Research* 31 (Autumn 1993): 246–271; Lang and Lundholm, "Corporate Disclosure Policy and Analysts," *The Accounting Review* 71 (October 1996): 467–492; M. Welker, "Disclosure Policy, Information Asymmetry and Liquidity in Equity Markets," *Contemporary Accounting Research* (Spring 1995); Christine Botosan, "The Impact of Annual Report Disclosure Level on Investor Base and the Cost of Capital," *The Accounting Review* (July 1997): 323–350; and Paul Healy, Amy Hutton, and Krishna Palepu, "Stock Performance and Intermediation Changes Surrounding Sustained Increases in Disclosure," *Contemporary Accounting Research* 16(3) (Fall 1999): 485–521. This research finds that firms are more likely to provide high levels of disclosure if they have strong earnings performance, issue securities, have more analyst following, and have less dispersion in analyst forecasts. In addition, firms with high levels of disclosure policies tend to have a lower cost of capital and bid-ask spread. Finally, firms that increase disclosure have accompanying increases in stock returns, institutional ownership, analyst following, and share liquidity. In "The Role of Supplementary Statements with Management's Earnings Forecasts," working paper, Harvard Business School, 2003, A. Hutton, G. Miller, and D. Skinner examine the market response to management earnings forecasts and find that bad news forecasts are always informative but that good news forecasts are informative only when they are supported by verifiable forward-looking statements.

15. See J. Cotter, I. Tuna, and P. Wysocki, "Expectations Management and Beatable Targets: How do Analysts React to Explicit Earnings Guidance," *Contemporary Accounting Research* 23(3) (Autumn 2006): 593–628.

16. The Seventh EU Company Law Directive, which governs the preparation of consolidated financial statements in the EU, defines large groups as those meeting at least two of the following three criteria in two consecutive years:

    1 Total assets above € 17.5 million.

    2 Annual turnover above € 35.0 million.

    3 More than 250 employees.

17. The Fourth EU Company Law Directive, which governs corporations' financial reporting in the EU, defines small corporations as those failing to meet two of the following three criteria in two consecutive years:

    1 Total assets above € 4.4 million.

    2 Annual turnover above € 8.8 million.

    3 More than 50 employees.

18. It should be noted that although the EU regulations have partly harmonized private corporations' accounting, the accessibility of public registers varies greatly and private corporations' financial statements are therefore in practice not equally available across the EU.

19. See R. Ball and L. Shivakumar, "Earnings Quality in UK Private Firms: Comparative Loss Recognition Timeliness," *Journal of Accounting and Economics* 39 (2005): 83–128, D. Burgstahler, L. Hail and C. Leuz, "The Importance of Reporting Incentives: Earnings Management in European Private and Public Firms," *The Accounting Review* 81 (2006): 983–1016, and E. Peek, R. Cuijpers and W. Buijink, "Creditors' and Shareholders' Reporting Demands in Public versus Private Firms: Evidence from Europe," *Contemporary Accounting Research* 27 (2010): 49–91.

20. The influence of tax rules is particularly strong on single company financial statements, which in many countries are the basis for tax computations. Although the influence of tax rules on consolidated financial statements is less direct, tax considerations may still affect the preparation of these statements. For example, companies may support their aggressive tax choices by having the consolidated statements conform to the single company statements.

21. See L. Bottazzi and M. Da Rin, "Venture Capital in Europe and the Financing of Innovative Companies," *Economic Policy*, April (2002): 231–269.

22. See L. Bottazzi and M. Da Rin, "Europe's 'New' Stock Markets," Working Paper, July 2002, and M. Goergen, A. Khurshed, J.A. McCahery and L. Renneboog, "The Rise and Fall of European New Markets: on the Short and Long-run Performance of High-tech Initial Public Offerings," Working Paper, European Corporate Governance Institute, September 2003. To be eligible for a listing on one of the two largest new markets, the Nouveau Marché and the Neuer Markt, companies had to meet all of the following admission requirements. First, companies' equity prior to the initial public offering (IPO) had to exceed €1.5 million. Second, companies had to issue more than 100,000 shares, which had to represent more than 20 percent of the companies'

nominal capital, at an amount exceeding €5 million. Third, not more than 50 percent of the shares issued were allowed to come from existing shareholders; more than 50 percent of the issued shares had to come from a capital increase. Fourth, managers were not allowed to trade their shares during a six-month period following the IPO on the Neuer Markt. Managers of companies listed on the Nouveau Marché could not trade 80 percent of their shares for a period of 12 months. The other new markets had very similar admission requirements.

23. For an illustration of the circumstances surrounding the IASB's decision to amend the reclassification rules, see P. André, A. Cazavan-Jeny, W. Dick, C. Richard and P. Walton, "Fair Value Accounting and the Banking Crisis in 2008: Shooting the Messenger," *Accounting in Europe*, 6 (2009): 3–24.

APPENDIX: DEFINING EUROPE

At various places in this book we refer to "Europe" and "European companies" without intending to imply that all European countries and companies are exactly alike. Because Europe's richness in diversity makes it impossible to describe the institutional details of each European country in detail, this book discusses primarily the commonalities between the countries that have chosen to harmonize the differences among their accounting systems. These countries are the 28 member states of the European Union as well as the three members of the European Economic Area (Iceland, Norway, and Liechtenstein), which are also committed to following EU accounting Directives. Of particular importance to the topic of this book is that, since 2005, companies from these 31 countries that have their shares publicly traded on a stock exchange are required to prepare their financial statements in accordance with IFRS. A special position is occupied by Switzerland, which is neither a member of the EU nor of the European Economic Area. Many of the issues that we address in this book also apply to a large group of Swiss listed companies, because Switzerland requires its listed companies with international operations to prepare IFRS-based financial statements.

In some of the chapters in this book we summarize the financial ratios, stock returns, and operational characteristics of a representative sample of listed European companies for illustrative purposes. This sample is composed of all domestic companies that were listed on one of the largest seven European stock exchanges (or their predecessors) between January 1992 (labeled the start of fiscal year 1992) and December 2011 (labeled the end of fiscal year 2011). Table 1.1 displays the seven largest European stock exchanges at the end of December 2011 and their countries of operation.

TABLE 1.1 European stock exchanges

Countries	Stock exchange	Total market capitalization of domestic companies at December 2011 (in € billions)
Belgium, France, the Netherlands, Portugal	Euronext Brussels – Paris – Amsterdam – Lisbon	1,884.7
Denmark, Estonia, Finland, Iceland, Latvia, Lithuania, Sweden	OMX Exchanges Copenhagen – Tallinn – Helsinki – Reykjavik – Riga – Vilnius – Stockholm	648.7
Germany	Deutsche Borse	912.4
Norway	Oslo Børs	169.7
Spain	Bolsa y Mercados Espanõles (BME)	794.2
Switzerland	SWX Swiss Exchange	837.1
United Kingdom, Italy	London Stock Exchange – Borsa Italiana (LSE Group)	2,516.1

Source: World Federation of Exchanges. Euronext is a Pan-European exchange that was formed from the merger of the exchanges of Amsterdam, Brussels, Lisbon and Paris. OMX Exchanges includes the exchanges of Copenhagen, Helsinki, Stockholm, Tallinn, Riga, and Vilnius. The reported market capitalizations of the Euronext exchange, the OMX Exchanges, and the London Stock Exchange Group represent the total sum of the sizes of the individual segments.

The role of capital market intermediaries in the dot-com crash of 2000

The rise and fall of the internet consultants

In the summer of 1999, a host of internet consulting firms made their debut on the Nasdaq. Scient Corporation, which had been founded less than two years earlier in March 1997, went public in May 1999 at an IPO price of $20 per share ($10 on a pre-split basis). Its close on the first day of trading was $32.63. Other internet consulting companies that went public that year included Viant Corporation, IXL Enterprises, and US Interactive **(see Exhibit 1)**.

The main value proposition of these companies was that they would be able to usher in the new internet era by lending their information technology and web expertise to traditional "old economy" companies that wanted to gain Web-based technology, as well as to the emerging dot-com sector. Other companies like Sapient Corporation and Cambridge Technology Partners had been doing IT consulting for years, but this new breed of companies was able to capitalize on the burgeoning demand for internet expertise.

Over the following months, the stock prices of the internet consultants rose dramatically. Scient traded at a high of $133.75 in March 2000. However, this was after a 2–1 split, so each share was actually worth twice this amount on a pre-split basis. This stock level represented a 1238 percent increase from its IPO price and a valuation of 62 times the company's revenues for the fiscal year 2000. Similar performances were put in by the other companies in this group. However, these valuation levels proved to be unsustainable. The stock prices of web consulting firms dropped sharply in April 2000 along with many others in the internet sector, following what was afterwards seen as a general "correction" in the Nasdaq. The prices of the web consultants seemed to stabilize for a while, and many analysts continued to write favorably about their prospects and maintained buy ratings on their stocks. But starting early in September 2000, after some bad news from Viant Corporation and many subsequent analyst downgrades, the stocks went into a free-fall. All were trading in single digits by February of 2001, representing a greater than 95 percent drop from their peak valuations **(see Exhibit 2)**.

The dramatic rise and fall of the stock prices of the Web consultants, along with many others in the internet sector, caused industry observers to wonder how this could have happened in a relatively sophisticated capital market like that of the United States. Several well-respected venture capitalists, investment banks, accounting firms, financial analysts, and money management companies were involved in bringing these companies to market and rating and trading their shares **(see Exhibit 3)**. Who, if anyone, caused the internet stock price bubble? What, if anything, could be done to avoid the recurrence of such stock market bubbles?

Gillian Elcock, MBA 2001, prepared this case from published sources under the supervision of Professor Krishna Palepu. HBS cases are developed solely as the basis for class discussion. Cases are not intended to serve as endorsements, sources of primary data, or illustrations of effective or ineffective management.

Context: The technology bull market

The 1980s and 1990s marked the beginning of a global technology revolution that started with the personal computer (PC) and led to the internet era. Companies like Apple, Microsoft, Intel, and Dell Computer were at the forefront of this new wave of technology that promised to enhance productivity and efficiency through the computerization and automation of many processes.

The capital markets recognized the value that was being created by these companies. Microsoft, which was founded in 1975, had a market capitalization of over $600 billion by the beginning of 2000, making it the world's most valuable company, and its founder, Bill Gates, one of the richest men in the world. High values were also given to many of the other blue-chip technology firms such as Intel and Dell (**Exhibit 4**).

The 1990s ushered in a new group of companies that were based on information networks. These included AOL, Netscape, and Cisco. Netscape was a visible symbol of the emerging importance of the internet: its browser gave regular users access to the World Wide Web, whereas previously the internet had been mostly the domain of academics and experts. In March 2000, Cisco Systems, which made the devices that routed information across the internet, overtook Microsoft as the world's most valuable company (based on market capitalization). This seemed further evidence of the value shift that was taking place from PC-focused technologies and companies to those that were based on the global information network.

It appeared obvious that the internet was going to profoundly change the world through greater computing power, ease of communication, and the host of technologies that could be built upon it. Opportunities to build new services and technologies were boundless, and they were global in scale. The benefits of the internet were expected to translate into greater economic productivity through the lowering of communication and transaction costs. It also seemed obvious that someone would be able to capitalize upon these market opportunities and that "the next Microsoft" would soon appear. No one who missed out on the original Microsoft wanted to do so the second time around.

A phrase that became popularized during this time was the "new economy." New economy companies, as opposed to old economy ones (exemplified by companies in traditional manufacturing, retail, and commodities), based their business models around exploiting the internet. They were usually small compared to their old economy counter parts, with little need for their real-world "bricks and mortar" structures, preferring to outsource much of the capital intensive parts of the business and concentrate on the higher value-added, information-intensive elements. Traditional companies, finding their market shares and business models attacked by a host of nimble, specialized dot-com start-ups, lived in danger of "being Amazoned." To many, the new economy was the future and old economy companies would become less and less relevant.

The capital markets seemed to think similarly. From July 1999 to February 2000, as the Nasdaq Composite Index (which was heavily weighted with technology and internet stocks) rose by 74.4 percent, the Dow Jones Industrial Average (which was composed mainly of old economy stocks) fell by 7.7 percent. Investors no longer seemed interested in anything that was not new economy.

Internet gurus and economists predicted the far-reaching effects of the internet. The following excerpts represent the mood of the time:

> *Follow the personal computer and you can reach the pot of gold. Follow anything else and you will end up in a backwater. What the Model T was to the industrial era ... the PC is to the information age. Just as people who rode the wave of automobile technology – from tire makers to fast food franchisers – prevailed in the industrial era, so the firms that prey on the passion and feed on the force of the computer community will predominate in the information era.*[1]
>
> – George Gilder, 1992

*****

> *Due to technological advances in PC-based communications, a new medium – with the internet, the World Wide Web, and TCP/IP at its core – is emerging rapidly. The market for internet-related products and services appears to be growing more rapidly than the early emerging markets for print*

---

[1] Mary Meeker, Chris DePuy, "U. S. Investment Research, Technology/New Media, The internet Report (Excerpt) from *Life After Television* by George Gilder, 1992" Morgan Stanley (February 1996).

publishing, telephony, film, radio, recorded music, television, and personal computers.... Based on our market growth estimates, we are still at the very early stages of a powerful secular growth cycle.[2]...

– Mary Meeker, Morgan Stanley Dean Witter, February 1996

*****

The easy availability of smart capital – the ability of entrepreneurs to launch potentially world-beating companies on a shoestring, and of investors to intelligently spread risk – may be the new economy's most devastating innovation. At the same time, onrushing technological change requires lumbering dinosaurs to turn themselves into clever mammals overnight. Some will. But for many others, the only thing left to talk about is the terms of surrender.[3]

– The *Wall Street Journal*, April 17, 2000

In the new economy, gaining market share was considered key because of the benefits of network effects. In addition, a large customer base was needed to cover the high fixed costs often associated with doing business. Profitability was of a secondary concern, and Netscape was one of the first of many internet companies to go public without positive earnings. Some companies deliberately operated at losses because it was essential to spend a lot early to gain market share, which would presumably translate at a later point into profitability. This meant that revenue growth was the true measure of success for many internet companies. Of course there were some dissenting voices, warning that this was just a period of irrational exuberance and the making of a classic stock market bubble. But for the most part, investors seemed to buy into the concept, as evidenced by the values given to several loss-making dotcoms (**Exhibit 5**).

Scient Corporation

The history of Scient, considered a leader in the internet consulting space, is representative of what happened to the entire industry. The firm was founded in November 1997. Its venture capital backers included several leading firms such as Sequioa Capital and Benchmark Capital (see **Exhibit 3**)

Scient described itself as "a leading provider of a new category of professional services called eBusiness systems innovation" that would "rapidly improve a client's competitive position through the development of innovative business strategies enabled by the integration of emerging and existing technologies."[4] Its aim was to provide services in information technology and systems design as well as high-level strategy consulting, previously the domain of companies such as McKinsey and The Boston Consulting Group.

The company grew quickly to almost 2,000 people within three years, primarily organically. Its client list included AT&T, Chase Manhattan, Johnson & Johnson, and Home-store.com.[5] As with any consulting firm, its ability to attract and retain talented employees was crucial, since they were its main assets.

By the fiscal year ending in March 2000, Scient had a net loss of $16 million on revenues of $156 million (see financial statements in **Exhibit 6**). These revenues represented an increase of 653 percent over the previous year. Analysts wrote glowingly about the firm's prospects. In February 2000 when the stock was trading at around $87.25, a Deutsche Banc Alex Brown report stated:

We have initiated research coverage of Scient with a BUY investment rating on the shares. In our view Scient possesses several key comparative advantages: (1) an outstanding management team; (2) a highly scalable and leverageable operating model; (3) a strong culture, which attracts the best and the brightest; (4) a private equity portfolio, which enhances long-term relationships and improves retention; and (5) an exclusive focus on the high-end systems innovation market with eBusiness and industry expertise, rapid time-to-market and an integrated approach.... Scient shares are currently trading at roughly 27x projected CY00 revenues, modestly ahead of pure play leaders like Viant (24x) and

The role of capital market intermediaries in the dot-com crash of 2000

---

[2]Mary Meeker, Chris DePuy, "U.S. Investment Research, Technology/New Media, The internet Report," *Morgan Stanley* (February 1996).

[3]John Browning, Spencer Reiss, "For the New Economy, the End of the Beginning," *The Wall Street Journal* (Copyright 2000 Dow Jones & Company, Inc).

[4]Scient Corporation Prospectus, May 1999. Available from Edgar Online.

[5]Scient Corporation website, <http://www.scient.com/non/content/clients/client_list/index.asp>.

Proxicom (25x), and ahead of our interactive integrator peer group average of just over 16x. Our 12-month price target is $120. It is a stock we would want to own.[6]

And in March 2000, when the stock was at $77.75, Morgan Stanley, which had an "outperform" rating, wrote:

All said we believe Scient continue [sic] to effectively execute on what is a very aggressive business plan.... While shares of SCNT trade at a premium valuation to its peer group, we continue to believe that such level is warranted given the company's high-end market focus, short but impressive record of execution, and deep/experienced management team. As well, in our view there is a high probability of meaningful upward revisions to Scient's model.[7]

Scient's stock reached a high of $133.75 in March 2000 but fell to $44 by June as part of the overall drop in valuation of most of the technology sector. In September the company announced it had authorized a stock repurchase of $25 million. But in December 2000 it lowered its revenue and earnings expectations for the fourth quarter due to the slowdown in demand for internet consulting services. The company also announced plans to lay off 460 positions worldwide (over 20 percent of its workforce) as well as close two of its offices, and an associated $40–$45 million restructuring charge. By February 2001 the stock was trading at $2.94.

Most of the analysts that covered Scient had buy or strong buy ratings on the company as its stock rose to its peak and even after the Nasdaq correction in April 2000. Then in September, a warning by Viant Corporation of results that would come in below expectations due to a slowdown in e-business spending from large corporate clients, prompted many analysts to downgrade most of the companies in the sector, including Scient **(see Exhibit 7)**. Several large mutual fund companies were holders of Scient as its stock rose, peaked, and fell **(see Exhibit 8)**.

As the major technology indices continued their slump during late 2000 and early 2001, and the stock prices of the internet consulting firms floundered in the single digits, they received increasing attention from the press:

Examining the downfall of the eConsultants provides an excellent case study of failed business models. Rose-colored glasses, a lack of a sustainable competitive advantage, and a "me too" mentality are just some of the mistakes these companies made.... The eConsultants failed to do the one thing that they were supposed to be helping their clients do – build a sustainable business model ... many eConsultants popped up and expected to be able to take on the McKinseys and Booz-Allens of the world. Now they are discovering that the relationships firmly established by these old economy consultants are integral to building a sustainable competitive advantage.[8]

Seems like everything dot-com is being shunned by investors these days. But perhaps no other group has experienced quite the brutality that Web consultancies have. Once the sweethearts of Wall Street, their stocks are now high-tech whipping boys. Even financial analysts, who usually strive to be positive about companies they cover, seem to have given up on the sector.... Many of these firms were built on the back of the dot-com boom. Now these clients are gone. At the same time, pressure on bricks-and-mortar companies to build online businesses has lifted, leading to the cancellation or delay of Web projects.[9]

The analysts who were formerly excited about Scient's prospects and had recommended the stock when it was trading at almost $80 per share now seemed much less enthusiastic. In January 2001, with the stock around $3.44, Morgan Stanley wrote:

We maintain our Neutral rating due to greater than anticipated market weakness, accelerating pricing pressure, the potential for increased turnover and management credibility issues. While shares of SCNT trade at a depressed valuation, we continuate [sic] to believe that turnover and pricing pressure

---

[6]F. Mark D'Annolfo, William S. Zinsmeister, Jeffrey A. Buchbinder, "Scient Corporation Premier Builder of eBusinesses," *Deutsche Banc Alex Brown* (February 14, 2000).

[7]Michael A. Sherrick, Mary Meeker, "Scient Corporation Quarter Update," *Morgan Stanley Dean Witter* (March 2, 2000).

[8]Todd N. Lebor, "The Downfall of internet Consultants," *Fool's Den*, Fool.com (December 11, 2000).

[9]Amey Stone, "Streetwise – Who'll Help the Web Consultants?" *BusinessWeek Online* (New York , February 15, 2001). From www.businessweek.com.

could prove greater than management's assumptions. While management indicated it would be "aggressive" to maintain its people, we still believe it will be difficult to maintain top-tier talent in the current market and company specific environment.[10]

Performance of the Nasdaq

The performance of the stock prices of Scient and its peers mirrored that of many companies in the internet sector. So dramatic was the drop in valuation of these companies, that this period was subsequently often referred to as the "Dot-com crash."

In the months following the crash, the equity markets essentially closed their doors to the internet firms. Several once high-flying dot-coms, operating at losses and starved for cash, filed for bankruptcy, or closed down their operations (see **Exhibit 9**).

The Nasdaq, which had reached a high of 5,132.52 in March of 2000 closed at 2470.52 in December 2000, a drop of 52 percent from its high. As of February 2001 it had not recovered, closing at 2151.83.

The role of intermediaries in a well-functioning market

In a capitalist economy, individuals and institutions have savings that they want to invest, and companies need capital to finance and grow their businesses. The capital markets provide a way for this to occur efficiently. Companies issue debt or equity to investors who are willing to part with their cash now because they expect to earn an adequate return in the future for the risk they are taking.

However, there is an information gap between investors and companies. Investors usually do not have enough information or expertise to determine the good investments from the bad ones. And companies do not usually have the infrastructure and know-how to directly receive capital from investors. Therefore, both parties rely on intermediaries to help them make these decisions. These intermediaries include accountants, lawyers, regulatory bodies (such as the SEC in the United States), investment banks, venture capitalists, money management firms, and even the media **(see Exhibit 10)**. The focus of this case is on the equity markets in the United States.

In a well-functioning system, with the incentives of intermediaries fully aligned in accordance with their fiduciary responsibility, public markets will correctly value companies such that investors earn a normal "required" rate of return. In particular, companies that go public will do so at a value which will give investors this fair rate of investment.

The public market valuation will have a trickle down effect on all intermediaries in the investment chain. Venture capitalists, who typically demand a very high return on investment, and usually exit their portfolio companies through an IPO, will do their best to ensure these companies have good management teams and a sustainable business model that will stand the test of time. Otherwise, the capital markets will put too low a value on the companies when they try to go public. Investment bankers will provide their expertise in helping companies to go public or to make subsequent offerings, and introducing them to investors.

On the other side of the process, portfolio managers acting on behalf of investors, will only buy companies that are fairly priced, and will sell companies if they become overvalued, since buying or holding an overvalued stock will inevitably result in a loss. Sell-side analysts, whose clients include portfolio managers and therefore investors, will objectively monitor the performance of public companies and determine whether or not their stocks are good or bad investment at any point in time. Accountants audit the financial statements of companies, ensuring that they comply with established standards and represent the true states of the firms. This gives investors and analysts the confidence to make decisions based on these financial documents.

The integrity of this process is critical in an economy because it gives investors the confidence they need to invest their money into the system. Without this confidence, they would not plough their money back into the economy, but instead keep it under the proverbial mattress.

---

[10]Michael A. Sherrick, Mary Meeker, Douglas Levine, "Scient Corporation. Outlook Remains Cloudy, Adjusting Forecasts," *Morgan Stanley Dean Witter* (January 18, 2001).

The role of capital market intermediaries in the dot-com crash of 2000

What happened during the dot-com bubble?

Many observers believed that something went wrong with the system during the dot-com bubble. In April 2001, *BusinessWeek* wrote about "The Great internet Money Game. How America's top financial firms reaped billions from the Net boom, while investors got burned."[11] The following month, *Fortune* magazine's cover asked "Can we ever trust Wall Street again?"[12] referring to the way in which, in some people's opinions, Wall Street firms had led investors and companies astray before and after the dot-com debacle.

The implications of the internet crash were far reaching. Many companies that needed to raise capital for investment found the capital markets suddenly shut to them. Millions of investors saw a large portion of their savings evaporate. This phenomenon was a likely contributor to the sharp drop in consumer confidence that took place in late 2000 and early 2001. In addition, the actual decrease in wealth threatened to dampen consumer spending. These factors, along with an overall slowing of the US economy, threatened to put the United States into recession for the first time in over 10 years.

On a more macro level, the dot-coms used up valuable resources that could have been more efficiently allocated within the economy. The people who worked at failed internet firms could have spent their time and energy creating lasting value in other endeavors, and the capital that funded the dot-coms could have been ploughed into viable, lasting companies that would have benefited the overall economy. However, it could be argued that there were benefits as well, and that the large investment in the technology sector positioned the United States to be a world leader in the future.

Nevertheless, the question remained: how could the dot-com bubble occur in a sophisticated capital market system like that of the United States? Why did the market allow the valuations of many internet companies to go so high? What was the role of the intermediaries in the process that gave rise to the stock market bubble?

The intermediaries

One way to try to answer some of these questions is to look more closely at some of the key players in the investing chain. Much of the material in the following section is derived from interviews with representatives from each sector.

Venture capitalists

Venture capitalists (VCs) provided capital for companies in their early stages of development. They sought to provide a very high rate of return to their investors for the associated risk. This was typically accomplished by selling their stake in their portfolio companies either to the public through an IPO, or to another company in a trade sale.

The partners in a VC firm typically had a substantial percentage of their net worth tied up in their funds, which aligned their interests with their investors. Their main form of compensation was a large share of profits (typically 20 percent) in addition to a relatively low fee based on the assets under management.

A large part of a VC's job was to screen good business ideas and entrepreneurial teams from bad ones. Partners at a VC firm were typically very experienced, savvy business people who worked closely with their portfolio companies to both monitor and guide them to a point where they have turned a business idea into a well-managed, fully functional company that could stand on its own. In a sense, their role was to nurture the companies until they reached a point where they were ready to face the scrutiny of the public capital markets after an IPO. Typically, companies would not go public until they had shown profits for at least three quarters.[13]

After the dot-com crash, some investors and the media started pointing fingers at the venture capitalists that had invested in many of the failed dot-coms. They blamed them for being unduly influenced by the euphoria of the market, and knowingly investing in and bringing public companies with questionable business models, or that had not yet proven themselves operationally. Indeed, many of the dot-coms went public

[11]Peter Elstrom, "The Great internet Money Game. How America's top financial firms reaped billions from the Net boom while investors got burned," *BusinessWeek e.biz* (April 16, 2001).

[12]*Fortune*, May 14, 2001.

[13]Peter Elstrom, "The Great internet Money Game. How America's top financial firms reaped billions from the Net boom while investors got burned," *BusinessWeek e.biz* (April 16, 2001).

within record time of receiving VC funding – a study of venture-backed initial public offerings showed that companies averaged 5.4 years in age when they went public in 1999, compared with eight years in 1995.[14]

Did the venture capital investing process change in a way that contributed to the internet bubble of 2000? According to a partner at a venture capital firm that invested in one of the internet consulting companies, the public markets had a tremendous impact on the way VCs invested during the late 1990s.[15] He felt that, because of expectations of high stock market valuations, VC firms invested in companies during late 1990s that they would not have invested in under ordinary circumstances. He also believed that the ready availability of money affected the business strategies and attitudes of the internet companies: "If the [management] team knows $50 million is available, it acts differently, e.g., 'go for market share'."

The VC partner acknowledged that VCs took many internet companies public very early, but he felt that the responsibility of scrutinizing these companies lay largely with the investors that subscribed to the IPOs: "If a mutual fund wants to invest in the IPO of a company that has no track record, profitability, etc. but sees it as a liquidity event, it has made a decision to become a VC. Lots of mutual funds thought 'VC is easy, I want a piece of it.'"

Investment bank underwriters

Entrepreneurs relied on investment banks (such as Goldman Sachs, Morgan Stanley Dean Witter, and Credit Suisse First Boston) in the actual process of doing an initial public offering, or "going public." Investment banks provided advisory financial services, helped the companies price their offerings, underwrite the shares, and introduce them to investors, often in the form of a road show.

Investment banks were paid a commission based on the amount of money that the company managed to raise in its offering, typically on the order of 7 percent.[16] Several blue-chip firms were involved in the capital-raising process of the internet consultants **(see Exhibit 3)**, and they also received a share of the blame for the dot-com crash in the months that followed it. In an article entitled *Just Who Brought Those Duds to Market?* the *New York Times* wrote:

> *… many Wall Street investment banks, from top-tier firms like Goldman Sachs … to newer entrants like Thomas Weisel Partners … have reason to blush. In one blindingly fast riches-to-rags story, Pets.com filed for bankruptcy just nine months after Merrill Lynch took it public.*
>
> *Of course, investment banks that took these underperforming companies public may not care. They bagged enormous fees, a total of more than $600 million directly related to initial public offerings involving just the companies whose stocks are now under $1.*
>
> *… How did investment banks, paid for their expert advice, pick such lemons?*[17]

Sell-side analysts

Sell-side analysts worked at investment banks and brokerage houses. One of their main functions was to publish research on public companies. Each analyst typically followed 15 to 30 companies in a particular industry, and his or her job involved forming relationships with and talking to the managements of the companies, following trends in the industry, and ultimately making buy or sell recommendations on the stocks. The recommendations analysts made could be very influential with investors. If a well-respected analyst downgraded a stock, the reaction from the market could be severe and swift, resulting in a same-day drop in the stock price. Sell-side analysts typically interacted with buy-side analysts and portfolio managers at money management companies (the buy-side) to market or "sell" their ideas. In addition, they usually provided support during a company's IPO process, providing research to the buy-side before the company actually went public. Sell-side analysts were usually partly compensated based on the amount of trading fees and investment banking revenue they helped the firm to generate through their research.

In the months following the dot-com crash, sell-side technology and internet analysts found themselves the target of criticism for having buy ratings on companies that had subsequently fallen drastically in price. Financial cable TV channel CNBC ran a report called "Analyzing the Analysts," addressing the issue of

[14]Shawn Neidorf, "Venture-Backed IPOs Make a Comeback," *Venture Capital Journal* (Wellesley Hills, Aug 1, 1999).

[15]Limited partners are the investors in a venture capital fund; the venture capital firm itself usually serves as the general partner.

[16]Source: casewriter interview.

[17]Andrew Ross Sorkin, "Just Who Brought Those Duds to Market?" *NYTimes.com* (Copyright 2001 The New York Times Company).

The role of capital market intermediaries in the dot-com crash of 2000

whether or not they were to blame for their recommendations of tech stocks. A March 2001 article in The *Wall Street Journal* raised similar issues after it was reported that J.P. Morgan Chase's head of European research sent out a memo requiring all the company's analysts to show their stock recommendation changes to the company involved and to the investment banking division.[18] The previously mentioned issue of *Forbes* featured an article criticizing Mary Meeker, a prominent internet analyst.[19] And a *Financial Times* article entitled "Shoot all the analysts" made a sweeping criticism of their role in the market bubble:

> *… instead of forecasting earnings per share, they were now in the business of forecasting share prices themselves. And those prices were almost always very optimistic. Now, at last, they have had their comeuppance. Much of what many of them have done in the past several years has turned out to be worthless. High-flying stocks that a year ago were going to be cheap at twice the price have halved or worse – and some analysts have been putting out buy recommendations all the way down.… They should learn a little humility and get back to analysis.[20]*

Responding to the media criticism of financial analysts, Karl Keirstead, a Lehman Brothers analyst who followed internet consulting firms, stated:

> *It is too easy as they do on CNBC to slam the analysts for recommending stocks when they were very expensive. In the case of the internet consulting firms, looking back before the correction in April 2000, the fundamentals were "nothing short of pristine." The companies were growing at astronomical rates, and it looked as though they would continue to do so for quite a while. Under these assumptions, if you modeled out the financials for these companies and discounted them back at a reasonable rate, they did not seem all that highly valued.[21]*

Keirstead also pointed out that there were times when it was legitimate to have a buy rating on a stock that was "overvalued" based on fundamentals:

> *The future price of a stock is not always tied to the discounted value of cash flow or earnings, it is equal to what someone is willing to pay. This is especially true in periods of tremendous market liquidity and huge interest in young companies with illiquid stocks and steep growth curves that are difficult to project. The valuation may seem too high, but if the fundamentals are improving and Street psychology and hype are building, the stock is likely to rally. Stock pickers must pay as much attention to these factors as the company and industry fundamentals.*

When asked his view on why the buy-side institutions went along with the high valuations that these companies were trading for, Keirstead commented that, "A lot of buy-side analysts and portfolio managers became momentum investors in disguise. They claimed in their mutual fund prospectus that they made decisions based on fundamental analysis. Truth is, they played the momentum game as well."

Keirstead also commented on the criticism analysts had received for being too heavily influenced by the possibility of banking deals when making stock recommendations. He stated that this claim was "completely over-rated." Though there was some legitimacy to the argument and some of analysts' compensation did come from investment banking fees, it was a limited component. Analysts also got significant fees from the trading revenue they generated and the published rankings.[22] He pointed out that critics' arguments were ludicrous because if analysts only made decisions based on banking fees, it would jeopardize their rankings and credibility with their buy-side clients. However, he did note that the potential deal flow could have distorted the view of some technology analysts during the boom.

Finally, Keirstead described the bias that was present on the sell-side to be bullish:

> *To be negative when you are a sell-side analyst is to be a contrarian, to stick your neck out. You take a lot of heat, it's tough. And it would have been the wrong call for the last four years. Had I turned short*

---

[18]Wade Lambert, Jathon Sapsford, "J.P. Morgan Memo to Analysts Raises Eyebrows," *The Wall Street Journal* (Thursday, March 22, 2001).

[19]Peter Elkind, "Where Mary Meeker Went Wrong," *Fortune* (May 14, 2001).

[20]"Shoot all the analysts," *Financial Times* (Tuesday, March 20, 2001).

[21]Source: casewriter interview.

[22]Several financial journals published analyst rankings. The most prominent ranking was by *Institutional Investor* magazine which published annual rankings of sell-side analysts by industry. These rankings were very influential in the analyst and investment community.

in 1999 when these stocks seemed overvalued, I would have missed a 200 percent increase in the stocks. My view was: I can't be too valuation-sensitive. The stocks are likely to rise as long as the fundamentals hold and that's the position a lot of analysts took.

Consistent with this optimistic bias, there were very few sell recommendations from analysts during the peak of the internet stock bubble. According to financial information company First Call, more than 70 percent of the 27,000 plus recommendations outstanding on some 6,000 stocks in November 2000 were strong buys or buys, while fewer than 1 percent were sells or strong sells.[23]

Buy-side analysts and portfolio managers

The "buy-side" refers to institutions that do the actual buying and selling of public securities, such as mutual fund companies, insurance companies, hedge funds, and other asset managers.

There were two main roles on the buy side: analysts and portfolio managers. Buy-side analysts had some of the same duties as their sell-side counterparts. They were usually assigned to a group of companies within a certain industry and were responsible for doing industry research, talking to the companies' management teams, coming up with earning estimates, doing valuation analysis, and ultimately rating the stock prices of the companies as either "buys" or "sells." The analyst's job was not yet complete, however. Though they did not publish their research, buy-side analysts needed to convince the portfolio managers within their company to follow their recommendations.

Portfolio managers were the ones who actually managed money, whether it was a retail mutual fund or an institutional account. Though they listened to the recommendations of the analysts, they were the ones who were ultimately responsible for buying or selling securities.

The compensation of the buy-side analysts was often linked to how well their stock recommendations do, and in the case of portfolio managers, compensation was determined by the performance of their funds relative to an appropriate benchmark return. These compensation schemes were designed to align the incentives of buy-side analysts and portfolio managers with the interests of investors.

Why then, did so many buy-side firms buy and hold on to the internet consulting firms during the market bubble? Did they really believe the companies were worth what they were trading for? Or did they know they were overvalued, but invest in them anyway for other reasons?

According to a former associate at a large mutual fund company, many people within his company knew that most of the internet companies were overvalued before the market correction, but they felt pressure to invest anyway:

My previous employer is known as a value investor, growth at a reasonable price. At first the general impression in the firm was that a lot of the internet firms would blow up, that they didn't deserve these valuations. But articles were written about my company … that it was being left behind because it was not willing to invest in the internet companies. Some of the analysts at the firm began to recommend companies simply because they knew that the stock prices would go up, even though they were clearly overvalued. And portfolio managers felt that if they didn't buy the stocks, they would lag their benchmarks and their competitors – they are rewarded on a one-year term horizon and three-year horizon. It is very important to meet their benchmark, it makes up a material part of their compensation. In addition, they compare against the performance of their peers for marketing purposes.[24]

The role of information

The accounting profession

Independent accountants audited the financial statements of public companies to verify their accuracy and freedom from fraud. If they were reasonably satisfied, they provided an unqualified opinion statement which was attached to the company's public filings. If auditors were not fully satisfied, this is noted as well.

---

[23]Walter Updegrave, "The ratings game," *Money* (New York , January 2001).
[24]Source: casewriter interview.

The role of capital market intermediaries in the dot-com crash of 2000

Investors usually took heed of the auditor's opinion as it provided an additional level of assurance of the quality of the information they were receiving from companies.

In the year 2000, the accounting profession in the United States was dominated by five major accounting firms, collectively referred to as "The Big Five" (PriceWaterhouseCoopers, Deloitte & Touche, KPMG, Ernst & Young, and Arthur Andersen.) The top 100 accounting firms had roughly a 50 percent share of the market and the Big Five account for about 84 percent of the revenues of the top 100.[25] However, the Big Five made up an even larger percentage of the auditing activity of internet IPOs. Of the 410 internet services and software IPOs between January 1998 and December 2000, 373 of them, or 91 percent were audited by one of the Big Five accountants.[26]

During the aftermath of the dot-com crash, these firms came under some criticism for not adequately warning investors about the precarious financial position of some of the companies. The *Wall Street Journal* wrote an article addressing the fact that many dotcoms that went bankrupt were not given "going concern" clauses by their auditors. A going concern clause was included by an auditor if it had a substantial doubt that the company would be able to remain in operation for another 12 months:

> In retrospect, critics say, there were early signs that the businesses weren't sustainable, including their reliance on external financing, rather than money generated by their own operations, to stay afloat. You wonder where some of the skepticism was … critics say many auditors appear to have presumed the capital markets would remain buoyant. For anybody to have assumed a continuation of those aberrant, irrational conditions was in itself irrational and unjustifiable whether it was an auditor, a board member or an investor....[27]

However, in the same article, accountants defended their actions by noting that going concern judgments were subjective, and that they were not able to predict the future any better than the capital markets.

Dr Howard Schilit, founder and CEO of CFRA, an independent financial research organization,[28] believed that accountants certainly had to take a part of the blame for what happened. In his opinion, they "looked the other way when they could have been more rigorous in doing their work."[29] However, he noted that the outcome may not have been materially different even if they did.

One particular criticism he had was that many accountants didn't look closely enough at the substance of transactions and didn't do enough questioning of the circumstances surrounding sales contracts. His hope was that accountants "go back and learn what the basic rules are of when revenues should be booked. The rules haven't changed whether this is the new economy or old economy."

FASB – A regulator

The Financial Accounting Standards Boards (FASB) was an independent regulatory body in the United States whose mission was to "establish and improve standards of financial accounting and reporting for the guidance and education of the public, including issuers, auditors, and users of financial information."[30] FASB standards were recognized by the Securities and Exchange Commission (SEC), which regulates the financial reporting of public companies in the United States.

The accounting practices of some new economy firms posed challenges for auditors and investors, and though some observers felt that the accountants were not doing a good enough job, others thought that the accounting rules themselves were too ambiguous, and this fact lent itself to exploitation by the companies.

Specific examples included the treatment of barter revenues in the case of companies that exchanged online advertising space, the practice of booking gross rather than net revenues in commission-based businesses (e.g., Priceline.com), and the issue of when to recognize revenues from long-term contracts (e.g., MicroStrategy Inc.) Given that the valuations of many internet firms were driven by how quickly they grew revenues,

[25]"Accounting Today Top 100 Survey Shows All is Well," The *CPA Journal* (May 1999).

[26]Information extracted from IPO.com website http://www.ipo.com.

[27]Johnathan Weil, "'Going Concerns': Did Accountants Fail to Flag Problems at Dot-Com Casualties?" The *Wall Street Journal* (February 9, 2001).

[28]CFRA's mission is to warn investors and creditors about companies experiencing operational problems and particularly those that employ unusual or aggressive accounting practices to camouflage such problems.

[29]Source: casewriter interview.

[30]FASB website: http://accounting.rutgers.edu/raw/fasb/.

there was a lot of incentive to inflate this number. In fact, the accounting practices of dot-coms became so aggressive that the SEC had to step in:

> *The Securities & Exchange Commission's crackdown on the aggressive accounting practices that have taken off among many dot-com firms really began ... when it quietly issued new guidelines to refocus corporate management and investors.... To rein in what it saw as an alarming trend in inflated revenue reports, the SEC required companies using lax accounting practices to restate financial results by the end of their next fiscal year's quarter....*
>
> *The SEC has also directed the Financial Accounting Standards Board to review a range of internet company accounting practices that could boost revenues or reduce costs unfairly. Under the scrutiny, more companies are likely to issue restatements of financial results....*[31]

In another spin on the issue, some questioned whether the accounting rules set out by the regulatory bodies had in fact become obsolete for the new economy. In July 2000, leaders in the accounting community told a Senate Banking subcommittee that the United States needed "a new accounting model for the New Economy." A major concern of theirs was that the current rules did not allow companies to report the value of intangible assets on their balance sheets, such as customers, employees, suppliers, and organizations.[32] Others argued that the accounting rules caused internet firms to appear unprofitable when they were actually making money. This was because old economy firms were allowed to capitalize their major investments such as factories, plants, and equipment, whereas the rules did not allow capitalization of expenditures on R&D and marketing, which created value for many dot-com companies:

> *While internet stocks may not be worth what they are selling for, the movement in their prices may not be as crazy as it seems. Many of these companies reporting losses actually make money – lots of it. It all has to do with accounting. Old-economy companies get to capitalize their most important investments, while new economy ones do not. While Amazon.com announces a loss almost every quarter, when it capitalizes its investments in intangibles that loss turns into a $400-million profit.*[33]

Retail investors

The role of the general public in the dot-com craze cannot be ignored. In addition to the people who poured money into mutual funds, many retail investors began trading on their own, often electronically. A group of avid day traders grew up, some of whom quit their regular jobs to devote all their time and energy to trading stocks. Analysts estimated that they made up almost 18 percent of the trading volume of the NYSE and Nasdaq in 2000.[34] Sites such as Yahoo Finance grew in popularity, while chat rooms devoted to stocks and trading proliferated.

The number of accounts of internet stock brokers like Etrade and Ameritrade grew rapidly (Etrade grew from 544 thousand brokerage accounts in 1998 to 3 million in 2000 and Ameritrade grew from 98 thousand accounts in 1997 to 1.2 million in 2000) as they slashed their commissions, some to as low as $8/trade compared to the $50-$300[35] charged by traditional brokerage firms. These companies were dot-coms themselves and they were able to slash prices partly because they were operating at losses that they were not penalized for by the capital markets. This gave rise to an interesting positive feedback loop: the Etrades of the world, funded by the dot-com frenzied capital markets slashed their prices and therefore encouraged more trading, which continued to fuel the enthusiasm of investors for the markets.

The financial press also became increasingly visible during this period. Several publications like *Barrons* and The *Wall Street Journal* had always been very influential in the financial community. However, a host of other information sources, often on the web, sprang up to support the new demand for information. CNBC and CNNfn, major network channels devoted to the markets, often featured analysts and portfolio managers making stock recommendations or giving their views on the market.

The role of capital market intermediaries in the dot-com crash of 2000

---

[31]Catherine Yang, "Earth to Dot-Com Accountants," *BusinessWeek* (New York , April 3, 2000).

[32]Stephen Barlas, "New accounting model demanded," *Strategic Finance* (Montvale, September 2000).

[33]Geoffrey Colvin, "The Net's hidden profits," *Fortune* (New York , April 17, 2000).

[34]Amy S. Butte, "Day Trading and Beyond. A New Niche Is Emerging," *Bear Stearns Equity Research*, April 2000.

[35]Lee Patterson, "If you can't beat 'em ...," *Forbes* (New York , August 23, 1999).

Many of the retail investors did not know much about finance or valuation, and often didn't understand much about the companies whose shares they were buying. They were therefore likely to be heavily influenced by some of the intermediaries previously described, especially the financial press, and the sell-side analysts that publicly upgraded and downgraded companies.

These investors were pointed to by some as having had a large role in driving internet valuations to the levels they went to. The reasoning was that other more sophisticated buyers such as the institutional money managers, may have bought overvalued companies because they thought they could easily sell them later at even higher valuations to "dumb retail investors."

The companies themselves

The entrepreneurs who founded the internet consulting companies, and the management teams who ran them, could almost be described as bystanders to the process that took the stock prices of their companies to such lofty highs and then punishing lows. However, they were profoundly affected by these changes in almost every aspect of their businesses.

Obviously there were many benefits to having a high stock price. According to a managing director (MD) at one of the internet consultants, the company was facing a very competitive labor market while trying to grow organically, and having a stock that was doing well helped with recruiting people since the option part of the compensation package was attractive.[36] He also explained that people were proud to be a part of the firm, partly because the stock was doing so well.

As the stock price of the company continued to rise higher and higher, the MD admitted that he did become afraid that the market was overvaluing the company, and that this doubt probably went all the way up to the CEO. As he put it "we were trading at just absurd levels."

When asked about his thoughts on his firm's current stock price, the MD thought that the market had over-reacted and gone to the other extreme. He remarked that investors were worried that the internet consulting firms were facing renewed competition from companies like IBM, the Big Five accounting firms, and the strategy consulting firms. Overall, though the rise and fall of the company's stock price was in many ways a painful experience, this MD thought that the market bubble presented a good opportunity that the company was able to capitalize upon. It was able to do a secondary offering at a high price and now had lots of cash on its balance sheet. His view was that "If you look at competitive sustainability [in this business], it could boil down to the company with the best balance sheet wins."

The blame game

In the aftermath of the dot-com crash, many tried to pinpoint whose fault it was that the whole bubble occurred in the first place. As mentioned previously, sell-side analysts, often the most visible group in the investment community, came under frequent attack in the media, as did, to some extent, venture capitalists, investment bankers, and even the accounting industry. Company insiders (including the founder of Scient) were also scrutinized for selling large blocks of shares when the stock prices of their companies were near their peaks.[37]

A *Wall Street Journal* article entitled "Investors, Entrepreneurs All Play the Blame Game," described how these various players were trying to blame each other for what happened:

> *With the tech-heavy Nasdaq Composite Index dancing close to the 2,000 mark – down from over 5,000 – internet entrepreneurs and venture capitalists have stepped up their finger-pointing about just who's at fault for the technology meltdown, which continues to topple businesses and once-cushy lifestyles.... Fingers pointed right and left – from entrepreneurs to venture capitalists, from analysts to day traders to shareholders – and back around again.*[38]

---

[36]Source: casewriter interview.

[37]Mark Maremont, John Hechinger, "If Only You'd Sold Some Stock Earlier – Say $100 Million Worth," The *Wall Street Journal* (March 22, 2001).

[38]Rebecca Buckman, "Investors, Entrepreneurs All Play the Blame Game," *The Wall Street Journal* (March 5, 2001).

The internet stock market bubble was certainly not the first one to occur. Other notables include the Tulip Craze of the seventeenth century and the Nifty Fifty boom of the 1970s. In all cases market valuations went to unsustainably high levels and ended with a sharp decrease in valuation that left many investors empty-handed.

But the question of what happened in this latest bubble remained: who, if anyone, could be blamed for the dot-com rise and crash? How did the various intermediaries described here affect or cause what happened? Was there really a misalignment of incentives in the system? If so, could it be fixed so that this sort of thing did not happen in the future? Or were market bubbles an inevitable part of the way the economy functioned?

Questions

1   What is the intended role of each of the institutions and intermediaries discussed in the case for the effective functioning of capital markets?

2   Are their incentives aligned properly with their intended role? Whose incentives are most misaligned?

3   Who, if anyone, was primarily responsible for the internet stock bubble?

4   What are the costs of such a stock market bubble? As a future business professional, what lessons do you draw from the bubble?

The role of capital market intermediaries in the dot-com crash of 2000

EXHIBIT 1   **Timeline of the internet consultants – founding and IPO**

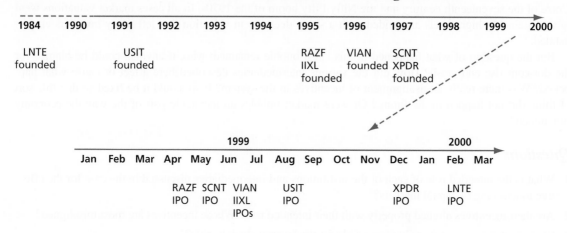

EXHIBIT 2   **Internet consultants – stock price highs and lows**

Company	IPO Price[a]	Peak Price	% Change IPO to Peak	Date of Peak	Price at End of Feb 2001	% Change from Peak
Scient	10	133.75	1,238%	10-Mar-00	2.94	−97.8%
Viant	8	63.56	695%	14-Dec-99	3.06	−95.2%
IXL Enterprises	12	58.75	390%	20-Jan-00	1.25	−97.9%
Lante	20	87.50	338%	29-Feb-00	1.81	−97.9%
Razorfish	8	56.94	612%	14-Feb-00	1.16	−98.0%
US Interactive	10	83.75	738%	4-Jan-00	0.56[b]	−99.3%
Xpedior	19	34.75	83%	10-Jan-00	0.69	−98.0%

[a]Split adjusted.

[b]Last trade on January 11, 2001. Filed for bankruptcy under Chapter 11 in January 2001.

Source: Bloomberg LP, The Center for Research in Security Prices (accessed via Wharton Research Database Services), Marketguide.com.

EXHIBIT 3   Intermediaries in the capital-raising process of the internet consultants

Company	Venture Capital Stage Investors	Investment Bank Underwriters	Auditors[a]	Analyst Coverage	Selected Institutional Holders	Venture Funding ($M)	IPO Amount Raised ($M)[b]	IPO Underwriting Fee ($M)	% Institutional Ownership[c]
Scient	Sequoia Capital, Benchmark Capital, Stanford Univ., Capital Research, Morgan Stanley Venture Partners, Amerindo Investment Advisors, Palantir Capital	Morgan Stanley Dean Witter, Hambrecht & Quist, Thomas Weisel Partners	PWC	Merrill Lynch, Morgan Stanley Dean Witter, CSFB, Lehman Brothers, UBS Warburg, SG Cowen, others	Capital Research, Putnam, Janus, Vanguard, Wellingon, State Street	31.2	60	4.2	34% (66% of float)
Viant	Kleiner Perkins Caufield & Byers, Mohr Davidow Ventures, Information Associates, Trident Capital, BancBoston Capital, General Motors, Technology Crossover Ventures	Goldman Sachs, Credit Suisse First Boston, WIT Capital Corporation	PWC	Goldman Sachs, Merrill Lynch, Lehman Brothers, CSFB, Wasserstein Perella, Bear Stearns, others	Fidelity, T Rowe Price, Putnam, Franklin, State Street, Vanguard, American Century, Goldman Sachs Asset Management	32.2	48	3.4	34% (67% of float)
IXL	Greylock Mgmt., Chase Capital Partners, Flatiron Partners, GE Capital, Kelso & Co., TTC Ventures, CB Capital, Portage Venture Partners, Transamerica Technology Finance	Merrill Lynch, BancBoston Robertson Stephens, DLJ, SG Cowen	PWC	Merrill Lynch, Robinson Humphrey, First Union Capital, others	Capital Research, State Street, Vanguard, Goldman Sachs Asset Management, GE Asset Management	91.0	72	5.0	29% (108% of float)
Lante	Frontenac Co., Dell Ventures, MSD Capital	Credit Suisse First Boston, Deutsche Bank Alex Brown, Thomas Weisel Partners	PWC	CSFB, Deutsche Bank, Thomas Weisel Partners, others	Fidelity, State Street, Vanguard, Goldman Sachs Asset Management	26.8	80	5.6	3% (21% of float)
Razorfish	N/A	Credit Suisse First Boston, BancBoston Robertson Stephens, BT Alex. Brown, Lehman Brothers	AA, PWC	CSFB, Lehman Brothers, SG Cowen, others	Janus, Capital Research, Fidelity, Vanguard, Goldman Sachs Asset Management	**N/A**	48	3.4	8% (14% of float)
US Interactive	Safeguard Scientific, Technology Leaders	Lehman Brothers, Hambrecht & Quist, Adams Harkness & Hill	KPMG	Lehman Brothers, Hambrecht & Quist, Deutsche Bank Alex Brown, others	T Rowe Price, Prudential, JP Morgan Investment Management, Credit Suisse Asset Mgmt.	**N/A**	46	2.0	4% (6% of float)
Xpedior	N/A	DLJ, First Union Securities, JP Morgan, The Robinson-Humphrey Group	E&Y	DLJ, First Union Securities, Robinson-Humphrey, others	Capital Research, T Rowe Price, Franklin, Vanguard, John Hancock	**N/A**	162	11.4	2% (10% of float)

[a]PWC stands for PriceWaterhouseCoopers; AA for Arthur Anderson; E&Y for Ernst & Young.

[b]Includes underwriting fee.

[c]As of April 2001.

Source: Compiled by casewriter.

The role of capital market intermediaries in the dot-com crash of 2000

EXHIBIT 4   **Market capitalization of major technology companies, January 2000**

Company	Market Capitalization ($ billions)[a]	Stock Price (January 3, 2000)
Microsoft	603	116.56
Intel	290	87.00
IBM	218	116.00
Dell Computer	131	50.88
Hewlett Packard	117	117.44
Compaq Computer	53	31.00
Apple Computer	18	111.94

[a]Based on share price close on January 3, 2000 and reported shares outstanding.

Sources: Bloomberg LP, The Center for Research in Security Prices (accessed via Wharton Research Database Services), Edgar Online.

EXHIBIT 5   **Market valuations given to loss-making dot-coms**

Company	Net Income ('99/'00)[a] ($ millions)	Market Capitalization ($ billions)[b]	Stock Price (January 3, 2000)
Amazon.com	−720	30.8	89.38
DoubleClick	−56	30.1	268.00
Akamai Technologies	−58	29.7	321.25
VerticalNet	−53	12.4	172.63
Priceline.com	−1,055	8.4	51.25
E*Trade	−57	7.1	28.06
EarthLink	−174	5.2	44.75
Drugstore.com	−116	1.6	37.13

[a]As of end of 1999 or early 2000, depending on fiscal year end.

[b]Based on share price close on January 3, 2000 and reported shares outstanding.

Sources: Bloomberg LP, The Center for Research in Security Prices (accessed via Wharton Research Database Services), Edgar Online.

EXHIBIT 6   **Scient – consolidated financial statements**

INCOME STATEMENT (in thousands except per-share amounts)

	November 7, 1997 (inception) through March 31, 1998	Year Ended March 31	
		1999	2000
Revenues	$179	$20,675	$155,729
Operating expenses:			
Professional services	102	10,028	70,207
Selling, general and administrative	1,228	15,315	90,854
Stock compensation	64	7,679	15,636
Total operating expenses	1,394	22,022	176,697
Loss from operations	(1,215)	(12,347)	(20,968)
Interest income and other, net	56	646	4,953
Net loss	$(1,159)	$(11,701)	$(16,015)
Net loss per share:			
Basic and diluted	$(0.10)	$(0.89)	$(0.29)
Weighted average shares	11,894	13,198	54,590

EXHIBIT 6   **Scient – consolidated financial statements** *(continued)*

BALANCE SHEET (in thousands except per-share amounts)

	March 31	
	1999	**2000**
ASSETS		
Current Assets:		
Cash and cash equivalents	$11,261	$108,102
Short-term investments	16,868	121,046
Accounts receivable, net	5,876	56,021
Prepaid expenses	811	4,929
Other	318	4,228
Total Current Assets	35,134	294,326
Long-term investments	—	3,146
Property and equipment, net	3,410	16,063
Other	268	219
	$38,812	$313,754
LIABILITIES AND STOCKHOLDERS' EQUITY		
Current Liabilities:		
Bank borrowings, current	$413	$1,334
Accounts payable	832	5,023
Accrued compensation and benefits	2,554	33,976
Accrued expenses	2,078	9,265
Deferred revenue	524	6,579
Capital lease obligations, current	625	2,624
Total Current Liabilities	7,026	58,801
Capital lease obligations, long-term	680	2,052
	8,835	61,718
Commitments and contingencies (Note 5)		
Stockholders' equity:		
Convertible preferred stock; issuable in series, $.0001 par value; 10,000 shares authorized; 9,012 and no shares issued and outstanding, respectively	1	—
Common stock: $.0001 par value; 125,000 shares authorized; 33,134 and 72,491 shares issues and outstanding, respectively	3	7
Additional paid-in capital	70,055	297,735
Accumulated other comprehensive loss	—	(47)
Unearned compensation	(27,222)	(16,784)
Accumulated deficit	(12,860)	(28,875)
Total Stockholders' Equity	29,977	252,036
	$38,812	$313,754

Sources: Scient Corporation 10-K; Edgar Online http://www.freedgar.com (May 11, 2001).

EXHIBIT 7 Analyst downgrades of the internet consultants

Company	Number of Analysts that Downgraded during August 30–September 8, 2000
Viant	13
Scient	7
IXL Enterprises	7
US Interactive	5
Xpedior	3
Lante	1
Razorfish	0

ANALYST DOWNGRADES OF SCIENT CORPORATION, AUGUST 30–SEPTEMBER 8, 2000

Institution	Previous Recommendation	New Recommendation	Date of Downgrade
Merrill Lynch	LT Buy	LT Accumulate	1-Sep-2000
Lehman Brothers	Buy	Outperform	1-Sep-2000
ING Barings	Buy	Hold	1-Sep-2000
SG Cowen	Buy	Neutral	1-Sep-2000
Legg Mason	Buy	Market Perform	1-Sep-2000
BB&T Capital Markets	Hold	Source of Funds	1-Sep-2000
First Union Securities	Strong Buy	Buy	31-Aug-2000

Source: I/B/E/S (accessed via Wharton Research Database Services).

EXHIBIT 8 Selected institutional holders of Scient Corporation, 1999–2000

Institution	Quarter Ended:						
	June 1999	September 1999	December 1999	March 2000	June 2000	September 2000	December 2000
Capital Research	—	—	—	265	1,079,911	586,442	586,706
Putnam Investments	5,000	—	625,900	2,209,200	4,800,800	5,749,200	—
Wellington Management	—	—	—	—	—	—	803,000
State Street	—	12,450	38,167	52,867	89,667	180,668	672,352
Janus	267,300	273,915	483,730	775,085	1,359,700	4,382,250	—

Source: Edgar (SEC).

The role of capital market intermediaries in the dot-com crash of 2000

EXHIBIT 9   **Dot-coms that filed for bankruptcy or closed operations**

(Selected List)

August 2000
Auctions.com
Hardware.com
Living.com
SaviShopper.com
GreatCoffee

September 2000
Clickmango.com
Pop.com
FreeScholarships.com
RedLadder.com
DomainAuction.com
Gazoontite.com
Surfing2Cash.com
Affinia.com

October 2000
FreeInternet.com
Chipshot.com
Stockpower.com
The Dental Store
More.com
WebHouse
UrbanFetch.com
Boxman.com
RedGorilla.com
Eve.com
MyLackey.com
BigWords.com

Mortgage.com
MotherNature.com
Ivendor
TeliSmart.com

November 2000
Pets.com
Caredata.com
Streamline.com
Garden.com
Furniture.com
TheMan.com
Ibelieve.com
eSociety
UrbanDesign.com
HalfthePlanet.com
Productopia.com
BeautyJungle.com
ICanBuy.com
Bike.com
Mambo.com
Babystripes.com
Thirsty.com
Checkout.com

December 2000
Quepasa.com
Finance.com
BizBuyer.com
Desktop.com
E-pods.com
Clickabid.com

HeavenlyDoor.com
ShoppingList.com
Babygear.com
HotOffice.com
Goldsauction.com
AntEye.com
EZBid
Admart
I-US.com
Riffage.com

January 2000
MusicMaker.com
Mercata
Send.com
CompanyLeader.com
Zap.com
Savvio.com
News Digital Media
TravelNow.com
Foodline.com
LetsBuyIt.com
e7th.cm
CountryCool.com
Ibetcha.com
Fibermarket.com
Dotcomix
New Digital Media
GreatEntertaining.com
AndysGarage.com
Lucy.com
US Interactive

Sources: Johnathan Weil, ''Going Concerns': Did Accountants Fail to Flag Problems at Dot-Com Casualties?'' *Wall Street Journal*, February 2001; Jim Battey, ''Dot-com details: The numbers behind the year's e-commerce shake-out,'' *Infoworld*, March 2001.

EXHIBIT 10   **Capital flows from investors to companies**

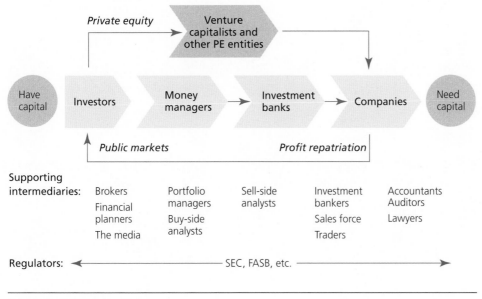

Supporting intermediaries:

Brokers	Portfolio	Sell-side	Investment	Accountants
Financial	managers	analysts	bankers	Auditors
planners	Buy-side		Sales force	Lawyers
The media	analysts		Traders	

Regulators: ⟵——————————— SEC, FASB, etc. ———————————⟶

Source: Created by casewriter.

The role of capital market intermediaries in the dot-com crash of 2000

BUSINESS ANALYSIS AND VALUATION TOOLS

Strategy Analysis

S trategy analysis is an important starting point for the analysis of financial statements. Strategy analysis allows the analyst to probe the economics of a firm at a qualitative level so that the subsequent accounting and financial analysis is grounded in business reality. Strategy analysis also allows the identification of the firm's profit drivers and key risks. This in turn enables the analyst to assess the sustainability of the firm's current performance and make realistic forecasts of future performance.

A firm's value is determined by its ability to earn a return on its capital in excess of the cost of capital. What determines whether or not a firm is able to accomplish this goal? While a firm's cost of capital is determined by the capital markets, its profit potential is determined by its own strategic choices:

1 The choice of an industry or a set of industries in which the firm operates (industry choice).

2 The manner in which the firm intends to compete with other firms in its chosen industry or industries (competitive strategy).

3 The way in which the firm expects to create and exploit synergies across the range of businesses in which it operates (corporate strategy).

Strategy analysis, therefore, involves **industry analysis**, **competitive strategy analysis**, and **corporate strategy analysis**.[1] In this chapter, we will briefly discuss these three steps and use the European airline industry, IKEA and the easyGroup, respectively, to illustrate the application of the steps.

INDUSTRY ANALYSIS

In analyzing a firm's profit potential, an analyst has to first assess the profit potential of each of the industries in which the firm is competing because the profitability of various industries differs systematically and predictably over time. For example, the median ratio of earnings before interest and taxes to the book value of assets for European listed companies between 1993 and 2011 was 5.5 percent. However, the average returns varied widely across specific industries: for the household furniture industry, the profitability ratio was five percentage points greater than the population average, and for the gold and silver ore mining industry it was 16 percentage points less than the population average.[2] What causes these profitability differences?

There is a vast body of research in industrial organization on the influence of industry structure on profitability.[3] Relying on this research, strategy literature suggests that the average profitability of an industry is influenced by the "five forces" shown in Figure 2.1.[4] According to this framework, the intensity of competition determines the potential for creating abnormal profits by the firms in an industry. Whether or not the potential profits are kept by the industry is determined by the relative **bargaining power** of the firms in the industry and their customers and suppliers. We will discuss each of these industry profit drivers in more detail below.

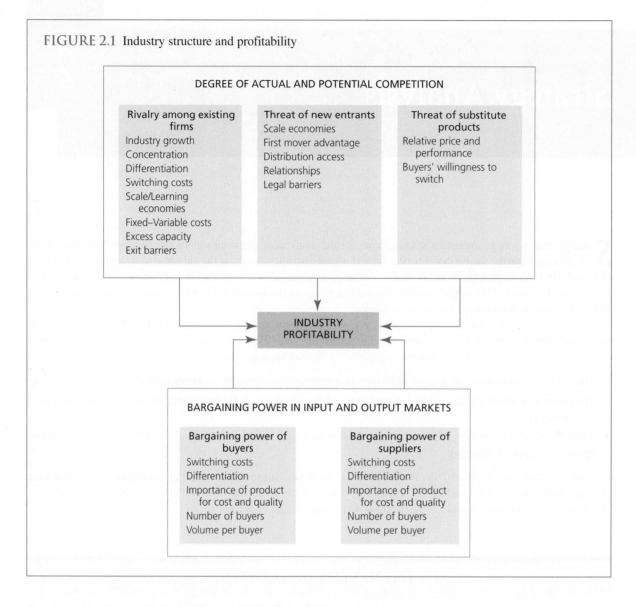

FIGURE 2.1 Industry structure and profitability

Degree of actual and potential competition

At the most basic level, the profits in an industry are a function of the maximum price that customers are willing to pay for the industry's product or service. One of the key determinants of the price is the degree to which there is competition among suppliers of the same or similar products (**industry competition**). At one extreme, if there is a state of perfect competition in the industry, micro-economic theory predicts that prices will be equal to marginal cost, and there will be few opportunities to earn supernormal profits. At the other extreme, if the industry is dominated by a single firm, there will be potential to earn monopoly profits. In reality, the degree of competition in most industries is somewhere in between perfect competition and monopoly.

There are three potential sources of competition in an industry:

1 Rivalry between existing firms.

2 Threat of entry of new firms.

3 Threat of substitute products or services.

We will discuss each of these **competitive forces** in the following paragraphs.

Competitive force 1: Rivalry among existing firms

In most industries the average level of profitability is primarily influenced by the nature of rivalry among existing firms in the industry. In some industries firms compete aggressively, pushing prices close to (and sometimes below) the marginal cost. In other industries firms do not compete aggressively on price. Instead, they find ways to coordinate their pricing, or compete on nonprice dimensions such as innovation, service, or brand image. Several factors determine the intensity of competition between existing players in an industry:

Industry growth rate If an industry is growing very rapidly, incumbent firms need not grab market share from each other to grow. In contrast, in stagnant industries the only way existing firms can grow is by taking share away from the other players. In this situation one can expect intense rivalry among firms in the industry.

Concentration and balance of competitors The number of firms in an industry and their relative sizes determine the degree of concentration in an industry.[5] The degree of concentration influences the extent to which firms in an industry can coordinate their pricing and other competitive moves. For example, if there is one dominant firm in an industry (such as Google in the search engine market in early 2010), it can set and enforce the rules of competition. Similarly, if there are only two or three equal-sized players (such as Procter & Gamble, Unilever, and Henkel in the laundry-detergent industry), they can implicitly cooperate with each other to avoid destructive price competition. If an industry is fragmented, competition is likely to be severe.

Excess capacity and exit barriers If capacity in an industry is larger than customer demand, there is a strong incentive for firms to cut prices to fill capacity. The problem of excess capacity is likely to be exacerbated if there are significant barriers for firms to exit the industry. Exit barriers are high when the assets are specialized or if there are regulations that make exit costly. The competitive dynamics of the steel industry demonstrate these forces at play.

Degree of differentiation and switching costs The extent to which firms in an industry can avoid head-on competition depends on the extent to which they can differentiate their products and services. If the products in an industry are very similar, customers are ready to switch from one competitor to another purely on the basis of price. Switching costs also determine customers' propensity to move from one product to another. When switching costs are low, there is a greater incentive for firms in an industry to engage in price competition. The PC industry, where the standardization of the software and microprocessor has led to relatively low switching costs, is extremely price competitive.

Scale/learning economies and the ratio of fixed to variable costs If there is a steep learning curve or there are other types of scale economies in an industry, size becomes an important factor for firms in the industry. In such situations, there are incentives to engage in aggressive competition for market share. Similarly, if the ratio of fixed to variable costs is high, firms have an incentive to reduce prices to utilize installed capacity. The airline industry, where price wars are quite common, is an example of this type of situation.

As indicated, companies can compete on various dimensions, including price and quality. Price competition is likely if customers' switching costs are low, if companies' fixed costs are significant or if products are subject to decay. Industry profitability comes under pressure especially when companies compete on the same dimension, and even more so when they compete on price. Through competing on different dimensions and targeting different customer groups, companies may succeed to segment the market and preserve industry profitability.

The relationship between rivalry factors and industry profitability is not perfect for various reasons. One reason is that some of the rivalry factors counterbalance each other. For example, in the European laundry-detergent industry the concentration of competitors is relatively high, as Procter & Gamble, Unilever, and Henkel share most of the European market. There is, however, intense rivalry among these companies because the market exhibits little to no growth. Another reason is the influence of the other competitive forces, such as the threat of new entrants or substitute products, which we will discuss below.

Competitive force 2: Threat of new entrants

The potential for earning abnormal profits will attract new entrants to an industry. The very threat of new firms entering an industry potentially forces incumbent firms to make additional investments in, for example, advertising or to keep prices low. Therefore the ease with which new firms can enter an industry is a key determinant of its profitability. Several factors determine the height of barriers to entry in an industry:

Scale When there are large economies of scale, new entrants face the choice of having either to invest in a large capacity which might not be utilized right away or to enter with less than the optimum capacity. Either way, new entrants will at least initially suffer from a cost disadvantage in competing with existing firms. Economies of scale might arise from large investments in research and development (the pharmaceutical or jet engine industries), in brand advertising (sportswear industry), or in physical plant and equipment (telecommunications industry). The scale of a firm may not only affect the cost per unit sold, it may also affect customers' demand for a product or service. Scale affects demand, for example, if the usefulness of a product or service increases with the number of users (Internet communication software such as Skype or MSN) or if the perceived reliability or reputation of a company increases with size and is valued by customers (insurance industry).

First mover advantage Early entrants in an industry may deter future entrants if there are first mover advantages. For example, first movers might be able to set industry standards, or enter into exclusive arrangements with suppliers of cheap raw materials. They may also acquire scarce government licenses to operate in regulated industries. Finally, if there are learning economies, early firms will have an absolute cost advantage over new entrants. First mover advantages are also likely to be large when there are significant switching costs for customers once they start using existing products. For example, switching costs faced by the users of Microsoft's Windows operating system make it difficult for software companies to market a new operating system.

Access to channels of distribution and relationships Limited capacity in the existing distribution channels and high costs of developing new channels can act as powerful barriers to entry. For example, a new entrant into the auto industry is likely to face formidable barriers because of the difficulty of developing a dealer network. Similarly, new consumer goods manufacturers find it difficult to obtain supermarket shelf space for their products. Existing relationships between firms and customers in an industry also make it difficult for new firms to enter an industry. Industry examples of this include auditing, investment banking, and advertising.

Legal barriers There are many industries in which legal barriers such as patents and copyrights in research-intensive industries limit entry. Similarly, licensing regulations limit entry into taxi services, medical services, broadcasting, and telecommunications industries.

Competitive force 3: Threat of substitute products

The third dimension of competition in an industry is the threat of substitute products or services. Relevant substitutes are not necessarily those that have the same form as the existing products but those that perform the same function. For example, airlines and high-speed rail systems might be substitutes for each other when it comes to travel over short distances. Similarly, plastic bottles and metal cans substitute for each other as packaging in the beverage industry. In some cases, threat of substitution comes not from customers' switching to another product but from utilizing technologies that allow them to do without, or use less of, the existing products. For example, energy-conserving technologies allow customers to reduce their consumption of electricity and fossil fuels. Similarly, e-mail allows customers to make less use of postal mail.

The threat of substitutes depends on the relative price and performance of the competing products or services and on customers' willingness to substitute. Customers' perception of whether two products are substitutes depends to some extent on whether they perform the same function for a similar price. If two products perform an identical function, then it would be difficult for them to differ from each other in price. However, customers' willingness to switch is often the critical factor in making this competitive dynamic work. For example, even when tap water and bottled water serve the same function, many customers may be unwilling to substitute the former for the latter, enabling bottlers to charge a price premium. Similarly, designer label clothing commands a price premium even if it is not superior in terms of basic functionality because customers place a value on the image offered by designer labels.

Bargaining power in input and output markets

While the degree of competition in an industry determines whether there is potential to earn abnormal profits, the *actual profits* are influenced by the industry's bargaining power with its suppliers and customers. On the input side, firms enter into transactions with suppliers of labor, raw materials and components, and finances. On the output side, firms either sell directly to the final customers or enter into contracts with intermediaries in the distribution chain. In all these transactions, the relative economic power of the two sides is important to the overall profitability of the industry firms.

Competitive force 4: Bargaining power of buyers

Two factors determine the power of buyers: price sensitivity and relative bargaining power. Price sensitivity determines the extent to which buyers care to bargain on price; relative bargaining power determines the extent to which they will succeed in forcing the price down.[6]

Price sensitivity Buyers are more price sensitive when the product is undifferentiated and there are few switching costs. The sensitivity of buyers to price also depends on the importance of the product to their own cost structure. When the product represents a large fraction of the buyers' cost (for example, the packaging material for soft-drink producers), the buyer is likely to expend the resources necessary to shop for a lower-cost alternative. In contrast, if the product is a small fraction of the buyers' cost (for example, windshield wipers for automobile manufacturers), it may not pay to expend resources to search for lower-cost alternatives. Further, the importance of the product to the buyers' own product quality also determines whether or not price becomes the most important determinant of the buying decision.

Relative bargaining power Even if buyers are price sensitive, they may not be able to achieve low prices unless they have a strong bargaining position. Relative bargaining power in a transaction depends, ultimately, on the cost to each party of not doing business with the other party. The buyers' bargaining power is determined by the number of buyers relative to the number of suppliers, volume of purchases by a single buyer, number of alternative products available to the buyer, buyers' costs of switching from one product to another, and the threat of backward integration by the buyers. For example, in the automobile industry, car manufacturers have considerable power over component manufacturers because auto companies are large buyers with several alternative suppliers to choose from, and switching costs are relatively low. In contrast, in the personal computer industry, computer makers have low bargaining power relative to the operating system software producers because of high switching costs.

Competitive force 5: Bargaining power of suppliers

The analysis of the relative power of suppliers is a mirror image of the analysis of the buyers' power in an industry. Suppliers are powerful when there are only a few companies and few substitutes available to their customers. For example, in the soft-drink industry, Coke and Pepsi are very powerful relative to the bottlers. In contrast, metal can suppliers to the soft-drink industry are not very powerful because of intense competition among can producers and the threat of substitution of cans by plastic bottles. Suppliers also have a lot of power over buyers when the suppliers' product or service is critical to buyers' business. For example, airline pilots have a strong bargaining power in the airline industry. Suppliers also tend to be powerful when they pose a credible threat of forward integration. For example, insurance companies are powerful relative to insurance intermediaries because of their own presence in the insurance-selling business.

APPLYING INDUSTRY ANALYSIS: THE EUROPEAN AIRLINE INDUSTRY

Let us consider the above concepts of industry analysis in the context of the European airline industry. In the early 1980s, the European airline industry was highly regulated. Bilateral agreements between European governments severely restricted competition by determining which airlines could operate which routes at what fares. During the ten years from 1987 to 1997, the European Union (EU) gradually liberalized the industry, and reduced government intervention. The industry exhibited steady growth. While the four largest European airlines carried 54 million passengers in 1980, the same airlines carried 147 million passengers in 2000.[7] Despite the steady growth in passenger traffic, however, many of the large European airlines, such as British Airways, KLM, Lufthansa, and SAS, reported volatile performance during the 2000s and on occasion were forced to undergo internal restructuring. Other national carriers, such as Sabena, Swissair, and Alitalia, went bankrupt. What accounted for this low profitability? What was the effect of liberalization on competition? What was the European airline industry's future profit potential?

Competition in the European airline industry

The competition was very intense for a number of reasons:

- Rivalry – industry growth. Between 2000 and 2010, the average annual industry growth was a moderate 2 percent. The industry growth was negative in the years immediately following the September 11 2001 terrorist attacks (−5 percent) and the start of the credit crisis (−8 percent), compared with an average of 5 percent in the other years.[8]

- Rivalry – concentration. The industry was fragmented. While several new airlines had entered the industry after the liberalization period, very few of the inefficient and loss-making national carriers left the industry. Several of these airlines were kept from bankruptcy or being taken over through government intervention or support. Further, in its attempt to promote competition on all routes, the European Union competition authority created regulatory hurdles that made mergers more complicated or economically less attractive.

- Rivalry – differentiation and switching costs. Services delivered by different airlines on short-haul flights, within Europe, were virtually identical, and, with the possible exception of frequent flyer programs, there were few opportunities to differentiate the products. Switching costs across different airlines were also low because in some areas airports were geographically close and code-sharing agreements increased the number of alternatives that passengers could consider.

- Rivalry – excess capacity. The European airlines had a structural excess capacity problem. Between 2000 and 2010, the average annual passenger load factor, which measures the percentage of passenger seats filled, was 75 percent. Because airlines lacked the opportunity to differentiate, they engaged in price competition in an attempt to fill the empty seats.

- Threat of new entrants – access to distribution channels/legal barriers. The system that most of the large European airports used to allocate their time slots among the airlines could have created barriers to entry. Slots are the rights to land at, or take off from, an airport at a particular date and time. In the twice-yearly allocation of time slots, priority was given to airlines that had slots in the previous season. After 1993, however, EU regulation promoted the entry of new airlines to the European market by requiring that at least 50 percent of the slots that became available were allocated to new entrants. New airlines also successfully managed to enter the European market by using alternative, smaller airports in the vicinity of those used by the established airlines. Most of these new entrants focused on offering low-fare, no-frills flights. Early new entrants were low-cost carriers easyJet and Ryanair, which experienced explosive growth and forced the incumbent airlines to start competing on price. In fact, the total number of passengers that easyJet and Ryanair carried increased from about 18.2 million passengers in 2001 to 120.9 million passengers in 2010.

- Threat of new entrants. New entrants had easy access to capital. Purchased aircraft served to securitize loans, or aircraft could be leased. Further, second-hand aircraft became cheap during industry downturns, when troubled airlines disposed of excess capacity.

- Threat of new entrants – legal barriers. After 1997, European airlines faced no legal barriers to enter European markets outside their domestic market. Measures taken by the EU to deregulate the industry made it possible for the airlines to freely operate on any route within the EU, instead of having to conform to bilateral agreements between countries.

- Threat of substitute products. High-speed rail networks were being expanded and provided a potential, not yet fully exploited, substitute for air travel over shorter distances.

The power of suppliers and buyers

Suppliers and buyers had significant power over firms in the industry for these reasons:

- Suppliers' bargaining power. Airlines' primary costs for operating passenger flights were airport fees and handling charges, aircraft depreciation and maintenance, fuel, and labor. Although competition among jet fuel suppliers helped to ensure that the fuel prices that suppliers charged to the airlines did not deviate much from market prices, the fluctuations in fuel market prices were beyond airlines' control. Further, during the 1990s, ground handling agents at several European airports were monopolist and charged higher handling fees than agents at airports with competition. Liberalization measures taken by the EU promoted competition among ground handling agents, but in the early 2000s, still very few airports had more than two competing agents. Finally, European airline employees had significant power over their employers since their job security tended to be well-protected and the threat of a strike was an efficient bargaining tool in labor negotiations.

Ninety percent of the aircraft that European airlines had acquired or leased came from two commercial aircraft manufacturers, Airbus and Boeing. The strong dependence of European airlines on only two aircraft suppliers potentially impaired airlines' bargaining power. However, because the overall demand for new aircraft was low, airlines remained relatively powerful in their negotiations with aircraft manufacturers.

- Buyers' bargaining power. Buyers gained more power because of the development of Web booking systems, which made market prices transparent. Buyers were price sensitive since they increasingly viewed air travel as a commodity. Being able to easily compare prices across different airlines substantially increased their bargaining power.

As a result of the intense rivalry and low barriers to entry in the European airline industry, there was severe price competition among different airlines. Further, government interference kept the national carriers from entering into mergers. Instead, they created alliances that did not sufficiently reduce or reallocate capacity. These factors led to a low profit potential in the industry. The power of suppliers and buyers reduced the profit potential further.

There were some indications of change in the basic structure of the European airline industry. First, most of the established airlines cut capacity in 2002, which led to a 3 percentage point improvement in the passenger load factor. The average load factor continued to increase from 73.7 percent in 2002 to 77.9 percent in 2010. Second, in 2003, the merger between two established airlines, Air France and KLM, was one of the first signs of consolidation in the industry. Consolidation progressed slowly when Lufthansa acquired Austrian Airlines, BMI (in 2009), and Brussels Airlines (in 2011) and British Airways and Iberia merged in 2010. Third, the EU was mandated to negotiate an "open skies" agreement with the US, which should substitute for all the bilateral agreements between European governments and the US, and open up a new market for European airlines. As a result, the profit potential of the European airline industry may gradually improve.

Limitations of industry analysis

A potential limitation of the industry analysis framework discussed in this chapter is the assumption that industries have clear boundaries. In reality, it is often not easy to clearly demarcate industry boundaries. For example, in analyzing the European airline industry, should one focus on the short-haul flight segment or the airline industry as a whole? Should one include charter flights and cargo transport in the industry definition? Should one consider only the airlines domiciled in Europe or also the airlines from other continents that operate flights to Europe? Inappropriate industry definition will result in incomplete analysis and inaccurate forecasts.

COMPETITIVE STRATEGY ANALYSIS

The profitability of a firm is influenced not only by its industry structure but also by the strategic choices it makes to cope with or change the industry's competitive forces. A firm may take strategic actions that aim at changing the industry's structure and profit potential. Examples of such actions are the mergers and acquisitions taking place in the European airline industry, which could ultimately reduce the industry's fragmentation and increase average profitability. Alternatively, a firm may take the industry structure as given and choose a set of activities that help it to carve out a profitable position within the industry. While there are many ways to characterize a firm's business strategy, as Figure 2.2 shows, there are two generic competitive strategies: (1) **cost leadership** and (2) **differentiation.**[9] Both these strategies can potentially allow a firm to build a sustainable competitive advantage. Strategy researchers have traditionally viewed cost leadership and differentiation as mutually exclusive strategies. Firms that straddle the two strategies are considered to be "stuck in the middle" and are expected to earn low

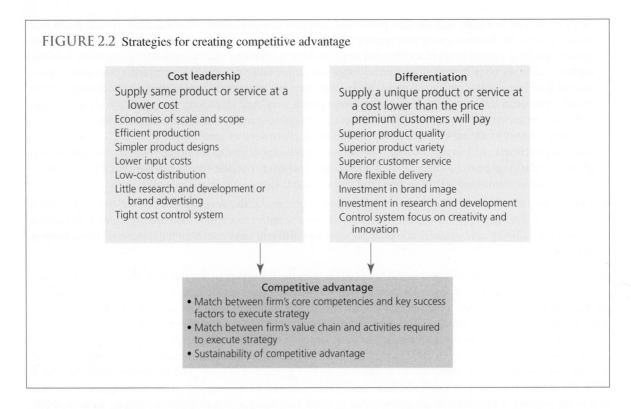

FIGURE 2.2 Strategies for creating competitive advantage

Cost leadership
Supply same product or service at a lower cost
Economies of scale and scope
Efficient production
Simpler product designs
Lower input costs
Low-cost distribution
Little research and development or brand advertising
Tight cost control system

Differentiation
Supply a unique product or service at a cost lower than the price premium customers will pay
Superior product quality
Superior product variety
Superior customer service
More flexible delivery
Investment in brand image
Investment in research and development
Control system focus on creativity and innovation

Competitive advantage
• Match between firm's core competencies and key success factors to execute strategy
• Match between firm's value chain and activities required to execute strategy
• Sustainability of competitive advantage

profitability.[10] These firms run the risk of not being able to attract price conscious customers because their costs are too high; they are also unable to provide adequate differentiation to attract premium price customers.

Sources of competitive advantage

Cost leadership enables a firm to supply the same product or service offered by its competitors at a lower cost. Differentiation strategy involves providing a product or service that is distinct in some important respect valued by the customer. As an example in food retailing, UK-based Sainsbury's competes on the basis of differentiation by emphasizing the high quality of its food and service, and by operating an online grocery store. In contrast, Germany-based Aldi and Lidl are discount retailers competing purely on a low-cost basis.

Competitive strategy 1: Cost leadership

Cost leadership is often the clearest way to achieve competitive advantage. In industries or industry segments where the basic product or service is a commodity, cost leadership might be the only way to achieve superior performance. There are many ways to achieve cost leadership, including economies of scale and scope, economies of learning, efficient production, simpler product design, lower input costs, and efficient organizational processes. If a firm can achieve cost leadership, then it will be able to earn above-average profitability by merely charging the same price as its rivals. Conversely, a cost leader can force its competitors to cut prices and accept lower returns, or to exit the industry. For example, the entry of low-cost carriers to the European airline industry at the end of the 1990s forced the incumbent airlines to change their strategy and focus more on competing through price.

Firms that achieve cost leadership focus on tight cost controls. They make investments in efficient scale plants, focus on product designs that reduce manufacturing costs, minimize overhead costs, make little investment in risky research and development, and avoid serving marginal customers. They have organizational structures and control systems that focus on cost control.

Competitive strategy 2: Differentiation

A firm following the differentiation strategy seeks to be unique in its industry along some dimension that is highly valued by customers. For differentiation to be successful, the firm has to accomplish three things. First, it needs to identify one or more attributes of a product or service that customers value. Second, it has to position itself to meet the chosen customer need in a unique manner. Finally, the firm has to achieve differentiation at a cost that is lower than the price the customer is willing to pay for the differentiated product or service.

Drivers of differentiation include providing superior intrinsic value via product quality, product variety, bundled services, or delivery timing. Differentiation can also be achieved by investing in signals of value such as brand image, product appearance, or reputation. Differentiated strategies require investments in research and development, engineering skills, and marketing capabilities. The organizational structures and control systems in firms with differentiation strategies need to foster creativity and innovation.

While successful firms choose between cost leadership and differentiation, they cannot completely ignore the dimension on which they are not primarily competing. Firms that target differentiation still need to focus on costs so that the differentiation can be achieved at an acceptable cost. Similarly, cost leaders cannot compete unless they achieve at least a minimum level on key dimensions on which competitors might differentiate, such as quality and service.

Achieving and sustaining competitive advantage

The choice of competitive strategy does not automatically lead to the achievement of competitive advantage. To achieve competitive advantage, the firm has to have the capabilities needed to implement and sustain the chosen strategy. Both cost leadership and differentiation strategy require that the firm makes the necessary commitments to acquire the core competencies needed, and structures its value chain in an appropriate way. Core competencies are the economic assets that the firm possesses, whereas the value chain is the set of activities that the firm performs to convert inputs into outputs. The uniqueness of a firm's core competencies and its value chain determine the sustainability of a firm's competitive advantage.[11] What makes a competitive strategy unique and thus successful in achieving a sustainable competitive advantage?[12]

- Unique core competencies. Important is that the resources supporting the core competencies cannot easily be acquired by competitors or substituted for by other resources. This tends to be the case if resources are, for example, physically unique (such as location or pharmaceutical patents), path dependent and the result of a long history of development (such as Microsoft's Windows operating system), or difficult to identify or comprehend for outsiders (what exactly determines Apple's success?).

- System of activities. Another important characteristic of a sustainable competitive strategy is that it comprises a *system* of activities that fit with the strategy and potentially reinforce each other. A coherent system of activities is difficult for competitors to imitate, especially when such activities require a trade-off. For example, when low-cost carriers like Ryanair and easyJet entered the European airline industry, traditional carriers initially responded by lowering service levels (and prices) on short-haul routes. The incumbent airlines would, however, not be able to effectively compete on price without trading off on, for example, the scope of flight networks, the diversity of ticket sales channels, and the quality of service levels in business class, thereby potentially alienating their traditional customer base. This focus on systems of activities distinguishes the concept of competitive strategy from operational effectiveness. Single tools that companies use to achieve operational effectiveness, such as incentive or inventory management systems, can be easily adopted by competitors and thus rarely help to create a sustainable competitive advantage.

- Positioning. To achieve a sustainable competitive advantage – or escape competition – firms often identify or carve out a profitable subsegment of an industry. The identification of such subsegments could be based on (1) particular product or service varieties (e.g., Porsche's focus on selling sports cars), (2) the needs of a particular customer group (e.g., Lenovo's focus on high-end business users), or (3) particular access and distribution channels (e.g., online sales versus physical stores).

To evaluate whether a firm is likely to achieve its intended competitive advantage, the analyst should ask the following questions:

- What are the key success factors and risks associated with the firm's chosen competitive strategy?
- Does the firm currently have the resources and capabilities (core competencies) to deal with the key success factors and risks?
- Has the firm made irreversible commitments to bridge the gap between its current capabilities and the requirements to achieve its competitive advantage?

- Has the firm structured its activities (such as research and development, design, manufacturing, marketing and distribution, and support activities) in a way that is consistent with its competitive strategy? Do these activities reinforce each other in some way?

- Has the company been able to identify or carve out a profitable subsegment of the industry?

- Is the company's competitive advantage sustainable? Are there any barriers that make imitation of the firm's strategy difficult?

- Are there any potential changes in the firm's industry structure (such as new technologies, foreign competition, changes in regulation, changes in customer requirements) that might dissipate the firm's competitive advantage? Is the company flexible enough to address these changes? Is the firm or its competitors taking any strategic actions that aim at changing the industry structure?

Applying competitive strategy analysis

Let us consider the concepts of competitive strategy analysis in the context of IKEA. In 2011, Sweden-based IKEA was the world's largest furniture retailer. The company, founded by Ingvar Kamprad as a mail-order company, bought its first furniture factory and showroom in 1953. During the 1960s, IKEA started to develop the operating concept that the company is still renowned for: selling flat-packed furniture through large warehouse stores. In those years, IKEA also started to expand internationally.

While continuously expanding its worldwide store base, IKEA firmly established itself in the furniture retailing industry by following a low-cost strategy. IKEA's average annual growth rate during the ten years between 2000 and 2011 was approximately 9 percent. During fiscal year 2010, IKEA generated a net profit margin of 11.6 percent on €23.1 billion in revenues. This margin was well above those of some of IKEA's larger competitors, such as US-based Target (4–5 percent). IKEA was one of the most successful and, presumably, one of the most profitable furniture retailers in the industry. How did IKEA achieve such performance?

IKEA's superior performance was based on a low-cost competitive strategy that consisted of the following key elements:[13]

- Global strategy. IKEA followed a purely global strategy. In each of the 41 countries where the retailer operated its stores, it targeted the same customer group – young families and young couples – and offered virtually the same selection of furniture. This strategy of strong economic integration and low responsiveness to national cultures helped the company to achieve economies of scale.

- Sourcing of production. IKEA did not own any production facilities other than Swedwood, which supplied 10 percent of its furniture. Instead, the company outsourced its production to manufacturers located throughout the world. Because IKEA had developed a network of 1,074 suppliers in 55 countries, the company could choose among a large number of manufacturers. Often, the company was a manufacturer's sole customer. Consequently, IKEA had substantial bargaining power in its dealings with its suppliers, which kept input costs to a minimum.

- Economic designs. Although IKEA outsourced its production, the company kept tight control of the design of its furniture. Its designers worked two to three years ahead of production to have sufficient time to find the most economic design solutions and review potential suppliers.

- Logistics. IKEA incorporated logistics into its strategy. The company operated large warehouse stores on relatively cheap locations outside the city centers. These warehouse stores sold furniture in flat-pack format that customers assembled at home. The integration of stores and warehouses and the use of flat-packs helped IKEA to economize on costs for storage and transportation.

- Sales. IKEA stores were able to employ a lower amount of sales staff than other stores because customers needed little assistance. All warehouse stores were designed such that customers, after having made their choice, picked the flat-packs from the shelves and paid for their purchases at a central location in the store. IKEA also provided its customers with limited after-sales service. Through this strategy, the company was able to keep personnel expenses to a minimum.

As a result of the above strategy, IKEA achieved a significant cost advantage over its competitors in the furniture retailing industry. Consequently, IKEA was able to continuously cut prices and maintain the price difference with its competitors. Because, over the years, the company had made large investments in knowledge of low-cost furniture design, store design, and logistics, the business model was difficult to replicate, making its competitive advantage sustainable. Although IKEA's brand image varied greatly across countries, in some countries it had become a cult brand. In 2011, Interbrand Corp. estimated the value of the IKEA brand at €11.9 billion. This value was similar to the value of brands such as Budweiser, Nescafé, and Sony. The strength of the retailer's brand name, the diversity in its assortment, and the distinctiveness of its designs illustrate that IKEA's strategy also exhibited some characteristics of a differentiation strategy.[14] However, the company's continuous focus on cost control was most likely the main driver of success. IKEA's success inspired some local competitors to attempt to replicate parts of its strategy. However no competitor to date has been able to replicate the business model on a similar scale.

CORPORATE STRATEGY ANALYSIS

So far in this chapter we have focused on the strategies at the individual business level. While some companies focus on only one business, many companies operate in multiple businesses. For example, of all companies that were listed on the seven largest European exchanges at the end of 2008, 46 percent operated in more than two business segments.[15] In the 1990s and 2000s, there has been an attempt by US and western European companies to reduce the diversity of their operations and focus on a relatively few "core" businesses. However, multi-business organizations continue to dominate the economic activity in many countries in the world.

When analyzing a multi-business organization, an analyst has to not only evaluate the industries and strategies of the individual business units but also the economic consequences – either positive or negative – of managing all the different businesses under one corporate umbrella. For example, General Electric has been very successful in creating significant value by managing a highly diversified set of businesses ranging from aircraft engines to light bulbs. In contrast, during the first half of the 2000s, shareholders of several German conglomerates, such as MAN and Siemens, pressured their companies to improve profitability by spinning off their "noncore" divisions.

Sources of value creation at the corporate level

Economists and strategy researchers have identified several factors that influence an organization's ability to create value through a broad corporate scope. Economic theory suggests that the optimal activity scope of a firm depends on the relative transaction cost of performing a set of activities inside the firm versus using the market mechanism.[16] Transaction cost economics implies that the multiproduct firm is an efficient choice of organizational form when coordination among independent, focused firms is costly due to market transaction costs.

Transaction costs can arise out of several sources. They may arise if the production process involves specialized assets such as human capital skills, proprietary technology, or other organizational know-how that is not easily available in the marketplace. Transaction costs also may arise from market imperfections such as information and incentive problems. If buyers and sellers cannot solve these problems through standard mechanisms such as enforceable contracts, it will be costly to conduct transactions through market mechanisms.

For example, as discussed in Chapter 1, public capital markets may not work well when there are significant information and incentive problems, making it difficult for entrepreneurs to raise capital from investors. Similarly, if buyers cannot ascertain the quality of products being sold because of lack of information, or cannot enforce warranties because of poor legal infrastructure, entrepreneurs will find it difficult to break into new markets. Finally, if employers cannot assess the quality of applicants for new positions, they will have to rely more on internal promotions rather than external recruiting to fill higher positions in an organization. Emerging economies often suffer from these types of transaction costs because of poorly developed intermediation infrastructure.[17] Even in many advanced economies, examples of high transaction costs can be found. For example, in many countries other than the US and western European nations, the venture capital industry is not highly developed, making it costly for new businesses in high technology industries to attract financing. Even in Europe and the US, transaction costs may vary across economic sectors. For example, until recently electronic commerce was hampered by consumer concerns regarding the security of credit card information sent over the Internet.

Transactions inside an organization may be less costly than market-based transactions for several reasons:

■ Information. Communication costs inside an organization are reduced because confidentiality can be protected and credibility can be assured through internal mechanisms.

- Enforcement. The headquarters office can play a critical role in reducing costs of enforcing agreements between organizational subunits.
- Asset sharing. Organizational subunits can share valuable nontradable assets (such as organizational skills, systems, and processes) or non-divisible assets (such as brand names, distribution channels, and reputation).

There are also forces that increase transaction costs inside organizations. Top management of an organization may lack the specialized information and skills necessary to manage businesses across several different industries. This lack of expertise reduces the possibility of actually realizing economies of scope, even when there is potential for such economies. This problem can be remedied by creating a decentralized organization, hiring specialist managers to run each business unit, and providing these managers with proper incentives. However, decentralization will also potentially decrease goal congruence among subunit managers, making it difficult to realize economies of scope.

Whether or not a multi-business organization creates more value than a comparable collection of focused firms is, therefore, context dependent.[18] Analysts should ask the following questions to assess whether an organization's corporate strategy has the potential to create value:

- Are there significant imperfections in the product, labor, or financial markets in the industries (or countries) in which a company is operating? Is it likely that transaction costs in these markets are higher than the costs of similar activities inside a well-managed organization?
- Does the organization have special resources such as brand names, proprietary know-how, access to scarce distribution channels, and special organizational processes that have the potential to create economies of scope?
- Is there a good fit between the company's specialized resources and the portfolio of businesses in which the company is operating?
- Does the company allocate decision rights between the headquarters office and the business units optimally to realize all the potential economies of scope?
- Does the company have internal measurement, information, and incentive systems to reduce agency costs and increase coordination across business units?

Empirical evidence suggests that creating value through a multi-business corporate strategy is hard in practice. Several researchers have documented that diversified companies trade at a discount in the stock market relative to a comparable portfolio of focused companies.[19] Studies also show that acquisitions of one company by another, especially when the two are in unrelated businesses, often fail to create value for the acquiring companies.[20] Finally, there is considerable evidence that value is created when multi-business companies increase corporate focus through divisional spin-offs and asset sales.[21]

There are several potential explanations for the above diversification discount:

- Empire building. Managers' decisions to diversify and expand are frequently driven by a desire to maximize the size of their organization rather than to maximize shareholder value.
- Incentive misalignment. Diversified companies often suffer from incentive misalignment problems. That is, business unit managers typically have incentives to make investment decisions that benefit their own units but may be suboptimal for the firm as a whole, thereby leading to poor operating performance.
- Monitoring problems. Capital markets find it difficult to monitor and value multi-business organizations because of inadequate disclosure about the performance of individual business segments.

In summary, while companies can theoretically create value through innovative corporate strategies, there are many ways in which this potential fails to get realized in practice. Therefore, it pays to be skeptical when evaluating companies' corporate strategies.

Applying corporate strategy analysis

Let us apply the concepts of corporate strategy analysis to easyGroup, a privately-owned company that licenses the "easy" brand name to, and holds shares in, various no-frills, low-cost businesses. EasyGroup's first and primary holding, easyJet, started operations as a low-fare short-haul airline company in 1995 and five years later placed 28 percent of its shares on the London Stock Exchange at an amount of £224 million. The company grew rapidly and began to pose a serious threat in the short-haul segment to the dominance of leading European airlines like Air France, British Airways, and Lufthansa. EasyJet's revenues increased from £46 million in 1997 to £2,973 million in 2010.

Flush with his success in selling cheap short-haul flights, Stelios Haji-Ioannou, the founder of easyJet and private owner of easyGroup, stretched the "easy" brand name to other industries. The new ventures that easyGroup started had a few common characteristics. They primarily sold services with high fixed costs and exploited the fact that the demand for a service could be highly elastic to its price. In fact, when demand was low, the ventures sold their services at often drastically reduced prices. Because the easyGroup ventures consistently offered their services through the Internet and rewarded customers for booking in advance, they were able to flexibly adjust prices to demand. Further, because of the no-frills character of services and the bypassing of intermediaries in industries such as the travel industry, the ventures were able to keep tight control over their costs. Following this strategy, easyGroup expanded into car rental, pizza delivery, bus transport, cruise travel, office space rental, cinemas, and hotels. In an interview, Haji-Ioannou emphasized his unique position: "Brand extension is very tricky. It's like starting another company, all the time. This is the privilege of entrepreneurs spending their own money."[22]

EasyGroup's diversification into unrelated businesses was not without risks. Haji-Ioannou claimed that easyGroup could create value through its broad corporate focus for the following reasons:[23]

- Through easyJet's rapid growth, its marketing strategy, and the innovations that the airline company had brought to the European airline industry, Haji-Ioannou had gained much exposure for his "easy" brand throughout Europe. Making use of easyJet's valuable brand name and its established reputation in offering no-frills services at low prices, Haji-Ioannou could economize on transaction costs in his new ventures. Customers are likely to have greater trust in new businesses that operate under a familiar brand name. Further, brand-stretching can help to economize on advertising. In fact, Haji-Ioannou admitted on occasions that, without the airline, the other businesses were not likely to survive.

- EasyGroup had been able to acquire critical expertise in flexible pricing and online selling. This is a general competency that can be exploited in many industries.

- EasyGroup's revenues came from licensing the "easy" brand and holding financial stakes in easyJet and the new ventures. Haji-Ioannou planned to take a venture public when it had proven to be successful, as he had done with easyJet. Because the easyGroup did not produce the services itself, the company shared the risks of production with the ventures' other stakeholders.

There were also signs that easyGroup was expanding too rapidly and that its diversification beyond air travel was likely to fail. Very few of the easyGroup's new business ventures were profitable during their first years of operation. For example, at the end of 2003, the losses incurred by easyGroup's Internet café chain added up to an estimated £100 million. In 2010, easyBus reported its first pre-tax profit since its inception in 2003. In many of the industries that easyGroup entered, incumbent companies also had valuable brand names, execution capabilities, and customer loyalty. Therefore these companies were likely to offer formidable competition to easyGroup's individual business lines. EasyGroup's critics also pointed out that expanding rapidly into so many different areas is likely to confuse customers, dilute easyGroup's brand value, and increase the chance of poor execution.

An interesting question to examine is whether there are systematic reasons to believe that a company such as easyGroup can succeed in pursuing a wide focus because its business model – online selling of no-frills services at demand-based prices under one common brand – somehow allows it to manage this diversity in a fundamentally different manner than a traditional company would be able to. The poor financial performance of some of Easy-Group's ventures during the 2000s casts some doubt on whether it can succeed as a diversified company.

SUMMARY

Strategy analysis is an important starting point for the analysis of financial statements because it allows the analyst to probe the economics of the firm at a qualitative level. Strategy analysis also allows the identification of the firm's profit drivers and key risks, enabling the analyst to assess the sustainability of the firm's performance and make realistic forecasts of future performance.

Whether a firm is able to earn a return on its capital in excess of its cost of capital is determined by its own strategic choices:

1 The choice of an industry or a set of industries in which the firm operates (industry choice).

2 The manner in which the firm intends to compete with other firms in its chosen industry or industries (competitive strategy).

3 The way in which the firm expects to create and exploit synergies across the range of businesses in which it operates (corporate strategy). Strategy analysis involves analyzing all three choices.

Industry analysis consists of identifying the economic factors that drive the industry profitability. In general, an industry's average profit potential is influenced by the degree of rivalry among existing competitors, the ease with which new firms can enter the industry, the availability of substitute products, the power of buyers, and the power of suppliers. To perform industry analysis, the analyst has to assess the current strength of each of these forces in an industry and make forecasts of any likely future changes.

Competitive strategy analysis involves identifying the basis on which the firm intends to compete in its industry. In general, there are two potential strategies that could provide a firm with a competitive advantage: cost leadership and differentiation. Cost leadership involves offering at a lower cost the same product or service that other firms offer. Differentiation involves satisfying a chosen dimension of customer need better than the competition, at an incremental cost that is less than the price premium that customers are willing to pay. To perform strategy analysis, the analyst has to identify the firm's intended strategy, assess whether the firm possesses the competencies required to execute the strategy, and recognize the key risks that the firm has to guard against. The analyst also has to evaluate the sustainability of the firm's strategy.

Corporate strategy analysis involves examining whether a company is able to create value by being in multiple businesses at the same time. A well-crafted corporate strategy reduces costs or increases revenues from running several businesses in one firm relative to the same businesses operating independently and transacting with each other in the marketplace. These cost savings or revenue increases come from specialized resources that the firm has that help it to exploit synergies across these businesses. For these resources to be valuable, they must be nontradable, not easily imitated by competition, and nondivisible. Even when a firm has such resources, it can create value through a multi-business organization only when it is managed so that the information and agency costs inside the organization are smaller than the market transaction costs.

The insights gained from strategy analysis can be useful in performing the remainder of the financial statement analysis. In accounting analysis the analyst can examine whether a firm's accounting policies and estimates are consistent with its stated strategy. For example, a firm's choice of functional currency in accounting for its international operations should be consistent with the level of integration between domestic and international operations that the business strategy calls for. Similarly, a firm that mainly sells housing to low-income customers should have higher than average bad debt expenses.

Strategy analysis is also useful in guiding financial analysis. For example, in a cross-sectional analysis the analyst should expect firms with cost leadership strategy to have lower gross margins and higher asset turnover than firms that follow differentiated strategies. In a time series analysis, the analyst should closely monitor any increases in expense ratios and asset turnover ratios for low-cost firms, and any decreases in investments critical to differentiation for firms that follow differentiation strategy.

Business strategy analysis also helps in prospective analysis and valuation. First, it allows the analyst to assess whether, and for how long, differences between the firm's performance and its industry (or industries) performance are likely to persist. Second, strategy analysis facilitates forecasting investment outlays the firm has to make to maintain its competitive advantage.

CORE CONCEPTS

Bargaining power in input and output markets One of the two main drivers of an industry's profit potential. The greater the bargaining power of buyers and suppliers, the lower is the industry's profit potential.

Competitive forces Five forces that together determine an industry's profit potential through their influence on the degree of actual and potential competition with the industry or the bargaining power in input and output markets.

Competitive strategy analysis Analysis of the strategic choices that a firm has made to position itself in the industry. Firms typically choose between two mutually exclusive strategies: (1) cost leadership or (2) differentiation. The competitive strategy that a firm has chosen and the industry's profit potential together affect the firm's profitability.

Corporate strategy analysis Analysis of a firm's business structure and processes to establish whether and how the firm has minimized, or can potentially minimize, its transaction costs.

Cost leadership Strategy in which a firm achieves a competitive advantage by producing and delivering its products or services at a lower cost than its competitors.

Differentiation Strategy in which a firm achieves a competitive advantage by producing and delivering products or services with unique features at premium prices.

Industry analysis Analysis of an industry's profit potential.

Industry competition One of the two main drivers of an industry's profit potential. The degree of actual and potential competition is determined by three competitive forces: (1) the rivalry among existing firms in the industry; (2) the threat of new entrants to the industry; and (3) the threat of substitute products.

QUESTIONS, EXERCISES AND PROBLEMS

1 Judith, an accounting student, states, "Strategy analysis seems to be an unnecessary detour in doing financial statement analysis. Why can't we just get straight to the accounting issues?" Explain to Judith why she might be wrong.

2 What are the critical drivers of industry profitability?

3 One of the fastest growing industries in the last 20 years is the memory chip industry, which supplies memory chips for personal computers and other electronic devices. Yet the average profitability for this industry has been very low. Using the industry analysis framework, list all the potential factors that might explain this apparent contradiction.

4 Joe argues, "Your analysis of the five forces that affect industry profitability is incomplete. For example, in the banking industry, I can think of at least three other factors that are also important; namely, government regulation, demographic trends, and cultural factors." His classmate Jane disagrees and says, "These three factors are important only to the extent that they influence one of the five forces." Explain how, if at all, the three factors discussed by Joe affect the five forces in the banking industry.

5 Examples of European firms that operate in the pharmaceutical industry are GlaxoSmithKline and Bayer. Examples of European firms that operate in the tour operating industry are Thomas Cook and TUI. Rate the pharmaceutical and tour operating industries as high, medium, or low on the following dimensions of industry structure:

   1 Rivalry.
   2 Threat of new entrants.
   3 Threat of substitute products.
   4 Bargaining power of suppliers.
   5 Bargaining power of buyers.

   Given your ratings, which industry would you expect to earn the highest returns?

6 In 2011, Puma was a profitable sportswear company. Puma did not produce most of the shoes, apparel, and accessories that it sold. Instead, the company entered into contracts with independent manufacturers, primarily in Asia. Puma also licensed independent companies throughout the world to design, develop, produce, and distribute a selected range of products under its brand name. Use the five-forces framework and your knowledge of the sportswear industry to explain Puma's high profitability in 2011.

7   In response to the deregulation of the European airline industry during the 1980s and 1990s, European airlines followed their US peers in starting frequent flyer programs as a way to differentiate themselves from others. Industry analysts, however, believe that frequent flyer programs had only mixed success. Use the competitive advantage concepts to explain why.

8   What are the ways that a firm can create barriers to entry to deter competition in its business? What factors determine whether these barriers are likely to be enduring?

9   Explain why you agree or disagree with each of the following statements:

   a   It's better to be a differentiator than a cost leader, since you can then charge premium prices.

   b   It's more profitable to be in a high technology than a low technology industry.

   c   The reason why industries with large investments have high barriers to entry is because it is costly to raise capital.

10   There are very few companies that are able to be both cost leaders and differentiators. Why? Can you think of a company that has been successful at both?

11   Many consultants are advising diversified companies in emerging markets such as India, Korea, Mexico, and Turkey to adopt corporate strategies proven to be of value in advanced economies like the US and western Europe. What are the pros and cons of this advice?

Problem 1   *The European airline industry*

The Association of European Airlines (AEA) is an association of 34 established European airlines, mostly national flag carriers such as Air France, Lufthansa, Finnair, and SAS, but also some cargo specialists such as TNT and Cargolux. The AEA continuously surveys its members and publishes reports and statistics about its members' passenger and cargo traffic and capacity, and operating performance. Although the members of the AEA do not represent the whole European airline industry, the AEA statistics are a useful source of information about the state of the industry. Following is a selection of statistics illustrating the developments in the industry during the years 2002–2007.

   Revenue passenger kilometers (RPK) is the number of passengers transported times the average number of kilometers flown. Cargo tonne kilometers (CTK) is the amount of cargo transported (in tonne) times the number of kilometers flown. Load factors are defined as the ratio of realized RPKs (or CTKs) and available seat kilometers (tonne kilometers). Note that the description of the European airline industry in this chapter covered the period 1995–2004. Use the above information to answer the following questions about whether and how competition in the European airline industry has changed after 2004:

1   Evaluate how the rivalry among existing firms has developed after 2004.

2   Evaluate the influence of rising fuel prices on the AEA airlines' profitability between 2003 and 2006. If fuel prices had not increased after 2003, what would have been the pre-interest breakeven load factor in 2006 (assuming all other factors constant)?

3   During the period examined, some airlines started to charge fuel surcharges to their customers. For example, late 2007 KLM charged its customers €27 on European flights and €80 on intercontinental flights. Other airlines had similar surcharges. How do such practices affect your answer to question 2?

4   The operating margins of the AEA airlines became positive, on average, in 2004 and gradually improved thereafter. What do you think are the most important drivers behind this development? (Also consider your answers to questions 2 and 3.)

TABLE 2.1

		2002	2003	2004	2005	2006	2007
AEA market share of the . . .							
. . . 4 largest AEA airlines	%	58.9%	58.8%	58.5%	58.2%	57.6%	56.5%
. . . 8 largest AEA airlines	%	79.8%	79.3%	79.4%	79.1%	78.3%	77.1%
Revenue passenger kilometers	mn.	589,575	598,454	656,677	699,515	741,608	781,165
RPK growth	%	−4.9%	1.5%	9.7%	6.5%	6.0%	5.3%
Cargo tonne kilometers	mn.	31,499	32,548	36,009	36,004	37,418	38,635
CTK growth	%	−0.3%	3.3%	10.6%	0.0%	3.9%	3.3%
Available seat kilometers	mn.	801,370	815,998	880,085	922,077	970,717	1,015,004
ASK growth	%	−8.8%	1.8%	7.9%	4.8%	5.3%	4.6%
Available tonne kilometers	mn.	87,371	88,952	97,869	102,398	107,568	112,477
ATK growth	%	−3.3%	1.8%	10.0%	4.6%	5.0%	4.6%
Passenger load factor	%	73.6%	73.3%	74.6%	75.9%	76.4%	77.0%
Cargo load factor	%	36.1%	36.6%	36.8%	35.2%	34.8%	34.3%
Overall load factor	%		68.6%	68.4%	68.9%	69.7%	
Revenue per kilometer	€c		79.1	80.0	82.2	84.5	
Cost per kilometer	€c		54.0	54.2	55.5	56.9	
Fuel cost to total cost	%		12.10%	15.20%		22.80%	
Pre-interest breakeven load factor	%		68.3%	67.8%	67.5%	67.3%	
Average AEA operating margins (before interest)	%	1.6%	−0.3%	2.0%	2.3%	3.4%	5.2%
Average AEA operating margins (after interest)	%	−1.2%	−2.1%	0.5%	1.1%	2.5%	4.6%
Millions weekly seats of low-cost carriers (non-AEA members)	mn.	0.9	1.5	1.9	2.6	3.1	3.9
Low-cost carriers growth	%	50.0%	66.7%	26.7%	36.8%	19.2%	25.8%

Source: Association of European Airlines

NOTES

1. The discussion presented here is intended to provide a basic background in strategy analysis. For a more complete discussion of the strategy concepts, see, for example, *Contemporary Strategy Analysis* by Robert M. Grant (Oxford: Blackwell Publishers, 2005); *Economics of Strategy* by David Besanko, David Dranove, and Mark Shanley (New York: John Wiley & Sons, 2004); *Strategy and the Business Landscape* by Pankaj Ghemawat (London: Pearson Education, 2005); and *Corporate Strategy: Resources and the Scope of the Firm* by David J. Collis and Cynthia Montgomery (Burr Ridge, IL: Irwin/McGraw-Hill, 1997).
2. The data to calculate these statistics come from Thomson Financial's Worldscope database. The statistics apply to all companies that were listed between January 1992 and December 2008 on one of the seven largest European stock exchanges (see the Appendix to Chapter 1 for more details about the sample of European companies).
3. For a summary of this research, see *Industrial Market Structure and Economic Performance*, second edition, by F.M. Scherer (Chicago: Rand McNally College Publishing Co., 1980).
4. See *Competitive Strategy* by Michael E. Porter (New York: The Free Press, 1980) and Michael E. Porter, "The Five Competitive Forces That Shape Strategy," *Harvard Business Review* (January 2008).

5. The four-firm concentration ratio is a commonly used measure of industry concentration; it refers to the market share of the four largest firms in an industry.

6. While the discussion here uses the buyer to connote industrial buyers, the same concepts also apply to buyers of consumer products. Throughout this chapter we use the terms buyers and customers interchangeably.

7. The industry statistics in this section are drawn from the Association of European Airlines (AEA) yearbooks and STAR database.

8. The growth rates represent the annual growth rates in passenger-kilometers (cumulative number of kilometers traveled by all passengers). These data come from the Association of European Airlines (AEA). Because the AEA collects data only from its members, which are primarily the established airlines, the growth rates may not reflect the growth that new entrants experienced.

9. For a more detailed discussion of these two sources of competitive advantage, see Michael E. Porter, *Competitive Advantage: Creating and Sustaining Superior Performance* (New York: The Free Press, 1985).

10. Ibid.

11. See *Competing for the Future* by Gary Hammel and C.K. Prahalad (Boston: Harvard Business School Press, 1994) for a more detailed discussion of the concept of core competencies and their critical role in corporate strategy.

12. See Michael E. Porter, "What Is Strategy?" *Harvard Business Review* (November-December 1996).

13. See Kenny Capell, "IKEA, How the Swedish Retailer Became a Global Cult Brand," *Business Week*, November 14 2005; K. Kling and I. Goteman, "IKEA CEO Anders Dahlvig on International Growth and IKEA's Unique Corporate Culture and Brand Identity," *Academy of Management Executive* (2003): 31–37; R. Normann and R. Ramirez, "From Value Chain to Value Constellation: Designing Interactive Strategy," *Harvard Business Review* 71 (1993): 65–77; Capell, op. cit.

14. One of the strategic challenges faced by corporations is having to deal with competitors who achieve differentiation with low cost. For example, Japanese auto manufacturers have successfully demonstrated that there is no necessary trade-off between quality and cost. The example of IKEA also suggests that combining low cost and differentiation strategies is possible when a firm introduces a significant technical or business innovation. However, such cost advantage and differentiation will be sustainable only if there are significant barriers to imitation by competitors.

15. Business segment data come from Thomson Financial's Worldscope database.

16. The following works are seminal to transaction cost economics: Ronald Coase, "The Nature of the Firm," *Economica* 4 (1937): 386–405; *Markets and Hierarchies: Analysis and Antitrust Implications* by Oliver Williamson (New York: The Free Press, 1975); David Teece, "Toward an Economic Theory of the Multi-product Firm," *Journal of Economic Behavior and Organization* 3 (1982): 39–63.

17. For a more complete discussion of these issues, see Krishna Palepu and Tarun Khanna, "Building Institutional Infrastructure in Emerging Markets," *Brown Journal of World Affairs,* Winter/Spring 1998, and Tarun Khanna and Krishna Palepu, "Why Focused Strategies May Be Wrong for Emerging Markets," *Harvard Business Review* (July/August 1997).

18. For an empirical study that illustrates this point, see Tarun Khanna and Krishna Palepu, "Is Group Affiliation Profitable in Emerging Markets? An Analysis of Diversified Indian Business Groups," *Journal of Finance* (April 2000): 867–891.

19. See Larry Lang and Rene Stulz, "Tobin's q, diversification, and firm performance," *Journal of Political Economy* 102 (1994): 1248–1280, and Phillip Berger and Eli Ofek, "Diversification's Effect on Firm Value," *Journal of Financial Economics* 37 (1994): 39–65.

20. See Paul Healy, Krishna Palepu, and Richard Ruback, "Which Takeovers Are Profitable: Strategic or Financial?" *Sloan Management Review* 38 (Summer 1997): 45–57.

21. See Katherine Schipper and Abbie Smith, "Effects of Recontracting on Shareholder Wealth: The Case of Voluntary Spinoffs," *Journal of Financial Economics* 12 (December 1983): 437–467; L. Lang, A. Poulsen and R. Stulz, "Asset Sales, Firm Performance, and the Agency Costs of Managerial Discretion," *Journal of Financial Economics* 37 (January 1995): 3–37.

22. "Stelios on Painting the World Orange," *Brand Strategy* (February 2005): 18–19.

23. Ibid.

VIZIO, Inc.

As William Wang, CEO and founder of VIZIO, Inc. (VIZIO), walked through the company's Irvine, California, headquarters, he couldn't help but smile. He took great pride in the company's brightly colored offices, with the state-of-the art viewing room and cutting-edge customer service operations. Wang founded the company in 2002 to create high-quality flat-panel televisions at affordable prices. He started the company with only $600,000 in capital. In five years, VIZIO had grown to roughly 120 employees and over $2 billion in revenue. The company's business model relied on volume sales with discount retailers and extremely lean operating expenses to drive profitability. By late 2007, VIZIO had joined well-established industry giants Sony Corp. (Sony) and Samsung Electronics Co. (Samsung) to become one of the top three flat-panel high-definition television (HDTV) brands sold in North America.

The company had developed out of Wang's engineering experience and personal connections in the computer display industry. Wang partnered with Taiwanese contractor manufacturing companies to source parts and assemble flat-panel TVs at significantly lower costs than VIZIO's more vertically integrated competitors. Two of VIZIO's suppliers owned a combined 31 percent equity stake in the company. VIZIO handled the design, marketing, and customer support functions for its products, and sold its liquid crystal display (LCD) and plasma televisions through warehouse and discount retailers such as Costco Wholesale Corp. (Costco), Wal-Mart Stores, Inc. (Wal-Mart), and BJ's Wholesale Club, Inc. (BJ's). VIZIO reached profitability relatively quickly for a start-up, and in the last few years had invested the bulk of its earnings in marketing and advertising initiatives to help develop its brand.

By the third quarter of 2008, the top three flat-panel brands held approximately 40 percent of the North American flat-panel TV market in terms of shipments. VIZIO ranked third, behind Samsung and Sony, with 9.0 percent. However, Wang recognized that the company's rapid growth would not last indefinitely. In fact, Sony and Samsung had recently launched low-priced flat-screen televisions designed to compete directly with VIZIO products in the discount and warehouse channels. Faced with intensifying price pressure from the established brands and an unprecedented economic crisis in the fall of 2008, Wang wondered how he should respond. As he thought beyond the recession and the company's immediate challenges, Wang also contemplated the longer-term sustainability of VIZIO's business model. He entered his office with the realization that he was facing two key questions: How could VIZIO continue its rapid growth, and how should the business be financed?

Background on William Wang and VIZIO

Background on William Wang

Born in Taiwan in 1963, Wang and his family moved to Hawaii when he was 12 and to California when he was 14. He came to the US with no knowledge of the English language. "It was a difficult adjustment because of language problems [and] cultural problems.... I originally

Professor Krishna Palepu and Senior Researcher Liz Kind prepared this case at the HBS California Research Center. HBS cases are developed solely as the basis for class discussion. Cases are not intended to serve as endorsements, sources of primary data, or illustrations of effective or ineffective management.

wanted to be an architect, but being an architect doesn't pay that much, so I got into electrical engineering."[1] Wang earned a bachelor's degree in electrical engineering from the University of Southern California in 1986.

After graduation, Wang was hired to work for Tatung Co. (Tatung) in Southern California, a Taiwanese company that made (among other things) computer monitors for International Business Machines Corp. (IBM). Wang started in Tatung's technical support group, answering customer service calls. He remarked: "After a while, I thought I could build a better computer monitor than the IBM standard … I was 26 – fearless, young, and foolish."[2] In 1990, with $350,000 Wang started MAG Innovision (MAG). In six years he grew the company to 400 employees and $600 million in revenue. However, as the industry became more commodity oriented, the company lost money and in 1998, Wang sold the business.

In 2000, Wang started another computer monitor company, Princeton Graphic Systems. He elaborated: "I started a research and development facility in Asia that worked on high-definition TVs. I tried doing custom video displays for slot machines, Internet-enabled high-definition TV sets, and a few other businesses, but none of them really worked out … Financially, it was a disaster."[3]

One of Wang's biggest life-changing events occurred in November of 2000, when his flight on Singapore Airlines took off on the wrong runway, struck a construction site, and crashed. Eighty-three passengers and crewmembers died. After Wang survived the crash and reflected on his life, he decided to shut down his businesses. He recalled, "… Several things went through my mind when the plane blew up. One thing was my family. The second thing was that all my headaches were gone. I was still stuck with all these bad businesses, but I had a better attitude. I mean at the end of the day, we're all going to die, right?"[4]

Background on VIZIO

Wang spent the next year or so unwinding his business operations. However, he did not sit idle for long. He explained the evolution of the concept for VIZIO:

I'd been in the computer industry for quite some time. In particular, I had been in the computer display industry for quite some time. I had close to 20 years of experience and knew a lot of people overseas who were involved in supplying the key components and parts.

The first time I saw a high-definition television, I thought, "Wow. I'd love to have a TV like that. This is a killer application that is going to change the industry and the way people look at television." With the US government mandating the transition from analog spectrum to digital, I saw an opportunity.

Coming from the display industry, I also quickly recognized that the technology behind TVs was no longer being controlled by traditional consumer electronics companies. In the 1980s and 1990s, large companies like Sony and Samsung owned all the technology. They manufactured everything from the glass to the knobs; they integrated the parts to put together TVs; and they owned both the supply chain and parts of the distribution chain in the US. However, by the early 2000s, a cathode ray tube (CRT) owned by Sony or whoever, was no longer the key component for a high-definition TV. Instead, the critical component was owned by the computer companies that sold LCD or plasma panels, and that technology was open and available to everyone.

In the early 2000s, the Sonys and Philips of the world were not actively pushing the technology envelope. They were happily selling their CRT TVs, and when they developed a flat-screen TV product, they targeted the absolute top of the market. The list price for one of their 40-inch flat-screen TVs was about $9,000. Now, I'm a geek. I love new gadgets. But when I'm shopping for a $9,000 flat TV, it doesn't make my wife very happy!

Given my background and those areas of opportunity, I decided to write a business plan. I was convinced there was a need for a company that could make inexpensive flat-screen TVs and I thought I could do it.

Wang borrowed from the personal computer (PC) industry, using an overseas contract-manufacturing model to build quality plasma flat-panel televisions at an affordable price. Wang showed his plan to Ted Waitt, then chairman of Gateway, Inc. (Gateway). Waitt had served as a mentor to Wang since the time Gateway had been

---

[1]William Wang and Mark Lacter, "How I did it: William Wang, CEO, VIZIO," *Inc. magazine*, June 2007, http://www.inc.com/magazine/20070701/hidi-wang.html, accessed September 17, 2008.

[2]Ibid.

[3]Ibid.

[4]Ibid.

a customer at MAG. In 2001, Gateway had approximately 500 retail stores and demand for the company's personal computers was so strong that they could not keep enough inventory on the stores' shelves. Waitt, eager to carry additional products, asked Wang to launch his idea for a $2,999 42-inch plasma TV through Gateway.

Wang recognized the advantages that the Gateway brand and retail distribution would provide and decided to work with the company on the project. He explained:

> *I knew it would be too risky to do a $2,999 plasma on my own without any retail. Who would buy a completely unknown brand compared to a Sony or something else? Gateway had the name and the retail shelves. In the first month after we launched, we sold 4,000 TVs and just like that, we were back-ordered for six months. We took the industry by storm. All the consumer electronics retailers thought we were crazy. At the time, plasma TVs were still selling for about $8,000, so the retailers wondered why we were coming in and ruining the market. Our project with Gateway proved that if you have a good price, customers will buy, and it doesn't have to be a Sony, a Panasonic, a Samsung, or an LG.*

However, in 2002, Gateway decided to close its retail stores and get out of the television business. Wang explained, "Gateway's PC margins were so low that even though we were doubling our sales every month for the TVs, we couldn't make up for the losses they had on their PCs." With Gateway out of the picture, Wang decided to develop the TV products under his own brand. He observed: "The experience with Gateway gave me the confidence to say, 'OK, I had a proven formula, now I'll go to Costco and ask them to carry our product under our own brand.'"

Wang started his company by mortgaging his house and borrowing money from friends and family. Initially, he planned to name the company "W," but after learning about the hotel company with the same name, Wang decided on "V" instead. Wang started with the same product concept but decided to use a different factory, again leveraging his overseas relationships for parts and assembly. He commented:

> *From the beginning, we decided to take a PC approach to building televisions. It wasn't like we had a whole lot of choice. My company had $600,000 and two employees. I couldn't go in and build another factory like Sony. I had to take some shortcuts. I knew all the parts guys from my time in the computer industry, so it was pretty easy to get started. I also know some of the retailers.*

In January 2003, Wang pitched a 46-inch plasma flat-panel TV for $3,800 to management at Costco and told them that within five years, he wanted to be the next Sony.[5] The executives laughed, but with the V television at half the price of competing models, they agreed to stock them in ten of Costco's warehouses.[6] By April 2003, Costco was carrying V televisions in all 320 of its warehouses.[7] Wang recounted:

> *The people at Costco thought I was crazy, but they took a chance on us and we've become their No. 1 supplier. We knew that we had to come up with a value proposition that buyers could not refuse. Our competitors were very vulnerable at that time because they were still enjoying 80 percent gross margins on their $8,000 high-end, flat-screen TVs. We came out of nowhere and took them by surprise by walking into retailers with a $3,000, 42-inch TV. It seemed obvious, but it was really also about the timing. We were the first ones in at those kinds of prices, so it seemed pretty obvious to us. We took advantage of the pricing umbrella to establish a foothold. If you tried to do this today, forget it.*

By 2004, the company had grown to six employees and changed its name to VIZIO. Revenue reached $18 million, and the company was profitable.[8] Wang decided to seek additional funding and started by approaching his manufacturing partners. In April 2004, Amtran Technology Co., Ltd. (Amtran), a Taiwanese maker of monitors, purchased an 8 percent stake in VIZIO for approximately $1 million. Later that month, Hon Hai Precision Industry Co. (Hon Hai), a large contract manufacturer of electronics, purchased an additional 8 percent in VIZIO.

Wang used the additional capital to broaden VIZIO's product line to five models and expand distribution beyond Costco to Wal-Mart's Sam's Club division and BJ's. By the end of 2005, VIZIO had grown to approximately $142 million in revenue. Six months later, Amtran bought an additional 15 percent stake in the company.

[5]Christopher Lawton, Yukari Iwatani Kane, and Jason Dean, "US Upstart Takes on TV Giants in Price War," *Wall Street Journal*, p. A1, April 15, 2008.

[6]Ibid.

[7]Ibid.

[8]Ibid.

VIZIO continued its rapid growth through 2006, earning $626 million in revenue, and continued to be profitable. Wang began plowing money into building the VIZIO brand. He explained, "I truly believe that any new technology or great product requires a good distribution channel and a strong brand." Wang began by building customer service and technology support call centers. In 2007, VIZIO signed National Football League star LaDainian Tomlinson as its spokesman. The company ran television ads during football season and the 2008 Beijing Olympics.

By the end of 2007, VIZIO reached $1.9 billion in revenue and shipped approximately 2,800,000 television sets. The company expected to break $2 billion in revenue and ship roughly 3,600,000 million units over the course of 2008. (See **Exhibit 1** for historical revenue data.) One analyst noted: "They are the fastest-growing TV maker in the market. They operate on razor-thin margins and they keep overhead to a minimum. They have very low inventory, and they turn their inventory very fast."[9] While VIZIO did not disclose detailed financial data, some industry observers estimated that consumer electronics products that were sold through discount and warehouse stores would generate margins in the range of 0.5 percent to 4 percent. Kyle Wescoat, VIZIO's chief financial officer, would not confirm those numbers, but noted that as of December 2008 total assets for VIZIO were approximately $500 million.

Most television sets were sold between "Black Friday," the Friday after Thanksgiving, and Super Bowl Sunday. As of November 2008, the company offered 27 different television products – five with plasma screens and 22 with LCD screens. Prices ranged from $399.99 to $1,699.99. (See **Exhibit 2** for full list of VIZIO television products.) Newer models featured 120 Hz smooth motion technology, full high-definition 1080p performance, and surround sound capabilities. In addition, the company recently began offering a variety of higher-margin television accessories including multimedia display monitors, wall mounts, remote control devices, high-definition sound systems, cables, and extended warranties.

During 2007 and 2008, VIZIO added Wal-Mart, Dell Inc. (Dell), Circuit City Stores, Inc. (Circuit City), Target.com, Sears Holding Corporation (Sears), and Kmart (owned by Sears) to its list of retail distributors. (See **Exhibit 3** for a chart depicting VIZIO's customer mix.) In August 2008, VIZIO began selling its TV sets in Costco stores in Japan, and that fall it expanded to Canada through Costco, Sam's Club, and Wal-Mart. VIZIO entered these new markets strategically, in conjunction with retail partners that the company knew and trusted. The company planned to continue its international expansion for the foreseeable future.

Many of the executives on VIZIO's senior management team had worked with Wang in the past. (See **Exhibit 4** for management biographies.) Several described the company's culture as "entrepreneurial," "fast paced," and "laser-focused." As one executive noted, "It can be a bit of a pressure cooker, but we all want VIZIO to succeed because we all love being part of a David and Goliath story." Wescoat added:

> Much of William's success is based on his knowledge and appreciation of the differences between people, cultures, and organizations, and his ability in getting them to collaborate. We like to think of ourselves as a reflection of our California base. We are multicultural and a true meritocracy. We have a good balance of young and seasoned men and women. We also have a mix of people with strong academic credentials working with and for people with passion and experience in global business. What really differentiates us from our competitors is our speed.

VIZIO won numerous awards including a #1 ranking in *Inc.* magazine's Inc. 500 for Top Companies in Computers and Electronics, *Fast Company's* Top 10 Most Innovative Consumer Electronics Companies, *Good Housekeeping's* Best Big Screen, CNET's Top 10 Holiday Gifts, and *PC World's* 100 Best Products of 2008. (**Exhibit 5** shows a breakdown of VIZIO's employees by department, and **Exhibit 6** shows revenue versus revenue per employee.)

Flat-panel television market overview

The term "flat panel" referred to the very thin display screens (generally less than three inches) that were used in modern computers and televisions. Various flat-screen technologies were under development, but the two main types available to the public were plasma and LCD. Plasma display monitors were first invented in 1964 at the University of Illinois and were originally used in computer terminals. It was not until 1997, when

[9]Alex Pham, "The Skinny on VIZIO: How this TV Seller Got Flat Down Pat," *The Virginian-Pilot*, October 20, 2007, p. D3.

Pioneer started selling the first plasma sets, that plasma television became available to the public. LCD technology, also over 40 years old, was introduced for television even later than plasma, with the commercial release of LCD sets by Panasonic, Sharp Corp. (Sharp), and Samsung in 2002.

Television companies began developing thin, flat-panel TVs as an alternative to bulkier CRT sets and to create larger-screen televisions. (The diagonal screen size of a CRT television was limited to about 40 inches due to the size of the cathode ray tube.) The picture and other aesthetic qualities of flat screen TVs were quickly recognized and appreciated by consumers, yet their high prices made them affordable to only a few. Most flat-panel televisions were manufactured by well-known, fully integrated consumer electronics companies that targeted the top of the market, selling through traditional electronics retailers and earning high margins. VIZIO and other players with competitive prices started entering the market in 2003.

Initially, plasma sets offered better brightness, faster response times, greater color range, and wider viewing angles than LCD sets. However, by 2003, technology improvements had greatly enhanced LCD product quality, and significant price reductions had generated strong demand for LCD sets, especially for smaller-screen sizes. In 2004, 73 percent of flat-panel TV sales were LCD products, and 27 percent were the larger plasma models.[10] As of the summer of 2008, LCD was more popular and outsold plasma by over five to one.

Competition in the LCD and plasma markets was dominated by a handful of technological giants, mostly based in Asia, including Samsung, Sony, Royal Philips Electronics (Philips), Panasonic, and Mitsubishi. (According to a 2007 *BusinessWeek* article, VIZIO's overhead costs were 0.7 percent of sales, compared with 10 percent–20 percent for the big, diversified electronics conglomerates, and its profit margins were approximately 2 percent of sales.[11] (More recent competitors included Syntax-Brillian's (Syntax's) Olevia brand and Westinghouse. Like VIZIO, both Syntax and Westinghouse were "virtual" companies that used contract manufacturing to assemble their televisions. Historically, Samsung and Sony led shipments in the LCD market, and Panasonic dominated the plasma segment of the market. (See **Exhibit 7** for quarterly market share data for the last 12 months.)

Total shipments for flat-screen TVs had grown dramatically since they were introduced in the late 1990s and early 2000s. In addition to keen interest in the technology and steadily declining prices, US government regulations played a role in increasing consumer demand. In the late 1990s, the US government mandated a transition from analog to digital TV by February 2009. In order to receive the new signals, consumers needed to purchase a DTV converter box (generally in the range of $40 to $60), or upgrade to a newer-model TV. Many consumers were replacing dated televisions with flat-screen models. By 2006, factory sales for digital televisions were $23 billion, up 64 percent over 2005 levels.[12] According to DisplaySearch, a TV monitoring firm, in North America shipments were still increasing 17 percent year-over-year.[13] One CNET reporter noted: "HDTV makers don't need their products to be a luxury any more. The industry has reached buyers that were wowed by the technology first, and now it's on to the people who need to upgrade to a digital TV, or who have been waiting for prices to drop."[14] Approximately one-half of US households had a high-definition television set, while less than 10 percent of households worldwide had HDTVs.

According to research firm Mintel International Group Ltd. (Mintel), US factory sales of digital televisions (including LCD, plasma, rear and front projection, and digital televisions) were expected to increase to $47.8 billion by 2010. LCD and plasma accounted for the largest percentages of total 2010 sales, at 55.1 percent and 23.4 percent, respectively.[15] (Rear projection, front projection, and direct view TVs accounted for the remaining 21.5 percent of 2010 forecast sales.) iSuppli Corporation (iSuppli) predicted that LCD TV shipments would expand at a compound annual growth rate of 8 percent between 2008 and 2013. (See **Exhibit 8** for a detailed forecast.)

[10]Eric A. Traub, "Signs of Glut and Lower Prices on Thin TV's," *The New York Times*, November 29, 2004, http://www.nytimes.com/, accessed September 30, 2008.

[11]Pete Engardio, "Flat Panel, Thin Margins," *BusinessWeek*, February 15, 2007, http://www.businessweek.com/print/globalbiz/content/feb2007/bg20070215_407935.html, accessed June 3, 2008.

[12]"Digital Television – US – April 2007," Mintel, accessed June 3, 2008.

[13]Erica Ogg, "HDTV Makers Turn to Budget Stores, Larger Screens," CNET.com, September 17, 2008, http://www.cnet.com/au/tvs/0,239035250,339292030,00.htm, accessed September 25, 2008.

[14]Ibid.

[15]"Digital Television – US – April 2007," Mintel, accessed June 3, 2008.

VIZIO, Inc.

VIZIO's supply chain relationships

Parts and suppliers

VIZIO's contract manufacturing model required aggressive procurement sourcing and supply chain management. While a typical flat-screen television included thousands of parts, the vast majority of the costs and ultimate performance were a function of two key components: the panel and the chipset. John Morriss, VIZIO's former vice president and general manager core products group, explained:

> The display industry is very unique. For PC monitors or flat-screen TVs, the panel accounts for some 85 percent–90 percent of the product's architecture and its performance. The second key component is the chipset or processor. Together, the two main parts make up about 94 percent of the costs. There are also mechanical parts, plastic components, and the rest of the architecture, but the bulk of the television set is driven by the panel and the chipset. If you don't have a handle on those top components, you're not going to be competitive. Your costs won't be optimized, you won't get products to market on time, and you'll end up with dated technology.

Samsung, LG Co. Ltd. (LG Display), and AU Optronics Corp. (AUO) were the top three suppliers of LCD panels, and Panasonic, Samsung, and LG Electronics were the leading suppliers of plasma panels. These firms controlled approximately 80 percent–90 percent of their respective panel markets. Digital television chipsets were supplied by a much broader spectrum of firms. Major suppliers included MediaTek Inc. (MediaTek), Broadcom Corporation (Broadcom), Trident MicroSystems, Inc., Genesis Microchip, Inc. (owned by STMicroelectronics), and LG.

Morriss stressed the need for strong relationships with the panel suppliers:

> On the panel side, you have to have strategic relationships with the right senior level executives. Large Asian-based display companies tend to be very structured. The CEOs and EVPs of the business units make the primary decisions. They prefer to work with their corresponding decision-maker, and everyone below them meets with their respective peers. Business is done both formally and informally. Formally, there are meetings – often two or three hours long – but then you have a four-hour dinner, and that's where all the decisions get made.
>
> At the end of the day the strategic relationships are absolutely critical. If your suppliers do not trust that you understand your business – the channels, the pricing, and the end-to-end value chain – you'll only get marginal results, but not the level that is required to make you a market leader. You'll be able to do business, but in order to get preferred pricing and advantaged time to market on panels, you need to break into the top-tier partner ranking.

Wang added:

> We have suppliers in Taiwan, Korea, Japan, and China, and we have to be sensitive to each of their needs and cultural preferences. For many of our suppliers, we are just a tiny portion of their business, so we need to work extra hard to get their attention and the best prices. Working with suppliers is an art, not a science.
>
> Our suppliers are worried about everything they read about the US recession. They are concerned about building capacity and then having us tell them we don't need as many parts as we initially projected.

In addition, another level of supplier relationship that VIZIO needed to manage was with the original design manufacturers (ODMs) or systems integrators. Those organizations served as contract manufacturers that ultimately purchased the panels and chipsets, and assembled the televisions. Morriss observed: "There is a triad of relationships between the panel makers, the ODMs, and VIZIO. The three of us need to be very, very coordinated." Leading ODMs in the digital TV business included Amtran (Taiwan), TPV Technology (Hong Kong), and Foxconn Technology Group (Foxconn), a subsidiary of Hon Hai (Taiwan).

Background on Amtran

Amtran was founded in 1994 in Taiwan as an ODM that produced computer display products branded by other firms. The company became known for its high-performance monitors, and it worked with a broad array of top-tier computer customers. In 2001, Amtran became publicly traded on the Taiwan Stock Exchange.

Wang knew Amtran's founder, Alpha Wu, from his days at Tantung, when Wu was then a founding executive of a Taiwanese monitor maker. In 2004, after wrestling with some product quality issues, Wang turned to Wu for assembly and manufacturing support. Morriss commented:

> *William had known the individuals at Amtran for a long, long time. In their prior lives, they knew each other both personally and professionally. It was natural that Amtran and VIZIO would become partners. William knew the key people at Amtran, and he knew the company had the capability to deliver the quality he wanted. At the same time, Amtran was starting to look at ways to expand its business. The monitor business is tough, especially if you're playing in the high-performance end. To cover overhead and grow, Amtran needed to build volume at the mid-range and entry levels.*

In addition to building digital televisions for VIZIO, Amtran also began building TVs for other companies such as Sony and Sharp. As of 2008, Amtran had over 3,000 employees and generated more than $2 billion in revenue. The company had two manufacturing sites – one in Suzhou, China and the other Hu-Kou, Taiwan. In September 2008, Amtran announced a joint venture with LG Display. Amtran and LG Display planned to base their joint venture in Amtran's China production facility, where they would invest $50 million of funding and expertise. Amtran owned 49 percent of the new company and LG Display owned the remaining 51 percent. Before the joint venture, Amtran received approximately 80 percent of its revenue from VIZIO.

Managing the Relationships

The vast majority of VIZIO's panels and chipsets were supplied by a handful of partners. Amtran provided about 80 percent of VIZIO's procurement and assembly work, with the remaining 20 percent performed by other ODMs including Foxconn and TPV Technology. Morriss described the challenges of coordinating the supply side:

> *Our production schedules need to be pulled together about 18 months in advance. We spend a tremendous amount of energy on the alignment of roadmaps and on trying to understand what can we do collectively to take cost out of the value chain. We constantly review our roadmaps, with weekly and monthly meetings to make sure they're on track as the markets change and new things happen. We're also continually monitoring all the other panel makers, all the other ODMs, and all the other chipmakers to ensure we have the optimum results.*
>
> *The sourcing process is our primary tool to create the best infrastructure for the supply base that supports our broader business model. That's the fundamental operational challenge, but we're also always thinking about picking and choosing the right partners. How many should we expand to? Which ones will have the infrastructure to support us as we become bigger and more global? How do we maintain our standard of quality as we grow? It takes a lot of effort to manage what we call our ODM strategy and our LCD or panel strategy, and it's very complicated. We also have to coordinate with our channel partners, look at what our competitors are doing, and review what the analysts are saying. But, if we do it correctly, picking and choosing the right partners will really allow us to round out our offerings and create best-in-class products.*

The Wall Street Journal described VIZIO's relationship with Amtran: "The arrangement gets VIZIO preferential treatment. Amtran sometimes swallows shipping costs and pushes component suppliers to ensure VIZIO's products are high quality and on time."[16] However, as Morriss explained, "We are such a big percentage of each other's business. There have been a lot of delicate discussions about how to mitigate the risk long term, and we've all agreed to reduce the percent over time. If we slowly add other manufacturers, and as long as the pie keeps getting bigger, it will be OK."

Distribution channel strategy

One of the cornerstone's of VIZIO's strategy was the decision to sell through wholesale clubs and discount retailers. Initially, Wang was able to leverage his relationships at Costco from his years of selling computer monitors. VIZIO's early focus on wholesale stores also fit with the company's value position and pricing

VIZIO, Inc.

---

[16]Christopher Lawton, Yukari Iwatani Kane, and Jason Dean, "US Upstart Takes on TV Giants in Price War," *Wall Street Journal*, p. Al, April 15, 2008.

strategy. By selling through wholesale clubs and discount stores, VIZIO was able to keeps its prices low. According to a CNET article: "These retailers … typically are looking for gross margins on their [TV] products only in the 10 percent range. Electronics retailers are looking for 25 percent or more. For VIZIO, that's a two-way benefit: the prices of its TVs are comparatively lower than those from major manufacturers at electronics stores, and major manufacturers can't participate as fully as they'd like to at places like Costco."[17] Jeff Schindler, VIZIO's vice president of business planning elaborated:

> I think the thing that sets us apart from all the other companies coming in and trying to get a flat-panel TV brand on the shelf is our distribution strategy. The typical approach is to buy or license an old brand and try to get into Best Buy because they have such a large percent of the market. However, the only way to get into Best Buy is to have a really, really low-priced product. So, companies will build the cheapest product they can to get it into the stores, and may even lose money on it just to get the business.
>
> Our approach was very different. Instead of buying an older brand, we created our own. We didn't go after traditional consumer electronics retailers, but after the channel that we thought had the greatest potential. Warehouse and wholesale clubs don't mark their products up as high as the consumer electronics retailers. They have lots of traffic and overhead is covered by paid memberships, so product margins can be very thin. So we started with Costco, in a channel that wasn't traditionally known for electronics, and that eventually helped us get into Sam's Club.
>
> The efficiencies in working with wholesale clubs also help us keep our inventories at really low levels. We get an order [from Costco] before the products arrive at the US border. Once the shipment arrives, the products get sorted [and shipped] to the customers within a week to ten days. The wholesale clubs don't hold much more than two-and-a-half weeks of inventory. The pallets go to their distribution centers; they get delivered to the stores; and the products are put on the shelves for customers to purchase. The clubs have high traffic, few SKUs, and a self-serve environment. You walk in, decide which product you want, and you're out.
>
> It's totally different with traditional consumer electronics retailers. They typically order a set amount for the month and hold about five to ten weeks of inventory. The products get shipped to their distribution centers. Some products get delivered to the retail stores, but most of the inventory is held at the distribution center. As the stores sell the products, they replenish their back rooms with stock from their distribution centers. The retailers are trying to hold less inventory to be more competitive, but if you run retail at less than four to five weeks, you're going to be out of stock in a lot of stores.
>
> The differences between the two channels are significant. As in the PC industry, costs are coming down every month. If you can keep your pipeline extremely thin and efficient, as soon as the cost of a panel drops, you can be the first one to take advantage of the price decrease. If you have a lot more inventory, you've just delayed your savings by the number of weeks of inventory you are carrying.

VIZIO's success in the warehouse channel with Costco, Sam's Club, and BJ's allowed it to sign on with Wal-Mart and Sears/Kmart in the spring of 2007. As of 2008, VIZIO was the leading digital television brand for Costco, Sam's Club, and Wal-Mart. According to Schindler, the three retailers accounted for the vast majority of VIZIO's business. In March 2008, VIZIO was named Wal-Mart's electronics supplier of the year.

By 2007, Mintel reported that consumers were just as likely to shop for TVs at mass merchants and club stores as they were at traditional consumer electronics stores. According to the research firm, 42 percent of consumers purchased televisions through mass merchandisers and warehouse clubs; 42 percent purchased TVs at consumer electronics retailers; and 4 percent of consumers bought their televisions online.[18] As consumers began to change their purchasing preferences, VIZIO responded by developing customized offerings for its various categories of retail accounts. Several retailers requested differentiated products, and VIZIO was able to fulfill their needs by offering different levels of features, technology, and prices. VIZIO also sold a small percentage of its televisions online to meet the growing demand of Internet shoppers.

---

[17]Michael Kanellos, The Secret of VIZIO's Success," CNET News.com, August 20, 2007, available from Factiva, http://www.factiva.com, accessed June 3, 2008.

[18]"Digital Television – US – April 2007," Mintel, accessed June 3, 2008.

The VIZIO brand

Wang believed that "at the end of the day, our biggest value is our brand." The company's strategy of creating a value-oriented product and its decision to sell through Costco helped provide credibility to an unknown brand. In fact, the company's motto, "Where Vision meets Value," was displayed prominently throughout the company's headquarters and was a constant source of focus. Schindler explained:

The whole key about our positioning is value. We didn't build the cheapest TV we could. Instead, we decided we would build good-quality TVs and did not include features that consumers wouldn't need. We focused on the technology that would provide a very high quality picture. Then we priced it really aggressively.

When you go into Costco or Sam's, the TVs are right in front when you walk in the door. That was a key move for them and a huge advantage for us. Maybe half of customers or less are planning to buy a TV when they go in the store. A lot of purchases are impulse buys. People look at all the TVs and compare the brands. Picture quality is the No. 1 reason why people buy one set over another. They see our sets and ask themselves, "If the picture quality looks the same and the price is so different, why would I spend all this extra money just for the brand I know?"

A lot of what we do is about finding ways for customers to trust our new brand. One thing that helped us is that the wholesale clubs have very liberal return policies. If the consumer buys this brand they've never heard of, they can bring it back if they don't like it. The return policies at traditional electronic retailers tend to be very strict. If you wait too long, they're not going to take the TV back.

In addition, in the retail channel, the boxes are not out on the sales floor. They're usually in the back room, so all you see on display are the TVs. The wholesale clubs are warehouses – all the products, with their boxes, are out on the floor. One of the things we did, and now everyone's copying us, was realize that we had this real estate and that there was no better place to market the brand. We were the first to come up with full-color boxes with descriptive information and great pictures that provided very attractive merchandising. The boxes were our main marketing approach in the beginning when we did not have the budget for much more. Instead of getting just a $3 \times 5''$ card on the shelf with a couple of lines of information, we were able to use the entire box to market the brand and communicate with consumers. Despite the fact that we use the highest-grade panels possible, we often find ourselves fighting rumors that the reason our TVs are so cheap is because we use lower-quality panels. One of the first things we put on the box is a zero pixel bright guarantee.

As VIZIO continued to grow and become profitable, the company began putting more money into building its brand. Wang believed strongly in providing VIZIO customers with a high level of support. He elaborated:

So much of our early success has been from word-of-mouth. We have to have a good-quality product, we have to offer a good value, and we have to make sure our customers are extremely happy. We don't have the same advertising and marketing budgets as our competitors, so we need to make sure that the money we spend has double the impact. One way to do that is to make sure our customers are happy. Until six months ago, most traditional consumer electronics companies didn't even have an 800 number, let alone a customer service group. We have a number of people here answering phones, as well as an outsource agent with significant resources dedicated to customer service and tech support.

In 2004, VIZIO added an in-house warranty. Schindler remarked, "We were the first to offer such a warranty, and on a product this big, people don't want to have to bring it back to a service center. The cost to send out labor for service in the home compared to paying to have the product shipped back was a wash." The company began its television advertising campaign in 2007 and spent $35 million in marketing and advertising for the year. (See **Exhibit 9** for advertising expenditures by competitors.)

Wang was pleased with the company's achievements to date, and especially with a December 2008 survey that ranked VIZIO as No. 1 in value. (See **Exhibit 10**.) He commented:

We've had a lot of things on our side. Without the government's mandate for digital TV by 2009, it would have taken about ten years to get the brand to where it is today. We were able to make huge strides in only three years because we hit things at the right time. Of course, as a newcomer going up against the top-tier brands, that's always the battle we'll have to fight. That won't go away until our brand awareness is up to

VIZIO, Inc.

95 percent, along the lines of Sony and some of our other large competitors. Currently we're only at 61 percent or 62 percent. So far it's been easy, because there's been a huge price gap between our products and theirs. As our competitors lower their prices, however, it's going to get a lot harder for us.

Financing the business

VIZIO had been able to grow without major capital infusions beyond the $600,000 that Wang raised to start the company and the two 2004 investments from Amtran and Hon Hai, totaling $2 million. Wang believed that VIZIO's success was in part due to the company's rigorous inventory management and its strict adherence to low overhead and a variable-oriented cost structure. CFO Wescoat described how VIZIO managed its inventory:

VIZIO uses what is known as a Vendor Managed Inventory (VMI) model. Our major suppliers ship product into distribution hubs at third-party logistic [3PL] warehouses in the US and maintain it for our use. We manage the overall structure of the supply chain, but the vendors maintain the inventory and carrying costs, as well as the returns. When we ship to our customer, a simultaneous transaction takes place where VIZIO bills its customer and purchases the product out of the hub. Our terms are such that we get paid by our customer at about the same time that we need to pay for the product. Our exposure occurs at this point of the transaction, or in some cases, between the time that VIZIO is responsible for shipping the product (taking ownership during transit) and the actual collection of the accounts receivable from the retailer.

VIZIO relied exclusively on its suppliers and their balance sheets for working capital funds. Wescoat explained: "While VIZIO generates positive cash flow, because of its thin margins, traditional sources of financing are not readily available to it. However, given the high credit ratings on our retail customers such as Wal-Mart and Costco, our suppliers have been very willing to provide working capital on the strength of our receivables."

For VIZIO's retail customers with lower credit ratings, the company took out credit insurance. In turn, VIZIO's suppliers mitigated their working capital risk by taking out credit insurance on VIZIO, or in the case of Amtran, taking a security interest in their accounts receivable to VIZIO. Wescoat commented: "Credit insurers are willing to support our model well beyond our capital levels because of the quality of our customer base, our limited exposure to inventory and returns, the suppliers' indemnification for intellectual property, and the fact that nearly all of our business is done in US dollars."

While VIZIO's gross and operating margins were slim, the company had been profitable for the last three years. Wescoat added:

We expect to be profitable throughout 2009 and in addition, our profitability levels have continued to improve as well. We think there are few, if any, other television companies that can claim this type of performance. The key to our success is our overhead structure and our ability to stay profitable at low margin levels. Our gross margins are in the mid single-digit to low double-digit range – 5 percent to 10 percent. Our overhead is in the 4 percent to 5 percent range, with 2 percent to 2½ percent allocated to marketing and the remainder to selling, general, and administrative expenses and other operating expenses, including engineering. Our operating margins are approximately in the range of 1 percent to 4 percent. We believe that all of our major competitors have overhead spending as a percent of revenue that is 4 to 5 times higher than VIZIO's. Most have comparable marketing expenditures (as a percent of revenue), although some like Sony and LG may have historically spent significantly more on marketing. [See Exhibit 11 for estimates on competitor margins.]

VIZIO had limited debt, a small equity base, and a relatively small number of employees given the company's substantial sales. As a result, the company generated a healthy cash flow and return on equity.

Market dynamics and challenges

By late 2008, the intense competition and price cutting in the industry was taking a toll on its participants. (See **Exhibit 12** for average selling price data.) In July 2008, Syntax-Brillian, the maker of Olevia TVs, filed for bankruptcy protection. Earlier in the year, Philips announced it was no longer manufacturing televisions for sale in the US and was licensing its brand to Funai Electric. In April 2008, Sony replaced its top television executive. Previously, Sony had initiated a $2 billion cost-cutting effort. Panasonic's parent company, Matsushita Electric Industrial Co., reorganized its US television business.

In the last few years, several companies decided to streamline their product offerings and/or outsource portions of their manufacturing to cut costs. Pioneer announced that it would buy its plasma panels rather than produce its own. Sony and Toshiba decided to drop their plasma lines in order to focus on LCD, and both companies began farming out more of their LCD TV production.

In 2007, Sony and Samsung introduced low-end, entry-level TV lines to compete directly against VIZIO's. Sony's no frills Bravia television sets, priced approximately $200 less than Sony's least expensive models, had the look and feel of a traditional Sony TV, but with a lower resolution than a full high-definition TV. Sony intended to sell Bravia sets at Wal-Mart, but the line was so successful that Best Buy and Circuit City also asked to carry them. A reporter for *BusinessWeek* noted the significance: "… this shows they are shedding the traditional if-we-build-it-they-will-buy mindset…."[19] A September 2008 article on Display-Search's HDTV Conference similarly reported:

> *The surprising story last year was VIZIO's stunning leap to the top of LCD TV sales in North America…. It's a different story this year. The big guys figured out what VIZIO was doing and responded by creating specific models of TVs for mass market stores like Wal-Mart and Target. By associating their brand names with the prices VIZIO and others were offering, the result has been that Samsung, Sharp, and Sony have leaped back into the lead, and VIZIO has fallen behind.[20]*

While VIZIO's market share of shipment in the 30″–34″ LCD category fell dramatically in the second quarter of 2008, the brand continued to rank among the top three in the overall LCD and plasma categories. A September 2008 survey generated by iSuppli found that among US consumers, screen size was overrated as a buying factor, and that price, picture quality, and brand name were the more important buying considerations.[21]

Perhaps the biggest uncertainty facing VIZIO in late 2008 was the state of the economy. Spurred by a collapse of the US sub-prime mortgage market, in September 2008 stock markets began to fall dramatically; large financial services institutions failed or were bought out; and governments around the world were forced to develop bailout programs to help stabilize the financial markets. US consumer spending dropped dramatically in October and the retail industry was particularly hard hit. On November 10, 2008, Circuit City announced that it was seeking bankruptcy protection. Two days later, Best Buy chief executive Brad Anderson sharply lowered its sales and earnings forecasts, stating that "Since mid-September, rapid, seismic changes in consumer behavior have created the most difficult climate we've ever seen."[22] Many retail industry analysts expected the upcoming holiday season to be the worst in decades.

Wal-Mart, however, had been faring relatively well compared with most other retailers. In October 2008, while consumer spending was down 1 percent – the largest decrease in a single month since September 11, 2001 – Wal-Mart US showed a sales increase of 5.3 percent and Sam's Club recorded a sales increase of 4.5 percent. Including its international business, Wal-Mart as a whole was up 2.3 percent. (See **Exhibit 13** for a comparison of retailer sales for October.) *Money Morning* noted, "There are a few retailers that … have managed to position themselves as offering more value for the money, which has allowed them to buck this downward spiral in consumer spending…. And that focus will continue in 2009. The best example of this value exception is Wal-Mart."[23] While the company was not without its vulnerabilities, Wal-Mart was the only stock in the Dow Jones Industrial Average to post gains for 2008.

[19]Knji Hall, "For Sony TVs, a New Downscale Front; An All-out Effort in Lower-end Models Should Result in Big Unit Sale Gains, But Some Wonder if Bravia Sets at Wal-Mart Will Hurt the Brand," *BusinessWeek.com*, May 16, 2008, via Factiva, accessed September 25, 2008.

[20]Erica Off, "HDTV Makers Turn to Budget Stores, Larger Screens," *CNET.com*, September 17, 2008, via Factiva, accessed September 25, 2008.

[21]Greg Tarr, "iSuppli: TV Screen Size Overrated As Buying Factor," *Twice*, September 15, 2008, http://www.twice.com/index.asp? layout=articlePrint&articleID=CA659088, accessed September 25, 2008.

[22]Miguel Bustillo, "Best Buy Warns of Dire Holiday Sales – Electronics Giant Says Profit and Revenue will Fall Short of Forecasts, Sending Shivers Through Markets," *Wall Street Journal*, November 13, 2008, via Factiva, accessed September 25, 2008.

[23]JenniferYousfi, "Retail Sales to Suffer in 2009 as US Consumers Curtail Spending," *Money Morning Outlook,* November 28, 2008, http://www.moneymorning.com/2008/11/28/retail-outlook-2009, accessed December 2, 2008.

Looking forward

Wang was convinced that many of the key elements of his strategy would help him weather the severe price competition and current economic downturn. He remained confident about the holiday season and about early 2009 when television stations were scheduled to switch from analog to digital broadcasts. He noted:

In some ways, a tough economy can be an advantage to a company like ours. People are very careful about how they spend money these days, but our products are still selling well and we are having trouble keeping up with demand. In the current environment, many of our competitors are worried about survival. Their focus is on bringing down costs. Our situation is very different because our fixed overhead is already very low. We need to figure out how to grow the top line.

We currently have about 12 percent of the flat-screen TV market. In the first quarter of 2009, we should be close to 20 percent market share. How big can we grow? Besides TV, what can we do? Outside of the US, where should we go? These are huge questions for us. Our competitors are scaling back, but I really think this is the time for us to aggressively move forward.

Wang felt that VIZIO could boost revenue through product enhancements and introductions, branding and marketing initiatives, and international growth. He was especially intrigued by further expansion in overseas markets, and was considering selling VIZIO products through Wal-Mart's stores in Brazil. Schindler explained the pressure that VIZIO was facing from its retail partners:

For some time, all three of our major customers have been asking us to expand internationally. In fact, the television buyer for Wal-Mart was recently promoted to run the company's international business. Wal-Mart is hoping that he will convince us to grow further overseas. In addition, the general manager of electronics for Sam's Club was promoted to run the Wal-Mart stores in Japan. She, too, is pushing us to provide products for them.

Wescoat added:

It was really through Costco's initiative that we entered Japan and Canada. We are doing our best to be accommodating, but we are only in the early stages of this. We launched in Canada late in the summer of 2008. We are still learning and working on getting the right approach and structure so that we can do this in a much bigger way.

There are so many things we need to assess. We need to think about the available markets and the degree of penetration of our technology in those markets. We have to understand the broadcast standards and how that will affect our product design. We need to understand each market within the context of our principal retailers and their respective market shares in those countries. We need to think about distribution – how easy or difficult it will be to source product and get it to retail outlets. How will we handle service on the back end? In some countries there are trademark issues related to protecting the brand that can be time-consuming to resolve. There's always a political dimension and an economic dimension. The list of considerations often feels endless.

As Wang contemplated VIZIO's next steps overseas, he reviewed the limited data he had available. (See **Exhibit 14** for the international operations of VIZIO's retail partners, **Exhibit 15** for HDTV penetration by region, and **Exhibit 16** for worldwide market share statistics.) While genuinely enthusiastic about the opportunity to follow Wal-Mart's success in Latin America and expand into Brazil, Wang wondered if VIZIO might be better off by focusing further on the foreign countries it was already in. There was clearly an argument for VIZIO to refine its overseas business model and add more products and stores in Japan and Canada before tackling a new geographic region.

At the same time, Wang couldn't help wondering about the risks of overseas expansion in the midst of a severe recession. Any international growth would be fairly capital intensive, and there was significant uncertainty about how the economic downturn would play itself out throughout the world. There was also a fair amount of uncertainty about VIZIO's ability to replicate its inventory management and working capital model overseas.

Regardless of how VIZIO approached international growth, Wang knew there were multiple challenges in the immediate term that would require ongoing attention. VIZIO would have to preserve its status with Costco and Wal-Mart and continue to focus on brand development and operating improvements. Riddhi

Patel, the television analyst for iSuppli, had argued that "VIZIO's survival will depend on their aggressiveness with pricing as well as incorporation of advanced features into their sets."[24] In addition, Wang wondered how VIZIO should decrease its dependency on Amtran, while still maintaining an advantageous and positive relationship. He also questioned what Amtran's joint venture with LG would mean over time for VIZIO.

As VIZIO sought to find the right balance between growth and profitability, Wang recognized the need to develop a long-term financing strategy for the company. Wescoat observed:

> While we've been increasing sales and profits significantly for some time, in order for our financial story to resonate, we've got to get our margins to levels that will intrigue a broader investor base. The pricing on televisions continues to erode to commodity levels. We think we have some opportunities with more growth and in providing content and higher-margin accessories, but the public markets may have to be convinced. Nonetheless, there is a lot of interest in our market share and in our brand. The consumer electronics industry and the venture capital and private equity markets have all been turned on their ears in the last few months. We will just have to be patient and see how things develop in the next 12 to 18 months.

With the company's financing strategy on his mind, before Wang shut down his computer for the day, he checked the stock market indexes and learned that the Dow Jones Industrial Average was down another 400 points. His heart sank as the reality of the economic slowdown hit home once again.

VIZIO, Inc.

---

[24]Riddhi Patel, "Will 2009 be the Year-of-Doom for TV Makers?" iSuppli Advanced Market Intelligence, p. 23.

EXHIBIT 1 Historical Revenue Data, 2003–2008

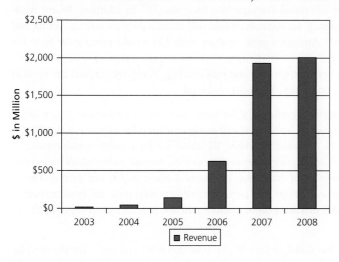

Source: Company.

EXHIBIT 2   **List of VIZIO Television Products**

Size	Product	Retail Price	Stores
50″ and Bigger			
VP505XVT	50″ Plasma 1080P Full HD	$1,699.99	Coming Soon
VP504F	50″ Plasma	1,699.99	Costco, Sears, BJ's
VP503	50″ Plasma HD	1,199.99	Costco, Circuit City
42″ to 49″			
V047LF	47″ LCD 1080P Full HD	1,399.99	Costco, Target, Sears, BJ's
SV470XVT	47″ LCD 1080P Full HD w/120 Hz	1,699.99	Costco, Sam's, Sears, Dell, Circuit City
GV47LF	47″ LCD 1080P Full HD	1,499.99	Costco, Sam's Sears, BJ's
VW46LF	46″ LCD 1080P Full HD	1,399.99	Wal-Mart
VW42LF	42″ LCD 1080P Full HD	1,099.99	Wal-Mart
VP422	42″ Plasma HD	799.99	Wal-Mart, Sears
V042LF	42″ LCD 1080P Full HD	1,099.99	Costco, Target, BJ's
SV20XVT	42″ LCD 1080P Full HD w/120 Hz	1,399.99	Costco, Sam's, Sears, Dell, Circuit City
GV42LF	42″ LCD 1080P Full HD	1,399.99	Sears, Circuit City
32″ to 41″			
VW37L	37″ LCD HD	789.99	Wal-Mart, Kmart
V0J370F	37″ LCD 1080P Full HD	849.99	Target, Dell
V037L	37″ LCD HD	799.99	Costco, Sam's, BJ's
V037LF	37″ LCD 1080P Full HD	849.99	Costco, Sears
VW32L	32″ LCD HD	629.99	Wal-Mart, Dell, Kmart
VP322	32″ Plasma HD	649.99	Costco, Wal-Mart
V0J320F	32″ LCD 1080P Full HD	649.99	Target, Dell
V032L	32″ LCD HD	649.99	Costco, BJ's
V032LF	32″ LCD 1080P Full HD	649.99	Costco, Sam's
20″ to 31″			
VW26L	26″ LCD HD	499.99	Costco, Wal-Mart, Kmart
VMM26	26″ Monitor Full HD	499.99	Costco, Sam's, BJ's
VA26L	26″ LCD HD	499.99	Costco, Sam's, Dell
VW22L	22″ LCD HD	399.99	Wal-Mart
V022L	22″ LCD HD	399.99	Costco, Sam's, BJ's
V022LF	22″ LCD 1080P Full HD	429.99	Coming Soon

Source: VIZIO website.

VIZIO, Inc.

EXHIBIT 3 **VIZIO Customer Mix (based on unit shipments)**

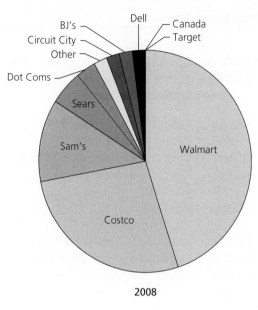

2008

Source: Company.

EXHIBIT 4 **Management Biographies**

Laynie Newsome – Vice President of Sales and Marketing and Co-founder

Newsome was an original employee and co-founder of VIZIO. Newsome began working with Wang as her first job after school in 1991. In over 18 years working with Wang, Newsome had been responsible for customer service, sales, and marketing communications. Ms Newsome was recognized as a leading voice in the HDTV industry and was a recent recipient of the prestigious Orange County Metro Businesswoman Under 40 award. She was known within VIZIO as the ''Champion of the Brand.''

Ken Lowe – Vice President of Product Engineering and Co-founder

Lowe was an original employee and co-founder of VIZIO with Wang and Newsome. He was an electrical engineer from Middlesex University and worked for over 30 years in the CRTs, monitors and displays business including over ten years at Philips. He was responsible for picture quality as well as features, usability, and consumer interface.

Jeff Schindler – Vice President of Business Planning

Schindler joined VIZIO in 2004. Schindler had over 25 years of experience in the consumer electronics and information technology businesses. He held several senior level product planning and marketing positions at Gateway Computers and was responsible for the development and launch of the first PC/TV by Gateway. He held a Bachelor of Science degree in electrical engineering from Western Michigan University.

Rob Brinkman – Vice President of Operations

Brinkman joined VIZIO in October of 2008. Brinkman held senior positions at several electronics and computer products companies, including four years as president of Princeton Digital (one of Wang's earlier companies). He was also executive vice president of operations at Micro Warehouse and spent eleven years at Insight Enterprises, Inc. He held a Bachelor of Science degree in mathematics from Northern Arizona University.

John Schindler – Vice President of New Products

Schindler joined VIZIO in November 2007. His twelve year tenure at Gateway included product management, product marketing, and the development of wireless home networking programs. He held a Bachelor of Science degree in electrical engineering from Western Michigan University.

Matt McRae – Vice President of Product Development

McRae joined VIZIO in August of 2008. Prior to VIZIO, he served as vice president of marketing and business development at Fabrik, Inc., and held executive positions at Cisco Systems, Linksys, and Viking Components. He held a business degree from the Wharton School of Business and a computer science engineering degree from the University of Pennsylvania.

Eunice Tseng – Vice President of Management Information Systems

Tseng joined VIZIO in October 2007, bringing her background in the implementation of computer accounting systems and supervising accounting departments. Tseng held the position of international accounting manager at Broadcom Corporation and had also served as the director of finance for MAG Innovision, one of Wang's earlier companies. She held a Bachelor of Science degree in business administration in data processing and accounting.

Kyle Wescoat – Vice President and Chief Financial Officer

Wescoat joined VIZIO in February 2008, with 25 years of CFO experience with several companies, including two NASDAQ listed consumer products companies, Vans and Cherokee. Most recently, Wescoat was the chief administrative officer for the Los Angeles Dodgers baseball team. Wescoat was a graduate of Drexel University and held an MBA in finance from the University of Michigan.

VIZIO, Inc.

Source: Company.

EXHIBIT 5   VIZIO Employees by Department

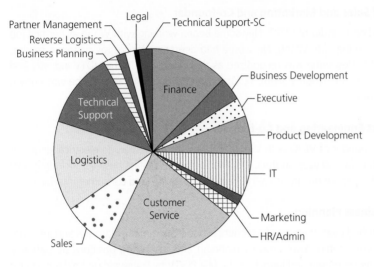

Employee Headcount: 128

Source: Company.

EXHIBIT 6   Revenue versus Revenue per Employee

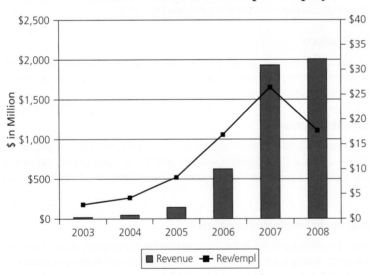

Source: Company.

EXHIBIT 7   **Latest 12 Months Quarterly Market Share Data (North America)**

Combined LCD and Plasma	Q4 '07	Q1 '08	Q2 '08	Q3 '08
Samsung	14.8%	14.0%	21.5%	22.5%
VIZIO	11.3%	12.7%	10.8%	10.4%
Sony	11.7%	11.7%	11.7%	14.2%
Sharp	8.1%	7.6%	7.0%	8.8%
LG Electronics	8.6	9.5%	7.3%	9.3%
Panasonic	6.2	4.2%	5.1%	7.3%
Philips	6.4%	4.2%	6.5%	1.9%
Other	33.0%	36.1%	30.1%	25.6%
TOTAL UNITS (000's)	**9,236**	**6,528**	**7,405**	**7,801**

Source: iSuppli, Television Systems Market Tracker, Q1 2009.

EXHIBIT 8   **Flat-Panel Television Unit Sales Forecast, 2008–2012 (000's)**

	2008	2009	2010	2011	2012	2013
Plasma	4,407	4,049	3,957	3,650	3,349	2,837
LCD	23,828	24,846	26,680	29,336	32,477	35,300
TOTAL	28,235	28,895	30,637	32,826	35,829	38,137

Source: iSuppi, Television Systems Market Tracker, Q1 2009.

EXHIBIT 9   **Advertising Expenditures by Competitor**

Brand	2004 Ad Spend ($ millions)	2005 Ad Spend ($ millions)	% Change
Sony	$21.6	$39.8	84%
Panasonic	17.1	34.8	103
Samsung	24.7	33.9	37
Sharp	30.5	33.0	8

Source: Mintel, "Digital Television – US – April 2007."

VIZIO, Inc.

EXHIBIT 10 **Brand Survey Results**

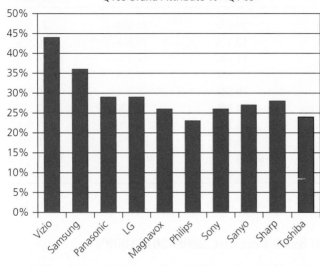

Brand	Q109
Vizio	44%
Samsung	36%
Panasonic	29%
LG	29%
Magnavox	26%
Philips	23%
Sony	26%
Sanyo	27%
Sharp	28%
Toshiba	24%

TV Brand Survey Conducted by Core Strategies Dec 30, 2008

Source: Company.

EXHIBIT 11 **Selected Comparative Financial Data – 2007, 2008 (estimated)**

	For the Latest 12 Months Ended 12/31/07			For the Latest 12 Months Ended 12/31/08		
	LCD Revenue[a]	LCD Operating Profit[a]	LCD Operating Margin	LCD Revenue[a]	LCD Operating Profit[a]	LCD Operating Margin
Sony	$10,826	$−671	−6.2%	$13,224	$−873	−6.6%
Samsung	$15,708	$2,102	13.4%	$15,751	$2,203	14.0%
Sharp	$9,788	$712	7.3%	$12,096	$558	4.6%

Source: America's Growth Capital.

[a]Adjusted for currency translations using an average annual exchange rate.

VIZIO, Inc.

EXHIBIT 12 **Average Selling Prices, North America 2002 through Third Quarter 2008**

	2002	2003	2004	2005	2006	2007	Q3 2008
Plasma TVs	$5,361	$4,997	$3,823	$2,741	$1,969	$1,540	$1,216
LCD TVs	$1,814	$1,455	$1,682	$1,352	$1,225	$1,098	$ 976

Source: iSuppli, Television Systems Market Tracker, Q1 2009.

EXHIBIT 13 **Retail Sales for October 2008**

	$ Millions	% Change from Prior Year
Discounters		
Wal-Mart	$28,565.0	+2.3%
Costco	5.300.0	+1 7
Target	4.415.0	−0.7
Department Stores		
J.C. Penney	$1,361.0	−11.8%
Kohl's	1,212,8	−4.8
Nordstrom	529.0	−15.5
Dillard's	406.1	−8.7
Neiman Marcus	286.0	−25.3
Saks	219.0	−16.6
Apparel		
TJX	$1,480.0	−2.0%
Gap	1,080.0	−16.0
Limited	580.4	−10.0
Teen Apparel		
Abercrombie & Fitch	$215.0	−14.0%
American Eagle	204.8	−2.6%

Source: Adapted by casewriter from Ann Zimmerman, "Retailers Wallow and See Only More Gloom," *Wall Street Journal*, November 7, 2008 via Factiva accessed December 2, 2008.

VIZIO, Inc.

VIZIO, Inc.

EXHIBIT 14 International Retailers

	BJ's	Costco	Kmart	Sam's	Sears	Target	Wal-Mart
# Total Stores	177	551	1,382	702	1,054	1,685	7,271
# US States	16	40	49	NA	50	48	50
# Members (000's)	8,800	53,500	NA	47,000	NA	NA	NA
Approx. Retail Sq. Ft.	19,203,000	77,691,000	131,159,000	79,464,000	134,000,000	207,945,000	589,299,876
Avg. Store Size	108,492	141,000	94,905	132,000	NA	130,700	138,398
# US Stores[a]	177	400	1,354	599	926	1,685	4,100
# International Stores	0	151	28	103	128	0	3,615
Net Revenue ($MM's)	$9,005.0	$72,483.0	$17,256.0	$44,357.0	$27,845.0[c]	$63,367.0	$239,529.0
International Revenue ($MM's)	None	$15,579.1[b]	NA	NA	$5,602.0[d]	None	$90,640.0
Operating Profit ($MM's)	$195.3	$1,968.8	$402.0	$1,618.0	$784.0[d]	$5,272.0	$17,516.0
International Op. Profit ($MM's)	None	$575.5	NA	NA	$400.0	None	$4,769.0
International Stores	None	Canada (76) Japan (8) Korea (6) Mexico (31) Puerto Rico (4) Taiwan (5) United Kingdom (21)	Guam (1) Puerto Rico (23) US Virgin Islands (4)	Brazil (15) Canada (6) China (3) Mexico (70) Puerto Rico (9)	Canada (121) Puerto Rico (9)	None	Argentina (28) Brazil (345) Canada (318) Chile (197) China (243) Costa Rica (164) Guatemala (160) Honduras (50) Japan (371) Mexico (1,197) Nicaragua (51) Puerto Rico (56) El Salvador (77) United Kingdom (358)

NA = Not applicable or not available.

Source: Adapted by casewriter from company websites and Form 10-Ks from the last available fiscal year.

[a] Excludes stores in Puerto Rico, which are included in international store numbers.

[b] Sears Canada only.

[c] Includes Puerto Rico.

[d] Excludes Kmart and Sears Canada.

EXHIBIT 15   **LCD and Plasma Shipment Forecasts by Region**

	2008	**2009**	**2010**	**2011**	**2012**	**2013**
Rest APAC	7,091	9,272	13,932	24,819	32,372	36,705
China	13,057	17,126	21,384	24,651	27,782	30,709
Eastern Europe	7,508	7,820	9,346	13,126	18,314	21,572
Western Europe	27,499	27,231	28,368	29,368	33,600	38,660
Japan	10,383	10,369	10,498	10,617	11,179	12,540
Latin America	4,985	6,886	9,619	13,104	16,591	19,827
Middle East & Africa	2,218	3,004	4,140	5,575	7,265	8,704
TOTAL	72,741	81,708	97,287	121,260	147,103	168,717

Source: iSuppli, Televisions Systems Market Tracker, Q1 2009.

EXHIBIT 16   **LCD and Plasma Market Share Worldwide Outside of the US (Third Quarter '08)**

	Shipments (000's)	**Market Share (%)**
Samsung	4,057	19.7
LG	2,277	11.0
Sharp	2,185	10.6
Sony	2,140	10.4
Philips	1,777	8.6
Panasonic	1,551	7.5
Toshiba	922	4.5
Others	5,734	27.8
TOTAL	20,643	100.00%

Source: iSuppli, Television Systems Market Tracker, Q1 2009.

VIZIO, Inc.

Accounting Analysis: The Basics

The purpose of accounting analysis is to evaluate the degree to which a firm's accounting captures its underlying business reality.[1] By identifying places where there is accounting flexibility, and by evaluating the appropriateness of the firm's accounting policies and estimates, analysts can assess the degree of distortion in a firm's accounting numbers. Another important skill is adjusting a firm's accounting numbers using cash flow information and information from the notes to the financial statements to "undo" any accounting distortions. Sound accounting analysis improves the reliability of conclusions from financial analysis, the next step in financial statement analysis.

FACTORS INFLUENCING ACCOUNTING QUALITY

Because the mechanisms that limit managers' ability to distort accounting data themselves add noise, it is not optimal to use accounting regulation to eliminate managerial flexibility completely. Therefore, real-world accounting systems leave considerable room for managers to influence financial statement data. The net result is that information in corporate financial reports is noisy and biased, even in the presence of accounting regulation and external auditing.[2] The objective of **accounting analysis** is to evaluate the degree to which a firm's accounting captures its underlying business reality and to "undo" any accounting distortions. When potential distortions are large, accounting analysis can add considerable value.[3]

There are three potential **sources of noise and bias in accounting data**:

1 That introduced by rigidity in accounting rules.

2 Random forecast errors.

3 Systematic reporting choices made by corporate managers to achieve specific objectives.

Each of these factors is discussed below.

Noise from accounting rules

Accounting rules introduce noise and bias because it is often difficult to restrict management discretion without reducing the information content of accounting data. For example, revised International Accounting Standard (IAS) 19 issued by the IASB requires firms to recognize pension expense net of a close to risk free return on the pension plan's investments. Clearly, if the firm's pension plan is making wise investments, in the long run we expect it to earn significantly more than the risk-free rate. However, because IAS 19 does not allow firms to recognize the true expected return on the plan's assets in their income statement, the application of the rule leads to a systematic distortion of reported accounting numbers. Broadly speaking, the degree of distortion introduced by accounting standards depends on how well uniform accounting standards capture the nature of a firm's transactions.

As a solution to the adverse effects of rigid accounting rules, the IASB often defines standards that are based more on broadly stated principles than on detailed rules. For example, most accountants agree that when a firm spends cash on research and development it essentially makes an investment that should be recorded as such on the balance sheet. In its standard for intangible assets, the IASB leaves much responsibility to the managers and auditors to decide what proportion of development outlays will likely generate future revenues and should thus be considered an asset. In contrast, the US accounting standard for intangible assets issued by the FASB prescribes that all research and development outlays are recognized as expense in the period that they are made. The US standard thus leaves managers much less discretion in the reporting of research and development than the international standard.

The research and development example illustrates what many see as an important difference in the approaches that the IASB and the FASB have been taking to standard-setting. Proponents of the principles-based approach claim that reporting in accordance with principles, instead of technical rules, ensures that the financial statements reflect the economic substance of firms' transactions, instead of their legal form. However, because principles-based standards provide less technical guidance than rules-based standards, they demand more professionalism from auditors in exercising their duties and are more difficult to enforce. Proponents of the rules-based approach therefore claim that using rules-based standards increases the verifiability of the information included in the financial statements, reduces managers' misuse of their reporting discretion, and increases the comparability of financial statements across firms. Because during recent years the FASB and IASB have intensively cooperated to eliminate differences between US GAAP and IFRS and to develop new common standards, the distinction between the two approaches to standard setting has gradually diminished, leaving some international standards to be more principles-based than others.

Forecast errors

Another source of noise in accounting data arises from pure forecast error, because managers cannot predict future consequences of current transactions perfectly. For example, when a firm sells products on credit, accrual accounting requires managers to make a judgment about the probability of collecting payments from customers. If payments are deemed "reasonably certain," the firm treats the transactions as sales, creating trade receivables on its balance sheet. Managers then make an estimate of the proportion of receivables that will not be collected. Because managers do not have perfect foresight, actual defaults are likely to be different from estimated customer defaults, leading to a forecast error. The extent of errors in managers' accounting forecasts depends on a variety of factors, including the complexity of the business transactions, the predictability of the firm's environment, and unforeseen economy-wide changes.

Managers' accounting choices

Corporate managers also introduce noise and bias into accounting data through their own accounting decisions. Managers have a variety of incentives to exercise their accounting discretion to achieve certain objectives:[4]

- **Accounting-based debt covenants.** Managers may make accounting decisions to meet certain contractual obligations in their debt covenants. For example, firms' lending agreements with banks and other debt holders require them to meet covenants related to interest coverage, working capital ratios, and net worth, all defined in terms of accounting numbers. Violation of these agreements may be costly because lenders can trigger penalties including demanding immediate payment of their loans. Managers of firms close to violating debt covenants have an incentive to select accounting policies and estimates to reduce the probability of covenant violation. The debt covenant motivation for managers' accounting decisions has been analyzed by a number of accounting researchers.[5]

- **Management compensation.** Another motivation for managers' accounting choice comes from the fact that their compensation and job security are often tied to reported profits. For example, many top managers receive bonus compensation if they exceed certain prespecified profit targets. This provides motivation for managers to choose accounting policies and estimates to maximize their expected compensation.[6] Stock option awards can also potentially induce managers to manage earnings. Options provide managers with incentives to understate earnings prior to option grants to lower the firm's current share price and hence the option exercise price, and to inflate earnings and share prices at the time of the option exercise.[7]

- **Corporate control contests.** In corporate control contests, such as hostile takeovers, competing management groups attempt to win over the firm's shareholders. Accounting numbers are used extensively in debating managers' performance in these contests. Therefore, managers may make accounting decisions to influence investor perceptions in corporate control contests. Also, when takeovers are not necessarily hostile but structured as a share-for-share merger, the acquiring firm may overstate its performance to boost its share price and by this reduce the share exchange ratio.[8]

■ Tax considerations. Managers may also make reporting choices to trade off between financial reporting and tax considerations. For example, US firms are required to use LIFO inventory accounting for shareholder reporting in order to use it for tax reporting. Under LIFO, when prices are rising, firms report lower profits, thereby reducing tax payments. Some firms may forgo the tax reduction in order to report higher profits in their financial statements. In countries where such a direct link between financial reporting and tax reporting does not exist, tax considerations may still indirectly affect managers' reporting decisions. For example, firms that recognize losses aggressively in their tax statements may support their aggressive tax choices by having the financial reporting treatment of these losses conform to their tax treatment. Having no divergence between the tax treatment and the financial reporting treatment could increase the probability that tax authorities allow the tax treatment.[9]

■ Regulatory considerations. Since accounting numbers are used by regulators in a variety of contexts, managers of some firms may make accounting decisions to influence regulatory outcomes. Examples of regulatory situations where accounting numbers are used include actions to end or prevent infringements of competition laws, import tariffs to protect domestic industries, and tax policies.[10]

■ Capital market considerations. Managers may make accounting decisions to influence the perceptions of capital markets. When there are information asymmetries between managers and outsiders, this strategy may succeed in influencing investor perceptions, at least temporarily.[11]

■ Stakeholder considerations. Managers may also make accounting decisions to influence the perception of important stakeholders in the firm. For example, since labor unions can use healthy profits as a basis for demanding wage increases, managers may make accounting decisions to decrease profit when they are facing union contract negotiations. In countries like Germany, where labor unions are strong, these considerations appear to play an important role in firms' accounting policy. Other important stakeholders that firms may wish to influence through their financial reports include suppliers and customers.[12]

■ Competitive considerations. The dynamics of competition in an industry might also influence a firm's reporting choices. For example, a firm's segment disclosure decisions may be influenced by its concern that disaggregated disclosure may help competitors in their business decisions. Similarly, firms may not disclose data on their margins by product line for fear of giving away proprietary information. Finally, firms may discourage new entrants by making profit-decreasing accounting choices.

In addition to accounting policy choices and estimates, the level of disclosure is also an important determinant of a firm's accounting quality. Corporate managers can choose disclosure policies that make it more or less costly for external users of financial reports to understand the true economic picture of their businesses. Accounting regulations usually prescribe minimum disclosure requirements, but they do not restrict managers from voluntarily providing additional disclosures. Managers can use various parts of the financial reports, including the Management Report and notes, to describe the company's strategy, its accounting policies, and its current performance. There is wide variation across firms in how managers use their disclosure flexibility.[13]

STEPS IN ACCOUNTING ANALYSIS

In this section we discuss a series of steps that an analyst can follow to evaluate a firm's accounting quality.

Step 1: Identify key accounting policies

As discussed in Chapter 1, a firm's industry characteristics and its own competitive strategy determine its key success factors and risks. One of the goals of financial statement analysis is to evaluate how well these success factors and risks are being managed by the firm. In accounting analysis, therefore, the analyst should identify and evaluate the policies and the estimates the firm uses to measure its critical factors and risks.

Key success factors in the banking industry include interest and credit risk management; in the retail industry, inventory management is a key success factor; and for a manufacturer competing on product quality and innovation, research and development and product defects after the sale are key areas of concern. A significant success factor in the leasing business is to make accurate forecasts of residual values of the leased equipment at the end of the lease terms. In each of these cases, the analyst has to identify the accounting measures the firm uses to capture these business constructs, the policies that determine how the measures are implemented, and the key estimates embedded in these policies. For example, the accounting measure a bank uses to capture credit risk is its loan loss reserves, and the accounting measure that captures product quality for a manufacturer is its warranty expenses and reserves. For a firm in the equipment leasing industry, one of the most important accounting policies is the way residual values are recorded. Residual values influence the company's reported profits and its asset base. If residual values are overestimated, the firm runs the risk of having to take large write-offs in the future.

CRITICAL ACCOUNTING ESTIMATES

When identifying a firm's key accounting policies, it is helpful that the IFRS mandate firms to explicitly identify the accounting methods and estimates that require most judgment and are of critical importance to the usefulness of their accounting information. For example, in its 2011 financial statements cruise company Carnival Corporation & plc reported that "… our most significant assets are our ships, ship improvements, and ships under construction, which represent 80 percent of our total assets. We make several critical accounting estimates dealing with our ship accounting. First, we compute our ships' depreciation expense, which represented approximately 11 percent of our cruise costs and expenses in fiscal 2011 and which requires us to estimate the average useful life of each of our ships as well as their residual values. Secondly, we account for ship improvement costs by capitalizing those costs which we believe will add value to our ships and depreciate those improvements over their or the ships' estimated useful lives, whichever is shorter, while the costs of repairs and maintenance, including minor improvement costs and dry-dock expenses, are charged to expense as they are incurred. Finally, when we record the retirement of a ship component that is included within the ship's cost basis, we may have to estimate its net book value." Other areas of significant judgment identified by Carnival were: (1) the determination of fair values of ships and trademarks for which no active market exists (in impairment tests) and (2) the valuation of potential liabilities related to lawsuits, environmental claims, guest and crew claims, and tax matters.

Step 2: Assess accounting flexibility

Not all firms have equal flexibility in choosing their key accounting policies and estimates. Some firms' accounting choice is severely constrained by accounting standards and conventions. For example, even though research and development is a key success factor for biotechnology companies, managers have no accounting discretion in reporting on research activities and, in practice, often make no distinction between development and research because the future benefits of development outlays are too difficult to assess. Similarly, even though marketing and brand building are key to the success of consumer goods firms, they are required to expense all their marketing outlays. In contrast, managing credit risk is one of the critical success factors for banks, and bank managers have the freedom to estimate expected defaults on their loans. Similarly, shipbuilding companies can adequately show the profitability status of their long-term projects because they have the flexibility to recognize proportions of the project revenues during the life of the project.

If managers have little flexibility in choosing accounting policies and estimates related to their key success factors (as in the case of biotechnology firms), accounting data are likely to be less informative for understanding the firm's economics. In contrast, if managers have considerable flexibility in choosing the policies and estimates (as in the case of banks), accounting numbers have the potential to be informative, depending upon how managers exercise this flexibility.

Regardless of the degree of accounting flexibility a firm's managers have in measuring their key success factors and risks, they will have some flexibility with respect to several other accounting policies. For example, all firms have to make choices with respect to depreciation policy (straight-line or accelerated methods), inventory accounting policy (FIFO or average cost), policy for amortizing intangible assets other than goodwill (write-off over 20 years or less), and policies regarding the estimation of pension and other post-employment benefits (expected return on plan assets, discount rate for liabilities, and rate of increase in wages and healthcare costs). Since all these policy choices can have a significant impact on the reported performance of a firm, they offer an opportunity for the firm to manage its reported numbers.

ACCOUNTING FLEXIBILITY

Carnival calculates the average useful life and residual value of its ships as the weighted average of the useful lives and residual values of the ships' major components, such as cabins and engines. Management's estimate of the average useful life of its ships is 30 years; the residual value is set at 15 percent of the ships' initial cost. In the notes to the financial statements, management illustrates its accounting flexibility as follows: "… if we change our assumptions in making our determinations as to whether improvements to a ship add value, the amounts we expend each year as repair and maintenance costs could increase, which would be partially offset by a decrease in depreciation expense, resulting from a reduction in capitalized costs. Our fiscal 2011 ship depreciation expense would have increased by approximately $37 million for every year we reduced our estimated average 30 year ship useful life. In addition, if our ships were estimated to have no residual value, our fiscal 2011 depreciation expense would have increased by approximately $190 million." In 2011, $37 million was equivalent to roughly 1.6 percent of the company's operating income.

Step 3: Evaluate accounting strategy

When managers have accounting flexibility, they can use it either to communicate their firm's economic situation or to hide true performance. Some of the strategy questions one could ask in examining how managers exercise their accounting flexibility include the following:

- **Reporting incentives.** Do managers face strong incentives to use accounting discretion to manage earnings? For example, is the firm close to violating bond covenants? Or are the managers having difficulty meeting accounting-based bonus targets? Does management own a significant amount of shares? Is the firm in the middle of a takeover battle or union negotiations? Managers may also make accounting decisions to reduce tax payments or to influence the perceptions of the firm's competitors.

- **Deviations from the norm.** How do the firm's accounting policies compare to the norms in the industry? If they are dissimilar, is it because the firm's competitive strategy is unique? For example, consider a firm that reports a lower provision for warranty costs than the industry average. One explanation is that the firm competes on the basis of high quality and has invested considerable resources to reduce the rate of product failure. An alternative explanation is that the firm is merely understating its warranty provision.

- **Accounting changes.** Has the firm changed any of its policies or estimates? What is the justification? What is the impact of these changes? For example, if warranty expenses decreased, is it because the firm made significant investments to improve quality?

- **Past accounting errors.** Have the company's policies and estimates been realistic in the past? For example, firms may overstate their revenues and understate their expenses during the year by manipulating quarterly or semi-annual reports, which are not subject to a full-blown external audit. However, the auditing process at the end of the fiscal year forces such companies to make large year-end adjustments, providing an opportunity for the analyst to assess the quality of the firm's interim reporting. Similarly, firms that depreciate fixed assets too slowly will be forced to take a large write-off later. A history of write-offs may be, therefore, a sign of prior earnings management.

- **Structuring of transactions.** Does the firm structure any significant business transactions so that it can achieve certain accounting objectives? For example, leasing firms can alter lease terms (the length of the lease or the bargain purchase option at the end of the lease term) so that the transactions qualify as sales-type leases for the lessors. Enron structured acquisitions of joint venture interests and hedging transactions with special purpose entities to avoid having to show joint venture liabilities, and to avoid reporting investment losses in its financial statements.[14] Such behavior may suggest that the firm's managers are willing to expend economic resources merely to achieve an accounting objective.

Step 4: Evaluate the quality of disclosure

Managers can make it more or less easy for an analyst to assess the firm's accounting quality and to use its financial statements to understand business reality. While accounting rules require a certain amount of minimum disclosure, managers have considerable choice in the matter. Disclosure quality, therefore, is an important dimension of a firm's accounting quality.

In assessing a firm's disclosure quality, an analyst could ask the following questions:

- Strategic choices. Does the company provide adequate disclosures to assess the firm's business strategy and its economic consequences? For example, some firms use management's narrative report in their financial statements to clearly lay out the firm's industry conditions, its competitive position, and management's plans for the future. Others use the report to puff up the firm's financial performance and gloss over any competitive difficulties the firm might be facing.

- Accounting choices. Do the notes to the financial statements adequately explain the key accounting policies and assumptions and their logic? For example, if a firm's revenue and expense recognition policies differ from industry norms, the firm can explain its choices in a note. Similarly, when there are significant changes in a firm's policies, notes can be used to disclose the reasons.

- Discussion of financial performance. Does the firm adequately explain its current performance? The Management Report section of the annual report provides an opportunity to help analysts understand the reasons behind a firm's performance changes. Some firms use this section to link financial performance to business conditions. For example, if profit margins went down in a period, was it because of price competition or because of increases in manufacturing costs? If the selling and general administrative expenses went up, was it because the firm is investing in a differentiation strategy, or because unproductive overhead expenses were creeping up?

- Non-financial performance information. If accounting rules and conventions restrict the firm from measuring its key success factors appropriately, does the firm provide adequate additional disclosure to help outsiders understand how these factors are being managed? For example, if a firm invests in product quality and customer service, accounting rules do not allow the management to capitalize these outlays, even when the future benefits are certain. The firm's review of its operations can be used to highlight how these outlays are being managed and their performance consequences. For example, the firm can disclose physical indexes of defect rates and customer satisfaction so that outsiders can assess the progress being made in these areas and the future cash flow consequences of these actions.

- Segment information. If a firm is in multiple business segments, what is the quality of segment disclosure? Some firms provide excellent discussion of their performance by product segments and geographic segments. Others lump many different businesses into one broad segment. The level of competition in an industry and management's willingness to share desegregated performance data influence a firm's quality of segment disclosure.

- Bad news. How forthcoming is the management with respect to bad news? A firm's disclosure quality is most clearly revealed by the way management deals with bad news. Does it adequately explain the reasons for poor performance? Does the company clearly articulate its strategy, if any, to address the company's performance problems?

- Investor relations. How good is the firm's investor relations program? Does the firm provide fact books with detailed data on the firm's business and performance? Is the management accessible to analysts?

Step 5: Identify potential red flags

In addition to the preceding steps, a common approach to accounting quality analysis is to look for "red flags" pointing to questionable accounting quality. These indicators suggest that the analyst should examine certain items more closely or gather more information on them. Some common red flags are the following:

- Unexplained changes in accounting, especially when performance is poor. This may suggest that managers are using their accounting discretion to "dress up" their financial statements.[15]

- Unexplained transactions that boost profits. For example, firms might undertake balance sheet transactions, such as asset sales or debt-for-equity swaps, to realize gains in periods when operating performance is poor.[16]

- Unusual increases in trade receivables in relation to sales increases. This may suggest that the company is relaxing its credit policies or artificially loading up its distribution channels to record revenues during the current period. If credit policies are relaxed unduly, the firm may face receivable write-offs in subsequent periods as a result of customer defaults. If the firm accelerates shipments to its distributors, it may either face product returns or reduced shipments in subsequent periods.

- Unusual increases in inventories in relation to sales increases. If the inventory build-up is due to an increase in finished goods inventory, it could be a sign that demand for the firm's products is slowing down, suggesting that the firm may be forced to cut prices (and hence earn lower margins) or write down its inventory. A build-up in work-in-progress inventory tends to be good news on average, probably signaling that managers expect an increase in sales. If the build-up is in raw materials, it could suggest manufacturing or procurement inefficiencies, leading to an increase in cost of sales (and hence lower margins).[17]

- An increasing gap between a firm's reported profit and its cash flow from operating activities. While it is legitimate for accrual accounting numbers to differ from cash flows, there is usually a steady relationship between the two if the company's accounting policies remain the same. Therefore, any *change* in the relationship between reported profits and operating cash flows might indicate subtle changes in the firm's accrual estimates. For example, a firm undertaking large construction contracts might use the percentage-of-completion method to record revenues. While earnings and operating cash flows are likely to differ for such a firm, they should bear a steady relationship to each other. Now suppose the firm increases revenues in a period through an aggressive application of the percentage-of-completion method. Then its earnings will go up, but its cash flow remains unaffected. This change in the firm's accounting quality will be manifested by a *change* in the relationship between the firm's earnings and cash flows.

- An increasing gap between a firm's reported profit and its tax profit. Once again, it is quite legitimate for a firm to follow different accounting policies for financial reporting and tax accounting as long as the tax law allows it. However, the relationship between a firm's book and tax accounting is likely to remain constant over time, unless there are significant changes in tax rules or accounting standards. Thus, an *increasing* gap between a firm's reported profit and its tax profit may indicate that financial reporting to shareholders has become more aggressive. For example, warranty expenses are estimated on an accrual basis for financial reporting, but they are recorded on a cash basis for tax reporting. Unless there is a big change in the firm's product quality, these two numbers bear a consistent relationship to each other. Therefore, a change in this relationship can be an indication either that product quality is changing significantly or that financial reporting estimates are changing.

- A tendency to use financing mechanisms like research and development partnerships, special purpose entities, and the sale of receivables with recourse. While these arrangements may have a sound business logic, they can also provide management with an opportunity to understate the firm's liabilities and/or overstate its assets.[18]

- Unexpected large asset write-offs. This may suggest that management is slow to incorporate changing business circumstances into its accounting estimates. Asset write-offs may also be a result of unexpected changes in business circumstances.[19]

- Large year-end adjustments. A firm's annual reports are audited by the external auditors, but its interim financial statements are usually only reviewed. If a firm's management is reluctant to make appropriate accounting estimates (such as provisions for uncollectible receivables) in its interim statements, it could be forced to make adjustments at the end of the year as a result of pressure from its external auditors. A consistent pattern of year-end adjustments, therefore, may indicate aggressive management of interim reporting.[20]

- Qualified audit opinions or changes in independent auditors that are not well justified. These may indicate a firm's aggressive attitude or a tendency to "opinion shop."

- Poor internal governance mechanisms. Internal governance agents, such as independent directors or supervisors, audit committees, and internal auditors, are responsible for assuring the flow of credible information to external parties. When a firm's supervising directors or audit committee lack independence from management or its internal control system has deficiencies, accounting may be of questionable quality.[21] A lack of independence can be the result of, for example, family bonds, economic relationships, or prior working relationships.

- Related-party transactions or transactions between related entities. These transactions may lack the objectivity of the marketplace, and managers' accounting estimates related to these transactions are likely to be more subjective and potentially self-serving.[22]

While the preceding list provides a number of red flags for potentially poor accounting quality, it is important to do further analysis before reaching final conclusions. Each of the red flags has multiple interpretations; some interpretations are based on sound business reasons, and others indicate questionable accounting. It is, therefore, best to use the red flag analysis as a starting point for further probing, not as an end point in itself.[23]

Step 6: Recast financial statements and undo accounting distortions

If the accounting analysis suggests that the firm's reported numbers are misleading, analysts should attempt to restate the reported numbers to reduce the distortion to the extent possible. It is, of course, virtually impossible to perfectly undo the distortion using outside information alone. However, some progress can be made in this direction by using the cash flow statement and the notes to the financial statements.

A firm's cash flow statement provides a reconciliation of its performance based on accrual accounting and cash accounting. If the analyst is unsure of the quality of the firm's accrual accounting, the cash flow statement provides an alternative benchmark of its performance. The cash flow statement also provides information on how individual line items in the income statement diverge from the underlying cash flows. For example, if an analyst is concerned that the firm is aggressively capitalizing certain costs that should be expensed, the information in the cash flow statement provides a basis to make the necessary adjustment.

The notes to the financial statements also provide information that is potentially useful in restating reported accounting numbers. For example, when a firm changes its accounting policies, it provides a note indicating the effect of that change if it is material. Similarly, some firms provide information on the details of accrual estimates such as the provision for doubtful receivables. The tax note usually provides information on the differences between a firm's accounting policies for shareholder reporting and tax reporting. Since tax reporting is often more conservative than shareholder reporting, the information in the tax note can be used to estimate what the earnings reported to shareholders would be under more conservative policies.

Undoing accounting distortions also entails recasting a firm's financial statements using standard reporting nomenclature and formats. Firms frequently use somewhat different formats and terminology for presenting their financial results. **Recasting the financial statements** using a standard template, therefore, helps ensure that performance metrics used for financial analysis are calculated using comparable definitions across companies and over time.

The following section shows how to recast the firm's financial statements into a template that uses standard terminology and classifications. In Chapter 4, we show how to make accounting adjustments for some of the most common types of accounting distortions.

RECASTING FINANCIAL STATEMENTS

Firms sometimes use different nomenclature and formats to present their financial results. For example, the asset goodwill can be reported separately using such titles as Goodwill, "Excess of cost over net assets of acquired companies," and "Cost in excess of fair value," or it can be included in the line item Other Intangible Assets. Interest Income can be reported as a subcategory of Revenues, shown lower down the income statement as part of Other Income and Expenses, or it is sometimes reported as Interest Expense, Net of Interest Income.

These differences in financial statement terminology, classifications, and formats can make it difficult to compare performance across firms, and sometimes to compare performance for the same firm over time. The first task for the analyst in accounting analysis is, therefore, to recast the financial statements into a common format. This involves designing a template for the balance sheet, income statement, cash flow statement, and statement of comprehensive income that can be used to standardize financial statements for any company.

Some complications

One particular obstacle that the analyst must overcome in recasting IFRS-based income statements is that the international standards allow firms to classify their operating expenses in two ways: by nature or by function. The classification by nature defines categories with reference to the cause of operating expenses. Firms using this classification typically distinguish between the cost of materials, the cost of personnel, and the cost of non-current assets (depreciation and amortization). In contrast, the classification by function defines categories with reference to the purpose of operating expenses. Under this classification, firms typically differentiate between costs that are incurred for the purpose of producing the products or services sold – labeled Cost of Sales – and costs for overhead activities such as administrative work and marketing – labeled Selling, General, and Administrative Expenses (SG&A). Only income statements that are prepared using the latter classification include the line item "**Gross Profit**," which is defined as the difference between Sales and Cost of Sales and measures the efficiency of a firm's production activities.

Although the **classification of operating expenses by function** potentially provides better information about the efficiency and profitability of a firm's operating activities, some analysts prefer the **classification of expenses by nature** because this classification is less arbitrary and requires less judgment from management. The coexistence of two classifications generally will not cause problems as long as the choice for a particular classification is industry-related. For example, firms that operate in the airline industry are more likely to classify their expenses by nature, whereas manufacturing firms are more likely to classify their expenses by function. Firms that operate in similar industries may, however, prefer different classifications.

A further complication may be that firms use similar terminology under different approaches. For example, in 2011 Hennes & Mauritz (H&M) reported that its Gross Profit was 60 percent of Sales, while Inditex, owner of brands such as Zara and Massimo Dutti and one of H&M's main competitors, reported that its Gross Profit was 59 percent of Sales. Because the two firms classified their expenses differently, however, these amounts were not comparable. Inditex's (mislabeled) Gross Profit was calculated by subtracting the nature-based cost of merchandise from sales, whereas H&M's Gross Profit reflected the difference between Sales and the function-based Cost of Sales, which included depreciation and the cost of procurement personnel. Fortunately, the IFRSs require that when firms classify their expenses by function, they should also report a classification of expenses by nature in the notes to the financial statements. Hence, the analyst can always recast H&M's income statement into the format that Inditex used.

Categories of financial statement items

Bearing in mind that the accounting analysis is one step in a larger process of analyzing a business, the design of standardized statements primarily depends on how such statements will be used in the following steps of the process. Although the use of standardized statements may vary according to the end objective of the business analysis – that is, whether a user is, for example, valuing investors' equity claim or assessing the firm's creditworthiness – two general rules apply to most common types of business analysis:

1 Business activities versus financing activities. Analysts typically analyze and value a firm's business activities separately from the firm's sources of financing because both have different value implications: whereas business activities affect the firm's creation of value, financing activities affect the allocation of value among the firm's capital providers more than the value itself. As we will see in a later chapter, for example, a common approach to equity valuation is to estimate equity value as the value of a residual claim on a firm's business assets or, alternatively stated, as the value of a firm's business assets after subtracting the value of its fixed financing obligations. To follow such an approach the standardized financial statements must clearly separate business from financial assets or liabilities.

2 Aggregation versus disaggregation. In many business analysis and valuation applications, a central task is to predict the amount, timing, and uncertainty of a firm's future cash flows or profits. Although aggregation of line items in the standardized financial statements generally helps to remove unnecessary details, the statements must be sufficiently disaggregated to enable users to separately analyze items that have materially different future performance consequences. This is why we distinguish, for example, operating from investment items, current from non-current items, and continued from discontinued operations.

In sum, following the above general rules, we classify balance sheet items along the following dimensions:

- Business (operating and investment) versus financial assets or liabilities.
- Current versus non-current assets or liabilities.
- Assets or liabilities from continued versus discontinued operations.

This classification is useful not only because managers' business and financing decisions have different valuation implications and thus must be separately analyzed, but also because the three categories of assets and liabilities receive different accounting treatments. For example, in contrast to most operating assets, several financial and discontinued assets are recognized at their fair values rather than at their historical cost. Consistent with the approach used for the balance sheet, in the income statement we distinguish business items, such as sales, cost of sales, and investment income, from financial items, such as interest expense, and income from discontinued operations.

Tables 3.1, 3.2, 3.3, 3.4, and 3.5 present the format used throughout the book to standardize the income statement, balance sheet, and cash flow statement, respectively.

To create standardized financials for a company, the analyst classifies each line item in that firm's financial statements using the appropriate account name from the templates set out in the tables. This may require using information from the notes to the financial statements to ensure that accounts are classified appropriately. An example, applying the templates to standardize the 2011 financial statements for apparel retailer Hennes & Mauritz AB, is shown in the Appendix at the end of this chapter.

TABLE 3.1 Standardized income statement format (classification of operating expenses by function)

Standard income statement accounts	Description	Sample line items classified in account
Business – Operating items		
Sales	Revenues generated through the use of operating assets.	Revenue(s) Turnover Membership fees Commissions Licenses
Cost of Sales (by function)	Expenses recognized to account for the use of operating assets in production or procurement activities.	Cost of merchandise sold Cost of products sold Cost of revenues Cost of services Depreciation on manufacturing facilities
SG&A (by function)	Expenses recognized to account for the use of operating assets in selling, distribution or overhead activities.	General and administrative Marketing and sales Distribution expenses Servicing and maintenance Depreciation on selling and administrative facilities Amortization of intangibles
Other Operating Income, Net of Other Operating Expense (by function)	Recurring income from non-core operating activities *minus* recurring expenses that are not directly related to current-period revenues but primarily incurred to generate other operating income or future revenues.	Research and development Start-up costs

(continued)

TABLE 3.1 Standardized income statement format (classification of operating expenses by function) *(Continued)*

Standard income statement accounts	Description	Sample line items classified in account
Business – Investment items		
Investment Income	Non-interest income generated from financial assets.	Result from associate companies Equity income from associates Dividend income Rental income
Interest Income	Interest accrued on investment assets during the period (net of the amortization of costs of acquiring the assets).	Interest income Interest earned
Financial items		
Interest Expense	Interest accrued on financial liabilities during the period (including the amortization of costs of issuing financial liabilities).	Interest expense Finance cost Interest charge on non-current provisions Amortization of issue costs on loans Dividend on preference shares
Minority Interest	Portion of net group income that is attributable to minority interests.	Non-controlling interests
Other items		
Other Income, Net of Other Expense	Gains *minus* losses from non-recurring transactions or events.	Foreign exchange gains/losses Special charges Gains/Losses on sale of investments/non-current assets Asset impairments Restructuring charges
Tax Expense	Current and deferred tax expense or credit (arising from business or financing activities).	Provision for taxes
Net Gain (Loss) from Discontinued Operations	Net after-tax profit or loss generated by operations that have been discontinued or will be sold.	
Net Profit/Loss to Ordinary Shareholders	Net profit or loss attributable to ordinary shareholders, i.e., excluding net gains/losses from discontinued operations and net profit/loss attributable to minority interests.	Net income

TABLE 3.2 Standardized income statement format (classification of operating expenses by nature)

Standard income statement accounts	Description	Sample line items classified in account
Business – Operating items		
Sales	Revenues generated through the use of operating assets.	Revenue(s) Turnover Membership fees Commissions Licenses
Cost of Materials (by nature)	Expenses recognized to account for the cost of inventories sold or used during the period.	Cost of outsourced work and services received Raw materials and work subcontracted Cost of components Changes in inventories and own work capitalized (correction)
Personnel Expense (by nature)	Expenses recognized to account for the cost of personnel during the period.	Salaries and wages Social security Post-employment/Pension benefits Share-based payments
Depreciation and Amortization (by nature)	Expenses recognized to account for the cost of non-current operating assets used during the period.	Depreciation on property, plant and equipment Amortization of intangibles
Other Operating Income, Net of Other Operating Expense (by nature)	Recurring income from non-core operating activities *minus* expenses that are: – recognized to account for operating expenditures or the use of operating assets; – recurring in nature, and – not classified as cost of materials, personnel expense or depreciation and amortization.	Transport and distribution costs Operating lease installments Insurance premiums
Investment, financial and other items	See Table 3.1	

TABLE 3.3 Standardized balance sheet format – assets

Standard balance sheet accounts	Description	Sample line items classified in account
Business – Operating items	Business assets related to the company's core business activities.	
Cash and Marketable Securities	Fair value of cash and cash equivalents used in the financing of short-term business activities.	Cash and cash equivalents Short-term investments Time deposits

(continued)

TABLE 3.3 Standardized balance sheet format – assets (*Continued*)

Standard balance sheet accounts	Description	Sample line items classified in account
Trade receivables	Claims against customers (to be settled within one year).	Accounts receivable Trade debtors
Inventories	Net cost of inventories produced or acquired.	Inventory Finished goods Raw materials Work-in-progress Stocks
Other Current Assets	Claims against others than customers (to be settled within one year) or expenditures incurred for next year's operations (other than the cost of inventories).	Prepaid expenses Claims for tax refunds Amounts due from affiliates Amounts due from employees
Derivatives – Asset	Fair value of investments in derivative financial instruments.	(Non-) current derivative financial Instruments
Non-Current Tangible Assets	Depreciated cost of tangible resources to be used in the long-term operations of the firm.	Property, plant and equipment Land and buildings
Non-Current Intangible Assets	Amortized cost of intangible resources to be used in the long-term operations of the firm.	Goodwill Software/product development costs Deferred financing costs Deferred subscriber acquisition costs Deferred catalog costs Deferred charges Trademarks and licenses
Business – Investment items	Business assets unrelated to the company's core business activities.	
Minority equity investments	Cost of minority investments in subsidiaries plus the accumulated share in subsidiaries' retained earnings.	Investments accounted for using the equity method Investments in associates
Other Non-Operating Investments	Cost or fair value of investments in (non-equity) assets that are not used in the company's core business activities.	Finance lease receivables Derivative financial Instruments Biological assets Investment property
Other items		
Deferred Tax Asset	Non-current tax claims arising from the company's business and financing activities.	
Assets Held For Sale	Assets that were used in operations that have been discontinued or will be sold.	Current assets classified as held for sale Non-current assets classified as held for sale

TABLE 3.4 Standardized balance sheet format – liabilities and equity

Standard balance sheet accounts	Description	Sample line items classified in account
Business – Operating items	(Non-interest bearing) liabilities arising from the company's business activities.	
Trade Payables	Suppliers' claims against the company (to be settled within one year).	Accounts payable Trade creditors
Other Current Liabilities	Claims against the company held by others than suppliers (to be settled within one year) or revenues to be earned in next year's operations.	Accrued expenses Amounts due to related parties Income tax liabilities Social security and payroll taxes Dividends payable Current deferred (unearned) revenue Current provisions
Derivatives – Liability	Fair value of investments in derivative financial instruments.	
Other Non-Current Liabilities (non-interest bearing)	Non-interest-bearing non-current liabilities arising from the company's business activities.	Non-current deferred (unearned) revenues Other non-current liabilities
Financial items	Liabilities incurred to finance the company's business activities	
Current Debt	Current interest-bearing liabilities or current portion of non-current interest-bearing liabilities.	Current borrowings Notes payable Bank overdrafts Current portion of non-current borrowings Current portion of finance lease obligation
Non-Current Debt	Non-current interest-bearing liabilities.	Long-term borrowings/financial liabilities Subordinated debentures Finance lease obligations Convertible debentures Provision for post-employment benefits Provision for decommissioning costs Other non-current provisions
Preference Shares	Preferred shareholders' investment in the company.	Preference shares Convertible preference shares
Minority Interest	Consolidated subsidiaries' minority shareholders' share in the company's net assets.	
Ordinary Shareholders' Equity	Ordinary shareholders' investment in the company.	Share capital Share premium Retained earnings Treasury share/Own share purchased but not canceled Other reserves

(continued)

TABLE 3.4 Standardized balance sheet format – liabilities and equity (*Continued*)

Standard balance sheet accounts	Description	Sample line items classified in account
Other items		
Deferred Tax Liability	Non-current tax claims against the company arising from the company's business and financing activities.	
Liabilities Held For Sale	Liabilities related to operations that have been discontinued or will be sold.	

TABLE 3.5 Standardized cash flow sheet format

Standard balance sheet accounts	Description	Sample line items classified in account
Business – Operating/ Investment items		
Profit Before Interest and Tax	Net profit/loss plus net interest expense and tax expense.	
Taxes Paid	Tax payments made during the current fiscal period.	
Non-Operating Gains (Losses)	Adjustment to profit for non-cash gains (and losses) resulting from non-operating activities.	Gain (loss) on disposal of investments/ non-current assets Cumulative effect of accounting changes Gain (loss) on foreign exchange
Non-Current Operating Accruals	Adjustment to profit for accruals related to changes in the book value of non-current assets or liabilities that result from the company's operating activities.	Depreciation and amortization Deferred revenues/costs Deferred taxes Impairment of non-current assets Other non-cash charges to operations Equity earnings of affiliates/ unconsolidated subs, net of cash received Minority interest Stock bonus awards
Interest received	Interest payments received on other non-operating investments.	
Dividends received	Dividend payments received from subsidiaries.	

(continued)

TABLE 3.5 Standardized cash flow sheet format (*Continued*)

Standard balance sheet accounts	Description	Sample line items classified in account
Net (Investments in) or Liquidation of Operating Working Capital	Net changes in working capital components arising from the company's operating activities.	Changes in: Trade receivables Other receivables Prepaid expenses Trade payables Accrued expenses (liabilities) Due from affiliates Accounts payable and accrued expenses Refundable/payable income taxes Inventories Provision for doubtful accounts Other current liabilities (excluding current debt)
Net (Investment in) or Liquidation of Non-Current Operating or Investment Assets	Net changes in the book value of non-current assets arising from the company's business activities.	Purchase/disposal of non-current assets Acquisition of research and development Acquisition/sale of business Capital expenditures Acquisition of subsidiaries and equity investments Capitalization of development costs Cost in excess of the fair value of net assets acquired Investment in financing leases
Financial items		
Interest Paid	Interest payments made on financial liabilities.	Interest paid Dividends paid on preference shares
Net Debt (Repayment) or Issuance	Net change in current and non-current debt arising from issuances and/or repayments.	Principal payments on debt Borrowings (repayments) under credit facility Issuance (repayment) of long-term debt Net increase (decrease) in short-term borrowings Notes payable Issue (redemption) of preferred securities
Dividend (Payments)	Dividend payments made during the current fiscal year.	Cash dividends paid on ordinary shares Distributions
Net Share (Repurchase) or Issuance	Net change in shareholders' equity arising from issuances and/or repurchases.	Proceeds from issuance of ordinary shares Issue of ordinary share for services Issue of subsidiary equity Purchase (issue) of treasury shares Capital contributions

EXTENSIBLE BUSINESS REPORTING LANGUAGE

An increasing number of firms worldwide prepare and report their financial statements using the Extensible Business Reporting Language (XBRL). These XBRL statements typically complement the traditional financial statements, but in future years XBRL reporting may start to replace the traditional way of financial reporting. XBRL is a language that supports the Internet-based communication of financial information. The basic idea underlying this language is that it provides a "tag" for every individual item in a company's financial statements, including the notes, which describes the main characteristics of the item. Tags contain information about, for example, the accounting standards that the company uses to prepare the item as well as the fiscal year and the broader category of items to which the item belongs. The data items including their tags are reported in an XBRL instance document, which the company makes publicly available through the Internet. By using the appropriate software that recognizes the tags, an analyst can then extract only the needed information from the instance document and ignore irrelevant items. One advantage of XBRL reporting is therefore that it substantially reduces the time that the analyst needs to collect and summarize financial statement information.

The process of tagging data items is somewhat similar to the process of recasting financial statements. Because companies use accepted taxonomies to categorize their financial statement items, they take over some of the analyst's work of standardizing the financial statements. The IASB XBRL Team has developed the IFRS taxonomy, which classifies all possible data items that may appear in an IFRS-based financial statement and defines the relationships among them. The use of the IFRS taxonomy for XBRL reporting by listed companies may therefore eventually reduce the importance of recasting IFRS-based financial statements.

ACCOUNTING ANALYSIS PITFALLS

There are several potential pitfalls and common misconceptions in accounting analysis that an analyst should avoid.

Conservative accounting is not "good" accounting

Some firms take the approach that it pays to be conservative in financial reporting and to set aside as much as possible for contingencies. This logic is commonly used to justify the expensing of research and advertising, and the rapid write-down of intangible assets other than goodwill. It is also used to support large loss reserves for insurance companies, for merger expenses, and for restructuring charges.

From the standpoint of a financial statement user, it is important to recognize that conservative accounting is not the same as "good" accounting. Financial statement users want to evaluate how well a firm's accounting captures business reality in an unbiased manner, and conservative accounting can be as misleading as aggressive accounting in this respect.

It is certainly true that it can be difficult to estimate the economic benefits from many intangibles. However, the intangible nature of some assets does not mean that they do not have value. Indeed, for many firms these types of assets are their most valued. For example, Swiss-based pharmaceutical Novartis' two most valued assets are its research capabilities that permit it to generate new drugs, and its sales force that enables it to sell those drugs to doctors. Yet neither is recorded on Novartis' balance sheet. From the investors' point of view, accountants' reluctance to value intangible assets does not diminish their importance. If they are not included in financial statements, investors have to look to alternative sources of information on these assets.

Further, conservative accounting often provides managers with opportunities for reducing the volatility of reported earnings, typically referred to as "earnings smoothing," which may prevent analysts from recognizing poor performance in a timely fashion. Finally, over time investors are likely to figure out which firms are conservative and may discount their management's disclosures and communications.

Not all unusual accounting is questionable

It is easy to confuse unusual accounting with questionable accounting. While unusual accounting choices might make a firm's performance difficult to compare with other firms' performance, such an accounting choice might be justified if the company's business is unusual. For example, firms that follow differentiated strategies or firms that structure their business in an innovative manner to take advantage of particular market situations, may make unusual accounting choices to properly reflect their business. Therefore it is important to evaluate a company's accounting choices in the context of its business strategy.

Similarly, it is important not to necessarily attribute all *changes* in a firm's accounting policies and accruals to earnings management motives.[24] Accounting changes might be merely reflecting changed business circumstances. For example, as already discussed, a firm that shows unusual increases in its inventory might be preparing for a new product introduction. Similarly, unusual increases in receivables might merely be due to changes in a firm's sales strategy. Unusual decreases in the allowance for uncollectible receivables might be reflecting a firm's changed customer focus. It is therefore important for an analyst to consider all possible explanations for accounting changes and investigate them using the qualitative information available in a firm's financial statements.

Common accounting standards are not the same as common accounting practices

Listed firms in the EU and elsewhere prepare their consolidated financial statements under a common set of accounting standards, IFRS. The adoption of IFRS makes financial statements more comparable across countries and lowers the barriers to cross-border investment analysis. It is important, however, not to confuse the adoption of common accounting *standards* such as IFRS with the introduction of common accounting *practices*.[25]

In Chapter 1 we discussed some international differences that have remained in place after the adoption of IFRS. For example, although the EU sets minimum standards for external auditing, it remains up to the member countries to implement and enforce such rules. Further, IFRS may not be similarly enforced throughout Europe because all European countries have their own public enforcement bodies. Finally, the role of financial reports in communication between managers and investors differs across firms and countries. In Chapter 1 we also discussed the reporting differences between private corporations and public corporations. Similar, potentially smaller differences exist between widely held and closely held listed firms. The analyst should therefore carefully consider these aspects of a firm's reporting environment.

VALUE OF ACCOUNTING DATA AND ACCOUNTING ANALYSIS

What is the value of accounting information and accounting analysis? Given the incentives and opportunities for managers to affect their firms' reported accounting numbers, some have argued that accounting data and accounting analysis are not likely to be useful for investors.

Researchers have examined the value of earnings and return on equity (ROE) by comparing stock returns that could be earned by an investor who has perfect foresight of firms' earnings, return on equity (ROE), and cash flows for the following year.[26] To assess the importance of earnings, the hypothetical investor is assumed to buy shares of firms with subsequent earnings increases and sell shares with subsequent earnings decreases. If this strategy had been followed each year during the period 1964 to 1996, the hypothetical investor would have earned an average return of 37.5 percent. If a similar investment strategy is followed using ROE, buying shares with subsequent increases in ROE and selling shares with ROE decreases, an even higher annual return, 43 percent, would be earned. In contrast, cash flow data appear to be considerably less valuable than earnings or ROE information. Annual returns generated from buying shares with increased subsequent cash flow from operations and selling shares with cash flow decreases would be only 9 percent. This suggests that next period's earnings and ROE performance are more relevant information for investors than cash flow performance.

Overall, this research suggests that the institutional arrangements and conventions created to mitigate potential misuse of accounting by managers are effective in providing assurance to investors. The research indicates that investors do not view earnings management so pervasive as to make earnings data unreliable.

A number of research studies have examined whether superior accounting analysis is a valuable activity. By and large, this evidence indicates that there are opportunities for superior analysts to earn positive stock returns. Studies show that companies criticized in the financial press for misleading financial reporting subsequently suffered an average share price drop of 8 percent.[27] Firms where managers appeared to inflate reported earnings prior to an equity issue and subsequently reported poor earnings performance had more negative share price performance after the offer than firms with no apparent earnings management.[28] Finally, US firms subject to SEC investigation for earnings management showed an average share price decline of 9 percent when the earnings management was first announced and continued to have poor share price performance for up to two years.[29]

These findings imply that analysts who are able to identify firms with misleading accounting are able to create value for investors. The findings also indicate that the stock market ultimately sees through earnings management. For all of these cases, earnings management is eventually uncovered and the share price responds negatively to evidence that firms have inflated prior earnings through misleading accounting.

SUMMARY

In summary, accounting analysis is an important step in the process of analyzing corporate financial reports. The purpose of accounting analysis is to evaluate the degree to which a firm's accounting captures the underlying business reality. Sound accounting analysis improves the reliability of conclusions from financial analysis, the next step in financial statement analysis.

There are six key steps in accounting analysis. The analyst begins by identifying the key accounting policies and estimates, given the firm's industry and its business strategy. The second step is to evaluate the degree of flexibility available to managers, given the accounting rules and conventions. Next, the analyst has to evaluate how managers exercise their accounting flexibility and the likely motivations behind managers' accounting strategy. The fourth step involves assessing the depth and quality of a firm's disclosures. The analyst should next identify any red flags needing further investigation. The final accounting analysis step is to restate accounting numbers to remove any noise and bias introduced by the accounting rules and management decisions.

Chapter 4 discusses how to implement these concepts and shows how to make some of the most common types of adjustments.

CORE CONCEPTS

Accounting analysis Evaluation of the potential accounting flexibility that management has and the actual accounting choices that it makes, focusing on the firm's key accounting policies. The accounting analysis consists of the following six steps:

1 Identification of the firm's key accounting policies.

2 Assessment of management's accounting flexibility.

3 Evaluation of management's reporting strategy.

4 Evaluation of the quality of management's disclosures.

5 Identification of potential red flags or indicators of questionable accounting quality.

6 Correction of accounting distortions.

Classification of operating expenses by function Classification in which firms distinguish categories of operating expense with reference to the *purpose* of the expense. This classification typically distinguishes (at least) the following categories of expenses: (a) Cost of Sales and (b) Selling, General, and Administrative Expenses.

Classification of operating expenses by nature Classification in which firms distinguish categories of operating expense with reference to the *cause* of the expense. This classification typically distinguishes the following categories of expenses: (a) Cost of Materials, (b) Personnel Expense, and (c) Depreciation and Amortization.

Gross profit Difference between Sales and Cost of Sales.

Recasting of financial statements Process of standardizing the formats and nomenclature of firms' financial statements (income statement, balance sheet, cash flow statement, comprehensive income statement).

Sources of noise and bias in accounting data Three potential sources of noise and bias in accounting data are:

a Rigid accounting standards.

b Management's forecast errors.

c Management's reporting strategy (accounting choices).

QUESTIONS, EXERCISES AND PROBLEMS

1 Many firms recognize revenues at the point of shipment. This provides an incentive to accelerate revenues by shipping goods at the end of the quarter. Consider two companies: one ships its product evenly throughout the quarter, and the other ships all its products in the last two weeks of the quarter. Each company's customers pay 30 days after receiving shipment. Using accounting ratios, how can you distinguish these companies?

2 a If management reports truthfully, what economic events are likely to prompt the following accounting changes?

   ■ Increase in the estimated life of depreciable assets.

   ■ Decrease in the allowance for doubtful accounts as a percentage of gross trade receivables.

   ■ Recognition of revenues at the point of delivery rather than at the point cash is received.

   ■ Capitalization of a higher proportion of research expenditures costs.

   b What features of accounting, if any, would make it costly for dishonest managers to make the same changes without any corresponding economic changes?

3 The conservatism (or prudence) principle arises because of concerns about management's incentives to overstate the firm's performance. Joe Banks argues, "We could get rid of conservatism and make accounting numbers more useful if we delegated financial reporting to independent auditors rather than to corporate managers." Do you agree? Why or why not?

4 A fund manager states, "I refuse to buy any company that makes a voluntary accounting change, since it's certainly a case of management trying to hide bad news." Can you think of any alternative interpretation?

5 On the companion website to this book there is a spreadsheet containing the financial statements of:

   a Vodafone plc for the fiscal year ended March 31, 2012.

   b The Unilever Group for the fiscal year ended December 31, 2011.

   c Audi AG for the fiscal year ended December 31, 2011.

   Use the templates shown in Tables 3.1–3.5 to recast these companies' financial statements.

Problem 1 Key accounting policies

Consider the following companies.

Juventus F.C. S.p.A. is an Italian publicly listed football club. The club's primary sources of revenue are:

a Season and single ticket sales.

b Television, radio, and media rights.

c Sponsorship and advertising contracts.

d The disposal of players' registration rights.

Players' registration rights are recognized on the balance sheet at cost and amortized over the players' contract terms. The club leases its stadium Stadio Delle Alpi under an operating lease arrangement; however, it has started the construction of a new stadium, which is cofinanced by an outside sponsor in exchange for exclusive naming rights.

Spyker Cars N.V. is a Netherlands-based publicly listed designer and manufacturer of exclusive sports cars. In 2008, the company's revenues amounted to €7,852 thousand, of which €5,772 thousand was related to car sales and €1,752 thousand was income from GT racing activities. In that year, Spyker produced 30 new cars and sold 37 cars. It held 42 cars in stock at the end of the year. Further, the company spent close to €6 million on development and €378,000 on research. Spyker had been loss-making since its initial public offering in 2004. At the end of 2008, the car manufacturer had €76 in tax-deductible carry forward losses.

J Sainsbury plc is a UK-based publicly listed retailer that operates 557 supermarkets and 377 convenience stores and has an estimated 16 percent market share in the UK. During the period 2007–2011, the company's operating profit margins steadily increased from 2.5 to 3.5 percent. At the end of March 2011, the net book value of Sainsbury's land and buildings was £7.1 billion. A part of the company's supermarket properties was pledged as security for long-term borrowings. In 2011 Sainsbury had 148,400 employees (99,300 full-time equivalents); many of them participated in one of the retailer's defined-benefit pension plans.

1 Identify the key accounting policies for each of these companies.

2 What are these companies' primary areas of accounting flexibility? (Focus on the key accounting policies.)

Problem 2 Fashion retailers' key accounting policies

In their 2010/2011 financial statements, eight European fashion retailers – i.e., Burberry, Inditex, Benetton, Marks & Spencer, Etam, Charles Voegele, French Connection, and Next – explicitly discussed their "key accounting policies." The following table summarizes the accounting policies that were denoted as "key" by at least one of the eight retailers (x = mentioned as key accounting policy; o = not mentioned):

	Burberry	Inditex	Benetton	Marks & Spencer	Etam	Charles Voegele	French Connection	Next
Depreciation and/or impairment of property, plant and equipment	x	x	x	x	x	o	x	o
Discontinued operations	o	o	o	o	o	o	x	o
Employee/post-retirement benefits	o	o	x	x	x	o	o	x
Impairment of assets in stores	o	x	x	o	x	x	x	x
Impairment of goodwill	x	x	x	x	x	x	x	o
Impairment of trade receivables	o	o	o	o	o	o	o	x
Income and deferred taxes	x	o	x	o	x	x	o	o
Other provisions	o	x	x	o	o	o	o	o
Provision for doubtful accounts	o	o	x	o	o	o	o	o
Provisions for litigation	o	x	o	o	o	x	o	o
Put option liability over non-controlling interests	x	o	x	o	o	o	o	o
Recoverability of deferred tax assets	o	x	o	o	o	o	o	o
Refunds and loyalty scheme accruals	o	o	o	x	o	o	o	o
Share-based payments	o	o	x	o	o	o	o	o

1 Based on your knowledge of the fashion retail industry, discuss for each of the above accounting policies why the accounting policy is considered as "key" by one or more of the eight fashion retailers.

2 Discuss which economic, industry, or firm-specific factors may explain the observed variation in key accounting policies across the eight retailers.

Problem 3 *Euro Disney and the first five steps of accounting analysis*

Euro Disney S.C.A. is a holding company, holding 82 percent of the shares of Euro Disney Associés S.C.A., which operates, amongst others, the Disneyland Park, Disneyland Hotel, and Davy Crockett Ranch in Paris and holds 99.99 percent of the shares of EDL Hotels S.C.A. EDL Hotels operates all of the Disney Hotels in Paris (except for the Disneyland Hotel and Davy Crockett Ranch).

Euro Disney Associés leases the Disneyland Park (including land) under a finance lease from Euro Disneyland S.N.C., which is owned by (1) a syndicate of banks and financial institutions (83 percent participation) and (2) a wholly-owned subsidiary of US-based The Walt Disney Company (17 percent participation). EDL Hotels S.C.A. rents land to a group of six special-purpose financing companies, who, in turn, own the hotels on the land and lease these hotels back to EDL Hotels. All special-purpose financing companies are fully consolidated in Euro Disney's financial statements, despite the absence of ownership in some cases. This is because, as the company reports in its 2011 annual report, "the substance of the relationship between the group and these financing companies is such that they are effectively controlled by the group." In fact, all special-purpose financing companies are managed by management companies that are directly or indirectly owned by The Walt Disney Company or Euro Disney Associés.

Euro Disney's primary sources of revenue are its two theme parks (entrance fees, merchandise, food and beverage, special events), its seven hotels and Disney Village (room rental, merchandise, food and beverage, dinner shows, convention revenues). Disney Village offers themed dining, entertainment, and shopping facilities. The company has, on average, 13,740 employees annually. The company and its subsidiaries are considered as one French economic and labor unit, regulated by the National Collective Bargaining Agreement signed in 2001 with six out of seven trade unions represented in the unit. The majority of the company's employees (about 90 percent) have a permanent contract. To cope with the seasonal nature of the business, Euro Disney is able to move employees from its theme parks to its hotels and vice versa. Approximately 5 percent of total personnel expenses consist of training costs.

In 2005, after a period of poor performance, Euro Disney began renegotiations with its lenders and The Walt Disney Company, obtained waivers for certain debt covenants and agreed to restructure its financial obligations. As part of the restructuring, the company would issue new share capital, obtain the option to defer certain payments to The Walt Disney Company, and receive authorization for a new investment plan. Further, the company would change its organizational structure to the one described above. Since the restructuring, Euro Disney's debt agreements include debt covenants requiring the company to maintain minimum ratios of adjusted operating income (before depreciation and amortization) to total debt service obligations. The adjusted operating income figure is also used to determine the amount of interest on the company's Walt Disney Studio Park loans and the royalties and management fees payable to The Walt Disney Company. In particular, if actual performance is less than the contractually agreed benchmark, the company can defer the payments of interest, royalties and management fees. The debt covenants also limit the amount of new debt capital that Euro Disney can attract to €50 million.

Euro Disney S.C.A. is publicly listed on the Euronext Paris stock exchange. By the end of 2011, 39.8 percent of its shares were owned by The Walt Disney Company, 10 percent were owned by Prince Alwaleed and 50.2 percent were in the hands of dispersed shareholders. The company has a Supervisory Board with ten members, two of which are representatives of The Walt Disney Company, an audit committee and a nominations committee. Euro Disney S.C.A. as well as both operating companies of Euro Disney S.C.A., i.e., Euro Disney Associés and Euro Disney Hotels, are managed by management company Euro Disney S.A.S. (referred to as the *Gérant),* an indirect wholly-owned subsidiary of The Walt Disney Company. At the end of fiscal year 2011, the CEO of the *Gérant* (Euro Disney S.A.S.) was Philippe Gas, who replaced Karl Holz on September 1, 2008. For the management services provided to the holding and operating companies, the *Gérant* receives management fees. The aggregate compensation for the eight independent Supervisory Board members was €276,041 in 2011. The two representatives of The Walt Disney Company received an annual fixed salary, a bonus, restricted stocks, and stock options from The Walt Disney Company. Philippe Gas' employment contract promised him:

1 An annual salary of €379,673.

2 A discretionary annual bonus based on individual performance relative to the objectives of the company and The Walt Disney Company Parks & Resorts operating segment.

3   Discretionary grants of the company's stock options, The Walt Disney Company's stock options, and The Walt Disney Company's restricted stock.

4   The use of a company car.

In addition to Philippe Gas, the Executive Committee of the *Gérant* consisted of five senior vice presidents and six vice presidents.

Euro Disney reported net losses in 2009, 2010, and 2011. Whereas the company's total revenues increased by 1.8 percent to €1,298 million in 2011, direct operating costs and marketing and sales expenses increased by 4.2 and 2.6 percent, respectively. Euro Disney's operating cash flows amounted to €124.1, €236.7, and €168.7 million in 2009, 2010, and 2011, respectively. In all three years, the cash flows used in investing activities were less than the operating cash flows. In 2011 Euro Disney used part of the surplus of operating over investment cash flows to repay some of its borrowings, thereby reducing the non-current debt to total assets ratio from 67.5 to 67.0 percent. The company's trade receivables to sales ratio decreased from 6.1 percent in 2009 to 5.6 percent in 2011. Liabilities for deferred revenues as a percentage of sales decreased from 2.4 percent in 2009 to 1.2 percent in 2011, after having amounted to 9.0 percent in 2008. The allowance for uncollectible receivables decreased from 3.2 percent (of gross trade receivables) in 2009 to 1.5 percent in 2011; the allowance for inventories obsolescence increased from 8.7 percent (of gross inventories) in 2009 to 9.2 percent in 2011. During fiscal year 2011, Euro Disney did not make any voluntary change in its accounting methods and did not recognize any asset write-offs. Related party transactions consisted primarily of the payment of royalties and management fees to the *Gérant* as well as payments to the *Gérant* to reimburse the direct and indirect costs of the technical and administrative services provided. Euro Disney's tax expense was zero in 2009, 2010, and 2011. At the end of fiscal year 2011, the company's unused tax loss carry forwards amounted to €1.8 billion and could be carried forward indefinitely. The company's 2011 financial statements received an unqualified audit opinion.

At the end of 2011, Euro Disney's share price was €3.54. The company's average share return since December 31, 2007 had been −21 percent (annually).

1   Identify the key accounting policies (step 1) and primary areas of accounting flexibility (step 2) for Euro Disney.

2   What incentives may influence management's reporting strategy (step 3)?

3   What disclosures would you consider an essential part of the company's annual report, given its key success factors and key accounting policies (step 4)?

4   What potential red flags can you identify (step 5)?

NOTES

1. Accounting analysis is sometimes also called quality of earnings analysis. We prefer to use the term accounting analysis because we are discussing a broader concept than merely a firm's earnings quality.

2. Thus, although accrual accounting is theoretically superior to cash accounting in measuring a firm's periodic performance, the distortions it introduces can make accounting data less valuable to users. If these distortions are large enough, current cash flows may measure a firm's periodic performance better than accounting profits. The relative usefulness of cash flows and accounting profits in measuring performance, therefore, varies from firm to firm. For empirical evidence on this issue, see P. Dechow, "Accounting Earnings and Cash Flows as Measures of Firm Performance: The Role of Accounting Accruals," *Journal of Accounting and Economics* 18 (July 1994): 3–42, and A. Charitou, C. Clubb, and A. Andreou, "The Effect of Earnings Permanence, Growth and Firm Size on the Usefulness of Cash Flows and Earnings in Explaining Security Returns: Empirical Evidence for the UK," *Journal of Business Finance and Accounting* 28 (June/July 2001): 563–594.

3. For example, a recent study shows that accounting adjustments made by Moody's (credit) analysts help to explain stock prices and analysts' target prices and recommendations (G. De Franco, F. Wong, and Y. Zhou, "Accounting Adjustments and the Valuation of Financial Statement Note Information in 10-K Filings," *Accounting Review* 86 (2011): 1577–1604). Further, Abraham Briloff wrote a series of accounting analyses of public companies in *Barron's* over several years. On average, the share prices of the analyzed companies changed by about 8 percent on the day these articles were published, indicating the potential value of performing such analysis. For a more complete discussion of this evidence, see G. Foster, "Briloff and the Capital Market," *Journal of Accounting Research* 17 (Spring 1979): 262–274.

4. For a complete discussion of these motivations, see *Positive Accounting Theory*, by R. Watts and J. Zimmerman (Englewood Cliffs, NJ: Prentice-Hall, 1986). A summary of this research is provided by P. Healy and J. Wahlen, "A Review of the Earnings Management Literature and Its Implications for Standard Setting," *Accounting Horizons* 13 (December 1999): 365–383 and

T. Fields, T. Lys and L. Vincent in "Empirical Research on Accounting Choice," *Journal of Accounting and Economics* 31 (September 2001): 255–307.

5. The most convincing evidence supporting the covenant hypothesis is reported in a study of the accounting decisions by firms in financial distress: A. Sweeney, "Debt-Covenant Violations and Managers' Accounting Responses," *Journal of Accounting and Economics* 17 (May 1994): 281–308.

6. Studies that examine the bonus hypothesis generally report evidence supporting the view that managers' accounting decisions are influenced by compensation considerations. See, for example, P. Healy, "The Effect of Bonus Schemes on Accounting Decisions," *Journal of Accounting and Economics* 7 (April 1985): 85–107; R. Holthausen, D. Larcker and R. Sloan, "Annual Bonus Schemes and the Manipulation of Earnings," *Journal of Accounting and Economics* 19 (February 1995): 29–74; and F. Guidry, A. Leone and S. Rock, "Earnings-Based Bonus Plans and Earnings Management by Business Unit Managers," *Journal of Accounting and Economics* 26 (January 1999): 113–142.

7. For empirical evidence that CEOs of firms with scheduled awards make opportunistic voluntary disclosures to maximize stock award compensation, see D. Aboody and R. Kasznik, "CEO Stock Option Awards and the Timing of Corporate Voluntary Disclosures," *Journal of Accounting and Economics* 29 (February 2000): 73–100.

8. L. DeAngelo, "Managerial Competition, Information Costs, and Corporate Governance: The Use of Accounting Performance Measures in Proxy Contests," *Journal of Accounting and Economics* 10 (January 1988): 3–36; and M. Erickson and S. Wang, "Earnings Management by Acquiring Firms in Stock for Stock Mergers," *Journal of Accounting and Economics* 27 (1999): 149–176.

9. The trade-off between taxes and financial reporting in the context of managers' accounting decisions is discussed in detail in *Taxes and Business Strategy* by M. Scholes and M. Wolfson (Englewood Cliffs, NJ: Prentice-Hall, 1992). Many empirical studies have examined firms' LIFO/FIFO choices.

10. Several researchers have documented that firms affected by such situations have a motivation to influence regulators' perceptions through accounting decisions. For example, J. Jones documents that firms seeking import protections make profit-decreasing accounting decisions in "Earnings Management During Import Relief Investigations," *Journal of Accounting Research* 29(2) (Autumn 1991): 193–228. Similarly, W. Beekes finds that UK water and electricity companies make profit-decreasing accounting choices in years of regulatory price reviews in "Earnings Management in Response to Regulatory Price Review. A Case Study of the Political Cost Hypothesis in the Water and Electricity Sectors in England and Wales," Working paper, Lancaster University, 2003. A number of studies find that banks that are close to minimum capital requirements overstate loan loss provisions, understate loan write-offs, and recognize abnormal realized gains on securities portfolios (see S. Moyer, "Capital Adequacy Ratio Regulations and Accounting Choices in Commercial Banks," *Journal of Accounting and Economics* 12 (1990): 123–154; M. Scholes, G.P. Wilson, and M. Wolfson, "Tax Planning, Regulatory Capital Planning, and Financial Reporting Strategy for Commercial Banks," *Review of Financial Studies* 3 (1990): 625–650; A. Beatty, S. Chamberlain, and J. Magliolo, "Managing Financial Reports of Commercial Banks: The Influence of Taxes, Regulatory Capital and Earnings," *Journal of Accounting Research* 33(2) (1995): 231–261; and J. Collins, D. Shackelford, and J. Wahlen, "Bank Differences in the Coordination of Regulatory Capital, Earnings and Taxes," *Journal of Accounting Research* 33(2) (Autumn 1995): 263–291). Finally, Petroni finds that financially weak property-casualty insurers that risk regulatory attention understate claim loss reserves: K. Petroni, "Optimistic Reporting in the Property Casualty Insurance Industry," *Journal of Accounting and Economics* 15 (December 1992): 485–508.

11. P. Healy and K. Palepu, "The Effect of Firms' Financial Disclosure Strategies on Stock Prices," *Accounting Horizons* 7 (March 1993): 1–11. For a summary of the empirical evidence, see P. Healy and J. Wahlen, "A Review of the Earnings Management Literature and Its Implications for Standard Setting," *Accounting Horizons* 13 (December 1999): 365–384.

12. R. Bowen, L. DuCharme, and D. Shores, "Stakeholders' Implicit Claims and Accounting Method Choice," *Journal of Accounting and Economics* 20 (December 1995): 255–295, argue that, based on theory and anecdotal evidence, managers choose long-run income-increasing accounting methods as a result of ongoing implicit claims between a firm and its customers, suppliers, employees, and short-term creditors.

13. Financial analysts pay close attention to managers' disclosure strategies; Standard and Poor's publishes scores that rate the disclosure of companies from around the world. For a discussion of these ratings, see, for example, T. Khanna, K. Palepu, and S. Srinivasan, "Disclosure Practices of Foreign Companies Interacting with US Markets," *Journal of Accounting Research* 42 (May 2004): 475–508.

14. See P. Healy and K. Palepu, "The Fall of Enron," *Journal of Economic Perspectives* 17(2) (Spring 2003): 3–26.

15. For detailed analyses of companies that made such changes, see R. Schattke and R. Vergoossen, "Barriers to Interpretation: A Case Study of Philips Electronics NV," *Accounting and Business Research* 27 (1996): 72–84, and K. Palepu, "Anatomy of an Accounting Change," in *Accounting and Management: Field Study Perspectives*, edited by W. Bruns, Jr. and R. Kaplan (Boston: Harvard Business School Press, 1987).

16. Examples of this type of behavior are documented by J. Hand in his study, "Did Firms Undertake Debt-Equity Swaps for an Accounting Paper Profit or True Financial Gain?" *The Accounting Review* 64 (October 1989): 587–623, and by E. Black, K. Sellers, and T. Manley in "Earnings Management Using Asset Sales: An International Study of Countries Allowing Noncurrent Asset Revaluation," *Journal of Business Finance and Accounting* 25 (November/December 1998): 1287–1317.

17. For an empirical analysis of inventory build-ups, see V. Bernard and J. Noel, "Do Inventory Disclosures Predict Sales and Earnings?" *Journal of Accounting, Auditing, and Finance* (Fall 1991).

18. For research on accounting and economic incentives in the formation of R&D partnerships, see A. Beatty, P. Berger, and J. Magliolo, "Motives for Forming Research and Development Financing Organizations," *Journal of Accounting and Economics*

19 (April 1995): 411–442. An overview of Enron's use of special purpose entities to manage earnings and window-dress its balance is provided by P. Healy and K. Palepu, "The Fall of Enron," *Journal of Economic Perspectives* 17(2) (Spring 2003): 3–26.

19. For an empirical examination of asset write-offs, see J. Elliott and W. Shaw, "Write-offs as Accounting Procedures to Manage Perceptions," *Journal of Accounting Research* 26 (1988): 91–119.

20. R. Mendenhall and W. Nichols report evidence consistent with managers taking advantage of their discretion to postpone reporting bad news until the year-end. See R. Mendenhall and W. Nichols, "Bad News and Differential Market Reactions to Announcements of Earlier-Quarter versus Fourth-Quarter Earnings," *Journal of Accounting Research*, Supplement (1988): 63–86.

21. K. Peasnell, P. Pope, and S. Young report evidence that independent outside directors prevent earnings management. See K. Peasnell, P. Pope, and S. Young, "Board Monitoring and Earnings Management: Do Outside Directors Influence Abnormal Accruals?," *Journal of Business Finance and Accounting* 32 (September 2005): 1311–1346.

22. The role of insider transactions in the collapse of Enron are discussed by P. Healy and K. Palepu, "The Fall of Enron," *Journal of Economic Perspectives* 17(2) (Spring 2003): 3–26.

23. This type of analysis is presented in the context of provisions for bad debts by M. McNichols and P. Wilson in their study, "Evidence of Earnings Management From the Provisions for Bad Debts," *Journal of Accounting Research*, Supplement (1988): 1–31.

24. This point has been made by several accounting researchers. For a summary of research on earnings management, see K. Schipper, "Earnings Management," *Accounting Horizons* (December 1989): 91–102.

25. See H. Daske, L. Hail, C. Leuz, and R. Verdi, "Mandatory IFRS Reporting around the World: Early Evidence on the Economic Consequences," *Journal of Accounting Research* 46 (2008): 1085–1142.

26. See J. Chang, "The Decline in Value Relevance of Earnings and Book Values," unpublished dissertation, Harvard University, 1998. Evidence is also reported by J. Francis and K. Schipper, "Have Financial Statements Lost Their Relevance?," *Journal of Accounting Research* 37(2) (Autumn 1999): 319–352; and W. E. Collins, E. Maydew, and I. Weiss, "Changes in the Value-Relevance of Earnings and Book Value over the Past Forty Years," *Journal of Accounting and Economics* 24 (1997): 39–67.

27. See G. Foster, "Briloff and the Capital Market," *Journal of Accounting Research* 17(1) (Spring 1979): 262–274.

28. See S. H. Teoh, I. Welch, and T. J. Wong, "Earnings Management and the Long-Run Market Performance of Initial Public Offerings," *Journal of Finance* 53 (December 1998a): 1935–1974; S. H. Teoh, I. Welch and T. J. Wong, "Earnings Management and the Post-Issue Underperformance of Seasoned Equity Offerings," *Journal of Financial Economics* 50 (October 1998): 63–99; and S. Teoh, T. Wong, and G. Rao, "Are Accruals During Initial Public Offerings Opportunistic?," *Review of Accounting Studies* 3(1–2) (1998): 175–208.

29. See P. Dechow, R. Sloan, and A. Sweeney, "Causes and Consequences of Earnings Manipulation: An Analysis of Firms Subject to Enforcement Actions by the SEC," *Contemporary Accounting Research* 13(1) (1996): 1–36; and M. D. Beneish, "Detecting GAAP Violation: Implications for Assessing Earnings Management among Firms with Extreme Financial Performance," *Journal of Accounting and Public Policy* 16 (1997): 271–309.

APPENDIX A: FIRST-TIME ADOPTION OF IFRS

The widespread use of IFRS to prepare financial statements is a fairly recent phenomenon. By the end of 2004, around 1,000 firms worldwide prepared their financial statements in conformity with IFRS. Since the mandated introduction of IFRS-based reporting in, amongst other countries, the EU, Australia (2005), New Zealand (2007), Brazil (2010), Canada and Korea (2011), however, the number of IFRS users has grown explosively to over 14,000 firms. Although the worldwide move to using one common set of accounting rules yields many advantages for the analyst, the switch from local to international accounting rules also complicates the accounting analysis a little.

In the first year that a firm applies IFRS, it is required to provide the current year's IFRS-based financial figures as well as restate prior year's balance sheet and income statement for comparative purposes. This means that the firm traces back every historical event and assumption that is relevant to a particular line item on the opening balance sheet of the prior year, recalculates the impact of these events and assumptions on the items, and essentially produces its first IFRS-based opening balance sheet as if it had applied IFRS all along (though applying current IFRSs). The firm then records all the events during the prior year and the current year in accordance with IFRS. To avoid the misuse of hindsight, when preparing its opening IFRS-based balance sheet the first-time IFRS adopter cannot use information that it received after the balance sheet date.

In their first IFRS-based financial statements firms have to disclose at least the following information to illustrate the effects of IFRS adoption on their financial figures:

- A description of the sources of differences between equity reported under previous accounting standards and under IFRS as well as the effects of these differences in quantitative terms. The firm must provide such reconciliations for equity in both its opening and its closing comparative balance sheets.

- A reconciliation of net profit reported under previous accounting standards and under IFRS for the prior year.

Some firms also voluntarily disclose the opening IFRS-based balance sheet of the prior year, improving the analyst's dataset, but they are not required to do so.

Unfortunately, in practice it is difficult for a first-time IFRS adopter to trace back every relevant historical event because it may not have collected or stored all the necessary data in the past. Further, the informational benefits of recalculating and restating certain line items may not outweigh the associated costs. For example, firms that consolidate the translated values of subsidiaries' foreign currency-denominated assets on their balance sheets, recognize the cumulative translation difference which arises because exchange rates fluctuate over the years, as a separate component in equity. When these firms adopt IFRS they would face the tedious task of recalculating all cumulative translation differences on their subsidiaries. Because separately reporting restated cumulative translation differences generates little additional information, however, first-time IFRS adopters can choose to add the cumulative translation differences to equity and reset the line item to zero upon adoption. To facilitate the first-time preparation of an IFRS-based opening balance sheet, the rules on the first-time IFRS application allow more of these exemptions and even prohibit some restatements.

APPENDIX B: RECASTING FINANCIAL STATEMENTS INTO STANDARDIZED TEMPLATES

The following tables show the financial statements for Hennes and Mauritz AB for the year ended November 30, 2011. The first column in each statement presents the recast financial statement classifications that are used for each line item. Note that the classifications are not applied to subtotal lines such as Total current assets or Net profit. The recast financial statements for Hennes and Mauritz are prepared by simply totaling the balances of line items with the same standard classifications. For example, on the recast balance sheet there are three line items classified as Non-Current Intangible Assets: brands, customer relations, and goodwill.

Hennes & Mauritz reported balance sheet (SEK millions)

Classifications	Fiscal year November 30	2011
	ASSETS	
Non-Current Intangible Assets	Brands	302.0
Non-Current Intangible Assets	Customer relations	84.0
Non-Current Tangible Assets	Leasehold rights	585.0
Non-Current Intangible Assets	Goodwill	64.0
Non-Current Tangible Assets	Buildings and land	804.0
Non-Current Tangible Assets	Equipment, tools, fixtures and fittings	16,589.0
Other Non-Operating Investments	Long-term receivables	608.0
Deferred Tax Assets	Deferred tax receivables	1,234.0
	Total fixed assets	**20,270.0**
Inventories	Stock-in-trade	13,819.0
Trade Receivables	Accounts receivable	2,337.0
Other Current Assets	Other receivables	919.0
Derivatives – Asset	Forward contracts	456.0
Other Current Assets	Prepaid expenses	1,110.0
Cash and Marketable Securities	Short-term investments	6,958.0
Cash and Marketable Securities	Liquid funds	14,319.0
	Total current assets	**39,918.0**
Total Assets	**Total assets**	**60,188.0**

(Continued)

Hennes & Mauritz reported balance sheet (SEK millions) (*Continued*)

Classifications	Fiscal year November 30	2011
LIABILITIES AND SHAREHOLDERS' EQUITY		
Ordinary Shareholders' Equity	Share capital	207.0
Ordinary Shareholders' Equity	Reserves	(487.0)
Ordinary Shareholders' Equity	Retained earnings	28,563.0
Ordinary Shareholders' Equity	Profit for the year	15,821.0
	Equity	**44,104.0**
Non-Current Debt	Provisions for pensions	377.0
Non-Current Debt	Other provisions	0.0
Deferred Tax Liabilities	Deferred tax liabilities	950.0
	Total noncurrent liabilities	**1,327.0**
Trade Payables	Accounts payable	4,307.0
Other Current Liabilities	Tax liabilities	1,851.0
Derivatives – Liability	Forward contracts	150.0
Other Current Liabilities	Other liabilities	2,278.0
Other Current Liabilities	Accrued expenses	6,171.0
	Total current liabilities	**14,757.0**
Total Liabilities and Shareholders' Equity	**Total liabilities and shareholders' equity**	**60,188.0**

Hennes & Mauritz reported income statement (SEK millions)

Classifications	Fiscal year ended November 30	2011
Sales	Sales, excluding VAT	109,999.0
Cost of Sales (function)	Cost of goods sold	(43,852.0)
	Gross profit	**66,147.0**
SG&A (function)	Selling expenses	(42,517.0)
SG&A (function)	Administrative expenses	(3,251.0)
	Operating profit	**20,379.0**
Interest Income	Interest income	568.0
Interest Expense	Interest expense	(5.0)
	Profit after financial items	**20,942.0**
Tax Expense	Tax	(5,121.0)
Net Profit/Loss to Ordinary Shareholders	**Profit for the year**	**15,821.0**
INCOME STATEMENT ITEMS BY NATURE		
Personnel Expenses (nature)	Salaries, other remuneration and payroll overheads	(18,534.0)
Depreciation and Amortization (nature)	Depreciation – within cost of goods sold	(366.0)
Depreciation and Amortization (nature)	Depreciation – within selling expenses	(2,698.0)
Depreciation and Amortization (nature)	Depreciation – within administrative expenses	(198.0)

Hennes & Mauritz reported cash flow statement (SEK millions)

Classifications	Fiscal year ended November 30	2011
Profit Before Interest and Tax	Profit after financial items	20,942.0
Profit Before Interest and Tax	Net interest expense	(563.0)
Interest Paid	Interest paid	(5.0)
Interest Received	Interest received	568.0
	Adjustment for:	
Non-Current Operating Accruals	Provisions for pensions	120.0
Non-Current Operating Accruals	Depreciation	3,262.0
Taxes Paid	Tax paid	(5,666.0)
Net (Investments in) or Liquidation of Operating Working Capital	Changes in current receivables	(244.0)
Net (Investments in) or Liquidation of Operating Working Capital	Changes in stock-in-trade	(2,331.0)
Net (Investments in) or Liquidation of Operating Working Capital	Changes in current liabilities	1,337.0
	Cash flow from current operations	**17,420.0**
Net (Investments in) or Liquidation of Operating or Investment Non-Current Assets	Investment in leasehold rights	(71.0)
Net (Investments in) or Liquidation of Operating or Investment Non-Current Assets	Sales of/investments in buildings and land	(157.0)
Net (Investments in) or Liquidation of Operating or Investment Non-Current Assets	Investments in fixed assets	(4,946.0)
Net (Investments in) or Liquidation of Operating or Investment Non-Current Assets	Adjustment of consideration/acquisition of subsidiaries	0.0
Net (Investments in) or Liquidation of Operating or Investment Non-Current Assets	Change in financial investments, 3-12 months	1,209.0
Net (Investments in) or Liquidation of Operating or Investment Non-Current Assets	Other investments	(91.0)
	Cash flow from investing activities	**(4,056.0)**
Dividend (Payments)	Dividend	(15,723.0)
	Cash flows from financing activities	**(15,723.0)**
	Exchange rate effect	(13.0)
	Cash flow for the year	(2,372.0)
	Liquid funds at beginning of year	16,691.0
	Liquid funds at end of year	**14,319.0**

The standardized financial statements for Hennes and Mauritz AB are as follows:

Hennes & Mauritz standardized balance sheet (SEK millions)

	2011
ASSETS	
Non-Current Tangible Assets	17,978.0
Non-Current Intangible Assets	450.0
Minority Equity Investments	0.0
Other Non-Operating Investments	608.0
Deferred Tax Assets	1,234.0
Derivatives – Asset	456.0
Total Non-Current Assets	**20,726.0**
Inventories	13,819.0
Trade Receivables	2,337.0
Other Current Assets	2,029.0
Cash and Marketable Securities	21,277.0
Total Current Assets	**39,462.0**
Assets Held For Sale	**0.0**
Total Assets	**60,188.0**
LIABILITIES AND SHAREHOLDERS' EQUITY	
Ordinary Shareholders' Equity	**44,104.0**
Minority Interest – Balance Sheet	**0.0**
Preference Shares	**0.0**
Non-Current Debt	377.0
Deferred Tax Liabilities	950.0
Derivatives – Liability	150.0
Other Non-Current Liabilities (non-interest bearing)	0.0
Non-Current Liabilities	**1,477.0**
Trade Payables	4,307.0
Other Current Liabilities	10,300.0
Current Debt	0.0
Current Liabilities	**14,607.0**
Liabilities Held For Sale	**0.0**
Total Liabilities and Shareholders' Equity	**60,188.0**

Hennes & Mauritz standardized income statement (SEK millions)

	2011
Sales	**109,999.0**
Operating expenses	(89,620.0)
Operating profit	20,379.0
Investment income	0.0
Other income, net of other expense	0.0
Net interest expense (income)	
Interest income	568.0
Interest expense	(5.0)
Profit before taxes	**20,942.0**

(Continued)

Hennes & Mauritz standardized income statement (SEK millions) (*Continued*)

	2011
Tax expense	(5,121.0)
Profit after taxes	**15,821.0**
Minority interest – Income statement	0.0
Net profit to ordinary shareholders	**15,821.0**

Operating expenses	**2011**
Classification by function:	
Cost of Sales (function)	(43,852.0)
SG&A (function)	(45,768.0)
Other Operating Income, Net of Other Operating Expenses (function)	0.0
Classification by nature:	
Cost of Materials (nature)	(43,486.0)
Personnel Expenses (nature)	(18,534.0)
Depreciation and Amortization (nature)	(3,262.0)
Other Operating Income, Net of Other Operating Expenses (nature)	(24,338.0)

Hennes & Mauritz standardized cash flow statement (SEK millions)

	2011
Profit Before Interest and Tax	20,379.0
Taxes Paid	(5,666.0)
Non-Operating Losses (Gains)	0.0
Non-Current Operating Accruals	3,382.0
Operating Cash Flow before Working Capital Investments	**18,095.0**
Net (Investments in) or Liquidation of Operating Working Capital	(1,238.0)
Operating Cash Flow before Investment in Non-Current Assets	**16,857.0**
Interest Received	568.0
Dividends received	0.0
Net (Investments in) or Liquidation of Operating or Investment Non-Current Assets	(4,056.0)
Free Cash Flow Available to Debt and Equity	**13,369.0**
Interest Paid	(5.0)
Net Debt (Repayment) or Issuance	0.0
Free Cash Flow Available to Equity	**13,364.0**
Dividend (Payments)	(15,723.0)
Net share (Repurchase) or Issuance	0.0
Net Increase (Decrease) in Cash Balance	**(2,359.0)**

Fiat Group's first-time adoption of IFRS

In June 2002, the Council of the European Union adopted new regulations that required companies listed in the EU to prepare their consolidated financial statements in accordance with International Financial Reporting Standards (IFRS). According to the new rules, companies must apply IFRS no later than in the fiscal year starting in 2005. Member states of the EU could, however, allow companies that were listed outside the EU and prepared their statements in accordance with US Generally Accepted Accounting Principles (US GAAP) to apply IFRS in either 2006 or 2007.

The decision of the European Council also affected Italy-based car manufacturer Fiat, which had its shares traded on the Italian Stock Exchange and reported its financial statements in accordance with Italian accounting standards (henceforth Italian GAAP). The Fiat Group decided not to apply IFRS earlier than required and reported its first IFRS-based annual report in fiscal year 2005.

Business description and financial performance[1]

In 2005 the Italy-based Fiat Group generated its revenues primarily from the production and sales of passenger vehicles, tractors, agricultural equipment, and light commercial vehicles. Its portfolio of passenger car brands included large-volume brands such as Fiat, Alfa Romeo, and Lancia (generating €19.5 billion in revenues), as well as luxury, high-margin brands such as Maserati and Ferrari (generating €1.8 billion in revenues). In addition to these activities, the Fiat Group produced components and production systems, provided administrative and financial services to its group companies, published a daily newspaper (*La Stampa*), and sold advertising space for multimedia customers. Total revenues amounted to €46.5 billion in 2005. The company's pretax profit was €1 billion.

The Fiat Group had its ordinary shares traded on the Italian Stock Exchange and had American Depository Receipts (ADRs) traded on the New York Stock Exchange. About one quarter of the group's ordinary shares were widely held, 45 percent were in the hands of banks and other institutional investors, and 30 percent were held by Fiat's primary shareholder, IFIL investments, which was controlled by the Agnelli family. Through IFIL Investments and several other investment vehicles, the Agnelli family, who were the founders of Fiat, held a substantial voting block in the group. Fiat Group's board of directors consisted of three executive directors and 12 non-executive directors, of which eight were considered "independent" from the company and its major shareholder. The company's chairman of the board of directors was Luca Cordero di Montezemolo, former protégé of Fiat's longtime boss Gianni Agnelli, chief executive officer (CEO) of Fiat's subsidiary Ferrari, and chairman of Italy's employers association Confindustria. Vice-chairman was John Elkann, who was a member of the Agnelli family, and CEO was Sergio Marchionne.

The first half of the 2000s had not been a successful period for the Fiat Group. Italian GAAP-based revenues had been declining from €57.5 billion in 2000 to €46.7 billion in 2004. Possible causes for the group's underperformance were the economic slowdown in Europe, the group's continued diversification into unrelated industries, and its lack of innovation and development of new car models. In fiscal 2005, however, the company

Professor Erik Peek prepared this case. The case is intended solely as the basis for class discussion and is not intended to serve as an endorsement, source of primary data, or illustration of effective or ineffective management.

[1]This section is primarily based on the Fiat Group's 2005 Annual Report and Report on Corporate Governance.

reported a slight increase in (IFRS-based) revenues of 2 percent and its first net profit since 2000, inducing management to designate the year 2005 as a "turning point" for Fiat. In spring 2006, analysts expected the Fiat Group's revenues to grow from €46.5 billion in 2005 to approximately €50.5 billion in 2006 and €52.2 billion in 2007. They also expected the Fiat Group to remain profitable in the next two years. Estimated pre-tax profits for 2006 and 2007 were €1.2 billion and €1.7 billion, respectively.[2] **Exhibit 1** shows the Fiat Group's stock price and accounting performance during the first half of the 2000s as well as its debt ratings in January 2006. In the first half of 2006 the Fiat Group made two Eurobond issues, each for €1 billion.

First-time adoption of IFRS

The general rule

In June 2003, the International Accounting Standards Board (IASB) issued IFRS 1 on firms' first-time adoption of IFRS. The objective of this new standard was to ensure that all firms preparing their financial statements for the first time in accordance with the IFRSs, (1) execute the transition to new reporting principles in a consistent manner and (2) provide sufficient additional disclosures to help the users of their statements understand the effects of the transition. IFRS 1 requires that a first-time adopter applies *retrospectively* the IFRSs that are *effective at the reporting date* of its first IFRS-based statements. Retrospective application of current IFRSs means that the firm recognizes all its assets and liabilities not only as if it has always applied IFRS but also as if the current IFRS version has always been effective and prior IFRS versions have never existed.[3] This illustrates that IFRS 1 aimed especially to improve comparability across first-time adopters, as opposed to improving comparability between first-time adopters and current users of IFRS, whose assets and liabilities are often affected by prior IFRS versions.

As well as the *reporting date* of the first IFRS statements, the *transition date* is important for the application of IFRS 1. The transition date is the beginning of the earliest fiscal year for which the first-time adopter prepares full IFRS-based comparative statements. Every first-time adopter is required to prepare an opening balance sheet at the transition date, although it is not required to publicly disclose this opening balance sheet. The accounting policies that a first-time adopter must use to prepare its opening balance sheet are the same policies that it uses to prepare its first IFRS-based financial statements (including the comparative statements).

Retrospective application of the IFRSs does not imply that on the transition date the first-time adopter can revise the estimates that it made for the same date under previous reporting standards. For example, if a first-time adopter receives information after the transition date that suggests that the economic life of one of its assets is three years instead of the previously assumed two years, the IFRS-based opening balance sheet on the transition date must reflect the "old" economic life assumption of two years. Hence, IFRS 1 explicitly forbids the first-time adopter modifying its prior financial statements with hindsight.

Exemptions

Retrospective application of current IFRSs may carry costs that exceed the benefits of the information that it produces. The IASB acknowledged the importance of a cost–benefit trade-off and included several exemptions from full retrospective application:

- The international standard on business combinations (IFRS 3) requires firms to recognize their acquisitions of other firms using purchase accounting. Under purchase accounting, a firm separately discloses on its balance sheet the fair value of the acquired assets as well as the excess of the purchase price over this amount (labeled goodwill). Under a few other accounting regimes, such as in the UK, firms can – or could – record some of their acquisitions using pooling accounting, whereby the acquirer recorded only the historical cost of the acquired assets on its balance sheet. Retrospective application would require a firm to restate all past business combinations that it recorded using the pooling method. IFRS 1 allows first-time adopters not to restate business combinations that occurred prior to the transition date. If a firm

---

[2]Source: Reuters consensus estimates.

[3]IFRS 1 allows first-time adopters to apply new IFRSs that will become effective on a date after the reporting date but that permit earlier application.

nevertheless chooses to restate a business combination that occurred on a date prior to the transition date, it must also restate all other business combinations that occurred after this particular date.

- When a firm records its property, plant and equipment, intangible assets, and investment property at their (depreciated) historical cost, IFRS 1 allows it to assume that these assets' fair values at the transition date are the assets' historical cost. IFRS 1 refers to this assumed value as the assets' "deemed cost." Alternatively, if the firm has revalued any of these assets prior to the adoption of IFRS and the revalued amount is broadly comparable to fair value under IFRS, it can use the revalued amount as deemed cost.

- A first-time adopter may choose to immediately recognize (into equity) the cumulative actuarial gains and losses on all its pension plans. By doing so, the first-time adopter avoids splitting the cumulative gains and losses that have arisen since the inception of the plans into a recognized and an unrecognized portion, which may be a difficult exercise when the firm uses the "corridor approach" for recognizing actuarial gains and losses.[4]

- A firm that consolidates the translated values of subsidiaries' foreign currency-denominated assets on its balance sheet, recognizes the cumulative translation difference, which arises because exchange rates fluctuate over the years, as a separate component in equity. Because separately reporting restated cumulative translation differences generates little additional information, a first-time adopter can choose to add the cumulative translation differences to equity and reset the line item to zero upon adoption.

- International accounting rules require a firm to separate the debt from the equity component of convertible debentures – or similar compound financial instruments – and account for these separately. Consequently, the equity component of compound financial instruments may remain on the firm's balance sheet after the debt component is no longer outstanding. IFRS 1 allows a first-time adopter not to separate the debt and equity components of compound financial instruments if the debt component is no longer outstanding on the transition date.

- A subsidiary that becomes a first-time adopter later than its parent can choose between reporting its assets and liabilities in accordance with IFRS 1 – using its own transition date – or reporting its assets and liabilities in accordance with the reporting principles used by its parent – using its parent's transition date. A parent that becomes a first-time adopter later than its subsidiary must report its subsidiary's assets and liabilities in its consolidated financial statements as they are reported in the subsidiary's financial statements.

- International rules require firms to report stock options using the fair value method, under which they record an expense for stock option compensation when the options are issued. The value of the options issued is estimated using a recognized option valuation model and is then expensed over the vesting period. A first-time adopter is, however, not required to use this method for options that it issued prior to November 7, 2002 or that vested before the later of (1) the transition date and (2) January 1, 2005.

This list of optional exemptions is nonexhaustive because every time that the IASB issues a new reporting standard, it may decide to exempt a first-time adopter from retrospective application of the new standard. In addition to these optional exemptions, IFRS 1 includes a few mandatory exemptions. For example, a first-time adopter cannot rerecognize assets and liabilities that it derecognized prior to January 1, 2004, under its previous accounting principles.

Required disclosures

According to IFRS 1, a first-time adopter needs to disclose at least the following information in its first-time IFRS-based financial statements:

- At least one year of comparative information under IFRSs. The comparative information of firms that adopted IFRS before January 1, 2006, such as the Fiat Group and most other listed firms in the EU, need

---

[4]Unrecognized actuarial losses arise, for example, when a change in a firm's actuarial assumptions increases its pension obligation, but the resulting change in the obligation is not recognized as a pension expense. Under the "corridor approach," the firm annually compares the cumulative unrecognized actuarial gains and losses to the greater of 10 percent of the pension obligation or 10 percent of the fair value of the pension plan assets. When the cumulative unrecognized actuarial gains and losses exceed their benchmark, the firm amortizes the difference over the remaining working lives of the active employees.

not comply with the international standards on financial instruments (IAS 32 and IAS 39) and on insurance contracts (IFRS 4). However, these firms must disclose the nature of the adjustments that would make the comparative information comply with these three reporting standards.

■ A reconciliation of equity under IFRS and equity under previous reporting standards at the transition date and at the end of the latest fiscal year prior to the first-time adoption of IFRS.

■ A reconciliation of the profit or loss under IFRS and under previous reporting standards in the latest fiscal year prior to the first-time adoption of IFRS.

■ The additional disclosures required by the international standard on the impairment of assets (IAS 36) if the firm recognized or reversed an impairment loss in its opening IFRS balance sheet.[5]

■ An explanation of the material adjustments made to the cash flow statement.

■ The aggregate adjustments that the firm made to the carrying amounts of the assets for which it uses the fair values as deemed cost.

The Fiat Group's first-time adoption of IFRS

For the Fiat Group the reporting date of its first IFRS statements was December 31, 2005. The company's transition date was January 1, 2004. Despite not being required to do so, the Fiat Group publicized its opening balance sheet for January 1, 2004 on May 11, 2005 in an appendix to the company's interim report for the first quarter of 2005. In addition to the 2004 opening balance sheet, the first-quarter report included an IFRS-based 2004 closing balance sheet, an IFRS-based 2004 income statement, and a reconciliation of IFRS-based and Italian GAAP-based opening and closing equity for fiscal 2004.

Exhibit 4 reports excerpts from appendix 1 to the 2005 financial statements of the Fiat Group. In this appendix, the group outlined the effects of the transition to IFRS on its balance sheet and income statement.

Questions

1 What are Fiat's key accounting policies? Which of Fiat's key accounting policies are affected by the adoption of IFRS?

2 Summarize the differences between Fiat's key accounting methods under Italian GAAP and those under IFRS. What characterizes the differences between the two sets of methods? From the perspective of a minority investor in the company's shares, which methods provide better information about the economic performance of Fiat?

3 Summarize the main factors that affect management's reporting incentives and strategy in fiscal year 2005. Which factors might reduce management's incentive to fully comply with the IFRSs?

[5]These disclosures are, for example, the amount of impairment, with an indication of the income statement item under which the impairment was categorized; the events that gave rise to the impairment (reversal); the nature of the impaired asset or cash generating unit, and the discount rate used to determine the value in use or the basis for determining the net selling price.

EXHIBIT 1   Market performance and accounting performance for the Fiat Group

Fiat's stock price and the MSCI World Automobiles Price Index from January 2000 to December 2005

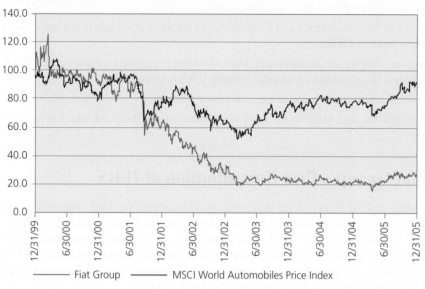

Source: Thomson Datastream.

Fiat's Accounting Performance from 2000 to 2005

(in € millions)	2005 (IFRS)	2004 (Italian GAAP)	2003 (Italian GAAP)	2002 (Italian GAAP)	2001 (Italian GAAP)	2000 (Italian GAAP)
Consolidated revenues	46,544	46,703	47,271	55,649	58,006	57,555
Operating result	2,215	−833	−510	−762	318	855
Group interest in net result	1,331	−1,586	−1,900	−3,948	−455	644
Group interest in stockholders' equity	8,681	5,099	6,793	7,641	12,170	13,320
Return on equity (in %)	15.3%	−26.7%	−26.3%	−39.9%	−3.5%	5.1%
Cash flow from operations	3,716	−358	−1,947	1,053	2,435	N.A.

Source: Annual reports of the Fiat Group.

Fiat's Debt Ratings in January 2006

Rating agency	Rating (long-term senior unsecured)	Date of rating	Rating (short-term senior unsecured)	Date of rating
Standard and Poor's	BB−	8/1/2005	B	8/2/2005
Fitch	BB−	1/20/2006	B	1/20/2006
Moody's	Ba3	1/31/2006		

Source: Reuters.

EXHIBIT 2   **Fiat Group's shareholders and directors**

On December 31, 2005, the Fiat Group had 1,092,246,316 ordinary shares, 103,292,310 preference shares and 79,912,800 savings shares outstanding and trading on public exchanges. All shares had a par value of €5. Holders of ordinary shares had voting rights but holders of preference shares and savings shares had limited or no voting rights. The ordinary shares were held by the following investors or investor groups:

Investor (group)	Percentage
IFIL Investments S.p.A. (controlled by IFI S.p.A., in turn controlled by Giovanni Agnelli & C. S.A.p.A.)	30.46%
Banca Intesa	6.08%
Unicredito	5.58%
Capitalia	3.80%
BNL	2.73%
Generali	2.38%
Libyan Arab Foreign Inv. Co.	2.28%
International Institutional Investors	approx. 12.5%
Italian Institutional Investors	approx. 10%
Other stockholders	approx. 24%

Source: Annual reports of the Fiat Group.

Director	Age	Position	Background
Luca Cordero di Montezemolo	59	Chairman of the Board[3]	Chairman and CEO of Ferrari S.p.A. since 1991; Director of La Stampa, Pinault-Printemps-Redoute S.A., Tod's, Indesit Company; Chairman of Bologna Fiere; President of Confindustria (the Federation of Italian Industries).
Andrea Agnelli	31	Director	Past positions at Iveco, Piaggio S.p.A., Auchan S.A., Juventus F.C. S.p.A., Ferrari S.p.A. and Philip Morris International Inc.
Roland Berger	68	Director[3]	Chairman of the Supervisory Board of Roland Berger Strategy Consultants, Munich.
Tiberto Brandolini d'Adda	58	Director	Chairman and CEO of Sequana Capital (formerly Worms & Cie); General Partner of Giovanni Agnelli & C.; Vice Chairman and Member of the Executive Committee of IFIL S.p.A.
John Philip Elkann	30	Vice Chairman of the Board[1,3]	Chairman of Itedi S.p.A., IFIL S.p.A. and Giovanni Agnelli & C. S.a.p.a.z.; Member of the Boards of Exor Group SA, IFI S.p.A. and RCS Media Group.
Luca Garavoglia	31	Director[1]	Chairman of Davide Campari-Milano S.p.A., parent company of the Campari Group.
Gian Maria Gros-Pietro	64	Director[1]	President of Federtrasporto (Italian association of transportation companies); Member of the Directive Committee and General Council of Assonime (Italian listed companies association), the Board of the Union of Industrialists of Rome, Confindustria's General Council, the Board of Edison S.p.A., the Board of SEAT Pagine Gialle S.p.A., the Executive Committee and the General Council of the Aspen Institute Italia, the International Business Council of the World Economic Forum and the Supervisory Board of Sofipa Equity Fund; Chairman of Autostrade S.p.A.; Vice President of I.G.I. (Istituto Grandi Infrastrutture); Senior Advisor for Italy of Société Générale Corporate& Investment Banking.

Fiat Group's first-time adoption of IFRS

(continued)

Director	Age	Position	Background
Hermann-Josef Lamberti	50	Director[2]	Chief Operating Officer and Member of the Board of Managing at Deutsche Bank AG; Chairman of the Supervisory Board of Deutsche Bank Privat und Geschaftskunden AG; Member of the Supervisory Board of Carl Zeiss AG and Deutsche Börse AG; Non-executive Director of Euroclear plc and Euroclear Bank SA.
Sergio Marchionne	54	CEO[3]	CEO of Fiat S.p.A., Fiat Auto Holding B.V. and Fiat Auto S.p.A.; Chairman of the Board of Directors of Lonza Group Ltd.; Director of Serono Ltd.; Member of the Supervisory Board of Hochtief; Chairman of Société Générale de Surveillance Holding SA, Banca Unione di Credito, CNH (Case New Holland) and ACEA (European Automobile Manufacturers Association); Member of the General Councils of Confindustria and Assonime (the Association of listed Italian companies); Permanent member of the Fondazione Giovanni Agnelli.
Virgilio Marrone	60	Director	General Manager and CEO of IFI S.p.A.; Member of the boards of SanPaolo IMI S.p.A. and the Exor Group.
Vittorio Mincato	70	Director[2]	Past CEO of Eni S.p.A; Chairman of Poste Italiane S.p.A.; Member of CNEL (the Italian National Committee for Economy and Labor); Chairman of Assonime, the Executive Board of Confindustria and the Boards of Directors of Parmalat S.p.A., the Teatro alla Scala Foundation, the Accademia Nazionale di Santa Cecilia, and the Accademia Olimpica; Vice President of the Union of Industrialists of Rome.
Pasquale Pistorio	70	Director[3]	Past President and CEO and Current Honory Chairman of SGS-THOMSON Microelectronics (STMicroelectronics); Member of numerous organizations, including the Internal Advisory Council of the Government of Singapore, the ICT Task Force of the United Nations, the International Business Council of the World Economic Forum, and the Boards of Telecom Italia S.p.A. and Chartered Semiconductor Manufacturing; Chairman of ENIAC, the technological platform for nanoelectronics of the EU; Vice President of Confindustria for innovation and research.
Carlo Sant'Albano	42	Director	Managing Director and General Manager of IFIL S.p.A; Member of the Boards of Sequana Capital, Juventus F.C. and Alpitour.
Ratan Tata	68	Director	Chairman of Tata Sons Limited, the holding company of the Tata Group; Chairman of the major Tata companies including Tata Steel, Tata Motors, Tata Power, Tata Consultancy Services, Tata Tea, Tata Chemicals, Indian Hotels and Tata Teleservices Limited; Associated with a number of important business and philanthropic organizations in India and abroad.
Mario Zibetti	67	Director[2]	Past senior partner at Arthur Andersen S.p.a.; Member of the Board of Directors of Ersel Finanziaria S.p.A., Comital – Cofresco S.p.a. and Fabio Perini S.p.A.

[1] Member of the Nominating and Compensation Committee
[2] Member of the Internal Control Committee
[3] Member of the Strategic Committee

Source: Form 20-F 2005 of the Fiat Group.

EXHIBIT 3   Letter from the chairman and the chief executive officer, December 2005

2005 marked a turning point for Fiat. We delivered on our commitments, we met all of our targets and we even exceeded a number of them. We had promised that 2004 would be Fiat's final year of net losses – and we achieved net income of over 1.4 billion euros in 2005. We had committed to a drastic cut in net industrial debt – and it was reduced by two-thirds. We had decided to focus on the relaunch of our Automobile activities, and in the last quarter of 2005 Fiat Auto posted a trading profit of 21 million euros after 17 consecutive quarters of losses. This has contributed to restoring Fiat's credibility, not only in Italy, but internationally, as evidenced by the improvement in our debt ratings and our ability to attract a large number of institutional investors in our debt raising activities. Our reputation has also benefited from the launch of new models across all brands that have been received extremely well by the public for their creativity, style, technology, and innovation, qualities that have distinguished the best Fiat cars since the firm was founded.

These breakthroughs, as well as all the other operational and financial improvements highlighted in this annual report, could not have been achieved without the strenuous efforts of the entire Fiat community, each and every one of whose members contributed to the relaunch of the Group with dedication and discipline. To do so, the Fiat people had to endorse fundamental changes in attitude, to assume greater responsibility and accountability, and to show their determination to deliver. We would like to express our sincere thanks to all of them.

During 2005, we also built a strong base for more effective and profitable operations in the future. First of all, we successfully resolved all pending strategic and financial issues: we settled our outstanding matters with General Motors and received a 1.56 billion euro cash payment; the Italenergia Bis transaction led to a 1.8 billion euro reduction in net industrial debt; and finally, conversion of the Mandatory Convertible Facility resulted in a 3 billion euro debt reduction and a sharp improvement in Group equity.

Fiat's business governance structure, especially in Automobiles, was right-sized to match realistic demand and market conditions. In Autos we have put in place a fully market-oriented organization, unbundling the brands: Fiat, Lancia, and Alfa Romeo now face the customer on their own, while sharing key functions such as manufacturing, quality and safety.

Everything is driven by the brands and for the brands. Similarly, in Agricultural and Construction

Equipment, Case New Holland was reorganized along four brands rather than regions. And we have begun to aggressively streamline processes throughout the organization. The Company will reap the benefits of these structural improvements in 2006 and beyond.

Last year, we made other important decisions that will shape the Group's future, in the form of targeted industrial alliances with major international partners. Seven such agreements were struck in the Automobile Sector – with Pars Industrial Development Foundation (PDIF), PSA-Tofas, Zastava, Suzuki, Ford, Severstal Auto, and Tata Motors – while another partnership was established in commercial vehicles and industrial engines, between Iveco and SAIC.

Though much was done in 2005 to set the Company on course towards a real, lasting rebirth of our Group, the process is far from over and much remains to be done. Nonetheless, today's Fiat is a much different company from what it was just a year ago. The Group improved all key financial indicators. Our cash position – about 7 billion euros at 2005 year end – is strong. The financial markets are showing increased confidence in our prospects, as demonstrated by the steady appreciation of the Fiat share price. We have nearly completed the process of making our Internal Control System fully Sarbanes Oxley compliant, a move that will further enhance confidence in the Group at the international level. The Fiat we are talking about is a Group with a reinvigorated managerial structure, a leaner organization, a solid financial structure, and stronger market positions thanks to new products. This new Fiat can achieve new, challenging targets in 2006.

At Group level, we aim to deliver positive cash flow from operations, a trading profit between 1.6 and 1.8 billion euros, and net income of about 700 million euros. While we do not expect market conditions for our operating Sectors to change materially this year, we have set high trading margin targets (trading profit as a percentage of revenues) for all of them: 7 percent to 7.5 percent at CNH, 5.5 percent to 6 percent at Iveco, and 3.5 percent to 4 percent in Components and Production Systems. The Automobile Sector should also turn in a positive performance, with a trading margin of 0.5 percent to 1 percent. This result will be supported by the full-year contribution of new models already rolled out. These will be joined in coming months by other new models, as we implement our aggressive product renewal plan calling for the launch of 20 new cars and the restyling of 23 current models between 2005 and 2008.

We made a clean break with the past, while respecting all commitments made to stakeholders. We

Fiat Group's first-time adoption of IFRS

are clearly within reach of recovering our position as a competitive automotive Group. This is why we are keeping up the pressure that has enabled us to get this far, demanding much from ourselves and from all the men and women of the Fiat community. We have no intention of lessening the momentum that has allowed Fiat to generate a series of steady improvements, quarter after quarter, throughout 2005. We will remain focused on reducing costs in non-essential areas, while continuing to invest in innovation. We will complement our advanced technological resources with better commercial organization and more efficient services. Finally, we will continue to seek new international opportunities, implementing our strategy of targeted alliances with key partners who will help us reduce capital commitments, and share investments and risks. It is for all these reasons that we feel confident about our future.

Turin, February 28, 2006
Luca Cordero di Montezemolo – Chairman
Sergio Marchionne – Chief Executive Officer

EXHIBIT 4 Excerpts from appendix 1 of Fiat's 2005 financial statements: Transition to international financial reporting standards

Following the coming into force of European Regulation No. 1606 dated July 19, 2002, starting from January 1, 2005, the Fiat Group adopted International Financial Reporting Standards (IFRS) issued by the International Accounting Standards Board (IASB). This Appendix provides the IFRS reconciliations of balance sheet data as of January 1 and December 31, 2004, and of income statement data for the year ended December 31, 2004, as required by IFRS 1 – First-time Adoption of IFRS, together with the related explanatory notes. This information has been prepared as part of the Group's conversion to IFRS and in connection with the preparation of its 2005 consolidated financial statements in accordance with IFRS, as adopted by the European Union.

Reconciliations required by IFRS 1

As required by IFRS 1, this note describes the policies adopted in preparing the IFRS opening consolidated balance sheet at January 1, 2004, the main differences in relation to Italian GAAP used to prepare the consolidated financial statements until December 31, 2004, as well as the consequent reconciliations between the figures already published, prepared in accordance with Italian GAAP, and the corresponding figures remeasured in accordance with IFRS. The 2004 restated IFRS consolidated balance sheet and income statement have been prepared in accordance with IFRS 1 – First-time Adoption of IFRS. In particular, the IFRS applicable from January 1, 2005, as published as of December 31, 2004, have been adopted, including the following:

■ IAS 39 – Financial Instruments: Recognition and Measurement, in its entirety. In particular, the Group adopted derecognition requirements retrospectively from the date on which financial assets and financial liabilities had been derecognized under Italian GAAP.

■ IFRS 2 – Share-based Payment, which was published by the IASB on February 19, 2004 and adopted by the European Commission on February 7, 2005.

Description of main differences between Italian GAAP and IFRS

The following paragraphs provide a description of the main differences between Italian GAAP and IFRS that have had effects on Fiat's consolidated balance sheet and income statement. Amounts are shown pre-tax and the related tax effects are separately summarized in the item R. Accounting for deferred income taxes.

A. Development costs

Under Italian GAAP applied research and development costs may alternatively be capitalised or charged to operations when incurred. Fiat Group has mainly expensed R&D costs when incurred. IAS 38 – Intangible Assets requires that research costs be expensed, whereas development costs that meet the criteria for capitalisation must be capitalised and then amortized from the start of production over the economic life of the related products.

Under IFRS, the Group has capitalised development costs in the Fiat Auto, Ferrari-Maserati, Agricultural and Construction Equipment, Commercial Vehicle and Components Sectors, using the retrospective approach in compliance with IFRS 1.

The positive impact of 1,876 million euros on the opening IFRS stockholders' equity at January 1, 2004, corresponds to the cumulative amount of qualifying development expenditures incurred in prior years by the Group, net of accumulated amortization. Consistently, intangible assets show an increase of 2,090 million euros and of 2,499 million euros at January 1, 2004, and at December 31, 2004, respectively.

The 2004 net result was positively impacted by 436 million euros in the year, reflecting the combined effect of the capitalisation of development costs incurred in the period that had been expensed under Italian GAAP, and the amortization of the amount that had been capitalised in the opening IFRS balance sheet at January 1, 2004. This positive impact has been accounted for in Research and Development costs.

In accordance with IAS 36 – Impairment of Assets, development costs capitalised as intangible assets shall be tested for impairment and an impairment loss shall be recognized if the recoverable amount of an asset is less than its carrying amount, as further described in the paragraph I. Impairment of assets.

B. Employee benefits

The Group sponsors funded and unfunded defined benefit pension plans, as well as other long term benefits to employees.

Under Italian GAAP, these benefits, with the exception of the Reserve for Employee Severance Indemnities ("TFR") that is accounted for in compliance with a specific Italian law, are mainly recorded in accordance with IAS 19 – Employee Benefits, applying the corridor approach, which consists of amortizing over the remaining service lives of active employees only the portion of net cumulative actuarial gains and losses that exceeds the greater of 10 percent of either the defined benefit obligation or the fair value of the plan assets, while the portion included in the 10 percent remains unrecognized.

With the adoption of IFRS, TFR is considered a defined benefit obligation to be accounted for in accordance with IAS 19 and consequently has been recalculated applying the Projected Unit Credit Method. Furthermore, as mentioned in the paragraph "Optional exemptions", the Group elected to recognize all cumulative actuarial gains and losses that existed at January 1, 2004, with a negative impact on opening stockholders' equity at that date of 1,247 million euros.

Consequently pension and other post-employment benefit costs recorded in the 2004 IFRS income statement do not include any amortization of unrecognized actuarial gains and losses deferred in previous years in the IFRS financial statements under the corridor approach, and recognized in the 2004 income statement under Italian GAAP, resulting in a benefit of 94 million euros.

The Group has elected to use the corridor approach for actuarial gains and losses arising after January 1, 2004.

Furthermore, the Group elected to state the expense related to the reversal of discounting on defined benefit plans without plan assets separately as Financial expenses, with a corresponding increase in Financial expenses of 127 million euros in 2004.

C. Business combinations

As mentioned above, the Group elected not to apply IFRS 3 – Business Combinations retrospectively to business combinations that occurred before the date of transition to IFRS.

As prescribed in IFRS 3, starting from January 1, 2004, the IFRS income statement no longer includes goodwill amortization charges, resulting in a positive impact on Other operating income and expense of 162 million euros in 2004.

D. Revenue recognition – sales with a buy-back commitment

Under Italian GAAP, the Group recognized revenues from sales of products at the time title passed to the customer, which was generally at the time of shipment. For contracts for vehicle sales with a buy-back commitment at a specified price, a specific reserve for future risks and charges was set aside based on the difference between the guaranteed residual value and the estimated realizable value of vehicles, taking into account the probability that such option would be exercised. This reserve was set up at the time of the initial sale and adjusted periodically over the period of the contract. The costs of refurbishing the vehicles, to be incurred when the buy-back option is exercised, were reasonably estimated and accrued at the time of the initial sale.

Under IAS 18 – Revenue, new vehicle sales with a buy-back commitment do not meet criteria for revenue recognition, because the significant risks and rewards of ownership of the goods are not necessarily transferred to the buyer. Consequently, this kind of contract is treated in a manner similar to an operating lease transaction. More specifically, vehicles sold with a buy-back commitment are accounted for as Inventory if they regard the Fiat Auto business (agreements with normally a short-term buy-back commitment) and as Property, plant and equipment if they regard the Commercial Vehicles business (agreements with normally a long-term buy-back commitment). The difference between the carrying value (corresponding to the manufacturing cost) and the estimated resale value (net of refurbishing costs) at the end of the buy-back period, is depreciated on a straight-line basis over the duration of the contract. The initial sale price received is accounted for as a liability. The difference between the initial sale price and the buy-back price is recognized as rental revenue on a straight-line basis over the duration of the contract.

Opening IFRS stockholders' equity at January 1, 2004 includes a negative impact of 180 million euros mainly representing the portion of the margin accounted for under Italian GAAP on vehicles sold with a buy-back commitment prior to January 1, 2004, that will be recognized under IFRS over the remaining buy-back period, net of the effects due to the adjustments to the provisions for vehicle sales with a buy-back commitment recognized under Italian GAAP.

This accounting treatment results in increases in the tangible assets reported in the balance sheet (1,001 million euros at January 1, 2004 and 1,106 million euros at December 31, 2004), in inventory (608 million euros at January 1, 2004 and 695 million euros at December 31, 2004), in advances from customers (equal to the operating lease rentals prepaid at the date of initial sale and recognized in the item Other payables), as well as in Trade payables, for the amount of the buy-back price, payable to the customer when the vehicle is bought back. In the income statement, a significant impact is generated on revenues (reduced by 1,103 million euros in 2004) and on cost of sales (reduced by 1,090 million euros in 2004), while no significant impact is generated on the net operating result; furthermore, the amount of these impacts in future years will depend on the changes in the volume and characteristics of these contracts year-over-year. Notwithstanding this, these changes are not expected to have a particularly significant impact on Group reported earnings in the coming years.

E. Revenue recognition – Other

Under Italian GAAP the recognition of disposals is based primarily on legal and contractual form (transfer of legal title).

Under IFRS, when risks and rewards are not substantially transferred to the buyer and the seller maintains a continuous involvement in the operations or assets being sold, the transaction is not recognized as a sale.

Consequently, certain disposal transactions, such as the disposal of the 14 percent interest in Italenergia Bis and certain minor real estate transactions, have been reversed retrospectively: the related asset has been recognized in the IFRS balance sheet, the initial gain recorded under Italian GAAP has been reversed and the cash received at the moment of the sale has been accounted for as a financial liability.

In particular, in 2001 the Group acquired a 38.6 percent shareholding in Italenergia S.p.A., now Italenergia Bis S.p.A. ("Italenergia"), a company formed between Fiat, Electricité de France ("EDF") and certain financial investors for the purpose of acquiring control of the Montedison – Edison ("Edison") group through tender offers. Italenergia assumed effective control of Edison at the end of the third quarter of that year and consolidated Edison from October 1, 2001. In 2002 the shareholders of Italenergia entered into agreements which resulted, among other things, in the transfer of a 14 percent interest in Italenergia from Fiat to other shareholders (with a put option that would require Fiat to repurchase the shares transferred in certain circumstances) and the assignment to Fiat of a put option to sell its shares in Italenergia to EDF in 2005, based on market values at that date, but subject to a contractually agreed minimum price in excess of book value.

Under Italian GAAP, Fiat accounted for its investments in Italenergia under the equity method, based on a 38.6 percent shareholding through September 30, 2002 and a 24.6 percent shareholding from October 1, 2002; in addition it recorded a gain of 189 million euros before taxes on the sale of its 14 percent interest in the investee to other shareholders effective September 30, 2002.

Under IFRS, the transfer of the 14 percent interest in Italenergia to the other shareholders was not considered to meet the requirements for revenue recognition set out in IAS 18, mainly due to the existence of the put options granted to the transferees and *de facto* constraints on the transferees' ability to pledge or exchange the transferred assets in the period from the sale through 2005. Accordingly, the gain recorded in 2002 for the sale was reversed, and the results of applying the equity method of accounting to the investment in Italenergia was recomputed to reflect a 38.6 percent interest in the net results and stockholders' equity of the investee, as adjusted for the differences between Italian GAAP and IFRS applicable to Italenergia.

This adjustment decreased the stockholders' equity at January 1, 2004 and at December 31, 2004 by an amount of 153 million euros and 237 million euros, respectively. Furthermore this adjustment increased the investment for an amount of 291 million euros at January 1, 2004 and of 341 million euros at December 31, 2004 and financial debt for amounts of 572 million euros at January 1, 2004 and of 593 million euros at December 31, 2004, as a consequence of the non-recognition of the transfer of the 14 percent interest in Italenergia.

F. Scope of consolidation

Under Italian GAAP, the subsidiary B.U.C. – Banca Unione di Credito – as required by law, was excluded from the scope of consolidation as it had dissimilar activities, and was accounted for using the equity method.

IFRS does not permit this kind of exclusion: consequently, B.U.C. is included in the IFRS scope of consolidation. Furthermore, under Italian GAAP investments that are not controlled on a legal basis or a *de facto* basis determined considering voting rights were excluded from the scope of consolidation.

Under IFRS, in accordance with SIC 12 – Consolidation – Special Purpose Entities, a Special Purpose Entity ("SPE") shall be consolidated when the substance of the relationship between an entity and the SPE indicates that the SPE is controlled by that entity.

This standard has been applied to all receivables securitisation transactions entered into by the Group (see the paragraph Q. Sales of receivables below), to a real estate securitisation transaction entered into in 1998 and to the sale of the Fiat Auto Spare Parts business to "Societá di Commercializzazione e Distribuzione Ricambi S.p.A." ("SCDR") in 2001.

In particular, in 1998 the Group entered in a real estate securitisation and, under Italian GAAP, the related revenue was recognized at the date of the legal transfer of the assets involved. In the IFRS balance sheet at January 1, 2004, these assets have been written back at their historical cost, net of revaluations accounted before the sale, if any. Cash received at the time of the transaction has been accounted for in financial debt for an amount of 188 million euros at January 1, 2004.

Fiat Group's first-time adoption of IFRS

The IFRS stockholders' equity at January 1, 2004 was negatively impacted for 105 million euros by the cumulative effect of the reversal of the capital gain on the initial disposal and of the revaluation previously recognized under Italian GAAP, net of the related effect of asset depreciation, as well as the recognition of financial charges on related debt, net of the reversal of rental fees paid, if any. The impact on the 2004 net result is not material.

Furthermore, in 2001 the Group participated with a specialist logistics operator and other financial investors in the formation of "Societá di Commercializzazione e Distribuzione Ricambi S.p.A." ("SCDR"), a company whose principal activity is the purchase of spare parts from Fiat Auto for resale to end customers. At that date Fiat Auto and its subsidiaries sold their spare parts inventory to SCDR recording a gain of 300 million euros. The Group's investment in SCDR represents 19 percent of SCDR's stock capital and was accounted for under the equity method for Italian GAAP.

Under IFRS, SCDR qualifies as a Special Purpose Entity (SPE) as defined by SIC 12 due to the continuing involvement of Fiat Auto in SCDR operations. Consequently, SCDR has been consolidated on a line by line basis in the IFRS consolidated financial statements, with a consequent increase in financial debt of 237 million euros and of 471 million euros at January 1, 2004 and at December 31, 2004, respectively. Opening stockholders' equity at January 1, 2004 was reduced by 266 million euros by the amount corresponding to the unrealized intercompany profit in inventory held by SCDR on that date; this amount did not change significantly at the end of 2004.

G. Property, plant and equipment

Under Italian GAAP and IFRS, assets included in Property, Plant and Equipment were generally recorded at cost, corresponding to the purchase price plus the direct attributable cost of bringing the assets to their working condition.

Under Italian GAAP, Fiat revalued certain Property, Plant and Equipment to amounts in excess of historical cost, as permitted or required by specific laws of the countries in which the assets were located. These revaluations were credited to stockholders' equity and the revalued assets were depreciated over their remaining useful lives.

Furthermore, under Italian GAAP, the land directly related to buildings included in Property, Plant and Equipment was depreciated together with the related building depreciation.

The revaluations and land depreciation are not permitted under IFRS. Therefore IFRS stockholders' equity at January 1, 2004 reflects a negative impact of 164 million euros, related to the effect of the elimination of the asset revaluation recognized in the balance sheet, partially offset by the reversal of the land depreciation charged to prior period income statements.

In the 2004 IFRS income statement, the above-mentioned adjustments had a positive impact of 14 million euros in 2004 due to the reversal of the depreciation of revalued assets, net of adjustments on gains and losses, if any, on disposal of the related assets, and to the reversal of land depreciation.

H. Write-off of deferred costs

Under Italian GAAP, the Group deferred and amortized certain costs (mainly start-up and related charges). IFRS require these to be expensed when incurred.

In addition, costs incurred in connection with share capital increases, which are also deferred and amortized under Italian GAAP, are deducted directly from the proceeds of the increase and debited to stockholders' equity under IFRS.

I. Impairment of assets

Under Italian GAAP, the Group tested its intangible assets with indefinite useful lives (mainly goodwill) for impairment annually by comparing their carrying amount with their recoverable amount in terms of the value in use of the asset itself (or group of assets). In determining the value in use the Group estimated the future cash inflows and outflows of the asset (or group of assets) to be derived from the continuing use of the asset and from its ultimate disposal, and discounted those future cash flows. If the recoverable amount was lower than the carrying value, an impairment loss was recognized for the difference.

With reference to tangible fixed assets, under Italian GAAP the Group accounted for specific write-offs when the asset was no longer to be used. Furthermore, in the presence of impairment indicators, the Group tested tangible fixed assets for impairment using the undiscounted cash flow method in determining the recoverable amount of homogeneous group of assets. If the recoverable amount thus determined was lower than the carrying value, an impairment loss was recognized for the difference. Under IFRS, intangible assets with indefinite useful lives are tested for impairment annually by a methodology substantially similar to the one required by Italian GAAP. Furthermore, development costs, capitalised under IFRS and expensed under Italian GAAP, are attributed to the related cash generating unit and tested for impairment together with the related tangible assets, applying the discounted cash flow method in determining their recoverable amount.

Consequently, the reconciliation between Italian GAAP and IFRS reflects adjustments due to both impairment losses on development costs previously capitalised for IFRS purposes, and the effect of discounting on the determination of the recoverable amount of tangible fixed assets.

L. Reserves for risks and charges

Differences between Italian GAAP and IFRS refer mainly to the following items:

■ Restructuring reserve: the Group provided restructuring reserves based upon management's best estimate of the costs to be incurred in connection with each of its restructuring programs at the time such programs were formally decided. Under IFRS the requirements to recognize a constructive obligation in the financial statements are more restrictive, and some restructuring reserves recorded under Italian GAAP have been eliminated.

■ Reserve for vehicle sales incentives: under Italian GAAP Fiat Auto accounted for certain incentives at the time at which a legal obligation to pay the incentives arose, which may have been in periods subsequent to that in which the initial sale to the dealer network was made. Under IAS 37 companies are required to make provision not only for legal, but also for constructive, obligations based on an established pattern of past practice. In the context of the IFRS restatement exercise, Fiat has reviewed its practice in the area of vehicle sales incentives and has determined that for certain forms of incentives a constructive obligation exists which should be provided under IFRS at the date of sale.

M. Recognition and measurement of derivatives

Beginning in 2001 the Fiat Group adopted – to the extent that it is consistent and not in contrast with general principles set forth in the Italian law governing financial statements – IAS 39 Financial Instruments: Recognition and Measurement. In particular, taking into account the restrictions under Italian law, the Group maintained that IAS 39 was applicable only in part and only in reference to the designation of derivative financial instruments as "hedging" or "non-hedging instruments" and with respect to the symmetrical accounting of the result of the valuation of the hedging instruments and the result attributable to the hedged items ("hedge accounting"). The transactions which, according to the Group's policy for risk management, were able to meet the conditions stated by the accounting principle for hedge accounting treat-

ment, were designated as hedging transactions; the others, although set up for the purpose of managing risk exposure (inasmuch as the Group's policy does not permit speculative transactions), were designated as "trading". The main differences between Italian GAAP and IFRS may be summarized as follows:

■ Instruments designated as "hedging instruments" – under Italian GAAP, the instrument was valued symmetrically with the underlying hedged item. Therefore, where the hedged item was not adjusted to fair value in the financial statements, the hedging instrument was also not adjusted. Similarly, where the hedged item had not yet been recorded in the financial statements (hedging of future flows), the valuation of the hedging instrument at fair value was deferred. Under IFRS:

■ In the case of a fair value hedge, the gains or losses from remeasuring the hedging instrument at fair value shall be recognized in the income statement and the gains or losses on the hedged item attributable to the hedge risk shall adjust the carrying amount of the hedged item and be recognized in the income statement. Consequently, no impact arises on net income (except for the ineffective portion of the hedge, if any) and on net equity, while adjustments impact the carrying values of hedging instruments and hedged items.

■ In the case of a cash flow hedge (hedging of future flows), the portion of gains or losses on the hedging instrument that is determined to be an effective hedge shall be recognized directly in equity through the statement of changes in equity; the ineffective portion of the gains or losses shall be recognized in the income statement. Consequently, with reference to the effective portion, only a difference in net equity arises between Italian GAAP and IFRS.

■ Instruments designated as "non-hedging instruments" (except for foreign currency derivative instruments) – under Italian GAAP, these instruments were valued at market value and the differential, if negative compared to the contractual value, was recorded in the income statement, in accordance with the concept of prudence. Under IAS 39 the positive differential should also be recorded. With reference to foreign currency derivative instruments, instead, the accounting treatment adopted under Italian GAAP was in compliance with IAS 39.

In this context, as mentioned in the consolidated financial statements as of December 31, 2003, Fiat was party to a Total Return Equity Swap contract on General Motors shares, in order to hedge the risk implicit in the Exchangeable Bond on General Motors shares.

Although this equity swap was entered into for hedging purposes it does not qualify for hedge accounting and accordingly it was defined as a non-hedging instrument. Consequently, the positive fair value of the instrument as of December 31, 2003, amounting to 450 million euros, had not been recorded under Italian GAAP. During 2004 Fiat terminated the contract, realizing a gain of 300 million euros.

In the IFRS restatement, the above mentioned positive fair value at December 31, 2003 has been recognized in opening equity, while, following the unwinding of the swap, a negative adjustment of the same amount has been recorded in the 2004 income statement.

N. Treasury stock

In accordance with Italian GAAP, the Group accounted for treasury stock as an asset and recorded related valuation adjustments and gains or losses on disposal in the income statement.

Under IFRS, treasury stock is deducted from stockholders' equity and all movements in treasury stock are recognized in stockholders' equity rather than in the income statement.

O. Stock options

Under Italian GAAP, with reference to share-based payment transactions, no obligations or compensation expenses were recognized.

In accordance with IFRS 2 – Share-based Payment, the full amount fair value of stock options on the date of grant must be expensed. Changes in fair value after the grant date have no impact on the initial measurement. The compensation expense corresponding to the option's fair value is recognized in payroll costs on a straight-line basis over the period from the grant date to the vesting date, with the offsetting credit recognized directly in equity.

The Group applied the transitional provision provided by IFRS 2 and therefore applied this standard to all stock options granted after November 7, 2002 and not yet vested at the effective date of IFRS 2 (January 1, 2005). No compensation expense is required to be recognized for stock options granted prior to November 7, 2002, in accordance with transitional provision of IFRS 2.

P. Adjustments to the valuation of investments in associates

These items represent the effect of the IFRS adjustments on the Group portion of the net equity of associates accounted for using the equity method.

Q. Sales of receivables

The Fiat Group sells a significant part of its finance, trade and tax receivables through either securitisation programs or factoring transactions.

A securitisation transaction entails the sale without recourse of a portfolio of receivables to a securitisation vehicle (special purpose entity). This special purpose entity finances the purchase of the receivables by issuing asset-backed securities (i.e., securities whose repayment and interest flow depend upon the cash flow generated by the portfolio). Asset-backed securities are divided into classes according to their degree of seniority and rating: the most senior classes are placed with investors on the market; the junior class, whose repayment is subordinated to the senior classes, is normally subscribed for by the seller. The residual interest in the receivables retained by the seller is therefore limited to the junior securities it has subscribed for.

Factoring transactions may be with or without recourse on the seller; certain factoring agreements without recourse include deferred purchase price clauses (i.e., the payment of a minority portion of the purchase price is conditional upon the full collection of the receivables), require a first loss guarantee of the seller up to a limited amount or imply a continuing significant exposure to the receivables cash flow.

Under Italian GAAP, all receivables sold through either securitisation or factoring transactions (both with and without recourse) had been derecognized. Furthermore, with specific reference to the securitisation of retail loans and leases originated by the financial services companies, the net present value of the interest flow implicit in the instalments, net of related costs, had been recognized in the income statement.

Under IFRS:

- As mentioned above, SIC 12 – Consolidation – Special Purpose Entities states that an SPE shall be consolidated when the substance of the relationship between the entity and the SPE indicates that the SPE is controlled by that entity; therefore all securitisation transactions have been reversed.

- IAS 39 allows for the derecognition of a financial asset when, and only when, the risks and rewards of the ownership of the assets are substantially transferred: consequently, all portfolios sold with recourse, and the majority of those sold without recourse, have been reinstated in the IFRS balance sheet.

The impact of such adjustments on stockholders' equity and on net income is not material. In particular, it refers mainly to the reversal of the gains arising from the related securitisation transactions on the retail portfolio of receivables of financial service companies, realized under Italian GAAP and not yet realized under IFRS.

With regards to financial structure, the reinstatement in the balance sheet of the receivables and payables involved in these sales transactions causes a significant increase in trade and financial receivables and in financial debt balances, and a worsening in net debt. In particular, in consequence of these reinstatements, trade receivables increase by 3,563 million euros and 2,134 euros at January 1, 2004 and at December 31, 2004, respectively; at the same dates, financial receivables increase by 6,127 million euros and 6,997 euros, and financial debt increased by 10,581 million euros and 10,174 million euros, respectively.

R. Accounting for deferred income taxes

This item includes the combined effect of the net deferred tax effects, after allowance, on the above mentioned IFRS adjustments, as well as other minor differences between Italian GAAP and IFRS on the recognition of tax assets and liabilities.

Effects of transition to IFRS on the consolidated balance sheet at January 1, 2004

(in € millions)	Italian GAAP	Reclassifi-cations	Adjust-ments	IAS/IFRS	
Intangible assets, ofwhich:	3,724		1,774	5,498	Intangible assets, of which:
Goodwill	*2,402*			*2,402*	*Goodwill*
Other intangible fixed assets	*1,322*		*1,774*	*3,096*	*Other intangible fixed assets*
Property, plant and equipment, of which:	9,675	(945)	817	9,547	Property, plant and equipment
Property, plant and equipment	*8,761*	*(31)*			
Operating leases	*914*	*(914)*			
		31		31	Investment property
Financial fixed assets	3,950	70	(121)	3,899	Investment and other financial assets
Financial receivables held as fixed assets	29	(29)			
		914	(50)	864	Leased assets
Deferred tax assets	1,879		266	2,145	Deferred tax assets
Total Non-Current assets	**19,257**	**41**	**2,686**	**21,984**	**Non-current assets**
Net inventories	6,484		1,113	7,597	Inventories
Trade receivables	4,553	(682)	2,678	6,549	Trade receivables
		12,890	7,937	20,827	Receivables from financing activities
Other receivables	3,081	(148)	541	3,474	Other receivables
		407	10	417	Accrued income and prepaid expenses
				2,129	Current financial assets, of which:
		32		*32*	*Current equity investments*
		515	*260*	*775*	*Current securities*
		430	*892*	*1,322*	*Other financial assets*
Financial assets not held as fixed assets	120	(120)			
Financial lease contracts receivable	1,797	(1,797)			
Financial receivables	10,750	(10,750)			
Securities	3,789	(3,789)			
Cash	3,211	3,214	420	6,845	Cash and cash equivalents
Total Current assets	**33,785**	**202**	**13,851**	**47,838**	**Current assets**
Trade accruals and deferrals	407	(407)			
Financial accruals and deferrals	386	(386)			
			21	21	Assets held for sale
TOTAL ASSETS	**53,835**	**(550)**	**16,558**	**69,843**	**TOTAL ASSETS**
Stockholders' equity	**7,494**	**(934)**		**6,560**	**Stockholders' equity**
				7,455	Provisions, of which:
Reserves for employee severance indemnities	*1,313*	*1,503*	*1,224*	*4,040*	*Employee benefits*
Reserves for risks and charges	*5,168*	*(1,550)*	*(203)*	*3,415*	*Other provisions*
Deferred income tax reserves	211	(211)			
Long-term financial payables	15,418	6,501	14,790	36,709	Debt, of which:
				10,581	Asset-backed financing
				26,128	Other debt
Total Non-current liabilities	**22,110**	**6,243**			

(continued)

Effects of transition to IFRS on the Consolidated Balance Sheet at January 1, 2004

(in € millions)	Italian GAAP	Reclassifi-cations	Adjust-ments	IAS/IFRS	
		568	(223)	345	Other financial liabilities
Trade payables	12,588		(297)	12,291	Trade payables
Others payables	2,742		1,948	4,690	Other payables
Short-term financial payables	6,616	(6,616)			
Total Current liabilities	**21,946**	**(6,048)**			
		211	274	485	Deferred tax liabilities
Trade accruals and deferrals	1,329		(21)	1,308	Accrued expenses and deferred income
Financial accruals and deferrals	956	(956)			
					Liabilities held for sale
TOTAL LIABILITIES AND STOCKHOLDERS' EQUITY	**53,835**	**(550)**	**(934)**	**69,843**	**TOTAL STOCKHOLDERS' EQUITY AND LIABILITIES**

Effects of transition to IFRS on the income statement for the year ended December 31, 2004

(in € millions)	Italian GAAP	Reclassifi-cations	Adjust-ments	IAS/IFRS	
Net revenues	46,703		(1,066)	45,637	Net revenues
Cost of sales	39,623	675	(1,177)	39,121	Cost of sales
Gross operating result	**7,080**				
Overhead	4,629	51	21	4,701	Selling, general and administrative costs
Research and development	1,810	1	(461)	1,350	Research and development costs
Other operating income (expenses)	(619)	346	(142)	(415)	Other income (expenses)
Operating result	**22**	**(381)**	**409**	**50**	**Trading profit**
		154	(4)	150	Gains (losses) on the disposal of equity investments
		496	46	542	Restructuring costs
		(243)		(243)	Other unusual income (expenses)
		(966)	**359**	**(585)**	**Operating result**
		(641)	(538)	(1,179)	Financial income
Result from equity investments	8		127	135	Result from equity investments
Non-operating income (expenses)	(863)	863			
EBIT	**(833)**				
Financial income (expenses)	(744)	744			
Income (loss) before taxes	**(1,577)**		**(52)**	**(1,629)**	**Result before taxes**
Income taxes	(29)		(21)	(50)	Income taxes
Net result of normal operations	**(1,548)**		**(31)**	**(1,579)**	**Net result of normal operations**
Result from discontinued Operations					Result from discontinued operations
Net result before minority interest	**(1,548)**		**(31)**	**(1,579)**	**Net result before minority interest**

Accounting Analysis: Accounting Adjustments

We learned in Chapter 3 that accounting analysis requires the analyst to adjust a firm's accounting numbers using cash flow information and information from the notes to the financial statements to "undo" any accounting distortions.

Once the financial statements have been standardized, the analyst is ready to identify any distortions in financial statements. The analyst's primary focus should be on those accounting estimates and methods that the firm uses to measure its key success factors and risks. If there are differences in these estimates and/or methods between firms or for the same firm over time, the analyst's job is to assess whether they reflect legitimate business differences and therefore require no adjustment, or whether they reflect differences in managerial judgment or bias and require adjustment. In addition, even if accounting rules are adhered to consistently, accounting distortions can arise because accounting rules themselves do a poor job of capturing firm economics, creating opportunities for the analyst to adjust a firm's financials in a way that presents a more realistic picture of its performance.

This chapter discusses the most common types of accounting distortions that can arise and shows how to make adjustments to the standardized financial statements to undo these distortions.

A balance sheet approach is used to identify whether there have been any distortions to assets, liabilities, or shareholders' equity. Once any asset and liability misstatements have been identified, the analyst can make adjustments to the balance sheet at the beginning and/or end of the current year, as well as any needed adjustments to revenues and expenses in the latest income statement. This approach ensures that the most recent financial ratios used to evaluate a firm's performance and forecast its future results are based on financial data that appropriately reflect its business economics.

In some instances, information taken from a firm's notes to the financial statements, cash flow statement, and statement of comprehensive income enables the analyst to make a precise adjustment for an accounting distortion. However, for many types of accounting adjustments the company does not disclose all of the information needed to perfectly undo the distortion, requiring the analyst to make an approximate adjustment to the financial statements.

RECOGNITION OF ASSETS

Accountants define assets as resources that a firm owns or controls as a result of past business transactions, and which are expected to produce future economic benefits that can be measured with a reasonable degree of certainty. Assets can take a variety of forms, including cash, marketable securities, receivables from customers, inventories, tangible assets, non-current investments in other companies, and intangibles.

Distortions in asset values generally arise because there is ambiguity about whether:

- The firm owns or controls the economic resources in question.

- The economic resources are likely to provide future economic benefits that can be measured with reasonable certainty.

- The fair values of assets fall below their book values.
- Fair value estimates are accurate.

Who owns or controls resources?

For most resources used by a firm, ownership or control is relatively straightforward: the firm using the resource owns the asset. However, some types of transactions make it difficult to assess who owns a resource. For example, who owns or controls a resource that has been leased? Is it the lessor or the lessee? Or consider a firm that discounts a customer receivable with a bank. If the bank has recourse against the firm should the customer default, is the real owner of the receivable the bank or the company? Or consider a firm owning 49 percent of another firm's ordinary shares. Does the firm control all of the investment's assets or only the net investment it legally owns?

Accounting rules often leave some discretion to managers and auditors in deciding whether their company owns or controls an asset. Leaving discretion to managers and auditors can be preferred over imposing detailed and mechanical rules if the latter solution causes managers to structure their transactions such that they avoid recognizing an asset. Following this idea, the IASB frequently takes a principles-based approach to setting accounting standards, thereby granting managers greater reporting discretion than under a rules-based approach. For example, the international standard for preparing consolidated financial statements (IAS 27) requires that firm A reports all the assets of firm B on its balance sheet when firm A has the power to govern the financial and operating policies of firm B. This broadly defined principle anticipates situations where firm A owns less than half of firm B's voting shares but has other ways to influence firm B's decisions, such as through board memberships or contractual agreements. The standard leaves much responsibility to managers and auditors to decide which subsidiaries are economically owned by the company.

While reporting discretion is necessary to benefit from managers' insider knowledge about the economic substance of their company's transactions, it also permits managers to misrepresent transactions and satisfy their own financial reporting objectives. Accounting analysis, therefore, involves assessing whether a firm's reported assets adequately reflect the key resources that are under its control, and whether adjustments are required to compare its performance with that of competitors. Although firms are generally inclined to understate the assets that they control, thereby inflating the return on capital invested, they may sometimes pretend to control subsidiaries for the sake of inflating asset and revenue growth. For example, in the period from 1999 to 2001, Dutch food retailer Royal Ahold fraudulently reported the assets, liabilities, revenues, and operating profits of jointly controlled joint ventures in its financial statements as if the company fully controlled the joint ventures. The correct accounting treatment would have been to report only half of the joint ventures' assets and liabilities on Ahold's balance sheet and only half of the joint ventures' revenues, expenses, and operating profits in Ahold's income statement. By fully consolidating the joint ventures, Royal Ahold overstated its revenues by a total amount of €27.6 billion and its annual sales growth by an average of 24 percent. Analyzing the accounting of a firm that follows a strategy of growing through acquisitions, such as Ahold, thus would include identifying subsidiaries that are fully consolidated but not fully owned and assessing their impact on the firm's net assets, revenues, and growth figures.

In situations where standard setters or auditors impose rigid and mechanical accounting rules on managers to reduce reporting discretion, accounting analysis is nevertheless also important because these detailed rules permit managers to "groom" transactions to satisfy their own reporting objectives. For example, although a significant change in the rules is imminent, current mechanical US rules on lease accounting permit two lease transactions with essentially the same but slightly different contract terms to be structured so that one is reported as an asset by the lessee, and the other is shown as an asset by the lessor. The analyst may attempt to correct for this distortion by adjusting the way in which the lessee and the lessor report these transactions.

Although a principles-based approach to standard setting may discourage the structuring of transactions, it cannot fully prevent it. In applying broadly defined reporting principles managers and auditors need guidance about, for example, the meaning of "carrying substantially all risks" or "controlling a subsidiary." When standard setters or standard interpretations committees, such as the International Financial Reporting Interpretations Committee (IFRIC), provide such guidance, they are bound to introduce some mechanical rules that auditors and public enforcers may hang on to. For example, the international standard for lease accounting includes several qualitative criteria for assessing whether the lessee is the economic owner of a leased asset. One example of a qualitative lease classification criterion is that leased assets are normally assumed to be owned by the lessee when the lease term covers the major part of the asset's economic useful life. Following the detailed US rules on lease accounting, auditors and public enforcers may themselves attach quantitative values to the term "major part," such as "greater than 75 percent." This practice of quantifying principles-based accounting standards could again encourage managers to structure transactions.

Asset ownership issues also arise indirectly from the application of rules for revenue recognition. Firms are permitted to recognize revenues only when their product has been shipped or their service has been provided to the customer. Revenues are then considered "earned," and the customer has a legal commitment to pay for the product or service. As a result, for the seller, recognition of revenue frequently coincides with "ownership" of a receivable that is shown as an asset on its balance sheet. Accounting analysis that raises questions about whether or not revenues have been earned therefore often affects the valuation of assets.

Ambiguity over whether a company owns an asset creates a number of opportunities for accounting analysis:

- Despite management's best intentions, financial statements sometimes do a poor job of reflecting the firm's economic assets because it is difficult for accounting rules to capture all of the subtleties associated with ownership and control.

- Accounting rules on ownership and control are the result of a trade-off between granting reporting discretion, which opens opportunities for earnings management, and imposing mechanical, rigid reporting criteria, which opens opportunities for the structuring of transactions. Because finding the perfect balance between discretion and rigidity is a virtually impossible task for standard setters, accounting rules cannot always prevent important assets being omitted from the balance sheet even though the firm bears many of the economic risks of ownership.

- There may be legitimate differences in opinion between managers and analysts over residual ownership risks borne by the company, leading to differences in opinion over reporting for these assets.

- Aggressive revenue recognition, which boosts reported earnings, is also likely to affect asset values.

Can economic benefits be measured with reasonable certainty?

It is almost always difficult to accurately forecast the future benefits associated with capital outlays because the world is uncertain. A company does not know whether a competitor will offer a new product or service that makes its own obsolete. It does not know whether the products manufactured at a new plant will be the type that customers want to buy. A company does not know whether changes in oil prices will make the oil drilling equipment that it manufactures less valuable.

Accounting rules deal with these challenges by stipulating which types of resources can be recorded as assets and which cannot. For example, the economic benefits from research and development are generally considered highly uncertain: research projects may never deliver promised new products, the products they generate may not be economically viable, or products may be made obsolete by competitors' research. International rules (IAS 38), therefore, require that research outlays be expensed and development outlays only be capitalized if they meet stringent criteria of technical and economic feasibility (which they rarely do in industries such as the pharmaceutical industry). In contrast, the economic benefits from plant acquisitions are considered less uncertain and are required to be capitalized.

Rules that require the immediate expensing of outlays for some key resources may be good accounting, but they create a challenge for the analyst – namely, they lead to less timely financial statements. For example, if all firms expense R&D, financial statements will reflect differences in R&D success only when new products are commercialized rather than during the development process. The analyst may attempt to correct for this distortion by capitalizing key R&D outlays and adjusting the value of the intangible asset based on R&D updates.[1]

Have fair values of assets declined below book value?

An asset is impaired when its fair value falls below its book value. In most countries accounting rules require that a loss be recorded for permanent asset impairments. International rules (IAS 36) specify that an impairment loss be recognized on a non-current asset when its book value exceeds the greater of its net selling price and the discounted cash flows expected to be generated from future use. If this condition is satisfied, the firm is required to report a loss for the difference between the asset's fair value and its book value.

Of course markets for many non-current operating assets are illiquid and incomplete, making it highly subjective to infer their fair values. Further, if the cash flows of an individual asset cannot be identified, IAS 36 requires that the impairment test be carried out for the smallest possible *group* of assets that has identifiable cash flows, called the cash generating unit. Consequently, considerable management judgment is involved in defining the boundaries of cash generating units, deciding whether an asset is impaired and determining the value of any impairment loss.

For the analyst, this raises the possibility that asset values are misstated. International accounting rules themselves permit a certain amount of asset overstatement since the test for asset impairment is typically applied to the cash-generating unit. This can create situations where no financial statement loss is reported for an individual asset that is economically impaired but whose impairment is concealed in the group.

Are fair value estimates accurate?

Managers estimate fair values of assets not only for asset impairment testing. One other use of fair value estimates is to adjust the book value of assets when firms use the revaluation method instead of the historical cost method. The international accounting rules for non-current assets (IAS 16) allow firms to record their non-current assets at fair value instead of their historical cost prices. When doing so, firms must regularly assess whether the reported book values deviate too much from the assets' fair values and, if necessary make adjustments. Although revaluation adjustments are recorded in the statement of comprehensive income (not in the income statement), revaluations do affect earnings through the depreciation expense because, under this method, depreciation is determined by reference to the assets' fair value.

Fair value estimates are also needed to calculate goodwill in business combinations. Specifically, the amount by which the acquisition cost exceeds the fair value of the acquired net assets is recorded on the balance sheet as goodwill. The international standard for business combinations (IFRS 3) requires that the amount of goodwill is not amortized but regularly tested for impairment. This may create the incentive for managers to understate the fair value of acquired net assets and, consequently, overstate goodwill.

Finally, new international rules on the recognition and measurement of financial instruments (IFRS 9) require a firm to recognize equity investments and debt investments held for trading (rather than for the purpose of collecting contractual cash flows till maturity) at their fair values. With a few exceptions, changes in the fair value of such assets are immediately recognized in profit or loss.

The task of determining fair values is delegated to management, with oversight by the firm's auditors, potentially leaving opportunities for management bias in valuing assets and for legitimate differences in opinion between managers and analysts over asset valuations. In most cases, management bias will lead to overstated assets since managers will prefer not to recognize an impairment or prefer to overstate nonamortized goodwill in business combinations. However, managers can also bias asset values downward by "taking a bath," reducing future expenses and increasing future earnings.

To reduce management's discretion in determining the fair value of financial assets, their values must be derived from quoted market prices if an active market for the assets exists (typically referred to as marking to market). If quoted market prices are not available, firms can use their own valuation technique to determine the assets' fair values (referred to as marking to model); however, their valuation should be based on assumptions that outside market participants would reasonably make, not management's own assumptions. During the credit market crisis of 2008 trading in asset-backed securities came to a halt because of the high uncertainty surrounding the value of these securities. As fewer transactions in asset-backed securities took place at increasingly volatile prices, financial institutions owning such securities argued that market prices could no longer be reliably used to determine the securities' fair values. Following the guidance of the IASB, many financial institutions started to adjust market prices or use their own valuations to assess fair value. Of course, this move away from using observable market prices increases managers' accounting flexibility and increases the importance as well as the difficulty of establishing whether financial institutions' fair value estimates are reliable.

In summary, distortions in assets are likely to arise when there is ambiguity about whether the firm owns or controls a resource, when there is a high degree of uncertainty about the value of the economic benefits to be derived from the resource, and when there are differences in opinion about the value of asset impairments. Opportunities for accounting adjustments can arise in these situations if:

- Accounting rules do not do a good job of capturing the firm's economics.
- Managers use their discretion to distort the firm's performance.
- There are legitimate differences in opinion between managers and analysts about economic uncertainties facing the firm that are reflected in asset values.

ASSET DISTORTIONS

Asset overstatements are likely to arise when managers have incentives to increase reported earnings. Thus, adjustments to assets also typically require adjustments to the income statement in the form of either increased expenses or reduced revenues. Asset understatements typically arise when managers have incentives to deflate reported earnings. This may occur when the firm is performing exceptionally well and managers decide to store away some of the current strong earnings for a rainy day. Income smoothing, as it has come to be known, can be implemented by overstating current period expenses (and understating the value of assets) during good times. Asset (and expense) understatements can also arise in a particularly bad year, when managers decide to "take a bath" by understating current period earnings to create the appearance of a turnaround in following years.

Accounting rules themselves can also lead to the understatement of assets. In many countries accounting standards require firms to expense outlays for research and advertising because, even though they may create future value for owners, their outcomes are highly uncertain. Also, until the early 2000s some acquisitions were accounted for using the pooling method, whereby the acquirer recorded the target's assets at their book value rather than their actual (higher) purchase price. In these cases the analyst may want to make adjustments to the balance sheet and income statement to ensure that they reflect the economic reality of the transactions.

Finally, asset understatements can arise when managers have incentives to understate liabilities. For example, if a firm records lease transactions as operating leases or if it discounts receivables with recourse, neither the assets nor the accompanying obligations are shown on its balance sheet. Yet in some instances this accounting treatment does not reflect the underlying economics of the transactions – the lessee may effectively own the leased assets, and the firm that sells receivables may still bear all of the risks associated with ownership. The analyst may then want to adjust the balance sheet (and also the income statement) for these effects.

Accounting analysis involves judging whether managers have understated or overstated assets (and also earnings) and, if necessary, adjusting the balance sheet and income statement accordingly. The most common items that can lead to overstatement or understatement of assets (and earnings) are the following:

- Depreciation and amortization on non-current assets.
- Impairment of non-current assets.
- Leased assets.
- Intangible assets.
- The timing of revenue (and receivables) recognition.
- Allowances (e.g., allowances for doubtful accounts or loan losses).
- Write-downs of current assets.

DEFERRED TAXES ON ADJUSTMENTS

Most firms use different accounting rules for business reporting and tax reporting. As a consequence, the assets and liabilities that firms report in their financial statements may differ in value from the assets and liabilities that they report in their tax statements. Consider a firm whose property, plant, and equipment have a book value of €300 in its financial statements but a tax base of €100 in its tax statements. Ignoring future investments, the firm will record a total amount of €300 in depreciation in its future financial statements, whereas it can only record an amount of €100 in tax-deductible depreciation in its future tax statements. Because the firm's tax statements are not publicly available, the analyst must estimate the firm's future tax deductions based on the book value of property, plant, and equipment as reported in the financial statements. This book value, however, overstates the firm's future tax deductions by an amount of €200 (€300 – €100). The IFRSs, therefore, require that the firm discloses the amount of overstatement of future tax deductions in its current financial statements. To do this, the firm recognizes a deferred tax liability on its balance sheet. Given a tax rate of 35 percent, the deferred tax liability equals €70 ([€300 – €100] × €0.35). This liability essentially represents the tax amount that the firm must pay in future years, in excess of the tax expense that the firm will report in its future financial statements. It also represents the tax amount that the firm would have to pay immediately were the firm to sell the asset for its current carrying amount. All additions to (reductions in) the deferred tax liability are accompanied by the recognition of a deferred tax expense (income) in the firm's income statement. Assets whose book values in the financial statements are below the tax bases recorded in the tax statements create a deferred tax asset.

When the analyst makes adjustments to the firm's assets or liabilities to undo any distortions, the deferred tax liability (or asset) is also affected. This is because the adjustments do not affect the tax statements and, consequently, change the difference between book values and tax bases. For example, when the analyst reduces the book value of property, plant, and equipment by €50, the deferred tax liability is reduced by an amount of €17.50 (€50 × €0.35) to €52.50 ([€250 − €100] × € 0.35).

The international accounting standard for income taxes requires that deferred taxes be recognized on any difference between book values and tax bases with the exception of a few differences, such as those related to:

- Nondeductible assets and nontaxable liabilities.
- Nondeductible goodwill and nontaxable negative goodwill.

We illustrate below some of the types of distortions that understate or overstate assets, and show corrections that the analyst can make to ensure that assets are reflected appropriately.

Note that some of the accounting methods that we describe can be used by managers to both understate and overstate assets. The corrections that we describe for asset understatement can of course be easily modified to undo the effects of asset overstatement (and vice versa).

Overstated depreciation for non-current assets

Because non-current assets such as manufacturing equipment decrease in value over time, accounting rules require that firms systematically depreciate the book values of these assets. The reduction in the book value of the assets must be recognized as depreciation or amortization expense in the income statement. Managers make estimates of asset lives, salvage values, and amortization schedules for depreciable non-current assets. If these estimates are optimistic, non-current assets and earnings will be overstated. This issue is likely to be most pertinent for firms in heavy asset businesses (e.g., airlines, utilities), whose earnings contain large depreciation components. Firms that use tax depreciation estimates of asset lives, salvage values, or amortization rates are likely to amortize assets more rapidly than justifiable given the assets' economic usefulness, leading to non-current asset understatements.

In 2011 Lufthansa, the German national airline, reported that it depreciated its aircraft over 12 years on a straight-line basis, with an estimated residual value of 15 percent of initial cost. These assumptions imply that Lufthansa's annual depreciation expense was, on average, 7.1 percent ([1 − 0.15]/12) of the initial cost of its aircraft. In contrast, British Airways (BA), the UK national carrier, reported that its aircraft depreciation was also estimated using the straight-line method but assuming an average annual depreciation percentage of 4.5 percent of initial cost.

For the analyst these differences raise several questions. Do Lufthansa and BA fly different types of routes, potentially explaining the differences in their depreciation policies? Alternatively, do they have different asset management strategies? For example, does Lufthansa use newer planes to attract more business travelers, to lower maintenance costs, or to lower fuel costs? If there do not appear to be operating differences that explain the differences in the two firms' depreciation rates, the analyst may well decide that it is necessary to adjust the depreciation rates for one or both firms to ensure that their performance is comparable.

To adjust for the effect of different depreciation policies, the analyst could decrease Lufthansa's depreciation rates to match those of BA's. The following financial statement adjustments would then be required in Lufthansa's financial statements:

1 Increase the book value of the fleet at the beginning of the year to adjust for the relatively high depreciation rates that had been used in the past. The necessary adjustment is equal to the following amount: original minus adjusted depreciation rate × average asset age × initial asset cost. At the beginning of 2011, Lufthansa reported in the notes to its financial statements that its fleet of aircraft had originally cost €21,699 million, and that accumulated depreciation was €11,699 million. This implies that the average age of Lufthansa's fleet was 7.6 years, calculated as follows:

€ (millions unless otherwise noted)

Aircraft cost, 1/1/2011	€21,699	Reported
Depreciable cost	€18,444.15	Cost × (1 − 0.15)
Accumulated depreciation, 1/1/2011	€11,699	Reported
Accumulated depreciation/Depreciable cost	63.43%	
Depreciable life	12 years	Reported
Average age of aircraft	7.612 years	12 × 0.6343 years

If Lufthansa used the same life and salvage estimates as BA, the annual depreciation rate would have been 4.5 percent, implying that given the average age of its fleet, accumulated depreciation would have been €7,433 (7.612 × 0.045 × 21,699) versus the reported €11,699. Consequently, the company's Non-Current Tangible Assets would have increased by €4,266 (11,699 − 7,433).

2 Calculate the offsetting increase in equity (retained earnings) and in the deferred tax liability. Given the 25 percent marginal tax rate, the adjustment to Non-Current Tangible Assets would have required offsetting adjustments of €1,066 (0.25 × 4,266) to the Deferred Tax Liability and €3,200 (0.75 × 4,266) to Shareholders' Equity.

3 Reduce the depreciation expense (and increase the book value of the fleet) to reflect the lower depreciation for the current year. Assuming that €1,215 million net new aircraft purchased in 2011 were acquired throughout the year, and therefore require only half a year of depreciation, the depreciation expense for 2011 (included in Cost of Sales) would have been €1,004 million {0.045 × [21,699 + (1,215/2)]} versus the €1,580 {(0.85/12) × [21,699 + (1,215/2)]} million reported by the company. Thus Cost of Sales would decline by €576 million.

4 Increase the tax expense, net profit, and the balance sheet values of equity and the deferred tax liability. Given the 25 percent tax rate for 2011, the Tax Expense for the year would increase by €144 million. On the balance sheet, these changes would increase Non-Current Tangible Assets by €576 million, increase Deferred Tax Liability by €144 million, and increase Shareholders' Equity by €432 million.

Note that these changes are designed to show Lufthansa's results as if it had always used the same depreciation assumptions as BA rather than to reflect a change in the assumptions for the current year going forward. This enables the analyst to be able to compare ratios that use assets (e.g., return on assets) for the two companies. By making the adjustments, the analyst substantially improves the comparability of Lufthansa's and BA's financial statements.

In summary, if Lufthansa were using the same depreciation method as BA, its financial statements for the years ended December 31, 2010 and 2011 would have to be modified as follows (references to the above described steps are reported in brackets):

€ (millions)	Adjustments December 31, 2010		Adjustments December 31, 2011	
	Assets	Liabilities	Assets	Liabilities
Balance sheet				
Non-Current Tangible Assets	+4,266 (1)		+4,266 (1)	
			+576 (3)	
Deferred Tax Liability		+1,066 (2)		+1,066 (2)
				+144 (4)
Shareholders' Equity		+3,200 (2)		+3,200 (2)
				+432 (4)
Income statement				
Cost of Sales				−576 (3)
Tax Expense				+144 (4)
Net Profit				+432 (4)

Leased assets off balance sheet

One of the objectives of the balance sheet is to report the assets for which a firm receives the rewards and bears the risks. These can also be assets the firm does not legally own but leases from another firm. Although significant changes in the international rules for lease accounting are imminent, there are currently two ways in which a firm can record its leased assets. Under the operating method, the firm recognizes the lease payment as an expense in the period in which it occurs, keeping the leased asset off its balance sheet. In contrast, under the finance method, the firm records the asset and an offsetting lease liability on its balance sheet. During the lease period, the firm then recognizes depreciation on the asset as well as interest on the lease liability.

Assessing whether a lease arrangement should be considered a rental contract (and hence recorded using the operating method) or equivalent to a purchase (and hence shown as a finance lease) is subjective. It depends on whether the lessee has effectively accepted most of the risks of ownership, such as obsolescence and physical deterioration. To guide the reporting of lease transactions, the international accounting rules include criteria for distinguishing between the two types. IAS 17 explains that a firm would normally consider a lease transaction equivalent to an asset purchase if any of the following conditions hold:

1 Ownership of the asset is transferred to the lessee at the end of the lease term.

2 The lessee has the option to purchase the asset for a bargain price at the end of the lease term.

3 The lease term is for the major part of the asset's expected useful life.

4 The present value of the lease payments is equal to substantially all of the fair value of the asset.

5 The asset cannot be used by other than the lessee without major modifications.

However, because the criteria for reporting leases are broadly defined and inconclusive, they create opportunities for management to circumvent the spirit of the distinction between capital and operating leases, potentially leading to the understatement of lease assets. This is likely to be an important issue for the analysis of heavy asset industries where there are options for leasing (e.g., airlines).[2] Debt rating analysts tend to consider the distinction between operating leases and finance leases as artificial and capitalize the present value of future operating lease payments before analyzing a firm's financial position. An example of how to capitalize operating lease commitments follows.[3]

Finnair, the Finnish airline company, accounts for part of its rented flight equipment using the operating method. These rented resources are therefore excluded from Finnair's balance sheet, making it difficult for an analyst to compare Finnair's financial performance with other airlines that have a different mixture of finance and operating leases. To correct this accounting, the analyst can use the information on noncancelable lease commitments presented in Finnair's lease note to estimate the value of the assets and liabilities that are omitted from the balance sheet. The leased equipment is then depreciated over the life of the lease, and the lease payments are treated as interest and debt repayment.

On December 31, 2011 and 2010, Finnair reports the following minimum future rental payments:

(€ millions)	December 31, 2011	December 31, 2010
Less than 1 year	65.8	70.2
1–2 years	48.7	62.2
2–3 years	32.6	45.4
3–4 years	29.9	29.9
4–5 years	22.0	27.2
More than 5 years	29.7	47.4
Total	228.7	282.3

Because Finnair does not show the present value of its operating lease commitments, the analyst must decide how to allocate the lump sum values of €29.7 and €47.4 over year 6 and beyond, and estimate a suitable interest rate on the lease debt. It is then possible to compute the present value of the lease payments.

Finnair indicates that its effective annual interest rate on outstanding interest-bearing debt is 2.9 percent and the lease expense reported in 2011 is €69.9 million. Assume that the annual rental payments in the sixth year is equal to the rental payment in the fifth year (€22.0 and €27.2) and the remainder of the lump sum values (€7.7 and

€20.2) is due in the seventh year. With a discount rate of 2.9 percent, the present values of the minimum rental payments for the years ended December 31, 2010 and 2011 are as follows:

(€ millions)	December 31, 2011	December 31, 2010
Within one year	63.9	68.2
Over one year	146.5	190.1
Total	210.4	258.3

Given this information, the analyst can make the following adjustments to Finnair's beginning and ending balance sheets, and to its income statement for the year ended December 31, 2011:

1 Capitalize the present value of the lease commitments for December 31, 2010, increasing Non-Current Tangible Assets and Non-Current Debt by €258.3.

2 Calculate the value of any change in lease assets and lease liabilities during the year from new lease transactions. On December 31, 2010, Finnair's liability for lease commitments in 2011 and beyond was €190.1. If there had been no changes in these commitments, one year later (on December 31, 2011), they would have been valued at €195.6 (190.1 × 1.029). Yet Finnair's actual lease commitment on December 31, 2008 was €210.4. Further, Finnair's actual lease expense in 2011 was €69.9, instead of the "anticipated" amount of €70.2 (see the table above showing the minimum future rental payments, third column). The unanticipated lower lease expense reflects a decrease in Finnair's lease commitments of €0.3 ([70.2 − 69.9]). In total, these differences indicate that the company increased its leased aircraft capacity by €14.5 ([210.4 − 195.6] + [69.9 − 70.2]). Finnair's Non-Current Tangible Assets and Non-Current Debt therefore increased by €14.5 during 2011.

3 Add back the operating lease expense in the income statement, included in Cost of Sales. As previously mentioned, the operating lease expense, which is equal to the lease payment that Finnair made to its lessors, is €69.9. When lease liabilities are recorded on the balance sheet, as under the finance method, the lease payment must be treated as the sum of interest and debt repayment (see next item), instead of being recorded as an expense.

4 Apportion the lease payment between Interest Expense and repayment of Non-Current Debt. The portion of this that is shown as Interest Expense is the interest rate (2.9 percent) multiplied by the beginning lease liability (€258.3) plus interest on the increase in the leased liability for 2011 (€14.5), prorated throughout the year. The interest expense for 2011 is therefore €7.7 (0.029 × 258.3 + 0.5 × 0.029 × 14.5). The Non-Current Debt repayment portion is then the remainder of the total lease payment, €62.2 (69.9 − 7.7).

5 Reflect the change in lease asset value and the expense from depreciation during the year. The depreciation expense for 2011 (included in Cost of Sales) is the depreciation rate multiplied by the beginning cost of leased equipment (€258.3) plus depreciation on the increase in leased equipment for 2011 (€14.5), prorated throughout the year. Unfortunately, the average lease term and the associated depreciation rate are not perfectly known to the outside analyst. A possible assumption to make is that the leased assets have remaining lease terms ranging from one to seven years – the number of years for which Finnair has operating lease commitments – with equal probabilities (for example, leased assets having a remaining lease term of two years and those having a remaining lease term of three years have the same total initial cost). Under this assumption, the depreciation rate is 0.25 (calculated as 7/[1 + 2 + 3 + 4 + 5 + 6 + 7], consistent with the sum-of-the-years' digits approach) and the depreciation expense for 2011 is €65.6 ([0.25 × 258.3] + [0.5 × 14.5 × 1/7]).

6 Make any needed changes to the Deferred Tax Liability to reflect differences in earnings under the finance and operating lease methods. Finnair's expenses under the finance lease method are €73.3 (€65.6 depreciation expense plus €7.7 interest expense) versus €69.9 under the operating lease method. Finnair will not change its tax books, but for financial reporting purposes it will show lower earnings before tax and thus a lower Tax Expense through deferred taxes. Given its 26 percent tax rate, the Tax Expense will decrease by €0.9 (0.26 × [69.9 − 73.3]) and the Deferred Tax Liability will decrease by the same amount.

In summary, the adjustments to Finnair's financial statements on December 31, 2010 and 2011, are as follows:

€(millions)	Adjustments December 31, 2010		Adjustments December 31, 2011	
	Assets	**Liabilities**	**Assets**	**Liabilities**
Balance sheet				
Non-Current Tangible Assets:				
Beginning capitalization	+258.3 (1)	+258.3 (1)	+258.3 (1)	
New leases			+14.5 (2)	
Annual depreciation			−65.6 (5)	
Non-Current Debt:				
Beginning debt				+258.3 (1)
New leases				+14.5 (2)
Debt repayment				−62.2 (4)
Deferred Tax Liability				−0.9 (6)
Shareholders' Equity				−2.5 (6)
Income statement				
Cost of Sales:				
Lease expense				−69.9 (3)
Depreciation expense				+65.6 (5)
Interest Expense				+7.7 (4)
Tax Expense				−0.9 (6)
Net Profit				−2.5 (6)

These adjustments increase Finnair's fixed assets by 18 and 14 percent in 2010 and 2011, respectively, reducing the company's fixed asset turnover (sales/fixed assets) from the reported value of 144 percent to 122 percent in 2010, and from 154 percent to 135 percent in 2011. Note that an alternative method for calculating depreciation (under item 5) is to assume that the scheduled debt repayments for the first to the seventh year following fiscal 2010 accurately reflect the consumption pattern of the future economic benefits arising from the leased assets. Under this method, which is sometimes referred to as the interest-based or present value method, the depreciation expense for 2011 is €62.2, as calculated under item 4, and the adjustment's effect on Net Profit is zero.

Recently, the IASB and FASB have decided to largely remove the distinction between the operating and finance methods and require firms to capitalize most leases under a new lease standard. After the (future) implementation of this standard, the above adjustments can be used to increase the comparability of financial statements that have been prepared under different lease rules.

THE SUM-OF-THE-YEARS' DIGITS METHOD

The above example of lease adjustments used the sum-of-the-years' digits method to calculate depreciation, even though Finnair depreciates its aircraft under finance leases on a straight line basis. To explain why this is, consider the following stylized situation. A firm purchases a new asset at the start of every year, for the same amount. The initial cost of the asset is €30, the asset's useful life is three years and depreciation is straight-line. The following table displays depreciation for years one through five for each asset and each year separately:

	Year 1	**Year 2**	**Year 3**	**Year 4**	**Year 5**
Asset 1	10	10	10		
Asset 2		10	10	10	
Asset 3			10	10	10
Asset 4				10	10
Asset 5					10
Total	10	20	30	30	30

As of year 3, total depreciation amounts to €30, which can be calculated by multiplying the depreciation rate (1/3) by the initial cost of the assets in place at the beginning of year 3 (€90). Note, however, that an alternative way of calculating depreciation is to apply the sum-of-the-years' digits method to the beginning-of-year book value (rather than the initial cost) of the assets in year 3. In particular, given the beginning-of-year book value of (€60), depreciation can be calculated as $3/[1 + 2 + 3] \times$ €60, which equals €30. Because in the lease example the analyst can only observe the estimate of the beginning-of-year book value of operating lease assets, not the assets' initial cost, the only possible way to calculate depreciation is by using the sum-of-the-years' digits method.

Key intangible assets off balance sheet

Some firms' most important assets are excluded from the balance sheet. Examples include investments in R&D, software development outlays, and brands and membership bases that are created through advertising and promotions. Accounting rules in most countries specifically prohibit the capitalization of research outlays, primarily because it is believed that the benefits associated with such outlays are too uncertain. New products or software may never reach the market due to technological infeasibility or to the introduction of superior products by competitors. Expensing the cost of intangibles has two implications for analysts. First, the omission of intangible assets from the balance sheet inflates measured rates of return on capital (either return on assets or return on equity).[4] For firms with key omitted intangible assets, this has important implications for forecasting long-term performance; unlike firms with no intangibles, competitive forces will not cause their rates of return to fully revert to the cost of capital over time. For example, pharmaceutical firms have shown very high rates of return over many decades, in part because of the impact of R&D accounting. A second effect of expensing outlays for intangibles is that it makes it more difficult for the analyst to assess whether the firm's business model works. Under the matching concept, operating profit is a meaningful indicator of the success of a firm's business model since it compares revenues and the expenses required to generate them. Immediately expensing outlays for intangible assets runs counter to matching and, therefore, makes it more difficult to judge a firm's operating performance. Consistent with this, research shows that investors view R&D and advertising outlays as assets rather than expenses.[5] Understated intangible assets are likely to be important for firms in pharmaceutical, software, branded consumer products, and subscription businesses.

How should the analyst approach the omission of intangibles? One way is to leave the accounting as is, but to recognize that forecasts of long-term rates of return will have to reflect the inherent biases that arise from this accounting method. A second approach is to capitalize intangibles and amortize them over their expected lives.

For example, consider the case of AstraZeneca, one of the largest pharmaceutical companies in the world. AstraZeneca does not capitalize most of its R&D costs because regulatory uncertainties surrounding the development and marketing of new products mean that the recognition criteria for research expenditures are rarely met. What adjustment would be required if the analyst decided to capitalize all of AstraZeneca's R&D and to amortize the intangible asset using the straight-line method over the expected life of R&D investments? Assume for simplicity that R&D spending occurs evenly throughout the year, that only half a year's amortization is taken on the latest year's spending, and that the average expected life of R&D investments is approximately five years. Given R&D outlays for the years 2005 to 2010, the R&D asset at the end of 2009 is $11.7 billion (rounded), calculated as follows:

Year	R&D Outlay	Proportion Capitalized 31/12/09	Asset 31/12/09	Proportion Capitalized 31/12/10	Asset 31/12/10
2010	$5.3b			(1 − 0.2/2)	$ 4.77b
2009	4.4	(1 − 0.2/2)	$ 3.96b	(1 − 0.2/2 − 0.2)	3.08
2008	5.2	(1 − 0.2/2 − 0.2)	3.64	(1 − 0.2/2 − 0.4)	2.60
2007	5.2	(1 − 0.2/2 − 0.4)	2.60	(1 − 0.2/2 − 0.6)	1.56
2006	3.9	(1 − 0.2/2 − 0.6)	1.17	(1 − 0.2/2 − 0.8)	0.39
2005	3.4	(1 − 0.2/2 − 0.8)	0.34		
Total			$11.71		$12.40

The R&D amortization expense (included in Other Operating Expenses) for 2009 and 2010 are $4.3 billion and $4.6 billion (rounded), respectively, and are calculated as follows:

Year	R&D Outlay	Proportion Amortized 31/12/09	Expense 31/12/09	Proportion Amortized 31/12/10	Expense 31/12/10
2010	$5.3b			0.2/2	$0.53b
2009	4.4	0.2/2	$0.44b	0.2	0.88
2008	5.2	0.2	1.04	0.2	1.04
2007	5.2	0.2	1.04	0.2	1.04
2006	3.9	0.2	0.78	0.2	0.78
2005	3.4	0.2	0.68	0.2/2	0.34
2004	3.5	0.2/2	0.35		
Total			$4.33		$4.61

Since AstraZeneca will continue to expense R&D immediately for tax purposes, the change in reporting method will give rise to a Deferred Tax Liability. Given a marginal tax rate of 28 percent, this liability will equal 28 percent of the value of the Intangible Asset reported, with the balance increasing Shareholders' Equity.

In summary, the adjustments required to capitalize R&D for AstraZeneca for the years 2009 and 2010 are as follows:

($ billions)	Adjustments December 31, 2009 Assets	Liabilities	Adjustments December 31, 2010 Assets	Liabilities
Balance sheet				
Non-Current Intangible Assets	+11.7		+12.4	
Deferred Tax Liability		+3.3		+3.5
Shareholders' Equity		+8.4		+8.9
Income statement				
Other Operating Expenses		−4.4		−5.3
Other Operating Expenses		+4.3		+4.6
Tax Expense		+0.0		+0.2
Net Profit		+0.1		+0.5

Accelerated recognition of revenues

Managers typically have the best information on the uncertainties governing revenue recognition – whether a product or service has been provided to customers and whether cash collection is reasonably likely. However, managers may also have incentives to accelerate the recognition of revenues, boosting reported earnings for the period. Earnings and trade receivables (or contracts in progress in case of long-term contracts) will then be overstated.

Consider UK-based Healthcare Locums plc, a company that recruits medical specialists for temporary or permanent placement at health and social care providers. In 2008, the recruitment company recognized revenue from permanent placements at the date that the candidate accepted the job offer. This acceptance date could be significantly earlier than the start date of the candidate, especially in the company's growing segment of international placements. In fact, in the US, lengthy visa applications could delay permanent placements by up to four years, leading some analysts to argue that Healthcare Locums' permanent placement revenue recognition policy was too aggressive.

During the years 2005 to 2008, Healthcare Locums recognized the following revenues and gross margins in its permanent placement segment:

(£ millions)	2008	2007	2006	2005
Revenues	5.3	4.0	3.2	1.0
Gross margin	4.5	3.6	2.8	0.9

Assume that an analyst estimates that candidates accepting a permanent position in 2005 start their new jobs in 2005, 2006, 2007, or 2008 with equal probabilities. The analyst's estimate of Healthcare Locums' 2008 revenues under a policy of recognizing revenues when candidates start (rather than when they accept) then equals £3.4 million (0.25 × 1.0 + 0.25 × 3.2 + 0.25 × 4.0 + 0.25 × 5.3). If the analyst decided to adjust for the distortions created by Healthcare Locums' aggressive revenue recognition policy, the following changes would have to be made to the company's 2008 financial reports:

1 Sales and Other Current Assets (in particular, accrued income) would both decline by £1.9 million (5.3 – 3.4).

2 Cost of Sales would decline and Other Current Assets (in particular, prepaid expenses) would increase to reflect the reduction in sales. The value of the Cost of Sales/Other Current Assets adjustment can be estimated from Healthcare Locums gross margin. For Healthcare Locums, the cost of permanent placement revenues is £0.8 million (5.3 – 4.5) under the current revenue recognition policy and would be £0.4 million (3.4 – [0.25 × 0.9 + 0.25 × 2.8 + 0.25 × 3.6 + 0.25 × 4.5]) under the adjusted policy. Hence, Cost of Sales would decline by £0.4 million (0.8 – 0.4).

3 The decline in pretax profit would result in a lower Tax Expense in the company's financial reporting books (but not in its tax books). Consequently, the Deferred Tax Liability would have to be reduced. Healthcare Locums' marginal tax rate was 28.5 percent, implying that the decline in the Tax Expense and Deferred Tax Liability was £0.4 million [(1.9 – 0.4) × 0.285].

The full effect of the adjustment on the quarterly financial statements would therefore be as follows:

(£ millions)	Adjustments	
	Assets	**Liabilities and Equity**
Balance sheet		
Trade Receivables	−1.9 (1)	
Other Current Assets	+0.4 (2)	
Deferred Tax Liability		−0.4 (3)
Shareholders' Equity		−1.1 (3)
Income statement		
Sales		−1.9 (1)
Cost of Sales		−0.4 (2)
Tax Expense		−0.4 (3)
Net Profit		−1.1 (3)

In 2009 Healthcare Locums voluntarily changed its revenue recognition policy for permanent placement revenues. Because of this accounting change the company restated its permanent placement revenues for prior years. The outcome was that revenues for 2008 were reduced by £1.9 million. Net profit was reduced by £1.4 million (or 12 percent of unrestated profit), leading to a significant drop in the company's stock price.

Accelerated revenue recognition is also a relevant concern when analyzing the financial statements of a company that engages into long-term contracts with its customers, agreeing to provide services or construct a product over a longer period of time. The international accounting rules on revenue recognition allow such a company to recognize revenues in increments during the contract period, as the company satisfies each of its contractual obligations. Under these rules, managers have an incentive to overstate the proportion of long-term contractual obligations satisfied at the end of a fiscal period.

Consider Denmark-based Vestas Wind Systems, a company specializing in developing, manufacturing, and installing wind turbines. In 2009 (and prior years), Vestas had several contracts requiring the company to supply and install wind turbines during periods that extended into the next fiscal year. At the end of the fiscal year, the company recognized revenues on such contracts in proportion to the contracts' rate of completion, despite the fact that the risks (and rewards) of owning the wind turbines would not be transferred to the customer before the contracts' completion. The effect of this accounting treatment on the company's financial statements was to:

■ Accelerate the recognition of revenues and

■ Create a non-current asset labeled 'construction contracts in progress', reflecting the difference between (1) revenues recognized and (2) billings made on contracts in progress.

In the notes to its financial statements Vestas disclosed the following information about revenues recognized on its projects in progress during the fiscal years 2008 and 2009:

(€ millions)	2009	2008
Sales value of construction contracts in progress	3,216	1,800
Progress billings	(2,782)	(2,701)
Net 'construction contracts in progress' asset (liability)	434	(901)

If there is significant uncertainty about the remaining risks of Vestas' projects in progress, the analyst may decide to recalculate revenues and earnings under the assumption that revenues on supply-and-installation projects are not recognized before completion. This would require making the following adjustments to the 2009 financial statements:

1 Reduce sales by the sales value of contracts in progress at the end of 2009, being €3,216 million. This adjustment would also require an offsetting adjustment to Other Current Assets (in particular, contracts in progress) of €3,216 million. To estimate the effect of the sales adjustment on the Vestas' Cost of Sales, assume that the gross margin on the contracts in progress is equal to the company's average gross margin in 2009 of 21.7 percent. Hence, decrease Cost of Sales and increase Inventories by €2,518 million ([1 – 0.217] × 3,216).

2 Under the new accounting treatment, prepayments on contracts in progress that Vestas received in 2009 give rise to a current liability. Therefore, increase Other Current Assets (in particular, contracts in progress) and increase Other Current Liabilities (in particular, prepayments from customers) by €2,782 million, being the amount of progress billings in 2009.

3 Assume that contracts in progress at the end of 2008 – with a sales value of €1,800 – have been completed during 2009, increasing sales in 2009 by €1,800 million. The value of the Cost of Sales adjustment can again be estimated based on the average gross margin in 2008, which was 19.5 percent. Hence, increase Cost of Sales by €1,449 million ([1 – 0.195] × 1,800).

4 The net effect on pretax profit of the adjustments to Sales and Cost of Sales is –€347 million ([1,800 – 1,449] – [3,216 – 2,518]). The decline in pretax profit would result in a lower Tax Expense. Thus, given Vestas' marginal tax rate of 25 percent, reduce the Tax Expense and the Deferred Tax Liability by €87 million (0.25 × 347).

5 As a result of these adjustments, Net Profit and Shareholders' Equity decrease by €260 million.

The full effect of the adjustment on the quarterly financial statements would therefore be as follows:

($ millions)	Adjustments	
	Assets	Liabilities and Equity
Balance sheet		
Other Current Assets	−3,216 (1)	
	+2,792 (2)	
Inventories	+2,518 (1)	
Other Current Liabilities		+2,792 (2)
Deferred Tax Liability		−87 (4)
Shareholders' Equity		−260 (5)
Income statement		
Sales		−3,216 (1)

($ millions)	Adjustments	
	Assets	Liabilities and Equity
		+1,800 (3)
Cost of Sales		−2,518 (1)
		+1,449 (3)
Tax Expense		−87 (4)
Net Profit		−260 (5)

Delayed write-downs of non-current assets

Deteriorating industry or firm economic conditions can affect the value of non-current assets as well as current assets. When the fair value of an asset falls below its book value, the asset is "impaired." Firms are required to recognize impairments in the values of non-current assets when they arise. However, since second-hand markets for non-current assets are typically illiquid and incomplete, estimates of asset valuations and impairment are inherently subjective. This is particularly true for intangible assets such as goodwill, which is the amount by which the cost of business acquisitions exceeds the fair value of the acquired assets. As a result, managers can use their reporting judgment to delay writedowns on the balance sheet and avoid showing impairment charges in the income statement.[6] This issue is likely to be particularly critical for heavily asset-intensive firms in volatile markets (e.g., airlines) or for firms that follow a strategy of aggressive growth through acquisitions and report substantial amounts of goodwill.[7] Warning signs of impairments in non-current assets include declining non-current asset turnover, declines in return on assets to levels lower than the weighted average cost of capital, write-downs by other firms in the same industry that have also suffered deteriorating asset use, and overpayment for or unsuccessful integration of key acquisitions. Managers may sometimes also have incentives to overstate asset impairment. Overly pessimistic management estimates of non-current asset impairments reduce current period earnings and boost earnings in future periods.

Consider discount airliner easyJet's acquisition of GB Airways. In January 2008 easy-Jet acquired all shares of GB Airways for an amount of £129.4 million. The airline estimated the fair value of GB's net assets (assets minus liabilities) at £79.2 million and, consequently, recorded £50.2 million (129.4 − 79.2) of goodwill in its balance sheet for the year ended September 30, 2008. The fair value estimate included fair value adjustments of £72.4 million for GB's landing rights at Gatwick airport and £30.0 million for GB's landing rights at Heathrow airport. It also included the fair value of GB's seven A321 Airbus aircraft, amounting to £83.4 million. In its 2008 financial statements easyJet reported that it would periodically test the amount of goodwill for impairment, together with its other assets, which easyJet considered all part of one cash generating unit.

On November 18, 2008, easyJet's non-executive director and primary shareholder Stelios Haji-Ioannou issued a press release stating that he could not approve easyJet's 2008 financial statements for several reasons. In particular, the director/shareholder argued that:

- The Gatwick landing rights have a zero fair value because the airport was not capacity constrained.

- Given that these landing rights have no value, goodwill on the GB acquisition amounts to £122.6 million (50.2 + 72.4). This amount should be tested for impairment separate from the other assets of easyJet because, like competitor Ryanair, easyJet could consider its routes as separate cash generating units.

- EasyJet needed to write down the value of the seven A321 Airbus aircraft that it had acquired.

The airline was trying to sell the seven aircraft but experienced some difficulty finding potential buyers during the economic downturn. On November 20, 2008, easyJet announced, however, that it had been able to sell two aircraft for a price that was in line with management's prior expectations. Although this announcement helped to ease outsiders' concerns about the fair value of the aircraft, an analyst might still decide that the landing rights are likely to have a zero fair value and need to be written down (rather than reclassified as goodwill). To record an additional write-down of £72.4 million in the September 2008 financials, it would be necessary to make the following balance sheet adjustments:

1 Reduce Non-Current Intangible Assets and increase Other Expenses by £72.4 million.

2 Reduce the Deferred Tax Liability and the Tax Expense for the tax effect of the write-down. Assuming a 28 percent tax rate, this amounts to £20.3 million.

3 Reduce Shareholders' Equity and Net Profit for the after-tax effect of the write-down (£52.1 million).

(£ millions)	Adjustment	
	Assets	Liabilities and Equity
Balance sheet		
Non-Current Intangible Assets	−72.4 (1)	
Deferred Tax Liability		−20.3 (2)
Shareholders' Equity		−52.1 (3)
Income statement		
Other Expenses		+72.4 (1)
Tax Expense		−20.3 (2)
Net Profit		−52.1 (3)

Note that the write-down of depreciable assets at the beginning of the year will require the analyst to also estimate the write-down's impact on depreciation and amortization expense for the year.

Delayed write-downs of current assets

If current assets become impaired – that is, their book values fall below their realizable values – accounting rules generally require that they be written down to their fair values. Current asset impairments also affect earnings since write-offs are charged directly to earnings. Deferring current asset write-downs is, therefore, one way for managers to boost reported profits.[8] Analysts that cover firms where management of inventories and receivables is a key success factor (e.g., the retail and manufacturing industries) need to be particularly cognizant of this form of earnings management. If managers over-buy or over-produce in the current period, they are likely to have to offer customers discounts to get rid of surplus inventories. In addition, providing customers with credit carries risks of default. Warning signs for delays in current asset write-downs include growing days' inventory and days' receivable, write-downs by competitors, and business downturns for a firm's major customers.

Managers potentially have an incentive to overstate current asset write-downs during years of exceptionally strong performance, or when the firm is financially distressed. By overstating current asset impairments and overstating expenses in the current period, managers can show lower future expenses, boosting earnings in years of sub-par performance or when a turnaround is needed. Overstated current asset write-downs can also arise when managers are less optimistic about the firm's future prospects than the analyst.

Allowances

Managers make estimates of expected customer defaults on trade receivables and loans. If managers underestimate the value of these allowances, assets and earnings will be overstated. Warning signs of inadequate allowances include growing days receivable, business downturns for a firm's major clients, and growing loan delinquencies. If managers overestimate allowances for doubtful accounts or loan losses, trade receivables and loans will be understated.

Consider the allowances for doubtful accounts reported by Luxemburg-based Metro International S.A. in the years 2008–2011. In these years, Metro International derived most of its revenues from selling advertisements in its international newspaper Metro, which it distributed free in more than 53 countries. To illustrate the low collection risk on its trade receivables, Metro reported in the notes to its financial statements that receivables came from "a large number of customers in different industries and geographical areas, none of whom are by themselves material in size." At the end of 2011, about 95 percent of Metro's receivables were less than 120 days old. From 2008 to 2011, Metro reported the following values for its gross trade receivables and allowances:

Year	Gross trade receivables	Allowances for doubtful accounts	Allowances / Gross receivables (%)
2008	67,213	9,281	13.8%
2009	44,410	6,028	13.6%
2010	51,633	5,305	10.3%
2011	36,142	1,636	4.5%

During these four years, the actual write-offs on Metro's receivables varied from 0 to 3 percent of the beginning balances of trade receivables, which may have motivated the firm to gradually reduce its allowance from 13.8 to 4.5 percent. Given the low collection risk on the company's receivables, Metro could have been overstating its allowances in earlier years, allowing the firm to recognize benefits from the recovery of doubtful debts in 2010 and 2011. If the analyst decided that allowances were indeed overstated, adjustments would have to be made to Trade Receivables and to Equity for the after-tax cost of the overstated provision for doubtful accounts.

On December 31, 2011, Metro reported the following values for its allowances and write-offs:

Allowances for doubtful accounts (€ thousands)	December 31, 2011	December 31, 2010	December 31, 2009
Balance at beginning of year	5,305	6,028	9,281
Allowance in companies (divested)/ acquired	(2,932)	(457)	(3,045)
Provision for/(recovery of) doubtful debts	(283)	(266)	1,738
Write-offs	(455)	0	(1,946)
Balance at end of year	1,635	5,305	6,028

If the analyst decided that receivable allowances for Metro in 2010 and 2011 should be 5 percent (in both years) rather than 10.3 and 4.5 percent, the following adjustments would have to be made:

1 Increase Trade Receivables on December 31, 2010 and 2011 by €2,723 thousand (5,305 – [0.050 × 51,633]) to reflect the adjustment to the allowance.

2 Given the company's marginal tax rate of 24 percent, increase Shareholders' Equity for 2010 by €2,069 thousand ([1 – 0.24] × 2,723), and increase the Deferred Tax Liability for 2010 by €654 thousand (0.24 × 2,723).

3 Adjust the allowance in companies divested to reflect the use of a lower provisioning percentage. Assuming that the divested allowance of €2,932 thousand was based on a provisioning percentage of 10.3 percent, decrease the allowance divested in 2011 by €1,509 thousand (2,932 – [2,932/.103] × .05). Because the amount of gross trade receivables divested remains unchanged, the decrease in the allowance divested automatically increase the amount of net trade receivables divested. Hence, the adjustment to the allowance divested results in a decrease in Trade Receivables for 2011 of €1,509 thousand and accompanying decreases in Shareholders' Equity for 2011 of €1,147 ([1 – 0.24] × 1,509) and the Deferred Tax Liability for 2011 of €362 thousand (0.24 × 1,509).

4 After adjustment, the beginning and ending balances of the allowance for 2011 are €2,582 thousand (5,305 – 2,723) and €1,807 thousand (0.050 × 36,142), respectively. Because the actual write-off on receivables for 2011 remains unchanged (€455 thousand) and the adjusted allowance divested amounts to (€1,423 thousand, calculated as [2,932/.103] × .05), the adjusted provision for bad debts is €1,103 thousand (1,807 – 2,582 + 455 + 1,423). Given the unadjusted provision (recovery of doubtful debt) for 2011 of –€283 thousand, decrease Trade Receivables and increase Cost of Sales for 2011 by €1,386 thousand (1,103 – [−283]).

5 Increase the tax expense, net profit, and the balance sheet values of equity and the deferred tax liability. Given the tax rate of 24 percent, the Tax Expense and Deferred Tax Liability for 2011 would decrease by €333 thousand (0.24 × 1,386), whereas Net Profit and Shareholders' Equity would decrease by €1,053 thousand ([1 – 0.24] × 1,386).

The adjustment to the December 31, 2010 and 2011, financial statements would, therefore, be as follows:

€ (millions)	Adjustments December 31, 2010		Adjustments December 31, 2011	
	Assets	Liabilities	Assets	Liabilities
Balance sheet				
Trade Receivables	+2,723 (1)		+2,723 (1)	
			−1,509 (3)	
			−1,386 (4)	
Deferred Tax Liability		+654 (2)		+654 (2)
				−362 (3)
				−333 (5)
Shareholders' Equity		+2,069 (2)		+2,069 (2)
				−1,147 (3)
				−1,053 (5)
Income statement				
Cost of Sales				+1,386 (4)
Tax Expense				−333 (5)
Net Profit				−1,053 (5)

This adjustment would decrease Metro's return on equity for 2011 by 2.7 percentage points (from 12.4 to 9.7 percent). Unfortunately, not all firms that report under IFRS separately disclose the allowances for doubtful accounts (or inventory obsolescence). This makes it sometimes difficult for the analyst to identify the overstatement or understatement of allowances.

Understated allowances are also a point of attention when analyzing the financial statements of loss-making firms. When a firm reports a loss in its tax statements, it does not receive an immediate tax refund but becomes the holder of a claim against the tax authorities, called a tax loss carryforward, which can be offset against future taxable profits. The period over which the firm can exercise this claim differs across tax jurisdictions. The international accounting standard for income taxes requires that firms record a deferred tax asset for a tax loss carryforward that is probable of being realized. Because changes in this deferred tax asset affect earnings through the tax expense, managers can manage earnings upwards by overstating the probability of realization.

During its first five years of operations, from 2001 to 2005, the Dutch manufacturer of exclusive cars Spyker Cars N.V. had been loss making. In December 2005 and December 2004, when Spyker reported net losses of €1.9 million and €5.0 million, respectively, the company reported the following losses carried forward and deferred tax assets:

(€ millions)	December 31, 2005	December 31, 2004
Total loss carried forward	19.822	15.687
× Tax rate	29.6%	34.5%
= Calculated deferred tax	5.867	5.412
− Allowance	(1.467)	(3.058)
= Recognized deferred tax asset	4.400	2.354

Spyker deducted an allowance from its calculated deferred tax assets because management deemed it not probable that the tax loss carryforwards could be fully realized in future years. The allowance, however, was substantially lower in 2005 than in 2004 because management expected an increase in Spyker's future profitability, justifying a decrease in the allowance from 56.5 percent of the deferred tax asset to 25 percent.

Any increase (decrease) in the deferred tax asset is offset by a decrease (increase) in the tax expense. If the analyst believed that management's optimism in 2005 was unwarranted and decided to increase the allowance to 56.5 percent, it would be necessary to reduce the Deferred Tax Asset, Shareholders' Equity, and Net Profit by €1.848 million ([0.565 -0.250] × 5.867) and increase the Tax Expense by the same amount.

(€ millions)	Adjustments	
	Assets	Liabilities and Equity
Balance sheet		
Deferred Tax Asset	−1.848	
Shareholders' Equity		−1.848
Income statement		
Tax Expense		+1.848
Net Profit		−1.848

In the years 2006–2008, Spyker kept reporting pre-tax losses. At the end of 2007, Spyker's management decided to deduct an allowance of 100 percent from its deferred tax asset, thereby removing the asset from its balance sheet in full, after being pressured by the Dutch enforcement body.

KEY ANALYSIS QUESTIONS

The following are some of the questions an analyst can probe when analyzing whether a firm's assets exhibit distortions:

- *Depreciation and amortization.* Are the firm's depreciation and amortization rates in line with industry practices? If not, is the firm aggressive or conservative in its estimates of the assets' useful lives? What does the deferred tax liability for depreciation and amortization suggest about the relationship between reported depreciation and tax depreciation?

- *Asset impairment.* Have industry or firm economic conditions deteriorated such that non-current assets' fair values could have fallen below their book values? Have industry peers recently recognized asset impairments? Does the firm have a history of regular write-downs, suggesting a tendency to delay?

- *Leased assets.* Does the firm have a material amount of off-balance sheet lease commitments? Is there a large variation in the proportion of operating leases to finance leases across industry peers?

- *Intangible assets.* Does the firm make material investments in non-current intangible assets, such as research and development, that are omitted from the balance sheet? If so, are these investments likely to yield future economic benefits? Does the immediate expensing of these investments lead to artificially permanent abnormal earnings?

- *Revenue recognition.* Are trade receivables abnormally high (relative to sales), suggesting aggressive revenue recognition?

- *Allowances.* Did the firm make unexplained changes in its allowance for doubtful accounts (or loan losses)? Is the size of the allowance in line with industry practices? Did the characteristics of the firm's receivables (e.g., concentration of credit risk) change such that the firm should adjust its allowance? Are the allowances that the firm recognizes systematically smaller or greater than its write-offs? Is it likely that the firm's deferred tax assets for losses carried forward can be realized?

RECOGNITION OF LIABILITIES

Liabilities are defined as economic obligations arising from benefits received in the past, and for which the amount and timing is known with reasonable certainty. Liabilities include obligations to customers that have paid in advance for products or services; commitments to public and private providers of debt financing; obligations to federal and local governments for taxes; commitments to employees for unpaid wages and post-employment benefits; and obligations from court or government fines or environmental clean-up orders.

Distortions in liabilities generally arise because there is ambiguity about whether (1) an obligation has really been incurred and/or (2) the obligation can be measured.

Has an obligation been incurred?

For most liabilities there is little ambiguity about whether an obligation has been incurred. For example, when a firm buys supplies on credit, it has incurred an obligation to the supplier. However, for some transactions it is more difficult to decide whether there is any such obligation. For example, if a firm announces a plan to restructure its business by laying off employees, has it made a commitment that would justify recording a liability? Or, if a software firm receives cash from its customers for a five-year software license, should the firm report the full cash inflow as revenues, or should some of it represent the ongoing commitment to the customer for servicing and supporting the license agreement?

Can the obligation be measured?

Many liabilities specify the amount and timing of obligations precisely. For example, a 20-year €100 million bond issue with an 8 percent coupon payable semiannually specifies that the issuer will pay the holders €100 million in 20 years, and it will pay out interest of €4 million every six months for the duration of the loan. However, for some liabilities it is difficult to estimate the amount of the obligation. For example, a firm that is responsible for an environmental clean-up clearly has incurred an obligation, but the amount is highly uncertain.[9] Similarly, firms that provide post-employment benefits for employees have incurred commitments that depend on uncertain future events, such as employee mortality rates, and on future inflation rates, making valuation of the obligation subjective. Future warranty and insurance claim obligations fall into the same category – the commitment is clear but the amount depends on uncertain future events.

Accounting rules frequently specify when a commitment has been incurred and how to measure the amount of the commitment. However, as discussed earlier, accounting rules are imperfect – they cannot cover all contractual possibilities and reflect all of the complexities of a firm's business relationships. They also require managers to make subjective estimates of future events to value the firm's commitments. Thus the analyst may decide that some important obligations are omitted from the financial statements or, if included, are understated, either because of management bias or because there are legitimate differences in opinion between managers and analysts over future risks and commitments. As a result, analysis of liabilities is usually with an eye to assessing whether the firm's financial commitments and risks are understated and/or its earnings overstated.

LIABILITY DISTORTIONS

Liabilities are likely to be understated when the firm has key commitments that are difficult to value and therefore not considered liabilities for financial reporting purposes. Understatements are also likely to occur when managers have strong incentives to overstate the soundness of the firm's financial position, or to boost reported earnings. By understating leverage, managers present investors with a rosy picture of the firm's financial risks. Earnings management also understates liabilities (namely deferred or unearned revenues) when revenues are recognized upon receipt of cash, even though not all services have been provided.

Accounting analysis involves judging whether managers have understated liabilities and, if necessary, adjusting the balance sheet and income statement accordingly. The most common forms of liability understatement arise when the following conditions exist:

- Unearned revenues are understated through aggressive revenue recognition.
- Provisions are understated.
- Non-current liabilities for leases are off-balance sheet.
- Post-employment obligations, such as pension obligations, are not fully recorded.

Unearned revenues understated

If cash has already been received but the product or service has yet to be provided, a liability (called unearned or deferred revenues) is created. This liability reflects the company's commitment to provide the service or product to the customer and is extinguished once that is accomplished. Firms that recognize revenues prematurely, after the receipt of cash but prior to fulfilling their product or service commitments to customers, understate deferred revenue liabilities and overstate earnings. Firms that bundle service contracts with the sale of a product are particularly prone to deferred revenue liability understatement since separating the price of the product from the price of the service is subjective.

Consider the case of MicroStrategy, a software company that bundles customer support and software updates with its initial licensing agreements. This raises questions about how much of the contract price should be allocated to the initial license versus the company's future commitments. In March 2000 MicroStrategy conceded that it had incorrectly overstated revenues on contracts that involved significant future customization and consulting by $54.5 million. As a result, it would have to restate its financial statements for 1999 as well as for several earlier years. To undo the distortion to 1999 financials, the following adjustments would have to be made:

1 In the quarter that the contracts were booked by the company, Sales would decline and unearned revenues (included in Other Current Liabilities) would increase by $54.5 million.

2 Cost of Sales would decline and prepaid expenses (inventory for product companies) would increase to reflect the lower sales. As noted earlier, MicroStrategy's cost of license revenues is only 3 percent of license revenues, implying that the adjustment to prepaid expenses (included in Other Current Assets) and Cost of Sales is modest ($1.6 million).

3 The decline in pretax profit would result in a lower Tax Expense in the company's financial reporting books (but presumably not in its tax books). Given MicroStrategy's marginal tax rate of 35 percent, the decline in the Tax Expense as well as in the Deferred Tax Liability is $18.5 million [($54.5 − 1.6) × 0.35].

The full effect of the adjustment on the quarterly financial statements would, therefore, be as follows:

($ millions)	Adjustments	
	Assets	Liabilities and Equity
Balance sheet		
Other Current Assets	+1.6 (2)	
Other Current Liabilities		+54.5 (1)
Deferred Tax Liability		−18.5 (3)
Shareholders' Equity		−34.4
Income statement		
Sales		−54.5 (1)
Cost of Sales		−1.6 (2)
Tax Expense		−18.5 (3)
Net Profit		−34.4

MicroStrategy's March 10 announcement that it had overstated revenues prompted the SEC to investigate the company. In the period when it announced its overstatements, MicroStrategy's stock price plummeted 94 percent, compared to the 37 percent drop by the NASDAQ in the same period.

Provisions understated

Many firms have obligations that are likely to result in a future outflow of cash or other resources but for which the exact amount is hard to establish. Examples of such uncertain liabilities are liabilities that arise from obligations to clean up polluted production sites or to provide warranty coverage for products sold. International accounting rules prescribe that a firm recognizes a provision – or nonfinancial liability – on its balance sheet for such uncertain liabilities when:

1 It is probable that the obligation will lead to a future outflow of cash.

2 The firm has no or little discretion to avoid the obligation.

3 The firm can make a reliable estimate of amount of the obligation.

When an uncertain liability does not meet these requirements for recognition, the firm discloses the liability only in the notes to the financial statements, as a "contingent liability." The international rules for the recognition of provisions may result in the understatement of a firm's liabilities. Because of the uncertainty surrounding the obligations, managers have much discretion in deciding whether obligations are probable as well as in estimating the amount of the obligation. Further, the use of a probability threshold below which uncertain liabilities are not recognized may lead to situations in which obligations with a relatively low probability but with a high expected value remain off-balance. An analyst may therefore decide that some of a firm's contingent liabilities are less uncertain than management asserts and undo the distortion by recognizing the liability on-balance as a provision. Additionally, the analyst may be of the opinion that low-probability obligations that nevertheless expose the firm to substantial risks because of their high expected value must also be recognized on the balance sheet.

At the end of the fiscal year 2011, British American Tobacco plc (BAT) – through some of its subsidiaries – was defendant in 8,688 US product liability cases, about which the company indicated that the "aggregate amounts involved in such litigation are significant, possibly totaling billions of US dollars." The company reported that in several cases that went to trial before the balance sheet date, judges had awarded substantial damages against BAT. Nevertheless, the company chose not to recognize a provision for potential damages because it considered it improbable that individual cases would result in an outflow of resources, even though in the aggregate the cases could have a material effect on the company's cash flow.

Assume that an analyst estimates the present value of future damages and settlements, discounted at BAT's incremental borrowing rate of 6 percent, to be £1 billion. In this particular situation, the analyst could base such an estimate on the historical probability that a tobacco company would lose a product liability case times the average damages awarded. Sometimes a firm's notes on contingent liabilities provide an indication of the size of the liability. For BAT, the following adjustments would have to be made to recognize the liability of £1 billion:

1 At the end of fiscal year 2010, the liability of £1 billion would be recognized as Non-Current Debt. Shareholders' Equity would decline by £0.74 billion (1.0 billion × [1 − 0.26]) and the Deferred Tax Liability would decline by £0.26 billion (1.0 billion × 0.26).

2 Because the non-current provision is a discounted liability, the provision increases as interest accrues. In 2011 BAT's income statement would include additional Interest Expense for an amount of £60 million (1.0 billion × 0.06). Tax Expense and the Deferred Tax Liability would decline by £16 million (60 million × 0.26) and Net Profit and Shareholders' Equity would decline by £44 million (60 million × [1 − 0.26]). The additional Interest Expense would result in an increase in Non-Current Debt.

The full effect of the adjustments would be as follows:

£ (millions)	Adjustments December 31, 2010		Adjustments December 31, 2011	
	Assets	**Liabilities**	**Assets**	**Liabilities**
Balance sheet				
Non-Current Debt		+1,000 (1)		+1,000 (1)
				+60 (2)
Deferred Tax Liability		−260 (1)		−260 (1)
				−16 (2)
Shareholders' Equity		−740 (1)		−740 (1)
				−44 (2)
Income statement				
Interest Expense				+60 (2)
Tax Expense				−16 (2)
Net Profit				−44 (2)

Non-current liabilities for leases are off balance sheet

As discussed earlier in the chapter, key lease assets and liabilities can be excluded from the balance sheet if the company structures lease transactions to fit the accounting definition of an operating lease. Firms that groom trans-actions to avoid showing lease assets and obligations will have very different balance sheets from firms with virtu-ally identical economics that either use finance leases or borrow from the bank to actually purchase the equivalent resources. For firms that choose to structure lease transactions to fit the definition of an operating lease, the analyst can restate the leases as finance leases, as discussed in the "Asset distortions" section. This will ensure that the firm's true financial commitments and risks will be reflected on its balance sheet, enabling comparison with peer firms.

Post-employment benefit obligations understated

Many firms make commitments to provide pension benefits and other post-employment benefits, such as health-care, to their employees. International accounting rules require managers to estimate and report the present value of the commitments that have been earned by employees over their years of working for the firm. This obligation is offset by any assets that the firm has committed to post-employment plans to fund future plan benefits. If the funds set aside in the post-employment plan are greater (less) than the plan commitments, the plan is overfunded (underfunded).

Estimating the post-employment benefit obligations is subjective – managers have to make forecasts of future wage and benefit rates, worker attrition rates, and the expected lives of retirees.[10] If these forecasts are too low, the firm's benefit obligations (as well as the annual expenses for benefits reported in the income statement) will be understated.[11] As a result, for labor-intensive firms that offer attractive post-employment benefits to employees, it is important that the analyst assesses whether reported post-employment plan liabilities reflect the firms' true commitments.

International accounting rules require that firms estimate the value of post-employment commitments, called the post-employment benefit obligation, as the present value of future expected payouts under the plans. The obli-gation under pension plans is the present value of plan commitments factoring in the impact of future increases in wage rates and salary scales on projected payouts. For other post-employment plans, such as post-employment healthcare or life insurance, the firm's obligation is calculated as the present value of expected future benefits for employees and their beneficiaries.

Each year the firm's post-employment obligations are adjusted to reflect the following factors:

- Current service cost. Defined benefit plans typically provide higher benefits for each additional year of service with the company. For example, a company may promise its employees pension benefits in the amount of 2 per-cent of their career-average pay for every year worked. The value of incremental benefits earned from another year of service is called the current service cost, and increases the firm's obligation each year.

- Interest cost. The passage of time increases the present value of the firm's obligation. The interest cost recog-nizes this effect, and it is calculated by multiplying the obligation at the beginning of the year by the discount rate.

- Actuarial gains and losses. Each year the actuarial assumptions used to estimate the firm's commitments are reviewed and, if appropriate, changes are made. The effect of these changes is shown as Actuarial Gains and Losses.

- Past service cost. Occasionally companies may decide to amend their post-employment plans. For example, during recent years some companies have switched from linking pension benefits to employees' career-end pay to linking pension benefits to employees' career-average pay. Because these amendments affect the future pay-outs under the plans, they also affect the current post-employment benefit obligation. The effect of these amendments is shown as Past Service Cost (or Benefit).

- Benefits paid. The plan commitments are reduced as the plan makes payments to retirees each year.

- Other. The post-employment obligations can change because of changes in foreign exchange rates, plan curtail-ments, and plan settlements.

For example, in the notes to its financial statements, brewing company Carlsberg provided the following infor-mation on its post-employment benefit obligation for the years ended December 31, 2011 and 2010:

DKK (millions)	December 31, 2011	December 31, 2010
Benefit obligation at beginning of year	9,330	7,974
Current service cost	176	150
Interest cost	376	390
Actuarial (gains)/losses	849	364
Benefits paid	(478)	(473)
Other	86	925
Benefit obligation at end of year	10,339	9,330

Carlsberg's obligation at the end of 2011 was DKK10.3 billion, a 10.8 percent decrease over the prior year.

To meet their commitments under post-employment plans, firms make contributions to the plans. These contributions are then invested in equities, debt, and other assets. Plan assets, therefore, are increased each year by new company (and employee) contributions. They are also increased or decreased by the returns generated each year from plan investments. Finally, plan assets decline when the plan pays out benefits to retirees. For the years ended December 31, 2011 and 2010, Carlsberg's post-employment assets were as follows:

DKK (millions)	December 31, 2011	December 31, 2010
Fair value of plan assets at beginning of year	6,904	5,823
Actual return on plan assets	83	522
Contributions to plans	331	187
Benefits paid	(391)	(380)
Other	172	752
Fair value of plan assets at end of year	7,099	6,904

Carlsberg had expected to earn a return of 4.74 percent on its beginning plan assets in 2011. The company's plan assets increased by a lower amount than expected because they generated an unexpected loss of DKK244 million (83 – [0.0474 × 6,904]) during the year. The difference between Carlsberg's post-employment plan obligations and the plan assets, DKK3.24 billion (10.339 – 7.099), represents the company's unfunded obligation to employees under the plan. The company reports a liability on its balance sheet for a similar amount.

Of course, estimating post-employment obligations is highly subjective. It requires managers to forecast the future payouts under the plans, which in turn involves making projections of employees' service with the firm, retirement ages, and life expectancies, as well as future wage rates. It also requires managers to select an interest rate to estimate the present value of the future benefits. For example, Carlsberg projected that future salaries would grow at 2.9 percent per year, on average. It also assumed that the appropriate discount rate was 3.6 percent. Under the simplified assumption that Carlsberg's retired workforce size remains constant throughout the next 30 years and then gradually decreases to zero over a period of 30 years, a 0.1 percent decrease in the discount rate (or a 0.1 percent increase in salary growth) would increase the post-employment benefit obligation by close to DKK225 million.[12] Given the management judgment involved in making these forecasts and assumptions, analysts should question whether reported obligations adequately reflect the firm's true commitments.

What does post-employment accounting imply for financial analysis? It is reasonable for the analyst to raise several questions about a firm's post-employment obligations, particularly for firms in labor-intensive industries.

1 Are the assumptions made by the firm to estimate its post-employment obligations realistic? These include assumptions about the discount rate, which is supposed to represent the current market interest rate for benefits, as well as assumptions about increases in wage and benefit costs. If these assumptions are optimistic, the obligations recorded on the books understate the firm's real economic commitment. As discussed above, the analyst may estimate that a 0.1 percent increase in expected salary growth increases Carlsberg's obligation by DKK225 million, and use this information to adjust for any optimism in management's assumptions. For example, if the analyst decided that Carlsberg's forecasts of future salaries were too low and needed to increase by 0.1 percent, the post-employment obligation would have to be increased by DKK225 million, with offsetting declines to

equity (for the after-tax effect) and to the deferred tax liability. The adjustment to Carlsberg's 2011 balance sheet, assuming a 24 percent tax rate, would be as follows:

	Adjustment	
DKK (millions)	Assets	Liabilities and Equity
Balance sheet		
Long-Term Debt		+225
Deferred Tax Liability		−54
Shareholders' Equity		−171

2 What effect do post-employment assumptions play in the income statement? The post-employment cost each year comprises:

a Current and past service cost, plus

b Interest cost on the net unfunded obligation.

For Carlsberg, in 2011 the post-employment cost equaled DKK277 million. Note that this cost is not equal to the change in Carlsberg's net unfunded obligation in 2011 of DKK814 million ([10,339 − 9,330] − [7,099 − 6,904]). This is because international accounting rules require companies to include several components of this change in other comprehensive income, a component of equity, rather than in the income statement. In particular, to mitigate the effect of fluctuations in the value of pension plans and commitments on companies' profits, the following components – labeled 'remeasurements' – are recognized outside the income statement:

a Actuarial gains and losses, plus

b Excess return on plan assets, calculated as the actual return minus the discount rate times the fair value of plan assets.

Although it makes sense to recognize such volatile remeasurements separate from the more persistent post-employment cost components, the differential treatment of the components strengthens managers' incentive to (temporarily) understate post-employment obligations. In fact, corrections on the obligation that follow a period of unwarranted optimism (e.g., low forecasts of future wage and benefit rates) will be classified as actuarial gains and losses and immediately recognized in equity, thus by-passing the income statement. To assess the risk that management is overly optimistic in its post-employment assumptions, the analyst could evaluate the company's history of amounts recognized in other comprehensive income.

Finally, past service cost relates to employees' prior service years rather than to the company's current performance. From an analyst's perspective, such costs should therefore not be considered as permanent and ideally excluded from profit (or classified as Other Income, Net of Other Expense) using the information from the notes to the financial statements.

KEY ANALYSIS QUESTIONS

The following are some of the questions an analyst can probe when analyzing whether a firm's liabilities exhibit distortions:

■ *Unearned revenues.* Has the firm recognized revenues for services or products that have yet to be provided?

■ *Provisions.* Did the firm disclose contingent liabilities that expose the firm to material risks? If so, can the expected value of such liabilities be estimated and recognized on the balance sheet? Did the firm make unexplained changes in its provisions? Is the size of the provisions in line with industry practices?

■ *Post-employment benefits.* Are the assumptions made by the firm to estimate its post-employment obligations realistic? Does the firm have a history of actuarial losses? Has the firm recognized past service cost?

EQUITY DISTORTIONS

Accounting treats stockholders' equity as a residual claim on the firm's assets, after paying off the other claimholders. Consequently, equity distortions arise primarily from distortions in assets and liabilities. For example, distortions in assets or liabilities that affect earnings also lead to **distortions in equity**. However, there are forms of equity distortions that would not typically arise in asset and liability analyses. One particular issue is how firms account for contingent claims on their net assets that they sometimes provide to outside stakeholders. Two examples of such contingent claims are employee stock options and conversion options on convertible debentures.

Contingent claims

A stock option gives the holder the right to purchase a certain number of shares at a predetermined price, called the exercise or strike price, for a specified period of time, termed the exercise period. In the 1990s, stock options became the most significant component of compensation for many corporate executives. Proponents of options argue that they provide managers with incentives to maximize shareholder value and make it easier to attract talented managers. Convertible debentures also contain a stock option component. Holders of these debentures have the right to purchase a certain number of shares in exchange for their fixed claim. When deciding on how to account for these contingent claims in a firm's financial statements, the following two factors are important to consider:

- Although providing a contingent claim does not involve a cash outflow for the firm, the claim is by no means costless to the firm's shareholders. The potential exercise of the option dilutes current shareholders' equity and as such imposes an economic cost on the firm's shareholders. To improve current net profit as a measure of the firm's current economic performance, the economic cost of contingent claims should therefore be included in the income statement in the same period in which the firm receives the benefits from these claims.

- The contingent claims are valuable to those who receive them. Employees are willing to provide services to the firm in exchange for employee stock options. Convertible debenture holders are willing to charge a lower interest rate to the firm in exchange for the conversion option. If, in future years, the firm wishes to receive similar services or similar low interest rates without providing contingent claims on its net assets, it must be willing to give up other resources. To improve current net profit as a predictor of the firm's future net profit the income statement should therefore include an expense that reflects the value of the contingent claims to the recipients.

These two factors underline the importance of accurately recording the cost of options in a firm's income statement. International rules require firms to report stock options using the fair value method (discussed in IFRS 2). The fair value method requires firms to record an expense for stock option compensation when the options are issued. The value of the options issued is estimated using a recognized valuation model, such as the Black-Scholes model, and is then expensed over the vesting period.[13] Prior to the European adoption of IFRS, the local accounting rules in most European countries permitted firms to report stock options using the intrinsic value method. Under the intrinsic value method, no compensation expense is reported at the grant date for the vast majority of stock options awarded, where the exercise price is equal to the firm's current stock price. If the options are subsequently exercised, there is also no expense recorded, and the new stock that is issued is valued at the exercise price rather than its higher market value.

Although there is no question that Black-Scholes valuations present a more accurate reflection of the economic cost of stock option awards to the firm's shareholders than the zero cost reported under the intrinsic value method, these valuations can be highly sensitive to management's assumptions about its share price characteristics. For example, when using the Black-Scholes model to value options, managers can understate the stock option expense by understating the expected future share price volatility or overstating the expected future dividend yield. One task of the analyst is therefore to assess the adequacy of management's valuation assumptions. Additionally, research suggests that employees attach much lower values than the Black-Scholes values to the nonmarketable options that they receive. This implies that when a firm plans to replace its stock option awards with cash-based forms of compensation, the analyst should assess whether a decrease in the compensation expense can be expected.

International accounting rules also require a firm to separate the debt from the equity component of convertible debentures. To do so, the firm first estimates what the fair value of the debentures would have been if the conversion option had not been attached to the debentures. This fair value is equal to the present value of the future fixed payments on the debentures, discounted at the firm's effective interest rate on nonconvertible debentures. The value of the equity component is then set equal to the proceeds of the debenture issue minus the fair value of the debt component. The economic cost of the conversion option is included in the income statement by calculating the interest expense on the debentures on the basis of the effective interest rate on nonconvertible debentures. Under these rules, firms may have the incentive to understate the effective interest rate on non-convertible debentures, thereby understating the convertible debentures' equity component and effective interest expense.

Recycling of gains and losses

In accordance with the international accounting rules on the measurement of financial instruments (IAS 39), firms typically record securities held available for sale at fair value and include any (unrealized) fair value gains or losses directly in the statement of comprehensive income. In the period in which these instruments are eventually sold, the cumulative unrealized gains and losses are taken from equity and recognized in the income statement. As a result, gains and losses that were previously included in comprehensive income (statement of comprehensive income) are "recycled" and re-included in net profit.

A disadvantage of recycling unrealized gains or losses on financial instruments held available for sale is that the discretionary timing of a firm's securities sales determines in which period gains or losses become realized. This contrasts, for example, with the way in which a firm treats unrealized gains and losses on securities that are held for short-term trading purposes. The difference between securities classified as available for sale and those held for short-term trading is that the former type of securities were originally designated by the firm as long-term investments. Consequently, international accounting rules require that only revaluation gains and losses on securities held for short-term trading be considered as profit from operating activities and directly included in the income statement. The analyst can, however, use the information from the statement of comprehensive income to incorporate unrealized gains and losses on financial instruments held available for sale in profits and undo the financial statements from any distortions caused by a firm's discretionary timing of securities sales.

In the notes to the financial statements for the fiscal years 2010 and 2011, Spain-based Banco Bilbao Vizcaya Argentaria (BBVA) disclosed the following amounts related to the valuation adjustments on its securities held available for sale:

€ (millions)	2010	2011
Balance at the beginning of the year	1,951	333
Revaluation gains (losses) on securities held available for sale	(1,952)	(1,349)
Revaluation (gains) losses transferred to the income statement	(206)	70
Income tax on revaluation gains/losses	540	264
Balance at the end of year	333	(682)

These disclosures show that recycling of unrealized gains and losses increased net profit by €1,618 million in 2010 (1,952 − (−206) − 540) and by €1,015 million in 2011 (1,349 − 70 − 264). For example, in 2011, the accounting treatment of available-for-sale securities helped BBVA to delay the recognition of losses on Spanish debt securities. To transfer current year's unrealized revaluation gains and losses (net of current realizations) to net income, the following adjustments would have to be made:

€ (millions)	2010	2011
Statement of comprehensive income		
Unrealized Revaluations, Net of Transfers to Income	+1,618	+1,015
Net Profit	−1,618	−1,015
Income statement		
Other Operating Income, Net of Other Operating Expense	−2,158	−1,279
Tax Expense	−540	−264
Net Profit	−1,618	−1,015

These adjustments would decrease BBVA's net profit by 32 and 29 percent in 2010 and 2011, respectively. The bank's return on equity would decrease by 4.3 percentage points (from 13.3 to 9.0 percent) in 2010 and by 2.5 percentage points (from 8.7 to 6.2 percent) in 2011.

Recently developed new rules on the measurement of financial instruments (IFRS 9), which replace IAS 39 after January 2015, require firms to recognize most fair value adjustments through profit or loss. These rules thus essentially eliminate recycling of fair value gains and losses. After the (future) implementation of the new standard, the above adjustments can be used to increase the comparability of financial statements that have been prepared under different rules.

SUMMARY

Once the financial statements are standardized, the analyst can determine what accounting distortions exist in the firm's assets, liabilities, and equity. Common distortions that overstate assets include delays in recognizing asset impairments, underestimated allowances, aggressive revenue recognition leading to overstated receivables, and optimistic assumptions on long-term asset depreciation. Asset understatements can arise if managers overstate asset write-offs, use operating leases to keep assets off the balance sheet, or make conservative assumptions for asset depreciation. They can also arise because accounting rules require outlays for key assets (e.g., research outlays and brands) to be immediately expensed.

For liabilities, the primary concern for the analyst is whether the firm understates its real commitments. This can arise from off-balance liabilities (e.g., operating lease obligations), from understated provisions, from questionable management judgment and limitations in accounting rules for estimating post-employment liabilities, and from aggressive revenue recognition that understates unearned revenue obligations. Equity distortions frequently arise when there are distortions in assets and liabilities.

Adjustments for distortions can, therefore, arise because accounting standards, although applied appropriately, do not reflect a firm's economic reality. They can also arise if the analyst has a different point of view than management about the estimates and assumptions made in preparing the financial statements. Once distortions have been identified, the analyst can use cash flow statement information and information from the notes to the financial statements to make adjustments to the balance sheet at the beginning and/or end of the current year, as well as any needed adjustments to revenues and expenses in the latest income statement. This ensures that the most recent financial ratios used to evaluate a firm's performance and to forecast its future results are based on financial data that appropriately reflect its business economics.

Several points are worth remembering when undertaking accounting analysis. First, the bulk of the analyst's time and energy should be focused on evaluating and adjusting accounting policies and estimates that describe the firm's key strategic value drivers. Of course this does not mean that management bias is not reflected in other accounting estimates and policies, and the analyst should certainly examine these. But given the importance of evaluating how the firm is managing its key success factors and risks, the bulk of the accounting analysis should be spent examining those policies that describe these factors and risks. Similarly, the analyst should focus on adjustments that have a material effect on the firm's liabilities, equity, or earnings. Immaterial adjustments cost time and energy but are unlikely to affect the analyst's financial and prospective analysis.

It is also important to recognize that many accounting adjustments can only be approximations rather than precise calculations, because much of the information necessary for making precise adjustments is not disclosed. The analyst should, therefore, try to avoid worrying about being overly precise in making accounting adjustments. By making even crude adjustments, it is usually possible to mitigate some of the limitations of accounting standards and problems of management bias in financial reporting.

CORE CONCEPTS

Examples of asset value distortions Examples of asset value distortions are:

a Non-current asset understatement resulting from overstated depreciation or amortization.

b Non-current asset understatement resulting from off-balance sheet operating leases.

c Non-current asset understatement resulting from the immediate expensing of investments in intangible assets (such as research).

d Current asset (receivables) understatement resulting from the sales of receivables.

e Current asset (receivables) overstatement resulting from accelerated revenue recognition.

f Non-current or current asset overstatement resulting from delayed write-downs, and

g Current asset overstatement resulting from underestimated allowances (e.g., for doubtful receivables or inventories obsolescence).

Examples of liability distortions Examples of liability distortions are:

a Liability understatement resulting from understated unearned revenues (e.g., revenues from long-term service contracts).

b Liability understatement resulting from understated provisions.

c Liability understatement resulting from the sales of receivables (with recourse).

d Non-current liability understatement resulting from off-balance sheet operating leases.

e Liability understatement resulting from post-employment obligations that are (partly) kept off-balance.

Sources of asset value distortions Managers may strategically bias or accounting rules may force them to bias the book values of assets if there is uncertainty about:

a Who owns or controls the economic resources that potentially give rise to the assets.

b Whether the economic resources will provide future economic benefits that can be reliably measured.

c What the fair value of the assets is.

d Whether the fair value of the asset is less than its book value.

Sources of liability distortions Managers may strategically bias or accounting rules may force them to bias the book values of liabilities if there is uncertainty about:

a Whether an obligation has been occurred.

b Whether the obligation can be reliably measured.

Sources and examples of equity distortions Distortions in assets and liabilities can lead to equity distortions. However, (a) contingent claims such as employee stock options or convertible debentures as well as (b) the recycling of unrealized fair value gains and losses can directly cause distortions in equity.

QUESTIONS, EXERCISES, AND PROBLEMS

1 Refer to the Lufthansa example on asset depreciation estimates in this chapter. What adjustments would be required if Lufthansa's aircraft depreciation was computed using an average life of 25 years and salvage value of 5 percent (instead of the reported values of 12 years and 15 percent)? Show the adjustments to the 2010 and 2011 balance sheets, and to the 2011 income statement.

2 At the beginning of 2011, the Rolls-Royce Group reported in its footnotes that its plant and equipment had an original cost of £2,538 million and that accumulated depreciation was £1,497. Rolls-Royce depreciates its plant and equipment on a straight-line basis under the assumption that the assets have an average useful life of 13 years (assume a 10 percent salvage value). Rolls-Royce's tax rate equals 26.5%. What adjustments should be made to Rolls-Royce's (i) balance sheet at the beginning of 2011; and (ii) income statement for the year 2011, if you assume that the plant and equipment has an average useful life of ten years (and a 10 percent salvage value)?

3 Car manufacturers Volvo and Fiat disclosed the following information in their 2008 financial statements:

	Volvo	Fiat
Property, plant and equipment (PP&E) at cost	SEK 119,089m	€36,239m
Accumulated depreciation on PP&E	SEK 61,819m	€23,632m
Deferred tax liability for depreciation of PP&E	SEK 3,885m	€ 679m
Statutory tax rate	28%	27.5%

Purely based on the companies' deferred tax liabilities, which of the two companies appears to be most conservative in its depreciation policy?

4 Dutch Food retailer Royal Ahold provides the following information on its finance leases in its financial statements for the fiscal year ended January 1, 2012:

Finance lease liabilities are principally for buildings. Terms range from 10 to 25 years and include renewal options if it is reasonably certain, at the inception of the lease, that they will be exercised. At the time of entering into finance lease agreements, the commitments are recorded at their present value using the interest rate implicit in the lease, if this is practicable to determine; if not the interest rate applicable for long-term borrowings is used.

The aggregate amounts of minimum lease liabilities to third parties, under noncancelable finance lease contracts for the next five years and thereafter are as follows:

(€ millions)	Future minimum lease payments	Present value of minimum lease payments
Within one year	€ 165	€ 67
Between one and five years	643	312
After five years	1,195	846
Total	2,003	1,225
Current portion of finance lease liabilities		67
Non-current portion of finance lease liabilities		1,158

What interest rate does Ahold use to capitalize its finance leases?

5 On January 1, 2012, Royal Ahold disclosed the following information about its operating lease commitments:

(€ millions)	2010	2011
Within one year	€ 655	€ 677
Between one and five years	2,194	2,245
After five years	3,130	3,016
Total	5,979	5,938

Ahold's operating lease expense in 2011 amounted to €635 million. Assume that Ahold records its finance lease liabilities at an interest rate of 8.4 percent. Use this rate to capitalize Ahold's operating leases at January 1, 2011 and 2012.

a Record the adjustment to Ahold's balance sheet at the end of 2010 (i.e., January 1, 2011) to reflect the capitalization of operating leases.

b How would this reporting change affect Ahold's income statement in 2011?

6 When bringing operating lease commitments to the balance sheet, some analysts assume that in each year of the lease term depreciation on the operating lease assets is exactly equal to the difference between (a) the operating lease payment and (b) the estimated interest expense on the operating lease obligation.

    a Explain how this simplifies the adjustments.

    b Do you agree that this is a valid assumption?

7 Refer to the AstraZeneca example on intangibles in this chapter. What would be the value of AstraZeneca's R&D asset at the end of fiscal years 2009 and 2010 if the average expected life of AstraZeneca's R&D investments is only three years?

8 Under IFRS firms can capitalize development outlays, whereas under US GAAP such outlays must be expensed as incurred. In its 2008 IFRS-based financial statements, Philips Electronics recognized a development asset of €357 million (€518 million in 2007). The company's development expenditures amounted to €233, €259, €295, €233, and €154 million in 2004, 2005, 2006, 2007, and 2008, respectively. In these years, total R&D expenditures were €1,615, €1,602, €1,659, €1,629, and €1,622 million, respectively. Philips' statutory tax rate is 25.5 percent.

    a Estimate the average expected life of Philips' investments in development at the end of 2008.

    b Using the estimate derived under a, what adjustments should an analyst make to the 2008 beginning balance sheet and 2008 income statement to immediately expense all development outlays and derecognize the development asset?

    c What adjustments should be made to the 2008 beginning balance sheet and 2008 income statement to recognize an asset for both research and development investments? Assume that the average expected life of Philips' investments in research at the end of 2007 and 2008 is equal to that of Philips' development investments at the end of 2008.

9 What approaches would you use to estimate the value of brands? What assumptions underlie these approaches? As a financial analyst, what would you use to assess whether the brand value of £5.2 billion reported by consumer goods company Reckitt Benckiser plc in 2011 for its health and personal care brands such as Strepsils and Clearasil was a reasonable reflection of the future benefits from these brands? What questions would you raise with the firm's CFO about the firm's brand assets?

10 In early 2003 Bristol-Myers Squibb announced that it would have to restate its financial statements as a result of stuffing as much as $3.35 billion worth of products into wholesalers' warehouses from 1999 through 2001. The company's sales and cost of sales during this period were as follows:

(millions)	2001	2000	1999
Net sales	$18,139	$17,695	$16,502
Cost of products sold	$ 5,454	$ 4,729	$ 4,458

    The company's marginal tax rate during the three years was 35 percent. What adjustments are required to correct Bristol-Myers Squibb's balance sheet for December 31, 2001? What assumptions underlie your adjustments? How would you expect the adjustments to affect Bristol-Myers Squibb's performance in the coming few years?

11 As the CFO of a company, what indicators would you look at to assess whether your firm's non-current assets were impaired? What approaches could be used, either by management or an independent valuation firm, to assess the value of any asset impairment? As a financial analyst, what indicators would you look at to assess whether a firm's non-current assets were impaired? What questions would you raise with the firm's CFO about any charges taken for asset impairment?

12 On December 31, 2011, Germany's largest retailer Metro AG reported in its annual financial statements that it held inventories for 52 days' sales. The inventories had a book value of €7,608 million.

a How much excess inventory do you estimate Metro is holding in December 2011 if the firm's optimal Days' Inventories is 45 days?

b Calculate the inventory impairment charge for Metro if 50 percent of this excess inventory is deemed worthless. Record the changes to Metro's financial statements from adjusting for this impairment.

13 On December 31, 2010 and 2011 Deutsche Telekom AG had net trade receivables in the amount of €6,766 million and €6,455 million, respectively. The following proportion of the receivables was past due on the reporting date:

	2010	2011
Not past due on the reporting date	(48.7%) 3,295	(49.4%) 3,190
Past due on the reporting date	(51.3%) 3,471	(50.6%) 3,265
Total	(100.0%) 6,766	(100.0%) 6,455

The changes in Deutsche Telekom's allowance for doubtful receivables were as follows:

Item	2010	2011
Allowance on January 1	1,178	1,323
Currency translation adjustments	15	(9)
Additions (allowance recognized as expense)	822	830
Use	(529)	(589)
Reversal	(163)	(323)
Allowance on December 31	1,323	1,232

Assume that Deutsche Telekom's statutory tax rate was 30.5 percent in 2010 and 2011. Further assume that an analyst wishes to recognize an additional allowance for 20 percent of the receivables that are past due on the reporting date.

a What adjustments should the analyst make to Deutsche Telekom's balance sheet at the end of 2010?

b What adjustments should the analyst make to Deutsche Telekom's 2011 income statement?

14 Refer to the British American Tobacco example on provisions in this chapter. The cigarette industry is subject to litigation for health hazards posed by its products. In the US, the industry has been negotiating a settlement of these claims with state and federal governments. As the CFO for UK-based British American Tobacco (BAT), which is affected through its US subsidiaries, what information would you report to investors in the annual report on the firm's litigation risks? How would you assess whether the firm should record a provision for this risk, and if so, how would you assess the value of this provision? As a financial analyst following BAT, what questions would you raise with the CFO over the firm's litigation provision?

15 Refer to the Carlsberg example on post-employment benefits in this chapter. Discuss the components of the pension expense. In your opinion, is it reasonable to exclude some components of the change in the unfunded obligation from earnings? Is the calculation of the pension charge in the income statement appropriate (from an analyst's perspective)?

16 Some argue that (1) because estimating the value of a contingent claims (such as executive stock options) is surrounded with uncertainty and (2) the claims do not represent a cash outlay, the value of these claims should not be included in the income statement as an expense. Do you agree with these arguments?

Problem 1 Merger accounting

International rules for merger accounting (IFRS 3) require that firms report mergers using the purchase method. Under this method the cost of the merger for the acquirer is the actual value of the consideration paid for the target firm's shares. The identifiable assets and liabilities of the target are then recorded on the acquirer's books at their fair values. If the value of the consideration paid for the target exceeds the fair value of its identifiable assets and liabilities, the excess is reported as goodwill on the acquirer's balance sheet. For example, when company A acquires company B for an amount of €1 billion (paid out in shares) and company B's net assets have a book value of €0.5 billion and a fair value of €0.7 billion, company A would record company B's net assets on its balance sheet for an amount of €0.7 billion and recognize €0.3 billion (1.0 – 0.7) of goodwill. The new rules require goodwill assets to be written off only if they become impaired in the future. However, as recently as 2003 some large acquisitions were reported using the pooling method. Under pooling accounting, the purchase of a target firm's shares is recorded at their historical book value rather than at their market value, so that no goodwill is recorded. For example, in the above example, company A would record company B's net assets on its balance sheet for an amount of €0.5 billion, ignoring the net assets' fair value and the amount of goodwill on the acquisition. This is likely to be a consideration for the analyst in evaluating the performance of serial share-for-share acquirers.

In December 2000 the pharmaceutical companies SmithKline Beecham and Glaxo Wellcome merged their activities to form UK-based GlaxoSmithKline. GlaxoSmithKline reported under UK Generally Accepted Accounting Principles (UK GAAP) and recorded the merger transaction using the pooling method. After the merger, the former shareholders of Glaxo Wellcome held close to 59 percent of GlaxoSmithKline's ordinary shares. Because GlaxoSmithKline's shares were listed on the New York Stock Exchange, the company also had to prepare a reconciliation of its UK GAAP statements with US GAAP. The US accounting rules did not, however, consider the transaction a merger of equals but an acquisition of SmithKline Beecham by Glaxo Wellcome. These rules did not permit, therefore, the use of the pooling method to record the transaction.

The additional disclosures that GlaxoSmithKline made as part of its reconciliation to US GAAP provide the analyst with much of the information that is needed to adjust for the distortion from using pooling accounting. Under the terms of the deal, the acquisition price of SmithKline Beecham was £43.9 billion. At the time of the acquisition, the book value of SmithKline Beecham's net assets was £2.7 billion and the fair value adjustments to SmithKline Beecham's net assets amounted up to £25.0 billion. The amount of goodwill thus equaled £16.2 billion (43.9 – 2.7 – 25.0). At the end of the fiscal year 2005, GlaxoSmithKline reported in its first IFRS-based financial statements that its goodwill on the acquisition of SmithKline Beecham had a remaining value of £15.9 billion, while fair value adjustments for acquired product rights were valued at £12.1 billion. The company did not, however, record these amounts on its balance sheet. The international rules on the first-time application of IFRS allow first-time adopters not to restate the accounting for business combinations (mergers and acquisitions) that took place prior to the start of the previous year because such restatements are complex and may require previously uncollected information. Like most first-time adopters, GlaxoSmithKline chose to apply this exemption. Pooling accounting therefore remained to affect GlaxoSmithKline's (and many other) IFRS-based financial statements.

1   Discuss why, from an analyst's point of view, purchase accounting is preferable over pooling accounting.

2   What adjustments should an analyst make to GlaxoSmithKline's 2006 beginning balance sheet to correct for the distortions from using pooling accounting? (Assume that GlaxoSmithKline's marginal tax rate is 30 percent. Note that the international accounting rules for income taxes prohibit the recognition of deferred taxes on nondeductible goodwill.)

3   What adjustments should an analyst make to GlaxoSmithKline's 2006 income statement?

Problem 2 *Impairment of non-current assets*

Consider the acquisitions by Germany-based media company EM.TV & Merchandising AG of the Jim Henson Company, creator of The Muppet Show, and Speed Investments Ltd., co-owner of the commercial rights to Formula One motor racing. At the end of the 1990s, EM.TV pursued a strategy of aggressive growth through the acquisitions of TV and marketing rights for well-known cartoon characters, such as the Flintstones, and popular sporting events. After its initial public offering on the Neuer Markt segment of the German Stock Exchange in October 1997, EM.TV's share price soared from €0.35 (split-adjusted) to a high of just above €120 in February 2000. Its high share price helped EM.TV to finance several acquisitions through a secondary stock offering and the issuance of convertible debt. In March and May 2000, respectively, the company made its two largest acquisitions with the intention of expanding its international reputation. The company acquired the Jim Henson Company for €699 million and Speed Investment for €1.55 billion. At the time of the acquisition, Speed Investment's book value of equity was negative and the amount of goodwill that EM.TV recognized on the investment was €2.07 billion. The rationale of capitalizing this amount of goodwill on EM.TV's balance sheet is that it could truly represent the future economic benefits that EM.TV expects to receive from its investment but that are not directly attributable to the investment's recorded assets and liabilities. However, the analyst should consider the possibility that EM.TV has overpaid for its new investments, especially in times where its managers are flush with free cash flow.

At the end of the fiscal year, when EM.TV's share price had already declined to €5.49, the company was forced to admit that it had overpaid for its latest acquisitions. Goodwill impairment charges for the year ending in December 2000 amounted to €340 million for the Jim Henson Company and €600 million for Speed Investment. In its annual report, EM.TV commented that "the salient factor for the write-offs was that, at the time of the acquisitions, the expert valuation was determined by the positive expectations of the capital markets. This was particularly expressed through the use of corresponding multiples." Despite the large write-offs, a considerable amount of goodwill, related to the acquisition of Speed Investment, remained part of EM.TV's assets. This amount of €1.41 billion was equal to 170 percent of EM.TV's book value of equity.

Given the questionable financial health of Speed Investment, did the initial €2.07 billion of goodwill ever represent a true economic asset? Was it reasonable to expect to receive €2.07 billion in future economic benefits from a firm that had not been able to earn profits in the past? If not, was the €600 million write-down adequate?

1   What balance sheet adjustments should an analyst make if she decided to record an additional write-down of €1.41 billion in the December 2000 financials?

2   What effect would this additional write-down have on EM.TV's depreciation expense in 2001? (Assume that the adjustments to EM.TV's balance sheet are in conformity with current IFRSs.)

Problem 3 *Audi, BMW and Skoda's research and development*

Car manufacturers Audi, BMW Group and Skoda Auto spend considerable amounts on research and development and capitalize a proportion of these amounts each year. Each manufacturer systematically amortizes development cost assets, presumably using the straight-line method, following the start of the production of a developed car model or component. In the notes to their financial statements, the firms report the following (average) estimated product lives:

- Audi: five to nine years;
- BMW: typically seven years,
- Skoda: two to ten years, according to the product life cycle.

In 2011 (2010), close to 99 (70) percent of Skoda's capitalized development expenditures capitalized concerned development costs for products under development (i.e., models or components that are not yet in production).

Audi and BMW both focus their activities on the premium sector of the automobile market. Skoda operates primarily in the lower segments of the market. Both Audi and Skoda are majority owned by Volkswagen Group and share car platforms and production facilities with their major shareholder. BMW is publicly listed and independent (from other car manufacturers).

The following table displays the firms' research and development expenditures and the amount capitalized and amortized during the years 2004–2011.

	2011	2010	2009	2008	2007	2006	2005	2004
BMW Group								
Research and development expense (€ millions)	3,610	3,082	2,587	2,825	2,920	2,544	2,464	2,334
Amortization and impairment	−1,209	−1,260	−1,226	−1,185	−1,109	−872	−745	−637
Development costs capitalized in the current year	972	951	1,087	1,224	1,333	1,536	1,396	1,121
Total R&D expenditure	3,373	2,773	2,448	2,864	3,144	3,208	3,115	2,818
Capitalized development costs (asset) at the end of the year	4,388	4,625	4,934	5,073	5,034	4,810	4,146	3,495

	2011	2010	2009	2008	2007	2006	2005	2004
End-of-year total assets	123,429	110,164	101,953	101,086	88,997	79,057	74,566	67,634
Sales	68,821	60,477	50,681	53,197	56,018	48,999	46,656	44,335
Operating profit	8,018	5,111	289	921	4,212	4,050	3,793	3,774
Audi								
Research and development expense (€ millions)	2,641	2,469	2,050	2,161	2,226	1,982	1,585	1,214
Amortization and impairment	−397	−567	−480	−530	−656	−905	−586	−461
Development costs capitalized in the current year	595	629	528	547	497	625	543	652
Total R&D expenditure	2,839	2,531	2,098	2,178	2,067	1,702	1,542	1,405
Capitalized development costs (asset) at the end of the year	2,249	2,051	1,989	1,940	1,923	2,082	2,362	2,405
End-of-year total assets	37,019	30,772	26,550	26,056	22,578	18,910	16,112	14,904
Sales	44,096	35,441	29,840	34,196	33,617	31,142	26,591	24,506
Operating profit	5,348	3,340	1,604	2,772	2,705	2,015	1,407	1,238
Skoda Auto								
Research and development expense (CZK millions)	9,133	8,222	7,139	5,721	4,812	4,307	4,633	4,252
Amortization and impairment	−3,072	−3,658	−2,899	−2,326	−2,450	−2,367	−2,081	−1,853
Development costs capitalized in the current year	3,306	3,093	1,493	2,066	3,097	2,762	2,862	2,453
Total R&D expenditure	9,367	7,657	5,733	5,461	5,459	4,702	5,414	4,852
Capitalized development costs (asset) at the end of the year	10,726	10,492	11,057	12,463	12,725	12,078	11,683	10,902
End-of-year total assets	153,557	135,736	118,376	122,456	115,781	105,212	83,979	88,206
Sales	252,562	219,454	187,858	200,182	221,967	203,659	177,822	155,396
Operating profit	18,257	11,316	5,924	13,620	19,784	14,602	10,004	5,289

A table presenting the manufacturers' production volumes by car type during the period 2004–2011 is available from the book's companion website.

1   Estimate the average economic lives of the car manufacturers' development assets. What assumptions make your estimates of the average economic lives consistent with those reported by the manufacturers?

2   The percentages of R&D expenditures capitalized fluctuate over time and differ between car manufacturers. Which factors may explain these fluctuations and differences? As an analyst, what questions would you raise with the CFO about the levels of and fluctuations in these capitalization percentages?

3   In accordance with IAS 38, the three car manufacturers do not capitalize research expenditures. From an analyst's perspective, which arguments would support capitalization (rather than immediate expensing) of research expenditures?

4   What adjustments to the car manufacturers' 2011 financial statements are required if you decide to capitalize (and gradually amortize) the firms' entire R&D? Which of the three manufacturers is most affected by these adjustments?

Problem 4   *H&M and Burberry's non-current assets*

Hennes & Mauritz AB (H&M) and Burberry Group plc (Burberry) are publicly listed apparel retailers. The following information is taken from their financial statements for the fiscal years ending on November 30, 2007 and March 31, 2008, respectively (hereafter referred to as fiscal 2007):

	H&M fiscal 2007	Burberry fiscal 2007
Land and buildings book value at the beginning of the year	SEK 420m	£58.2m
Book value of land, buildings, and equipment leased under finance leases at the beginning of the year	SEK 222m	£0.0m
Equipment at cost at the beginning of the year	SEK 13,605m	£192.8m
Equipment book value at the beginning of the year	SEK 7,134m	£99.2m
Cost of equipment acquired during the year	SEK 3,466m	£38.3m
Buildings depreciation expense	SEK 14m	£1.9m
Equipment depreciation expense	SEK 1,750m	£27.0m
Sales	SEK 78,346m	£995.4m

Both retailers had non-cancellable operating leases related to land, buildings and equipment. Under the operating lease agreements, the companies were committed to paying the following amounts:

	H&M		Burberry	
Due in ...	fiscal 2007	fiscal 2006	fiscal 2007	fiscal 2006
Year 1	SEK 6,801m	SEK 6,169m	£39.1m	£31.5m
Years 2–5	SEK 19,732m	SEK 17,689m	£112.9m	£86.0m
After year 5	SEK 12,478m	SEK 11,593m	£167.5m	£103.8m
Actual lease payment made during the year	SEK 7,810m	SEK 7,030m	£43.0m	£31.0m

The incremental borrowing rate of H&M in fiscal years 2006 and 2007 was 4.4 percent; the incremental borrowing rate of Burberry in fiscal years 2006 and 2007 was 5.4 percent. The statutory tax rates of H&M and Burberry were 28 and 30 percent, respectively.

Assume that all land, buildings and equipment have zero residual values. Further assume that both retailers recognize half a year of depreciation on assets acquired during the year.

1   Two measures of the efficiency of a firm's investment policy are (a) the ratio of land, buildings and equipment to sales and (b) the ratio of depreciation to sales. Calculate both ratios for H&M and Burberry based on the reported information. Which of the two companies appears to be relatively more efficient in its investment policy?

2   Calculate the depreciation rates that H&M and Burberry use for their equipment.

3   What adjustments to (a) the beginning book value of H&M's equipment and (b) the equipment depreciation expense would be required if you assume that H&M uses Burberry's depreciation rate?

4   What adjustments to (a) the beginning book value of H&M's and Burberry's land, buildings and equipment and (b) H&M's and Burberry's depreciation expense would be required if you capitalize the retailers' operating leases?

5   Recalculate the investment efficiency measures using the adjusted data. Do the adjustments affect your assessment of the retailers' investment efficiency?

NOTES

1. See P. Healy, S. Myers, and C. Howe, "R&D Accounting and the Tradeoff Between Relevance and Objectivity," *Journal of Accounting Research* 40 (June 2002): 677–711, for analysis of the value of capitalizing R&D and then annually assessing impairment.

2. V. Beattie, K. Edwards, and A. Goodacre show that adjustments to capitalize operating leases have a significant impact on leverage and other key financial ratios of UK firms. See "The Impact of Constructive Operating Lease Capitalisation on Key Accounting Ratios," *Accounting and Business Research* 28 (Autumn 1998): 233–254.

3. Some research suggests that the distinction between finance and operating lease obligation is not fully arbitrary. In their study "Recognition Versus Disclosure: An Investigation of the Impact on Equity Risk Using UK Operating Lease Disclosures," *Journal of Business Finance and Accounting* 27 (November/December 2000): 1185–1224, V. Beattie, A. Goodacre, and S. Thomson find that UK investors interpret the operating lease obligation as an obligation that increases a firm's equity risk but less so than ordinary debt.

4. P. Healy, S. Myers, and C. Howe, "R&D Accounting and the Tradeoff Between Relevance and Objectivity," *Journal of Accounting Research* 40 (June 2002): 677–711, show that the magnitude of this bias is sizable.

5. See e.g., B. Bublitz and M. Ettredge, "The Information in Discretionary Outlays: Advertising, Research and Development," *The Accounting Review* 64 (1989): 108–124; M. Hirschey and J. Weygandt, "Amortization Policy for Advertising and Research and Development Expenditures," *Journal of Accounting Research* 23 (1985): 326–335; B. Lev and T. Sougiannis, "The Capitalization, Amortization, and Value-Relevance of R&D," *Journal of Accounting and Economics* 21 (1996): 107–138; P. Green, A. Stark, and H. Thomas, "UK Evidence on the Market Valuation of Research and Development Expenditures," *Journal of Business Finance and Accounting* 23 (March 1996): 191–216; D. Aboody and B. Lev, "The Value-Relevance of Intangibles: The Case of Software Capitalization," *Journal of Accounting Research* 36 (1998): 161–191; and M. Ballester, M. Garcia-Ayuso, and J. Livnat, "The Economic Value of the R&D Intangible Asset," *European Accounting Review* 12 (2003): 605–633.

6. J. Francis, D. Hanna, and L. Vincent find that management is more likely to exercise judgment in its self-interest for goodwill write-offs and restructuring charges than for inventory or PP&E write-offs. See "Causes and Effects of Discretionary Asset Write-Offs," *Journal of Accounting Research* 34, Supplement, 1996.

7. P. Healy, K. Palepu, and R. Ruback find that acquisitions add value for only one-third of the 50 largest acquisitions during the early 1980s, suggesting that acquirers frequently do not recover goodwill. See "Which Takeovers Are Profitable – Strategic or Financial?" *Sloan Management Review*, Summer 1997. Studying a sample of 519 UK acquirers between 1983 and 1995, S. Sudarsanam and A. Mahate find in their study "Glamour Acquirers, Method of Payment and Post-acquisition Performance: The UK Evidence," *Journal of Business Finance and Accounting* 30 (January 2003): 299–341, that the risk of not recovering goodwill is especially large for glamour acquirers, who have experienced a large share price run-up prior to the acquisition.

8. J. Elliott and D. Hanna find that the market anticipates large write-downs by about one quarter, consistent with managers being reluctant to take write-downs on a timely basis. See "Repeated Accounting Write-Offs and the Information Content of Earnings," *Journal of Accounting Research* 34, Supplement, 1996.

9. Mary E. Barth and Maureen McNichols discuss ways for investors to estimate the value of environmental liabilities. See "Estimation and Market Valuation of Environmental Liabilities Relating to Superfund Sites," *Journal of Accounting Research* 32, Supplement, 1994.

10. Defined contribution plans, where companies agree to contribute fixed amounts today to cover future benefits, require very little forecasting to estimate their annual cost since the firm's obligation is limited to its annual obligation to contribute to the employees' pension funds.

11. E. Amir and E. Gordon show that firms with larger post-retirement benefit obligations and more leverage tend to make more aggressive estimates of post-retirement obligation parameters. See "A Firm's Choice of Estimation Parameters: Empirical Evidence from SFAS No. 106," *Journal of Accounting, Auditing and Finance* 11, No. 3, Summer 1996.

12. The annuity of a €1 payout that grows at rate g_a during n_a years and then gradually declines to zero over a period of n years can be calculated as follows:

$$\text{Annuity} = \frac{1 - ([1+g_a]/[1+r])^{n_a}}{(r-g_a)} + \left(\frac{1 - ([1-1/n_b]/[1+r])^{n_b}}{(r+1/n_b)}\right)\left(\frac{(1+g_a)^{n_a}}{(1+r)^{n_a}}\right)$$

Given a discount rate (r) of 3.6 percent, g_a equal to 2.9 percent, and n_a and n_b equal to 30 years, the annuity is equal to €36.59. Decreasing the discount rate from 3.6 percent to 3.5 percent increases the annuity by €0.80, or 2.18 percent. 2.18 percent of Carlsberg's post-employment obligation of DKK 10.339 billion is approximately DKK225 million.

13. The Black-Scholes option pricing model estimates the value of an option as a nonlinear function of the exercise price, the remaining time to expiration, the estimated variance of the underlying stock, and the risk-free interest rate. Studies of the valuation of executive stock options include T. Hemmer, S. Matsunaga, and T. Shevlin, "Optimal Exercise and the Cost of Granting Employee Stock Options with a Reload Provision," *Journal of Accounting Research* 36(2) (1998); C. Cuny and P. Jorion, "Valuing Executive Stock Options with Endogenous Departure," *Journal of Accounting and Economics* 20 (September 1995): 193–206; and S. Huddart, "Employee Stock Options," *Journal of Accounting and Economics* 18 (September 1994): 207–232.

Marks and Spencer's accounting choices

On March 2, 2009, Credit Suisse analyst Tony Shiret issued a new research report about clothing retailer Marks and Spencer Group plc (M&S), setting a target price of 160 pence – which was substantially less than the company's share price of 265 pence – and reiterating his sell recommendation. The more than one hundred pages long report sharply criticized the strategic choices of M&S's management during the past year, claimed that the company's recent performance was not as good as it appeared, and called upon management to change the company's course. In addition, Shiret and his team critically analyzed management's reporting strategy and showed how past discretionary accounting choices might have helped management to overstate M&S's accounting performance. The report explicitly discussed the company's accounting for pension liabilities, intangible assets, and depreciation.

Marks and Spencer's current chief executive officer and chairman of the board, Sir Stuart Rose, had been appointed in May 2004. During Rose's tenure, M&S had reported steadily increasing sales and net profits, positive abnormal profits, and consistently positive cash flows from operations. Rose joined Marks and Spencer after a period in which the company's share price had underperformed. In the year of his appointment, the new chairman implemented a new strategic plan aimed at modernizing the company's stores, tightening cost control, and improving the efficiency of inventory management and procurement. The new plan led to a significant improvement in operating margins.

In addition to questioning some of M&S's accounting practices in his report, analyst Tony Shiret argued that since Rose's appointment M&S had made limited performance improvements and that the company was still too reliant on older customers. On the day that Shiret issued his research report, M&S's share price dropped by 4 percent.

On May 19, 2009, M&S published its financial statements for the fiscal year ending on March 31, 2009 (hereafter referred to as fiscal year 2009/2008). The retailer's profitability had declined since the prior year, primarily due to the economic downturn, forcing management to cut the company's dividend. M&S had been able to keep its leverage ratio relatively constant, but only because of a somewhat unusual transaction that helped the company to reclassify one of its liabilities as equity. This liability had been the result of a transaction in January 2007, when the company sold (and leased back) £1.1 million of its property portfolio to a new partnership that it jointly owned with its pension fund. Part of the transaction was that the partnership promised to pay £50m annually (financed through the annual rental payments made by M&S) to M&S's pension fund during a period of 15 years. Because M&S had full control over the financing and operating decisions of the partnership, it had to consolidate the partnership in its financial statement, thus recognizing the liability to the pension fund. The transaction helped the pension fund to increase its pension plan assets and reduce M&S's pension deficit. In fiscal years 2009/2008 and 2008/2007, M&S also changed the terms of its defined benefit plans to recognize an exceptional pension credit and further reduce the pension deficit.

Professor Erik Peek prepared this case. The case is intended solely as the basis for class discussion and is not intended to serve as an endorsement, source of primary data, or illustration of effective or ineffective management.

Three days after the publication date, Shiret and his team issued a new report, increasing the target price to 195 pence but keeping the sell recommendation unchanged. In this report as well as another report following a few weeks later, the analyst repeated his concerns about some of M&S's accounting choices. Adding to these concerns was the reclassification as equity of a liability that Shiret continued to see as debt.

Questions

1 **Exhibits 1 and 2** report the income statements and excerpts from the notes to Marks and Spencer's financial statements for the fiscal years ending between March 31, 2005 and March 31, 2009. Critically analyze M&S's accounting choices. What choices may have helped the company to overstate its net profits between 2005 and 2009?

2 **Exhibit 3** provides information about the liability that Marks and Spencer reclassified as equity. Do you agree with the decision to reclassify? What will be the effect of this decision on future financial statements?

EXHIBIT 1 Marks and Spencer Group – (comprehensive) income statements

(£ millions)	2009/2008	2008/2007	2007/2006	2006/2005	2005/2004
Revenue	**9,062.1**	**9,022.0**	**8,588.1**	**7,797.7**	**7,490.5**
Cost of sales	(5,690.2)	(5,535.2)	(5,246.9)	(4,812.1)	(4,884.3)
Gross profit	**3,371.9**	**3,486.8**	**3,341.2**	**2,985.6**	**2,606.2**
Selling and marketing expenses	(2,074.4)	(1,912.7)	(1,779.2)	(1,625.7)	(1,493.0)
Administrative expenses	(570.1)	(534.5)	(584.1)	(522.7)	(476.8)
Other operating income	41.5	49.7	66.1	18.6	12.7
Profit on property disposals	6.4	27.0	1.9	(5.7)	30.7
Exceptional costs (strategic restructure)	(135.9)	0.0	0.0	0.0	(81.7)
Exceptional pension credit	231.3	95.0	0.0	0.0	0.0
Operating profit	**870.7**	**1,211.3**	**1,045.9**	**850.1**	**598.1**
Finance income	50.0	64.4	33.8	30.5	27.9
Finance costs	(214.5)	(146.6)	(112.6)	(134.9)	(120.9)
Exceptional finance costs	0.0	0.0	(30.4)	0.0	0.0
Profit on ordinary activities before taxation	**706.2**	**1,129.1**	**936.7**	**745.7**	**505.1**
Income tax expense	(199.4)	(308.1)	(277.5)	(225.1)	(150.1)
Profit for the year	**506.8**	**821.0**	**659.2**	**520.6**	**355.0**
Taxation:					
Current tax	(121.8)	(117.4)	(179.5)	(153.6)	(103.7)
Deferred tax from					
– fixed assets temporary differences	(2.0)	13.7	4.4	(2.7)	1.9
– accelerated capital allowances	17.3	(41.4)	(18.2)	(10.7)	0.8
– pension temporary differences	(87.0)	(150.5)	(71.4)	(42.4)	(48.3)
– other short-term temporary differences	(5.7)	(12.9)	(12.5)	(14.9)	(4.1)
– overseas deferred tax	(0.2)	0.4	(0.3)	(0.8)	0.3
Other information:					
Net cash flow from operating activities	1,290.6	1,069.8	1,292.5	1,096.0	1,435.1
Inventories	536.0	488.9	416.3	374.3	338.9
Trade and other receivables (including prepayments and accrued income)	285.2	307.6	196.7	210.5	213.8
Total assets	7,258.1	7,161.0	5,381.0	5,210.5	4,867.3
Total equity	2,100.6	1,964.0	1,648.2	1,155.3	909.2
Comprehensive income statement:					
Profit for the year	**506.8**	**821.0**	**659.9**	**523.1**	**586.2**
Foreign currency translation difference	33.1	21.3	(14.0)	11.1	0.0
Actuarial (losses)/gains on retirement benefit schemes	(927.1)	605.4	(8.6)	(169.3)	(78.1)
Cash flow and net investment hedges					
– fair value movements in equity	304.8	(33.5)	(7.4)	(3.1)	0.0
– recycled and reported in net profit	(206.8)	1.3	10.7	(1.4)	0.0
– amount recognized in inventories	(8.6)	2.4	2.1	(3.8)	0.0
Tax on items taken directly to equity	225.8	(185.7)	24.5	80.7	24.9
Net (losses)/gains not recognized in the income statement	**(578.8)**	**411.2**	**7.3**	**(85.8)**	**(53.2)**
Total recognized income and expense for the year	**(72.0)**	**1,232.2**	**667.2**	**437.3**	**533.0**

Source: 2009/2008 – 2005/2004 annual reports of Marks and Spencer.

Marks and Spencer's accounting choices

EXHIBIT 2 **Marks and Spencer Group – excerpts from the notes to the financial statements (2009/2008 – 2005/2004)**

Property, plant, and equipment

The Group's policy is to state property, plant, and equipment at cost less accumulated depreciation and any recognized impairment loss. Assets in the course of construction are held at cost less any recognized impairment loss.

Depreciation is provided to write off the cost of tangible non-current assets (including investment properties), less estimated residual values, by equal annual installments as follows:

■ freehold land – not depreciated.

■ freehold and leasehold buildings with a remaining lease term over 50 years – depreciated to their residual value over their estimated remaining economic lives.

■ leasehold buildings with a remaining lease term of less than 50 years – over the remaining period of the lease.

■ fixtures, fittings and equipment – 3 to 25 years according to the estimated life of the asset.

Residual values and useful economic lives are reviewed annually. Depreciation is charged on all additions to, or disposals of, depreciating assets in the year of purchase or disposal. Any impairment in value is charged to the income statement.

(£ millions)	2009/2008	2008/2007	2007/2006	2006/2005	2005/2004
Land and buildings:					
Cost at year-end	2,566.6	2,525.2	2,468.2	2,392.2	2,412.0
Accumulated depreciation at year-end	(108.6)	(103.8)	(95.3)	(82.2)	(82.7)
Net book value at year-end	2,458.0	2,421.4	2,372.9	2,310.0	2,329.3
Additions (other than acquisitions)	45.7	82.6	63.9	34.7	
Disposals	58.4	73.8	6.4	34.1	
Depreciation charge	9.2	8.5	13.9	10.7	
Other changes in the net book value (exchange differences, acquisitions, etc.)	58.5	48.2	19.3	(9.2)	
Fixtures, fittings & equipment:					
Cost at year-end	4,811.9	4,473.3	3,653.3	3,287.1	3,162.1
Accumulated depreciation at year-end	(2,546.4)	(2,377.0)	(2,089.2)	(2,061.8)	(1,926.8)
Net book value at year-end	2,265.5	2,096.3	1,564.1	1,225.3	1,235.3
Additions (other than acquisitions)	395.2	692.8	578.7	251.8	
Disposals	17.3	5.2	10.7	6.2	
Depreciation charge	372.5	287.8	254.9	256.9	
Other changes in the net book value (exchange differences, acquisitions, etc.)	163.8	132.4	25.7	1.3	
Deferred tax assets/(liabilities) for tangible assets:					
Deferred tax asset/(liability) at year-end	(78.9)	(76.9)	(90.6)	(95.0)	(97.3)
Credited/(charged) to the income statement during the year	(2.0)	13.7	4.4	(2.7)	
Statutory tax rate	28.0%	28.0%	30.0%	30.0%	

Intangible assets

Software intangibles: Where computer software is not an integral part of a related item of computer hardware, the software is treated as an intangible asset.

Capitalised software costs include external direct costs of material and services and the payroll and payroll-related costs for employees who are directly associated with the project.

Capitalised software development costs are amortized on a straight-line basis over their expected economic lives, normally between three to five years.

Computer software under development is held at cost less any recognized impairment loss.

(£ millions)	2009/2008	2008/2007	2007/2006	2006/2005	2005/2004
Goodwill:					
Cost at year-end	**119.2**	**117.9**	**69.5**	**69.5**	**69.5**
Accumulated depreciation at year-end	0.0	0.0	0.0	0.0	0.0
Net book value at year-end	**119.2**	**117.9**	**69.5**	**69.5**	**69.5**
Additions (other than acquisitions)	1.3	48.4	0.0	0.0	
Disposals	0.0	0.0	0.0	0.0	
Depreciation charge	0.0	0.0	0.0	0.0	
Other changes in the net book value (exchange differences, acquisitions, etc.)	(0.0)	0.0	0.0	0.0	
Computer software:					
Cost at year-end	**102.9**	**82.9**	**51.2**	**42.3**	**32.8**
Accumulated depreciation at year-end	(56.6)	(34.6)	(18.7)	(27.0)	(19.8)
Net book value at year-end	**46.3**	**48.3**	**32.5**	**15.3**	**13.0**
Additions (other than acquisitions)	1.9	18.6		0.2	
Transfers (from computer software under development)	18.0	12.5		9.5	
Depreciation charge	22.0	15.9		7.4	
Other changes in the net book value (exchange differences, acquisitions, etc.)	0.1	0.6	17.2	0.0	
Computer software under development:					
Cost at year-end	**178.8**	**78.0**	**25.4**	**6.7**	**5.6**
Accumulated depreciation at year-end	0.0	0.0	0.0	0.0	0.0
Net book value at year-end	**178.8**	**78.0**	**25.4**	**6.7**	**5.6**
Additions (other than acquisitions)	118.8	65.1	46.2	10.7	
Transfers (to computer software)	18.0	12.5	25.9	9.5	
Depreciation charge	0.0	0.0	0.0	0.0	
Other changes in the net book value (disposals etc.)	0.0	0.0	(1.6)	(0.1)	

Leases

(£ millions)	2009/2008	2008/2007	2007/2006	2006/2005	2005/2004
Finance leases:					
Minimum lease payments, not later than one year	18.3	11.6	7.1	4.8	5.5
Minimum lease payments, later than one year but not later than five years	51.3	45.4	19.5	9.8	13.6
Minimum lease payments, later than five years	209.4	214.9	196.0	197.7	201.2
Total minimum lease payments	**279.0**	**271.9**	**222.6**	**212.3**	**220.3**

Marks and Spencer's accounting choices

(continued)

(£ millions)	2009/2008	2008/2007	2007/2006	2006/2005	2005/2004
Present value of finance lease obligations:					
– current	13.7	6.2	4.4	2.7	4.4
– non-current	88.2	77.3	57.2	47.5	49.5
Operating leases:					
Minimum lease payments, not later than one year	44.0	17.9	10.6	10.2	13.3
Minimum lease payments, later than one year but not later than five years	178.5	90.4	57.4	49.9	62.1
Minimum lease payments, later than five years but not later than 25 years	2,464.4	2,223.6	1,778.3	1,724.4	1,658.1
Minimum lease payments, later than 25 years	1,488.0	1,551.1	1,527.6	1,515.4	1,554.7
Total minimum lease payments	**4,174.9**	**3,883.0**	**3,373.9**	**3,299.9**	**3,288.2**

Post-retirement benefits

(£ millions)	2009/2008	2008/2007	2007/2006	2006/2005	2005/2004
A. Pensions and other post-retirement assets/liabilities:					
Total market value of assets	3,977.0	5,045.5	5,227.5	4,606.2	3,956.8
Present value of scheme liabilities	(4,112.4)	(4,542.3)	(5,487.0)	(5,381.3)	(4,611.0)
Net funded pension plan (deficit)/asset	**(135.4)**	**503.2**	**(259.5)**	**(775.1)**	**(654.2)**
Unfunded retirement benefits	(1.0)	(1.3)	(1.2)	(1.7)	(2.5)
Postretirement healthcare	(15.8)	(18.4)	(22.6)	(18.1)	(19.3)
Net retirement benefit (deficit)/asset	**(152.2)**	**483.5**	**(283.3)**	**(794.9)**	**(676.0)**
B. Pensions and other post-retirement benefits/expenses:					
Current service cost	72.2	106.1	113.9	109.9	113.8
Curtailment gain	(5.0)	(3.0)	(2.0)	(13.0)	(14.0)
Exceptional pension credit	(231.3)	(95.0)	0.0	0.0	0.0
Operating cost	**(164.1)**	**8.1**	**111.9**	**96.9**	**99.8**
Expected return on plan assets	(334.6)	(342.7)	(282.0)	(265.5)	(248.3)
Interest on scheme liabilities	299.2	283.8	261.2	248.0	236.9
Finance cost	**(35.4)**	**(58.9)**	**(20.8)**	**(17.5)**	**(11.4)**
Service cost and finance cost of discontinued operations	0.0	0.0	0.0	1.3	3.4
Curtailment gain on disposal of Financial Services	0.0	0.0	0.0	0.0	(7.0)
Total (operating + finance cost)	**(199.5)**	**(50.8)**	**91.1**	**80.7**	**84.8**
C. Assumptions:					
Rate of increase in salaries	1.0%	3.1 – 4.5%	3.7%	3.7%	3.7%
Discount rate	6.8%	6.8%	5.3%	4.9%	5.5%
Inflation rate	2.9%	3.5%	3.0%	2.9%	2.9%
Long-term healthcare cost increase	7.9%	8.5%	8.0%	7.9%	7.9%

Marks and Spencer's accounting choices

(continued)

(£ millions)	2009/2008	2008/2007	2007/2006	2006/2005	2005/2004
D. Pension plan assets and expected rates of return					
Property partnership interest	13.3%	10.0%	9.5%	0%	0%
	(7.1%)	(6.0%)	(5.5%)	(–)	(–)
UK equities	12.1%	15.6%	15.8%	17%	26%
	(8.0%)	(8.3%)	(8.4%)	(8.0%)	(8.1%)
Overseas equities	16.2%	22.0%	26.5%	30%	27%
	(8.0%)	(8.3%)	(8.4%)	(8.0%)	(8.4%)
Government bonds	3.2%	9.6%	6.9%	16%	31%
	(4.2%)	(4.6%)	(4.7%)	(4.3%)	(4.8%)
Corporate bonds	57.3%	40.6%	41.2%	27%	13%
	(6.8%)	(6.0%)	(5.3%)	(4.9%)	(5.5%)
Cash and other	2.1%	2.1%	0.1%	10%	3%
	(4.2%)	(5.0%)	(5.5%)	(4.5%)	(3.8%)
	100%	**100%**	**100%**	**100%**	**100%**
	(7.2%)	**(6.7%)**	**(6.6%)**	**(6.2%)**	**(6.7%)**
E. Other information:					
Participants: active members	21000	24000	27000	31000	35000
Participants: deferred members	57000	58000	57000	57000	56000
Participants: pensioners	42000	39000	37000	38000	36000
Employer contributions	92.1	111.1	611.3	130.2	156.4
Employee contributions	2.0	1.0	0.0	0.0	0.0
Benefits paid	226.5	220.4	191.8	164.2	160.1
Actual return on plan assets	(945.7)	(79.9)	201.6	720.2	326.3
Cumulative actuarial (gains) and losses recognized in equity at year end	(1,257.3)	(330.2)	(935.6)	(927.0)	(757.7)

Marks and Spencer's accounting choices

EXHIBIT 3   Marks and Spencer Group – notes about the partnership liability

Note 22 Partnership liability to the Marks & Spencer UK Pension Scheme (2007/2006 financial statements)

The partnership liability to the Marks & Spencer UK Pension Scheme of £496.9m (last year £nil) relates to the amortizing liability in respect of the obligations of the Marks and Spencer Scottish Limited Partnership to the Marks & Spencer UK Pension Scheme. The Group has agreed a plan with the Pension Scheme Trustee to address the majority of the deficit by transferring properties with a current market value of £1.1bn into a partnership established by the Group. A limited interest in this partnership was contributed to the Pension Scheme on 13 March 2007. The Group retains control over these properties, including the flexibility to substitute alternative properties. The properties held in the partnership have been leased back to Marks and Spencer plc. The pension scheme is entitled to a distribution from the profits of the partnership of £50m per annum for 15 years from July 2008. The Group has the right to buy out the Trustee's partnership interest at any point for an amount equal to the net present value of the remaining annual distributions due to the pension scheme.

Each year the obligation will reduce as payments are made to the pension scheme by the partnership and an interest charge will be taken to the income statement representing the unwinding of the discounted obligation at an implied interest rate of 5.32 percent. The fair value of this liability was £495.3m (last year £nil).

Note 21 Partnership liability to the Marks & Spencer UK Pension Scheme (2009/2008 financial statements)

Last year the partnership liability of £723.2m related to an amortizing liability in respect of obligations of the Marks and Spencer Scottish Limited Partnership to the Marks & Spencer UK Pension Scheme. During the year an interest charge of £38.0m was taken to the income statement representing the unwinding of the discount included in this obligation at an implied average interest rate of 5.7 percent (last year 5.7 percent).

On 25 March 2009 the terms of the Scottish Limited Partnership agreement were amended to make the payment by the Scottish Limited Partnership of annual distributions to the Pension Scheme discretionary at the instance of Marks and Spencer plc in relation to financial years 2010/11 onwards. This discretion is exercisable if the Group does not pay a dividend or make any other form of return to its shareholders. As a result, the distributions to the Pension Scheme in 2009 and 2010 remain as financial liabilities, while the remaining financial instrument is now an equity instrument (see note 26).

The agreement includes a clause such that, following a default event (including the appointment of an administrator, liquidator, receiver, or similar officer in respect of Marks and Spencer plc or Marks and Spencer Group plc and the winding up or dissolution of Marks and Spencer plc or Marks and Spencer Group plc) or on a relevant change of law, the net present value of the outstanding distributions becomes payable to the Pension Scheme by the Scottish Limited Partnership at the option of the Pension Scheme. On the basis of the expected cash flows associated with such an event, the related financial liability has been fair valued at nil.

Financial Analysis

The goal of financial analysis is to assess the performance of a firm in the context of its stated goals and strategy. There are two principal tools of financial analysis: ratio analysis and cash flow analysis. **Ratio analysis** involves assessing how various line items in a firm's financial statements relate to one another. Cash flow analysis allows the analyst to examine the firm's liquidity, and how the firm is managing its operating, investment, and financing cash flows.

Financial analysis is used in a variety of contexts. Ratio analysis of a company's present and past performance provides the foundation for making forecasts of future performance. As we will discuss in later chapters, financial forecasting is useful in company valuation, credit evaluation, financial distress prediction, security analysis, and mergers and acquisitions analysis.

RATIO ANALYSIS

The value of a firm is determined by its profitability and growth. As shown in Figure 5.1, the firm's growth and profitability are influenced by its product market and financial market strategies. The product market strategy is implemented through the firm's competitive strategy, operating policies, and investment decisions. Financial market strategies are implemented through financing and dividend policies.

Thus the four levers managers can use to achieve their growth and profit targets are:

1 Operating management.
2 Investment management.
3 Financing strategy.
4 Dividend policies.

The objective of ratio analysis is to evaluate the effectiveness of the firm's policies in each of these areas. Effective ratio analysis involves relating the financial numbers to the underlying business factors in as much detail as possible. While ratio analysis may not give all the answers to an analyst regarding the firm's performance, it will help the analyst frame questions for further probing.

In ratio analysis, the analyst can:

1 Compare ratios for a firm over several years (a time-series comparison).
2 Compare ratios for the firm and other firms in the industry (cross-sectional comparison).
3 Compare ratios to some absolute benchmark.

In a **time-series comparison**, the analyst can hold firm-specific factors constant and examine the effectiveness of a firm's strategy over time. **Cross-sectional comparison** facilitates examining the relative performance of a firm within its industry, holding industry-level factors constant. For most ratios there are no absolute benchmarks. The exceptions are measures of rates of return, which can be compared to the cost of the capital associated with the investment. For example, subject to distortions caused by accounting, the rate of return on equity (ROE) can be compared to the cost of equity capital.

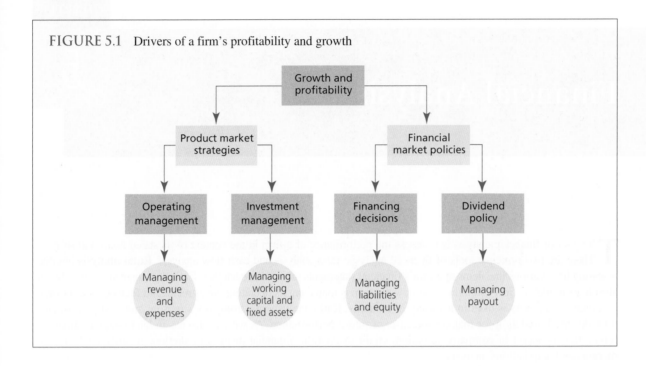

FIGURE 5.1 Drivers of a firm's profitability and growth

In the discussion below, we will illustrate these approaches using the example of apparel retailer Hennes & Mauritz AB (H&M). We will compare H&M's ratios for the fiscal year ending November 30, 2011, with its own ratios for the fiscal year ending November 30, 2010, and with the ratios of a group of competitors for the same fiscal years.[1] After seeing years of high growth and profitability, H&M's growth has slowed and its return on equity has fallen by 8 percentage points in 2011. Analyzing the company's performance over time therefore allows us to assess which factors contributed to the retailer's decreasing financial performance. Comparison of Hennes & Mauritz with its industry peers allows us to see the impact of different strategies on financial ratios. While pursuing a different competitive strategy, H&M also follows different investment and financing strategies than many of its industry peers. H&M holds, on average, more cash and securities to finance future acquisitions and uses less debt financing and shorter term leases than its peers. Further, Hennes & Mauritz outsources more of its production and invests less in inventories than its peers. We will illustrate how these differences among the companies affect their ratios. We will also try to see which strategy is delivering better performance for shareholders.

In order to facilitate replication of the ratio calculations presented below, we present in the Appendix to this chapter three versions of the financial statements of H&M. The first version is the one reported by the company in its annual reports. The second set of financial statements is presented in the standardized format described in Chapter 3. These "standardized and adjusted financial statements" not only put industry peers' financials in one standard format to facilitate direct comparison but also have been adjusted for one form of asset/liability understatement: the omission from the balance sheet of operating lease assets and liabilities. We also present H&M's financial statements in a third format in the appendices. These statements, labeled "Condensed Financial Statements," are essentially a recasting of the standardized and adjusted financial statements to facilitate the calculation of several ratios discussed in the chapter. We will discuss later in the chapter how this recasting process works.[2]

BACKGROUND INFORMATION ON HENNES & MAURITZ AND ITS INDUSTRY

General information

Sweden-based Hennes & Mauritz AB (occasionally referred to as H&M) is an internationally operating apparel retailer that is publicly listed on the Stockholm Stock Exchange. During the fiscal year ended November 30, 2011 (labeled fiscal 2011), the company employed close to 65,000 employees, operated

2,472 stores in more than 32 countries around the world, and generated close to €11.9 billion (SEK110 billion) of sales. In 2011 H&M derived about 66 percent of its total revenues from selling apparel within Europe. Sales in the US and the rest of the world accounted for 8 and 25 percent of total sales, respectively. In Scandinavia, Austria, Germany, the Netherlands, and the UK the apparel retailer also sold its products through catalogue and the Internet. At the end of 2011, H&M had plans to open 275 new stores worldwide and start Internet sales in the US in 2012.

Some of H&M's publicly listed European industry peers are: Benetton (Italy), Burberry (UK), Charles Voegele (Switzerland), Etam (France), French Connection (UK), Inditex (Spain), and Next (UK). With the exception of Inditex (109,512 employees; €13.8 billion sales in 2011), these competitors are significantly smaller than H&M, having between 7,312 and 52,569 employees and between €0.8 and €4.1 billion sales in 2011. H&M and its peers differ on some important dimensions other than size. Specifically, some peers, such as Benetton and Inditex, manage own manufacturing facilities to produce (part of) their assortment. In addition, whereas H&M operates on a global scale, some of its peers have focused their activities within a smaller group of countries (Charles Voegele, Etam, Next). Inditex, the Spain-based apparel retailer with brands such as Zara, Pull & Bear, and Massimo Dutti, most closely resembles H&M in terms of strategy and scale. Like H&M, Inditex follows a fast fashion strategy, which we describe below. Further, Inditex has a worldwide store network, just as H&M. In this chapter we therefore compare H&M's performance with that of Inditex and the average performance of six other peers (Benetton, Burberry, Charles Voegele, Etam, French Connection, and Next) separately.

The industry

H&M and its peers operate in the branded apparel segment of the retail industry. The apparel retail industry is a cyclical industry, implying that the demand for apparel typically depends on consumers' discretionary spending and varies with economic cycles. Accordingly, industry growth rates were negatively affected by the economic slowdown that followed the credit crisis of 2008.

The apparel retail industry is competitive. Around 2011, the following factors contributed to the industry's profit potential:

- Moderate growth. Industry growth was moderate to low because of the economic slowdown. Future growth rates of the global apparel retail industry were expected to be similar to recent growth rates, which had been close to 3 percent. Growth opportunities arose primarily in emerging markets and the online sales segment.
- Importance of pricing and supply chain management. With growth slowing, pricing decisions and inventory and supply chain management became even more important in preserving margins than they had been in the past.
- Perishable nature of fashion. Consumers' fastly changing tastes and expectations demanded from apparel retailers that they keep design and production cycles efficient and short. Only by doing so, could the retailers avoid inventory markdowns or write-offs.
- Sourcing of production. Motivated by the need to be price competitive, apparel retailers outsourced much of their production to low-cost labor markets. Production outsourcing introduced some risks. For example, it made quality control more challenging, complicated supply chain management, and made companies potentially subject to reputational damage from poor labor practices and conditions.
- Private labels and specialty retailing. One of the primary ways to differentiate was through branding. Related to this, selling private labels and specialty retailing had become increasingly popular. Private labels help apparel retailers to capture a bigger portion of the margin, become more flexible in responding to fashion trends, and build brand equity.
- Increasing input prices. Apparel retailers' product costs increased significantly during 2010 and 2011 as cotton prices reached historical levels.

The strategy

Hennes & Mauritz pursues a differentiation strategy, focusing on "fast fashion" retailing. The fast fashion retailing strategy is characterized by the following two features: the retailer (1) sells trendy, affordable products and (2) is able to respond quickly to changing trends by maintaining short production and lead times. Core competencies that help H&M to achieve this strategy are the following:

- In-house design. H&M employs more than 100 in-house designers. The retailer's designer teams work on several collections simultaneously and continuously monitor customer preferences to spot and anticipate new fashion trends.
- Competitive pricing. H&M is able to keep its prices affordable by being cost efficient. It does so, for example, by outsourcing production to about 700 independent manufacturers coordinated by self-operated production offices around the world.
- Brand. The H&M brand has high customer awareness, achieved through high-profile advertising campaigns and collaborations with star designers and celebrities. One of the brand values that H&M increasingly communicates to customers is that of a sustainable brand, being committed to supporting social development in production countries and reducing the environmental impact of its activities.
- Size and growth. H&M is pursuing a growth strategy, implying that it plans to expand its store network by 10 to 15 percent every year. This growth strategy helps H&M to achieve economies of scale in, for example, design, production (sourcing), and advertising. The expansion of H&M into emerging markets also helps the company to become less dependent on saturated mature markets. H&M's currently low dependence on debt financing and high profitability provides the retailer with the financial flexibility it needs to realize its growth plans.

Some of the activities that H&M undertakes as part of its strategy potentially reinforce each other, thus contributing to the strategy's sustainability. In particular, the retailer's carefully developed brand identity helps it to build customer loyalty, especially among its target group of young, fashion conscious customers. In addition, because of its superior design competencies H&M is able to frequently renew its assortment during a season and entice its target customers to make return visits to its stores, which further supports customer loyalty creation. Finally, the retailer's size and growth strategy help create the economies of scale that make it price competitive. H&M's strong brand name, high customer loyalty, superior fast fashion design team, and price competitiveness thus jointly contribute to achieving high inventory turnover, little to no inventory markdowns, and superior margins. By the end of 2011 the sustainability of H&M's strategy was, however, not undisputed. In fact, analysts of Morgan Stanley argued that H&M's declining performance signaled that the retailer's superior performance was the result of high operational efficiency rather than a sustainable competitive advantage.

H&M's strategy is, of course, not without risks. The retailer's international expansion and production make its profitability sensitive to foreign exchange rate fluctuations, as evidenced by the 6 percent negative impact of exchange rate changes on 2011 sales. H&M is also strongly dependent on its 700 suppliers. Unexpected interruptions in deliveries could seriously increase production and lead times and impair the company's fast fashion strategy. Further, after a decrease in demand during 2008 and 2009 cotton suppliers had reduced production, which resulted in increasing cotton prices when the demand for cotton recovered in 2010 and 2011. Because H&M uses much cotton in its garments, inflation in cotton prices adversely affects the retailer's profit margin. Finally, H&M's focus on the low-priced segment of the market makes the retailer vulnerable to competition from general merchandise retailers or discount apparel retailers such as Primark. To counter this risk, the company had started to introduce new brands and store concepts (such as "& Other Stories"), typically focused on the higher priced segments of the market.

Measuring overall profitability

The starting point for a systematic analysis of a firm's performance is its return on equity (ROE), defined as

$$\text{ROE} = \frac{\text{Net profit}}{\text{Shareholders' equity}}$$

ROE is a comprehensive indicator of a firm's performance because it provides an indication of how well managers are employing the funds invested by the firm's shareholders to generate returns. On average, over long periods, large publicly traded firms in Europe generate ROEs in the range of 8 to 10 percent.

In the long run, the value of the firm's equity is determined by the relationship between its ROE and its cost of equity capital. That is, those firms that are expected over the long run to generate ROEs in excess of the cost of equity capital should have market values in excess of book value, and vice versa. (We will return to this point in more detail in Chapter 7 on valuation.)

A comparison of ROE with the cost of capital is useful not only for contemplating the value of the firm but also in considering the path of future profitability. The generation of consistent supernormal profitability will, absent significant barriers to entry, attract competition. For that reason, ROEs tend over time to be driven by competitive forces toward a "normal" level – the cost of equity capital. Thus one can think of the cost of equity capital as establishing a benchmark for the ROE that would be observed in a long-run competitive equilibrium. Deviations from this level arise for two general reasons. One is the industry conditions and competitive strategy that cause a firm to generate supernormal (or subnormal) economic profits, at least over the short run. The second is distortions due to accounting.

In computing ROE, one can either use the beginning equity, ending equity, or an average of the two. Conceptually, the average equity is appropriate, particularly for rapidly growing companies. However, for most companies, this computational choice makes little difference as long as the analyst is consistent. Therefore, in practice most analysts use ending balances for simplicity. This comment applies to all ratios discussed in this chapter where one of the items in the ratio is a flow variable (items in the income statement or cash flow statement) and the other item is a stock variable (items in the balance sheet). Because of its conceptual superiority, throughout this chapter we use the average balances of the stock variables.

Table 5.1 shows the ROE based on reported earnings for Hennes & Mauritz and its industry peers. Hennes & Mauritz's ROE declined from 44.1 to 35.8 percent between 2010 and 2011 despite a moderate increase in sales (of 1.4 percent), suggesting that the unfavorable market conditions affected the company's performance disproportionally compared to its sales. Compared to historical trends of ROE in the European economy, Hennes & Mauritz's earnings performance in 2011 can be viewed as being significantly above average. Further, its ROE in 2011 is more than adequate to cover reasonable estimates of its cost of equity capital.[3]

TABLE 5.1 Return on equity for Hennes & Mauritz and its industry peers

Ratio	H&M 2011	H&M 2010	Inditex 2011	Other peers 2011
Return on equity	35.8%	44.1%	28.0%	22.8%

In 2011 Hennes & Mauritz's performance was also ahead of its peers' ROE. In particular, Inditex's ROE was 28.0 percent, a decrease from 29.5 percent in 2010. The average ROE of H&M's other peers showed a moderate decrease from 23.3 to 22.8 percent. At that performance the industry peers were also earning excess returns relative to the historical trends of ROE in the economy, as well as to their own cost of equity. Hennes & Mauritz's superior performance relative to its peers is reflected in the difference in the companies' ratio of market value of equity to book value. As we will discuss in Chapter 7, ROE is a key determinant of a company's market to book ratio. As of November 30, 2011, Hennes & Mauritz's market value to book value ratio was 8.0, while the same ratio was 5.6 for Inditex and 3.7 for the other apparel retailers.

Decomposing profitability: Traditional approach

A company's ROE is affected by two factors: how profitably it employs its assets and how big the firm's asset base is relative to shareholders' investment. To understand the effect of these two factors, ROE can be decomposed into return on assets (ROA) and a measure of financial leverage, the equity multiplier, as follows:

$$\text{ROE} = \text{ROA} \times \text{Equity multiplier}$$
$$= \frac{\text{Net profit}}{\text{Total assets}} \times \frac{\text{Total assets}}{\text{Equity}}$$

ROA tells us how much profit a company is able to generate for each euro of assets invested. The equity multiplier indicates how many euros of assets the firm is able to deploy for each euro invested by its shareholders.

The ROA itself can be decomposed as a product of two factors:

$$\text{ROA} = \frac{\text{Net profit}}{\text{Sales}} \times \frac{\text{Sales}}{\text{Total assets}}$$

The ratio of net profit to sales is called net profit margin or return on sales (ROS); the ratio of sales to total assets is known as asset turnover. The profit margin ratio indicates how much the company is able to keep as profits for each euro of sales it makes. Asset turnover indicates how many sales euros the firm is able to generate for each euro of its assets.

Table 5.2 displays the three drivers of ROE for our apparel retailers: net profit margins, asset turnover, and equity multipliers. In 2011 Hennes & Mauritz's decrease in ROE is largely driven by a decrease in its net profit margin and, to a lesser extent, a decrease in its asset turnover. In fact, its financial leverage slightly increased, which weakly helped to cushion its deteriorating operating performance. Despite the decline in performance, H&M has superior operating performance relative to the other industry peers, as indicated by its higher ROA. The retailer's ROA is lower than Inditex's ROA because after a decrease in asset turnover from 1.05 to 1.01 H&M currently generates six cents of sales less than Inditex for each euro invested in assets. H&M's operating performance is, however, leveraged by its more aggressive financial management relative to Inditex, which causes its ROE to exceed that of Inditex.

TABLE 5.2 Traditional decomposition of ROE

Ratio	H&M 2011	H&M 2010	Inditex 2011	Other peers 2011
Net profit margin (ROS)	14.4%	17.2%	14.1%	7.4%
× Asset turnover	1.01	1.05	1.07	0.84
= Return on assets (ROA)	14.6%	18.0%	15.1%	6.2%
× Equity multiplier	2.46	2.45	1.86	3.71
= Return on equity (ROE)	35.8%	44.1%	28.0%	22.8%

Decomposing profitability: Alternative approach

Even though the above approach is popularly used to decompose a firm's ROE, it has several limitations. In the computation of ROA, the denominator includes the assets claimed by all providers of capital to the firm, but the numerator includes only the earnings available to equity holders. The assets themselves include both operating assets and investment assets such as minority equity investments and excess cash. Further, net profit includes profit from operating and investment activities, as well as interest income and expense, which are consequences of financing decisions. Often it is useful to distinguish between these sources of performance for at least two reasons:

1 As we will see in Chapters 6 through 8, valuing operating assets requires different tools from valuing investment assets. Specifically, financial statements include much detailed information about the financial and risk consequences of operating activities, which enables the analyst to take an informed approach to the analysis and valuation of such activities. In contrast, what comprises the investment assets and drives their profitability is often not easily identified from the financial statements, thus forcing the analyst to use shortcut methods or rely on a firm's own fair value disclosures to assess the value of such assets.

2 Operating, investment, and financing activities contribute differently to a firm's performance and value and their relative importance may vary significantly across time and firms. For example, as we will show in this chapter, whereas close to 16 percent of H&M's business assets consist of investment assets that earn an average return of less than 3 percent, the retailer's industry peers have only 7 percent of their capital invested in such low-performing investment assets. Mixing operating with investment assets would obfuscate the effect that these investments have on retailers' performance. Further, an increase in financial leverage may not only have a direct positive effect on return on equity but also an indirect negative effect through increasing a firm's financial risk and borrowing costs. The traditional decomposition of ROE does not make this explicit: whereas the equity multiplier reflects the direct effect of leverage, the net profit margin reflects the indirect effect.

Finally, the financial leverage ratio used above does not recognize the fact that some of a firm's liabilities are in essence non-interest-bearing operating liabilities. These issues are addressed by an alternative approach to decomposing ROE discussed below.

Before discussing this alternative ROE decomposition approach, we need to define some terminology (see Table 5.3) used in this section as well as in the rest of this chapter.

TABLE 5.3 Definitions of accounting items used in ratio analysis

Item	Definition
Income statement items	
Interest expense after tax	Interest expense × (1 − Tax rate)[a]
Net investment profit after tax (NIPAT)	(Investment income + Interest income) × (1 − Tax rate)
Net operating profit after taxes (NOPAT)	Net profit − Net investment profit after tax + Net interest expense after tax
Balance sheet items	
Operating working capital	(Current assets − Excess cash and marketable securities) − (Current liabilities − Current debt and current portion of non-current debt)[b]
Net non-current operating assets	Non-current tangible and intangible assets + Derivatives − (Net) deferred tax liability − Non-interest-bearing non-current liabilities
Investment assets	Minority equity investments + Other non-operating investments + Excess cash and marketable securities
Operating assets	Operating working capital + Net non-current operating assets
Business assets	Operating assets + Investment assets
Debt	Total interest-bearing non-current liabilities + Current debt and current portion of non-current debt
Capital	Debt + Group equity

a. This calculation treats interest expense as absolute value, independent of how this figure is reported in the income statement.
b. Excess cash and marketable securities is defined as total cash and marketable securities minus the cash balance needed for operations. In the analysis of Hennes & Mauritz and its peers, we set the cash balance needed for operations equal to 8 percent of sales, the long-term average cash balance in the European apparel retail industry.

We use the terms defined in Table 5.3 to recast the financial statements of Hennes & Mauritz and industry peers. H&M's recast financial statements, which are shown in the appendices to this chapter, are used to decompose ROE in the following manner:

$$ROE = \frac{NOPAT + NIPAT}{Equity} - \frac{Interest\ expense\ after\ tax}{Equity}$$

$$= \frac{NOPAT + NIPAT}{Business\ assets} \times \frac{Business\ assets}{Equity} - \frac{Interest\ expense\ after\ tax}{Debt} \times \frac{Debt}{Equity}$$

$$= \frac{NOPAT + NIPAT}{Business\ assets} \left(1 + \frac{Debt}{Equity}\right) - \frac{Interest\ expense\ after\ tax}{Debt} \times \frac{Debt}{Equity}$$

= Return on business assets

+ (Return on business assets − Effective interest rate after tax) × Financial leverage

= Return on business assets + Spread × Financial leverage

Return on business assets is a measure of how profitably a company is able to deploy its operating and investment assets to generate profits. This would be a company's ROE if it were financed with all equity. Spread is the incremental economic effect from introducing debt into the capital structure. This economic effect of borrowing is positive as long as the return on business assets is greater than the cost of borrowing. Firms that do not earn adequate business returns to pay for interest cost, reduce their ROE by borrowing. Both the positive and negative effect is magnified by the extent to which a firm borrows relative to its equity base. The ratio of debt to equity provides a measure of this financial leverage. A firm's spread times its financial leverage, therefore, provides a measure of the financial leverage gain to the shareholders.

To separate the effect on profitability of a firm's investments from its operating activities the return on business assets (ROBA) can be split up into an operating and an investment component:

$$
\begin{aligned}
ROBA &= \frac{NOPAT}{Business\ Assets} + \frac{NIPAT}{Business\ Assets} \\
&= \frac{NOPAT}{Operating\ assets} \times \frac{Operating\ assets}{Business\ assets} + \frac{NIPAT}{Investment\ assets} \times \frac{Investment\ assets}{Business\ assets} \\
&= Return\ on\ operating\ assets \times \frac{Operating\ assets}{Business\ assets} + Return\ on\ investment\ assets \times \frac{Investment\ assets}{Business\ assets}
\end{aligned}
$$

In words, the return that a firm earns on its business assets is a weighted average of its return on operating assets and its return on non-operating investments. For the average European firm the return on investment assets is lower than the return on operating assets. Therefore, non-operating investments typically decrease the return on business assets relative to the return on operating assets.

Finally, return on operating assets can be further decomposed into NOPAT margin and operating asset turnover as follows:

$$
Return\ on\ operating\ assets = \frac{NOPAT}{Sales} \times \frac{Sales}{Operating\ assets}
$$

NOPAT margin is a measure of how profitable a company's sales are from an operating perspective. Operating asset turnover measures the extent to which a company is able to use its operating assets to generate sales.

Table 5.4 presents the decomposition of ROE for Hennes & Mauritz and its peers. The ratios in this table show that there is a significant difference between H&M's ROA and its return on business assets (ROBA). In 2011, for example, H&M's ROA was 14.6 percent, while its ROBA was 18.2 percent. This difference between the retailer's ROBA and ROA can be largely attributed to the company's current operating liabilities, such as trade payables, and (non-interest-bearing) deferred tax liabilities, which reduce the amount of net operating assets relative to the amount of total assets. The difference between H&M's ROA and its return on operating assets is even more remarkable: its return on operating assets in 2011 was 21.1 percent, or 6.5 percentage points above the ROA. One of the reasons that H&M's return on operating assets is dramatically larger than its ROA is that the firm holds a significant amount of excess cash and marketable securities (of estimably 11 percent of sales), most likely to finance its future expansion investments. As indicated, we classify excess cash as a (non-operating) investment asset. At 28.7 percent, Inditex's return on operating assets is significantly larger than Hennes & Mauritz's. This superior operating performance of

TABLE 5.4 Distinguishing operating, investment and financing components in ROE decomposition

Ratio	H&M 2011	H&M 2010	Inditex 2011	Other peers 2011
Net operating profit margin	15.0%	18.1%	14.4%	9.2%
× Operating asset turnover	1.41	1.46	1.99	1.18
= Return on operating assets	21.1%	26.5%	28.7%	10.9%
Return on operating assets	21.1%	26.5%	28.7%	10.9%
× (Operating assets/business assets)	0.84	0.83	0.72	0.93
+ Return on investment assets	2.8%	1.7%	0.5%	1.8%
× (Investment assets/business assets)	0.16	0.17	0.28	0.07
= Return on business assets	18.2%	22.2%	20.9%	10.3%
Spread	15.9%	19.6%	18.7%	6.9%
× Financial leverage	1.11	1.11	0.38	1.83
= Financial leverage gain	17.6%	21.8%	7.1%	12.6%
ROE = Return on business assets				
+ financial leverage gain	35.8%	44.0%	28.0%	22.8%

Inditex would have been obscured by using the simple ROA measure. This shows that, for at least some firms, it is important to adjust the simple ROA to take into account non-operating investments and financial structure.

The decomposition of returns on business assets into investment and operating returns shows that the returns on operating assets of H&M and Inditex were substantially larger than their returns on business assets in 2011. This is because the retailers invested 16 and 28 percent, respectively, in low-earning investment assets such as marketable securities. Although these typically liquid and low-risk investments were likely needed to finance the firms' growth plans, their immediate effect was to reduce overall business performance.

The appropriate benchmark for evaluating return on business assets is the weighted average cost of debt and equity capital, or WACC.[4] In the long run, the value of the firm's assets is determined by where return on business assets stands relative to this norm. Moreover, over the long run and absent some barrier to competitive forces, return on business assets will tend to be pushed toward the weighted average cost of capital. Since the WACC is lower than the cost of equity capital, return on business assets tends to be pushed to a level lower than that to which ROE tends. The average return on business assets for large firms in Europe, over long periods of time, is in the range of 7 to 9 percent. Hennes & Mauritz's return on business assets in 2011 exceeds this range, indicating that its operating and investment performance is above average.

Although the NOPAT margins of Inditex and Hennes & Mauritz were similar in 2011, one year earlier H&M still had a substantially better NOPAT margin than Inditex. Because H&M is operating in the lower-priced segment of the apparel industry and presumably is not asking significantly higher premium prices than Inditex, H&M's higher NOPAT margin seems to be the result of its higher operating efficiency. Inditex's higher operating asset turnover shows that the company is able to utilize its operating assets efficiently enough to compensate for the lower margins on its sales.

Hennes & Mauritz is also able to create shareholder value through its financing strategy. In 2010 the spread between H&M's return on business assets and its after-tax interest cost was 19.6 percent; its debt as a percent of its equity was 111 percent. Both these factors contributed to a net increment of 21.8 percent to its ROE. Thus, while H&M's return on business assets in 2011 was 22.2 percent, its ROE was 44.0 percent. In 2011 H&M's spread decreased to 15.9 percent, its financial leverage remained constant at 111 percent, leading to an 18.2 percent net increment to ROE due to its debt policy. With a return on business assets of 18.2 percent in that year, its ROE went down to 35.8 percent.

Inditex had low leverage in 2011, to the tune of 38 percent. As a result, even though Inditex had a positive spread of 18.7 percent, it had a relatively modest financial leverage gain of 7.1 percent. This financial leverage gain helped to produce a ROE of 28.0 percent, which was less than H&M's ROE in spite of Inditex's superior operating performance. With a higher level of leverage, Inditex could have exploited its spread to produce an even higher ROE. Note that an increase in Inditex's financial leverage would also raise its equity risk and, consequently, increase its cost of equity, thus reducing the benefits of leverage. Given the large spread, however, the higher cost of equity would not likely offset the higher financial leverage gain. We will discuss the relationship between leverage and the cost of equity in more detail in Chapter 8.

Assessing operating management: Decomposing net profit margins

A firm's net profit margin or ROS shows the profitability of the company's operating activities. Further decomposition of a firm's ROS allows an analyst to assess the efficiency of the firm's operating management. A popular tool used in this analysis is the common-sized income statement in which all the line items are expressed as a ratio of sales revenues. This type of analysis is also referred to as vertical analysis.

Common-sized income statements make it possible to compare trends in income statement relationships over time for the firm, and trends across different firms in the industry. Income statement analysis allows the analyst to ask the following types of questions:

1 Are the company's margins consistent with its stated competitive strategy? For example, a differentiation strategy should usually lead to higher gross margins than a low-cost strategy.

2 Are the company's margins changing? Why? What are the underlying business causes-changes in competition, changes in input costs, or poor overhead cost management?

3 Is the company managing its overhead and administrative costs well? What are the business activities driving these costs? Are these activities necessary?

To illustrate how the income statement analysis can be used, common-sized income statements for Hennes & Mauritz, Inditex and the other industry peers are shown in Table 5.5. The table also shows some commonly used

TABLE 5.5 Common-sized income statement and profitability ratios

Ratio	H&M 2011	H&M 2010	Inditex 2011	Other peers 2011
Line items as a percentage of sales				
Sales	100.0%	100.0%	100.0%	100.0%
Net operating expense	(80.1%)	(75.7%)	(81.1%)	(85.5%)
Other income/expense	0.0%	0.0%	0.1%	(0.8%)
Net operating profit before tax	19.9%	24.3%	19.0%	13.6%
Investment income	0.0%	0.0%	(0.1%)	0.0%
Interest income	0.5%	0.3%	0.2%	0.0%
Interest expense	(1.4%)	(1.6%)	(0.6%)	(2.7%)
Tax expense	(4.7%)	(5.8%)	(4.4%)	(3.6%)
Net profit	14.4%	17.2%	14.1%	7.4%
Net operating expense line items as a percent of sales (by nature)				
Personnel expense	(16.8%)	(15.3%)	(16.2%)	(18.5%)
Cost of materials	(39.5%)	(36.8%)	(40.7%)	(39.1%)
Depreciation and amortization	(13.4%)	(13.2%)	(13.3%)	(8.9%)
Other operating income/expense	(10.9%)	(10.4%)	(10.9%)	(19.0%)
Operating expense line items as a percent of sales (by function)				
Cost of sales	(39.9%)	(37.1%)	N.A.	N.A.
Selling, general, and administrative expense	(40.2%)	(38.7%)	N.A.	N.A.
Key profitability ratios				
Gross profit margin	60.1%	62.9%	N.A.	N.A.
EBITDA margin	33.8%	37.8%	32.5%	22.1%
NOPAT margin	15.0%	18.1%	14.4%	9.2%
Net profit margin	14.4%	17.2%	14.1%	7.4%

profitability ratios. We will use the information in Table 5.5 to investigate why Hennes & Mauritz had a net profit margin (or return on sales) of 14.4 percent in 2011 and 17.2 percent in 2010, while Inditex and the other industry peers had net margins of 14.1 and 7.4 percent, respectively, in 2011. Hennes & Mauritz classifies its expenses by function in the income statement and discloses a classification of its expenses by nature in the notes to the financial statements. In contrast, Inditex and some of the other peers classify their expenses by nature only. Consequently, we can decompose H&M's net profit margins both by function and by nature, but can only compare expenses by nature.

Decomposition by function

Although not required to do so by the international accounting rules, some firms classify their operating expensing according to function. The decomposition of operating expenses by function is potentially more informative than the decomposition by nature. This is because the functional decomposition requires the firm to use judgment in dividing total operating expenses into expenses that are directly associated with products sold or services delivered (cost of sales) and expenses that are incurred to manage operations (selling, general, and administrative expense).

The difference between a firm's sales and cost of sales is gross profit. Gross profit margin is an indication of the extent to which revenues exceed direct costs associated with sales, and it is computed as

$$\text{Gross profit margin} = \frac{\text{Sales} - \text{Cost of Sales}}{\text{Sales}}$$

Gross margin is influenced by two factors: (1) the price premium that a firm's products or services command in the marketplace and (2) the efficiency of the firm's procurement and production process. The price premium a firm's products or services can command is influenced by the degree of competition and the extent to which its products are unique. The firm's cost of sales can be low when it can purchase its inputs at a lower cost than competitors and/or run its production processes more efficiently. This is generally the case when a firm has a low-cost strategy.

Table 5.5 indicates that Hennes & Mauritz's gross margin in 2011 decreased significantly to 60.1 percent. In 2011 steadily increasing cotton prices raised the production costs of fashion manufacturers and thus made it more expensive for H&M to source its products. In contrast, H&M's procurement costs were relatively low in 2010, also in comparison with previous years, because of temporary excess capacity at H&M's suppliers and low transportation costs. Given H&M's strategy of selling fashion at affordable prices, the retailer could not easily compensate for higher input prices by raising its selling prices. In fact, as a consequence of the economic slowdown H&M was forced to more frequently mark down its inventory to stimulate sales. Further, the appreciation of the Swedish Krona, H&M's reporting currency, relative to local currencies in several of H&M's output markets, negatively affected the retailer's sales by close to 6 percent. Increased input prices, more frequent inventory markdowns, and adverse currency exchange rate changes thus jointly contributed to an increase in H&M's cost of sales relative to sales in 2011. In addition to these external influences on the gross margin, in the second half of 2010 H&M's management had decided to improve the quality and design of its products and reduce selling prices of part of its assortment. This decision was intended to improve the retailer's asset turnover but at the same time reduce the retailer's gross margin.

A company's selling, general, and administrative (SG&A) expenses are influenced by the operating activities it has to undertake to implement its competitive strategy. As discussed in Chapter 2, firms with differentiation strategies have to undertake activities to achieve differentiation. A company competing on the basis of quality and rapid introduction of new products is likely to have higher R&D costs relative to a company competing purely on a cost basis. Similarly, a company that attempts to build a brand image, distribute its products through full-service retailers, and provide significant customer service, is likely to have higher selling and administration costs relative to a company that sells through warehouse retailers or direct mail and does not provide much customer support.

A company's SG&A expenses are also influenced by the efficiency with which it manages its overhead activities. The control of operating expenses is likely to be especially important for firms competing on the basis of low cost. However, even for differentiators, it is important to assess whether the cost of differentiation is commensurate with the price premium earned in the marketplace.

The ratio of SG&A expense to sales in Table 5.5 allows us to evaluate the effectiveness with which Hennes & Mauritz managed its SG&A expenses. This ratio shows how much a company is spending to generate each euro of sales. In 2011 H&M's SG&A-to-sales ratio increased from 38.7 percent to 40.2 percent. This increase continued a trend of growing SG&A expenses, which had been 36.0 percent of sales in 2007. One factor that potentially explains the increase in the SG&A-to-sales ratio is the stickiness of SG&A expenses. In particular, in periods during which sales per store decline, changes in selling expenditures typically lag behind sales changes, thus increasing the ratio of these costs to sales. This is because it is costly for firms to temporarily cut capacity in down periods and bring back capacity when sales recover. For example, in many countries labor regulations make it difficult to lay off personnel. Also, temporarily cutting back on personnel could be difficult in stores that require a minimum amount of staffing to function efficiently. To illustrate the effect of cost stickiness, consider H&M's SG&A expense on a per-store basis. In 2011 the ratio of SG&A to the average number of stores operated decreased by almost 6 percent, from SEK20.8 million to SEK19.6 million. This observation indicates that H&M's management kept its SG&A in control and underlines the usefulness of non-financial data, such as measures of store space, in dissecting the changes in cost-to-sales ratios.

Note that a retailer's expenditures on procurement can be just as sticky as selling expenditures. However, procurement costs that are related to unsold products end up on the firm's balance sheet as part of inventories. The temporary capitalization of these costs dampens the positive effect of sales declines on the cost of sales to sales ratio, though it leads to an increase in the inventories to sales ratio. We will return to this issue in the section on asset turnover.

Decomposition by nature

The international accounting rules require that all firms reporting under IFRS classify and disclose their operating expenses by nature, either in the income statement or in the notes to the financial statements. Like most firms, Hennes & Mauritz, Inditex, and the other industry peers distinguish four expense categories:

1 Cost of materials.
2 Personnel expense.
3 Depreciation and amortization.
4 Other operating expenses.

Table 5.5 indicates that Hennes & Mauritz experienced an increase in personnel expense in 2011. As argued earlier, this is possibly because personnel expenses tend to exhibit stickiness in the presence of a sales-per-store decline, given that it is costly to lay off personnel and often difficult to cut salaries. The increase in personnel costs worsened the operating margin by 1.5 percent. An advantage of classifying operating expenses by nature is that these expenses can be more easily related to their main drivers, such as the number of employees or the number of stores operated. This helps us to further analyze the development in Hennes & Mauritz's personnel expenses.

In 2011 Hennes & Mauritz's average workforce grew by 9.1 percent to 64,874 employees, which given the slowdown in sales growth, led to a reduction in employee productivity. In particular, sales per employee decreased by 7.1 percent to SEK1.7 million (or €183 thousand). In contrast, H&M's personnel cost per employee increased by 2.1 percent to SEK286 thousand per employee (which is equal to €31 thousand per employee), which in combination with the decrease in employee productivity led to the increase in the personnel expense-to-sales ratio. In 2011 Inditex spent on average €20.4 thousand per employee, up 1.7 percent from €20.1 thousand per employee in 2010, which illustrates that the company had a less expensive workforce than H&M. The difference in average cost per employee between H&M and Inditex can be partly attributed to the fact that Inditex operates its own manufacturing facilities and thus employs more low-cost production employees than H&M. Because of these manufacturing activities Inditex also needs a larger workforce than H&M, making Inditex's average employee productivity significantly lower at €126 thousand in sales per employee.

Note that, given Hennes & Mauritz outsources its production and therefore does not employ production personnel, one would expect that its personnel expense-to-sales ratio is lower than that of Inditex. This holds true if one takes into account the potential stickiness of personnel expenses. In particular, if H&M's sales per store in 2011 had remained constant at its 2010 level of SEK51.73 million, the retailer's 2011 total sales would have amounted to SEK121 billion and its personnel expense-to-sales ratio would have been 15.3 percent (18.5/121). This ratio is less than that of Inditex in 2011 (which was 16.2 percent) and equal to H&M's personnel expense-to-sales ratio in 2010. The increase in H&M's per-employee wage expense thus seems to be largely due to the stickiness of these expenses in times of a sales growth slowdown.

Hennes & Mauritz experienced a small increase in its depreciation and amortization expense of roughly 0.2 percent. An explanation for this increase, in addition to the decrease in store productivity, is that during 2010 and 2011 H&M invested in the refurbishment of many of its stores, as part of its efforts to improve asset turnover. H&M's and Inditex's depreciation and amortization-to-sales ratios are almost equal. The retailers' ratios are, however, significantly higher than those of their other industry peers. One factor explaining this is that H&M and Inditex tend to lease their stores at more central and hence more expensive locations. Because we capitalize leased assets, following the methods discussed in Chapter 4, before calculating ratios, the higher lease payments that H&M and Inditex make are reflected in the higher depreciation and amortization-to-sales ratios.

Hennes & Mauritz saw its cost of materials to sales ratio increase in 2011 from 36.8 to 39.5 percent, most likely because of an increase in the price for cotton. When we compare Hennes & Mauritz's with Inditex's cost of materials, we see that H&M's cost of materials as a percent of sales is slightly lower. This difference between the two retailers is somewhat surprising given that H&M purchases only finished products, whereas Inditex purchases both finished products and raw materials, which it uses in its production. The difference in cost of materials suggests that H&M has a greater price markup on its products or has more bargaining power over its suppliers, making its outsourcing strategy relatively efficient compared with Inditex's strategy to self-manufacture part of its assortment.

NOPAT margin and EBITDA margin

Given that Hennes & Mauritz and its peers are pursuing different pricing, distribution, marketing and production strategies, it is not surprising that they have different cost structures. The question is, when these costs are netted out, which company is performing better? Two ratios provide useful signals here: net operating profit margin (NOPAT margin) and EBITDA margin:

$$\text{NOPAT margin} = \frac{\text{NOPAT}}{\text{Sales}}$$

$$\text{EBITDA margin} = \frac{\text{Earnings before interest, taxes, depreciation and amortization}}{\text{Sales}}$$

NOPAT margin provides a comprehensive indication of the operating performance of a company because it reflects all operating policies and eliminates the effects of debt policy. EBITDA margin provides similar information, except that it excludes depreciation and amortization expense, a significant noncash operating expense. Some analysts prefer to use EBITDA margin because they believe that it focuses on "cash" operating items. While this is to some extent true, it can be potentially misleading for two reasons. EBITDA is not a strictly cash concept because sales, cost of sales, and SG&A expenses often include noncash items. Also, depreciation is a real operating expense, and it reflects to some extent the consumption of resources. Therefore, ignoring it can be misleading.

From Table 5.5 we see that H&M's NOPAT margin and EBITDA margin worsened between 2010 and 2011. Because of this development, in 2011 the company is able to retain only 15 cents in net operating profits for each euro of sales, which is still more than the 14.4 and 9.2 cents that Inditex and the other industry peers are able to retain. H&M also has a higher EBITDA margin than Inditex and the other industry peers.

Recall that in Table 5.3 we define NOPAT as net profit plus interest expense and minus investment profit after tax. Therefore, NOPAT is influenced by any non-operating income (expense) items included in net profit. We can calculate a "recurring" NOPAT margin by eliminating these items, which we labeled "Other Income, Net of Other Expense" in the standardized income statement. For the other industry peers, the average recurring NOPAT margin was 9.6 percent in 2011. The 2011 margin is higher than the NOPAT margin number we discussed above, suggesting that a portion of the retailers' expenses are related to sources other than its core, recurring operations and investments. These sources include impairment and foreign exchange rate losses that some of the firms reported in their financial statements. Recurring NOPAT may be a better benchmark to use when one is extrapolating current performance into the future because it reflects margins from the core business activities of a firm.

Tax expense

Taxes are an important element of firms' total expenses. Through a wide variety of tax planning techniques, firms can attempt to reduce their tax expenses.[5] There are two measures one can use to evaluate a firm's tax expense. One is the ratio of tax expense to sales, and the other is the ratio of tax expense to earnings before taxes (also known as the average tax rate). The firm's tax note provides a detailed account of why its average tax rate differs from the statutory tax rate.

When evaluating a firm's tax planning, the analyst should ask two questions: (1) Are the company's tax policies sustainable, or is the current tax rate influenced by one-time tax credits? (2) Do the firm's tax planning strategies lead to other business costs? For example, if the operations are located in tax havens, how does this affect the company's profit margins and asset utilization? Are the benefits of tax planning strategies (reduced taxes) greater than the increased business costs?

Table 5.5 shows that Hennes & Mauritz's tax rate decreased significantly between 2010 and 2011. Hennes & Mauritz's taxes as a percentage of sales were higher than those of Inditex and the other industry peers. One reason for this is that H&M's pretax profits as a percent of sales were higher. Further, despite the fact that the statutory tax rate of 30 percent in Inditex's country of domicile is higher than the statutory rate of 26.3 percent in H&M's country of domicile, Inditex is able to effectively pay a lower average rate than H&M by earning a greater proportion of its profits in low-tax countries. Specifically, in 2011 Inditex's effective tax rate was 24.0 percent (calculated as tax/[net profit + tax], i.e., 4.45%/[14.11% + 4.45%]), whereas H&M's and the other industry peers' effective tax rates were 24.5 percent (4.66%/[14.38% + 4.66%]) and 30.2 percent (3.18%/[7.37% + 3.18%]).

In summary, we conclude that Hennes & Mauritz's reduction in return on sales is primarily driven by an increase in the cost of sales-to-sales ratio – as the result of increased inventory markdowns, higher input prices, adverse exchange rate changes, and management's decision to improve product quality – and an increase in the SG&A-to-sales ratio – most likely as a result of selling costs' sticky behavior in the presence of a decline in store productivity. The company was able to reduce its tax expense, not only as a consequence of earning a lower pretax profit but also because it reduced its effective tax rate from 25.3 to 24.5 percent. In comparison with Inditex and the other industry peers, Hennes & Mauritz has a higher gross profit margin and a higher NOPAT margin, resulting from the retailer's high operating efficiency.

Evaluating investment management: Decomposing asset turnover

Asset turnover is the second driver of a company's return on equity. Since firms invest considerable resources in their assets, using them productively is critical to overall profitability. A detailed analysis of asset turnover allows the analyst to evaluate the effectiveness of a firm's investment management.

There are two primary areas of asset management: (1) working capital management and (2) management of non-current operating assets. Working capital is defined as the difference between a firm's current assets and current liabilities. However, this definition does not distinguish between operating components (such as trade receivables, inventories, and trade payables) and the financing and investment components (such as excess cash, marketable securities, and notes payable). An alternative measure that makes this distinction is operating working capital, as defined in Table 5.3:

$$\text{Operating working capital} = (\text{Current assets} - \text{Excess cash and marketable securities})$$
$$- (\text{Current liabilities} - \text{Current debt and current portion of non-current debt})$$

Working capital management

The components of operating working capital that analysts primarily focus on are trade receivables, inventories, and trade payables. A certain amount of investment in working capital is necessary for the firm to run its normal operations. For example, a firm's credit policies and distribution policies determine its optimal level of trade receivables. The nature of the production process and the need for buffer stocks determine the optimal level of inventories. Finally, trade payables are a routine source of financing for the firm's working capital, and payment practices in an industry determine the normal level of trade payables.

The following ratios are useful in analyzing a firm's working capital management: operating working capital as a percentage of sales, operating working capital turnover, trade receivables turnover, inventories turnover, and trade payables turnover. The turnover ratios can also be expressed in number of days of activity that the operating working capital (and its components) can support. The definitions of these ratios are as follows:

$$\text{Operating working capital to sales ratio} = \frac{\text{Operating working capital}}{\text{Sales}}$$

$$\text{Operating working capital to sales turnover} = \frac{\text{Sales}}{\text{Operating working capital}}$$

$$\text{Trade receivables turnover} = \frac{\text{Sales}}{\text{Trade receivables}}$$

$$\text{Inventories turnover} = \frac{\text{Cost of sales}}{\text{Inventories}} \quad \text{or} \quad \frac{\text{Cost of materials}}{\text{Inventories}}$$

$$\text{Trade payables turnover} = \frac{\text{Purchases}}{\text{Trade payables}} \quad \text{or} \quad \frac{\text{Cost of sales}}{\text{Trade payables}} \quad \text{or} \quad \frac{\text{Cost of materials}}{\text{Trade payables}}$$

$$\text{Days' receivables} = \frac{\text{Trade receivables}}{\text{Average sales per day}}$$

$$\text{Days' inventories} = \frac{\text{Inventories}}{\text{Average cost of sales per day}} \quad \text{or} \quad \frac{\text{Inventories}}{\text{Average cost of materials per day}}$$

$$\text{Days' payables} = \frac{\text{Trade payables}}{\text{Average purchases per day}} \quad \text{or} \quad \frac{\text{Trade payables}}{\text{Average cost of sales per day}}$$
$$\text{or} \quad \frac{\text{Trade payables}}{\text{Average cost of materials per day}}$$

Operating working capital turnover indicates how many euros of sales a firm is able to generate for each euro invested in its operating working capital. Trade receivables turnover, inventories turnover, and trade payables turnover allow the analyst to examine how productively the three principal components of working capital are being used. Days' receivables, days' inventories, and days' payables are another way to evaluate the efficiency of a firm's working capital management.[6]

Non-current assets management

Another area of investment management concerns the utilization of a firm's non-current operating assets. It is useful to define a firm's investment in non-current operating assets as follows:

$$\text{Net non-current operating assets} = (\text{Total non-current operating assets}$$
$$- \text{Non-interest-bearing non-current liabilities})$$

Non-current operating assets generally consist of net property, plant, and equipment (PP&E), intangible assets such as goodwill, and derivatives used to hedge operating risks. Non-interest-bearing non-current liabilities include such items as (net) deferred taxes.

The efficiency with which a firm uses its net non-current assets is measured by the following two ratios: net non-current assets as a percentage of sales and net non-current asset turnover. Net non-current operating asset turnover is defined as:

$$\text{Net non-current operating asset turnover} = \frac{\text{Sales}}{\text{Net non-current operating assets}}$$

PP&E is the most important non-current asset in a firm's balance sheet. The efficiency with which a firm's PP&E is used is measured by the ratio of PP&E to sales, or by the PP&E turnover ratio:

$$\text{PP\&E turnover} = \frac{\text{Sales}}{\text{Net property, plant and equipment}}$$

The ratios listed above allow the analyst to explore a number of business questions in four general areas:

1 How well does the company manage its inventories? Does the company use modern manufacturing techniques? Does it have good vendor and logistics management systems? If inventories ratios are changing, what is the underlying business reason? Are new products being planned? Is there a mismatch between the demand forecasts and actual sales?

2 How well does the company manage its credit policies? Are these policies consistent with its marketing strategy? Is the company artificially increasing sales by loading the distribution channels?

3 Is the company taking advantage of trade credit? Is it relying too much on trade credit? If so, what are the implicit costs?

4 Are the company's investment in plant and equipment consistent with its competitive strategy? Does the company have a sound policy of acquisitions and divestitures?

Table 5.6 shows the asset turnover ratios for Hennes & Mauritz and its peers. Between 2010 and 2011 Hennes & Mauritz became less efficient in its working capital management, as can be seen from the increase in operating working capital as a percentage of sales and the decrease in operating working capital turnover. Working capital management worsened because of decreases in trade receivables turnover and inventories turnover and an increase in trade payables turnover. The decrease in inventories turnover is consistent with the information disclosed by H&M that it experienced difficulty in selling its products and needed to mark down its inventory more frequently in 2011. In addition to the decrease in working capital turnover, Hennes & Mauritz's non-current operating asset utilization significantly worsened in 2011: both its net non-current operating asset turnover and its PP&E turnover decreased. These decreases in turnover signal that management's investments in the quality and design of H&M's apparel did not immediately deliver the sought-after improvements in store productivity.

TABLE 5.6 Asset management ratios

Ratio	H&M 2011	H&M 2010	Inditex 2011	Other peers 2011
Operating working capital/Sales	10.5%	10.0%	1.7%	16.5%
Net non-current operating assets/Sales	60.7%	58.3%	48.5%	68.2%
PP&E/Sales	59.8%	57.9%	48.8%	63.0%
Operating working capital turnover	9.56	9.96	58.61	6.04
Net non-current operating asset turnover	1.65	1.71	2.06	1.47
PP&E turnover	1.67	1.73	2.05	1.59
Trade receivables turnover	47.88	51.07	27.23	5.91
Days' receivables	7.5	7.0	13.2	61.0
Inventories turnover	3.44	3.67	4.50	2.90
Days' inventories	104.7	98.1	79.9	124.0
Trade payables turnover	10.51	10.45	2.26	3.89
Days' payables	34.2	34.4	159.0	92.5

Inditex managed its inventories more efficiently than H&M in 2011. Although the two retailers followed a similar fast fashion strategy, having its own manufacturing facilities helped Inditex to more promptly respond to changes in customers' tastes and demands. As a consequence, Inditex appeared more successful in the execution of the fast fashion strategy than H&M, as evidenced by its lower days' inventories. Consistent with this difference in success, Inditex also achieved better non-current operating asset utilization ratios in 2011 relative to Hennes & Mauritz. Because not all retailers in the group of other industry peers follow the same fast fashion strategy as Inditex and H&M, the other industry peers have lower inventory turnover and net non-current operating asset turnover (on average) than Inditex and H&M.

Evaluating financial management: Financial leverage

Financial leverage enables a firm to have an asset base larger than its equity. The firm can augment its equity through borrowing and the creation of other liabilities like trade payables, provisions, and deferred taxes. Financial leverage increases a firm's ROE as long as the cost of the liabilities is less than the return from investing these funds. In this respect it is important to distinguish between interest-bearing liabilities such as notes payable, other forms of current debt and non-current debt that carry an explicit interest charge, and other forms of liabilities. Some of these other forms of liability, such as trade payables or deferred taxes, do not carry any interest charge at all. Other liabilities, such as finance lease obligations or pension obligations, carry an implicit interest charge. Finally, some firms carry large cash balances or investments in marketable securities. These balances reduce a firm's net debt because conceptually the firm can pay down its debt using its cash and short-term investments.

While financial leverage can potentially benefit a firm's shareholders, it can also increase their risk. Unlike equity, liabilities have predefined payment terms, and the firm faces risk of financial distress if it fails to meet these commitments. There are a number of ratios to evaluate the degree of risk arising from a firm's financial leverage.

Current liabilities and short-term liquidity

The following ratios are useful in evaluating the risk related to a firm's current liabilities:

$$\text{Current ratio} = \frac{\text{Current assets}}{\text{Current liabilities}}$$

$$\text{Quick ratio} = \frac{\text{Cash and marketable securities} + \text{Trade receivables (net)}}{\text{Current liabilities}}$$

$$\text{Cash ratio} = \frac{\text{Cash and marketable securities}}{\text{Current liabilities}}$$

$$\text{Operating cash flow ratio} = \frac{\text{Cash flow from operations}}{\text{Current liabilities}}$$

All these ratios attempt to measure the firm's ability to repay its current liabilities. The first three compare a firm's current liabilities with its current assets that can be used to repay those liabilities. The fourth ratio focuses on the ability of the firm's operations to generate the resources needed to repay its current liabilities.

Since both current assets and current liabilities have comparable duration, the current ratio is a key index of a firm's short-term liquidity. Analysts view a current ratio of more than one to be an indication that the firm can cover its current liabilities from the cash realized from its current assets. However, the firm can face a short-term liquidity problem even with a current ratio exceeding one when some of its current assets are not easy to liquidate. Further, firms whose current assets have high turnover rates, such as food retailers, can afford to have current ratios below one. Quick ratio and cash ratio capture the firm's ability to cover its current liabilities from liquid assets. Quick ratio assumes that the firm's trade receivables are liquid. This is true in industries where the creditworthiness of the customers is beyond dispute, or when receivables are collected in a very short period. When these conditions do not prevail, cash ratio, which considers only cash and marketable securities, is a better indication of a firm's ability to cover its current liabilities in an emergency. Operating cash flow is another measure of the firm's ability to cover its current liabilities from cash generated from operations of the firm.

The liquidity ratios for Hennes & Mauritz and its peers are shown in Table 5.7. H&M's liquidity situation in 2010 was comfortable, thanks to its large cash balance and a sound operating cash flow. All of H&M's liquidity ratios worsened in 2011 but remained at acceptable levels. Also in 2011 the industry peers' current and quick ratios were significantly lower than those of H&M.

TABLE 5.7 Liquidity ratios

Ratio	H&M 2011	H&M 2010	Inditex 2011	Other peers 2011
Current ratio	2.83	3.12	1.98	1.47
Quick ratio	1.79	2.09	1.47	0.89
Cash ratio	1.63	1.92	1.28	0.33
Operating cash flow ratio	2.08	2.78	1.32	0.41

Debt and long-term solvency

A company's financial leverage is also influenced by its debt financing policy. There are several potential benefits from debt financing. First, debt is typically cheaper than equity because the firm promises predefined payment terms to debt holders. Second, in most countries, interest on debt financing is tax deductible whereas dividends to shareholders are not tax deductible. Third, debt financing can impose discipline on the firm's management and motivate it to reduce wasteful expenditures. Fourth, it is often easier for management to communicate their proprietary information on the firm's strategies and prospects to private lenders than to public capital markets. Such communication can potentially reduce a firm's cost of capital. For all these reasons, it is optimal for firms to use at least some debt in their capital structure. Too much reliance on debt financing, however, is potentially costly to the firm's shareholders. The firm will face financial distress if it defaults on the interest and principal payments. Debt holders also impose covenants on the firm, restricting the firm's operating, investment, and financing decisions.

The optimal capital structure for a firm is determined primarily by its business risk. A firm's cash flows are highly predictable when there is little competition or there is little threat of technological changes. Such firms have low business risk and hence they can rely heavily on debt financing. In contrast, if a firm's operating cash flows are highly volatile and its capital expenditure needs are unpredictable, it may have to rely primarily on equity financing. Managers' attitude toward risk and financial flexibility also often determine a firm's debt policies.

There are a number of ratios that help the analyst in this area. To evaluate the mix of debt and equity in a firm's capital structure, the following ratios are useful:

$$\text{Liabilities-to-equity ratio} = \frac{\text{Total liabilities}}{\text{Shareholders' equity}}$$

$$\text{Debt-to-equity ratio} = \frac{\text{Current debt} + \text{Non-current debt}}{\text{Shareholders equity}}$$

$$\text{Debt-to-capital ratio} = \frac{\text{Current debt} + \text{Non-current debt}}{\text{Current debt} + \text{Non-current debt} + \text{Shareholders' equity}}$$

The first ratio restates the assets-to-equity ratio (one of the three primary ratios underlying ROE) by subtracting one from it. The second ratio provides an indication of how many euros of debt financing the firm is using for each euro invested by its shareholders. The third ratio measures debt as a proportion of total capital. In calculating all the above ratios, it is important to include all interest-bearing obligations, whether the interest charge is explicit or implicit. Recall that examples of line items that carry an implicit interest charge include capital lease obligations and pension obligations. Analysts sometimes include any potential off-balance sheet obligations that a firm may have, such as noncancelable operating leases, in the definition of a firm's debt.

The ease with which a firm can meet its interest payments is an indication of the degree of risk associated with its debt policy. The interest coverage ratio provides a measure of this construct:

$$\text{Interest coverage (earning basis)} = \frac{\text{Net profit} + \text{Interest expense} + \text{Tax expense}}{\text{Interest expense}}$$

$$\text{Interest coverage (cash flow basis)} = \frac{\text{Cash flow from operations} + \text{Interest expense} + \text{Taxes paid}}{\text{Interest expense}}$$

One can also calculate coverage ratios that measure a firm's ability to measure all fixed financial obligations, such as interest payments, lease payments, and debt repayments, by appropriately redefining the numerator and denominator in the above ratios. In doing so it is important to remember that while some fixed charge payments, such as interest and lease rentals, are paid with pretax euros, others, such as debt repayments, are made with after-tax euros.

The earnings-based coverage ratio indicates the euros of earnings available for each euro of required interest payment; the cash flow-based coverage ratio indicates the euros of cash generated by operations for each euro of required interest payment. In both these ratios, the denominator is the interest expense. In the numerator we add taxes back because taxes are computed only after interest expense is deducted. A coverage ratio of one implies that the firm is barely covering its interest expense through its operating activities, which is a very risky situation. The larger the coverage ratio, the greater the cushion the firm has to meet interest obligations.

KEY ANALYSIS QUESTIONS

Some of the business questions to ask when the analyst is examining a firm's debt policies are:

- Does the company have enough debt? Is it exploiting the potential benefits of debt – interest tax shields, management discipline, and easier communication?

- Does the company have too much debt given its business risk? What type of debt covenant restrictions does the firm face? Is it bearing the costs of too much debt, risking potential financial distress and reduced business flexibility?

- What is the company doing with the borrowed funds? Investing in working capital? Investing in fixed assets? Are these investments profitable?

- Is the company borrowing money to pay dividends? If so, what is the justification?

We show debt and coverage ratios for Hennes & Mauritz and its peers in Table 5.8. Hennes & Mauritz's liabilities-to-equity and debt-to-capital ratios remained close to unchanged in 2011. The company's interest coverage decreased but remained at a comfortable level. Inditex's debt ratios indicate that it has been following a less aggressive debt policy than Hennes & Mauritz and the other industry peers. Its interest coverage ratios in 2011 are far above the other retailer's ratios. Overall, the interest coverage ratios illustrate that the apparel retailers' current earnings and cash flows are, on average, more than sufficient to cover their interest expenses.

TABLE 5.8 Debt and coverage ratios

Ratio	H&M 2011	H&M 2010	Inditex 2011	Other peers 2011
Liabilities-to-equity	1.46	1.44	0.86	2.70
Debt-to-equity	1.11	1.11	0.38	1.83
Debt-to-capital	0.53	0.53	0.28	0.65
Interest coverage (earnings based)	14.54	15.87	32.22	4.84
Interest coverage (cash flow based)	32.24	32.77	77.73	6.71

Ratios of disaggregated data

So far we have discussed how to compute ratios using information in the financial statements. Analysts often probe these ratios further by using disaggregated financial and physical data. For example, for a multi-business company, one could analyze the information by individual business segments. Such an analysis can reveal potential differences in the performance of each business unit, allowing the analyst to pinpoint areas where a company's strategy is working and where it is not. It is also possible to probe financial ratios further by computing ratios of physical data pertaining to a company's operations. The appropriate physical data to look at varies from industry to industry. As an example in retailing, one could compute productivity statistics such as sales per store, sales per square meter, customer transactions per store, and amount of sales per customer transaction; in the hotel industry, room occupancy rates provide important information; in the cellular telephone industry, acquisition cost per new subscriber and subscriber retention rate are important. These disaggregated ratios are particularly useful for young firms and young industries such as Internet firms, where accounting data may not fully capture the business economics due to conservative accounting rules.

Putting it all together: Assessing sustainable growth rate

Analysts often use the concept of sustainable growth as a way to evaluate a firm's ratios in a comprehensive manner. A firm's **sustainable growth rate** is defined as:

$$\text{Sustainable growth rate} = \text{ROE} \times (1 - \text{Dividend payout ratio})$$

We have already discussed the analysis of ROE in the previous four sections. The dividend payout ratio is defined as:

$$\text{Dividend payout ratio} = \frac{\text{Cash dividends paid}}{\text{Net profit}}$$

A firm's dividend payout ratio is a measure of its dividend policy. Firms pay dividends for several reasons. They provide a way for the firm to return to its shareholders any cash generated in excess of its operating and investment needs. When there are information asymmetries between a firm's managers and its shareholders, dividend payments can serve as a signal to shareholders about managers' expectation of the firm's future prospects. Firms may also pay dividends to attract a certain type of shareholder base.

Sustainable growth rate is the rate at which a firm can grow while keeping its profitability and financial policies unchanged. A firm's return on equity and its dividend payout policy determine the pool of funds available for growth. Of course the firm can grow at a rate different from its sustainable growth rate if its profitability, payout policy, or financial leverage changes. Therefore, the sustainable growth rate provides a benchmark against which a firm's growth plans can be evaluated. Figure 5.2 shows how a firm's sustainable growth rate can be linked to all

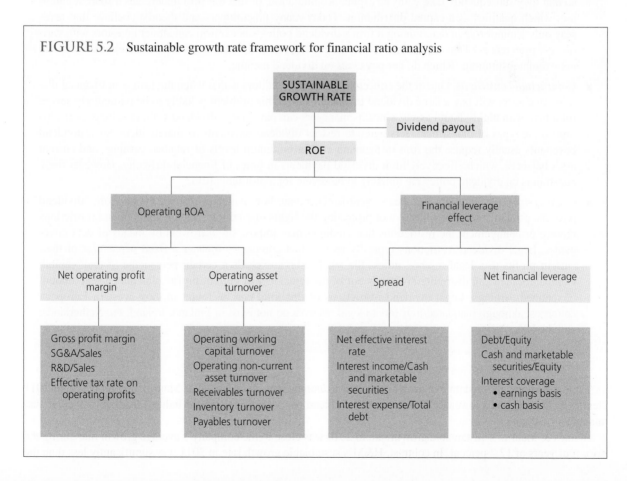

FIGURE 5.2   Sustainable growth rate framework for financial ratio analysis

the ratios discussed in this chapter. These linkages allow an analyst to examine the drivers of a firm's current sustainable growth rate. If the firm intends to grow at a higher rate than its sustainable growth rate, one could assess which of the ratios are likely to change in the process. This analysis can lead to asking business questions such as these: Where is the change going to take place? Is management expecting profitability to increase? Or asset productivity to improve? Are these expectations realistic? Is the firm planning for these changes? If the profitability is not likely to go up, will the firm increase its financial leverage or cut dividends? What is the likely impact of these financial policy changes?

Conflicts of interest between managers and shareholders can also have implications for dividend policy decisions. Shareholders of a firm with high profits and free cash flows and few profitable investment opportunities want managers to adopt a dividend policy with high payouts, thus reducing the sustainable growth rate. This will deter managers from growing the firm by investing in new projects that are not valued by shareholders or from spending the free cash flows on management perks. If a firm's sustainable growth rate is much higher than warranted by the firm's growth opportunities, one could evaluate the possible reasons for why management has not changed its dividend policy: Is management expecting profitability to decrease? If profitability is not expected to decline, has the firm reduced or will it reduce leverage? Are there contractual or legal constraints preventing the firm from paying higher dividends?

CONSTRAINTS ON DIVIDEND POLICIES

A firm's dividend policy affects its sustainable growth, financing decisions and conflicts with its shareholders. The following factors impose some constraints on dividend policy:

- *Tax costs of dividends.* Classical models of the tax effects of dividends predict that if the capital gains tax rate is less than the rate on dividend income, investors will prefer that the firm either pays no dividends, so that they subsequently take gains as capital accumulation, or that the firm undertakes a share repurchase, which qualifies as a capital distribution. Today many practitioners and theorists believe that taxes play only a minor role in determining a firm's dividend policy since a firm can attract investors with various tax preferences. Thus a firm that wishes to pay high dividend rates will attract shareholders that are tax-exempt institutions, which do not pay taxes on dividend income.

- *Contractual constraints.* One of the concerns of a firm's creditors is that when the firm is in financial distress, managers will pay a large dividend to shareholders. This problem is likely to be particularly severe for a firm with highly liquid assets, since its managers can pay a large dividend without selling assets. To limit these types of ploys, managers agree to restrict dividend payments to shareholders. Such dividend covenants usually require the firm to maintain certain minimum levels of retained earnings and current asset balances, which effectively limit dividend payments in times of financial difficulty. However these constraints on dividend policy are unlikely to be severe for a profitable firm.

- *Legal constraints.* In many European countries corporate law mandates restrictions on firms' dividend payouts, primarily with the objective of protecting the rights of creditors. Such legal dividend restrictions replace or complement the restrictions that creditors may impose on borrowers by means of debt covenants.[7] Legal dividend restrictions typically require that companies transfer a fixed percentage of their current profits to a legal reserve, unless the legal reserve exceeds a certain percentage of total capital. Companies then can distribute dividends out of the remainder of current profits plus the current amount of retained earnings. Legal dividend restrictions of this kind can be found in most western European countries, although mandated transfers to legal reserves do not exist in Finland, Ireland, the Netherlands, and the UK.

Table 5.9 shows the sustainable growth rate and its components for Hennes & Mauritz and its peers. In 2011 Hennes & Mauritz had a lower ROE and a higher dividend payout ratio relative to Inditex, leading to a lower sustainable growth rate.

Hennes & Mauritz's sustainable growth rate in 2010 was close to the company's average growth rate during the prior four years of 12.2 percent. In contrast, H&M's sustainable growth rate in 2011 was significantly less than the

TABLE 5.9 Sustainable growth rate

Ratio	H&M 2011	H&M 2010	Inditex 2011	Other peers 2011
ROE	35.8%	44.1%	28.0%	22.8%
Dividend payout ratio	99.4%	70.9%	51.6%	39.2%
Sustainable growth rate	0.2%	12.8%	13.6%	13.9%

retailer's historical growth rates as well as reasonable expectations of its future growth. This observation raises the question of whether the company's 2011 dividend payout is sustainable. One reason for management not to cut dividends, and thus bring the sustainable growth rate in line with expected growth, is that it expects that the current decrease in profitability will not persist. Alternatively, management may have decided to gradually increase financial leverage by keeping future sustainable growth rates below the expected growth rate.

Historical patterns of ratios for European firms

To provide a benchmark for analysis, Table 5.10 reports historical values of the key ratios discussed in this chapter. These ratios are calculated using financial statement data for our sample of 7,015 publicly listed European companies. The table shows the median values of ROE, its key components, and the sustainable growth rate for

TABLE 5.10 Historical values of key financial ratios

Year	ROE	NOPAT margin	Operating asset turnover	Return on operating assets	Return on business assets	Spread	Net financial leverage	Sustainable growth rate
1992	8.9%	5.2%	1.87	9.8%	9.6%	4.1%	0.85	4.9%
1993	9.2%	5.3%	1.86	9.7%	9.5%	4.2%	0.83	5.2%
1994	11.2%	5.6%	1.91	10.3%	9.9%	5.2%	0.76	7.0%
1995	11.5%	5.6%	1.93	10.5%	10.0%	5.2%	0.78	7.2%
1996	11.4%	5.4%	1.95	10.1%	9.4%	5.2%	0.77	7.3%
1997	12.7%	5.5%	1.98	10.8%	10.0%	5.9%	0.71	8.3%
1998	12.5%	5.4%	1.99	10.4%	9.8%	5.6%	0.68	8.4%
1999	11.2%	5.0%	1.90	9.4%	8.7%	5.0%	0.66	7.3%
2000	9.2%	4.5%	1.84	8.5%	7.8%	3.9%	0.63	6.1%
2001	5.6%	3.4%	1.71	6.4%	6.0%	1.8%	0.63	3.0%
2002	4.3%	2.9%	1.67	5.2%	5.0%	1.0%	0.67	1.7%
2003	5.7%	3.2%	1.72	6.0%	5.5%	1.9%	0.65	2.6%
2004	8.5%	3.9%	1.83	7.4%	6.7%	3.3%	0.62	4.9%
2005	10.3%	4.7%	1.80	9.0%	8.0%	4.6%	0.59	6.5%
2006	11.0%	5.1%	1.76	9.6%	8.4%	4.9%	0.59	7.3%
2007	10.7%	5.6%	1.70	9.8%	8.4%	4.5%	0.57	6.9%
2008	7.0%	4.3%	1.65	7.4%	6.6%	2.6%	0.61	4.6%
2009	3.7%	3.0%	1.48	4.8%	4.2%	1.0%	0.63	1.8%
2010	7.4%	4.2%	1.56	6.9%	5.9%	3.1%	0.58	4.8%
2011	9.5%	4.9%	1.71	8.2%	7.0%	4.0%	0.45	6.3%
Average	9.1%	4.6%	1.79	8.5%	7.8%	3.9%	0.66	5.6%

Source: Financial statement data for all nonfinancial companies publicly listed on one of the seven major European exchanges (Compustat Global database).

each of the years 1992 to 2011, and the average for this 20-year period. The data in the table show that the average ROE during this period has been 9.1 percent, average return on business assets has been 7.8 percent, and the average spread between operating ROA and net borrowing costs after tax has been 3.9 percent. The average sustainable growth rate for European companies during this period has been 5.6 percent. Of course an individual company's ratios might depart from these economy-wide averages for a number of reasons, including industry effects, company strategies, and management effectiveness. Nonetheless, the average values in the table serve as useful benchmarks in financial analysis.

CASH FLOW ANALYSIS

The ratio analysis discussion focused on analyzing a firm's income statement (net profit margin analysis) or its balance sheet (asset turnover and financial leverage). The analyst can get further insights into the firm's operating, investing, and financing policies by examining its cash flows. Cash flow analysis also provides an indication of the quality of the information in the firm's income statement and balance sheet. As before, we will illustrate the concepts discussed in this section using Hennes & Mauritz's and Inditex's cash flows.

Cash flow and funds flow statements

All companies reporting in conformity with IFRSs are required to include a statement of cash flows in their financial statements under IAS 7. In the reported cash flow statement, firms classify their cash flows into three categories: cash flow from operations, cash flow related to investments, and cash flow related to financing activities. Cash flow from operations is the cash generated by the firm from the sale of goods and services after paying for the cost of inputs and operations. Cash flow related to investment activities shows the cash paid for capital expenditures, intercorporate investments, acquisitions, and cash received from the sales of non-current assets. Cash flow related to financing activities shows the cash raised from (or paid to) the firm's shareholders and debt holders.

Firms use two cash flow statement formats: the direct format and the indirect format. The key difference between the two formats is the way they report cash flow from operating activities. In the direct cash flow format, which is used by only a small number of firms in practice, operating cash receipts and disbursements are reported directly. In the indirect format, firms derive their operating cash flows by making accrual adjustments to net profit. Because the indirect format links the cash flow statement with the firm's income statement and balance sheet, many analysts and managers find this format more useful.

You may recall from Chapter 3 that net profit differs from operating cash flows because revenues and expenses are measured on an accrual basis. There are two types of accruals embedded in net profit. First, there are current accruals like credit sales and unpaid expenses. Current accruals result in changes in a firm's current assets (such as trade receivables, inventories, and prepaid expenses) and current liabilities (such as trade payables and current provisions). The second type of accruals included in the income statement is non-current accruals such as depreciation, deferred taxes, and equity income from unconsolidated subsidiaries. To derive cash flow from operations from net profit, adjustments have to be made for both these types of accruals. In addition, adjustments have to be made for non-operating gains included in net profit such as profits from asset sales.

The indirect cash flow format explicitly details the accrual adjustments that need to be made to net profit in order to arrive at operating cash flows. If a firm uses the direct cash flow format, it is useful for analysts to know how to prepare an approximate indirect cash flow statement. The first step to doing so is to calculate a firm's working capital from operations, defined as net profit adjusted for non-current accruals, and gains from the sale of non-current assets. Information about non-current accruals such as depreciation and deferred taxes or non-operating gains can typically be taken from the income statement or the notes to the financial statements. The second step is to convert working capital from operations to cash flow from operations by making the relevant adjustments for current accruals related to operations.

Information on current accruals can be obtained by examining changes in a firm's current assets and current liabilities. Typically, operating accruals represent changes in all the current asset accounts other than cash and cash equivalents, and changes in all the current liabilities other than notes payable and the current portion of non-current debt.[8] Cash from operations can be calculated as follows:

Working capital from operations
- Increase (or + decrease) in trade receivables
- Increase (or + decrease) in inventories
- Increase (or + decrease) in other current assets excluding cash and cash equivalents
+ Increase (or − decrease) in trade payables
+ Increase (or − decrease) in other current liabilities excluding debt.

In most cases working capital from operations adjusted for changes in the balance sheet values of current assets and liabilities will not be exactly equal to the operating cash flow disclosed in the direct cash flow statement. Therefore, the analyst needs to add a category of other, unexplained accruals to the self-constructed indirect cash flow statement to make the operating cash flows in the two cash flow statements match. This complication arises because year-to-year changes in the balance sheet values of current assets and liabilities are affected by events such as changes in consolidation or foreign currency exchange rate changes, whereas the current accruals in the indirect cash flow statement are not.

Analyzing cash flow information

Cash flow analysis can be used to address a variety of questions regarding a firm's cash flow dynamics:

- How strong is the firm's internal cash flow generation? Is the cash flow from operations positive or negative? If it is negative, why? Is it because the company is growing? Is it because its operations are unprofitable? Or is it having difficulty managing its working capital properly?

- Does the company have the ability to meet its short-term financial obligations, such as interest payments, from its operating cash flow? Can it continue to meet these obligations without reducing its operating flexibility?

- How much cash did the company invest in growth? Are these investments consistent with its business strategy? Did the company use internal cash flow to finance growth, or did it rely on external financing?

- Did the company pay dividends from internal free cash flow, or did it have to rely on external financing? If the company had to fund its dividends from external sources, is the company's dividend policy sustainable?

- What type of external financing does the company rely on? Equity, current debt, or non-current debt? Is the financing consistent with the company's overall business risk?

- Does the company have excess cash flow after making capital investments? Is it a long-term trend? What plans does management have to deploy the free cash flow?

While the information in reported cash flow statements can be used to answer the above questions directly in the case of some firms, it may not be easy to do so always for a number of reasons. First, even though IAS 7 provides broad guidelines on the format of a cash flow statement, there is still significant variation across firms in how cash flow data are disclosed. Therefore, to facilitate a systematic analysis and comparison across firms, analysts often recast the information in the cash flow statement using their own cash flow model. Second, firms may choose to include interest expense in computing their cash flow from operating activities. However, this item is not strictly related to a firm's operations but a function of financial leverage. Therefore it is useful to restate the cash flow statement to take this into account.

Analysts use a number of different approaches to restate the cash flow data. One such model is shown in Table 5.11. This presents cash flow from operations in two stages. The first step computes cash flow from operations before operating working capital investments. In computing this cash flow, the model excludes interest expense. To compute this number starting with a firm's profit before interest and taxes, an analyst subtracts or adds back three types of items:

1 Subtract taxes paid adjusted for the tax shield on interest payments, i.e., taxes paid plus (1 − tax rate) × interest paid. The tax shield adjustment is made to ensure that the restated cash flow from operations does not depend on the financing structure of the firm.

2 Add back non-operating gains or losses typically arising out of asset disposals or asset write-offs because these items are investment related and will be considered later.

3 Add back non-current operating accruals such as depreciation and deferred taxes because these are noncash operating charges.

TABLE 5.11 Cash flow analysis

Line item (SEK or € millions)	H&M 2011	H&M 2010	Inditex 2011
Profit before Interest and Tax	21,920.7	26,333.5	2,610.7
Taxes Paid plus Tax Shield on Interest Paid	(6,072.8)	(5,893.2)	(717.8)
Non-Operating Losses (Gains)	0.0	0.0	13.2
Non-Current Operating Accruals	14,833.3	14,280.5	1,835.4
Operating Cash Flow before Working Capital Investments	30,681.2	34,720.8	3,741.5
Net (Investments in) or Liquidation of Operating Working Capital	(1,238.0)	(783.0)	(204.2)
Operating Cash Flow before Investment in Non-Current Assets	29,443.2	33,937.8	3,537.4
Interest Received	568.0	356.0	30.2
Dividends received	0.0	0.0	0.0
Net (Investments in) or Liquidation of Operating or Investment Non-Current Assets	(18,033.3)	(22,398.0)	(2,595.4)
Free Cash Flow Available to Debt and Equity	11,977.9	11,895.8	972.2
Interest Paid After Tax	(1,139.9)	(1,239.3)	(57.4)
Net Debt (Repayment) or Issuance	2,526.0	1,052.5	108.1
Free Cash Flow Available to Equity	13,364.0	11,709.0	1023.0
Dividend (Payments)	(15,723.0)	(13,239.0)	(1,003.9)
Net share (Repurchase) or Issuance	0.0	0.0	0.0
Net Increase (Decrease) in Cash Balance	(2,359.0)	(1,530.0)	19.1

Several factors affect a firm's ability to generate positive cash flow from operations. Healthy firms that are in a steady state should generate more cash from their customers than they spend on operating expenses. In contrast, growing firms – especially those investing cash in research and development, advertising and marketing, or building an organization to sustain future growth – may experience negative operating cash flow. Firms' working capital management also affects whether they generate positive cash flow from operations. Firms in the growing stage typically invest some cash flow in operating working capital items like accounts receivable, inventories, and accounts payable. Net investments in working capital are a function of firms' credit policies (trade receivables), payment policies (trade payables, prepaid expenses, and provisions), and expected growth in sales (inventories). Thus, in interpreting firms' cash flow from operations after working capital, it is important to keep in mind their growth strategy, industry characteristics, and credit policies.

The cash flow analysis model next focuses on cash flows related to long-term investments. These investments take the form of capital expenditures, intercorporate investments, and mergers and acquisitions. Any positive operating cash flow after making operating working capital investments allows the firm to pursue long-term growth opportunities. If the firm's operating cash flows after working capital investments are not sufficient to finance its long-term investments, it has to rely on external financing to fund its growth. Such firms have less flexibility to pursue long-term investments than those that can fund their growth internally. There are both costs and benefits from being able to fund growth internally. The cost is that managers can use the internally generated free cash flow to fund unprofitable investments. Such wasteful capital expenditures are less likely if managers are forced to rely on external capital suppliers. Reliance on external capital markets may make it difficult for managers to undertake long-term risky investments if it is not easy to communicate to the capital markets the benefits from such investments.

Any excess cash flow after these long-term investments is free cash flow that is available for both debt holders and equity holders. Payments to debt holders include interest payments and principal payments. Firms with negative free cash flow have to borrow additional funds to meet their interest and debt repayment obligations, or cut some of their investments in working capital or long-term investments, or issue additional equity. This situation is clearly financially risky for the firm.

Cash flow after payments to debt holders is free cash flow available to equity holders. Payments to equity holders consist of dividend payments and share repurchases. If firms pay dividends despite negative free cash flow to equity holders, they are borrowing money to pay dividends. While this may be feasible in the short-term, it is not prudent for a firm to pay dividends to equity holders unless it has a positive free cash flow on a sustained basis. On the other hand, firms that have a large free cash flow after debt payments run the risk of wasting that money on unproductive investments to pursue growth for its own sake. An analyst, therefore, should carefully examine the investment plans of such firms.

The model in Table 5.11 suggests that the analyst should focus on a number of cash flow measures:

1 Cash flow from operations before investment in working capital and interest payments, to examine whether or not the firm is able to generate a cash surplus from its operations.

2 Cash flow from operations after investment in working capital, to assess how the firm's working capital is being managed and whether or not it has the flexibility to invest in non-current assets for future growth.

3 Free cash flow available to debt and equity holders, to assess a firm's ability to meet its interest and principal payments.

4 Free cash flow available to equity holders, to assess the firm's financial ability to sustain its dividend policy and to identify potential agency problems from excess free cash flow.

These measures have to be evaluated in the context of the company's business, its growth strategy, and its financial policies. Further, changes in these measures from year to year provide valuable information on the stability of the cash flow dynamics of the firm.

KEY ANALYSIS QUESTIONS

The cash flow model in Table 5.11 can also be used to assess a firm's earnings quality, as discussed in Chapter 3. The reconciliation of a firm's net profit with its cash flow from operations facilitates this exercise. The following are some of the questions an analyst can probe in this respect:

- Are there significant differences between a firm's net profit and its operating cash flow? Is it possible to clearly identify the sources of this difference? Which accounting policies contribute to this difference? Are there any one-time events contributing to this difference?

- Is the relationship between cash flow and net profit changing over time? Why? Is it because of changes in business conditions or because of changes in the firm's accounting policies and estimates?

- What is the time lag between the recognition of revenues and expenses and the receipt and disbursement of cash flows? What type of uncertainties need to be resolved inbetween?

- Are the changes in receivables, inventories, and payables normal? If not, is there adequate explanation for the changes?

Finally, as we will discuss in Chapter 7, free cash flow available to debt and equity and free cash flow available to equity are critical inputs into the cash flow-based valuation of firms' assets and equity, respectively.

Analysis of Hennes & Mauritz's and Inditex's cash flow

Hennes & Mauritz and Inditex reported their cash flows using the indirect cash flow statement. Table 5.11 recasts these statements using the approach discussed above so that we can analyze the two companies' cash flow dynamics.

Cash flow analysis presented in Table 5.11 shows Hennes & Mauritz had an operating cash flow before working capital investments of SEK30.7 billion in 2011, a decrease from SEK34.7 billion in 2010. The difference between earnings and these cash flows is primarily attributable to the depreciation and amortization charge included in the company's income statement. Hennes & Mauritz's decrease in operating cash flow is smaller than its decrease in profitability. The company's decrease in net profit was partly due to an increase in the depreciation and amortization charge, which is a non-current operating accrual, presumably caused by the firm's investments in new stores. H&M increased its investment in operating working capital. The firm's largest working capital investment in was its inventories investment. This investment was not only the result of the firm's store network expansion but also a consequence of the difficulties that the firm experienced in selling its apparel in 2011. The negative impact on cash of the inventories investment was partly offset by the positive cash flow effect of H&M's reduction of current liabilities.

Both Hennes & Mauritz and Inditex generated more than adequate cash flow from operations to meet their total investments in non-current assets. Consequently, in 2011 Hennes & Mauritz had SEK12.0 billion of free cash flow available to debt and equity holders; Inditex's free cash flow to debt and equity holders was €972.2 million.

In 2011 Hennes & Mauritz was a net borrower, increasing the free cash flow available to equity holders. The company utilized this free cash flow to pay dividends in 2010 and 2011. As a result, distributions to equity holders exceeded the free cash flow in both years and Hennes & Mauritz gradually drew down its cash balance from its extraordinarily high level at the beginning of these years. Doing so helped the company also to gradually decrease its emphasis on non-operating investments and will improve its return on business assets when profitability recovers.

Inditex paid €57.4 million in interest (net of taxes) and was a net issuer of debt, leaving it with €1,023 million in free cash flow available to equity holders. The company distributed close to the same amount of cash to its shareholders – €1,004 million in dividends – leaving a small cash increase of about €19 million. Inditex's dividend payout thus seems to be consistent with its growth rate; that is, also after making all necessary investments in non-current assets and working capital to support the company's growth plans, the excess cash flow left is sufficient to sustain its dividend policy.

SUMMARY

This chapter presents two key tools of financial analysis: ratio analysis and cash flow analysis. Both these tools allow the analyst to examine a firm's performance and its financial condition, given its strategy and goals. Ratio analysis involves assessing the firm's income statement and balance sheet data. Cash flow analysis relies on the firm's cash flow statement.

The starting point for ratio analysis is the company's ROE. The next step is to evaluate the three drivers of ROE, which are net profit margin, asset turnover, and financial leverage. Net profit margin reflects a firm's operating management, asset turnover reflects its investment management, and financial leverage reflects its liability management. Each of these areas can be further probed by examining a number of ratios. For example, common-sized income statement analysis allows a detailed examination of a firm's net margins. Similarly, turnover of key working capital accounts like accounts receivable, inventories, and accounts payable, and turnover of the firm's fixed assets allow further examination of a firm's asset turnover. Finally, short-term liquidity ratios, debt policy ratios, and coverage ratios provide a means of examining a firm's financial leverage.

A firm's sustainable growth rate – the rate at which it can grow without altering its operating, investment, and financing policies – is determined by its ROE and its dividend policy. The concept of sustainable growth provides a way to integrate the ratio analysis and to evaluate whether or not a firm's growth strategy is sustainable. If a firm's plans call for growing at a rate above its current sustainable rate, then the analyst can examine which of the firm's ratios is likely to change in the future.

Cash flow analysis supplements ratio analysis in examining a firm's operating activities, investment management, and financial risks. Firms reporting in conformity with IFRSs are currently required to report a cash flow statement summarizing their operating, investment, and financing cash flows. Since there are wide variations across firms in the way cash flow data are reported, analysts often use a standard format to recast cash flow data. We discussed in this chapter one such cash flow model. This model allows the analyst to assess whether a firm's operations generate cash flow before investments in operating working capital, and how much cash is being invested in the firm's working capital. It also enables the analyst to calculate the firm's free cash flow after making long-term investments, which is an indication of the firm's ability to meet its debt and dividend payments. Finally, the cash flow analysis shows how the firm is financing itself, and whether its financing patterns are too risky.

The insights gained from analyzing a firm's financial ratios and its cash flows are valuable in forecasts of the firm's future prospects.

CORE CONCEPTS

Alternative approach to ROE decomposition Decomposition of return on equity into NOPAT margin, asset turnover, return on investment assets, financial spread, and net financial leverage. Return on operating assets is the product of NOPAT margin and asset turnover. Return on business assets is the weighted average of the returns on operating and investment assets. The financial leverage gain is the product of financial spread and financial leverage.

$$
\begin{aligned}
\text{ROE} &= \left[\frac{\text{NOPAT}}{\text{Sales}} \times \frac{\text{Sales}}{\text{Operating assets}}\right] \times \frac{\text{Operating assets}}{\text{Business assets}} + \left[\frac{\text{NIPAT}}{\text{Investment assets}}\right] \times \frac{\text{Investment assets}}{\text{Business assets}} \\
&\quad + \text{Spread} \times \frac{\text{Debt}}{\text{Equity}} \\
&= \text{Return on operating assets} \times \frac{\text{Operating assets}}{\text{Business assets}} + \text{Return on investment assets} \times \frac{\text{Investment assets}}{\text{Business assets}} \\
&\quad + \text{Spread} \times \frac{\text{Debt}}{\text{Equity}} \\
&= \text{Return on business assets} + \text{Spread} \times \frac{\text{Debt}}{\text{Equity}} \\
&= \text{Return on business assets} + \text{Financial leverage gain}
\end{aligned}
$$

where

$$
\text{Spread} = \text{Return on business assets} - \frac{\text{Interest expense after tax}}{\text{Debt}}
$$

Asset turnover analysis Decomposition of asset turnover into its components, with the objective of identifying the drivers of (changes in) a firm's asset turnover and assessing the efficiency of a firm's investment management. The asset turnover analysis typically distinguishes between working capital turnover (receivables, inventories, and payables) and non-current operating assets turnover (PP&E and intangible assets).

Cross-sectional comparison Comparison of the ratios of one firm to those of one or more other firms from the same industry.

Financial leverage analysis Analysis of the risk related to a firm's current liabilities and mix of non-current debt and equity. The primary considerations in the analysis of financial leverage are whether the financing strategy (1) matches the firm's business risk and (2) optimally balances the risks (e.g., financial distress risk) and benefits (e.g., tax shields, management discipline).

Profit margin analysis Decomposition of the profit margin into its components, typically using common-sized income statements. The objective of profit margin analysis is to identify the drivers of (changes in) a firm's margins and assess the efficiency of a firm's operating management. The operating expenses that impact the profit margin can be decomposed by function (e.g., cost of sales, SG&A) or by nature (e.g., cost of materials, personnel expense, depreciation, and amortization).

Ratio analysis Analysis of financial statement ratios to evaluate the four drivers of firm performance:

1 Operating policies.
2 Investment policies.
3 Financing policies.
4 Dividend policies.

Sustainable growth rate The rate at which a firm can grow while keeping its profitability and financial policies unchanged.

$$
\text{Sustainable growth rate} = \text{ROE} \times \left(1 - \frac{\text{Cash dividends paid}}{\text{Net profit}}\right)
$$

Time-series comparison Comparison of the ratios of one firm over time.

Traditional approach to ROE decomposition Decomposition of return on equity into profit margin, asset turnover, and financial leverage:

$$\text{ROE} = \frac{\text{Net profit}}{\text{Sales}} \times \frac{\text{Sales}}{\text{Assets}} \times \frac{\text{Assets}}{\text{Shareholders' equity}}$$

QUESTIONS, EXERCISES AND PROBLEMS

1 Which of the following types of firms do you expect to have particularly high or low asset turnover? Explain why.
   - A supermarket.
   - A pharmaceutical company.
   - A jewelry retailer.
   - A steel company.

2 Which of the following types of firms do you expect to have high or low sales margins? Why?
   - A supermarket.
   - A pharmaceutical company.
   - A jewelry retailer.
   - A software company.

3 Sven Broker, an analyst with an established brokerage firm, comments: "The critical number I look at for any company is operating cash flow. If cash flows are less than earnings, I consider a company to be a poor performer and a poor investment prospect." Do you agree with this assessment? Why or why not?

4 In 2005 France-based food retailer Groupe Carrefour had a return on equity of 19 percent, whereas France-based Groupe Casino's return was only 6 percent. Use the decomposed ROE framework to provide possible reasons for this difference.

5 Joe Investor asserts, "A company cannot grow faster than its sustainable growth rate." True or false? Explain why.

6 What are the reasons for a firm having lower cash from operations than working capital from operations? What are the possible interpretations of these reasons?

7 ABC Company recognizes revenue at the point of shipment. Management decides to increase sales for the current quarter by filling all customer orders. Explain what impact this decision will have on:
   - Days' receivable for the current quarter.
   - Days' receivable for the next quarter.
   - Sales growth for the current quarter.
   - Sales growth for the next quarter.
   - Return on sales for the current quarter.
   - Return on sales for the next quarter.

8 What ratios would you use to evaluate operating leverage for a firm?

9 What are the potential benchmarks that you could use to compare a company's financial ratios? What are the pros and cons of these alternatives?

10 In a period of rising prices, how would the following ratios be affected by the accounting decision to select LIFO, rather than FIFO, for inventory valuation?

- Gross margin.
- Current ratio.
- Asset turnover.
- Debt-to-equity ratio.
- Average tax rate.

Problem 1 ROE decomposition

Inditex S.A. is the Spain-based parent company of a large number of clothing design, manufacturing and retail subsidiaries. The company's brands include Zara, Pull & Bear, and Massimo Dutti. At the end of the fiscal year ending on January 31, 2009 (fiscal year 2008), the subsidiaries of Inditex operated 4,359 stores across 73 countries, making Inditex one of the three largest clothing retailers in the world.

The following tables show the standardized and adjusted income statements and balance sheets for Inditex, for the years ended January 31, 2007 and 2008. Operating lease obligations have been capitalized and the operating lease expense has been replaced with depreciation and interest expense, following the procedure described in Chapter 4:

Standardized and adjusted income statement

(€ millions)	2008	2007
Sales	**10,407**	**9,435**
Cost of materials	(4,493)	(4,086)
Personnel expense	(1,703)	(1,473)
Depreciation and amortization	(910)	(803)
Other operating income, net of other operating expense	(1,168)	(1,039)
Operating profit	**2,133**	**2,033**
Investment income	0	(9)
Net interest expense	(84)	(72)
Profit before taxes	**2,050**	**1,953**
Tax expense	(455)	(474)
Profit after taxes	**1,595**	**1,479**
Minority interest	(8)	(7)
Net profit	**1,587**	**1,471**

Standardized and adjusted balance sheet

(€ millions)	2008	2007
Non-current tangible assets	6,325	6,000
Non-current intangible assets	148	139
Deferred tax asset	203	133
Other non-current assets	188	165
Total non-current assets	**6,863**	**6,437**
Trade receivables	585	464
Inventories	1,055	1,007
Other current assets	158	45
Cash and marketable securities	1,466	1,466
Total current assets	**3,264**	**2,982**
TOTAL ASSETS	**10,127**	**9,418**

(continued)

Standardized and adjusted balance sheet (€ millions)	2008	2007
Shareholders' equity	5,055	4,414
Minority interest	27	24
Non-current debt	2,003	2,095
Deferred tax liability	343	197
Other non-current liabilities (non-interest bearing)	308	229
Total non-current liabilities	2,655	2,522
Current debt	234	371
Trade payables	2,073	1,975
Other current liabilities	84	112
Total current liabilities	2,391	2,458
TOTAL LIABILITIES AND SHAREHOLDERS' EQUITY	10,127	9,418

1   Calculate Inditex's net operating profit after taxes, operating working capital, net non-current assets, net debt, and net assets in 2007 and 2008. (Use the effective tax rate [tax expense/profit before taxes] to calculate NOPAT.)

2   Decompose Inditex's return on equity in 2007 and 2008 using the traditional approach.

3   Decompose Inditex's return on equity in 2007 and 2008 using the alternative approach. What explains the difference between Inditex's return on assets and its operating return on assets?

4   Analyze the underlying drivers of the change in Inditex's return on equity. What explains the decrease in return on equity? How strongly does Inditex appear to be affected by the economic crisis of 2008? (In your answer, make sure to address issues of store productivity, cost control, pricing and leverage.)

Problem 2   Ratio analysis and acquisitions

TomTom is a Netherlands-based designer and manufacturer of portable GPS car navigation systems that it sells across the world. The company's initial public offering in 2005 helped boost the company's revenues from €192 million in 2004 to €1,364 million in 2006. In the fourth quarter of 2007, TomTom acquired 29.9 percent of the shares of Tele Atlas, a provider of digital maps. The company completed the acquisition in 2008. The following tables show the components of return on equity and balance sheet items as a percentage of sales for TomTom N.V. for 2006, 2007, and 2008. The ratios have been calculated after removing the margin effect of a one-time impairment charge in 2008:

Ratio	2008	2007	2006
Net business profit after tax/sales	12.6%	17.5%	15.9%
× Sales/business assets	1.03	1.87	11.11
= Return on business assets	12.9%	32.6%	176.7%
Spread	9.7%	29.2%	175.4%
× Financial leverage	2.21	−0.31	−0.78
= Financial leverage gain	21.5%	−9.1%	−136.4%
ROE = Return on business assets + Financial leverage gain	34.5%	23.5%	40.3%

Ratio	2008	2007	2006
Operating working capital/Sales	5.9%	8.2%	10.6%
Net non-current assets/Sales	91.5%	45.4%	−1.6%
Non-current intangible assets/Sales	111.5%	3.2%	2.9%
. . . . . . of which Goodwill/Sales	51.1%	0.0%	0.0%
Investment assets/Sales	0.3%	47.0%	0.0%
PP&E/Sales	3.2%	1.0%	0.6%
Days' accounts receivable	62.4	83.5	70.2
Days' inventory	58.6	48.4	56.4
Days' accounts payable	61.3	56.2	30.6

1   Summarize the main factors behind the decrease in TomTom's ROE in 2007 and the increase in the company's ROE in 2008.

2   What effect did the acquisition of a 29.9 percent stake in Tele Atlas have on the components of TomTom's ROE in 2007?

3   What effect did the acquisition of a majority stake in Tele Atlas have on the components of TomTom's ROE in 2008?

Problem 3 *Ratios of three fashion retailers*

Exhibit P3 displays a selected set of financial ratios for the years 2008–2011 of three European fashion retailers: Italy-based Benetton Group, France-based Etam Group, and UK-based French Connection. Using this set of ratios, analyze the retailers' financial performance. (Note: More information about these three retailers is available on the companion website to this book.)

1   The return on equity (ROE) decomposition shows that the underlying drivers of ROE performance vary across retailers. Which economic or strategic factors may explain these differences in the components of ROE?

2   How did performance trends (during the period 2008 to 2011) differ among the three retailers? Which factors contributed most to these differences?

EXHIBIT P3   **Ratio analysis of Benetton, Etam, and French Connection**

ROE decomposition	Benetton				Etam				French Connection			
	2011	2010	2009	2008	2011	2010	2009	2008	2011	2010	2009	2008
Net operating profit margin	5.8%	7.0%	7.7%	9.8%	2.3%	3.3%	3.5%	2.7%	3.8%	5.7%	−1.7%	−5.4%
× Operating asset turnover	0.66	0.67	0.67	0.71	1.69	1.73	1.57	1.45	1.24	1.17	0.99	1.08
= Return on operating assets	3.8%	4.7%	5.2%	7.0%	3.8%	5.7%	5.5%	3.9%	4.7%	6.7%	−1.7%	−5.8%
Return on operating assets	3.8%	4.7%	5.2%	7.0%	3.8%	5.7%	5.5%	3.9%	4.7%	6.7%	−1.7%	−5.8%
× (Operating assets/Business assets)	0.97	0.97	0.98	0.97	0.97	0.97	0.96	0.97	0.89	0.90	0.91	0.89
+ Return on investment assets	1.7%	−0.3%	2.9%	1.2%	−0.8%	−6.4%	−2.1%	3.0%	4.0%	5.9%	1.7%	3.9%
× (Investment assets/Business assets)	0.03	0.03	0.02	0.03	0.03	0.03	0.04	0.03	0.11	0.10	0.09	0.11
= Return on business assets	3.7%	4.6%	5.1%	6.8%	3.7%	5.3%	5.2%	3.9%	4.6%	6.6%	−1.4%	−4.8%
Spread	1.2%	2.2%	2.6%	3.6%	0.7%	2.0%	2.0%	0.3%	0.9%	3.1%	−5.3%	−7.6%
× Financial leverage	1.14	1.13	1.21	1.20	1.35	1.05	0.86	0.91	1.64	1.85	1.71	1.33
= Financial leverage gain	1.4%	2.4%	3.2%	4.3%	0.9%	2.1%	1.7%	0.2%	1.5%	5.6%	−9.2%	−10.0%
ROE = Return on business assets + financial leverage gain	5.1%	7.0%	8.3%	11.1%	4.6%	7.4%	6.9%	4.1%	6.1%	12.2%	−10.6%	−14.8%

Line items as a percentage of sales	Benetton				Etam				French Connection			
	2011	2010	2009	2008	2011	2010	2009	2008	2011	2010	2009	2008
Sales	100.0%	100.0%	100.0%	100.0%	100.0%	100.0%	100.0%	100.0%	100.0%	100.0%	100.0%	100.0%
Net operating expense	−90.6%	−88.0%	−86.9%	−86.5%	−96.3%	−94.8%	−94.4%	−94.5%	−95.6%	−95.3%	−97.2%	−101.3%
Other income/expense	−0.6%	−1.0%	−1.2%	0.1%	−0.5%	−0.5%	−1.1%	−0.7%	0.3%	1.6%	−3.4%	−4.0%
Net operating profit before tax	8.8%	11.0%	11.9%	13.6%	3.2%	4.7%	4.4%	4.8%	4.6%	6.4%	−0.6%	−5.3%
Investment income	0.0%	−0.1%	0.1%	0.0%	0.0%	−0.2%	−0.1%	0.0%	0.4%	0.7%	0.2%	0.1%
Interest income	0.1%	0.1%	0.0%	0.1%	0.0%	0.0%	0.0%	0.1%	0.1%	0.1%	0.0%	0.5%
Interest expense	−3.1%	−2.8%	−3.0%	−3.7%	−1.6%	−1.5%	−1.5%	−1.8%	−2.8%	−3.0%	−3.8%	−2.3%
Tax expense	−2.1%	−3.2%	−3.3%	−2.6%	−0.4%	−0.9%	−0.4%	−1.5%	−0.2%	−0.1%	−0.1%	0.4%
Net profit	3.8%	5.0%	5.8%	7.3%	1.2%	2.2%	2.4%	1.5%	2.1%	4.1%	−4.3%	−6.6%

Line items as a percentage of sales	Benetton				Etam				French Connection			
	2011	2010	2009	2008	2011	2010	2009	2008	2011	2010	2009	2008
Operating expense line items as a percent of sales												
Personnel expense	−12.7%	−12.4%	−12.4%	−12.0%	−20.1%	−19.5%	−20.5%	−20.8%	−19.8%	−21.5%	−25.2%	−20.6%
Cost of materials	−50.4%	−47.6%	−47.3%	−46.9%	−42.2%	−40.8%	−40.2%	−38.5%	−51.9%	−48.3%	−48.7%	−48.8%
Depreciation and amortization	−10.9%	−10.7%	−10.7%	−10.0%	−10.0%	−9.4%	−9.2%	−10.3%	−0.1%	−2.1%	−2.7%	−3.1%
Other operating income/expense	−16.5%	−17.4%	−16.5%	−17.6%	−24.0%	−25.2%	−24.6%	−25.0%	−23.9%	−23.4%	−20.7%	−28.9%

Asset management ratios	Benetton				Etam				French Connection			
	2011	2010	2009	2008	2011	2010	2009	2008	2011	2010	2009	2008
Operating working capital/Sales	38.9%	36.9%	37.7%	36.3%	7.8%	5.4%	7.6%	9.6%	18.3%	16.3%	22.4%	23.8%
Net non-current assets/Sales	113.3%	111.9%	112.2%	104.3%	51.3%	52.3%	56.0%	59.3%	62.3%	68.8%	78.8%	69.0%
PP&E/Sales	94.3%	92.4%	91.8%	84.8%	36.3%	37.2%	38.8%	41.1%	59.6%	66.2%	76.2%	64.7%
Operating working capital turnover	2.57	2.71	2.65	2.76	12.84	18.43	13.19	10.37	5.46	6.12	4.47	4.21
Net non-current asset turnover	0.88	0.89	0.89	0.96	1.95	1.91	1.79	1.69	1.61	1.45	1.27	1.45
PP&E turnover	1.06	1.08	1.09	1.18	2.75	2.69	2.58	2.44	1.68	1.51	1.31	1.55
Trade receivables turnover	2.41	2.59	2.61	2.91	14.81	17.17	18.05	18.97	21.43	25.45	19.50	17.84
Days' receivables	149.5	138.9	137.7	123.7	24.3	21.0	19.9	19.0	16.8	14.1	18.5	20.2
Inventories turnover	3.12	3.29	2.94	2.87	2.38	2.46	2.61	2.57	2.56	2.55	2.00	2.09
Days' inventories	115.3	109.3	122.5	125.4	151.4	146.5	137.9	140.3	140.4	141.5	180.0	172.0
Trade payables turnover	2.16	2.31	2.37	2.49	2.39	2.30	2.43	2.62	5.20	5.47	4.39	4.67
Days' payables	166.7	155.7	152.2	144.6	150.8	156.6	148.0	137.6	69.2	65.8	82.0	77.1

Problem 4 The Fiat Group in 2008

In 2009, following the worldwide credit crisis, several US-based car manufacturers, such as Chrysler and General Motors, approached bankruptcy and needed to be bailed out by the US government and private investors. Italy-based Fiat Group SpA. decided to help rescue Chrysler by acquiring 20 to 35 percent of the car manufacturer's shares. In exchange, Fiat would get access to Chrysler's vehicle platforms and manufacturing facilities, which could eventually help the Italian manufacturer to re-enter the US market. Following the initial rumors about private negotiations between Fiat and Chrysler and Fiat's (coinciding) announcement that it would not pay a dividend for 2008, Fiat's share price dropped by more than 25 percent in one week. The question arose whether Fiat's performance was really stronger than Chrysler's.

The following tables show the financial statements of the Fiat Group SpA. for the fiscal years 2006–2008. In all three years, Fiat earned a return on equity in excess of 12 percent. Decompose Fiat's return on equity and evaluate the drivers of the company's performance during the period 2006–2008. What trends can you identify in the company's performance? What has been the likely effect of the credit crisis on Fiat?

Income statement (€ millions)	2008	2007	2006
Net revenues	59,380	58,529	51832
Cost of sales	(49,423)	(48,924)	(43,888)
Selling, general, and administrative costs	(5,075)	(4,924)	(4,697)
Research and development costs	(1,497)	(1,536)	(1,401)
Other income (expenses)	(23)	88	105
Trading profit	**3,362**	**3,233**	**1,951**
Gains (losses) on the disposal of investments	20	190	607
Restructuring costs	(165)	(105)	(450)
Other unusual income (expenses)	(245)	(166)	(47)
Operating profit/(loss)	**2,972**	**3,152**	**2,061**
Financial income (expenses)	(947)	(564)	(576)
Result from investments	162	185	156
Profit before taxes	**2,187**	**2,773**	**1,641**
Income taxes	(466)	(719)	(490)
Profit from continuing operations	**1,721**	**2,054**	**1,151**
Profit from discontinued operations	0	0	0
Net profit/(loss)	**1,721**	**2,054**	**1,151**

Balance sheet (€ millions)	2008	2007	2006
Intangible assets	7,048	6,523	6,421
Property, plant, and equipment	12,607	11,246	10,540
Investment property	0	10	19
Investments and other financial assets	2,177	2,214	2,280
Leased assets	505	396	247
Defined benefit plan assets	120	31	11
Deferred tax assets	2,386	1,892	1,860
Total non-current assets	**24,843**	**22,312**	**21,378**
Inventories	11,346	9,990	8,548
Trade receivables	4,390	4,384	4,944
Receivables from financing activities	13,136	12,268	11,743
Current tax receivables	770	1,153	808
Other current assets	2,600	2,291	2,278
Current financial assets	967	1,016	637
Cash and cash equivalents	3,683	6,639	7,736
Total current assets	**36,892**	**37,741**	**36,694**

Balance sheet (€ millions)	2008	2007	2006
Assets held for sale	37	83	332
TOTAL ASSETS	**61,772**	**60,136**	**58,404**
Shareholders' equity	10,354	10,606	9,362
Minority interest	747	673	674
Employee benefits	3,366	3,597	3,761
Other provisions	4,778	4,965	4,850
Asset-backed financing	6,663	6,820	8,344
Other debt	14,716	11,131	11,844
Other financial liabilities	1,202	188	105
Trade payables	13,258	14,725	12,603
Current tax payables	331	631	311
Deferred tax liabilities	170	193	263
Other current liabilities	6,185	6,572	5,978
Liabilities held for sale	2	35	309
TOTAL SHAREHOLDERS' EQUITY AND LIABILITIES	**61,772**	**60,136**	**58,404**

Cash flow statement (€ millions)	2008	2007	2006
Net profit/(loss)	1,721	2,054	1,151
Amortization and depreciation (net of vehicles sold under buy-back commitments)	2,901	2,738	2,969
(Gains) losses on disposal	(50)	(297)	(575)
Other non-cash items	253	(138)	7
Dividends received	84	81	69
Change in provisions	(161)	6	229
Change in deferred taxes	(490)	(157)	(26)
Change in items due to buy-back commitments	(88)	34	(18)
Change in working capital	(3,786)	1,588	812
Cash flows from (used in) operating activities	**384**	**5,909**	**4,618**
Cash flows from (used in) investment activities	**(6,310)**	**(4,601)**	**(1,390)**
Cash flows from (used in) financing activities	**3,127**	**(2,375)**	**(1,731)**
Translation exchange differences	(159)	(33)	(173)
Total change in cash and cash equivalents	**(2,958)**	**(1,100)**	**(1,324)**

NOTES

1. For Hennes & Mauritz, we will call the fiscal year ending November 2011 as the year 2011, and the fiscal year ending November 2010 as the year 2010.
2. A spreadsheet containing the three versions of the financial statements of Hennes & Mauritz and Inditex as well as all ratios described throughout this chapter is available on the companion website of this book. This spreadsheet also shows how we capitalized omitted operating lease assets on Hennes & Mauritz's and Inditex's balance sheet before calculating all ratios.
3. We discuss in greater detail in Chapter 8 how to estimate a company's cost of equity capital. Analysts following Hennes & Mauritz and Inditex estimated their equity betas at close to 0.8 in 2011. The yield on long-term treasury bonds was approximately 4.5 percent. If one assumes a risk premium of 5 percent, the two firms' cost of equity is 8.5 percent; if the risk premium is assumed to be 7 percent, then their cost of equity is close to 10 percent. Lower assumed risk premium will, of course, lead to lower estimates of equity capital.

4. Both Hennes & Mauritz and Inditex have a solid financial position and a relatively low cost of debt. Given the level of leverage, the weighted average cost of capital will be lower than the cost of equity. We will discuss in Chapter 8 how to estimate a company's weighted average cost of capital.

5. See *Taxes and Business Strategy* by Myron Scholes and Mark Wolfson (Englewood Cliffs, NJ: Prentice-Hall, 1992).

6. Average sales (or average cost of sales) is calculated as annual sales (or annual cost of sales) divided by the number of days in the year. There are a number of issues related to the calculation of turnover ratios in practice. First, in calculating all the turnover ratios, the assets used in the calculations can either be beginning of the year values, year-end values or an average of the beginning and ending balances in a year. We use the average values in our calculations. Second, strictly speaking, one should use credit sales to calculate trade receivables turnover and days' receivables. But since it is usually difficult to obtain data on credit sales, total sales are used instead. Similarly, in calculating trade payables turnover or days' payables, cost of sales (or cost of materials) is substituted for purchases for data availability reasons. Third, the ratios for income statements classified by function differ from those for income statements classified by nature. Turnover ratios for the two types of statements are therefore not perfectly comparable.

7. See Christian Leuz, Dominic Deller, and Michael Stubenrath, "An international comparison of accounting-based payout restrictions in the United States, United Kingdom, and Germany," *Accounting and Business Research* 28 (1998): 111–129.

8. Changes in cash and marketable securities are excluded because this is the amount being explained by the cash flow statement. Changes in current debt and the current portion of non-current debt are excluded because these accounts represent financing flows, not operating flows.

APPENDIX: HENNES & MAURITZ AB FINANCIAL STATEMENTS

Consolidated Statements of Earnings (SEK Millions)

Fiscal year ended November 30	2011	2010	2009
Sales, excluding VAT	109,999	108,483	101,393
Cost of goods sold	(43,852)	(40,214)	(38,919)
Gross profit	**66,147**	**68,269**	**62,474**
Selling expenses	(42,517)	(40,751	(38,224)
Administrative expenses	(3,251)	(2,859)	(2,606)
Operating profit	**20,379**	**24,659**	**21,644**
Interest income	568	356	467)
Interest expense	(5)	(7)	(8)
Profit after financial items	**20,942**	**25,008**	**22,103**
Tax	(5,121)	(6,327)	(5,719)
Profit for the year	**15,821**	**18,681**	**16,384**
Operating expense items by nature			
Salaries, other remuneration and payroll overheads	(18,534)	(16,640)	(17,518)
Depreciation – within cost of goods sold	(366)	(336)	(310)
Depreciation – within selling expenses	(2,698)	(2,540)	(2,350)
Depreciation – within administrative expenses	(198)	(185)	(170)

Source: 2011 and 2010 Annual Report, Hennes & Mauritz AB.

Consolidated Balance Sheets (SEK millions)

Fiscal year ended November 30	2011	2010	2009
ASSETS			
Brands	302	349	396
Customer relations	84	97	110
Leasehold rights	585	688	744
Goodwill	64	64	424
Buildings and land	804	656	492
Equipment, tools, fixtures and fittings	16,589	14,813	14,319
Long-term receivables	608	518	551
Deferred tax receivables	1,234	1,065	1,246
Total fixed assets	**20,270**	**18,250**	**18,282**
Stock-in-trade	13,819	11,487	10,240
Accounts receivable	2,337	2,258	1,990
Other receivables	919	996	629
Forward contracts	456	457	260
Prepaid expenses	1,110	876	937
Short-term investments	6,958	8,167	3,001
Liquid funds	14,319	16,691	19,024
Total current assets	**39,918**	**40,932**	**36,081**
Total assets	**60,188**	**59,182**	**54,363**
LIABILITIES AND SHAREHOLDERS' EQUITY			
Share capital	207	207	207
Reserves	−487	−369	1,514
Retained earnings	28,563	25,653	22,508
Profit for the year	15,821	18,681	16,384
Equity	**44,104**	**44,172**	**40,613**
Provisions for pensions	377	257	254
Other provisions	0	0	0
Deferred tax liabilities	950	906	2,038
Total non-current liabilities	**1,327**	**1,163**	**2,292**
Accounts payable	4,307	3,965	3,667
Tax liabilities	1,851	2,304	439
Forward contracts	150	176	335
Other liabilities	2,278	2,026	2,196
Accrued expenses	6,171	5,376	4,453
Total current liabilities	**14,757**	**13,847**	**11,090**
Total liabilities and shareholders' equity	**60,188**	**59,182**	**53,995**

Source: 2011 and 2010 Annual Report, Hennes & Mauritz AB.

Consolidated Statements of Cash Flows (SEK millions)

Fiscal year ended November 30	2011	2010	2009
OPERATING ACTIVITIES			
Profit after financial items	20,942	25,008	22,103
Net interest expense	(563)	(349)	(459)
Interest paid	(5)	(7)	(8)
Interest received	568	356	467
Adjustment for:			
Provisions for pensions	120	3	26
Depreciation	3,262)	3,061	2,830
Tax paid	(5,666)	(5,451)	(6,468)
Changes in current receivables	(244)	(778)	(71)
Changes in stock-in-trade	(2,331)	(1,557)	(1,740)
Changes in current liabilities	1,337	1,552	1,293
Cash flow from current operations	**17,420**	**21,838**	**17,973**
INVESTING ACTIVITIES			
Investment in leasehold rights	(71)	(147)	(180)
Sales of/investments in buildings and land	(157)	(209)	(25)
Investments in fixed assets	(4,946)	(4,603)	(5,481)
Adjustment of consideration/acquisition of subsidiaries	0	(8)	7
Change in financial investments, 3–12 months	1,209	(5,166)	(3,001)
Other investments	(91)	4	(75)
Cash flow from investing activities	**(4,056)**	**(10,129)**	**(8,755)**
FINANCING ACTIVITIES			
Dividend	(15,723)	(13,239)	(12,825)
Cash flows from financing activities	**(15,723)**	**(13,239)**	**(12,825)**
Exchange rate effect	(13)	(803)	(95)
Cash flow for the year	**(2,372)**	**(2,333)**	**(3,702)**
Liquid funds at beginning of year	16,691	19,024	22,726
Liquid funds at end of year	**14,319**	**16,691**	**19,024**

Source: 2011 and 2010 Annual Report, Hennes & Mauritz AB.

Standardized and Adjusted Statements of Earnings (SEK millions)

Fiscal year ended November 30	2011	2010	2009
Sales	**109,999**	**108,483**	**101,393**
Operating expenses	(88,078.3)	(82,149.5)	(78,215.5)
Operating profit	21,920.7	26,333.5	23,177.5
Investment income	0	0	0
Other income, net of other expense	0	0	0
Net interest expense (income)			
Interest income	568	356	467
Interest expense	(1,546.7)	(1,681.5)	(1,541.5)
Profit before taxes	**20,942**	**25,008**	**22,103**
Tax expense	(5,121)	(6,327)	(5,719)
Profit after taxes	**15,821**	**18,681**	**16,384**
Minority interest – Income statement	0	0	0
Net profit to ordinary shareholders	15,821	18,681	16,384
OPERATING EXPENSES			
Classification by function:			
Cost of sales (function)	(43,852)	(40,214)	(38,919)
SG&A (function)	(45,768)	(43,610)	(40,830)
Other operating income, net of other operating expenses (function)	0	0	0
Classification by nature:			
Personnel expenses (nature)	(18,534)	(16,640)	(17,518)
Depreciation and amortization (nature)	(3,262)	(3,061)	(2,830)
Other operating income, net of other operating expenses (nature)	(24,338)	(24,245)	(20,792)

Source: Authors' calculations.

Standardized and Adjusted Balance Sheets (SEK millions)

Fiscal year ended November 30	2011	2010	2009
ASSETS			
Non-current tangible assets	67,941.5	63,594.5	61,940
Non-current intangible assets	450	510	930
Minority equity investments	0	0	0
Other non-operating investments	608	518	551
Deferred tax assets	1,234	1,065	1,246
Derivatives – asset	456	457	260
Total non-current assets	**70,689.5**	**66,144.5**	**64,927**
Inventories	13,819	11,487	10,240
Trade receivables	2,337	2,258	1,990
Other current assets	2,029	1,872	1,566
Cash and marketable securities	21,277	24,858	22,025
Total current assets	**39,462**	**40,475**	**35,821**
Assets held for sale	**0**	**0**	**0**
Total assets	**110,151.5**	**106,619.5**	**100,748**
LIABILITIES AND SHAREHOLDERS' EQUITY			
Ordinary shareholders' equity	**44,104**	**44,172**	**40,613**
Minority interest – balance sheet	**0**	**0**	**0**
Preference shares	**0**	**0**	**0**
Non-current debt	50,340.5	47,694.5	46,639
Deferred tax liabilities	950	906	2,038
Derivatives – liability	150	176	335
Other non-current liabilities (non-interest bearing)	0	0	0
Non-current liabilities	**51,440.5**	**48,776.5**	**49,012**
Trade payables	4,307	3,965	3,667
Other current liabilities	10,300	9,706	7,088
Current debt	0	0	0
Current liabilities	**14,607**	**13,671**	**10,755**
Liabilities held for sale	**0**	**0**	**0**
Total liabilities and shareholders' equity	**110,151.5**	**106,619.5**	**100,380**

Source: Authors' calculations.

Standardized and Adjusted Statements of Cash Flows (SEK millions)

Fiscal year ended November 30	2011	2010	2009
Profit before interest and tax	21,920.7	26,333.5	23,177.5
Taxes paid plus tax shield on interest paid	(6,072.8)	(5,893.2)	(6,899.6)
Non-operating losses (gains)	0	0	0
Non-current operating accruals	14,833.3	14,280.5	13,571.5
Operating cash flow before working capital investments	**30,681.2**	**34,720.8**	**29,849.4**
Net (investments in) or liquidation of operating working capital	(1,238)	(783)	(518)
Operating cash flow before investment in non-current assets	**29,443.2**	**33,937.8**	**29,331.4**
Interest received	568	356	467
Dividends received	0	0	0
Net (investments in) or liquidation of operating or investment non-current assets	(18,033.3)	(22,398)	(19,385.1)
Free cash flow available to debt and equity	**11,977.9**	**11,895.8**	**10,413.2**
Interest paid after tax	(1,139.9)	(1,239.3)	(1,109.9)
Net debt (repayment) or issuance	2,526	1,052.5	(85.3)
Free cash flow available to equity	**13,364.0**	**11,709.0**	**9,218.0**
Dividend (payments)	(15,723)	(13,239)	(12,825)
Net share (repurchase) or issuance	0	0	0
Net increase (decrease) in cash balance	**2,359.0**	**1,530.0**	**3,607.0**

Source: Authors' calculations.

Condensed Statements of Earnings (SEK millions)

Fiscal year ended November 30	2011	2010	2009
Sales	**109,999.0**	**108,483.0**	**101,393.0**
Net operating profit after tax	**16,542.3**	**19,657.9**	**17,157.7**
Net profit	15,821.0	18,681.0	16,384.0
− Investment profit after tax	(418.6)	(262.4)	(336.2)
+ Interest expense after tax	1,139.9	1,239.3	1,109.9
= **Net operating profit after tax**	**16,542.3**	**19,657.9**	**17,157.7**
of which: Net other expense after tax	**0.0**	**0.0**	**0.0**
= Net other expense (income)	0.0	0.0	0.0
× (1 − Tax rate)	73.7%	73.7%	72.0%
= **Net other expense after tax**	**0.0**	**0.0**	**0.0**
+ **Net investment profit after tax**	**418.6**	**262.4**	**336.2**
= Investment and interest income	568.0	356.0	467.0
× (1 − Tax rate)	73.7%	73.7%	72.0%
= **Net interest expense after tax**	**418.6**	**262.4**	**336.2**
− **Interest expense after tax**	**1,139.9**	**1,239.3**	**1,109.9**
= Interest expense	1,546.7	1,681.5	1,541.5
× (1 − Tax rate)	73.7%	73.7%	72.0%
= **Interest expense after tax**	**1,139.9**	**1,239.3**	**1,109.9**
= **Net profit**	**15,821.0**	**18,681.0**	**16,384.0**

Source: Authors' calculations.

Condensed Balance Sheets (SEK millions)

Fiscal year ended November 30	2011	2010	2009
Ending net working capital			
Operating cash	8,799.9	8,678.6	8,111.4
+ Trade receivables	2,337.0	2,258.0	1,990.0
+ Inventories	13,819.0	11,487.0	10,240.0
+ Other current assets	2,029.0	1,872.0	1,566.0
− Trade payables	4,307.0	3,965.0	3,667.0
− Other current liabilities	10,300.0	9,706.0	7,088.0
= **Ending net working capital**	**12,377.9**	**10,624.6**	**11,152.4**
+ **Ending net non-current operating assets**			
Non-current tangible assets	67,941.5	63,594.5	61,940.0
+ Non-current intangible assets	450.0	510.0	930.0
+ Derivatives (assets net of liabilities)	306.0	281.0	−75.0
− Deferred tax liabilities (net of assets)	−284.0	−159.0	792.0
− Other non-current liabilities (non-interest-bearing)	0.0	0.0	0.0
= **Ending net non-current operating assets**	**68,981.5**	**64,544.5**	**62,003.0**
+ **Ending investment assets**			
Excess cash	12,477.1	16,179.4	13,913.6
Minority equity investments	0.0	0.0	0.0
+ Other non-operating investments	608.0	518.0	551.0
= **Ending investment assets**	**13,085.1**	**16,697.4**	**14,464.6**
= **Total business assets**	**94,444.5**	**91,866.5**	**87,620.0**
Ending Debt			
Current debt	0.0	0.0	0.0
+ Non-current debt	50,340.5	47,694.5	46,639.0
+ Preference shares	0.0	0.0	0.0
= **Ending debt**	**50,340.5**	**47,694.5**	**46,639.0**
+ **Ending group equity**			
Ordinary shareholders' equity	44,104.0	44,172.0	40,613.0
+ Minority interests	0.0	0.0	0.0
− Net assets held for sale	0.0	0.0	0.0
= **Group equity**	**44,104.0**	**44,172.0**	**40,613.0**
= **Total capital**	**94,444.5**	**91,866.5**	**87,252.0**

Source: Authors' calculations.

Carrefour S.A.

Analyst Chrystelle Moreau of Leblanc Investissements, a small Paris-based investment firm, glanced through the annual report of Groupe Carrefour for the fiscal year 2011 that she had just received. The past year had been a worrisome year for Carrefour's shareholders; during the year the company's share price had decreased by close to 43 percent. The analyst was considering various European large cap stocks for possible inclusion in her firm's high-dividend yield fund. Although Carrefour's management had proposed a reduction in dividends per share from €1.08 in 2010 to €0.52 in 2011, the recent decline in the company's market capitalization could make Carrefour an attractive addition to the fund. In fact, Moreau estimated that even if dividends would remain at 52 cents in 2012, Carrefour's dividend yield would still be close to a respectable level of 3 percent.

In January 2012, Lars Olofsson had stepped down as Carrefour's Chairman and Chief Executive Officer (CEO) to make place for Georges Plassat, the former Chairman and CEO of France-based apparel company Vivarte. Olofsson had led Carrefour for close to three years, during which his main task had been to turnaround the company's growth and financial performance. Carrefour's core strengths had long been its low prices, its wide product offering, and the convenience of finding all of its products in one place, i.e., in its hypermarkets.[1] However, the company's business model had gradually become outdated, also as a result of the increasing popularity of shopping on the internet where the selection of low-priced (non-food) products was still growing and potentially limitless. Carrefour also lost market share in the food segment of the retail market, presumably because, as some analysts argued, the company's relatively expensive hypermarkets prevented it from being sufficiently price competitive. Olofsson's expertise in marketing and consumer behavior and his experience at Nestlé, where he had helped building the success of Nespresso, potentially made him the right person to develop a new strategy that would win back customers to Carrefour's hypermarkets.

During the 1990s, Carrefour had been one of Moreau's favorite shares. The company had created a great reputation for its broad assortment and low prices, and had shown an outstanding share price performance. During the first half of the 2000s, however, Carrefour's share price had fallen from about €80 to €40, despite the fact that the company had consistently earned returns on equity in excess of 17 percent. In 2005, Jose Luis Duran took over from Daniel Bernard as the CEO of Carrefour, planning to put an end to Carrefour's over-aggressive expansion abroad and its incoherent pricing strategy in France.[2] However, in 2008, soon after the privately-held investment firm Colony Capital and French billionaire Bernard Arnault had acquired a 14 percent stake in Carrefour (and 20 percent of the voting rights), they forced out Duran and welcomed Olofsson as the new CEO in an effort to speed up the company's change process. Two pillars of Olofsson's turnaround plan were the offering and marketing of competitive low prices and the realization of cost savings, as the new CEO discussed in Carrefour's 2008 annual report:

In 2009, we are tailoring our plan to the current economic climate because the year may not be easy. For that reason, we have three top priorities: customers, costs, and

Professor Erik Peek prepared this case. The case is intended solely as the basis for class discussion and is not intended to serve as an endorsement, source of primary data, or illustration of effective or ineffective management.

[1] See "Bread, Cheese, New Boss?" *The Economist*, January 14, 2012.

[2] See "Carrefour at Crossroads," *The Economist,* October 20, 2005.

cash. In this environment, we must, more than ever, have a close relationship with our customers. We plan to invest €600 million in our retail business, in our price competitiveness, including its promotion to customers, and in our Carrefour brand offering, with a 40 percent increase in products. That is our strategy for gaining market share. At the same time, we intend to reduce our operating costs by €500 million as part of our transformation plan. That means we'll save three times more than we did in 2008, and the savings should increase over time to ensure our competitive advantage and improve our profitability. We will continue to generate cash through sound management, particularly by reducing our stock levels from 37 to 35 days to free up the resources we need for growth. Our 2009 objectives are clear, but I will remain vigilant and ready to respond as the situation demands.

In addition, Olofsson introduced a new store concept, labeled "Carrefour Planet," and developed plans to streamline the company, resulting in, for example, the spin-off the retailer's hard discount division (Dia) in 2011. Olofsson's actions did, however, not help to improve Carrefour's financial performance. During the fiscal years 2009 through 2011 the retailer's share price decreased by 26 percent (adjusted for the Dia spin-off). Having seen the value of their investment more than halve since acquisition, Arnault and Colony Capital intervened and replaced Olofsson with Plassat early 2012.

Being aware of these developments, a few questions arose for the analyst. In particular, she wanted to get a better understanding of what had caused Carrefour's performance decline during the past years as well as the company's current financial position. Further, she wanted to find out what could have driven Carrefour to cut its dividends for 2011, also with an eye on future dividend decisions.

Company background

France-based food and non-food retailer Carrefour was established in 1959 by the Fournier and Defforey families and opened its first hypermarket in Sainte-Geneviéve-de-Bois in 1963. The hypermarket concept was the store concept that Carrefour would eventually become most famous for. The typical characteristic of such hypermarkets is that they offer a wide assortment of food as well as nonfood products at economic prices and are of a much greater size than the traditional supermarkets. Specifically, the size of hypermarkets can range from 2,400 to 23,000 square meters. In comparison, Carrefour's regular supermarkets, operating under the name Carrefour Market, and convenience stores, such as the Carrefour City and Carrefour Express stores, have sales areas ranging from 90 to 4,000 square meters.

In 1979 Carrefour opened its first hard discount stores under the "Ed" banner in France and under the "Dia" banner in Spain. The hard discount stores sold a much smaller variety of products than the hypermarkets (on average 800 products versus 20,000 to 80,000) on a much smaller store space (between 200 and 800 square meters) at discount prices. Some of the discount products were sold under own brand names, such as the Dia brand name. After having transformed its Ed stores into Dia stores at the end of the 2000s, Carrefour spun off its hard discount division in 2011. To achieve this, the company paid out a special dividend of one Dia share for each ordinary Carrefour share on July 5, 2011, leading to a decrease in the company's market capitalization by close to €2.3 billion (or 12 percent).

During the 1970s and 1980s, Carrefour expanded across the oceans and established hypermarkets in, for example, Brazil (1975), Argentina (1982), and Taiwan (1989). The international and intercontinental expansion of Carrefour took off especially in the 1990s when Carrefour opened a large number of hypermarkets in southern Europe (Greece, Italy, and Turkey), eastern Europe (Poland), Asia (China, Hong Kong, Korea, Malaysia, Singapore, and Thailand), and Latin America (Mexico, Chile, and Colombia). The company's intercontinental expansion primarily occurred through the opening of hypermarkets. Most of Carrefour's smaller supermarkets were located throughout Europe. **Exhibit 1** provides information about Carrefour's operations by geographic segment and by store format.

In addition to its traditional food and nonfood retailing activities, the company soon offered traveling, financial, and insurance services to its customers in Brazil, France, and Spain. For example, Carrefour has its own payment card, the "Pass" card, which it introduced in the early 1980s. In the beginning, the Pass card offered customers priority at store check-outs and allowed them to pay their bills in installments. Later, the card became linked to a credit card and customers could borrow money for out-of-store purchases. By the end of 2011, Carrefour's financial services unit had €5.6 billion in credit outstanding throughout the world.

One of the key events in Carrefour's history took place in 1999, when it merged with Promodès, a large French food retailer that owned the Champion supermarket chain. At the time of the merger, Carrefour and Promodès were, respectively, the sixth and ninth largest retailers in the world and held market shares of around 18 and 12 percent in France. After the merger, the combined company, which continued under the name Carrefour, became Europe's largest retailer, the world's second largest retailer, and the world's most international supermarket chain. An important trigger for the merger was that in the late 1990s, US-based Wal-Mart, the world's largest retailer, was expanding its operations to Europe and posed a potential threat to the French retailer's strong position in their home market.

The integration of the operations of Promodès and Carrefour went slowly and the merger of the two retailers was the start of a difficult period. Immediately following the merger, Carrefour acquired a few other supermarket chains, such as Norte in Argentina, GS in Italy, and GB in Belgium, emphasizing its desire to aggressively expand its operations and become the leading international retailer. However, over the years, competition in the food retailing industry substantially increased and all retailers came under pressure to cut prices. Carrefour's sales growth in its home market suffered from the competition of France-based Leclerc and Auchan, which focused their strategy on cutting prices and gaining market share. Although Carrefour did join its French rivals in cutting prices, the company aimed much more at improving its margins than increasing sales volumes. Only in 2003, when Carrefour's sales growth in France approached zero, did the company start to put more emphasis on competing on price, gaining market share, and stimulating customer loyalty.

Between 2005 and 2008, Carrefour's then-CEO Jose Luis Duran managed to restore the retailer's (organic) sales and profit growth. During this period, Carrefour redesigned its store layout, further widened its product offering, and expanded its assortment of Carrefour-branded products. Carrefour also abandoned its multi-banner strategy and gradually brought all store concepts under the Carrefour banner, with the exception of the retailer's hard discount division, to improve branding. Further, the retailer withdrew operations from some of its less profitable geographic segments. However, being unsatisfied with the speed of change and Carrefour's profitability, the company's primary shareholders, Arnault and Colony Capital, forced out Duran at the end 2008.

Carrefour had been listed on the Paris Stock Exchange (Euronext) since 1970. The company's stock price performance during the years 2005 through 2012 is summarized in **Exhibit 2**.

Carrefour from 2009 to 2011

In 2009, Lars Olofsson took over as the CEO of Carrefour and introduced a new three-year transformation plan. The transformation plan involved increasing customers' awareness of Carrefour's price competitiveness. Furthermore, the plan aimed at achieving significant cost savings, gradually reducing days inventories (by seven days), and revitalizing the hypermarket concept. To achieve the latter, Carrefour launched the Carrefour Planet concept in 2010. Carrefour Planet stores were redesigned, more spacious hypermarkets organized in distinct product areas: market, organic, frozen, beauty, fashion, baby, home, and leisure-multimedia. The primary goals of this redesign were to provide a more focused offering of non-food products, improve the hypermarkets' attractiveness, win back customers, and improve store traffic. After a successful pilot with the conversion of two hypermarkets in 2010, Carrefour decided to convert around 250 additional hypermarkets into Carrefour Planet stores between 2011 and 2013. At the end of 2011, Carrefour had opened 81 Carrefour Planet stores, of which 29 and 39 were located in France and Spain, respectively.

In 2009, 2010, and 2011, Carrefour realized costs savings of €590, €495, and €449 million (excluding Dia's cost savings), respectively, although part of these cost savings were offset by the effect concurrent cost inflation. The retailer maintained the amount that it spent on expansion. In particular, capital expenditures for expansion were €665 million (excluding Dia) and €660 million in 2010 and 2011, respectively. In contrast, amounts spent on remodeling and maintenance increased from €838 million in 2010 to €1,303 million in 2011. Further, IT spending increased from €329 million (excluding Dia) in 2010 to €367 million in 2011.

In March 2011, Carrefour's management announced its intention to spin off its hard discount unit Dia. Management argued that Dia's business model was significantly different from Carrefour's, which reduced the synergies from combining the two companies. In addition, management revealed its plans to spin off its property into a separate publicly listed entity. However, while Carrefour did complete the spin-off of Dia on July 5, 2011, the retailer decided to postpone its property spin-off plans under pressure from activist investors who feared that the spin-off would be too costly and value-destroying.

Carrefour S.A.

Carrefour in 2012

In its 2011 financial statements Carrefour's management disclosed the following outlook for 2012:

In 2012, the Group intends to maintain strict financial discipline in response to a still challenging busi-ness environment. It will pursue initiatives deployed since the introduction of the Transformation Plan in 2009 with the goal of reducing costs by approximately 400 million euros. The Group has also set an objective of reducing inventory turnover by two days. Expenditure for the deployment of the new Car-refour Planet hypermarket concept will be sharply reduced in 2012, with priority going to expanding the store network in key growth markets. Investments for the year will total between 1,600 million euros and 1,700 million euros.

For comparison, in 2011 investments in tangible and intangible fixed assets had amounted to €2,330 mil-lion, of which €369 million had resulted from remodeling expenditures incurred for the development of Car-refour Planet hypermarkets in Europe. Because the performance of the Carrefour Planet stores had been lower than expected in 2011, management decided to significantly scale down the investment in hypermarket conversions. In fact, it planned to convert only 11 hypermarkets into Carrefour Planet stores (compared with 81 in 2011) and put a further roll out of the conversion plan on hold, or, alternatively, lower the conversion costs before any further roll out. Some of the other strategic actions that management planned to take in 2012 were to further improve Carrefour's price positioning, revamp a large selection of Carrefour-branded products, accelerate cost savings and investments in e-commerce, including the expansion of the number of Drives where customers can pick up their online orders, and increase the number of (smaller) convenience stores.

At the beginning of 2012, Carrefour also disclosed that its expected payout policy for 2012 was to pay out approximately 45 percent of net group income (adjusted for exceptional items) as dividends, with a max-imum cash payout of €340 million.

Casino

One of Carrefour's French competitors was Groupe Casino. Though being significantly smaller than Carre-four in terms of revenues (€34.4 billion sales in 2011), the retailer was fairly comparable in terms of strategy. In particular, like Carrefour, Casino had adopted a multi-format strategy, operating hypermarkets (Géant), supermarkets (Casino and Monoprix), convenience stores (Petite Casino and Franprix), and discount stores (Leader Price). More than 80 percent of Casino's stores were located in France, where Casino was the third largest food retailer; however, in 2011 the retailer earned 55 percent of its revenues outside France. The retailer's key international markets were Brazil, Colombia, Thailand, and Vietnam. In 2011, Casino's hyper-markets accounted for 30 percent and supermarkets for 19 percent of the company's revenues.

Casino held a 50.4 percent equity stake in Mercialys, a publicly listed real estate investment company that owned the Casino group's 120 shopping centres, and a controlling interest in banking subsidiary Banque Ca-sino, which helped the company to offer financial services through its stores. Although retailing was its pri-mary focus, Casino aimed to create additional value by developing a valuable real estate portfolio through its subsidiary Mercialys and other property development subsidiaries. In 2011, Casino's return on equity was 8.4 percent. **Exhibit 7** shows a summary of Casino's financial performance in fiscal years 2009 through 2011.

Tesco

One of Carrefour's European industry peers was UK-based Tesco, one of the world's largest retailers, to-gether with Carrefour and Wal-Mart. The strategies of Carrefour and Tesco exhibited some similarities. Par-ticularly, both retailers engaged in international expansion and reserved a substantial amount of store space for nonfood products. Tesco's operations were less international than Carrefour's. In 2011, 57 percent of Carrefour's revenues came from outside France, whereas 41 percent of Tesco's revenues were earned outside the UK. Like Carrefour, Tesco offered financial services, such as banking and insurance services, to its cus-tomers. Tesco also operated a successful online grocery store, with sales over £2 billion.

The company had different store formats, which all operated under the Tesco banner. Tesco Express and Metro stores were the smallest type of stores (with up to 5,000 square meters) and focused on selling food products. Tesco's Superstores occupied between 7,000 and 16,000 square meters and offered both food and nonfood products. Since 1997, Tesco also operated Extra stores, which offered a wide range of food and nonfood lines, including electrical equipment, clothing, and health and pharmaceutical products. These stores had store spaces of approximately 20,000 square meters. Tesco's Superstores and Extra stores were thus comparable, at least in size and assortment, to Carrefour's Hypermarkets.

In the fiscal year ending on February 25, 2012, Tesco's return on equity was 17.6 percent. **Exhibit 7** shows a summary of Tesco's financial performance in fiscal years 2009 through 2011.

Carrefour S.A.

Carrefour S.A.

EXHIBIT 1   Carrefour's operations by geographic segment and store format

(in € millions)	Fiscal year	France	Rest of Europe	Latin America	Asia	Hard discount
Net sales	2011	35,179	23,699	15,082	7,312	9,753
	2010	34,907	24,597	13,919	6,923	9,600
	2009	34,266	25,058	10,598	6,441	9,600
	2008	35,150	26,674	9,560	5,955	9,629
Recurring operating income	2011	862	508	554	258	232
	2010	1,284	726	441	289	171
	2009	1,084	805	472	244	195
	2008	1,469	1,000	384	258	
Tangible and intangible fixed assets	2011	4,677	5,110	3,453	1,497	1,643
	2010	4,604	5,224	3,510	1,417	1,746
	2009	4,488	5,362	3,092	1,437	1,655
	2008	4,528	5,724	2,508	1,401	
Capital expenditures	2011	928	683	463	256	290
	2010	744	452	418	218	341
	2009	718	405	372	301	442
	2008	759	810	546	351	
Depreciation and amortization expense	2011	688	517	290	216	250
	2010	648	536	278	210	242
	2009	606	569	227	213	225
	2008	646	585	218	195	
Sales area of consolidated stores (in square meters, thousands)	2011	3,093	4,469	2,340	2,636	1,983
	2010	3,126	4,467	2,304	2,459	2,134
	2009	3,103	4,499	2,203	2,517	2,101
	2008	3,055	4,334	2,113	2,210	

EXHIBIT 2   **Carrefour's stock price and the MSCI Europe price index
from December 1995 to December 2011 (price on December 31,
1995 = 100)**

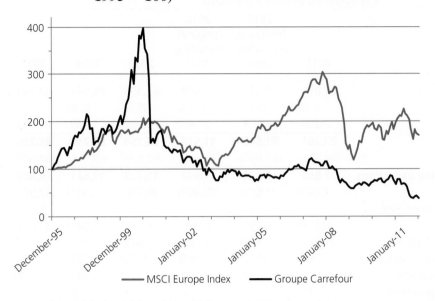

EXHIBIT 3   **Carrefour's consolidated income statements, balance sheets, and cash flow statements, 2006 to 2011 (in € millions)**

Consolidated Income Statements

IFRS – € millions	2011	2010 (restated, excluding Dia)	2010 (original, including Dia)	2009	2008	2007
Net sales	81,271	80,511	90,099	85,366	86,967	82,149
Loyalty program costs	(816)	(774)	(774)	(602)	(626)	–
Other revenue	2,309	2,103	2,187	1,990	1,899	1,147
Total revenue	**82,764**	**81,840**	**91,512**	**86,754**	**88,240**	**83,296**
Cost of sales	(64,912)	(63,969)	(71,640)	(67,626)	(68,719)	(64,609)
Gross margin from recurring operations	**17,852**	**17,871**	**19,872**	**19,128**	**19,521**	**18,686**
Labour costs	(7,843)	(7,699)	(8,493)	(8,290)	(8,307)	(7,988)
Other sales, general and administrative expenses	(6,126)	(5,795)	(6,486)	(6,269)	(6,045)	(5,685)
Depreciation of tangible fixed assets	(1,427)	(1,427)	(1,664)	(1,645)	(1,651)	(1,517)
Amortization of intangible fixed assets	(267)	(232)	(240)	(214)	(198)	(183)
Depreciation – investment properties	(18)	(19)	(19)	(20)	(20)	(18)
Allocations and reversals of provisions	10	2	2	31	9	(5)
Recurring operating income	**2,181**	**2,701**	**2,972**	**2,721**	**3,309**	**3,291**
Net gains (losses) on sales of assets	255	54	–	–	–	–
Impairment losses	(2,161)	(135)	(223)	(761)	(396)	(23)
Restructuring costs	(209)	(346)	(415)	(237)	(72)	(92)
Other non-recurring items	(547)	(571)	(498)	(67)	(52)	162
Operating income	**(481)**	**1,703**	**1,836**	**1,656**	**2,789**	**3,338**
Finance income	80	47	76	30	27	43
Finance costs	(666)	(614)	(617)	(638)	(713)	(628)
Changes in the fair value or gains/losses on sales of financial assets	(171)	(81)	(116)	2	125	59
Income before taxes	**(1,238)**	**1,055**	**1,179**	**1,050**	**2,228**	**2,812**
Income tax expense	(1,002)	(610)	(697)	(635)	(740)	(807)
Net income from companies accounted for by the equity method	64	34	35	38	52	43
Income attributable to non-controlling interests	(33)	(135)	(135)	(110)	(266)	(180)
Net income from continuing operations	**(2,209)**	**344**	**382**	**343**	**1,274**	**1,869**
Net income from discontinued operations	2,580	89	51	(67)	(5)	431
Net income	**371**	**433**	**433**	**276**	**1,269**	**2,299**

Carrefour S.A.

Consolidated Balance Sheets

IFRS – € millions	2011	2010 (original, including Dia)	2009	2008	2007	2006
ASSETS						
Inventories	6,848	6,994	6,607	6,867	6,867	6,051
Commercial receivables	2,781	2,555	2,336	3,226	3,424	3,620
Consumer credit granted by the financial services companies – short term	3,384	3,444	3,215	2,708	2,713	2,586
Other current financial assets	911	1,811	2,051	245	–	–
Tax receivables	468	621	564	673	582	553
Other receivable and prepaid expenses	941	988	964	1,056	956	815
Loans	28	55	12	–	–	–
Cash and cash equivalents	3,849	3,271	3,300	5,316	4,164	3,697
Assets held for sale	44	471	241	151	670	25
Total current assets	**19,254**	**20,210**	**19,290**	**20,242**	**19,376**	**17,347**
Goodwill	8,740	11,829	11,473	11,363	11,674	10,852
Other intangible assets	966	1,100	1,075	1,050	1,173	1,038
Tangible fixed assets	13,770	15,299	15,031	14,793	14,751	13,735
Other non-current financial assets	1,433	1,542	1,310	1,306	1,119	1,111
Investments in companies accounted for by the equity method	280	256	201	430	436	417
Deferred tax assets	745	766	713	682	944	922
Investment property	507	536	455	346	500	455
Consumer credit granted by the financial services companies – long term	2,236	2,112	2,005	2,097	1,959	1,656
Total non-current assets	**28,677**	**33,440**	**32,263**	**32,067**	**32,556**	**30,186**
Total assets	**47,931**	**53,650**	**51,553**	**52,309**	**51,932**	**47,533**
EQUITY AND LIABILITIES						
Short-term borrowings	2,149	2,715	2,158	2,785	3,247	2,474
Suppliers and other creditors	15,362	16,796	16,800	17,544	17,077	16,450
Consumer credit financing – short term	4,482	4,527	4,061	4,044	3,989	3,427
Tax payables	1,319	1,298	1,325	1,467	1,193	1,172
Other payables	2,785	2,824	2,747	2,875	3,114	2,910
Liabilities related to assets held for sale	–	321	93	25	227	13
Total current liabilities	**26,097**	**28,481**	**27,184**	**28,740**	**28,847**	**26,446**
Long-term borrowings	9,523	10,365	9,794	9,505	8,276	7,532
Post-employment benefit obligations	734	777	689	668	674	707
Other provisions	2,946	2,411	1,927	1,709	2,147	2,256
Deferred tax liabilities	586	560	496	424	462	280
Consumer credit financing – long term	419	493	592	451	430	516
Total liabilities	**14,208**	**14,606**	**13,498**	**12,757**	**11,315**	**10,584**
Shareholders' equity attributable to non-controlling interests	**1,009**	**979**	**798**	**789**	**1,107**	**1,017**
Share capital	1,698	1,698	1,762	1,762	1,762	1,762
Consolidated reserves and (loss)/income for the year	4,919	7,886	8,311	8,261	8,901	7,724
Shareholders' equity – group share	**6,617**	**9,584**	**10,073**	**10,023**	**10,663**	**9,486**
Total shareholders' equity and liabilities	**47,931**	**53,650**	**51,553**	**52,309**	**51,932**	**47,533**

Carrefour S.A.

Consolidated Cash Flow Statements

IFRS – € millions	2011	2010 (restated, excluding Dia)	2010 (original, including Dia)	2009	2008	2007
(Loss)/Income before taxes	**(1,238)**	**1,055**	**1,179**	**1,052**	**2,228**	**2,812**
Depreciation and amortization expense	1,795	1,740	2,033	1,965	1,946	1,790
Taxes	(712)	(589)	(678)	(618)	(624)	(660)
Capital gains/losses on sales of assets	(155)	(74)	(30)	8	(225)	(139)
Change in provisions and impairment	2,643	771	804	937	642	98
Dividends received from companies accounted for by the equity method	26	12	12	38	50	7
Impact of discontinued operations	217	478	73	(1)	(12)	10
Change in working capital requirement	(117)	(730)	(598)	294	972	(89)
Impact of discontinued operations	(111)	158	26	11	21	40
Change in consumer credit granted by the financial services companies	(229)	(84)	(84)	(256)	(111)	43
Net cash from operating activities	**2,119**	**2,737**	**2,737**	**3,430**	**4,887**	**3,912**
Acquisitions of property and equipment and intangible assets	(2,330)	(1,832)	(2,122)	(2,074)	(2,908)	(3,069)
Acquisitions of financial assets	(30)	(46)	(48)	(38)	(143)	(101)
Acquisitions of subsidiaries	(41)	(97)	(97)	(116)	(296)	(1,388)
Proceeds from the disposal of subsidiaries	7	15	15	47	191	684
Proceeds from the disposal of property and equipment and intangible assets	495	196	203	128	742	505
Proceeds from disposals of investments in non-consolidated companies	21	51	51	7	12	33
Other cash flows from investing activities	151	(274)	(284)	(215)	(171)	(50)
Impact of discontinued operations	1,329	(320)	(25)	(115)	(23)	(105)
Net cash used in investing activities	**(398)**	**(2,307)**	**(2,307)**	**(2,376)**	**(2,596)**	**(3,491)**
Proceeds from share issues	37	17	17	7	3	14
Acquisitions and disposals of investments without any change of control	(13)	218	218	–	–	–
Dividends paid by Carrefour (parent company)	(708)	(740)	(740)	(741)	(740)	(722)
Dividends paid by consolidated companies to non-controlling interests	(103)	(124)	(124)	(161)	(202)	(106)
Change in treasury stock and other equity instruments	(126)	(943)	(943)	1	(404)	(507)
Change in current financial assets	853	221	221	(1,860)	(233)	–
Issuance of bonds	500	1,978	1,978	510	–	–
Repayments of bonds	(1,442)	(1,000)	(1,000)	(1,000)	–	–
Other changes in borrowings	(190)	(71)	(53)	75	561	1,298
Impact of discontinued operations	22	100	83	67	(13)	69
Net cash used in financing activities	**(1,170)**	**(344)**	**(344)**	**(3,102)**	**(1,028)**	**46**
Effect of changes in exchange rates	27	(115)	(115)	31	(110)	–
Net change in cash and cash equivalents	**578**	**(29)**	**(29)**	**(2,017)**	**1,153**	**467**
Cash and cash equivalents at beginning of period	3,271	3,300	3,300	5,316	4,164	3,697
Cash and cash equivalents at end of period	**3,849**	**3,271**	**3,271**	**3,300**	**5,317**	**4,164**

Carrefour S.A.

EXHIBIT 4 Excerpts from Carrefour's annual report for the fiscal year ending December 31, 2011

Note 2: Summary of significant accounting policies

2.2 Segment information

IFRS 8 – Operating Segments requires the disclosure of information about an entity's operating segments extracted from the internal reporting system and used by the entity's chief operating decision maker to make decisions about resources to be allocated to the segment and assess its performance. Based on the IFRS 8 definition, the Group's operating segments are the countries in which it conducts its business through consolidated stores.

These countries have been combined to create four geographical segments:

- France;
- Rest of Europe: Spain, Italy, Belgium, Greece, Poland, Turkey, and Romania;
- Latin America: Brazil, Argentina, and Colombia;
- Asia: China, Taiwan, Malaysia, Indonesia, India, and Singapore.

The hard discount operating segment for which information was disclosed in 2010 no longer exists following the loss of control of the Dia sub-group on July 5, 2011.

2.8 Banking activities

To support its core retailing business, the Group offers banking and insurance services to customers through its subsidiary Carrefour Banque. Due to its specific financial structure, this secondary business is presented separately in the Consolidated Financial Statements:

- consumer credit granted by the financial services companies (payment card receivables, personal loans, etc.) is presented in the statement of financial position under "Consumer credit granted by the financial services companies – long-term" and "Consumer credit granted by the financial services companies – short-term" as appropriate;
- financing for these loans is presented under "Consumer credit financing – long-term" and "Consumer credit financing – short term" as appropriate;
- revenues from banking activities are reported in the income statement under "Other revenue";
- cash flows generated by banking activities are reported in the statement of cash flows under "Change in consumer credit granted by the financial services companies".

2.15 Non-current assets and disposal groups held for sale and discontinued operations

A discontinued operation is a component of an entity that has been either disposed of or classified as held for sale, and:

- represents a separate major line of business or geographical area of operations; and
- is part of a single coordinated plan to dispose of a separate major line of business or geographical area of operations; or
- is a subsidiary acquired exclusively with a view to resale.

It is classified as a discontinued operation at the time of sale or earlier if its assets and liabilities meet the criteria for classification as "held for sale." When a component of an entity is classified as a discontinued operation, comparative income statement and cash flow information are restated as if the entity had met the criteria for classification as a discontinued operation on the first day of the comparative period.

In addition, all the assets and liabilities of the discontinued operation are presented on separate lines on each side of the statement of financial position, for the amounts at which they would be reported at the time of sale after eliminating intra-group items.

2.17 Other revenue

Other revenue, corresponding mainly to sales of financial services and travel, rental revenues and franchise fees, is reported on a separate line below "Net sales" in the income statement.

Financial services revenues correspond mainly to bank card fees and arranging fees for traditional and revolving credit facilities, which are recognized over the life of the contract.

Note 3: Significant events of the year

Economic environment

The Group operated in a challenging macro-economic environment in 2011, particularly in Southern Europe.

In response to the deepening crisis in the second half and the introduction of successive austerity plans in the various European countries, the Group revised its business plan projections to reflect the new environment. The downgrading of the Group's growth forecasts in Greece and Italy led to the recognition of significant impairment losses on goodwill, in the

Carrefour S.A.

amounts of 188 million euros and 1,750 million euros respectively, representing total non-recurring expense for the year of 1,938 million euros.

Distribution of Dia shares

The Shareholders Meeting of June 21, 2011 approved the distribution on July 5, 2011 of 100 percent of Dia's share capital to Carrefour shareholders, in the form of a special dividend in kind. At that date, there were 679,336,000 Carrefour shares outstanding and the same number of Dia shares, so that shareholders received one Dia share for each Carrefour share held.

Also on July 5, 2011, Dia SA was listed on the Madrid Stock Exchange at an IPO price of 3.40 euros per share. [...]

Consequently, in the interim financial statements at June 30, 2011, the dividend was recognized by recording a liability towards shareholders. In the absence of a more reliable indicator at June 30, 2011, the fair value of Dia shares at that date was considered as being equal to the initial fair value of 3.40 euros per share, corresponding to the July 5, 2011 IPO price.

In the financial statements at December 31, 2011, the Group recorded:

- in shareholders' equity – Group share, the dividend recorded in Carrefour SA's accounts, i.e. 2,230 million euros (unchanged from June 30, 2011);
- in cash and cash equivalents, the proceeds from the sale of Dia shares held in treasury stock at the time of the distribution (79 million euros);
- in net income from discontinued operations, the 1,909 million euros capital gain corresponding to the difference between the fair value of the Dia shares (2,309 million euros) and their carrying amount, including disposal costs and the tax effect (400 million euros).

Dia and its subsidiaries were consolidated by Carrefour up to the date when control of the companies was lost, on July 5, 2011. In accordance with IFRS 5, the following reclassifications were made in the 2011 annual financial statements:

- Dia's net income for the period up to the date when control was lost (32 million euros) was included in the carrying amount at June 30 and therefore presented under "Net income from discontinued operations" as part of the 1,909 million euros capital gain referred to above. To permit meaningful comparisons, Dia's 2010 net income was also reclassified to this line;
- in the statement of cash flows, all of Dia's cash flows for the first half of 2011 were presented on the lines "Impact of discontinued operations." Its 2010 cash flows were reclassified accordingly.

Disposal of operations in Thailand

Pursuant to an agreement signed on November 15, 2010, on January 7, 2011 Carrefour sold its operations in Thailand to Big C, a subsidiary of the Casino Group, for a total of 816 million euros net of transaction costs. The capital gain on the transaction, in the amount of 667 million euros, is reported in the 2011 income statement under "Net income from discontinued operations."

Other significant events

On December 27, 2011, the Group sold a portfolio of 97 supermarket properties owned by Carrefour Property for 365 million euros. The supermarkets will continue to be operated under the Carrefour Market banner under long-term fixed rent leases with an indexation clause.

The transaction qualifies as a sale-and-leaseback transaction under IAS 17 – Leases. The leases with the new owner of the properties, for an initial term of 12 years with multiple renewal options, fulfill the criteria for classification as operating leases, as substantially all the risks and rewards incidental to ownership of the asset are retained by the lessor.

The properties were sold at market price and the capital gain, net of transaction costs, was recognized in full in the 2011 income statement in the amount of 229 million euros.

Note 14: Net income from discontinued operations

Net income from discontinued operations in 2011 comprises:

- the net gain on the sale of operations in Thailand, for 667 million euros;
- the net gain on the sale of the Dia entities and their contribution to consolidated income for the period up to the sale date, for 1,909 million euros.

Net income from discontinued operations in 2010 comprises:

- the contribution to 2010 consolidated income of operations in Thailand, for 44 million euros;
- the contribution to 2010 consolidated income of the Dia subsidiaries, for 38 million euros;
- the contribution to 2010 consolidated income of the Russian subsidiary, for a negative 3 million euros;
- the reversal of a provision set aside at the time of the 2005 sale of the out-of-home dining business, for 11 million euros.

Note 19: Investment property

Investment property consists mainly of shopping malls located adjacent to the Group's stores.

(in millions of euros)	12/31/2011	12/31/2010
Investment property at cost	702	709
Depreciation	(195)	(173)
Total	507	536

Rental revenue generated by investment property, reported in the income statement under "Other revenue," totaled 104.6 million euros in 2011 (2010: 100 million euros). Operating costs directly attributable to the properties amounted to 12.1 million euros in 2011 (2010: 14.7 million euros).

The estimated fair value of investment property was 1,346 million euros at December 31, 2011 (December 31, 2010: 1,343 million euros).

Note 22: Inventories

(in millions of euros)	12/31/2011	12/31/2010
Inventories at cost	7,150	7,282
Impairment	(302)	(289)
Inventories net	6,848	6,994

Note 23: Commercial receivables

(in millions of euros)	12/31/2011	12/31/2010
Commercial receivables	1,446	1,263
Impairment	(240)	(259)
Commercial receivables, net	1,207	1,004
Receivables from suppliers	1,575	1,551
Total	2,782	2,555

Commercial receivables correspond for the most part to amounts due by franchisees. Receivables from suppliers correspond to rebates and supplier contributions to marketing costs.

Note 35: Other payables

(in millions of euros)	12/31/2011	12/31/2010
Accrued employee benefits expense	1,615	1,702
Due to suppliers of non-current assets	763	669
Deferred revenue	72	59
Other payables	336	394
Total	2,785	2,824

Note 42: Subsequent events

Guyenne & Gascogne

On December 12, 2011, the Group announced that it planned to file a cash offer with a stock alternative for Guyenne & Gascogne, its historical partner in south-western France.

The offer terms are as follows:

- cash offer: one Guyenne & Gascogne share (cum dividend) for 74.25 euros in cash (as adjusted for any dividend payment in addition to the interim dividend described below);
- alternative stock offer: one Guyenne & Gascogne share for 3.90 Carrefour shares (cum dividend). The stock alternative will be available for a maximum of 4,986,786 Guyenne & Gascogne shares.

Guyenne & Gascogne has stated that it will pay an interim dividend of seven euros before the close of the offer period. This interim dividend has been taken into account in determining the offer price.

Guyenne & Gascogne operates six Carrefour hypermarkets and 28 Carrefour Market supermarkets under franchise agreements. In 2011, these stores generated sales of 623 million euros including VAT. Guyenne & Gascogne is also a 50/50 shareholder of Sogara alongside Carrefour, which exercises management control. Sogara owns and operates 13 hypermarkets, which generated sales of 1.6 billion euros including VAT in 2011 and also holds an 8.2 percent stake in Centros Comerciales Carrefour, the holding company for Carrefour's operating activities in Spain.

Carrefour's draft information memorandum was filed with France's securities regulator, Autorité des Marchés Financiers (AMF), on February 14, 2012. It was approved by the AMF on February 28 under visa no. 12-095.

New financial services partnership in Brazil

On April 14, 2011, the Group announced that it had signed an agreement for the sale to Itaù Unibanco of 49 percent of BSF Holding, the company that controls Carrefour's financial services and insurance operations in Brazil. The partnership with Itaù Unibanco will enable Carrefour to bolster its financial services and insurance businesses by leveraging the major potential synergies between the two groups and expanding its financial product and service offering.

On June 30, 2011, Carrefour notified Cetelem, its current partner in BSF Holding, that it intended to exercise its call option on Cetelem's 40 percent interest at a total price of 132.5 million euros.

The buyout of its current partner and the sale of shares to Itaù Unibanco are subject to the usual regulatory provisions, including the requirement to obtain an authorization from the Brazilian central bank.

On completion of the transactions, Carrefour will hold a 51 percent majority stake in BSF Holding along with the 315 million euros proceeds from the sale of the 49 percent interest.

The deal is expected to close during the first half of 2012.

Carrefour S.A.

EXHIBIT 5   **Carrefour's operating leases, post-employment benefit obligations, and other revenues during the fiscal years 2006 through 2011**

Future minimum operating lease payments

€ millions	2011	2010	2009	2008	2007	2006
Within one year	957	1,081	1,002	859	800	788
In one to five years	1,888	1,850	2,183	2,076	1,626	1,905
Beyond five years	1,714	2,231	3,014	2,928	2,473	2,704
Total future minimum lease payments	4,559	5,162	6,199	5,863	4,899	5,397
Present value of future minimum lease payments	3,150					
Minimum lease payment made during the period	1,015	1,287	1,167	1,152	1,039	891

Post-employment benefit obligations – defined benefit plans

€ millions	2011	2010	2009	2008	2007	2006
Fair value of plan assets	214	228	234	223	292	308
Defined benefit obligation	(1,119)	(1,105)	(990)	(835)	(918)	(950)
Funding status	(905)	(877)	(756)	(612)	(626)	(642)

Other revenue by nature

€ millions	2011	2010 (restated, excluding Dia)	2010 (original, including Dia)	2009	2008	2007
Financing fees	1,292	1,184	1,184	1,125	1,055	NA
Rental revenue	299	278	278	246	246	225
Revenue from sub-leases	204	170	198	175	149	124
Other revenue	515	471	527	444	449	798
	2,309	2,103	2,187	1,990	1,899	1,147

Note: Financing fees are revenues generated by the financial services companies. Other revenues are mainly franchise fees, business lease fees, and related revenue. In 2007, other revenues include financing fees.

Other information

	2011	2010	2009	2008	2007	2006
Statutory tax rate	34.40%	34.40%	34.40%	34.40%	34.40%	34.40%
Average number of employees	407,861	464,148	469,666	479,072	461,260	434,205
Number of employees at the end of the period	412,443	471,755	475,976	495,287	490,042	456,295

Note: In 2010, Carrefour's average (end-of-year) number of employees excluding Dia's employees was 419,063 (419,417).

Carrefour S.A.

EXHIBIT 6   **Assets and liabilities of Distribuidora Internacional de Alimentación, S.A. (Dia) in fiscal year 2010**

€ millions	2010
ASSETS	
Property, plant, and equipment	1,597.4
Goodwill	414.4
Other intangible assets	45.4
Investments accounted for using the equity method	0.1
Non-current financial assets	51.7
Consumer loans by finance companies	3.2
Deferred tax assets	29.3
Non-current assets	**2,141.5**
Inventories	539.3
Trade and other receivables	179.0
Consumer loans by finance companies	5.6
Current tax assets	38.4
Other current financial assets	21.6
Other assets	11.1
Cash or cash equivalents	316.8
Current assets	**1,111.9**
Total assets	**3,253.4**
LIABILITIES AND EQUITY	
Equity attributable to equityholders of the parent	**430.3**
Non-controlling interests	**(7.8)**
Non-current borrowings	28.0
Provisions	184.4
Deferred tax liabilities	10.4
Non-current liabilities	**222.8**
Current borrowings	540.5
Trade and other payables	1,726.1
Refinancing of consumer loans	0.5
Current tax liabilities	106.8
Current income tax liabilities	23.5
Other financial liabilities	208.2
Liabilities directly associated with non-current assets held for sale	2.5
Current liabilities	**2,608.1**
Total equity and liabilities	**3,253.4**

Source: 2011 financial report Distribuidora Internacional de Alimentación, S.A.

Carrefour S.A.

EXHIBIT 7   **Summary of industry peers' accounting performance in the fiscal years 2009 to 2011[a]**

	Casino			Tesco		
	2011	2010	2009	2011	2010	2009
Panel A: ROE decomposition						
Net operating profit margin	2.4%	2.4%	2.2%	5.0%	4.8%	4.6%
× Net operating asset turnover	2.61	2.40	2.38	1.68	1.73	1.85
= Return on Operating Assets	6.3%	5.8%	5.3%	8.4%	8.4%	8.5%
Return on Operating Assets	6.3%	5.8%	5.3%	8.4%	8.4%	8.5%
× (Operating Assets/Business Assets)	0.65	0.72	0.71	0.83	0.81	0.88
+ Return on Investment Assets	6.1%	7.5%	6.3%	5.8%	5.5%	9.2%
× (Investment Assets/Business Assets)	0.35	0.28	0.29	0.17	0.19	0.12
= Return on Business Assets	6.2%	6.3%	5.6%	8.0%	7.8%	8.6%
Spread	1.8%	2.2%	1.4%	5.4%	5.3%	5.1%
× Net financial leverage	1.19	1.10	1.10	1.75	2.01	1.70
= Financial leverage gain	2.1%	2.5%	1.5%	9.5%	10.6%	8.6%
ROE = Return on Business Assets + Financial leverage gain	8.4%	8.7%	7.1%	17.4%	18.5%	17.2%
Panel B: Other ratios						
Personnel expense	−12.1%	−11.7%	−11.7%	−10.6%	−11.0%	−10.9%
Cost of materials	−72.3%	−73.4%	−72.7%	−75.8%	−74.7%	−74.7%
Operating working capital/Sales	−7.5%	−6.9%	−7.2%	−5.4%	−5.0%	−5.0%
Net non-current assets/Sales	45.9%	48.5%	49.1%	65.0%	62.8%	59.1%
PP&E/Sales	23.2%	25.5%	25.7%	58.7%	56.2%	54.6%
Days' receivables	8.9	10.9	13.2	9.1	7.4	6.4
Days' inventories	45.1	48.5	48.0	24.9	23.2	22.0
Days' payables	74.9	79.7	81.9	43.7	42.1	38.6
Current ratio	0.68	0.71	0.76	0.47	0.48	0.55
Quick ratio	0.37	0.33	0.39	0.26	0.29	0.32
Cash ratio	0.30	0.24	0.28	0.17	0.22	0.24
Debt-to-equity	1.19	1.10	1.10	1.75	2.01	1.70
Debt-to-capital	0.54	0.52	0.52	0.64	0.67	0.63
Interest coverage (earnings based)	2.32	2.77	2.58	4.78	4.46	3.98

[a]Source: Reuters Fundamentals and author's own calculations. The ratios in this table have been calculated (a) using the average balances of balance sheet items, (b) after adjusting the financial statements for off-balance operating lease and pension commitments, and (c) after excluding other income and expense from NOPAT and net income.

Carrefour S.A.

Prospective Analysis: Forecasting

Most financial statement analysis tasks are undertaken with a forward-looking decision in mind – and, much of the time, it is useful to summarize the view developed in the analysis with an explicit forecast. Managers need forecasts to formulate business plans and provide performance targets; analysts need forecasts to help communicate their views of the firm's prospects to investors; and bankers and debt market participants need forecasts to assess the likelihood of loan repayment. Moreover, there are a variety of contexts (including but not limited to security analysis) where the forecast is usefully summarized in the form of an estimate of the firm's value. This estimate can be viewed as an attempt to best reflect in a single summary statistic the manager's or analyst's view of the firm's prospects.

Prospective analysis includes two tasks – forecasting and valuation – that together represent approaches to explicitly summarizing the analyst's forward-looking views. In this chapter we focus on forecasting; valuation is the topic of the next two chapters. Forecasting is not so much a separate analysis as it is a way of summarizing what has been learned through business strategy analysis, accounting analysis, and financial analysis. However, there are certain techniques and knowledge that can help a manager or analyst to structure the best possible forecast, conditional on what has been learned in the previous steps. Below we summarize an approach to structuring the forecast, offer information useful in getting started, explore the relationship between the other analytical steps and forecasting, and give detailed steps to forecast earnings, balance sheet data, and cash flows. The key concepts discussed in this chapter are illustrated using a forecast for Hennes & Mauritz, the apparel retailer examined in Chapter 5.

THE OVERALL STRUCTURE OF THE FORECAST

The best way to forecast future performance is to do it comprehensively – producing not only an earnings forecast, but also a forecast of cash flows and the balance sheet. A **comprehensive forecasting approach** is useful, even in cases where one might be interested primarily in a single facet of performance, because it guards against unrealistic implicit assumptions. For example, if an analyst forecasts growth in sales and earnings for several years without explicitly considering the required increases in working capital and plant assets and the associated financing, the forecast might possibly imbed unreasonable assumptions about asset turnover, leverage, or equity capital infusions.

A comprehensive approach involves many forecasts, but in most cases they are all linked to the behavior of a few key "drivers." The drivers vary according to the type of business involved, but for businesses outside the financial services sector, the sales forecast is nearly always one of the key drivers; profit margin is another. When asset turnover is expected to remain stable – often a realistic assumption – working capital accounts and investment in plant should track the growth in sales closely. Most major expenses also track sales, subject to expected shifts in profit margins. By linking forecasts of such amounts to the sales forecast, one can avoid internal inconsistencies and unrealistic implicit assumptions.

In some contexts the manager or analyst is interested ultimately in a forecast of cash flows, not earnings *per se*. Nevertheless, even forecasts of cash flows tend to be grounded in practice on forecasts of accounting numbers, including sales, earnings, assets, and liabilities. Of course it would be possible in principle to move *directly* to forecasts of cash flows – inflows from customers, outflows to suppliers and laborers, and so forth – and in some businesses this is a convenient way to proceed. In most cases, however, the growth prospects, profitability, and investment and financing needs of the firm are more readily framed in terms of accrual-based sales, operating earnings, assets, and liabilities. These amounts can then be converted to cash flow measures by adjusting for the effects of non-cash expenses and expenditures for working capital and plant.

A practical framework for forecasting

The most practical approach to forecasting a company's financial statements is to focus on projecting **"condensed" financial statements**, as used in the ratio analysis in Chapter 5, rather than attempting to project detailed financial statements that the company reports. There are several reasons for this recommendation. First, this approach involves making a relatively small set of assumptions about the future of the firm, so the analyst will have more ability to think about each of the assumptions carefully. A detailed line item forecast is likely to be very tedious, and an analyst may not have a good basis to make all the assumptions necessary for such forecasts. Further, for most purposes condensed financial statements are all that are needed for analysis and decision making. We therefore approach the task of financial forecasting with this framework.

Recall that the condensed income statement that we used in Chapter 5 consists of the following elements: sales, net operating profit after tax (NOPAT), net investment profit after tax (NIPAT), interest expense after tax, and net profit. The condensed balance sheet consists of: net operating working capital, net non-current operating assets, investment assets, debt, and equity. Also recall that we start with a balance sheet at the beginning of the forecasting period. Assumptions about investment in working capital and non-current assets, and how we finance these assets, results in a balance sheet at the end of the forecasting period; assumptions about how we use the average assets available during the period and run the firm's operations will lead to the income statement for the forecasting period.

In Chapter 5 we learned how to decompose return on equity in order to separately analyze the consequences on profitability of management's (1) operating, (2) non-operating investment, and (3) financing decisions. To make full use of the information generated through the return on equity decomposition the forecasting task should follow the same process, forecasting operating items first, then non-operating investment items, and finally financing items.

Operating items

To forecast the operating section of the condensed income statement, one needs to begin with an assumption about next-period sales. Beyond that an assumption about NOPAT margin is all that is needed to prepare the operating income statement items for the period. To forecast the operating section of the condensed balance sheet for the end of the period (or the equivalent, the beginning of the next period), we need to make the following additional assumptions:

1　The ratio of operating working capital to sales to estimate the level of working capital needed to support those sales.
2　The ratio of net operating non-current assets to sales to calculate the expected level of net operating non-current assets.

Non-operating investment items

Forecasting the investment sections of the condensed income statement and balance sheet requires that one makes assumptions about the following two items:

1　The ratio of investment assets to sales to calculate the expected level of net operating non-current assets.
2　The return on investment assets.

NIPAT margin then follows as the product of the ratio of investment assets to sales and the return on investment assets (after tax).

Financing items

To forecast the financing sections of the condensed income statement and balance sheet, one needs to make assumptions about:

1 The ratio of debt to capital to estimate the levels of debt and equity needed to finance the estimated amount of assets in the balance sheet.

2 The average interest rate (after tax) that the firm will pay on its debt.

Using these forecasts, net interest expense after tax can be calculated as the product of the average interest rate after tax and the debt to capital ratio. Note that a ninth forecast, that of the firm's tax rate, is implicit in three of the above forecasts (NOPAT margin, NIPAT margin, and interest rate after tax).

Once we have the condensed income statement and balance sheet, it is relatively straightforward to compute the condensed cash flow statement, including cash flow from operations before working capital investments, cash flow from operations after working capital investments, free cash flow available to debt and equity, and free cash flow available to equity.

Information for forecasting

The three levels of analysis that precede prospective analysis – strategy, accounting, and financial analysis – can lead to informed decisions by an analyst about expected performance, especially in the short and medium term. Specifically, the primary goal of financial analysis is to understand the historical relationship between a firm's financial performance and economic factors identified in the strategy and accounting analysis, such as the firm's macroeconomic environment, industry and strategy, and accounting decisions. Forecasting can be seen as performing a reverse financial analysis, primarily addressing the question of what the effect will be of anticipated changes in relevant economic factors on the firm's future performance and financial position, conditional on the historical relationships identified in the financial analysis. Thus, much of the information generated in the strategic, accounting and financial analysis is of use when going through the following steps of the forecasting process.

Step 1: Predict changes in environmental and firm-specific factors

The first step in forecasting is to assess how the firm's economic environment, such as macroeconomic conditions and industry competitiveness, will change in future years and how the firm may respond to such changes. Throughout this chapter we will use the example of Hennes & Mauritz, the apparel retailer discussed in Chapter 5, to illustrate the mechanics of forecasting. A thorough step 1 analysis of H&M for the year 2012 must be grounded in an understanding of questions such as these:

- From a macroeconomic analysis. How will the economic situation in H&M's geographic segments develop?

- From industry and business strategy analysis. Will slow growth in the industry motivate apparel retailers to intensify price competition with each other? Is it expected that new discount retailers or general merchandise retailers will enter the lower-priced segment of the apparel retail industry, thereby increasing competition in H&M's primary segment? Will H&M's brand recognition and strong advertising campaigns help the firm to preserve customer loyalty and avoid price competition? Or will the firm's recent increase in inventory markdowns persist into next year? Will H&M's bargaining power over its suppliers decrease if its need for production flexibility, which is inherent to the fast fashion strategy, requires the retailer to develop longer term and more integrated relationships with its suppliers? How will the average labor costs in production countries develop in the near future? What will be the effect of consumers' increased demand for ethical and sustainable clothing on the costs of outsourced production? How long will H&M maintain its policy of outsourcing all production to independent suppliers? Will H&M be able to successfully replicate its strategy in emerging markets? What will be the near-term importance of H&M's higher-priced brands? What will be the performance consequences of H&M's foreign currency risk exposure?

- From accounting analysis. Are there any aspects of H&M's accounting that suggest past earnings and assets are misstated, or expenses or liabilities are misstated? If so, what are the implications for future accounting statements?

Step 2: Assess the relationship between step 1 factors and financial performance

After having obtained a thorough understanding of what economic factors are relevant and how these factors are expected to change in future years, the next step of the forecasting process is to assess how such future changes will translate into financial performance trends. This second step strongly builds on the financial analysis. In particular, observations on how sensitive Hennes & Mauritz's past ratios have been to variations in, for example, economic growth, price competition and input prices can help the analyst to learn what will happen to the firm's ratios if the anticipated changes crystallize. The financial analysis of H&M helps to understand questions that include the following: What were the sources of H&M's superior performance in 2010? Which economic factors caused the firm's profitability to decrease in 2011 (and by how much)? Are these factors and their performance effects permanent or transitory? Is there any discernible longer term pattern in H&M's past performance? If so, are there any reasons why this trend is likely to continue or change?

Step 3: Forecast condensed financial statements

Based on the outcomes of steps 1 and 2, one can produce forecasts of the line items in the firm's condensed financial statements, most particularly of the operating statement items. For Hennes & Mauritz, the key challenge in building forecasts is to predict whether the firm will be able to maintain its superior margins and turnover and grow its sales at the same rate at which it expands its store network or whether competition, the economic downturn, increasing input prices, or the continuing store network expansion will lead to a further decline in operating performance. Forecasts of non-operating investment performance and financing structure typically rely less on business strategy information and build strongly on firm-specific information about investment and financing plans as well as historical trends in these measures, which we will discuss in the next section.

PERFORMANCE BEHAVIOR: A STARTING POINT

The above described forecasting framework implicitly assumes that sufficient information is available, or generated in prior steps of the business analysis process, to produce detailed, informed forecasts. Quite often such information is not or not sufficiently obtainable, especially when preparing longer term forecasts. Therefore, every forecast has, at least implicitly, an initial "benchmark" or point of departure – some notion of how a particular ratio, such as sales growth or profit margins, would be expected to behave in the absence of detailed information. By the time one has completed a business strategy analysis, an accounting analysis, and a detailed financial analysis, the resulting forecast might differ significantly from the original point of departure. Nevertheless, simply for purposes of having a starting point that can help anchor the detailed analysis, it is useful to know how certain key financial statistics behave "on average" for all firms. As a general rule, the lower the quality and richness of the available information, the more emphasis one ultimately places on the initial benchmark.

In the case of some key statistics, such as earnings, a point of departure based only on prior behavior of the number is more powerful than one might expect. Research demonstrates that some such benchmarks for earnings are almost as accurate as the forecasts of professional security analysts, who have access to a rich information set (we return to this point in more detail below). Thus the benchmark is often not only a good starting point but also close to the amount forecast after detailed analysis. Large departures from the benchmark could be justified only in cases where the firm's situation is demonstrably unusual.

Reasonable points of departure for forecasts of key accounting numbers can be based on the evidence summarized below. Such evidence may also be useful for checking the reasonableness of a completed forecast.

Sales growth behavior

Sales growth rates tend to be "mean-reverting": firms with above-average or below-average rates of sales growth tend to revert over time to a "normal" level (historically in the range of 6 to 9 percent for European firms) within three to ten years. Figure 6.1 documents this effect for 1992 through 2011 for all the publicly traded European (nonfinancial) firms covered by the Compustat Global database. All firms are ranked in terms of their sales growth in 1992 (year 1) and formed into five portfolios based on the relative ranking of their sales growth in that year. Firms in portfolio 1 are in the top 20 percent of rankings in terms of their sales growth in 1992, those in portfolio 2 fall into the next 20 percent, while those in portfolio 5 are in the bottom 20 percent when ranked by sales growth. The sales growth rates of firms in each of these five portfolios are traced from 1992 through the subsequent nine years (years 2 to 10). The same experiment is repeated with every year between 1993 and 2002 as the base year

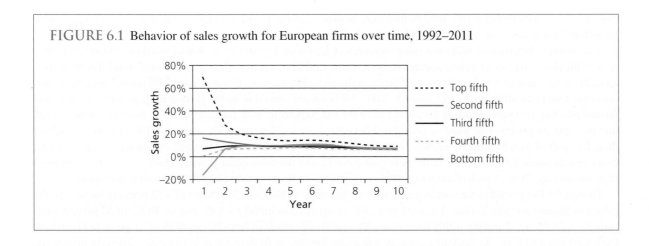

FIGURE 6.1 Behavior of sales growth for European firms over time, 1992–2011

(year 1). The results are averaged over the eleven experiments and the resulting sales growth rates of each of the five portfolios for years 1 through 10 are plotted in the figure.

The figure shows that the group of firms with the highest growth initially – sales growth rates of just over 69 percent – experience a decline to about 19 percent growth rate within two years and are never above 19 percent in the next seven years. Those with the lowest initial sales growth rates, minus 15 percent, experience an increase to about a 10 percent growth rate by year 3, and average about 9 percent annual growth in years 4 through 10. One explanation for the pattern of sales growth seen in Figure 6.1 is that as industries and companies mature, their growth rate slows down due to demand saturation and intra-industry competition. Therefore, even when a firm is growing rapidly at present, it is generally unrealistic to extrapolate the current high growth indefinitely. Of course, how quickly a firm's growth rate reverts to the average depends on the characteristics of its industry and its own competitive position within an industry.

Earnings behavior

Earnings have been shown on average to follow a process that can be approximated by a "random walk" or "random walk with drift." Thus the prior year's earnings figure is a good starting point in considering future earnings potential. As will be explained, it is reasonable to adjust this simple benchmark for the earnings changes of the most recent quarter (that is, changes relative to the comparable quarter of the prior year after controlling for the long-run trend in the series). Even a simple random walk forecast – one that predicts next year's earnings will be equal to last year's earnings – is surprisingly useful. One study documents that professional analysts' year-ahead forecasts are only 22 percent more accurate, on average, than a simple random walk forecast.[1] Thus a final earnings forecast will usually not differ dramatically from a random walk benchmark.

The implication of the evidence is that, in beginning to contemplate future earnings possibilities, a useful number to start with is last year's earnings; the average level of earnings over several prior years is not useful. Long-term trends in earnings tend to be sustained on average, and so they are also worthy of consideration. If quarterly or semiannual data are also included, then some consideration should usually be given to any departures from the long-run trend that occurred in the most recent quarter or half year. For most firms, these most recent changes tend to be partially repeated in subsequent quarters or half years.[2]

Returns on equity behavior

Given that prior earnings serves as a useful benchmark for future earnings, one might expect the same to be true of rates of return on investment, like ROE. That, however, is not the case for two reasons. First, even though the *average* firm tends to sustain the current earnings level, this is not true of firms with unusual levels of ROE. Firms with abnormally high (low) ROE tend to experience earnings declines (increases).[3]

Second, firms with higher ROEs tend to expand their investment bases more quickly than others, which causes the denominator of the ROE to increase. Of course, if firms could earn returns on the new investments that match the returns on the old ones, then the level of ROE would be maintained. However, firms have difficulty pulling that off. Firms with higher ROEs tend to find that, as time goes by, their earnings growth does not keep pace with growth in their investment base, and ROE ultimately falls.

The resulting behavior of ROE and other measures of return on investment is characterized as "mean-reverting": firms with above-average or below-average rates of return tend to revert over time to a "normal" level (for ROE, historically in the range of 8 to 10 percent for European firms) within no more than ten years.[4] Figure 6.2 documents this effect for European firms from 1992 through 2011. All firms are ranked in terms of their ROE in 1992 (year 1) and formed into five portfolios. Firms in portfolio 1 have the top 20 percent ROE rankings in 1992, those in portfolio 2 fall into the next 20 percent, and those in portfolio 5 have the bottom 20 percent. The average ROE of firms in each of these five portfolios is then traced through nine subsequent years (years 2 to 10). The same experiment is repeated with every year between 1993 and 2002 as the base year (year 1), and the subsequent years as years +2 to +10. Figure 6.2 plots the average ROE of each of the five portfolios in years 1 to 10 averaged across these eleven experiments.

Though the five portfolios start out in year 1 with a wide range of ROEs (−33 percent to +32 percent), by year 10 the pattern of **mean-reversion** is clear. The most profitable group of firms initially – with average ROEs of 32 percent – experience a decline to 18 percent within three years. By year 10 this group of firms has an ROE of 11 percent. Those with the lowest initial ROEs (−33 percent) experience a dramatic increase in ROE and then level off at −2 percent in year 10.

The pattern in Figure 6.2 is not a coincidence; it is exactly what the economics of competition would predict. The tendency of high ROEs to fall is a reflection of high profitability attracting competition; the tendency of low ROEs to rise reflects the mobility of capital away from unproductive ventures toward more profitable ones.

Despite the general tendencies documented in Figure 6.2, there are some firms whose ROEs may remain above or below normal levels for long periods of time. In some cases the phenomenon reflects the strength of a sustainable competitive advantage (e.g., Wal-Mart), but in other cases it is purely an artifact of conservative accounting methods.

A good example of the latter phenomenon is pharmaceutical firms, whose major economic asset, the intangible value of research and development, is not recorded on the balance sheet and is therefore excluded from the denominator of ROE. For those firms, one could reasonably expect high ROEs – in excess of 20 percent – over the long run, even in the face of strong competitive forces.

The behavior of components of ROE

The behavior of rates of return on equity can be analyzed further by looking at the behavior of its key components. Recall from Chapter 5 that ROEs and profit margins are linked as follows:

$$\text{ROE} = \text{Return on business assets} + (\text{Return on business assets} - \text{Interest rate after tax})$$
$$\times \text{Financial leverage}$$
$$= (\text{NOPAT margin} \times \text{Operating asset turnover}) \times (\text{Operating assets/Business assets})$$
$$+ \text{Return on investment assets} \times (\text{Investment assets/Business assets}) + \text{Spread} \times \text{Financial leverage}$$

Thus, the primary components of ROE are: NOPAT margin, operating asset turnover, return on investment assets, spread, and financial leverage. The time-series behavior of the components of ROE for European companies for

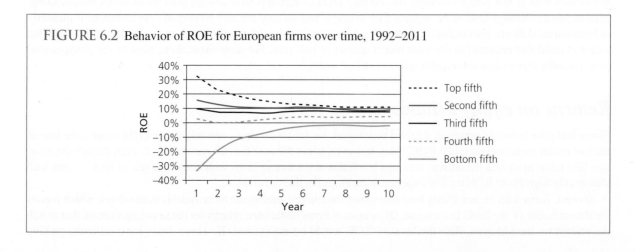

FIGURE 6.2 Behavior of ROE for European firms over time, 1992–2011

1992 through 2011 are shown in a series of figures in the Appendix to this chapter. Some major conclusions can be drawn from these figures:

1 Operating asset turnover tends to be rather stable, in part because it is so much a function of the technology of the industry. The only exception to this is the set of firms with very high asset turnover, which tends to decline somewhat over time before stabilizing.

2 Net financial leverage also tends to be stable, simply because management policies on capital structure aren't often changed.

3 NOPAT margin and spread stand out as the most variable component of ROE; if the forces of competition drive abnormal ROEs toward more normal levels, the change is most likely to arrive in the form of changes in profit margins and the spread. The change in spread is itself driven by changes in NOPAT margin, because the cost of borrowing is likely to remain stable if leverage remains stable.

To summarize, profit margins, like ROEs, tend to be driven by competition to "normal" levels over time. What constitutes normal varies widely according to the technology employed within an industry and the corporate strategy pursued by the firm, both of which influence turnover and leverage.[5] In a fully competitive equilibrium, profit margins should remain high for firms that must operate with a low turnover, and vice versa.

The above discussion of rates of return and margins implies that a reasonable point of departure for forecasting such a statistic should consider more than just the most recent observation. One should also consider whether that rate or margin is above or below a normal level. If so, then without detailed information to the contrary, one would expect some movement over time to that norm. Of course this central tendency might be overcome in some cases – for example, where the firm has erected barriers to competition that can protect margins, even for extended periods. The lesson from the evidence, however, is that such cases are unusual.

In contrast to rates of return and margins, it is reasonable to assume that asset turnover, financial leverage, and net interest rate remain relatively constant over time. Unless there is an explicit change in technology or financial policy being contemplated for future periods, a reasonable point of departure for assumptions for these variables is the current period level. The only exceptions to this appear to be firms with either very high asset turnover that experience some decline in this ratio before stabilizing, or those firms with very low (usually negative) net debt to capital that appear to increase leverage before stabilizing.

As we proceed with the steps involved in producing a detailed forecast, the reader will note that we draw on the above knowledge of the behavior of accounting numbers to some extent. However, it is important to keep in mind that a knowledge of *average* behavior will not fit all firms well. The art of financial statements analysis requires not only knowing what the "normal" patterns are but also having expertise in identifying those firms that will *not* follow the norm.

FORECASTING ASSUMPTIONS

In this section we apply the above described forecasting framework to the example of Hennes & Mauritz. After providing some background information about macroeconomic and industry factors, we will forecast the line items of H&M's condensed financial statements following the order outlined in the previous section. For each line item, we will go through the three steps of the forecasting process, thereby relying on the outcomes of H&M's business strategy and financial analyses. In cases where we lack information, we will discuss whether it is more appropriate to rely on forecasts implied by the historical time series patterns of European financial ratios. Although our forecasts are grounded in realistic assumptions, we emphasize that rather than providing a full-fledged forecasting analysis, the main purpose of the example is to illustrate the basics of the forecasting process and provide a sound basis for the next step of the prospective analysis, the valuation of H&M. Therefore, at some points in the analysis we take the liberty of making some necessary simplifying assumptions.

Background: macroeconomic and industry growth

In the first half of 2012, the European economy was still in an economic downturn. Following the worldwide credit crisis and the associated economic slowdown, several European countries started to experience difficulties repaying the huge debts that they had been running up during the prior decade. The drastic government budget cuts

TABLE 6.1 Realized and expected economic growth rates

	2010	2011e	2012e	2013e
European Union	1.0%	0.4%	0.4%	1.1%
Weighted average of H&M's European markets	1.5%	0.8%	0.9%	1.3%
Weighted average of H&M's World markets	1.7%	1.2%	1.2%	1.6%

Source: European Economic Forecast Autumn 2011 – Directorate-General for Economic and Financial Affairs.

that necessarily followed, reduced consumers' discretionary income. Further, the significant uncertainty about the consequences of one of the countries defaulting or restructuring its debt impaired consumer confidence and deepened the economic slowdown that had started a few years earlier. During the autumn of 2011, the Directorate-General for Economic and Financial Affairs of the European Commission revised down its growth projections for 2012. The Directorate-General forecast that annual Private Consumption growth in the EU – an aggregate measure of the growth in households' purchases – would be 0.4 and 1.1 percent for 2012 and 2013, respectively. Table 6.1 shows the realized and predicted Private Consumption growth rates for (1) the EU, (2) H&M's European markets, and (3) all countries where H&M operates. These growth rates illustrate that while economy-wide growth declined during 2011, an increase in growth was not expected until 2013. The growth rates further illustrate that in 2011 H&M operated in European countries with growth rates and growth prospects above the European Union average. Finally, realized growth rates and growth prospects in H&M's non-European markets exceeded those in the European markets, suggesting that H&M worldwide expansion helped the retailer to be less exposed to the economic consequences of the European sovereign debt crisis.

The apparel retail industry is a cyclical industry. Because consumers tend to delay their purchases of apparel during periods of economic uncertainty, apparel retailers' sales typically vary with economic cycles. Table 6.2 shows the realized and predicted near-term industry growth rates for the apparel industry. The industry growth rates are moderate to low, though slightly higher than the economy-wide growth rates. In line with the cyclicality of the apparel retail industry, future industry growth rates are expected to follow the decline in private consumption.

Sales growth

A good starting point for developing a forecast of short-term sales growth is management's outlook. Management typically provides guidance about future sales and margins in the Management Report section of the annual report but sometimes also in interim reports, press releases, or analyst conferences. The analyst's task is to critically challenge the assumptions underlying management's expectations, using information about macro-economic, industry and firm-specific factors.

At the presentation of the 2011 annual report H&M's management expressed the expectation that the firm would grow its store network by approximately 275 stores in 2012 and by 10 to 15 percent per annum in the immediate years thereafter. H&M plans to expand its operations especially in China, the UK and the US. Based on

TABLE 6.2 Realized and expected industry growth rates

	2010	2011e	2012e	2013e
Annual growth rate	3.5%	3.4%	2.7%	2.9%

Source: Marketline.

TABLE 6.3 Expected growth in H&M's store network

	2010	2011	2012e	2013e	2014e
Growth rate	11.0%	12.1%	11.1%	12.0%	12.0%
Number of stores added during the year	218	266	275	330	369
Number of stores at the end of the year	2,206	2,472	2,747	3,077	3,446
Average number of stores	2,097.0	2,339.0	2,609.5	2,912.0	3,261.5

this information, it is relatively straightforward to predict the number of stores that H&M will operate during the next two to three years. Table 6.3 displays our estimates of the worldwide number of H&M stores during the years 2012–2014, calculated under the assumption that in 2013 and 2014 the store growth rate will be 12.0 percent.

The number of stores is, however, not H&M's only sales driver; the other driver, which certainly is more challenging to predict, is the amount of sales per store. Recall that our analysis of H&M's past financial performance revealed that H&M's sales per store –calculated as the ratio between total sales and the average number of stores operated during the year – has been gradually declining from SEK54.4 million per store in 2009 to SEK47.0 million per store in 2011. Key questions at this point in the analysis therefore are: What economic factors explain the recent decline in H&M's store productivity? How will these factors develop during the next three years?

The following factors contributed to the recent decrease of H&M's sales per store:

■ Foreign currency exchange rate changes. Hennes & Mauritz operates stores in 32 different countries and, consequently, is exposed to exchange rate risk. In 2010 and 2011, the exchange rates of most currencies in which H&M transacted, including the euro and the US dollar, depreciated against the firm's reporting currency, the Swedish Krona (SEK), primarily because of the relative strength of the Swedish economy. In fact, the sales-weighted average percentage changes in the local currency-to-SEK exchange rate amounted to −5.48 percent in 2011 and −6.86 percent in 2010, suggesting that exchange rate changes were the single most important contributor to the observed declines in sales per store.

■ Changes in consumer demand and inventory markdowns. In 2010 and 2011 the economic downturn negatively affected consumer demand in many of H&M's geographic segments. Not only did H&M's inventories turnover decrease during these years, the retailer also needed to mark down its inventories more frequently. The impact of increased competition on H&M's sales per store seemed to be moderate. For example, in the UK, where discount retailer Primark was considered to be a potentially strong competing entrant, H&M was able to improve store productivity (in local currency) by 1.6 and 3.0 percent in 2010 and 2011, respectively.

■ Changes in H&M's store portfolio. Because store productivity varies across markets and H&M is continuously expanding its store network, changes in the composition of H&M's store network unavoidably lead to changes in the retailer's average store productivity.

Table 6.4 summarizes the quantitative impact of these three factors on H&M's average store productivity. The next step in forecasting sales growth is to assess the persistence of each of the effects in future years. When doing so, the following considerations are particularly important:

■ Foreign currency exchange rate changes. Much research suggests that exchange rates between currencies can be reasonably modeled as a random walk, implying that the current exchange rate is the best possible estimate of next year's exchange rate. If the exchange rates between the Swedish Krona and other major currencies indeed follow a random walk, the change in H&M's store productivity that is due to changes in exchange rates should be considered as permanent. It may be reasonable, however, to expect that the Swedish Krona will depreciate against, for example, the euro as soon as the Eurozone economies start to recover.

■ Changes in consumer demand and inventory markdowns. As indicated above, early 2012 the expectation is that economic growth in the European Union will be close to its level in 2011. Given the cyclical nature of the apparel retail industry, it is reasonable to expect that consumer demand will not pick up until 2013.

TABLE 6.4 Decomposition of changes in H&M's store productivity

	2009	*2010*	*2011*
Sales (in SEK millions)	101,393	108,483	109,999
Average number of stores	1,863	2097	2105
Sales per store (in SEK millions)	54.42	51.73	47.03
Percentage change in sales per store, consisting of:		−4.95%	−9.09%
− the effect of currency exchange rate changes		−6.86%	−5.48%
− the effect of changes in H&M's store portfolio		−0.06%	−0.24%
− the effect of changes in consumer demand and inventory markdowns		+2.11%	−3.59%

■ Changes in H&M's store portfolio. Without detailed information, it is reasonable to assume that the 2011 change in sales per store that is due to the change in H&M's store portfolio is a permanent change.

Given these considerations, we assume that the consumer demand-driven reduction in sales per store will gradually revert during the years 2012 to 2014. In contrast, we assume that the effects of exchange rate changes and changes in the store portfolio will persist in the near term. Table 6.5 summarizes the consequences of these assumptions for H&M's sales growth forecasts between 2012 and 2014.

The above growth forecasts assume that in the near term Hennes & Mauritz will maintain high growth, backed by its brand equity and ability to enter new markets. While long-term trends in the apparel retail market are uncertain, it is reasonable to assume that Hennes & Mauritz will not be immune to the long-run forces of competition and mean reversion. Two factors that may lead to increased future competition are the consistently moderate growth in the apparel retail industry and the market entrance of new discount retailers and general merchandise stores. Consequently, without detailed information we assume that sales growth forecasts after 2014 gradually revert to the average growth rate of the world economy, from 12 percent in 2015 to 3 percent in 2021.

TABLE 6.5 Expected sales growth for H&M

	2011	*2012e*	*2013e*	*2014e*
(Expected) effect on sales per store of:				
− currency exchange rate changes	−5.48%	−5.48%	−5.48%	−5.48%
− changes in H&M's store portfolio	−0.24%	−0.24%	−0.24%	−0.24%
− changes in consumer demand and inventory markdowns	−3.59%	−3.59%	−1.80%	0.00%
(a) Total (expected) effect on sales per store	−9.09%	−9.09%	−7.40%	−5.71%
(b) Sales per store in 2010 (in SEK millions)	51.73	51.73	51.73	51.73
+ (Expected) change in sales per store (a × b)	−4.70	−4.70	−3.83	−2.95
= (Expected) sales per store	47.03	47.03	47.90	48.78
× (Expected) average number of stores (from Table 6.3)	2,339.0	2,609.5	2,912.0	3,261.5
= (Expected) sales	109,999	122,725	139,485	159,096
Implied sales growth rate		11.6%	13.7%	14.1%

NOPAT margins

In 2011, Hennes & Mauritz's NOPAT margin decreased to 15.0 percent, after an increase from 16.9 percent to 18.1 percent in 2010. The following economic factors, which we discussed in Chapter 5, contributed to the changes in H&M's margins:

■ Input prices. In 2009 cotton suppliers cut capacity to cope with the economic decline. This capacity reduction led to an increase in cotton prices when clothing manufacturers' demand for cotton recovered in 2010 and 2011. In fact, the average cotton price increased from 61 US cents per pound to 96 cents in 2010 and 161 cents in 2011. Based on the historical association between quarterly changes in cotton prices and quarterly changes in H&M's gross margin, we estimate that a 10 percent increase in the average cotton price reduces the firm's NOPAT margin by close to 0.2 percentage points. Hence, the 57 percent cotton price increase in 2010 presumably led to a 1.15 percentage points decrease in NOPAT margin, whereas the following 68 percent price increase in 2011 caused an additional 1.35 percentage points decrease in NOPAT margin.

■ Inventory markdowns. In January 2012, H&M's management indicated during a conference call with financial analysts that the net effect of inventory markdowns on the firm's gross margin for the fourth quarter of 2011 had been 0.6 percentage points. Because inventory markdowns occurred less frequently in the first three-quarters of the year, we assume that the average effect of such markdowns on H&M's 2011 margin was 0.3 percentage points, or 0.2 percentage points after tax.

■ SG&A cost stickiness. We discussed in Chapter 5 that in periods of store productivity declines (such as in 2011) or small increases (such as in 2010), stickiness of SG&A expenses can lead to a change in the SG&A-to-sales ratio. To illustrate the impact of this effect, if in 2010 and 2011 H&M's SG&A expense on a per-store basis had remained constant at its 2009 level of SEK21.91 million, the firm's SG&A-to-sales ratio – adjusted for exchange rate changes – would have decreased by 0.8 percentage points in 2010 and increased by 2.5 percentage points in 2011. At a tax rate of 26.3 percent, the firm's NOPAT margin would, consequently, have increased by 0.6 percentage points in 2010 and decreased by 1.9 percentage points in 2011.

■ Net effect of SG&A cost savings and margin investments. In 2010 and 2011, Hennes & Mauritz's management had been able to achieve significant SG&A cost savings. However, management also gave up some of its margin to invest in the improvement of product quality and design. We assume that the portions of the NOPAT decrease that cannot be explained by the above three economic factors can be attributed to the net effect of SG&A cost savings and margin investments.

Table 6.6 summarizes the effects of the above described factors on H&M's NOPAT margins in 2010 and 2011. In assessing the persistence of each of the NOPAT effects in future years, we take the following considerations into account:

TABLE 6.6 Decomposition of changes in H&M's NOPAT margin

	2009	2010	2011
Sales (in SEK millions)	101,393	108,483	109,999
NOPAT (in SEK millions)	17,157.7	19,657.9	16,542.3
NOPAT margin	16.9%	18.1%	15.0%
Annual percentage change in NOPAT margin, consisting of:		+1.20%	−3.10%
– the effect of input prices		−1.15%	−1.35%
– the effect of inventory markdowns		−0.00%	−0.20%
– the effect of SG&A cost stickiness		+0.60%	−1.90%
– the net effect of SG&A cost savings and margin investments		+1.75%	+0.35%

- Input prices. During the first quarter of 2012 the average cotton price decreased to a level of 99 US cents per pound. It is reasonable to expect that it will take another year before cotton prices have reached their 2009 level. We therefore assume that in 2012 the cotton price-induced NOPAT margin effect will be equal to its level in 2010, whereas in 2013 the NOPAT margin effect will revert to its 2009 level.

- Inventory markdowns. In January 2012, H&M's management indicated that it expected further inventory markdowns during the first part of 2012. We assume that the NOPAT margin effect of inventory markdowns will remain at −0.2 percent in 2012, but will be zero in 2013 and beyond.

- SG&A cost stickiness. Because we predict that store productivity will only slowly revert to a higher level, we also expect that the cost stickiness effect will largely persist in the near term.

- Net effect of SG&A cost savings and margin investments. H&M's management has committed to keeping tight control of the firm's SG&A costs. Further, is has announced the margin investments (in quality and design) as part of a long-term strategy. We therefore assume that the NOPAT margin effect of SG&A cost savings and margin investments is persistent, at least in the near term.

Table 6.7 shows what these assumptions imply for H&M's NOPAT margin between 2012 and 2014. Based on our assumptions, NOPAT margin would gradually increase from 15 percent in 2011 to 18.1 percent in 2014.

Recall that the NOPAT margin of H&M's competitor Inditex was 14.3 percent in 2011; the average NOPAT margin of the other industry peers was 9.2 percent. Based on the historical trends in the European economy, we expect that in the long run H&M's NOPAT margin will gradually move closer to that of its industry peers. An important factor that may contribute to the mean reversion of H&M's margin is, for example, that consumers' increasing demand for sustainable products, rising labor costs in production countries and H&M's need for developing long-term relationships with its suppliers will make it gradually more expensive for H&M to outsource its production. Hence, we expect that the firm's NOPAT margin will gradually decrease from 18.1 percent in 2014 to 12 percent in 2021.

Working capital to sales

Hennes & Mauritz's working capital consists of the following components: (1) operating cash, (2) trade receivables, (3) inventories, (4) trade payables, and (5) other current assets and liabilities. In 2011, days' receivables and day's payables were 7.5 and 34 days, respectively. The ratios varied marginally during the prior four years and their 2011 values were close to the five-year averages. Therefore, without detailed information we consider it reasonable to assume that during the forecasting period days' receivables and days' payables will remain constant at 7 and 34 days, respectively.

In 2011, H&M's days' inventories increased from its 2010 level of 97.3 days to 103.9 days. The firm's average days' inventories was 87.8 days between 2007 and 2009. The decrease in inventories turnover reflects that H&M experienced difficulties in selling its products during the second half of 2011, presumably because of the economic slowdown and an unusually warm autumn season. Because both factors driving the decrease in inventory turnover are non-permanent factors and H&M has been investing in quality improvements and store refurbishments to

TABLE 6.7 Expected NOPAT margins for H&M

	2011	2012e	2013e	2014e
NOPAT margin in 2010	18.1%	18.1%	18.1%	18.1%
(Expected) effect on NOPAT margin of:				
– input prices	−1.35%	0.00%	+1.15%	+1.15%
– inventory markdowns	−0.20%	−0.20%	+0.00%	+0.00%
– SG&A cost stickiness	−1.90%	−1.90%	−1.70%	−1.50%
– SG&A cost savings and margin investments	+0.35%	+0.35%	+0.35%	+0.35%
= (Expected) NOPAT margin	15.0%	16.4%	17.9%	18.1%

TABLE 6.8 Working capital-to-sales forecasts for H&M

	2011	2012e	2013e	2014e
(a) Days' receivables	7.5	7.5	7.5	7.5
(b) Days' inventories	103.9	100.0	95.0	90.0
(c) Days' payables	34.0	34.0	34.0	34.0
Receivables to sales [(a)/365]		2.1%	2.1%	2.1%
Inventories to sales [0.4 × (b)/365]		11.0%	10.4%	9.9%
Payables to sales [−0.4 × (c)/365]		−3.7%	−3.7%	−3.7%
Operating cash to sales		8.0%	8.0%	8.0%
Net other current assets/liabilities to sales		−7.3%	−7.3%	−7.3%
Working capital to sales		10.1%	9.5%	9.0%

stimulate inventory turnover, we predict that during the next three years days' inventories will gradually revert to a level of 90 days.

Finally, without information to the contrary we assume that average operating cash and net other current assets/liabilities as a percentage of sales remain at a level of 8.0 and −7.3 percent, respectively. Table 6.8 details the calculation of our working capital-to-sales forecasts. Note that, technically speaking, the inventories-to-sales and payables-to-sales ratios also depend on the gross margin forecasts, as both days' inventories and days' payables are a function of cost of sales instead of sales. However, to simplify calculations and because the effect is non-material, we calculate the inventories-to-sales and payables-to-sales forecasts using a constant cost of sales-to-sales ratio (of 40 percent).

Non-current assets to sales

The forecasts of net non-current operating assets to sales are closely linked with the above-described forecasts of H&M's store productivity. Specifically, under an assumption that the investment in net non-current operating assets per store will remain constant in the next few years, store productivity (sales per store) and net non-current operating to sales will follow the same trend. Between 2009 and 2011 net non-current operating assets per store gradually decreased from SEK32.6 million per store to SEK28.5 million per store. Much of this decrease can, however, be ascribed to the appreciation of the Swedish Krona during this period. Because we have no clear expectation about the future exchange rates of the Swedish Krona, we assume that the non-current operating investment per store will remain constant at SEK28.5 million per store between 2012 and 2014. Table 6.9 shows what this assumption, in combination with our earlier forecasts of store productivity, implies for our net non-current assets-to-sales forecasts. Because we assumed that store productivity will slightly increase between 2012 and 2014, net non-current operating assets as a percentage of sales will decrease from 60.7 percent in 2012 to 58.4 percent in 2014. Without detailed information to the contrary, we assume that in the years beyond 2014 store productivity and investments per store will remain constant (or both increase at the inflation rate), which implies that net non-current operating assets-to-sales ratio remains constant at 58.4 percent.

TABLE 6.9 Net non-current operating assets-to-sales forecasts for H&M

	2011	2012e	2013e	2014e
(a) Net non-current operating assets per store	SEK28.5m	SEK28.5m	SEK28.5m	SEK28.5m
(b) Sales per store (see Table 6.5)	47.03	47.03	47.90	48.78
Net non-current operating assets to sales [(a)/(b)]	60.7%	60.7%	59.5%	58.4%

Non-operating investments

At the end of fiscal year 2011 Hennes & Mauritz had a substantial amount of excess cash, which we classified as non-operating investments. Assuming that the company needs a cash balance of 8 percent of sales to finance its daily operations, excess cash amounted to close to 13 percent of business assets (or 11 percent of sales). It is uncertain which actions the company will undertake to dispose of its excess cash. It is likely that in the near term H&M will use the amount to finance the expansion of its store network. In the long run when, as we assumed previously, H&M's growth opportunities will gradually decline, the company will likely redistribute the amount of excess cash to its shareholders, either through share repurchases or dividends. Consequently, we assume that the investment assets-to-sales ratio will remain steady between 2012 and 2014, at its current level of 11.9 percent, and then gradually decrease, in line with the firm's growth decline. We further assume that the (after-tax) return on investment assets remains constant at 2.8 percent, which is close to the European average.

Capital structure

Between 2008 and 2011 H&M's debt-to-capital ratio ranged from 0.53 to 0.55. Given the low variance in leverage and without any concrete information that management plans to change the firm's capital structure, we assume that the debt-to-capital ratio will be 52.6 percent throughout the forecasting period. In 2011, Hennes & Mauritz's after-tax interest rate was low, at 2.3 percent, as a consequence of the economic downturn. Because at the end of 2011 the yield curve was steep, indicating that investors expected that market interest rates would increase in the medium term, we let H&M's after-tax interest rate gradually increase from 2.3 percent in 2012 to 3.5 percent in 2017.

FROM ASSUMPTIONS TO FORECASTS

The analysis of Hennes & Mauritz's performance in Chapter 5, and the preceding discussions about general market behavior and H&M's strategic positioning, leads to the conclusion that in the near and medium term it is likely that the company can defy the forces of competition and, at least temporarily, earn substantial abnormal profits.

Table 6.10 shows the forecasting assumptions for years 2012 to 2021. Table 6.11 shows the forecasted income statements for these same fiscal years, and beginning of the year balance sheets for years 2013 to 2022. Recall that the balance sheet at the beginning of fiscal 2012 is the same as the balance sheet reported by the company for the year ending November 30, 2011. Further note that, technically speaking, our forecasts of assets-to-sales ratios express average (rather than ending or beginning) assets as a percentage of sales. To simplify calculations when translating these ratios into monetary values we treat all ratios as forecasts of ending assets to sales. In other words, we implicitly assume that all required investments are made immediately after the start of the fiscal year.

We have chosen a ten-year forecasting period because we believe that the firm should reach such a steady state of performance by the end of the period that a few simplifying assumptions about its subsequent performance are sufficient to estimate firm value (discussed in further detail in Chapter 8). For example, as we will discuss in Chapter 8, a reasonable assumption for the period following the forecasting period is that a portion of the firm's abnormal profits will be competed away and the performance of the firm will revert towards the mean, as has been the general trend that we have seen earlier in the chapter.

Our strategic analysis led to an expectation of significant sales growth, primarily because of H&M's store network expansion and the presumed absence of negative exchange rate effects. As shown in Table 6.10, we assume that sales will increase at 11.6 percent, which is substantially higher than the 1.4 percent sales growth that the company achieved in 2011. This growth rate leads to an expected sales level in 2012 of SEK122,725 million, up from SEK109,999 million in 2011 as Table 6.11 shows. The assumptions together lead to a projected SEK19,385 million net profit in fiscal year 2012 compared with a reported net profit of SEK15,821 million in 2011.

In making longer-term forecasts, in this instance for years 2 to 10, we have relied on our analysis of the firm and its prospects as well as the time-series behavior of various performance ratios discussed earlier. Given our assumptions of increased store productivity, we assume that H&M will be able to slightly increase its sales growth rate to 14,1 percent in years 2 and 3. Thereafter, sales growth will gradually decline as the effect of competition gets stronger.

TABLE 6.10 Forecasting assumptions for Hennes & Mauritz

Forecast year	2012	2013	2014	2015	2016	2017	2018	2019	2020	2021
Sales growth rate	11.6%	13.7%	14.1%	12.0%	10.0%	8.0%	6.0%	4.0%	3.0%	3.0%
NOPAT margin	16.4%	17.9%	18.1%	18.0%	17.0%	16.0%	15.0%	14.0%	13.0%	13.0%
Net working capital/ sales	10.1%	9.5%	9.0%	9.0%	9.0%	9.0%	9.0%	9.0%	9.0%	9.0%
Net non-current operating assets/ sales	60.7%	59.5%	58.4%	58.4%	58.4%	58.4%	58.4%	58.4%	58.4%	58.4%
Investment assets/sales	12.0%	12.0%	12.0%	10.0%	9.0%	8.0%	7.0%	6.0%	5.0%	5.0%
After tax return on investment assets	2.8%	2.8%	2.8%	2.8%	2.8%	2.8%	2.8%	2.8%	2.8%	2.8%
After tax cost of net debt	2.3%	2.5%	2.7%	2.9%	3.1%	3.3%	3.5%	3.5%	3.5%	3.5%
Debt to capital	52.6%	52.6%	52.6%	52.6%	52.6%	52.6%	52.6%	52.6%	52.6%	52.6%

In addition to these assumptions, we also assume that sales will continue to grow at 3.0 percent in 2022 and all the balance sheet ratios remain constant, to compute the beginning balance sheet for 2022 and cash flows for 2021.

We assume a pattern of moderately increasing and then declining NOPAT margins over time. The assumption that the NOPAT margin increases in the medium-term is consistent with our assessment of the effects of decreasing input prices and inventory markdowns. The assumed time-series trend for the second half of the forecasting period is consistent with that documented earlier in the chapter for firms with initially high NOPAT. While Hennes & Mauritz clearly has a significant competitive advantage over its rivals, it is prudent to assume, given the history of European firms, that this advantage will decline over time. Overall, we assume that the company's NOPAT margin reaches its peak of 18.1 percent in year 3 and then declines to reach a value of 13 percent by year 9.

H&M currently has a working capital to sales ratio of 10.5 percent. Based on the inventories turnover assumption for years 1 and 2, this ratio is projected to decline to 9.0 percent. The forecast assumes that a ratio of 9.0 percent is maintained throughout the forecast horizon. Based on the assumed improvement in store productivity, the ratio of net non-current assets to sales is expected to decrease to 58.4 percent in year 3 and remain steady thereafter. As H&M's need for excess cash to finance new stores is assumed to decrease, the investment assets-to-sales ratio steadily decreases from 12 percent in year 1 to 5 percent in year 10.

Hennes & Mauritz's capital structure remains relatively unchanged. As a result, the ratio of debt to book value of capital of 52.6 percent is maintained for the duration of the forecast horizon. This assumption of a constant capital structure policy is consistent with the general pattern observed in the historical data discussed earlier in the chapter. The forecast assumes that H&M's cost of debt increase from 3.2 percent, or an after-tax cost of 2.3 percent, to 4.7 percent, or an after-tax cost of 3.5 percent.

Having made this set of key assumptions, it is a straightforward task to derive the forecasted income statements and beginning balance sheets for years 2012 through 2021 as shown in Table 6.11. Under these forecasts, H&M's sales will grow to SEK247,575 million, more than double the level in 2011. By 2021, the firm will have net operating assets of SEK162,006 million and shareholders' equity of SEK82,454 million. Consistent with market-wide patterns of mean-reversion in returns, H&M's return on beginning equity will decline from 51.8 percent in 2014 to 35.6 percent by 2021, and return on beginning operating assets will show a similar pattern.

Cash flow forecasts

Once we have forecasted income statements and balance sheets, we can derive cash flows for the years 2012 through 2021. Note that we need to forecast the beginning balance sheet for 2022 to compute the cash flows for

TABLE 6.11 Forecasted financial statements for Hennes & Mauritz

Fiscal year	2012	2013	2014	2015	2016	2017	2018	2019	2020	2021
Beginning balance sheet (SEK millions)										
Beginning net working capital	12,377.9	12,395.2	13,251.1	14,318.6	16,036.9	17,640.6	19,051.8	20,194.9	21,002.7	21,632.8
+ Beginning net non-current operating assets	68,981.5	74,494.1	82,993.6	92,912.1	104,061.5	114,467.7	123,625.1	131,042.6	136,284.3	140,372.8
+ Beginning investment assets	13,085.1	14,727.0	16,738.2	19,091.5	17,818.8	17,640.6	16,934.9	15,707.2	14,001.8	12,018.2
= Business assets	94,444.5	101,616.3	112,982.9	126,322.2	137,917.1	149,748.8	159,611.8	166,944.7	171,288.8	174,023.8
Debt	49,695.8	53,469.5	59,450.5	66,469.5	72,570.6	78,796.3	83,986.2	87,844.6	90,130.5	91,569.6
+ Group equity	44,748.7	48,146.8	53,532.4	59,852.7	65,346.5	70,952.5	75,625.7	79,100.0	81,158.3	82,454.2
= Capital	94,444.5	101,616.3	112,982.9	126,322.2	137,917.1	149,748.8	159,611.8	166,944.7	171,288.8	174,023.8
Income statement (SEK millions)										
Sales	122,725.0	139,485.0	159,096.0	178,187.5	196,006.3	211,686.8	224,388.0	233,363.5	240,364.4	247,575.3
Net operating profit after tax	20,126.9	24,967.8	28,796.4	32,073.8	33,321.1	33,869.9	33,658.2	32,670.9	31,247.4	32,184.8
+ Net investment profit after tax	414.0	470.5	536.7	500.9	495.9	476.1	441.6	393.6	337.9	348.0
= Net business profit after tax	20,540.9	25,438.4	29,333.1	32,574.7	33,817.0	34,346.0	34,099.8	33,064.5	31,585.2	32,532.8
− Net interest expense after tax	−1,155.7	−1,336.7	−1,605.2	−2,060.6	−2,394.8	−2,757.9	−2,939.5	−3,074.6	−3,154.6	−3,204.9
= Net profit	19,385.2	24,101.6	27,727.9	30,514.1	31,422.1	31,588.1	31,160.2	29,989.9	28,430.7	29,327.8
Return on business assets	21.7%	25.0%	26.0%	25.8%	24.5%	22.9%	21.4%	19.8%	18.4%	18.7%
ROE	43.3%	50.1%	51.8%	51.0%	48.1%	44.5%	41.2%	37.9%	35.0%	35.6%
BV of equity growth rate	1.3%	7.6%	11.2%	11.8%	9.2%	8.6%	6.6%	4.6%	2.6%	1.6%
Net profit	19,385.2	24,101.6	27,727.9	30,514.1	31,422.1	31588.1	31,160.2	29,989.9	28,430.7	29,327.8
− Change in net working capital	−17.3	−855.9	−1,067.6	−1,718.2	−1,603.7	−1,411.2	−1,143.1	−807.8	−630.1	−649.0
− Change in net non-current operating assets	−5,512.6	−8,499.5	−9,918.5	−11,149.4	−10,406.2	−9,157.4	−7,417.5	−5,241.7	−4,088.5	−4,211.2
− Change in investment assets	−1,641.9	−2,011.2	−2,353.3	1,272.8	178.2	705.6	1,227.8	1,705.3	1,983.6	−360.5
+ Change in debt	3,773.7	5,981.0	7,019.0	6,101.1	6,225.7	5,189.8	3,858.5	2,285.8	1,439.1	2,747.1
= Free cash flow to equity	15,987.1	18,716.0	21,407.6	25,020.3	25,816.2	26,914.9	27,685.9	27,931.6	27,134.8	26,854.2
Net operating profit after tax	20,126.9	24,967.8	28,796.4	32,073.8	33,321.1	33,869.9	33,658.2	32,670.9	31,247.4	32,184.8
− Change in net working capital	−17.3	−855.9	−1,067.6	−1,718.2	−1,603.7	−1,411.2	−1,143.1	−807.8	−630.1	−649.0
− Change in net non-current operating assets	−5,512.6	−8,499.5	−9,918.5	−11,149.4	−10,406.2	−9,157.4	−7,417.5	−5,241.7	−4,088.5	−4,211.2
= Free cash flow from operations	14,597.0	15,612.5	17,810.3	19,206.1	21,311.2	23,301.2	25,097.6	26,621.4	26,528.8	27,324.6

We do not show the beginning balance sheet forecasted for 2022 here, but it is implicit in the calculation of cash flows for 2021. As stated in Table 6.10, we assume that sales continue to grow in 2022 and that all the balance sheet ratios continue to be the same, to derive the beginning balance sheet for 2022.

2021. This balance sheet is not shown in Table 6.11. For the purpose of illustration, we assume that all the sales growth and the balance sheet ratios remain the same in 2022 as in 2021. Based on this, we project a beginning balance sheet for 2022 and compute the cash flows for 2021. Free cash flow from operations is equal to net operating profit after tax (NOPAT) minus increases in net working capital and net non-current operating assets. Cash flow to equity is cash flow to capital minus interest after tax plus increase in debt. These two sets of forecasted cash flows are presented in Table 6.11. As the table shows, the free cash flow from operating assets increases from SEK14,597 million to SEK27,325 million by 2021. In addition, the firm is expected to increase the free cash flow it generates to its equity holders from SEK15,987 million in 2012 to SEK26,854 million by 2021.

SENSITIVITY ANALYSIS

The projections discussed thus far represent nothing more than an estimation of a most likely scenario for Hennes & Mauritz. Managers and analysts are typically interested in a broader range of possibilities. For example, an analyst estimating the value of Hennes & Mauritz might consider the sensitivity of the projections to the key assumptions about sales growth, profit margins, and asset utilization. What if rising labor costs in H&M's production countries lead to a substantial increase in cost of sales? Alternatively, what if H&M's investments in product quality and design pay off significantly and store productivity grows at a faster rate than assumed in the above forecasts? It is wise to also generate projections based on a variety of assumptions to determine the sensitivity of the forecasts to these assumptions.

There is no limit to the number of possible scenarios that can be considered. One systematic approach to **sensitivity analysis** is to start with the key assumptions underlying a set of forecasts and then examine the sensitivity to the assumptions with greatest uncertainty in a given situation. For example, if a company has experienced a variable pattern of gross margins in the past, it is important to make projections using a range of margins. Alternatively, if a company has announced a significant change in its expansion strategy, asset utilization assumptions might be more uncertain. In determining where to invest one's time in performing sensitivity analysis, it is therefore important to consider historical patterns of performance, changes in industry conditions, and changes in a company's competitive strategy.

In the case of Hennes & Mauritz, two likely alternatives to the forecast can be readily envisioned. The forecast presented above expects that H&M's sales per store will only moderately improve during the year 2012 to 2014. An upside case for H&M would have the firm improve store productivity at a greater rate. On the downside, the projected decrease in H&M's sourcing costs could turn out to be too optimistic, flattening the improvement in the company's NOPAT margin.

Seasonality and interim forecasts

Thus far we have concerned ourselves with annual forecasts. However, traditionally for security analysts in the US and increasingly for security analysts in Europe, forecasting is very much a quarterly exercise. Forecasting quarter by quarter raises a new set of questions. How important is seasonality? What is a useful point of departure for **interim forecasts** – the most recent quarter's performance? The comparable quarter of the prior year? Some combination of the two? How should quarterly data be used in producing an annual forecast? Does the item-by-item approach to forecasting used for annual data apply equally well to quarterly data? Full consideration of these questions lies outside the scope of this chapter, but we can begin to answer some of them.

Seasonality is a more important phenomenon in sales and earnings behavior than one might guess. It is present for more than just the retail sector firms that benefit from holiday sales. Seasonality also results from weather-related phenomena (e.g., for electric and gas utilities, construction firms, and motorcycle manufacturers), new product introduction patterns (e.g., for the automobile industry), and other factors. Analysis of the time-series behavior of earnings for US firms suggests that at least some seasonality is present in nearly every major industry.

The implication for forecasting is that one cannot focus only on performance of the most recent quarter as a point of departure. In fact the evidence suggests that, in forecasting earnings, if one had to choose only one quarter's performance as a point of departure, it would be the comparable quarter of the prior year, not the most recent quarter. Note how this finding is consistent with the reports of analysts or the financial press; when they discuss a quarterly earnings announcement, it is nearly always evaluated relative to the performance of the comparable quarter of the prior year, not the most recent quarter.

Research has produced models that forecast sales, earnings, or EPS, based solely on prior quarters' observations. Such models are not used by many analysts, because analysts have access to much more information than such simple models contain. However, the models are useful for helping those unfamiliar with the behavior of earnings data to understand how it tends to evolve through time. Such an understanding can provide useful general background, a point of departure in forecasting that can be adjusted to reflect details not revealed in the history of earnings, or a "reasonableness" check on a detailed forecast.

One model of the earnings process that fits well across a variety of industries is the so-called Foster model.[6] Using Q_t to denote earnings (or EPS) for quarter t, and $E(Q_t)$ as its expected value, the Foster model predicts that:

$$E(Q_t) = Q_{t-4} + \delta + \varphi(Q_{t-1} - Q_{t-5})$$

Foster shows that a model of the same form also works well with quarterly sales data.

The form of the Foster model confirms the importance of seasonality because it shows that the starting point for a forecast for quarter t is the earnings four quarters ago, Q_{t-4}. It states that, when constrained to using only prior earnings data, a reasonable forecast of earnings for quarter t includes the following elements:

- The earnings of the comparable quarter of the prior year (Q_{t-4}).
- A long-run trend in year-to-year quarterly earnings increases (δ).
- A fraction (ϕ) of the year-to-year increase in quarterly earnings experienced most recently ($Q_{t-1} - Q_{t-5}$).

The parameters δ and ϕ can easily be estimated for a given firm with a simple linear regression model available in most spreadsheet software.[7] For most firms the parameter ϕ tends to be in the range of 0.25 to 0.50, indicating that 25 to 50 percent of an increase in quarterly earnings tends to persist in the form of another increase in the subsequent quarter. The parameter δ reflects in part the average year-to-year change in quarterly earnings over past years, and it varies considerably from firm to firm.

Research indicates that the Foster model produces one-quarter-ahead forecasts that are off by $.30 to $.35 per share, on average.[8] Such a degree of accuracy stacks up surprisingly well with that of security analysts, who obviously have access to much information ignored in the model. As one would expect, most of the evidence supports analysts being more accurate, but the models are good enough to be "in the ball park" in most circumstances. While it would certainly be unwise to rely completely on such a naïve model, an understanding of the typical earnings behavior reflected by the model is useful.

SUMMARY

Forecasting represents the first step of prospective analysis and serves to summarize the forward-looking view that emanates from business strategy analysis, accounting analysis, and financial analysis. Although not every financial statement analysis is accompanied by such an explicit summarization of a view of the future, forecasting is still a key tool for managers, consultants, security analysts, investment bankers, commercial bankers, and other credit analysts, among others.

The best approach to forecasting future performance is to do it comprehensively – producing not only an earnings forecast but a forecast of cash flows and the balance sheet as well. Such a comprehensive approach provides a guard against internal inconsistencies and unrealistic implicit assumptions. The approach described here involves line-by-line analysis, so as to recognize that different items on the income statement and balance sheet are influenced by different drivers. Nevertheless, it remains the case that a few key projections – such as sales growth and profit margin – usually drive most of the projected numbers.

The forecasting process should be embedded in an understanding of how various financial statistics tend to behave on average, and what might cause a firm to deviate from that average. Without detailed information to the contrary, one would expect sales and earnings numbers to persist at their current levels, adjusted for overall trends of recent years. However, rates of return on investment (ROEs) tend, over several years, to move from abnormal to normal levels – close to the cost of equity capital – as the forces of competition come into play. Profit margins also tend to shift to normal levels, but for this statistic "normal" varies widely across firms and industries, depending on the levels of asset turnover and leverage. Some firms are capable of creating barriers to entry that enable them to fight these tendencies toward normal returns, even for many years, but such firms are the unusual cases.

Forecasting should be preceded by a comprehensive business strategy, accounting, and financial analysis. It is important to understand the dynamics of the industry in which the firm operates and its competitive positioning within that industry. Therefore, while general market trends provide a useful benchmark, it is critical that the analyst incorporates the views developed about the firm's prospects to guide the forecasting process.

For some purposes, including short-term planning and security analysis, forecasts for quarterly periods are desirable. One important feature of quarterly data is seasonality; at least some seasonality exists in the sales and earnings data of nearly every industry. An understanding of a firm's intra-year peaks and valleys is a necessary ingredient of a good forecast of performance on a quarterly basis.

Forecasts provide the input for estimating a firm's value, which can be viewed as the best attempt to reflect in a single summary statistics the manager's or analyst's view of the firm's prospects. The process of converting a forecast into a value estimate is labeled valuation and is discussed next.

CORE CONCEPTS

Comprehensive forecasting approach Forecasting of the (condensed) income statement, balance sheet, and cash flow statement to make sure that the performance forecast does not imbed unreasonable assumptions about future asset turnover, leverage, or equity changes.

Condensed financial statements Recommended focus of the forecasting task. The condensed financial statements consist of the following elements:

1 Income statement: Sales, net operating profit after tax, net interest expense after tax, net profit.
2 Balance sheet: Net working capital, net non-current assets, net operating assets, net debt, shareholders' equity, net capital.
3 Cash flow statement: Net profit (net operating profit after taxes), change in net working capital, change in net non-current assets, change in net debt.

Interim forecasts Forecasts of quarterly performance. A key issue in interim forecasting is the seasonality of performance, i.e., the tendency of quarterly performance to exhibit within-year time-series patterns that repeat themselves across years.

Mean-reversion Tendency of financial ratios to revert to the industry or economy average over time. Financial ratios or indicators that tend to revert to the mean are: sales growth, return on equity, return on assets, and financial spread. Financial ratios that have a low tendency to revert to the mean are: operating asset turnover and net financial leverage.

Prospective analysis Fourth and final step of financial statement analysis, which focuses on forecasting a firm's future financial performance and position. The forecasts can be used for various purposes, such as estimating firm value or assessing creditworthiness.

Sensitivity analysis Analysis of how sensitive performance forecasts are to (realistic) changes in the key assumptions made to produce the forecast. In a sensitivity analysis, the analyst typically produces forecasts under various scenarios.

QUESTIONS, EXERCISES AND PROBLEMS

1 GlaxoSmithKline is one of the largest pharmaceutical firms in the world, and over an extended period of time in the recent past it consistently earned higher ROEs than the pharmaceutical industry as a whole. As a pharmaceutical analyst, what factors would you consider to be important in making projections of future ROEs for GlaxoSmith-Kline? In particular, what factors would lead you to expect GlaxoSmithKline to continue to be a

superior performer in its industry, and what factors would lead you to expect GlaxoSmithKline's future performance to revert to that of the industry as a whole?

2   An analyst claims, "It is not worth my time to develop detailed forecasts of sales growth, profit margins, etcetera, to make earnings projections. I can be almost as accurate, at virtually no cost, using the random walk model to forecast earnings." What is the random walk model? Do you agree or disagree with the analyst's forecast strategy? Why or why not?

3   Which of the following types of businesses do you expect to show a high degree of seasonality in quarterly earnings? Explain why.
   ■   A supermarket.
   ■   A pharmaceutical company.
   ■   A software company.
   ■   An auto manufacturer.
   ■   A clothing retailer.

4   What factors are likely to drive a firm's outlays for new capital (such as plant, property, and equipment) and for working capital (such as receivables and inventory)? What ratios would you use to help generate forecasts of these outlays?

5   How would the following events (reported this year) affect your forecasts of a firm's future net profit?
   ■   An asset write-down.
   ■   A merger or acquisition.
   ■   The sale of a major division.
   ■   The initiation of dividend payments.

6   Consider the following two earnings forecasting models:

$$\text{Model: } E_t(EPS_{t+1}) = EPS_t$$

$$\text{Model: } E_t(EPS_{t+1}) = \frac{1}{5}\sum_{i=0}^{4} EPS_{t-i}$$

$E_t(EPS)$ is the expected forecast of earnings per share for year $t + 1$, given information available at t. Model 1 is usually called a random walk model for earnings, whereas Model 2 is called a mean-reverting model. The earnings per share for Telefónica for the period 2000 to 2004 are as follows:

Year	1	2	3	4	5
EPS	€0.61	€0.43	€(1.08)	€0.40	€0.58

   a   What would be the year 6 forecast for earnings per share for each model?
   b   Actual earnings per share for Telefónica in year 6 were €0.91. Given this information, what would be the year 7 forecast for earnings per share for each model? Why do the two models generate quite different forecasts? Which do you think would better describe earnings per share patterns? Why?

7   An investment banker states, "It is not worth my while to worry about detailed long-term forecasts. Instead, I use the following approach when forecasting cash flows beyond three years. I assume that sales grow at the rate of inflation, capital expenditures are equal to depreciation, and that net profit margins and working capital to sales ratios stay constant." What pattern of return on equity is implied by these assumptions? Is this reasonable?

Problem 1 *Predicting Tesco's 2009/2010 earnings*

On April 21, 2009, UK-based retailer Tesco plc presented its preliminary financial statements for the fiscal year ending on March 31, 2009. The following tables show a selection of Tesco's financial figures for the fiscal years 2007/2008 and 2008/2009 (i.e., the fiscal years ending on March 31, 2008 and 2009, respectively):

Income statement (£ millions)	2008/2009	2007/2008
Sales	54,327	47,298
Operating expenses	(51,121)	(44,507)
Interest expense	(284)	(112)
Investment income	32	124
Tax expense	(788)	(673)
Net profit	**2,166**	**2,130**

Balance sheet (£ millions)	2008/2009	2007/2008
Net working capital	**(4,912)**	**(3,885)**
Non-current tangible assets	23,152	19,787
Non-current intangible assets	4,027	2,336
Other non-current assets	3,469	1,725
Non-interest bearing liabilities	(888)	(954)
Total business assets	**29,760**	**22,894**
Debt	11,910	7,194
Equity	12,938	11,815
Total capital	**24,848**	**19,009**

Other information (£ millions)	2008/2009	2007/2008
Depreciation of non-current tangible assets	1,036	876
Amortization of non-current intangible assets	153	116
Non-current tangible assets at cost	29,844	25,550
Non-current intangible assets at cost	4,790	2,944
Dividends paid	883	792

In addition to disclosing the financial statements, Tesco's management also provided guidance about future investment plans, financing strategies, and performance expectations. In particular, the following information became available to investors and analysts on the publication date:

- In 2008/2009, Tesco opened 9 million square feet of new store space. The retailer plans to open 8 million square feet of new store space in 2009/2010.

- Revenues in 2008/2009 were the revenues of 53 weeks. The fiscal year 2009/2010 will include 52 weeks.

- Group capital expenditure during 2008/2009 was GBP 4.7 billion, a little more than planned (GBP 4.5b) due to currency movements. Tesco's management indicates that capital expenditures in 2009/2010 will be around GBP 3.5 billion. One reason for why capital expenditures can be reduced is that in the current economic downturn, Tesco can buy more new store space for less.

- Tesco's effective tax rate in 2008/2009 was 26.7 percent versus 24.0 percent in 2007/2008. The increase in tax rate was primarily the result of one-time tax benefits in 2007/2008. Management expects the effective tax rate for 2009/2010 to be around 27 percent.

- In 2008/2009, Tesco was able to realize cost saving of close to GBP 550 million through its Step-Change program. Management expects these cost savings to persist.

- In 2008/2009, Tesco's net finance cost, including the company's return on pension assets, was GBP 284 million. The underlying interest charge was GBP 309 million, up from GBP 159 million in 2007/2008. The weighted average coupon rate of Tesco's debt was 5.6 percent.

- Tesco's debt rose substantially during 2008/2009 as a result of:

  1 Increased capital expenditures.

  2 An increased pension deficit (GBP 0.65 billion increase).

  3 The significant depreciation in the sterling-dollar/euro exchange rates (with a debt impact of approximately GBP 1 billion).

If exchange rates remain stable, management intends to bring down debt by approximately GBP 1 billion during 2009/2010. Further, management disclosed the following information about realized and planned store openings:

(£ millions)	UK	Rest of Europe	Asia	US
2008/2009 (Realized):				
Revenues	38,191	8,862	7,068	206
Operating profit	2,540	479	343	(156)
Square feet store space (× 1,000):				
Beginning-of-year	29,549	22,517	23,363	530
Openings, extensions, adjustments	1,773	3,502	3,006	620
Acquisitions	239	3,015	0	0
Closures/disposals	(276)	(196)	(190)	0
End-of-year	31,285	28,838	26,179	1,150
2009/2010 (Expected):				
Square feet store space (× 1,000):				
Beginning-of-year	31,285	28,838	26,179	1,150
Openings, extensions, adjustments	1,897	2,697	2,733	600
Acquisitions	98	0	0	0
Closures/disposals	(225)	0	(63)	0
End-of-year	33,055	31,535	28,849	1,750

1 Predict Tesco's 2009/2010 sales using the information about the company's store space and revenues (per geographical segment).

2 Predict the 2009/2010 book values of Tesco's non-current assets and working capital using the information about the company's investment plans. Make simplifying assumptions where necessary.

3 During fiscal year 2008/2009, at least two factors influenced Tesco's operating expenses: (a) the increase in depreciation and (b) the cost savings of approximately GBP 550 million. Assume that all other changes in the company's operating profit margin were caused by the economic downturn.

   a What was the net effect of the downturn on Tesco's operating margins?

   b Estimate Tesco's 2009/2010 operating expense under the assumption that the effect of the economic downturn fully persists in 2009/2010. (Estimate the company's depreciation and amortization expense separately from the other operating expenses.)

4 Estimate Tesco's 2009/2010 interest expense and debt-to-equity ratio under the assumption that the company reduces its debt in 2009/2010, as planned.

5 What do the above estimates (and your estimate of Tesco's 2009/2010 tax expense) imply for the company's free cash flow to equity holders in 2009/2010? How likely is it that Tesco will be able to reduce its debt in 2009/2010?

NOTES

1. See Patricia O'Brien, "Analysts' Forecasts as Earnings Expectations," *Journal of Accounting and Economics* (January 1988): 53–83.
2. See George Foster, "Quarterly Accounting Data: Time Series Properties and Predictive Ability Results," *The Accounting Review* (January 1977): 1–21.
3. See Robert Freeman, James Ohlson, and Stephen Penman, "Book Rate-of-Return and Prediction of Earnings Changes: An Empirical Investigation," *Journal of Accounting Research* (Autumn 1982): 639–653.
4. See Stephen H. Penman, "An Evaluation of Accounting Rate-of-Return," *Journal of Accounting, Auditing, and Finance* (Spring 1991): 233–256; Eugene Fama and Kenneth French, "Size and Book-to-Market Factors in Earnings and Returns," *Journal of Finance* (March 1995): 131–156; and Victor Bernard, "Accounting-Based Valuation Methods: Evidence on the Market-to-Book Anomaly and Implications for Financial Statements Analysis," University of Michigan, working paper (1994). Ignoring the effects of accounting artifacts, ROEs should be driven in a competitive equilibrium to a level approximating the cost of equity capital.
5. A "normal" profit margin is that which, when multiplied by the turnover achievable within an industry and with a viable corporate strategy, yields a return on investment that just covers the cost of capital. However, as mentioned above, accounting artifacts can cause returns on investment to deviate from the cost of capital for long periods, even in a competitive equilibrium.
6. See Foster, op. cit. A somewhat more accurate model is furnished by Brown and Rozeff, but it requires interactive statistical techniques for estimation – Lawrence D. Brown and Michael Rozeff, "Univariate Time Series Models of Quarterly Accounting Earnings per Share," *Journal of Accounting Research* (Spring 1979): 179–189.
7. To estimate the model, we write in terms of realized earnings (as opposed to expected earnings) and move Q_{t-4} to the left-hand side:

$$Q_t - Q_{t-4} = \delta + \varphi(Q_{t-1} - Q_{t-5}) + e_t$$

We now have a regression where $(Q_t - Q_{t-4})$ is the dependent variable, and its lagged value – $(Q_{t-1} - Q_{t-5})$ – is the independent variable. Thus, to estimate the equation, prior earnings data must first be expressed in terms of year-to-year changes; the change for one quarter is then regressed against the change for the most recent quarter. The intercept provides an estimate of δ, and the slope is an estimate of ϕ. The equation is typically estimated using 24 to 40 quarters of prior earnings data.
8. See O'Brien, op. cit.

APPENDIX : THE BEHAVIOR OF COMPONENTS OF ROE

In Figure 6A we show that ROEs tend to be mean-reverting. In this appendix we show the behavior of the key components of ROE – return on operating assets, operating margin, operating asset turnover, return on investment assets, spread, and net financial leverage. These ratios are computed using the same portfolio approach described in the chapter, based on the data for all European firms for the time period 1992 through 2011.

FIGURE 6A.1 Behavior of return on operating assets for European firms over time, 1992–2011

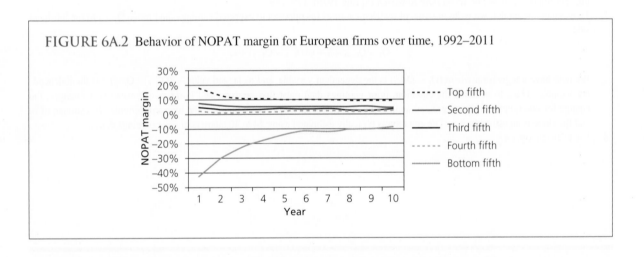

FIGURE 6A.2 Behavior of NOPAT margin for European firms over time, 1992–2011

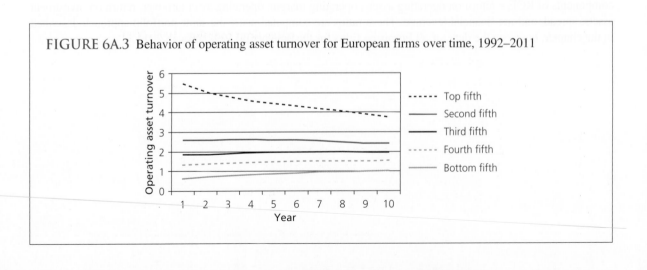

FIGURE 6A.3 Behavior of operating asset turnover for European firms over time, 1992–2011

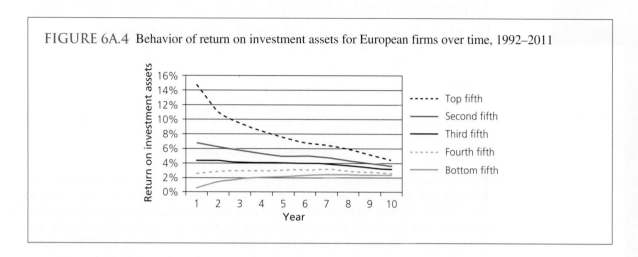

FIGURE 6A.4 Behavior of return on investment assets for European firms over time, 1992–2011

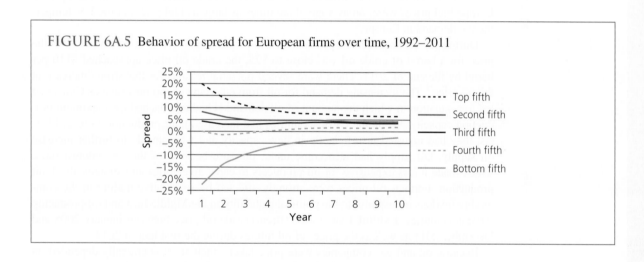

FIGURE 6A.5 Behavior of spread for European firms over time, 1992–2011

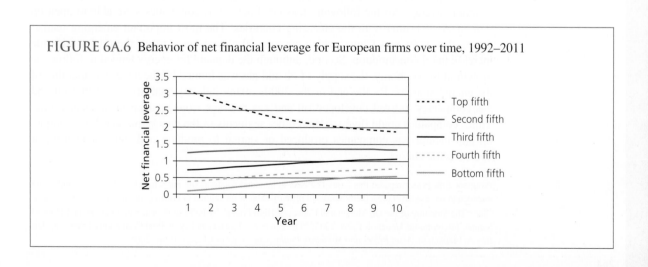

FIGURE 6A.6 Behavior of net financial leverage for European firms over time, 1992–2011

Forecasting earnings and earnings growth in the European oil and gas industry

Industry overview

In 2011 the largest companies operating in the European oil exploration and production industry all tended to operate on a global scale. They were typically categorized as "price takers" because they had little control over the prices that they could ask from their customers. One reason for this small influence on prices was that the 12 oil-producing developing countries that coordinated their production activities through the OPEC organization had a strong influence on the worldwide oil supply and crude oil prices. Although the OPEC countries possessed close to 80 percent of the worldwide proved oil reserves, they supplied only 42 percent of the worldwide oil production to stabilize prices at higher levels. National taxes also influenced local prices and demand for oil. For example, in Europe fuel prices were, on average, three times as large as fuel prices in the US, tempering the demand in Europe.

During the 2000s, crude oil prices soared to record levels. While at the end of 1999 the price for a barrel of crude oil was close to $25, the crude oil price approached $110 per barrel by the end of 2011. There were several potential reasons for this strong increase in the oil price.[1] The increasing demand for oil from emerging economies such as China had led to a situation in which the amount of oil demanded had approached the maximum production capacity. While the OPEC countries had increased their production to record levels, they had invested insufficiently in new capacity and were unable to further increase oil supply. Oil supply had also come under pressure because of the low interest rates, which made it less expensive for oil producers to carry inventories and strategically limit production. Further, oil prices were strongly affected by speculative trading in the commodity markets in response to the political instability in the Middle East and oil-producing African countries. **Exhibit 1** shows the (Brent) crude oil price between January 2005 and December 2011 as well as the prices of oil futures during the first half of 2012.

Because oil and gas companies were price takers, their success critically depended on (1) their ability to grow and (2) the efficiency of their exploration and production activities. Although the growth of the energy markets typically followed the growth in gross domestic product, oil and gas companies could grow at a faster or slower rate than the economy average for the following reasons. First, some companies were able to open up new markets, primarily in the emerging countries. The most important emerging market during the 2000s was China, which contributed almost one-third to the total worldwide increase in oil consumption. Second, although the demand for energy tended to follow the growth of the economy, the supply of oil and gas was limited by the natural availability of the energy sources. By the end of the 2000s, many industry analysts feared that oil and gas companies' proved developed oil and gas reserves would reduce in the near future. Third, companies could diversify into other segments of the energy market. For example, oil and natural gas companies produced or started to produce coal, nuclear energy, or hydroelectric energy.

Professor Erik Peek prepared this case. The case is intended solely as the basis for class discussion and is not intended to serve as an endorsement, source of primary data, or illustration of effective or ineffective management.

[1]See "The Structure of the Oil Market and Causes of High Prices" by Pelin Berkmen, Sam Ouliaris, and Hossein Samiei, *International Monetary Fund,* 2005; "The Effect of Monetary Policy on Real Commodity Prices" by Jeffrey A. Frankel, in: *Asset Prices and Monetary Policy*, University of Chicago Press, 2008.

The increasing oil price tended to have a positive impact on oil and gas companies' profits in the 2000s. Nonetheless, various other developments put pressure on the companies' profit margins. First, because oil was traded in US dollars, the weak dollar implied that it was expensive for oil companies to buy resources in other currencies. Second, steel prices were also rising, making oil and gas companies' capital investments more expensive. Third, and most importantly, during the first half of the 2000s exploration costs per barrel of oil equivalent (BOE) had risen sharply.[2]

Oil and gas companies that had operations in developing countries were also subject to a substantial degree of country risk. Many companies were extending their operations to developing countries in, for example, West Africa or around the Caspian Sea, because they were running out of reserves in the developed countries. Operations in such developing countries could, however, be disrupted by political crises, acts of war, and expropriation or nationalization of reserves and production facilities by governments. For example, in 2006 Bolivia announced plans to nationalize its oil and gas fields, which were then owned by several international oil and gas producers. Similarly, early 2012 Argentina decided to take back control of YPF, the Argentinian operating branch of Spain-based oil producer Repsol.

Oil and gas companies' accounting and disclosure

As argued, because oil and gas companies are price takers, their future profitability depends primarily on (1) the quantity and quality of their current oil and gas reserves, (2) their ability to efficiently extract and produce oil and gas, and (3) their ability to replace extracted reserves. Some inherent characteristics of oil and gas companies' exploration and development activities, however, make accounting for these activities a difficult exercise. Particularly, because the future economic benefits of current exploration and development expenditures are hard to establish, deciding on which expenditures must be capitalized as assets and which expenditures must be categorized as "unsuccessful" and immediately written-off can be problematic.

Most oil and gas companies use the "successful efforts method" of accounting for exploration and development activities. Under this method, the key financial reporting estimate is for proved oil and gas reserves. Accounting standards consider oil and gas reserves to be proved when the company has government and regulatory approval for the extraction of reserves and is able to bring the reserves quickly to the market in a commercially viable manner. Companies make these estimates using geological information about each reservoir, reservoir production histories, and reservoir pressure histories. The distinction between proved and unproved reserves is important because only exploration expenditures that are associated with proved reserves are capitalized as assets. Specifically, under the successful efforts method, companies capitalize their exploration expenditures for a short period, after which they choose between continued capitalization and immediate amortization based on whether the exploration has successfully led to the booking of proved reserves. In addition, oil companies' depreciation, depletion, and amortization of production plants are typically calculated using the unit-of-production method, where the expected production capacity is derived from the proved reserves. The following paragraphs from BP plc's 2011 Annual Report describe how BP accounts for exploration and development expenditures and illustrates the basic idea underlying the successful efforts method:

> *Exploration license and leasehold property acquisition costs are capitalized within intangible assets and are reviewed at each reporting date to confirm that there is no indication that the carrying amount exceeds the recoverable amount. This review includes confirming that exploration drilling is still under way or firmly planned or that it has been determined, or work is under way to determine, that the discovery is economically viable based on a range of technical and commercial considerations and sufficient progress is being made on establishing development plans and timing. If no future activity is planned, the remaining balance of the license and property acquisition costs is written off. [...]*
>
> *Geological and geophysical exploration costs are charged against income as incurred. Costs directly associated with an exploration well are initially capitalized as an intangible asset until the drilling of the well is complete and the results have been evaluated. These costs include employee remuneration, materials and fuel used, rig costs, and payments made to contractors. If potentially commercial quantities of hydrocarbons are not found, the exploration well is written off as a dry hole. If*

Forecasting earnings and earnings growth in the European oil and gas industry

---

[2]See "Oil Companies' Profits: Not Exactly What They Seem to Be," *The Economist*, October 28, 2004.

hydrocarbons are found and, subject to further appraisal activity, are likely to be capable of commercial development, the costs continue to be carried as an asset. [...]

When proved reserves of oil and natural gas are determined and development is approved by management, the relevant expenditure is transferred to property, plant, and equipment. [...]

Expenditure on the construction, installation, and completion of infrastructure facilities such as platforms, pipelines, and the drilling of development wells, including service and unsuccessful development or delineation wells, is capitalized within property, plant, and equipment and is depreciated from the commencement of production as described below in the accounting policy for property, plant, and equipment. [...]

Oil and natural gas properties, including related pipelines, are depreciated using a unit-of-production method. The cost of producing wells is amortized over proved developed reserves. License acquisition, common facilities, and future decommissioning costs are amortized over total proved reserves.

The method that BP uses to account for its exploration and development expenditures is similar to the method used by many other oil and gas companies, including Royal Dutch Shell and Statoil. Most oil and gas companies also provide supplemental disclosures about their oil and gas reserves. These disclosures typically show (1) the exploration and development costs that the company incurred during the year, (2) the exploration and development costs that the company capitalized over the years, (3) the results of the company's oil and gas exploration and development activities, and (4) the movements in the company's proved and unproved oil and gas reserves during the year. **Exhibit 2** summarizes the supplemental information that BP, Royal Dutch Shell, and Statoil provided in annual reports for the fiscal year ended on December 31, 2011.

A description of three European oil and gas companies

Following are the descriptions of three European companies that operated in the oil and gas industry in 2011: BP, Royal Dutch Shell, and Statoil.

BP

At the end of the 2000s, BP was one the world's largest publicly listed oil and gas company's in terms of revenues. The company had upstream (oil exploration and production) and downstream (sales and distribution) operations in more than 30 countries, in which it employed approximately 83,000 people. Between December 31, 2004 and December 31, 2011, BP's share price decreased by 9.3 percent, which in combination with an average annualized dividend yield of 3.2 percent yielded an average annual return of 2.0 percent. By the end of 2011, BP's market value was close to £88 billion.

BP's shares were widely held. In 2011, the company's largest shareholder owned less than 6 percent of BP's ordinary shares outstanding. Like many other oil and gas companies, during the 2000s BP had excess cash that it returned to its shareholders through share repurchases and dividends. Between 2000 and 2008, the company repurchased ordinary shares for an amount of £51.1 billion; however, BP halted its buy-back program in 2009. BP was a financially healthy company, evidenced by the fact that Standard and Poor's had rated BP's public debt at A.

Although BP's primary activities were the exploration, development, and production of oil and natural gas, the company also operated in other product segments. However, in 2011 less than 1 percent of the company's revenues came from its alternative energy business. BP's primary geographical segment was the US and Europe, where it generated 35 percent of its revenues, followed by the UK (20 percent of its revenues).

Fiscal years 2010 and 2011 had been a turbulent period for BP. In the first half of 2010 an oil spill caused by an explosion at one of BP's operations had caused significant environmental damage in the Gulf of Mexico. Following the oil spill, BP had committed to an extensive clean up, to supporting the economic restoration of the area affected by the oil spill, and to creating a $20 billion Deepwater Horizon Oil Spill Trust from which individual claims and settlements could be funded. BP's income statement for fiscal 2010 included a pre-tax charge of $40.8 billion resulting from its oil spill-related commitments; the company's 2011 income statement included an oil spill-related pre-tax gain (reversal) of $3.8 billion.

BP's capital expenditures in the exploration and production segment totaled $25.5 billion in 2011.[3] The company's proved developed and undeveloped reserves increased by 411 million barrels of oil equivalent (BOE) because of discoveries and improvements in recovery techniques. BP's daily production in 2011 was approximately 2.1 million BOEs.

Royal Dutch Shell

By the beginning of 2012, Royal Dutch Shell plc was, like BP, one of the world's largest publicly listed energy and petrochemical group and larger than BP in terms of revenues and market capitalization. The company employed around 90,000 people in more than 80 countries. The shares of Royal Dutch Shell were widely held. The company's largest shareholder held less than 5 percent of the company's ordinary share capital.

Royal Dutch Shell's core activities were the production, development, and retailing of oil and natural gas. Forty percent of Royal Dutch Shell's revenues in 2011 came from its European operations, 20 percent of its revenues came from its US operations, and 32 percent of its sales was made in non-European countries from the eastern hemisphere.

In the period from 2005 to 2011, Royal Dutch Shell's returns on its equity ranged from 9.2 percent to 28.6 percent. During this period, the company realized an average total share return of 0.7 percent, reaching a market capitalization of €174 billion on December 31, 2011. Rating agency Standard and Poor's had rated Royal Dutch Shell's debt at AA.

In 2004, Royal Dutch Shell had surprised investors with the announcement that its proved oil and gas reserves were about 20 percent smaller than it had previously disclosed. Specifically, the company reclassified 2.7 billion barrels of oil and natural gas liquids as well as 7.2 trillion standard cubic feet of natural gas as "probable but not proved." The estimated value of the reclassified reserves was close to €6 billion. To restore credibility after the restatements of its oil and gas reserves, Royal Dutch Shell undertook several steps. The company improved its internal control systems, replaced some of its directors, abandoned its practice of evaluating business unit's performance and calculating managers' bonuses based on reserve bookings, and changed its governance structure.

In 2011, Royal Dutch Shell reported a return on operating assets of 15.3 percent, up by 4.3 percentage points compared to 2010, partly because of higher oil prices and asset sales and despite lower refining margins. In that year, the company's share price increased by close to 15 percent. Royal Dutch Shell's capital expenditures in the exploration and production segments were $19.1 billion in 2011, when its daily oil and gas production level had declined from 2.4 million to 2.3 million BOEs. Management planned to raise capital investments by close to 25 percent in 2012, anticipating a 25 percent increase in production between 2011 and 2017-2018.

Statoil

Of the three described European oil and gas companies – BP, Royal Dutch Shell, and Statoil – Statoil was a smallest. In 2011, the company operated in more than 41 countries, employing approximately 21,000 people. Between 2005 and 2011, Statoil's return on equity ranged from 9 to 37 percent. During these years, the company's share price had increased by an average of 12.1 percent (including dividends), to reach a market value of NOK488.2 billion (€62.8 billion) on December 31, 2011. Statoil had one large shareholder, the government of Norway, who held close to 67 percent of the company's ordinary share capital. In 2011, Statoil's dividends totaled NOK20.7 billion; the company had not repurchased ordinary shares. Standard and Poor's rated Statoil's public debt at AA.

Statoil's operating activities were focused on exploring for, producing, and retailing oil and natural gas. The company had most of its operations located in Norway and North America and was less geographically diversified than BP and Royal Dutch Shell. Specifically, it had 49 percent of its non-current assets located in Norway, 25 percent in the US and Canada, and 17 percent in Angola, Brazil, and Azerbaijan.

Fiscal year 2011 had been a profitable year for Statoil. The company's profitability had benefited from the rising oil prices, gains on the sale of assets and unrealized gains on derivatives. For the years 2012, Statoil's management targeted a 3 percent growth in production. In 2011, the company made capital

[3]Note that BP's reporting currency was US dollars, whereas the company's shares were traded in British pounds.

expenditures of NOK85.1 billion, up by 24 percent compared to 2010, and anticipated a further increase in capital spending by 20 percent in the next year. In its 2011 Annual Report, the company identified as one of its primary ambitions to remain in the top quartile of its peer group for unit of production cost.

Questions

1 What are the European oil and gas companies' drivers of profitability? What are their key risks?

2 Using the supplemental information summarized in **Exhibit 2**, analysts can produce several ratios that provide insight into the efficiency of the companies' exploration, development, and production activities as well as their growth opportunities. Develop a set of ratios that provide such insights. How efficient are the three oil and gas companies in exploration and production?

3 **Exhibit 3** summarizes analysts' one-year-horizon (2012), two-year-horizon (2013), and three-year-horizon (2014) forecasts of sales growth and profit margins. For each of the three oil and gas companies, provide arguments justifying the most pessimistic scenarios as well as arguments justifying the most optimistic scenarios.

4 Given your answers to the previous questions, what are your forecasts of the oil and gas companies' net profits for fiscal year 2012? What are your expectations about each of the companies' long-term earnings growth (i.e., growth in 2013 and 2014)?

EXHIBIT 1   **Crude Brent oil prices**

Crude Brent spot price from December 2004 to December 2011

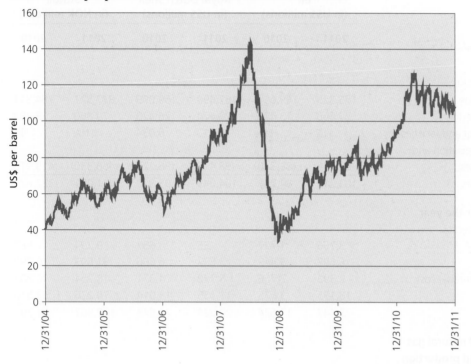

Source: Thomson Datastream.

Crude Brent oil futures for delivery in	Crude Brent oil futures prices during the first half of 2012		
	Price in US$ per barrel on December 31, 2011	Price in US$ per barrel on March 31, 2012	Price in US$ per barrel on June 30, 2012
December 2012	103.89	117.75	97.79
December 2013	99.30	110.07	96.94
December 2014	95.73	102.66	94.80
December 2015	93.24	97.35	93.10
December 2016	91.74	94.40	91.51

Source: Thomson Datastream.

Forecasting earnings and earnings growth in the European oil and gas industry

EXHIBIT 2   **Supplementary information about BP's, Royal Dutch Shell's, and Statoil's oil and natural gas reserves**

	BP (in US$ millions)		Royal Dutch Shell (in US$ millions)		Statoil (in NOK millions)	
	2011	2010	2011	2010	2011	2010
Capitalized costs						
Gross capitalized costs:						
Proved properties	175,325	159,655	167,690	159,099	827,521	704,311
Unproved properties	20,666	13,473	28,474	26,420	79,860	38,283
Auxiliary equipment and facilities	NA	NA	6,313	6,034	NA	NA
Accumulated depreciation and impairment losses	(92,779)	(88,340)	(98,428)	(96,223)	(466,330)	(419,919)
Net capitalized costs	103,212	84,788	104,049	95,330	441,051	322,675
Costs incurred for the year						
Acquisition of properties:						
Proved	3,156	1,777	35	657	9,294	587
Unproved	6,698	3,469	3,632	6,606	31,693	10,390
Exploration and appraisal costs	2,398	2,706	5,722	4,371	18,754	16,803
Development costs	10,195	9,675	11,135	13,014	70,226	53,516
Total costs	22,447	17,627	20,524	24,648	129,967	81,296
Results of oil and natural gas exploration and production activities						
Sales and other operating revenues:						
To third parties	11,450	10,492	18,038	14,899	11,461	5,966
To group companies	41,922	37,364	49,316	37,059	248,444	207,978
Total sales	53,372	47,856	67,354	51,958	259,905	213,944
Exploration expenditure	(1,520)	(843)	(2,266)	(2,036)	(13,838)	(15,773)
Production costs	(7,704)	(6,158)	(10,617)	(8,989)	NA	NA
Production taxes	(8,307)	(5,269)	(3,016)	(2,193)	NA	NA
Production costs (including taxes)	(16,011)	(11,427)	(13,633)	(11,182)	(30,652)	(29,910)
Other operating costs	(5,078)	(4,091)	(4,951)	(2,696)	NA	NA
Depreciation, depletion, and amortization	(8,114)	(8,021)	(8,367)	(10,738)	(43,397)	(42,367)
Impairment and gains (losses) on sale of business and fixed assets	2,120	3,721	NA	NA	NA	NA
Profit before taxation	24,769	27,195	38,137	25,306	172,018	125,894
Taxes	(9,906)	(10,032)	(23,642)	(14,815)	(120,138)	(88,885)
Results of operations	14,863	17,163	14,495	10,491	51,880	37,009

Forecasting earnings and earnings growth in the European oil and gas industry

(continued)

EXHIBIT 2   **Supplementary information about BP's, Royal Dutch Shell's, and Statoil's oil and natural gas reserves**

	BP (in US$ millions)		Royal Dutch Shell (in US$ millions)		Statoil (in NOK millions)	
	2011	2010	2011	2010	2011	2010
Proved developed and undeveloped reserves of crude oil and natural gas liquids (in million barrels)						
Reserves at the beginning of the year:						
Developed reserves	2,902	3,070	2,883	2,171	1,322	1,414
Undeveloped reserves	2,657	2,588	2,296	2,522	701	656
Total reserves	5,559	5,658	5,179	4,693	2,023	2,070
Revision of previous estimates	(159)	(146)	84	723	310	123
Increase due to improvements in recovery techniques	206	421	2	62	NA	NA
Extensions and discoveries	21	131	311	147	132	174
Purchases of reserves-in-place	21	77	0	59	120	4
Sales of reserves-in-place	(140)	(143)	(34)	(42)	(66)	0
Production	(355)	(439)	(444)	(463)	(338)	(348)
Reserves at the end of the year						
Developed reserves	2,616	2,902	3,282	2,883	1,344	1,322
Undeveloped reserves	2,537	2,657	1,816	2,296	837	701
Total reserves	5,153	5,559	5,098	5,179	2,181	2,023
Proved developed and undeveloped reserves of natural gas (in billion cubic feet)						
Reserves at the beginning of the year:						
Developed reserves	20,766	21,032	11,182	10,170	14,700	14,990
Undeveloped reserves	17,043	19,356	17,801	19,791	3,265	3,158
Total reserves	37,809	40,388	28,983	29,961	17,965	18,148
Revision of previous estimates	554	(2,206)	639	331	359	332
Increase due to improvements in recovery techniques	803	1,659	0	41	NA	NA
Extensions and discoveries	266	2,171	3,322	1,104	563	948
Purchases of reserves-in-place	418	146	0	189	227	45
Sales of reserves-in-place	(995)	(1,514)	(359)	(227)	0	0
Production	(2,474)	(2,835)	(2,299)	(2,416)	(1,433)	(1,508)
Reserves at the end of the year						
Developed reserves	19,900	20,766	18,564	11,182	13,730	14,700
Undeveloped reserves	16,481	17,043	11,722	17,801	3,951	3,265
Total reserves	36,381	37,809	30,286	28,983	17,681	17,965
Conversion rate: x billion cubic feet of gas = 1 million barrel of oil equivalents	5.80	5.80	5.80	5.80	5.80	5.80

Source: Annual Reports for the fiscal year ended on December 31, 2011 of BP, Royal Dutch Shell, and Statoil. Average exchange rates in 2011 (2010): €1 = $1.39; €1 = NOK7.80 (€1 = $1.32; €1 = NOK8.02).

Forecasting earnings and earnings growth in the European oil and gas industry

EXHIBIT 3   **Analysts' forecasts for fiscal years 2012, 2013, and 2014 at mid-2012**

Forecasts of sales growth

Fiscal year 2012 relative to fiscal year 2011	Most pessimistic forecast	Consensus forecast	Most optimistic forecast
BP	−30.6%	−6.3%	10.8%
Royal Dutch Shell	−32.6%	−3.2%	15.1%
Statoil	−37.8%	1.4%	19.3%

Fiscal year 2013 relative to fiscal year 2011	Most pessimistic forecast	Consensus forecast	Most optimistic forecast
BP	−22.1%	−4.7%	20.6%
Royal Dutch Shell	−32.6%	−4.9%	23.7%
Statoil	−38.9%	−4.3%	22.0%

Fiscal year 2014 relative to fiscal year 2011	Most pessimistic forecast	Consensus forecast	Most optimistic forecast
BP	−21.1%	−7.0%	12.2%
Royal Dutch Shell	−20.8%	−5.1%	17.6%
Statoil	−37.9%	−2.9%	19.5%

Forecasts of net profit margins

Fiscal year 2012	Most pessimistic forecast	Consensus forecast	Most optimistic forecast
BP	4.4%	5.6%	7.8%
Royal Dutch Shell	4.9%	6.2%	9.1%
Statoil	7.0%	8.5%	12.3%

Fiscal year 2013	Most pessimistic forecast	Consensus forecast	Most optimistic forecast
BP	4.3%	6.1%	9.1%
Royal Dutch Shell	4.8%	6.4%	7.5%
Statoil	5.3%	9.1%	12.5%

Fiscal year 2014	Most pessimistic forecast	Consensus forecast	Most optimistic forecast
BP	3.7%	6.1%	10.1%
Royal Dutch Shell	5.4%	6.3%	7.5%
Statoil	5.3%	9.1%	15.0%

Source: Thomson One.

Forecasting earnings and earnings growth in the European oil and gas industry

EXHIBIT 4   **Standardized financial statements and financial ratios of BP, Royal Dutch Shell, and Statoil for the fiscal year ended December 31, 2011**

CONSOLIDATED INCOME STATEMENTS – BP ($ millions)

Fiscal year ended December 31,	2011	2010	2009
Sales	375,517.0	297,107.0	239,272.0
Operating expenses	(347,824.9)	(269,086.9)	(217,058.9)
Operating profit	27,692.1	28,020.1	22,213.1
Investment income	6,288.0	4,448.0	4,508.0
Other income, net of other expense	5,872.0	(36,164.0)	(160.0)
Net interest expense (income)			
Interest income	596.0	681.0	792.0
Interest expense	(1,616.1)	(1,812.1)	(2,231.1)
Profit before taxes	38,832.0	(4,827.0)	25,122.0
Tax expense	(12,737.0)	1,501.0	(8,365.0)
Profit after taxes	26,095.0	(3,326.0)	16,757.0
Minority interest – Income statement	(397.0)	(395.0)	(181.0)
Net profit to ordinary shareholders	25,698.0	(3,721.0)	16,576.0

CONSOLIDATED BALANCE SHEETS – BP ($ millions)

Fiscal year ended December 31,	2011	2010	2009	2008
ASSETS				
Non-current tangible assets	132,810.7	121,637.0	120,121.6	117,916.1
Non-current intangible assets	33,202.0	22,896.0	20,168.0	20,138.0
Minority equity investments	28,809.0	25,621.0	28,259.0	27,826.0
Other non-operating investments	13,648.0	16,201.0	11,097.0	10,690.0
Deferred tax assets	611.0	528.0	0516.0	0.0
Total non-current assets	209,080.7	186,883.0	180,161.6	176,570.1
Inventories	25,661.0	26,218.0	22,605.0	16,821.0
Trade receivables	43,526.0	36,549.0	29,531.0	29,261.0
Other current assets	5,622.0	6,870.0	7,178.0	12,105.0
Cash and marketable securities	14,355.0	20,088.0	8,339.0	8,197.0
Total current assets	89,164.0	89,725.0	67,653.0	66,384.0
Assets held for sale	8,420.0	7,128.0	0.0	0.0
Total assets	306,664.7	283,736.0	247,814.6	242,954.1
LIABILITIES AND SHAREHOLDERS' EQUITY				
Ordinary shareholders' equity	111,465.0	94,987.0	101,613.0	91,303.0
Minority interest – Balance sheet	1,017.0	904.0	500.0	806.0
Preference shares	0.0	0.0	0.0	0.0
Non-current debt	87,187.7	74,459.0	60,344.6	54,719.1
Deferred tax liabilities	15,078.0	10,908.0	18,662.0	16,198.0
Other non-current liabilities (non interest bearing)	7,599.0	18,599.0	7,375.0	10,135.0
Non-current liabilities	109,864.7	103,966.0	86,381.6	81,052.1
Trade payables	32,284.0	29,583.0	23,882.0	20,716.0
Other current liabilities	42,452.0	38,623.0	26,329.0	33,337.0
Current debt	9,044.0	14,626.0	9,109.0	15,740.0
Current liabilities	83,780.0	82,832.0	59,320.0	69,793.0
Liabilities held for sale	538.0	1,047.0	0.0	0.0
Total liabilities and shareholders' equity	306,664.7	283,736.0	247,814.6	242,954.1

Source: Annual financial statements of BP (standardized and adjusted for operating leases). Average exchange rate in 2011 (2010): €1 = $1.39 (€1 = $1.32).

Forecasting earnings and earnings growth in the European oil and gas industry

EXHIBIT 4 **Standardized financial statements and financial ratios of BP, Royal Dutch Shell, and Statoil for the fiscal year ended December 31, 2011**

ROE DECOMPOSITION – BP

Ratio	2011	2010	2009
Net operating profit margin	6.2%	−1.7%	6.3%
× Operating asset turnover	2.56	2.23	1.87
= Return on operating assets	15.9%	−3.8%	11.8%
Return on Operating assets	15.9%	−3.8%	11.8%
× (Operating assets/Business assets)	0.77	0.76	0.77
+ Return on investment assets	8.6%	6.6%	7.4%
× (Investment assets/business assets)	0.23	0.24	0.23
= Return on business assets	14.2%	−1.3%	10.8%
Spread	13.3%	−2.6%	9.0%
× Financial leverage	0.95	0.83	0.72
= Financial leverage gain	12.6%	−2.1%	6.5%
ROE = Return on business assets + Financial leverage gain	26.8%	−3.5%	17.3%

Source: Author's own calculations.

CONSOLIDATED INCOME STATEMENTS – ROYAL DUTCH SHELL ($ millions)

Fiscal year ended December 31,	2011	2010	2009
Sales	**470,171.0**	**368,056.0**	**278,188.0**
Operating expenses	(426,681.9)	(338,176.3)	(259,702.9)
Operating profit	43,489.1	29,879.7	18,485.1
Investment income	9,567.0	6,352.0	5,246.0
Other income, net of other expense	4,625.0	763.0	(1,659.0)
Net interest expense (income)			
Interest income	209.0	153.0	384.0
Interest expense	(2,230.1)	(1,803.7)	(1,436.1)
Profit before taxes	**55,660.0**	**35,344.0**	**21,020.0**
Tax expense	(24,475.0)	(14,870.0)	(8,302.0)
Profit after taxes	**31,185.0**	**20,474.0**	**12,718.0**
Minority interest – Income statement	(267.0)	(347.0)	(200.0)
Net profit to ordinary shareholders	30,918.0	20,127.0	12,518.0

CONSOLIDATED BALANCE SHEETS – ROYAL DUTCH SHELL ($ millions)

Fiscal year ended December 31,	2011	2010	2009	2008
ASSETS				
Non-current tangible assets	168,335.3	156,780.4	144,864.3	127,723.3
Non-current intangible assets	4,521.0	5,039.0	5,356.0	5,021.0
Minority equity investments	37,990.0	33,414.0	31,175.0	28,327.0
Other non-operating investments	26,156.0	23,147.0	23,041.0	17,027.0
Deferred tax assets	4,732.0	5,361.0	4,533.0	3,418.0
Total non-current assets	**241,734.3**	**223,741.4**	**208,969.3**	**181,516.3**

EXHIBIT 4   **Standardized financial statements and financial ratios of BP, Royal Dutch Shell, and Statoil for the fiscal year ended December 31, 2011**

CONSOLIDATED BALANCE SHEETS – ROYAL DUTCH SHELL ($ millions)

Fiscal year ended December 31,	2011	2010	2009	2008
Inventories	28,976.0	29,348.0	27,410.0	19,342.0
Trade receivables	51,538.0	40,418.0	31,970.0	32,618.0
Other current assets	27,971.0	29,684.0	27,358.0	49,422.0
Cash and marketable securities	11,292.0	13,444.0	9,719.0	15,188.0
Total current assets	**119,777.0**	**112,894.0**	**96,457.0**	**116,570.0**
Assets held for sale	**0.0**	**0.0**	**0.0**	**0.0**
Total assets	**361,511.3**	**336,635.4**	**305,426.3**	**298,086.3**
LIABILITIES AND SHAREHOLDERS' EQUITY				
Ordinary shareholders' equity	**169,517.0**	**148,013.0**	**136,431.0**	**127,285.0**
Minority interest – Balance sheet	**1,486.0**	**1,767.0**	**1,704.0**	**1,581.0**
Preference shares	**0.0**	**0.0**	**0.0**	**0.0**
Non-current debt	68,279.3	68,665.4	64,078.3	47,496.3
Deferred tax liabilities	14,649.0	13,388.0	13,838.0	12,518.0
Other non-current liabilities (non interest bearing)	4,921.0	4,250.0	4,586.0	3,677.0
Non-current liabilities	**87,849.3**	**86,303.4**	**82,502.3**	**63,691.3**
Trade payables	50,006.0	38,858.0	32,791.0	29,584.0
Other current liabilities	45,554.0	51,366.0	47,366.0	66,065.0
Current debt	7,099.0	10,328.0	4,632.0	9,880.0
Current liabilities	**102,659.0**	**100,552.0**	**84,789.0**	**105,529.0**
Liabilities held for sale	**0.0**	**0.0**	**0.0**	**0.0**
Total liabilities and shareholders' equity	**361,511.3**	**336,635.4**	**305,426.3**	**298,086.3**

Source: Annual financial statements of Royal Dutch Shell (standardized and adjusted for operating leases). Average exchange rate in 2011 (2010): €1 = $1.39 (€1 = $1.32).

ROE DECOMPOSITION – ROYAL DUTCH SHELL

Ratio	2011	2010	2009
Net operating profit margin	5.8%	4.9%	3.8%
× Operating asset turnover	2.65	2.27	1.90
= Return on operating assets	15.3%	11.0%	7.1%
Return on operating assets	15.3%	11.0%	7.1%
× (Operating assets/Business assets)	0.75	0.75	0.75
+ Return on investment assets	8.7%	6.3%	6.1%
× (Investment assets/business assets)	0.25	0.25	0.25
= Return on business assets	13.6%	9.8%	6.9%
Spread	12.1%	8.5%	5.6%
× Financial leverage	0.48	0.51	0.47
= Financial leverage gain	5.8%	4.4%	2.7%
ROE = Return on Business Assets + Financial leverage gain	19.4%	14.2%	9.5%

Source: Author's own calculations.

Forecasting earnings and earnings growth in the European oil and gas industry

EXHIBIT 4 **Standardized financial statements and financial ratios of BP, Royal Dutch Shell, and Statoil for the fiscal year ended December 31, 2011**

CONSOLIDATED INCOME STATEMENTS – STATOIL (NOK millions)

Fiscal year ended December 31,	2011	2010	2009
Sales	**668,941.0**	**528,515.0**	**463,655.0**
Operating expenses	(456,082.3)	(390,677.7)	(341,748.8)
Operating profit	212,858.7	137,837.3	121,906.2
Investment income	1,401.0	1,265.0	1,844.0
Other income, net of other expense	6,008.0	1,435.0	(3,725.0)
Net interest expense (income)			
Interest income	2,467.0	2,383.0	2,767.0
Interest expense	(8,893.7)	(6,104.3)	(7,902.2)
Profit before taxes	**213,841.0**	**136,816.0**	**114,890.0**
Tax expense	(135,398.0)	(99,169.0)	(97,175.0)
Profit after taxes	**78,443.0**	**37,647.0**	**17,715.0**
Minority interest – Income statement	344.0	435.0	598.0
Net profit to ordinary shareholders	78,787.0	38,082.0	18,313.0

CONSOLIDATED BALANCE SHEETS –STATOIL (NOK millions)

Fiscal year ended December 31,	2011	2010	2009	2008
ASSETS				
Non-current tangible assets	474,930.4	403,232.5	377,515.2	375,267.8
Non-current intangible assets	92,674.0	39,695.0	54,253.0	66,036.0
Minority equity investments	9,217.0	13,884.0	10,056.0	12,640.0
Other non-operating investments	55,339.0	41,185.0	33,605.0	23,792.0
Deferred tax assets	5,704.0	1,878.0	1,960.0	1,302.0
Total non-current assets	**637,864.4**	**499,874.5**	**477,389.2**	**479,037.8**
Inventories	27,770.0	23,627.0	20,196.0	15,151.0
Trade receivables	103,261.0	80,649.0	64,642.0	69,931.0
Other current assets	6,583.0	7,150.0	5,548.0	31,345.0
Cash and marketable securities	60,474.0	41,846.0	31,745.0	28,385.0
Total current assets	**198,088.0**	**153,272.0**	**122,131.0**	**144,812.0**
Assets held for sale	**0.0**	**44,890.0**	**0.0**	**0.0**
Total assets	**835,952.4**	**698,036.5**	**599,520.2**	**623,849.8**
LIABILITIES AND SHAREHOLDERS' EQUITY				
Ordinary shareholders' equity	**278,916.0**	**219,542.0**	**198,319.0**	**214,079.0**
Minority interest – Balance sheet	**6,239.0**	**6,853.0**	**1,799.0**	**1,976.0**
Preference shares	**0.0**	**0.0**	**0.0**	**0.0**
Non-current debt	293,244.4	244,845.5	209,618.2	179,929.8
Deferred tax liabilities	82,520.0	78,052.0	76,322.0	68,144.0
Other non-current liabilities (non interest bearing)	3,904.0	3,386.0	1,657.0	0.0
Non-current liabilities	**379,668.4**	**326,283.5**	**287,597.2**	**248,073.8**
Trade payables	93,967.0	73,551.0	59,801.0	61,200.0
Other current liabilities	57,315.0	50,854.0	43,854.0	77,826.0
Current debt	19,847.0	11,730.0	8,150.0	20,695.0
Current liabilities	**171,129.0**	**136,135.0**	**111,805.0**	**159,721.0**
Liabilities held for sale	**0.0**	**9,223.0**	**0.0**	**0.0**
Total liabilities and shareholders' equity	**835,952.4**	**698,036.5**	**599,520.2**	**623,849.8**

Source: Annual financial statements of Statoil (standardized and adjusted for operating leases). Average exchange rate in 2011 (2010): €1 = NOK7.80 (€1 = NOK8.02).

EXHIBIT 4   **Standardized financial statements and financial ratios of BP, Royal Dutch Shell, and Statoil for the fiscal year ended December 31, 2011**

ROE DECOMPOSITION – STATOIL

Ratio	2011	2010	2009
Net operating profit margin	12.3%	7.5%	4.3%
× Operating asset turnover	1.49	1.40	1.24
= Return on operating assets	18.3%	10.5%	5.4%
Return on operating assets	18.3%	10.5%	5.4%
× (Operating assets/Business assets)	0.86	0.87	0.90
+ Return on investment assets	3.7%	4.7%	7.9%
× (Investment assets/Business assets)	0.14	0.13	0.10
= Return on business assets	16.2%	9.7%	5.6%
Spread	14.0%	7.9%	2.9%
× Financial leverage	1.20	1.21	1.01
= Financial leverage gain	16.7%	9.5%	2.9%
ROE = Return on business assets + Financial leverage gain	33.0%	19.3%	8.5%

Source: Author's own calculations.

Forecasting earnings and earnings growth in the European oil and gas industry

Prospective Analysis: Valuation Theory and Concepts

The previous chapter introduced forecasting, the first stage of prospective analysis. In this and the following chapter we describe valuation, the second and final stage of prospective analysis. This chapter focuses on valuation theory and concepts, and the following chapter discusses implementation issues.

Valuation is the process of converting a forecast into an estimate of the value of the firm's assets or equity. At some level, nearly every business decision involves valuation, at least implicitly. Within the firm, capital budgeting involves consideration of how a particular project will affect firm value. Strategic planning focuses on how value is influenced by larger sets of actions. Outside the firm, security analysts conduct valuation to support their buy/sell decisions, and potential acquirers (often with the assistance of investment bankers) estimate the value of target firms and the synergies they might offer. Even credit analysts, who typically do not explicitly estimate firm value, must at least implicitly consider the value of the firm's equity "cushion" if they are to maintain a complete view of the risk associated with lending activity.

In practice, a wide variety of valuation approaches are employed. For example, in evaluating the fairness of a takeover bid, investment bankers commonly use five to ten different methods of valuation. Among the available methods are the following:

- Discounted dividends. This approach expresses the value of the firm's equity as the present value of forecasted future dividends.

- Discounted cash flow (DCF) analysis. This approach involves the production of detailed, multiple-year forecasts of cash flows. The forecasts are then discounted at the firm's estimated cost of capital to arrive at an estimated present value.

- Discounted abnormal earnings. Under this approach the value of the firm's equity is expressed as the sum of its book value and the present value of forecasted **abnormal earnings**.

- Discounted abnormal earnings growth. This approach defines the value of the firm's equity as the sum of its capitalized next-period earnings forecast and the present value of forecasted **abnormal earnings growth** beyond the next period.

- Valuation based on price multiples. Under this approach a current measure of performance or single forecast of performance is converted into a value by applying an appropriate price multiple derived from the value of comparable firms. For example, firm value can be estimated by applying a price-to-earnings ratio to a forecast of the firm's earnings for the coming year. Other commonly used multiples include price-to-book ratios and price-to-sales ratios.

These methods are developed throughout the chapter, and their pros and cons discussed. All of the above approaches can be structured in two ways. The first is to directly value the equity of the firm, since this is usually the variable the analyst is directly interested in estimating. The second is to value the operating and investment assets of the firm, that is, the claims of equity and debt, and then to deduct the value of debt to arrive at the final equity estimate. Theoretically, both approaches should generate the same values. However, as we will see in the next chapter, there are implementation issues in reconciling the approaches. In this chapter we illustrate valuation using an all-equity firm to simplify the discussion. A brief discussion of the theoretical issues in valuing a firm's assets is included in Appendix A.

DEFINING VALUE FOR SHAREHOLDERS

How should shareholders think about the value of their equity claims on a firm? Finance theory holds that the value of any financial claim is simply the present value of the cash payoffs that its claimholders receive. Since shareholders receive cash payoffs from a company in the form of dividends, the value of their equity is the present value of future dividends (including any liquidating dividend).[1]

$$\text{Equity value} = \text{PV of expected future dividends}$$

If we denote r_e as the cost of equity capital (the relevant discount rate), the **equity value** is as follows:

$$\text{Equity value}_0 = \frac{\text{Dividend}_1}{(1 + r_e)^2} + \frac{\text{Dividend}_2}{(1 + r_e)^2} + \frac{\text{Dividend}_3}{(1 + r_e)^3} + \dots$$

Notice that the valuation formula views a firm as having an indefinite life. But in reality firms can go bankrupt or get taken over. In these situations shareholders effectively receive a terminating dividend on their shares.

If a firm had a constant dividend growth rate (g^{div}) indefinitely, its value would simplify to the following formula:

$$\text{Equity value}_0 = \frac{\text{Dividend}_1}{r_e - g^{div}}$$

To better understand how the discounted dividend approach works, consider the following example. At the beginning of year 1, Down Under Company raises €60 million of equity and uses the proceeds to buy a fixed asset. Operating profits before depreciation (all received in cash) and dividends for the company are expected to be €40 million in year 1, €50 million in year 2, and €60 million in year 3, at which point the company terminates. The firm pays no taxes. If the cost of equity capital for this firm is 10 percent, the value of the firm's equity is computed as follows:

Year	Dividend	PV factor	PV of dividend
	(a)	(b)	(a) × (b)
1	€40m	0.9091	€ 36.4m
2	50	0.8264	41.3
3	60	0.7513	45.1
Equity value			€122.8m

The above valuation formula is called the dividend discount model. It forms the basis for most of the popular theoretical approaches for equity valuation. Despite its theoretical importance, the dividend discount model is not a very useful valuation model in practice. This is because equity value is created primarily through the investment and operating activities of a firm. Dividend payments tend to be a by-product of such activities and their timing and amount depends strongly on the firm's investment opportunities. Within a period of five to ten years, which tends to be the focus of most prospective analyses, dividends may therefore reveal very little about the firm's equity value. For example, high-growth start-up firms tend not to pay out dividends until later into their life cycle but they nonetheless have value when they start their operations. Predicting long-run dividends for these firms is a tedious, virtually impossible task. As the first stage of the prospective analysis, as discussed in Chapter 6, typically produces comprehensive, detailed forecasts for the near term but unavoidably makes simplifying assumptions for the longer term, useful valuation models value near-term profitability and growth directly rather than indirectly through long run dividends. The remainder of this chapter discusses how the dividend discount model can be recast to generate such useful models. The models that we discuss are the discounted cash flow, discounted abnormal earnings, discounted abnormal earnings growth, and price multiple models of value.

THE DISCOUNTED CASH FLOW MODEL

As we described in the previous section, the value of an asset or investment is the present value of the net cash payoffs that the asset generates. The **discounted cash flow** valuation model clearly reflects this basic principle of finance. The model defines the value of a firm's business assets as the present value of cash flows generated by these assets (OCF) minus the investments made in new assets (Investment), or, alternatively stated, as the sum of the **free cash flows to debt and equity** holders discounted at the weighted average cost of debt and equity (WACC).

$$\text{Asset value}_0 = \text{PV of free cash flows to debt and equity claim holders}$$
$$= \frac{\text{OCF}_1 - \text{Investment}_1}{(1 + \text{WACC})} + \frac{\text{OCF}_2 - \text{Investment}_2}{(1 + \text{WACC})^2} + \ldots$$

Note that in this equation OCF excludes interest payments (unlike the operating cash flows reported in IFRS-based cash flow statements), as these are distributions to debt holders.

The cash flows that are available to equity holders are the cash flows generated by the firm's business assets minus investment outlays, adjusted for cash flows from and to debt holders, such as interest payments, debt repayments, and debts issues. As discussed in Chapter 5, operating cash flows to equity holders are simply net profit plus depreciation and amortization less changes in working capital. Investment outlays are expenditures for noncurrent operating and investment assets less asset sales. Finally, net cash flows from debt owners are issues of new debt less retirements. By rearranging these terms, the free cash flows to equity can be written as follows:

$$\text{Free cash flows to equity} = \text{Net profit} - \Delta \text{BVA} + \Delta \text{BVD}$$

where ΔBVA is the change in book value of business assets (changes in working capital plus investment expenditures less depreciation and amortization expense), and ΔBVD is the change in book value of (interest-bearing) debt. Using the discounted cash flow model, equity value is thus estimated as follows:

$$\text{Equity value}_0 = \text{PV of free cash flow to equity holders}$$
$$= \frac{\text{Net profit}_1 - \Delta \text{BVA}_1 + \Delta \text{BVD}_1}{(1 + r_e)}$$
$$+ \frac{\text{Net profit}_2 - \Delta \text{BVA}_2 + \Delta \text{BVD}_2}{(1 + r_e)^2} + \ldots$$

Valuation under this method therefore involves the following three steps:

Step 1: Forecast free cash flows available to equity holders over a finite forecast horizon (usually five to ten years).

Step 2: Forecast free cash flows beyond the terminal year based on some simplifying assumption.

Step 3: Discount free cash flows to equity holders at the cost of equity. The discounted amount represents the estimated value of free cash flows available to equity.

Returning to the Down Under Company example, there is no debt, so that the free cash flows to owners are simply the operating profits before depreciation. Since the company's cost of equity is assumed to be 10 percent, the present value of the free cash flows is as follows:

Year	Net profit	Change in book value of net assets	Change in book value of net debt	Free cash flows to equity	PV factor	PV of free cash flows
	(a)	(b)	(c)	(d) = (a) − (b) + (c)	(e)	(d) × (e)
1	€20m	−€20m	€0m	€40m	0.9091	€ 36.4m
2	30	−20	0	50	0.8264	41.3
3	40	−20	0	60	0.7513	45.1
Equity value						€122.8m

Earlier we indicated that the discounted cash flow model can be obtained by recasting the dividend discount model. To see how this works, recall our formulation of the free cash flows to equity holders in terms of net profit, the change in the book value of business assets (ΔBVA) and the change in the book value of debt (ΔBVD). In the recast financial statements, which we described in Chapter 5 and use throughout this book, the change in the book value of business assets minus the change in the book value of debt is equal to the change in the book value of equity (ΔBVE). The free cash flows to equity can therefore be written as:

$$\text{Free cash flow to equity} = \text{Net profit} - \Delta\text{BVA} + \Delta\text{BVD}$$
$$= \text{Net profit} - \Delta\text{BVE}$$
$$= \text{Dividends}$$

which illustrates the relationship between free cash flows to equity and dividends.[2]

As discussed in Chapter 6, the key ingredient to an accurate prediction of future free cash flows is a full set of predicted future (condensed) income statements and balance sheets. Given the prominence of earnings forecasts in most prospective analyses, models have been developed that express equity value directly in terms of expected earnings, book values of equity, and cost of equity, thus further sharpening the focus of the valuation exercise. The following sections describe two of these accounting-based valuation models: the **discounted abnormal earnings model** and the **discounted abnormal earnings growth model**. In a later section, we also show that these accounting-based valuation models can help in better understanding the rationale underlying valuation based on price multiples.

THE DISCOUNTED ABNORMAL EARNINGS MODEL

As discussed in Chapter 3, there is a link between dividends, earnings, and equity. At the end of each accounting period net profit for the period is added to retained earnings, a component of equity. Dividends are taken out of retained earnings. Stated differently, if all equity effects (other than capital transactions) flow through the income statement,[3] the expected book value of equity for existing shareholders at the end of year 1 (BVE_1) is simply the book value at the beginning of the year (BVE_0) plus expected net profit (Net profit$_1$) less expected dividends (Dividend$_1$).[4] This relation can be written as follows:

$$\text{Dividend}_1 = \text{Net profit}_1 + \text{BVE}_0 - \text{BVE}_1$$

By substituting this identity for dividends into the dividend discount formula and rearranging the terms, equity value can be rewritten as follows:[5]

$$\text{Equity value} = \text{Book value of equity} + \text{PV of expected future abnormal earnings}$$

Abnormal earnings are net profit adjusted for a capital charge, which is computed as the discount rate multiplied by the beginning book value of equity. Abnormal earnings incorporate an adjustment to reflect the fact that accountants do not recognize any opportunity cost for equity funds used. Thus, the discounted abnormal earnings valuation formula is:

$$\text{Equity value}_0 = \text{BVE}_0 + \frac{\text{Net profit}_1 - r_e \cdot \text{BVE}_0}{(1 + r_e)} + \frac{\text{Net profit}_2 - r_e \cdot \text{BVE}_1}{(1 + r_e)^2} + \cdots$$

The earnings-based formulation has intuitive appeal. If a firm can earn only a normal rate of return on its book value, then investors should be willing to pay no more than book value for its shares. Investors should pay more or less than book value if earnings are above or below this normal level. Thus, the deviation of a firm's market value from book value depends on its ability to generate "abnormal earnings." The formulation also implies that a firm's equity value reflects the cost of its existing net assets (that is, its book equity) plus the net present value of future growth options (represented by cumulative abnormal earnings).

To illustrate the earnings-based valuation approach, let's return to the Down Under Company example. Assuming the company depreciates its fixed assets using the straight-line method, its accounting-based earnings will be €20 million lower than dividends in each of the three years. Further, the book value of equity at the beginning of years 2 and 3 equals prior year's beginning book value plus prior year's earnings minus prior year's dividends. The firm's beginning book equity, earnings, abnormal earnings, and valuation will be as follows:

Year	Beginning book value	Earnings	Capital charge	Abnormal earnings	PV factor	PV of abnormal earnings
	(a)	(b)	(c)	(d) = (b) − (c)	(e)	(d) × (e)
1	€60m	−€20m	€6m	€14m	0.9091	€ 12.7m
2	40	30	4	26	0.8264	21.5
3	20	40	2	38	0.7513	28.6
Cumulative PV of abnormal earnings						62.38
+ Beginning book value						60.0
= Equity value						€122.8m

Notice that the value of Down Under's equity is exactly the same as that estimated using the discounted cash flow method. This should not be surprising. Both methods are derived from the dividend discount model. And in estimating value under the two approaches, we have used the same underlying assumptions to forecast earnings and cash flows.

KEY ANALYSIS QUESTIONS

Valuation of equity under the discounted abnormal earnings method requires the analyst to answer the following questions:

- What are expected future net profit and book values of equity (and therefore abnormal earnings) over a finite forecast horizon (usually five to ten years) given the firm's industry competitiveness and the firm's positioning?
- What is expected future abnormal net profit beyond the final year of the forecast horizon (called the "terminal year") based on some simplifying assumption? If abnormal returns are expected to persist, what are the barriers to entry that deter competition?
- What is the firm's cost of equity used to compute the present value of abnormal earnings?

Accounting methods and discounted abnormal earnings

One question that arises when valuation is based directly on earnings and book values is how the estimate is affected by managers' choice of accounting methods and accrual estimates. Would estimates of value differ for two otherwise identical firms if one used more conservative accounting methods than the other? We will see that, provided analysts recognize the impact of differences in accounting methods on future earnings (and hence their earnings forecasts), the accounting effects *per se* should have no influence on their value estimates. There are two reasons for this. First, accounting choices that affect a firm's current earnings also affect its book value, and therefore they affect the capital charges used to estimate future abnormal earnings. For example, conservative accounting not only lowers a firm's current earnings and book equity but also reduces future capital charges and inflates its future abnormal earnings. Second, double-entry bookkeeping is by nature self-correcting. Inflated earnings for one period have to be ultimately reversed in subsequent periods.

To understand how these two effects undo the effect of differences in accounting methods or accrual estimates, let's return to Down Under Company and see what happens if its managers choose to be conservative and expense some unusual costs that could have been capitalized as inventory in year 1. This accounting decision causes earnings and ending book value to be lower by €10 million. The inventory is then sold in year 2. For the time being, let's say the accounting choice has no influence on the analyst's view of the firm's real performance.

Managers' choice reduces abnormal earnings in year 1 and book value at the beginning of year 2 by €10 million. However, future earnings will be higher, for two reasons. First, future earnings will be higher (by €10 million) when the inventory is sold in year 2 at a lower cost of sales. Second, the benchmark for normal earnings (based on book value of equity) will be lower by €10 million. The €10 million decline in abnormal earnings in year

1 is perfectly offset (on a present value basis) by the €11 million higher abnormal earnings in year 2. As a result, the value of Down Under Company under conservative reporting is identical to the value under the earlier accounting method (€122.8 million).

Year	Beginning book value	Earnings	Capital charge	Abnormal earnings	PV factor	PV of abnormal earnings
	(a)	(b)	(c) = $r_e \times$ (a)	(d) = (b) − (c)	(e)	(d) × (e)
1	€60m	€10m	€6m	€ 4m	0.9091	€ 3.6m
2	30	40	3	37	0.8264	30.6
3	20	40	2	38	0.7513	28.6
Cumulative PV of abnormal earnings						62.8
+ Beginning book value						60.0
= Equity value						€122.8m

Provided the analyst is aware of biases in accounting data that arise from managers' using aggressive or conservative accounting choices, abnormal earnings-based valuations are unaffected by the variation in accounting decisions. This shows that strategic and accounting analyses are critical precursors to abnormal earnings valuation. The strategic and accounting analysis tools help the analyst to identify whether abnormal earnings arise from sustainable competitive advantage or from unsustainable accounting manipulations. For example, consider the implications of failing to understand the reasons for a decline in earnings from a change in inventory policy for Down Under Company. If the analyst mistakenly interpreted the decline as indicating that the firm was having difficulty moving its inventory, rather than that it had used conservative accounting, she might reduce expectations of future earnings. The estimated value of the firm would then be lower than that reported in our example. To avoid such mistakes, the analyst would be wise to go through all steps of the accounting analysis, including step 6 (undo accounting distortions), and then perform the financial and prospective analyses using the restated financial statements.

THE DISCOUNTED ABNORMAL EARNINGS GROWTH MODEL

As discussed above, abnormal earnings are the amount of earnings that a firm generates in excess of the opportunity cost for equity funds used. The annual change in abnormal earnings is generally referred to as abnormal earnings growth and can be rewritten as follows:

Abnormal earnings growth = change in abnormal earnings

$$= (\text{Net profit}_2 - r_e \cdot \text{BVE}_1) - (\text{Net profit}_1 - r_e \cdot \text{BVE}_0)$$
$$= (\text{Net profit}_2 - r_e \cdot [\text{BVE}_0 + \text{Net profit}_1 - \text{Dividends}_1]) - (\text{Net profit}_1 - r_e \cdot \text{BVE}_0)$$
$$= \text{Net profit}_2 + r_e \cdot \text{Dividends}_1 - (1 + r_e) \cdot \text{Net profit}_1$$
$$= \Delta\text{Net profit}_2 - r_e \cdot (\text{Net profit}_1 - \text{Dividends}_1)$$
$$(= \text{abnormal change in earnings})$$

This formula shows that abnormal earnings growth is actual earnings growth benchmarked against normal earnings growth. Normal earnings growth is calculated as the portion of prior period earnings that is retained in the firm times a normal rate of return. When abnormal earnings growth is zero, the firm functions like a savings account. In this particular case, the firm earns an abnormal return on its existing investment but is only able to earn a normal rate of return on the additional investments that it finances from its retained earnings. Consequently, an investor would be indifferent between reinvesting earnings in the firm and receiving all earnings in dividends.

The discounted dividend model can also be recast to generate a valuation model that defines equity value as the capitalized sum of (1) next-period earnings and (2) the discounted value of abnormal earnings growth beyond the next period. The **discounted abnormal earnings** growth valuation formula is:[6]

$$\text{Equity value}_0 = \frac{\text{Net profit}_1}{r_e} + \frac{1}{r_e}\left[\frac{\Delta\text{Net profit}_2 - r_e \cdot (\text{Net profit}_1 - \text{Dividend}_1)}{(1 + r_e)}\right.$$

$$\left. + \frac{\Delta\text{Net profit}_3 - r_e \cdot (\text{Net profit}_2 - \text{Dividend}_2)}{(1 + r_e)^2} + \ldots\right]$$

This approach, under which valuation starts with capitalizing next-period earnings, has practical appeal because investment analysts spend much time and effort on estimating near-term earnings as the starting point of their analysis. The valuation formula shows that differences between equity value and capitalized next-period earnings are explained by abnormal changes in earnings – or changes in abnormal earnings – beyond the next period. Notice that this formula also views the firm as having an indefinite life. However, the formula can be easily used for the valuation of a finite-life investment by extending the investment's life by one year and setting earnings and dividends equal to zero in the last year. For example, consider the earnings and dividends of the Down Under Company during its three years of existence. Capitalized year 1 earnings are equal to €200.0 million (20.0/0.1). Abnormal earnings growth equals €12.0 million in year 2 (30.0 + 40.0 × 0.1 – 20.0 × 1.1) and €12.0 million in year 3 (40.0 + 50.0 × 0.1 – 30.0 × 1.1). In year 4, when earnings and dividends are zero, abnormal earnings growth is –€38.0 million (0.0 + 60.0 × 0.1 – 40.0 × 1.1). The total value of the firm's equity is computed as follows:

Year	Earnings	Retained earnings	Normal earnings growth	Abnormal earnings growth	PV factor	PV of abnormal earnings growth
	(a)	(b) = (a) – Dividends	(c) = $r_e \times$ (b)$_{t-1}$	(d) = Δ(a) – (c)	(e)	(d) × (e)
1	€20m	–€20 m				
2	30	–20	–€2m	€12	0.9091	€ 10.91m
3	40	–20	–2	12	0.8264	9.92
4	0	0	–2	–38	0.7513	–28.55
Cumulative PV of abnormal earnings growth						–7.72
+ Earnings in year 1						20.00
=						€ 12.28m
× 1/r_e						10.00
= Equity value						€ 122.8m

Note that the Down Under Company gradually reduces its investment because the annual dividend payments exceed annual earnings. Consequently, normal earnings growth is negative and the firm's abnormal earnings growth is greater than its actual earnings growth in every year.

Like the abnormal earnings method, the value estimate from the abnormal earnings growth model is not affected by the firm's accounting choices. For example, recall the situation where the Down Under Company reports conservatively and expenses unusual costs that could have been capitalized in year 1, thereby reducing earnings by €10.0 million. Under conservative accounting, the value of capitalized year 1 earnings decreases from €200.0 million to €100.0 million. This reduction, however, is exactly offset by an increase in the discounted value of abnormal earnings growth, as shown in the following table:

Year	Earnings	Retained earnings	Normal earnings growth	Abnormal earnings growth	PV factor	PV of abnormal earnings growth
	(a)	(b) = (a) – Dividends	(c) = $r_e \times$ (b)$_{t-1}$	(d) = Δ(a) – (c)	(e)	(d) × (e)
1	€10m	–€30 m				
2	40	–10	–€3m	€33	0.9091	€ 30.00m
3	40	–20	–1	1	0.8264	0.83
4	0	0	–2	–38	0.7513	–28.55
Cumulative PV of abnormal earnings growth						2.28
+ Earnings in year 1						10.00
=						€ 12.28m
× 1/r_e						10.00
= Equity value						€ 122.8m

This value is again identical to the value estimated under the discounted dividends and abnormal earnings approaches.

DEMONSTRATION CASE: HENNES & MAURITZ AB

During the first week following the publication of the financial statements for the fiscal year ending on November 30, 2011, several analysts updated their forecasts of H&M's 2012 and 2013 sales and net profit. Analysts' average expectations were as follows:

	2011 realized	2012 expected	2013 expected
Sales	SEK110.0b	SEK121.7b	SEK135.4b
Net profit	15.8	18.0	20.5

Required:

1 These forecasts are not sufficient to estimate the value of H&M's equity. Forecast H&M's ending net working capital, net non-current assets, debt and group equity under the simplifying assumption that the future growth in these items follows sales growth.

2 Assume that H&M's cost of equity is 10 percent. Calculate:

   a Dividends in 2012 and 2013.

   b Abnormal earnings in 2012 and 2013.

   c Abnormal earnings growth in 2013.

   d Free cash flows to equity in 2012 and 2013.

3 To estimate H&M's equity value, we need to make an assumption about what will happen to H&M's profits, dividends, equity, debt, and assets after 2013. In the next chapter we will discuss several assumptions that the analyst can make. For now, we assume that in 2014 H&M liquidates all its assets at their book values, uses the proceeds to pay off debt and pays out the remainder to its equity holders. What does this assumption imply about:

   a The book value of H&M's assets and liabilities at the end of 2014?

   b H&M's net profit in 2014?

   c H&M's final dividend payment in 2014?

   d H&M's free cash flow to equity holders in 2014?

   e H&M's abnormal earnings growth in 2014 and 2015 (!)?

4 Estimate H&M's equity value at the end of 2011 using:

   a The discounted dividends model and the discounted cash flow model.

   b The discounted abnormal earnings model.

   c The discounted abnormal earning growth model.

Answers:

1 Expected sales growth in 2012 and 2013 is 10.6 percent (11.7/110.0) and 11.3 percent (13.7/121.7), respectively. The values of the four balance sheet items at the end of 2011 are known. Based on the expected sales growth rates, the expected values at the end of 2012 and 2013 are:

Ending . . .	2011 realized	2012 expected	2013 expected
Net working capital	SEK 15.7b	SEK 17.4b	SEK 19.3b
Net non-current assets	78.7	87.1	96.9
Debt	50.3	55.7	61.9
Group equity	44.1	48.8	54.3
Assets / capital	94.4	104.5	116.2

2 Calculations:

  a $\text{Dividends}_{2012} = \text{Equity}_{2011} + \text{Profit}_{2012} - \text{Equity}_{2012} = 44.1 + 18.0 - 48.8 = 13.3$

       $\text{Dividends}_{2013} = \text{Equity}_{2012} + \text{Profit}_{2013} - \text{Equity}_{2013} = 48.8 + 20.5 - 54.3 = 15.0.$

  b $\text{Abnormal Earnings}_{2012} = \text{Profit}_{2012} - r_e \times \text{Equity}_{2011} = 18.0 - 10\% \times 44.1 = 13.6.$

       $\text{Abnormal Earnings}_{2013} = \text{Profit}_{2013} - r_e \times \text{Equity}_{2012} = 20.5 - 10\% \times 48.8 = 15.6.$

  c $\text{Abnormal Earnings growth}_{2013} = \Delta\text{Profit}_{2013} - r_e \times (\text{Profit}_{2012} - \text{Dividends}_{2012}) = 2.5 - 10\% \times (18.0 - 13.3) = 2.0.$

       (Check that Abnormal earnings growth = ΔAbnormal earnings (see b).)

  d $\text{FCF to Equity}_{2012} = \text{Profit}_{2012} - \Delta\text{Assets}_{2012} + \Delta\text{Debt}_{2012} = 18.0 - 10.1 + 5.4 = 13.3.$

       $\text{FCF to Equity}_{2013} = \text{Profit}_{2013} - \Delta\text{Assets}_{2013} + \Delta\text{Debt}_{2013} = 20.5 - 11.7 + 6.2 = 15.0.$

       (Note that the free cash flows to equity holders is equal to the dividends paid out to equity holders.)

3 Calculations:

  a   H&M's assets and liabilities will have book values of zero at the end of 2014.

  b   H&M's net profit will be zero in 2014 because all assets have been sold at their book values (i.e., profit on the sale = 0).

  c   The final dividend payment in 2014 will be equal to the ending book value in 2013: $\text{Dividends}_{2014} = \text{Equity}_{2013} + \text{Profit}_{2014} - \text{Equity}_{2014} = 54.3 + 0 - 0 = 54.3.$

  d $\text{FCF to Equity}_{2014} = \text{Profit}_{2014} - \Delta\text{Assets}_{2014} + \Delta\text{Debt}_{2014} = 0 - (-116.2) + (-61.9) = 54.3.$

       (Note that the final free cash flow to equity holders is equal to the final dividend.).

  e $\text{Abnormal Earnings}_{2014} = \text{Profit}_{2014} - r_e \times \text{Equity}_{2013} = 0 - 10\% \times 54.3 = -5.4.$

  f $\text{Abnormal Earnings growth}_{2014} = \Delta\text{Profit}_{2014} - r_e \times (\text{Profit}_{2013} - \text{Dividends}_{2013}) = -20.5 - 10\% \times (20.5 - 15.0) = -21.0.$

       $\text{Abnormal Earnings growth}_{2015} = \Delta\text{Profit}_{2015} - r_e \times (\text{Profit}_{2014} - \text{Dividends}_{2014}) = 0 - 10\% \times (0 - 54.3) = 5.4.$

       (Check that Abnormal earnings growth = ΔAbnormal earnings (see e and 2b).)

4 Calculations:

  a   Note that H&M's expected dividends are exactly equal to its free cash flows to equity holders. Using the discounted dividends (DIV) model (or discounted cash flow model), H&M's equity value is calculated as follows:

$$\text{Equity value}_{\text{end 2011}} = \frac{\text{DIV}_{2012}}{(1 + r_e)} + \frac{\text{DIV}_{2013}}{(1 + r_e)^2} + \frac{\text{DIV}_{2014}}{(1 + r_e)^3}$$

$$= \frac{13.3}{(1.1)} + \frac{15.0}{(1.1)^2} + \frac{54.3}{(1.1)^3} = 65.3$$

  b   Using the discounted abnormal earnings (AE) model, H&M's equity value is calculated as follows:

$$\text{Equity value}_{\text{end 2011}} = \text{BVE}_{\text{end 2011}} + \frac{\text{AE}_{2012}}{(1 + r_e)} + \frac{\text{AE}_{2013}}{(1 + r_e)^2} + \frac{\text{AE}_{2014}}{(1 + r_e)^3}$$

$$= 44.1 + \frac{13.6}{(1.1)} + \frac{15.6}{(1.1)^2} + \frac{-5.4}{(1.1)^3} = 65.3$$

  c   Using the discounted abnormal earnings growth (AE) model, H&M's equity value is calculated as follows:

$$\text{Equity value}_{\text{end 2011}} = \frac{\text{Profit}_{2012}}{r_e} + \frac{1}{r_e}\left[\frac{\text{AEG}_{2013}}{(1 + r_e)} + \frac{\text{AEG}_{2014}}{(1 + r_e)^2} + \frac{\text{AEG}_{2015}}{(1 + r_e)^3}\right]$$

$$= \frac{18.0}{(0.1)} + \frac{1}{(0.1)}\left[\frac{2.0}{(1.1)} + \frac{-2.0}{(1.1)^2} + \frac{5.4}{(1.1)^3}\right] = 65.3$$

At the end of 2011, H&M had 1,655,072 thousand shares outstanding. The equity value estimate of SEK65.3 billion thus corresponds with an estimate of SEK39.45 per share. On January 27, 2012, one day after H&M's preliminary annual earnings announcement, the company's closing share price was SEK221.40. Our estimate of equity value per share is substantially lower than the actual share price because we made very conservative assumptions about H&M's performance after 2013. In the next chapter we will discuss methods to arrive at more realistic (less conservative) equity value estimates.

VALUATION USING PRICE MULTIPLES

Valuations based on price multiples are widely used by analysts. The primary reason for the popularity of this method is its simplicity. Unlike the discounted dividend, discounted abnormal earnings (growth), and discounted cash flow methods, **multiple-based valuations** do not require detailed multiyear forecasts of a number of parameters such as growth, profitability, and cost of capital.

Valuation using multiples involves the following three steps:

Step 1: Select a measure of performance or value (e.g., earnings, sales, cash flows, book equity, book assets) as the basis for multiple calculations. The two most commonly used metrics are based on earnings and book equity.

Step 2: Calculate price multiples for comparable firms, i.e., the ratio of the market value to the selected measure of performance or value.

Step 3: Apply the comparable firm multiple to the performance or value measure of the firm being analyzed.

Under this approach, the analyst relies on the market to undertake the difficult task of considering the short- and long-term prospects for growth and profitability and their implications for the values of the comparable firms. Then the analyst assumes that the pricing of those other firms is applicable to the firm at hand.

Main issues with multiple-based valuation

On the surface, using multiples seems straightforward. Unfortunately, in practice it is not as simple as it would appear. Identification of "comparable" firms is often quite difficult. There are also some choices to be made concerning how multiples will be calculated. Finally, understanding why multiples vary across firms, and how applicable another firm's multiple is to the one at hand, requires a sound knowledge of the determinants of each multiple.

Selecting comparable firms

Ideally, price multiples used in a comparable firm analysis are those for firms with similar operating and financial characteristics. Firms within the same industry are the most obvious candidates. But even within narrowly defined industries, it is often difficult to identify comparable firms. Many firms are in multiple industries, making it difficult to identify representative benchmarks. In addition, firms within the same industry frequently have different strategies, growth opportunities, and profitability, creating selection problems.

One way of dealing with these issues is to average across *all* firms in the industry. The analyst implicitly hopes that the various sources of noncomparability cancel each other out, so that the firm being valued is comparable to a "typical" industry member. Another approach is to focus on only those firms within the industry that are most similar.

For example, consider using multiples to value Hennes & Mauritz (H&M). Business and financial databases classify the company in the Apparel Retail industry. Its competitors include Benetton, Burberry, Charles Voegele, Etam, French Connection, Inditex, and Next. The average price-earnings ratio for a profitable subset of these direct competitors was 13.6 and the average price-to-book ratio was 4.9. However, it is unclear whether these multiples are useful benchmarks for valuing H&M. Not all of these competitors follow a fast fashion strategy like H&M and some of them operate on a significantly smaller scale, both in terms of revenue and geographic reach. In addition, not all competitors exhibit similar growth rates as H&M.

A potential problem of choosing comparable firms from different countries is that a variety of factors that influence multiples may differ across countries. For example, the cost of equity, which is inversely related to the price-earnings multiple, is affected by the risk-free interest rate. Further, the expected earnings growth rate, which positively affects the price-earnings multiple, partly depends on a country's future economic growth. Consequently, international differences in risk-free interest rates and growth expectations lead to international differences in price-earnings multiples. In addition, international differences in accounting practices may lead to systematic international differences in net profits, which is the denominator in price-earnings multiples. The most obvious way to get around this problem is to choose comparable firms from one country. This is, however, often not feasible in smaller equity markets. The alternative solution is to explicitly take into account the country factors that affect multiples. For example, when using the multiples of the above group of competitors, it is important to realize that at the time that the multiples were calculated, risk-free interest rates in Spain and Italy (domicile of Inditex and Benetton) were higher than the risk-free interest rate in France, Switzerland, and the UK (domicile of the other industry peers). This may have caused the average price-earnings multiple of H&M's Southern European competitors to be relatively low.

Multiples for firms with poor performance

Price multiples can be affected when the denominator variable is performing poorly. This is especially common when the denominator is a flow measure, such as earnings or cash flows. For example, one of H&M's competitors, Charles Voegele, reported losses in 2011, making the price-earnings ratios negative. Because negative price-earnings ratios have no sensible meaning, these were ignored in the calculation of the average price-earnings ratio.

What are analysts' options for handling the problems for multiples created by transitory shocks to the denominator? One option is to simply exclude firms with large transitory effects from the set of comparable firms, as we did above. If poor performance is due to a one-time write down or special item, analysts can simply exclude that effect from their computation of the comparable multiple. For example, in 2009 Burberry recorded a small profit of £0.03 per share, including close to £0.32 per share (after tax) in impairment and restructuring charges. If these charges were excluded, Burberry's net profit would be £0.35 per share and its price-earnings ratio would change from an unrealistically high value of 90.7 to a more informative value of 7.8. This change shows the sensitivity of price-earnings multiples to transitory shocks. Finally, analysts can reduce the effect on multiples of temporary problems in past performance by using a denominator that is a forecast of future performance rather than the past measure itself. Multiples based on forecasts are termed *leading* multiples, whereas those based on historical data are called *trailing* multiples. Leading multiples are less likely to include one-time gains and losses in the denominator, simply because such items are difficult to anticipate.

Adjusting multiples for leverage

Price multiples should be calculated in a way that preserves consistency between the numerator and denominator. Consistency is an issue for those ratios where the denominator reflects performance *before* servicing debt. Examples include the price-to-sales multiple and any multiple of operating earnings or operating cash flows. When calculating these multiples, the numerator should include not just the market value of equity but the value of debt as well.

Determinants of value-to-book and value-earnings multiples

Even across relatively closely related firms, price multiples can vary considerably. The abnormal earnings valuation method provides insight into factors that lead to differences in value-to-book multiples across firms. Similarly, the abnormal earnings growth valuation method helps to explain why value-to-earnings multiples vary across firms.

If the abnormal earnings formula is scaled by book value, the left-hand side becomes the equity value-to-book ratio as opposed to the equity value itself. The right-hand side variables now reflect three multiple drivers: (1) earnings deflated by book value, or our old friend return on equity (ROE), discussed in Chapter 5, (2) the growth in equity book value over time, and (3) the firm's cost of equity. The actual valuation formula is as follows:

$$\text{Equity value-to-book ratio}_0 = 1 + \frac{\text{ROE}_1 - r_e}{(1 + r_e)} + \frac{(\text{ROE}_2 - r_e)(1 + g_1^{\text{equity}})}{(1 + r_e)^2}$$

$$+ \frac{(\text{ROE}_3 - r_e)(1 + g_1^{\text{equity}})(1 + g_2^{\text{equity}})}{(1 + r_e)^3} + \dots$$

where g_t^{equity} = growth in book value of equity (BVE) from year t−1 to year t or:

$$\frac{BVE_t - BVE_{t-1}}{BVE_{t-1}}$$

A firm's value-to-book ratio is largely driven by the magnitude of its future abnormal ROEs, defined as ROE less the cost of equity capital ($ROE - r_e$). Firms with positive abnormal ROE are able to invest their net assets to create value for shareholders and will have price-to-book ratios greater than one. In contrast, firms with negative abnormal ROEs are unable to invest shareholder funds at a rate greater than their cost of capital and have ratios below one.

The magnitude of a firm's value-to-book multiple also depends on the amount of growth in book value. Firms can grow their equity base by issuing new equity or by reinvesting profits. If this new equity is invested in positive valued projects for shareholders – that is, projects with ROEs that exceed the cost of capital – the firm will boost its equity value-to-book multiple. Conversely, for firms with ROEs that are less than the cost of capital, equity growth further lowers the multiple.

The valuation task can now be framed in terms of two key questions about the firm's "value drivers":

- Will the firm be able to generate ROEs that exceed its cost of equity capital? If so, for how long?
- How quickly will the firm's investment base (book value) grow?

If desired, the equation can be rewritten so that future ROEs are expressed as the product of their components: profit margins, sales turnover, and leverage. Thus the approach permits us to build directly on projections of the same accounting numbers utilized in financial analysis (see Chapter 5) without the need to convert projections of those numbers into cash flows. Yet in the end, the estimate of value should be the same as that from the dividend discount model.[7]

Returning to the Down Under Company example, the implied equity value-to-book multiple can be estimated as follows:

	Year 1	Year 2	Year 3
Beginning book value	€60m	€40m	€20m
Earnings	€20m	€30m	€40m
ROE	0.33	0.75	2.00
− Cost of capital	0.10	0.10	0.10
= Abnormal ROE	0.23	0.65	1.90
× (1 + cumulative book value growth)	1.00	0.67	0.33
= Abnormal ROE scaled by book value growth	0.23	0.43	0.63
× PV factor	0.909	0.826	0.751
= PV of abnormal ROE scaled by book value growth	0.212	0.358	0.476
Cumulative PV of abnormal ROE scaled by book value growth	1.046		
+ 1.00	1.000		
= Equity value-to-book multiple	2.046		

The equity value-to-book multiple for Down Under is therefore 2.046, and the implied equity value is €122.8 (€60 times 2.046), once again identical to the dividend discount model value.

The equity value-to-book formulation can also be used to construct the equity value-earnings multiple as follows:

$$\text{Equity value-to-earnings multiple} = \text{Equity value-to-book multiple} \times \frac{\text{Book value of equity}}{\text{Earnings}}$$

$$= \frac{\text{Equity value-to-book multiple}}{\text{ROE}}$$

In other words, the same factors that drive a firm's equity value-to-book multiple also explain its equity value-earnings multiple. The key difference between the two multiples is that the value-earnings multiple is affected by the firm's current level of ROE performance, whereas the value-to-book multiple is not. Firms with low current ROEs therefore have very high value-earnings multiples and vice versa. If a firm has a zero or negative ROE, its PE multiple is not defined. Value-earnings multiples are therefore more volatile than value-to-book multiples.

The following data for a subset of firms in the Apparel Retail industry illustrate the relation between ROE, the price-to-book ratio, and the price-earnings ratio:

Company	ROE	Price-to-book ratio	Price-earnings ratio
Benetton	4.9%	0.36	7.36
Burberry	31.4%	7.03	22.61
French Connection	6.1%	0.64	10.55

Both the price-to-book and price-earnings ratios are high for Burberry. Investors therefore expect that in the future Burberry will generate higher ROEs than its current level (31.4 percent). In contrast, French Connection has a price-to-book ratio smaller than one (0.64) and a moderate price-earnings ratio (10.55). This indicates that investors expect that French Connection will continue to generate negative abnormal ROEs but that the current level of ROE (6.1 percent) is sustainable. Finally, Benetton has a relatively low price-to-book ratio, 0.36, and a low price-earnings multiple. Investors apparently do not expect Benetton to sustain its already low performance and earn abnormal ROEs in the future.

The effect of future growth in net profit on the price-earnings multiple can also be seen from the model that arises when we scale the abnormal earnings growth valuation formula by next-period net profit. The valuation formula then becomes:

Leading equity value-to-earnings ratio $=$

$$\frac{1}{r_e} + \frac{1}{r_e}\left[\frac{g_2^{profit} + (d_1 - 1)r_e}{(1 + r_e)} + \frac{\left(1 + g_2^{profit}\right)\left[g_3^{profit} + (d_2 - 1)r_e\right]}{(1 + r_e)^2} \cdots\right]$$

where d_t = dividend payout ratio in year t

g_t^{profit} = growth in net profit (NP) from year t $-$ 1 to year t or

$$\frac{NP_t - NP_{t-1}}{NP_{t-1}}$$

In this formula, future earnings growth rates and dividend payouts are the basis for estimating price-earnings multiples.[8] Consider the earnings growth rates and dividend payout ratios of the Down Under Company. The earnings growth rates (g_t^{profit}) are 50, 33, and -100 percent in years 2, 3, and 4, respectively. Dividend payouts are 200 percent, 167 percent, and 150 percent in years 1, 2, and 3, respectively. Substituting these percentages in the leading price-earnings formula yields:

Leading equity value-to-earnings ratio $=$

$$\frac{1}{r_e} + \frac{1}{r_e}\left[\frac{g_2^{profit} + (d_1 - 1)r_e}{(1 + r_e)} + \frac{\left(1 + g_2^{profit}\right)\left[g_3^{profit} + (d_2 - 1)r_e\right]}{(1 + r_e)^2}\right.$$
$$\left. + \frac{\left(1 + g_2^{profit}\right)\left(1 + g_3^{profit}\right)\left[g_4^{profit} + (d_3 - 1)r_e\right]}{(1 + r_e)^3}\right]$$
$$= \frac{1}{.1} + \frac{1}{.1}\left[\frac{.5 + .1}{1.1} + \frac{1.5 \times [.33 + 0.067]}{1.1^2} + \frac{1.5 \times 1.33 \times [-1 + .05]}{1.1^3}\right] = 6.14$$

The price-earnings multiple of 6.14 is consistent with a value of equity of €122.8 (6.14 × €20).

KEY ANALYSIS QUESTIONS

To value a firm using multiples, an analyst must assess the quality of the variable used as the multiple basis and determine the appropriate peer firms to include in the benchmark multiple. Analysts are therefore likely to be interested in answering the following questions:

- How well does the denominator used in the multiple reflect the firm's performance? For example, if earnings or book equity are used as the denominator, has the firm made conservative or aggressive accounting choices that are likely to unwind in the coming years? Is the firm likely to show strong growth in earnings or book equity? If earnings are the denominator, does the firm have temporarily poor or strong performance?

- What is the sustainability of the firm's growth and ROE based on the competitive dynamics of the firm's industry and product market and its own competitive position?

- Which are the most suitable peer companies to include in the benchmark multiple computation? Have these firms had growth (earnings or book values), profitability, and quality of earnings comparable to the firm being analyzed? Do they have the same risk characteristics?

SHORTCUT FORMS OF EARNINGS-BASED VALUATION

The discounted abnormal earnings valuation formula can be simplified by making assumptions about the relation between a firm's current and future abnormal earnings. Similarly, the equity value-to-book formula can be simplified by making assumptions about long-term ROEs and growth.

Abnormal earnings (growth) simplification

Several assumptions about the relation between current and future abnormal earnings are popular for simplifying the abnormal earnings model and the abnormal earnings growth model. First, abnormal earnings are assumed to follow a random walk. The random walk model for abnormal earnings implies that an analyst's best guess about future expected abnormal earnings are current abnormal earnings. The model assumes that past shocks to abnormal earnings persist forever, but that future shocks are random or unpredictable. The random walk model can be written as follows:

$$\text{Forecasted AE}_1 = \text{AE}_0$$

Forecasted AE_1 is the forecast of next year's abnormal earnings and AE_0 is current period abnormal earnings. Under the model, forecasted abnormal earnings for two years ahead are simply abnormal earnings in year 1, or once again current abnormal earnings. In other words, the best guess of abnormal earnings in any future year is just current abnormal earnings. It is also possible to include a drift term in the model, allowing earnings to grow by a constant amount, or at a constant rate in each period.

How does the above assumption about future abnormal earnings simplify the discounted abnormal earnings valuation model? If abnormal earnings follow a random walk, all future forecasts of abnormal earnings are simply current abnormal earnings. Consequently, the present value of future abnormal earnings can be calculated by valuing the current level of abnormal earnings as a perpetuity. It is then possible to rewrite value as follows:

$$\text{Equity value} = \text{BVE}_0 + \frac{\text{AE}_0}{r_e}$$

Equity value is the book value of equity at the end of the year plus current abnormal earnings divided by the cost of capital. The perpetuity formula can be adjusted to incorporate expectations of constant growth in future abnormal earnings.

A logical consequence of the above assumption is also that future abnormal earnings growth equals zero. When abnormal earnings growth in any future year is zero, the abnormal earnings growth valuation model can be rewritten as follows:

$$\text{Equity value} = \frac{\text{Net profit}_1}{r_e}$$

Equity value is then set equal to the capitalized value of next-period net profit.

In reality, shocks to abnormal earnings are unlikely to persist forever. Firms that have positive shocks are likely to attract competitors that will reduce opportunities for future abnormal performance. Firms with negative abnormal earnings shocks are likely to fail or to be acquired by other firms that can manage their resources more effectively. The persistence of abnormal performance will therefore depend on strategic factors such as barriers to entry and switching costs, discussed in Chapter 2. To reflect this, analysts frequently assume that current shocks to abnormal earnings decay over time. Under this assumption, abnormal earnings are said to follow an autoregressive model. Forecasted abnormal earnings are then:

$$\text{Forecasted AE}_1 = \beta\text{AE}_0$$

β is a parameter that captures the speed with which abnormal earnings decay over time. If there is no decay, β is one and abnormal earnings follow a random walk. If β is zero, abnormal earnings decay completely within one year. Estimates of β using actual company data indicate that for a typical firm, β is approximately 0.6. However, it varies by industry, and is smaller for firms with large accruals and onetime accounting charges.[9]

Note that if the rate of decay in abnormal earnings, β, is constant, the perpetual growth rate in abnormal earnings equals $(\beta - 1$. The autoregressive model therefore implies that equity values can again be written as a function of current abnormal earnings and book values:[10]

$$\text{Equity value} = \text{BVE}_0 + \frac{\beta\text{AE}_0}{r_e - (\beta - 1)}$$

This formulation implies that equity values are simply the sum of current book value plus current abnormal earnings weighted by the cost of equity capital and persistence in abnormal earnings.

Under the assumption that abnormal earnings follow an autoregressive model, abnormal earnings growth, or the change in abnormal earnings, in year 1 can be rewritten as $(\beta - 1)AE_0$ and the abnormal earnings growth model simplifies to:

$$\text{Equity value} = \frac{\text{Net profit}_1}{r_e} + \frac{(1 + r_e)}{r_e}\left[\frac{(\beta - 1)\text{AE}_1}{r_e - (\beta - 1)}\right]$$

This formula illustrates that equity values can be expressed as the sum of capitalized next-period earnings plus next-period abnormal earnings weighted by the cost of equity capital and persistence in abnormal earnings.

An advantage of the abnormal earnings growth model over the abnormal earnings model is that the former model can be simplified by making assumptions about the change in abnormal earnings. This can be useful in situations where the analyst believes, for example, that a firm has a sustainable competitive advantage but expects that the growth in abnormal earnings will gradually decay over time. Under the assumption that:

$$\text{Forecasted }(\text{AE}_2 - \text{AE}_1) = \beta(\text{AE}_1 - \text{AE}_0)$$

the abnormal earnings growth model simplifies to:

$$\text{Equity value} = \frac{\text{Net profit}_1}{r_e} + \frac{(1 + r_e)}{r_e}\left[\frac{\beta(\text{AE}_1 - \text{AE}_0)}{r_e - (\beta - 1)}\right]$$

ROE and growth simplifications

It is also possible to make simplifications about long-term ROEs and equity growth to reduce forecast horizons for estimating the equity value-to-book multiple. Firms' long-term ROEs are affected by such factors as barriers to entry in their industries, change in production or delivery technologies, and quality of management. As discussed in Chapter 6, these factors tend to force abnormal ROEs to decay over time. One way to model this decay is to assume that ROEs revert to the mean. Forecasted ROE after one period then takes the following form:

$$\text{Forecasted ROE}_1 = \text{ROE}_0 + \beta\left(\text{ROE}_0 - \overline{\text{ROE}}\right)$$

$\overline{ROE}$ is the steady state ROE (either the firm's cost of capital or the long-term industry ROE) and β is a "speed of adjustment factor" that reflects how quickly it takes the ROE to revert to its steady state.[11]

Growth rates in the book value of equity are driven by several factors. First, the size of the firm is important. Small firms can sustain very high growth rates for an extended period, whereas large firms find it more difficult to do so. Second, firms with high rates of growth are likely to attract competitors, which reduces their growth rates. As a result, steady-state rates of growth in book equity are likely to be similar to rates of growth in the overall economy, which have averaged 2–4 percent per year.

The long-term patterns in ROE and book equity growth rates imply that for most companies there is limited value in making forecasts for valuation beyond a relatively short horizon, generally five to ten years. Powerful economic forces tend to lead firms with superior or inferior performance early in the forecast horizon to revert to a level that is comparable to that of other firms in the industry or the economy. For a firm in steady state, that is, expected to have a stable ROE and book equity growth rate (g^{equity}), the value-to-book multiple formula simplifies to the following:

$$\text{Equity value-to-book multiple} = 1 + \frac{ROE_0 - r_e}{r_e - g^{equity}}$$

Of course, analysts can make a variety of simplifying assumptions about a firm's ROE and growth. For example, they can assume that they decay slowly or rapidly to the cost of capital and the growth rate for the economy. They can assume that the rates decay to the industry or economy average ROEs and book value growth rates. The valuation formula can easily be modified to accommodate these assumptions.

COMPARING VALUATION METHODS

We have discussed four methods of valuation derived from the dividend discount model: discounted dividends, discounted abnormal earnings (or abnormal ROEs), discounted abnormal earnings growth, and discounted cash flows. Since the methods are all derived from the same underlying model, no one version can be considered superior to the others. As long as analysts make the same assumptions about firm fundamentals, value estimates under all four methods will be identical. However, we discuss below important differences between the models.

Focus on different issues

The methods frame the valuation task differently and can in practice focus the analyst's attention on different issues. The earnings-based approaches frame the issues in terms of accounting data such as earnings and book values. Analysts spend considerable time analyzing historical income statements and balance sheets, and their primary forecasts are typically for these variables.

Defining values in terms of ROEs has the added advantage that it focuses analysts' attention on ROE, the same key measure of performance that is decomposed in a standard financial analysis. Furthermore, because ROEs control for firm scale, it is likely to be easier for analysts to evaluate the reasonableness of their forecasts by benchmarking them with ROEs of other firms in the industry and the economy. This type of benchmarking is more challenging for free cash flows and abnormal earnings.

Differences in required structure

The methods differ in the amount of analysis and structure required for valuation. The discounted abnormal earnings and ROE methods require analysts to construct both *pro forma* income statements and balance sheets to forecast future earnings and book values. In contrast, the discounted abnormal earnings growth model requires analysts to forecast future earnings and dividends. The discounted cash flow method requires analysts to forecast income statements and changes in working capital and long-term assets to generate free cash flows. Finally, the discounted dividend method requires analysts to forecast dividends.

The discounted abnormal earnings (growth), ROE, and free cash flow models all require more structure for analysis than the discounted dividend approach. They therefore help analysts to avoid structural inconsistencies in their forecasts of future dividends by specifically allowing for firms' future performance and investment opportunities. Similarly, the discounted abnormal earnings/ROE method requires more structure and work than the discounted cash flow method and the discounted abnormal earnings growth method to build full *pro forma* balance sheets. This permits analysts to avoid inconsistencies in the firm's financial structure.

Differences in terminal value implications

A third difference between the methods is in the effort required for estimating terminal values. Terminal value estimates for the abnormal earnings, abnormal earnings growth, and ROE methods tend to represent a much smaller fraction of total value than under the discounted cash flow or dividend methods. On the surface, this would appear to mitigate concerns about the aspect of valuation that leaves the analyst most uncomfortable. Is this apparent advantage real? As explained below, the answer turns on how well value is already reflected in the accountant's book value.

The abnormal earnings and abnormal earnings growth valuations do not eliminate the discounted cash flow terminal value problem, but they do reframe it. Discounted cash flow terminal values include the present value of *all* expected cash flows beyond the forecast horizon. Under abnormal earnings valuation, that value is broken into two parts: the present values of *normal* earnings and *abnormal* earnings beyond the terminal year. The terminal value in the abnormal earnings technique includes only the *abnormal* earnings. The present value of normal earnings is already reflected in the original book value. Similarly, under the abnormal earnings growth approach the present value of near-term abnormal earnings is already reflected in next-period earnings or the growth in earnings over the forecast horizon. The terminal value includes only the *changes in abnormal* earnings that are expected to occur in the years beyond the terminal year.

The abnormal earnings and abnormal earnings growth approaches, then, recognize that current book value and earnings over the forecast horizon already reflect many of the cash flows expected to arrive after the forecast horizon. The approaches build directly on accrual accounting. For example, under accrual accounting, book equity can be thought of as the minimum recoverable future benefits attributable to the firm's net assets. In addition, revenues are typically realized when earned, not when cash is received. The discounted cash flow approach, on the other hand, "unravels" all of the accruals, spreads the resulting cash flows over longer horizons, and then reconstructs its own "accruals" in the form of discounted expectations of future cash flows. The essential difference between the two approaches is that abnormal earnings (growth) valuation recognizes that the accrual process may already have performed a portion of the valuation task, whereas the discounted cash flow approach ultimately moves back to the primitive cash flows underlying the accruals.

The usefulness of the accounting-based perspective thus hinges on how well the accrual process reflects future cash flows. The approach is most convenient when the accrual process is "unbiased," so that earnings can be abnormal only as the result of economic rents and not as a product of accounting itself.[12] The forecast horizon then extends to the point where the firm is expected to approach a competitive equilibrium and earn only normal earnings on its projects. Subsequent abnormal earnings would be zero, and the terminal value at that point would be zero. In this extreme case, *all* of the firm's value is reflected in the book value and earnings projected over the forecast horizon.

Of course accounting rarely works so well. For example, many firms expense research and development costs, and book values fail to reflect any research and development assets. As a result, firms that spend heavily on research and development – such as pharmaceuticals – tend on average to generate abnormally high earnings even in the face of stiff competition. Purely as an artifact of research and development accounting, abnormal earnings would be expected to remain positive indefinitely for such firms, and, under the abnormal earnings approach, the terminal value could represent a substantial fraction of total value.

If desired, the analyst can alter the accounting approach used by the firm in his or her own projections. "Better" accounting would be viewed as that which reflects a larger fraction of the firm's value in book values and earnings over the forecast horizon.[13] This same view underlies analysts' attempts to "normalize" earnings; the adjusted numbers are intended to provide better indications of value, even though they reflect performance only over a short horizon.

Research has focused on the performance of abnormal earnings-based valuation relative to discounted cash flow and discounted dividend methods. The findings indicate that over relatively short forecast horizons (ten years or less), valuation estimates using the abnormal earnings approach generate more precise estimates of value than either the discounted dividend or discounted cash flow models. This advantage for the abnormal earnings-based approach persists for firms with conservative or aggressive accounting, indicating that accrual accounting does a reasonably good job of reflecting future cash flows.[14] The performance of the abnormal earnings growth valuation model has not yet been extensively studied. However, the model's close relationship to the abnormal earnings model makes it subject to many of the same practical advantages.

Research also indicates that abnormal earnings estimates of value outperform traditional multiples, such as price-earnings ratios, price-to-book ratios, and dividend yields, for predicting future share price movements.[15] Firms that have high abnormal earnings model estimates of value relative to current price show positive abnormal future stock returns, whereas firms with low estimated value-to-price ratios have negative abnormal share price performance.

KEY ANALYSIS QUESTIONS

The above discussion on the trade-offs between different methods of valuing a company raises several questions for analysts about how to compare methods and to consider which is likely to be most reliable for their analysis:

- What are the key performance parameters that the analyst forecasts? Is more attention given to forecasting accounting variables, such as earnings and book values, or to forecasting cash flow variables?

- Has the analyst linked forecasted income statements and balance sheets? If not, is there any inconsistency between the two statements, or in the implications of the assumptions for future performance? If so, what is the source of this inconsistency and does it affect discounted earnings-based and discounted cash flow methods similarly?

- How well does the firm's accounting capture its underlying assets and obligations? Does it do a good enough job that we can rely on book values as the basis for long-term forecasts? Alternatively, does the firm rely heavily on off-balance sheet assets, such as R&D, which make book values a poor lower bound on long-term performance?

- Has the analyst made very different assumptions about long-term performance in the terminal value computations under the different valuation methods? If so, which set of assumptions is more plausible given the firm's industry and its competitive positioning?

SUMMARY

Valuation is the process by which forecasts of performance are converted into estimates of price. A variety of valuation techniques are employed in practice, and there is no single method that clearly dominates others. In fact, since each technique involves different advantages and disadvantages, there are gains to considering several approaches simultaneously.

For shareholders, a firm's equity value is the present value of future dividends. This chapter described four valuation techniques directly based on this dividend discount definition of value: discounted dividends, discounted abnormal earnings/ROEs, discounted abnormal earnings growth, and discounted free cash flows. The discounted dividend method attempts to forecast dividends directly. The abnormal earnings approach expresses the value of a firm's equity as book value plus discounted expectations of future abnormal earnings. The abnormal earnings growth approach defines equity value as capitalized next-period earnings plus the present value of future changes in abnormal earnings. Finally, the discounted cash flow method represents a firm's equity value by expected future free cash flows discounted at the cost of capital.

Although these four methods were derived from the same dividend discount model, they frame the valuation task differently. In practice they focus the analyst's attention on different issues and require different levels of structure in developing forecasts of the underlying primitive, future dividends.

Price multiple valuation methods were also discussed. Under these approaches, analysts estimate ratios of current price to historical or forecasted measures of performance for comparable firms. The benchmarks are then used to value the performance of the firm being analyzed. Multiples have traditionally been popular, primarily because they do not require analysts to make multiyear forecasts of performance. However, it can be difficult to identify comparable firms to use as benchmarks. Even across highly related firms, there are differences in performance that are likely to affect their multiples.

The chapter discussed the relation between two popular multiples, value-to-book and value-earnings ratios, and the discounted abnormal earnings valuation. The resulting formulations indicate that value-to-book multiples are a function of future abnormal ROEs, book value growth, and the firm's cost of equity. The value-earnings multiple is a function of the same factors and also the current ROE.

CORE CONCEPTS

Abnormal earnings Difference between net profit and a capital charge. The capital charge is calculated as the cost of equity times the beginning of the period book value of equity.

Abnormal earnings growth Change in abnormal earnings. The change in abnormal earnings can be rewritten as the abnormal change in earnings, which is calculated as the difference between the actual period change in net profit and the expected change in net profit. The expected change in net profit is calculated as the cost of equity times prior period's retained net profit:

$$\text{Abnormal earnings growth (AEG)} = \Delta\text{Net profit}_2 - r_e \cdot (\text{Net profit}_1 - \text{Dividend}_1)$$

Discounted abnormal earnings growth model Model expressing equity value as a function of next-period net profit and the present value of abnormal earnings growth (AEG) beyond the next period:

$$\text{Equity value} = \frac{\text{Net profit}_1}{r_e} + \frac{1}{r_e}\left[\frac{\text{AEG}_2}{(1+r_e)} + \frac{\text{AEG}_3}{(1+r_e)^2} + \dots\right]$$

Discounted abnormal earnings model Model expressing equity value as the sum of the beginning book value of equity and the present value of future abnormal earnings (AE):

$$\text{Equity value} = \text{BVE}_0 + \frac{\text{AE}_1}{(1+r_e)} + \frac{\text{AE}_1}{(1+r_e)^2} + \dots$$

Discounted cash flow model Model expressing equity value as the present value of future free cash flows to equity (FCFE):

$$\text{Equity value} = \frac{\text{FCFE}_1}{(1+r_e)} + \frac{\text{FCFE}_2}{(1+r_e)^2} + \dots$$

Equity value Present value of expected future dividends (DIV):

$$\text{Equity value} = \frac{\text{DIV}_1}{(1+r_e)} + \frac{\text{DIV}_2}{(1+r_e)^2} + \frac{\text{DIV}_3}{(1+r_e)^3} + \dots$$

This dividend-discount model can be recast to generate the discounted abnormal earnings model, the discounted abnormal earnings growth model, and the discounted free cash flow model.

Free cash flow to debt and equity Cash flow available for distribution to creditors and shareholders. The free cash flow to debt and equity is equal to: net profit + after tax net interest expense – change in net working capital – change in net non-current assets.

Free cash flow to equity Cash flow available for distribution to shareholders. The free cash flow to equity is equal to: net profit – change in net working capital – change in net non-current assets + change in net debt.

Multiple-based valuation Use of price multiples – ratios of market value to a measure of firm performance (e.g., net profit) or value (e.g., book value of equity) – of comparable firms to value equity.

SUMMARY OF NOTATIONS USED IN THIS CHAPTER

AE	Abnormal earnings
AEG	Abnormal earnings growth
BVA	Book value of operating net assets
BVE	Book value of equity
BVND	Book value of net debt
DIV	Dividends
EBIT	Earnings before interest and taxes
g^{div}	Dividend growth rate
g^{equity}	Growth rate in the book value of equity
g^{profit}	Growth rate in net profit
NP	Net profit
OCF	Operating cash flow
PV	Present value
r_e	Cost of equity
WACC	Weighted average cost of capital (debt and equity)

QUESTIONS, EXERCISES, AND PROBLEMS

1   Jonas Borg, an analyst at EMH Securities, states: "I don't know why anyone would ever try to value earnings. Obviously, the market knows that earnings can be manipulated and only values cash flows." Discuss.

2   Explain why terminal values in accounting-based valuation are significantly less than those for DCF valuation.

3   Manufactured Earnings is a "darling" of European analysts. Its current market price is €15 per share, and its book value is €5 per share. Analysts forecast that the firm's book value will grow by 10 percent per year indefinitely, and the cost of equity is 15 percent. Given these facts, what is the market's expectation of the firm's long-term average ROE?

4   Given the information in question 3, what will be Manufactured Earnings' share price if the market revises its expectations of long-term average ROE to 20 percent?

5   Analysts reassess Manufactured Earnings' future performance as follows: growth in book value increases to 12 percent per year, but the ROE of the incremental book value is only 15 percent. What is the impact on the market-to-book ratio?

6   How can a company with a high ROE have a low PE ratio?

7   What types of companies have:

   a   A high PE and a low market-to-book ratio?

   b   A high PE ratio and a high market-to-book ratio?

   c   A low PE and a high market-to-book ratio?

   d   A low PE and a low market-to-book ratio?

8   Free cash flows (FCF) used in DCF valuations discussed in the chapter are defined as follows:

$$\begin{aligned}
\text{FCF to debt and equity} = {}& \text{Earnings before interest and taxes} \times (1 - \text{tax rate}) + \\
& \text{Depreciation and deferred taxes} - \text{Capital} \\
& \text{expenditures} - / + \text{Increase/decrease} \\
& \text{in working capital}
\end{aligned}$$

$$\begin{aligned}
\text{FCF to equity} = {}& \text{Net profit} + \text{Depreciation and deferred taxes} - \\
& \text{Capital expenditures} - / + \text{Increase/decrease} \\
& \text{in working capital} + / - \text{Increase/decrease in debt}
\end{aligned}$$

Which of the following items affect free cash flows to debt and equity holders? Which affect free cash flows to equity alone? Explain why and how.

   ■   An increase in trade receivables.

   ■   A decrease in gross margins.

   ■   An increase in property, plant, and equipment.

   ■   An increase in inventories.

   ■   Interest expense.

   ■   An increase in prepaid expenses.

   ■   An increase in notes payable to the bank.

9   Starite Company is valued at €20 per share. Analysts expect that it will generate free cash flows to equity of €4 per share for the foreseeable future. What is the firm's implied cost of equity capital?

10 Janet Stringer argues that "the DCF valuation method has increased managers' focus on short-term rather than long-term performance, since the discounting process places much heavier weight on short-term cash flows than long-term ones." Comment.

Problem 1   *Estimating Hugo Boss's equity value*

Hugo Boss AG is a German designer, manufacturer and distributor of men's and women's clothing, operating in the higher end of the clothing retail industry. During the period 2001–2008, the company consistently earned returns on equity in excess of 18 percent, grew its book value of equity (before special dividends) by 5.5 percent per year, on average, and paid out 65–70 percent of its net profit as dividends. In 2008, the company paid out a special dividend of €345.1 million. Consequently, the company's book value of equity decreased from €546.8 million in 2007 to €199.0 million in 2008.

   On April 1, 2009, one month before the publication of the first-quarter results, when Hugo Boss's 70.4 million common shares trade at about €11 per share, an analyst produces the following forecasts for Hugo Boss.

Income statement (€ millions)		2009E	2010E	2011E
Sales		1548.1	1493.9	1561.2
Gross profit		897.9	875.1	923.7
EBIT		179.6	176.9	196.2
Interest expense		(45)	(40)	(35)
EBT		134.6	136.9	161.2
Tax expense		(36.3)	(37)	(43.5)
Net profit		98.3	99.9	117.7

Balance sheet (€ millions)	2008R	2009E	2010E	2011E
Total non-current assets	459.2	480.8	499.1	512.0
Inventories	381.4	325.1	304.3	305.3
Trade receivables	201.0	175.4	160.8	156.1
Cash and cash equivalents	24.6	33.5	32.5	47.2
Other current assets	95.4	136.5	172.5	203.2
Total current assets	702.4	670.5	670.1	711.8
Shareholders' equity	199.0	200.2	221.6	259.0
Non-current provisions	27.9	25.6	24.7	25.8
Non-current debt	588.5	576.7	565.2	553.9
Other non-current liabilities (non-interest bearing)	26.7	24.5	23.6	24.8
Deferred tax liabilities	17.9	18.3	18.7	19.0
Total non-current liabilities	661.0	645.1	632.2	623.5
Current provisions	59.3	59.3	59.3	59.3
Current debt	40.2	40.2	40.2	40.2
Other current liabilities	202.1	206.5	215.9	241.8
Total current liabilities	301.6	306.0	315.4	341.3
TOTAL EQUITY AND LIABILITIES	1161.6	1151.3	1169.2	1223.8

Assume that Hugo Boss's cost of equity equals 12 percent.

1   Calculate free cash flows to equity, abnormal earnings, and abnormal earnings growth for the years 2009–2011.

2   Assume that in 2012 Hugo Boss AG liquidates all its assets at their book values, uses the proceeds to pay off debt and pays out the remainder to its equity holders. What does this assumption imply about the company's:

   a   Free cash flow to equity holders in 2012 and beyond?

   b   Abnormal earnings in 2012 and beyond?

   c   Abnormal earnings growth in 2012 and beyond?

3   Estimate the value of Hugo Boss's equity on April 1, 2009, using the above forecasts and assumptions. Check that the discounted cash flow model, the abnormal earnings model, and the abnormal earnings growth model yield the same outcome.

4   The analyst estimates a target price of €20 per share. What is the expected value of Hugo Boss's equity at the end of 2011 that is implicit in the analysts' forecasts and target price?

5   Under the assumption that the historical trends in the company's ROE (i.e., approximately 18 percent), payout ratio (70 percent) and book value growth (5.5 percent) continue in the future, what would be your estimate of Hugo Boss's equity value-to-book ratio *before the company paid out its special dividend?* How does the special dividend payment change your estimate of the equity value-to-book ratio?

Problem 2 *Estimating Adidas's equity value*

Germany-based Adidas is one of the world's largest producers of sportswear. During 2011, Adidas showed strong operational performance and saw its equity value increase by 3 percent to close to €10.5 billion. On April 1, 2012, one month before the publication of the first-quarter results, an analyst produces the following forecasts of Adidas's 2012–2014 performance and financial position:

Income statement (€ millions)	2012E	2013E	2014E
Sales	14917.0	15915.8	17029.7
Gross profit	7042.3	7532.9	8046.5
EBIT	1192.4	1380.6	1609.9
Net interest expense	−74.7	−55.0	−39.6
Profit before tax	1117.7	1325.6	1570.3
Tax expense	−313.0	−371.2	−439.7
Group profit	804.7	954.4	1130.6
Minority interest	−1.5	−1.7	−1.8
Net profit	803.2	952.7	1128.8

Balance sheet (€ millions)	2011R	2012E	2013E	2014E
Fixed assets	4717.0	5273.0	5626.1	6019.9
Current operating assets	4649.0	5197.0	5545.0	5933.1
Investment assets	2014.0	2251.4	2402.2	2570.3
Total assets	11380.0	12721.5	13573.3	14523.2
Shareholders' equity	5327.0	5878.5	6520.0	7272.2
Minority interest	4.0	5.0	6.1	7.0
Debt	1589.0	1852.2	1727.6	1552.2
Current operating liabilities	3992.0	4462.6	4761.4	5094.6
Non-current operating liabilities	468.0	523.2	558.2	597.3
Total equity and liabilities	11380.0	12721.5	13573.3	14523.2

Other estimates	2011R	2012E	2013E	2014E
Dividends		251.7	311.3	376.6

Assume that Adidas's cost of equity equals 10 percent.

1   Check whether all changes in the book value of equity that the analyst predicts can be fully explained through earnings and dividends. Why is this an important property of the analyst's equity estimates?

2   When using these forecasts to estimate the value of equity, the analyst can deal with minority interests in the following ways:

a   (1) Classify minority interests on the balance sheet as a non-interest-bearing liability (and hence as a negative operating asset) and (2) exclude income from minority interests from earnings (i.e., focus on net profit).

b   (1) Classify minority interests on the balance sheet as (group) equity, (2) include income from minority interests in earnings (i.e., focus on group profit), and (3) subtract the book value of minority interests from the estimated value of group equity to arrive at the value of shareholders' equity.

These approaches may yield different values. Discuss potential drawbacks of both approaches.

3   Based on a market value of €12,247 million on March 30, 2012 and the analyst's estimates, Adidas's leading market value-to-earnings ratio is 15.2. What does this ratio suggest about the analyst's expectations about future abnormal earnings growth?

4   Calculate abnormal earnings for the years 2012–2014.

5   Assume that abnormal earnings in 2015 and beyond are zero. Estimate the value of Adidas's group equity (group equity is the sum of shareholders' equity and minority interests). What might explain the difference between your equity value estimate and Adidas's actual market value (of €12,247 million)?

NOTES

1.   From a theoretical perspective, it is preferred to express equity *per share* as a function of dividends *per share*. This is because only the discounted dividends *per share* model accurately accounts for the wealth transfer from new shareholders to the current shareholders that occurs when a firm offers shares to new shareholders in future years at a price that is not equal to the prevailing market price. To simplify the discussion of the other valuation models, however, we describe all models on a "total equity value basis," thereby implicitly assuming that future capital transactions do not affect the firm's current equity value per share – i.e., are value neutral.

2.   In practice, firms do not have to pay out all of their free cash flows as dividends; they can retain surplus cash in the business. The conditions under which a firm's dividend decision affects its value are discussed by M. H. Miller and F. Modigliani in "Dividend Policy, Growth, and the Valuation of Shares," *Journal of Business* 34 (October 1961): 411–433.

3.   The incorporation of all nonowner changes in equity into profit is called clean surplus accounting. It is analogous to "recognized income and expense," the concept defined in IAS 1.

4.   Changes in book value also include new capital contributions. However the dividend discount model assumes that new capital is issued at fair value. As a result, any incremental book value from capital issues is exactly offset by the discounted value of future dividends to new shareholders. Capital transactions therefore do not affect firm valuation.

5.   Appendix B to this chapter provides a simple proof of the earnings-based valuation formula.

6.   The abnormal earnings growth model and its properties are extensively discussed in the following articles: J. A. Ohlson and B. E. Juettner-Nauroth, "Expected EPS and EPS Growth as Determinants of Value," *Review of Accounting Studies* (2005): 349–365; J. A. Ohlson, "On Accounting-Based Valuation Formulae," *Review of Accounting Studies* (2005): 323–347; S. H. Penman, "Discussion of 'On Accounting-Based Valuation Formulae' and 'Expected EPS and EPS Growth as Determinants of Value'," *Review of Accounting Studies* (2005): 367–378.

7.   It may seem surprising that one can estimate value with no explicit attention to two of the cash flow streams considered in DCF analysis – investments in working capital and capital expenditures. The accounting-based technique recognizes that these investments cannot possibly contribute to value without impacting abnormal earnings, and that therefore only their earnings impacts need be considered. For example, the benefit of an increase in inventory turnover surfaces in terms of its impact on ROE (and thus, abnormal earnings), without the need to consider explicitly the cash flow impacts involved.

8.   This model must not be confused with the PEG ratio. The PEG ratio, which is defined as the price-earnings ratio divided by the short-term earnings growth rate, is a rule-of-thumb used by some analysts to determine whether a share is overpriced. The rule suggests that shares whose PEG ratio is above one are overpriced. Valuation using the PEG ratio has, however, no clear theoretical basis.

9.   See P. M. Dechow, A. P. Hutton, and R. G. Sloan, "An Empirical Assessment of the Residual Income Valuation Model," *Journal of Accounting and Economics* 23 (January 1999).

10. This formulation is a variant of a model proposed by James Ohlson, "Earnings, Book Values, and Dividends in Security Valuation," *Contemporary Accounting Research* 11 (Spring 1995). Ohlson includes in his forecasts of future abnormal earnings a variable that reflects relevant information other than current abnormal earnings. This variable then also appears in the equity valuation formula. Empirical research by Dechow, Hutton, and Sloan, "An Empirical Assessment of the Residual Income Valuation Model," *Journal of Accounting and Economics* 23 (January 1999), indicates that financial analysts' forecasts of abnormal earnings do reflect considerable information other than current abnormal earnings, and that this information is useful for valuation.

11. This specification is similar to the model for dividends developed by J. Lintner, "Distribution of Incomes of Corporations Among Dividends, Retained Earnings, and Taxes," *American Economic Review* 46 (May 1956): 97–113.

12. Unbiased accounting is that which, in a competitive equilibrium, produces an expected ROE equal to the cost of capital. The actual ROE thus reveals the presence of economic rents. Market value accounting is a special case of unbiased accounting that produces an expected ROE equal to the cost of capital, even when the firm is *not* in a competitive equilibrium. That is, market value accounting reflects the present value of future economic rents in book value, driving the expected ROEs to a normal level. For a discussion of unbiased and biased accounting, see G. Feltham and J. Ohlson, "Valuation and Clean Surplus Accounting for Operating and Financial Activities," *Contemporary Accounting Research* 11(2) (Spring 1995): 689–731.

13.   In Bennett Stewart's book on EVA valuation, *The Quest for Value* (New York: HarperBusiness, 1999), he recommends a number of accounting adjustments, including the capitalization of research and development.

14.   S. Penman and T. Sougiannis, "A Comparison of Dividend, Cash Flow, and Earnings Approaches to Equity Valuation," *Contemporary Accounting Research* (Fall 1998): 343–383, compares the valuation methods using actual realizations of earnings, cash flows, and dividends to estimate prices. J. Francis, P. Olsson, and D. Oswald, "Comparing Accuracy and Explainability of Dividend, Free Cash Flow, and Abnormal Earnings Equity Valuation Models," *Journal of Accounting Research* 38 (Spring 2000): 45–70, estimates values using *Value Line forecasts*.

15.   See C. Lee and J. Myers, "What is the Intrinsic Value of the Dow?" *The Journal of Finance* 54 (October 1999): 1693–1741.

APPENDIX A: ASSET VALUATION METHODOLOGIES

All of the valuation approaches discussed in this chapter can also be structured to estimate the value of a firm's net operating assets rather than its equity. Switching from equity valuation to asset valuation is often as simple as substituting financial measures related to equity for financial measures related to the entire firm. For example, in the earnings-based valuation model, net income (the earnings flow to equity) is replaced by NOPAT plus NIPAT (the earnings generated through operations and investments), and book values of business assets replace the book value of equity. Value multiples are based on ROEs for the equity formulation and on returns on operating assets for valuing asset multiples. And the discount rate for equity models is the cost of equity compared to the weighted average cost of capital (or WACC) for asset valuation models.

The formulas used for asset valuation under the various approaches are presented below.

Abnormal earnings valuation

Under the earnings-based approach, the value of business assets (operating plus investment assets) is:

$$\text{Business asset value}_0 = \text{BVA}_0 + \frac{\text{NOPAT}_1 + \text{NIPAT}_1 - \text{WACC} \cdot \text{BVA}_0}{(1 + \text{WACC})}$$
$$+ \frac{\text{NOPAT}_2 + \text{NIPAT}_2 - \text{WACC} \cdot \text{BVA}_1}{(1 + \text{WACC})^2} + \ldots$$

BVA is the book value of the firm's business assets, NOPAT is net operating profit (before interest) after tax, NIPAT is net investment profit after tax, and WACC is the firm's weighted-average cost of debt and equity. From this asset value the analyst can deduct the (after-tax) market value of debt to generate an estimate of the value of equity.

Similarly, the value of the operating assets is:

$$\text{Operating asset value}_0 = \text{BVNOA}_0 + \frac{\text{NOPAT}_1 - r_{\text{NOA}} \cdot \text{BVNOA}_0}{(1 + r_{\text{NOA}})} + \frac{\text{NOPAT}_2 - r_{\text{NOA}} \cdot \text{BVNOA}_1}{(1 + r_{\text{NOA}})^2} + \ldots$$

where BVNOA is the book value of the firm's net operating assets, NOPAT is net operating profit after tax, and r_{NOA} is the firm's required return on operating assets.

Valuation using price multiples

The multiple valuation can be structured as the debt plus equity value-to-book assets ratio by scaling the above business asset valuation formula by the book value of business assets. The valuation formula then becomes:

$$\text{Debt plus equity value-to-book ratio}_0 = 1 + \frac{\text{ROBA}_1 - \text{WACC}}{(1 + \text{WACC})} + \frac{(\text{ROBA}_2 - \text{WACC})(1 + g_1{}^{\text{assets}})}{(1 + \text{WACC})^2}$$
$$+ \frac{(\text{ROBA}_3 - \text{WACC})(1 + g_1{}^{\text{assets}})(1 + g_2{}^{\text{assets}})}{(1 + \text{WACC})^3} + \ldots$$

where

ROBA = return on business assets, as defined in Chapter 5.
WACC = weighted average cost of debt and equity
g_t^{assets} = growth in book value of business assets (BVA) from year $t-1$ to year t or

$$\frac{BVA_t - BVA_{t-1}}{BVA_{t-1}}$$

The value of a firm's business assets to the book value of the assets therefore depends on its ability to generate asset returns that exceed its WACC, and on its ability to grow its asset base. The value of equity under this approach is then the estimated multiple times the current book value of business assets less the (after-tax) market value of debt.

Discounted cash flow model

The free cash flow formulation can be structured by estimating the value of claims to net debt and equity and then deducting the market value of net debt. The value of debt plus equity is computed as follows:

Debt plus equity value$_0$ = PV of free cash flows from business assets

$$= \frac{NOPAT_1 + NIPAT_1 - \Delta BVA_1}{(1 + WACC)} + \frac{NOPAT_2 + NIPAT_2 - \Delta BVA_2}{(1 + WACC)^2} + \cdots$$

The firm's asset valuation therefore depends on the expected free cash flows from business assets during the forecast horizon, the forecasted terminal value of the free cash flows, and the weighted average cost of capital.

APPENDIX B: RECONCILING THE DISCOUNTED DIVIDENDS, DISCOUNTED ABNORMAL EARNINGS, AND DISCOUNTED ABNORMAL EARNINGS GROWTH MODELS

To derive the abnormal earnings model from the dividend discount model, consider the following two-period valuation:

$$\text{Equity value}_0 = \frac{\text{Dividend}_1}{(1 + r_e)} + \frac{\text{Dividend}_2}{(1 + r_e)^2}$$

With clean surplus accounting, dividends (*DIV*) can be expressed as a function of net profit (*NP*) and the book value of equity (*BVE*):

$$\text{Dividend}_t = \text{Net profit}_t + BVE_{t-1} - BVE_t$$

Substituting this expression into the dividend discount model yields the following:

$$\text{Equity value}_0 = \frac{\text{Net profit}_1 + BVE_0 - BVE_1}{(1 + r_e)} + \frac{\text{Net profit}_2 + BVE_1 - BVE_2}{(1 + r_e)^2}$$

This can be rewritten as follows:

$$\text{Equity value}_0 = \frac{\text{Net profit}_1 - r_e BVE_0 + (1 + r_e)BVE_0 - BVE_1}{(1 + r_e)}$$

$$+ \frac{\text{Net profit}_2 - r_e BVE_1 + (1 + r_e)BVE_1 - BVE_2}{(1 + r_e)^2}$$

$$= BVE_0 + \frac{\text{Net profit}_1 - r_e BVE_0}{(1 + r_e)} + \frac{\text{Net profit}_2 - r_e BVE_1}{(1 + r_e)^2} - \frac{BVE_2}{(1 + r_e)^2}$$

The value of equity is therefore the current book value plus the present value of future abnormal earnings. As the forecast horizon expands, the final term (the present value of liquidating book value) becomes inconsequential under the assumption that the long-term growth in the book value of equity is less than the cost of equity. A simple and appealing condition under which this assumption holds is when the firm has a constant dividend payout ratio.

To derive the abnormal earnings growth model from the dividend discount model consider the same two-period dividend model and express dividends in the second (and final) period as a function of net profit and first-period dividends:

$$\text{Dividend}_2 = \text{Net profit}_2 + \text{Net profit}_1 - \text{Dividend}_1$$

Substituting this expression into the dividend discount model yields the following:

$$\text{Equity value}_0 = \frac{\text{Net profit}_1 + \text{Dividend}_1 - \text{Net profit}_1}{(1 + r_e)} + \frac{\text{Net profit}_1 + \text{Net profit}_2 - \text{Dividend}_1}{(1 + r_e)^2}$$

This can be rewritten as follows:

$$\text{Equity value}_0 = \frac{\text{Net profit}_1}{(1 + r_e)} + \frac{\text{Net profit}_1}{(1 + r_e)^2} - \frac{(\text{Net profit}_1 - \text{Dividend}_1)(1 + r_e)}{(1 + r_e)^2}$$

$$+ \frac{(\text{Net profit}_2 - \text{Dividend}_1)}{(1 + r_e)^2}$$

$$= \frac{\text{Net profit}_1}{(1 + r_e)} + \frac{\text{Net profit}_1}{(1 + r_e)^2} + \frac{\text{Net profit}_2 + r_e\text{Dividend}_1 - (1 + r_e)\text{Net profit}_1}{(1 + r_e)^2}$$

The value of equity is therefore the capitalized value of first-period earnings plus the present value of second-period abnormal earnings growth. Note that in contrast to the abnormal earnings model, the abnormal earnings growth model does not assume clean surplus accounting.

TomTom's initial public offering: dud or nugget?

A pril 2005. Klaas van der Mullen was a bit dumbfounded. He had always put a lot of trust in the investment banks' opinions about the technology companies in which he was interested in investing. However, this time, the analyst's report was anything but useful. In essence, the author of the report practically acknowledged that he had no clue what the company was really worth – not a very comforting thought. From his ninth floor office in Amsterdam, Klaas managed a €500 million portfolio of high-technology, publicly listed companies. The fund's core strategy for outperforming its benchmark index was to invest selectively in the initial public offerings (IPOs) of high-potential companies. This buy-and-hold approach, often with investment horizons of five to seven years, had proven quite successful over the years. But, the IPO in front of him seemed to defy all traditional valuation approaches.

TomTom, a Dutch electronics company, had taken the European navigation market by storm with a series of recently launched commercial satellite navigation devices, also known as global positioning systems (GPSs). TomTom pioneered the concept of the fully integrated, handheld GPS, ready to use out of the box. With its ease of use, TomTom significantly enhanced the driving experience and the feeling of security in foreign cities; it effectively brought GPS to the masses, and its approach facilitated worldwide acceptance. The global market, which stood at some €800 million in 2004, was set to grow to €5 billion by 2010. With a 23 percent global market share, TomTom held a commanding lead in this exciting market.

Overall, the company seemed to have exactly what Klaas was looking for in a potential investee: It was a technology leader with strong potential in rapidly growing markets. The pending IPO would finally offer an opportunity to capitalize on TomTom. But was the initial offering price appropriate? Klaas was puzzled by the extreme range of the valuation provided by his favorite analyst at Fortis Bank: It valued the company from €1.8 billion to €3.1 billion. Klaas decided he would have to go through the whole valuation exercise on his own before deciding whether to invest in the IPO.

Klaas van der Mullen's track record as investment manager was stellar. Over the years, his approach to investing had generated peer-beating performances that helped him increase Assets under Management (AuM) to close to €500 million. The portfolio focused on high-technology, publicly-listed companies and relied on a proprietary screening approach, a combination of fundamental and momentum analyses, with a long-term buy-and-hold approach, to generate superior returns.

One of Klaas's favorite plays was to invest in IPOs of select technology companies, where he thought he had two significant advantages. First, he felt he was better able than anyone else was to analyze the true market potential of new, potentially disruptive technologies, and second, he had developed exceptional relationships with some of the lead technology underwriters in Europe over the years. These relationships were based on mutual respect. Klaas would freely discuss his insights on particular companies about to go public with the underwriters. In return, they would give him and his fund access to the IPOs they

IMD for the case study "TomTom's Initial Public Offering: Dud or Nugget?" by Benoit Leleux & Kudzanai Samushonga, IMD, Lausanne, Switzerland, 12 April 2011, copyright © 2009 by IMD, Lausanne, Switzerland. Reproduced with permission.

The case borrows from and builds on the case "TomTom: Building and Marketing A New Business Concept" (IMD-5-0735) by Dr Dominique Turpin, President and Nestle Professor at IMD.

were handling. He was also privileged to receive their early valuation reports on pending IPOs. In general, these reports provided expert opinions as to the probable valuation for a company going public. Combined with the IPO offering memorandum (a rather dull and legalistic document) and in-depth industry analyses, the analysts' reports helped validate Klaas's professional opinions.

The case of TomTom was a bit different, though, and definitely challenging. The company had enjoyed a beautiful run in the market for portable navigation devices (GPS). It pioneered the all-in-one product that was truly "plug-and-play" and easy to use. Consequently, sales had exploded, growing 400 percent in 2004 alone. In March 2005, TomTom's new products were the stars of CeBIT,[1] and the company hired an experienced CFO, clearly indicating it was on the road to a public listing. Sure enough, rumors quickly turned into facts when TomTom filed for an April 2005 IPO on the Amsterdam Stock Exchange. TomTom's impending floatation was a perfect fit with Klaas's investment strategy, so the company prominently featured on his radar screen.

The satellite navigation market: industry overview

Satellite navigation involved the transmission of GPS[2] signals from a network of 24 dedicated satellites (maintained by the US government) to appropriately configured receiver devices that translated the signals into position and direction data. Satellite navigation systems allowed a user to access real-time position information and features, such as route directions, instantaneous speed, time to destination, and mileage calculations, using a GPS receiver. The system consisted of a hardware device, a satellite signal receiver, and a highly accurate three-dimensional road map that allowed the digital position to be interpreted in terms of the local environment. These were integrated using navigational software that allowed locations and route calculations to be delivered through a user-friendly interface.

Two main segments existed in this industry:

1 **In-car navigation systems,** which were built into motor vehicle dashboards during assembly.
2 **Personal and portable navigation systems,** which were respectively electronic devices such as smartphones[3] and PDAs with installed navigation software or dedicated machines serving no other function but navigation.

Several technical factors limited the effectiveness of GPS technology. Because the signals transmitted by the GPS satellites were relatively weak, an accurate position reading required line-of-sight visibility between the receiver and at least three satellites. GPS signals could be blocked or disturbed by buildings, hills, dense vegetation, or tunnels or distorted by atmospheric conditions.

Since the late 1990s, the European Space Agency was also developing a new positioning network called Galileo that would be inter-operable with the GPS satellites. The first Galileo satellite was expected to be launched in 2006, with the full system of 30 dedicated positioning satellites to be fully deployed by 2010. Galileo's network was expected to augment the overall GPS signal accuracy. The impact Galileo would ultimately have on the market for positioning devices was still unknown.

In 2004, the market value for navigation devices was estimated at €800 million, but it was set to grow to €5 billion by 2010. While in-car navigation systems had been most popular so far, it was envisaged that personal and portable navigation would increase in popularity over the years owing to a combination of factors, such as: (1) technological improvements in memory and processing power; (2) increased affordability; (3) increased availability; (4) ease of use; and (5) the emergence of dynamic navigation, which allowed users to get updates on weather or traffic information while on the road through subscription services.

---

[1] CeBIT is the world's largest trade fair showcasing digital IT and telecommunications solutions for home and work environments. It offers an international platform for comparing notes on current industry trends, networking and product presentations. Deutsche Messe AG had been organizing the fair in Hannover each spring since 1986.

[2] GPS (global positioning system) is the global system that uses a number of satellite signals to calculate the exact location of the receiver. Usually GPS receivers use the signals of 7 to 12 satellites. In 2002, the US government stopped scrambling the satellite signals (for military reasons) and as a result, the signals became much more accurate (locating is now possible on a sub-five meter accuracy).

[3] A smartphone is a mobile phone offering advanced capabilities, often with PC-like functionality.

In-car Navigation

While industry analysts in general favored portable and smartphones as the navigational devices of the future, in-car navigation was expected to grow through factory-installed systems. Figure 7.1 illustrates the expected evolution of the market over the next three years.

The European market was much larger than its American counterpart. However, competition from personal navigation devices was increasing, so the market was expected to decrease over time (refer to Figures 7.2 and 7.3).

The in-car navigation market was further broken down into factory installed (line-fitted) systems and after-sales (retrofitted) systems. The proportion of new cars sold with factory fitted systems in 2004 stood at around 10 percent, despite massive promotional efforts by car producers. The adoption rate was expected to increase steadily, especially as the satellite navigation systems became an integrated part of the cars electronics. At this point, though, only 4 percent of the cars on European roads had line-fitted systems. The largest hold-up for growth in this industry was the prohibitive price of the systems, often billed to clients between €1,500 and €2,500 per system.

Personal navigation

While handheld navigation devices had been used in niche markets such as outdoor hiking and marine/aerospace applications, the mass market for such devices in cars remained largely untapped, with around €300 million in 2003 sales. With an estimated compound annual growth rate of 35 percent between 2005 and

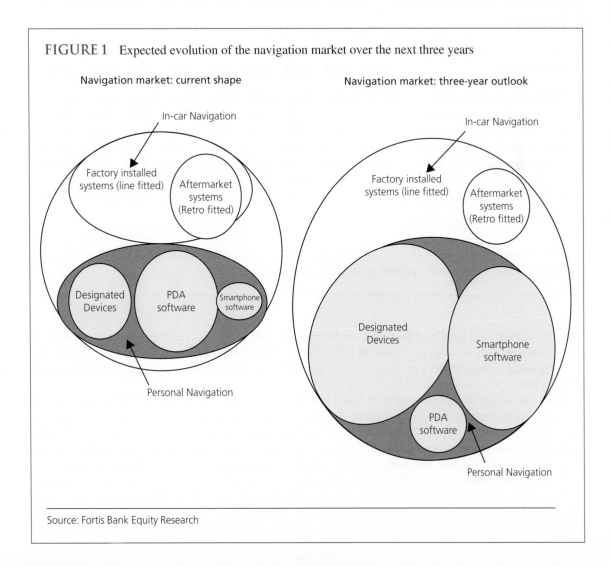

FIGURE 1   Expected evolution of the navigation market over the next three years

Source: Fortis Bank Equity Research

TomTom's initial public offering: dud or nugget?

FIGURE 2   European car park and navigation penetration

Million units	2002	2003	2004	2005	2006	2007	2008	2009	2010
Number of cars on the road	192.0	195.0	198.0	201.0	204.0	207.0	210.1	213.3	216.5
Installed base in-car navigation	3.8	5.7	7.9	9.5	11.4	13.6	16.1	19.1	22.5
Installed base personal navigation	0.4	1.2	3.2	6.0	10.1	15.6	23.6	34.8	50.2
% in-car navigation penetration	2.0%	2.9%	4.0%	4.7%	5.6%	6.6%	7.7%	8.9%	10.4%
% total navigation penetration	2.2%	3.5%	5.6%	7.8%	10.5%	14.1%	18.9%	25.3%	33.6%
number of new cars sold	14.0	14.2	14.5	14.7	14.9	15.0	15.1	15.1	15.1
% in-car navigation take rate (line fitted)	5.6%	7.4%	10.0%	12.0%	14.3%	17.0%	20.6%	24.8%	29.6%

Source: Fortis Bank

FIGURE 3   North American car park and navigation penetration

Million units	2002	2003	2004	2005	2006	2007	2008	2009	2010
Number of cars on the road	215.0	218.0	221.0	224.1	227.0	230.4	233.6	236.9	240.2
Installed base in-car navigation	0.6	1.3	2.2.	3.3	4.7	6.5	9.0	12.2	16.1
Installed base personal navigation	1.3	1.7	2.4	2.8	3.4	4.3	5.4	6.9	8.7
% in-car navigation penetration	0.3%	0.6%	1.0%	1.5%	2.0%	2.8%	3.8%	5.1%	6.7%
% total navigation penetration	0.9%	1.4%	2.1%	2.7%	3.5%	4.7%	6.2%	8.0%	10.3%
number of new cars sold	15.8	15.6	15.7	15.9	15.9	16.0	16.1	16.1	16.1
% in-car navigation take rate (line fitted)	1.9%	3.5%	5.4%	7.3%	9.7%	13.1%	18.2%	23.7%	29.6%

Source: JD Power, ACEA, ANFAC, Tele Atlas, NavTeq. Fortis Bank estimates

2010, the market was tipped to grow to sales of €5 billion by 2010. This was definitely the market TomTom intended to capitalize on with the TomTom GO – the windshield-mounted dedicated portable device. The use of personal navigation devices outside of cars by pedestrians and cyclists for example was expected to remain small for the foreseeable future.

Much like the mobile phone revolution had taken the mobile phone out of vehicles and onto the streets with evolving technology, navigation software ported onto PDAs and smartphones was expected to take satellite navigation out of the car (Figure 7.4). This would potentially bring huge gains for software vendors such as TomTom, but the Fortis valuation remained conservative on the estimates. It assumed that as prices dropped below €500 by 2006, the market for dedicated devices would begin to exceed that for software.

The **dedicated (integrated) device** was a sub-segment of the personal navigation market. It was envisioned that this would be the fastest growing segment of the navigation market, and it was forecasted to grow from 2004 sales of about 1 million units per year to 17 million units by 2010. In value terms, assuming 10 percent price erosion over this period, the market would grow from €550 million to €4.4 billion (Figure 7.5).

FIGURE 4   In-car navigation market – annual units sold

1,000 units	2002	2003	2004	2005	2006	2007	2008	2009	2010
European market									
Line fitted systems	790	1,050	1,450	1,760	2,124	2,562	3,108	3,742	4,479
Retrofitted systems	420	420	461	495	515	525	504	484	465
Total in-car systems	1,210	1,470	1,911	2,255	2,639	3,087	3,612	4,226	4,944
North American market									
Line fitted systems	300	550	850	1,150	1,553	2,096	2,934	3,814	4,768
Retrofitted systems	20	40	60	80	100	100	100	100	100
Total in-car systems	320	590	910	1,230	1,653	2,196	3,034	3,914	4,868

Source: NavTeq. Tele Atlas, JD Power, Fortis Bank estimates

FIGURE 5   Dedicated device market projection (1,000 units)

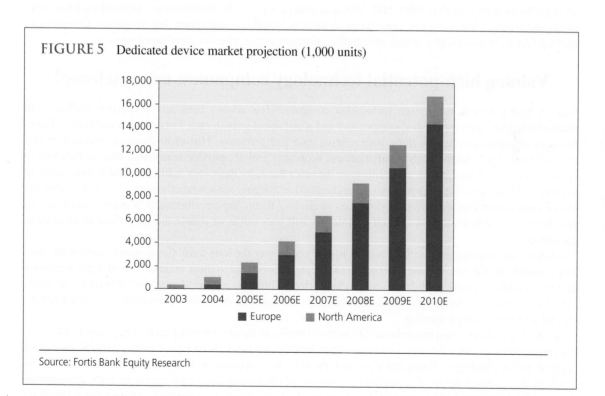

Source: Fortis Bank Equity Research

The devices generally shared their software with that used in PDAs and smartphones. However, they also featured larger, higher resolution touch screens, better sound systems, and user-friendly interfaces, which made them more popular for drivers. They were set to gain market share at the expense of in-car navigation because of their shorter product cycles, i.e., they could easily be upgraded whenever innovations in hardware and software were introduced, while in-car systems followed the car life cycles and generally lagged behind. They were also a lot cheaper, with an average price of €500 compared to the €1,000 to €2,000 that was common for in-car services.

TomTom's initial public offering: dud or nugget?

TomTom and the navigation market: 2002 to 2005

In 2002, TomTom launched its first satellite navigation software package for PDAs, the TomTom Navigator, just as US President Bill Clinton opened up the GPS system technology for non-military applications. The company's breakthrough was its ability to gain access to major European retailers, such as FNAC in France, Dixon's in the UK, and MediaMarkt in Germany and Switzerland. The first "bundled product" was launched in the Netherlands, and then rolled out to the UK, France, and Germany. By the end of 2002, the company had sold 45,000 units worth some €8.8 million. At that point, the company realized it had turned itself into a personal navigation company, not an "add-on to PDA" specialist. It was time to sever its linkages with the PDA platform and create an all-in-one navigation product.

Alexander Ribbink, a former vice president of brand development at Unilever and later a European portfolio director at Mars Inc., joined TomTom in November 2003 to drive the marketing of the growing range of products. The TomTom Navigator 2 reached the market in 2003. In the spring of 2004 the TomTom GO, the easiest to use and most portable stand-alone car navigation device ever, was introduced. The following autumn, TomTom launched MOBILE, a new navigation solution designed to turn smartphones into in-car navigators. The TomTom GO emerged as a best selling product with warm reception from customers and trade magazines. In the May-December 2004 period, 250,000 GO devices were sold, generating €115 million in sales. The company closed 2004 with revenues of €192 million, five times their 2003 revenues (€39 million).

In February 2005, Marina Wyatt joined the company as Chief Financial Officer (CFO). She had previous work experience with Colt Telecom and Psion in the UK, and joined TomTom to help it go public. At the March 2005 CeBIT, the company outlined a complete product range overhaul. The 2004 GO model was replaced by four new models (300, 500, 700, and Rider), varying by functionality, targeted customer segments and pricing. One of the key innovations in the new model line was connected navigation. Connectivity enabled GO users to subscribe to real-time traffic information and other location-based services.

Valuing high-potential technology companies: art or science?

Valuing high-potential, early-stage technology companies has always been an exceptional challenge. In mature industries, with established competitors and a stabilized growth rate, forecasting a company's future revenues or costs can often be done with relative ease and precision. Historical financial information and external market parameters, such as inflation and economic growth, provide reasonable base from which to support forecasts. Rapid growth companies, on the other hand, by their very nature, are much more difficult to predict. Their initial super-growth period and attractive margins are a winner's curse, and they eventually attract competition that will ultimately weaken or destroy them. Superperformance is often temporary and self-destructive. When and how the self-destruction will play out is of course the most difficult element to guesstimate.

Markets are dynamic entities; no situation is ever stable over the long term. Competitors continually challenge market incumbents, and the latter try to anticipate and respond to those attacks. The strategic responses to new entrants and new products affect product prices, volumes, market shares, and economies of scale. Establishing forecasts for revenues and costs becomes a complicated science of predicting consumer behavior and corporate strategic gaming.

Technology adds its own unpredictability to the exercise. In rapidly evolving technology-based industries, exciting inventions often become obsolete within months, giving way to newer generations of ever-more sophisticated technologies. Releasing a product ahead of the competition does not guarantee success; it can result in the cannibalization of a successful existing product portfolio. In the world of GPS navigational devices, the European Galileo project, for example, had the ability to completely change the technology landscape.

The regulatory framework in which companies operate also influences the industry's competitiveness. Trade unions for example could have an impact on the labor cost structure. On the one hand, the European Union opened a new and much bigger market with limited trade restrictions for TomTom products. On the other hand, it also meant that the social, political, and economic affairs of other countries within the union would have a bearing on interest and exchange rates across the region. This would impact the competitiveness of Euro zone exports in international markets.

The challenges did not stop at the forecasted cash flows. Once those were established with reasonable accuracy, they would have to be discounted back at an appropriate discount rate. Appropriate in this case meant that the discount rate accounted for both the riskiness of the cash flow projections as well as the consequent costs of the capital employed. Factored into this cost of capital are elements such as the expected risk-free rate of return, the expected market risk premium (MRP), and the beta – a measure of how the company's share price is moving relative to the market, or its systematic risk. In general, beta risk was evaluated for listed companies by simply measuring the historical relative volatility of the company vis-a-vis the market. For non-listed companies, the exercise was made more difficult by the need to identify exchange-listed "comparable" companies, and using their estimated betas as proxies for the unlisted company, with qualitative adjustments made to correct for the specific aspects that differentiated the company in question. In an emerging industry with few pure-play comparable listed companies, the game turned quickly into a sophisticated guesstimate.

TomTom and the Fortis valuation

What bothered Klaas on this particular target investment was the fact that the analysts seemed to be utterly puzzled by the company's future prospects. While they all agreed on the historical success of the firm and its unique positioning in the promising navigational systems market, they seemed to diverge massively on key assessments, particularly around value drivers. Not only did they disagree materially among themselves, but there were also instances of a single analyst providing an extremely broad range of valuations for the firm! The case at hand was the valuation report Klaas had received from the research department at Fortis Bank, one of the underwriters. Using multiples based on its peer companies, the report suggested valuations for TomTom from €1,879 million to €3,065 million. Using the popular discounted cash flow (DCF) method, the report showed enterprise values of between €1,993 million and €2,483 million, or a 25 percent estimation error. This range was at least twice as large as anything he had seen before on these pre-IPO analyst reports, and it was the direct result of the different valuation assumptions that were made, as highlighted in **Exhibit 7.1**. In general, people considered DCF a better valuation method to use in circumstances where comparable listed companies were either not available, were considered unreliable (for example due to insufficient liquidity) or just too different in terms of key operating parameters (such as growth rates). In all instances, DCF forced the evaluator to make explicit assumptions about the value drivers of a company, which was more desirable than the assumptions implicit in the valuations of listed companies. In a way, DCF was seen as more robust because it required a formal deconstruction of the valuation drivers for the company.

Fortis's valuation of TomTom led to a base case enterprise value of €2,231 million, detailed in Figures 7.6 to 7.8. The DCF model is presented in **Exhibit 7.2**. Klaas knew all too well that he should never rely on the analysts' assumptions when investigating the pricing of a particular IPO, particularly when the analyst was potentially conflicted, as was the case with Fortis, which was underwriting the IPO. Klaas felt he would

---

FIGURE 6   TomTom's 10-year forecast

Beta[4]	1.22
Risk free rate of return (10-year treasury bond)	4%
Market risk premium (MRP)[5]	4.5%
Weighted average cost of capital*	9.5%
Present value of discounted cash flows	€1,019m

* The weighted average cost of capital (WACC) was derived using the capital asset pricing model (CAPM). which can be presented as:
$$R_e = R_f + \beta\,(R_m - Rf) \text{ or } R_e = R_f + \beta\,(MRP)$$

---

[4]As the entity was financed completely by equity an unlevered beta was used based on an industry average sourced from Stem Stewart.
[5]The risk premium used is consistent for all valuations carried out by Fortis.

FIGURE 7 TomTom's terminal value

Cash flow in final forecast year	2,690
Expected annual growth in perpetuity	0%
Discount rate	9.5%
Discounted terminal value	€1,172m

FIGURE 8 TomTom's enterprise value

	€ million
Present value of discounted cash flows	1,019
Present value of terminal cash flow	1,172
Excess cash and marketable security	40
Enterprise value	2,231

---

have to go through the whole valuation exercise on his own, assessing the reasonableness of each and every assumption in light of his own understanding of the market.

Figure 7.9 shows the road map that Klaas drew up to guide him in navigating through the key external and internal assumptions he would consider challenging in the industry and company analyses. While the road map seemed to suggest that a step-by-step analysis could be carried out for each of the factors, the reality was that all aspects were so closely intertwined that they had to be evaluated jointly. Altering any one variable would have a bearing on one or more of the others. For example, assuming erosion in the average selling price would in reality result in a probable increase in sales volumes and a likely change in the market shares across competitors. No one factor, therefore, could be considered in isolation.

In addition, even though he prided himself for his extensive access to valuation and industry information, he was certainly no match for the much-celebrated Fortis research department. Fortis had an edge, so he would have to focus on the assumptions he considered the most relevant. All in all, he still hoped that his template would offer a good start for the exercise.

The revenue forecasts provided in the company's prospectus were based on market share estimates.[6] They reflected aggressive growth over the next ten years and made the -simple assumption that there would be no subsequent growth thereafter. While unsatisfactory, that assumption was required because there were no credible scenarios as to the likely growth rates beyond a ten-year horizon.

The market shares were derived by assessing TomTom's product portfolio and how well it had been doing in each product sub-category. The future growth rates were then predicted using current market shares as the base. Of course, these assumptions were easily challenged. A further decomposition of the revenue was necessary in order to show the relative contributions of the different products in the company's portfolio.[7] The assumptions regarding volumes and average sales prices also had to be re-evaluated.

Practically, the business was expected to experience an annual growth rate of 37 percent per annum between 2004 and 2010, with non-integrated software ultimately representing only 8 percent of revenues. The installed base revenues, initially insignificant, would overtake non-integrated software by 2008 to become the second largest revenue earner. Integrated devices would ultimately contribute approximately 80 percent of the revenues.

---

[6]The detailed market share estimates underlying the revenue forecasts can be found under **Exhibits 7.1** and **7.2** under the "penetration" tab in the electronic spreadsheet that accompanies the case, available from the authors.

[7]The relative contributions of the different products in the company's portfolio to revenues, as well as the estimates of sales prices and volumes, can be found in **Exhibit 7.3** under the "penetration" tab in the case electronic spreadsheet that accompanies the case, available from the authors.

FIGURE 9   Analysis of valuation assumptions

External considerations	Internal considerations
Markets	**Management team**
■ Geographies	■ Experience
■ Political and regulatory environments	■ Vision
■ Economic growth rates	■ Working relationship
■ Electronics industry growth forecasts	
■ Advances in technology	
Customers	**Revenue and growth rate**
■ Segments	■ Sales volumes
■ Trends	■ Average selling price
■ Buyer behavior and purchasing criteria	■ Product mix
■ Availability of substitute products and associated switching costs	■ Quality
	■ Geographic market
Competition	**Cost structure**
■ Market share	■ Key suppliers
■ Product offering	■ Sales and distribution channels
■ Key strategy	■ Advertising and promotion
■ Barriers to entry and exit	■ General administrative costs
	Operational
	■ Supply chain
	■ Outsourcing
	■ Investment in increased capacity

TomTom's initial public offering: dud or nugget?

For valuation purposes, this last point was clearly the most important: While a good understanding of the assumptions regarding all products was necessary, a detailed analysis of TomTom's product and market strategy in the integrated devices segment was clearly imperative to improve the valuation estimates.

TomTom GO

The TomTom GO became commercially available in May 2004. It integrated all hardware and software components into a single navigation device, providing a user interface based on touch screen, and route guidance instructions transmitted verbally and visually. Following a highly successful introduction, it was revamped in March 2005 when the new generation "GO 2005" models reached the market. Four products were created to serve four distinct segments: the 300, 500, 700, and Rider. The characteristics of each offering are summarized in Figure 7.10.

Rider was the most innovative new offering, a GO version for the motorcycle market. It offered larger, "glove ready" buttons and enhancements allowing motorcyclists to store and exchange routes with each other. All products shared a set of novel features: (1) subscription-based dynamic navigation or location services, which provided traffic, weather and safety camera information; (2) hands free calling and SMS functionality; and (3) easy software updates.

FIGURE 10   Expansion of the TomTom GO product family

Product type	2004 model	GO 300	GO 500	GO 700	Rider
Commercial Availability	May-04	April-05	2005 Q2	2005 Q2	Jun-05
Recommended retail price (€)	699	499	649	799	699
Map	Door to door within country/ region	Door to door within country/ region	Door to door within country/ region and cross border to towns and major roads across Europe	Door to door across Europe	Door to door within country/ region and cross border to towns and major roads across Europe
Hands-free calling			X	X	X
Remote control			optional	X	X
Ready for TomTom Plus		X	X	X	X
Enhanced software		X	X	X	X
Navigate out of the box	X	X	X	X	X

Source: Company brochures

Pricing strategy

In Q2 2004, TomTom set the recommended retail prices for its GO range of devices between €600 and €800 (*refer to* Figure 7.11), with an introductory price of €799 for the GO2004. This was in line with the competition and provided a healthy margin, of 27 percent for the retailer. As e-tailers started to undercut these prices, margins were subsequently reduced until the price settled around €650 in Q4 2004, translating into an average selling price for a TomTom device of €465.

While prices settled and demand remained high in the fourth quarter, TomTom reduced its prices even further to clear the distribution channel ahead of the launch of the GO2005 range. The average selling price of the GO2004 dropped to €434.

FIGURE 11   TomTom G0 2004 pricing strategy

	2004 Q2	2004 Q3	2004 Q4	2005 Q1
End user retail price	€799	€700	€650	€619
Retail price exc. VAT	€699	€586	€544	€518
TomTom net ASP	€487	€463	€435	€434
Retail gross margin	27%	21%	15%	16%

Source: Fortis prospectus

FIGURE 12   TomTom G0 2005 pricing strategy

Model	Unit share of sales	Recommended retail price €	Net average selling price €
GO300	35%	€499	€324
GO500	27%	€649	€422
GO700	35%	€799	€519
Rider	3%	€699	€454
Blended ASP			**€423**

Source: Fortis prospectus

Pricing for the GO2005 range was based on the results of the GO2004 campaign, and is shown in Figure 7.12.

A different sales mix from that predicted would result in a different average selling price (ASP). Changes in consumer purchasing power and the availability of cheaper substitutes would also impact the selling price. Generally, it was assumed that there would be an average erosion of 8 percent in 2006 and that this would increase to 12 percent by 2010.

Competition

The most significant competitors in the dedicated devices segment in Europe and the United States were Garmin, Magellan, Navigon, and Navman (*refer to* Figure 7.13). TomTom enjoyed the largest brand awareness while Garmin came second as a well-recognized supplier of quality navigation equipment. In its home market – the United States – Garmin enjoyed the greatest brand awareness. Magellan was a close second owing to a deal struck with car rental companies to install its device in their vehicles. Though no credible source for the North American market shares could be located, TomTom was believed to hold only a 2 percent market share in North America. It was, however, considered by its peers as a credible competitor due to its successful strategy in Europe (*refer to* Figure 7.14).

While considerable competition existed in this segment, TomTom was well ahead of its peers in terms of innovation. The majority of competing products still largely featured technology used in the TomTom GO2004. Enhanced services such as dynamic navigation were still to come.

TomTom Navigator

TomTom Navigator was the software product for third party personal digital assistants (PDAs). The product's sales revenues had grown in value from €5 million in 2002 to nearly €70 million in 2004 mainly as a result of successful bundle deals with all major PDA vendors.

Competition

Though TomTom enjoyed a 20 percent market share of the PDA software segment, management acknowledged that growth in this segment was likely to stagnate – 40 percent of PDA software buyers had not bought navigation software. A software deal had been struck with Hewlett Packard in early 2005 to bundle the software with the iPac Pocket PC. This was expected to sustain revenues, but growth was not forecasted to be significant in this segment.

TomTom's initial public offering: dud or nugget?

FIGURE 13   Dedicated device vendors

Manufacturer	Model	Software	Map provider
Garmin	Streetpilot c320	Garmin	Navteq
	Streetpilot c330	Garmin	Navteq
	Quest	Garmin	Navteq
	Streetpilot III	Garmin	Navteq
	Streetpilot 2620	Garmin	Navteq
	Streetpilot 2610	Garmin	Navteq
	Streetpilot 2650	Garmin	Navteq
	Streetpilot 2660	Garmin	Navteq
	Motorrad Navigator II	Garmin	Navteq
	Navus (GM Mopar)	Garmin	Navteq
Navman	ICN510	SmartST V3	TeleAtlas
	ICN630	SmartST V2	Tele Atlas
	ICN635	SmartST V3	TeleAtlas
	ICN650	SmartST V3	TeleAtlas
Navigon	Transonic 4000	MobileNavigator 5	Navteq,Tele Atlas
Magellan	Roadmate 300	Magellan	Navteq
	Roadmate 500	Magellan	Navteq
	Roadmate 700	Magellan	Navteq
	Roadmate 750	Magellan	Navteq

Source: Fortis Bank

TomTom Mobile

As smartphones gained popularity, TomTom introduced compatible navigation software through TomTom Mobile in September 2004. This was essentially the smartphone version of the PDA. Bundling deals with mobile operators such as Orange and Vodafone were used for distribution. The market's low adoption rate of smartphones meant that this market segment was not forecasted to provide significant growth. A foothold in the market was however necessary in order to ensure recognition if the mobile market were to take off in a few years.

Competition

The competition in the PDA software and smartphone software vendor segments was quite intense. The main vendors in the latter were TomTom, Navigon, Destinator, and ViaMichelin. TomTom stood out as having the most user-friendly products in various consumer tests; it also had superior access to the market through the bundle deals it had entered into with PDA vendors.

Fewer competitors existed in the smaller smartphone segment owing to its smaller market size. Distribution was again thought to be crucial as the distribution power resided with the mobile operators. Though TomTom had a bundle deal with Nokia, deals with Vodafone and Orange, actual telephone operators, were expected to be more potent given the large subsidies they provided on handsets.

TomTom Plus

TomTom Plus was the true innovation of 2005: a data subscription service that allowed dynamic navigation. Customers could obtain instantaneous updates on traffic conditions, weather or speed cameras, creating the

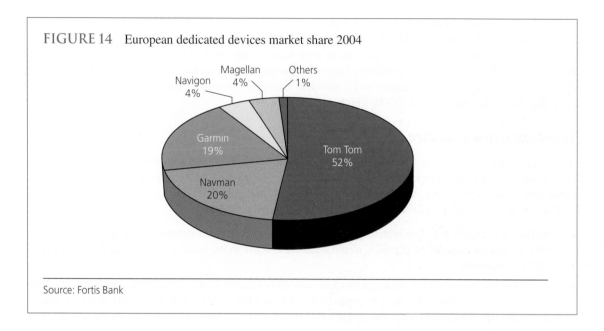

FIGURE 14 European dedicated devices market share 2004

Source: Fortis Bank

new concept of "connected navigation." The technology worked by creating a link between each TomTom device and a TomTom host server via a GPRS mobile phone with a standard Bluetooth connection.

Customers could sign up for a yearly subscription through their mobile phone providers. Competitors were bound to respond to this novelty, but TomTom planned to remain ahead by further enhancing the service, for example offering celebrity voices (Tom Selleck warning you about speed traps, President Chirac announcing a one-star Michelin restaurant coming up on the right, etc.), speed limit announcements or other value-adding services.

Services were expected over time to overtake the software business and generate at least €100 million in revenues by 2010. While management would aim to make the product a profit center on its own, it was viewed as key to driving hardware sales through packaged deals.

Competition

TomTom's main competitors, Garmin and Navman, did not offer such service yet. Some smaller players had developed a similar offering, but nobody else provided an integrated offering, and it was unlikely that customers would buy TomTom Plus for use with a different vendor's hardware.

In-car Navigation

Car dealers and manufacturers were acutely aware of the success of portable navigation devices (PND) over original equipment manufacturers (OEM) or retrofitted in-car navigation options. Since satellite navigation systems represented the most profitable optional item for many of them, the thought was extremely distressful. TomTom, for its part, believed that the cheaper and fancy PNDs could stimulate lower-end vehicle sales. Bundling deals had already been struck with Toyota and Opel for the Aygo and Corsa models respectively.

Competition

The market was best characterized as non-competitive. The multi-year deals that system vendors signed with vehicle manufacturers locked competition out. In Europe, Blaupunkt delivered systems to Mercedes-Benz and had the largest market share. Siemens' VDO served BMW and occupied the third position in terms of market share. Harman/Becker, a relative newcomer to the sector, had managed to gain market share mainly from Blaupunkt and established itself in second position. The incumbents were not totally free of worry. Serious competitive threats were appearing from a number of angles: Japanese vendors such as Pioneer, Melco, Alpine, and Denso were starting to bring in lower priced products and personal navigation vendors were providing cheaper substitutes that were upgraded more regularly.

The North American market had a similar profile, with Denso clinching the Toyota/Lexus contract, Alpine signing on with Honda, and Garmin with General Motors.

The retrofitted in-car systems were thought to pose more competition as the consumer purchased one of these only after buying a car. The prohibitive prices, however, made them less attractive. A system featuring dynamic navigation, hands-free calling and a seamless European coverage map would cost up to €1,900 – more than twice the price of the GO700, which retailed for €799.

TomTom's cost structure

Having analyzed the entity's revenue base, Klaas focused his attention on the expense and' margin forecasts. This would have a material bearing on the anticipated free cash flows that were used in the DCF valuation. Costs were forecasted as a percentage of revenue as depicted in Figure 7.15:

The following key assumptions were made to compute these numbers:

- TomTom was expected to continue to operate with an outsourced manufacturing, assembly, and logistics model, so that the majority of expenses would continue to relate to the costs of the contract manufacturers – the bills of materials.

- These bills of materials were expected to increase from 42 percent to 50 percent over the period 2004 to 2010 as the average selling price of a unit was expected to fall from €466 to €247. TomTom could, however, benefit from a reduction in manufacturing costs as GPS chip prices were also likely to go down over the period.

FIGURE 15 TomTom's cost structure

	2004	2005	2006	2007	2008	2009	2010
Cost of sales	**55.7%**	**56.0%**	**58.5%**	**59.3%**	**59.7%**	**59.9%**	**60.1%**
including							
Bill of material	42.1%	44.5%	47.7%	48.9%	49.3%	49.4%	49.5%
map royalties	10.0%	7.5%	6.8%	6.4%	6.4%	6.5%	6.6%
other	3.7%	4.0%	4.0%	4.0%	4.0%	4.0%	4.0%
Operating expenses	**21.7%**	**19.2%**	**20.5%**	**20.3%**	**20.1%**	**19.4%**	**19.3%**
including							
SGA	16.8%	15.2%	15.0%	14.9%	14.9%	14.8%	14.7%
of which marketing	10.2%	11.0%	11.0%	10.5%	10.2%	10.0%	10.0%
R&D	2.5%	3.2%	4.0%	4.1%	4.1%	4.1%	4.1%
Depreciation	0.4%	0.4%	30.0%	0.3%	0.4%	0.4%	0.3%
Amortization	1.9%	0.2%	1.1%	0.8%	0.6%	0.0%	0.0%
Other	0.2%	0.1%	0.1%	0.1%	0.1%	0.1%	0.2%
Total gross margin	44.3%	44.0%	41.5%	40.7%	40.3%	40.1%	39.9%
EBITDA margin	25.0%	25.6%	22.5%	21.7%	21.3%	21.2%	21.1%
REBIT margin	24.6%	25.2%	22.2%	21.4%	20.9%	20.8%	20.8%
EBIT margin	22.6%	24.8%	21.0%	20.4%	20.2%	20.7%	20.6%
Pre tax margin	22.2%	25.2%	21.4%	20.9%	20.9%	21.5%	21.5%
Net margin	**14.4%**	**17.4%**	**14.8%**	**14.7%**	**14.6%**	**15.1%**	**15.1%**

Source: Fortis estimates

[8]Tele Atlas estimated that up to 15 percent of road data changes every given year. Source: TomTomweb site.

- As a result of the falling average sales price, a decrease in the gross margin from 44 percent to 40 percent was anticipated.

- Map royalty fees were charged based on the number of devices sold. These fees were likely to fall as increases in sales volumes over the period enabled TomTom to re-negotiate quantity discounts.

- Marketing costs were expected to remain in line with sales as TomTom aggressively promoted its products to reach its growth targets.

- The historical research and development spend at 2.5 percent of sales was considered relatively low, and Fortis had anticipated this would have to be increased to 4.1 percent of sales by 2010.

Decision time

Armed with this information, Klaas now had to make a decision about what to do with the forthcoming IPO. Clearly, he liked the story behind TomTom. This had been one of the most remarkable technological success stories in The Netherlands. Growth rates were truly outstanding, and the company clearly had a long way to go. But exactly how long would these extravagant growth rates persist? How long would it take the competition to wake up and challenge TomTom's dominance? Yes, the company had been able to identify and serve its customers' needs better than anyone else. It had revolutionized the portable navigation device market, and brought it to the masses. Success is, however, a self-destructive force: it carries the seeds of its own demise. Growth attracts attention and jealousy. Second movers learn and improve from the first mover's mistakes and attack at a later stage with a superior product. Now that TomTom had shown the way, many companies could pounce and challenge the incumbent.

The challenges were numerous. First and foremost, what would be the navigation platform of the future? TomTom's winning formula was based on individuals preferring a dedicated, self-standing GPS device. Alternatives, such as GPS on smartphones or PDAs, were still rudimentary. How long would it take for Nokia, Sony Ericsson or Apple to take a run at the navigation market?

Second, the raw navigation data was, so far, provided by only two global competitors – Tele Atlas and Navteq. In other words, TomTom was dependent on third party providers for content. What if these companies ceased to exist or were acquired by competitors?

Third, while the content needed frequent updating,[8] the hardware was actually quite robust, requiring replacement only every five to seven years. What would happen once the population was significantly equipped?

Fourth, pressure on prices was intensifying. The days of €200 devices or lower were clearly closing in, pressuring margins further. Would they continue to be able to squeeze a margin out of such low prices? The reliance on third-party manufacturers had so far been a blessing, but would it continue to give them sufficient leverage to negotiate low enough prices?

Finally, Google successfully launched its internet map service in 2004. Rumors were circulating that a mobile version of Google Maps would be out by the third or fourth quarter of 2005. What would that do to the market? Some technology insiders were talking about Google actively trying to develop technologies using cell phone tower ID information to provide the triangulation needed to support location services, freeing the user from the satellite constraints altogether.

Putting all these dynamic (and elusive) assumptions into a single valuation model was less than obvious. Klaas was left with the unsavory feeling that the Fortis research team had relied a bit too much on history to predict the future. In the case of technology companies, history was most definitely a poor predictor of the future. TomTom had unleashed a dramatic industry shakedown, but would that shakedown turn it from instigator to victim? From experience, Klaas knew that companies were good at timing their IPOs to match the peak of their investor appeal. Furthermore, what would TomTom do with the IPO money? Would they start to invest in their own manufacturing facilities, new R&D capacities or what? What about the production of content, i.e., the maps on which the devices were based? Would Google be successful with the development of its mobile-signal based location services, rendering GPS devices obsolete?

Klaas hoped that uncertainty or, to be more precise, information asymmetries were tilted in his favor. This was, after all, the source of the superior performance of his fund so far. Practically, though, he still found the

[8]Tele Atlas estimated that up to 15 percent of road data changes every given year. Source: TomTomweb site.

degree of unpredictability of many of the value drivers in the TomTom business model disconcerting. He used to get a real kick out of off-the-wall companies, but not anymore. Maybe he was just growing older or simply more mature!

It was time for a well-deserved glass of Advocaat, a Dutch liqueur made from egg yolks, brandy, vanilla, and sugar. The sugar boost would most definitely carry him through the evening.

EXHIBIT 1 TomTom discounted cash flow analysis

	2004	2005	2006	2007	2008	2009	2010	2011	2012	2013	2014
Total revenue	192,429	408,766	649,824	829,986	1,015,881	1,166,193	1,316,536	1,448,189	1,571,285	1,689,132	1,773,589
% change	391.8%	112.4%	59.0%	27.7%	22.4%	14.8%	12.9%	10.0%	8.5%	7.5%	5.0%
EBITA	43,729	99,814	136,988	170,307	206,708	243,023	273,369	300,706	324,695	347,358	364,726
% change	331.1%	128.3%	37.2%	24.3%	21.4%	17.6%	12.5%	10.0%	8.0%	7.0%	5.0%
Adjusted cash tax	(3,730)	(23,063)	(38,408)	(49,089)	(61,386)	(73,709)	(83,468)	(90,212)	(97,408)	(104,207)	(109,418)
% tax rate	8.5%	23.1%	28.0%	28.8%	29.7%	30.3%	30.5%	30.0%	30.0%	30.0%	30.0%
NOPLAT	39,999	76,751	98,580	121,218	145,322	169,315	189,901	210,494	227,286	243,150	255,308
% change	331.2%	91.9%	28.4%	23.0%	19.9%	16.5%	12.2%	10.8%	8.0%	7.0%	5.0%
Change in working capital	(6,635)	(12,179)	(13,521)	(6,709)	(4,786)	(1,258)	2,632	(1,052)	(1,136)	(1,216)	(1,277)
Change in provisions	324										
Depreciation	836	1,786	2,222	2,800	3,675	4,210	4,420	4,420	4,420	4,420	4,420
Investments	(2,321)	(5,000)	(4,000)	(4,200)	(4,410)	(4,631)	(4,862)	(4,420)	(4,420)	(4,420)	(4,420)
Investments / Depreciation	277.6%	280.0%	180.0%	150.0%	120.0%	110.0%	110.0%	100.0%	100.0%	100.0%	100.0%
Intangible investments & acquisitions	(653)	(848)	(1,103)	(1,434)	(1,720)	(2,064)	(2,477)	(2,746)	(2,965)	(3,172)	(3,330)
Free cash flow	31,550	60,510	82,178	111,675	138,081	165,572	189,614	206,696	223,185	238,762	250,701
% change	358.2%	91.8%	35.8%	35.9%	23.6%	19.9%	14.5%	9.0%	8.0%	7.0%	5.0%
Discount factor	100.0%	98.5%	90.0%	82.2%	75.0%	68.5%	62.6%	57.2%	52.2%	47.7%	43.6%
Discounted free cash flow	31,550	59,602	73,960	91,797	103,561	113,417	118,698	118,230	116,503	113,889	109,306
Present value of free cash flows	**1,050,513**										

Source: Fortis Bank Equity Research

TomTom's initial public offering: dud or nugget?

EXHIBIT 2   **DCF sensitivity analysis base on integrated devices business (shareholder value in € million)**

CAGR ASP decline	Average market share of integrated devices in 2005–2011)						
	34%	35%	36%	37%	38%	39%	40%
2005–2010							
−8	2,381	2,394	2,412	2,429	2,446	2,459	2,483
−9	2,287	2,299	2,314	2,330	2,343	2,362	2,383
−10	2,187	2,200	2,215	2,331	2,244	2,262	2,284
−11	2,090	2,108	2,136	2,141	2,154	2,171	2,192
−12	1,990	2,008	2,045	2,060	2,079	2,139	2,156

Source: Fortis Bank

TomTom's initial public offering: dud or nugget?

EXHIBIT 3 TomTom profit & loss account (€1,000)

EUR 1,000	2005 Q1	2005 Q2	2005 Q3	2005 Q4	2004 E	2005 E	2006 E	2007 E
Integrated devices	46,970	92,400	82,485	112,718	115,624	334,573	564,004	721,617
Non-integrated software	16,337	16,380	13,440	10,474	68,760	56,631	53,721	55,305
Services and other	2,850	3,563	4,453	6,696	8,045	17,561	32,099	53,064
Total revenue	**66,157**	**112,343**	**100,378**	**129,888**	**192,429**	**408,766**	**649,824**	**829,986**
Cost of sales	35,028	63,474	55,710	74,697	107,192	228,909	380,147	492,181
Total gross profit	31,129	48,869	44,668	55,191	85,237	179,857	269,677	337,804
Sales, general & administrative	10,472	17,975	14,956	18,729	32,267	62,132	97,474	123,668
Research & development	1,764	2,664	3,744	4,909	4,796	13,081	25,993	34,029
Other operating expenses	–	330	330	340	3,609	1,000	7,000	7,000
Total operating expenses	12,236	20,969	19,030	23,978	40,672	76,213	130,466	164,697
EBITDA	**18,893**	**27,900**	**25,638**	**31,213**	**44,565**	**103,644**	**139,211**	**173,107**
Depreciation, amortization, impairments	454	552	552	651	1,128	2,210	2,835	3,696
Extraordinary income/expense	–	–	–	–				
Operating profit	**18,439**	**27,348**	**24,085**	**30,562**	**43,437**	**101,434**	**136,376**	**169,411**
Financial income (expense)	1,742	–1,000	300	698	–774	1,740	2,612	4,460
Pre-tax profit	20,181	26,348	25,385	31,260	42,663	103,174	138,988	173,870
Income tax expense	6,421	8,300	7,996	9,473	14,946	32,190	42,669	52,161
Net profit	**13,760**	**18,048**	**17,389**	**21,787**	**27,717**	**70,984**	**96,318**	**121,709**
REBIT	18,893	28,230	25,968	31,553	47,338	102,858	143,988	177,307

TomTom's initial public offering: dud or nugget?

TomTom's initial public offering: dud or nugget?

EXHIBIT 3 TomTom profit & loss account (€1,000)

EUR 1,000	2005 Q1	2005 Q2	2005 Q3	2005 Q4	2004 E	2005 E	2006 E	2007 E
Per share (EUR)	**2005 Q1**	**2005 Q2**	**2005 Q3**	**2005 Q4**	**2004 E**	**2005 E**	**2006 E**	**2007 E**
Avg. number of shares (1,000)	100,000	100,000	100,000	100,000	100,000	100,000	100,250	100,751
Net current EPS excl. extr.	0.14	0.19	0.18	0.22	0.29	0.73	0.99	1.24
% growth	585.0%	226.2%	118.1%	75.6%	339.6%	153.7%	35.1%	25.8%
EPS incl. extr. and amortization	0.14	0.18	0.17	0.22	0.28	0.71	0.96	1.21
% growth	621.2%	233.0%	118.9%	76.0%	348.4%	156.1%	35.4%	25.7%
Sales mix (%)								
Integrated devices	71.0%	82.2%	82.2%	86.8%	60.1%	81.8%	86.8%	86.9%
Non-integrated devices	24.7%	14.6%	13.4%	8.1%	35.7%	13.9%	8.3%	6.7%
Services and other	4.3%	3.2%	4.4%	5.2%	4.3%	4.3%	4.9%	6.4%
Total revenue	**100.0%**	**100.0%**	**100.0%**	**100.0%**	**100.0%**	**100.0%**	**100.0%**	**100.0%**
% change								
Integrated devices	17.7%	737.0%	142.7%	59.7%		189.4%	68.6%	27.9%
Non-integrated devices		−29.9%	−15.9%	−32.6%	83.9%	83.9%	−5.1%	2.9%
Services and other	936.4%	150.9%	54.5%	93.1%	365.3%	118.3%	82.8%	65.3%
Total revenue	**367.5%**	**213.5%**	**90.0%**	**45.0%**	**391.8%**	**112.4%**	**59.0%**	**27.7%**
Margin analysis								
Total gross margin	47.1%	43.5%	44.5%	42.6%	44.3%	44.0%	41.5%	40.7%
EBITDA margin	28.6%	24.8%	25.5%	24.0%	23.2%	25.4%	21.4%	20.9%
REBIT margin	28.6%	25.1%	25.9%	24.3%	24.6%	25.2%	22.2%	24.4%
EBIT margin	27.9%	24.3%	25.0%	23.5%	22.6%	24.8%	21.0%	20.4%
Net margin excl. extr	20.8%	16.1%	17.3%	16.8%	14.4%	17.%	14.8%	14.7%
Tax rate	31.8%	31.5%	31.5%	30.3%	35.0%	31.2%	30.7%	30.0%

Source: Fortis Bank estimates

EXHIBIT 4 TomTom balance sheet

EUR 1,000	2003	2004	2005 E	2006 E	2007 E	2008 E	2009 E	2010 E
Tangible fixed assets	565	2,050	5,264	7,042	8,442	9,177	9,598	10,040
Intangible fixed assets	600	959	1,383	1,873	2,411	2,902	3,246	3,246
Total fixed assets	1,165	3,009	6,648	8,915	10,853	12,079	12,844	13,286
Inventory	2,218	13,402	26,878	40,948	50,027	58,448	63,901	68,532
Trade receivables	9,076	29,383	64,955	103,260	131,888	160,036	182,118	201,989
Other receivables & tax assets	1,508	4,436	4,436	4,436	4,436	4,436	4,436	4,436
Prepaid expenses	97	539	539	539	539	539	539	539
Total current assets	12,899	47,760	96,807	149,182	186,890	223,459	250,994	275,496
Cash & cash equivalents	6,896	40,168	104,697	196,473	319,593	470,459	645,594	847,971
Total assets	**20,960**	**90,937**	**208,152**	**354,571**	**517,336**	**705,998**	**909,433**	**1,136,754**
Shareholders' equity	7,593	37,806	109,790	213,108	341,818	496,413	672,030	870,599
Minority interest	–	–	–	–	–	–	–	–
Total shareholders' equity	7,593	37,806	109,790	213,108	341,818	496,413	672,030	870,599
Trade creditors	6,982	25,608	55,995	89,017	113,697	139,162	159,753	180,347
Taxes and social securities	2,952	12,867	21,231	25,477	28,534	30,817	32,357	33,975
Bank debt	–	–	–	–	–	–	–	–
Other liabilities	3,363	12,961	19,442	25,274	31,592	37,911	43,598	50,137
Total current liabilities	13,297	51,436	96,667	139,768	173,823	207,889	235,707	264,460
Provisions	70	394	394	394	394	394	394	394
Long-term interest-bearing debt	–	–	–	–	–	–	–	–
Deferred tax liabilities	–	1,301	1,301	1,301	1,301	1,301	1,301	1,301
Total non-current liabilities	70	1,695	1,695	1,695	1,695	1,695	1,695	1,695
Total liabilities & equity	**20,960**	**90,937**	**208,152**	**354,571**	**517,336**	**705,998**	**909,433**	**1,136,754**
Net DSO	85	56	58	58	58	57.5	57	56
Creditor days, year end	65	49	50	50	50	50	50	50
Inventory days	21	25	24	23	22	21	20	19

Source: Fortis Bank estimates

TomTom's initial public offering: dud or nugget?

EXHIBIT 5 TomTom cash flow statement

	2003	2004	2005 E	2006 E	2007 E	2008 E	2009 E	2010 E
EBIT	9,969	4,347	101,434	136,375	169,411	205,479	241,303	270,892
Depreciation & amortization	381	1,128	2,210	2,835	3,696	4,904	5,930	6,897
Net working capital movement	−1,684	−6,635	−12,179	−13,521	−6,709	−4,786	−1,258	2,632
Tax, provisions, interest, other	−1,219	1,669	21,087	28,811	−37,644	48,601	−64,146	−70,705
Operating cash flow	**7,447**	**36,261**	**70,378**	**96,878**	**128,753**	**156,996**	**181,830**	**209,716**
Investments in intangibles	−438	−653	−848	−1,103	−1,434	−1,720	−2,064	−2,477
Purchase of property, plant and equipment	−545	−2,321	−5,000	−4,000	−4,200	−4,410	−4,631	−4.862
Investing cash flow	−983	−2,974	−5,848	−5,103	−5,634	−6,130	−6,695	−7,339
Free cash flow	**6,464**	**33,288**	**64,529**	**91,776**	**123,120**	**150,866**	**175,135**	**202,377**
Distribution of dividend	−400	–	–	–	–	–	–	–
Issue of common stock	–	–	–	–	–	–	–	–
Change in minority interest	–	–	–	–	–	–	–	–
Change in interest bearing debt	−6	–	–	–	–	–	–	–
Legal & translation adjustment	30	−15	–	–	–	–	–	–
Financing cash flow	−376	−15	–	–	–	–	–	–
Net increase in cash	**6,088**	**33,273**	**64,529**	**91,776**	**123,120**	**150,866**	**175,135**	**202,377**

Source: Fortis Bank estimates

EXHIBIT 6   **Garmin – key financials (US$1,000)**

US $1,000	2002	2003	2004	2005 E
Total group operations				
Total revenue (US $1,000)	465,144	572,989	762,549	900,000
% change	26.0%	23.2%	33.1%	18.0%
Total units sold (1,000)	1,557	2,066	2,306	
% change	0.0%	32.7%	11.6%	
ASP (US$)	299	277	331	
% change	0.0%	–7.2%	19.2%	
Gross margin	54.8%	57.7%	53.9%	53.0%
EBIT margin	38.1%	39.6%	35.5%	33.5%
Net cash from operations (US$ 1,000)	175,408	175,180	204,100	
as % of revenue	37.7%	30.6%	26.8%	
DSO	46	53	53	
Inventory days	45	62	74	
R&D expenses	32,163	43,706	61,580	75,436
as % of revenue	6.9%	7.6%	8.1%	8.4%
Advertising costs	16,670	22,071	29,577	
as % of revenue	3.6%	3.9%	3.9%	
Consumer segment	**2002**	**2003**	**2004**	**2005 E**
Net sales	350,674	452,437	591,023	697,407
% change	33.2%	29.0%	30.6%	18.0%
Gross profit	184,544	253,153	304,217	341,729
SG&A	35,114	47,113	60,942	71,912
R&D	18,863	22,195	31,684	38,813
Total operating expenses	53,977	69,308	92,626	110,724
EBIT	130,567	183,845	211,591	231,005
Pre-tax income	134,859	182,701	196,326	231,005
Gross margin	52.6%	56.0%	51.5%	49.0%
Operating margin	37.2%	40.6%	35.8%	33.1%
Pre-tax margin	38.5%	40.4%	33.2%	33.1%
SG&A as % of net sales	10.0%	10.4%	10.3%	10.3%
R&D as % of net sales	5.4%	4.9%	5.4%	5.6%
DSO	46	53	53	
Inventory days	45	62	74	

Source: Garmin, Fortis Bank estimates

TomTom's initial public offering: dud or nugget?

TomTom's initial public offering: dud or nugget?

EXHIBIT 7   Navigation markets

European Navigation Market

1,000 units	2001	2002	2003	2004	2005 E	2006 E	2007 E	2008 E	2009 E	2010 E
In-car navigation	980	1,210	1,470	1,911	2,255	2,638	3,087	3,612	4,226	4,944
of which line-fitted	650	790	1,050	1,450	1,760	2,124	2,562	3,108	3,742	4,479
of which retro-fitted	330	420	420	461	495	515	525	504	484	465
Personal navigation		100	900	2,652	3,832	5,845	8,498	12,710	18,324	25,807
of which dedicated devices		–	100	452	1,483	3,113	5,137	7,706	10,788	14,671
of which non-integrated software		100	800	2,200	2,349	2,732	3,361	5,004	7,537	11,136
Total navigation market	**980**	**1,310**	**2,370**	**4,563**	**6,087**	**8,484**	**11,585**	**16,321**	**22,550**	**30,751**
% mix										
In-car navigation	100%	92%	62%	42%	37%	31%	27%	22%	19%	16%
of which line-fitted	66%	60%	44%	32%	29%	25%	22%	19%	17%	15%
of which retro-fitted	34%	32%	18%	10%	8%	6%	5%	3%	2%	2%
Personal navigation	0%	8%	38%	58%	63%	69%	73%	78%	81%	84%
of which dedicated devices	0%	0%	4%	10%	24%	37%	44%	47%	48%	48%
of which non-integrated software	0%	8%	34%	48%	39%	32%	29%	31%	33%	36%
Total navigation market	**100.0%**	**100.0%**	**100.0%**	**100.0%.**	**100.0%**	**100.0%**	**100.0%**	**100.0%**	**100.0%**	**100.0%**
% change										
In-car navigation	24.1%	23.5%	21.5%	30.0%	18.0%	17.0%	17.0%	17.0%	17.0%	17.0%
of which line-fitted	22.6%	21.5%	32.9%	38.1%	21.4%	20.7%	20.6%	21.3%	20.4%	19.7%
of which retro-fitted	26.9%	27.3%	0.0%	9.8%	7.4%	4.0%	2.0%	-4.0%	-4.0%	-4.0%
Personal navigation			800.0%	194.7%	44.5%	52.5%	45.4%	49.6%	44.2%	40.8%
of which dedicated devices				352.0%	228.0%	110.0%	65.0%	50.0%	40.0%	36.0%
of which non-integrated software			700.0%	175.0%	6.8%	16.3%	23.0%	48.9%	50.6%	47.8%
Total navigation market	**24.1%**	**33.7%**	**80.9%**	**92.5%**	**33.4%**	**39.4%**	**36.6%**	**40.9%**	**38.2%**	**36.4%**

EXHIBIT 7   Navigation markets

North American Navigation Market

1,000 units	2001	2002	2003	2004	2005 E	2006 E	2007 E	2008 E	2009 E	2010 E
In-car navigation	185	320	590	910	1,230	1,653	2,196	3,034	3,914	4,868
of which line-fitted	175	300	550	850	1,150	1,553	2,096	2,934	3,814	4,768
of which retro-fitted	10	20	40	60	80	100	100	100	100	100
Personal navigation	–	–	300	700	1,050	1,450	1,913	2,415	3,066	3,914
of which dedicated devices			205	540	800	1,050	1,313	1,575	1,890	2,268
of which non-integrated software			95	160	250	400	600	840	1,176	1,646
Total navigation market	**185**	**320**	**890**	**1,610**	**2,280**	**3,103**	**4,108**	**5,449**	**6,980**	**8,783**
% mix										
In-car navigation	100.0%	100.0%	66.3%	56.5%	53.9%	53.3%	53.4%,	55.7%	56.1%	55.4%
of which line-fitted	94.6%	93.8)	61.8%	52.8%	50.4%	50.0%	51.0%	53.8%	54.6%	54.3%
of which retro-fitted	5.4%	6.3%	4.5%	3.7%	3.5%	3.2%	2.4%	1.8%	1.4%	1.1%
Personal navigation	0.0%	0.0%	33.7%	43.5%	46.1%	46.7%	46.6%	44.3%	43.9%	44.6%
of which dedicated devices	0.0%	0.0%	23.0%	33.5%	35.1%	33.8%	31.9%	28.9%	27.1%	25.8%
of which non-integrated software	0.0%	0.0%	10.7%	9.9%	11.0%	12.9%	14.6%	15.4%,	16.8%	18.7%
Total navigation market	**100.0%**	**100.0%**	**100.0%**	**100.0%**	**100.0%**	**100.0%**	**100.0%**	**100.0%**	**100.0%**	**100.0%**
% change										
In-car navigation	32.1%	73.0%	84.4%	54.2%	35.2%	34.3%	32.9%	38.2%	29.0%	24.4%
of which line-fitted	29.6%	71.4%	83.3%	54.5%	35.3%	35.0%	35.0%	40.0%	30.0%	25.0%
of which retro-fitted				50.0%	33.3%	25.0%	0.0%	0.0%	0.0%	0.0%,
Personal navigation					50.0%	38.1%	31.9%	26.3%	27.0%	27.7%
of which dedicated devices				163.4%	48.1%	31.3%	25.0%	20.0%	20.0%	20.0%
of which non-integrated software					56.3%	60.0%	50.0%	40.0%	40.0%,	40.0%
Total navigation market	**32.1%**	**73.0%**	**178.1%**	**80.9%**	**41.6%**	**36.1%**	**32.4%**	**32.6%**	**28.1%**	**25.8%**

Source: NavTeq. Tele Atlas, Canalys. JD Power. ABI and Fortis Bank estimates

TomTom's initial public offering: dud or nugget?

8

Prospective Analysis: Valuation Implementation

To move from the valuation theory discussed in the previous chapter to the actual task of valuing a company, we have to deal with three key issues. First, we have to estimate the cost of capital to discount our forecasts. Second, we have to make forecasts of financial performance stated in terms of abnormal earnings and book values, or free cash flows, over the life of the firm. And third, we need to choose between an equity valuation or an asset valuation approach and understand the consequences of this choice. Figure 8.1 displays a condensed "fair-value" balance sheet, including the (primary) performance forecasts and discount rates used to value assets and claims. This figure shows that there are various approaches that an analyst can follow to value a firm's equity. Possible valuation approaches are:

- To value the firm's equity directly as, for example, the sum of its book value of equity and the present value of forecasted net profits, discounted at the cost of equity.

- To value the firm's business assets as the sum of these assets' book values and the present value of forecasted NOPAT plus NIPAT – discounted at the weighted average cost of capital – first and then calculate equity value as the difference between the value of business assets and the after-tax value of debt claims. As we will discuss in this chapter, this (business) asset valuation approach is a useful alternative to the equity valuation approach, especially if the analyst anticipates significant changes in leverage over the forecast horizon.

- To separately value operating assets as the sum of these assets' book values and the present value of forecasted NOPAT – discounted at the **required return on operating assets** – first and then calculate equity value as the sum of the value of operating assets and the value of investment assets minus the after-tax value of debt claims. This (operating) asset valuation approach is especially useful if the value of investment assets can be easily obtained from the financial statements and/or if the analyst anticipates significant changes in the relative size of investment assets over the forecast horizon.

The first part of this chapter provides guidance on calculating the discount rates used under each of these three approaches: the cost of equity (equity valuation), the weighted average cost of capital (business asset valuation), and the required return on operating assets (operating asset valuation). The second part of this chapter explains that the forecasting task itself is divided into two subcomponents: (1) detailed forecasts over a finite number of years and (2) a forecast of terminal value, which represents a summary forecast of performance beyond the period of detailed forecasts. This part builds on the forecast developed in Chapter 6 and provides guidance on computing a terminal value and synthesizing the different pieces of the analytical process to estimate firm or equity value.

COMPUTING A DISCOUNT RATE

To value a company's equity (directly), the analyst discounts abnormal earnings (growth), abnormal ROE, or cash flows available to equity holders. The proper discount rate to use is the cost of equity.

FIGURE 8.1 Condensed fair-value balance sheet

	Assets			Claims	
Asset	Primary performance forecast	Discount rate	Claim	Primary performance forecast	Discount rate
Value of operating assets	NOPAT	Required return on operating assets (r_{NOA})	After-tax value of debt claims	(1 – tax rate) × Interest expense	Cost of debt (r_D)
+ Value of investment assets	+ NIPAT	Required return on investment assets (r_{NIA})	+ Value of equity claim	+ Net profit	Cost of equity (r_E)
= Total value of business assets	= NOPAT + NIPAT	Weighted average cost of capital (WACC)	= Total value of capital claims	= Net profit + (1 – tax rate) × Interest expense	Weighted average cost of capital (WACC)

Estimating the cost of equity

Estimating the **cost of equity** (r_e) can be difficult, and a full discussion of the topic lies beyond the scope of this chapter. In any case, even an extended discussion would not supply answers to all the questions that might be raised in this area because the field of finance is in a state of flux over what constitutes an appropriate measure of the cost of equity.

The capital asset pricing model

One common approach to estimating the cost of equity is to use the **capital asset pricing model** (CAPM). The main idea of the CAPM is that investors holding a portfolio of investments (only) care about – and thus want to be compensated for – the risk that an asset contributes to the portfolio. This type of risk, labeled beta or systematic risk, is the risk created by the correlation between the asset's return and the returns of the other investments in the portfolio. The CAPM therefore expresses the cost of equity as the sum of a required return on riskless assets plus a premium for beta or systematic risk:

$$r_e = r_f + \beta[E(r_m) - r_f]$$

where r_f is the riskless rate; $[E(r_m) - r_f]$ is the risk premium expected for the market as a whole, expressed as the excess of the expected return on the market index over the riskless rate; and β is the systematic risk of the equity.

To compute r_e one must estimate three parameters: the riskless rate, r_f, the market risk premium $[E(r_m) - r_f]$, and systematic risk, β. To estimate the required return on riskless assets, analysts often use the rate on intermediate-term government bonds, based on the observation that it is cash flows beyond the short-term that are being discounted.[1] Theory calls for the use of a short-term rate, but if that rate is used here, a difficult practical question arises: how does one reflect the premium required for expected inflation over long horizons? While the premium could, in principle, be treated as a portion of the term $[E(r_m) - r_f]$, it is probably easier to use an intermediate- or long-term riskless rate that presumably reflects expected inflation.

The systematic or beta risk (β) of a share reflects the sensitivity of its cash flows and earnings (and hence stock price) to economy-wide market movements.[2] A firm whose performance increases or decreases at the same rate as changes in the economy as a whole will have a beta of one. Firms whose performance is highly sensitive to economy-wide changes, such as luxury goods producers, capital goods manufacturers, and construction firms, will have beta risks that exceed one. And firms whose earnings and cash flows are less sensitive to economic changes, such as regulated utilities or supermarkets, will have betas that are lower than one. Financial services firms, such as Bloomberg and Thomson Financial, provide estimates of beta for publicly-listed companies that are based on the historical relation between the firm's stock returns and the returns on the market index. These estimates provide a useful way to assess publicly-traded firms' beta risks. For firms that are not publicly-traded, analysts can use betas for publicly-traded firms in the same industries, adjusting for any differences in financial leverage, as an indicator of the likely beta risk.

APPAREL RETAILERS' BETAS

One way to estimate systematic risk is to regress the firm's stock returns over some recent time period against the returns on the market index. In this regression the slope coefficient on the market index represents an estimate of a company's (historical) β. Using monthly returns on the MSCI World index as the measure for market returns, the estimated relationship between Hennes & Mauritz's monthly stock returns and the market index between January 2007 and December 2011 is as follows:

$$\text{Monthly return H\&M} = 0.13 + 0.43 \times \text{Monthly market return} \ (R^2 = 13.5\%)$$

This equation indicates that H&M's historical beta estimate is 0.43. When changing the starting year of the estimation period from 2007 to years between 2000 and 2006, the beta estimate remains relatively stable and averages to 0.49. Based on these results, we assume that the best estimate of H&M's future beta is 0.45.

Similar regressions estimated using the monthly stock returns of Inditex and the other industry peers indicate than Inditex's equity beta is close to 0.65. The value-weighted average equity beta of the other industry peers is approximately 0.9, confirming the cyclicality of the apparel industry.

Finally, the market risk premium is the amount that investors demand as additional return for bearing beta risk. It is the excess of the expected return on the market index over the riskless rate r_f. When r_f is measured as the rate on intermediate-term government bonds, then average worldwide common stock returns (based on the returns to a 19-country, common-currency equity index) have exceeded that rate by 5.0 percent over the 1900–2010 period.[3] This excess return constitutes an estimate of the market risk premium $[E(r_m) - r_f]$. Based on the risk premium's historical means and variances between 1900 and 2010, one study reports that plausible estimates of future market risk premiums for the "world market," Europe, and the UK are somewhere around 5.0, 5.3, and 5.4 percent, respectively. However, it is important to realize that the market risk premium has varied substantially across countries and will likely continue to do so, albeit to a lesser degree when worldwide stock markets will further integrate and worldwide disclosure and securities regulation will be further harmonized.[4] In addition, while the historical risk premium has been calculated over a long time period, the premium is likely to change over time because of, for example, the changing risk preferences of investors.

HENNES & MAURITZ'S RISK PREMIUM

At the end of 2011, the yield on ten-year government bonds in the euro area was close to 4.3 percent (Source: Eurostat). The long-term historical average return on European governments bonds between 1900 and 2010 has been approximately 4.8 percent. Using the long-term average bond return as a measure for the risk-free rate and assuming that the market risk premium equals 5.3 percent, the CAPM-based estimate of H&M's cost of equity equals,

$$\text{Cost of equity} = 4.8 \text{ percent } (r_f) + 0.45(\beta) \times 5.3 \text{ percent } (E(r_m) - r_f) = 7.19 \text{ percent}$$

The firm size effect

Although the above CAPM is often used to estimate the cost of capital, the evidence indicates that the model is incomplete. Assuming stocks are priced competitively, stock returns should be expected just to compensate investors for the cost of their capital. Thus long-run average returns should be close to the cost of capital and should (according to the CAPM) vary across stocks according to their systematic risk. However, factors beyond just systematic risk seem to play some role in explaining variation in long-run average returns. The most important such factor is labeled the "size effect": smaller firms (as measured by market capitalization) tend to generate higher returns in subsequent periods.[5] Why this is so is unclear. It could mean either that smaller firms are riskier than indicated by the CAPM or that they are underpriced at the point their market capitalization is measured, or some combination of both.

Average stock returns for European firms (from the 17 European countries described in Chapter 1) varied across size deciles from 1990 to 2010 as shown in Table 8.1. The table shows that, historically, investors in firms in the two smallest size deciles of the size distribution have realized returns that are, on average, 5.1 to 9.1 percent higher than the returns earned in the top size decile. Note, however, that if we use firm size as an indicator of the cost of capital, we are implicitly assuming that large size is indicative of lower risk. Yet finance theorists have not developed a well-accepted explanation for why that should be the case.

One method for combining the cost of capital estimates is based on the CAPM and the "size effect." The approach calls for adjustment of the CAPM-based cost of capital, based on the difference between the average return on the market index used in the CAPM and the average return on firms of size comparable to the firm being evaluated. The resulting cost of capital is:

$$r_e = r_f + \beta[E(r_m) - r_f] + r_{SIZE}$$

In light of the continuing debate on how to measure the cost of capital, it is not surprising that managers and analysts often consider a range of estimates. In addition to the question about whether or not the historical risk premium of about 5 percent is valid today,[6] there is debate over whether beta is a relevant measure of risk, and whether other metrics such as size should be reflected in cost of capital estimates. Since these debates are still unresolved, it is prudent for analysts to use a range of risk premium estimates in computing a firm's cost of capital.

TABLE 8.1 European firms' stock returns and firm size

Size deciles	Market value of largest company in decile, in 2010 (€ millions)	Average premium 1990–2010 (% return differential with decile 10)
1-small	7.9	9.1%
2	17.3	5.1%
3	29.5	1.8%
4	52.3	3.2%
5	91.5	2.1%
6	179.4	1.3%
7	377.7	1.6%
8	864.7	0.3%
9	2,698.6	1.3%
10-large	128,885.9	0.0%

Source: Duff & Phelps' European Risk Premium Report 2011.

HENNES & MAURITZ'S SIZE PREMIUM

At the end of 2011, the market value of H&M's shares was approximately €38,309 million (SEK354,185 million), down from €42,529 million in 2010 due to the overall market decline. Although the equity value that we estimate for Hennes & Mauritz may deviate from its market price, this value is likely to fall within the top size decile of the European market. Consequently, it is unnecessary to adjust H&M's cost of equity estimate for a size effect.

Adjusting the cost of equity for changes in leverage

The beta risk of a firm's equity changes as a function of its leverage. As the leverage increases, the sensitivity of the firm's equity performance to economy-wide changes also increases. To see this, recall from Chapter 5 that return on equity (ROE) can be decomposed in the following manner:

$$\text{ROE} = \text{Return on business assets} +$$

$$(\text{Return on business assets} - \text{Effective interest rate after tax}) \times \frac{\text{Net debt}}{\text{Equity}}$$

This equation shows that if net debt equals equity, a 2 percent increase in return on business assets (ROBA) after an economy-wide recovery will increase ROE by 4 percent, all else equal. In contrast, if net debt is two times equity, the same increase in ROBA will increase ROE by 6 percent. Hence, the equity beta of a firm does not only reflect the sensitivity of its assets' performance to economy-wide movements (labeled **asset beta**) but also the net financial leverage effect on its equity performance. If an analyst is contemplating changing capital structure during the forecasting period relative to the historical capital structure of the firm, or changing the capital structure over time during the forecasting period, it is important to re-estimate the equity beta and to take these changes into account. We describe below a simple approach to this task.

We begin with the observation that the beta of a portfolio of assets is the weighted average of the assets' individual betas. Similarly, the beta of a firm's business assets is equal to the weighted average of its debt and equity betas, weighted by the proportion of debt and equity in its capital structure, taking into account the tax shield on debt:

$$\beta_{\text{BUSINESS ASSETS}} = \frac{(1 - \text{Tax rate}) \times \text{Debt}}{(1 - \text{Tax rate}) \times \text{Debt} + \text{Equity}} \beta_{\text{DEBT}} + \frac{\text{Equity}}{(1 - \text{Tax rate}) \times \text{Debt} + \text{Equity}} \beta_{\text{EQUITY}}$$

A firm's equity beta can be estimated directly using its stock returns and the capital asset pricing model. Its debt beta can be inferred from the capital asset pricing model if we have information on its current interest rate and the risk-free rate, using the CAPM formula. From these estimated equity and debt betas at the current capital structure, we can infer the firm's asset beta.

When the firm's capital structure changes, its equity and debt betas will change, but its asset beta remains the same. We can take advantage of this fact to estimate the expected equity beta for the new capital structure. We first have to get an estimate of the interest rate on debt at the new capital structure level. Once we have this information, we can estimate the implied debt beta using the capital asset pricing model and the risk-free rate. Now we can estimate the equity beta for the new capital structure using the identity that the new equity beta and the new debt beta, weighted by the new capital structure weights, have to add up to the asset beta estimated earlier.

For many firms that have a low probability of bankruptcy, the current interest rate will be close to the risk-free rate and the debt beta will be close to zero. To simplify the calculation of leverage-adjusted betas, many analysts thus assume that the debt beta equals zero. Under this assumption, the equity and asset betas have the following relationship:

$$\beta_{\text{EQUITY}} = \left[1 + (1 - \text{Tax rate}) \times \frac{\text{Debt}}{\text{Equity}}\right] \beta_{\text{BUSINESS ASSETS}}$$

Note that in this equation, debt and equity are measured in terms of economic values rather than book values. We will next discuss some of the complications involved in obtaining these economic values.

Adjusting the cost of equity for changes in non-operating investments

In the previous discussion we conveniently ignored the fact that the business assets of some firms consist for a significant part of non-operating investment assets and, just as importantly, that the relevance of such assets may change during the forecasting period. For example, in Chapter 6 we described that at the end of 2011 Hennes & Mauritz held a significant amount of excess cash – a non-operating investment asset – which would likely be reduced during the forecasting period. Because the beta of excess cash and marketable (fixed income) securities is close to zero and therefore significantly different from the average beta of the other business assets, changes in the holdings of excess cash and similar non-operating investments will also lead to changes in the firm's equity beta. We describe below how the equity beta can be re-estimated to take such changes into account.

Because the beta of a portfolio of assets is the weighted average of the assets' individual betas, the following equation – which sets the weighted average of the two types of asset betas equal to the weighted average of the debt and equity beta – should hold:

$$\beta_{\text{BUSINESS ASSETS}} = \frac{\text{Net operating assets}}{\text{Business assets}} \beta_{\text{OPERATING ASSETS}} + \frac{\text{Investment assets}}{\text{Business assets}} \beta_{\text{INVESTMENT ASSETS}}$$

$$= \frac{(1 - \text{Tax rate}) \times \text{Debt}}{(1 - \text{Tax rate}) \times \text{Debt} + \text{Equity}} \beta_{\text{DEBT}} + \frac{\text{Equity}}{(1 - \text{Tax rate}) \times \text{Debt} + \text{Equity}} \beta_{\text{EQUITY}}$$

Rearranging the equation leads to the following relationship between the equity beta and the betas of net operating assets, investment assets, and debt:

$$\beta_{\text{EQUITY}} = \left[1 + \frac{(1 - \text{Tax rate}) \times \text{Debt} - \text{Investment assets}}{\text{Equity}} \right] \beta_{\text{OPERATING ASSETS}}$$

$$+ \left[\frac{\text{Investment assets}}{\text{Equity}} \right] \beta_{\text{INVESTMENT ASSETS}} - \left[\frac{(1 - \text{Tax rate}) \times \text{Debt}}{\text{Equity}} \right] \beta_{\text{DEBT}}$$

In this equation debt, equity, and investment assets are all measured in terms of economic values, not book values. When analyzing a financially healthy industrial (non-financial) firm whose investment assets consist mostly of cash and marketable fixed income securities, such as Hennes & Mauritz, it is reasonable to assume that the betas of the investment assets and debt equal zero, such that the equity beta only depends on the beta of the operating assets.

Estimating the weighted average cost of capital

To value a company's business assets, the analyst discounts abnormal NOPAT plus NIPAT, or cash flows available to both debt and equity holders. The proper discount rate to use is therefore the **weighted average cost of capital (WACC)**. The WACC is calculated by weighting the costs of debt and equity capital according to their respective market values:

$$\text{WACC} = \frac{\text{Debt}}{\text{Debt} + \text{Equity}} (1 - \text{Tax rate}) \times \text{Cost of debt} + \frac{\text{Equity}}{\text{Debt} + \text{Equity}} \text{Cost of equity}$$

Estimating the cost of debt

The cost of debt is the interest rate on the debt. It can be used to calculate the WACC, value debt capital, or calculate the present value of the tax shield on debt in asset valuation. If the assumed capital structure in future periods is the same as the historical structure, then the current interest rate on debt will be a good proxy for this. However, if the analyst assumes a change in capital structure, then it is important to estimate the expected interest rate given the new level of debt ratio. One approach to this would be to estimate the expected credit rating of the company at the new level of debt and use the appropriate interest rates for that credit category. We discuss the estimation of credit ratings in further detail in Chapter 10.

It is also worth noting that the cost of debt will change over time if market interest rates are expected to change. This can arise if investors expect inflation to increase or decrease over the forecast horizon. Since we typically discount nominal earnings or cash flows, the cost of debt is a nominal rate, and will change over time to reflect changes in inflation. This can be handled by scaling the cost of debt up or down over time to reflect expected changes in interest rates each year. If interest rates are projected to rise by 3 percent as a result of expected inflation, the cost of debt for the firm we are analyzing should also increase by 3 percent. The yield curve, which shows how investors expect interest rates to change over time can be used to assess whether time-varying interest rates are likely to be important in the analysis.

Finally, in the WACC calculation, the cost of debt should be expressed on a net-of-tax basis because it is after-tax cash flows that are being discounted. In most settings the market rate of interest can be converted to a net-of-tax basis by multiplying it by one minus the marginal corporate tax rate.

Weights of debt and equity

The weights assigned to debt and equity in the above equations represent their respective fractions of total capital provided, measured in terms of economic values. Computing an economic value for debt should not be difficult. International accounting standards (IFRS 7) require that firms disclose the economic value of their liabilities in the notes to the financial statements. Further, if interest rates have not changed significantly since the time the debt was issued, it is reasonable to use book values rather than economic values in the beta leverage-adjustment. If interest rates have changed and economic value information is not available from the financial statements, the value of the debt can be estimated by discounting the future payouts at current market rates of interest applicable to the firm.

The tricky problem we face is assigning an economic value to equity. That is the very amount we are trying to estimate in the first place! How can the analyst possibly assign a market value to equity at this intermediate stage, given that the estimate will not be known until all steps in the valuation analysis are completed? One common approach to the problem is to insert at this point "target" ratios of debt to capital and equity to capital. For example, one might expect that a firm will, over the long run, maintain a capital structure that is 40 percent debt and 60 percent equity. The long-run focus is reasonable because we are discounting cash flows over the long horizon.

Another way around the problem is to start with book value of equity as a weight for purposes of calculating an initial estimate of the leverage-adjusted equity beta, which in turn can be used in the discounting process to generate an initial estimate of the value of equity. That initial estimate can then be used in place of the guess to arrive at a new equity beta, and a second estimate of the value of equity can be produced. This process can be repeated until the value used to calculate the leverage-adjusted equity beta and the final estimated value converge.

Estimating the required return on operating assets

To value a company's operating assets, the analyst discounts abnormal net operating profit after tax (NOPAT), abnormal return on operating assets (ROA), or free cash flows from operating assets. The proper discount rate to use therefore depends on the beta of the firm's operating assets. Based on the theoretical relationship between the equity beta and the betas of the operating and investment assets, which we described earlier, this beta can be calculated as:

$$\beta_{\text{OPERATING ASSETS}} = \left[\frac{\text{Equity}}{(1 - \text{Tax rate}) \times \text{Debt} + \text{Equity} - \text{Investment assets}} \right] \beta_{\text{EQUITY}}$$

$$+ \left[\frac{(1 - \text{Tax rate}) \times \text{Debt}}{(1 - \text{Tax rate}) \times \text{Debt} + \text{Equity} - \text{Investment assets}} \right] \beta_{\text{DEBT}}$$

$$- \left[\frac{\text{Investment assets}}{(1 - \text{Tax rate}) \times \text{Debt} + \text{Equity} - \text{Investment assets}} \right] \beta_{\text{INVESTMENT ASSETS}}$$

For financially healthy firms whose investment assets consist of low risk instruments such as excess cash or fixed income securities, like Hennes & Mauritz, the calculation can again be simplified by setting the beta of the investment assets equal to zero. After having derived the beta of the operating assets, one can plug the beta into the CAPM formula to calculate the required return on operating assets.

HENNES & MAURITZ'S REQUIRED RETURN ON OPERATING ASSETS

During the years 2007–2011, the ratio of H&M's after-tax book value of debt to market value of equity ranged from 0.07 to 0.14 and averaged at 0.10.

	2011	2010	2009	2008	2007
Book/market value of net debt	SEK50.34b	SEK47.69b	SEK46.64b	SEK47.07b	SEK32.54b
× (1 − Tax rate)	73.7%	73.7%	72.0%	72.0%	72.0%
After-tax value of net debt	37.10b	35.15b	33.58b	33.89b	23.43b
Market value of equity	354.19b	392.91b	341.19b	246.61b	330.19b
Leverage ratio	10.5%	8.9%	9.8%	13.7%	7.1%

Given H&M's low leverage and high creditworthiness, it is safe to assume that the market value of the company's debt is close to its book value. Footnote disclosures in the company's financial statements, made in accordance with international accounting standard IFRS 7, also confirm this. Using the average after-tax leverage ratio of 0.10 and our previous equity beta estimate of 0.45 (and assuming that the H&M's debt beta equals zero), H&M's asset beta can be easily derived:

$$\beta_{\text{BUSINESS ASSETS}} = \frac{1}{[0.10 + 1]} \times \beta_{\text{EQUITY}} = \frac{1}{1.1} \times 0.45 = 0.41$$

Between 2007 and 2011, the ratio between the market/book value of H&M's investment assets to the market value of its equity ranged from 0.04 to 0.06 and averaged at 0.05.

	2011	**2010**	**2009**	**2008**	**2007**
Book/market value of investment assets	SEK13.09b	SEK16.70b	SEK14.46b	SEK16.12b	SEK14.95b
Market value of equity	354.19b	392.91b	341.19b	246.61b	330.19b
Investment ratio	3.7%	4.2%	4.2%	6.5%	4.5%

Using this information (and assuming that the H&M's investment assets and debt betas equal zero), the net operating asset beta of H&M can be calculated as follows:

$$\beta_{\text{OPERATING ASSETS}} = \left[\frac{\text{Equity}}{(1 - \text{Tax rate}) \times \text{Debt} + \text{Equity} - \text{Investment assets}} \right] \beta_{\text{EQUITY}}$$

$$= \left[\frac{1}{0.10 + 1 - 0.05} \right] 0.45 = 0.43$$

In our forecasts we assume that H&M's leverage ratio will remain steady; however, we assume that investment assets will decrease by approximately 58 percent (0.05/0.12 − 1). Consequently, we assume that H&M's equity beta will increase, though only marginally to 0.46 ([0.10 + 1 − (1 − 0.58) × 0.05] × 0.43), leaving its cost of equity capital almost unchanged at 7.25 percent.

Using the beta of the operating assets and the CAPM formula, one can also calculate the required return on net operating assets (r_{NOA}):

$$r_{\text{NOA}} = 4.8 \text{ percent } (r_f) + 0.43(\beta_{\text{NOA}}) \times 5.3 \text{ percent } (E(r_m) - r_f) = 7.08 \text{ percent}$$

USING INDUSTRY BETAS

The previous estimates of H&M's cost of equity and required return on operating assets were based on our firm-specific estimate of H&M's equity beta. H&M's equity beta appears to be low relative to the equity betas of its industry peers. An obvious explanation for this difference in equity betas is that H&M's current strategy has reduced the retailer's exposure to economy-wide fluctuations, thus lowering its systematic risk relative to the other peers'. In our forecasting analysis we assumed, however, that over time H&M's superior performance would decline and the firm would gradually become more similar to its peers. Given this assumption, it makes sense to also assume that in the long run the systematic risk of H&M's operating assets will approach the industry average. Consequently, the industry asset beta should be used as the basis for calculating H&M's cost of equity and required return on operating assets. To do so, we take the following approach.

First, we calculate the industry equity beta as the equity value-weighted average of the retailers' individual betas. Using the equity beta estimation procedure described earlier, the weighted average equity beta of the eight European apparel retailers that we examined in Chapter 5 is 0.60.

Second, we estimate the industry beta of operating assets by adjusting the equity beta for the average degree of leverage and the proportion of investment assets in the industry. During the years 2007–2011, the ratio of eight retailers' after-tax book value of debt to market value of equity ranged from 0.12 to 0.21 and averaged at 0.14.

	2011	2010	2009	2008	2007
After tax book/market value of net debt	€10.63b	€ 9.99b	€10.09b	€10.05b	€ 8.64b
Market value of equity	€91.82b	€86.23b	€68.28b	€48.79b	€67.31b
Industry leverage ratio	11.6%	11.6%	14.8%	20.6%	12.8%

Given industry's low leverage and high creditworthiness, it is safe to assume that the market value of the industry's debt is close to its book value. Between 2007 and 2011, the ratio between the market/book value of the industry's investment assets to the market value of its equity ranged from 0.04 to 0.06 and averaged at 0.05.

	2011	2010	2009	2008	2007
Book/market value of investment assets	€ 4.70b	€ 5.15b	€ 3.62b	€ 2.77b	€ 2.73b
Market value of equity	€91.82b	€86.23b	€68.28b	€48.79b	€67.31b
Investment ratio	5.1%	6.0%	5.3%	5.7%	4.1%

Using this information (and assuming that the industry's investment assets and debt betas equal zero), the average net operating asset beta of the eight retailers can be calculated as follows:

$$\beta_{\text{OPERATING ASSETS}} = \left[\frac{\text{Equity}}{(1 - \text{Tax rate}) \times \text{Debt} + \text{Equity} - \text{Investment assets}} \right] \beta_{\text{EQUITY}}$$

$$= \left[\frac{1}{0.14 + 1 - 0.05} \right] 0.60 = 0.55$$

Third, assuming that the industry average operating assets beta is a more appropriate measure of the systematic risk of H&M's operating assets than the firm's individual beta, we can calculate H&M's required return on net operating assets (r_{NOA}) as:

$$r_{\text{NOA}} = 4.8 \text{ percent } (r_f) + 0.55(\beta_{\text{NOA}}) \times 5.3 \text{ percent } (E(r_m) - r_f) = 7.72 \text{ percent}$$

Fourth and finally, taking into account (1) H&M's leverage ratio of 0.10, (2) H&M's investment ratio of 0.05, and (3) our expectation that H&M's investment assets to sales ratio will decrease by 58 percent, we can derive H&M's equity beta from the industry's operating assets beta:

$$\beta_{\text{EQUITY}} = \left[1 + \frac{(1 - \text{Tax rate}) \times \text{Debt} - \text{Investment assets}}{\text{Equity}} \right] \beta_{\text{OPERATING ASSETS}}$$

$$= \left[1 + \frac{0.10 - (1 - 0.58) \times 0.05}{1} \right] 0.55 = 0.59$$

Consequently, our estimate of H&M's cost of equity is:

$$\text{Cost of equity} = 4.8 \text{ percent } (r_f) + 0.59(\beta) \times 5.3 \text{ percent } (E(r_m) - r_f) = 7.93 \text{ percent}$$

Throughout this chapter we will use this cost of equity estimate to value H&M's equity.

DETAILED FORECASTS OF PERFORMANCE

The horizon over which detailed forecasts are to be made is itself a choice variable. We will discuss later in this chapter how the analyst might make this choice. Once it is made, the next step is to consider the set of assumptions regarding a firm's performance that are needed to arrive at the forecasts. We described in Chapter 6 the general framework of financial forecasting and illustrated the approach using Hennes & Mauritz.

The key to sound forecasts is that the underlying assumptions are grounded in a company's business reality. Strategy analysis provides a critical understanding of a company's value proposition, and whether current performance is likely to be sustainable in future. Accounting analysis and ratio analysis provide a deep understanding of a company's current performance, and whether the ratios themselves are reliable indicators of performance. It is, therefore, important to see the valuation forecasts as a continuation of the earlier steps in business analysis rather than as a discreet exercise not connected from the rest of the analysis.

Since valuation involves forecasting over a long time horizon, it is not practical to forecast all the line items in a company's financial statements. Instead, the analyst has to focus on the key elements of a firm's performance. Specifically, we forecasted H&M's condensed income statement, beginning balance sheet, and free cash flows for a period of ten years starting in fiscal year 2012 (year beginning in December 2011). We will use these same forecasting assumptions and financial forecasts, which are repeated here in Tables 8.2 and 8.3, as a starting point to value Hennes & Mauritz as of December 1, 2011. A spreadsheet containing H&M's actual and forecasted financial statements as well as the valuation described in this chapter is available on the companion website of this book.

TABLE 8.2 Forecasting assumptions for Hennes & Mauritz

Forecast year	2012	2013	2014	2015	2016	2017	2018	2019	2020	2021
Sales growth rate	11.6%	13.7%	14.1%	12.0%	10.0%	8.0%	6.0%	5.0%	4.0%	4.0%
NOPAT margin	16.4%	17.9%	18.1%	18.0%	17.0%	16.0%	15.0%	14.0%	13.0%	13.0%
Net working capital/sales	10.1%	9.5%	9.0%	9.0%	9.0%	9.0%	9.0%	9.0%	9.0%	9.0%
Net non-current operating assets/sales	60.7%	59.5%	58.4%	58.4%	58.4%	58.4%	58.4%	58.4%	58.4%	58.4%
Investment assets/sales	12.0%	12.0%	12.0%	10.0%	9.0%	8.0%	7.0%	6.0%	5.0%	5.0%
After tax return on investment assets	2.8%	2.8%	2.8%	2.8%	2.8%	2.8%	2.8%	2.8%	2.8%	2.8%
After tax cost of net debt	2.3%	2.5%	2.7%	2.9%	3.1%	3.3%	3.5%	3.5%	3.5%	3.5%
Debt to capital	52.6%	52.6%	52.6%	52.6%	52.6%	52.6%	52.6%	52.6%	52.6%	52.6%

Making performance forecasts for valuing H&M

As discussed in Chapter 7, the forecasts required to convert the financial forecasts shown above into estimates of value differ depending on whether we wish to value a firm's equity or its assets. To value equity, the essential inputs are:

- Abnormal earnings: net profit less shareholders' equity at the beginning of the year times cost of equity.
- Abnormal ROE: the difference between ROE and the cost of equity.
- Abnormal earnings growth: the change in net profit less the cost of equity times prior period's change in equity (or the change in abnormal earnings).
- Free cash flow to equity: net income less the increase in operating working capital less the increase in net non-current assets plus the increase in net debt.

TABLE 8.3 Forecasted financial statements for Hennes & Mauritz

Fiscal year	2012	2013	2014	2015	2016	2017	2018	2019	2020	2021
Beginning balance sheet (SEK millions)										
Beginning net working capital	12,377.9	12,395.2	13,251.1	14,318.6	16,036.9	17,640.6	19,051.8	20,194.9	21,002.7	21,632.8
+ Beginning net non-current operating assets	68,981.5	74,494.1	82,993.6	92,912.1	104,061.5	114,467.7	123,625.1	131,042.6	136,284.3	140,372.8
+ Beginning investment assets	13,085.1	14,727.0	16,738.2	19,091.5	17,818.8	17,640.6	16,934.9	15,707.2	14,001.8	12,018.2
= **Business assets**	**94,444.5**	**101,616.3**	**112,982.9**	**126,322.2**	**137,917.1**	**149,748.8**	**159,611.8**	**166,944.7**	**171,288.8**	**174,023.8**
Debt	49,695.8	53,469.5	59,450.5	66,469.5	72,570.6	78,796.3	83,986.2	87,844.6	90,130.5	91,569.6
+ Group equity	44,748.7	48,146.8	53,532.4	59,852.7	65,346.5	70,952.5	75,625.7	79,100.0	81,158.3	82,454.2
= **Capital**	**94,444.5**	**101,616.3**	**112,982.9**	**126,322.2**	**137,917.1**	**149,748.8**	**159,611.8**	**166,944.7**	**171,288.8**	**174,023.8**
Income statement (SEK millions)										
Sales	122,725.0	139,485.0	159,096.0	178,187.5	196,006.3	211,686.8	224,388.0	233,363.5	240,364.4	247,575.3
Net operating profit after tax	20,126.9	24,967.8	28,796.4	32,073.8	33,321.1	33,869.9	33,658.2	32,670.9	31,247.4	32,184.8
+ Net investment profit after tax	414.0	470.5	536.7	500.9	495.9	476.1	441.6	393.6	337.9	348.0
= **Net business profit after tax**	**20,540.9**	**25,438.4**	**29,333.1**	**32,574.7**	**33,817.0**	**34,346.0**	**34,099.8**	**33,064.5**	**31,585.2**	**32,532.8**
– Net interest expense after tax	–1,155.7	–1,336.7	–1,605.2	–2,060.6	–2,394.8	–2,757.9	–2,939.5	–3,074.6	–3,154.6	–3,204.9
= **Net profit**	**19,385.2**	**24,101.6**	**27,727.9**	**30,514.1**	**31,422.1**	**31,588.1**	**31,160.2**	**29,989.9**	**28,430.7**	**29,327.8**
Return on operating assets	24.7%	28.7%	29.9%	29.9%	27.7%	25.6%	23.6%	21.6%	19.9%	19.9%
Return on business assets	21.7%	25.0%	26.0%	25.8%	24.5%	22.9%	21.4%	19.8%	18.4%	18.7%
ROE	43.3%	50.1%	51.8%	51.0%	48.1%	44.5%	41.2%	37.9%	35.0%	35.6%
BV of operating assets growth rate	8.2%	6.8%	10.8%	11.4%	12.0%	10.0%	8.0%	6.0%	4.0%	3.0%
BV of business assets growth rate	2.8%	7.6%	11.2%	11.8%	9.2%	8.6%	6.6%	4.6%	2.6%	1.6%
BV of equity growth rate	1.3%	7.6%	11.2%	11.8%	9.2%	8.6%	6.6%	4.6%	2.6%	1.6%
Net profit	19385.2	24101.6	27727.9	30514.1	31422.1	31588.1	31160.2	29989.9	28430.7	29327.8
– Change in net working capital	–17.3	–855.9	–1067.6	–1718.2	–1603.7	–1411.2	–1143.1	–807.8	–630.1	–649.0
– Change in net non-current operating assets	–5512.6	–8499.5	–9918.5	–11149.4	–10406.2	–9157.4	–7417.5	–5241.7	–4088.5	–4211.2
– Change in investment assets	–1641.9	–2011.2	–2353.3	1272.8	178.2	705.6	1227.8	1705.3	1983.6	–360.5
+ Change in debt	3773.7	5981.0	7019.0	6101.1	6225.7	5189.8	3858.5	2285.8	1439.1	2747.1
= **Free cash flow to equity**	**15987.1**	**18716.0**	**21407.6**	**25020.3**	**25816.2**	**26914.9**	**27685.9**	**27931.6**	**27134.8**	**26854.2**
Net operating profit after tax	20126.9	24967.8	28796.4	32073.8	33321.1	33869.9	33658.2	32670.9	31247.4	32184.8
– Change in net working capital	–17.3	–855.9	–1067.6	–1718.2	–1603.7	–1411.2	–1143.1	–807.8	–630.1	–649.0
– Change in net non-current operating assets	–5512.6	–8499.5	–9918.5	–11149.4	–10406.2	–9157.4	–7417.5	–5241.7	–4088.5	–4211.2
= **Free cash flow from operations**	**14597.0**	**15612.5**	**17810.3**	**19206.1**	**21311.2**	**23301.2**	**25097.6**	**26621.4**	**26528.8**	**27324.6**

Alternatively, to value a company's operating assets, the significant performance forecasts would be:

- Abnormal NOPAT: Net operating profit after tax (NOPAT) less total net operating assets at the beginning of the year times the required return on operating assets.
- Abnormal ROA: the difference between the forecasted and required return on operating assets (ROA).
- Abnormal NOPAT growth: the change in NOPAT less the required return on operating assets times prior period's change in net operating assets (or the change in abnormal NOPAT).
- Free cash flow from operating assets: NOPAT less the increase in operating working capital less the increase in net non-current operating assets.

Table 8.4 shows H&M's performance forecasts for all eight of these financial statement variables for the ten-year period 2012–2021.

As discussed earlier, to derive cash flows in 2021, we need to make assumptions about the sales growth rate and balance sheet ratios in 2022. The cash flow forecasts shown in Table 8.4 are based on the simple assumption that the sales growth and beginning balance sheet ratios in 2022 remain the same as in 2021. We discuss the sensitivity of this assumption and the terminal value assumption later in the chapter.

Hennes & Mauritz's projected abnormal ROE increases from 35.4 percent in 2012 to 43.9 percent in 2014 and then declines again due to the forces of competition. Abnormal operating ROA, abnormal NOPAT, and abnormal earnings show a similar trend. A slightly different pattern is shown for cash flow to equity and cash flow from operations. Projected cash flows gradually increase and become steady after 2019.

TERMINAL VALUES

Explicit forecasts of the various elements of a firm's performance generally extend for a period of five to ten years. The final year of this forecast period is labeled the *terminal year* (selection of an appropriate terminal year is discussed later in this section). **Terminal value** is then the present value of either abnormal earnings or free cash flows occurring beyond the terminal year. Since this involves forecasting performance over the remainder of the firm's life, the analyst must adopt some assumption that simplifies the process of forecasting. A key question is whether it is reasonable to assume a continuation of the terminal year performance or whether some other pattern is expected.

Clearly, the continuation of a sales growth that is significantly greater than the average growth rate of the economy is unrealistic over a very long horizon. That rate would likely outstrip inflation in the euro and the real growth rate of the world economy. Over many years, it would imply that the firm would grow to a size greater than that of all the other firms in the world combined. But what would be a suitable alternative assumption? Should we expect the firm's sales growth rate to ultimately settle down to the rate of inflation? Or to a higher rate, such as the nominal GDP growth rate? And perhaps equally important, will a firm that earns abnormal profits continue to do so by maintaining its profit margins on a growing, or even existing, base of sales?

To answer these questions, we must consider how much longer the rate of growth in industry sales can outstrip overall economic growth, and how long a firm's competitive advantages can be sustained. Clearly, looking 11 or more years into the future, any forecast is likely to be subject to considerable error. Below we discuss a variety of alternative approaches to the task of calculating a terminal value.

Terminal values with the competitive equilibrium assumption

Fortunately, in many if not most situations, how we deal with the seemingly imponderable questions about long-range growth in sales simply *does not matter very much!* In fact, under plausible economic assumptions, there is no practical need to consider sales growth beyond the terminal year. Such growth may be *irrelevant*, so far as the firm's current value is concerned!

How can long-range growth in sales *not* matter? The reasoning revolves around the forces of competition. One impact of competition is that it tends to constrain a firm's ability to identify, on a consistent basis, growth opportunities that generate supernormal profits. The other dimension that competition tends to impact is a firm's margins.

TABLE 8.4 Performance forecasts for Hennes & Mauritz

Fiscal year	2012	2013	2014	2015	2016	2017	2018	2019	2020	2021
Equity valuation (SEK millions)										
Abnormal earnings	15,836.6	20,283.6	23,482.8	25,767.8	26,240.2	25,961.6	25,163.1	23,717.3	21,994.8	22,789.2
Abnormal ROE	35.4%	42.1%	43.9%	43.1%	40.2%	36.6%	33.3%	30.0%	27.1%	27.6%
Free cash flow to equity	15,987.1	18,716.0	21,407.6	25,020.3	25,816.2	26,914.9	27,685.9	27,931.6	27,134.8	26,854.2
Abnormal earnings growth		4447.0	3199.2	2285.0	472.4	−278.6	−798.4	−1445.8	−1722.5	794.4
Asset valuation (SEK millions)										
Abnormal NOPAT	13,846.0	18,260.0	21,366.3	23,795.5	24,049.5	23,671.1	22,643.5	20,995.4	19,104.8	19,678.0
Abnormal ROA	17.0%	21.0%	22.2%	22.2%	20.0%	17.9%	15.9%	13.9%	12.1%	12.1%
Free cash flow from operations	14,597.0	15,612.5	17,810.3	19,206.1	21,311.2	23,301.2	25,097.6	26,621.4	26,528.8	27,324.6
Abnormal NOPAT growth		4414.0	3106.3	2429.3	253.9	−378.3	−1027.6	−1648.2	−1890.5	573.1
Discount rates:										
Equity	0.927	0.858	0.795	0.737	0.683	0.633	0.586	0.543	0.503	0.466
Net operating assets	0.928	0.862	0.800	0.743	0.689	0.640	0.594	0.552	0.512	0.475
Growth factors:[a]										
Equity	1.00	1.08	1.20	1.34	1.46	1.59	1.69	1.77	1.81	1.84
Net operating assets	1.00	1.07	1.18	1.32	1.48	1.62	1.75	1.86	1.93	1.99

a. The growth factor is relevant only for calculating the present value for abnormal ROA and ROE.

Ultimately, we would expect high profits to attract enough competition to drive down a firm's margins, and therefore its returns, to a normal level. At this point, the firm will earn its cost of capital, with no abnormal returns or terminal value. (Recall the evidence in Chapter 6 concerning the reversion of ROEs to normal levels over horizons of five to ten years.)

Certainly a firm may at a point in time maintain a competitive advantage that permits it to achieve returns in excess of the cost of capital. When that advantage is protected with patents or a strong brand name, the firm may even be able to maintain it for many years, perhaps indefinitely. With hindsight, we know that some such firms – like Coca-Cola – were able not only to maintain their competitive edge but to expand it across dramatically increasing investment bases. However, with a few exceptions, it is reasonable to assume that the terminal value of the firm will be zero under the **competitive equilibrium assumption**, obviating the need to make assumptions about long-term growth rates.

Competitive equilibrium assumption only on incremental sales

An alternative version of the competitive equilibrium assumption is to assume that a firm will continue to earn abnormal earnings forever on the sales it had in the terminal year, but there will be no abnormal earnings on any incremental sales beyond that level. If we invoke the competitive equilibrium assumption on incremental sales for years beyond the terminal year, then it does not matter what sales growth rate we use beyond that year, and we may as well simplify our arithmetic by treating sales *as if* they will be constant at the terminal year level. Then return on business assets, ROE, NOPAT, net profit, free cash flow to debt and equity, and free cash flow to equity will all remain constant at the terminal year level. For example, by treating Hennes & Mauritz as if its competitive advantage can be maintained only on the nominal sales level achieved in the year 2021, we will be assuming that in *real* terms its competitive advantage will shrink. Under this scenario, it is simple to estimate the terminal value by dividing the 2021 level of each of the variables by the appropriate discount rate. Under the abnormal earnings (NOPAT) growth valuation method, H&M's abnormal earnings (NOPAT) growth beyond 2021 and its terminal value will be zero. As one would expect, terminal values in this scenario will be higher than those with no abnormal returns on all sales in years 2022 and beyond. This is entirely due to the fact that we are now assuming that H&M can retain indefinitely its superior performance on its existing base of sales.

Terminal value with persistent abnormal performance and growth

Each of the approaches described above appeals in some way to the "competitive equilibrium assumption." However, there are circumstances where the analyst is willing to assume that the firm may defy competitive forces and earn abnormal rates of return on new projects for many years. If the analyst believes supernormal profitability can be extended to larger markets for many years, it can be accommodated within the context of valuation analysis.

One possibility is to project earnings and cash flows over a longer horizon, i.e., until the competitive equilibrium assumption can reasonably be invoked. In the case of Hennes & Mauritz, for example, we could assume that the supernormal profitability will continue for five years beyond 2021 (for a total forecasting horizon of 15 years from the beginning of the forecasting period), but after that period, the firm's ROE and return on operating assets will be equal to its cost of equity and its required return on operating assets.

Another possibility is to project growth in abnormal earnings or cash flows at some constant rate. For instance, one could expect H&M to maintain its advantage on a sales base that remains constant in *real* terms, implying that sales grow beyond terminal year 2021 at the expected long-run European inflation rate of between 2 and 4 percent. Beyond our terminal year, 2021, as the sales growth rate remains constant at the inflation rate, abnormal earnings (growth), free cash flows, and book values of assets and equity also grow at the constant inflation rate. This is simply because we held all other performance ratios constant in this period. As a result, abnormal return on operating assets and abnormal ROE remain constant at the same level as in the terminal year.

This approach is more aggressive than the preceding assumptions about terminal value, but it may be more realistic. After all, there is no obvious reason why the *real* size of the investment base on which H&M earns abnormal returns should depend on inflation rates. The approach, however, still relies to some extent on the competitive equilibrium assumption. The assumption is now invoked to suggest that supernormal profitability can be extended only to an investment base that remains constant in real terms. In rare situations, if the company has established a market dominance that the analyst believes is immune to the threat of competition, the terminal value can be based on both positive real sales growth and abnormal profits.

When we assume that the abnormal performance persists at the same level as in the terminal year, projecting abnormal earnings (growth) and free cash flows is a simple matter of growing them at the assumed sales growth rate. Since the rate of abnormal earnings and cash flows growth is constant starting in the year after the terminal year, it is also straightforward to discount those flows. The present value of the flow stream is the flow at the end of the first year (after the terminal year) divided by the difference between the discount rate and steady-state growth rate, provided that the discount rate exceeds the growth rate. There is nothing about this valuation method that requires reliance on the competitive equilibrium assumption, so it could be used with *any* rate of growth in sales. The question is not whether the arithmetic is available to handle such an approach but rather how realistic it is.

Terminal value based on a price multiple

A popular approach to terminal value calculation is to apply a multiple to abnormal earnings, cash flows, or book values of the terminal period. The approach is not as *ad hoc* as it might at first appear. Note that under the assumption of no sales growth, abnormal earnings or cash flows beyond the terminal year remain constant. Capitalizing these flows in perpetuity by dividing by the cost of capital is equivalent to multiplying them by the inverse of the cost of capital. For example, in the case of Hennes & Mauritz, capitalizing free cash flows to equity at its cost of equity of 7.9 percent is equivalent to assuming a terminal cash flow multiple of 12.6 (1/0.079). Thus, applying a multiple in this range to H&M is similar to discounting all free cash flows beyond 2021 while invoking the competitive equilibrium assumption on incremental sales.

The mistake to avoid here is to capitalize the future abnormal earnings or cash flows using a multiple that is too high. The earnings or cash flow multiples might be high currently because the market anticipates abnormally profitable growth. However, once that growth is realized, the price-earnings multiple should fall to a normal level. It is that normal price-earnings ratio, applicable to a stable firm or one that can grow only through zero net present value projects, that should be used in the terminal value calculation. Thus multiples in the range of 7 to 12 – close to the reciprocal of cost of equity and required return on operating assets – should be used here. Higher multiples are justifiable only when the terminal year is closer and there are still abnormally profitable growth opportunities beyond that point. A similar logic applies to the estimation of terminal values using book value multiples.

Selecting the terminal year

A critical question posed by the above discussion is how long to make the detailed forecast horizon. When the competitive equilibrium assumption is used, the answer is whatever time is required for the firm's returns on incremental investment projects to reach that equilibrium – an issue that turns on the sustainability of the firm's competitive advantage. As indicated in Chapter 6, historical evidence indicates that most firms in Europe should expect ROEs to revert to normal levels within five to ten years. But for the typical firm, we can justify ending the forecast horizon even earlier – note that the return on *incremental* investment can be normal even while the return on *total* investment (and therefore ROE) remains abnormal. Thus a five- to ten-year forecast horizon should be more than sufficient for most firms. Exceptions would include firms so well insulated from competition (perhaps due to the power of a brand name) that they can extend their investment base to new markets for many years and still expect to generate supernormal returns.

Estimates of Hennes & Mauritz's terminal value

Choosing terminal year

In the case of Hennes & Mauritz, the terminal year used is ten years beyond the current one. Table 8.3 shows that the ROE (and operating ROA) is forecasted to decline at the end of these ten years, from the unusually high 51.8 percent in 2014 to 35.6 percent (rounded) by 2021. At this level the company will earn an abnormal return on equity of 27.6 percent (rounded), since its cost of equity is estimated to be 7.9 percent.

Based on the foregoing strategic assessment of Hennes & Mauritz, we believe that the firm has created a competitive advantage that should be sustainable in the long term. Consequently, we assume that the firm will have reached a steady state of performance in 2021 and extending the forecast horizon will not lead to further insights into how market dynamics will impact H&M's performance. The overall projection, therefore, expects that while H&M's current level of abnormal performance is not sustainable and that growth will slow and margins will get squeezed, the firm has created a market position that will allow it to make some level of abnormal earnings in the long-term. Based on this logic, we will fix 2021 as the terminal year for H&M and attempt to estimate its terminal value at that time.

Terminal value under varying assumptions

Table 8.5 shows H&M's terminal value under the various theoretical approaches we discussed above. Scenario 1 of this table shows the terminal value if we assume that H&M will continue to grow its sales at 3.0 percent beyond fiscal year 2021, and that it will continue to earn the same level of abnormal returns as in 2021 (that is, we assume that all the other forecasting assumptions will be the same as in 2021). Under this scenario, terminal values in the abnormal earnings model (TV_{AE}), the abnormal earnings growth model (TVAEG), and the free cash flow model (TV_{FCF}) are as follows:

$$TV_{AE} = \frac{1.03 \times AE_{2021}}{(0.079 - 0.03) \times (1.079)^{10}}$$

$$TV_{AEG} = \frac{1}{0.079} \times \frac{0.03 \times AE_{2021}}{(0.079 - 0.03) \times (1.079)^{9}}$$

$$TV_{FCF} = \frac{1.03 \times FCFE_{2021}}{(0.079 - 0.03) \times (1.079)^{10}}$$

where AE_{2021} and $FCFE_{2021}$ are expected abnormal earnings and free cash flow to equity for fiscal 2021, respectively. Using the abnormal earnings methodology this scenario leads to a terminal value of SEK222 billion.

TABLE 8.5 Terminal values for Hennes & Mauritz under various assumptions (using abnormal earnings methodology)

Scenario number	Approach	Scenario	Terminal sales growth	Terminal NOPAT margin	Value beyond the forecast horizon (AE terminal value)
1	Persistent abnormal performance	Sales growth and margins based on detailed analysis and forecast	3.0%	13.0%	SEK222.0b
2	Abnormal returns on constant sales (real terms)	Sales grow at the rate of inflation, margins maintained	2.0%	13.0%	SEK182.7b
3	Abnormal returns on constant sales (nominal terms)	Essentially zero sales growth, margins maintained	0.0%	13.0%	SEK134.0b
4	Competitive equilibrium	Margins reduced so no abnormal earnings	3.0%	3.8%	SEK0.0b

Scenario 2 calculates the terminal value assuming that H&M will maintain its margins only on sales that grow at the long-run expected rate of inflation, assumed to be 2 percent, dropping the terminal value in the abnormal earnings model to SEK182.7 billion. Scenario 3 shows the terminal value if we assume that the company's competitive advantage can be maintained only on the nominal sales level achieved in 2021. As a result, sales growth beyond the terminal year is assumed to be zero, which is equivalent to assuming that incremental sales do not produce any abnormal returns. The terminal value under this scenario drops to SEK134.0 billion.

The final scenario invokes the competitive equilibrium assumption, i.e., margins will be eroded such that the firm will have no abnormal returns irrespective of the rate of sales growth, leading to no terminal value in the abnormal earnings model. For the sake of illustration, the expected sales growth of 4.0 percent is maintained. To portray the competitive equilibrium, margins are lowered to eliminate any competitive advantage that H&M will have. In this final scenario, the terminal values are as follows:

$$TV_{AE} = 0$$

$$TV_{AEG} = \frac{1}{0.079} \times \frac{-1 \times AE_{2021}}{(1.079)^{10}}$$

$$TV_{FCF} = \frac{BVE_{2021}}{(1.079)^{10}}$$

where BVE_{2021} is H&M's end-of-year book value of equity in fiscal 2021.

COMPUTING ESTIMATED VALUES

Table 8.6 shows the estimated value of Hennes & Mauritz's net operating assets and equity, each using four different methods discussed in Chapter 7. The value of net operating assets is estimated using abnormal return on operating assets (ROA), abnormal NOPAT, abnormal NOPAT growth, and free cash flows from operations. The value of equity is estimated using operating ROE, abnormal earnings, abnormal earnings growth, and free cash flow to equity. These values are computed using the financial forecasts in Table 8.4 and the terminal value forecast under the persistent abnormal performance scenario.

In Table 8.6, present values of abnormal NOPAT (growth) and free cash flow from operations are computed using a required return on operating assets of 7.7 percent; present values of abnormal earnings (growth) and free cash flow to equity are computed using a cost of equity of 7.9 percent. Note that under the abnormal earnings (NOPAT) growth valuation approach, abnormal earnings (NOPAT) growth values in year t are multiplied by the corresponding discount factors in year $t–1$. To calculate the present values of abnormal returns on operating assets and abnormal ROE, the values for each year are first multiplied by the corresponding growth factor, as shown in the formulae in Chapter 7, and then they are discounted using the required return on operating assets and cost of equity, respectively. Under the assumptions and forecasts we have made, Hennes & Mauritz's estimated equity value per share is SEK253.85 and the total value of the firm's operating assets is SEK424.7 billion.

TABLE 8.6 Valuation summary for Hennes & Mauritz using various methodologies

	Beginning book value	Value from forecast period 2012–2021	Value beyond forecast horizon (terminal value)	Total value	Value per share (SEK)
Equity value (SEK billions)					
Abnormal earnings	44.7	153.4	222.0	420.1	253.85
Abnormal ROE	44.7	153.4	222.0	420.1	253.85
Abnormal earnings growth	N.A.	332.1	88.0	420.1	253.85
Free cash flows to equity	N.A.	158.6	261.6	420.1	253.85
Operating assets value (SEK billions)					
Abnormal NOPAT	81.4	139.3	204.1	424.8	N.A.
Abnormal ROA	81.4	139.3	204.1	424.8	N.A.
Abnormal NOPAT growth	N.A.	341.8	283.5	424.8	N.A.
Free cash flows to capital	N.A.	141.3	83.0	424.8	N.A.

Value estimates presented in each scenario show that the abnormal returns method, abnormal earnings method, abnormal earnings growth method, and the free cash flow method result in the same value, as claimed in Chapter 7. Note also that H&M's terminal value represents a larger fraction of the total value of assets and equity under the free cash flow method relative to the other methods. As discussed in Chapter 7, this is due to the fact that the abnormal returns and earnings methods rely on a company's book value of assets and equity, so the terminal value estimates are estimates of incremental values over book values. Similarly, under the abnormal earnings growth method, the terminal value estimates reflect only the changes in abnormal earnings that are expected to occur beyond the terminal year. In contrast, the free cash flow approach ignores the book values, so the terminal value forecasts are estimates of total value during this period.

The primary calculations in the above estimates treat all flows as if they arrive at the end of the year. Of course, they are likely to arrive throughout the year. If we assume for the sake of simplicity that cash flows will arrive mid-year, then we should adjust our value estimates upward by the amount $[1 + (r/2)]$, where r is the discount rate.

From asset values to equity values

The net operating asset value estimates displayed in Table 8.6 can also be used to derive an estimate of H&M's equity value. To calculate equity value we should make the following adjustments to the net operating assets value:

	Value of net operating assets
Add:	Value of investment assets
Add:	Value of net assets held for sale
Add:	Present value of the tax shield on debt
Subtract:	Value of debt
Subtract:	Value of minority interests
=	Equity value

The asset value estimate that we calculated reflects the value of the firm's net operating assets had the firm been financed with 100 percent equity. The introduction of debt into the firm's capital structure can, however, increase firm value because the associated interest payments create a valuable tax shield. We therefore include the present value of the tax shield on debt in our calculation of firm value, in addition to the value of investment assets and net assets held for sale, to calculate the total value of the firm (also referred to as the enterprise value). To derive the value of ordinary shareholders' equity, we subtract the value of all non-equity claims.

Value of investment assets

In accordance with the International Financial Reporting Standards, firms disclose the economic values of their investment assets either on the balance sheet or in the notes to their financial statements. Determining the economic values of, for example, marketable securities or long-term receivables is therefore relatively straightforward. At least two types of investment assets are potentially more complicated to value. These assets are (1) investment property and (2) minority equity investments.

Under IAS 40, firms can choose between recognizing their investment property at fair value or at cost. If recognized at cost, the fair value of the investment property must be disclosed in the notes to the financial statements. To obtain the economic value of investment property, an analyst should therefore check the firm's accounting policy for investment property and use information from the notes, if necessary, to adjust the investment property's book value.

The IFRS require that a firm use the equity method to account for minority equity investments (also referred to as associates) over which it has significant influence (but not control). The equity method requires that the equity investment is recorded at its initial cost and in subsequent periods adjusted for the firm's share in the investment's net profits. Consequently, the balance sheet value of the minority equity investment reflects what portion the firm owns of the investment's book value of equity, not its economic value. An analyst therefore has the challenging task of estimating the value of minority equity investment based on very limited information.

Consider the associates of Next plc, one of H&M's industry peers. In the notes to its financial statements, Next discloses that at the end of 2011 its investment in associates had a book value of £6.1 million (£5.1 million in 2010), consisting of £12.1 million total assets and £6.0 million total liabilities. Further, in 2011, Next's share in the associates' revenues amounted to £36.3 million, up from £33.5 million in 2010; the firm's share in its associates' net profits was £1.5 million, down from £1.8 million in 2010. Given the low materiality of the investment, relative to Next's market value of £4.45 billion, a simple, acceptable solution would be to assume that the associates' economic value is equal to its book value of £6.1 million. An alternative, conceptually preferred approach is to use one of the shortcut valuation formulae from Chapter 7. For example, note that the associates' average return on equity decreased from 35 percent in 2010 (1.8/5.1) to 25 percent in 2011 (1.5/6.1). The associates' average sales growth was 8 percent (6.1/5.1). Assuming a future return on equity of 25 percent (as in 2011), a long-run growth rate of 3 percent (as for H&M), and a cost of equity of 9 percent, the theoretical equity value-to-book multiple for Next's associates can be calculated as:

$$\text{Equity value-to-book multiple} = 1 + \frac{ROE_0 - r_e}{r_e - g^{equity}} = 1 + \frac{0.25 - 0.09}{0.09 - 0.03} = 3.67$$

Based on a multiple of 3.67 the economic value of Next's investment in associates equals £22.4 million. Whether this multiple approach is preferred over using the book value of the investment should be decided based on factors such as the volatility of the associates' performance and the materiality of the investment.

In the notes to its financial statements Hennes & Mauritz discloses that the fair value of its investment assets is not significantly different from their book value. We therefore assume that the firm's investment assets have a book value and an economic value of SEK13,085 million.

Value of net assets held for sale

Because we removed net assets held for sale from the balance sheet before calculating financial ratios and valuing the net operating assets of Hennes & Mauritz, we must add back the assets' economic value to the value of the firm. IFRS 5 requirements imply that non-current assets held for sale are often recorded on the balance sheet at values close to their fair values. Therefore, we can set the economic value estimate of net assets held for sale equal to the assets' book values.

In 2011, Hennes & Mauritz did not have any non-current assets that the firm classified as held for sale.

Present value of the tax shield on debt

The present value of the tax shield on debt can be written as follows:

$$\text{Present value of tax shield} = \frac{\text{Interest expense}_1 \times \text{tax rate}_1}{(1 + r_d)} + \frac{\text{Interest expense}_2 \times \text{tax rate}_2}{(1 + r_d)^2} + \ldots$$

where interest expense is the pre-tax interest expense forecast, tax rate is the expected future tax rates, and r_d is the cost of debt. Note that cost of debt used in the calculation can vary over the forecasting period. For example, we assumed that the pre-tax interest rate of Hennes & Mauritz gradually increases from 3.1 to 4.7 percent. In such case, discount rates should be based on future interest rates. In particular, for H&M, the discount factor would be $1/(1+3.1\%)$ in 2012, $1/[(1+3.1\%)(1+3.4\%)]$ in 2013, $1/[(1+3.1\%)(1+3.4\%)(1+3.7\%)]$ in 2014, and so on.

Table 8.7 displays the calculation of the present value of the tax shield on debt for Hennes & Mauritz. Note that the discount factor in 2021 includes the effect of the terminal value, which is based on a terminal growth rate of 3 percent and a terminal cost of debt of 4.7 percent. The calculation shows that the present value of the tax shield at the beginning of 2012 is equal to SEK22,952.1 million.

Value of debt

As indicated earlier in this chapter, international accounting standards (IFRS 7) require that firms disclose the economic value of their liabilities in the notes to the financial statements. If interest rates have not changed significantly since the time the debt was issued, it is reasonable to assume that the economic value of debt is equal to its book value. If interest rates have changed and economic value information is not available from the financial statements, the value of the debt can be estimated by discounting the future payouts at current market rates of interest applicable to the firm.

TABLE 8.7 Present value of the tax shield on debt for Hennes & Mauritz

Fiscal year	2012	2013	2014	2015	2016	2017	2018	2019	2020	2021
Interest expense	1,568.1	1,813.8	2,178.0	2,795.9	3,249.4	3,742.0	3,988.5	4,171.7	4,280.3	4,348.6
Tax rate	26.3%	26.3%	26.3%	26.3%	26.3%	26.3%	26.3%	26.3%	26.3%	26.3%
Tax shield	412.4	477.0	572.8	735.3	854.6	984.2	1,049.0	1,097.2	1,125.7	1,143.7
Discount factor	0.969	0.938	0.904	0.868	0.831	0.793	0.757	0.723	0.690	14.947

Total present value SEK22,952.1m

Value of minority interests

The balance sheet item minority interests reflects the share of the net assets that is attributable to outside shareholders. The economic value of this outside claim on the value of the firm should thus be excluded from the value of ordinary shareholders' equity. In most cases, the economic value of minority interest is not material relative to the value of the firm. If so, it is reasonable to set the economic value equal to the book value of the claim. If the claim is sufficiently large, an alternative approach to valuing the claim is to use a multiple approach, like the one we used to value the investment in associates earlier. When using a multiple approach the share of profit that is attributable to minority shareholders can be taken from the income statement.

For Hennes & Mauritz, the book value of minority interests equals zero.

Deriving Hennes & Mauritz's equity value

Based on the foregoing discussion, we can derive Hennes & Mauritz's equity value as follows:

	Value of net operating assets:	SEK424,754.5m
Add:	Value of investment assets	+13,085.1m
Add:	Value of net assets held for sale	+0m
Add:	Present value of the tax shield on debt	+22,952.1m
Subtract:	Value of debt	−49,695.8m
Subtract:	Value of minority interests	−0m
=	Equity value	SEK411,095.9m

Based on this approach, our estimate of H&M's equity value equals SEK411.1 billion, or SEK248.39 per share, which is slightly less than our equity value estimate under the direct approach discussed earlier.

Asset valuation versus equity valuation

The example of Hennes & Mauritz shows that asset-based approach to valuation (i.e., valuing net operating assets first, then deriving equity value) does not always produce the same equity value estimate as the equity-based approach (i.e., directly valuing equity). In fact, the asset-based approach has one advantage over the equity-based approach that tends to make this approach the more accurate of the two: discount factors in the asset-based approach are based on the required return on operating assets, whereas discount factors in the equity-based approach are based on the cost of equity. As we discussed earlier, the cost of equity varies as a function of a firm's degree of leverage and the proportion of funds invested in investment assets. If leverage or the importance of investment assets changes over the forecast horizon, future cost of equity estimates should be adjusted accordingly. Unfortunately, this is a difficult task, leading most analysts to use a constant cost of equity instead. In contrast, the required return on operating assets only depends on the systematic risk of a firm's operating assets, at least in theory, and is presumably insensitive to changes in leverage or investment assets. Consequently, the asset-based approach to valuation makes use of the fact that the economic values of several claims and assets can be easily taken from the financial statements and circumvents some of the complications associated with cost of equity estimation.

Value estimates versus market values

As the discussion above shows, valuation involves a substantial number of assumptions by analysts. Therefore the estimates of value will vary from one analyst to another. The only way to ensure that one's estimates are reliable is to make sure that the assumptions are grounded in the economics of the business being valued. It is also useful to check the assumptions against the time-series trends for performance ratios discussed in Chapter 6. While it is quite legitimate to make assumptions that differ markedly from these trends in any given case, it is important for the analyst to be able to articulate the business and strategy reasons for making such assumptions.

When a company being valued is publicly traded, it is possible to compare one's own estimated value with the market value of a company. When an estimated value differs substantially from a company's market value, it is useful for the analyst to understand why such differences arise. A way to do this is to redo the valuation exercise and figure out what valuation assumptions are needed to arrive at the observed stock price. One can then examine whether the market's assumptions are more or less valid relative to one's own assumptions. As we discuss in the next chapter, such an analysis can be invaluable in using valuation to make buy or sell decisions in the security analysis context.

In the case of Hennes & Mauritz, our estimated value of the firm's equity per share (SEK253.85) is above the observed value, of SEK222.70, at the end of January 2012, when the market had assimilated the announced results for the quarter and fiscal year ended November 30, 2011. In the months following the announcement, H&M's share price fluctuated between SEK220 and SEK250. Analysts' target prices ranged from SEK195 to SEK250. Clearly the market was making less optimistic assumptions than our own. Although part of the discrepancy can surely be attributed to the uncertainty in stock markets at the beginning of 2012, the differences in the two sets of assumptions might also be related to growth rates, NOPAT margins, or asset turns. One could run different scenarios regarding each of these variables and test the sensitivity of the estimated value to these assumptions.

Sensitivity analysis

Recall that in Chapter 6, we developed what we believed to be a reasonable assessment of H&M's expected future performance. The resulting valuation seems to be more optimistic than the market's expectations, as the imputed value per share exceeds the traded value per share at the time. However, we acknowledged that the company's future could play out in multiple ways and proposed two alternative scenarios. As shown in Table 8.8, if H&M is able to improve its store productivity at a greater rate (to SEK 48, 49, and 50 million per store in 2012, 2013, and 2014, respectively, resulting in sales growth rates of 13.8, 13.9, and 14.3 percent), its value per share would be SEK259.53. If, on the other hand, H&M's sourcing costs would decrease at a lower rate, resulting in an overall decrease of the firm's NOPAT margin by, say, 1 percent, its shares would be worth only SEK231.70 per share. The changes in equity value in these scenarios are driven primarily by changes in sales growth and margins, performance measures that are most strongly affected by the forces of competition.

TABLE 8.8 Equity valuation under various scenarios using abnormal earnings

Scenario	Beginning book value	Value from forecast period 2012–2021	Value beyond forecast horizon (terminal value)	Total value	Value per share (SEK)
Greater improvement in store productivity between 2012 and 2014	44.7	157.3	227.5	429.5	259.53
Slower reduction in sourcing costs, decreasing the NOPAT margin by 1 percent	44.7	140.9	197.9	383.5	231.70

SOME PRACTICAL ISSUES IN VALUATION

The above discussion provides a blueprint for doing valuation. In practice, the analyst has to deal with a number of other issues that have an important effect on the valuation task. We discuss below three frequently encountered complications – accounting distortions, negative book values, and excess cash.

Dealing with accounting distortions

We know from the discussion in Chapter 7 that accounting methods *per se* should have no influence on firm value (except as those choices influence the analyst's view of future real performance). Yet the abnormal returns and earnings valuation approaches used here are based on numbers that vary with accounting method choices.

Since accounting choices must affect both earnings *and* book value, and because of the self-correcting nature of double-entry bookkeeping (all "distortions" of accounting must ultimately reverse), estimated values will not be affected by accounting choices, *as long as the analyst recognizes the accounting distortions.*[7]

If accounting reliability is a concern, the analyst has to expend resources on accounting adjustments. When a company uses "biased" accounting – either conservative or aggressive – the analyst needs to recognize the bias to ensure that value estimates are not biased. If a thorough analysis is not performed, a firm's accounting choices can influence analysts' perceptions of the real performance of the firm and hence the forecasts of future performance. Accounting choice would affect expectations of future earnings and cash flows, and distort the valuation, regardless of whether the valuation is based on DCF or discounted abnormal earnings. For example, if a firm overstates current revenue growth through aggressive revenue recognition, failure to appreciate the effect is likely to lead the analyst to overstate future revenues, affecting both earnings and cash flow forecasts.

An analyst who encounters biased accounting has two choices – either to adjust current earnings and book values to eliminate managers' accounting biases, or to recognize these biases and adjust future forecasts accordingly. Whereas both approaches lead to the same estimated firm value, the choice will have an important impact on what fraction of the firm's value is captured within the forecast horizon, and what remains in the terminal value. Holding forecasting horizon and future growth opportunities constant, higher accounting quality allows a higher fraction of a firm's value to be captured by the current book value, earnings, and the abnormal earnings within the forecasting horizon.

Dealing with negative book values

A number of firms have negative earnings and book values of book equity. Firms in the start-up phase have negative equity, as do those in high technology industries. These firms incur large investments whose payoff is uncertain. Accountants write off these investments as a matter of conservatism, leading to negative book equity. Examples of firms in this situation include biotechnology firms, Internet firms, telecommunication firms, and other high technology firms. A second category of firms with negative book equity are those that are performing poorly, resulting in cumulative losses exceeding the original investment by the shareholders.

Negative book equity and negative earnings make it difficult to use the accounting-based approach to value a firm's equity. There are several possible ways to get around this problem. The first approach is to value the firm's assets (using, for example, abnormal return on operating assets or abnormal NOPAT) rather than equity. Then, based on an estimate of the value of the firm's debt, one can estimate the equity value. Another alternative is to "undo" accountants' conservatism by capitalizing the investment expenditures written off. This is possible if the analyst is able to establish that these expenditures are value creating. A third alternative, feasible for publicly traded firms, is to start from the observed share price and work backwards. Using reasonable estimates of cost of equity and steady-state growth rate, the analyst can calculate the average long-term level of abnormal earnings or abnormal earnings growth needed to justify the observed share price. Then the analytical task can be framed in terms of examining the feasibility of achieving this abnormal earnings (growth) "target."

It is important to note that the value of firms with negative book equity often consists of a significant option value. For example, the value of high tech firms is not only driven by the expected earnings from their current technologies, but also the payoff from technology options embedded in their research and development efforts.

Similarly, the value of troubled companies is driven to some extent by the "abandonment option" – shareholders with limited liability can put the firm to debt holders and creditors. One can use the options theory framework to estimate the value of these "real options."[8]

Dealing with excess cash flow

Firms with large free cash flows also pose a valuation challenge. In our projections in Table 8.3, we implicitly assumed that cash beyond the level required to finance a company's operations will be paid out to the firm's shareholders. Excess cash flows are assumed to be paid out to shareholders either in the form of dividends or share repurchases. Notice that these cash flows are already incorporated into the valuation process when they are earned, so there is no need to take them into account when they are paid out.

It is important to recognize that both the accounting-based valuations and the discounted cash flow valuation assume a dividend payout that can potentially vary from period to period. This dividend policy assumption is required as long as one wishes to assume a constant level of financial leverage, a constant cost of equity, and a constant required return on operating assets used in the valuation calculations. As discussed in a later chapter, firms rarely have such a variable dividend policy in practice. However, this in itself does not make the valuation approaches invalid, as long as a firm's dividend policy does not affect its value. That is, the valuation approaches assume that the well known Modigliani-Miller theorem regarding the irrelevance of dividends holds.

A firm's dividend policy can affect its value if managers do not invest free cash flows optimally. For example, if a firm's managers are likely to use excess cash to undertake value-destroying acquisitions, then our approach overestimates the firm's value. If the analyst has these types of concerns about a firm, one approach is to first estimate the firm according to the approach described earlier and then adjust the estimated value for whatever agency costs the firm's managers may impose on its investors. One approach to evaluating whether or not a firm suffers from severe agency costs is to examine how effective its corporate governance processes are.

SUMMARY

We illustrate in this chapter how to apply the valuation theory discussed in Chapter 7. The chapter explains the set of business and financial assumptions one needs to make to conduct the valuation exercise. It also illustrates the mechanics of making detailed valuation forecasts and terminal values of earnings, free cash flows, and accounting rates of return. We also discuss how to compute cost of equity and the required return on operating assets. Using a detailed example, we show how a firm's equity values and asset values can be computed using earnings, cash flows, and rates of return. The sensitivity of equity and firm value to the assumptions, both during the forecast horizon and for the terminal value, are highlighted. Finally, we offer ways to deal with some commonly encountered practical issues, including accounting distortions, negative book values, and excess cash balances.

CORE CONCEPTS

Asset beta Sensitivity of a firm's assets' performance to economy-wide movements. The asset beta can be derived from the firm's equity beta, its debt to equity ratio and its tax rate:

$$\beta_{\text{BUSINESS ASSETS}} = \frac{(1 - \text{Tax rate}) \times \text{Debt}}{(1 - \text{Tax rate}) \times \text{Debt} + \text{Equity}} \beta_{\text{DEBT}}$$
$$+ \frac{\text{Equity}}{(1 - \text{Tax rate}) \times \text{Debt} + \text{Equity}} \beta_{\text{EQUITY}}$$

The asset beta remains constant if leverage changes and can be used to calculate the effect of a change in leverage on the equity beta.

Capital asset pricing model Model expressing the cost of equity as a function of (1) the risk-free rate (r_f) and (2) a risk premium for systematic risk ($[E(r_m) - r_f]$):

$$r_e = r_f + \beta[E(r_m) - r_f]$$

The risk-free rate is typically the rate of return on intermediate-term government bonds. Systematic or beta risk (β) is the risk from correlation of the firm's return and the market return.

Competitive equilibrium assumption Assumption that competitive forces will drive down a firm's abnormal earnings until it reaches an equilibrium stage in which the firm's return on equity equals it cost of equity. If it is assumed that the firm reaches this equilibrium stage in or before the terminal year, the terminal value is equal to zero in the abnormal earnings (growth) model and is equal to the discounted terminal-year book value of equity in the free cash flow model.

Cost of equity Rate of return that equity investors demand on their investment and discount rate in the equity valuation model. One way to estimate the cost of equity is to use the capital asset pricing model. Firm size may also affect the cost of equity: small firms tend to have higher (required) rates of return.

Required return on operating assets Rate of return that equity and debt investors demand on their operating investments and discount rate in the (operating) asset valuation model. The required return on operating assets can be calculated using the CAPM model and an estimate of the operating asset beta:

$$\beta_{\text{OPERATING ASSETS}} = \left[\frac{\text{Equity}}{(1 - \text{Tax rate}) \times \text{Debt} + \text{Equity} - \text{Investment assets}}\right]\beta_{\text{EQUITY}}$$
$$+ \left[\frac{(1 - \text{Tax rate}) \times \text{Debt}}{(1 - \text{Tax rate}) \times \text{Debt} + \text{Equity} - \text{Investment assets}}\right]\beta_{\text{DEBT}}$$
$$- \left[\frac{\text{Investment assets}}{(1 - \text{Tax rate}) \times \text{Debt} + \text{Equity} - \text{Investment assets}}\right]\beta_{\text{INVESTMENT ASSETS}}$$

The weights must be calculated using the market values of debt, equity, and investment assets.

Terminal value Present value of abnormal earnings (growth) or free cash flows occurring beyond the last year of the forecasting period (labeled terminal year).

Weighted average cost of capital (WACC) Rate of return that equity and debt investors demand on their investment and discount rate in the (business) asset valuation model. The WACC is the weighted average of the *after*-tax cost of debt and the cost of equity:

$$\text{WACC} = \frac{\text{Debt}}{\text{Debt} + \text{Equity}}(1 - \text{Tax rate}) \times \text{Cost of debt} + \frac{\text{Equity}}{\text{Debt} + \text{Equity}}\text{Cost of equity}$$

The weights must be calculated using the market values of debt and equity.

QUESTIONS, EXERCISES, AND PROBLEMS

1 A spreadsheet containing Hennes & Mauritz's actual and forecasted financial statements as well as the valuation described in this chapter is available on the companion website of this book. How will the forecasts in Table 8.3 for Loewe change if the assumed growth rate in sales from 2012 to 2019 remains at 5 percent (and all the other assumptions are kept unchanged)?

2 Recalculate the forecasts in Table 8.3 assuming that the NOPAT profit margin declines by 1 percentage point per year between fiscal 2015 and 2019 (keeping all the other assumptions unchanged).

3 Recalculate the forecasts in Table 8.4 assuming that the ratio of net operating working capital to sales is 15 percent, and the ratio of net non-current operating assets to sales is 65 percent for all the years from fiscal 2012 to fiscal 2021. Keep all the other assumptions unchanged.

4   Calculate H&M's cash payouts to its shareholders in the years 2012–2021 that are implicitly assumed in the projections in Table 8.3.

5   How will the abnormal earnings calculations in Table 8.4 change if the cost of equity assumption is changed to 10 percent?

6   How will the terminal values in Table 8.6 change if the sales growth in years 2022 and beyond is 4 percent, and the company keeps forever its abnormal returns at the same level as in fiscal 2021 (keeping all the other assumptions in the table unchanged)? If sales growth is 3 percent in 2021 and 4 percent in 2022, why are the equity value estimates of the free cash flow model and the abnormal earnings model no longer the same?

7   Calculate the proportion of terminal values to total estimated values of equity under the abnormal earnings method, the abnormal earnings growth method, and the discounted cash flow method. Why are these proportions different?

8   Under the competitive equilibrium assumption the terminal value in the discounted cash flow model is the present value of the end-of-year book value of equity in the terminal year. Explain.

9   Under the competitive equilibrium assumption the terminal value in the discounted abnormal earnings growth model is the present value of abnormal earnings in the terminal year times minus one, capitalized at the cost of equity. Explain.

10   What will be H&M's cost of equity if the equity market risk premium is 6 percent?

11   Assume that H&M changes its capital structure so that its market value weight of debt to capital increases to 45 percent, and its after-tax interest rate on debt at this new leverage level is 4 percent. Assume that the equity market risk premium is 7 percent. What will be the cost of equity at the new debt level? What will be the weighted average cost of capital?

12   Nancy Smith says she is uncomfortable making the assumption that H&M's dividend payout will vary from year to year. If she makes a constant dividend payout assumption, what changes does she have to make in her other valuation assumptions to make them internally consistent with each other?

Problem 1 Hugo Boss's and Adidas's terminal values

Refer to Problem 1 in Chapter 7 (see p. 298).

1   The analyst following Hugo Boss estimates a target price of €20 per share. Under the assumption that the company's profit margins, asset turnover, and capital structure remain constant after 2011, what is the terminal growth rate that is implicit in the analysts' forecasts and target price?

2   Using the analyst's forecasts, estimate Hugo Boss's equity value under the following three scenarios:
   a   Hugo Boss enters into a competitive equilibrium in 2012.
   b   After 2011, Hugo Boss's competitive advantage can only be maintained on the nominal sales level achieved in 2011.
   c   After 2011, Hugo Boss's competitive advantage can be maintained on a sales base that remains constant in real terms.

3   Using the analyst's forecasts, estimate Hugo Boss's equity value under the assumption that the company's profitability gradually reverts to its required level (i.e., $AE_t = 0.75 \times AE_{t-1}$) after the terminal year.
   Refer to Problem 2 in Chapter 7.

4   Using the analyst's forecasts, estimate Adidas's terminal values in the discounted cash flow and the abnormal earnings growth models under the assumption that the company enters into a competitive equilibrium in 2015.

Problem 2 *Anheuser-Busch InBev S.A.*

In November 2008, the Belgian InBev S.A. completed the acquisition of US-based Anheuser-Busch. The brewer acquired Anheuser-Busch for close to €40 billion, of which it classified approximately €25 billion as goodwill. At the end of the fiscal year ending on December 31, 2008, Anheuser-Busch InBev's (AB InBev) net assets amounted to €61,357 million, consisting of €64,183 million in non-current assets and –€2,826 million in working capital. The company's book value of equity amounted to €16,126 million.

Early May, 2009, when AB Inbev's 1,593 million common shares trade at about €24 per share, an analyst produces the following forecasts for the company and issues an "overweight" (buy) recommendation.

Forecasts (€ millions)	2009	2010	2011	2012	2013	2014	2015	2016	2017	2018
Sales	28,475	26,688	27,909	29,047	30,089	31,011	31,810	32,470	32,311	32,658
NOPAT	6,169	6,294	6,729	7,003	7,254	7,476	7,669	7,828	7,790	7,874
Depreciation and amortization	2,297	2,158	2,228	2,318	2,402	2,475	2,539	2,592	2,579	2,607
Investment in non-current assets	−1,529	−1,441	1,549	−1,743	−1,805	−1,860	−1,909	−1,948	−1,939	−1,959
Investment in working capital	485	580	669	435	451	465	477	487	485	490
Free cash flow to debt and equity	7,425	7,590	8,077	8,014	8,301	8,556	8,777	8,958	8,915	9,011

1 The analyst estimates that AB InBev's weighted average cost of capital is 9 percent and assumes that the free cash flow to debt and equity grows indefinitely at a rate of 1 percent after 2018. Show that under these assumptions, the equity value per share estimate exceeds AB InBev's share price.

2 Calculate AB InBev's expected abnormal NOPATs between 2009 and 2018 based on the above information. How does the implied trend in abnormal NOPAT compare with the general trends in the economy?

3 Estimate AB InBev's equity value using the abnormal NOPAT model (under the assumption that the WACC is 9 percent and the terminal growth rate is 1 percent). Why do the discounted cash flow model and the abnormal NOPAT model yield different outcomes?

4 What adjustments to the forecasts are needed to make the two valuation models consistent?

NOTES

1. See T. Copeland, T. Koller, and J. Murrin, *Valuation: Measuring and Managing the Value of Companies*, 2nd edition (New York: John Wiley & Sons, 1994).
2. One way to estimate systematic risk is to regress the firm's stock returns over some recent time period against the returns on the market index. The slope coefficient represents an estimate of β. More fundamentally, systematic risk depends on how sensitive the firm's operating profits are to shifts in economy-wide activity, and the firm's degree of leverage. Financial analysis that assesses these operating and financial risks should be useful in arriving at reasonable estimates of β.
3. The average return reported here is the arithmetic mean as opposed to the geometric mean. Ibbotson and Associates explain why this estimate is appropriate in this context (see *Stocks, Bonds, Bills, and Inflation*, 2002 Chicago Yearbook,). This estimate of the worldwide equity risk premium comes from E. Dimson, P. Marsh, and M. Staunton, "Credit Suisse Global Investment Returns Sourcebook," which updates the evidence in "Global Evidence on the Equity Risk Premium," *Journal of Applied Corporate Finance* 15(4) (2003): 8–19.
4. E. Dimson, P. Marsh, and M. Staunton (2003), op. cit., argue that when estimating future equity risk premiums, it is preferred to take a global approach than a country-by-country approach. Reasons for taking a global approach are, for example, that many country-specific events that affected historical risk premiums are nonrecurring and that worldwide capital markets have integrated significantly. In their study "International Differences in the Cost of Equity Capital: Do Legal Institutions and Securities Matter," *Journal of Accounting Research* 44(3) (2006): 485–531, L. Hail and C. Leuz provide evidence that international differences in

the strictness of disclosure and securities regulation and enforcement also create international differences in firms' cost of equity. Harmonization of such regulations within, for example, the European Union may therefore also reduce the country variations in risk premiums.

5. See Mathijs A. van Dijk, "Is size dead? A review of the size effect in equity returns," *Journal of Banking and Finance* 35 (2011): 3263–3274.

6. See William R. Gebhardt, Charles M. C. Lee, and Bhaskaran Swaminathan, "Toward an Ex-Ante Cost of Capital," *Journal of Accounting Research* 39 (2001): 135–176; and James Claus and Jacob Thomas, "Equity Premia as Low as Three Percent? Evidence from Analysts' Earnings Forecasts for Domestic and International Stock Markets," *The Journal of Finance* 56 (October 2001): 1629–1666.

7. Valuation based on discounted abnormal earnings does require one property of the forecasts: that they be consistent with "clean surplus accounting." Such accounting requires the following relation:

End-of-period book value = Beginning book value + earnings − dividends ± capital contributions/withdrawals

Clean surplus accounting rules out situations where some gain or loss is excluded from earnings but is still used to adjust the book value of equity. For example, under IFRS, gains and losses on foreign currency translations are handled this way. In applying the valuation technique described here, the analyst would need to deviate from IFRS in producing forecasts and treat such gains/losses as a part of earnings. However, the technique does *not* require that clean surplus accounting has been applied *in the past* – so the existing book value, based on IFRS or any other set of principles, can still serve as the starting point. All the analyst needs to do is apply clean surplus accounting in his/her forecasts. That much is not only easy but is usually the natural thing to do anyway.

8. If negative earnings are likely to be transitory, this may be a reason to extend the forecast horizon. P. Joos and G. Plesko find that the probability of losses being transitory is negatively related to the size of the loss and positively related to the size of the firm, sales growth, whether or not the loss is the first loss, and whether or not the firm pays out dividends. If a loss is likely to be permanent, the value of the firm is driven by the value of the abandonment option. See P. Joos and G. Plesko, "Valuing Loss Firms," *The Accounting Review* 80 (2005): 847–870.

Ryanair Holdings plc

R yanair is a low-cost, low-fare airline headquartered in Dublin, Ireland, operating over 200 routes in 20 countries. The company has directly challenged the largest airlines in Europe and has built a 20-year-plus track record of incredibly strong passenger growth while progressively reducing fares. It is not unusual for one-way tickets (exclusive of taxes) to sell on Ryanair's website for less than €1.00. See **Exhibit 1** for an excerpt of Ryanair's website, where fares between London and Stockholm, for example, are available for 19 pence (approximately US$0.33). CEO Michael O'Leary, formerly an accountant at KPMG, described the airline as follows: "Ryanair is doing in the airline industry in Europe what Ikea has done. We pile it high and sell it cheap…. For years flying has been the preserve of rich [people]. Now everyone can afford to fly."[1] Having created profitable operations in the difficult airline industry, Ryanair, as did industry analysts, likened itself to US carrier Southwest Airlines, and its common stock has attracted the attention of investors in Europe and abroad.

Low-fare airlines

Historically the airline industry has been a notoriously difficult business in which to make consistent profits. Over the past several decades, low-fare airlines have been launched in an attempt to operate with lower costs, but with few exceptions, most have gone bankrupt or been swallowed up by larger carriers (see **Exhibit 2** for a list of failed airlines). Given the excess capacity in the global aircraft market in more recent years, barriers to entry in the commercial airline space have never been so low. Price competition in the US and Europe, along with rising fuel costs, has had a deleterious effect on both profits and margins at most carriers. The current state of the industry can be described for most carriers as, at best, tumultuous.

The introduction of the low-fare sector in the United States predated its arrival in Europe. An open-skies policy was introduced through the Airline Deregulation Act of 1978, which removed controls of routes, fares, and schedules from the control of the Civil Aeronautics Board.[2] This spurred 22 new airlines to be formed between 1978 and 1982, each hoping to stake its claim in the newly deregulated market.[3] These airlines maximized their scheduling efficiencies, which, in combination with lower staff-to-plane ratios and a more straightforward service offering, gave them a huge cost advantage over the big

Professor Mark T. Bradshaw prepared this case with the assistance of Fergal Naugton and Jonathan O'Grady (MBAs 2005). This case was prepared from published sources. HBS cases are developed solely as the basis for class discussion. Cases are not intended to serve as endorsements, sources of primary data, or illustrations of effective or ineffective management.

[1] G. Bowley, "How Low Can You Go?" FT.com website, June 20, 2003.

[2] US Centennial of Flight Commission report, www.centennialofflight.gov/essay/Commercial_Aviation/Dereg/Tran8.htm.

[3] N. Donohue and P. Ghemawat, "The US Airline Industry, 1978–1988 (A)," HBS No. 390-025.

airlines. This led to the current two-tier industry structure, with the low-fare airlines waging fare wars with the larger established carriers.

This was, however, a challenging time for the start-ups. First, the Federal Reserve raised the funds rate from 7.93 percent in 1978 to 12.26 percent in 1982. This had a dramatic effect on the financing costs for the start-up airlines, making financing of capital expenditures excessively costly. In addition, at this time the incumbent airlines were generally in relatively strong financial positions. Their deep pockets made it possible for them to run at a loss on certain routes in order to undercut the start-ups where necessary. As a result, many of the new companies failed.

One notable exception, however, was Southwest Airlines. By focusing on secondary airports, lightning-fast turnarounds, information technology, and a strong firm culture, it managed to gain passenger share and profitability. Within a decade, ticket prices in the US had fallen by 33 percent, and the volume of passengers had more than doubled.[4]

In Europe, it was not until 1992, with the signing of the Maastricht Treaty, that years of protectionism by the governments of the so-called flag carriers began to be dismantled. In 1993, European Union (EU) national carriers were for the first time permitted to offer international services from other EU countries. By 1997, this was broadened to include domestic destinations and opened to any certified EU airline. Open skies had arrived in Europe.

Even before then, start-up airlines had begun to enter the European space. These companies would typically negotiate with their country's flag carrier for the right to fly to secondary airports only. Ticket sales were handled by agents, and the resulting cost structure forced the start-ups to compete with the incumbents, primarily on service. Because they were not competing to provide traffic for the major hubs but rather targeting customers who had not previously considered flights for travel, they were in effect growing the market and were thus not seen as a major threat to the legacy carriers. However, with the Maastricht Treaty, the number of new airlines entering the industry greatly increased, and these start-ups were now free to compete solely on cost, looking across the Atlantic to the Southwest model.

Subsequently, as the new entrants vied for market space, prices fell, encouraging previously untapped demand. European passenger volumes had a strong upward trajectory (5 percent-plus compound annual growth rate between 1998 and 2003). However, while low-cost passenger numbers soared, the long-haul operators faced reduced traffic and higher fuel costs due to events such as the SARS virus and the September 11 attacks. The flag carriers, now financially constrained, were forced to renegotiate, and even cancel, contracts for the delivery of new aircraft from Airbus and Boeing. The two aerospace giants were left with significant numbers of planes for which the start-ups proved to be welcome customers.

Unlike the arrangements legacy carriers negotiated with major airports, start-up airlines negotiated dramatically lower landing and facility charges with secondary airports. They argued that, because they were bringing a significant number of passengers through these airports on a regular basis, the airports would be able to substantially increase the rents they received from concession stands and other retailers. As the low-fare airlines had no particular loyalty to one airport over another, the threat that they could simply stop flying to a particular airport was real.

Ryanair

Ryanair was Europe's first low-fare carrier, with an initial route between Waterford, Ireland and London. The initial cabin crew had to be no taller than 5′ 2″ because the aircraft being deployed were among the smallest being flown on commercial routes. The company immediately challenged incumbents Aer Lingus and British Airways and obtained approval for a Dublin–London (Luton) route, charging less than half of what the large carriers were charging. A price war ensued, but over the next decade Ryanair eventually overtook Aer Lingus and British Airways on this route, the largest international route in Europe at that time.[5] (See **Exhibit 3** for Ryanair's remarkable passenger growth from 1985 through 2004.)

The company went public on May 9, 1997, and shortly thereafter was voted "Airline of the Year" by the Irish Air Transport Users Committee, "Best Managed National Airline" in the world by *International Aviation Week* magazine, "Best Value Airline" by the UK's *Which* consumer magazine, and most popular airline

[4] "Freedom in the Air," *The Economist*, April 3, 1997.
[5] Company website.

on the Web by Google. Relative to that of other airlines, Ryanair's common stock has performed reasonably well since the company went public, despite negative events such as the Iraq war and significant increases in fuel prices. The company emphasizes that it defines customer service by low airfares and safety, rather than by the quality of food, pleasantness of staff, and other peripheral items.

See **Exhibit 4** for the stock price performance of Ryanair and selected European airlines since Ryanair's initial public offering. Additionally, see **Exhibits 5–7** for Ryanair's 2004 financial statements and supplemental revenue and cost information. The financial statements were prepared under Irish and UK accounting standards. Because the company has shares trading on the NASDAQ in the US, they also provide a reconciliation of major line items from Irish and UK accounting standards to US accounting standards (see **Exhibit 8**).

Ryanair's objectives, as set forth in its 2004 annual report, include:

- Increasing passenger traffic by 20 percent each year.
- Reducing fares by 5 percent each year.
- Reducing costs by 5 percent each year.
- Realizing a profit margin of 20 percent or more.

To date, there are numerous factors that have contributed to the company's profitability, including the following:

1 *Cut-price deals.* Ryanair will frequently sell a large number of seats in advance for a nominal fee, for example, €1.00 or less. Indeed, currently approximately 25 percent of passenger tickets are free, and Mr O'Leary has a goal of eventually bringing this figure to 50 percent by 2010. This attracts immense publicity as customers scramble to log in and purchase seats. For each seat purchased, tax and duties must also be paid, which typically amount to €30–€40. The tickets are sold on a nonrefundable basis. Because they are so cheap, many buy multiple seats to gain flexibility, and the "no show" rate is therefore much higher for these types of tickets. Average fares reflect these cut-price deals as well as higher fares that travelers pay to secure seats on routes in higher demand.

2 *Point-to-point flights.* Each route is a mini-business unit. Capacity is tailored to fit demand according to computer-simulated models. If a route is unprofitable, it can simply be cut from the schedule. Passengers may not buy connecting flights so must check in for each Ryanair flight individually. This reduces the firm's liability in the event of a delay and reduces instances of lost baggage.

3 *Flights to secondary airports.* By avoiding the large hubs, Ryanair is able to negotiate reduced landing charges. There is the added benefit of lower congestion at such airports. This allows the aircraft to complete the journey in the shortest possible time. The downside to passengers is that sometimes these airports are located in locations far from the intended destination. For example, the company flies to Frankfurt-Hahn, not Frankfurt, which is 100 kilometers away. As O'Leary states, "For the price-sensitive customers, distance is no problem."[6]

4 *Quick turnaround.* Ryanair aircraft are expected to land and take off again from an airport inside 25 minutes. This is only possible because they fly into secondary airports. This allows the firm to maximize the number of flights per day.

5 *No overnighting of staff.* By flying point to point, a Ryanair plane ends the day where it started. This means that crew can return to their homes, and expensive hotel bills and per diems are avoided.

6 *Internet bookings.* The firm sells over 97 percent of its tickets via the internet at its website, www.ryanair.com, which is now the most popular European travel site. This cuts out travel agent commission costs (averaging approximately 10 percent of the ticket cost) and gives the airline maximum control over scheduling and capacity. Moreover, it funnels customers towards other services such as car hire and rail tickets, for which Ryanair collects a commission itself. O'Leary is not bashful about this substantial source of cost savings and revenues, having stated, "Screw the travel agent. Take the [agents] out and shoot them. What have they done for passengers over the years?"[7]

Ryanair Holdings plc

---

[6]G. Bowley, "How Low Can You Go?"
[7]Ibid.

7 *One class.* Ryanair does not offer passengers the choice of business and economy class, eliminating the requirement for food to be delivered to the aircraft when it lands, thus facilitating low turnaround times. Moreover, offering only one class of service furthers the goal of providing low fares, which the company believes is the ultimate in customer service. According to its passenger service and lowest fares charter, "Ryanair believes that any passenger service commitment must involve a commitment on pricing and punctuality, and should not be confined to less important aspects of 'service' which is the usual excuse the high fare airlines use for charging high air fares."[8]

8 *One aircraft type.* The company flies Boeing 737 planes exclusively. This reduces maintenance training costs and allows for bulk buying of spare parts. The strong financial position of the company allowed it to purchase many of the aircraft that had been canceled by incumbent airlines. These new airplanes are more fuel efficient and have a higher passenger capacity. As of the end of fiscal 2004, the company had fully hedged fuel costs through September 2004, but were largely unhedged thereafter. Subsequently, the company hedged its fuel through the end of fiscal 2006 at US$49 per barrel, while market values topped US$70 per barrel. Additionally, the company has ordered winglets that will be retrofitted on all aircraft, which will reduce fuel burn by approximately 2.5 percent, which translates into savings of approximately US$10,000–14,000 per aircraft per month.

9 *Personnel costs and incentives.* Because the aircraft that Ryanair pilots fly are new, the firm claims that their pilots' experience is of value to the competition. Therefore, it charges pilots for training, the cost of which is earned back by the pilots through years of service. Pilots have financial incentives for smooth landings, not so much for passenger comfort but for reduced maintenance costs. Additionally, the airline does not provide food or beverages for free but does offer items for sale on each flight. Flight attendants are paid a commission based on the total of beverage and other sales in flight.

Ryanair has an entrepreneurial culture and takes great pride in breaking with old conventions. This spirit is disseminated from the top by the swashbuckling manner of CEO O'Leary. Irish business folklore has it that when he first decided to employ the internet to sell seats, O'Leary did not hire a firm of IT consultants and Web designers. He instead visited a local technical college and offered the project as a challenge to the eager students in the computer lab. They learned by doing, and O'Leary got a website with the necessary functionality at a fraction of list price. He is also known for wild publicity stunts, such as driving a tank to easyJet's headquarters in England and broadcasting the theme to the television show "The A-Team." He taunts the competition even with the painting of aircraft. One of Ryanair's airplanes is painted with the message, "Arrivederci Alitalia."[9]

O'Leary is not bashful of his company's achievements, and has a unique demeanor for a company CEO, often charmingly foul-mouthed and offensive. In a recent interview, he stated "I don't give a [*&%#] if nobody likes me. I am not a cloud bunny, I am not an aerosexual. I don't like aeroplanes. I never wanted to be a pilot like those other platoons of goons who populate the air industry."[10] Attacking competitors is not out of the question either, as he recently said of Jurgen Weber, CEO of Lufthansa, "Weber says Germans don't like low fares. How the [*&%#] does he know? He never offered them any."[11]

He positions the airline as a champion against inefficiencies and monopolies, and his manner has been described as arrogant and dismissive. Even in financial reports for investors, he often leads off with tirades against airports that charge too much or other issues that adversely affect Ryanair. For example, the 2005 road show included several slides titled "Stansted Airport: The Rip-Off," which highlighted costs of a cross-subsidization plan across airports run by the British Airport Authority. Similarly, in discussing 2005 financial results, the company report stated:

In Ireland, the situation at Dublin Airport has descended into a farce. The Dublin Airport Authority which is responsible for this third world facility is to be rewarded for its incompetence by being allowed to build the second terminal. This facility will not be available until 2009 at the earliest and in the mean time passengers at Dublin will be forced to endure long queues and intolerable overcrowding while the Government protects this failed monopoly by blocking competition.... The [prime minister]

---

[8]Company website.

[9]G. Bowley, "How Low Can You Go?"

[10]A. Clark, "The Guardian profile: Michael O'Leary," *The Guardian*, June 24, 2005.

[11]M. Ridley, "The World's Favourite 'Despot'," *Daily Express*, June 1, 2005.

recently demonstrated how hopelessly out of touch he is by claiming that the present overcrowded terminal has the capacity for 6 million more passengers per annum. It would appear that there aren't any queues at the VIP escort to the Government jet.... Had the Government heeded Ryanair's calls for a competing second terminal seven years ago, this current embarrassment for Irish tourism would have been avoided. As always in Ireland the ordinary passengers suffer, while the politicians fudge.[12]

Turbulence in 2004

Just after reporting third-quarter profit increases of 10 percent (quarter ended December 31, 2003), Ryanair issued a profit warning in January 2004 for the company's upcoming full-year results for the fiscal year ending March 31, 2004. O'Leary stated, "While we now expect after-tax profits for the current year to dip slightly, our annualized profit margin will still be in excess of 20 percent, and Ryanair will continue to be the world's most profitable airline by margin." Ryanair's share price dropped 30 percent on the news (see **Exhibit 9**). The expected fall in profits for the fourth quarter was attributed to lower yields (i.e., average passenger fares) and lower load factors (i.e., seats with paying passengers as a fraction of total seats available). According to O'Leary, the lower yields were due to Ryanair's strategy of steadily lowering fares as part of its battle plan. He argued, "This is not due to overcapacity. It's the result of the ongoing fare wars under way across Europe, and we're winning them. It's like Southwest in the US. When they first went into California, their stock price fell by 40 percent to 50 percent due to fare wars with the likes of the United [Airlines] shuttle and other California carriers. Ten years later, Southwest owned California."[13]

More bad news followed immediately after the profit warning, when Ryanair received an unfavorable ruling from the European Commission (EC) regarding $18 million in financial incentives it had received from Charleroi Airport in Belgium between 2001 and 2003. The commissioners indicated that the ruling was an attempt to encourage economic growth while simultaneously ending state subsidies that have been declared illegal under the EU. The ruling put additional pressure on Ryanair's stock price. In response, O'Leary explained, "Any share price jumps up and down, and ours is no exception. But as long as the basic business model is sound and you're executing it properly, nothing will stop you – certainly not a bunch of EU commissioners who think everyone should pay higher fares."[14]

Financial performance

Prior to the profit warnings in early 2004, Ryanair had been profitable every quarter and reported annual increases in sales, operating profit, and net income in every year (see **Exhibit 10**). As forewarned in January 2004, despite an increase in sales for fiscal 2004, net income declined for the fiscal year ended March 31, 2004, relative to the fiscal 2003 level. This was the first reported year-over-year downturn in profits since the company went public.

Nevertheless, Ryanair continued to add capacity in 2004, increasing available seat kilometers by 64 percent. The overall load factor for 2004 exceeded 80 percent, relative to a break-even level of 59 percent. The company's fleet of planes had 189 seats, implying that, on average, 111 seats had to be filled for the company to break even. Ryanair has the lowest cost structure of any comparable airline, as seen in **Exhibit 11**. The company is obsessive about low costs, down to details such as making employees provide their own pens and not allowing the charging of cell phones in corporate facilities. Low costs permit Ryanair to charge lower fares and still provide a high return on investment. See **Exhibit 12** for average revenue per passenger, return on equity (ROE), and other financial metrics for 15 airlines. Ryanair's average revenue per passenger (in US$) is just $49. The only other airlines with similarly low fares include UK-based easyJet (US$77 per passenger) and Southwest Airlines (US$89). Nearly half of the airlines listed (all US-based incumbent carriers) report losses and/or have meaningless ROE because the denominator of the calculation (i.e., book value of equity) is negative. For 2004, Ryanair reports the highest ROE, 17 percent. The only other airline with profitability approaching that of Ryanair is Japan Airlines, but the duPont decomposition of ROE

Ryanair Holdings plc

---

[12]Company press release, May 31, 2005.

[13]"Airing Ryanair's Beef with the EC," BusinessWeek Online, February 16, 2004.

[14]Ibid.

indicates that this is largely driven by Japan Airlines' use of significant leverage, relative to limited leverage at Ryanair. Even with the relatively strong profitability, the stock market values Ryanair at just a modest level relative to other airlines, trading at a price-to-earnings ratio of 20.8 relative to 50.5 for newcomer Jet-Blue Airways and 40.7 for veteran low-fare airline Southwest.

Valuation

Following the series of bad news announcements in early 2004, the investor community split into two camps: those that saw the downturn in profits and cash flows as the end of Ryanair's strong performance run versus those that believed the stock price drop to be an overreaction to a company that retained strong fundamentals. **Exhibit 13** provides an analysis of Ryanair's profitability and operating, investment, and financing activities over the most recent three years. The overall picture is that of a financially healthy company with strong sales growth, high profitability, and negative net debt (i.e., interest-bearing liabilities less than cash and liquid resources).

Exhibit 14 summarizes equity analyst reports released during the first six months of 2004 that encompass the profit warnings in January, the EU decision in February, and the announcement of earnings in June. The recommendations span the range from sell, with target prices below the current trading price (e.g., target price of €4.40 when the current stock price was €4.65), to buy, with target prices at lofty levels up to 35 percent above the current trading price (e.g., target price of €6.00 when the current stock price was €4.41).

Clearly, discrepancies in valuations reflect divergent opinions on numerous issues that plague the airline sector, such as fare competition, cost containment, regulation, and macroeconomic vulnerability. Perhaps not surprisingly, in contrast to many market observers in the airline industry, Ryanair continues to have a bullish outlook, signing purchase agreements for an additional 140 Boeing 737 aircraft in February 2005. Each aircraft will have an approximate cost of US$51 million. With the addition of these aircraft to the 91 in service already, the company expects to grow annual passenger traffic to 70 million by 2012, almost triple the number in 2004.

Ryanair Holdings plc

EXHIBIT 1 **Ryanair website**

Source: www.ryanair.com, July 8, 2005.

EXHIBIT 2 Failed airlines in the US and Europe

US	People's Express	**Italy**	Volare
	Frontier Airlines		Agent Air
	Texas Air		Air Freedom
	New York Air		Free Airways
			Windjet
Great Britain	Duo		
	Now	**Poland**	Air Polonia
Ireland	Fresh Aer		DreamAir
	JetMagic		GetJet
	JetGreen		Silesian Air
	Skynet		White Eagle
Germany	Berlinjet	**Finland**	Flying Finn
	Low Fare Jet	**Norway**	Goodjet
	V-Bird	**Bosnia**	Air Bosnia
France	Aeris	**Spain**	Air Cataluyna
	Air Littoral		
	Airlib Express		
	Fly Eco		

Source: Merrion Stockbrokers Irish Equity Research report, January 21, 2005.

Ryanair Holdings plc

EXHIBIT 3 **Annual Ryanair passenger traffic (number of passengers), 1985–2006 (estimate)**

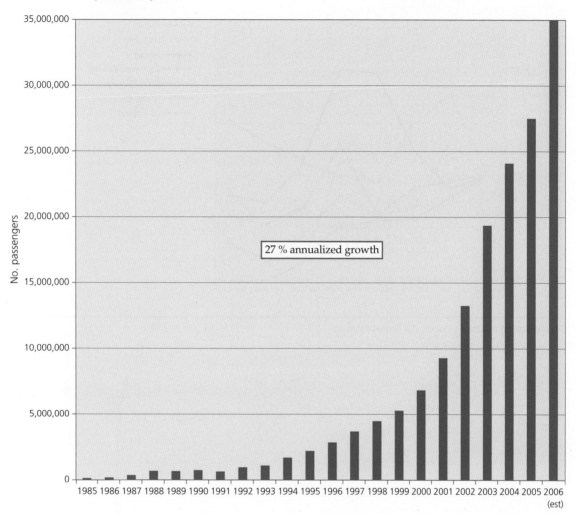

Source: Ryanair investor relations website.

EXHIBIT 4 **Relative stock price performance of selected European and US airlines: 1997–2003**

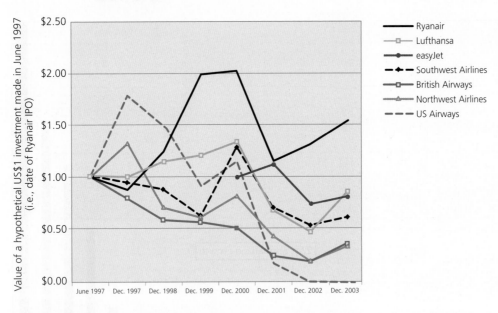

Source: Standard & Poor's Compustat Global database.

EXHIBIT 5   **Financial statements**

Consolidated Profit and Loss Account
(all amounts in €000, except per share and share amounts)

	2004	2003	2002
Operating revenue			
Scheduled revenues	924,566	731,951	550,991
Ancillary revenues	149,658	110,557	73,059
Total operating revenue – continuing operations	1,074,224	842,508	624,050
Operating expenses			
Staff costs	(123,624)	(93,073)	(78,240)
Depreciation and amortization	(101,391)	(76,865)	(59,010)
Other operating expenses	(597,922)	(409,096)	(323,867)
Total operating expenses excluding goodwill	(822,937)	(579,034)	(461,117)
Operating profit – continuing operations before amortization of goodwill	251,287	263,474	162,933
Amortization of goodwill	(2,342)	—	—
Operating profit – continuing operations after amortization of goodwill	248,945	263,474	162,933
Other (expenses)/income			
Foreign exchange gains	3,217	628	975
(Loss) on disposal of fixed assets	(9)	(29)	527
Interest receivable and similar income	23,891	31,363	27,548
Interest payable and similar charges	(47,564)	(30,886)	(19,609)
Total other (expenses)/income	(20,465)	1,076	9,441
Profit on ordinary activities before tax	228,480	264,550	172,374
Tax on profit on ordinary activities	(21,869)	(25,152)	(21,999)
Profit for the financial year	206,611	239,398	150,375
Earnings per ordinary share (€ cents)			
Basic	27.28	31.71	20.64
Diluted	27.00	31.24	20.32
Weighted average number of ordinary shares (000's)			
Basic	757,447	755,055	728,726
Diluted	759,300	766,279	739,961

Ryanair Holdings plc

EXHIBIT 5 Financial statements *(continued)*

Consolidated Balance Sheet (all amounts in €000)

	2004	2003
Fixed assets		
Intangible assets	44,499	0
Tangible assets	1,576,526	1,352,361
Total fixed assets	1,621,025	1,352,361
Current assets		
Cash and liquid resources	1,257,350	1,060,218
Accounts receivable	14,932	14,970
Other assets	19,251	16,370
Inventories	26,440	22,788
Total current assets	1,317,973	1,114,346
Total assets	2,938,998	2,466,707
Current liabilities		
Accounts payable	67,936	61,604
Accrued expenses and other liabilities	338,208	251,328
Current maturities of long term debt	80,337	63,291
Short term borrowings	345	1,316
Total current liabilities	486,826	377,539
Other liabilities		
Provisions for liabilities and charges	94,192	67,833
Accounts payable due after one year	30,047	5,673
Long term debt	872,645	773,934
Total other liabilities	996,884	847,440
Shareholders' funds-equity		
Called-up share capital	9,643	9,588
Share premium account	560,406	553,512
Profit and loss account	885,239	678,628
Total shareholders' funds-equity	1,455,288	1,241,728
Total liabilities and shareholders' funds	2,938,998	2,466,707

Ryanair Holdings plc

EXHIBIT 5 Financial statements *(continued)*

Consolidated Cash Flow Statement (all amounts in €000)

	2004	2003	2002
Net cash inflow from operating activities	462,062	351,003	309,109
Return on investments and servicing of finance			
Interest received	26,292	30,171	30,193
Interest paid	(46,605)	(29,563)	(19,833)
Net cash (outflow)/inflow from return on investments and servicing of finance	(20,313)	608	10,360
Taxation			
Corporation tax paid	(2,056)	(3,410)	(5,071)
Capital expenditure			
Purchase of tangible fixed assets	(331,603)	(469,878)	(372,587)
Sale of tangible fixed assets	4	31	563
Net cash (outflow) from capital expenditure	(331,599)	(469,847)	(372,024)
Acquisitions			
Purchase consideration	(20,795)	—	—
Onerous lease payments	(11,901)	—	—
Net cash (outflow) from acquisition of subsidiary undertakings	(32,696)	—	—
Net cash inflow/(outflow) before financing and management of liquid resources	75,398	(121,646)	(57,626)
Financing			
Loans raised	187,035	331,502	175,746
Loans repaid	(71,278)	(44,779)	(27,886)
Issue of share capital	6,948	56	188,331
Share issue costs	—	—	(6,330)
Capital element of finance leases	—	(1)	(107)
Net cash inflow from financing	122,705	286,778	329,754
Management of liquid resources			
(Increase) in liquid resources	(249,220)	(166,329)	(251,241)
Net cash (outflow)/inflow from financing and management of liquid resources	(126,515)	120,449	78,513
Increase (decrease) in cash	(51,117)	(1,197)	20,887

Ryanair Holdings plc

EXHIBIT 5   **Financial statements** *(continued)*

Consolidated Statement of Changes in Shareholders' Funds-equity (all amounts in €000)

	Called-up share capital	Share premium account	Profit and loss account	Total
Balance at March 31, 2002	9,587	553,457	439,230	1,002,274
Issue of ordinary equity shares (net of issue) costs)	1	55	—	56
Profit for the financial year	—	—	239,398	239,398
Balance at March 31, 2003	9,588	553,512	678,628	1,241,728
Issue of ordinary equity shares	55	6,894	—	6,949
Profit for the financial year	—	—	206,611	206,611
Balance at March 31, 2004	9,643	560,406	885,239	1,455,288

Source: 2004 and 2003 Ryanair annual reports.

EXHIBIT 6   **Supplemental revenue information (€000)**

Ancillary revenues comprise:	2004	2003
Nonflight scheduled	66,616	35,291
Car hire	35,110	27,615
Inflight	30,100	23,142
Internet income	17,721	12,159
Charter	111	12,350
	149,658	110,557

All of the group's operating profit arises from airline-related activities. Nonflight-scheduled revenue arises from the sale of rail and bus tickets, hotel reservations, and other revenues. Inflight revenues reflect sales of refreshments (e.g., peanuts, drinks) and other items (e.g., duty-free sales etc.). Internet income comprises revenue generated from Ryanair.com excluding internet car hire revenue which is included under the heading 'Car hire.'

Ancillary revenue increased by 35 percent to €149.7 million and reflects strong growth in nonflight scheduled revenue, car hire, and hotel revenue, offset, by the cessation of the charter program as Ryanair replaced charter capacity with scheduled services. Ancillary revenues were also negatively impacted by the strengthening of the euro versus sterling in the year, as 65 percent of ancillary revenues are denominated in sterling. Ancillary revenue, excluding charters increased by 52 percent, higher than the growth in passenger numbers, and accounted for 14 percent of total revenues compared to 13 percent in the year ended March 31, 2003.

Source: 2004 Ryanair annual report.

EXHIBIT 7 Supplemental cost information (€000)

STAFF NUMBER AND COSTS

Average weekly number of employees, including the executive director, during the year, analyzed by category:	2004	2003
Flight and cabin crew	1,530	983
Sales, operations, and administration	758	763
	2,288	1,746

Aggregate payroll costs of these persons:	2004	2003
Wages, salaries, and related costs	112,258	82,633
Social welfare costs	9,660	7,835
Other pension costs	1,706	2,605
	123,624	93,073

OTHER OPERATING EXPENSES

Other operating expenses comprise:	2004	2003
Fuel and oil	174,991	128,842
Airport and handling charges	147,221	107,994
Route charges	110,271	68,406
Maintenance, materials, and repairs	43,420	29,709
Marketing and distribution costs	16,141	14,623
Aircraft rentals	11,541	—
Other costs	78,034	59,522
	582,619	409,096
Exceptional costs		
Aircraft rentals	13,291	—
Buzz reorganization	3,012	—
	16,303	—
	598,922	409,096

Other costs include, among other things, certain direct costs of providing inflight service, car hire costs, and other non-flight scheduled costs.

Exceptional items are those items that are material items which derive from events or transactions that fall within the ordinary activities of the group but which need to be disclosed by virtue of their size or incidence. The exceptional costs relate to the closure of Buzz for one month post acquisition to restructure the business and integrate it into Ryanair and the exceptional lease costs associated with the early permanent retirement of six Boeing 737-200 aircraft which are no longer operated due to scratch marks which occurred during an aircraft painting program. The costs are treated as exceptional as they are material to the results for the year.

Source: 2004 Ryanair annual report.

Ryanair Holdings plc

EXHIBIT 8 Summary of differences between Irish/United Kingdom and US GAAP (€000)

	2004	2003	2002
Profit for financial year as reported in the consolidated profit and loss account and in accordance with Irish and UK GAAP	206,611	239,398	150,375
Adjustments			
Pensions	89	697	751
Derivative financial instruments (net of tax)	—	(4,189)	—
Amortization of goodwill	2,342	—	—
Employment grants	—	469	464
Capitalized interest regarding aircraft acquisition programme	7,213	5,262	5,027
Darley Investments Limited	88	88	88
Taxation – effect of above adjustments	(913)	85	(1,156)
Net income in accordance with US GAAP	215,430	241,810	155,549
Total assets as reported in the consolidated balance sheets and in accordance with Irish and UK GAAP	2,938,998	2,466,707	1,889,572
Adjustments			
Pensions	3,200	3,111	2,414
Amortization of goodwill	2,342	—	—
Capitalized interest regarding aircraft acquisition programme	17,502	10,289	5,027
Darley Investments Limited	(151)	(239)	(327)
Total assets as adjusted to accord with US GAAP	2,961,891	2,479,868	1,896,686
Shareholders' equity as reported in the consolidated balance sheets and in accordance with Irish and UK GAAP	1,455,288	1,241,728	1,002,274
Adjustments			
Pension	3,200	3,111	2,414
Amortization of goodwill	2,342	—	—
Employment grants	—	—	(469)
Capitalized interest regarding aircraft acquisition programme	17,502	10,289	5,027
Darley Investments Limited	(151)	(239)	(327)
Minimum pension liability (net of tax)	(2,631)	(2,656)	—
Unrealized (losses) on derivative financial instruments (net of tax)	(116,681)	(73,371)	12,448
Tax effect of adjustments (excluding pension and derivative adjustments)	(2,588)	(1,675)	(1,760)
Shareholders' equity as adjusted to accord with US GAAP	1,356,281	1,177,187	1,019,607

Source: 2004 and 2003 Ryanair annual reports.

Ryanair Holdings plc

EXHIBIT 9   **Ryanair stock price: January–June 2004**

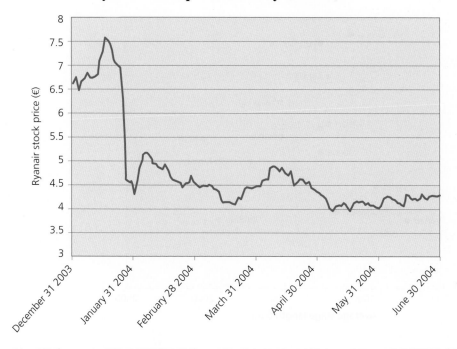

Source: Center for Research on Security Prices database.

EXHIBIT 10   **Ryanair financial performance 1997–2004 (€000)**

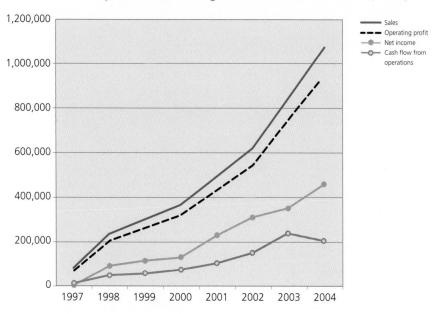

Source: Thomson Financial Datastream.

Ryanair Holdings plc

EXHIBIT 11 **Comparison of costs per available seat kilometre for various airlines**

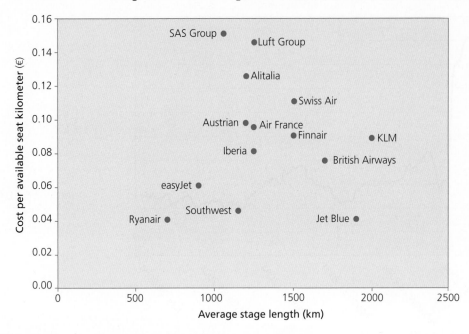

Source: Davy Stockbroker report on Ryanair, February 16, 2004.

EXHIBIT 12 **Financial and operating metrics for selected airlines**

	P/E	Market Value (000 $US)	Average Revenue/ Passenger ($US)	Load Factor	Margin	Turnover	Leverage	ROE
JetBlue Airways	50.5	2420	104	0.83	0.04	0.45	3.70	0.06
Southwest Airlines	40.7	1,2780	89	0.69	0.05	0.58	2.05	0.06
British Airways	24.2	5,501	330	0.73	0.03	0.67	4.60	0.10
Japan Airlines	24.2	6,752	201	0.64	0.01	0.98	11.10	0.15
Ryanair	20.8	4,273	49	0.74	0.20	0.44	1.99	0.17
Lufthansa	13.1	6,564	280	0.74	0.02	0.86	4.55	0.09
easyJet	12.4	917	77	0.85	0.04	0.82	1.68	0.05
Qantas Airways	9.8	4,526	208	0.78	0.06	0.62	3.02	0.11
Singapore Airlines	9.6	8,000	540	0.73	0.12	0.54	1.76	0.11
SAS	n.m.	1,486	137	0.64	−0.03	0.91	5.16	−0.15
American Airlines	n.m.	1,765	185	0.75	−0.04	0.65	n.m.	n.m.
Delta Air Lines	n.m.	1,046	125	0.75	−0.35	0.69	n.m.	n.m.
Northwest Airlines	n.m.	952	152	0.80	−0.08	0.80	n.m.	n.m.
United Airlines	n.m.	151	176	0.79	−0.10	0.79	n.m.	n.m.
US Airways	n.m.	60	151	0.76	−0.09	0.85	n.m.	n.m.

Notes: n.m. = not meaningful.
   Load factor = Revenue passenger miles (or kilometers)/Available seat miles (or kilometers).
   Margin = Net income/Sales.
   Turnover = Sales/Total assets.
   Leverage = Total assets/Stockholders' equity.

Source: Jane's World Airlines, company annual reports.

Ryanair Holdings plc

EXHIBIT 13   **Ratio analysis, 2002–2004[a]**

Decomposing Profitability: Dupont Alternative	2001	2002	2003	2004
NOPAT/Sales	20.1%	23.0%	28.4%	21.2%
× Sales/Net Assets	2.3	1.4	1.3	1.1
= **Operating ROA**	**46.2%**	**31.8%**	**36.3%**	**22.4%**
Financial Spread[b]	43.4%	28.6%	36.1%	32.0%
× Net Financial Leverage[c]	−0.5	−0.3	−0.3	−0.2
= Financial Leverage Gain	−22.6%	−9.4%	−12.4%	−5.7%
ROE (Operating ROA + Financial Spread * Net Financial Leverage)	**23.7%**	**22.4%**	**23.9%**	**16.6%**

Evaluating Operating Management	2001	2002	2003	2004
Key Growth Rates:				
Annual Sales Growth	**31.7%**	**28.0%**	**35.0%**	**27.5%**
Annual Net Income Growth	**44.1%**	**43.9%**	**59.2%**	**13.7%**
Key Profitability Ratios:				
Sales/Sales	**100.0%**	**100.0%**	**100.0%**	**100.0%**
Cost of Sales/Sales	76.6%	73.9%	68.7%	76.6%
Gross Margin	**23.4%**	**26.1%**	**31.3%**	**23.4%**
SG&A/Sales	0.0%	0.0%	0.0%	0.0%
Other Operating Expense/Sales	0.0%	0.0%	0.0%	0.0%
Investment Income/Sales	0.0%	0.0%	0.0%	0.0%
Other Income, net of Other Expense/Sales	0.3%	0.2%	0.1%	0.1%
Minority Interest/Sales	0.0%	0.0%	0.0%	0.0%
EBIT Margin	**23.7%**	**26.3%**	**31.3%**	**23.5%**
Net Interest Expense (Income)/Sales	−1.6%	−1.3%	−0.1%	2.2%
Pre-Tax Income Margin	25.3%	27.6%	31.4%	21.3%
Taxes/Sales	3.9%	3.5%	3.0%	2.0%
Unusual Gains, Net of Unusual Losses (after tax)/Sales	0.0%	0.0%	0.0%	0.0%
Net Income Margin	**21.4%**	**24.1%**	**28.4%**	**19.2%**
EBITDA Margin	35.9%	35.8%	43.3%	37.1%
NOPAT Margin	20.1%	23.0%	28.4%	21.2%
Recurring NOPAT Margin	19.8%	22.8%	28.3%	21.2%

Ryanair Holdings plc

EXHIBIT 13   **Ratio analysis, 2002–2004[a]** *(continued)*

Evaluating Investment Management	2001	2002	2003	2004
Working Capital Management:				
Operating Working Capital/Sales	−18.0%	−21.2%	−26.8%	−24.1%
Operating Working Capital Turnover	−5.5	−4.7	−3.7	−4.2
Accounts Receivable Turnover	22.2	71.8	81.6	71.8
Inventory Turnover	26.8	28.9	33.8	36.1
Accounts Payable Turnover	16.3	15.4	12.4	13.4
Days' Receivables	16.5	5.1	4.5	5.1
Days' Inventory	13.6	12.6	10.8	10.1
Days' Payables	22.3	23.7	29.5	27.3
Long-Term Asset Management:				
Net Long-Term Assets Turnover	1.6	1.1	1.0	0.8
Net Long-Term Assets / Sales	61.5%	93.5%	105.0%	119.0%
PP&E Turnover	1.5	1.0	0.9	0.8
Depreciation & Amortization / Sales	12.1%	9.5%	11.9%	13.6%

Evaluating Financial Management	2001	2002	2003	2004
Short-Term Liquidity:				
Current Ratio	2.77	3.28	3.04	2.95
Quick Ratio	2.63	3.14	2.95	2.85
Cash Ratio	2.47	3.10	2.92	2.81
Operating Cash Flow Ratio	1.04	1.03	1.13	1.22
Debt and Long-Term Solvency:				
Liabilities-to-Equity	0.61	0.91	0.89	0.99
Debt-to-Equity	0.28	0.61	0.55	0.68
Net-Debt-to-Equity	−0.52	−0.33	−0.34	−0.18
Debt-to-Capital	0.22	0.38	0.36	0.40
Net-Debt-to-Net Capital	−1.08	−0.49	−0.52	−0.22
Interest Coverage Ratio	11.31	9.79	9.57	5.80
Dividend Payout Ratio	n/a	n/a	n/a	n/a
Sustainable Growth Rate:	23.7%	22.4%	23.9%	16.6%

[a]All ratios incorporating balance sheet measures are computed using beginning-of-year values.

[b]Operating ROA – effective after-tax interest rate.

[c]Net Debt/Net Equity, where Net Debt = Interest-bearing liabilities – cash and marketable equity securities.

Source: Ryanair annual reports.

Ryanair Holdings plc

EXHIBIT 14 **Equity analyst reports on Ryanair, January–June 2004**

Ryanair Holdings plc

Report date	Equity Research Firm	Report title	Recommendation	Price (€ per share, except where noted)	Target price
28-Jan-04	ABN Amro	The Emperor Falls Off His Throne	Sell	4.75	5.15
29-Jan-04	UBS	More Questions than Answers	Reduce 2 (Sell)	4.72	6.25
29-Jan-04	BNP/Paribas	Reach for the Alka-Selzer? Buy Instead	Outperform	4.75	6.10
2-Feb-04	UBS	Business Model Under the Microscope	Reduce 2 (Sell)	4.87	4.50
3-Feb-04	Deutsche Bank	Stop Talking and Do Your Business – Upgrade to Buy	Buy	4.66	5.70
3-Feb-04	Smith Barney Citigroup	Talk of Its Demise is Greatly Exaggerated	Hold (2)	4.95	5.50
4-Feb-04	BNP/Paribas	No Lasting Damage (But a Slap on the Wrist!)	Outperform	4.95	6.10
4-Feb-04	ABN Amro	Imperial Lather	Reduce	4.66	4.40
4-Feb-04	Raymond James	EU Decision Announced	Market Perform	$35.75	–
5-Feb-04	NCB Group	Commission Ruling Will Not Derail the Model	Buy	–	6.00
11-Feb-04	CSFB	Profits Shock	Underperform	5.20	4.42
12-Feb-04	Raymond James	Raising Rating to Outperform	Outperform	$37.68	$45.00
3-Mar-04	NCB Group	All to Play For in March	Buy	4.84	6.00
9-Mar-04	Raymond James	February Traffic Results; Establishing FY05 Quarterly Estimates	Outperform 2	$34.28	$40.00
6-Apr-04	ABN Amro	Yields Set to Improve	Add	4.97	5.50
3-May-04	NCB Group	It Isn't Broken – It's Just More Visibly Seasonal	Buy	4.80	6.00
6-May-04	Panmure Gordon	easyJet and Ryanair Passenger Growth and Load Factors	Hold	4.45	5.00
21-May-04	UBS	Full Year Results – June 1st	Reduce 2 (Sell)	4.65	4.40
21-May-04	CSFB	FY Results Preview	Underperform	4.55	4.42
25-May-04	Deutsche Bank	FY03/04 Results Preview	Buy	4.53	5.70
27-May-04	Smith Barney Citigroup	FY04 Results Expectations – Outlook Uncertain	Hold (2)	4.39	5.50
1-Jun-04	Deutsche Bank	Good Results but Competition Remains Tough	Buy	4.38	5.70
1-Jun-04	Smith Barney Citigroup	Results in Line, Outlook Slightly Better	Hold (2)	4.38	5.50
1-Jun-04	William deBroe	Ryanair Results	Sell	4.45	–
2-Jun-04	ABN Amro	Walking a tightrope	Add	4.38	5.00
2-Jun-04	NCB Group	No Major Surprises – Forecasts Creep Up on Stronger Summer Trading	Buy	4.41	6.00
3-Jun-04	CSFB	Challenging Outlook	Underperform	4.41	4.42

Source: Investext.

BUSINESS ANALYSIS AND VALUATION APPLICATIONS

Equity Security Analysis

Equity **security analysis** is the evaluation of a firm and its prospects from the perspective of a current or potential investor in the firm's shares. Security analysis is one step in a larger investment process that involves:

1 Establishing the objectives of the investor.

2 Forming expectations about the future returns and risks of individual securities.

3 Combining individual securities into portfolios to maximize progress toward the investment objectives.

Security analysis is the foundation for the second step, projecting future returns and assessing risk. Security analysis is typically conducted with an eye toward identification of mispriced securities in hopes of generating returns that more than compensate the investor for risk. However, that need not be the case. For analysts who do not have a comparative advantage in identifying mispriced securities, the focus should be on gaining an appreciation for how a security would affect the risk of a given portfolio, and whether it fits the profile that the portfolio is designed to maintain.

Security analysis is undertaken by individual investors, by analysts at brokerage houses (sell-side analysts), and by analysts that work at the direction of fund managers for various institutions (buy-side analysts). The institutions employing buy-side analysts include collective investment funds, pension funds, insurance companies, universities, and others.

A variety of questions are dealt with in security analysis:

■ A sell-side analyst asks: Is the industry I am covering attractive, and if so why? How do different firms within the industry position themselves? What are the implications for my earnings forecasts? Given my expectations for a firm, do its shares appear to be mispriced? Should I recommend this share as a buy, a sell, or a hold?

■ A buy-side analyst for a "value share fund" asks: Does this security possess the characteristics we seek in our fund? That is, does it have a relatively low ratio of price to earnings, low price-to-book value, and other fundamental indicators? Do its prospects for earnings improvement suggest good potential for high future returns on the security?

■ An individual investor asks: Does this security offer the risk profile that suits my investment objectives? Does it enhance my ability to diversify the risk of my portfolio? Is the firm's dividend payout rate low enough to help shield me from taxes while I continue to hold the security?

As the above questions underscore, there is more to security analysis than estimating the value of equity securities. Nevertheless, for most sell-side and buy-side analysts, the key goal remains the identification of mispriced securities.

INVESTOR OBJECTIVES AND INVESTMENT VEHICLES

The investment objectives of individual savers in the economy are highly idiosyncratic. For any given saver they depend on such factors as income, age, wealth, tolerance for risk, and tax status. For example, savers with many years until retirement are likely to prefer to have a relatively large share of their portfolio invested in equities, which offer a higher expected return than fixed income (or debt) securities and higher short-term variability. Investors in high tax brackets are likely to prefer to have a large share of their portfolio in shares that generate tax-deferred capital gains rather than shares that pay dividends or interest-bearing securities.

Collective investment funds (mutual funds, unit trusts, OEICs, SICAVs, or BEVEKs as they are termed in some countries) have become popular investment vehicles for savers to achieve their investment objectives.[1] Collective investment funds sell shares in professionally managed portfolios that invest in specific types of equity and/or fixed income securities. They therefore provide a low-cost way for savers to invest in a portfolio of securities that reflects their particular appetite for risk.

The major classes of collective investment funds include:

1 Money market funds that invest in commercial paper, certificates of deposit, and treasury bills.
2 Bond funds that invest in debt instruments.
3 Equity funds that invest in equity securities.
4 Balanced funds that hold money market, bond, and equity securities.
5 Real estate funds that invest in commercial real estate.

Within the bond and equities classes of funds, however, there are wide ranges of fund types. For example, bond funds include:

■ *Corporate bond funds* that invest in investment-grade rated corporate debt instruments.[2]
■ *Government bond funds* that invest in government debt instruments.
■ *High yield funds* that invest in non-investment-grade rated corporate debt.
■ *Mortgage funds* that invest in mortgage-backed securities.

Equity funds include:

■ *Income funds* that invest in equities that are expected to generate dividend income.
■ *Growth funds* that invest in equities expected to generate long-term capital gains.
■ *Income and growth funds* that invest in equities that provide a balance of dividend income and capital gains.
■ *Value funds* that invest in equities that are considered to be undervalued.
■ *Short funds* that sell short equity securities that are considered to be overvalued.
■ *Index funds* that invest in equities that track a particular market index, such as the MSCI World Index or the DJ Euro Stoxx 50.
■ *Sector funds* that invest in equities in a particular industry segment, such as the technology or health sciences sectors.
■ *Regional funds* that invest in equities from a particular country or geographic region, such as Japan, the Asia-Pacific region, or the US.

Since the 1990s, hedge funds have gained increased prominence and the assets controlled by these funds have grown significantly. While generally open only to institutional investors and certain qualified wealthy individuals, hedge funds are becoming an increasingly important force in the market. Hedge funds employ a variety of investment strategies including:

■ *Market neutral funds* that typically invest equal amounts of money in purchasing undervalued securities and shorting overvalued ones to neutralize market risk.
■ *Short-selling funds*, which short-sell the securities of companies that they believe are overvalued.
■ *Special situation funds* that invest in undervalued securities in anticipation of an increase in value resulting from a favorable turn of events.

These fund types employ very different strategies. But, for many, fundamental analysis of companies is the critical task. This chapter focuses on applying the tools we have developed in Part 2 of the book to analyze equity securities.

EQUITY SECURITY ANALYSIS AND MARKET EFFICIENCY

How a security analyst should invest his or her time depends on how quickly and efficiently information flows through markets and becomes reflected in security prices. In the extreme, information would be reflected in security prices fully and immediately upon its release. This is essentially the condition posited by the *efficient markets hypothesis*. This hypothesis states that security prices reflect all available information, as if such information could be costlessly digested and translated immediately into demands for buys or sells without regard to frictions imposed by transactions costs. Under such conditions, it would be impossible to identify mispriced securities on the basis of public information.

In a world of efficient markets, the expected return on any equity security is just enough to compensate investors for the unavoidable risk the security involves. Unavoidable risk is that which cannot be "diversified away" simply by holding a portfolio of many securities. Given efficient markets, the investor's strategy shifts away from the search for mispriced securities and focuses instead on maintaining a well-diversified portfolio. Aside from this, the investor must arrive at the desired balance between risky securities and risk-free short-term government bonds. The desired balance depends on how much risk the investor is willing to bear for a given increase in expected returns.

The above discussion implies that investors who accept that share prices already reflect available information have no need for analysis involving a search for mispriced securities. If all investors adopted this attitude, of course no such analysis would be conducted, mispricing would go uncorrected, and markets would no longer be efficient![3] This is why the efficient markets hypothesis cannot represent an equilibrium in a strict sense. In equilibrium there must be just enough mispricing to provide incentives for the investment of resources in security analysis.

The existence of some mispricing, even in equilibrium, does not imply that it is sensible for just anyone to engage in security analysis. Instead, it suggests that securities analysis is subject to the same laws of supply and demand faced in all other competitive industries: it will be rewarding only for those with the strongest comparative advantage. How many analysts are in that category depends on a number of factors, including the liquidity of a firm's shares and investor interest in the company.[4] For example, there are about 45 sell-side professional analysts who follow British Petroleum, a company with highly liquid shares and considerable investor interest. There are many other buy-side analysts who track the firm on their own account without issuing any formal reports to outsiders. For the smallest publicly traded firms in Europe, there is typically no formal following by analysts, and would-be investors and their advisors are left to form their own opinions on a security.

Market efficiency and the role of financial statement analysis

The degree of **market efficiency** that arises from competition among analysts and other market agents is an empirical issue addressed by a large body of research spanning the last four decades. Such research has important implications for the role of financial statements in security analysis. Consider for example the implications of an extremely efficient market, where information is fully impounded in prices within minutes of its revelation. In such a market, agents could profit from digesting financial statement information in two ways. First, the information would be useful to the select few who receive newly announced financial data, interpret it quickly, and trade on it within minutes. Second, and probably more important, the information would be useful for gaining an understanding of the firm, so as to place the analyst in a better position to interpret other news (from financial statements as well as other sources) as it arrives.

On the other hand, if securities prices fail to reflect financial statement data fully, even days or months after its public revelation, market agents could profit from such data by creating trading strategies designed to exploit any systematic ways in which the publicly available data are ignored or discounted in the price-setting process.

Market efficiency and managers' financial reporting strategies

The degree to which markets are efficient also has implications for managers' approaches to communicating with their investment communities. The issue becomes most important when the firm pursues an unusual strategy, or when the usual interpretation of financial statements would be misleading in the firm's context. In such a case, the communication avenues managers can successfully pursue depend not only on management's credibility, but also on the degree of understanding present in the investment community.

Evidence of market efficiency

There is an abundance of evidence consistent with a high degree of efficiency in securities markets.[5] In fact, during the 1960s and 1970s, the evidence was so one-sided that the efficient markets hypothesis gained widespread acceptance within the academic community and had a major impact on the practicing community as well.

Evidence pointing to very efficient securities markets comes in several forms:

- When information is announced publicly, the markets react very quickly.
- It is difficult to identify specific funds or analysts who have consistently generated abnormally high returns.
- A number of studies suggest that share prices reflect a rather sophisticated level of fundamental analysis.

While a large body of evidence consistent with efficiency exists, recent years have witnessed a re-examination of the once widely accepted thinking. A sampling of the research includes the following:

- On the issue of the speed of share price response to news, a number of studies suggest that even though prices react quickly, the initial reaction tends to be incomplete.[6]
- A number of studies point to trading strategies that could have been used to outperform market averages.[7]
- Some related evidence – still subject to ongoing debate about its proper interpretation – suggests that, even though market prices reflect some relatively sophisticated analyses, prices still do not fully reflect all the information that could be garnered from publicly available financial statements.[8]

The controversy over the efficiency of securities markets is unlikely to be resolved soon. However, there are some lessons that are accepted by most researchers. First, securities markets not only reflect publicly available information, but they also anticipate much of it before it is released. The open question is what fraction of the response remains to be impounded in price once the day of the public release comes to a close. Second, even in most studies that suggest inefficiency, the degree of mispricing is relatively small for large firms.

Finally, even if some of the evidence is currently difficult to align with the efficient markets hypothesis, it remains a useful benchmark (at a minimum) for thinking about the behavior of security prices. The hypothesis will continue to play that role unless it can be replaced by a more complete theory. Some researchers are developing theories that encompass the existence of market agents who are forced to trade for unpredictable "liquidity" reasons, and prices that differ from so-called "fundamental values," even in equilibrium. Also, behavioral finance models recognize that cognitive biases can affect investor behavior.[9]

APPROACHES TO FUND MANAGEMENT AND SECURITIES ANALYSIS

Approaches used in practice to manage funds and analyze securities are quite varied. One dimension of variation is the extent to which the investments are actively or passively managed. Another variation is whether a quantitative or a traditional fundamental approach is used. Security analysts also vary considerably in terms of whether they produce formal or informal valuations of the firm.

Active versus passive management

Active portfolio management relies heavily on security analysis to identify mispriced securities. The passive portfolio manager serves as a price taker, avoiding the costs of security analysis and turnover while typically seeking to hold a portfolio designed to match some overall market index or sector performance. Combined approaches are also possible. For example, one may actively manage 20 percent of a fund balance while passively managing the remainder. The growing popularity of passively managed funds in Europe over the past 20 years serves as testimony to the growing belief that it is difficult to consistently earn returns that are superior to broad market indices.

Quantitative versus traditional fundamental analysis

Actively managed funds must depend on some form of security analysis. Some funds employ "technical analysis," which attempts to predict share price movements on the basis of market indicators (prior share price movements, volume, etc.). In contrast, "fundamental analysis," the primary approach to security analysis, attempts to evaluate the current market price relative to projections of the firm's future earnings and cash flow generating potential. Fundamental analysis involves all the steps described in the previous chapters of this book: business strategy analysis, accounting analysis, financial analysis, and prospective analysis (forecasting and valuation). In recent years, some analysts have supplemented traditional fundamental analysis, which involves a substantial amount of subjective judgment, with more quantitative approaches.

The quantitative approaches themselves are quite varied. Some involve simply "screening" shares on the basis of some set of factors, such as trends in analysts' earnings revisions, price-earnings ratios, price-book ratios, and so on. Whether such approaches are useful depends on the degree of market efficiency relative to the screens. Quantitative approaches can also involve implementation of some formal model to predict future stock returns. Longstanding statistical techniques such as regression analysis and probit analysis can be used, as can more recently developed computer-intensive techniques such as neural network analysis. Again, the success of these approaches depends on the degree of market efficiency and whether the analysis can exploit information in ways not otherwise available to market agents as a group.

Quantitative approaches play a more important role in security analysis today than they did a decade or two ago. However, by and large, analysts still rely primarily on the kind of fundamental analysis involving complex human judgments, as outlined in our earlier chapters.

Formal versus informal valuation

Full-scale, formal valuations based on the methods described in Chapter 7 have become more common, especially in recent years. However, less formal approaches are also possible. For example, an analyst can compare his or her long-term earnings projection with the consensus forecast to generate a buy or sell recommendation. Alternatively, an analyst might recommend a share because his or her earnings forecast appears relatively high in comparison to the current price. Another possible approach, that might be labeled "marginalist," involves no attempt to value the firm. The analyst simply assumes that if he or she has unearthed favorable (or unfavorable) information believed not to be recognized by others, the share should be bought (or sold).

Unlike many security analysts, investment bankers produce formal valuations as a matter of course. Investment bankers, who estimate values for purposes of bringing a private firm to the public market, for evaluating a merger or buyout proposal, for issuing a fairness opinion or for making a periodic managerial review, must document their valuation in a way that can readily be communicated to management and, if necessary, to the courts.

THE PROCESS OF A COMPREHENSIVE SECURITY ANALYSIS

Given the variety of approaches practiced in security analysis, it is impossible to summarize all of them here. Instead, we briefly outline **steps to be included in a comprehensive security analysis**. The amount of attention focused on any given step varies among analysts.

Selection of candidates for analysis

No analyst can effectively investigate more than a small fraction of the securities on a major exchange, and thus some approach to narrowing the focus must be employed. Sell-side analysts are often organized within an investment house by industry or sector. Thus they tend to be constrained in their choices of firms to follow. However, from the perspective of a fund manager or an investment firm as a whole, there is usually the freedom to focus on any firm or sector.

As noted earlier, funds typically specialize in investing in shares with certain risk profiles or characteristics (e.g., growth shares, "value" shares, technology shares, cyclical shares). Managers of these types of funds seek to focus the energies of their analysts on identifying shares that fit their fund objective. In addition, individual investors who seek to maintain a well-diversified portfolio without holding many shares also need information about the nature of a firm's risks and how they fit with the risk profile of their overall portfolio.

An alternative approach to security selection is to screen firms on the basis of some potential mispricing followed by a detailed analysis of only those shares that meet the specified criteria. For example, one fund managed by a large insurance company screens shares on the basis of recent "earnings momentum," as reflected in revisions in the earnings projections of sell-side and buy-side analysts. Upward revisions trigger investigations for possible purchase. The fund operates on the belief that earnings momentum is a positive signal of future price movements. Another fund complements the earnings momentum screen with one based on recent short-term share price movements, in the hopes of identifying earnings revisions not yet reflected in share prices.

KEY ANALYSIS QUESTIONS

Depending on whether fund managers follow a strategy of targeting equities with specific types of characteristics, or of screening shares that appear to be mispriced, the following types of questions are likely to be useful:

- What is the risk profile of a firm? How volatile is its earnings stream and share price? What are the key possible bad outcomes in the future? What is the upside potential? How closely linked are the firm's risks to the health of the overall economy? Are the risks largely diversifiable, or are they systematic?

- Does the firm possess the characteristics of a growth share? What is the expected pattern of sales and earnings growth for the coming years? Is the firm reinvesting most or all of its earnings?

- Does the firm match the characteristics desired by "income funds"? Is it a mature or maturing company, prepared to "harvest" profits and distribute them in the form of high dividends?

- Is the firm a candidate for a "value fund"? Does it offer measures of earnings, cash flow, and book value that are high relative to the price? What specific screening rules can be implemented to identify misvalued shares?

Inferring market expectations

If the security analysis is conducted with an eye toward the identification of mispricing, it must ultimately involve a comparison of the analyst's expectations with those of "the market." One possibility is to view the observed share price as the reflection of market expectations and to compare the analyst's own estimate of value with that price. However, a share price is only a "summary statistic." It is useful to have a more detailed idea of the market's expectations about a firm's future performance, expressed in terms of sales, earnings, and other measures. For example, assume that an analyst has developed new insights about a firm's near-term sales. Whether those insights represent new information for the stock market, and whether they indicate that a "buy" recommendation is appropriate, can be easily determined if the analyst knows the market consensus sales forecast.

Around the world a number of agencies summarize analysts' forecasts of sales and earnings. Forecasts for the next year or two are commonly available, and for many firms, a "long-run" earnings growth projection is also available – typically for three to five years. Some agencies provide continuous online updates to such data, so if an analyst revises a forecast, that can be made known to fund managers and other analysts within seconds.

As useful as analysts' forecasts of sales and earnings are, they do not represent a complete description of expectations about future performance, and there is no guarantee that consensus analyst forecasts are the same as those reflected in market prices. Further, financial analysts typically forecast performance for only a few years, so that even if these do reflect market expectations, it is helpful to understand what types of long-term forecasts are reflected in share prices. Armed with the models in Chapters 7 and 8 that express price as a function of future cash flows or earnings, an analyst can draw some educated inferences about the expectations embedded in share prices.

For example, consider the valuation of apparel retailer Burberry plc. On June 29 2012, Burberry's share price was 1,325 pence. For the year ended March 31 2012, the company reported that earnings per share increased from 49 pence the prior year to 62 pence, reflecting the company's improved store productivity and operating margins. Burberry's book value of equity per share was 198 pence. By the end of June analysts were forecasting that Burberry would experience a slowdown in earnings growth in 2013, with earnings projected to grow by 16 percent to 72 pence. Gradually decreasing growth was projected for the following years: 17 percent in 2014 (84 pence), 12 percent in 2015 (94 pence), and 12 percent in 2016 (105 pence).[10] Analysts expected Burberry to pay out approximately 40 percent of its annual earnings in dividends.

How do consensus forecasts by analysts reconcile with the market valuation of Burberry? What are the market's implicit assumptions about the short-term and long-term earnings growth for the company? By altering the amounts for key value drivers and arriving at combinations that generate an estimated value equal to the observed market price, the analyst can infer what the market might have been expecting for Burberry in June 2012. Table 9.1 summarizes the combinations of earnings growth, book value growth, and cost of capital that generate prices comparable to the market price of 1,325 pence.

Burberry has an equity beta of 0.9. Given the long-term return on European government bonds rates of 4.8 percent and a market risk premium of 5–6 percent, Burberry's cost of equity capital probably lies between 9.3 and 10.2 percent. Critical questions for judging the market valuation of Burberry include how quickly will the company's abnormal profitability erode, and how quickly will earnings growth revert to the same level as average firms in the economy, historically around 4 percent. The analysis reported in Table 9.1 presents three scenarios for Burberry's earnings growth that are consistent with an observed market price of 1,325 pence. The three scenarios assume that earnings growth reverts to the economy average after 2016 and that Burberry's dividend payout ratio between 2013 and 2016 is 40 percent.

Table 9.1 shows the implications for Burberry's earnings growth in 2015 and 2016 if competition drives down earnings in 2013 and 2014. This analysis indicates that with a 9.3 percent cost of equity and a rapid return to pre-2012 performance (i.e., 10 percent decline in 2013 and 2014), earnings need to grow by close to 40 percent per year in 2015 and 2016 to justify the 1,325 pence share price. However, if growth is 16 and 17 percent in 2013 and 2014 respectively, as the consensus predicts, expected earnings growth approaches the economy average (of 4 percent) during the next three years. The 1,325 pence share price is also consistent with a scenario that predicts constant earnings growth of 11.6 percent between 2013 and 2016. The value of Burberry's equity is computed as in Table 9.2. Because one quarter of the fiscal year has passed on June 30, two adjustments must be made in the

TABLE 9.1 Alternative assumptions about value drivers for Burberry consistent with the observed market price of 1,325 pence

	2013	2014	2015	2016	After 2016	Implied earnings per share in 2016
Assumed equity costs of capital of 9.3%						
Earnings growth:						
Scenario 1	16.0%	17.0%	9.0%	5.0%	4.0%	98 pence
Scenario 2	−10.0%	−10.0%	38.4%	38.4%	4.0%	98 pence
Scenario 3	11.6%	11.6%	11.6%	11.6%	4.0%	98 pence
Assumed equity cost of capital of 10.2%						
Earnings growth:						
Scenario 1	16.0%	17.0%	15.7%	15.7%	4.0%	114 pence
Scenario 2	−10.0%	−10.0%	49.9%	49.9%	4.0%	115 pence
Scenario 3	16.1%	16.1%	16.1%	16.1%	4.0%	114 pence

TABLE 9.2 Computing the value of Burberry's equity

Year	Beginning book value	Earnings (11.6% annual growth)	Abnormal earnings (9.3% cost of equity)	PV factor	PV of abnormal earnings
2013	198.0p	70.3p	51.9p	0.9354	48.54
2014	240.2	78.5	56.1	0.8558	48.03
2015	287.3	87.6	60.9	0.7830	47.64
2016	339.8	97.7	66.1	0.7163	47.37
After 2016			68.8	13.5159	929.44
Cumulative PV of abnormal earnings					1121.02
+ Book value on June 30, 2012					202.43
= Equity value per share					1323.45p

analysis. First, the present value factor for the first five years equals $(1 - r_e)^{-(t - 0.25)}$. Second, the book value on June 30 is set equal to the book value on April 1 times $(1 + r_e)^{0.25}$.

Unless the analyst has good indications that Burberry's abnormal profitability will rebound after two years, given the company's 1,325 pence share price it is unlikely that the market anticipates that earnings will be hit by competition in 2013 and 2014. Burberry's share price more likely reflects the expectation that earnings growth will gradually revert to the economy average in future years. This type of scenario analysis provides the analyst with insights about investors' expectations for Burberry, and is useful for judging whether the share is correctly valued. Security analysis need not involve such a detailed attempt to infer market expectations. However, whether or not an explicit analysis, a good analyst understands what economic scenarios could plausibly be reflected in the observed price.

KEY ANALYSIS QUESTIONS

By using the discounted abnormal earnings/ROE valuation model, analysts can infer the market's expectations for a firm's future performance. This permits analysts to ask whether the market is overvaluing or undervaluing a company. Typical questions that analysts might ask from this analysis include the following:

- What are the market's assumptions about long-term ROE and growth? For example, is the market forecasting that the company can grow its earnings without a corresponding level of expansion in its asset base (and hence equity)? If so, how long can this persist?

- How do changes in the cost of capital affect the market's assessment of the firm's future performance? If the market's expectations seem to be unexpectedly high or low, has the market reassessed the company's risk? If so, is this change plausible?

Developing the analyst's expectations

Ultimately, a security analyst must compare his or her own view of a share with the view embedded in the market price. The analyst's view is generated using the same tools discussed in Chapters 2 through to 8. The final product of this work is, of course, a forecast of the firm's future earnings and cash flows and an estimate of the firm's value. However, that final product is less important than the understanding of the business and its industry that the analysis provides. It is such understanding that enables the analyst to interpret new information as it arrives and to infer its implications.

In developing expectations about the firm's future performance using the financial analysis tools discussed throughout this book, the analyst is likely to ask the following types of questions:

■ How profitable is the firm? In light of industry conditions, the firm's corporate strategy, and its barriers to competition, how sustainable is that rate of profitability?

■ What are the opportunities for growth for this firm?

■ How risky is this firm? How vulnerable are operations to general economic downturns? How highly levered is the firm? What does the riskiness of the firm imply about its cost of capital?

■ How do answers to the above questions compare to the expectations embedded in the observed share price?

The final product of security analysis

For financial analysts, the final product of security analysis is a recommendation to buy, sell, or hold the share (or some more refined ranking). The recommendation is supported by a set of forecasts and a report summarizing the foundation for the recommendation. Analysts' reports often delve into significant detail and include an assessment of a firm's business as well as a line-by-line income statement, balance sheet, and cash flow forecasts for one or more years.

In making a recommendation to buy or sell a share, the analyst has to consider the investment time horizon required to capitalize on the recommendation. Are anticipated improvements in performance likely to be confirmed in the near-term, allowing investors to capitalize quickly on the recommendation? Or do expected performance improvements reflect long-term fundamentals that will take several years to play out? Longer investment horizons impose greater risk on investors that the company's performance will be affected by changes in economic conditions that cannot be anticipated by the analyst, reducing the value of the recommendation. Consequently, thorough analysis requires not merely being able to recognize whether a share is misvalued, but being able to anticipate when a price correction is likely to take place.

Because there are additional investment risks from following recommendations that require long-term commitments, security analysts tend to focus on making recommendations that are likely to pay off in the short-term. This potentially explains why so few analysts recommended selling dot-com and technology shares during the late 1990s when their prices would be difficult to justify on the basis of long-term fundamentals. It also explains why analysts recommended Enron's share at its peak, even though the kind of analysis performed in this chapter would have shown that the future growth and ROE performance implied by this price would be extremely difficult to achieve. It also implies that to take advantage of long-term fundamental analysis can often require access to patient, long-term capital.

PERFORMANCE OF SECURITY ANALYSTS AND FUND MANAGERS

There has been extensive research on the performance of security analysts and fund managers during the last three decades. A few of the key findings are summarized below.

Performance of security analysts

Despite the recent failure of security analysts to foresee the dramatic price declines for dot-com and telecommunications shares, and to detect the financial shenanigans and overvaluation of companies such as Ahold, Enron, and Parmalat, research shows that analysts generally add value in the capital market. Analyst earnings forecasts are more accurate than those produced by time-series models that use past earnings to predict future earnings.[11] Of course this should not be too surprising since analysts can update their earnings forecasts between quarters to incorporate new firm and economy information, whereas time-series models cannot. In addition, share prices tend to respond positively to upward revisions in analysts' earnings forecasts and recommendations, and negatively to downward revisions.[12] Finally, recent research finds that analysts play a valuable role in improving market efficiency. For example, share prices for firms with higher analyst following more rapidly incorporate information on accruals and cash flows than prices of less followed firms.[13]

Several factors seem to be important in explaining analysts' earnings forecast accuracy. Not surprisingly, forecasts of near-term earnings are much more accurate than those of long-term performance.[14] This probably explains why analysts typically make detailed forecasts for only one or two years ahead. Studies of differences in earnings forecast accuracy across analysts find that analysts that are more accurate tend to specialize by industry and by country and work for large well-funded firms that employ other analysts who follow the same industry.[15]

Although analysts perform a valuable function in the capital market, research shows that their forecasts and recommendations tend to be biased. Early evidence on bias indicated that analyst earnings forecasts tended to be optimistic and that their recommendations were almost exclusively for buys.[16] Several factors potentially explain this finding. First, security analysts at brokerage houses are typically compensated on the basis of the trading volume that their reports generate. Given the costs of short selling and the restrictions on short selling by many institutions, brokerage analysts have incentives to issue optimistic reports that encourage investors to buy shares rather than to issue negative reports that create selling pressure. Second, analysts that work for investment banks are rewarded for promoting public issues by current clients and for attracting new banking clients, creating incentives for optimistic forecasts and recommendations. Studies show that analysts that work for lead underwriters make more optimistic long-term earnings forecasts and recommendations for firms raising equity capital than unaffiliated analysts.[17]

Evidence indicates that during the late 1990s there was a marked decline in analyst optimism for forecasts of near-term earnings.[18] One explanation offered for this change is that during the late 1990s analysts relied heavily on private discussions with top management to make their earnings forecasts. Management allegedly used these personal connections to manage analysts' short-term expectations downward so that the firm could subsequently report earnings that beat analysts' expectations. In response to concerns about this practice, in October 2000 the US SEC approved Regulation Fair Disclosure, which prohibits management from making selective disclosures of nonpublic information. In Europe, the EU Transparency and Market Abuse Directives, adopted in 2004, may counter such practices, albeit less directly.

There also has been a general decline in sell-side analysts' optimistic recommendations during the past few years. Many large investment banks now require analysts to use a forced curve to rate shares, leading to a greater number of the lower ratings. Factors that underlie this change include a sharp rise in trading by hedge funds, which actively seek shares to short-sell. In contrast, traditional money management firms are typically restricted from short-selling, and are more interested in analysts' buy recommendations than their sells. Second, regulatory changes require tight separation between investment banking and equity research at investment banks.

Performance of fund managers

Measuring whether collective investment and pension fund managers earn superior returns is a difficult task for several reasons. First, there is no agreement about how to estimate benchmark performance for a fund. Studies have used a number of approaches – some have used the capital asset pricing model (CAPM) as a benchmark while others have used multifactor pricing models. For studies using the CAPM, there are questions about what type of market index to use. For example, should it be an equal- or value-weighted index, an exchange-related index, or a broader market index? Second, many of the traditional measures of fund performance abstract from market-wide performance, which understates fund abnormal performance if fund managers can time the market by reducing portfolio risk prior to market declines and increasing risks before a market run-up. Third, given the overall volatility of stock returns, statistical power is an issue for measuring fund performance. Finally, tests of fund performance are likely to be highly sensitive to the time period examined. Value or momentum investing could therefore appear to be profitable depending on when the tests are conducted.

Perhaps because of these challenges, there is no consistent evidence that actively managed collective investment funds generate superior returns for investors. While some studies find evidence of positive abnormal returns for the industry, others conclude that returns are generally negative.[19] Of course, even if collective investment fund managers on average can only generate "normal" returns for investors, it is still possible for the best managers to show consistently strong performance. Some studies do in fact document that funds earning positive abnormal returns in one period continue to outperform in subsequent periods. However, more recent evidence suggests that these findings are caused by general momentum in stock returns and fund expenses rather than superior fund manager ability.[20] Researchers have also examined which, if any, investment strategies are most successful. However, no clear consensus appears – several studies have found that momentum and high turnover strategies generate superior returns, whereas others conclude that value strategies are better.[21]

Finally, recent research has examined whether fund managers tend to buy and sell many of the same shares at the same time. They conclude that there is evidence of "herding" behavior, particularly by momentum fund managers.[22] This could arise because managers have access to common information, because they are affected by similar cognitive biases, or because they have incentives to follow the crowd.[23] For example, consider the calculus of a fund manager who holds a share but who, through long-term fundamental analysis, estimates that it is misvalued. If the manager changes the fund's holdings accordingly and the share price returns to its intrinsic value in the next quarter, the fund will show superior relative portfolio performance and will attract new capital. However, if the share continues to be misvalued for several quarters, the informed fund manager will underperform the benchmark and capital will flow to other funds. In contrast, a risk-averse manager who simply follows the crowd will not be rewarded for detecting the misvaluation, but neither will this manager be blamed for a poor investment decision when the share price ultimately corrects, since other funds made the same mistake.

There has been considerably less research on the performance of pension fund managers. Overall, the findings show little consistent evidence that pension fund managers either over perform or under perform traditional benchmarks.[24]

SUMMARY

Equity security analysis is the evaluation of a firm and its prospects from the perspective of a current or potential investor in the firm's shares. Security analysis is one component of a larger investment process that involves:

1 Establishing the objectives of the investor or fund.

2 Forming expectations about the future returns and risks of individual securities.

3 Combining individual securities into portfolios to maximize progress toward the investment objectives.

Some security analysis is devoted primarily to assuring that a share possesses the proper risk profile and other desired characteristics prior to inclusion in an investor's portfolio. However, especially for many professional buy-side and sell-side security analysts, the analysis is also directed toward the identification of mispriced securities. In equilibrium, such activity will be rewarding for those with the strongest comparative advantage. They will be the ones able to identify any mispricing at the lowest cost and exert pressure on the price to correct the mispricing. What kinds of efforts are productive in this domain depends on the degree of market efficiency. A large body of evidence exists that is supportive of a high degree of efficiency in stock markets, but recent evidence has reopened the debate on this issue.

In practice, a wide variety of approaches to fund management and security analysis are employed. However, at the core of the analyses are the same steps outlined in Chapters 2 through to 8 of this book: business strategy analysis, accounting analysis, financial analysis, and prospective analysis (forecasting and valuation). For the professional analyst, the final product of the work is, of course, a forecast of the firm's future earnings and cash flows, and an estimate of the firm's value. But that final product is less important than the understanding of the business and its industry that the analysis provides. It is such understanding that positions the analyst to interpret new information as it arrives and infer its implications.

Finally, the chapter summarizes some key findings of the research on the performance of both sell-side and buy-side security analysts.

CORE CONCEPTS

Active versus passive portfolio management Active portfolio management involves the use of security analysis to identify mispriced securities; passive portfolio management implies holding a portfolio of securities to match the risk and return of a market or sector index.

Collective investment funds Funds selling shares in professionally managed portfolios of securities with similar risk, return and/or style characteristics.

Market efficiency Degree to which security prices reflect all available information. Market inefficiencies can lead to security mispricing and increase opportunities for earning abnormal investment returns through the use of comprehensive security analysis.

Security analysis Projecting future returns and assessing risks of a security with the objective of identifying mispriced securities or understanding how the security affects the risk, return, and style characteristics of a portfolio.

Steps of security analysis Comprehensive security analysis consists of the following steps:

1 Selection of candidates for analysis on the basis of risk, return, or style characteristics, industry membership or mispricing indicators.

2 Inferring market expectations about the firm's future profitability and growth from the current security price.

3 Developing expectations about the firm's profitability and growth using the four steps of business analysis.

4 Making an investment decision after comparing own expectations with those of the market.

QUESTIONS

1 Despite many years of research, the evidence on market efficiency described in this chapter appears to be inconclusive. Some argue that this is because researchers have been unable to link company fundamentals to share prices precisely. Comment.

2 Geoffrey Henley, a professor of finance, states: "The capital market is efficient. I don't know why anyone would bother devoting their time to following individual shares and doing fundamental analysis. The best approach is to buy and hold a well-diversified portfolio of shares." Do you agree? Why or why not?

3 What is the difference between fundamental and technical analysis? Can you think of any trading strategies that use technical analysis? What are the underlying assumptions made by these strategies?

4 Investment funds follow many different types of investment strategies. Income funds focus on shares with high dividend yields, growth funds invest in shares that are expected to have high capital appreciation, value funds follow shares that are considered to be undervalued, and short funds bet against shares they consider to be overvalued. What types of investors are likely to be attracted to each of these types of funds? Why?

5 Intergalactic Software Plc went public three months ago. You are a sophisticated investor who devotes time to fundamental analysis as a way of identifying mispriced shares. Which of the following characteristics would you focus on in deciding whether to follow this share?

- The market capitalization.
- The average number of shares traded per day.
- The bid–ask spread for the share.
- Whether the underwriter that took the firm public is a Top Five investment banking firm.
- Whether its audit company is a Big Four firm.
- Whether there are analysts from major brokerage firms following the company.
- Whether the share is held mostly by retail or institutional investors.

6 There are two major types of financial analysts: buy-side and sell-side. Buy-side analysts work for investment firms and make recommendations that are available only to the management of funds within that firm. Sell-side analysts work for brokerage firms and make recommendations that are used to sell shares to the brokerage firms' clients, which include individual investors and managers of investment funds. What would be the differences in tasks and motivations of these two types of analysts?

7 Many market participants believe that sell-side analysts are too optimistic in their recommendations to buy shares and too slow to recommend sells. What factors might explain this bias?

8 Joe Klein is an analyst for an investment banking firm that offers both underwriting and brokerage services. Joe sends you a highly favorable report on a share that his firm recently helped go public and for which it currently makes the market. What are the potential advantages and disadvantages in relying on Joe's report in deciding whether to buy the share?

9 Intergalactic Software's shares have a market price of €20 per share and a book value of €12 per share. If its cost of equity capital is 15 percent and its book value is expected to grow at 5 percent per year indefinitely, what is the market's assessment of its steady state return on equity? If the share price increases to €35 and the market does not expect the firm's growth rate to change, what is the revised steady state ROE? If instead the price increase was due to an increase in the market's assessments about long-term book value growth rather than long-term ROE, what would the price revision imply for the steady state growth rate?

10 Joe states, "I can see how ratio analysis and valuation help me do fundamental analysis, but I don't see the value of doing strategy analysis." Can you explain to him how strategy analysis could be potentially useful?

NOTES

1. OEIC stands for "Open-Ended Investment Company" and is a UK collective investment fund. SICAV stands for "Société d'Investissement à Capital Variable" and is an open-ended collective investment fund in France and Luxembourg. BEVEK stands for "Beleggingsvennootschap met Veranderlijk Kapitaal" and is an open-ended collective investment fund in Belgium.

2. Investment-grade rated bonds have received a credit rating by Moody's of Baa or above and/or a credit rating by Standard & Poor's of BBB or above. We discuss these rating categories in more detail in Chapter 10.

3. P. Healy and K. Palepu, "The Fall of Enron," *Journal of Economic Perspectives* 17(2) (Spring 2003): 3–26, discuss how weak money manager incentives and long-term analysis contributed to the share price run-up and subsequent collapse for Enron. A similar discussion on factors affecting the rise and fall of dot-com shares is provided in "The Role of Capital Market Intermediaries in the Dot-Com Crash of 2000," Harvard Business School Case 9–101–110, 2001.

4. See R. Bhushan, "Firm Characteristics and Analyst Following," *Journal of Accounting and Economics* 11(2/5), July 1989: 255–275, and P. O'Brien and R. Bhushan, "Analyst Following and Institutional Ownership," *Journal of Accounting Research* 28, Supplement (1990): 55–76.

5. Recent reviews of evidence on market efficiency are provided by E. Fama, "Efficient Capital Markets: II," *Journal of Finance* 46 (December 1991): 1575–1617; S. Kothari, "Capital Markets Research in Accounting," *Journal of Accounting and Economics* 31 (September 2001): 105–231; and C. Lee, "Market Efficiency in Accounting Research," *Journal of Accounting and Economics* 31 (September 2001): 233–253.

6. For example, see V. Bernard and J. Thomas, "Evidence That Stock Prices Do Not Fully Reflect the Implications of Current Earnings for Future Earnings," *Journal of Accounting and Economics* 13 (December 1990): 305–341.

7. Examples of studies that examine a "value share" strategy include J. Lakonishok, A. Shleifer, and R. Vishny, "Contrarian Investment, Extrapolation, and Risk," *Journal of Finance* 49 (December 1994): 1541–1578, and R. Frankel and C. Lee, "Accounting Valuation, Market Expectation, and Cross-Sectional Stock Returns," *Journal of Accounting and Economics* 25 (June 1998): 283–319.

8. For example, see J. Ou and S. Penman, "Financial Statement Analysis and the Prediction of Stock Returns," *Journal of Accounting and Economics* 11 (November 1989): 295–330; R. Holthausen and D. Larcker, "The Prediction of Stock Returns Using Financial Statement Information," *Journal of Accounting and Economics* 15 (June/September 1992): 373–412; and R. Sloan, "Do Stock Prices Fully Reflect Information in Accruals and Cash Flows about Future Earnings?" *The Accounting Review* 71 (July 1996): 298–325.

9. For an overview of research in behavioral finance, see *Advances in Behavioral Finance* by R. Thaler (New York: Russell Sage Foundation, 1993), and *Inefficient Markets: An Introduction to Behavioral Finance* by A. Shleifer (Oxford: Oxford University Press, 2000).

10. These forecasts were taken from I/B/E/S.

11. Time-series model forecasts of future annual earnings are the most recent annual earnings (with or without some form of annual growth), and forecasts of future quarterly earnings are a function of growth in earnings for the latest quarter relative to both the last quarter and the same quarter one year ago. See L. Brown and M. Rozeff, "The Superiority of Analyst Forecasts as Measures of Expectations: Evidence from Earnings," *Journal of Finance* 33 (1978): 1–16; L. Brown, P. Griffin, R. Hagerman, and M. Zmijewski, "Security Analyst Superiority Relative to Univariate Time-Series Models in Forecasting Quarterly Earnings," *Journal of Accounting and Economics* 9 (1987): 61–87; and D. Givoly, "Financial Analysts' Forecasts of Earnings: A Better Surrogate for Market Expectations," *Journal of Accounting and Economics* 4(2) (1982): 85–108.

12. See D. Givoly and J. Lakonishok, "The Information Content of Financial Analysts' Forecasts of Earnings: Some Evidence on Semi-Strong Efficiency," *Journal of Accounting and Economics* 2 (1979): 165–186; T. Lys and S. Sohn, "The Association Between Revisions of Financial Analysts' Earnings Forecasts and Security Price Changes," *Journal of Accounting and Economics* 13 (1990): 341–364; and J. Francis and L. Soffer, "The Relative Informativeness of Analysts' Stock Recommendations and Earnings Forecast Revisions," *Journal of Accounting Research* 35(2) (1997): 193–212.

13. See M. Barth and A. Hutton, "Information Intermediaries and the Pricing of Accruals," working paper, Stanford University, 2000.

14. See P. O'Brien, "Forecasts Accuracy of Individual Analysts in Nine Industries," *Journal of Accounting Research* 28 (1990): 286–304.

15. See G. Bolliger, "The Characteristics of Individual Analysts' Forecasts in Europe," *Journal of Banking and Finance* 28 (2004): 2283–2309; M. Clement, "Analyst Forecast Accuracy: Do Ability, Resources, and Portfolio Complexity Matter?" *Journal of Accounting and Economics* 27 (1999): 285–304; J. Jacob, T. Lys, and M. Neale, "Experience in Forecasting Performance of Security Analysts," *Journal of Accounting and Economics* 28 (1999): 51–82; and S. Gilson, P. Healy, C. Noe, and K. Palepu, "Analyst Specialization and Conglomerate Stock Breakups," *Journal of Accounting Research* 39 (December 2001): 565–573.

16. See L. Brown, G. Foster, and E. Noreen, "Security Analyst Multi-Year Earnings Forecasts and the Capital Market," *Studies in Accounting Research*, No. 23 (Sarasota, FL), American Accounting Association, 1985. M. McNichols and P. O'Brien, in "Self-Selection and Analyst Coverage," *Journal of Accounting Research*, Supplement (1997): 167–208, find that analyst bias arises primarily because analysts issue recommendations on firms for which they have favorable information and withhold recommending firms with unfavorable information.

17. See H. Lin and M. McNichols, "Underwriting Relationships, Analysts' Earnings Forecasts and Investment Recommendations," *Journal of Accounting and Economics* 25(1) (1998): 101–128; R. Michaely and K. Womack, "Conflict of Interest and the Credibility of Underwriter Analyst Recommendations," *Review of Financial Studies* 12(4) (1999): 653–686; and P. Dechow, A. Hutton, and R. Sloan, "The Relation Between Analysts' Forecasts of Long-Term Earnings Growth and Stock Price Performance Following Equity Offerings," *Contemporary Accounting Research* 17(1) (2000): 1–32.

18. See L. Brown, "Analyst Forecasting Errors: Additional Evidence," *Financial Analysts' Journal* (November/December 1997): 81–88, and D. Matsumoto, "Management's Incentives to Avoid Negative Earnings Surprises," *The Accounting Review* 77 (July 2002): 483–515.

19. For example, evidence of superior fund performance is reported by M. Grinblatt and S. Titman, "Mutual Fund Performance: An Analysis of Quarterly Holdings," *Journal of Business* 62 (1994), and by D. Hendricks, J. Patel, and R. Zeckhauser, "Hot Hands in Mutual Funds: Short-Run Persistence of Relative Performance," *The Journal of Finance* 48 (1993): 93–130. In contrast, negative fund performance is shown by M. Jensen, "The Performance of Mutual Funds in the Period 1945–64," *The Journal of Finance* 23 (May 1968): 389–416, and B. Malkiel, "Returns from Investing in Equity Mutual Funds from 1971 to 1991," *Journal of Finance* 50 (June 1995): 549–573.

20. M. Grinblatt and S. Titman, "The Persistence of Mutual Fund Performance," *Journal of Finance* 47 (December 1992): 1977–1986, and D. Hendricks, J. Patel, and R. Zeckhauser, "Hot Hands in Mutual Funds: Short-Run Persistence of Relative Performance," *Journal of Finance* 48 (March 1993): 93–130, find evidence of persistence in mutual fund returns. However, M. Carhart, "On Persistence in Mutual Fund Performance," *The Journal of Finance* 52 (March 1997): 57–83, shows that much of this is attributable to momentum in stock returns and to fund expenses; B. Malkiel, "Returns from Investing in Equity Mutual Funds from 1971 to 1991," *The Journal of Finance* 50 (June 1995): 549–573, shows that survivorship bias is also an important consideration.

21. See M. Grinblatt, S. Titman, and R. Wermers, "Momentum Investment Strategies, Portfolio Performance, and Herding: A Study of Mutual Fund Behavior," *The American Economic Review* 85 (December 1995): 1088–1105.

22. For example, J. Lakonishok, A. Shleifer, and R. Vishny, "Contrarian Investment, Extrapolation, and Risk," *Journal of Finance* 49 (December 1994): 1541–1579, find that value funds show superior performance, whereas M. Grinblatt, S. Titman, and R. Wermers, "Momentum Investment Strategies, Portfolio Performance, and Herding: A Study of Mutual Fund Behavior," *The American Economic Review* 85 (December 1995): 1088–1105, find that momentum investing is profitable.

23. See D. Scharfstein and J. Stein, "Herd Behavior and Investment," *The American Economic Review* 80 (June 1990): 465–480, and P. Healy and K. Palepu, "The Fall of Enron," *Journal of Economic Perspectives* 17(2) (Spring 2003): 3–26.

24. For evidence on performance by pension fund managers, see J. Lakonishok, A. Shleifer, and R. Vishny, "The Structure and Performance of the Money Management Industry," *Brookings Papers on Economic Activity*, Washington, DC American Accounting Association (1992): 339–392; T. Coggin, F. Fabozzi, and S. Rahman, "The Investment Performance of US Equity Pension Fund Managers: An Empirical Investigation," *The Journal of Finance* 48 (July 1993): 1039–1056; and W. Ferson and K. Khang, "Conditional Performance Measurement Using Portfolio Weights: Evidence for Pension Funds," *Journal of Financial Economics* 65 (August 2002): 249–282.

Valuation at Novartis

I n early 2007, Novartis announced record annual earnings of $7.2 billion for the year ended December 31, 2006, representing a 17 percent increase over the prior year. The company's return on beginning book equity of 21.7 percent far exceeded the company's estimate of its cost of equity (8.5 percent). Further, since 2003, the company had grown earnings by an average of 17 percent per year, and its return on beginning book equity had increased steadily from 16.8 percent. Despite this superior performance, the company's stock performance had lagged that of the S&P500 and Swiss Market indexes, growing by an average of 10 percent per year (see **Exhibit 9.1**). In addition, its price-to-earnings multiple had declined steadily from 22.9 2003 to 19.4 in 2006 (see **Exhibit 9.9**).

Several explanations for the gap between the company's earnings and stock performance were plausible. First, given the sustained strong performance of the pharmaceutical industry and the company's past success, market expectations were likely to be high. Merely meeting those heady expectations would generate only normal stock price appreciation. A second explanation was that the market questioned whether Novartis could sustain such strong performance, perhaps because of heightened regulatory oversight and proposed changes in the US medical system, or as a result of concerns about the viability of the company's unique strategy of investing in both branded pharmaceuticals and generics. Finally, it was possible that investors had under-estimated Novartis and the stock was undervalued. For Novartis's management, understanding which of these best explained the company's situation was a necessary first step before deciding on an appropriate course of action.

The pharmaceutical industry

The pharmaceutical industry had an impressive track record of generating strong growth and returns for shareholders over an extended period. From 2003 to 2006, the industry reported revenue and earnings growth of 11 percent per year, and had an average return on book equity of 17.5 percent.[1] Two forces had combined to help create this sustained high performance. First, the industry had been remarkably successful in creating new innovative drugs to address patient needs. This was a costly process. Only one in 5,000 to 10,0000 compounds tested in the laboratory reached the market, and of these only 30 percent were a commercial success.[2] As a result of extensive testing and regulatory approval to ensure drug efficacy and safety, total drug development time lasted around fourteen years and cost more than $800 million per drug. On average, in 2006 pharmaceutical

Professor Paul Healy prepared this case. This case was developed from published sources. HBS cases are developed solely as the basis for class discussion. Cases are not intended to serve as endorsements, sources of primary data, or illustrations of effective or ineffective management.

[1]Source: Capital IQ.

[2]See "Pharmaceutical Industry Profile 2007," Pharmaceutical Research and Manufacturers of America website, www.phrma.org/publications.

companies spent $55.2 billion (17.5 percent of sales) on research and development.[3] However, patent protection of new compounds prevented competitors from copying successful new innovations and enabled innovators to recover the heavy costs of drug discovery and development. The average effective patent life for branded drugs was 11.5 years.[4]

A second factor behind the industry's performance was its strong sales and marketing capability. On average, pharmaceutical companies spent around 30 percent of sales on sales and marketing costs. In many markets, drug companies employed an army of sales reps who visited doctors to convince them to prescribe their firms' drugs. However, given the time constraints faced by physicians, sales rep visits were typically short, enabling the reps to drop off promotional materials and free sample drugs. Drug companies therefore frequently organized educational conferences, dinners, and other events to enable sales reps to spend time with doctors. Firms also appealed directly to patients by consumer advertising. By 2005, direct-to-consumer advertising was $4.2 billion.[5]

In early 2007, the pharmaceutical industry faced a number of challenges. Public concern over the cost of medical care and drugs had escalated, particularly in the US, the most expensive (and also most profitable) health care market in the world. For the first time in fifteen years politicians had seriously begun debating whether the health care system in the US needed to be changed. Candidates for the 2008 presidential elections from both political parties were in the process of developing new health care initiatives to solve dual problems of a large uninsured population and the increased cost of health care. While increased access to health care could potentially benefit the pharmaceutical industry, there was also a significant risk that changes would increase the power of health care providers (including federal and state governments) which would use their leverage to obtain price cuts of as much as 40 percent, reducing the industry's profitability and the financial resources available for developing new drugs.

A second challenge had emerged following publication of research showing adverse cardiac risks for patients using Merck's blockbuster Vioxx painkiller. Merck had voluntarily withdrawn Vioxx from the market in September 2004 following the publication. However, research findings from a 2001 study presented to the company also showed cardiac risks, leading critics to allege that the company had over-promoted the drug and underplayed its risks. By early 2007, roughly 22,000 lawsuits in US state and federal courts had been filed against Merck. Analysts estimated that company's legal liabilities could range from $4 billion to more than $25 billion. Merck opted to defend each suit separately on its merits. Of the 17 cases tried as of March 28, 2007, Merck won ten, lost five, and two had ended in mistrials.[6] Merck planned to or had appealed the cases it had lost. However, the problems had increased pressure on the Food and Drug Administration, which regulated drug approvals in the US, to be more cautious in approving new drugs and to respond more promptly to drug safety questions.

In addition, it appeared that the industry was becoming less productive in discovering and commercializing new drugs to replace those going off patent. Drug development costs had increased from $54 million per new drug in 1976 to $231 million in 1987 and to $802 million in 2001.[7] A study by Bain & Co. discovered that by 2003, only one in thirteen drugs that reached animal testing actually reached the market, down from one in eight in the late 1990s. Opinions were divided on the causes of this decline. Some argued that it was becoming more difficult to discover breakthrough drugs. Others pointed to increased regulatory oversight to improve drug safety. Despite questions about research productivity, spending on R&D continued to grow, both in dollar terms and as a percentage of sales. In 2006, industry R&D totaled $55.2 billion, a 7.8 percent increase over the prior year. As a percentage of sales, R&D increased from 12.9 percent in 1985 to 17.5 percent in 2006.[8]

[3]Ibid.

[4]Ibid.

[5]Julie M. Donohue, Marisa Cevasco, and Meredith B. Rosenthal, "A Decade of Direct-to-Consumer Advertising of Prescription Drugs," *New England Journal of Medicine*, Vol. 357 (August 16, 2007): 673–681.

[6]Standard & Poor's Healthcare, "Pharmaceuticals Industry Survey," May 10,2007.

[7]"Pharmaceutical Industry Profile 2007," Pharmaceutical Research and Manufacturers of America website, www.phrma.org/publications.

[8]Ibid.

Finally, the industry faced increased pricing pressure from generics companies that produced and marketed drugs for which patent protection had expired. Generics drugs sold at 30 percent to 90 percent discounts relative to prices of brand-name drugs prior to patent expiration. Analysts estimated that in the first year after patent expiration, a brand-name drug could lose more than 80 percent of its volume to generics. The generics share of the US prescription drug market had grown from 19 percent in 1994, to 47 percent in 2000, and 54 percent in 2005.[9] This growth was driven by managed care providers, which substituted generics drugs for the brand names to reduce costs. Generics companies followed a very different business model than traditional pharma companies. They spent much less on research and development, and on marketing and sales. Their focus was on aggressively challenging existing brand name drugs about to lose patent protection since the first to market was granted six-month period of market exclusivity. Once this six-month period ended, however, other generics firms were free to enter the market, leading to intense competition.

Novartis

Novartis was founded in 1996 through the merger of Ciba-Geigy and Sandoz. Under the leadership of Daniel Vasella, who was appointed CEO in 1999, Novartis grew through a combination of successful new drug discoveries and selected acquisitions. From 1999 to 2006, revenues increased from $20.4 billion to $36 billion, and operating earnings grew from $4.6 to $8.1 billion (see **Exhibit 9.2** for Novartis's income statement and balance sheet data for the period 1999 to 2006).[10] During this period Novartis was among the industry leaders in introducing new drugs, including Femura (for breast cancer), Excelon (for Alzheimers), Dio-van/Co-Diovan (for hypertension), Visudyne (for age-related macular degeneration), Glee-vac/Gilvec (for chronic myeloid leukemia), and Zometa (for cancer complications).[11] It also successfully refocused by divesting its agribusiness and made several key acquisitions, including contact lens maker Wesley Jessen for $845 million in 2000, generics companies Lek ($959 million in 2002), Eon and Hexal ($8.4 billion in 2005), and Chiron, a biopharmaceutical, vaccine, and diagnostics firm for $6.3 billion in 2006.[12]

By early 2007, Novartis comprised four divisions: Pharmaceuticals, Sandoz (its generics business), Consumer Health, and Vaccines and Diagnostics. The company's strategy was to provide customers with a full complement of the health care products they needed, including branded drugs, generic drugs, vaccines, and over-the-counter medicines.

Pharmaceuticals, the largest division with sales of $26.6 billion, boasted highly successful drugs in the cardiovascular, oncology, and neuroscience areas (see **Exhibit 9.3** for data on the company's top twenty drug sales and **Exhibit 9.4** for sales by drug maturity). Sales growth at Pharma exceeded 12 percent for 2006 with profit margins of 28.7 percent. The unit's strong performance was expected to continue in 2007 and 2008 with approvals pending in the US and Europe for a number of new drugs, including Exforge and Tekturna (hypertension), Galvus (type 2 diabetes), and Lucentis (for blindness). A total of 138 new projects were in progress at the end of 2006, 36 percent classified as new molecular entities, and the remainder as life cycle management projects. Fifteen projects had been submitted to regulatory authorities, thirteen were in phase III (large clinical trials), and another 76 were in phase II clinical trials.[13] The company's major competitors in this sector included GlaxoSmithKline, Johnson & Johnson, Merck, and Pfizer (see **Exhibit 9.5** for data on the performance of these firms).

Sandoz, with sales of $5.6 billion in 2006, was the world's second-largest generics business. In 2003, Novartis consolidated its different generics businesses using the Sandoz brand. It subsequently invested in building the generics business with acquisitions of Lek, Hexal, and Eon. Novartis was the only major pharma company with a generics drug business. In commenting on the strategy, CEO Vasella explained that the company viewed "generic medicines as a critical complement to innovative medicines. Large purchasers like Wal-Mart, and private and state-run health care providers want to buy a range of generic and patented

[9]"Insights 2006, Highlights from the Pharmaceutical Industry Profile," Pharmaceutical Research and Manufacturers of America website, www.phrma.org/publications.

[10]Source: Novartis annual reports, 1999 to 2006.

[11]Ibid.

[12]Source: Capital IQ.

[13]Source: Novartis 2006 annual report.

products."[14] Also, generic drugs were projected to increase their market share as patents for many large drug companies were scheduled to expire in the US market. However, some analysts expressed doubts about the move, pointing out that "competition is high in the (generics) sector, fueled by the entry of low-cost producers from emerging markets like India which (has) hurt (generic drug) margins and profitability."[15] In 2006, Sandoz sales grew by 27 percent and operating profit margins increased to 12 percent as a result of the completion of the Hexal and Eon acquisitions, and rapid growth in the US and Eastern European markets. Key competitors in this sector included Teva Pharmaceutical Industries, Watson Pharmaceuticals, and a range of smaller companies (see **Exhibit 9.6** for data on the performance of key competitors in the industry).

The Consumer Health division included several businesses, Over-the Counter (OTC), Animal Health, CIBA Vision, and Gerber. In 2006, the group's Medical Nutrition unit was sold to Nestle for $2.5 billion. Consumer Health sales from continuing operations grew by 8 percent to $6.5 billion. This was led by strong performance in OTC, which jumped from sixth largest in sales to the fourth largest in the world, and in Animal Health which jumped three positions to number five. The group's other major business units included eye lens firm CIBA Vision and Gerber, the leading baby nutrition company in the US Key competitors in this sector included Johnson & Johnson, Schering-Plough, Reckitt and Benkiser, and Pfizer (see **Exhibit 9.7** for data on the performance of key competitors).

The Vaccines and Diagnostics unit arose from the acquisition of Chiron. 2006 sales for the post-acquisition eight months were $956 million, up 42 percent over the comparable period for 2005. This increase was driven by a sharp increase in influenza vaccines in the US market. Novartis reported that given novel new products and innovations in manufacturing technologies it anticipated double digit growth in this segment during the following decade. Key competitors in this sector included Johnson & Johnson, Sanofi-Aventis, Merck, and Abbott Laboratories (see **Exhibit 9.8** for data on the performance of competitors).

Valuation

The health care industry had experienced declining stock multiples from 2003 to 2006. Price-to-earnings multiples during the period had dropped steadily from 47.8 to 33.0, despite strong earnings growth in 2006. Price-to-book multiples had declined from 6.0 to 4.0 during the same period despite sustained strong returns on book equity (see **Exhibit 9.9**).

In early 2007, Novartis's price to earnings multiple was higher than that of three of its five leading competitors (GlaxoSmithKline, Pfizer, and Johnson & Johnson). Yet its price to book multiple was lower than that all but Pfizer (see **Exhibit 9.10**). Despite continued strong earnings performance, its record of new drug introductions, and its strong pipeline of future new drugs, management was puzzled by the stock's three-year record of merely tracking the S&P index. What assumptions was the market making about Novartis's future performance? How were questions about the future of the industry, and the company's unique strategy affecting its valuation? And what actions if any should the company's management team take to respond to market's assessments?

[14]Tom Wright, "Novartis to become generics leader," *International Herald Tribune*, February 22, 2005.
[15]Ibid.

EXHIBIT 1 **Stock performance for Novartis and indexes for the period 2003 to 2006**

	Novartis	Swiss Market Index	S&P 500 Index	Morgan Stanley World Pharmaceutical Index
2003	13%	21%	26%	3%
2004	4%	5%	9%	−8%
2005	22%	36%	3%	19%
2006	2%	17%	14%	7%
Average	10%	20%	13%	5%

Source: Novartis 2006 annual report for performance of Novartis stock, Swiss market index, and Pharmaceutical Index, and Standard & Poor's for S&P500 Index.

Valuation at Novartis

EXHIBIT 2 Novartis's income statement for the years ended December 31, 1999 to 2006 in $US millions

	1999	2000	2001	2002	2003	2004	2005	2006
Total Revenue	20,380	21,846	18,762	20,877	24,930	27,277	31,319	36,749
Cost of Goods Sold	6,166	6,321	4,744	4,994	6,457	6,700	8,259	10,299
Gross Profit	**14,214**	**15,525**	**14,018**	**15,883**	**18,473**	**20,577**	**23,060**	**26,450**
Selling General & Administrative Expense	6,939	7,785	7,153	7,883	9,235	9,989	11,078	12,411
R&D Expense	2,665	2,874	2,528	2,843	3,729	4,152	4,493	5,349
Other Operating Expense	—	—	—	65	15	270	350	548
Operating Income	**4,609**	**4,865**	**4,337**	**5,092**	**5,494**	**6,166**	**7,139**	**8,142**
Interest Expense	(340)	(315)	(218)	(194)	(243)	(261)	(294)	(266)
Interest and Invest. Income	725	705	404	484	340	400	408	375
Net Interest Expense	**385**	**391**	**186**	**290**	**97**	**139**	**114**	**109**
Income/(loss) from Affiliates	240	60	83	(7)	(279)	68	193	264
Currency Exchange Gains (Loss)	(213)	(124)	(152)	69	64	95	115	38
Other Non-Operating Inc. (Expense)	(68)	(77)	(86)	333	272	(66)	(107)	(316)
EBT Excl. Unusual Items	4,953	5,115	4,368	5,777	5,648	6,402	7,454	8,237
EBT Incl. Unusual Items	5,347	5,599	4,692	5,698	5,734	6,410	7,162	8,301
Income Tax Expense	1,151	1,123	844	959	947	1,045	1,090	1,282
Minority Int. in Earnings	(17)	(26)	(12)	(14)	(44)	(15)	(11)	(27)
Earnings from Continuing Operations	**4,180**	**4,450**	**3,836**	**4,725**	**4,743**	**5,350**	**6,061**	**6,992**
Earnings of Discontinued Operations	—	—	—	—	—	15	69	183
Net Income	**4,180**	**4,450**	**3,836**	**4,725**	**4,743**	**5,365**	**6,130**	**7,175**
Per Share Items								
Basic EPS	$1,575	$1,703	$1,492	$1,878	$1,993	$2,278	$2,628	$3,059
Basic EPS Excluding Extra Items	1.575	1.703	1.492	1.878	1.993	2.271	2.598	2.981
Weighted Average Basic Shares Outstanding	2,653.8	2,613.5	2,571.7	2,515.3	2,380.1	2,355.5	2,332.8	2,345.2
Dividends per Share	$0.5	$0.52	$0.54	$0.68	$0.8	$0.86	$0.94	$1.11
Payout Ratio %	29.1%	28.6%	33.1%	28.9%	35.0%	35.3%	34.4%	28.6%

Source: Standard & Poor's Capital IQ data.

EXHIBIT 2   Novartis's income statement for the years ended December 31, 1999 to 2006 in $US millions

	1999	2000	2001	2002	2003	2004	2005	2006
ASSETS								
Cash and Short-Term Investments	10,250	12,667	13,346	12,542	13,259	13,358	10,449	7,848
Accounts Receivable	4,420	3,261	3,223	4,982	5,480	6,334	6,663	8,041
Inventory	4,323	2,544	2,477	2,963	3,346	3,558	3,725	4,498
Other Current Assets	2,776	1,858	1,544	328	188	670	606	1,017
Total Current Assets	21,770	20,330	20,590	20,815	22,273	23,920	21,443	21,404
Net Property, Plant & Equipment	7,323	5,573	5,458	6,321	7,597	8,497	8,679	10,945
Long-term Investments	4,967	1,864	5,362	7,789	8,362	9,206	8,996	8,424
Goodwill	963	1,276	1,382	1,704	1,477	1,899	7,279	10,659
Other Intangibles	1,044	2,313	2,563	2,691	3,231	3,430	5,177	8,205
Deferred Charges, Long Term	11	9	—	—	—	300	838	2,366
Other Long-Term Assets	2,896	2,547	2,917	3,527	3,976	3,001	2,757	4,468
Total Assets	41,134	35,919	40,222	45,025	49,317	52,488	57,732	68,008
LIABILITIES								
Accounts Payable	1,237	982	1,090	1,266	1,665	2,020	1,961	2,487
Short-term Borrowings	4,197	2,287	2,281	2,399	2,235	3,142	5,768	5,220
Current Portion of Long-Term Debt	498	46	776	111	45	680	1,122	1,340
Other Current Liabilities	4,999	3,870	4,407	4,496	5,375	6,007	6,477	7,187
Total Current Liabilities	10,931	7,184	8,553	8,272	9,320	11,849	15,328	16,234
Long-Term Debt	1,534	1,409	1,506	2,729	3,191	2,736	1,319	656
Minority Interest	139	48	63	66	90	138	174	183
Pension & Other Post-Retirement Benefits	1,543	965	1,084	1,342	1,573	2,706	2,797	2,679
Deferred Tax Liability, Non-Current	2,289	2,153	2,341	2,821	3,138	2,340	3,472	5,290
Other Non-Current Liabilities	1,336	1,408	1,223	1,526	1,576	1,542	1,652	1,855
Total Liabilities	17,772	13,168	14,770	16,756	18,888	21,311	24,742	26,897
Total Common Equity	23,362	22,751	25,452	28,269	30,429	31,177	32,990	41,111
Total Liabilities and Equity	41,134	35,919	40,222	45,025	49,317	52,488	57,732	68,008

Source: Standard & Poor's Capital IQ data.

Valuation at Novartis

Valuation at Novartis

EXHIBIT 3   Sales for Novartis pharmaceutical division's top 20 drugs in 2006

Brands	Therapeutic Area	USA USD millions	% change in local currencies	Rest of world USD millions	% change in local currencies	Total USD millions	%change in USD	%change in local currencies
Diovan/Co-Diovan	Hypertension	1858	20	2365	12	4223	15	15
Gleevec/Glivec	Chronic myeloid leukemia	630	20	1924	16	2554	18	17
Lotrel	Hypertension	1352	26			1352	5	4
Zometa	Cancer complications	696	-1	587	12	1283	5	4
Lamisil (group)	Fungal infections	574	7	404	-31	978	-14	-13
Neural/Sandimmun	Transplantation	125	-17	793	-1	918	-4	-4
Sandostatin (incl. LAR)	Acromegaly	367	-2	548	4	915	2	2
Lescol	Cholesterol reduction	256	0	469	-8	725	-5	-5
Trileptal	Epilepsy	549	19	172	11	721	17	17
Femara	Breast cancer	338	40	381	27	719	34	33
Top ten products total		**6745**	**15**	**7643**	**7**	**14388**	**10**	**10**
Voltaren (group)	Inflammation/pain	8	60	682	0	690	0	1
Zelnorm/Zelmac	Irritable bowel syndrome	488	37	73	20	561	34	34
Exelon	Alzheimer's disease	187	9	338	12	525	12	11
Tegretol (incl. CR/XR)	Epilepsy	120	10	271	-5	391	-1	-1
Visudyne	Macular degeneration	70	-62	284	-6	354	-27	-27
Miacalcic	Osteoporosis	199	-13	140	3	339	-7	-7
Comtan/Stalevo Group	Parkinson's disease	157	18	182	24	339	22	21
Foradil	Asthma	14	0	317	-1	331	0	-1
Ritalin/Focalin (group)	Attention deficit/ hyperactive disorder	264	47	66	6	330	37	37
Famvir	Viral infections	166	10	102	-3	268	6	5
Top twenty products total		**8418**	**14**	**10098**	**5**	**18516**	**9**	**9**
Rest of portfolio		1054	43	3006	14	4060	21	21
Total Division net sales		**9472**	**17**	**13104**	**7**	**22576**	**11**	**11**

Source: Novartis 2006 annual report.

EXHIBIT 4   **2006 sales for Novartis pharmaceutical division by drug maturity**

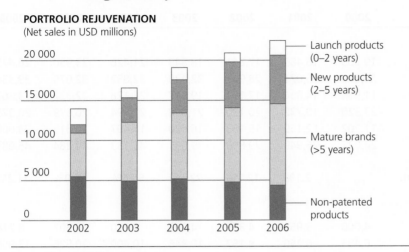

PORTROLIO REJUVENATION
(Net sales in USD millions)

Launch products (0–2 years)

New products (2–5 years)

Mature brands (>5 years)

Non-patented products

Source: Novartis 2006 annual report.

Valuation at Novartis

EXHIBIT 5 **Performance of key competitors in the pharmaceutical industry (in $US millions)**

	2000	2001	2002	2003	2004	2005	2006
Revenues							
AstraZeneca plc	19,200	16,480	17,841	18,849	21,426	23,950	26,475
GlaxoSmithKline plc	23,074	25,021	28,963	32,439	32,852	32,075	39,334
Johnson & Johnson	11,954	14,851	17,151	19,517	22,128	22,322	23,267
Merck & Co. Inc.	23,320	19,732	20,130	21,038	21,494	20,679	20,375
Novartis	11,202	12,159	15,183	16,020	18,497	20,515	23,000
Pfizer	24,027	26,949	29,843	39,631	46,133	44,284	45,083
Weighted average sales growth		2.1%	12.1%	22.1%	53.6%	6.0%	11.2%
EBIT							
AstraZeneca plc	4,008	3,954	4,356	4,202	4,770	6,502	8,216
GlaxoSmithKline plc	6,455	6,256	8,157	10,348	10,400	10,586	13,958
Johnson & Johnson	4,175	4,928	5,787	5,896	7,376	6,365	6,894
Merck & Co. Inc.	11,564	12,200	12,723	13,250	13,507	13,158	13,649
Novartis	3,334	3,420	4,353	4,423	5,253	6,014	6,703
Pfizer	8,859	10,936	12,920	6,837	21,510	19,594	20,718
Weighted average EBIT margin	34.0%	36.2%	37.4%	30.5%	35.0%	34.2%	34.8%
Net Operating Assets							
AstraZeneca plc	na	na	21,576	23,573	25,616	24,840	29,932
GlaxoSmithKline plc	29,017	26,278	29,950	33,927	36,165	28,242	33,179
Johnson & Johnson	9,209	10,591	11,112	15,351	16,058	16,091	18,799
Merck & Co. Inc.	na	na	na	na	na	na	na
Novartis	10,423	11,225	12,118	13,836	14,914	14,655	20,418
Pfizer	15,854	16,881	18,541	81,522	81,651	74,406	72,497
Weighted average revenues to net operating assets	1.09	1.22	1.17	0.75	0.81	0.90	0.90

Notes: Data are actual reported segment data reported at each year end. Changes in the performance measures therefore include the effect of any acquisitions or divestitures, such as Pfizer's acquisition of Pharmacia in mid-2003. EBIT are earnings before interest and taxes. Net operating assets are operating assets less non-interest-bearing liabilities.
Source: Standard & Poor's Capital IQ data.

EXHIBIT 6   **Performance of key competitors in the generics industry (in $US millions)**

	2000	2001	2002	2003	2004	2005	2006
Revenues							
Novartis	1,973	2,433	2,809	2,906	3,045	4,712	5,983
Teva Pharmaceutical Inds. Ltd.	1,548	1,838	2,240	2,885	4,276	4,703	7,821
Watson Pharmaceuticals Inc.	423	552	650	749	1,239	1,247	1,517
Weighted average sales growth rate		22.3%	18.2%	14.8%	30.9%	24.6%	43.7%
EBIT							
Novartis	242	281	406	473	235	342	736
Teva Pharmaceutical Inds. Ltd.	223	297	427	692	307	981	372
Watson Pharmaceuticals Inc.	na	na	na	na	na	356	321
Weighted average EBIT margin	13.2%	13.5%	16.5%	20.1%	7.4%	15.8%	9.3%
Net Operating Assets							
Novartis	2,575	3,362	4,673	4,321	5,379	14,057	15,009
Teva Pharmaceutical Inds. Ltd.	1,439	1,367	2,521	3,205	5,973	6,094	na
Watson Pharmaceuticals Inc.	na	na	na	na	na	na	na
Weighted average revenues to net operating assets	0.88	0.90	0.70	0.77	0.64	0.47	0.40

Notes: Data are actual reported segment data reported at each year end. Changes in the performance measures therefore include the effect of any acquisitions or divestitures, such as Novartis's acquisition of Hexal and Eon in mid-2005. EBIT are earnings before interest and taxes. Net operating assets are operating assets less non-interest-bearing liabilities.
Source: Standard & Poor's Capital IQ data.

Valuation at Novartis

EXHIBIT 7 **Performance of key competitors in the consumer health industry (in $US millions)**

	2000	2001	2002	2003	2004	2005	2006
Revenues							
GlaxoSmithKline plc	3,963	4,776	5,178	5,817	6,156	5,155	6,165
Johnson & Johnson	6,904	6,320	6,564	7,431	8,333	9,096	9,774
Novartis	4,880	5,098	5,532	5,938	5,595	6,092	6,579
Pfizer Animal Health	5,547	5,310	2,530	4,640	5,469	6,084	2,311
Reckit & Benkiser	na	4,665	5,334	6,279	7,053	6,848	9,262
Schering Plough (Consumer & Animal Health)	na	1,341	1,412	1,662	1,855	1,944	2,033
Average sales growth rate		1.0%	−3.5%	19.6%	8.5%	2.2%	2.6%
EBIT							
GlaxoSmithKline plc	618	628	777	1,056	1,268	1,229	1,338
Johnson & Johnson	867	1,004	1,229	1,393	1,444	1,592	1,374
Novartis	598	659	886	821	919	952	1,068
Pfizer Animal Health	813	787	546	671	1,019	1,103	419
Reckitt & Benckiser	na	675	861	1,140	1,358	1,363	1,979
Schering Plough (Consumer & Animal Health)		281	267	195	322	355	348
Weighted average EBIT margin	13.6%	14.7%	17.2%	16.6%	18.4%	18.7%	18.1%
Net Operating Assets							
GlaxoSmithKline plc	3,271	5,596	5,986	8,850	7,095	4,204	5,423
Johnson & Johnson	4,761	4,209	5,056	5,371	6,142	6,275	25,380
Novartis	4,688	4,576	5,136	5,417	6,155	6,863	6,480
Pfizer Animal Health	3,840	3,553	2,105	7,514	7,878	8,158	1,951
Reckitt & Benckiser	na	na	na	na	5,737	5,370	10,634
Schering Plough (Consumer & Animal Health)	na	na	na	na	na	na	na
Weighted average revenues to net operating assets	1.29	1.20	1.08	0.88	0.99	1.08	0.68

Notes: Data are actual reported segment data reported at each year end. Changes in the performance measures therefore include the effect of any acquisitions or divestitures, such as Proctor & Gamble's acquisition of Gillette in 2005, Pfizer's acquisition of its animal health business in 2003 and the sale of its consumer health business to Johnson & Johnson in 2006. Net operating assets are operating assets less non-interest-bearing liabilities. EBIT are earnings before interest and taxes.
Source: Standard & Poor's Capital IQ data.

EXHIBIT 8 **Performance of key competitors in the vaccines and diagnostics industry (in $US millions)**

	2000	2001	2002	2003	2004	2005	2006
Revenues							
Abbot Labs Vaccines	2,924	2,929	2,897	3,040	3,378	3,756	3,979
J&J Medical Devices & Diagnostics	10,281	11,146	12,583	14,914	16,887	19,096	20,283
Merck Vaccines	na	na	na	na	973	984	1,706
Novartis	na	na	na	na	na	na	1,187
Sanofi-Aventis Vaccines	na	na	na	na	925	2,512	3,436
Weighted average sales growth rate	33.2%	6.6%	10.0%	16.0%	12.9%	18.9%	11.6%
EBIT							
Abbot Labs Vaccines	331	357	220	249	378	495	431
J&J Medical Devices & Diagnostics	1,696	2,001	2,489	3,370	3,924	5,240	6,126
Merck Vaccines	na	na	na	na	881	767	893
Novartis	na	na	na	na	na	na	(26)
Sanofi-Aventis Vaccines	na	na	na	na	(1,374)	220	673
Weighted average EBIT margin	15.4%	16.8%	17.5%	20.2%	17.2%	25.5%	26.5%
Net Operating Assets							
Abbot Labs Vaccines	na	na	na	na	3,691	3,742	4,073
J&J Medical Devices & Diagnostics	12,745	13,645	15,052	16,082	15,805	16,540	18,601
Merck Vaccines	na	na	na	na	na	na	na
Novartis	na	na	na	na	na	na	5,609
Sanofi-Aventis Vaccines	na	na	na	na	7,099	8,130	8,582
Weighted average sales to net operating assets	0.81	0.82	0.84	0.93	0.80	0.89	0.78

Notes: Data are actual reported segment data reported at each year end. Changes in the performance measures therefore include the effect of any acquisitions or divestitures, such as Novartis's acquisition of Chiron in 2006, and Sanofi's acquisition of Aventis in 2004. Net operating assets are operating assets less non-interest-bearing liabilities. EBIT are earnings before interest and taxes. Source: Standard & Poor's Capital IQ data.

Valuation at Novartis

EXHIBIT 9 **Health care industry and Novartis valuation multiples for the period 2003 to 2006**

	2003	2004	2005	2006
Health care Industry				
Price-to-earnings multiple	47.8	40.1	34.4	33.0
Price-to-book multiple	6.0	4.7	4.3	4.0
Return on equity %	13.3%	12.7%	12.7%	13.4%
Revenue growth %	14.4%	13.6%	8.8%	16.0%
Earnings growth	26.5%	19.1%	12.6%	21.7%
Novartis AG				
Price to Earnings Multiple	22.9	21.2	21.0	19.4
Price to Book Multiple	3.4	3.3	3.9	3.3

Note: Multiples are based on year-end financial information and stock price data from March 31 the following year.
Source: Standard & Poor's Capital IQ data.

Valuation at Novartis

EXHIBIT 10   Valuation and multiples for leading pharmaceutical companies based on financial statement data for fiscal year-end 2006 and stock price data on March 31, 2007

Company	Stock Price ($US)	Market Equity Capitalization ($US million)	Enterprise Value ($US million)	Book Equity	Price-Book Multiple	Diluted EPS ($US)	PE Multiple	ROE	Beta
Johnson & Johnson	60.26	174,451	176,960	39,318	4.4	3.734	16.1	28.3%	0.33
Pfizer Inc.	25.26	178,761	159,169	71,217	2.5	1.515	16.7	16.1%	0.69
Roche Holding AG	177.64	153,227	146,024	32,590	4.7	7.46	23.8	21.6%	0.16
GlaxoSmithKline plc	27.37	153,337	158,650	18,388	8.3	1.85	14.8	64.6%	0.27
Novartis AG	57.59	135,233	134,780	41,111	3.3	2.962	19.4	17.5%	0.33
Merck & Co. Inc.	44.17	95,848	96,377	17,560	5.5	2.027	21.8	25.0%	0.96
Weighted average					4.7		18.4	24.1%	0.43

Notes: Market capitalization is the stock price multiplied by the number of shares outstanding. Earnings per share are diluted earnings per share excluding extraordinary items. Enterprise value is the market equity capitalization plus the book value of interest-bearing debt and minority interest, less cash and marketable securities and earnings. ROE is net income as a percentage of average book equity. Beta is the systematic risk of the stock, estimated by regressing the firm's stock for the previous 36 months on the S&P 500 index returns. The weighted average price-book and PE multiples are weighted by the market capitalizations of the firms, whereas the weighted ROE is weighted by their relative book equity values. Data for GlaxoSmithKline plc and Roche Holding AG are translated into $US using exchange rates on March 31, 2007.
Source: Standard & Poor's Capital IQ data.

Valuation at Novartis

10 Credit Analysis and Distress Prediction

Credit analysis is the evaluation of a firm from the perspective of a holder or potential holder of its debt, including trade payables, loans, and public debt securities. A key element of credit analysis is the prediction of the likelihood a firm will face financial distress. Credit analysis is involved in a wide variety of decision contexts:

- A commercial banker asks: Should we extend a loan to this firm? If so, how should it be structured? How should it be priced?

- If the loan is granted, the banker must later ask: Are we still providing the services, including credit, that this firm needs? Is the firm still in compliance with the loan terms? If not, is there a need to restructure the loan, and if so, how? Is the situation serious enough to call for accelerating the repayment of the loan?

- A potential investor asks: Are these debt securities a sound investment? What is the probability that the firm will face distress and default on the debt? Does the yield provide adequate compensation for the default risk involved?

- An investor contemplating purchase of debt securities in default asks: How likely is it that this firm can be turned around? In light of the high yield on this debt relative to its current price, can I accept the risk that the debt will not be repaid in full?

- A potential supplier asks: Should I sell products or services to this firm? The associated credit will be extended only for a short period, but the amount is large and I should have some assurance that collection risks are manageable.

Finally, there are third parties – those other than borrowers and lenders – who are interested in the general issue of how likely it is that a firm will avoid financial distress:

- An auditor asks: How likely is it that this firm will survive beyond the short run? In evaluating the firm's financials, should I consider it a going concern?

- An actual or potential employee asks: How confident can I be that this firm will be able to offer employment over the long-term?

- A potential customer asks: What assurance is there that this firm will survive to provide warranty services, replacement parts, product updates, and other services?

- A competitor asks: Will this firm survive the current industry shakeout? What are the implications of potential financial distress at this firm for my pricing and market share?

This chapter develops a framework to evaluate a firm's creditworthiness and assess the likelihood of financial distress.

WHY DO FIRMS USE DEBT FINANCING?

Before discussing the credit market and credit analysis, it is worth understanding why firms use debt financing. Debt financing is attractive to firms for two key reasons:

- Corporate interest tax shields. In many countries tax laws provide for the corporate tax deductibility of interest paid on debt. No such corporate tax shield is available for dividend payments or retained earnings. Therefore, corporate tax benefits should encourage firms with high effective tax rates and few forms of tax shields other than interest to favor debt financing.

- Management incentives for value creation. Firms with relatively high leverage face pressures to generate cash flows to meet payments of interest and principal, reducing resources available to fund unjustifiable expenses and investments that do not maximize shareholder value. Debt financing, therefore, focuses management on value creation, reducing conflicts of interest between managers and shareholders.

However, in addition to these **benefits of debt**, there are also **costs of debt** financing. As a firm increases its use of debt financing, it increases the likelihood of financial distress, where it is unable to meet interest or principal repayment obligations to creditors. When a firm is in serious financial distress, its owners' claims are likely to be restructured. This can take place under formal bankruptcy proceedings or out of bankruptcy, depending on the jurisdiction in which the firm operates. Financial distress has multiple negative consequences for the firm:

- Legal costs of financial distress. Restructurings are likely to be costly, since the parties involved have to hire lawyers, bankers, and accountants to represent their interests, and to pay court costs if there are formal legal proceedings. These are often called the direct costs of financial distress.

- Costs of foregone investment opportunities. Distressed firms face significant challenges in raising capital as potential new investors and creditors will be wary of becoming embroiled in the firm's legal disputes. Thus, firms in distress are often unable to finance new investments even though they may be profitable for its owners.

- Costs of conflicts between creditors and shareholders. When faced with financial distress, creditors focus on the firm's ability to service its debt while shareholders worry that their equity will revert to the creditors if the firm defaults. Thus, managers face increased pressure to make decisions that typically serve the interests of the stockholders, and creditors react by increasing the costs of borrowing for the firm's stockholders.

DEBT FINANCING AND FREE CASH FLOW

The debt introduced as a result of leveraged buyouts (LBOs) is viewed by many as an example of debt creating pressure for management to refocus on value creation for shareholders. The increased debt taken with the LBO forces management to eliminate unnecessary perks, to limit diversification into unrelated industries, and to cancel unprofitable projects. For example, in 2011 Poland-based mobile-phone operator Polkomtel S.A. was one of the few large European firms being acquired in a leveraged buyout for €4.6 billion (18.1 billion zloty). The funds used to finance this largest leveraged buyout in Europe included about €2.6 billion of term loans, €140 million of payment in kind loans, €150 million of revolving loans, and €900 million of 12.5 percent yield bonds, which Standard and Poor's had rated at B+. In comparison with the company's global competitors, Polkomtel had relatively stable cash flows and good growth prospects because its domestic market was characterized by low smartphone penetration and poor fixed broadband roll-outs.

Financial ratio and prospective analysis can help analysts assess whether there are currently free cash flow inefficiencies at a firm as well as risks of future inefficiencies. Symptoms of excessive management perks and investment in unprofitable projects include the following:

- *High ratios of general and administrative expenses and overhead to sales.* If a firm's ratios are higher than those for its major competitors, one possibility is that management is wasting money on perks.

- *Significant new investments in unrelated areas.* If it is difficult to rationalize these new investments, there might be free cash flow problems.

- *High levels of expected operating cash flows (net of essential capital expenditures and debt retirements) from pro forma income and cash flow statements.*

- *Poor management incentives to create additional shareholder value*, evidenced by a weak linkage between management compensation and firm performance.

Firms are more likely to fall into financial distress if they have high business risks and their assets are easily destroyed in financial distress. For example, firms with human capital and brand intangibles are particularly sensitive to financial distress since dissatisfied employees and customers can leave or seek alternative suppliers. In contrast, firms with tangible assets can sell their assets if they get into financial distress, providing additional security for lenders and lowering the costs of financial distress. Firms with intangible assets are therefore less likely to be highly leveraged than firms whose assets are mostly tangible.

The above discussion implies that a firm's long-term decisions on the use of debt financing reflect a trade-off between the corporate interest tax shield and incentive benefits of debt against the costs of financial distress. As the firm becomes more highly leveraged, the costs of leverage presumably begin to outweigh the tax and monitoring benefits of debt.

Table 10.1 shows median leverage ratios for publicly-traded stocks in selected industries for the fiscal years 1992–2011. Median ratios are reported for all listed companies and for large companies (with market capitalizations greater than €300 million) only.

Median debt-to-book equity ratios are highest for the electric services and auto leasing industries, which are typically not highly sensitive to economy risk and whose core assets are primarily physical equipment and property that are readily transferable to debt holders in the event of financial distress. In contrast, the software and pharmaceutical industries' core assets are their research staffs and sales force representatives. These types of assets can easily be lost if the firm gets into financial difficulty as a result of too much leverage. In all likelihood, management would be forced to cut back on R&D and marketing, allowing their most talented researchers and sales representatives to be subject to offers from competitors. To reduce these risks, firms in these industries have relatively conservative capital structures.[1] Construction and air transportation firms have leverage in-between these extremes, reflecting the need to balance the impact of having extensive physical assets and being subject to more volatile revenue streams.

It is also interesting to note that large firms tend to have higher leverage than small firms in the same industries. This probably reflects the fact that larger firms tend to have more product offerings and to be more diversified geographically, reducing their vulnerability to negative events for a single product or market, and enabling them to take on more debt.

TABLE 10.1 Median net interest-bearing debt-to-book equity and net interest-bearing debt-to-market equity for selected European industries in 1992–2011

Industry	Interest-bearing debt-to-book equity	
	All listed firms	Large listed firms
Computer programming and data processing	17%	24%
Pharmaceutical	40%	47%
Heavy construction	92%	147%
Air transportation	114%	131%
Electric services	140%	148%
Truck, auto rental and leasing	244%	229%

THE MARKET FOR CREDIT

An understanding of **credit analysis** requires an appreciation of the various players in the market for credit. We briefly describe below the major **suppliers of debt financing**.

Commercial banks

Commercial banks are very important players in the market for credit. Since banks tend to provide a range of services to a client, and have intimate knowledge of the client and its operations, they have a comparative advantage in extending credit in settings where (1) knowledge gained through close contact with management reduces the perceived riskiness of the credit and (2) credit risk can be contained through careful monitoring of the firm. This is even more so in countries where commercial banks also provide investment banking services to their clients. Examples of investment banking services are asset management, investment advice, and the underwriting of clients' securities. Banks that engage in investment banking sometimes hold substantial equity stakes in other companies, including their clients. The combination of commercial banking and investment banking services, which is called universal banking, therefore not only helps banks to become better informed about their clients' operations but also makes banks more influential over their clients through the equity stakes that they control. Universal banking activities are especially common among the larger banks in Continental European countries such as Germany and Switzerland.[2]

Bank lending operations are constrained by a low tolerance for risk to ensure that the overall loan portfolio will be of acceptably high quality to bank regulators. Because of the importance of maintaining public confidence in the banking sector and the desire to shield government deposit insurance from risk, governments have incentives to constrain banks' exposure to credit risk. Banks also tend to shield themselves from the risk of shifts in interest rates by avoiding fixed-rate loans with long maturities. Because banks' capital mostly comes from short-term deposits, such long-term loans leave them exposed to increases in interest rates, unless the risk can be hedged with derivatives. Thus, banks are less likely to play a role when a firm requires a very long-term commitment to financing. However, in some cases banks place the debt with investors looking for longer-term credit exposure.

Non-bank financial institutions

Banks face competition in the commercial lending market from a variety of sources. Finance companies compete with banks in the market for asset-based lending (i.e., the secured financing of specific assets such as receivables, inventory, or equipment). Insurance companies are also involved in a variety of lending activities. Since life insurance companies face obligations of a long-term nature, they often seek investments of long duration (e.g., long-term bonds or loans to support large, long-term commercial property and development projects). Investment bankers are prepared to place debt securities with private investors or in the public markets (discussed below). Various government agencies are another source of credit.

Public debt markets

Some firms have the size, strength, and credibility necessary to bypass the banking sector and seek financing directly from investors, either through sales of commercial paper or through the issuance of bonds. Such debt issues are facilitated by the assignment of a **public debt rating**, which measures the underlying credit strength of the firm and determines the yield that must be offered to investors.

Banks often provide financing in tandem with a public debt issue or other source of financing. In highly levered transactions, such as leveraged buyouts, banks commonly provide financing along with public debt that has a lower priority in case of bankruptcy. The bank's "senior financing" would typically be scheduled for earlier retirement than the public debt, and it would carry a lower yield. For smaller or start-up firms, banks often provide credit in conjunction with equity financing from venture capitalists. Note that in the case of both the leveraged buyout and the start-up company, the bank helps provide the cash needed to make the deal happen, but it does so in a way that shields it from risks that would be unacceptably high in the banking sector.

Sellers who provide financing

Another sector of the market for credit is manufacturers and other suppliers of goods and services. As a matter of course, such firms tend to finance their customers' purchases on an unsecured basis for periods of 30 to 60 days. Suppliers will, on occasion, also agree to provide more extended financing, usually with the support of a secured note. A supplier may be willing to grant such a loan in the expectation that the creditor will survive a cash shortage and remain an important customer in the future. However the customer would typically seek such an arrangement only if bank financing is unavailable because it could constrain flexibility in selecting among and/or negotiating with suppliers.

COUNTRY DIFFERENCES IN DEBT FINANCING

Country factors and credit types

The above described suppliers of credit are not equally important in every country. One source of differences across countries is the extent to which national bankruptcy laws protect credit providers. A stylized classification of bankruptcy laws involves two groups: laws that provide extensive creditor protection in the case of default, versus laws that are oriented toward keeping the company in default a going concern and shielding the company from the influence of creditors. The former types of laws typically offer creditors a first right to repossess collateral and enforce other contractual rights when their borrower is in default. These laws therefore increase the probability that creditors recover their loans but reduce the probability that borrowers survive bankruptcy. The latter types of laws typically impose court-administered bankruptcy procedures on the borrower in default and its creditors as well as an automatic stay on the borrower's assets. An automatic stay on the assets means that creditors cannot repossess their collateral during the period in which the borrower's financial obligations are being restructured. The UK is an example of a European country that has strong creditor protection laws. Examples of European countries that have weak creditor protection laws, or borrower-friendly bankruptcy laws, are France, Italy, and Portugal. Germany takes a position in-between these two extremes. In Germany, courts impose bankruptcy procedures on the borrower and its creditors, but there is no automatic stay on the borrower's assets and creditors have considerable influence on the borrower's reorganization process.[3]

The orientation of a country's bankruptcy laws can affect the characteristics of credit provided in various ways. A few examples of how legal differences matter are the following:

■ Multiple-bank borrowing. In countries where the legal rights of banks are weakly protected and banks experience difficulties in repossessing collateral when a borrower defaults, they are likely to be hesitant in extending long-term credit. As an alternative, companies may borrow smaller proportions of debt from multiple banks. Because it is more difficult for a company in default to renegotiate its loans with multiple banks than with one bank, multiple-bank borrowing reduces the company's incentive to strategically default. Research has found that multiple-bank borrowing is most common in Belgium, France, Italy, Spain, and Portugal, where banks are indeed weakly protected in case of bankruptcy.[4]

■ Supplier financing. Supplier financing is also an efficient alternative form of debt financing when creditor rights are weakly protected.[5] A reason for this is that suppliers are often well informed about their debtors' operations and they have a straightforward way to discipline their debtors. That is, in case of default of payment, suppliers can repossess the delivered goods and withhold future deliveries. In fiscal year 2011, public companies in Belgium, France, Italy, Spain, and Portugal had an average payables-to-sales ratio of 19.5 percent. The ratio ranged from 16.0 percent in Portugal to 26.0 percent in Italy. In contrast, public companies in Denmark, Finland, Germany, the Netherlands, Norway, Sweden, Switzerland, and the UK had an average payables-to-sales ratio of 10.9 percent.

■ Off-balance sheet financing. Research has indicated that in countries where companies' access to bank debt is restricted or relatively expensive, companies may also resort to off-balance sheet financing.[6] One example of off-balance sheet financing is the factoring of receivables, where companies sell their customer receivables to a lender at a discount. In the first half of the 2000s, the use of factoring was fastest growing in Eastern Europe,

TABLE 10.2 The importance of public debt markets in the economy (end-2011 data)

Country	Market value of (bank-owned) public corporate debt securities as a percentage of GDP
Belgium	12.7%
Denmark	5.7%
Finland	15.5%
France	27.4%
Germany	14.7%
Italy	21.2%
Netherlands	25.7%
Portugal	26.7%
Spain	3.3%
Sweden	15.7%
Switzerland	8.6%
UK	14.2%

Source: International Banking Statistics of the Bank for International Settlements.

where bankruptcy laws were weak. Further, companies in Italy made relatively more use of factoring than companies in other parts of Europe.

■ Public debt. Public debt markets are also not equally developed in all parts of the world. Table 10.2 shows the value of (bank-owned) public debt securities as a percentage of national gross domestic product (GDP) in 12 European countries at the end of 2011. These percentages show that public debt markets were especially large in France, Italy, the Netherlands, and Portugal, suggesting that public debt is sometimes used as an alternative to bank debt in countries with borrower-friendly bankruptcy laws.

Country factors and the optimal mix of debt and equity

In summary, the above discussion shows that in countries with borrower-friendly, creditor-unfriendly bankruptcy laws:

■ Creditors extend more short-term debt because this allows them to frequently review the borrower's financial position and adjust the terms of the loan when necessary.

■ Companies make greater use of supplier financing.

■ Companies make greater use of off-balance sheet financing such as the factoring of customer receivables.

■ Public debt markets tend to be more developed.

The net effect of these country differences in loan maturity, off-balance sheet financing, supplier financing, and public debt markets' importance on country differences in leverage, is unfortunately anything but straightforward. For example, we showed that Belgian, French, and Italian companies have, on average, greater amounts of trade payables on their balance sheets. In these three countries, however, equity markets are still not as well developed as in some other parts of Europe. Thus, supplier financing might just as well serve as a substitute for long-term debt and equity, leaving the net debt to net capital ratio unchanged.

To provide a rough indication of how the mix of debt and equity financing varies across Europe, Table 10.3 shows median debt-to-equity, cash-to-equity, and net debt-to-equity ratios for 13 European countries in 2011. Sweden, Switzerland, and the UK tend to have the lowest net debt-to-equity ratios. Cash and marketable securities holdings of the median company in these countries tend to be close to the book value of its interest-bearing debt. Maybe surprisingly, the net interest-bearing debt-to-equity ratios are highest in countries with borrower-friendly, creditor-unfriendly bankruptcy laws, such as Italy, Portugal, and Spain. Two reasons may explain this.

TABLE 10.3 Median cash and marketable securities holdings and leverage for 13 European countries in 2011

Country	Interest-bearing debt-to-book equity	Cash and marketable securities-to-book equity	Net interest-bearing debt-to-book equity	Interest-bearing debt-to-market equity
Portugal	212%	28%	148%	227%
Spain	123%	26%	104%	95%
Italy	117%	23%	99%	97%
Belgium	76%	21%	50%	54%
Norway	75%	25%	48%	55%
Finland	66%	18%	47%	34%
Netherlands	65%	18%	47%	37%
Germany	62%	31%	26%	38%
France	57%	29%	29%	41%
Denmark	55%	16%	29%	33%
Switzerland	41%	29%	13%	22%
UK	35%	21%	17%	24%
Sweden	35%	19%	18%	20%

First, in countries where bankruptcy laws shield management from its creditors in situations of financial distress, the threat of creditors intervening in the company's operations and repossessing collateral is less severe. Consequently, managers in these countries may feel comfortable with taking on more debt. As argued, despite being weakly protected, creditors are willing to extend debt because they can force borrowers to borrow smaller proportions of debt from multiple banks and can choose to extend loans with short maturities.

Second, the net debt-to-equity ratios are lowest in the countries where equity markets are most developed, such as the UK and Switzerland. Companies from these countries can more easily use equity financing as an alternative to debt financing than companies from countries with weakly developed equity markets, such as Portugal and Italy.

THE CREDIT ANALYSIS PROCESS IN PRIVATE DEBT MARKETS

Credit analysis is more than just establishing the creditworthiness of a firm, that is, its ability to pay its debts at the scheduled times. The decision to extend credit is not a binary one – the firm's exact value, its upside potential, and its distance from the threshold of creditworthiness are all equally important. There are ranges of creditworthiness, and it is important for purposes of pricing and structuring a loan to understand where a firm lies within that range. While downside risk must be the primary consideration in credit analysis, a firm with growth potential offers opportunities for future income-generating financial services from a continuing relationship.

This broader view of credit analysis involves most of the issues already discussed in the prior chapters on business strategy analysis, accounting analysis, financial analysis, and prospective analysis. Perhaps the greatest difference is that credit analysis rarely involves any explicit attempt to estimate the value of the firm's equity. However, the determinants of that value are relevant in credit analysis because a larger equity cushion translates into lower risk for the creditor.

Below we describe a representative but comprehensive series of steps that is used by commercial lenders in credit analysis. However, not all credit providers follow these guidelines. For example, when compared to a banker, manufacturers conduct a less extensive analysis on their customers since the credit is very short-term and the manufacturer is willing to bear some credit risk in the interest of generating a profit on the sale.

We present the steps in a particular order, but they are in fact all interdependent. Thus, analysis at one step may need to be rethought depending on the analysis at some later step.

Step 1: Consider the nature and purpose of the loan

Understanding the purpose of a loan is important not just for deciding whether it should be granted but also for structuring the loan based on duration, purpose, and size. Loans might be required for only a few months, for several years, or even as a permanent part of a firm's capital structure. Loans might be used for replacement of other financing, to support working capital needs, or to finance the acquisition of long-term assets or another firm.

The required amount of the loan must also be established. When bankruptcy laws provide a bank sufficient protection, it would typically prefer to be the sole financier of small and medium-sized companies. This preference is not only to gain an advantage in providing a menu of financial services to the firm but also to maintain a superior interest in case of bankruptcy. If other creditors are willing to subordinate their positions to the bank, that would of course be acceptable so far as the bank is concerned.

Often the commercial lender deals with firms that may have parent-subsidiary relations, posing the question of the appropriate counterparty. In general, the entity that owns the assets that will serve as collateral (or that could serve as such if needed in the future) acts as the borrower. If this entity is the subsidiary and the parent presents some financial strength independent of the subsidiary, a guarantee of the parent could be considered.

National bankruptcy laws in the country where the potential borrower is located also affect the maturity of the loan. When the bankruptcy laws provide weak protection to the credit provider it may decide only to extend a loan with a short maturity. Short-term loans carry the advantage that the lender can frequently review the borrower and make adjustments to the terms of the loan when necessary.[7] Commercial lenders are inclined to shorten loan maturities especially when lending to firms with little collateral, such as in tangible-intensive firms.[8]

Step 2: Consider the type of loan and available security

The type of loan is a function of not only its purpose but also the financial strength of the borrower. Thus, to some extent, the loan type will be dictated by the financial analysis described in step 3. Some of the possibilities are as follows:

- Open line of credit. An open line of credit permits the borrower to receive cash up to some specified maximum on an as-needed basis for a specified term, such as one year. To maintain this option, the borrower pays a fee (e.g., 3/8 of 1 percent) on the unused balance, in addition to the interest on any used amount. An open line of credit is useful in cases where the borrower's cash needs are difficult to anticipate.

- Revolving line of credit. When it is clear that a firm will need credit beyond the short run, financing may be provided in the form of a "revolver." The terms of a revolver, which is sometimes used to support working capital needs, require the borrower to make payments as the operating cycle proceeds and inventory and receivables are converted to cash. However it is also expected that cash will continue to be advanced so long as the borrower remains in good standing. In addition to interest on amounts outstanding, a fee is charged on the unused line.

- Working capital loan. Such a loan is used to finance inventory and receivables, and it is usually secured. The maximum loan balance may be tied to the balance of the working capital accounts. For example, the loan may be allowed to rise to no more than 80 percent of receivables less than 60 days old.

- Term loan. Term loans are used for long-term needs and are often secured with long-term assets such as plant or equipment. Typically, the loan will be amortized, requiring periodic payments to reduce the loan balance.

- Mortgage loan. Mortgages support the financing of real estate, have long-terms, and require periodic amortization of the loan balance.

- Lease financing. Lease financing can be used to facilitate the acquisition of any asset but is most commonly used for equipment, including vehicles, and buildings. Leases may be structured over periods of 1 to 15 years, depending on the life of the underlying asset.

Much bank lending is done on a secured basis, especially with smaller and more highly leveraged companies. Security will be required unless the loan is short-term and the borrower exposes the bank to minimal default risk. When security is required, an important consideration is whether the amount of available security is sufficient to support the loan. The amount that a bank will lend on given security involves business judgment, and it depends on a variety of factors that affect the liquidity of the security in the context of a situation where the firm is distressed. It also depends on the extent to which creditor protection laws permit banks to quickly repossess collateral in the event of default. In countries where bankruptcy laws provide weak creditor protection, such as France, banks typically require more collateral for a given loan amount.[9] The following are some rules of thumb often applied in commercial lending to various categories of security:

- Receivables. Trade receivables are usually considered the most desirable form of security because they are the most liquid. An average bank allows loans of 50 to 80 percent of the balance of nondelinquent accounts. The percentage applied is lower when:

  1 There are many small accounts that would be costly to collect in case the firm is distressed.

  2 There are a few very large accounts, such that problems with a single customer could be serious.

  3 Bankruptcy laws are creditor-unfriendly and preclude the bank claiming and collecting the receivables while the borrower in default is being restructured.

  4 The customer's financial health is closely related to that of the borrower, so that collectibility is endangered just when the borrower is in default.

On the latter score, banks often refuse to accept receivables from affiliates as effective security.

- Inventory. The desirability of inventory as security varies widely. The best-case scenario is inventory consisting of a common commodity that can easily be sold to other parties if the borrower defaults. More specialized inventory, with appeal to only a limited set of buyers, or inventory that is costly to store or transport is less desirable. An average bank typically lends up to 60 percent on raw materials, 50 percent on finished goods, and 20 percent on work in process.

- Machinery and equipment. Machinery and equipment is less desirable as collateral. It is likely to be used, and it must be stored, insured, and marketed. Keeping the costs of these activities in mind, banks typically will lend only up to 50 percent of the estimated value of such assets in a forced sale such as an auction.

- Real estate. The value of real estate as collateral varies considerably. Banks will often lend up to 80 percent of the appraised value of readily saleable real estate. On the other hand, a factory designed for a unique purpose would be much less desirable.

Even when a loan is not secured initially, a bank can require a "negative pledge" on the firm's assets – a pledge that the firm will not use the assets as security for any other creditor. In that case, if the borrower begins to experience difficulty and defaults on the loan, and if there are no other creditors in the picture, the bank can demand the loan become secured if it is to remain outstanding.

Step 3: Conduct a financial analysis of the potential borrower

This portion of the analysis involves all the steps discussed in our chapters on business strategy analysis, accounting analysis, and financial analysis. The emphasis, however, is on the firm's ability to service the debt at the scheduled rate. All the factors that could impact that ability, such as the presence of off-balance-sheet lease obligations and the sustainability of the firm's operating profit stream, need to be carefully examined. The focus of the analysis depends on the type of financing under consideration. For example, if a short-term loan is considered to support seasonal fluctuations in inventory, the emphasis would be on the ability of the firm to convert the inventory into cash on a timely basis. In contrast, a term loan to support plant and equipment must be made with confidence in the long-run earnings prospects of the firm. This step incorporates both an assessment of the potential borrower's financial status using ratio analysis and a forecast to determine future payment prospects.

Ratio analysis

Ultimately, since the key issue in the financial analysis is the likelihood that cash flows will be sufficient to repay the loan, lenders focus much attention on solvency ratios: the magnitude of various measures of profits and cash flows relative to debt service and other requirements. Therefore, ratio analysis from the perspective of a creditor differs somewhat from that of an owner. There is greater emphasis on cash flows and earnings available to *all* claimants (not just owners) *before* taxes (since interest is tax-deductible and paid out of pretax euros). The *funds flow coverage ratio* illustrates the creditor's perspective:

$$\text{Funds flow coverage} = \frac{\text{EBIT} + \text{Depreciation}}{\text{Interest} + \dfrac{\text{Debt repayment}}{(1 - \text{tax rate})} + \dfrac{\text{Preference dividends}}{(1 - \text{tax rate})}}$$

Earnings before both interest and taxes in the numerator is compared directly to the interest expense in the denominator, because interest expense is paid out of pretax euros. In contrast, any payment of principal scheduled for a given year is nondeductible and must be made out of after-tax profits. In essence, with a 50 percent tax rate, one euro of principal payment is "twice as expensive" as a one-euro interest payment. Scaling the payment of principal by (1 – tax rate) accounts for this. The same idea applies to preference dividends, which are not tax-deductible.

The funds flow coverage ratio provides an indication of how comfortably the funds flow can cover unavoidable expenditures. The ratio excludes payments such as dividend payments to ordinary shareholders and capital expenditures on the premise that they could be reduced to zero to make debt payments if necessary.[10] Clearly, however, if the firm is to survive in the long run, funds flow must be sufficient to not only service debt but also maintain plant assets. Thus, long-run survival requires a funds flow coverage ratio well in excess of 1.[11]

To the extent that the ratio exceeds 1, it indicates the "margin of safety" the lender faces. When such a ratio is combined with an assessment of the variance in its numerator, it provides an indication of the probability of nonpayment. However, it would be overly simplistic to establish any particular threshold above which a ratio indicates a loan is justified. A creditor clearly wants to be in a position to be repaid on schedule, even when the borrower faces a reasonably foreseeable difficulty. That argues for lending only when the funds flow coverage is expected to exceed 1, even in a recession scenario – and higher if some allowance for capital expenditures is prudent.

The financial analysis should produce more than an assessment of the risk of nonpayment. It should also identify the nature of the significant risks. At many commercial banks it is standard operating procedure to summarize the analysis of the firm by listing the key risks that could lead to default and factors that could be used to control those risks if the loan were made. That information can be used in structuring the detailed terms of the loan so as to trigger default when problems arise, at a stage early enough to permit corrective action.

Forecasting

Implicit in the discussion of ratio analysis is a forward-looking view of the firm's ability to service the loan. Good credit analysis should also be supported by explicit forecasts. The basis for such forecasts is usually management, though lenders perform their own tests as well. An essential element of this step is a sensitivity analysis to examine the ability of the borrower to service the debt under a variety of scenarios such as changes in the economy or in the firm's competitive position. Ideally, the firm should be strong enough to withstand the downside risks such as a drop in sales or a decrease in profit margins.

At times it is possible to reconsider the structure of a loan so as to permit it to "cash flow." That is, the term of the loan might be extended or the amortization pattern changed. Often a bank will grant a loan with the expectation that it will be continually renewed, thus becoming a permanent part of the firm's financial structure (labeled an "evergreen" loan). In that case the loan will still be written as if it is due within the short-term, and the bank must assure itself of a viable "exit strategy." However, the firm would be expected to service the loan by simply covering interest payments.

Step 4: Assemble the detailed loan structure, including loan covenants

If the analysis thus far indicates that a loan is in order, the final step is to assemble the detailed structure. Having previously determined the type of loan and repayment schedule, the focus shifts to the loan covenants and pricing.

Writing loan covenants

Loan covenants specify mutual expectations of the borrower and lender by specifying actions the borrower will and will not take. Covenants generally fall into three categories:

1 Those that require certain actions such as regular provision of financial statements.

2 Those that preclude certain actions such as undertaking an acquisition without the permission of the lender.

3 Those that require maintenance of certain financial ratios.

Loan covenants must strike a balance between protecting the interests of the lender and providing the flexibility management needs to run the business. The covenants represent a mechanism for ensuring that the business will remain as strong as the two parties anticipated at the time the loan was granted.

The principal covenants that govern the management of the firm include restrictions on other borrowing, pledging assets to other lenders, selling substantial assets, engaging in mergers or acquisitions, and paying of dividends. The financial covenants should seek to address the significant risks identified in the financial analysis, or to at least provide early warning that such risks are surfacing. Some commonly used financial covenants include:

- Maintenance of minimum net worth. This covenant assures that the firm will maintain an "equity cushion" to protect the lender. Covenants typically require a level of net worth rather than a particular level of profit. In the final analysis, the lender may not care whether that net worth is maintained by generating profit, cutting dividends, or issuing new equity. Tying the covenant to net worth offers the firm the flexibility to use any of these avenues to avoid default.

- Minimum coverage ratio. Especially in the case of a long-term loan, such as a term loan, the lender may want to supplement a net worth covenant with one based on coverage of interest or total debt service. The funds flow coverage ratio presented above would be an example. Maintenance of some minimum coverage helps assure that the ability of the firm to generate funds internally is strong enough to justify the long-term nature of the loan.

- Maximum ratio of total liabilities to net worth. This ratio constrains the risk of high leverage and prevents growth without either retaining earnings or infusing equity.

- Minimum net working capital balance or current ratio. Constraints on this ratio force a firm to maintain its liquidity by using cash generated from operations to retire current liabilities (as opposed to acquiring long-lived assets).

- Maximum ratio of capital expenditures to earnings before depreciation. Constraints on this ratio help prevent the firm from investing in growth (including the illiquid assets necessary to support growth) unless such growth can be financed internally, with some margin remaining for debt service.

Required financial ratios are typically based on the levels that existed at the time that the agreement was executed, perhaps with some allowance for deterioration but often with some expected improvements over time. Violation of a covenant represents an event of default that could cause immediate acceleration of the debt payment, but in most cases the lender uses the default as an opportunity to re-examine the situation and either waive the violation or renegotiate the loan.

Covenants are included not only in private lending agreements but also in public debt agreements. However, public debt agreements tend to have less restrictive covenants for two reasons. First, since negotiations resulting from a violation of public debt covenants are costly (possibly involving not just the trustee, but bondholders as well), the covenants are written to be triggered only in serious circumstances. Second, public debt is usually issued by stronger, more creditworthy firms, though there is a large market for high-yield debt. For the most financially healthy firms with strong debt ratings, very few covenants will be used, generally only those necessary to limit dramatic changes in the firm's operations, such as a major merger or acquisition.

Dividend payout restrictions are not only included in debt contracts, but may also be mandated by law. For example, in several Continental European countries firms are legally obliged to transfer a proportion of their profits to a legal reserve, out of which they cannot distribute dividends. The law then prescribes the minimum legal reserve that a company must maintain.

Loan pricing

A detailed discussion of loan pricing falls outside the scope of this text. The essence of pricing is to assure that the yield on the loan is sufficient to cover:

1 The lender's cost of borrowed funds.

2 The lender's costs of administering and servicing the loan.

3 A premium for exposure to default risk.

4 At least a normal return on the equity capital necessary to support the lending operation.

The price is often stated in terms of a deviation from a bank's base rate – the rate charged to stronger borrowers. For example, a loan might be granted at base rate plus 2 percent. An alternative base is LIBOR, or the London Interbank Offered Rate, the rate at which large banks from various nations lend large blocks of funds to each other.

Banks compete actively for commercial lending business, and it is rare that a yield includes more than 2 percentage points to cover the cost of default risk. If the spread to cover default risk is, say, 1 percent, and the bank recovers only 50 percent of amounts due on loans that turn out bad, then the bank can afford only 2 percent of their loans to fall into that category. This underscores how important it is for banks to conduct a thorough analysis and to contain the riskiness of their loan portfolio.

FINANCIAL STATEMENT ANALYSIS AND PUBLIC DEBT

Fundamentally, the issues involved in analysis of public debt are no different from those of bank loans and other private debt issues. Institutionally, however, the contexts are different. Bankers can maintain very close relations with clients so as to form an initial assessment of their credit risk and monitor their activities during the loan period. In the case of public debt, the investors are distanced from the issuer. To a large extent, they must depend on professional debt analysts, including debt raters, to assess the riskiness of the debt and monitor the firm's ongoing activities. Such analysts and debt raters thus serve an important function in closing the information gap between issuers and investors.

The meaning of debt ratings

A firm's debt rating influences the yield that must be offered to sell the debt instruments. After the debt issue, the rating agencies continue to monitor the firm's financial condition. Changes in the rating are associated with fluctuation in the price of the securities. The three major debt rating agencies in the world are Moody's, Standard and Poor's, and Fitch Ratings.

Using the Standard and Poor's labeling system, the highest possible rating is AAA. Proceeding downward from AAA, the ratings are AA, A, BBB, BB, B, CCC, CC, C, and D, where D indicates debt in default. Table 10.4 presents examples of firms in rating categories AA through CCC, as well as the average interest expense as a percentage of total debt across all firms in each category. As of early 2011, none of the European public non-financial companies rated by Standard & Poor's had the financial strength to merit an AAA rating. Among the few that had an AAA rating but received a downgrade in 2007 or 2008 are the European firms Novartis and Nestlé – both among the largest, most profitable firms in the world. AA firms are also very strong and include Astra-Zeneca, Roche, and Royal Dutch Shell. Firms rated AAA and AA have the lowest costs of debt financing; in fiscal year 2010 their average interest expense was roughly 3.0 percent of total debt.

To be considered investment grade, a firm must achieve a rating of BBB or higher. Many funds are precluded by their articles from investing in any bonds below that grade. Even to achieve a grade of BBB is difficult. Deutsche Telekom, one the largest telecommunications companies in Europe, was rated as "only" BBB, or barely investment grade in 2011. Car manufacturers Fiat and Renault were in the BB category. The B category includes Alcatel Lucent, Continental, and Petroplus, all of which were facing financial difficulty. Alcatel Lucent, which was the result of the 2006 merger between France-based Alcatel and US-based Lucent Technologies, was the world's largest telecom equipment manufacturer. However, after the merger the company had struggled to integrate the operations of the two units and had to cope with an industry-wide downturn in equipment spending. Consequently, Alcatel Lucent had reported losses in almost every year since the merger. In Europe, only a few of the industrial companies rated by Standard & Poor's are in a category below the B category. An example of a firm that was rated CCC in 2011 is the French electronics company Technicolor, which was close to bankruptcy but whose rating was upgraded to B later in the year.

Table 10.4 shows that the cost of debt financing rises markedly once firms' debt falls below investment grade. For example, between 2005 and 2010 the interest expenses of companies with BBB rated debt were 3.9 percent of total debt, on average; interest rates for BB rated companies were 5.2 percent; and interest rates for firms with B rated debt were 6.8 percent.

Table 10.5 shows median financial ratios for firms by debt rating category. Firms with AAA and AA ratings have very strong earnings and cash flow performance as well as minimal leverage. Firms in the BBB class are only moderately leveraged, with about 58 percent of capital coming in the form of debt. Earnings tend to be relatively strong, as indicated by a pretax interest coverage (EBIT/interest) of 4.7 and a EBITDA debt coverage (EBITDA/total debt) of nearly 28 percent. Firms with B or CCC ratings, however, face significant risks: they typically report small profits or losses, have high leverage, and have interest coverage ratios close to 1.

TABLE 10.4 Debt ratings: European example firms and average interest expense by category

S&P debt rating	Example firms early 2011	Percentage of European companies given same rating by S&P	Average interest expense to total debt, fiscal 2005–2010 (%)
AA	AstraZeneca Nestlé Novartis Roche Royal Dutch Shell	6.5	3.03
A	Aeroports de Paris Carrefour GlaxoSmithKline Groupe Danone Philips Electronics Vodafone	32.0	3.38
BBB	Adecco British American Tobacco Daimler Electrolux Marks & Spencer Suedzucker	42.0	3.90
BB	Cable & Wireless Fiat Ladbrokes Piaggio Renault	14.2	5.20
B	Alcatel Lucent Continental Evraz Petroplus	4.1	6.83
CCC	Head Technicolor	1.2	8.44

Source: Standard and Poor's and Compustat Global.

Factors that drive debt ratings

Research demonstrates that some of the variation in debt ratings can be explained as a function of selected financial statement ratios, even as used within a quantitative model that incorporates no subjective human judgment. Some debt rating agencies rely heavily on quantitative models, and such models are commonly used by insurance companies, banks, and others to assist in the evaluation of the riskiness of debt issues for which a public rating is not available.

Table 10.6 lists the factors used by three different firms in their quantitative debt rating models. The firms include one insurance company and one bank, which use the models in their private placement activities, and an investment research firm, which employs the models in evaluating its own debt purchases and holdings. In each case profitability and leverage play an important role in the rating. One firm also uses firm size as an indicator, with larger size associated with higher ratings.

Several researchers have estimated quantitative models used for debt ratings. Two of these **debt rating prediction models**, developed by Kaplan and Urwitz and shown in Table 10.7, highlight the relative importance

TABLE 10.5 Debt ratings: Median financial ratios by category

S&P debt rating	Median ratios for overall category between March 2005 and March 2011 (European non-financial companies only)			
	Return on business assets	Pretax interest coverage	EBITDA to total debt	Debt to Capital
AAA	12.2%	23.8 times	71.7%	31.2%
AA	12.3	16.3	58.5	47.8
A	9.4	6.2	31.9	57.3
BBB	8.6	4.7	27.8	57.9
BB	7.3	3.0	24.3	60.4
B	4.9	1.5	19.6	66.1

Source: Standard & Poor's and Compustat Global.

of the factors.[12] Model 1 has the greater ability to explain variation in bond ratings. However, it includes some factors based on equity market data, which are not available for all firms. Model 2 is based solely on financial statement data.

The factors in Table 10.7 are listed in the order of their statistical significance in Model 1. An interesting feature is that the most important factor explaining debt ratings is not a financial ratio at all – it is simply firm size! Large firms tend to get better ratings than small firms. Whether the debt is subordinated or unsubordinated is next most important, followed by a leverage indicator. Profitability appears less important, but in part that reflects the presence in the model of multiple factors (ROA and interest coverage) that capture profitability. It is only the explanatory power that is *unique* to a given variable that is indicated by the ranking in Table 10.7. Explanatory power common to the two variables is not considered.

When applied to a sample of bonds that were not used in the estimation process, the Kaplan-Urwitz Model 1 predicted the rating category correctly in 44 of 64 cases, or 63 percent of the time. Where it erred, the model was never off by more than one category, and in about half of those cases its prediction was more consistent with the market yield on the debt than was the actual debt rating. The discrepancies between actual ratings and those

TABLE 10.6 Factors used in quantitative models of debt ratings

	Firm 1	Firm 2	Firm 3
Profitability measures	Return on net capital	Return on net capital	Return on net capital
Leverage measures	Non-current debt to capitalization	Non-current debt to capitalization Total debt to total capital	Non-current debt to capitalization
Profitability and leverage	Interest coverage Cash flow to non-current debt	Interest coverage Cash flow to non-current debt	Fixed charge coverage Coverage of current debt and fixed charges
Firm size	Sales	Total assets	
Other		Standard deviation of return Subordination status	

TABLE 10.7 Kaplan-Urwitz models of debt ratings

Firm or debt characteristic	Variable reflecting characteristic	Coefficients	
		Model 1	Model 2
	Model intercept	5.67	4.41
Firm size	Total assets[a]	0.0009	0.0011
Subordination status of debt	1 = subordinated; 0 = unsubordinated	−2.36	−2.56
Leverage	Non-current debt to total assets	−2.85	−2.72
Systematic risk	Market model beta, indicating sensitivity of share price to market-wide movements (1 = average)[b]	−0.87	—
Profitability	Net profit to total assets	5.13	
Unsystematic risk	Standard deviation of residual from market model (average = .10)	−2.90	—
Riskiness of profit stream	Coefficient of variation in net profit over 5 years (standard deviation/mean)	—	−0.53
Interest coverage	Pretax funds flow before interest to interest expense	0.007	0.006

The score from the model is converted to a bond rating as follows:

If score > 6.76, predict AAA

   score 6.76 – 5.19, predict AA

   score 5.19 – 3.28, predict A

   score 3.28 – 1.57, predict BBB

   score 1.57 – 0.00, predict BB

   score < 0.00, predict B

a. The coefficient in the Kaplan-Urwitz model was estimated at 0.005 (Model 1) and 0.006 (Model 2). Its scale has been adjusted to reflect that the estimates were based on assets measured in US dollars from the early 1970s. Given that $1 from 1972 is approximately equivalent to $5.40 in 2012, the original coefficient has been divided by 5.40. On December 31, 2011, $1 was approximately equal to £0.65, €0.77, DKK5.74, and SEK6.89.

b. Market model is estimated by regressing stock returns on the market index, using monthly data for the prior five years.

estimated using the Kaplan-Urwitz model indicate that rating agencies incorporate factors other than financial ratios in their analysis. These are likely to include the types of strategic, accounting, and prospective analyses discussed throughout this book.

We have also estimated a debt ratings prediction model that is conceptually similar to the Kaplan-Urwitz model but includes the factors from Table 10.5 (plus firm size) as predictors. The sample of companies that we used to estimate the model is the sample of 262 European non-financial companies that were rated by Standard & Poor's at least once between March 2005 and March 2011. Table 10.8 lists the factors and their coefficients in order of their statistical significance. Note that one important difference between this model and the Kaplan-Urwitz model is that this model predicts company-specific debt ratings instead of bond-issue-specific ratings. When applied to the sample of 262 European companies, the model predicted the debt rating category correctly for 53 percent of the companies. The model was off by one category for 43 percent of the companies and off by two categories for 4 percent of the companies. The model was never off by more than two categories.

In the "European" debt ratings prediction model, factors similar to those in the Kaplan-Urwitz model are most significant. That is, Standard and Poor's European debt ratings between 2005 and 2011 were primarily driven by firm size, riskiness of the profit stream, profitability, and leverage (in order of statistical significance). We did not include equity market data in the model to make it usable for privately-held firms, which may be one of the reasons why this model predicts debt ratings slightly less accurately than the Kaplan-Urwitz model.

Given that debt ratings can be explained reasonably well in terms of a handful of financial ratios, one might question whether ratings convey any news to investors – anything that could not already have been garnered from publicly available financial data. The answer to the question is yes, at least in the case of debt rating downgrades.

TABLE 10.8 Debt ratings prediction model estimated on a sample of European companies

Firm or debt characteristic	Variable reflecting characteristic	Coefficients
	Model intercept	2.597
Firm size	Natural logarithm of total assets (in € billions)	0.519
Riskiness of profit stream	Standard deviation of return on business assets over 5 years	−6.842
Profitability	Return on business assets	4.909
Interest coverage	EBIT to interest expense	0.044
Leverage	Debt to capital	−0.765
Cash flow performance	EBITDA to total debt	−0.004

The score from the model is converted to a debt rating as follows:

If score > 7.73, predict AAA
   score 7.73 – 5.88, predict AA
   score 5.88 – 4.21, predict A
   score 4.21 – 2.68, predict BBB
   score 2.68 – 1.36, predict BB
   score 1.36 – 0.00, predict B
   score < 0.00, predict CCC

That is, downgrades are greeted with drops in both bond and share prices.[13] To be sure, the capital markets anticipate much of the information reflected in rating changes. But that is not surprising, given that the changes often represent reactions to recent known events and that the rating agencies typically indicate in advance that a change is being considered.

PREDICTION OF DISTRESS AND TURNAROUND

The key task in credit analysis is assessing the probability that a firm will face financial distress and fail to repay a loan. A related analysis, relevant once a firm begins to face distress, involves considering whether it can be turned around. In this section we consider evidence on the predictability of these states.

The prediction of either distress or turnaround is a complex, difficult, and subjective task that involves all of the steps of analysis discussed throughout this book: business strategy analysis, accounting analysis, financial analysis, and prospective analysis. Purely quantitative models of the process can rarely serve as substitutes for the hard work the analysis involves. However, research on such models does offer some insight into which financial indicators are most useful in the task. Moreover, there are some settings where extensive credit checks are too costly to justify, and where quantitative distress prediction models are useful. For example, the commercially available "Zeta" model is used by some manufacturers and other firms to assess the creditworthiness of their customers.[14]

Models for distress prediction

Several **financial distress prediction models** have been developed over the years.[15] They are similar to the debt rating models, but instead of predicting ratings, they predict whether a firm will face some state of distress, typically defined as bankruptcy, with a specified period such as one year. One study suggests that the factors most useful (on a stand-alone basis) in predicting bankruptcy one year in advance are the firm's level of profitability, the volatility of that profitability (as measured by the standard deviation of ROE), and its leverage.[16] Interestingly, liquidity measures turn out to be much less important. Current liquidity won't save an unhealthy firm if it is losing money at a fast pace.

A number of more robust, multifactor models have also been designed to predict financial distress. One such model, the Altman Z-score model, weights five variables to compute a bankruptcy score.[17] For public companies the model is as follows:[18]

$$Z = 1.2(X_1) + 1.4(X_2) + 3.3(X_3) + 0.6(X_4) + 1.0(X_5)$$

where X_1 = net working capital/total assets (measure of liquidity)

X_2 = retained earnings/total assets (measure of cumulative profitability)

X_3 = EBIT/total assets (measure of return on assets)

X_4 = market value of equity/book value of total liabilities (measure of market leverage)

X_5 = sales/total assets (measure of sales generating potential of assets)

The model predicts bankruptcy when $Z < 1.81$. The range between 1.81 and 2.67 is labeled the "gray area." The following table presents calculations for two apparel retailers, French Connection and Hennes & Mauritz:

	Model coefficient	French Connection plc		Hennes & Mauritz AB	
		Ratio	Score	Ratio	Score
Net working capital/assets	1.2	0.175	0.210	0.112	0.135
Retained earnings/Total assets	1.4	0.246	0.344	0.259	0.363
EBIT/Total assets	3.3	0.045	0.150	0.199	0.657
Market value of equity/Book value of total liabilities	0.6	0.293	0.176	5.363	3.218
Sales/Total assets	1.0	0.909	0.909	0.999	0.999
			1.789		5.371

The table shows a performance gap between the two companies. H&M's Z score demonstrates its financial strength. H&M has delivered steady sales growth and abnormal profitability over the past five years, and the book value of its liabilities is substantially lower than the market value of its equity. French Connection's Z-score, on the other hand, highlights its relatively poor performance. In the past few years, difficult market conditions in the traditional segment of the apparel retail industry drove down the retailer's margins and made it report below-normal returns on equity. Further, French Connection's liabilities are more than three times larger than its market capitalization, an indication of its precarious financial state.

Such models have some ability to predict failing and surviving firms. Altman reports that when the model was applied to a holdout sample containing 33 failed and 33 nonfailed firms (the same proportion used to estimate the model), it correctly predicted the outcome in 63 of 66 cases. However, the performance of the model would degrade substantially if applied to a holdout sample where the proportion of failed and nonfailed firms was not forced to be the same as that used to estimate the model.

The Altman Z-score model was estimated on a sample of US firms. When applying this model to a sample of non-US firms, the following complications must be considered. First, accounting practices may differ from country to country. In particular, under some accounting systems total liabilities may be substantially understated because of firms' use of off-balance sheet financing. When comparing the Altman Z-scores of two firms with different accounting practices, the preferred approach would be to undo these firms' financial statements from accounting distortions and bring all off-balance sheet liabilities on the balance sheet before calculating the scores. Second, although the model may be equally useful across countries in predicting financial distress, the likelihood that financial distress leads to bankruptcy depends on national bankruptcy laws and thus varies from country to country.

One way to overcome the above problems is to use distress prediction models that were estimated in a particular firm's home country. An international survey of distress prediction models suggests that more than 40 variants of such models exist worldwide.[19] A common characteristic of these models is that they all include some measures of profitability and leverage. For example, one model that was developed by Taffler and is commonly used in the UK calculates Z-scores as follows:[20]

$$Z = 3.20 + 12.18(X_1) + 2.50(X_2) - 10.68(X_3) + 0.0289(X_4)$$

where X_1 = profit before tax/current liabilities

X_2 = current assets/total liabilities

X_3 = current liabilities/total assets

X_4 = no-credit interval (in days).

The no-credit interval is defined as immediate assets (current assets excluding inventories and prepaid expenses) minus current liabilities, divided by total operating expenses excluding depreciation and multiplied by 365 days. This variable measures how long the firm can finance its current operations when other sources of short-term finance are unavailable. The model predicts bankruptcy when $Z < 0$.

While simple distress prediction models like the Altman and the Taffler models cannot serve as a replacement for in-depth analysis of the kind discussed throughout this book, they do provide a useful reminder of the power of financial statement data to summarize important dimensions of the firm's performance. In addition, they can be useful for screening large numbers of firms prior to more in-depth analysis of corporate strategy, management expertise, market position, and financial ratio performance.

Investment opportunities in distressed companies

The debt securities of firms in financial distress trade at steep discounts to par value. Some hedge fund managers and investment advisors specialize in investing in these securities – even purchasing the debt of firms operating under bankruptcy protection. Investors in these securities can earn attractive returns if the firm recovers from its cash flow difficulties.

Distressed debt investors assess whether the firm is likely to overcome its immediate cash flow problems and whether it has a viable long-run future. Two elements of the framework laid out in Part 2 of this book are particularly relevant to analyzing distressed opportunities. The first is a thorough analysis of the firm's industry and competitive positioning and an assessment of its business risks. This is followed by the construction of well reasoned forecasts of its future cash flow and earnings performance in light of the business analysis.

CREDIT RATINGS, DEFAULT PROBABILITIES, AND DEBT VALUATION

Debt rating prediction models and financial distress prediction models can help in estimating the value of debt. To illustrate how, consider the following debt valuation formula, which defines debt value as a function of future contractual coupon and face value payments, the expected return on debt (denoted as r_d), and the expected cumulative probabilities that a firm will default on its debt payments within one to T years (denoted as $\pi_1, \ldots, \pi_T$).

$$\text{Debt value} = \frac{(1 - \pi_1) \times \text{Coupon}_1}{(1 + r_d)} + \frac{(1 - \pi_2) \times \text{Coupon}_2}{(1 + r_d)^2} + \ldots + \frac{(1 - \pi_T) \times \text{Coupon}_T + (1 - \pi_T) \times \text{Face value}}{(1 + r_d)^T}$$

Note that, for simplicity, this formula assumes that debtholders will receive nothing if the firm defaults on its loans. In practice, however, recovery rates on defaulting debt are often greater than zero. Some studies estimate recovery rates on, for example, senior unsecured bonds at close to 50 percent. It is possible to adjust the debt valuation formula for such non-zero recovery rates, albeit at the expense of making calculations somewhat more complicated. Including the possibility that in case of default debtholders receive ρ percent of face value, changes the debt valuation formula to:

$$\text{Debt value} = \frac{(1 - \pi_1) \times \text{Coupon}_1 + \pi_1 \times \rho \times \text{Face value}}{(1 + r_d)} + \frac{(1 - \pi_2) \times \text{Coupon}_2 + (\pi_2 - \pi_1) \times \rho \times \text{Face value}}{(1 + r_d)^2} + \ldots$$

$$+ \frac{(1 - \pi_T) \times \text{Coupon}_T + (1 - \pi_T) \times \text{Face value} + (\pi_T - \pi_{T-1}) \times \rho \times \text{Face value}}{(1 + r_d)^T}$$

Assuming for the moment that the contractual payments and the required return on default risk-free debt are known, there are essentially two practical approaches to estimating debt value. First, an analyst can explicitly estimate expected default probabilities and recovery rates (if relevant), and use the above formulas to calculate debt value. Second, and alternatively, as a short-cut approach an analyst can discount the contractual payments at the effective yield on debt with similar default risk characteristics, as in the following debt valuation formula.

$$\text{Debt value} = \frac{\text{Coupon}_1}{(1+y)} + \frac{\text{Coupon}_2}{(1+y)^2} + \ldots + \frac{\text{Coupon}_T + \text{Face value}}{(1+y)^T}$$

Under this approach the effective yield (y) conveniently summarizes the analyst's expectations about future default ($\pi_1, \ldots, \pi_T$), recovery rates (ρ) and the required return on debt (r_d) into one rate of return (y). Debt rating and financial distress prediction models can thus contribute to debt valuation by informing the analyst on either expected default probabilities and required returns on debt or effective yields.

Table 10.9 shows Standard and Poor's estimates of the percentage of firms that default within one to eight years in seven debt rating categories ranging from AAA to CCC. The debt rating agency derives these percentages from European companies' historical default rates between 1996 and 2011. The percentages in Table 10.9 indicate that firms with CCC ratings have a 43.4 percent probability to default within three years, compared with a 12.5 percent probability for firms with B ratings. In the lower rating categories the marginal probability to default (measured as the year-to-year change in the cumulative probability) decreases over time. For example, firms with CCC ratings that do not default during the first year, have an average marginal probability of only 4.93 percent (39.62 − 34.69) to default in the second year (compared with a default probability of 34.69 percent in the first year). This is because some of the low-rated firms that survive the first year improve their financial health and move up to higher rating categories.

One complication in estimating debt value using the above default probability percentages is that the expected return on debt − r_d in the debt valuation formula − is not simply equal to the riskless rate of return. Instead, the expected return on debt depends on the debt's systematic risk and various other (non-default) risk factors, all of which in turn may be a function of a firm's financial health. In a manner analogous to the calculation of the cost of equity, the expected return on debt can be estimated using an extended version of the CAPM model (see Chapter 8), which expresses the expected return on debt as the sum of a required return on riskless assets plus (1) a premium for beta or systematic risk and (2) a premium for other risk factors:

$$r_d = r_f + \beta[E(r_m) - r_f] + r_{\text{OTHER}}$$

where r_f is the riskless rate; $[E(r_m)-r_f]$ is the risk premium expected for the market as a whole, expressed as the excess of the expected return on the market index over the riskless rate, β is the systematic risk of the debt; and r_{OTHER} is the premium for other risks.

Contrary to equity betas, debt betas cannot be easily obtained for each individual firm. To circumvent the complication of estimating firm-specific betas some analysts therefore assume that financial health is the main driver of debt betas and set the firm-specific debt beta equal to the average debt beta in the firm's debt rating category. Such debt beta estimates typically range from close to zero for low-risk AAA-rated debt to 0.4 or higher for high-risk

TABLE 10.9 European companies' default probabilities by debt rating category

| S&P debt rating | Cumulative probability that the firm defaults within . . . year(s) | | | | | | | |
	1	2	3	4	5	6	7	8
AAA	0.00%	0.00%	0.00%	0.00%	0.00%	0.00%	0.00%	0.00%
AA	0.00	0.04	0.08	0.18	0.28	0.39	0.46	0.46
A	0.05	0.11	0.18	0.28	0.41	0.54	0.71	0.75
BBB	0.12	0.35	0.60	0.76	0.90	1.05	1.24	1.24
BB	0.64	2.04	3.19	3.83	4.55	5.36	6.14	6.53
B	3.70	9.00	12.57	14.81	16.55	17.68	18.15	18.15
CCC	34.69	39.62	43.40	43.40	43.40	43.40	43.40	43.40

Source: Standard & Poor's. Reproduced with permission.

TABLE 10.10 Effective yield spreads by debt rating category

S&P debt rating	Median spread between the effective yields in the debt rating category and those on AAA-rated debt between 2005 and 2011	
	Europe	United States
AAA	0.000%	0.000%
AA	0.168	0.230
A	0.377	0.934
BBB	0.804	1.609
BB	3.668	3.455
B	5.548	4.824
CCC (or lower)	11.355	7.976

Source: Bank of America – Merrill Lynch Corporate Bond Indices

CCC-rated debt. Much research has shown, however, that default risk probabilities and systematic risk do fully explain the observed variation in bond prices or expected returns on debt (r_d). Which other risk factors are relevant in debt valuation remains a topic of debate, although many researchers agree that the risk of incurring losses from debt instruments' low liquidity (referred to as liquidity risk) is a significant determinant of the expected return on debt.[21]

The uncertainty about the exact effect of systematic risk, liquidity risk and other risk factors on debt value explains the popularity of using effective yields as an alternative (short-cut) approach to debt valuation. To follow this approach all that an analyst needs to assess is the average effective yield in the firm's debt rating category. If for a particular firm a debt rating is unavailable, the debt rating prediction models, which we described in one of the previous sections, can be used to produce an approximate estimate of the firm's creditworthiness. Table 10.10 shows the average spread (difference) between the effective yields in six debt rating categories ranging from AA to CCC and that in category AAA. During the period 2005 to 2011, the median effective yield on AA-rated European bonds was 0.17 percent higher than the effective yield on AAA-rated European bonds; the median effective yield spread between B-rated bonds and AAA-rated bond was 5.55 percent. Similar patterns were observed in the United States. Note that the effective yield increases sharply once firms' debt falls below investment grade (BBB). This yield increase compensates debtholders for the substantially higher default risk, higher beta risk and potentially higher liquidity risk. Further, keep in mind that the effective yields in Table 10.10 are those of long-term bonds with average maturities greater than five years. Because the marginal default probabilities of lower-rated bonds tend to decrease over the forecast horizon (as can be seen from Table 10.9) the effective yields on lower-rated short-term bonds likely exceed those reported in Table 10.10.

Consider the following example to illustrate how debt rating prediction models and effective yield spreads can be used to value debt. At the end of the fiscal year ending on January 2012, the debt rating prediction model rates the debt of apparel retailer Next plc at BBB. The following table presents the calculation of apparel retailer Next plc's debt rating score of 3.87 at the end of the fiscal year ending on January 2012:

	Model coefficient	Next plc	
		Ratio	Score
Intercept	2.597	1.000	2.597
Natural logarithm of total assets (in € billions)	0.519	1.348	0.699
Standard deviation of return on business assets over five years	−6.842	0.020	−0.135
Return on business assets	4.909	0.228	1.120
EBIT to interest expense	0.044	6.331	0.279
Debt to capital	−0.765	0.899	−0.688
EBITDA to total debt	−0.004	0.451	−0.002
			3.870

The debt rating score of 3.870 corresponds with a debt rating of BBB. At the end of fiscal 2012, Next plc had three bonds outstanding, one of which was a £325 million 5.375 percent coupon bond due on October 26, 2021. This bond had been issued at an effective yield of 4.75 percent. At the end of January 2012, the effective yield on AAA-rated UK corporate bonds was close to 3.5 percent. Given an expected yield spread of 0.8 percent for European BBB-rated bonds, Next's effective yield at the end of January 2012 can therefore be estimated at 4.3 percent and the value of the retailer's £325 million bond is:

Payment date	Coupon (5.375% × £325) and face value (a)	Discount factor (b)	(a) × (b)
Oct 2012	£17.469	$1/(1+0.043)^{9/12}$	£16.926
Oct 2013	17.469	$1/(1+0.043)^{21/12}$	16.228
Oct 2014	17.469	$1/(1+0.043)^{33/12}$	15.559
Oct 2015	17.469	$1/(1+0.043)^{45/12}$	14.917
Oct 2016	17.469	$1/(1+0.043)^{57/12}$	14.302
Oct 2017	17.469	$1/(1+0.043)^{69/12}$	13.713
Oct 2018	17.469	$1/(1+0.043)^{81/12}$	13.147
Oct 2019	17.469	$1/(1+0.043)^{93/12}$	12.605
Oct 2020	17.469	$1/(1+0.043)^{105/12}$	12.086
Oct 2021	342.469	$1/(1+0.043)^{117/12}$	227.169
			£356.653

This bond value estimate of £356.7 million is approximately 4 percent higher than the bond's balance sheet value and close to 10 percent above par value. For comparison, at the end of January 2012, Next's £325 million bond traded at a price of close to 103 percent of par value. The difference between the observed market price and our debt value estimate illustrates that fundamental estimates of debt value need not be equal to transaction prices that are subject to the influence of investor sentiment. In fact, a possible explanation for the difference may be that on the valuation date credit yield spreads of lower-rated bonds, such as those issued by Next, were temporarily above their historical averages.

SUMMARY

Debt financing is attractive to firms with high marginal tax rates and few non-interest tax shields, making interest tax shields from debt valuable. Debt can also help create value by deterring management of firms with high, stable profits/cash flows and few new investment opportunities from over-investing in unprofitable new ventures.

However, debt financing also creates the risk of financial distress, which is likely to be particularly severe for firms with volatile earnings and cash flows, and intangible assets that are easily destroyed by financial distress.

Prospective providers of debt use credit analysis to evaluate the risks of financial distress for a firm. Credit analysis is important to a wide variety of economic agents – not just bankers and other financial intermediaries but also public debt analysts, industrial companies, service companies, and others.

At the heart of credit analysis lie the same techniques described in Chapters 2 through 8: business strategy analysis, accounting analysis, financial analysis, and portions of prospective analysis. The purpose of the analysis is not just to assess the likelihood that a potential borrower will fail to repay the loan. It is also important to identify the nature of the key risks involved, and how the loan might be structured to mitigate or control those risks. A well structured loan provides the lender with a viable "exit strategy," even in the case of default. Properly designed accounting-based covenants are essential to this structure.

Fundamentally, the issues involved in analysis of public debt are no different from those involved in evaluating bank loans or other private debt. Institutionally, however, the contexts are different. Investors in public debt are usually not close to the borrower and must rely on other agents, including debt raters and other analysts, to assess creditworthiness. Debt ratings, which depend heavily on firm size and financial measures of performance, have an important influence on the market yields that must be offered to issue debt.

The key task in credit analysis is the assessment of the probability of default. The task is complex, difficult, and to some extent, subjective. A few financial ratios can help predict financial distress with some accuracy. The most important indicators for this purpose are profitability, volatility of profits, and leverage. While there are a number of models that predict distress based on financial indicators, they cannot replace the in-depth forms of analysis discussed in this book.

CORE CONCEPTS

Benefits of debt Two benefits of debt financing are:

1 The tax deductibility of interest payments creates a corporate tax shield.
2 Debt reduces the free cash flow that is available to management and, consequently, strengthens managerial incentives for value creation.

Costs of debt Three potential costs of debt financing are:

1 Too much debt can lead to financial distress and costly debt restructurings.
2 Financial distress can make a firm forego valuable investment opportunities.
3 Financial distress creates conflicts between creditors, who wish to maximize the value of the firm's assets, and shareholders, who wish to maximize the value of equity.

Country differences in debt financing The use of debt financing differs across countries because of institutional differences, such as differences in the legal protection of creditors' interests. Institutional differences affect, amongst others, the occurrence of multiple-bank borrowing, the use of supplier financing, the use of off-balance sheet financing (such as factoring of receivables), and the development of public debt markets. The ultimate effect of institutional differences on firms' leverage ratios is complex and uncertain.

Credit analysis Credit analysis includes assessing the creditworthiness of a firm; determining the type of loan, loan structure, and the necessity of security and/or loan covenants; and assessing whether the firm's future growth opportunities can be valuable to the lender. The credit analysis process consists of the following four steps:

1 Understanding why the firm applies for a loan and for what purpose the loan will be used.
2 Determining the type of loan on the basis of the purpose of the loan and the firm's financial strength. This step also includes determining the type of security that will be required to reduce the lender's risk (and thereby the cost of debt).
3 Analyzing the creditworthiness of the firm using ratio analysis and forecasting.
4 Determining the loan structure, including loan covenants and price (interest rate).

Debt rating prediction models Quantitative models explaining firms' public debt ratings on the basis of observable firm and debt characteristics. An example of a debt rating prediction model is the Kaplan-Urwitz model. The primary firm characteristics used to predict debt ratings are: firm size, profitability, leverage, and interest coverage.

Financial distress prediction models Quantitative models predicting the likelihood that a firm will become financially distressed within a period of typically one year (on the basis of observable firm characteristics). An example of a financial distress prediction model is the Altman Z-score model. Some firm characteristics used to predict financial distress are: (cumulative) profitability, leverage, and liquidity.

Public debt ratings Scores assigned to the financial condition of firms issuing public debt by debt rating agencies such as Fitch, Moody's and Standard and Poor's.

Suppliers of debt financing Major suppliers of debt financing are: commercial banks, non-bank financial institutions such as finance and insurance companies, public debt markets, and suppliers of goods and services.

QUESTIONS

1 What are the critical performance dimensions for (a) a retailer and (b) a financial services company that should be considered in credit analysis? What ratios would you suggest looking at for each of these dimensions?

2 Why would a company pay to have its public debt rated by a major rating agency (such as Fitch, Moody's or Standard & Poor's)? Why might a firm decide not to have its debt rated?

3 Some have argued that the market for original-issue junk bonds developed in the US in the late 1970s as a result of a failure in the rating process. Proponents of this argument suggest that rating agencies rated companies too harshly at the low end of the rating scale, denying investment-grade status to some deserving companies. What are proponents of this argument effectively assuming were the incentives of rating agencies? What economic forces could give rise to this incentive?

4 Many debt agreements require borrowers to obtain the permission of the lender before undertaking a major acquisition or asset sale. Why would the lender want to include this type of restriction?

5 Betty Li, the Finance Director of a company applying for a new loan, states, "I will never agree to a debt covenant that restricts my ability to pay dividends to my shareholders because it reduces shareholder wealth." Do you agree with this argument?

6 A bank extends three loans to the following companies: an Italy-based biotech firm; a France-based car manufacturer; and a UK-based food retailer. How may these three loans differ from each other in terms of loan maturity, required collateral, and loan amount?

7 Cambridge Construction Plc follows the percentage-of-completion method for reporting long-term contract revenues. The percentage of completion is based on the cost of materials shipped to the project site as a percentage of total expected material costs. Cambridge's major debt agreement includes restrictions on net worth, interest cover age, and minimum working capital requirements. A leading analyst claims that "the company is buying its way out of these covenants by spending cash and buying materials, even when they are not needed." Explain how this may be possible.

8 Can Cambridge improve its Z score by behaving as the analyst claims in Question 7? Is this change consistent with economic reality?

9 A banker asserts, "I avoid lending to companies with negative cash from operations because they are too risky." Is this a sensible lending policy?

10 A leading retailer finds itself in a financial bind. It doesn't have sufficient cash flow from operations to finance its growth, and it is close to violating the maximum debt-to-assets ratio allowed by its covenants. The Marketing Director suggests, "We can raise cash for our growth by selling the existing stores and leasing them back. This source of financing is cheap since it avoids violating either the debt-to-assets or interest coverage ratios in our covenants." Do you agree with his analysis? Why or why not? As the firm's banker, how would you view this arrangement?

NOTES

1. Rahim Bah and Pascal Dumontier provide empirical evidence that R&D-intensive firms in Europe, Japan, and the US have lower debt and pay out lower dividends than non-R&D firms. See Rahim Bah and Pascal Dumontier, "R&D Intensity and Corporate Financial Policy: Some International Evidence," *Journal of Business Finance and Accounting* 28 (June/July 2001): 671–692.
2. Some arguments that have been raised in other countries against universal banking are the following. First, because of their investment banking activities, universal banks may incur greater risks than other commercial banks and, consequently, jeopardize the stability of a country's financial system. Second, universal banks may become too powerful because of their size and hold back competition in the banking industry. Third, universal banks could potentially misuse inside information about clients that they obtained through their lending activities in securities trading. In the US, these concerns led to ban on universal banking until 1999. For a discussion of the potential advantages and disadvantages of universal banking, see, for example, George J. Benston, "Universal Banking," *Journal of Economic Perspectives* (1994): 121–143.
3. See Sergei A. Davydenko and Julian R. Franks, "Do Bankruptcy Codes Matter? A Study of Defaults in France, Germany and the UK," working paper, University of Toronto and London Business School, 2005.
4. See Steven Ongena and David C. Smith, "What Determines the Number of Bank Relationships? Cross-Country Evidence," *Journal of Financial Intermediation* (2000): 26–56.
5. See Asli Demirgüç-Kunt and Vojislav Maksimovic, "Firms as Financial Intermediaries: Evidence from Trade Credit Data," working paper, World Bank and University of Maryland, 2001.
6. See Marie H. R. Bakker, Leonora Klapper, and Gregory F. Udell, "Financing Small and Medium-Sized Enterprises with Factoring: Global Growth and Its Potential In Eastern Europe," working paper, World Bank and Indiana University, 2004.
7. See Asli Demirgüç-Kunt and Vojislav Maksimovic, "Institutions, Financial Markets, and Firm Debt Maturity," *Journal of Financial Economics* 54 (1999): 295–336.
8. See Mariassunta Giannetti, "Do Better Institutions Mitigate Agency Problems? Evidence from Corporate Finance Choices," *Journal of Financial and Quantitative Analysis* 38 (2003): 185–212.
9. Sergei A. Davydenko and Julian R. Franks, op. cit.
10. The same is true of preference dividends. However, when preference shares are cumulative, any dividends missed must be paid later, when and if the firm returns to profitability.
11. Other relevant coverage ratios are discussed in Chapter 5.
12. Robert Kaplan and G. Urwitz, "Statistical Models of Bond Ratings: A Methodological Inquiry," *Journal of Business* (April 1979): 231–261.
13. See Robert Holthausen and Richard Leftwich, "The Effect of Bond Rating Changes on Common Stock Prices," *Journal of Financial Economics* (September 1986): 57–90; and John Hand, Robert Holthausen, and Richard Leftwich, "The Effect of Bond Rating Announcements on Bond and Stock Prices," *Journal of Finance* (June 1992): 733–752.
14. See *Corporate Financial Distress* by Edward Altman (New York: John Wiley, 1993).
15. See Edward Altman, "Financial Ratios, Discriminant Analysis, and the Prediction of Corporate Bankruptcy," *Journal of Finance* (September 1968): 589–609; Altman, *Corporate Financial Distress*, op. cit.; William Beaver, "Financial Ratios as Predictors of Distress," *Journal of Accounting Research*, Supplement (1966): 71–111; James Ohlson, "Financial Ratios and the Probabilistic Prediction of Bankruptcy," *Journal of Accounting Research* (Spring 1980): 109–131; and Mark Zmijewski, "Predicting Corporate Bankruptcy: An Empirical Comparison of the Extant Financial Distress Models," working paper, SUNY at Buffalo, 1983.
16. Zmijewski, op. cit.
17. Altman, *Corporate Financial Distress*, op. cit.
18. For private firms, Altman, ibid., adjusts the public model by changing the numerator for the variable X_4 from the market value of equity to the book value. The revised model follows:

$$Z = 0.717(X_1) + 0.847(X_2) + 3.107(X_3) + 0.420(X_4) + 0.998(X_5)$$

where X_1 = net working capital/total assets
X_2 = retained earnings/total assets
X_3 = EBIT/total assets
X_4 = book value of equity/book value of total liabilities
X_5 = sales/total assets

The model predicts bankruptcy when $Z < 1.20$. The range between 1.20 and 2.90 is labeled the "gray area."

19. See E. Altman and P. Narayanan, "An International Survey of Business Failure Classification Models," *Financial Markets, Institutions and Instruments* (May 1997): 1–57, for an extensive description of various non-US bankruptcy prediction models.
20. The Taffler model and tests of its predictive accuracy are described in R. Taffler, "The Assessment of Company Solvency and Performance Using a Statistical Model," *Accounting and Business Research* (1983): 295–307 and R. Taffler, "Empirical Models for the Monitoring of UK Corporations," *Journal of Banking and Finance* (1984): 199–227.
21. See, for example, E. Elton, M. Gruber, D. Agrawal, and D. Mann, "Explaining the Rate Spread on Corporate Bonds." *Journal of Finance* (2001): 247–277, P. Collin-Dufresne, R. Goldstein, and J. Spencer Martin, "The Determinants of Credit Spread Changes," *Journal of Finance* (2001): 2177–2207, and L. Chen, D. Lesmond, and J. Wei, "Corporate Yield Spreads and Bond Liquidity," *Journal of Finance* (2007): 119–149 for discussions of what factors explain corporate bond spreads.

Getronics' debt ratings

Getronics NV is a Netherlands-based provider of Information and Communication Technology (ICT) services. The company originates from a leveraged management buyout of Geveke Electronics NV and was taken public by its privately held owner SHV Holdings NV in 1985. Following its initial public offering, the company adopted a strategy of aggressive expansion through internal growth, acquisitions, and strategic investments. Between 1985 and 1999, Getronics managed to double its sales and earnings every three years, on average. In 1999, the company turned from a moderate player in the European ICT industry into one of the world's largest ICT service providers through its acquisition of US-based Wang Global. This acquisition more than doubled Getronics' revenues (from €1.5 billion to €3.7 billion) and almost tripled the company's employee base.

To finance the acquisition of Wang Global, Getronics needed to issue new shares and attract a substantial amount of new debt. Therefore, the company entered into a €500 million syndicated revolving variable-rate credit facility, which would mature on April 2004, and issued €350 million of subordinated convertible bonds. The subordinated convertible bonds bore an annual interest rate of 0.25 percent but would be redeemed at 113.21 percent of their face value if they remained unconverted until the maturity date (April 2004). Hence, the yield to maturity of unconverted bonds was 2.75 percent. The bonds' conversion price was €14.53 per ordinary share, while Getronics' share price on December 31, 1999 had reached €26.40.

At the end of fiscal year 1999, Getronics had 343,724,237 ordinary shares and 21,950,000 cumulative preference shares outstanding. The preference shares earned cumulative dividend, paid annually in arrears, at 5.7 percent and had been issued at €10.75 per share (€236 million in total).

During fiscal year 2000, Getronics issued €500 million of new subordinated convertible bonds (with an annual interest rate of 0.25 percent, a redemption price of 116.01 percent, and a conversion price of €36.98), maturing in March 2005, and reduced its debt under the revolving credit facility by €150 million. Getronics' share price at the end of 2000 was €6.26; by the end of 2001, it had dropped further to €3.64.

During fiscal year 2001, Getronics temporarily lowered the conversion price of its subordinated convertible bonds to persuade its bondholders to convert their bonds into ordinary shares. As a result, convertible debt with a total book value €295 million was converted into equity, increasing the number of outstanding shares with 61,078,827. In 2003, Getronics eventually redeemed its outstanding subordinated convertible bonds by paying the bondholders €325 million in cash and agreeing to repay the remaining €250 million through quarterly installment payments during a five-year period. The interest rate on the new installment bonds equaled 13 percent. To finance the redemption, Getronics issued new unsubordinated convertible bonds, maturing in five years, for an amount of €100 million (with an annual interest rate of 5.5 percent, a redemption price of 100 percent, and a conversion price of €1.58). At the end of 2003, Getronics' share price was €1.66.

In 2004 and 2005, Getronics issued 100 million and 48.5 million new shares. The company used the proceeds of the 2004 issue to redeem its installment bonds early. In

Professor Erik Peek prepared this case. The case is intended solely as the basis for class discussion and is not intended to serve as an endorsement, source of primary data, or illustration of effective or ineffective management.

addition, the company obtained a new €175 credit facility in 2004 – which got replaced by a €300 credit facility in 2005 – to help finance the redemption as well as replace a €100 credit facility and issued new unsubordinated convertible bonds (with an annual interest rate of 5.5 percent and a redemption price of 100 percent) in 2005. As a consequence of the adoption of IFRS in 2005, Getronics reclassified its cumulative preference shares from equity to debt. The par value and premium reserve of these shares (i.e., the book value of the new debt) amounted to €235 million.

Fiscal year 2006 was another challenging year for Getronics. The company incurred unexpected losses in Italy, had to recognize an impairment charge of €65 million on goodwill relating to the Wang Global acquisition and, consequently, reported a significant net loss. During 2006, Getronics did not change much to its borrowings other than replacing maturing bonds with new unsubordinated convertible bonds. The losses continued in 2007, when competitors started to consider the company as a takeover candidate. On July 31, 2007, Royal KPN NV announced its interest in acquiring Getronics. On October 22, 2007, KPN completed its acquisition.

EXHIBIT 1   Getronics NV – summary of events

Date	Event/announcement
May 5, 1999	Getronics acquires US-based industry peer Wang Global; the company finances the acquisition through a mixture of new equity (€0.7 billion common and €0.3 billion preferred) and debt (€0.5 billion loans and €0.3 billion convertible bonds). The amount of goodwill that Getronics recognized on the transaction is close to €2.4 billion.
February 9, 2000	Getronics sells its ATM business, realizing a profit on the sale.
March 3, 2000	Annual results 1999 announcement. The acquisition of Wang Global boosts the company's results. Getronics announces ambitious growth plans.
March 16, 2000	Getronics issues €450 million in subordinated convertible debt (to replace maturing debt).
First half 2000	End of the dot-com bubble. Technology shares decline.
August 17, 2000	First half-year report.
November 22, 2000	Getronics announces that this year's earnings will be below expectations. Getronics' share price declines by 42 percent.
February 5, 2001	Getronics signs €75 million contract with Shell.
February 28, 2001	Annual results 2000 announcement
June 1, 2001	Getronics' CEO Cees van Luijk resigns and is succeeded by Peter van Voorst.
August 16, 2001	First half-year report
December 11, 2001	Getronics exchanges €295.3 million of subordinated convertible bonds for equity.
December 18, 2001	Getronics signs €90 million contract with Barclays.
March 5, 2002	Annual results 2001 announcement. Getronics decides to freeze wages of its employees after incurring a record loss.
April 22, 2002	Getronics announces that it plans to repurchase some of its outstanding convertible bonds
August 13, 2002	Getronics' share price drops by close to 40 percent after rumors that the company is close to applying for bankruptcy.
August 15, 2002	First half-year report
December 31, 2002	Getronics repays all its amounts outstanding under the €500 million credit facility.
February 12, 2003	Getronics offers (mostly institutional) subordinated convertible bondholders equity in exchange for their bonds. Convertible bondholders deny the offer, resulting in a conflict between management and bondholders.
February 21, 2003	CEO Peter van Voorst and CFO Jan Docter step down. The new CEO of Getronics is Klaas Wagenaar.
March 4, 2003	Annual results 2002 announcement
March 21, 2003	Getronics announces to reduce debt by selling assets rather than offering bondholders equity.
April 22, 2003	Getronics sells Getronics HR Solutions for €315 million in cash (and realizes a profit on the sale of €270 million).
June 10, 2003	Getronics immediately repays bondholders €325 million (in cash) and agrees for the repayment of the remaining €250 million in installments. The agreement resolves the company's conflict with its convertible bondholders.
July 1, 2003	Getronics obtains a loan of €100 million, which will be used to replace a €200 million credit facility.
August 13, 2003	First half-year report
October 13, 2003	Getronics issues €100 million in convertible debt (to replace maturing debt).
February 4, 2004	Getronics sells 100 million new shares to institutional investors (proceeds: €233 million). The proceeds are used to repay €250 million in subordinated installment bonds on March 30, 2004.
March 2, 2004	Annual results 2003 announcement
April 19, 2004	Getronics obtains a new credit facility of €175 million from a consortium of banks.

Getronics' debt ratings

EXHIBIT 1   Getronics NV – summary of events *(continued)*

Date	Event/announcement
August 11, 2004	First half-year report
November 1, 2004	Getronics announces the acquisition of industry peer PinkRoccade N.V for the amount of €350 million. The company will obtain a new credit facility of €125 million that, together with the credit facility obtained in April, will be used to finance the acquisition.
March 3, 2005	Annual results 2004 announcement
April 11, 2005	Getronics issues new shares (proceeds: €388 million).
August 3, 2005	First half-year report.
September 29, 2005	Getronics issues €150 million in unsecured convertible debt (to replace maturing bonds).
March 2, 2006	Annual results 2005 announcement. Getronics also announces that its Italian subsidiary has committed fraud, hiding €15 million in expenses.
April 20, 2006	Getronics receives four bids for its Italian subsidiary.
June 23, 2006	Getronics sells its Italian subsidiary to Eutelia for an estimated amount of €135 million, realizing a loss of €50 million. The sale helps the company to meet its debt covenants again.
August 1, 2006	First half-year report. Disappointing results cause share prices to decline by close to 24 percent. Getronics announces restructuring plans.
November 15, 2006	CFO Theo Janssen resigns unexpectedly. Two other Board Members follow his example.
December 14, 2006	Getronics issues €95 million in convertible bonds (to replace maturing bonds).
February 27, 2007	Annual results 2006 announcement. Getronics announces its annual results early. The company realized an unexpected loss of €145 million.
July 30, 2007	Royal KPN acquires Getronics.

Getronics' debt ratings

Getronics' debt ratings

EXHIBIT 2   Getronics NV – financial information (in € millions)

	2007 H2	2007 H1	2006 H2	2006 H1	2005 H2	2005 H1	2004 H2	2004 H1	2003 H2	2003 H1	2002 H2	2002 H1	2001 H2	2001 H1	2000 H2	2000 H1
Revenue	1224	1280	1319	1308	1271	1322	918	1188	1308	1363	1757	1838	2048	2101	2214	1913
Cost of sales	−996	−1051	−1040	−1062	−988	−1079	−740	−981	−1103	−1131	−1463	−1495	−1703	−1723	−1768	−1514
Gross profit	**228**	**229**	**279**	**246**	**283**	**243**	**178**	**207**	**205**	**232**	**294**	**343**	**345**	**378**	**446**	**399**
Selling expenses	−91	−97	−99	−108	−95	−98	−68	−86	−84	−92	−124	−132	−135	−131	−131	−125
General and administrative expenses	−153	−108	−111	−106	−98	−106	−67	−94	−105	−128	−126	−151	−148	−162	−180	−161
Other operating expenses/income	0	−13	−2	−11	−43	−3	−6	6	15	−62	−33	0	3	—	—	—
Amortization/impairment of intangible assets	−13	−88	−65	0	0	0	0	0	−22	−21	−403	−30	−983	−49	−50	−48
Earnings before interest and taxes (EBIT)	**−29**	**−77**	**2**	**21**	**47**	**36**	**37**	**33**	**9**	**−71**	**−392**	**30**	**−918**	**36**	**85**	**65**
Financial income and expenses	−29	−22	−40	−23	−17	−46	−2	−21	−23	−35	−13	−15	−17	−30	−24	−19
Earnings before taxes (EBT)	**−58**	**−99**	**−38**	**−2**	**30**	**−10**	**35**	**12**	**−14**	**−106**	**−405**	**15**	**−935**	**6**	**61**	**46**
Income taxes	6	−9	−38	24	24	0	60	−4	22	74	−9	−11	−12	−14	−26	−22
Income from unconsolidated investments and discontinued operations (net of income taxes)	1	0	−28	−63	−40	0	−47	0	9	261	0	0	−8	−76	−28	31
Net earnings	**−51**	**−108**	**−104**	**−41**	**14**	**−10**	**48**	**8**	**17**	**229**	**−414**	**4**	**−955**	**−84**	**7**	**55**
Intangible fixed assets	517	534	681	896	913	925	530	553	623	—	654	1213	1238	2196	2201	2258
Tangible fixed assets	109	102	95	107	113	143	73	76	83	—	144	177	185	240	223	202
Other non-current assets	322	281	281	352	283	241	147	191	160	214	91	79	88	100	168	161
Total non-current assets	**948**	**917**	**1057**	**1355**	**1309**	**1309**	**750**	**820**	**866**	**833**	**889**	**1469**	**1511**	**2536**	**2592**	**2621**
Total current assets	**701**	**714**	**793**	**841**	**907**	**963**	**889**	**872**	**1087**	**1042**	**1287**	**1564**	**1752**	**1805**	**1882**	**1604**
– of which cash and cash equivalents	134	122	174	144	251	141	236	217	409	214	296	269	387	250	292	150
Assets held for sale	**0**	**161**	**90**	**22**	**181**	—	—	—	—	—	—	—	—	—	—	—
Total assets	**1649**	**1792**	**1940**	**2218**	**2397**	**2272**	**1639**	**1692**	**1953**	**1875**	**2176**	**3033**	**3263**	**4341**	**4474**	**4225**

Getronics' debt ratings

	1	2	3	4	5	6	7	8	9	10	11	12	13	14	15	16
Shareholders' equity	409	321	408	524	597	602	357	386	299	320	122	522	532	1209	1257	1317
Minority interests	0	0	0	0	0	0	0	2	2	1	2	2	3	3	4	3
Subordinated convertibles	—	—	—	—	—	—	—	—	—	—	520	522	554	849	849	849
Short-term interest bearing debt	67	223	137	85	100	10	6	2	105	38	15	12	24	20	15	15
Long-term debt	347	340	323	551	337	453	197	199	330	301	80	367	427	542	435	395
Provisions	—	—	—	—	—	—	—	—	—	—	337	391	411	413	458	452
Employee benefit plans	95	110	119	155	160	185	202	237	126	286	—	—	—	—	—	—
Provisions for liabilities and charges	27	16	26	51	39	40	22	23	81	—	—	—	—	—	—	—
Deferred income tax liabilities	10	7	6	20	12	72	12	51	50	—	—	—	—	—	—	—
Other non-current liabilities	13	29	24	6	15	0	4	0	0	—	—	—	—	—	—	—
Non-current liabilities and short-term debt	559	725	635	868	663	760	443	512	692	625	432	770	862	975	908	862
Current liabilities (excl. short-term debt)	681	684	862	814	888	910	839	792	960	929	1100	1217	1312	1305	1456	1194
Liabilities from discontinued activities	0	62	35	12	249	—	—	—	—	—	—	—	—	—	—	—
Total equity and liabilities	1649	1792	1940	2218	2397	2272	1639	1692	1953	1875	2176	3033	3263	4341	4474	4225
Cash flow from operations	12	−148	144	−142	95	−160	34	−141	96	−103	175	5	229	−27	−16	−13
Cash flow from capital expenditures	13	−26	65	−81	−28	−344	−19	−1	32	259	150	−17	22	−83	−29	−127
Cash flow from financing activities	−20	115	−203	127	48	403	9	−53	92	−231	−307	−97	−114	68	181	130
Market capitalization at year end		753		1392		846		679		237		1489		2152		
Statutory tax rate	25.50%	25.50%	29.60%	29.60%	31.50%	31.50%	34.50%	34.50%	34.50%	34.50%	34.50%	34.50%	34.50%	34.50%	34.50%	34.50%

Source: 2000–2007 annual and semiannual reports of Getronics NV.

Mergers and Acquisitions

Mergers and acquisitions have long been a popular form of corporate investment, particularly in countries with Anglo-American forms of capital markets. There is no question that these transactions provide a healthy return to target shareholders. However, their value to acquiring shareholders is less understood. Many skeptics point out that given the hefty premiums paid to target shareholders, acquisitions tend to be negative-valued investments for acquiring shareholders.[1]

A number of questions can be examined using financial analysis for mergers and acquisitions:

- Securities analysts can ask: Does a proposed acquisition create value for the acquiring firm's shareholders?
- Risk arbitrageurs can ask: What is the likelihood that a hostile takeover offer will ultimately succeed, and are there other potential acquirers likely to enter the bidding?
- Acquiring management can ask: Does this target fit our business strategy? If so, what is it worth to us, and how can we make an offer that can be successful?
- Target management can ask: Is the acquirer's offer a reasonable one for our shareholders? Are there other potential acquirers that would value our company more than the current bidder?
- Investment bankers can ask: How can we identify potential targets that are likely to be a good match for our clients? And how should we value target firms when we are asked to issue fairness opinions?

In this chapter we focus primarily on the use of financial statement data and analysis directed at evaluating whether a merger creates value for the acquiring firm's shareholders. However, our discussion can also be applied to these other merger contexts. The topic of whether acquisitions create value for acquirers focuses on evaluating:

1 Motivations for acquisitions.
2 The pricing of offers.
3 Forms of payment.
4 The likelihood that an offer will be successful.

Throughout the chapter we use US-based DuPont's acquisition of Denmark-based Danisco in 2011 to illustrate how financial analysis can be used in a merger context.

MOTIVATION FOR MERGER OR ACQUISITION

There are a variety of reasons why firms merge or acquire other firms. Some acquiring managers may want to increase their own power and prestige. Others, however, realize that business combinations provide an opportunity to create new economic value for their shareholders. **Merger or acquisition benefits** include the following:

1 Taking advantage of economies of scale. Mergers are often justified as a means of providing the two participating firms with increased economies of scale. Economies of scale arise when one large firm can perform a function more efficiently than two smaller firms. For example, Danisco and DuPont were both R&D-intensive

companies, were partners in a biofuel-producing joint venture and had overlap between their industrial enzymes and cultures (Danisco) and health and nutrition (DuPont) segments. The merger may therefore provide operating synergies from eliminating duplicate functions and from reducing research costs. At the time of the merger, management estimated that it would save $130 million annually by 2013, for example, by sharing research and development and sales facilities.

2 Improving target management. Another common motivation for acquisition is to improve target management. A firm is likely to be a target if it has systematically underperformed its industry. Historical poor performance could be due to bad luck, but it could also be due to the firm's managers making poor investment and operating decisions, or deliberately pursuing goals that increase their personal power but cost shareholders. In the years 2006 through 2009 Danisco had reported low growth, negative abnormal profitability, and market-to-book ratios below one. However, during the last fiscal year ending prior to the merger announcement, Danisco had managed to grow revenues by 5.5 percent and increase its market-to-book ratio to 1.5. Further, for the following three fiscal years, analysts reckoned that Danisco's revenues would increase by an average of 8 percent and return on equity would revert to a normal level of 10.5 percent, making it less likely that DuPont's motive to acquire Danisco was to replace its management.

3 Combining complementary resources. Firms may decide that a merger will create value by combining complementary resources of the two partners. For example, a firm with a strong research and development unit could benefit from merging with a firm that has a strong distribution unit. In the DuPont–Danisco merger, the two firms appeared to have complementary capabilities and resources. DuPont was strong in biomass processing and microbe engineering, whereas Danisco was the world's second-largest manufacturer of enzymes. Combining these activities would help the companies to obtain a stronger position in biotechnology and, for example, develop cost-effective biofuels. Further, through a strong sales organization and close collaboration with customers Danisco had managed to become the global leader in several (bio-based) segments of the competitive food ingredients industry. Danisco's sales organization could thus help to strengthen DuPont's access to several food application markets.

4 Capturing tax benefits. Companies may obtain several tax benefits from mergers and acquisitions. The major benefit is the acquisition of operating tax losses. If a firm does not expect to earn sufficient profits to fully utilize operating loss carryforward benefits, it may decide to buy another firm that is earning profits, provided that these profits are made in the same tax jurisdiction as where the loss carryforwards arose. The operating losses and loss carryforwards of the acquirer can then be offset against the target's taxable profit. A second tax benefit often attributed to mergers is the tax shield that comes from increasing leverage for the target firm. That is, the interest expense on the additional debt is tax-deductible and lowers the target firm's tax payments. This was particularly relevant for leveraged buyouts in the 1980s.[2]

5 Providing low-cost financing to a financially constrained target. If capital markets are imperfect, perhaps because of information asymmetries between management and outside investors, firms can face capital constraints. Information problems are likely to be especially severe for newly formed, high-growth firms. These firms can be difficult for outside investors to value since they have short track records, and their financial statements provide little insight into the value of their growth opportunities. Further, since they typically have to rely on external funds to finance their growth, capital market constraints for high-growth firms are likely to affect their ability to undertake profitable new projects. Public capital markets are therefore likely to be costly sources of funds for these types of firms. An acquirer that understands the business and is willing to provide a steady source of finance may therefore be able to add value.[3]

6 Creating value through restructuring and break-ups. Acquisitions are often pursued by financial investors such as leveraged buy-out firms that expect to create value by breaking up the firm. The break-up value is expected to be larger than the aggregate worth of the entire firm. Often, a consortium of financial investors will acquire a firm with a view of unlocking value from various components of the firm's asset base.

7 Increasing product-market rents. Firms also can have incentives to merge to increase product-market rents. By merging and becoming a dominant firm in the industry, two smaller firms can collude to restrict their output and raise prices, thereby increasing their profits. This circumvents problems that arise in cartels of independent firms, where firms have incentives to cheat on the cartel and increase their output. DuPont focused its activities on biotechnology and chemicals. Danisco operated primarily in the food ingredients and industrial enzymes industries. Because the companies operated in related segments but were not directly competing, the merger

was not expected to significantly increase product-market rents other than through a possible increase in the companies' bargaining power over their suppliers.

While product-market rents make sense for firms as a motive for merging, the two partners are unlikely to announce their intentions when they explain the merger to their investors, since most countries have competition (antitrust) laws which regulate mergers between two firms in the same industry. For example, in the EU large mergers must be approved by the European Commission, which examines whether mergers do not impede effective competition by creating a dominant market position. National mergers are generally reviewed by national competition authorities. In the US there are three major antitrust statutes – The Sherman Act of 1890, The Clayton Act of 1914, and The Hart Scott Rodino Act of 1976.

Anti-competitive concerns were less significant for the DuPont-Danisco merger because the merging companies were not directly competing in the same markets. Merger approval was obtained from the US Federal Trade Commission (FTC), China's Ministry of Commerce, and the European Commission.

While many of the motivations for acquisitions are likely to create new economic value for shareholders, some are not. Firms that are flush with cash but have few new profitable investment opportunities are particularly prone to using their surplus cash to make acquisitions. Shareholders of these firms would probably prefer that managers pay out any surplus or "free" cash flows as dividends, or use the funds to repurchase their firm's shares. However, these options reduce the size of the firm and the assets under management's control. Management may therefore prefer to invest the free cash flows to buy new companies, even if they are not valued by shareholders. Of course managers will never announce that they are buying a firm because they are reluctant to pay out funds to shareholders.

They may explain the merger using one of the motivations discussed above, or they may argue that they are buying the target at a bargain price.

Another motivation for mergers that is valued by managers but not shareholders is diversification. Diversification was a popular motivation for acquisitions in the 1960s and early 1970s. Acquirers sought to dampen their earnings volatility by buying firms in unrelated businesses. Diversification as a motive for acquisitions has since been widely discredited. Modern finance theorists point out that in a well-functioning capital market, investors can diversify for themselves and do not need managers to do so for them. In addition, diversification has been criticized for leading firms losing sight of their major competitive strengths and expanding into businesses where they do not have expertise.[4] These firms eventually recognize that diversification-motivated acquisitions do not create value, leading to divestitures of business units.

KEY ANALYSIS QUESTIONS

In evaluating a proposed merger, analysts are interested in determining whether the merger creates new wealth for acquiring and target shareholders, or whether it is motivated by managers' desires to increase their own power and prestige. Key questions for financial analysis are likely to include:

- *What is the motivation(s) for an acquisition and any anticipated benefits disclosed by acquirers or targets?*

- *What are the industries of the target and acquirer?* Are the firms related horizontally (the firms are suppliers of similar products) or vertically (one firm is the other firm's supplier)? How close are the business relations between them? If the businesses are unrelated, is the acquirer cash-rich and reluctant to return free cash flows to shareholders?

- *What are the key operational strengths of the target and the acquirer?* Are these strengths complementary? For example, does one firm have a renowned research group and the other a strong distribution network?

- *Is the acquisition a friendly one, supported by target management, or hostile?* A hostile takeover is more likely to occur for targets with poor-performing management who oppose the acquisition to preserve their jobs. However, as discussed below, this typically reduces acquirer management's access to information about the target, increasing the risk of overpayment.

- *What is the premerger performance of the two firms?* Performance metrics are likely to include ROE, gross margins, general and administrative expenses to sales, and working capital management ratios. On the basis of these measures, is the target a poor performer in its industry, implying that there are opportunities for improved management? Is the acquirer in a declining industry and searching for new directions?

■ *What is the tax position of both firms?* What are the average and marginal current tax rates for the target and the acquirer? Does the acquirer have operating loss carryforwards and the target taxable profits?

This analysis should help the analyst understand what specific benefits, if any, the merger is likely to generate.

ACQUISITION PRICING

A well thought out economic motivation for a merger or acquisition is a necessary but not sufficient condition for it to create value for acquiring shareholders. The acquirer must be careful to avoid overpaying for the target. Overpayment makes the transaction highly desirable and profitable for target shareholders, but it diminishes the value of the deal to acquiring shareholders. A financial analyst can use the following methods to assess whether the acquiring firm is overpaying for the target.

Analyzing premium offered to target shareholders

One popular way to assess whether the acquirer is overpaying for a target is to compare the premium offered to target shareholders to premiums offered in similar transactions. If the acquirer offers a relatively high **acquisition premium**, the analyst is typically led to conclude that the transaction is less likely to create value for acquiring shareholders.

Premiums differ significantly for friendly and hostile acquisitions. Premiums tend to be about 30 percent higher for hostile deals than for friendly offers, implying that hostile acquirers are more likely to overpay for a target.[5] There are several reasons for this. First, a friendly acquirer has access to the internal records of the target, making it much less likely that it will be surprised by hidden liabilities or problems once it has completed the deal. In contrast, a hostile acquirer does not have this advantage in valuing the target and is forced to make assumptions that may later turn out to be false. Second, the delays that typically accompany a hostile acquisition often provide opportunities for competing bidders to make an offer for the target, leading to a bidding war.

Comparing a target's premium to values for similar types of transactions is straightforward to compute, but it has several practical problems. First, it is not obvious how to define a comparable transaction. European takeover premiums differ on various dimensions. As argued, average premiums are greater in hostile takeovers than in friendly takeovers. Further, takeover premiums vary by means of payment. Equity-financed acquisitions (share-for-share mergers) require lower premiums than cash-financed acquisitions because the former type makes the target firms' shareholders also shareholders of the new company. Target shareholders thereby keep benefiting – through capital gains – from the synergies created by the merger. Takeover premiums may also depend on the target firms' country of domicile. When a target firm is located in a country with strict takeover rules, the target firm's shareholders may have more power to negotiate higher premiums. Research has indicated that during the years 1993 to 2001 takeover premiums in the UK, where hostile takeover were more common and takeover rules were stricter, were on average higher than in Continental Europe.[6]

A second problem in using premiums offered to target shareholders to assess whether an acquirer overpaid is that measured premiums can be misleading if an offer is anticipated by investors. The share price run-up for the target will then tend to make estimates of the premium appear relatively low. This limitation can be partially offset by using target share prices one month prior to the acquisition offer as the basis for calculating premiums. However, in some cases offers may have been anticipated for even longer than one month.

Finally, using target premiums to assess whether an acquirer overpaid ignores the value of the target to the acquirer after the acquisition. The acquirer expects to benefit from the merger by improving the target firm's operating performance through a combination of economies of scale, improved management, tax benefits, and spillover effects derived from the acquisition. Clearly, acquirers will be willing to pay higher premiums for targets that are expected to generate higher merger benefits. Thus, examining the premium alone cannot determine whether the acquisition creates value for the acquiring shareholder.

Analyzing value of the target to the acquirer

A second and more reliable way of assessing whether the acquirer has overpaid for the target is to compare the offer price to the estimated value of the target to the acquirer. This latter value can be computed using the valuation techniques discussed in Chapters 7 and 8. The most popular methods of valuation used for mergers and acquisitions are earnings multiples and discounted cash flows. Since a comprehensive discussion of these techniques is provided earlier in the book, we focus here on implementation issues that arise for valuing targets in mergers and acquisitions.

We recommend first computing the value of the target as an independent firm. This provides a way of checking whether the valuation assumptions are reasonable, because for publicly listed targets we can compare our estimate with premerger market prices. It also provides a useful benchmark for thinking about how the target's performance, and hence its value, is likely to change once it is acquired.

Earnings multiples

To estimate the value of a target to an acquirer using earnings multiples, we have to forecast earnings for the target and decide on an appropriate earnings multiple, as follows:

- Step 1: Forecasting earnings. Earnings forecasts are usually made by first forecasting next year's net profit for the target assuming no acquisition. Historical sales growth rates, gross margins, and average tax rates are useful in building a *pro forma* earnings model. Once we have forecasted the profit for the target prior to an acquisition, we can incorporate into the *pro forma* model any improvements in earnings performance that we expect to result from the acquisition. Performance improvements can be modeled as:

  - Higher operating margins through economies of scale in purchasing, or increased market power.

  - Reductions in expenses as a result of consolidating research and development staffs, sales forces, and/or administration.

  - Lower average tax rates from taking advantage of operating tax loss carryforwards.

- Step 2: Determining the price-earnings multiple. How do we determine the earnings multiple to be applied to our earnings forecasts? If the target firm is listed, it may be tempting to use the preacquisition price-earnings multiple to value postmerger earnings. However, there are several limitations to this approach. First, for many targets earnings growth expectations and risk characteristics are likely to change after a merger, implying that there will be a difference between the pre- and postmerger price-earnings multiples. Post-merger earnings should then be valued using a multiple for firms with comparable growth and risk characteristics (see the discussion in Chapter 7). A second problem is that premerger price-earnings multiples are unavailable for unlisted targets. Once again it becomes necessary to decide which types of listed firms are likely to be good comparables. In addition, since the earnings being valued are the projected earnings for the next 12 months or the next full fiscal year, the appropriate benchmark ratio should be a forward price-earnings ratio. Finally, if a premerger price-earnings multiple is appropriate for valuing postmerger earnings, care is required to ensure that the multiple is calculated prior to any acquisition announcement because the price will increase in anticipation of the premium to be paid to target shareholders.

Table 11.1 summarizes how price-earnings multiples are used to value a target firm before an acquisition (assuming it will remain an independent entity), and to estimate the value of a target to a potential acquirer.

TABLE 11.1 Summary of price-earnings valuation for targets

Value of target as an independent firm	Target earnings forecast for the next year, assuming no change in ownership, multiplied by its *premerger* PE multiple
Value of target to potential acquirer	Target *revised* earnings forecast for the next year, incorporating the effect of any operational changes made by the acquirer, multiplied by its *postmerger* PE multiple

Limitations of price-earnings valuation

As explained in Chapter 7, there are serious limitations to using earnings multiples for valuation. In addition to these limitations, the method has two more that are specific to merger valuations:

1 PE multiples assume that merger performance improvements come either from an immediate increase in earnings or from an increase in earnings growth (and hence an increase in the postmerger PE ratio). In reality, improvements and savings can come in many forms – gradual increases in earnings from implementing new operating policies, elimination of overinvestment, better management of working capital, or paying out excess cash to shareholders. These types of improvements are not naturally reflected in PE multiples.

2 PE models do not easily incorporate any spillover benefits from an acquisition for the acquirer because they focus on valuing the earnings of the target.

Discounted abnormal earnings, abnormal earnings growth, or cash flows

As discussed in Chapters 7 and 8, we can also value a company using the discounted abnormal earnings, discounted abnormal earnings growth, and discounted free cash flow methods. These require us to first forecast the abnormal earnings, abnormal earnings growth, or free cash flows for the firm and then discount them at the cost of capital, as follows.

- Step 1: Forecast abnormal earnings/abnormal earnings growth/free cash flows. A *pro forma* model of expected future profits and cash flows for the firm provides the basis for forecasting abnormal earnings, abnormal earnings growth, and free cash flows. As a starting point, the model should be constructed under the assumption that the target remains an independent firm. The model should reflect the best estimates of future sales growth, cost structures, working capital needs, investment and research and development needs, and cash requirements for known debt retirements, developed from financial analysis of the target. The abnormal earnings (growth) method requires that we forecast earnings or net operating profit after tax (NOPAT) for as long as the firm expects new investment projects to earn more than their cost of capital. Under the free cash flow approach, the *pro forma* model will forecast free cash flows to either the firm or to equity, typically for a period of five to ten years. Once we have a model of the abnormal earnings, abnormal earnings growth or free cash flows, we can incorporate any improvements in earnings/free cash flows that we expect to result from the acquisition. These will include the cost savings, cash received from asset sales, benefits from eliminating overinvestment, improved working capital management, and paying out excess cash to shareholders.

- Step 2: Compute the discount rate. If we are valuing the target's postacquisition NOPAT or cash flows to the firm, the appropriate discount rate is the required return on operating assets for the target, using its expected *postacquisition* capital structure. Alternatively, if the target equity cash flows are being valued directly or if we are valuing abnormal earnings, the appropriate discount rate is the target's *postacquisition cost of equity* rather than its required return on operating assets. Two common mistakes are to use the acquirer's cost of capital or the target's *preacquisition* cost of capital to value the postmerger earnings/cash flows from the target.

  The computation of the target's postacquisition cost of capital can be complicated if the acquirer plans to make a change to the target's capital structure after the acquisition, since the target's costs of debt and equity will change. As discussed in Chapter 8, this involves estimating the asset beta for the target, calculating the new equity and debt betas under the modified capital structure, and finally computing the revised cost of equity capital or weighted cost of capital. As a practical matter, the effect of these changes on the weighted average cost of capital is likely to be quite small unless the revision in leverage has a significant effect on the target's interest tax shields or its likelihood of financial distress.

  Table 11.2 summarizes how the discounted abnormal earnings/cash flow methods can be used to value a target before an acquisition (assuming it will remain an independent entity), and to estimate the value of a target firm to a potential acquirer.

TABLE 11.2 Summary of discounted abnormal earnings/abnormal earnings growth/cash flow valuation
for targets

Value of target without an acquisition	a. Present value of abnormal earnings/abnormal earnings growth/free cash flows to target equity assuming no acquisition, discounted at *premerger* cost of equity; or
	b. present value of abnormal NOPAT/abnormal NOPAT growth/free cash flows to target debt and equity assuming no acquisition, discounted at *premerger* required return on operating assets, plus value of investment assets less value of debt.
Value of target to potential acquirer	(a) Present value of abnormal earnings/abnormal earnings growth/free cash flows to target equity, *including benefits from merger*, discounted at *postmerger* cost of equity; or
	(b) present value of abnormal abnormal NOPAT/abnormal NOPAT growth/free cash flows to target, *including benefits from merger*, discounted at *postmerger* required return on operating assets, plus value of investment assets less value of debt.

- Step 3: Analyze sensitivity. Once we have estimated the expected value of a target, we will want to examine the sensitivity of our estimate to changes in the model assumptions. For example, answering the following questions can help the analyst assess the risks associated with an acquisition:

  - What happens to the value of the target if it takes longer than expected for the benefits of the acquisition to materialize?

  - What happens to the value of the target if the acquisition prompts its primary competitors to respond by also making an acquisition? Will such a response affect our plans and estimates?

KEY ANALYSIS QUESTIONS

To analyze the pricing of an acquisition, the analyst is interested in assessing the value of the acquisition benefits to be generated by the acquirer relative to the price paid to target shareholders. Analysts are therefore likely to be interested in answers to the following questions:

- What is the premium that the acquirer paid for the target's shares? What does this premium imply for the acquirer in terms of future performance improvements to justify the premium?

- What are the likely performance improvements that management expects to generate from the acquisition? For example, are there likely to be increases in the revenues for the merged firm from new products, increased prices, or better distribution of existing products? Alternatively, are there cost savings as a result of taking advantage of economies of scale, improved efficiency, or a lower cost of capital for the target?

- What is the value of any performance improvements? Values can be estimated using multiples or discounted abnormal earnings/cash flow methods.

DuPont's pricing of Danisco

The DuPont-Danisco acquisition was structured as a cash tender offer. For each share they held, Danisco shareholders would receive DKK665. DuPont's DKK32.3 ($5.8) billion price for Danisco represented a 29 percent premium to target shareholders over the market value on December 17, 2010, one day after Danisco's most recent quarterly earnings announcement and a few weeks prior to the disclosure of the cash tender offer.

With average takeover premiums in cash financed acquisitions of 26 percent, the premium that DuPont offered to Danisco shareholders is slightly above average. Prior to the acquisition announcement, Danisco's leading PE multiple (based on expected earnings for the next fiscal year) was close to 18. Given management's estimate that the acquisition would create cost savings of about DKK0.5 billion (after tax), analysts' consensus (pre-merger) earnings forecast for 2011 of DKK1.4 billion, and a PE multiple of 18, Danisco's post-merger value could be estimated at DKK34.2 billion (18 × [1.4 + 0.5]). This multiple-based value estimate is more than the offer price of DKK32.3 billion, which suggests that DuPont's management expected that the anticipated cost savings would not persist or were somewhat uncertain.

The market reaction to the acquisition announcement on January 10, 2011 suggests that analysts believed that the deal would not create value for DuPont's shareholders – DuPont's share price decreased by 1.5 percent, during the 11 days prior to the announcement through to the actual announcement day. By the tenth trading day after the announcement, DuPont's share was still down 1.5 percent, or $0.7 billion. Given the $1.3 billion premium that DuPont paid for Danisco, investors believed that the merger would create value of $0.6 billion.

ACQUISITION FINANCING AND FORM OF PAYMENT

Even if an acquisition is undertaken to create new economic value and is priced judiciously, it may still destroy shareholder value if it is inappropriately financed. Several financing options are available to acquirers, including issuing shares or warrants to target shareholders, or acquiring target shares using surplus cash or proceeds from new debt. The trade-offs between these options from the standpoint of target shareholders usually hinge on their tax and transaction cost implications. For acquirers, they can affect the firm's capital structure and provide new information to investors.

As we discuss below, the financing preferences of target and acquiring shareholders can diverge. Financing arrangements can therefore increase or reduce the attractiveness of an acquisition from the standpoint of acquiring shareholders. As a result, a complete analysis of an acquisition will include an examination of the implications of the financing arrangements for the acquirer.

Effect of form of payment on acquiring shareholders

From the perspective of the acquirer, the form of payment is essentially a financing decision. As discussed in Chapter 10, in the long-term firms choose whether to use debt or equity financing to balance the tax and incentive benefits of debt against the risks of financial distress. For acquiring shareholders the costs and benefits of different financing options usually depend on how the offer affects their firm's capital structure, any information effects associated with different forms of financing.

Capital structure effects of the form of financing

In acquisitions where debt financing or surplus cash are the primary form of consideration for target shares, the acquisition increases the net financial leverage of the acquirer. This increase in leverage may be part of the acquisition strategy, since one way an acquirer can add value to an inefficient firm is to lower its taxes by increasing interest tax shields. However, in many acquisitions an increase in postacquisition leverage is a side effect of the method of financing and not part of a deliberate tax-minimizing strategy. The increase in leverage can then potentially reduce shareholder value for the acquirer by increasing the risk of financial distress.

To assess whether an acquisition leads an acquirer to have too much leverage, financial analysts can assess the acquirer's financial risk following the proposed acquisition by these methods:

■ Analyze the business risks and the volatility of the combined, postacquisition cash flows against the level of debt in the new capital structure, and the implications for possible financial distress.

■ Assessing the *pro forma* financial risks for the acquirer under the proposed financing plan. Popular measures of financial risk include debt-to-equity and interest coverage ratios, as well as projections of cash flows available to meet debt repayments. The ratios can be compared to similar performance metrics for the acquiring and target firms' industries to determine whether postmerger ratios indicate that the firm's probability of financial distress has increased significantly.

■ Examining whether there are important off-balance sheet liabilities for the target and/or acquirer that are not included in the *pro forma* ratio and cash flow analysis of post-acquisition financial risk.

■ Determining whether the *pro forma* assets for the acquirer are largely intangible and therefore sensitive to financial distress. Measures of intangible assets include such ratios as market to book equity and tangible assets to the market value of equity.

Information problems and the form of financing

In the short-term, information asymmetries between managers and external investors can make managers reluctant to raise equity to finance new projects. Managers' reluctance arises from their fear that investors will interpret the decision as an indication that the firm's equity is overvalued. In the short-term, this effect can lead managers to deviate from the firm's long-term optimal mix of debt and equity. As a result, acquirers are likely to prefer using internal funds or debt to finance an acquisition, because these forms of consideration are less likely to be interpreted negatively by investors.[7]

The information effects imply that firms forced to use equity financing are likely to face a share price decline when investors learn of the method of financing.[8] From the viewpoint of financial analysts, the financing announcement may, therefore, provide valuable news about the preacquisition value of the acquirer. On the other hand, it should have no implications for analysis of whether the acquisition creates value for acquiring shareholders, since the news reflected in the financing announcement is about the *preacquisition* value of the acquirer and not about the *postacquisition* value of the target to the acquirer.

A second information problem arises if the acquiring management does not have good information about the target. Equity financing then provides a way for acquiring shareholders to share the information risks with target shareholders. If the acquirer finds out after the acquisition that the value of the target is less than previously anticipated, the accompanying decline in the acquirer's equity price will be partially borne by target shareholders who continue to hold the acquirer's shares. In contrast, if the target's shares were acquired in a cash offer, any postacquisition loss would be fully borne by the acquirer's original shareholders. The risk-sharing benefits from using equity financing appear to be widely recognized for acquisitions of private companies, where public information on the target is largely unavailable.[9] In practice it appears to be considered less important for acquisitions of large public corporations.[10]

Corporate control and the form of payment

There is a significant difference between the use of cash and shares in terms of its impact on the voting control of the combined firm postacquisition. Financing an acquisition with cash allows the acquirer to retain the structure and composition of its equity ownership. On the other hand, depending on the size of the target firm relative to the acquirer, an acquisition financed with shares could have a significant impact on the ownership and control of the firm postacquisition. This could be particularly relevant to a family-controlled acquirer. Therefore, the effects of control need to be balanced against the other costs and benefits when determining the form of payment.

Research has found that European acquirers whose primary shareholder controls between 40 and 60 percent of the equity votes indeed have a preference for cash as the primary form of consideration.[11] For shareholders who hold an equity stake between 40 and 60 percent, the threat of losing control after a share-for-share exchange is most imminent.

Effect of form of payment on target shareholders

The key payment considerations for target shareholders are the tax and transaction cost implications of the acquirer's offer.

Tax effects of different forms of consideration

Target shareholders care about the after-tax value of any offer they receive for their shares. In many countries, whenever target shareholders receive cash for their shares, they are required to pay capital gains tax on the difference between the takeover offer price and their original purchase price. Alternatively, if they receive shares in the acquirer as consideration, they can defer any taxes on the capital gain until they sell the new shares. To qualify for the deferral of capital gains taxes, governments may require additional conditions to be met.[12] In the UK, taxes on capital gains from takeovers can only be deferred when the acquirer and the target firm operate in the same industry. In the US, the acquisition must be undertaken as a tax-free reorganization. Within the EU, not only capital gains on national, within-border share-for-share exchanges can be deferred. The EU Merger Directive guarantees that the option to defer capital gains taxes, if allowed for national mergers, applies also to cross-border share-for-share exchanges.

Tax laws that allow the deferral of capital gains taxes appear to cause target shareholders to prefer a share offer to a cash one. This is certainly likely to be the case for a target founder who still has a significant stake in the company. If the company's share price has appreciated over its life, the founder will face substantial capital gains tax on a cash offer and will therefore probably prefer to receive shares in the acquiring firm. However, cash and share offers can be tax-neutral for some groups of shareholders. For example, consider the tax implications for risk arbitrageurs, who take a short-term position in a company that is a takeover candidate in the hope that other bidders will emerge and increase the takeover price. They have no intention of holding shares in the acquirer once the takeover is completed and will pay ordinary income tax on any short-term trading gain. Cash and share offers therefore have identical after-tax values for risk arbitrageurs. Similarly, tax-exempt institutions are likely to be indifferent to whether an offer is in cash or shares.

Transaction costs and the form of payment

Transaction costs are another factor related to the form of financing that can be relevant to target shareholders. Transaction costs are incurred when target shareholders sell any shares received as consideration for their shares in the target. These costs will not be faced by target shareholders if the bidder offers them cash. Transaction costs are unlikely to be significant for investors who intend to hold the acquirer's shares following a share acquisition. However they may be relevant for investors who intend to sell, such as risk arbitrageurs.

KEY ANALYSIS QUESTIONS

For an analyst focused on the acquiring firm, it is important to assess how the method of financing affects the acquirer's capital structure and its risks of financial distress by asking the following questions:

- What is the leverage for the newly created firm? How does this compare to leverage for comparable firms in the industry?

- What are the projected future cash flows for the merged firm? Are these sufficient to meet the firm's debt commitments? How much of a cushion does the firm have if future cash flows are lower than expected? Is the firm's debt level so high that it is likely to impair its ability to finance profitable future investments if future cash flows are below expectations?

DuPont's financing of Danisco

DuPont offered Danisco shareholders DKK665 in cash for each Danisco share. Given Danisco's 48,574 shares outstanding, this implied a total offer of DKK32.3 billion. By using cash to finance the acquisition, DuPont increased its financial leverage and let its shareholders fully bear any future losses arising from the acquisition. The choice for cash to finance the acquisition suggests that the risk of postacquisition losses was small, presumably because of Danisco's public status and transparency as well as the company's relatively small size.

ACQUISITION OUTCOME

The final question of interest to the analyst evaluating a potential acquisition is whether it will indeed be completed. If an acquisition has a clear value-based motive, the target is priced appropriately, and its proposed financing does not create unnecessary financial risks for the acquirer, it may still fail because the target receives a higher competing bid, there is opposition from **entrenched target management**, or the transaction fails to receive necessary regulatory approval. Therefore, to evaluate the likelihood that an offer will be accepted, the financial analyst has to understand whether there are potential competing bidders who could pay an even higher premium to target shareholders than is currently offered. They also have to consider whether target managers are entrenched and, to protect their jobs, likely to oppose an offer, as well as the political and regulatory environment in which the target and the acquirer operate.

Other potential acquirers

If there are other potential bidders for a target, especially ones who place a higher value on the target, there is a strong possibility that the bidder in question will be unsuccessful. Target management and shareholders have an incentive to delay accepting the initial offer to give potential competitors time to also submit a bid. From the perspective of the initial bidder, this means that the offer could potentially reduce shareholder value by the cost of making the offer (including substantial investment banking and legal fees). In practice, a losing bidder can usually recoup these losses and sometimes even make healthy profits from selling to the successful acquirer any shares it has accumulated in the target.

KEY ANALYSIS QUESTIONS

The financial analyst can determine whether there are other potential acquirers for a target and how they value the target by asking the following questions:

- Are there other firms that could also implement the initial bidder's acquisition strategy? For example, if this strategy relies on developing benefits from complementary assets, look for potential bidders who also have assets complementary to the target. If the goal of the acquisition is to replace inefficient management, what other firms in the target's industry could provide management expertise?

- Who are the acquirer's major competitors? Could any of these firms provide an even better fit for the target?

Target management entrenchment

If target managers are entrenched and fearful for their jobs, it is likely that they will oppose a bidder's offer. Some firms have implemented "golden parachutes" for top managers to counteract their concerns about job security at the time of an offer. Golden parachutes provide top managers of a target firm with attractive compensation rewards should the firm get taken over. However, many firms do not have such schemes, and opposition to an offer from entrenched management is a very real possibility.

In some European countries the entrenchment of management is facilitated by legal provisions that allow a company to install various takeover defenses. For example, in most countries, firms can limit the number of votes that a shareholder can exercise at a shareholders' meeting. A voting cap effectively reduces the voting power that a potential acquirer can obtain. Another example of a takeover defense mechanism, which is commonly used in the Netherlands, is the issuance of depository receipts by an administrative office that is controlled by the firm whose shares the office holds.[13] Holders of depository receipts have the right to receive dividends but no voting rights. Instead, the administrative office retains and exercises the voting rights. This construction makes it difficult for an acquiring firm to obtain any voting power.

While the existence of takeover defenses for a target indicates that its management is likely to fight a bidding firm's offer, defenses do not often prevent an acquisition from taking place. Instead, they tend to cause delays, which increase the likelihood that there will be competing offers made for the target, including offers by friendly parties solicited by target management, called "white knights." Takeover defenses therefore increase the likelihood that the bidder in question will be outbid for the target, or that it will have to increase its offer significantly to win a bidding contest. These risks may discourage acquirers from embarking on a potentially hostile acquisition. Nonetheless, in recent years hostile takeovers have become more rather than less popular in Europe. For example, in 2006, steel producer Mittal Steel was engaged in a hostile takeover attempt for industry peer Arcelor. Arcelor called in the help of "white knight" Severstal, but eventually was forced by its shareholders to accept Mittal's offer. The takeover battle had caused a delay of five months and had driven up the takeover price by 49 percent, or €8.4 billion.

Takeover regulations have the objectives of preventing management entrenchment and protecting minority shareholders during European takeovers. During the 1990s, national takeover regulations in Europe began converging toward the UK regime model. In 2004 the European Commission issued a heavily debated Takeover Directive, which applies to companies whose shares are traded on a (regulated) public exchange. The most important rules in this Directive (effective since May 2006) are the following:[14]

- The equal-treatment rule and the mandatory-bid rule aim at protecting minority shareholders in takeovers. The mandatory-bid rule prescribes that the acquiring firm makes an offer for all remaining shares, once its equity stake exceeds a predefined threshold. In Denmark, Italy, and the UK, this threshold is, for example, 30 percent. The equal-treatment rule requires that the acquiring firm makes equally favorable offers to the controlling and minority shareholders of the target firm.

- Under the squeeze-out rule, the acquiring firm can force the remaining minority shareholders to sell their shares at the tender offer price, once the firm holds a predefined equity stake of, usually, between 80 and 95 percent. Under the sell-out rule, the remaining shareholders can force the acquiring firm to buy their shares at a fair price.

- The board-neutrality rule requires that during takeovers management will not take actions that may frustrate the takeover.

Another proposed rule, the breakthrough rule, did make it into the final Directive but can be opted out of by individual countries. The breakthrough rule mandates that a firm that has acquired a predefined percentage of shares can exercise votes on its shares as if all outstanding shares, including the firm's shares, carry one vote per share. For example, the break through rule guarantees that an acquiring firm that owns 90 percent of the target firm's ordinary shares can exercise exactly 90 percent of the votes during a shareholders' meeting of the target firm, irrespective of the takeover defense mechanisms that are in place.

The rules in the EU Takeover Directive can affect the analysis of a takeover offer. For example, in some jurisdictions the laws prescribe that when the mandatory-bid rule comes into effect, the acquiring firm must offer the remaining shareholders no less than the highest price it has paid to other shareholders. This rule, of course, invites the investor to strategically wait until the last moment before accepting the offer. The board-neutrality rule reduces management entrenchment through postbid takeover defenses and therefore reduces the probability that a target firm will oppose an acquisition. The breakthrough rule, if implemented, can remove firms' prebid takeover defenses, such as voting caps.

KEY ANALYSIS QUESTIONS

To assess whether the target firm's management is entrenched and therefore likely to oppose an acquisition, analysts can ask the following questions:

- Does the target firm have takeover defenses designed to protect management? If so, do national takeover rules reduce the effect of such defenses? Further, do national takeover rules regulate that minority shareholders receive a fair price?

- Has the target been a poor performer relative to other firms in its industry? If so, management's job security is likely to be threatened by a takeover, leading it to oppose any offers.

- Is there a golden parachute plan in place for target management? Golden parachutes provide attractive compensation for management in the event of a take over to deter opposition to a takeover for job security reasons.

Antitrust and security issues

Regulators such as the European Commission's DG for Competition Analysts and the Federal Trade Commission in the US assess the effects of an acquisition on the competitive dynamics of the industry in which the firms operate. The objective is to ensure that no one firm, through mergers and acquisitions, creates a dominant position that can impede effective competition in specific geographies or product markets.

Analysis of outcome of DuPont's offer for Danisco

Analysts covering Danisco had little reason to question whether Danisco would be sold to DuPont. The offer was a friendly one that had received the approval of Danisco's management and board of directors. There probably was some risk of another biotech or chemical firm entering the bidding for Danisco. For example, following the merger announcement there were rumors that Netherlands-based DSM, which owned a 5 percent equity stake in Danisco, would launch a competing bid. However, DSM's management considered DuPont's bid too high and sold its equity stake to DuPont in May 2011. Eventually, none of DuPont's competitors made a bid for Danisco.

In Denmark, takeover regulations require the acquirer to hold at least 90 percent of the target's shares before it can squeeze out the remaining shareholders. Following the acquisition announcement US-based hedge fund Elliott International gradually increased its stake in Danisco to 10.02 percent, making the acquisition outcome uncertain and pressuring DuPont to raise its bid from DKK 665 per share to DKK700 per share. After calling the DKK700 bid "final," Elliott ended its activism and surrendered its shares to DuPont. Elliott's interference in the DuPont-Danisco merger raised the premium received by Danisco's shareholders and thus illustrates how European takeover regulations can support shareholder activism and, consequently, protect shareholders' interests during a takeover.

REPORTING ON MERGERS AND ACQUISITIONS: PURCHASE PRICE ALLOCATIONS

The acquisition price that an acquiring firm pays to the target firm's shareholders compensates these for the transfer of a potentially wide collection of assets and liabilities. For example, in the DuPont-Danisco acquisition DuPont's management paid Danisco's shareholders DKK32.3 billion in cash and assumed Danisco's liabilities in exchange for receiving ownership of not only Danisco's physical equipment and buildings but also its technology, in-process research and development, customer relationships, and sales force. The international accounting standards on business combinations (IFRS 3) require that acquiring firms separately identify and value the assets and liabilities that are transferred in a merger or acquisition to provide a basis for reporting the transaction in the acquirer's post-merger consolidated financial statements. The process of doing so is typically referred to as a **purchase price allocation** and relies strongly on the valuation tools discussed in previous chapters.[15]

The objective of a purchase price allocation is essentially twofold. First, the exercise aims to allocate the acquisition price, being the fair value of the consideration transferred to the target firm's shareholders, to the separately identifiable assets (and liabilities), such as buildings, machinery, or patents. Second, the allocation aims to determine the remaining proportion of the acquisition price that cannot be allocated to individual assets and as such is assumed to be the fair value of the synergies created from using all assets in combination. This remaining proportion is labeled "goodwill" and reported as a separate line item in the acquirer's post-acquisition consolidated financial statements. Consequently, a purchase price allocation helps outside investors to assess whether the acquisition price is reasonable given the identifiable assets acquired or whether the amount of goodwill arising from the merger or acquisition is too large to be justified by the expected M&A synergies. Further, the distinction between goodwill and other intangible assets is relevant because it affects future financial statements. Accountants assume that goodwill has an indefinite economic useful life and must therefore be regularly tested for impairment rather than amortized over a predefined period. In contrast, most other intangible assets have finite economic lives and must thus be systematically amortized, thereby creating periodic charges to future income statements. Given the differences in accounting treatments, managers are not likely to be indifferent to the choice between goodwill and other intangibles in a purchase price allocation.

Purchase price allocations consist of the following five steps:

- Step 1: Determine the value of the target firm. The first step in a purchase price allocation is to determine the value of the target firm as the sum of the fair values of (1) the consideration transferred to the target firm's shareholders and (2) the target firm's interest-bearing debt. In the following steps, this target firm value will be allocated among the separately identifiable assets and goodwill.

- Step 2: Estimate the rate of return implicit in the M&A transaction. The second step of a purchase price allocation is to estimate the discount rate that sets the target firm value equal to the sum of: (a) the fair value of the target firm's investment assets plus (b) the present value of the target firm's *postacquisition* free cash flows from operations. Benchmarking this internal rate of return estimate against the target firm's normally required return on operating assets provides an initial assessment of whether the acquirer overpaid for the target. In particular, if the internal rate of return is significantly lower than the normally required return, this may indicate that the acquisition price is too high to be justified by expected M&A synergies and warrants further investigation of whether goodwill on the transaction is impaired.

■ Step 3: Identify the contributory assets. The third step identifies the target firm's assets that are separately identifiable and contribute to the target firm's *postacquisition* free cash flows. These assets are commonly referred to as the "contributory assets." Contributory assets can be working capital components (such as trade receivables, inventories, and trade payables), non-current tangible assets (such as property, plant, and equipment), or non-current intangible assets (such as trademarks, software, customer relationships, and the assembled workforce).

Part of this step is also to determine the required return on each of the identified contributory assets. These required returns have at least two purposes. First, following the idea that the required return on a portfolio of assets is a weighted average of the required returns on the individual assets in the portfolio, the asset value-weighted average of the required returns on the contributory assets must be equal to the internal rate of return estimated under step 2. This equality helps to derive the implied required return on goodwill, thereby providing an initial indication of the riskiness of the transaction. Second, the required returns help to estimate each asset's contribution to future free cash flows, also referred to as contributory asset charges, which become relevant in the next step.

■ Step 4: Value the contributory assets. Different types of contributory assets may require different valuation techniques. For example, whereas the valuation of property, plant, and equipment typically relies on external appraisers' value estimates, the value of brand names must be derived from royalty rates that companies pay to make use of a brand. The following set of valuation approaches can be used in purchase price allocations:

■ Cost approach. The value of an asset can be assumed equal to the cost of replacing it with a similar asset or reproducing the asset, thereby taking into account the age and condition of the asset.

■ Market approach. If there is an active market on which similar assets are frequently traded, transaction prices from this market can be used to determine the current market value of an asset.

■ Income approach. If the net cash flows generated by an individual asset can be reliably measured, the value of the asset can be derived from the present value of its cash flows. The international accounting rules describe various methods to estimate the cash flows of an individual asset, such as:

■ The direct cash flow forecast method, under which the asset's value is the present value of the cash flows directly attributable to the asset. This method is especially appropriate for assets that generate predictable and separable cash flows, such as financial assets;

■ The relief-from-royalty method, under which the asset's value is the present value of future royalties saved by owning the asset. This method tends to be used for valuing brands (trademarks), patent rights, or technologies;

■ The multi-period excess earnings method, under which the asset's value is the present value of future cash flows generated by the asset *in excess of* charges for the unavoidable use of other contributory assets. This method helps to value, for example, customer relationships.

The international accounting standards on business combinations set a clear order of priority, preferring the market approach over the income approach and preferring the income approach over the cost approach. In addition, the rules prescribe that similar approaches are used for similar types of assets or liabilities.

Note that the multi-period excess earnings method requires the calculation of contributory asset charges, which are defined as the product of the required return on a contributory asset and the contributory asset's value. For example, when valuing Danisco's customer relationships the contributory asset charges reflect the economic cost of capital tied up in assets that are needed to serve the existing customers, such as working capital, property, plant and equipment, or the assembled workforce. Consequently, assets that are valued using the multi-period excess earnings method can only be valued after all other contributory assets have been valued.

■ Step 5: Calculate and evaluate goodwill. The final step in the purchase price allocation process calculates goodwill as the difference between the value of the target firm, as derived in step 1, and the sum of the values of the contributory assets, as calculated in step 4. The derived goodwill amount can be evaluated for reasonableness in various ways. First, the amount of goodwill is not likely to be (significantly) smaller than the premium paid in the acquisition. This is because all other assets identified in the purchase price allocation process were owned by the target firm and must have been valued by investors – at least theoretically – also prior to the merger or acquisition. Consequently, the acquisition premium imposes a (soft) lower bound on the goodwill calculation. Second, purchase price allocations of prior comparable mergers and acquisitions, usually in the same industry, serve as a useful benchmark against which to compare proportions of the acquisition price allocated to the various intangible assets and goodwill. Third, as indicated, the expected return on goodwill that is implicit in the purchase price allocation can be derived from the overall internal rate of return and the individual required returns of contributory assets. As a rule of thumb, if the difference between this expected return on goodwill and the target firm's normally required return on operating assets is small, some of the risk and uncertainty surrounding the realization of presented synergies may have been ignored in the purchase price allocation, which makes it more likely that goodwill is impaired.

In the next section we will illustrate each of the above steps using the example of the DuPont-Danisco acquisition.

Danisco's purchase price allocation

Target firm value

To acquire Danisco, DuPont paid Danisco's shareholders DKK32.30 billion in cash and assumed interest-bearing debt and other non-current liabilities to the amount of DKK4.45 billion. This offer thus valued Danisco's assets at DKK36.75 billion.

On April 29, 2011, DuPont announced that close to 48 percent of Danisco's shareholders had tendered their shares and that it would raise the price of its tender offer. DuPont's offer would become unconditional only if more than 80 percent of Danisco's shareholders would tender their shares before May 13. On May 19, 2011, DuPont announced that it had completed the acquisition of 92.2 percent of Danisco's share capital, thereby obtaining formal control over Danisco's operations. Prior to this date, the relevant regulatory authorities, including China's Ministry of Commerce and the European Commission, had given their approval to the acquisition. Following the international accounting rules on business combinations, we denote the date on which DuPont obtained control (May 19) as the "acquisition date" and consider this date as the date of valuation in the purchase price allocation.

Internal rate of return

Danisco's equity beta, estimated over a ten-year period immediately prior to the acquisition date, is close to 0.8. The firm's operating asset beta, estimated using the procedures described in Chapter 8, is close to 0.6. Given a long-term risk free rate of 4.8 percent and a market risk premium of 5.3 percent (see Chapter 8), Danisco's required return on operating assets can thus be estimated at approximately 8 percent ($4.8\% + 0.6 \times 5.3\%$).

Table 11.3 displays the estimation of the internal rate of return on the acquisition. In this table, forecasts of Danisco's future sales and free cash flows are based on analyst forecasts issued closely before DuPont announced its intention to acquire Danisco. The estimation shows that the internal rate of return on the Danisco acquisition is approximately 7.852 percent. This internal rate of return is very close to the estimate of Danisco's required return on operating assets, which suggests that Danisco is reasonably priced, albeit under the assumption that the anticipated synergy effects are justified.

Contributory assets

In DuPont's acquisition of Danisco, the following identifiable assets were transferred:

- Tangible assets: working capital and property, plant and equipment.
- Intangible assets: customer relationships, brand names, technology, and in-process research and development.

The risk of the intangible assets can be considered equal to the average risk of Danisco's operations. It is therefore reasonable to assume that the required return on intangible assets is equal to the average required return on operating assets, which is 8 percent.[16] In contrast, the risk of tangible assets is lower. A typical assumption made in purchase price allocations is that the required return on property, plant, and equipment is equal to the yield on long-term corporate bonds, whereas the required return on working capital is equal to the yield on short-term debt.

TABLE 11.3 Estimation of the internal rate of return on DuPont's acquisition of Danisco

Forecast year	2011/ 2012	2012/ 2013	2013/ 2014	2014/ 2015	2015/ 2016	2016/ 2017	2017/ 2018	2018/ 2019
Sales	16.44	17.21	18.01	18.85	19.74	20.68	21.30	21.94
Operating profit	2.41	2.55	2.72	2.86	3.01	3.17	3.26	3.36
− Tax (30 percent)	−0.72	−0.77	−0.81	−0.86	−0.90	−0.95	−0.98	−1.01
NOPAT	1.68	1.79	1.90	2.00	2.11	2.22	2.28	2.35
− Change in net operating assets	0.41	0.47	0.49	0.47	0.49	0.52	0.63	0.64
Pre-acquisition free cash flow	1.28	1.32	1.42	1.53	1.61	1.70	1.66	1.71
+ M&A synergies	0.20	0.40	0.50	0.52	0.53	0.55	0.56	0.58
Post-acquisition free cash flow	1.48	1.72	1.92	2.04	2.14	2.25	2.22	2.29
× Partial year factor	0.8667	1.0000	1.0000	1.0000	1.0000	1.0000	1.0000	1.0000
× Discount factor @ 7.852%	0.9678	0.9019	0.8362	0.7753	0.7189	0.6665	0.6180	0.5730
Present value of post-acquisition free cash flows	1.07	1.19	1.18	1.18	1.16	1.13	1.02	0.98
Value between May 19, 2011 and March 31, 2019								8.93
Terminal value								27.82
Target firm value (in DKK billions)								36.75

Assumptions:

- Forecasts of sales, operating profits, and free cash flows (until 2016/2017) are based on analyst forecasts issued closely before the acquisition announcement date.
- The acquisition increases free cash flows by DKK0.2 billion in fiscal 2011/2012, by DKK0.4 billion in fiscal 2012/2013, and by DKK0.5 billion in fiscal 2013/2014. This assumption is based on management's expectation that the acquisition will help to achieve annual cost savings to the amount of DKK0.5 billion (after tax) by 2013.
- After 2013/2014, the cash flow effect of the acquisition grows at an annual rate of 3 percent, being the long-run growth rate of the economy.
- The terminal growth rate equals 3 percent. Forecasts in 2017/2018 and 2018/2019 are based on the assumption that all income statement and balance sheet items grow at an annual rate of 3 percent to impose a steady state prior to the terminal year.
- The valuation date is May 19, 2011. Cash flows in year 1 occur halfway between May 19, 2011 and March 31, 2012. Cash flows in the other years occur halfway through the fiscal year, which runs from April 1 to March 31.
- The partial year factor in 2011/2012 is the number of days between May 19, 2011 and March 31, 2012, divided by 366.

In May 2011, the one-year EURIBOR rate was 2.1 percent; the yield on long-term AAA corporate bonds was 5.0 percent. Given a model-based credit rating for Danisco of BBB (see Chapter 10) and an associated yield spread of about 1 percent, we estimate Danisco's required returns on working capital and property, plant and equipment at 3 and 6 percent, respectively, before tax and 2.1 and 4.2 percent, respectively, after tax.

Valuation of tangible assets

External appraisers valued Danisco's working capital at DKK3.98 billion and its property, plant, and equipment at DKK8.60 billion. In its third quarter financial statements, for the quarter ended on January 31, 2011, the book values of working capital and property, plant, and equipment were DKK3.10 billion DKK5.60 billion, respectively.

The fair value of working capital can sometimes be assumed equal to its book value; however, inventories are likely subject to revaluation. The difference between the fair value and the book value of Danisco's working capital of DKK0.88 billion (3.98 – 3.10) is close to 33 percent of the May 19 book value of Danisco's inventories. This revaluation percentage seems reasonable but conservative given Danisco's past year's gross profit margin of 47 percent of sales and selling costs of 17.5 percent of sales. In particular, these ratios suggest a revaluation percentage of 56 percent, estimated as follows:

Gross profit as a percentage of sales:	47.0 percent
Less: cost to sell	17.5 percent
= markup as a percentage of selling price:	29.5 percent
Divide by: (1 − gross profit margin):	53.0 percent
= markup as a percentage of cost:	55.7 percent

The fair value estimates and required returns on working capital and property, plant and equipment can be used to estimate future contributory asset charges only after making some necessary additional assumptions. Specifically, to calculate the future annual averages of the fair values of working capital and property, plant and equipment we must assume the following:

■ The annual growth in the fair value of working capital follows sales growth;

■ The annual changes in the book value of property, plant, and equipment are as predicted by analysts (closely before the acquisition announcement date),

■ The difference between the fair value and the book value of property, plant, and equipment grows at a constant rate of 3 percent annually to reflect the effect of inflation.

Table 11.4 summarizes the implications of these assumptions for the contributory asset charges between 2011/2012 and 2018/2019. The contributory asset charges (after tax) for working capital are close to 0.52 percent of sales; the contributory asset charges for property, plant, and equipment range from 2.20 to 2.29 percent.

Valuation of trade names and technology

The most commonly used method to value intellectual property rights such as trademarks, patents, or copyrights is the relief-from-royalty method. The rationale of this method is that intellectual property rights derive their value from the royalties that a firm would be willing to pay to acquire the right to use the intellectual property or, alternatively, from the royalties that a firm would be relieved from by owning the intellectual property rights. Possible sources of royalty rates are industry peers' financial statements, management estimates, or commercial databases.

DuPont's 2011 financial statement disclosures regarding the Danisco acquisition indicate that the fair value of Danisco's trade names was estimated at DKK2.92 billion. Table 11.5 shows how the relief-from-royalty method can be used to value Danisco's trade names or, alternatively, estimate what royalty rate is implicit in the value that DuPont assigned to these trade names. The calculations show that a value estimate of DKK2.92 billion is consistent with a (pre-tax) royalty rate of 1.13 percent. This royalty rate seems low but reasonable given that trade names are significantly less valuable in Danisco's business-to-business industry than in consumer-to-business industries.

When valuing Danisco's technology, DuPont distinguished and separately valued two categories: indefinite-lived technology (microbial cell factories), with an estimated value of DKK1.54 billion, and definite-lived technology (such as patents), with an estimated value of DKK2.96 billion. Table 11.6 shows the calculation of royalty rates that are consistent with these value estimates. We estimate the royalty rate of Danisco's indefinite-lived technology at 0.60 percent. Further, under the assumption that the average useful life of Danisco's definite-lived technology is eight years, we estimate that the royalty rate of this technology gradually decreases from 6.53 percent in fiscal 2011/2012 to 0.82 percent (rounded) in fiscal 2018/2019.

Note that in the above calculations we assume that the amortization on acquired intangible assets is not tax-deductible. If, in contrast to our assumption, such amortization would be tax-deductible, the value estimates would need to be upwardly adjusted to account for the tax amortization benefit. For example, if Danisco's definite-lived technology would be tax-deductible on a straight-line basis over a five year period, we would need to increase the technology's value by a factor of 1.3219. Table 11.7 shows how this factor can be calculated by considering a hypothetical asset with a pre-tax value of 100, which is amortized over five years.

TABLE 11.4 Estimation of the contributory asset charges for working capital and property, plant and equipment

		2011/ 2012	2012/ 2013	2013/ 2014	2014/ 2015	2015/ 2016	2016/ 2017	2017/ 2018	2018/ 2019
Sales growth rate (see Table 11.3)	(a)	4.26%	4.63%	4.66%	4.69%	4.72%	4.75%	3.00%	3.00%
Beginning fair value of working capital	(b)	3.98	4.15	4.34	4.54	4.76	4.98	5.22	5.37
Annual change in the fair value of working capital	(a) × (b) = (c)	0.17	0.19	0.20	0.21	0.22	0.24	0.16	0.16
Average fair value of working capital	(b) + 0.5×(c) = (d)	4.06	4.25	4.44	4.65	4.87	5.10	5.30	5.46
Contributory charge @ 2.1 percent	0.021×(d) = (e)	0.09	0.09	0.09	0.10	0.10	0.11	0.11	0.11
Contributory charge as a percentage of sales	(e)/sales = (f)	0.52%	0.52%	0.52%	0.52%	0.52%	0.52%	0.52%	0.52%
Beginning book value of PP&E	(g)	5.60	5.87	6.19	6.52	6.83	7.14	7.47	7.98
Change in book value of PP&E	Forecasts = (h)	0.27	0.32	0.33	0.31	0.32	0.33	0.50	0.52
Average book value of PP&E	(g) + 0.5×(h) = (i)	5.74	6.03	6.35	6.67	6.98	7.31	7.73	8.24
Beginning PP&E fair-book value difference	(j)	3.00	3.09	3.18	3.28	3.38	3.48	3.58	3.69
Change in fair-book value difference	0.03 × (j) = (k)	0.09	0.09	0.10	0.10	0.10	0.10	0.11	0.11
Average PP&E fair-book value difference	(j) + 0.5×(k) = (l)	3.05	3.14	3.23	3.33	3.43	3.53	3.64	3.74
Average fair value of PP&E	(i) + (l) = (m)	8.78	9.17	9.58	10.00	10.41	10.84	11.36	11.98
Contributory charge @ 4.2 percent	0.042 × (m) = (n)	0.37	0.39	0.40	0.42	0.44	0.46	0.48	0.50
Contributory charge as a percentage of sales	(n)/sales = (o)	2.24%	2.24%	2.24%	2.23%	2.22%	2.20%	2.24%	2.29%

TABLE 11.5 Estimation of Danisco's trade names royalty rate

		2011/ 2012	2012/ 2013	2013/ 2014	2014/ 2015	2015/ 2016	2016/ 2017	2017/ 2018	2018/ 2019
Sales	Given	16.44	17.21	18.01	18.85	19.74	20.68	21.30	21.94
× Royalty rate (%)	Plug-in	1.134%	1.134%	1.134%	1.134%	1.134%	1.134%	1.134%	1.134%
= Royalties saved (pre-tax)		0.19	0.20	0.20	0.21	0.22	0.23	0.24	0.25
× (1 − tax rate)	30%	0.70	0.70	0.70	0.70	0.70	0.70	0.70	0.70
= Royalties saved (after tax)		0.13	0.14	0.14	0.15	0.16	0.16	0.17	0.17
× Partial year factor		0.8667	1.0000	1.0000	1.0000	1.0000	1.0000	1.0000	1.0000
× Discount factor	8 %	0.9672	0.9002	0.8335	0.7717	0.7146	0.6616	0.6126	0.5673
= Present value of royalties saved		0.11	0.12	0.12	0.12	0.11	0.11	0.10	0.10

Present value of royalties saved between May 19, 2011 and March 31, 2019	0.89
Terminal value	2.03
Value of trade names	2.92

TABLE 11.6 Estimation of Danisco's definite-lived and indefinite-lived technology royalty rates

		2011/ 2012	2012/ 2013	2013/ 2014	2014/ 2015	2015/ 2016	2016/ 2017	2017/ 2018	2018/ 2019
Indefinite-lived technology									
Sales	Given	16.44	17.21	18.01	18.85	19.74	20.68	21.30	21.94
× Royalty rate (%)	Plug-in	0.597%	0.597%	0.597%	0.597%	0.597%	0.597%	0.597%	0.597%
= Royalties saved (pre-tax)		0.10	0.10	0.11	0.11	0.12	0.12	0.13	0.13
× (1 − tax rate)	30%	0.70	0.70	0.70	0.70	0.70	0.70	0.70	0.70
= Royalties saved (after tax)		0.07	0.07	0.08	0.08	0.08	0.09	0.09	0.09
× Partial year factor		0.8667	1.0000	1.0000	1.0000	1.0000	1.0000	1.0000	1.0000
× Discount factor	8 %	0.9672	0.9002	0.8335	0.7717	0.7146	0.6616	0.6126	0.5673
= Present value of royalties saved		0.06	0.06	0.06	0.06	0.06	0.06	0.05	0.05
Present value of royalties saved between May 19, 2011 and March 31, 2019									0.47
Terminal value									1.07
Value of indefinite-lived technology									1.54
Definite-lived technology									
Sales	Given	16.44	17.21	18.01	18.85	19.74	20.68	21.30	21.94
× Royalty rate (%)	Plug-in	6.528%	5.712%	4.896%	4.080%	3.264%	2.448%	1.632%	0.816%
= Royalties saved (pre-tax)		1.07	0.98	0.88	0.77	0.64	0.51	0.35	0.18
× (1 − tax rate)	30%	0.70	0.70	0.70	0.70	0.70	0.70	0.70	0.70
= Royalties saved (after tax)		0.75	0.69	0.62	0.54	0.45	0.35	0.24	0.13
× Partial year factor		0.8667	1.0000	1.0000	1.0000	1.0000	1.0000	1.0000	1.0000
× Discount factor	8 %	0.9672	0.9002	0.8335	0.7717	0.7146	0.6616	0.6126	0.5673
= Present value of royalties saved		0.63	0.62	0.51	0.42	0.32	0.23	0.15	0.07
Present value of royalties saved between May 19, 2011 and March 31, 2019									2.96
Terminal value (assumed average useful life is eight years)									0.00
Value of definite-lived technology									2.96

TABLE 11.7 Calculation of the tax amortization benefit factor

		Year 1	Year 2	Year 3	Year 4	Year 5
Tax amortization	1/5 per year	20.00	20.00	20.00	20.00	20.00
Tax amortization benefit (TAB)	30 %	6.00	6.00	6.00	6.00	6.00
× Partial year factor		0.8667	1.0000	1.0000	1.0000	1.0000
× Discount factor	@8 %	0.9672	0.9002	0.8335	0.7717	0.7146
= Present value of TABs		5.03	5.40	5.00	4.63	4.29
Asset tax base	(a)					100
− Total value of TABs	(b)					24.35
= After-tax value	(a) − (b) = (c)					75.65
Tax amortization benefit factor	(a) / (c)					1.3219

Assembled workforce

Danisco's workforce is an intangible asset that is of significant value to DuPont. Although the international accounting rules do not allow DuPont to recognize the value of Danisco's assembled workforce as a separate line item in its postacquisition financial statements, the valuation of the workforce is relevant as an input to the valuation of customer relationships later in the purchase price allocation exercise. Purchase price allocation experts typically assume that the target firm's assembled workforce has value to an acquirer for the following reasons:

- Experienced employees are more efficient than newly hired employees. For example, in fiscal 2009/2010 Danisco had an average of 6,853 employees and spent DKK2.5 billion on salaries. Assuming that 90 percent of Danisco's employees were experienced employees and that inexperienced employees are only 80 percent as efficient as experienced employees during a period of six months, the company's experienced workforce helped it to avoid inefficiencies for an amount of DKK0.225 billion (90% × 20% × 6/12 × 2.5), or 1.6 percent of sales;

- Companies incur recruitment and training costs when hiring new employees. Assuming that the average recruitment and training costs for Danisco were DKK37 thousand (€5 thousand) per employee, having 90 percent experienced employees helped the company to avoid recruitment and training costs of DKK0.228 billion (90% × 6,853 × 37), or 1.7 percent of sales, in 2009/2010.

Under the above assumptions, the cost to replace Danisco's assembled workforce is 3.3 percent of sales. That is, using the cost method the value of the company's workforce can be estimated as a fixed percentage of its sales, as shown in Table 11.8.

Note that the valuation of Danisco's assembled workforce affects the valuation of its customer relationships in two ways. First, the growth in the annual values of the assembled workforce can be considered an investment that needs to be added back to the cash flows from customer relationships. Second, the assembled workforce is a contributory asset that helps to generate cash flows from customer relationships and therefore should give rise to contributory charges. In Table 11.8, we calculate the contributory charges under the assumption that the required return on Danisco's assembled workforce is equal to the average required return on operating assets of 8 percent.

Customer relationships

The previous steps of the purchase price allocation exercise have laid the groundwork for the valuation of Danisco's customer relationships. To value customer relationships using the multi-period excess earnings method we must first determine which proportion of Danisco's sales, operating expenses, and growth investments can be

TABLE 11.8 Estimation of the contributory asset charges for and investments in Danisco's assembled workforce

		2011/ 2012	2012/ 2013	2013/ 2014	2014/ 2015	2015/ 2016	2016/ 2017	2017/ 2018	2018/ 2019
Sales	(a)	16.44	17.21	18.01	18.85	19.74	20.68	21.30	21.94
Assembled workforce [AWF] value as a percentage of sales	(b)	3.30%	3.30%	3.30%	3.30%	3.30%	3.30%	3.30%	3.30%
Beginning AWF value	$(a)_{t-1} \times (b)_{t-1} = (c)$	0.52	0.54	0.57	0.59	0.62	0.65	0.68	0.70
Ending AWF value	$(a) \times (b) = (d)$	0.54	0.57	0.59	0.62	0.65	0.68	0.70	0.72
Investment in AWF (add back)	$(d) - (c) = (e)$	0.02	0.03	0.03	0.03	0.03	0.03	0.02	0.02
Average AWF value	$(c) + 0.5 \times (d) = (f)$	0.53	0.56	0.58	0.61	0.64	0.67	0.69	0.71
Contributory charge @ 8 percent	$0.08 \times (f) = (g)$	0.04	0.04	0.05	0.05	0.05	0.05	0.06	0.06
Contributory charge as a percentage of sales	$(g)/sales = (h)$	0.26%	0.26%	0.26%	0.26%	0.26%	0.26%	0.26%	0.26%

attributed to the company's existing customers. A common method of doing so is to (a) establish one attrition rate, being the average rate per year at which customers switch between suppliers, and (b) estimate customer relationships' remaining economic life. Because Danisco is the market leader in many of its segments, sells several highly specialized and patented products, and has invested significantly in developing close relationships with customers and creating customer loyalty, we can expect that the company's customer attrition rate is relatively low, to the tune of less than 10 percent. In Table 11.9, which details the valuation of Danisco's customer relationships, we therefore assume that Danisco's customer relationships attrite by 8.25 percent annually over a remaining economic life of 25 years. To estimate free cash flows from existing customers before contributory add backs and charges, we further assume that the company's gross profit margin, selling and administrative costs-to-sales ratio, and tax rate (for sales from existing customers) remain constant at 41.5, 17.5, and 30.0 percent, respectively. These percentages are close to the average ratios forecasted by analysts.

As a next step in calculating excess earnings we must subtract the contributory asset charges that we estimated earlier from the free cash flows from existing customers. We account for the following charges:

- Trade names royalty charges: 0.794 percent of sales from existing customers. This after-tax percentage is equivalent to a pre-tax percentage of 1.134 percent, as estimated in Table 11.5.

- Indefinite-lived technology royalty charges: 0.418 percent of sales from existing customers (or 0.597 percent before tax, as estimated in Table 11.6).

- Definite-lived technology royalty charges: 4.570 percent of sales from existing customers (or 6.528 percent before tax, as estimated in Table 11.6). This after-tax percentage is the percentage estimated for fiscal 2011/2012. We use this percentage throughout the forecasting period under the assumption that in future years Danisco will reinvest to maintain its 2011/2012 technology level.

- Returns on working capital and property, plant and equipment, calculated as the annual contributory charges (as a percentage of sales) for working capital and PP&E, taken from Table 11.4, times sales from existing customers.

- Return on the assembled workforce, calculated as the annual contributory charges (as a percentage of sales) for the assembled workforce, taken from Table 11.8, times sales from existing customers. In addition to subtracting the return, we add back the annual growth investment in the assembled workforce that is attributable to existing customers, as described earlier.

Table 11.9 displays the excess earnings from customer relationships that result after subtracting the above charges. Because the remaining economic life of Danisco's customer relationships is 25 years but we have detailed forecasts for only eight years, we must make some simplifying for the 17-year period after the terminal year 2018/2019. Specifically, we assume that excess earnings decrease at a constant rate between 2018/2019 and 2035/2036 and that excess earnings are equal to zero after 2035/2036. Under these assumptions, the terminal value is defined as:

$$\text{TV}_{\text{Customer relationships}} = \frac{(1+g) \times \text{Excess earnings}_{2018/2019}}{(1+r)^T (r-g)} - \frac{(1+g)^{18} \times \text{Excess earnings}_{2018/2019}}{(1+r)^{T+17} (r-g)}$$

where r is the required return on operating assets and g is the terminal growth rate. Given a sales growth rate of 3 percent and an attrition rate of 8.25 percent, the terminal growth rate equals −5.24 percent ([1 + 0.03] × [1 − 0.0825]).

The calculations displayed in Table 11.9 show that our estimate of the value of Danisco's customer relationships is DKK6.62 billion. This value estimate is equal to the value disclosed in DuPont's 2011 financial statements.

Goodwill

The fair value estimates derived in the previous sections help us to estimate goodwill. Goodwill is defined as the difference between the total value of Danisco and the sum of the fair values of the identifiable assets. Recall that goodwill includes the fair value of Danisco's assembled workforce because the international accounting rules on business combinations do not allow DuPont to separately recognize this asset. Table 11.10 shows that based on the above fair value estimates and Danisco's value of DKK36.75 billion the value of goodwill can be estimated at DKK9.39 billion. This value is slightly greater than the acquisition premium. The implied expected return on

TABLE 11.9 Valuation of Danisco's customer relationships

	Given	2011/2012	2012/2013	2013/2014	2014/2015	2015/2016	2016/2017	2017/2018	2018/2019
Sales	Given	16.44	17.21	18.01	18.85	19.74	20.68	21.30	21.94
End-of-year customer retention rate		92.00%	84.64%	77.87%	71.64%	65.91%	60.64%	55.78%	51.32%
Average customer retention rate		96.00%	88.32%	81.25%	74.75%	68.77%	63.27%	58.21%	53.55%
Sales from existing customers		15.79	15.20	14.63	14.09	13.58	13.08	12.40	11.75
Gross profit	41.50%	6.55	6.31	6.07	5.85	5.63	5.43	5.15	4.88
Selling and administrative costs	17.50%	−2.76	−2.66	−2.56	−2.47	−2.38	−2.29	−2.17	−2.06
Operating profit		3.79	3.65	3.51	3.38	3.26	3.14	2.98	2.82
Tax	30.00%	−1.14	−1.09	−1.05	−1.01	−0.98	−0.94	−0.89	−0.85
NOPAT		2.65	2.55	2.46	2.37	2.28	2.20	2.08	1.97
Change in operating assets		V0.39	−0.41	−0.39	−0.35	−0.34	−0.33	−0.36	−0.35
Free cash flows from existing customers before add backs/CACs		2.26	2.14	2.06	2.01	1.94	1.87	1.72	1.63
Add backs:									
Assembled workforce growth investment		0.02	0.02	0.02	0.02	0.02	0.02	0.01	0.01
Contributory asset charges:									
Return on working capital		−0.08	−0.08	−0.08	−0.07	−0.07	−0.07	−0.06	−0.06
Return on property, plant and equipment		−0.35	−0.34	−0.33	−0.31	−0.30	−0.29	−0.28	−0.27
Trade names royalties saved	0.794%	−0.13	−0.12	−0.12	−0.11	−0.11	−0.10	−0.10	−0.09
Technology royalties saved	5.099%	−0.79	−0.76	−0.73	−0.70	−0.68	−0.65	−0.62	−0.59
Return on the assembled workforce		−0.04	−0.04	−0.04	−0.04	−0.04	−0.03	−0.03	−0.03
Excess earnings		0.89	0.83	0.80	0.80	0.77	0.75	0.64	0.60
Partial year factor		0.8667	1.0000	1.0000	1.0000	1.0000	1.0000	1.0000	1.0000
Discount factor		0.9672	0.9002	0.8335	0.7717	0.7146	0.6616	0.6126	0.5673
Present value of excess earnings		0.75	0.74	0.66	0.61	0.55	0.49	0.39	0.33

Present value of excess earnings between May 19, 2011 and March 31, 2019   4.52

Terminal value   2.10

Value of trade names   6.62

TABLE 11.10 Calculation of goodwill

	Fair value	Return
Total value of Danisco (as implied by the acquisition price)	36.75	7.85%
Less: fair values of . . .		
Working capital	3.98	2.10%
Property, plant and equipment	8.60	4.20%
Other assets (including in-process R&D)[a]	0.75	8.00%
Trade names	2.92	8.00%
Indefinite-lived technology	1.54	8.00%
Definite-lived technology	2.96	8.00%
Customer relationships	6.62	8.00%
= Goodwill (including assembled workforce), net of deferred tax	9.39	13.40%
Add: Deferred taxes	5.17	
= Goodwill (as reported)	14.55	

[a] Taken from DuPont's 2011 annual financial statements.

goodwill, which can be derived from the required returns on the identifiable assets and the internal rate of return on the acquisition, equals 13.40 percent.

Note that the goodwill estimate shown in Table 11.10 is net of deferred taxes. Although the identifiable assets are revalued to their fair values for financial reporting purposes, the assets' tax bases may not change by the same amount, depending on the tax jurisdiction. If the amount of revaluation exceeds the change in the assets' tax base, this will give rise to a deferred tax liability.[17] The international accounting rules prescribe that such increase in the deferred tax liability is accompanied by an increase in goodwill of the same amount. In the example of the Danisco acquisition, DuPont recognized deferred tax liabilities for the amount of DKK5.17 billion. Consequently, the total value of goodwill equaled DKK14.55 billion (9.39 + 5.17).

SUMMARY

This chapter summarizes how financial statement data and analysis can be used by financial analysts interested in evaluating whether an acquisition creates value for an acquiring firm's shareholders. Obviously, much of this discussion is also likely to be relevant to other merger participants, including target and acquiring management and their investment banks.

For the external analyst, the first task is to identify the acquirer's acquisition strategy. We discuss a number of strategies. Some of these are consistent with maximizing acquirer value, including acquisitions to take advantage of economies of scale, improve target management, combine complementary resources, capture tax benefits, provide low-cost financing to financially constrained targets, and increase product-market rents.

Other strategies appear to benefit managers more than shareholders. For example, some unprofitable acquisitions are made because managers are reluctant to return free cash flows to shareholders, or because managers want to lower the firm's earnings volatility by diversifying into unrelated businesses.

The financial analyst's second task is to assess whether the acquirer is offering a reasonable price for the target. Even if the acquirer's strategy is based on increasing shareholder value, it can overpay for the target. Target shareholders will then be well rewarded but at the expense of acquiring shareholders. We show how the ratio, *pro forma*, and valuation techniques discussed earlier in the book can all be used to assess the worth of the target to the acquirer.

The method of financing an offer is also relevant to a financial analyst's review of an acquisition proposal. If a proposed acquisition is financed with surplus cash or new debt, it increases the acquirer's financial risk. Financial analysts can use ratio analysis of the acquirer's postacquisition balance sheet and *pro forma* estimates of cash flow volatility and interest coverage to assess whether demands by target shareholders for consideration in cash lead the acquirer to increase its risk of financial distress.

Finally, the financial analyst is interested in assessing whether a merger is likely to be completed once the initial offer is made, and at what price. This requires the analyst to determine whether there are other potential bidders, and whether target management is entrenched and likely to oppose a bidder's offer.

CORE CONCEPTS

Acquisition financing Methods of acquisition financing are through equity issues, debt issues or the use of surplus cash. The latter two methods increase net financial leverage and potentially increase distress risk. Information problems make acquirers reluctant to use equity to finance the acquisition. Different forms of payment may have different tax effects across countries.

Acquisition premium Premium offered to target shareholders. Acquisition premiums tend to be:

1 Higher for hostile than friendly takeovers.

2 Higher for cash-financed than equity-financed (share-for-share) acquisitions.

3 Higher when the target's country's takeover rules are stricter.

Entrenched target management Target management's use of takeover defense mechanisms to deter the acquisition. The use of takeover defense mechanisms may discourage acquisitions or drive up acquisition premiums.

Merger and acquisition benefits Mergers or acquisitions can create value through:

1 Increasing economies of scale.

2 Improving the target firm's management.

3 Combining complementary resources.

4 Capturing tax benefits such as operating tax losses or interest tax shields.

5 Providing a source of finance to the target.

6 Restructuring.

7 Increasing product market rents.

Purchase price allocation Allocation of the total value of a target firm, as implied by the acquisition price, to individual identifiable assets, with the primary objectives of explaining the acquisition price and calculating goodwill.

Takeover regulations Rules aimed at preventing target management entrenchment, such as the EU Takeover Directive.

Target value analysis Target value analysis includes estimating the value of a target both as an independent firm and to the potential acquirer, using earnings multiples or using discounted abnormal earnings of cash flow methods. Earnings multiple-based valuations tend to ignore the long-term effects of the acquisition.

QUESTIONS

1 Since the year 2000, there has been a noticeable increase in mergers and acquisitions between firms in different countries (termed cross-border acquisitions). What factors could explain this increase? What special issues can arise in executing a cross-border acquisition and in ultimately meeting your objectives for a successful combination?

2   Private equity firms have become an important player in the acquisition market. These private investment groups offer to buy a target firm, often with the cooperation of management, and then take the firm private. Private equity buyers tend to finance a significant portion of the acquisition with debt.

   a   What types of firms would make ideal candidates for a private equity buyout? Why?

   b   How might the acquirer add sufficient value to the target to justify a high buyout premium?

3   Kim Silverman, Finance Director of the First Public Bank, notes: "We are fortunate to have a cost of capital of only 10 percent. We want to leverage this advantage by acquiring other banks that have a higher cost of funds. I believe that we can add significant value to these banks by using our lower cost financing." Do you agree with Silverman's analysis? Why or why not?

4   The Munich Beer Company plans to acquire Liverpool Beer Co. for £60 per share, a 50 percent premium over the current market price. Jan Höppe, the Financial Director of Munich Beer, argues that this valuation can easily be justified, using a price-earnings analysis. "Munich Beer has a price-earnings ratio of 15, and we expect that we will be able to generate long-term earnings for Liverpool Beer of £5 per share. This implies that Liverpool Beer is worth £75 to us, well above our £60 offer price." Do you agree with this analysis? What are Höppe's key assumptions?

5   You have been hired by GS Investment Bank to work in the merger department. The analysis required for all potential acquisitions includes an examination of the target for any off-balance sheet assets or liabilities that have to be factored into the valuation. Prepare a checklist for your examination.

6   A target company is currently valued at €50 in the market. A potential acquirer believes that it can add value in two ways: €15 of value can be added through better working capital management, and an additional €10 of value can be generated by making available a unique technology to expand the target's new product offerings. In a competitive bidding contest, how much of this additional value will the acquirer have to pay out to the target's shareholders to emerge as the winner?

7   A leading oil exploration company decides to acquire an Internet company at a 50 percent premium. The acquirer argues that this move creates value for its own shareholders because it can use its excess cash flows from the oil business to help finance growth in the new Internet segment. Evaluate the economic merits of this claim.

8   Under current International Financial Reporting Standards, acquirers are required to capitalize goodwill and report any subsequent declines in value as an impairment charge. What performance metrics would you use to judge whether goodwill is impaired?

NOTES

1.   In a review of studies of merger returns, Michael Jensen and Richard Ruback, "The Market for Corporate Control: The Scientific Evidence," *Journal of Financial Economics* 11 (April 1983): 5–50, conclude that target shareholders earn positive returns from takeovers, but that acquiring shareholders only break even.

2.   See Steven Kaplan, "Management Buyouts: Evidence on Taxes as a Source of Value," *Journal of Finance* 44 (1989): 611–632.

3.   Krishna Palepu, "Predicting Takeover Targets: A Methodological and Empirical Analysis," *Journal of Accounting and Economics* 8 (March 1986): 3–36.

4.   Chapter 2 discusses the pros and cons of corporate diversification and evidence on its implications for firm performance.

5.   See Paul Healy, Krishna Palepu, and Richard Ruback, "Which Mergers Are Profitable – Strategic or Financial?," *Sloan Management Review* 38(4) (Summer 1997): 45–58. For empirical evidence on European target firms' cumulative stock returns around the takeover announcement, see Martina Martynova and Luc Renneboog, "Mergers and Acquisitions in Europe," Working Paper, Tilburg University, 2006. This study reports that 60 days after a hostile takeover announcement European target firms' share

prices have run up by, on average, 45 percent since 60 days prior to the announcement. In contrast, after friendly takeover announcements, share prices have run up by, on average, 10 percent. The average difference in price run up of 35 percent can be interpreted as the average difference in (expected) takeover premiums.

6. See, for example, Martina Martynova and Luc Renneboog, op. cit.

7. See Stewart Myers and Nicholas Majluf, "Corporate Financing and Investment Decisions When Firms Have Information That Investors Do Not," *Journal of Financial Economics* (June 1984): 187–221.

8. For evidence see Nicholas Travlos, "Corporate Takeover Bids, Methods of Payments, and Bidding Firms' Stock Returns," *Journal of Finance* 42 (1987): 943–963.

9. See S. Datar, R. Frankel, and M. Wolfson, "Earnouts: The Effects of Adverse Selection and Agency Costs on Acquisition Techniques," *Journal of Law, Economics, and Organization* 17 (2001): 201–238.

10. See Mara Faccio and Ronald W. Masulis, "The Choice of Payment Method in European Mergers and Acquisitions," *Journal of Finance* 60 (2005): 1345–1388.

11. See Mara Faccio and Ronald W. Masulis, op. cit.

12. In several European countries, such as in Belgium, Denmark, and Germany, individual shareholders pay no or little taxes on the capital gains that they make from selling or exchanging their shares in a takeover, provided that they have held the shares for a defined period, typically being a period of one or two years. For these shareholders the after-tax value of a takeover offer does not depend on whether they receive cash or shares as consideration.

13. See Rezaul Kabir, Dolph Cantrijn, and Andreas Jeunink, "Takeover Defenses, Ownership Structures, and Stock Returns in the Netherlands: An Empirical Analysis," *Strategic Management Journal* 18 (1997): 97–109.

14. Marc Goergen, Marina Martynova, and Luc Renneboog give a complete description of the most important rules in the EU Takeover Directive in their study "Corporate Governance Convergence: Evidence from Takeover Regulation Reforms in Europe," *Oxford Review of Economic Policy* 21 (2005): 243–268.

15. The Appraisal Foundation summarizes some of the best practices in purchase price allocations in "The Identification of Contributory Assets and Calculation of Economic Rents" (May 2010).

16. Purchase price allocation experts have debated on whether one should use the required return on operating assets or the internal rate of return on the acquisition to measure the required return on intangible assets. Some experts prefer using the internal rate of return because of the complexities surrounding the estimation of required returns on operating assets (see Chapter 8).

17. See Chapter 4 for a discussion of deferred taxes.

PPR – PUMA: A successful acquisition?

"I am delighted to have reached an agreement with Mayfair supported by PUMA which creates the basis for a combined future for our two Groups. This friendly transaction represents an exciting development for PPR and a milestone in our strategy of profitable growth. I am confident that PPR is the ideal partner to support PUMA in its current development phase to become a global iconic sport-lifestyle company."

François-Henri Pinault, Chairman and CEO, PPR Group

"As we continue the execution of our Phase IV strategy, we are convinced that PPR's proposal is a unique opportunity to get additional long term support to achieve our global targets and our mission to become the most desirable sport-lifestyle company in the world. My colleagues and I have carefully considered this proposal by PPR and subject to review of the offer document we will recommend it to our shareholders. We strongly believe that this friendly transaction is in the best interests of the company and that the offer price is fair to all PUMA shareholders."

Jochen Zeitz, Chairman and CEO, PUMA

Merger overview

On April 10th 2007 PPR announced a tender offer to purchase the remaining 73 percent of the Puma shares, after a friendly agreement with Mayfair, major Puma shareholder, to purchase its 27.1 percent stake. The offer price for both the stake purchase and the tender offer was €330, with a premium of 15.8 percent (ex-dividend) to the closing price on April 4th, the day before press speculation on an offer emerged. The €330 offer was also at the upper end of the 12 month trading range of €256–€333. According to the numbers provided by the companies in their press release,[1] the implied multiples of the offer price were equal to 12.2 × 2006EBITDA and 13.4 × 2006EBIT.

The acquisition was finalized in July with a total 62.1 percent acceptance by Puma shareholders. The acquisition was considered from a huge part of the financial arena to be "not compliant" with the PPR strategy, given that PPR was believed to position itself in the luxury market. The top management of the two companies strongly supported the view that the deal was based on a sound strategic rationale and that the synergies derived from the acquisition might explain the surprising fit between Puma and PPR.

The financial market reaction to the announcement of the deal has been extremely positive, as illustrated in **Exhibit 1** and **Exhibit 2**. Puma share price rose from €278.04 to €350.10 (+25 percent) in the three days following the deal announcement. Also PPR share prices seemed to reflect a positive valuation of the deal, rising from 128.94 to 133.03 (+3 percent) in the first three days following the announcement and gaining +20 percent in the two following months.

This case is based on real facts and data. Every valuation or judgment on the company's business policy and financial condition is a personal opinion of the authors, as resulting from interpretation and analysis of publicly available information. The authors, Massimo Buongiorno and Barbara Rovetta, gratefully acknowledge the help of Jimena Cisneros in the preparation of the earlier versions of this case.

ECCH for the case study "PPR – PUMA: A Successful Acquisition" by Massimo Buongiorno and Barbara Rovetta, October 2009. Printed with permission from SDA Bocconi and www.ecch.com

[1] "PPR & Puma. The Perfect Match" Company Presentation, April 10th 2007.

EXHIBIT 1   **Puma share price performance**

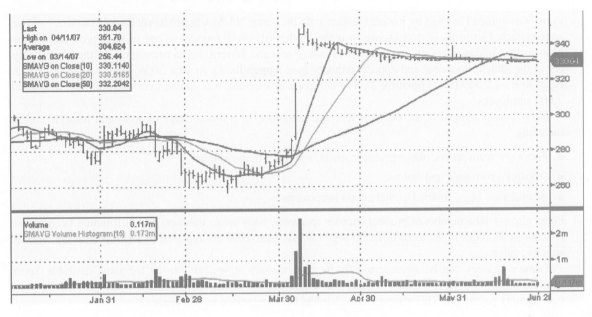

Source: Bloomberg

EXHIBIT 2   **PPR share price performance**

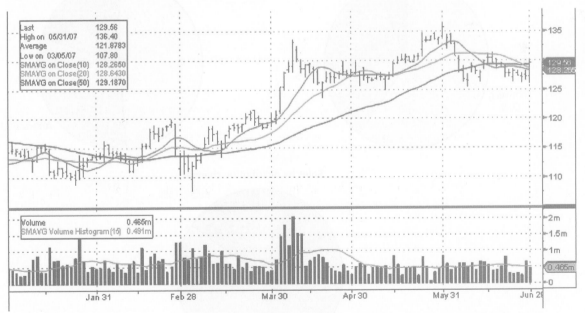

Source: Bloomberg

The target company: PUMA

Puma was founded in 1948 by Rudolf Dassler, with the name "PUMA Schuhfabrik Rudolf Dassler," in Herzogenaurach, Germany. Rudolf Dassler was the brother of Adolf, founder of one of its biggest competitors historically, Adidas. Through two different brands, Puma and Tretorn, Puma became one of the biggest players in the athletic footwear and apparel industry (see **Appendix 1**). In year 2006, consolidated sales were equal to € ml 2.369 (see **Appendix 2**). The company distribution was spread over 80 countries, with about 7,800 employees.

PUMA was engaged in the development and marketing of a broad range of sport and lifestyle articles including:

■ Footwear: team sports, running, motor sports, and other training shoes

■ Apparel: sportswear and fashion

■ Accessories: bags, footballs, other sports accessories

Puma also issued a number of product licenses (perfume, body wear, watches) and distribution licenses (not consolidated). Sales in the three different segments for year 2006 are reported in **Exhibit 3**, along with the split by region.

Puma's strategy can be summarized by its own mission statement: "to be the most desirable Sport-lifestyle Company." In 2006, the company was aware that the restructuring process of the previous 10 years was strongly paying off. This restructuring plan had been organized in four phases.

EXHIBIT 3   **Sales by region, by segment and by distribution channel (2006)**

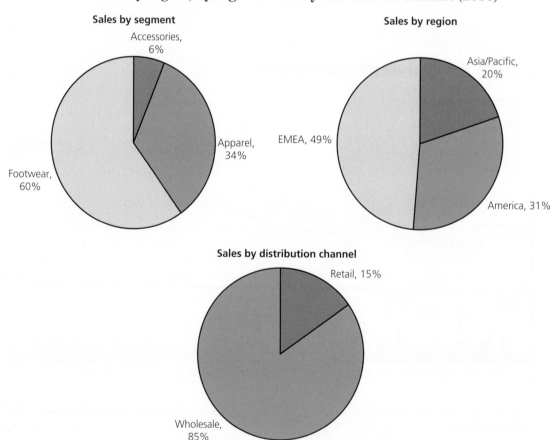

Source: Company Annual Report

- ***Phase I*** began in year 1993, after serious financial troubles. The objective was to restructure the company from a financial point of view. One of the main actions implemented by the executives moved production activity into low-cost geographical markets, such as South-Eastern Asia and Eastern Europe.

- ***Phase II*** began in 1997 and focused on improving the company's Brand Equity, especially through prestigious sponsorships and testimonials. This, combined with a major strategic partnership and the acquisition of the Swedish brand Tretorn helped the company to achieve its objective.

- ***Phase III*** started in year 2002 and aimed at strengthening the Puma brand together with maximizing company profitability. In this period, the company experienced a major expansion moment, with double digit growth in sales and a significant increase in margins. In year 2005, the German holding Mayfair Wealth Management brought its shareholdings up to 25 percent of the total equity.

- In January 2006, Puma's management started implementing *Phase IV* of its strategy, a five-year plan for the years 2006–2010. Their goal was to "position itself as one of the few true multi-category brands making effective use of the many opportunities offered by the Sport-lifestyle market in all categories and regions." Being a multi-category brand, Puma aimed at filling those categories and business segments able to offer the possibility of achieving sustained value increases through utilization of its unique brand positioning. To do that, the company was planning significant investments in supporting the brand, particularly within marketing, sales (including its own retail), product development and design.

As shown in **Exhibit 4**, the company has experienced a very strong growth since 1993.

To achieve the objectives of the IV Phase of the restructuring plan, the company needed to work on three main areas:

EXHIBIT 4   Puma historical performance

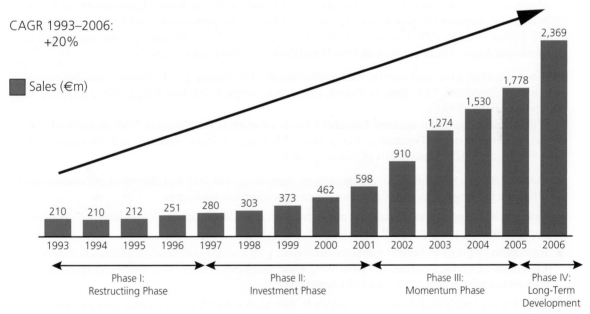

Source: Company Presentation, April 10th, 2007.

- ***Expansion of product categories:*** the company wanted to launch new products and new product lines with the objective of covering all the segments of the Sport-lifestyle market (both sports and casual lines and fashion lines). To achieve this objective the company planned to create new product categories, such as Golf apparel, Denim, and Motorsport apparel and accessories, and was also considering selected licensing agreements (especially in US and Asian markets). In addition, the company focused on developing country specific design-based skills and competences, and on cooperating with internationally renowned fashion designers (such as Alexander McQueen).

- **Regional expansion:** one of Puma's main goals was strengthening its international presence mainly by increasing the number of DOS (the company was operating about 100 retail stores). In stable and mature markets, these stores have been able to help the company become extremely market responsive and constantly align its offerings with new trends and market momentum. In addition, this choice was able to significantly help in strengthening and protecting the brand. Through the international retail expansion and the vertical integration, the company aimed to significantly increase the average weight of retail distribution upon the total consolidated revenues. In 2006, 85 percent of the company sales were realized through wholesale distribution and the company was planning a progressive reduction of the number of concessions to limit the role of strong footwear retailers, such as Footlocker.

- **Non-Puma brand expansion:** in 2006, the company had no plans for additional acquisitions but industry analysts were not excluding the opportunity for this to change at any time.

In addition, Puma aimed at achieving a more flexible network of suppliers, looking for new contractual agreements with a larger suppliers' base and developing relationships based on a new strategic approach towards supplying. As the raw materials and work in progress impacted significantly on the total production cost, the company was working to minimize its level of dependency on a small set of suppliers – this would also achieve economic advantages.

The bidder company: PPR

"An adventure of enterprise

  Above all, PPR is the incarnation of a state of mind: the desire and willingness to display entrepreneurship. With boldness and a sense of risk, PPR invests and commits itself to its various businesses, always directed at the same goal: to grow its activities and become the leader. It imposes on each of its brands and companies its own demanding culture of growth and performance. With revenues of nearly €18 billion in 2006, PPR is a world leader in two different, but complementary universes: Luxury Goods and Retail. The diversity of its brands and businesses drives its success."[2]

PPR was a luxury goods and general retail conglomerate. The Luxury goods division included numerous brands including Gucci, YSL, Bottega Veneta, Boucheron, Sergio Rossi, Balenciaga, Alex McQueen, Stella McCartney, and Bedat&Co.

  Within Retail, the group operated household goods superstores (Conforama), Multimedia/Books stores (Fnac), department stores (Printemps), a large Home Shopping business (Redcats), and wholesaling operations in Africa (CFAO). More details of this are given below:

- Conforama was a major player in European home furnishing, operating as a discounter and multispecialist offering a full range of furniture, decorative items, and electrical appliances.

- Fnac was a leading retailer of "cultural and technological products" operating in Europe with bookstores, music stores and a very powerful and widely known website.

- Redcats was a player in fashion and home decoration with a wide portfolio of prestigious brands (such as La Redoute, Cyrillus, Avenue, The Gold Warehouse, and others), effectively combining speciality stores with an extensive use of catalogues and internet sites.

- CFAO was a specialized distributor in Africa in four main industries: automobile, pharmaceutical, technologies, and consumer products.

Established in 1963 by François Pinault in the timber and building material businesses, in the mid 1990s the PPR group positioned itself in the Retail business, soon becoming one of its main players. The purchase of a controlling stake in Gucci Group in 1999 and the establishment of a multi-brand Luxury Goods group marked a new stage in the development of the Group. In 2006, the company continued to expand its activities in high-growth markets through powerful and recognized brands. The company stated itself to be driven by the objective of maximizing sustainable growth and continuing to expand internationally in a spirit of "achievement and creativity."

---

[2]Source: PPR Annual Report, 2006

EXHIBIT 5　**Evolution of PPR as a listed company – from timber trading to manager of global brands**

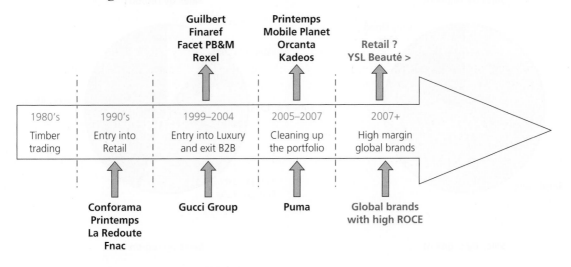

Source: Deutsche Bank, Equity Report, August 2007

Exhibit 5 shows how PPR has evolved over the past twenty years. There are five distinct "chapters" to its history:

1　1980s – A predominantly timber trading and business-to-business (B2B) operator

2　1990s – Entry into the Retail sector starting with the purchase of Conforama

3　1999–2004 – Entry into the Luxury Goods sector and the exit of B2B operations

4　2005–2007 – Disposal of non-core Retail activities and purchase of Puma

5　2007 on – Focus on managing global brands

In 2006, the consolidated sales of the group were close to € ml 18.000 (see **Appendix 4**). With approximately 78,000 employees in 75 countries, PPR was considered a truly global player (see **Exhibit 6**). According to the top management, Gucci Group gave PPR a global presence in high-growth markets. On the other hand, the Retail companies were major players in stable and mature consumer markets. By combining both universes, PPR achieved a special balance in terms of products, sales formats, brands and geographic locations, driving higher-than-average growth in international markets.

As shown in **Exhibit 5**, PPR has dramatically changed its portfolio structure in the last ten years. The company pursued a strategy based on building a portfolio of brands with global opportunities, high margins and high return on capital. **Exhibit 7** shows the average improvement in EBIT margin that occurred between 1998 and 2002 thanks to acquisitions and disposals of businesses.

The Group always considered its size a major competitive advantage: because of the size and diversity of its activities, the company had no single proper competitor. The company explained the choice to combine Luxury Goods and Retail with the belief that both these two businesses base their success on brand management, customer service quality, and control of distribution.

The luxury goods business unit

Each of the brands included in this business unit has been acquired by the company over time.

Gucci Group has consolidated its positions and developed in all regions where its brands were present, in particular in those regions where the growth potential was showing the most promise, such as China, India, and Russia. Management of brands and brand image were tightly controlled through the group distribution network.

PPR – PUMA: A successful acquisition?

EXHIBIT 6   Sales by region and by segment (2005 and 2006)

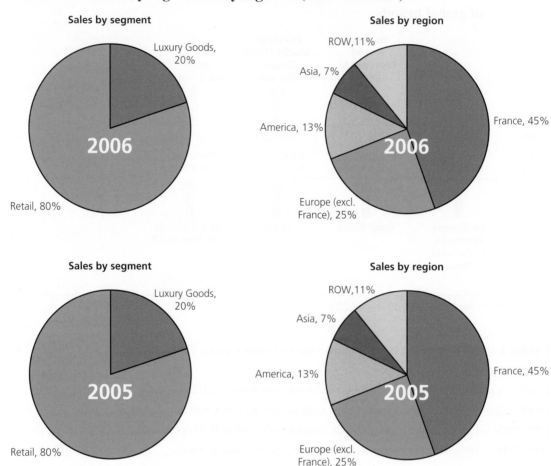

Source: Company Annual Report

EXHIBIT 7   PPR – Portfolio diversification and EBIT margin (1998–2002)

	1998	2002
B2B weight on cons. sales	53%	50%
Retail weight on cons. sales	47%	33%
Luxury weight on cons. sales	0%	17%
PPR – Ebit Margin	**5.52%**	**6.67%**

Source: Company Annual Report

The carefully controlled development of an integrated distribution network with a sound geographical basis has been a key strategic focus for Gucci Group. Fashion goods and accessories were primarily sold in directly-operated stores, designed according to a specific concept for each brand, ensuring consistency in terms of product display and service quality around the world. In 2006, the 454 directly operated stores generated 55 percent of Gucci Group revenue. Gucci Group's products were also distributed through selected exclusive franchise stores, duty-free boutiques, department, and specialty stores.

Founded in 1921, the Gucci brand celebrated its 85th anniversary during 2006, further enhancing its reputation as a world leader in fashion and luxury goods. As Gucci Group's flagship brand, Gucci was one of the most prominent and profitable brands in the luxury sector, with a focus on manufacturing and selling leather goods (handbags, small leather goods, and luggage), shoes, ready-to-wear, ties and scarves, timepieces, and jewellery. Moreover, Gucci was able to grant licenses for the production and distribution of eyewear and fragrances by global industry leaders for these categories. The products were sold exclusively through directly-operated stores and exclusive Gucci franchise stores, department stores and specialty stores around the world.

Gucci group acquired Bottega Veneta (66.7 percent stake, increased to 82.28 percent by 2006) in 2001 for an estimated €156mn and turned it into the second most successful brand in the portfolio. Created in 1966 and acclaimed for the superior quality of its products and its "discreet elegance," Bottega Veneta was positioned at the high end of the luxury spectrum.

At the time of the acquisition, Bottega had sales of €58mn and a 7 percent margin, but with a very different mix. Wholesale accounted for 59 percent of sales. To take control of its distribution, Bottega ramped up its store-opening program, culminating in a loss of €18mn in 2003 following a tripling of its store base to 61. By 2006, Bottega Veneta achieved excellent returns and the brand started to become a real star in the portfolio.

PPR bought YSL via the Gucci group as part of the US$1.2bn Sanofi deal at the end of 1999. It was bought on a vision and proved to be the most costly acquisition for the Gucci group. Although the brand was good and with great history (it was a mythical brand of the late 20th century), known globally and with high potential, it had been damaged by years of over-licensing and product proliferation, similar to what happened to Gucci. PPR and Gucci believed that with the help of star designer Tom Ford, the Gucci group could establish YSL as a premier luxury business, the same way management had turned around Gucci in the early 1990s. Management and analysts believed that YSL could become "a €1bn business and achieve margins of 15–20 percent" with a breakeven point set at €300–350mn to be achieved in 2004–05. In 2005, after investing a total of €416mn, YSL struggled to sell more than €162mn (half of what it needed to breakeven) and was losing €66mn.

Not one of the many – and very costly – actions (involving the acquisition of most of the brand's key strategic licenses, taking control of distribution by building a global network of DOS in all the major key markets and repositioning the brand from a stylistic standpoint) made by the new owners helped in turning the brand profitable.

No matter what, the brand kept performing poorly, with weak wholesale sales and low sales densities at DOS, both symptoms of the lack of commercial success and the failure to translate its brand heritage into best-selling products. Similarly, in 2006, the other brands of the group were still struggling to positively contribute to the Luxury Goods business operating margin (see **Exhibit 8**). This evidence shows how PPR used its multi-brand strategy to enter into non-core businesses. However, the company actually chose to capitalize on the star brand in its portfolio, in line with what is done by LVMH with the Louis Vuitton brand.

The expectations from the deal

"External growth may offer excellent opportunities to accelerate PPR's development towards more international higher-margin businesses generating significant cash flow. Puma fits this description and is consistent with our strategic criteria. It is clearly a leading brand in its category. This status provides it with global visibility, an exceptional growth profile and strong margins."

Francois – Henri Pinault, Chairman & CEO, PPR (Conference Call – 10 April 2007)

At the time of the acquisition, the bidding company was well aware of the major changes that the integration of Puma within PPR's portfolio would cause (see **Exhibit 9**). As a matter of fact, PPR would benefit from the high sales growth rates of the target company, and would also achieve a broader geographic diversification (see **Exhibit 10**). The analysis of the *pro-forma* key figures also suggested that the deal would be accretive for margins and cash flow generation capacity (see **Exhibit 11**).

When the Puma deal was announced to the markets, many people argued that this could not be considered a perfectly integrated acquisition in the PPR long-term strategy. That is because, after the dismissal of some non-core Retail activities (i.e., MobilePlanet, Orcanta) during 2005–2006, PPR was seen by financial practitioners and analysts as pursuing a strategy to become a Luxury company.

EXHIBIT 8   **Gucci Group – Sales and EBIT margin by brand (2004–2006)**

	Sales (ml €)			% of total sales		
Brand	**2004**	**2005**	**2006**	**2004**	**2005**	**2006**
Gucci	1,590	1,807	2,101	59%	60%	59%
Bottega Veneta	100	160	267	4%	5%	7%
Yves Saint Laurent	169	162	194	6%	5%	5%
Other brands	232	294	380	9%	10%	11%
YSL Beaute	619	611	626	23%	20%	18%
Total	2,710	3,034	3,568			

	EBIT (ml €)			% of total EBIT		
Brand	**2004**	**2005**	**2006**	**2004**	**2005**	**2006**
Gucci	423	485	612	145.4%	123.7%	108.3%
% on sales	*27%*	*27%*	*29%*			
Bottega Veneta	7	14	55	−2.4%	3.6%	9.7%
% on sales	*−7%*	*9%*	*21%*			
Yves Saint Laurent	71	66	49	−24.4%	−16.8%	−8.7%
% on sales	*−42%*	*−41%*	*−25%*			
Other brands	80	59	85	−27.5%	−15.1%	−15.0%
% on sales	*−34%*	*−20%*	*−22%*			
YSL Beaute	26	18	32	8.9%	4.6%	57%
% on sales	*4%*	*3%*	*5%*			
Total	291	392	565			
	11%	*13%*	*16%*			

Source: Company Annual Report

EXHIBIT 9   **Puma and PPR together**

Pro-forma Key Figures (2006)	PPR	Puma	Combined
Net sales	17,948	2,369	**20,317**
EBITDA	1,630	405	**2,035**
% margin	*9.1%*	*17.1%*	***10.0%***
EBIT	1,275	366	**1,641**
% margin	*7.1%*	*15.4%*	***8.1%***
Employees	78,453	7,742	**86,195**

Source: Based on Company Annual Reports

However, some investment banks provided reassuring recommendations on the deal and expressed very positive valuations on the target company:

> *"Lots of opportunities*
> *Our Puma analysts have a Buy recommendation and €380 price target on Puma. They see it as an attractively valued growth company (it now trades at €314.25) with average earnings growth of 15 percent between 2006–09E. This should be driven by market share gains in new regions, strong apparel growth and expansion into new product categories."*
> *(Deutsche Bank, Equity Report, April 10th 2007)*

EXHIBIT 10 **Puma and PPR together: sales growth and breakdown**

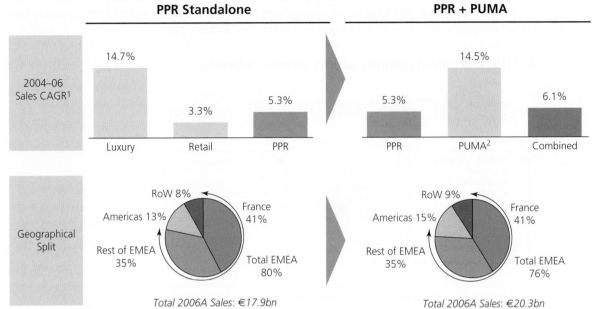

^{1}PPR 2004 sales adjusted for the reporting period of Gucci
^{2}PUMA's 2006 sales on a like for like basis (12.9 percent growth vs. 2005 excluding regional expansion)

Source: "PPR & Puma. The Perfect Match," Company Presentation, April 10th, 2007

EXHIBIT 11 **Puma and PPR together: margins and cash flows**

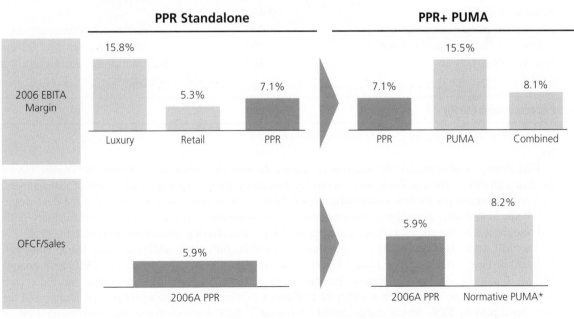

Source: "PPR & Puma. The Perfect Match," Company Presentation, April 10th, 2007

According to the analysts covering Puma stocks, in 2006 Puma's next steps to achieve could be summarized as follows: (i) the acquisition of important licenses (such as China, Japan apparel, and Argentina); (ii) the foundation of new operations in Dubai to get a bridgehead for Africa and India; and (iii) the expansion into new product categories, such as golf, denim, and motorsport (see **Exhibit 12**).

EXHIBIT 12 **Puma multi-category product offering**

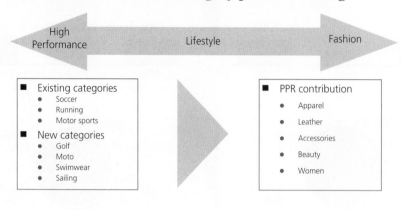

Source: "PPR & Puma. The Perfect Match," Company Presentation, April 10th, 2007

On the basis of these expected next strategic moves, analysts' consensus was aligned on the achievement of €4 billion turnover by 2010, as shown in **Exhibit 13**. This assumption was the main driver in building up the projections for the company on a ten year time horizon (see **Appendix 5** for detailed projections).

EXHIBIT 13 **Puma's revenue potential (2006–2010)**

	€ ml	Notes
Actual sales (2006)	2.400	
Sales by new product categories	400	*i.e., golf, denim, motorsport, etc.*
Expansions in new geographical markets	900	*i.e., Asia and US*
Growth of other brands	300	*both from Treton and future acquisitions*
Expected sales (2010)	**4.000**	

Source: Authors' calculation based on equity analysts consensus

PPR management explained the decision to acquire the sport-life brand as supporting the consistency of the deal with PPR's strategy. Puma was a company with an excellent long-term track record of management, with solid financial results and a successful growth history. In addition, they believed that the deal would help Puma in its further development process thanks to the opportunity to access PPR's complementary skills and resources. Last but not least, Puma's management team was offering unanimous support to the deal.

The deal would be financed by existing financial facilities plus some additional bank loans. However, Standard & Poor's rating agency placed its corporate credit ratings on PPR on watch. S&P credit analyst Nicolas Baudouin said in a statement that the rating reflected "uncertainties regarding the bid's cash impact, which in turn depends on whether all of Puma's existing shareholders pledge their shares, and the final price paid by PPR, which could exceed €5 billion."[3] S&P also pointed to the benefits for PPR of buying Puma. "Acquiring Puma would provide PPR with an international brand carrying strong worldwide

[3]Source: "PPR launches friendly takeover offer for Puma", *International Herald Tribune*, April 10th 2007

recognition, as well as diversification into the sportswear industry, which enjoys strong growth prospects," the agency said.

According to the PPR management, the changing consumer behavior would drive an accelerating convergence between fast fashion, sports, and lifestyle. It was a common belief in the fashion and luxury business that the boundaries between traditional categories (high-street, fast fashion, sports, premium, and luxury) were in fact getting blurry and that in this scenario there would be new room for trading up and down. **Exhibit 14** shows the company view of the target company positioning after the merge.

EXHIBIT 14   **Puma within PPR**

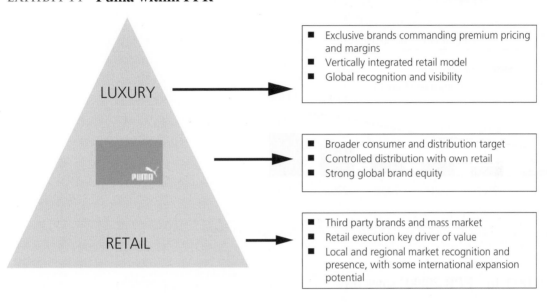

Source: "PPR & Puma. The Perfect Match," Company Presentation, April 10th, 2007

Among its peers, Puma was the company with the most evident design and fashion orientation in its DNA. Several designers in the PPR portfolio, such as Stella McCartney and Alexander McQueen, were already involved in the athletic footwear industry.

On a different note, the branded consumer market was becoming increasingly global, with winning brands transcending borders, cultures, and trends. As a consequence, global brand awareness was drawing upon international symbols, icon products, and store concepts, thus transforming retail distribution into a key success factor for a growing number of companies.[4] On the basis of this belief, the bidding company also declared that Puma's retail capabilities would be significantly expanded thanks to the acquisition. PPR was planning to support concept store roll-out, strengthen wholesale business through the optimization of the relationship with key accounts, and finally enhance e-commerce thanks to its strong expertise in logistic, inventory management, data collection, and consumer interface. In this way, PPR was expecting to further increase the weight of retail sales over the total consolidated revenues of Puma (see **Exhibit 15**).

On average, financial analysts and institutions expressed a positive valuation of the transaction. In particular, many sources claimed that the acquisition of Puma would be in line with PPR's choice to remain committed to its retail activities, grounded on the defensiveness of this structure compared to being a pure-play luxury player. **Exhibits 16 and 17** show what PPR would have looked like in terms of sales and operating profit mix by 2008.

On a longer time horizon, the benefits in terms of contribution to the EBIT margin of the group were expected to be even higher (see **Exhibit 18**).

[4]For additional details on this aspect, see "Fashion and Luxury Insight" (2007)

PPR – PUMA: A successful acquisition?

EXHIBIT 15 **Puma retail capabilities over time**

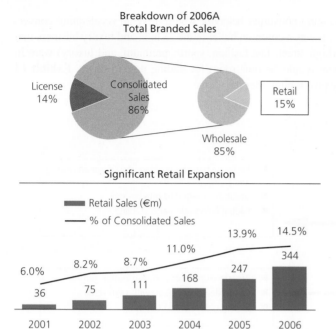

Source: "PPR & Puma. The Perfect Match," Company Presentation, April 10th, 2007

EXHIBIT 16 **PPR 2008E sales mix**

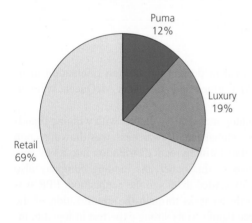

Source: Deutsche Bank, Equity Report, August 2007

Real or imaginary synergies?

The day the acquisition was announced, PPR issued a note with the following comments:

> "*PPR's strategy is based on achieving superior growth through a focus on international expansion, global brands and retail operations. The ambition is to strengthen PPR's portfolio with higher growth and higher margin businesses and the PUMA transaction is entirely consistent with these strategic priorities.*
>
> *PUMA is a leading company in the sport-lifestyle market with a strong international presence and an attractive financial profile. The PUMA brand is product driven, consumer focused with a high*

EXHIBIT 17 PPR 2008E EBIT (Excuding potential synergies)

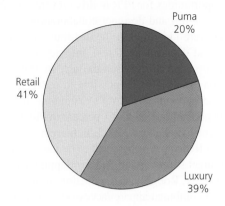

EXHIBIT 18 Group EBIT margin development including and excluding Puma

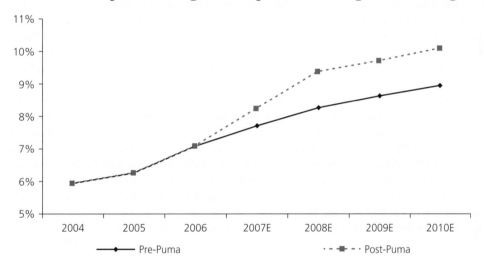

Source: Deutsche Bank, Equity Report, August 2007

global recognition, and therefore fits perfectly within PPR's global brand portfolio. PUMA's historical performance has been driven by a highly-skilled management and PPR believes that this team will find additional resources within the PPR group, in particular to (…) access PPR's in-house design and sourcing skills to expand high end product lines and benefit from PPR's experience in managing multiple brands while maximizing the value of each individual brand."[5]

PPR was perfectly aware that changing consumer behaviour was driving an accelerating convergence between fast fashion, sports, and lifestyle. In this regard, they were seeing the trend towards more fashion and lifestyle products as a key driver of out-performance for Puma versus its competitors. According to the financial analysts' opinion, within increasingly global branded consumer markets, a winning brand such as Puma could easily transcend borders, cultures, and trends. As global brand awareness draws upon international symbols, icon products, and store concepts, Puma could also benefit from PPR's expertise in dealing with these issues.

As usually happens in acquisitions, the most interesting synergies were expected on the top-line. However, revenue synergies are always the most difficult to quantify. PPR was believed to be capable of

[5]Source: PPR, Press Release, April 10th 2007

accelerating gains in the US and Asia, where the company had strong visibility and deep local knowledge. At first analysis, analysts claimed that the main opportunities for PPR to drive revenue synergies would be in luxury footwear (such as the Alexander McQueen tie-up) and designer collaborations (especially in apparel and accessories). In addition, major opportunities were identified in the distribution area, through access to higher quality US wholesale accounts (i.e., high-end department stores), internet retailing (where Redcats' strength could help Puma to improve its poor results) and distribution through Redcats catalogues. Finally, some sources claimed that geographical expansion would also be possible in relatively new countries, for example in Africa, thanks to the cooperation and support of CFAO's. Summing up, analysts agreed in assuming that, on a conservative basis, PPR could add an incremental 3 percent to Puma's top-line over three years. This would mean about €16 million incremental Ebit at the 2006 Ebit margin.

On the costs side, the combination of Puma and Redcats was believed to be the major source of potential synergies, as the two companies massively used direct sourcing and had overlapping experience in sourcing regions, such as China, India, Bangladesh, and Turkey. Roughly, the reduction in this overlap was believed to bring to the group savings of around 1 percent of combined apparel/accessories cost of goods sold.

In addition, one of the main points of discussion in the presentation to the market on April 10th, 2007 was that, according to the company's executives, Puma could exploit the strong expertise in leather goods manufacturing deriving from leaders in the sector like Gucci and Bottega Veneta, especially for its high-end lines (Black station, Platinum, 24hours, etc). Furthermore, they were confident that, in some cases, the purchasing power for good quality leather might be increase substantially by combining the demand of different companies inside the PPR group.[6] In addition, they also seemed to strongly believe that many PPR luxury brands could achieve additional synergies in specific sport shoes components, such as rubber soles (in particular Gucci's sneakers). Unfortunately, this saving opportunity was considered extremely difficult to quantify.

Last but not least, some possible savings were expected at the head office / corporate level and in logistics. Although most of the head office at the acquired companies tended to remain untouched in the fashion and luxury world, removal of some duplications was expected (especially in the supporting functions such as accounting and legal). At the same time, PPR was expected to achieve considerable benefits from the renegotiation of its global UPS contract. This carrier was used both by PPR and Puma long before the acquisition took place.[7] On the basis of previous PPR experience in the acquisition of Sportsman's Guide,[8] the equity analysts were assuming that the savings in this area could be equal to at least €16 million a year, including some potential benefits in warehousing and freight costs.

On the basis of this information, the synergies expected by the major investment banks rating PPR stocks could be prudentially quantified at about €56 million by the end of year 2010 (see **Exhibit 19**).

EXHIBIT 19 **PPR and Puma synergies forecast (2008–2010)**

Synergy totals	2007	2008	2009	2010
Revenue synergies:	0	27	61	102
– EBIT	0	4	10	16
Cost synergies:				
– Head office / corporate	0	5	5	5
– Buying	0	8	13	19
– Logistics	0	16	16	16
Cumulative total	**0**	**34**	**44**	**56**

Source: Deutsche Bank, Equity Report, August 2007

[6]This was an area of significant gain in Adidas' acquisition of Reebok.

[7]Puma outsources almost all of its logistics requirements to UPS.

[8]After the acquisition of Sportsman's Guide in 2006 (about 0.1 × the size of Puma), PPR yielded benefits of about €6 million thanks to merging logistics requirements

The valuation of the deal

Directly after the announcement of the deal, the equity analysts covering the two stocks started to dig into the available information and press releases to better understand what was going on between the two players.

Was the PPR management right to offer €330 per Puma share? At a first glance, numbers suggested different views depending on the valuation methodology used (DCF, Comparable Companies Multiples, and Precedent Transactions Multiples).

The common sentiment on the market was that Puma expected to achieve some important synergies from the deal. Was this assumption reasonable and were the synergies actually going to have a substantial impact on the aggregated entity?

Annexes

Appendix 1
Strategic Overview of the Athletic Footwear and Apparel Industry

The global athletic footwear and apparel market was a huge market (€61 billion at the end of 2005), with a global CAGR of 8.7 percent between 2003 and 2005 (6.2 percent CAGR for athletic footwear and 14.4 percent for apparel). In terms of players in the market, the footwear and the apparel market were very different. The former was very concentrated, with Nike and Adidas being the major players (with Nike controlling 37 percent of the market share and Adidas 22 percent), while the latter was very fragmented, with Nike and Adidas still in a leading market position (both containing a 9 percent market share). Exhibit 1.1 reports the 2005 global market share for both markets in more detail.

At that time, the market growth was boosted by the impressive success of the premium branded segment that met two new customers' needs and trends: latest technologies and fashion oriented products. The latest

EXHIBIT 1.1   **2005 Global market share**

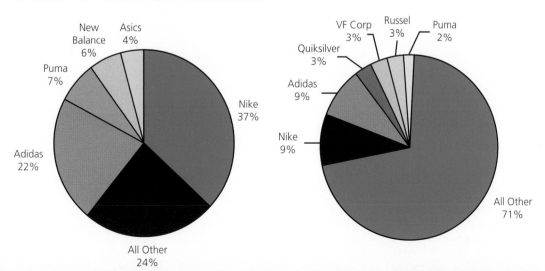

PPR – PUMA: A successful acquisition?

EXHIBIT 1.2 **Proliferation of directly-owned stores (2002–2006)**

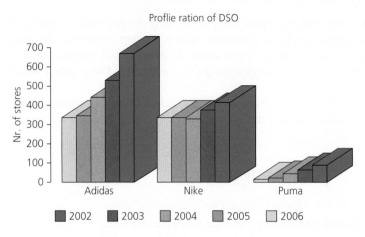

Proflie ration of DSO

technologies met the requirements of the specialists, more and more oriented toward high performances, while the fashion oriented products have been in line with the convergence of fashion and design within the sport segment (cross-over between fashion and function).

Among the players, Nike has been more oriented towards the "specialists" segment, Puma has been more active in the fashion sector (i.e., Yohji Yamamoto's at the ManCat footwear line by Puma; cooperation between Puma and Alexander McQueen, launched in Spring 2006; yoga clothes line designed by Christy Turlington for Puma), and Adidas has diversified its business in both segments (i.e., agreement with Stella McCartney for special items).

Regarding this last trend, the athletic apparel and footwear industry are not alone in trying to move towards the fashion industry, it is also happening the other way around. Many luxury brands started positioning themselves in this new market niche (i.e., Prada Sport and Polo Sport) and some others have added to their catalogues products for this new segment (i.e., sneakers). The industry was also increasingly shifting towards direct distribution. As shown in Exhibit 1.2, the leading brands opened a large number of Directly Operated Stores (DOS) in 2002–2005. As such, the specialty retail stores have been negatively impacted. Footlocker remained the biggest athletic specialty retailer with approximately 15 percent of the market share, although with a very significant dependency on Nike (that represented 49 percent of Foot Locker's purchases at the end of 2005).

Appendix 2
Puma historical income statements & selected key financial data

Sales	2001	%	2002	%	2003	%	2004	%	2005	%	2006	%	*CAGR*
€ million													
Sales by product													
Footwear	384.1	64.2	613.0	67.4	859.3	67.4	1011.4	66.1	1175.0	66.1	1420.0	59.9	**30%**
Apparel	169.5	28.3	238.5	26.2	337.0	26.5	416.0	27.2	473.9	26.7	795.4	33.6	**36%**
Accessories	44.5	7.4	58.3	6.4	77.7	6.1	102.9	6.7	128.6	7.2	153.8	6.5	**28%**
Total Net Sales	**598.1**	**100**	**909.8**	**100**	**1274.0**	**100**	**1530.3**	**100**	**1777.5**	**100**	**2369.2**	**100**	**32%**
Y-o-Y growth	*N/A*		*52.1%*		*40.0%*		*20.1%*		*16.2%*		*33.3%*		
Sales by channel													
Licensee	413.6		470.2		417.5		486.2		610.0		385.9		
Puma Group	598.1		909.8		1274.0		1530.3		1777.5		2369.2		
Total Worldwide Sales	**1011.7**		**1380.0**		**1691.5**		**2016.5**		**2387.5**		**2755.1**		
Sales by region													
EMEA	275.1		464.0		881.5		1047.0		1104.9		1158.7		
Americas	107.7		154.7		255.0		302.3		476.3		724.1		
Asia / Pacific	215.3		291.1		137.5		181.0		196.3		486.5		
Total Sales	**598.1**		**909.8**		**1274.0**		**1530.3**		**1777.5**		**2369.3**		
Net Sales	**598.1**		**909.8**		**1274.0**		**1530.3**		**1777.5**		**2369.2**		**32%**
Y-o-Y growth	*N/A*		*52.1%*		*40.0%*		*20.1%*		*16.2%*		*33.3%*		
EBITDA	**67.4**		**137.5**		**283.3**		**384.2**		**421.9**		**404.5**		**43%**
EBITDA %	*11.3%*		*15.1%*		*22.2%*		*25.1%*		*23.7%*		*17.1%*		
EBIT	**59.0**		**125.0**		**263.2**		**359.0**		**397.7**		**366.2**		**44%**
EBIT%	*9.9%*		*13.7%*		*20.7%*		*23.5%*		*22.4%*		*15.5%*		
PBT	**57.4**		**124.4**		**264.1**		**364.7**		**404.1**		**374.0**		**45%**
PBT%	*9.6%*		*13.7%*		*20.7%*		*23.8%*		*22.7%*		*15.8%*		
Net Income	**39.7**		**84.9**		**179.3**		**258.7**		**285.8**		**263.2**		**46%**
Net income %	*6.6%*		*9.3%*		*14.1%*		*16.9%*		*16.1%*		*11.1%*		
Earnings per share [euro]	2.58		5.44		11.26		16.14		17.79		16.39		
Shareholders' equity per share [euro]	11.45		15.92		24.04		34.3		548		65.1		
Dividend per share [euro]	0.30		0.55		0.70		1.00		2.00		2.50		
Pay out ratio [%]	11.6		10.3		6.2		6.2		11.1		15.3		
End year price of share [euro]	34.1		65.0		140.0		202.3		246.5		295.7		
Average outstanding shares [million]	15.392		15.611		15.932		16.026		16.066		16.054		
Market capitalization [euro million]*	525.4		1030.5		2248.2		3249.3		3,938		4,764		

PPR – PUMA: A successful acquisition?

* Calculated with average number of shares outstanding

Appendix 3
Puma historical balance sheets

Balance Sheets	2005A mn. Euro	2006A mn. Euro	Δ
Assets			
Cash and cash equivalents	475.5	459.2	−16.3
Inventories	238.3	364.0	125.7
Trade receivables	277.5	373.8	96.3
Other current assets	80.1	105.8	25.7
Current Assets	**1,071.4**	**1,302.8**	231.4
Property, plant and equipment	121.9	155.0	33.1
Intangible Assets	59.4	180.5	121.1
Other non-current assets	68.4	76.5	8.1
Non-current Assets	**249.7**	**412.0**	162.3
Total Assets	**1,321.1**	**1,714.8**	393.7
Liabilities and Equity			
Current bank debt	45.1	65.5	20.4
Trade payables	178.7	208.7	30.0
Other non interest bearing liabilities	123.9	171.9	48.0
Current liabilities	**347.8**	**446.1**	98.3
Provision for liabilities and charges	97.9	119.5	21.6
Mediun term loans	0.0	100.3	100.3
Non-current liabilities	**97.9**	**219.8**	121.9
Subscribed capital	43.2	44.1	0.9
Group reserves	307.0	423.4	116.4
Accumulated profits	680.3	799.3	119.0
Treasury stock	−159.6	−225.6	−66.0
Minority interest	4.5	7.7	3.2
Shareholder's equity	**875.4**	**1,048.9**	173.5
Total liabilities and equity	**1,321.1**	**1,714.8**	**393.7**

PPR – PUMA: A successful acquisition?

Appendix 4
PPR historical income statements & selected key financial data

Sales	2004	%	2005	%	2006	%	CAGR
€ million							
Sales							
Conforama	3,102.5	18%	3,140.0	18%	3,274.9	19%	*3%*
Redcats	4,390.8	26%	4,377.3	26%	4,332.2	25%	*−1%*
Fnac	4,138.9	24%	4,381.9	26%	4,538.4	27%	*5%*
CFAO	1,861.5	11%	2,034.3	12%	2,219.4	13%	*9%*
Luxury	3,212.2	19%	3,036.2	18%	3,568.2	21%	*5%*
Other	336.1	2%	795.4	5%	15.0	0%	
Total Net Sales	**17,042.0**		**17,765.1**		**17,948.1**		*3%*
Y-o-Y growth			*4.2%*		*1.0%*		
EBITDA	**1,939.9**		**1,410.8**		**1,629.9**		
EBITDA%	*11.4%*		*7.9%*		*9.1%*		
EBIT							
Conforama	226.0	15%	177.1	16%	181.7	14%	*−10%*
Redcats	229.3	16%	231.3	21%	225.1	18%	*−1%*
Fnac	150.6	10%	154.0	14%	170.2	13%	*6%*
CFAO	163.4	11%	167.0	15%	182.4	14%	*6%*
Luxury	394.4	27%	392.0	36%	565.2	44%	*20%*
Intercompany		–	32.0	–	50.1		
Total EBIT	**1,466.7**		**1,089.4**		**1,274.5**		*−7%*
Y-o-Y growth			*−25.7%*		*17.0%*		
PBT	**1,535.9**		**782.0**		**984.6**		*−20%*
PBT%	*9.0%*		*4.4%*		*5.5%*		
Net Income	**940.4**		**555.1**		**679.9**		*−15%*
Net income %	*5.5%*		*3.1%*		*3.8%*		
Earnings per share [euro]	4.74		4.18		5.58		
Dividend per share [euro]	2.52		2.71		3.00		
Average outstanding shares [million]	132.700		132.800		121.800		

PPR – PUMA: A successful acquisition?

Appendix 5
Puma projected figures (2007–2016)

To complete the valuation considerations, the analysts performed a DCF analysis (see Exhibit 5.1). The DCF projections were based on the following assumptions:

- For the period running from 2007 to 2009, Puma's income statement projections were based on brokers' consensus. For the following years, estimates have been based on authors' assumptions.

- Top line growth is expected to level down to terminal growth rate of 2 percent in 2016E.

- Ebitda Margin is expected to gradually decrease to a constant 17.5 percent after the peak of 18.2 percent forecasted in 2009 on the basis of analysts' consensus.

- Capex are expected to level down to 120 percent of depreciation in 2016E. The depreciation is assumed constant at 10 percent of the previous year operating fixed assets.

- Working Capital is expected to be driven by top line growth and to keep constant at 16 percent of sales.

- A 30 percent stable tax rate is assumed for the entire period running from 2008 to 2016. In 2007, the expected tax rate is equal to 32 percent.

EXHIBIT 5.1 Puma cash flow projections

Unlevered Free Cash Flow Calculation

(€ in millions)	Actual	Brokers' consensus				Authors' estimates						CAGR	
	2006A	2007E	2008E	2009E	2010E	2011E	2012E	2013E	2014E	2015E	2016E	06–16	TV
Sales	2,369.2	2,556	2,876	3,244.0	3,650	3,941	4,139	4,304	4,433	4,522	4,612.3	6.9%	4,705
% growth	33.3%	7.9%	12.5%	12.8%	12.5%	8.0%	5.0%	4.0%	3.0%	2.0%	2.0%		2.0%
EBIT	366	435	492	566	633	671	697	724	746	761	776	7.8%	791
% margin	15.5%	17.0%	17.1%	17.5%	17.3%	17.0%	16.8%	16.8%	16.8%	16.8%	16.8%		16.8%
+ Depreciation	38	22	23	24	24	27	28	29	30	31	32	**-1.9%**	32
% sales	1.6%	0.9%	0.8%	0.7%	0.7%	0.7%	0.7%	0.7%	0.7%	0.7%	0.7%		0.7%
= **EBITDA**	**405**	**458**	**515**	**590**	**657**	**698**	**724**	**753**	**776**	**791**	**807**	7.2%	**823**
% margin	17.1%	17.9%	17.9%	18.2%	18.0%	17.7%	17.5%	17.5%	17.5%	17.5%	17.5%		17.5%
./. Cash Taxes	(139)	(139)	(148)	(170)	(190)	(201)	(209)	(217)	(224)	(228)	(233)	5.3%	(237)
% effective tax rates	38.0%	32.0%	30.0%	30.0%	30.0%	30.0%	30.0%	30.0%	30.0%	30.0%	30.0%		30.0%
./. Capex	(193)	(51)	(49)	(41)	(36)	(38)	(39)	(39)	(39)	(38)	(38)	– **15.0%**	(39)
% sales	8.1%	-2.0%	-1.9%	-1.6%	-1.4%	-1.5%	-1.5%	-1.5%	-1.5%	-1.5%	-1.5%		-1.5%
% depreciation	-503%	-230%	-220%	-184%	-164%	-173%	-175%	-175%	-175%	-173%	-170%		-174%
./. Change in working capital	(148)	(86)	(45)	(45)	(65)	(47)	(32)	(26)	(21)	(14)	(14)		–15
% sales growth	-25.0%												
= FCFO	(75)	181	273	335	366	411	445	470	493	511	522		533

Source: Authors' calculation based on equity analysts consensus

PPR – PUMA: A successful acquisition?

Appendix 6
Cost of Capital information

The cost of capital calculation can be based on the data shown in Exhibits 6.1 and 6.2. With a prudential approach, analysts applied a target debt to equity ratio of 10 percent to Puma, assuming that the company would have raised debt to finance its expansion and to use tax shield for reducing its cost of capital. Exhibit 6.3 reports the key WACC assumptions of the main brokers as published in the research over the two months preceding the closure of the deal.

EXHIBIT 6.1 Comparables' levered beta and leverage

Comparables' Beta*

	Levered Beta	Debt to Equity	Unlevered Beta
Puma	0.64	0%	0.64
Adidas	0.32	47%	0.24
Asics	1.09	19%	0.96
K-Swiss	1.02	0%	1.02
Nike	0.56	8%	0.53
Billlabong	1.55	27%	1.30
Columbia Sportwear	0.97	0%	0.97
Sketchers	2.05	17%	1.83
Timberland	1.14	0%	1.14
Geox	1.28	4%	1.25
Industry Average	**1.11**	**14%**	**1.03**

* As of March 2007

EXHIBIT 6.2 Key data for cost of capital calculation

Puma WACC Calculation

Tax rate	30.00%
D/E (market value)	10%
Industry Unlevered Beta	1.03
Risk-free rate*	4.10%
MRP**	5.00%
Debt spread	1.00%

* Yield of ten years German Treasury Bonds as of March 2007
**Average Brokers' consensus

EXHIBIT 6.3   Key brokers' WACC assumptions

Brokers' Key WACC Assumptions*

Company	MRP	Beta	WACC
Credit Suisse	5.50%	na	10.90%
Deutsche Bank	4.50%	1.001	8.50%
Goldman Sachs	na	na	6.90%
Societe Generale	4.54%	1.20	9.85%
Industry Average	**4.85%**	**1.10**	**9.04%**

* As of March 2007

Appendix 7
Multiples analysis: comparable companies multiples

Below, Exhibit 7.1 reports comparables companies trading multiples as of March 2007.

EXHIBIT 7.1   Comparable companies trading multiples

(As from March 2007) Company	Trading Currency	Market Cap (ml)	Enterprise Value	EV/EBITDA			P/E		
				FY2006	FY2007	FY2008	FY2006	FY2007	FY2008
Athletic Footwear									
Adidas	EUR	8,478	10,718	9.8	9.1	7.8	17.5	15.6	12.7
Asics	JPY	281,748	281,938	13.0	11.4	10.0	20.4	18.9	16.2
K-Swiss	USD	989	729	7.2	12.8	10.1	12.8	19.9	16.3
Nike	USD	27,426	25,702	10.5	9.7	8.7	19.0	17.2	15.2
Average				*10.1*	*10.8*	*9.2*	*17.4*	*17.9*	*15.1*
Outdoor and Activewear									
Billabong	AUD	3,508	3,761	14.7	12.5	10.6	21.9	18.7	15.9
Columbia Sportswear	USD	2,338	2,122	10.4	9.6	8.5	19.3	17.1	15.2
Quicksilver	USD	1,589	2,465	10.1	10.4	8.3	17.6	21.3	14.0
Average				*11.7*	*10.8*	*9.1*	*19.6*	*19.0*	*15.0*
Fashion brands									
Geox	EUR	3,533	3,470	22.6	15.7	12.4	36.2	27.6	23.0
Hugo Boss	EUR	3,208	3,390	14.5	12.3	10.9	24.9	21.0	18.4
Tod's	EUR	2,046	2,002	14.5	12.3	10.7	29.8	24.3	20.6
Average				*17.2*	*13.4*	*11.3*	*30.3*	*24.3*	*20.7*
Average (all comparables)				*12.7*	*11.6*	*9.8*	*21.9*	*20.2*	*16.8*
Puma	**EUR**	**5,027**	**4,873**	**12.0**	**10.6**	**9.5**	**19.1**	**17.4**	**14.7**

Source: Company reports and market data

PPR – PUMA: A successful acquisition?

Appendix 8
Multiples analysis: precedent transactions multiples

The industry has undergone a substantial consolidation. As a consequence, nine transactions starting from 2002 have been included in the pooling. They all regard the acquisition of a target operating in similar businesses to Puma (see Exhibit 8.1).

EXHIBIT 8.1   **Precedent transactions multiples**

Announcement date	Bidder	Target	Enterprise value (ml)	EV/EBITDA
17/04/2006	Berkshire Hathaway	Russell Corporation	961	7.0
23/12/2005	Apax Partners	Tommy Hilfiger	1,600	8.1
03/08/2005	Adidas	Reebok	3,831	11.4
02/06/2005	Stride Rite	Saucony	142	8.0
29/04/2004	PPR	Gucci	8,820	13.8
27/04/2004	VF Corporation	Vans	335	15.3
09/07/2003	Nike	Converse	324	8.4
07/07/2003	VF Corporation	Nautica	517	6.5
01/03/2002	Cerberus	Fila	351	8.5

Source: Authors' research on company data

ADDITIONAL CASES

1 Enforcing Financial Reporting Standards: The Case of White Pharmaceuticals AG

Abstract

A s a consequence of accounting scandals, Germany – like many other countries – set up a supervisory body to control the compliance of capital market oriented companies with accounting regulations. The Financial Reporting Enforcement Panel (FREP) assumed their duty in July 2005 and has forced a number of companies to restate their financial statements. This case study adapts one of the real cases of the FREP and invites students to reflect on the enforcement of financial reporting standards: White Pharmaceuticals AG enters a strategic alliance to profit from the research and development of their partner. The company charges all payments that it conducts in the course of the alliance to their expense accounts. The FREP, however, finds that the final lump-sum payment should have been capitalized by White. The case reviews the accounting for research and development expenditure and also discusses the convergence of financial reporting standards in the US and Europe.

Keywords: Financial Reporting Enforcement, Research and Development, IFRS

The Case

Introduction

Peter Schmidt, head of the accounting department of Germany-based White Pharmaceuticals AG,[1] had been waiting for the letter for quite a while now. When it finally came, his hands started shaking as he read "Financial Reporting Enforcement Panel" on the envelope. Opening the letter he recalled the painfully long days in his office during which he tried to answer countless questions to the panel's satisfaction. As he read through the letter, his face grew paler. This was exactly what he had warned the CFO of White Pharmaceuticals AG of and exactly what he had described as a worst case scenario. In the letter, dated November 18th 2009, the Financial Reporting Enforcement Panel (FREP) requested a restatement of White's financial statements for the year 2006. Income as well as intangible assets had been understated by 55 million Euros as White Pharmaceuticals AG had expensed a payment made to acquire research results. With the letter in his hand, Peter slowly walked to the office of Alexander Muller, White's Chief Financial Officer, and reflected on the events that had led to the examination by the FREP.

White Pharmaceuticals AG was founded in 1956 by Paul White and his brother Roland. Since its inception, the company had been headquartered in a small town near Frankfurt, Germany, and had specialized in various fields of pharmaceutical research. In recent years, White Pharmaceuticals AG had benefited from major breakthroughs with drugs for

The sole responsibility for the content of the HHL Working Paper lies with the authors, Henning Zülch and Dominic Detzen. We encourage the use of the material for teaching or research purposes with reference to the source. The reproduction, copying and distribution of the paper for non-commercial purposes is permitted on condition that the source is clearly indicated. Any commercial use of the document or parts of its content requires the written consent of the author/s.

For further HHL publications see www.hhl.de/publications.

[1]All names, dates and locations have been changed, as have the "characters" involved in the case.

neurological diseases and subsequently experienced a remarkable growth with revenues that soon exceeded 1 billion Euros. In 2000, the current CEO and son of Paul White, Richard, decided to use the momentum to have his company listed on the German stock exchange. The initial public offering (IPO) was a huge success for Richard White who also took the opportunity to reward his employees for their contribution to White's recent success. At the same time, he made his intention quite clear that he did not want to rest but that he wanted to challenge the big pharmaceutical companies.

The Cooperation Agreement

In a meeting subsequent to the IPO, Mr. White asked his managerial staff for options to grow further and to expand into additional markets. His CFO, Alex Muller, proposed to sustain the recent growth by entering strategic alliances with other research companies. Richard White agreed with his CFO as he saw a huge potential for his company to both profit from joint research results and from entering new markets. His considerations also based on the fact that, following the IPO, White Pharmaceuticals AG had enough money to make strategic alliances attractive to potential partners. Thus, Mr. White encouraged his staff to follow this idea and find research companies that fit into their portfolio.

Soon, a US-based company called Neurocentral, Inc. was identified and offered a partnership which the company gratefully accepted as they had been facing serious funding problems recently. Neurocentral, Inc. was a medium-sized pharmaceutical company that also specialized in the development of neurological drugs. According to the terms of the partnership, White Pharmaceuticals AG received access to Neurocentral's research results by obtaining the sole rights to sell the jointly developed drugs worldwide. White would therefore be able to expand into additional markets while profiting from Neurocentral's good ties to the US Food and Drug Administration (FDA). For Neurocentral, Inc., on the other hand, the alliance meant that their funding problems were solved. Simultaneously, they could increase their competitiveness which had also suffered lately. Both companies were delighted with the alliance and signed the contract in 2001 feeling like they were getting the most out of the deal.

Thus, the companies jointly agreed on the development of a transdermal patch that treats a common form of epilepsy. Neurocentral, Inc. had made a lot of progress in the research and expected to start clinical studies in the near future. To fund this R&D project, White Pharmaceuticals AG was to provide its US counterpart with three forms of compensation that corresponded to the typical steps in a drug development process[2]: After signing the contract, Neurocentral, Inc. was to receive a non-refundable upfront payment of five million Euros that was directly linked to the development of the transdermal patch. Using this money, the American company could increase their research efforts and complete the research and the pre-clinical phase in the year 2001, a little earlier than expected. In addition, White Pharmaceuticals AG would make two milestone payments of ten million Euros each as soon as Neurocentral, Inc. reached pre-defined targets in the development of the patch. The payments would become due when Neurocentral completed Phase I and II of the clinical studies which would be when preliminary testing of the new drug provided first results on central characteristics like dosage range, efficacy and side effects. Provided that no complications arose, Neurocentral, Inc. estimated to finalize Phase I in 2002 and Phase II in 2004. The final component of the compensation package would include a lump-sum payment of 55 million Euros that White would transfer when Neurocentral, Inc. completed the final clinical studies (Phase III) successfully. Early estimations by Neurocentral's researchers showed that they expected the drug ready for approval in 2006. In exchange for their payments, White Pharmaceuticals AG received worldwide commercialization rights for the transdermal patch. Consequently, White would use their own resources to file for approval of the patch with both FDA and European Medicines Agency (EMA). The post-approval studies (Phase IV) would also be undertaken by White who would then continue to market the new drug.

Accounting for the Agreement

Soon after the contract was signed and the corresponding upfront payment was made, Peter Schmidt was confronted with analyzing the partnership from an accounting perspective. For him, the key issue concerning the payments was quite clear. The subject revolved around the question whether to recognize an intangible asset or whether to expense the costs as the payments were made. He knew that IAS 38 sets the rules for the treatment of intangible assets and research and development expenditures. Here, he read that he needed to

---

[2]See Appendix for a depiction of the drug development process and the payment structure.

distinguish between separately acquired and internally generated intangible assets. The former are usually capitalized as the definition and recognition criteria of IAS 38 are fulfilled. Concerning internally generated intangibles, however, IAS 38 differentiates between a research and a development phase. While costs for research are to be expensed, costs that are incurred in the development phase are recognized as intangible assets if an additional set of criteria is fulfilled.

With these abstract explanations in mind, Peter sought to assess the upfront payment concerning a possible capitalization. He remembered that when he first started his job, Alex Muller told him that "we expense almost all of our R&D costs. That's what everyone does in the pharmaceutical industry. Besides, we never know if we will receive approval by EMA or FDA. Only if we have the authorization do we recognize the costs for the development of the approved drug. And we only capitalize those costs that we incur after the approval." Still unsure about what to do Peter called his colleague at Neurocentral, Inc. and asked him to assess the situation. Jeff Hudson, head of accounting at Neurocentral, Inc., was about to go to a meeting when his phone rang. Jeff was surprised by the question but did not have too much time to get involved with the issue. Thus, he simply said: "Look, Peter, I am kind of busy at the moment. But I can tell you that, here, in the US, we don't recognize costs that we incur when doing research for new drugs. SFAS No. 2 doesn't allow a capitalization. However, if we acquire R&D, that's a different story. In that case, we follow SFAS No. 141 and SFAS No. 142 and capitalize the acquired in-process R&D. But I'm not really sure what I would do in your situation. Besides, you're an IFRS guy and, as far as I know, R&D accounting still differs on our continents." Peter didn't feel like his American counterpart had fully understood his problem but was still thankful for Jeff's quick assessment of the situation.

Feeling that he had to solve the issue himself, Peter considered the nature of the upfront compensation. White Pharmaceuticals AG conducted the payment to profit from the research carried out by Neurocentral, Inc. While White Pharmaceuticals AG received all rights to the research performed, Peter did not perceive the five million Euros as an acquisition of an intangible asset. Instead, he felt that White only provided Neurocentral with the funding for research activities that the company performed. Following this reasoning, the payment had to be regarded as if White's researchers were conducting the research. And, considering the status the research was in at that time, no one could tell if the project would eventually yield a product that White would be able to sell. Therefore, the up-front payment would fall under the definition of research expenditure which IAS 38 prohibits from capitalizing. Although being skeptical of his argumentation, he charged the five million Euros to White's R&D expenses.

Thereafter, the project proceeded as expected and Neurocentral, Inc. started the clinical studies in 2002. In the same year, they were able to complete the first phase of the studies which provided them with a safety profile of the transdermal patch. Acting upon their role in the collaboration agreement, White transferred the first milestone payment of ten million Euros as soon as they received the latest research report from their partner. As a consequence of the payment, Peter was again confronted with the accounting for the alliance. Considering that the project had progressed to the development phase which, according to IAS 38, meant that incurred costs should be recognized, he wanted to discuss a possible capitalization of the payment with his CFO. In their meeting, Peter outlined his train of thought and explained that a capitalization may be necessary. He argued that White received all rights to the research performed and to the development carried out thus far. Therefore, the ten million Euros could be considered part of the intangible asset that White acquired in the course of the collaboration. Besides, Peter told Mr. Muller that IAS 38 required enterprises to recognize expenses that they incur in the development phase. Alex Muller listened carefully to what Peter Schmidt told him. However, he made clear that he assessed the payment differently: "I understand your reasoning, Peter, but I don't share your opinion. I believe that assessing the agreement is a two-step-process. First, we have to judge whether or not the transaction is an acquisition of R&D. I don't consider the agreement as an acquisition, but as an outsourcing of our R&D because we just fund the research and development conducted by Neurocentral. Thus, the second and central question that we have to ask is: Would we capitalize our expenses if we conducted the R&D in-house? And the answer is: No, we would not. At this point in the development process, we do not know if we will ever get a marketable product. And, if you read IAS 38, the standard tells you that an enterprise should only capitalize R&D if it can demonstrate that the intangible asset will yield future economic benefits. But as we don't have approval by either FDA or EMA yet, we cannot reasonably expect future economic benefits from the product. All this leads me to the conclusion that we don't have to capitalize the milestone payment." Although Peter felt that he had made a valid point, Alex Muller's argumentation also sounded convincing. In the end, he decided to follow his CFO's reasoning as

Mr. Muller had been in the business longer than Peter and could therefore reasonably be expected to know the relevant accounting practices in the industry. Thus, he recorded the milestone payment as part of White's expenses.

While Peter had struggled with the accounting treatment of the ten million Euros, Neurocentral, Inc. had begun with the second phase of the development. In the years 2003 and 2004, the transdermal patch was tested with 250 patients who were closely monitored to observe possible side effects of the drug. At the same time, these tests provided Neurocentral with first indications of the actual efficacy of the patch. Researchers at the American company and their counterparts in Europe were both delighted with the progress with which the project advanced. In 2004, Neurocentral, Inc. proudly notified White Pharmaceuticals AG that the second phase was completed successfully. In return, White transferred another ten million Euros expecting to soon receive a fully developed product. For Peter who still had his CFO's reasoning in mind, the milestone payment seemed of a similar nature as the one made in 2002. Concluding that no intangible asset was received in return for the ten million Euros, he again expensed the milestone payment as he had done with the previous one.

Subsequently, Neurocentral, Inc. conducted Phase III of the development process which typically is of much larger scale. As the company had not observed any severe side effects from the patch so far, they were able to limit the final clinical study to 1,000 patients. Over the course of two years, Neurocentral again tested the transdermal patch and observed a great effectiveness of the drug. What's more, no complications or additional side effects arose. Accordingly, the development process was completed in 2006 which was celebrated at both companies. After receiving all documents associated with the transdermal patch, White Pharmaceuticals AG went on to make the final lump-sum payment of 55 million Euros to Neurocentral, Inc. In addition, they used the documents received to compile the application for FDA and EMA approval. Thus, the project had been completed and Peter faced the last payment resulting from the agreement. He realized that Mr. Muller's argumentation was still valid – White had filed for approval but not received an authorization for the drug yet. As a consequence, he again charged the 55 million Euros to White's expense accounts. Nevertheless, the official termination of the agreement made him reconsider the accounting treatment and he decided to openly discuss the issue with White's auditors.

The Discussion with White's Auditors

At year's end, Peter sat down with the auditors and was asked if any extraordinary transactions had occurred. He described the circumstances of the alliance with Neurocentral, Inc. and asked the auditors for their opinion on the lump-sum payment. A few days later, after the auditors had analyzed the issue, they discussed whether White had acquired an intangible asset or whether the payment was part of White's R&D expense. The auditors, however, suggested that the issue may be open to interpretation. On the one hand, they shared Alex Muller's assessment and acknowledged that the lack of an official approval indeed made a capitalization questionable. On the other hand, they shared Peter's doubts and indicated that the approval only seemed to remain a legal formality. The clinical studies had been completed without any complications and White could present the necessary paperwork for an approval by FDA or EMA. This would lead to the conclusion that all criteria in IAS 38 were fulfilled and the costs incurred in the last stage of the development phase, i.e., 55 million Euros, should be recognized. In addition, the auditors declared that the transaction could also be interpreted as an acquisition of an intangible asset. Consequently, the price White had paid for the R&D could be seen to reflect White's expectations concerning an inflow of economic benefits. According to IAS 38, such a separate acquisition always resulted in an intangible asset that had to be recognized by the acquirer. Regardless of these discussions, Alex Muller who joined Peter and the auditors at the meeting insisted on the fact that White only compensated Neurocentral, Inc. for the research and did not acquire an asset. He claimed that he had researched similar transactions and found that engaging another entity to conduct research did not constitute an acquisition of an asset. Thus, he asserted that the arrangement with Neurocentral, Inc. had to be evaluated as an outsourcing of research and development. Following this argumentation, he demanded to apply the same criteria as would be the case if the R&D was conducted in-house, i.e., by White's own research department. And, in that situation, they had to evaluate if all criteria of development costs were fulfilled. He, again, negated that White could already expect future economic benefits as White still did not have an approval by either FDA or EMA. Therefore, he pushed for an expense charge of the lump-sum payment. As the auditors could not provide an unequivocal interpretation that asserted the contrary and as they had specifically asked for managerial judgment, they eventually decided to follow Mr. Muller's reasoning and approved the expense charges.

The Examination

Although the transdermal patch turned out to be a huge success and the executive teams of both White Pharmaceuticals AG and Neurocentral, Inc. were eager to extend the alliance, they could not agree on a follow-up project and the collaboration was terminated. Consequently, Peter slowly forgot about his struggle of how to treat the payments to Neurocentral, Inc. Thus, in the summer of 2008, Peter was not in the least worried when White Pharmaceuticals AG received a letter by the Financial Reporting Enforcement Panel. In their letter, the FREP told White Pharmaceuticals AG that the company was chosen at random to be inspected by the new supervising authority. They would like to examine White's financial statements for the year 2006. Mr. Muller did not really know what was coming at them but he put Peter in charge of the FREP investigation as "this is an accounting thing and it's clearly your job to handle this." As a first task, Peter was to provide the FREP with White's annual as well as quarterly financial statements including auditor's report and their summary of unadjusted audit differences. When two months passed without an additional notification by FREP, Peter started wondering what the examination would bring about. A little while later, White received another letter from the enforcement institution that indicated areas that the FREP would put an emphasis on in their examination. At the same time, they requested a number of documents to be sent back to the FREP within the next two weeks. The short time frame surprised Peter and he was glad that he could rely on his team to help him provide all documents necessary and answer all questions. Still, they struggled with several of the panel's queries and, in the end, barely made the deadline to send the material back. Relieved from this stress, he turned back to his routine business at White which had suffered in the prior weeks. While having hoped that the examination was over, he was proved wrong by another notification that came about two months later. The institution requested more material and asked even more questions than before. Holding the letter in his hands, he started to realize that this would be a tough year for him. Over a period of ten months, Peter repeatedly received notifications and letters that he was to respond to in a very short period of time. Again and again, his usual habit of working eight to nine hours a day turned into a frenzy of long nights that often lasted until midnight. As soon as he had finished the latest request by FREP, he needed to take care of his usual work and started worrying when the next letter was coming.

On a regular basis, he met with Mr. Muller to talk about the status of the examination and to discuss how they should handle the panel's investigation. How should they communicate with the capital market? Should they openly inform investors of what was going on or should they wait until they received the results of the investigation? After long debates, Mr. Muller decided to wait and assured Peter that "everything will work out eventually" and that "investors don't need to know everything." While pondering this issue, Peter realized that the FREP's questions soon circled around White Pharmaceuticals' payments to Neurocentral, Inc. and he recalled his insecurity concerning the treatment of the compensation. Looking at White's financial statements for the year 2006, he saw that the company expensed a total amount of 240 million Euros for research and development. This amount included 55 million Euros which represented the final lump-sum payment to Neurocentral, Inc. Suddenly it dawned on Peter that they might have made a mistake.

With FREP's concluding letter in his hand, Peter Schmidt was walking towards Mr. Muller's office. He prepared to tell his boss what had gone wrong. The FREP stated that White Pharmaceuticals AG had incorrectly expensed 55 million Euros in 2006. This amount should have been recognized because it represented the costs of a separately acquired intangible asset. In exchange for their payment, White had received a fully developed product which could reasonably be expected to result in an inflow of economic benefits. Therefore, White's income and assets had been understated by 55 million Euros. In addition, the FREP indicated that they had serious doubts about the treatment of the milestone payments. However, these doubts did not result in an additional finding. The letter further read that if White Pharmaceuticals AG accepted the statement, the error would be released in the electronic German Federal Gazette. If White wanted to object, they had to address this issue with the Financial Supervisory Authority (*Bundesanstalt für Finanzdienstleistungsaufsicht*, BaFin) who would then carry out their own investigation. Knocking on the CFO's door, Peter wondered how investors would react upon learning that the examination had been concealed from them.

Requirements

Research and Development Costs

1 The central issue of the case is the treatment of White Pharmaceuticals' payments to Neurocentral, Inc.

    1 How are research and development costs treated (a) according to IFRS and (b) according to US-GAAP?

    2 How are separately acquired intangible assets treated (a) according to IFRS and (b) according to US-GAAP?

    3 Assess the payments made by White according to the criteria set out in IAS 38. Which payment would you have recognized in Peter's place?

2 Costs for research and development are a major part of a pharmaceutical company's spending.

    1 Why does capitalizing R&D seem to be an area of managerial discretion, although there are explicit rules of how to treat R&D?

    2 Are there advantages (disadvantages) of capitalizing R&D?

    3 White's CFO tells Peter Schmidt that the pharmaceutical industry charges most of their R&D costs to expenses. Table 1 shows the ratio of capitalized R&D to total R&D expenditures in different industries. Can you imagine why industries differ in their treatment of R&D?

    4 The IFRS Framework constitutes qualitative characteristics that financial statements are to fulfill. Do you think that the accounting for research and development costs corresponds to the qualitative characteristics of relevance and reliability?

TABLE 1 Capitalizing Development Costs in Germany.

Industry	ATL	BCU	CPH	FBI	IND	MTST	RCF
Capitalized R&D/ Total Costs for R&D	29.73%	36.66%	1.66%	31.01%	13.60%	45.54%	15.99%

Note: (ATL=Automobile, Transportation, Logistics; BCU=Basic Resources, Construction, Utilities; CPH=Chemicals, Pharmaceuticals, Healthcare; FBI=Financial Services, Banks, Insurance; IND=Industrial; MTST=Media, Technology, Software, Telecommunication; RCF=Retail, Consumer, Food&Beverages; Hagerand Hitz 2007).

Global Accounting Standards: IFRS and US-GAAP

The case study reviewed the different treatment of R&D costs according to IFRS and US-GAAP. As the IASB and the FASB want to create uniform global accounting standards, many financial reporting standards will change and many companies face a complex process to adapt their accounting systems (see, for example, Gornik-Tomaszewski and Jermakowicz, 2010).

1 Can you think of advantages (disadvantages) of global accounting standards?

2 What is the impact on reporting entities that have to adapt their accounting?

3 The IASB and the FASB also plan to converge the rules for R&D expenditures. However, the project has been set on hold in 2009. Outline the boards' approach concerning the convergence. Can you imagine possible hindrances to the convergence of R&D accounting?

Enforcement of Financial Reporting Standards

1 In Germany, an institution that enforces financial reporting standards was only established in recent years.

    1 What is the reasoning behind an institution that enforces financial reporting standards?

    2 How are companies that are to be inspected selected? What does the German enforcement process look like?

2 At the end of our case, Peter receives a final letter by the FREP that presents an error finding to him. He is wondering what the consequences of this finding are.

    1 What are White's possible responses to the finding? Which way would you pursue? Why?

    2 How do you think investors will react to the error finding? How should White Pharmaceuticals AG have best reacted to the examination by the FREP?

    3 Who is to take responsibility for the restatements? Which role do you attribute to White's auditors?

    4 Imagine that Alex Muller asked Peter to appeal FREP's finding. What would be his motivations to do so? In your answer, outline arguments that Peter could use to successfully appeal the decision.

    5 Now, imagine that White's CFO decided to accept the finding. How would Peter go about restating White's financial statements?[3] In your answer, refer to IAS 8 and examine what decisions Peter has to make. Also, consider how White best let investors know about the restatement. What role do tax authorities play?

References

S. Gornik-Tomaszewski and E. K. Jermakowicz, "Adopting IFRS – Guidance for U.S. Entities Under IFRS 1," *CPA Journal* 80(3) (2010): 12–18.

S. Hager and J.-M. Hitz, "Immaterielle Vermögenswerte in der Bilanzierung und Berichterstattung – eine empirische Bestandsaufnahme für die Geschäftsberichte deutscher IFRS-Bilanzierer 2005" (Accounting for and Reporting of Intangible Assets – An Empirical Survey of German IFRS Accounts in 2005). *Zeitschrift für internationale und kapitalmarktorientierte Rechnungslegung* (2007)(4): 205–218.

---

[3] Assume that White's financial year ends December 31st. Also, assume that White only presents one prior period in their annual report.

Appendix

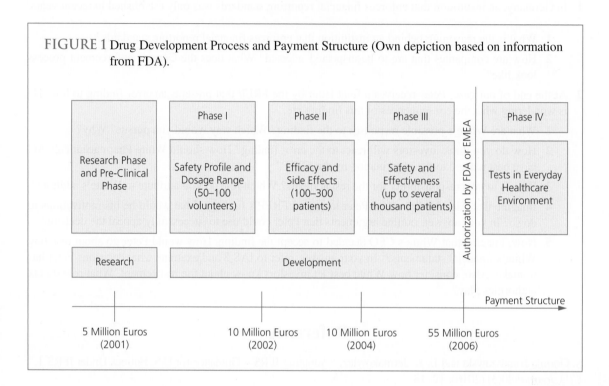

FIGURE 1 Drug Development Process and Payment Structure (Own depiction based on information from FDA).

2 KarstadtQuelle AG

Credit analyst Felix Brüggen glanced through the latest annual and quarterly reports of the German publicly listed company KarstadtQuelle AG. He was given the task to assess the creditworthiness of KarstadtQuelle, determine whether the company could bear the burden of another loan, and, if so, determine the maximum loan amount and set the appropriate interest rate on the new loan. KarstadtQuelle was a German diversified company that operated 90 German department stores and 32 German sport stores, provided European mail order services under the brand names neckermann.de and Quelle, held a 50 percent stake in tour operator Thomas Cook AG, and held investments in real estate through its subsidiary Karstadt Immobilien.[1] The company had been close to bankruptcy in 2004, but had shown a remarkable turnaround in 2005. In March 2006, KarstadtQuelle announced that it was debt-free, which suggested that the company had been able to substantially improve its creditworthiness.

KarstadtQuelle in 2004[2]

In the second half of 2004, KarstadtQuelle was on the verge of bankruptcy. The company did not reach its financial targets for that year and struggled under the debt load it had built up over the years, while lacking access to new long-term financing. The main reasons for the company's problems, which KarstadtQuelle's (new) management outlined in the company's 2005 Annual Report, were mismanagement and difficult market circumstances. The poor financial situation required drastic measures. In 2004, KarstadtQuelle's Management Board changed composition – by replacing the managing and finance directors – and the company reorganized the Management Boards of many of its subsidiaries. In addition, the company negotiated a new three-year credit facility of €1.75 billion with a syndicate of 16 banks, agreed with its current shareholders to issue new shares for an amount of approximately €500 million, and issued €140 million in convertible bonds. These capital increases were supported by the announcement of a new restructuring plan that was to be carried out in fiscal 2005. During 2004, KarstadtQuelle's share price decreased, however, by 61 percent, from €19.70 to €7.60.

KarstadtQuelle in 2005

Fiscal year 2005 was labeled by management "the year of restructuring." KarstadtQuelle's restructuring program had the following components:

- *Divestments in retail.* The company would strengthen its 88 larger department stores – with sales space above 8,000 square meters and total revenues of €4.5 billion – and divest its 77 smaller department stores – with sales space below 8,000 square meters and total revenues of €0.7 billion. It also planned to divest its specialty store chains,

Professor Erik Peek prepared this case. The case is intended solely as the basis for class discussion and is not intended to serve as an endorsement, source of primary data, or illustration of effective or ineffective management.

[1]Thomas Cook AG has been proportionally consolidated in KarstadtQuelle's financial statements.

[2]This and the following sections are primarily based on material from KarstadtQuelle's 2005 Annual Report, its Interim Reports of March 2006 and June 2006, and its press releases issued during 2004, 2005, and 2006.

such as sports stores RunnersPoint and GolfHouse. These divestments should help KarstadtQuelle to expand its high-margin products in the department store business.

- *Focus within mail order.* In the mail order business, KarstadtQuelle would focus its efforts on growth in the specialty mail order segment and in the e-commerce segment.[3] The company would further strategically reorient its traditionally strong universal mail order business in Germany.

- *Cost savings.* KarstadtQuelle expected to be able to achieve €210 million in cost savings in its department store business and €150 million in cost savings in its universal mail order business by the year 2006.

- *Real estate.* The company considered segregating its real estate business from its department store (retail) business.

- *Reorientation of the group.* KarstadtQuelle would streamline its portfolio, abandon marginal operations and outsource some of its processes in the retail business.

Although the financial and operational state of the company's mail order business appeared worse than anticipated, KarstadtQuelle's management had been able to make some important changes to the segment in 2005. Mail order companies Quelle and neckermann.de were converted into limited liability companies and started to operate separately under their own management to improve these subsidiaries' decision processes. In the mail order segment the company also positioned Quelle and neckermann.de in the market as two sharply distinct brands and combined several separately operating service units into one to reduce costs.

KarstadtQuelle also sold several specialty stores as well as its small department stores. The divestiture program also resulted in the sale of Karstadt Hypothekenbank AG to the company's pension fund. After the sale, Karstadt Hypothekenbank AG took over from KarstadtQuelle's finance companies the financing of the company's hire purchase business in its mail order segment, thereby helping KarstadtQuelle to derecognize its discounted installment receivables (in accordance with IAS 39). The sale of Karstadt Hypothekenbank reduced KarstadtQuelle's net non-current liabilities by approximately €1 billion. The sale of the company's marginal operations and smaller department stores yielded close to €1.1 million. In addition, KartstadtQuelle sold and leased back its mail order logistics real estate at a price of over €400 million. As a result of the restructuring, KarstadtQuelle was able to reduce its workforce by roughly one-fifth, or 25,000 employees.

In KarstadtQuelle's 2005 Annual Report, management reported that although performance in the mail order segment was still below plan, the company had reached its targets. In 2005, sales had declined from €17.2 billion to €15.8 billion, but the company had been able to cut its net loss from €1.6 billion to €316 million. During the fiscal year 2005, KarstadtQuelle's share price increased by 68 percent, from €7.60 to €12.74, to imply a market value of €2.69 billion.

KarstadtQuelle in the first half of 2006

After the financial restructuring of the company in 2005, KarstadtQuelle's management considered the company's equity position too vulnerable. To reduce leverage further, the company sold its real estate portfolio – consisting of department stores, car parks, sport stores, and office buildings – for an amount of €4.5 billion. The real estate was sold to and leased back from an entity that was jointly owned by a subsidiary of Goldman Sachs – the Whitehall Fund – and KarstadtQuelle. KarstadtQuelle had a participation of 49 percent in the joint entity but, as it reported, carried no other risks than arising from its equity contribution of €120 million. The operational management of the joint entity was in the hands of the Whitehall Fund. The first payment under the real estate transaction – €2.7 billion – was received on July 3, 2006. The second payment – the remaining €1.8 billion – would be received later in the year 2006.

According to KarstadtQuelle, the real estate transaction had several positive effects. First, it yielded a high short-term cash inflow that helped the company to quickly reduce its financial liabilities. Second, it improved important balance sheet ratios such as the equity-to-assets ratio. Third, it resulted in a high non-recurring income component for fiscal 2006. Fourth and finally, it led to a lasting improvement in pretax profits to the order of €100 million.

---

[3]Specialty mail order companies focus on selling one product type, such as baby products or fashion products, whereas universal mail order companies offer a broad assortment of product categories.

The company continued to restructure its business. It repositioned its department stores by distinguishing "Premium" stores that sold high-margin products at prime locations from "Boulevard" stores that focused on selling brands in the middle to higher price segment. Further, KarstadtQuelle increased its purchase volume in Asia and set up local design centers in Europe and Asia to develop fashionable and timely products. To facilitate procurement in Asia, the company signed an agreement to cooperate with the Chinese export company Li & Fung. These actions aimed to reduce purchase expenses and increase inventory turnover, thereby reducing working capital by an estimated €500 million. The proceeds from the real estate transaction further helped KarstadtQuelle to invest another €200 million in restructuring its universal mail order business.

In the first half of 2006, KarstadtQuelle managed to report a net profit of €558.1 million. During this half year, KarstadtQuelle's share price increased by 62 percent, from €12.74 to €20.59, to reach a market value of €4.34 billion.

Questions

1 When preparing a report that summarizes the main factors affecting KarstadtQuelle's creditworthiness, which factors should the credit analyst focus on? How do these factors affect KarstadtQuelle's creditworthiness?

2 Assess whether KarstadtQuelle could bear the burden of another €500 million loan. If so, what would be the appropriate interest rate on this new loan?

2 KarstadtQuelle AG

EXHIBIT 1　KarstadtQuelle's consolidated financial statements

INCOME STATEMENTS (€ thousands)

	Half year ending June 30, 2006	Year ending December 31, 2005	Half year ending June 30, 2005	Year ending December 31, 2004
Sales	6,474,551	15,845,032	7,166,102	17,199,007
Cost of sales and expenses for tourism services	(3,614,132)	(8,911,823)	(3,911,755)	(9,631,912)
Gross income	2,860,419	6,933,209	3,254,347	7,567,095
Other capitalized own costs	13,987	50,691	22,242	53,519
Operating income	1,315,470	1,102,555	388,286	819,669
Staff costs	(1,180,843)	(2,630,323)	(1,382,563)	(3,109,417)
Operating expenses	(2,321,642)	(5,152,129)	(2,245,903)	(5,575,730)
Other taxes	(10,702)	(29,344)	(13,644)	(30,262)
Earnings before interest, tax and depreciation and amortization (EBITDA)	676,689	274,659	22,765	(275,126)
Depreciation and amortization (not including amortization of goodwill)	(145,297)	(343,329)	(171,828)	(425,115)
Impairment loss	(507)	(48,193)	(57,550)	(101,641)
Earnings before interest, tax and amortization of goodwill (EBITA)	530,885	(116,863)	(206,613)	(801,882)
Amortization of goodwill	0	(8,399)	205	(152,446)
Earnings before interest and tax (EBIT)	530,885	(125,262)	(206,408)	(954,328)
Income from investments	2,740	(9,454)	2,259	1,314
Income from investments in associates	4,259	16,681	8,535	12,481
Net interest income	(192,055)	(292,953)	(153,537)	(326,863)
Other financial results	19,634	15,783	(12,911)	(165,371)
Earnings before tax (EBT)	365,463	(395,205)	(362,062)	(1,432,767)
Taxes on income	194,500	81,180	117,053	178,008
Earnings from continuing operations	559,963	(314,025)	(245,009)	(1,254,759)
Result from discontinued operations	0	(258)	(25,352)	(370,531)
Net profit/loss before minority interests	559,963	(314,283)	(270,361)	(1,625,290)
Profit/loss due to minority interests	(1,847)	(2,199)	(1,515)	(24)
Net loss after minority interests	558,116	(316,482)	(271,876)	(1,625,314)

2 KarstadtQuelle AG

EXHIBIT 1 **KarstadtQuelle's consolidated financial statements** *(continued)*

BALANCE SHEETS (€ thousands)

	Half year ending June 30, 2006	Year ending December 31, 2005	Half year ending June 30, 2005	Year ending December 31, 2004
Intangible assets	1,087,878	1,104,831	1,117,732	1,100,986
Tangible assets	1,061,660	2,452,839	2,659,840	2,786,185
Shares in associates	86,343	98,398	110,226	105,877
Other financial assets	624,494	535,220	1,032,739	1,405,772
Other non-current assets	96,764	94,167	129,746	116,313
Deferred taxes	220,891	228,249	283,529	164,914
Non-current assets	3,178,030	4,513,704	5,333,812	5,680,047
Inventories	1,547,838	1,621,095	1,700,643	1,823,904
Trade receivables	795,267	844,385	1,400,712	1,295,494
Tax receivables	127,316	50,430	89,381	61,800
Other receivables and other assets	1,011,858	1,139,128	1,046,039	911,201
Purchase price receivable from real estate transaction	2,690,203	0	0	0
Cash and cash equivalents and securities	770,550	707,163	657,504	661,156
Current assets	6,943,032	4,362,201	4,894,279	4,753,555
Assets classified as held for sale	481,506	262,658	1,942,263	1,209,587
Balance sheet total	10,602,568	9,138,563	12,170,354	11,643,189
Subscribed share capital	514,544	510,398	510,398	510,398
Reserves	790,711	(237,068)	(196,053)	58,663
Minority interests	12,192	16,745	31,595	26,783
Equity	1,317,447	290,075	345,940	595,844
Long-term capital of minority interests	0	0	53,203	58,983
Non-current financial liabilities	1,007,146	3,012,793	3,361,517	3,372,376
Other non-current liabilities	485,925	566,606	596,024	549,694
Pension provisions	886,923	906,756	859,101	891,911
Other non-current provisions	368,220	383,784	350,802	365,483
Deferred taxes	18,880	11,673	8,483	12,533
Non-current liabilities	2,767,094	4,881,612	5,229,130	5,250,980
Current financial liabilities	3,062,043	724,776	2,164,105	2,062,517
Trade payables	1,331,760	1,600,870	1,424,662	1,554,497
Current tax liabilities	180,695	201,746	151,775	229,840
Other current liabilities	1,405,913	768,855	1,286,692	799,186
Current provisions	506,277	609,677	564,313	626,136
Current liabilities	6,486,688	3,905,924	5,591,547	5,272,176
Liabilities from assets classified as held for sale	31,339	60,952	1,003,737	524,189
Balance sheet total	10,602,568	9,138,563	12,170,354	11,643,189

2 KarstadtQuelle AG

EXHIBIT 1 KarstadtQuelle's consolidated financial statements *(continued)*

CASH FLOW STATEMENTS (€ thousands)

	Half year ending June 30, 2006	Year ending December 31, 2005	Half year ending June 30, 2005	Year ending December 31, 2004
EBITDA	676,689	274,659	22,765	(275,126)
Profit/loss from the disposal of fixed assets	(906,419)	(155,154)	(24,278)	(1,304)
Profit/loss from foreign currency	(4,457)	(1,907)	3,038	4,919
Decrease of non-current provisions (not including pension and tax provisions)	(2,178)	(95,099)	(18,760)	(59,880)
Addition to (Utilization of) restructuring provision	(130,367)	255,853	(84,830)	583,809
Other expenses/income not affecting cash flow	146,904	168,307	98,454	146,161
Gross cash flow	(219,828)	446,659	(3,611)	398,579
Changes in working capital	(68,114)	1,006,822	(173,859)	93,576
Changes in other current assets and liabilities	317,002	(231,280)	114,760	165,831
Dividends received	1,165	13,278	2,803	24,958
Payments/refunds of taxes on income	(46,068)	(8,253)	(37,395)	(46,452)
Cash flow from operating activities	(15,843)	1,227,226	(97,302)	636,492
Cash flow from acquisitions/divestments of subsidiaries less cash and cash equivalents disposed of	79,572	250,388	10,080	(3,060)
Purchase of tangible and intangible assets	(81,127)	(258,785)	(84,686)	(331,475)
Purchase of investments in non-current financial assets	(140,295)	(7,953)	(69,020)	(83,283)
Cash receipts from sale of tangible and intangible assets	62,133	703,648	133,560	119,356
Cash receipts from sale of non-current financial assets	8,522	43,723	40,665	32,835
Cash flow from investing activities	(71,195)	731,021	30,599	(265,627)
Interest received	72,957	134,202	62,773	131,533
Interest paid	(185,698)	(377,162)	(190,584)	(331,834)
Pension payments	(54,135)	(62,272)	(90,365)	(95,867)
Cash receipts/payments under mortgage bond program and for (financial) loans	334,309	(1,546,621)	297,971	(192,959)
Payment of liabilities due under finance lease	(9,729)	(47,264)	(16,208)	(39,489)
Cash payments/cash receipts for dividends and capital increase	3,979	(1,520)	(571)	473,006
Cash flow from financing activities	161,683	(1,900,637)	63,016	(55,610)
Changes in cash and cash equivalents affecting cash flow	74,645	57,610	(3,687)	315,255
Changes in cash and cash equivalents due to changes in exchange rates or other changes caused by the consolidated companies	(11,258)	(14,856)	(1,020)	(14,367)
Cash and cash equivalents at the beginning of the period	707,163	653,162	662,211	352,274
Cash and cash equivalents at the end of the period	770,550	695,916	657,504	653,162

EXHIBIT 2 Excerpts from the notes to the consolidated financial statements KarstadtQuelle's annual report 2005

2 KarstadtQuelle AG

Consolidation

In the year under review the shares in Karstadt Hypothekenbank AG were exchanged for shares held by the II.KarstadtQuelle Pension Trust e.V. In Quelle Neckermann Versand Finanz GmbH & Co. KG and Karstadt Hypothekenbank AG deconsolidated. During the year the company was treated as a disposal group and its assets and liabilities recognized under Assets qualified as held for sale and Liabilities in connection with assets classified as held for sale. Impairment of €51,440 thousand resulting within the year from estimated sales proceeds from company assets has proved to be no longer necessary in connection with this exchange.

Sale of receivables

Individual group companies are selling trade receivables to Karstadt Hypothekenbank AG, which was transferred to the II.KarstadtQuelle Pension Trust e.V. under the CTA program. Karstadt Hypothekenbank AG at the end of the fiscal year took over from the finance companies the purchase of receivables being sold by these companies under the ABS programs. In this connection, the sale of receivables was classified as an actual derecognition under IAS 39. International companies in mail order are continuing to sell under asset-backed securitization (ABS) transactions their receivables to a finance company, which refinances the purchases on the capital market. Under the ABS program the purchasers of these receivables withhold part of the purchase price as security until receipt of the payments. If there is sufficient likelihood of realization, the anticipated payment is shown as a separate financial asset.

The vendors must assume responsibility for collecting the debts. At the balance sheet date adequate provisions are set aside for these commitments. For the assumption of the risks and interim financing the vendors pay a program fee, which, depending on the classification of the sales, is shown as a true sale or a sale which does not qualify for derecognition under other operating expenses or interest.

Operating income

Amounts shown in € thousands	2005	2004
Income from the disposal of assets classified as held for sale	167,613	12,949
Income from advertising cost subsidies	154,738	169,702
Earnings from rental income and commissions	131,155	103,239
Income from charged-on goods and services	57,800	55,283
Income from the disposal of non-current assets	52,080	11,885
Income from the reversal of other liabilities	37,514	27,883
Income from exchange rate differences	28,157	44,121
Income from the reversal of other provisions	27,697	19,851
Income from deconsolidation	20,471	10,659
Income from other services	18,779	21,569
Income from the reversal of allowances	9,783	8,310
Other income	396,768	334,218
	1,102,555	819,669

Operating expenses

Amounts shown in € thousands	2005	2004
Logistics costs	1,431,003	1,459,007
Catalog costs	893,853	861,938
Operating and office/workshop costs	693,058	777,016
Advertising	615,761	648,103
Administrative costs	559,386	479,393
Restructuring costs	269,342	651,455
Allowances on and derecognition of trade receivables	223,506	256,577
Losses from the disposal of assets classified as held for sale	60,050	1,894
Outside staff	32,435	23,632
Expenses due to currency differences and losses	26,250	49,040
Losses from the disposal of fixed assets	4,491	21,636
Other expenses	342,994	346,039
	5,152,129	5,575,730

Net interest income

Amounts shown in € thousands	2005	2004
Interest costs from pension expense	(133,384)	(137,104)
Other interest and similar income	254,790	217,699
Other interest and similar expenses	(414,359)	(407,458)
	(292,953)	(326,863)

The previous year's value included non-recurring charges of €51.9 million from restructuring.

Through application of the new IAS 39 the Group's receivables sales were classified as non-disposal of receivables. Accordingly, the corresponding expenses from pre-financing of receivables (so-called program fees) are recognized under interest expenses. These amount to €55,641 thousand (previous year: €41,165 thousand) for the 2005 financial year. The previous year's amounts were adjusted accordingly for better comparability.

Leases

Finance lease agreements have a firmly agreed basic leasing period of between 20 and 25 years and include a purchase option for the lessee after expiry of the basic leasing period. Assets under finance lease agreements have a carrying amount of €237,783 thousand (previous year: €262,686 thousand) at the balance sheet date. These assets relate to buildings, aircraft and reserve engines where the carrying value of the future minimum lease payments covers the material purchase costs. For aircraft financing normally a purchase option for the residual value plus an amount

equal to 25 percent of the amount by which the fair value exceeds the residual value exists after the expiry of the lease period. If the purchase option is not exercised, the aircraft is sold by the lessor. If the proceeds from the sale are lower than the residual value, the lessee must pay the difference to the lessor. The lessee is entitled to up to 75 percent of the amount by which the sales proceeds exceed the residual value.

The operating lease agreements comprise mainly building leases without purchase option or aircraft leases where the assessment of the criteria of IAS 17 resulted in classification as operating lease.

	Up to 1 year		1 to 5 years		Over 5 years	
Amounts shown in € thousands	**2005**	**2004**	**2005**	**2004**	**2005**	**2004**
Finance lease agreements:						
Lease payments due in future	38,328	65,875	320,653	185,498	138,313	131,161
Discount	(759)	(36,209)	(35,783)	(48,924)	(31,598)	(14,162)
Present value	37,569	29,666	284,870	136,574	106,715	116,999
Lease payments under subleases	1,152	0	4,606	0	5,758	0
Operating lease agreements:						
Lease payments due in future	343,359	311,629	919,291	863,627	1,221,619	842,697
Discount	(11,072)	(16,953)	(124,498)	(131,195)	(600,007)	(364,210)
Present value	332,287	294,676	794,793	732,432	621,612	478,487
Lease payments under subleases	23,847	22,694	63,318	43,098	75,363	15,940

Trade receivables

Breakdown of trade receivables by business segment (Amounts shown in € thousands)	2005	2004
Karstadt	82,441	41,324
Mail order	602,074	1,093,715
Thomas Cook	82,113	73,508
Services	76,626	79,287
Other	1,131	7,660
	844,385	1,295,494

In connection with the application of IAS 39 sales of receivables under ABS programs were not subject to any further disposals at the beginning of the 2005 financial year. Accordingly, the previous year's figures of

€622 million have been adjusted to suit the change in recognition. The reorganization of the receivables sale program at home with the sale of receivables amounting to €613 million to Karstadt Hypothekenbank AG at the end of the financial year, however, resulted in an actual disposal and thus to a marked reduction in trade receivables.

To secure claims under a global agreement for the sale of receivables, security was provided to Karstadt Hypothekenbank AG on existing and future trade receivables.

Under the syndicated loan agreement and the second lien financing amounts totaling €243,414 thousand owed by customers to various Group companies were assigned as security for debtors' liabilities.

Financial liabilities

Amounts shown in € thousands	Up to 1 year		1 to 5 years		Over 5 years	
	2005	2004	2005	2004	2005	2004
Bank loans and overdrafts	231,438	734,047	797,776	694,086	326,934	469,513
Liabilities under leasing agreements	18,800	33,249	244,719	145,809	68,013	163,177
Other financial liabilities	474,538	1,295,221	200,511	677,130	1,374,840	1,222,661
Total	724,776	2,062,517	1,243,006	1,517,025	1,769,787	1,855,351

Interest-bearing bank loans and overdraft loans are recognized at the amount paid out less directly assignable issue costs. Financing costs, including premiums payable as repayments or redemption, are allocated with effect for income. Liabilities under lease agreements are shown at present value.

The terms and conditions of the facility were adjusted in December 2005 mainly with regard to the conclusion of the secondary loan facility explained below with regard to adherence to financial ratios. €275 million of the loan facility had been utilized at the balance sheet date. The financial ratios to be adhered to relate to adjusted EBITDA, interest coverage, debt coverage and the level of equity. For the mail order segment there is a further financial ratio relating to adjusted EBITDA.

To secure the Group's finances for the long term, in December of the financial year the KarstadtQuelle Group also agreed a further secondary loan facility amounting to nominally €309 million, which had been fully utilized by the balance sheet date. The security provided for the liabilities is for the most part identical with the security underlying the syndicated loan facility, although ranking below the syndicated facility.

The loans secured by mortgage bear interest rates between 2.75 percent p.a. and 7.24 percent p.a. at the balance sheet date. The syndicated loan facility taken up the previous year and the recently concluded second-ranking loan facility bear interest on the basis of EURIBOR (or LIBOR, if drawing in currencies other than euros) plus margin and regulatory costs. In the case of the syndicated loan facility the bullet facility is initially subject to a margin of 3.5 percent p.a., which will rise to 4.5 percent p.a. in 2006 and to 5.5 percent p.a. in 2007. For the seasonal facility and the revolving loan facility initially a margin of 3.75 percent p.a. has been agreed from December 10, 2005, for the period of one year. Thereafter under certain circumstances it will rise to 4.75 percent p.a. The second-ranking loan facility bears interest with a margin of 12 percent.

Financial liabilities also include liabilities to customers of the KarstadtQuelle Bank from savings deposits, night money, balances on card accounts, promissory notes and savings certificates amounting to €77,642 thousand.

Of first-ranking financial liabilities €484,675 thousand (previous year: €742,172 thousand) are secured by mortgages and €350,372 thousand by other rights. In addition, there is first-ranking mortgage security amounting to €1,249,465 thousand (previous year: €1,419,737 thousand) under the Karstadt Hypothekenbank AG's (Essen) mortgage bond program. Liabilities of €91,238 thousand proportionate (previous year €74,060 thousand) arising from real estate financing at Thomas Cook are likewise supported by mortgage or similar security.

KarstadtQuelle AG has undertaken a guarantee to the Karstadt Hypothekenbank AG, Essen, for loans of Karstadt Finance B.V., Hulst, Netherlands, amounting to €1.8 billion, which translates to €1.3 billion at the balance sheet date.

Under the agreed syndicated loan facility a partial land charge assignment declaration was agreed with real estate management companies, and the creation of overall land charges and in some cases binding security pledges in respect of land charges was agreed. Furthermore, shares in Thomas Cook AG and various fully consolidated Group companies and amounts due from customers of the various Group companies were assigned. Furthermore, unrecognized brands held by KarstadtQuelle AG, Karstadt Warenhaus GmbH, Quelle GmbH and neckermann.de GmbH were assigned as security for liabilities of KarstadtQuelle AG.

Liabilities of €350,273 thousand (previous year: €391,850 thousand) arising from aircraft financing are secured by aircraft mortgages or are subject to availability limitations resulting from the financing structure.

Leasing liabilities carried as liabilities are effectively secured by the lessor's rights to buildings or aircraft specified in the finance lease.

2 KarstadtQuelle AG

Pension provisions

The recognized amount from pension obligations results as follows:

Amounts shown in € thousands	Commitments financed from funds	Commitments financed from provisions	2005	2004
Present value of future pension commitments (DBO)	1,564,743	1,019,941	2,584,684	2,602,586
Unrecognized actuarial gains/losses	(71,678)	(117,610)	(189,288)	(72,217)
Unrecognized past service costs	(119)	(336)	(455)	(634)
Fair value of plan assets	(1,485,424)	0	(1,485,424)	(1,504,939)
	7,522	901,995	909,517	1,024,796
Pension provisions in connection with disposal groups	0	(2,761)	(2,761)	(132,885)
	7,522	899,234	906,756	891,911

Pension costs are as follows:

Amounts shown in € thousands	Commitments financed from funds	Commitments financed from provisions	2005	2004
Service costs	3,856	8,378	12,234	15,126
Interest costs	70,151	39,009	109,160	141,735
Expected return on plan assets	(84,723)	0	(84,723)	(83,865)
Actuarial gains/losses with effect on income	32	305	337	113,424
Past service costs	1,255	2,386	3,641	99
Income from changes in plans/expenses from deconsolidation	4,987	3,201	8,188	351
	(4,442)	53,279	48,837	186,168

Whereas the cost of pension claims acquired during the financial year is shown under staff costs, the interest and the expected return on plan assets and the actuarial losses affecting plan assets are recorded with effect for income and shown under financial results.

The composition of plan assets is calculated from the following table:

Amounts shown in € thousands	2005	2004
Real estate, incl. dormant holdings	987,966	1,091,060
Corporate investments	351,000	348,674
Financial resources	146,458	65,205
	1,485,424	1,504,939

The Group utilizes parts of real estate assets itself. The lease payments are made on the basis of usual market estimates. Furthermore, under their articles of incorporation the pension trusts may lend up to 10 percent of their assets back to the Group in the form of cash and cash equivalents. An amount of €72,982 thousand (previous year: €26,971 thousand) results here at the balance sheet date.

Other non-current provisions

Amounts shown in € thousands	Staff	Guarantees/ warranties	Contingent losses resulting from pending transactions	Restructuring effects	Other
As at 01.01.2005	31,866	958	298	235,295	34,659
Changes in consolidated companies	(123)	0	0	(626)	(128)
Currency differences	(8)	(2)	0	8	0
Recourse	(705)	(642)	276	(43,444)	(1,804)
Reversal	(13,283)	(23)	(248)	(6,704)	(678)
Appropriation	965	647	0	72,227	11,660
Reclassification acc. to IFRS 5	(285)	(1)	0	8,694	(701)
As at 31.12.2005	18,427	937	326	265,450	43,008

Staff provisions include provisions for severance payments and jubilee payments and death benefits.

Other provisions relate mainly to litigation risks and restoration liabilities.

3 Oddo Securities – ESG Integration

I n January of 2009, John Keyes, portfolio manager for a medium-sized UK fund, reviewed the analyst report on the telecommunications industry he had just received from the French brokerage firm Oddo Securities (Oddo). Keyes was intrigued by Oddo's research, which provided two ratings of stocks covered, a financial rating and an environmental, social and governance (ESG) rating. Keyes was particularly struck by the returns generated by Oddo's ESG recommendations, which had outperformed most major stocks indices over the last five years. He reviewed the recommendations and analysis for two telecom stocks he was considering adding to his portfolio, British Telecom (BT) and France Telecom (FT). The Oddo analysis assigned BT its highest ESG rating (a Strong Opportunity) but rated the company as a "Reduce" in the financial recommendation. In contrast, FT was rated as a Moderate Risk under the ESG rating and a "Buy" for the financial rating. Keyes wondered how he should interpret these conflicting ratings, and which deserved more of his attention.

Background on Oddo Securities

Oddo Securities was owned by Oddo & Cie – an independent investment services firm that in 2010 had 900 employees, offices in Paris, Dubai, Madrid, and New York, and over €17 billion in assets under management. The firm was 80 percent owned by management, employees, and the Oddo family, and 20 percent by German-based insurer Allianz. It was headed by Philippe Oddo, whose family had been in the stockbroker business for five generations. In addition to its brokerage business, Oddo & Cie owned an investment bank, a financial advisory business, options and commodity businesses, a private bank, and an asset management unit.

Oddo Securities was one of France's top brokers. The unit catered to an international institutional clientele providing brokerage services and research on a broad product range, including shares, futures, options and fixed income/credit. The research team, with 60 analysts, economists, and strategists, focused on the French and European market – equities, corporate bonds, and derivatives. The five-member credit research team focused on fixed-income securities and covered more than 120 European companies. The equity research team had more than 45 sector analysts and covered 320 European companies, including 220 French stocks. Oddo's equity research covered 98 percent of the market capitalization of the France CAC 40 index, 89 percent of the DJ STOXX Euro 50 index and 60 percent of the DJ STOXX 600 index.[1]

Professors George Serafeim and Paul M. Healy and Senior Researcher Aldo Sesia of the Global Research Group prepared this case. HBS cases are developed solely as the basis for class discussion. Cases are not intended to serve as endorsements, sources of primary data, or illustrations of effective or ineffective management.

[1]The CAC 40 was an index of 40 stocks traded on the Paris Stock Exchange. The Dow Jones STOXX Euro 50 Index represented 50 super sector market leaders in the 12 Eurozone countries: Austria, Belgium, Finland, France, Germany, Greece, Ireland, Italy, Luxemburg, the Netherlands, Portugal and Spain. The Dow Jones STOXX 600 Index was comprised of 600 highly capitalized and actively traded stocks listed and traded on stock exchanges from 17 European countries.

ESG investing and analysis

The use of ESG criteria for investing was a relatively recent innovation in the investment management industry and fell under the umbrella of socially responsible investing (SRI). SRI strategies could be broadly classified into five categories: negative screening, positive screening, integration, thematic, and engagement. Under negative screening, companies were excluded from investment portfolios based on ethical concerns about the safety of their products (e.g., tobacco, weapons, etc.) and their ethical standards of behavior. Positive screening identified companies with best-in-class ESG performance as investment candidates. Integration strategies focused on relations between ESG data, cash flows and/or cost of capital, and then embedded those relationships into valuation models. Thematic strategies followed either a multi-theme approach focusing on a broad range of long-term environmental or social issues (e.g., ageing societies, sustainable nutrition, clean energy, low-income solutions, urbanization, health, sustainable resources), or a hybrid approach combining a large cap "best in class" universe with a thematic overlay. Finally, engagement represented a form of shareholder activism where investors sought to influence how companies addressed material ESG issues to protect and enhance the value of their investments.

SRI investing experienced dramatic growth in the 1990s and 2000s. Between 2001 and 2007 assets under management of socially responsible investors grew by $400 billion in the US, $600 billion in the UK, and $400 billion in Canada.[2] In 2007, mutual funds that invested in socially conscious firms had assets under management of more than $2.5 trillion in the United States, $2 trillion in Europe, $500 billion in Canada, $100 billion in Japan and $64 billion in Australia.

ESG Analysis at Oddo

In June 2005, Oddo hired Jean-Phillippe Desmartin to head its SRI initiative. Desmartin, who had started his career in financial engineering at Credit du Nord, a subsidiary of Societe Generale, and subsequently worked for several social and environmental rating agencies, was charged with developing a systematic methodology for SRI analysis at Oddo. He subsequently hired Sebastien Thevoux-Chabuel as a senior analyst in the initiative. Thevoux-Chabuel had been with Oddo since 2005 as a sell-side analyst on the European Technology sector and he had experience at Deutsche Bank and BFT, a subsidiary of Credit Agricole, as a buy-side analyst.

ESG research at Oddo was divided into three broad areas, Environmental, Social, and Governance (**Exhibit 1**). Environmental factors included environmental management, risks, and opportunities. Social factors covered regulatory risks, the management of the firm's human resources, its reputational capital and brands, and its supplier and partner relationships. Governance factors included the firm's commitment to sustainable development (i.e., using resources to meet human needs while also preserving the environment), adherence to corporate governance best practices, and business ethics.

The Oddo SRI Research team, working in collaboration with the firm's sector analysts, used a multi-step approach to build separate ESG models for each sector. Under the first step, the analyst team assessed which ESG factors were likely to be relevant and material for firms in the sector. Once these constructs were identified, the team developed quantitative and qualitative metrics for each material factor. Finally, the analyst team determined appropriate sector-specific weightings for the metrics, enabling them to be aggregated into separate environmental, social, and governance performance scores, and into a total ESG score. In explaining how the weightings were created, Desmartin noted that they are "intended to reflect the degree to which our ESG performance factors correlate with returns." Weights were estimated using historical relations between the sector's metrics/factors and its stock returns. The time horizon over which the historical relations were estimated ranged between one and five years depending on the availability of data.

The ESG analysts at Oddo then used the sector metrics and weightings generated from this process to construct ESG scores for individual companies within the sector. Based on a company's aggregate score, Oddo issued one of four ESG recommendations (Strong Opportunity, Opportunity, Moderate Risk, or High Risk).

[2]The authors calculated these numbers from information provided by national and international organizations that track socially conscious funds, such as Eurosif, Social Investment Forum, Responsible Investment Association Australasia, Social Responsible Organization, and SRI funds in Asia.

Around 25 percent of Oddo's non-ESG analysts believed that the firm's ESG research was a useful input into their company research and equity valuations. These analysts typically estimated how the opportunities and risks associated with the ESG scores would affect the future cash flow projections and/or the cost of capital for the companies they covered. Desmartin observed that: "the best financial analysts are most eager to use ESG research in their analysis and recommendations. The analysts who have the best reputation in the market are always trying to find ways to innovate and stay ahead of the curve." He added that "10 percent of financial analysts are skeptical about the value of ESG research." Thevoux-Chabuel explained that these analysts "are reluctant to incorporate ESG factors into their valuation models because they do not fully understand ESG analysis and do not have control over the analysis."

Oddo's ESG approach was designed to provide investors with insights into a firm's management capabilities, identify its key risks and opportunities, and drivers of its long-term sustainable financial performance. The goal of the ESG analysis, therefore, was to allow clients to optimize the ratio of returns to risk. Desmartin explained the firm's approach and the type of clients it sought to attract:

> *In practice we are very far from some of the ethical approaches used in the US. We do not exclude companies, we do not exclude activities, and we do not say what is good and what is bad. Ours is not a religious or moral approach. We simply want to find the best investment opportunities for our clients in the long-term.... We want 80 percent of our SRI research business to come from mainstream investors, not explicitly socially-conscious investors. Already, 50 percent of our business is coming from mainstream investors.*

SRI research was targeted to large institutional investors with long-term time horizons such as pension funds and insurance companies. However, Desmartin observed "we have seen some recent interest in SRI from hedge funds. I would not say it is a trend, yet it is very interesting because their focus is exclusively on making money."

Oddo's ESG recommendations reflected the expected performance of each stock over a long-term horizon (i.e., beyond 12 months). As reported in **Exhibit 2**, the stocks included in Oddo's SRI Strong Opportunity portfolio had outperformed the market for both the five-year and one-year horizons. Oddo calculated that from 2005 to 2010, its Strong Opportunity portfolio beat market indices by between 1,476 and 2,401 basis points (bps), depending on the index. For 2010, the portfolio beat the market by 181 to 970 bps, again depending on the index.

Oddo's telecom sector report

Oddo's study of the telecom sector covered major equipment makers and service providers in the US and Europe.

ESG Model

Desmartin and Thevoux-Chabuel created a model to evaluate and score telecommunication companies based on the three ESG factors. The environmental factor was labeled Health, Safety and Environment and covered whether the firm had an environmental management system, the environmental impact of telecom products and services, and the safety of products and services. Social factors included regulatory risks and opportunities, and intellectual capital (reflecting customer relationships and branding, human resource management, and supplier and partner relationships). Governance covered commitment to a sustainable development strategy, corporate governance, and business ethics. For each of these factors, Oddo analysts identified lower level quantitative and qualitative metrics. The weights assigned to each of these factors are shown in **Exhibit 3**. For operators, intellectual capital accounted for 40 percent and governance for 38 percent of ESG scoring.

Health/safety/environment (HSE)

Oddo analysts rated HSE factors as less important for the telecom sector than other sectors (e.g., energy, transportation, etc.). Telecom companies contributed less than 1 percent of CO_2 emissions, and telecom products and services could lower transportation demand, paper consumption, etc. The principal HSE risk identified was exposure to potential electromagnetic waves, which insurance companies were hesitant to cover. Risk exposure to electromagnetic waves was driven by exposure to mobile communications (80 percent) and by prevention measures (20 percent).

Social Factors

For telecom operators, the most important social factors identified were regulatory risks, and intellectual capital generated from the management of human resources and customer, supplier, and partner relationships (termed social ecosystem). On the human resources side the Oddo analysis attempted to identify companies characterized by a workforce that was productive and economically efficient but at the same time paid well. On the social ecosystem side the analysts assess the innovation capacity, brand value, supply chain efficiency, the quality, durability, growth potential and diversification of distributed networks, product and service quality, and customer satisfaction. The criteria used to generate scores for human resource and social ecosystem factors are shown in **Exhibits 4 and 5**.

Governance

The sustainable development and corporate governance criteria used in the ESG model are shown in **Exhibits 6 and 7**. The sustainable development criteria distinguished between companies that factored corporate social responsibility (CSR) and sustainable development into their internal and external communications and those that integrated CSR and sustainable development into their strategies and business models. The weightings used for corporate governance criteria differed for large-cap and mid to small sized firms, for firms with a controlling interest and for those with diversified owners, and for family-owned businesses.

Exhibit 8 shows the scores that BT and FT received by Oddo analysts in each of the factors. BT scored higher by more than 20 points and outperformed FT in all three categories.

Industry Drivers

Oddo's SRI analysis of the telecom industry identified five long-term performance drivers: sustainable development, regulation, sector consolidation, emerging countries, and technological advances or breakthroughs.

Sustainable Development

The analysts rated the sector highly for sustainable development, primarily because they assessed that it was well-positioned to create dematerialized growth (defined as making more products using fewer resources), facilitate entrepreneurial activities, open new markets, and help other organizations and industries become more sustainable.

Regulation

Because the telecom operator sector was viewed as a natural monopoly, it had been subject to regulation. Oddo analysts perceived this to be a key industry risk, particularly for many European telecom operators as regulators focused on increasing competition to lower prices and offer more services options for retail consumers.

Consolidation

Oddo analysts argued that countries with fragmented operator markets could see more consolidations to take advantage of economies of scale. Consolidations had already occurred in France, reducing the number of operators from nine to three, and in the Netherlands, where the number had fallen from five to three. However, Oddo analysts cautioned that cross-border acquisitions, although popular, presented political and implementation risks that made synergies elusive.

Emerging countries

According to Oddo's analysis, with little growth opportunities in home markets, operators and equipment makers would seek opportunities in emerging markets in Africa, Asia, and Latin America where penetration rates remained low.

Technological advances or breakthroughs

Advances in telecommunication technology were perceived to generate opportunities and threats. Equipment makers that failed to keep up with technological change were likely to face product obsolescence and financial failure. Operators also relied on technology so they needed to ensure that their offerings delivered the newest services, which often required heavy investment.

Results and Recommendations

Using the latest iteration of its ESG model, SRI Research analyzed 25 companies, assigning each an ESG score, rank, recommendation and outlook (see **Exhibit 9**). A summary of the findings is presented in **Exhibit 10**. Of those companies that were covered by Oddo's financial analysts and given a recommendation, only three – Iliad, Telefonica, and Vivendi – had ESG recommendations that matched the financial recommendation. Desmartin explained:

> *The first reason there may be a difference is because we are looking at different time horizons. The SRI team looks at long-term prospects, usually between 12 to 60 months, while the financial analysts typically are looking more short-term. The other reason for differences is when there is a mismatch between the SRI team and the financial analyst covering the sector or the company, about what is material for the sector or the company. Our aim is not to cover all ESG indicators but those that are most relevant and the most material from a financial standpoint. Our goal is to be right 50 percent of the time or more.*

In looking at the past performance of the 25 stocks, those that SRI Research identified as strong opportunity or opportunity outperformed the DJ Stoxx Telecommunications index by 171 percent; while those companies SRI Research identified as having moderate to high risk, underperformed the same index by 32 percent (**Exhibit 11**).

Keyes' decision

John Keyes reflected on the Oddo SRI Telecom report. The ESG and financial recommendations for British Telecom and France Telecom led him to the opposite conclusions. He reviewed the recent financial performance (see **Exhibit 12**) and stock market performance (see **Exhibit 13**) of the two companies. The performance of BT was impressively strong in 2006 and 2007 where earnings-per-share increased significantly and the company proposed an increase in dividends. However, BT's performance was completely reversed as the financial crisis hit and investors' expectations adjusted. How should he proceed? Should he follow the ESG recommendation and buy BT stock, or the financial recommendation and take a position in FT?

EXHIBIT 1 **Integrating ESG into Valuation Models**

ESG Research	→	Materiality	→	Measurement	→	Valuation Model
	L					
Environment	O					
Management	N					Opportunities
Risks	G	Business Model		ESG KPI's		↓
Opportunities						Performance
	T			+		
Social	E					
Regulation	R					Cash flow
IC – Human Capital	M	Management		ESG Events		Cost of Capital
IC – License to Operate/Reputation						Risk Premium
IC – Ecosystem, Quality, non-compliance	D			+		
	R					
Governance	I					Volatility
Sustainable development strategy	V	Statements		Monetary Value		↑
Corporate Governance	E					Risks
Business Ethics	R					
	S					

Source: Company documents.

Note "Management" refers to "Management quality." "Statements" refers to "Financial statements." "IC" is "Intellectual Capital".

EXHIBIT 2   **One-year and five-year performance comparison: Oddo SRI vs industry indices as of December 2010**

Index	Since Dec-31-2009	Since Dec-31-2005
Oddo SRI List (non-weighted)	7.96%	1.69%
France CAC 40	−1.74	−17.95
France SBF 120	0.77	−13.96
DJ STOXX Euro 50	−0.85	−22.32
DJ STOXX 600	6.15	−13.07

CAC 40 Compagnie des Agents de Change 40 Index

Owner/publisher/sponsor: Association of French Stock Exchanges – Paris Stock Exchange
   Number of constituents: 40 French companies listed on the Paris Stock Exchange that were also traded on the options market
   Construction principle: Capitalization-weighted value ratio

SBF 120 Société des Bourses Françaises 120 Index

Owner/publisher/sponsor: Association of French Stock Exchanges – Paris Stock Exchange
Number of constituents: 120 French companies listed on the Paris Stock Exchange
Construction principle: Capitalization-weighted value ratio

DJ STOXX Euro 50 Index

Europe's leading blue-chip index provided a representation of super sector leaders in Europe. The index covered 50 stocks from 18 European countries: Austria, Belgium, Denmark, Finland, France, Germany, Greece, Iceland, Ireland, Italy, Luxembourg, the Netherlands, Norway, Portugal, Spain, Sweden, Switzerland and the UK.

DJ STOXX 600 Index

Derived from the STOXX Europe Total Market Index (TMI) and was a subset of the STOXX Global 1800 Index. With a fixed number of 600 components, the STOXX Europe 600 Index represented large, mid and small capitalization companies across 18 countries of the European region: Austria, Belgium, Denmark, Finland, France, Germany, Greece, Iceland, Ireland, Italy, Luxembourg, the Netherlands, Norway, Portugal, Spain, Sweden, Switzerland, and the UK.

Source: Company documents.

EXHIBIT 3   **Overview of the ESG scoring model for the telecom sector**

ESG Criteria/Positioning	Equipment Makers	Operators
EMS (Environmental Management System)	3%	1%
Products and services (environmental impacts)	6	2
Industrial accidents (frequency rate)	2	0
Risk of exposure to electromagnetic waves	5	5
HSE (Health/Safety/Environment)	**16**	**8**
Regulation	1	14
Intellectual capital		
Human resources	15	15
Organizational	1	2
Ecosystem	29	23
Social	**46**	**54**
Sustainable development strategy	10	10
Corporate governance	25	25
Business ethics	3	3
Governance	**38**	**38**
Total ESG	100%	100%

Source: Company documents.

EXHIBIT 4   **Human resources indicators and criteria for the telecom sector**

Indicator	Criteria	Weighting	Nature of Criterion
Governance and HR profile	Growth model	10%	Quantitative & qualitative
	Age pyramid management	6	Quantitative & qualitative
	HR representation on executive board	4	Qualitative
	HR transparency	2	Quantitative & qualitative
Attractiveness and recruitment	Size-related attractiveness	5	Quantitative
	International presence-related attractiveness	4	Quantitative
	Economic attractiveness	2	Quantitative
	Average wage costs	2	Quantitative
	Employee share of ownership	5	Quantitative
Career integration and planning	Growth in headcount	2	Quantitative
	Integration, annual review rate, career planning	4	Quantitative & qualitative
	Training quality and effectiveness	2	Quantitative & qualitative
Motivation and satisfaction	Management of reorganizational/ restructuring measures	10	Mainly Qualitative
	Departure/arrival of key personnel	5	Qualitative
	Staff turnover	3	Quantitative
	Absenteeism	3	Quantitative
	Workplace climate and dialogue	10	Mainly Qualitative
Operational HR management	Payroll management	2	Quantitative
	Quality of local management	5	Qualitative
	Operating margin per employee	5	Quantitative
	Social liabilities (pension funds, healthcare, class actions)	9	Quantitative
Total		100%	

Source: Company documents.

EXHIBIT 5   **Ecosystem criteria for the telecom sector**

Criteria	Equipment Makers	Operators	Nature of Criteria
Corporate culture, internal organization	4.0%	2.0%	Qualitative
Innovation/R&D/patents	11.0	4.0	Quantitative & qualitative
Brand	2.0	3.0	Quantitative & qualitative
Supply chain, logistics, industrial partnerships	4.0	2.0	Qualitative
Distribution network	2.0	5.0	Qualitative
Product and service quality	3.0	3.0	Quantitative & qualitative
Customer satisfaction	3.0	4.0	Quantitative & qualitative
Total	29.0%	23.0%	

Source: Company documents.

EXHIBIT 6   **Sustainable development strategy criteria for the telecom sector**

Criteria	Equipment Makers	Operators	Nature of Criteria
Length of sustainable development track record and learning curve	1.0%	1.0%	Quantitative & qualitative
Sustainable development organization: Direct reporting; Director profile; Resources allocated; Interactions across functions	1.0	1.0	Qualitative
Sustainable development information systems	2.0	2.0	Quantitative & qualitative
Products and services with sustainable development added value	3.0	3.0	Quantitative & qualitative
Sustainable development objectives and results	3.0	3.0	Quantitative & qualitative
Total	10.0%	10.0%	

EXHIBIT 7 Corporate governance criteria for the telecom sector

Criteria	Large Cap		Mid-Small Cap		
	Non-Controlled	Controlled	Non-Controlled	Controlled	Family-owned
1. Minority shareholder rights (one share – one vote; anti-takeover measures)	17%	12%	18%	11%	12%
2. Separation of functions CEO-Chairman	13	10	13	10	5
3. Separation of roles (executives/shareholders/board members)	2	10	2	10	13
4. Executive succession planning	10	10	15	15	20
5. Transparency and cohesion of executive pay	3	3	3	3	3
6. Assessment of executive pay and long-term performance	5	5	5	5	5
7. Board effectiveness (composition, functioning)	20	20	20	21	16
8. Committees reporting to the board	5	5	6	5	5
9. Audit processes; degree of accountability, legal and tax transparency and complexity	13	13	7	9	9
10. Quality of financial communication	12	12	11	11	12
Total	100%	100%	100%	100%	100%

Source: Company documents.

EXHIBIT 8 Overview of the ESG Scoring Model for the Telecom Sector

ESG criteria/positioning	British Telecom	France Telecom
EMS (Environmental Management System)	1.0	0.5
Products and services (environmental impacts)	2.0	1.5
Industrial accidents (frequency rate)	0.0	0.0
Risk of exposure to electromagnetic waves	5.0	2.0
HSE (health/safety/environment)	**8.0**	**4.0**
Regulation	9.0	4.0
Intellectual capital		
Human resources	8.8	8.4
Organizational	1.5	0.5
Ecosystem	15.5	15.4
Social	**34.8**	**28.3**
Sustainable development strategy	10.0	5.5
Corporate governance	18.8	14.0
Business ethics	2.5	2.0
Governance	**31.3**	**21.5**
Total ESG	**74.1**	**53.8**

Source: Company documents.

EXHIBIT 9 Telecom sector: summary of ESG scores, rank, recommendation, outlook, financial recommendation, and target prices

Company	ESG Score	ESG Rank	ESG Recommendation*	ESG Outlook	Financial Recommendation*	Target Price
Equipment Makers						
Alcatel-Lucent	51.5	7	3	Positive	2	€3.5
Cisco	66.6	3	2	na	Not followed	na
Ericsson	65.3	4	2	Negative	3	SEK 65.0
Gemalto	59.8	5	2	na	1	€29.0
Motorola	50.3	8	3	na	Not followed	na
Nokia	77.1	1	1	Stable	2	€16.0
Oberthur	57.1	6	3	na	Accept the offer	€6.7
Tandberg	70.7	2	1	na	Not followed	na
Operators						
AT&T	61.7	3	2	na	Not followed	na
Belgacom	53.2	12	3	na	2	€25.5
Bouygues	55.5	9	3	Positive	1	€51.0
British Telecom	74.0	1	1	Stable	3	€170.0
Deutsche Telekom	51.4	13	3	Negative	2	€14.0
France Telecom	53.3	11	3	Positive	1	€24.0
Iliad	62.1	6	2	Stable	2	€79.0
KPN	61.6	5	2	Stable	1	€13.0
Maroc Telecom	51.0	15	3	na	2	€16.5
Mobistar	50.8	14	3	na	1	€60.0

EXHIBIT 9 **Telecom sector: summary of ESG scores, rank, recommendation, outlook, financial recommendation, and target prices** *(continued)*

Company	ESG Score	ESG Rank	ESG Recommendation*	ESG Outlook	Financial Recommendation*	Target Price
OTE	47.8	16	4	na	1	€24.0
Sprint	38.7	17	4	na	Not followed	na
Telecom Italia	54.1	10	3	Negative	3	€1.0
Telefonica	59.2	8	2	Stable	2	€17.5
Verizon	60.7	7	2	na	Not followed	na
Vivendi	63.2	2	2	Positive	2	€33.0
Vodafone	61.7	4	2	Stable	3	£115

Averages	
Equipment Makers	62.3
Operators	56.5
Telecom Sector	58.3
Maximum possible score	100.0

* Recommendation
1 = Strong opportunity
2 = Opportunity
3 = Moderate risk
4 = High risk

Source: Company documents.
SEK=Swedish Krona

EXHIBIT 10 **Results of Oddo ESG analysis for telecom sector health/safety/ environment: emphasis on usage-related energy consumption and exposure to electromagnetic waves (EMW)**

Environmental impact of products and services

Our model addresses the management of operator-related and, especially, equipment maker-related environmental impacts via environmental management systems (EMS). The Telecom sector produces palpable environmental effects, especially from a broader perspective embracing, for example, environmental life cycle issues (production process, usage impacts, and recycling). However, direct impacts from telecom players (elimination of dangerous substances during the production process, recycling) are modest compared with the effects associated with product and service usage. As in other sectors (automobile, capital goods, etc.), the impact is at least 80 percent indirect (usage) and 20 percent direct (production and end of life). The key issue for the Telecom sector is energy consumption linked to the usage of fixed-line and mobile telephony, the internet, and so forth.

Accordingly, our environmental analysis model emphasizes the criterion of product- and service-related environmental added value, particularly as measured by energy efficiency. This means that priority is given to efforts by equipment makers and operators to provide telecom products and services that are increasingly energy-efficient. Since 2005, equipment makers have stepped up the launch of offerings that have yielded 20–50 percent cuts in base-station energy consumption. At end-2007, the recently-formed Nokia-Siemens joint venture announced plans for an ambitious product/software offering with the potential to slash base-station energy consumption by up to 70 percent. This would be achieved by decreasing the number of base stations and reducing air-conditioning requirements for base stations. Experts like market research firm Gartner estimate potential energy savings at 50 percent. In the case of telecom operators, too, a "green" slant would make sense financially: energy consumption is operators' third-largest expenditure item after payroll expense and office space.

To avoid ecological gloom-mongering, which would lead to dispersion and undermine priority-setting, we again stress that "green" opportunities amply outweigh environmental risks in the Telecom sector. This contrasts sharply with the situation in other sectors like steel, chemicals, cement, extraction, oil, air, and road transport, and electricity production based on fossil fuels like coal and lignite. According to Ericsson, CO_2 emissions from mobile telephone usage average 25kg annually. As concerns recycling and end-of-life issues in the Telecom context, recycling is factored into our model, but to a much lesser extent than for the IT hardware industry (PCs, servers, etc.).

Risk of exposure to electromagnetic waves (EMW)

The potential risk to human health posed by electromagnetic waves has been a recurring theme for more than a decade. A large body of scientific material has been published both nationally (Agence Française de Sécurité sanitaire de l'environnement et du travail (Afsset) in France, University of Louvain in Belgium, publications in Denmark and Sweden, etc.) and internationally (European Commission, World Health Organisation, the Interphone epidemiological study conducted in 13 countries under the supervision of the International Agency for Research on Cancer (IARC), etc.). Numerous research projects are also in progress. As far as we are aware, no definitive conclusion has yet been reached concerning public health risks, such as an increased risk of a benign tumor on the auditory nerve or interference with the hemato-encephalic barrier. The debate is likely to continue, as the widespread usage of mobile telephones is a recent development and any symptoms might take as long as 10–15 years to emerge. It is also possible that the focus of discussions, currently mobile telephony, will broaden to include Wi-Fi equipment.

The sole proven risk concerns the use of a mobile telephone when driving; the rest is still subject to debate. Encouragingly, advances made over the past ten years with regard to SAR (specific absorption rate) reference values for mobile telephones have resulted in the reduction of this potential risk from one year to the next. The specific absorption rate measures the amount of radio frequencies emitted by a mobile telephone to the user when functioning at full capacity and under less than optimal conditions. The SAR is measured in watts per kilogram (W/kg) of tissue. A comparative study on the French website guerir.fr gives average SAR values for the products marketed by leading equipment makers (LG, Motorola, Nokia, Samsung, Sony-Ericsson, etc.), which range from 0.70 to 0.94.

The issue of human health risks still crops up regularly, however. In France, on September 18, 2008, telecom operator Bouygues Telecom was ordered to remove one of its masts in accordance with the "precautionary principle" on the grounds that there was a "potential health risk." The general scientific community is more concerned about intensive mobile telephone usage and advises taking precautions. Accordingly, 80 percent of our scoring model for the risk of exposure to electromagnetic waves is concerned with mobile-related exposure (mobile revenues as a percentage of total sales). Communication and awareness-raising initiatives by equipment makers and operators with regard to prevention account for the remaining 20 percent. Key prevention issues include:

- age limits (minimum age requirement of 12 years to promote moderate use, but the mobile telephone take-up rate for 12 year olds is currently close to 50 percent or 60 percent in many European countries);
- the systematic use of earphones (hand-free kits); =/ the non-use of a mobile telephone when driving (with or without hand-free kit);
- limitation of usage time in areas with poor coverage, where the emitted signal is all the stronger since the mast is far away.

Insurance companies have reservations concerning the principle of providing insurance for companies in the sphere of exposure to electromagnetic waves. In substance, as the risk associated with radio waves from mobile telephones is still uninsurable, EMW risks are generally excluded from corporate insurance contracts. From a purely EMW perspective, the best-positioned stocks as per our model are British Telecom, Iliad and Tandberg. The worst-positioned stocks are Ericsson, Gemalto, Maroc Telecom, Mobistar, Nokia, Sprint, and Vodafone.

3 Oddo Securities – ESG Integration

Nanotechnologies

The use of nanotechnologies is another public health issue. We see the potential for nanotechnological risks mainly in chemicals (production risk), construction materials (production risk), cosmetics (usage risk), and food (usage risk). In contrast, the aerospace, semi-conductor, environmental, and healthcare sectors should benefit from significant nanotechnology opportunities in the coming years. In the case of the Telecom sector, we see little potential exposure from a production or usage perspective. Rather, the Telecom sector might benefit from nanotechnologies in future, particularly in terms of energy efficiency. The nanotechnologies theme is dealt with in detail in an earlier study published in 2006.

Two stocks – British Telecom and Tandberg – rate highly on the HSE criterion.

Social issues: regulation, few outright winners, human resources, productivity at all stages, ecosystem, strategic innovation by equipment makers

Regulation: Smartcard manufacturers and operators British Telecom and Iliad are best positioned

In the case of equipment makers, smartcard makers like Gemalto operate within a structurally favorable regulatory framework in their two main outlets – telecommunications and, especially, banking. Players in this category also have the benefit of increased investment by governments worldwide in security and biometry programmes. On the operator side, regulation in Europe and elsewhere is one of the five key long-term drivers identified, as discussed earlier in this study. Although regulation represents a potential risk for telecom operators in Europe and, to a lesser extent, the US, we expect British Telecom and Iliad to fare well.

Human resources: quest for productivity at all levels

In our opinion, human resources risks for the Telecom sector do not include major risks like fundamental rights, exposure to dangerous products, industrial accident frequency and gravity, and the difficult working conditions associated with such sectors as construction, automotive component suppliers, industrial cleaning, textiles, toys, hotel and catering, and distribution. The Telecom sector offers abundant employment opportunities in most major functions like development, sales, marketing, R&D, and production. The sector is attractive, particularly to young graduates and non-graduates, who identify with its products and services. The sector has a long history of organized labor and houses large industrial and service groups with structured social relations. Above all, collective bargaining agreements at incumbent operators in both Europe and the US have so far been favorable.

Nevertheless, two areas bear watching from a human resources risk perspective: the management of activities at call centers, and productivity and employment imperatives at equipment makers and, especially, operators.

In developed and emerging countries alike, call centers have staff turnover rates of 20–25 percent at the low end and 50–60 percent at the high end. Turnover rates of as much as 100 percent have been encountered. These turnover levels are largely attributable to low pay (which spurs mobility), a high level of stress occasioned by consistently demanding productivity objectives, a sometimes inadequate work environment, irregular and inadequately planned working hours, and insufficiently diversified tasks. In addition, the internal promotion and mobility policy might not be properly structured. Note, however, that the employment situation at call centers is gradually improving and that many operators choose to outsource part or all of their call-centre activity, although Bouygues Telecom and a few others have adopted an integrated approach. Note, too, that telecom operators rarely speak "naturally" of working conditions at their call centers.

Since the beginning of the 2000s, the Telecom sector – in particular, incumbent operators – has been in the throes of a restructuring process characterized by continual reorganizations and job cuts. This state of affairs is typical for incumbent operators and should continue for at least another five years. Productivity gains will no doubt be forthcoming, but the social climate might be adversely affected in some cases (cf. recent events at Belgacom, Deutsche Telekom, and France Telecom), with a tangible impact on quality, customer satisfaction and, therefore, financial performance. This is precisely what happened in 2007 to Deutsche Telekom in Germany, where the deterioration of the social climate (as reflected by strike action) was detrimental to quality and customer satisfaction.

Our HR database for the Telecom sector (2,200,000 employees, of which 400,000 employed by equipment makers and 1,800,000 by operators) indicates that over the 2003–2007 period, head-count for the 25 groups covered by this study increased 3.2 percent overall (including acquisition growth; +6.5 percent for equipment makers and +2.6 percent for operators). However, the database also shows that with the exception of Telefonica, head-count declined for all European incumbent operators (even when employees added through acquisitions are included). At Telecom Italia, for example, the average number of employees fell more than 5 percent annually between 2003 and 2007. The quest for workforce productivity is aided by incumbent operators' typically unbalanced age pyramids, with retirement-induced attrition helping to cushion the social impact of restructuring. Productivity gains should continue to accrue over the next four to five years. More detailed information on this subject may be found in our June 2007 cross-sector age pyramid study, which focused in particular on the three incumbent operators Deutsche Telekom, France Telecom, and Telecom Italia.

Our findings for equipment makers and operators are similar. Based on a human capital approach, our four preferred stocks are Cisco, Nokia, Tandberg, and Vodafone. Our least preferred stocks are Motorola, OTE, and Sprint.

Ecosystem – strategic innovation by equipment makers

Our ESG model reflects the importance that we attach to the ecosystem criterion as applied to the Telecom sector (see above). The seven ecosystem criteria (corporate culture/internal organization, innovation/R&D/patents, brand, supply chain/logistics/industrial partners, distribution network, product and service quality, and customer satisfaction) account for 23 percent of our model for operators and 29 percent of our model for equipment makers. From an ecosystem perspective, the stocks rated Strong Opportunity (1) are equipment makers Cisco and Nokia, and operators Iliad, AT&T and Vivendi. We have a more cautious stance on Motorola, Alcatel, Bouygues, Deutsche Telekom, Sprint, and Telecom Italia.

Innovation capacity accounts for 11 percent of our ESG model for equipment makers. The weighting of innovation is lower in the case of operators, for which innovation is an opportunity, but also a constraint in terms of network replacement costs.

Regrettably, disclosure of ecosystem-related readings is scant; the general preference is to withhold information concerning, for example, R&D and churn, which is deemed "sensitive." This, we believe, vindicates our choice of applied methodologies and indicators. The full innovation-related results are presented in Appendix 10 and a summary of the innovation-related information (R&D, patents, etc.) obtained for analysis purposes is provided in Appendix 11. Our preferred stocks from an innovation perspective are equipment makers Cisco and Tandberg, and operators Iliad and Telefonica. Note that the positive correlation between innovation capacity and sustainable development (overall ESG results) is again corroborated by the findings presented in this Telecom sector study.

The rate of correlation between general ESG scores and innovation scores is 0.67 for the entire Telecom sector, 0.86 for equipment makers and 0.48 for operators.

Intellectual capital summary

Our model for the analysis of intellectual capital covers the three themes of human capital, license to operate/reputation and ecosystem. The five highest-ranked stocks on this criterion are Nokia, Cisco, Iliad, Vodafone, and Vivendi. We have a more cautious stance on Motorola, Alcatel, Deutsche Telekom, Sprint, OTE, and Telecom Italia.

Governance: Blue Chips at the Top of the League

Sustainable development strategy: advantage blue chips

Four stocks score particularly well from a sustainable development strategy perspective – equipment maker Nokia,and operators British Telecom, Telecom Italia, and Vodafone. Mobistar and Iliad have the lowest scores. Blue chips are well placed. Average readings for equipment makers and operators are identical. Except for AT&T and Verizon, US stocks are slightly behind on the learning curve and with regard to formalization and reporting in the field of sustainable development strategies.

Corporate governance: large-caps lead the way

Nokia, BT, KPN, and Vodafone score highest on the corporate governance criterion. We have a more cautious stance on Alcatel-Lucent, OTE, and Maroc Telecom. Average readings for equipment makers and operators are quite similar. There is, however, a bias in favor of large-caps, as we have observed since 2006 in our corporate governance research based on data for 130 European large-caps and 150 European mid-caps. Our results do not reveal any clear discrepancy in corporate governance performance between the European stock universe (19 companies) and the US stock universe (five companies) as covered in this study.

Overall governance assessment: Northern Europe is the frontrunner

In our opinion, Nokia, BT, and Vodafone have the best overall governance (combination of the three themes of sustainable development strategy, corporate governance, and business ethics). We have a more cautious stance on Alcatel, Bouygues, Maroc Telecom, Mobistar, and OTE. There are no marked discrepancies between readings for equipment makers and readings for operators.

Source: Company documents.

EXHIBIT 11   **Long-term stock market performances of Oddo's 13 eligible telecom stocks and 12 ineligible telecom stocks vs industry indices**

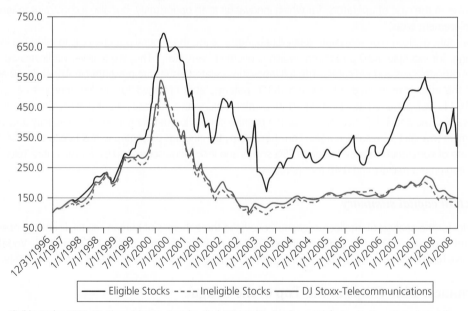

Eligible stocks: AT&T, BT, Cisco, Ericsson, Gemalto, Iliad, KPN, Nokia, Tandberg, Telefonica, Verizon, Vivendi, Vodafone
Ineligible stocks: Alcatel-hucent, Belgacom, Bouygues, Deutsche Telecom, France Telecom, Maroc Telecom, Mobistar, Motorola, Oberthur, OTE, Sprint, Telecom Italia

Source: Company documents.

EXHIBIT 12   Financial performance of France Telecom and British Telecom

France Telecom, for year ended December 31 (in € million)	2006	2007	2008
Total revenue	51,702	46,568	46,712
Revenue growth	7.5%	−9.9%	0.3%
NOPAT margin	10.3%	18.4%	12.3%
Asset turnover	0.71	0.68	0.70
ROA	7.2%	12.6%	8.6%
Spread	4.8%	7.1%	4.1%
Leverage	194.6%	154.8%	126.2%
Impact of leverage	9.4%	10.9%	5.2%
ROE	16.6%	23.5%	13.8%
Percent of revenues			
Gross profit	43.6%	44.7%	42.4%
Operating expenses	23.6%	23.0%	19.7%
Unusual income (expenses)	−0.3%	−7.5%	1.4%
Discontinued operations	1.3%	6.9%	0.4%
Valuation multiples			
Price-to-earnings	11.82	31.23	9.40
Price-to-book value	2.28	2.37	1.77

British Telecom, for the year ended March 31 (£ million)	2007	2008	2009
Total revenue	20,223	20,704	21,390
Revenue growth	3.6%	2.4%	3.3%
NOPAT margin	17.0%	11.6%	2.4%
Asset turnover	1.73	1.71	1.43
ROA	29.3%	19.8%	3.4%
Spread	23.5%	11.4%	−4.0%
Leverage	653.5%	186.5%	177.0%
Impact of leverage	153.8%	21.2%	−7.0%
ROE	183.2%	41.0%	−3.6%
Percent of revenues			
Gross profit	61.9%	61.8%	61.4%
Operating expenses	45.7%	45.5%	55.9%
Unusual income (expenses)	−1.3%	−2.9%	−2.6%
Discontinued operations	0.0%	0.0%	0.0%
Valuation multiples			
Price- to-earnings	10.48	8.32	6.66
Price-to-book value	7.47	4.02	2.20

Source: Capital IQ, accessed July 2011.
Note NOPAT is net operating profit after taxes. NOPAT margin is NOPAT over Net Assets. Asset turnover is total revenue over assets. Spread is NOPAT margin minus the interest on all interest paying liabilities. Leverage is total debt minus cash, over shareholder's equity. Impact of leverage is spread times leverage.

3 Oddo Securities – ESG Integration

EXHIBIT 13 **Stock market performance of France Telecom vs British Telecom**

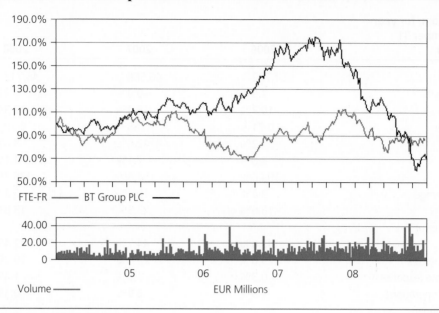

FTE-FR ——— BT Group PLC ———

Volume ———   EUR Millions

Source: Thomson Reuters Datastream, accessed July 2011.

4 Accounting for the iPhone at Apple Inc.

On October 21, 2008, Apple Inc. announced financial results for its fiscal 2008 fourth quarter ended September 27, 2008. (See **Exhibit 1**.) Under the US GAAP (generally accepted accounting principles), Apple reported quarterly revenue of $7.9 billion and net profit of $1.1 billion. For the first time, the Cupertino, California-based company included in its earnings announcement non-GAAP measures to supplement its US GAAP financial results. Apple's non-GAAP quarterly revenue and net profit were $11.7 billion and $2.4 billion, respectively. As Apple CEO Steve Jobs noted, "As you can see, the non-GAAP financial results are truly stunning."[1] He explained the change in a rare appearance on the company's earnings conference call later that day:

> I would like to … talk about the non-GAAP financial results, because I think this is a pretty big deal. In addition to reporting an outstanding quarter, today we are also introducing non-GAAP financial results which eliminate the impact of subscription accounting. Because by its nature subscription accounting spreads the impact of iPhone's contribution to Apple's overall sales, gross margin and net income over two years, it can make it more difficult for the average Apple manager or the average investor to evaluate the company's overall performance. As long as our iPhone business was small relative to our Mac and music businesses, this didn't really matter much, but the past quarter, as you heard, our iPhone business has grown to about $4.6 billion, or 39 percent of Apple's total business, clearly too big for Apple management or investors to ignore.[2]

Jobs also noted that in terms of non-GAAP mobile phone revenue, in just 15 months, Apple had become the world's third largest phone manufacturer behind Nokia and Samsung but ahead of Sony Ericsson, LG, Motorola, and RIM.

Company background

Jobs and Steve Wozniak launched the personal computer revolution in the 1970s with the Apple II. In 1984, the Apple Macintosh, with its ease-of-use and brilliant design, redefined the personal computer. Shortly thereafter, Jobs left the company, returning in 1997. Under Jobs, Apple catalyzed the digital media industry with the launch of its iPod portable musical player in October 2001, followed by the introduction of its iTunes online store in April 2003.

In June 2007, the company entered the highly competitive mobile phone market with its iPhone, the first smartphone (a combination of a phone and a mini-computer) with a touch screen interface and the company's new mobile operating system iOS. Several months later, Apple released the iPod touch (an iPhone without the phone capability).

Professors Francois Brochet and Krishna G. Palepu and Research Associate Lauren Barley prepared this case. This case was developed from published sources. HBS cases are developed solely as the basis for class discussion. Cases are not intended to serve as endorsements, sources of primary data, or illustrations of effective or ineffective management.

Apple released its iPhone 3G in July 2008 along with its second generation mobile operating system (iOS 2). Also in July 2008, Apple introduced its App Store that offered iPhone and iPod touch users a wide variety of mobile applications ranging from games to social networking to productivity tools, mostly priced under $10. On July 14, 2008, Jobs noted, "The App Store is a grand slam, with a staggering 10 million applications downloaded in just three days. Developers have created some extraordinary applications, and the App Store can wirelessly deliver them to every iPhone and iPod touch user instantly."[3] Many of the applications took advantage of the more robust iOS 2. By October 2008, Apple was best known for its technical and design innovation, its "walled garden" approach (i.e., its mostly proprietary ecosystem of hardware, operating and application software, and peripherals), and its premium-priced products.

iPhone business model

The original iPhone 8GB model had a US retail price of $399 and was available through Apple and AT&T, the iPhone's exclusive US mobile carrier. In the US, mobile carriers typically provided subsidies to phone manufacturers, which lowered the purchase price of the new phone. In exchange, most consumers signed a two-year service contract with the carriers. Apple and AT&T agreed to a different arrangement, but did not disclose its specifics. AT&T did not subsidize the iPhone; instead, Apple signed a revenue sharing agreement with AT&T that gave Apple a share of the subscribers' monthly service fees. Needham & Co. analyst Charles Wolf believed AT&T paid Apple $10 per month over a typical two-year contract.[4] In addition, although Apple did not disclose how much it sold the iPhone for to AT&T, it was believed that Apple made an estimated $120 in gross profit on every iPhone sold.[5]

At the iPhone's launch, Apple announced it might periodically offer new software updates and upgrades free of charge to its iPhone customers. In contrast, Mac and iPod users did not receive free software features and upgrades. For example, users were charged $129 to upgrade to the new Mac operating system (Mac OS X Leopard) in October 2007, whereas Apple planned to provide newer versions of the iPhone operating systems free of charge to all iPhone users. Apple's chief financial officer Peter Oppenheimer explained, "Since iPhone customers will likely be our best advocates for the product, we want to get them many of these new features and applications at no additional charge as they become available."[6]

Apple's management knew that smartphone users were slow to update their software, and few opted to buy upgrades. Therefore, the company believed it was necessary to offer new software features free of charge to increase user acceptance. In contrast, most other mobile software vendors reserved new software updates for new hardware (i.e., phone) releases.[7] Apple, AT&T, third-party application developers, and users would benefit from consumers' use of the latest operating system and applications, giving Apple and its ecosystem a competitive advantage. AT&T would run a more effective and efficient mobile network; third-party software developers would have a stable hardware and software roadmap; Apple could delist applications from its App Store that weren't written for its latest operating system; and all the while, iPhone users would benefit from an evolving and differentiated set of features and functionality. Many users of competing mobile phone platforms could not upgrade to newer operating systems and applications because of compatibility issues with their phones.

When Apple launched the iPhone 3G in July 2008, it revamped its business model, bringing it more in line with industry practices. Apple gave up its share of the monthly service revenue in exchange for AT&T subsidizing the price of the iPhone 3G, which sold for $199 at retail. Again, the two parties chose not to disclose the specifics of their arrangement, but the subsidy was estimated at $300 per phone sold.[8] Apple continued to differ from most other industry participants when it offered existing iPhone users upgrades to its second-generation operating system at no cost.

By August 2008, a month after Apple introduced its App Store, Jobs noted that users downloaded more than 60 million programs for the iPhone, and Apple was averaging $1 million a day in application software revenue. Apple received 30 percent of the App Store revenue from the sale of an iPhone application and the developer received the remaining 70 percent.[9] Jobs stated, "Phone differentiation used to be about radios and antennas and things like that. We think, going forward, the phone of the future will be differentiated by software."[10]

Also in August 2008, *The New York Times* reported that T-Mobile would be the first carrier to launch mobile phones using Google's Android mobile operating system, which were expected to hit shelves in late October 2008. On October 21, 2008, Google announced that Android was now "the first free, open source, and fully customizable mobile platform."[11]

iPhone revenue recognition

Software-enabled hardware devices (also known as "bundled components"), such as Apple's iPhone, Macs, and iPods, fell under the software revenue recognition rules pursuant to American Institute of Certified Public Accountants (AICPA) Statement of Position (SOP) No. 97-2, Software Revenue Recognition. When Apple first introduced the iPhone in 2007, the company announced it would use the "subscription method of accounting" under SOP No. 97-2 to book revenue for its new iPhone. Oppenheimer explained:

> *Since we will be periodically providing new software features to iPhone customers free of charge, we will use subscription accounting and recognize the revenue and product cost of goods sold associated with iPhone handset sales on a straight line basis over 24 months. So while the cash from iPhone sales will be collected at the time of sale, we will be recording deferred revenue and costs of goods sold on our balance sheet, and amortizing both of them into our earnings on a straight line basis over 24 months. We will continue to expense our iPhone engineering, sales and marketing costs as we incur them. This accounting policy will have no impact on cash flow or the economics of our business.[12]*

In contrast, Apple generally recognized revenue and cost of sales for its other software-enabled hardware products such as Macs and iPods at the time of sale (i.e., immediate revenue recognition) under SOP No. 97-2. This was because the company did not provide new features or software applications for those products free of charge. (See **Exhibit 2** for FY 2008 financial statement note relating to Apple's revenue recognition policies under GAAP.)

Apple's decision to use subscription accounting for the iPhone came soon after the company faced consumer backlash over a $5 upgrade fee (later reduced to $1.99) it charged new MacBook buyers.[13] In 2006, Apple sold its latest MacBooks with a wireless chip that would allow users to access the new and better Wi-Fi 802.11n technology once it became available and the chip was activated with software. Apple did not tell MacBook buyers about the chip's existence, and it also recognized all revenue at the time the MacBooks sold. Thus, the chip and its activation software were an unspecified, future upgrade that did not have an established, objective, separate value (which would have allowed it to be accounted for separately) at the time of the MacBook sale. To comply with GAAP, Apple faced two options: 1) restate its financials to recognize the MacBook revenue under subscription accounting, or 2) charge users for the upgrade. The company chose the latter option.

Technology companies such as Apple were increasingly facing the issue of how to account for bundled components as the software and hardware in these products became more integrated and integral to the products' function. This placed US technology companies on unequal footing with their overseas competitors because International Financial Reporting Standards (IFRS) allowed companies to use a more subjective measure – cost-plus margin – when an objective and separate value could not be established for a future deliverable such as a free software upgrade. Consequently, an overseas company did not have to report only a fraction of its revenue when it sold a bundled component with the promise of a future deliverable such as a free upgrade. Company management could estimate the cost and the margin of the upgrade and defer just that portion of the bundled component's sale until the upgrade was delivered.[14]

Subscription accounting

The software and magazine publishing industries were well known for their use of subscription accounting. Magazine publishers reported the cash received for a subscription at the time that the subscription was purchased, but only recorded the revenue as each issue was delivered. The remaining balance was deferred into a liability account called unearned (or deferred) revenue. For example, if a year's subscription of a monthly magazine cost $12, then the magazine publisher would recognize $1 per month in revenue for 12 months as the unearned revenue account decreased by $1 per month.

Under subscription accounting, Apple recognized the associated revenue and cost of goods sold for the iPhone on a straight-line basis over the product's estimated 24-month economic life (the typical length of a mobile phone service contract). When Apple announced its quarterly results from iPhone sales, its reported revenues (and other related metrics) reflected only an eighth of the revenue from iPhone sales during that quarter. This resulted in a deferral of the remaining revenue and cost of sales relating to iPhones units sold, although the company received and reported the cash in the quarter of the sale. Each quarter, Apple also reported a share of iPhone sales (both the revenue and the associated cost of goods sold) for iPhones sold in previous quarters. (See **Exhibit 3** for illustration of iPhone subscription accounting.) As long as the number of iPhone sales increased each quarter, the deferral balance increased. Costs incurred for engineering, sales, marketing, and warranty were expensed as incurred.

Reactions

In July 2008, iPhone users validated Apple's decision to offer free upgrades when they quickly adopted the free iOS 2. Apple never intended to give iPod touch users upgrades at no charge, and its users expressed confusion and dissatisfaction with their $9.95 upgrade fee for the same software.[15] At the same time, Apple's use of subscription accounting drew mixed reviews from the business community. A *Business Finance* article praised Apple's "smoother revenue curve" that resulted from its use of subscription accounting and continued, "Apple shows how a mature, astute organization can use revenue accounting rules to its benefit."[16] However, an *Apple 2.0 Fortune Tech* post stated:

> More than seven months have passed [since Apple's use of subscription accounting began] and nobody – not the analysts, not the investors, and certainly not Wall Street – has quite wrapped their mind around what this bookkeeping oddity means for Apple's bottom line. That's in part because it's complicated, and in part because Apple hasn't provided all the data you would need to fully assess its impact.
>
> But those so-called deferred earnings are adding up, and some professional Apple watchers are starting to realize that their impact could be substantial. And to the dismay of Apple shareholders, the fact that these deferred earnings are piling up seems to have gone right over the heads of the institutional investors who have driven Apple shares down nearly 75 points since December.[17] *(See* **Exhibit 4** *for quarterly deferred earning balances.)*

Non-GAAP supplements

By the fourth quarter of 2008, Apple's management believed the impact of subscription accounting on its financials was too big for the company to ignore. Apple released select Q4 2008 non-GAAP financial results as supplements that gave Apple watchers their first look at its revenue numbers without the use of subscription accounting. Research suggested that companies issued non-GAAP supplementary disclosures to communicate adjusted accounting numbers that better predicted future performance, but also for opportunistic reasons.[18] On average, investors appeared to weight non-GAAP numbers more heavily compared to GAAP numbers when they formed their expectations for future earnings, assuming they found the non-GAAP numbers informative and credible. Not surprisingly, research also showed that companies tended to emphasize measures that portrayed the most favorable performance.[19]

In 2003, the Securities and Exchange Commission (SEC) issued new non-GAAP disclosure rules to address concerns about the lack of oversight on these disclosures. The SEC's Regulation G required companies that disclosed non-GAAP financial measures to use the most comparable GAAP measures when preparing their non-GAAP disclosures, in addition to providing a reconciliation of the GAAP and non-GAAP results.[20] Recent studies indicated that since the passage of Regulation G, firms were less likely to provide non-GAAP earnings that excluded expenses of a recurring nature.[21]

In describing Apple's non-GAAP financials, Jobs noted that iPhone non-GAAP sales were a staggering $4.6 billion, 39 percent of Apple's total revenue in the fourth quarter of 2008. See Table c4.A.

Apple cautioned that its non-GAAP calculations did not adjust for the estimated costs associated with its plan to provide new features and software upgrades to iPhone buyers free of charge. It also warned investors that these figures were not prepared under a comprehensive set of rules or principles, since no standards existed for making these calculations. (See **Exhibit 5** for Apple's cautions on use of its non-GAAP supplements.)

Apple also announced iPhone Q4 2008 GAAP sales that just missed Wall Street's estimates, but total income that easily beat the Street's estimates.[22] Apple's first quarter 2009 guidance was well below the Street's forecast. Apple's stock closed down for the day.

Q4 2008	GAAP ($ billions)	Non-GAAP ($ billions)	% Increase
Total Sales	$7.9	$11.7	48%
Total Income	1.1	2.4	115%
iPhone Sales	0.8	4.6	475%
iPhone as % of Sales	10%	39%	

Source: Casewriter.

Conclusion

The immediate analyst reaction to Apple's Q4 2008 financial results and conservative Q1 2009 guidance was largely positive, although Maynard Um of UBS downgraded his rating from "Buy" to "Neutral" and cut his share price target to $115 (from $125), citing "potential macro-economic issues impacting Mac sales."[23] In contrast, Shebly Seyrafi of Calyon Securities raised his rating from "Add" to "Buy" and increased his price target to $150 (from $130), noting that Apple's earnings-per-share (EPS) would have more than doubled had it not been for the company's use of subscription accounting for iPhone sales.[24] (See **Exhibit 6** for share price performance.)

Reaction to Apple's decision to provide non-GAAP supplements was more mixed. Proponents of Apple's use of non-GAAP supplements argued that these results were more consistent with Apple's $24.5 billion in cash and short-term investments. They also pointed out that under GAAP, the iPhone's strong shipments in Q4 2008 were not fully reflected in Apple's results. They also argued that valuations using non-GAAP measures were better indicators of the company's true financial performance.[25]

In contrast, GAAP proponents asserted that the Street penalized technology companies reporting non-GAAP results. They argued that Apple's management clearly believed future, free software upgrades were critical to an iPhone buyer's initial purchase decision and necessitated Apple's use of subscription accounting. Further, they argued that non-GAAP supplements gave the iPhone too much weight, pointing to the fact that Apple's quarterly numbers became more sensitive to iPhone unit sales, which were more volatile and difficult for analysts to predict. Perhaps most importantly, they maintained that investors knew to use cash revenue numbers for valuations and ratios, and that changing to non-GAAP measures should have no impact on the economic value of Apple shares.[26]

Apple announced it would provide non-GAAP supplements ongoing during earnings releases. Only time would reveal their effects, if any, on Apple's share pricing.

4 Accounting for the iPhone at Apple Inc.

4 Accounting for the iPhone at Apple Inc.

EXHIBIT 1   Apple Inc. Select Historical Financial Data

1a. Apple Inc. Q4 2008 Unaudited Summary Data

| | Q3 2008 | | Q4 2007 | | Q4 2008 | | Sequential Change | | Year/Year Change | |
	CPU Units (K)	Revenue ($M)	CPU Units (K)	Revenue ($M)	CPU Units K	Revenue ($M)	CPU Units	Revenue	CPU Units	Revenue
Product summary										
Desktops[a]	943	$1,373	817	$1,195	936	$1,363	−1%	−1%	15%	14%
Portables[b]	1,553	2,237	1,347	1,908	1,675	2,257	8%	1%	24%	18%
Subtotal CPUs	**2,496**	**3,610**	**2,164**	**3,103**	**2,611**	**3,620**	**5%**	**0%**	**21%**	**17%**
iPod	11,011	1,678	10,200	1,619	11,052	1,660	0%	−1%	8%	3%
Other music-related products and services[c]		819		601		832		2%		38%
iPhone and related products and services[d]	717	419	1,119	118	6,892	806	861%	92%	516%	583%
Peripherals and other hardware		437		346		428		−2%		24%
Software, service, and other sales		501		430		549		10%		28%
Total Apple		**$7,464**		**$6,217**		**$7,895**		**6%**		**27%**

Source: "Apple Reports Fourth Quarter Results," October 21, 2008, http://www.apple.com/pr/library/2008/10/21results.html, accessed 6/22/10.

Note: K = units in thousands; $M=amounts in millions.

[a]Includes iMac, Mac mini, Mac Pro, PowerMac and Xserve product lines.

[b]Includes MacBook, iBook, MacBook Air, MacBook Pro and PowerBook product lines.

[c]Consists of iTunes Store sales, iPod services, and Apple-branded and third-party iPod accessories.

[d]Units consist of iPhone handset sales; Revenue is derived from handset sales, carrier agreements, and Apple-branded and third-party iPhone accessories.

1b. Apple Inc. Unaudited Condensed Consolidated Statement of Operations (in millions, except share amounts which are reflected in thousands and per share amounts)

	Three Months Ended:		Twelve Months Ended:	
	September 27, 2008	September 29, 2007	September 27, 2008	September 29, 2007
Net sales	$7,895	$6,217	$32,479	$24,006
Cost of sales[a]	5,156	4,127	21,334	15,852
Gross margin	2,739	2,090	11,145	8,154
Operating expenses:				
Research and development[a]	298	207	1,109	782
Selling, general, and administrative[a]	999	823	3,761	2,963
Total operating expenses	1,297	1,030	4,870	3,745
Operating income	1,442	1,060	6,275	4,409
Other income and expense	140	170	620	599
Income before provision for income taxes	1,582	1,230	6,895	5,008
Provision for income taxes	446	326	2,061	1,512
Net income	$1,136	$904	$4,834	$3,496
Earnings per common share:				
Basic	$1.28	$1.04	$5.48	$4.04
Diluted	$1.26	$1.01	$5.36	$3.93
Shares used in computing earnings per share:				
Basic	887,110	870,881	881,592	864,595
Diluted	904,786	895,666	902,139	889,292
[a]Includes stock-based compensation expense as follows:				
Cost of sales	$21	$10	$80	$35
Research and development	$52	$21	$185	$77
Selling, general, and administrative	$68	$37	$251	$130

Source: "Apple Reports Fourth Quarter Results," October 21, 2008, http://www.apple.com/pr/library/2008/10/21results.html, accessed 6/22/10.

4 Accounting for the iPhone at Apple Inc.

1c. Unaudited Condensed Balance Sheets (in millions, except share amounts)

	September 27, 2008	September 29, 2007
ASSETS:		
Current Assets:		
Cash and cash equivalents	$11,875	$9,352
Short-term investments	12,615	6,034
Accounts receivable, less allowances of $47 in each period	2,422	1,637
Inventories	509	346
Deferred tax assets	1,447	782
Other current assets[a]	5,822	3,805
Total current assets	34,690	21,956
Property, plant and equipment, net	2,455	1,832
Goodwill	207	38
Acquired intangible assets, net	285	299
Other assets[b]	1,935	1,222
Total Assets	$39,572	$25,347
LIABILITIES AND SHAREHOLDERS' EQUITY:		
Current Liabilities:		
Accounts payable	$5,520	$4,970
Accrued expenses[c]	8,572	310
Total current liabilities	14,092	9,280
Non-current liabilities[d]	4,450	1,535
Total Liabilities	18,542	10,815
Commitments and contingencies		
Shareholders' Equity:		
Common stock, no par value;	7,177	5,368
Retained earnings	13,845	9,101
Accumulated other comprehensive income	8	63
Total Shareholders' Equity	21,030	14,532
Total Liabilities and Shareholders' Equity	$39,572	$25,347

Source: "Apple Reports Fourth Quarter Results," October 21, 2008, http://www.apple.com/pr/library/2008/10/21results.html, accessed 6/22/10.

[a]Includes current portion of deferred costs under subscription accounting of $1,931 and $247, respectively.
[b]Includes non-current portion of deferred costs under subscription accounting of $1,089 and $214, respectively.
[c]Includes current portion of deferred revenue under subscription accounting of $4,853 and $1,391, respectively.
[d]Includes non-current portion of deferred revenue under subscription accounting of $3,029 and $849, respectively.

1d. Unaudited Condensed Consolidated Statements of Cash Flows (in millions)

Twelve Months Ended:	September 27, 2008	September 29, 2007
Cash and cash equivalents, beginning of the period	$9,352	$6,392
Operating Activities:		
Net income	4,834	3,496
Adjustments to reconcile net income to cash generated by operating activities:		
Depreciation, amortization, and accretion	473	317
Stock-based compensation expense	516	242
Provision for deferred income taxes	(368)	78
Loss on disposition of property, plant, and equipment	22	12
Changes in operating assets and liabilities:		
Accounts receivable, net	(785)	(385)
Inventories	(163)	(76)
Other current assets	(1,958)	(1,540)
Other assets	(492)	81
Accounts payable	596	1,494
Deferred revenue	5,642	1,139
Other liabilities	1,279	612
Cash generated by operating activities	9,596	5,470
Investing Activities:		
Purchases of short-term investments	(22,965)	(11,719)
Proceeds from maturities of short-term investments	11,804	6,483
Proceeds from sales of short-term investments	4,439	2,941
Purchases of long-term investments	(38)	(17)
Payments made in connection with business acquisitions, net of cash acquired	(220)	—
Payment for acquisition of property, plant, and equipment	(1,091)	(735)
Payment for acquisition of intangible assets	(108)	(251)
Other	(10)	49
Cash used in investing activities	(8,189)	(3,249)
Financing Activities:		
Proceeds from issuance of common stock	483	365
Excess tax benefits from stock-based compensation	757	377
Cash used to net share settle equity awards	(124)	(3)
Cash generated by financing activities	1,116	739
Increase in cash and cash equivalents	2,523	2,960
Cash and cash equivalents, end of the period	$11,875	$9,352
Supplemental cash flow disclosure:		
Cash paid for income taxes, net	$1,267	$863

Source: "Apple Reports Fourth Quarter Results," October 21, 2008, http://www.apple.com/pr/library/2008/10/21results.html, accessed 6/22/10.

1e. Unaudited Condensed Schedule of Deferred Revenue (in millions)

	September 27, 2008	June 28, 2008	September 29, 2007
Deferred revenue – Current:			
iPhone and Apple TV	$3,518	$1,389	$346
AppleCare	599	547	430
Other	736	791	615
Total deferred revenue – Current	4,853	2,727	1,391
Deferred revenue – Noncurrent:			
iPhone and Apple TV	2,262	632	290
AppleCare	651	597	495
Other	116	107	64
Total deferred revenue – Noncurrent	3,029	1,336	849
Total deferred revenue	$7,882	$4,063	$2,240

Source: ''Apple Reports Fourth Quarter Results,'' October 21, 2008, http://www.apple.com/pr/library/2008/10/21results.html, accessed 6/22/10.

4 Accounting for the iPhone at Apple Inc.

1f. Unaudited Reconciliation of Non-GAAP to GAAP Results of Operations (in millions, except share amounts which are reflected in thousands and per share amounts)

	Three Months Ended September 27, 2008		
	As Reported	Non-GAAP Adjustments	Non-GAAP
Net sales	$7,895	$3,787[a]	$11,682
Cost of sales	5,156	1,975[b]	7,131
Gross margin	2,739	1,812[c]	4,551
Operating expenses	1,297	—	1,297
Operating income	1,442	1,812	3,254
Other income and expense	140	—	140
Income before provision for income taxes	1,582	1,812	3,394
Provision for income taxes	446	511[d]	957
Net income	$1,136	$1,301[e]	$2,437
Earnings per diluted common share	$1.26	$1.43[f]	$2.69
Shares used in computing diluted earnings per share	904,786		904,786

Source: "Apple Reports Fourth Quarter Results," October 21, 2008, http://www.apple.com/pr/library/2008/10/21results.html, accessed 6/22/10.

[a]Non-GAAP adjustment to net sales reflect (i) the reversal of the current period's amortization of deferred revenue derived from iPhone handsets and Apple TV units shipped in current and prior periods and (ii) the inclusion of amounts generally due to Apple at the time of sale related to iPhone handsets and Apple TV units shipped in the current period.
[b]Non-GAAP adjustment to cost of sales reflect (i) the reversal of the current period s amortization of deferred cost related to iPhone handsets and Apple TV units shipped in current and prior periods and (ii) the inclusion of the total cost of iPhone handsets and Apple TV units shipped in the current period. In addition, the non-GAAP adjustment to cost of sales reflects the estimate of the warranty expense in the period when the related product is sold, rather than when the expense is incurred. The non-GAAP adjustment to cost of sales does not reflect the cost of providing unspecified additional software products and upgrades.
[c]Non-GAAP adjustments to gross margin, operating income and income before provision for income taxes are the difference between non-GAAP adjustments to net sales and non-GAAP adjustments to cost of sales [(a) − (b)].
[d]Represents the application of the period's effective tax rate to the non-GAAP adjustments to income before provision for income taxes.
[e]Represents the after-tax effect of the non-GAAP adjustments to gross margin, operating income and income before provision for income taxes.
[f]Represents the per share impact of the non-GAAP adjustments to net income.

4 Accounting for the iPhone at Apple Inc.

EXHIBIT 2   Apple Inc. FY 2008 Revenue Recognition Policy

Notes to Consolidated Financial Statements

Note 1 – Summary of Significant Accounting Policies

Revenue Recognition

Net sales consist primarily of revenue from the sale of hardware, software, music products, digital content, peripherals, and service and support contracts. For any product within these groups that either is software, or is considered software-related in accordance with the guidance in Emerging Issues Task Force ("EITF") No. 03-5, *Applicability of AICPA Statement of Position 97-2 to Non-Software Deliverables in an Arrangement Containing More-Than-Incidental Software* (e.g., Mac computers, iPod portable digital music players and iPhones), the Company accounts for such products in accordance with the revenue recognition provisions of American Institute of Certified Public Accountants ("AICPA") Statement of Position ("SOP") No. 97-2, *Software Revenue Recognition*, as amended. The Company applies Staff Accounting Bulletin ("SAB") No. 104, *Revenue Recognition*, for products that are not software or software-related, such as digital content sold on the iTunes Store and certain Mac, iPod and iPhone supplies and accessories.

   The Company recognizes revenue when persuasive evidence of an arrangement exists, delivery has occurred, the sales price is fixed or determinable, and collection is probable. Product is considered delivered to the customer once it has been shipped and title and risk of loss have been transferred. For most of the Company's product sales, these criteria are met at the time the product is shipped. For online sales to individuals, for some sales to education customers in the US, and for certain other sales, the Company defers revenue until the customer receives the product because the Company legally retains a portion of the risk of loss on these sales during transit. If at the outset of an arrangement the Company determines the arrangement fee is not, or is presumed not to be, fixed or determinable, revenue is deferred and subsequently recognized as amounts become due and payable and all other criteria for revenue recognition have been met.

   Revenue from service and support contracts is deferred and recognized ratably over the service coverage periods. These contracts typically include extended phone support, repair services, web-based support resources, diagnostic tools, and extend the service coverage offered under the Company's one-year limited warranty.

   The Company sells software and peripheral products obtained from other companies. The Company generally establishes its own pricing and retains related inventory risk, is the primary obligor in sales transactions with its customers, and assumes the credit risk for amounts billed to its customers. Accordingly, the Company generally recognizes revenue for the sale of products obtained from other companies based on the gross amount billed.

   The Company accounts for multiple element arrangements that consist only of software or software-related products in accordance with SOP No. 97-2. If a multiple-element arrangement includes deliverables that are neither software nor software-related, the Company applies EITF No. 00-21, *Revenue Arrangements with Multiple Deliverables*, to determine if those deliverables constitute separate units of accounting from the SOP No. 97-2 deliverables. If the Company can separate the deliverables, the Company applies SOP No. 97-2 to the software and software-related deliverables and applies other appropriate guidance (e.g., SAB No. 104) to the deliverables outside the scope of SOP No. 97-2. Revenue on arrangements that include multiple elements such as hardware, software, and services is allocated to each element based on the relative fair value of each element. Each element's allocated revenue is recognized when the revenue recognition criteria for that element have been met. Fair value is generally determined by vendor specific objective evidence ("VSOE"), which is based on the price charged when each element is sold separately. If the Company cannot objectively determine the fair value of any undelivered element included in a multiple-element arrangement, the Company defers revenue until all elements are delivered and services have been performed, or until fair value can objectively be determined for any remaining undelivered elements. When the fair value of a delivered element has not been established, the Company uses the residual method to recognize revenue if the fair value of all undelivered elements is determinable. Under the residual method, the fair value of the undelivered elements is deferred and the remaining portion of the arrangement fee is allocated to the delivered elements and is recognized as revenue.

   The Company records reductions to revenue for estimated commitments related to price protection and for customer incentive programs, including reseller and end-user rebates, and other sales programs and volume-based incentives. The estimated cost of these programs is accrued as a reduction to revenue in the period the Company

EXHIBIT 2   **Apple Inc. FY 2008 Revenue Recognition Policy** *(continued)*

has sold the product and committed to a plan. The Company also records reductions to revenue for expected future product returns based on the Company's historical experience. Revenue is recorded net of taxes collected from customers that are remitted to governmental authorities, with the collected taxes recorded as current liabilities until remitted to the relevant government authority.

Generally, the Company does not offer specified or unspecified upgrade rights to its customers in connection with software sales or the sale of extended warranty and support contracts. When the Company does offer specified upgrade rights, the Company defers revenue for the fair value of the specified upgrade right until the future obligation is fulfilled or when the right to the specified upgrade expires. Additionally, a limited number of the Company's software products are available with maintenance agreements that grant customers rights to unspecified future upgrades over the maintenance term on a when and if available basis. Revenue associated with such maintenance is recognized ratably over the maintenance term.

In 2007, the Company began shipping Apple TV and iPhone. For Apple TV and iPhone, the Company indicated it may from time-to-time provide future unspecified features and additional software products free of charge to customers. Accordingly, Apple TV and iPhone handsets sales are accounted for under subscription accounting in accordance with SOP No. 97-2. As such, the Company's policy is to defer the associated revenue and cost of goods sold at the time of sale, and recognize both on a straight-line basis over the currently estimated 24-month economic life of these products, with any loss recognized at the time of sale. Costs incurred by the Company for engineering, sales, marketing and warranty are expensed as incurred.

Source: Apple Inc. 10-K, November 05, 2008.

EXHIBIT 3   **Illustration of iPhone Subscription Accounting**

Assume Apple sold the iPhone 3G for $500 (AT&T subsidy of $300 + retail price of $200) and the gross profit was $150 per unit (30 percent) The subscription accounting for the sale would be as follows:

Q1 (QUARTER IN WHICH IPHONE WAS SOLD TO CONSUMER):		
Dr. Cash	500	
Cr. Revenue		62.5
Cr. Deferred Revenue under Subscription Accounting		437.5
Dr. COGS	43.75	
Dr. Deferred Costs under Subscription Accounting	306.25	
Cr. Inventory		350

Q2 TO Q8 (REMAINING QUARTERS OF IPHONE'S ECONOMIC LIFE):		
Dr. Deferred Revenue under Subscription Accounting	62.5	
Cr. Revenue		62.5
Dr. COGS	43.75	
Cr. Deferred Costs under Subscription Accounting		43.75

Source: Casewriter.
Note: iPhone costs incurred for engineering, sales, marketing, and warranty were expensed as incurred.

EXHIBIT 4 **Apple Inc. Quarterly Deferred Revenue Balances ($ millions)**

	9/08	6/08	3/08	12/07	9/07	6/07	3/07	9/06
Current deferred revenue	4,853	2,727	2,416	2,059	1,391	1,063	903	718
Noncurrent deferred revenue	3,029	1,336	1,409	1,229	849	561	433	383
Total deferred revenue	7,882	4,063	3,825	3,288	2,240	1,624	1,336	1,101

Source: Casewriter from Apple Inc. Quarterly 10Qs.
Note: Apple did not include quarterly deferred cost balances in its 10Qs.

EXHIBIT 5 **Apple's "Cautions on Use of Non-GAAP Measures"**

As noted previously, these non-GAAP financial measures are not consistent with GAAP because they do not reflect the deferral of revenue and product costs for recognition in later periods. These non-GAAP financial measures do not adjust for the costs associated with the Company's intention to provide unspecified new features and software to purchasers of iPhone and Apple TV products. These costs are expensed as incurred under GAAP's subscription accounting model, and are not adjusted in these non-GAAP financial measures. As such, these non-GAAP financial measures are not intended to reflect in a given period all of the costs of sales made in that period. Rather, the non-GAAP financial measures presented below are intended for the limited purpose of presenting performance measures that include the total sales, related product costs, and resulting income for iPhones and Apple TVs in the period those products are sold to customers.

Management believes investors will benefit from greater transparency in referring to these non-GAAP financial measures when assessing the Company's operating results, as well as when forecasting and analyzing future periods. However, management recognizes that:

- these non-GAAP financial measures are limited in their usefulness and should be considered only as a supplement to the Company's GAAP financial measures;

- these non-GAAP financial measures should not be considered in isolation from, or as a substitute for, the Company's GAAP financial measures;

- these non-GAAP financial measures should not be considered to be superior to the Company's GAAP financial measures; and

- these non-GAAP financial measures were not prepared in accordance with GAAP and investors should not assume that the non-GAAP financial measures presented in this earnings release were prepared under a comprehensive set of rules or principles.

Further, these non-GAAP financial measures may be unique to the Company, as they may be different from non-GAAP financial measures used by other companies. As such, this presentation of non-GAAP financial measures may not enhance the comparability of the Company's results to the results of other companies.

Source: "Apple Reports Fourth Quarter Results," October 21, 2008, http://www.apple.com/pr/library/2008/10/21results.html, accessed 2/8/11

EXHIBIT 6 **Apple Inc. Share Price Performance (October 15, 2008–October 29, 2008)**

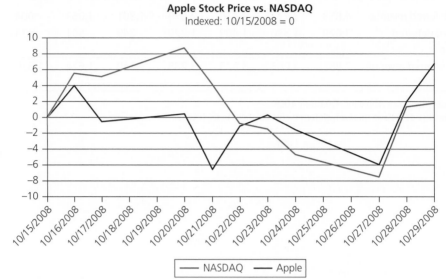

Note: Apple share price performance versus the Nasdaq Composite Index over the time period surrounding Apple's fiscal 2008 fourth quarter earnings announcement on October 21, 2008 that included non-GAAP supplements.

Endnotes

1. "Q4 2008 Apple Inc. Earnings Conference Call," Voxant FD Wire, ASC Partners, LLC, October 21, 2008 (accessed by Factiva 5/14/2010).
2. Ibid.
3. "iPhone App Store Downloads Top 10 Million in First Weekend," July 14, 2008, http://wdirect.apple.com/pr/library/2008/07/14appstore.html, accessed 5/14/2010.
4. Olga Kharif and Peter Burrows, "On the Trail of the Missing iPhones," *BusinessWeek*, February 11, 2008, p. 25, accessed by Factiva, February 4, 2011.
5. Ibid.
6. Daniel Eran Dilger, "Inside Apple's iPhone Subscription Accounting Changes," AppleInsider, October 21, 2009, http://www.appleinsider.com/print/09/10/21inside_apples_iphone_subscription_accounting_changes, accessed 6/22/2010.
7. Ibid.
8. M.G. Siegler, "AT&T iPhone Deal Extended to 2010. Did Apple Mortgage Its Future for a Subsidy?", August 1, 2008.
9. Nick Wingfield, "iPhone Software Sales Take Off: Apple's Job," *The Wall Street Journal*, August 11, 2008, accessed by Factiva January 25, 2011.
10. Ibid.
11. "Android is Now Open Source," October 21, 2008, http://googlesystem.blogspot.com/2008/10/android-is-now-open-source.html, accessed 1/20/2011.
12. Daniel Eran Dilger, "Inside Apple's iPhone Subscription Accounting Changes," AppleInsider, October 21, 2009, http://www.appleinsider.com/print/09/10/21inside_apples_iphone_subscription_accounting_changes, accessed 6/22/2010.
13. Ibid.
14. PricewaterhouseCoopers Global Software Practice, "A Shifting Software Revenue Recognition Landscape?," 2008, http://www.pwc.com/en_GX/gx/technology/pdf/shiftingsoftware.pdf, accessed 2/24/2011.
15. Daniel Eran Dilger, "Inside Apple's iPhone Subscription Accounting Changes," AppleInsider, October 21, 2009, http://www.appleinsider.com/print/09/10/21inside_apples_iphone_subscription_accounting_changes, accessed 6/22/2010.
16. Alok Ajmera and Reed Kingston, "Giving Revenue Recognition Its Due," *Business Finance*, October 1, 2008 (accessed by Factiva 5/27/10).

17. Philip Elmer-DeWitt, "Deferred Earnings: Apple's Hidden Revenue Bonus," *Apple 2.0 Fortune Tech*, CNNMoney.com, February 11, 2008, http:tech.fortune.cnn.com/2008/02/11/deferred-earnings-apples-hidden-revenue-bonus, accessed 6/25/10.

18. Beyer, A., Cohen, D., Lys, T., Walther, B., 2010 "The financial reporting environment: Review of the recent literature," *Journal of Accounting and Economics* 50: 296–343.

19. Bowen, R., Davis, A., Matsumoto, D. "Emphasis on proforma versus GAAP earnings in quarterly press releases," *The Accounting Review* 80: 1011–1038.

20. http://www.sec.gov/rules/final/33-8176.htm.

21. Kolev, K., Marquardt, C., McVay, S., 2008. "SEC scrutiny and the evolution of non-GAAP reporting," *The Accounting Review* 83: 157–184.

22. Tiernan Ray, "Apple Stock Rises 12 percent Despite Q4 Revenue Miss, Lower-Than-Expected-Forecast; 69 Mil iPhones Sold," *Barron's*, October 21, 2008 (accessed by Factiva 5/14/2010).

23. Eric Savitz, "Apple Rallies on Earnings Beat; Ests Fall on Conservative Guidance, UBS Downgrades; Calyon Upgrades," *Barron's*, October 22, 2008 (accessed by Factiva 5/14/2010).

24. Ibid.

25. Mike Abramsky, Paul Treiber, Mark Sue, "Apple: the Non-GAAP Trap," RBC Capital Markets Equity Research, October 23, 2008.

26. Ibid.

CASE

5 Air Berlin's IPO

Introduction

During the first few days of May 2006, Joachim Hunold, co-founder and CEO of Air Berlin, was faced with two decisions: Should he delay Air Berlin's initial public offering (IPO)? And should he lower the price range of the IPO?

Originally scheduled for shares to begin trading on May 5, 2006, with net proceeds at approximately €290 million, the Air Berlin offer was receiving mixed reviews from the investment community. One of the IPO's most prominent detractors, Jurgen Pieper from Frankfurt's Bankhaus Metzler, stated: "It is my view that the shares are definitely priced too high. I am telling my customers not to buy the shares because they are too expensive and the risks are too high."[1] Analysts also pointed to other factors such as the absence of profits for the last two years, the ascending price of fuel costs, high capital expenditure, and a low likelihood that the company would be cash-flow positive before 2008. In addition, shareholder advocates with the German Association for the Protection of Security Holdings were questioning how the proceeds would be used. One lawyer stated: "Because of the lack of transparency and risks involved, we're telling investors to be very careful."[2]

Air Berlin, along with its joint bookrunners for the deal – Commerzbank and Morgan Stanley – attempted to quell fears by stating that the inflow from the issue would be used to finance a business expansion, including the purchase of 55 new planes, and to pay off debt. Air Berlin and its advisors predicted a net profit of €51 million for 2006, emphasizing cost savings through the reduction of on-board catering costs, airport handling expenses and fees paid to agencies.

As the listing date of May 5, 2006 came closer, Hunold wondered what would be the most appropriate course of action, considering the ground swell against Air Berlin's debut on the Frankfurt Stock Exchange.

European airline industry and the proliferation of low-cost airlines

The European airline industry was valued at €83.7 billion at the close of 2005. Airline travel had grown at a compound annual growth rate (CAGR) of 2.8 percent from 2000 to 2005. The growth in the number of passengers grew at a CAGR of 4.2 percent during the same period. In 2005, the total number of passengers surpassed the one billion mark,

IESEP Publishing for the case study "Air Berlin's IPO" by Ahmad Rahnema & Prof. Jordan Mitchell, IESE Business School, University of Navarra, 28 May 2007, copyright © IESEP Publishing. Reproduced with permission.

No part of this publication may be reproduced, stored in a retrieval system, used in a spreadsheet, or transmitted in any form or by any means – electronic, mechanical, photocopying, recording, or otherwise – without the permission of IESE.

[1]William Boston, "Air Berlin's…The German low-cost carrier," *BusinessWeek Online*, May 5, 2006.
[2]Ibid.

ending up at 1,030.3 million passengers. Future growth prospects by Datamonitor were 4.6 percent in industry sales and 6 percent in the number of passengers.[3] See **Exhibit 1** for predictions of industry growth by country.

The widespread growth of low-cost carriers had been a defining characteristic of air travel in Europe and a key driver for the industry's growth. The concept of low-cost airlines was based on the model from Southwest Airlines in the US, which called for a homogenous fleet making short and medium-haul point-to-point flights to and from secondary airports. Combined with a stripped-down no frills flying experience, the low-cost model permitted airlines to offer passengers reduced prices in contrast to full-service alternatives. As of 2006, the interpretation of "low-cost" had taken on many forms. Some low-cost airlines charged for on-board snacks and beverages, whereas others did not. Other airlines maintained strict luggage allowances and levied fees for check-in bags over a low weight threshold, while some chose to give passengers luggage allowances comparable to full-service airlines. Airlines rallied to position themselves at different points along the "low-cost" continuum. At one end, Ryanair offered no frills and flew to secondary airports. At the other end, Germanwings offered service to primary airports and complimentary snacks.

Low-cost carriers in Europe dated back to the early 1990s, when RyanAir changed its business model to follow the Southwest approach. Other airlines such as easyJet and Virgin Express entered the segment in the mid-1990s, mostly offering connections between the United Kingdom and destinations around Europe. From 2000, a spate of other small airlines purveying the low-cost model began springing up throughout the continent. Examples included bmibaby (founded in the UK in 2002), flybe (founded in the UK in 1979 and repositioned as a low-cost airline in 2002), Helvetic (founded in Switzerland in 2002), Transavia (founded in Holland in 1966 and repositioned to a low-cost airline in 1998), Wizz Air (founded in Hungary in 2003), and Vueling (founded in Barcelona in 2004). In Germany, new low-cost airlines included Germania Express, DBA, Germanwings, and Hapag-Lloyd Express.

The number of passengers flying on low-cost airlines increased from 7 million in 1998 to 80 million in 2004. It was expected that as the low-cost segment became more mature and more saturated, passenger growth rates would slow. McKinsey predicted that the number of passengers flying low-cost would reach 170 million by 2010, which would represent a CAGR of 13 percent from 2004. Thus, passenger growth in the low-cost segment would outpace that of charter and legacy carriers at 4 percent CAGR by 2010. In 2010, it was predicted that low-cost carriers would carry 24 percent of passengers in Europe versus 16 percent in 2004.

Many of the larger low-cost airlines had placed orders for new aircraft to be delivered over the next few years. It was estimated that Ryanair, easyJet, Air Berlin, DBA, and Germanwings had fixed orders for 360 new aircraft and options for an additional 370 aircraft in the near future. Industry observers believed that the number of new aircraft would leave the low-cost segment exposed to overcapacity and increased competition on several routes. Furthermore, many of the legacy carriers had their own "low-cost" airlines. For example, Transavia was owned by KLM-Air France and Iberia planned on launching Clickair in 2006. At the same time, some legacy airlines had either sold their "low-cost" arms (such as British Airways' sale of Go Fly to easyJet) or had completely withdrawn from the market.

Background on Air Berlin[4]

Air Berlin's first incarnation was in 1978, when former PanAm captain, Kim Lundgren established Air Berlin, Inc. in the US. The rationale for the US incorporation was due to rules under the Potsdam Treaty of August 1945, stating that only aircraft operated by Western Allies were permitted to fly into West Berlin. 1990 marked the end of the treaty and Air Berlin converted into a limited partnership under German law. The co-founders were Lundgren and Joachim Hunold. In 1993, European Union (EU) regulations came into force allowing airlines more freedom on setting airfares. During the same year, Air Berlin formed a purchase agreement with Boeing for 26 new aircraft for delivery between 1998 and 2003. The company's next major milestone was in 1997 when its flights appeared on international reservation systems through its membership of the International Air Transport Association (IATA). Air Berlin also began offering single-seat one-way ticket sales and fixed commissions for travel agents, making it a first for a non-legacy Germany carrier. This

---

[3]*Air Berlin plc Prospectus*, April 19, 2006, p. 81.

[4]*Air Berlin plc Prospectus*, April 19, 2006, p. 65.

move signaled a shift away from its historical operations as a charter service to a single-seat model.[5] The company continued its expansion by establishing the Mallorca Shuttle; a service with daily flights from 12 destinations around Germany to Mallorca, Spain. The success of the shuttle led the company to launch the City Shuttle, a similar service to destinations around Europe.

In 2004, Air Berlin purchased 24 percent of NIKI, an Austrian low-cost airline established by the famous Formula 1 world champion, Niki Lauda. In the same year, Air Berlin agreed to buy 60 Airbus A320 planes by 2011, with options to purchase another 40 planes. In 2005, Air Berlin combined Mallorca Shuttle with City Shuttle under the umbrella of "Euro Shuttle." The company also changed its corporate structure, moving from a limited partnership (a "KG" in Germany) by establishing a holding company, Air Berlin plc (public limited company) registered in Bristol, UK. The plc structure was to permit Air Berlin to be governed by one managing body, as opposed to a combination of management and supervisory boards under similar German structures.

As of 2006, Air Berlin was Germany's largest low-cost carrier, the country's second-largest airline behind Lufthansa and the third-largest low-cost airline in Europe (next to Ryanair and easyJet) in terms of aircraft fleet size, passenger numbers and revenues. The number of seats sold had increased steadily in the last few years from 10 million in 2003 to 12.1 in 2004 to 13.5 million in 2005. Revenues grew from €863 million in 2003 to €1.0 billion in 2004 and €1.2 billion in 2005. **Exhibit 2** shows Air Berlin's financial statements. The company had 2,581 employees, of which 497 were pilots. Air Berlin was led by a four-person board of directors. All four held executive positions. The company was seeking non-executive directors to join the board. **Exhibit 3** shows profiles of Air Berlin's management.

Strategy

Air Berlin positioned itself between low-cost carriers and full-service airlines. Its premise was to differentiate its services by offering some of the frills of full-service flights such as flying to primary airports and offering select in-flight snacks and beverages while still delivering an average lower fare than full-service airlines. The company estimated that it enjoyed strong brand recognition of 76 percent in Germany (up from 25 percent in 1999). It had also been rated by British newspaper, *The Guardian*, as "Best Short-Haul Airline." Air Berlin wanted to use its current strengths to expand by increasing its frequency on existing routes and opening up its route network to areas such as Eastern Europe and Scandinavia.

Moving away from its historical reliance on charter flights, the company also intended to strengthen its position in the business traveler market through offering the Air Berlin Corporate program and the Top Bonus frequent flyer point system. Part of the plan was to offer more early morning and late afternoon return flights to accommodate business travel. Already, 25 percent to 30 percent of the company's traffic was attributable to corporate travel, which was substantially higher than its two main competitors, easyJet, and Ryanair.[6] Additionally, Air Berlin planned on using its customer base (both business and pleasure travelers) to increase commissions earned from car rentals, hotel stays, travel insurance, tourist attractions, and credit card surcharges.

The company's approach was predicated upon its efficient cost structure. A breakdown of Air Berlin's major costs in comparison to Ryanair and easyJet is shown in **Exhibit 4**. The exhibit also shows other comparative peer data by different analysts.

Routes and fares[7]

With 350 flights per day, Air Berlin offered 135 routes and flew to 74 destinations throughout Europe and parts of northern Africa. Air Berlin's average fare was €86 compared to €65.10 for easyJet and €48.80 for Ryanair. Its route network included the following 17 countries: Germany, Spain, Austria, the UK, Switzerland, Italy, Greece, Egypt, Portugal, Turkey, Hungary, Tunisia, Holland, Morocco, France, Denmark, and Finland. See **Exhibit 5** for a map of the routes. At the beginning of a booking phase (usually six to nine

---

[5] As of 2006, single seat sales were the most common for low-cost carriers.

[6] "Air Berlin: Betting on Business Traffic and a World Cup Boost," Analyst Report, Morgan Stanley, June 21, 2006, p. 9.

[7] *Air Berlin plc Prospectus*, April 19, 2006, pp. 78–79.

months ahead of the departure date), Air Berlin offered standard one-way prices of €29 within Germany and €49 to Palma de Mallorca and the Spanish mainland.

Air Berlin relied heavily on traffic between Germany and Palma de Mallorca in Spain. In 2005, 25 percent of Air Berlin's arrivals and departures were attributable to Palma de Mallorca. See **Exhibit 6** for a list of the top 15 most important airports. Air Berlin offered 200 flights per week from 18 German airports to Palma de Mallorca as well as flights connecting Palma de Mallorca with 11 mainland Spanish airports. As the date moved closer, the price usually increased except during special promotions. As of 2006, Air Berlin was the largest airline operating in Palma de Mallorca. One of every four passengers landing or taking off from Palma de Mallorca was on an Air Berlin flight. The company considered Palma de Mallorca to be one of its most important hubs and a key competitive strength. The airline's other two hubs were Nuremberg Airport and London Stansted Airport.

An analyst from Morgan Stanley talked about Air Berlin's route network:

> *As Air Berlin's main service base is concentrated out of Germany and Spain (Palma), there is limited overlap in direct competition with Ryanair and easyJet. The cross-over in German flights is relatively low, as Ryanair only serves seven airports in Germany (base only in Frankfurt Hahn) and easyJet only serves six German airports – with the most overlap in Berlin Schonefeld, Bremen, and Dortmund.*[8]

Fleet[9]

Air Berlin had a fleet of 56 aircraft with a weighted average of 176 seats as of mid-2006. The average age of the fleet was 5.6 years and was split between owned and operating leases. The majority of the fleet comprised Boeing 737s (the same airplane used by Southwest Airlines), but Air Berlin was planning to make the transition to the Airbus A320 family over the next decade. Air Berlin had formed a purchase agreement with Airbus for 60 planes until 2011 with options for an additional 40 planes before the end of 2012. Air Berlin talked about the fleet composition in its IPO prospectus:

> *Air Berlin believes a mixed Boeing and Airbus fleet will provide additional economic benefits as well as with access to a broader pool of pilots to fly its aircraft.*[10] *Although additional type certification and spare part requirements create certain additional costs, Air Berlin believes that these costs will be mitigated as it gradually transforms each of its airports in Germany into either solely Boeing-operated airports or solely Airbus-operated airports.*[11]

See **Exhibit 7** for Air Berlin's fleet.

Sales and distribution[12]

In 2005, 56 percent of the company's sales were derived from single-seat ticket sales via Air Berlin's website, the company's service centre, ticket counters, and travel agencies. Bulk ticket sales to charter and package and tour operators made up the remaining 44 percent of all sales. Tour operators included large groups such as Alltours, ITS, TUI, Thomas Cook, and FTI. See **Exhibit 8** for a list of Air Berlin's distribution channels. One analyst saw Air Berlin's reliance on charter sales as an investment negative stating:

> *Around 44 percent of passengers are still sourced from package tour operators (TUI, Thomas Cook, ITS, and AllTours). This exposes the company to more fluctuations in travel demand – particularly to destinations in North Africa and Turkey.*[13]

[8]"Air Berlin: Betting on Business Traffic and a World Cup Boost," Analyst Report, Morgan Stanley, June 21, 2006, p. 6.

[9]*Air Berlin plc Prospectus*, April 19, 2006, p. 80.

[10]Under flight regulatory bodies, all pilots were required to complete required training courses for each type of airplane.

[11]*Air Berlin plc Prospectus*, April 19, 2006, p. 74.

[12]*Air Berlin plc Prospectus*, April 19, 2006, pp.74–75.

[13]"Air Berlin: Betting on Business Traffic and a World Cup Boost," Analyst Report, Morgan Stanley, June 21, 2006, p. 9.

Marketing and alliances[14]

Cited for marketing on billboards with "scantily clad women in bikinis,"[15] Air Berlin emphasized its low fares, premium service, and extensive route network. The company used most mediums such as newspapers, magazines, and television (often in coordination with weather reports). To take advantage of the hysteria surrounding the World Cup 2006, Air Berlin also connected itself to football; the company sponsored two prominent German football clubs.

Air Berlin had strategic cooperation agreements with Austrian low-cost airline NIKI and tour operator TUI's Hapagfly airline. Air Berlin had a 24 percent stake in NIKI and the two airlines coordinated flight schedules. Air Berlin also provided marketing, sales, and logistics for NIKI. The two airlines offered joint services from Austria to Eastern European destinations. The two companies had also participated in the negotiations with Airbus to secure lower prices.

Air Berlin's agreement with Hapagfly involved coordinating flight schedules and offering code-sharing flights whereby the non-operating airline could sell tickets under its own name for the other airline. As of 2006, Air Berlin was in discussions with Germania and DBA to enter into management agreements for joint technical, purchasing, and insurance arrangements.

The IPO

The IPO would be made in Germany on the Frankfurt Stock Exchange (owned by Deutsche-Boerse and referred to as the "Frankfurter Wertpapierbörse" in German). The Frankfurt Stock Exchange was the largest of the eight exchanges in Germany, accounting for 96 percent of stock trading in Germany. It was also the third largest stock market in the world with €5.2 trillion in market capitalization. It had two trading platforms: an electronic exchange called Xetra® and a traditional floor trading exchange. There were 6,823 companies quoted on the exchange, 77,000 securities listed and 260,000 trades processed daily as of the end of 2005.[16]

Air Berlin's offering was expected to raise gross proceeds of approximately €350 million and after underwriting charges, €290 million. The reason for the IPO was to fund growth of the business and pay off debt. Approximately 50 percent of the net proceeds would be applied to the equity portion of the purchase price for the 55 new Airbus airplanes delivered up to 2011. 10 percent or €29 million of the net proceeds would be used to pay off the company's net financial indebtedness to banks of €345.4 million. The remaining 40 percent would be used to fund organic growth such as launching new routes and general corporate expenses. In the case that Air Berlin followed through with the option to buy the additional 40 Airbus planes, they would use part of the 40 percent towards the purchase price of the planes. While Air Berlin did not have any immediate takeover plans for other airlines, the company mentioned the possibility of future acquisitions in its prospectus.

The schedule[17]

Air Berlin's original IPO schedule was:

[14]*Air Berlin plc Prospectus*, April 19, 2006, pp. 76–78.

[15]LEX COLUMN, "Air Berlin," *Financial Times*, May 3, 2006, Page 18.

[16]ADVFN, http://www.advfn.com/StockExchanges/about/FSE/FrankfurtStockExchange.html, Accessed December 14, 2006.

[17]*Air Berlin plc Prospectus*, April 19, 2006, p. 33.

April 19	Approval of Prospectus by Financial Service Authority		May 4	Admission to trading by Frankfurt Stock Exchange and close of offer period
April 20–21	Publication of Prospectus		May 5	Listing, first day of trading
April 21	Start of marketing (roadshow)		May 6 or 8	Publication of offer price
April 27–28	Approval and publication of Price Range Supplement		May 9	Book-entry delivery of shares
May 3	Preferential allocation to employees and business partners			

Air Berlin had had its prospectus approved by the Financial Service Authority (FSA) on April 19, 2006. The FSA notified the German Federal Financial Supervisory Authority *(Bundesanstalt für Finanzdiensteleistung-saufischt* or BaFin) of its approval. The company had begun marketing the IPO via an investor road show on April 21, 2006. The road show involved top Air Berlin executives and book runners presenting parts of the prospectus to institutional investors. On April 27, 2006 the company published the price range supplement (see the next section below) and a day later the commencement of the offer period began.

The offer period had been scheduled to close on May 4, 2006, with the first day of trading on Friday, May 5, 2006. Employees and Air Berlin's business partners who wanted preferential allocation were required to submit their orders by the end of the business day on May 3, 2006.

Price ranges and shares[18]

Air Berlin's range of share value was targeted between €15 and €17.50. The company planned to offer a total of 49,833,333 shares – 20,000,000 were from the current selling shareholders and the remaining 23,333,333 were from a capital increase to be approved by the board of directors in early May 2006. Of the 20,000,000 shares held by the selling shareholders, there was a possible greenshoe option of up to 6,500,000 shares. The greenshoe[19] option allowed the underwriters to buy additional shares at the offer price.

At the end of the issue, the company would be left with a total of 59.8 million shares. Thus, about 83 percent of the shares would be in free float including the greenshoe and approximately 72 percent without the greenshoe option.

Air Berlin's top executives were subject to a lock-up period of six months whereby no selling shareholder would issue or sell more shares for this period. Hunold, who would not be selling any of his shares in the flotation, committed to not sell his shares for at least 18 months after the IPO. See **Exhibit 9** for a list of the current shareholders.

---

[18]"Bookbuilding for Air Berlin shares ranges from €15.00 to €17.50," Air Berlin Press Release, April 27, 2006.

[19]Greenshoe agreements allowed the underwriters to buy a certain portion of the shares (usually about 15 percent) at the offering price for a set period of time (usually a couple of months) after the offering. Greenshoe agreements were also referred to as the overallotment and were used when the IPO was oversubscribed and the trading price of the stock was higher than the offer price.

Conditions

In allocating the shares, Air Berlin would follow the principles laid out by the Exchange Commission of Experts of the German Federal Ministry of Finance. At the end of the offer period, Air Berlin would determine the details of the allocation method. Preferential allocation would be given to employees, members of Air Berlin's Top Bonus Card program and specific business partners. About 5 percent of the offer shares would be made available to these three groups. No discounts would be given on the offer price.[20]

All shareholders in the offer would be given one vote per share held at the company's shareholder meeting. The existing shares of the existing shareholders were subject to the same voting rights as the other shares.[21]

The dividend policy of the shares was to be determined. Under the plc structure (which had been established on December 31, 2005), the company had not distributed dividends to its existing shareholders. It was likely that the company would retain future profits for business expansion.[22]

Should the price be lowered and should the IPO be delayed?

During the marketing of the IPO, Air Berlin had found that many analysts, institutional investors, and business journalists were skeptical about the price of the offering. **Exhibit 10** shows one analyst's future financial projections for Air Berlin along with discounted cash flow (DCF) assumptions and weighted average cost of capital (WACC) calculations. One journalist reflected on Air Berlin's offer in the *Financial Times*:

> *Air Berlin's advertisements have been known to feature models in scanty bikinis. The proposed price range for its initial public offering is similarly cheeky … The need for an equity injection is clear. Air Berlin is more highly leveraged than its larger rivals, Ryanair and Easyjet, and hopes to use some of the flotation proceeds to pay off debt. It will also buy new planes and add new routes. The airline hopes that expansion into Scandinavia and Eastern Europe will help offset growing competition in its main markets of Germany and Spain.*
>
> *The strategy is reasonably convincing. So too are Air Berlin's plans to increase revenues from so-called "ancillaries" such as car hire or hotel bookings, currently only 3 percent of sales, compared with 15 percent at Ryanair and 7 percent at Easyjet. Other goals seem less realistic. Like every other carrier, Air Berlin hopes to increase the proportion of business travellers using its services, but achieving this will be challenging. Similarly, cutting costs could also prove difficult. Air Berlin's non-unionised workforce means labour costs are already less than 10 percent of sales.*
>
> *Morgan Stanley, one of the IPO co-ordinators, forecasts that Air Berlin will increase earnings before interest, tax, depreciation, amortisation, and rent[23] from Euros 153m in 2005 to Euros 250m this year. At the low end of the proposed price range, this implies an enterprise value to 2006 EBITDA of 6.4 times. The discount to Easyjet's 8 times seems more than justified.[24]*

Air Berlin's shares traded in the grey or unofficial market had been soft over the first few days of May and some predicted that they had fallen below the lower band of the target price of €15.[25] Should the management of Air Berlin be concerned? Would it be better to delay the offer by a week or more? If so, what would potentially happen? Would it be most sensible to lower the range of the offer price? If so, to what price range?

---

[20]*Air Berlin plc Prospectus*, April 19, 2006, p. 35.

[21]Ibid., p. 34.

[22]Ibid., p. 39.

[23]On the financial statements in **Exhibit 10**, rent is referred to as "operating leases."

[24]LEX COLUMN, "Air Berlin," *Financial Times*, May 3, 2006, Page18.

[25]"Air Berlin denies market talk of IPO cancellation," AFX International Focus, May 4, 2006.

EXHIBIT 1 **Industry growth**

	2000	2004	2005E	2006E	2007E	2008E	2009E
European Airline Industry							
Sales (in € billion)	72.9	79.8	83.7	87.4	91.5	95.7	99.8
Passengers (million)	836.8	964.4	1030.3	1095.9	1160.7	1224.9	1288.8
German Airline Industry							
Sales (in € billion)	14.9	15.7	16	16.5	17	17.5	18
Passengers (million)	142.4	160.3	172.1	183.5	193.9	203.6	212
Spanish Airline Industry							
Sales (in € billion)	5	5.9	6.2	6.6	6.9	7.3	7.7
Passengers (million)	136.7	163.9	176.4	189.2	202.2	215.4	228.9
Scandinavian Airline Industry							
Sales (in € billion)	5.4	5.8	6.2	6.6	6.9	7.3	7.7
Passengers (million)	74.9	83	89.5	95.1	100.2	104.9	109.6
Eastern European Airline Industry							
Sales (in € billion)	1.5	2.1	2.2	2.4	2.6	2.9	3.1
Passengers (million)	16.2	25	28.3	31.5	34.4	37	39.8

Source: *Air Berlin plc Prospectus*, April 19, 2006, p. 64.

5 Air Berlin's IPO

EXHIBIT 2   **Operating data**[1]

	2005	2004	2003
Number of seats sold, in thousands	13,537	12,055	10,019
RPKs[2] in million	20,527	18,782	16,613
ASKs[3] in million	26,102	23,619	21,656
Average passenger carrying capacity (Pax) in thousands	17,295	15,223	13,111
Passenger load factor	78.6%	79.5%	76.7%
Passenger revenue per ASK (€ cents)	4.33	4.11	3.75
Operating expenses per ASK excluding fuel costs (€ cents)	3.78	3.71	3.63
Revenue scheduled departures	99,823	87,370	75,626
Average price per US gallon of fuel ($)	1.83	1.24	0.99
US gallons of fuel consumed, in thousands	164,509	148,946	135,687
Average length of aircraft flights, in kilometers	1,509	1,554	1,626
Average revenue block hours per aircraft per day	11.47	11.52	11.17
Total revenues block hours	210,134	188,546	168,908
Total kilometres flown in millions	151.4	136.5	123.8
Aircraft in service at end of period	50	47	46
Full-time equivalent employees at end of period	2,488	2,146	1,956

[1] The data in this table have been taken from Air Berlin's management accounts.

[2] RPKs, or revenue passenger kilometres, are the average number of revenue sold seats per flight stage multiplied by the total number of kilometres flown.

[3] ASKs, or available seat kilometres, are the average number of seats available for sale per flight stage multipled by the total number of kilometres flown.

Source: *Air Berlin plc Prospectus*, April 19, 2006, p. 64.

EXHIBIT 2 Operating data (continued)

PROFIT AND LOSS			
in €000s	2005	2004	2003
Revenue	1,215,240	1,033,880	863,230
Other operating income	4,731	13,395	4,059
Expenses for materials and services	(864,145)	(705,270)	(588,103)
Personnel expenses	(116,903)	(100,825)	(90,091)
Depreciation and amortization	(62,558)	(74,939)	(75,659)
Other operating expenses	(181,908)	(166,915)	(166,247)
Operating expenses	(1,225,514)	(1,047,949)	(920,100)
Results from operating activities	(5,543)	(674)	(52,811)
Financial expenses	(19,026)	(13,325)	(13,633)
Financial income	2,851	1,556	2,643
Foreign exchange gains, net	(49,192)	29,058	108,612
Net financing costs	(65,367)	17,289	97,622
Share of profit (loss) of associates	39	332	(53)
Profit (loss) before tax	(70,871)	16,947	44,758
Income tax expenses	(45,029)	(19,869)	(8,018)
Profit (loss) for the year	(115,900)	(2,922)	36,740
Attributable to:			
Equity holders of the parent	(115,900)	(2,992)	11,987
Minority interest	–	–	24,753
Profit (loss) for the year	(115,900)	(2,992)	36,740
Basic and diluted earnings per share in €	(11.59)	(0.29)	1.20

Source: *Air Berlin plc Prospectus*, April 19, 2006, p. 112.

BALANCE SHEET			
in €000s	2005	2004	2003
Assets			
Non current assets			
Software licenses and other rights	1,317	1,443	1,396
Aircraft and engines	712,133	706,412	761,977
Technical equipment and machinery	30,319	22,638	21,374
Office equipment	10,306	8,184	8,677
Investments in associates	660	984	579
Non-current assets	754,735	739,661	794,003

EXHIBIT 2   Operating data (continued)

in €000s	2005	2004	2003
Current assets			
Inventories	3,201	2,556	2,229
Trade receivables	26,708	20,821	12,444
Other current assets	79,888	28,300	19,933
Prepaid expenses	8,147	5,428	876
Investment securities	125	138	127
Cash and cash equivalents	189,051	87,552	45,000
Current assets	307,120	144,795	80,609
Total assets	**1,061,855**	**884,456**	**874,612**
Equity and liabilities			
Shareholders' equity			
Share capital	10,073	30	30
Limited partners' capital	–	41,300	41,000
Other capital reserves	217,056	55,551	–
Retained earnings and profit (loss) for the year	(29,779)	86,932	7,993
Fair value reserve	(127)	(114)	(118)
Equity attributable to equity holders of the parent	197,223	183,699	48,905
Minority interest	–	–	142,042
Equity	**197,223**	**183,699**	**190,947**
Non-current liabilities			
Deferred tax liabilities	96,833	52,880	34,057
Liabilities due to bank from assignment of future lease payments	350,829	370,163	472,664
Interest-bearing liabilities	30,154	9,459	5,466
Non-current liabilities	477,816	432,502	512,187
Current liabilities			
Liabilities due to bank from assignment of future lease payments	99,893	47,514	54,275
Interest-bearing liabilities	17,477	2,156	250
Accrued taxes	662	267	2,302
Other provisions	1,048	586	–
Accrued liabilities	45,867	17,181	11,920
Trade payables	61,164	61,403	52,514
Other liabilities	15,372	27,666	22,050
Deferred income	14,003	9,501	7,964
Advanced payments	131,330	101,981	20,204
Current liabilities	386,816	268,255	171,479
Total equity and liabilities	**1,061,855**	**884,456**	**874,613**

Source: *Air Berlin plc Prospectus*, April 19, 2006, p. 113.

EXHIBIT 2 Operating data (continued)

CASH FLOW STATEMENT

in €000s	2005	2004	2003
Profit (loss) for the year	(115,900)	(2,922)	36,740
Adjustments to reconcile profit or loss to cash flows from operating activities:			
Depreciation and amortization of non-current assets	62,558	74,939	75,659
Impairment losses	–	250	–
Loss on disposal of tangible and intangible assets	5,367	1,161	24,367
(Increase) decrease in inventories	(645)	(327)	433
Increase in trade accounts receivable	(5,887)	(8,376)	(6,862)
Increase in other assets and prepaid expenses	(32,616)	(8,110)	(6,002)
Increase in deferred income taxes	43,954	18,822	7,546
Increase (decrease) in accrued liabilities and provisions	28,419	5,848	(3,531)
Increase in other current liabilities	36,198	58,756	26,966
Foreign exchange (gains) losses	59,685	(15,801)	(75,774)
Interest expenses	19,026	13,325	13,633
Income tax expenses	1,076	1,048	472
Share of (profit) loss of associates	(2)	(332)	53
Changes in fair value of derivatives	(16,571)	11,369	1,056
Cash generated from operations	84,662	149,650	94,756
Interest paid	(18,238)	(13,007)	(11,650)
Income taxes paid	(681)	(3,294)	(484)
Net cash flows from operating activities	**65,743**	**133,349**	**82,622**
Purchases of tangible and intangible assets	(103,999)	(21,179)	(60,115)
Advanced payments for non-current items	(29,077)	(6,696)	(206)
Proceeds from sale of tangible and intangible assets	29,898	31	123,741
Advanced payments for sale of tangible assets	–	31,099	–
Dividends received from associates	332	–	–
Acquisition of investments in associates	(6)	(322)	–
Cash flow from investing activities	**(102,852)**	**2,933**	**63,420**
Principal payments on interest-bearing liabilities	(64,218)	(97,144)	(234,749)
Proceeds from long-term borrowings	73,389	9,582	75,717
Increase in other capital reserves	130,000	–	–
Increase in share capital	–	–	4
Partners' distributions	(563)	(4,330)	(1,487)
Principle payments on loans due to related parties	–	(1,838)	(1,731)
Cash flow from financing activities	**138,608**	**(93,730)**	**(162,246)**
Change in cash and cash equivalents	**101,499**	**42,552**	**(16,204)**
Cash and cash equivalents at beginning of period	**87,552**	**45,000**	**61,204**
Cash and cash equivalents at end of period	**189,051**	**87,552**	**45,000**

Source: *Air Berlin plc Prospectus*, April 19, 2006, p. 115.

5 Air Berlin's IPO

EXHIBIT 3   Board of Directors profiles

Joachim Hunold – Chief Executive Officer

- Born on September 5, 1949 in Düsseldorf, Germany
- Studied law beginning in 1970
- Began career in 1978 with the handling firm Braathens Air Transport
- 1982 to 1990: Sales and marketing director at LTU Group
- 1991: Co-founded Air Berlin GmbH & Co.
- 1991-2005: Managing director of Air Berlin
- December 2005–present: CEO of the reorganized Air Berlin Group

Ulf Hüttmeyer – Chief Financial Officer

- Born on July 9, 1973 in Visbek, Germany
- Holds a bachelor of arts in business administration from the Berfuskadamie Vechta and a degree in business studies from the Fachhochschule für Wirtschaft und Technik in Vechta
- 1999–2003: Relationship manager for transportation and energy for Commerzbank in Singapore
- 2003–2006: Group manager of Commerzbank's corporate client services in Berlin
- February 2006–present: CFO of Air Berlin

Karl Friedrich Lotz – Chief Operating Officer

- Born on December 26, 1949 in Wuppertal, Germany
- Began career in the aviation industry in 1969 as a ramp agent at LTU Fluggesellschaft GmbH & Co KG
- Subsequently held management positions at LTU with responsibilities for flight operations staff, crew allocation, traffic management and flight operation support
- 1995–1999: Managing director of CHS Cabin and Handling Service GmbH
- July 1999–present: COO of Air Berlin

Elke Schütt – Chief Commercial Officer

- Born on February 19, 1956 in Sandbostel, Germany
- Trained business reporter and licensed dispatcher
- 1976–1979: assistant at Aeroamerica airline
- 1980: joined Air Berlin as assistant to flight operations manager
- 1983: Became manager of the operations department at Air Berlin
- July 1999: Became managing director and vice-chair of Air Berlin KG
- December 2005–present: Chief commercial officer of Air Berlin

---

Note: There are no family relationships between the directors.

Source: Summarized from IPO Prospectus, April 19, 2006, pp. 91–92.

EXHIBIT 4 Peer comparison

Low-cost Carrier Cost Comparison

in € millions	Ryanair			easyJet			Air Berlin		
	2005	2006E	2007E	2005	2006E	2007E	2005	2006E	2007E
Passengers (m)	27.6	35	42.1	29.6	34	39.1	13.5	15.4	17.6
Revenues per Pax[1]	48.4	48.5	48.9	66.3	67.2	68	90.1	95.9	99
Employees	2,800	3,363	3,958	4,152	4,721	5,355	2,488	2,861	3,147
Total revenues	1,337	1,699	2,058	1,958	2,284	2,659	1,220	1,479	1,741
Passenger revenues	1,128	1,439	1,736	1,831	2,116	2,446	1,129	1,364	1,602
Ancillary revenues	208	260	322	127	168	213	34	54	74
Labour	141.7	171.0	207.2	198.8	219.4	256.3	116.9	140	161.9
Pay per employee	9,855	10,422	10,624	7,119	7,200	7,300	5,441	5,394	5,590
Cost per employee	50,598	50,581	52,344	47,888	46,472	47,867	46,987	48,917	51,449
Employees per aircraft	32.2	31.4	29.5	38.1	38.7	38.8	49.8	53	49.2
% sales	10.6%	10.1%	10.1%	10.2%	9.6%	9.6%	9.6%	9.5%	9.3%
Fuel	265.3	463.7	614.1	379.9	568.9	641.8	239.5	314.1	437.3
% sales	20%	27%	30%	19%	25%	24%	20%	21%	25%
Airport charges	178.4	219.8	258.4	526.4	584.5	658.4	333.4	372.5	411.9
per Pax	6.5	6.3	6.1	17.8	17.2	16.8	24.6	24.1	23.4
% sales	13%	13%	13%	27%	26%	25%	27%	25%	24%
Maintenance	37.9	45.2	55.3	174	171.3	192.8	27.5	32	37.2
per Pax	1.4	1.3	1.3	5.9	5	4.9	2	2.1	2.1
% sales	2.8%	2.7%	2.7%	8.9%	7.5%	7.3%	2.3%	2.2%	2.1%
Navigation	135.7	165.4	196.5	158.5	173.1	199	109	120.6	133.3
% sales	10.2%	9.7%	9.6%	8.1%	7.6%	7.5%	8.9%	8.1%	7.7%
Advertising	19.6	15	16.1	47.9	45.7	53.2	66.4	71.9	77.9
% sales	1.5%	0.9%	0.8%	2.4%	2.0%	2.0%	5.4%	4.9%	4.5%
Other	97	86.3	98.3	171.2	182.8	206.3	174	178.5	190.2
per Pax	3.5	2.5	2.3	5.8	5.4	5.3	12.9	11.6	10.8
% sales	7.3%	5.1%	4.8%	8.7%	8.0%	7.8%	14.3%	12.1%	10.9%
Total costs before fuel	610	703	832	1,277	1,377	1,566	827	915	1,012
per Pax	22.1	20	19.8	43.2	40.5	40.1	61.1	59.3	57.5
% sales	45.7%	41.3%	40.4%	65.2%	60.3%	58.9%	67.8%	61.9%	58.2%
Total operating costs	876	1,166	1,446	1,657	1,946	2,208	1,067	1,229	1,450
per Pax	31.7	33.3	34.4	56.1	57.2	56.5	78.8	79.7	82.4
% sales	65.5%	68.6%	70.3%	84.6%	85.2%	83.0%	87.4%	83.1%	83.3%
EBITDAR	461	533	612	301	339	451	153	250	291
% sales	34.0%	31.0%	30.0%	15.0%	15.0%	17.0%	13.0%	17.0%	17.0%
Aircraft rentals	33.5	45.2	51.8	180.6	182.5	197.7	96.2	85.9	67.8
% sales	2.5%	2.7%	2.5%	9.2%	8.0%	7.4%	7.9%	5.8%	3.9%
EBITDA	**428**	**488**	**560**	**121**	**156**	**253**	**57**	**164**	**223**
% sales	32.0%	29.0%	27.0%	6.0%	7.0%	10.0%	5.0%	11.0%	13.0%
Depreciation	98.7	110.5	143.2	24.2	49.1	57.3	62.6	82.9	119.7
% sales	7.4%	6.5%	7.0%	1.2%	2.1%	2.2%	5.1%	5.6%	6.9%
Operating income (EBIT)	**328.8**	**377.3**	**416.5**	**96.6**	**107.2**	**196**	**−5.5**	**81**	**103.7**
Margin	24.6%	22.2%	20.2%	4.9%	4.7%	7.4%	−0.4%	5.5%	6.0%

[1] Pax refers to the average passenger carrying capacity.

Source: ''Air Berlin: Betting on Business Traffic and a World Cup Boost,'' Analyst Report, Morgan Stanley, June 21, 2006, p. 8.

5 Air Berlin's IPO

PEER ANALYSIS BY MORGAN STANLEY
Comparative Ratio Analysis

	Ryanair				easyJet				Air Berlin			
	2005	2006E	2007E	2008E	2005	2006E	2007E	2008E	2005	2006E	2007E	2008E
Sales/assets	0.87	0.95	1.02	1.09	0.82	0.83	0.88	0.91	1.15	1.08	1.17	1.23
Working capital (% of sales)	(43.7)	(41.5)	(40.7)	(39.6)	(14.2)	(15.3)	(16.5)	(16.4)	(21.9)	(20.4)	(19.9)	(19.7)
Leverage (net debt/EBITDA)	0.45	0.54	0.71	0.96	1.65	1.09	1.25	1.36	5.42	0.6	0.97	0.6
ROCE %	20.1	17.7	18.1	20.5	3.9	3.1	5.2	8.6	7	6.5	7.1	8.9
ROE%	15.8	14	13.6	15.2	3.5	3.1	4.7	7.2	(13.2)	5.1	6	8.6
Price to earnings ratio			13.6	10.8			14.5	9.5			8.1	5.6

	South west				Air Asia				Virgin I Blue			
	2005	2006E	2007E	2008E	2005	2006E	2007E	2008E	2005	2006E	2007E	2008E
Sales/assets	0.53	0.65	0.67	0.68	0.59	0.31	0.26	0.28	0.84	0.97	0.95	0.91
Working capital (% of sales)	(36.5)	(27.2)	25.2	(23.4)	60.9	60.1	59.1	59.3	(26.0)	(20.7)	(20.6)	(20.5)
Leverage (net debt/EBITDA)	1.55	1.05	0.8	0.7	−2.03	3.86	7.71	7.36	2.96	3.95	2.7	1.75
ROCE %	5.3	5.6	6.2	6.6	15.5	11.7	10.6	10.9	6.8	5.1	6.9	11.1
ROE%	8.2	8.4	9.2	9.7	11.7	12.9	9.3	12	10.2	6.8	9.5	16.4
Price to earnings ratio			19.4	17.3			73.9	32.8				

Source: "Air Berlin: Betting on Business Traffic and a World Cup Boost," Analyst Report, Morgan Stanley, June 21, 2006, p. 5, 11.

PEER ANALYSIS BY DEUTSCHE BANK

Year to Dec 31	Market Capitalization (millions of euros)	PE	EV/ EBITDAR	EV/IC	EV/Sales	EBITDAR margin (%)	Rev Traffic CAGR % 06-08E
Air France	4,596.0	8.4	4.6	0.8	0.7	15.6	5.1
Alitalia	1,188.4	−64.2	5.9	0.9	0.7	11.3	6.0
Austrian	213.5	not avail.	5.3	0.9	0.7	12.6	1.2
BA	3,764.9	8.9	4.4	0.8	0.7	16.9	1.0
Iberia	1,867.9	22.6	5.4	0.9	0.8	14.2	3.5
Lufthansa	6,502.2	17.0	5.7	0.7	0.5	19.3	2.9
Flag sector average (weighted)	**18,132.9**	**8.2**	**5.1**	**0.8**	**0.7**	**13.1**	**3.3**
Easyjet	1,618.2	20.9	9.1	1.4	1.4	15.0	15.5
Ryanair	5,410.2	17.4	10.0	2.0	2.9	29.2	18.1
LCC[1]sector average (weighted)	**7,577.6**	**17.6**	**9.5**	**1.8**	**2.5**	**25.3**	**1.1**

[1] LCC stands for Low Cost Carriers.

Source: "Air Berlin," Analyst Report, Deutsche Bank, June 30, 2006, p. 9.

EXHIBIT 5 **Map of route network**

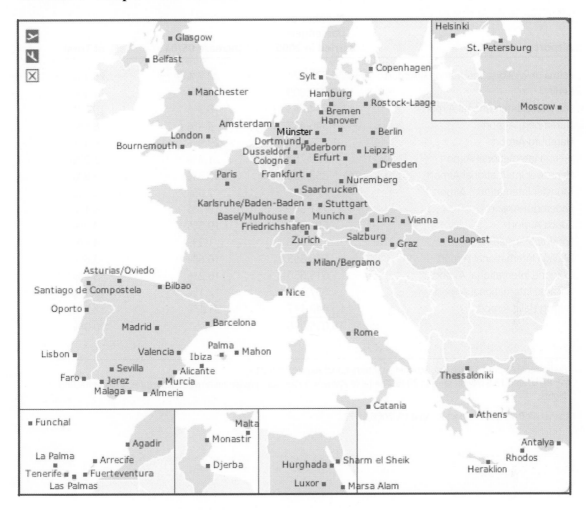

Source: Air Berlin Website, www.airberlin.com.

EXHIBIT 6   **Top 15 airports**

Airport	Number of passengers carried in 2005	Increase 05/04	% of Total
Palma de Mallorca International Airport	4,529,321	22.7%	25.1%
Berlin[1]	2,072,009	8.0%	11.5%
Dusseldorf International Airport	1,794,643	18.3%	10.0%
Nuremberg Airport	1,546,433	4.4%	8.6%
Hamburg Airport	1,153,171	29.9%	6.4%
Vienna International Airport	929,702	21.7%	5.2%
Hannover International Airport	858,750	36.3%	4.8%
Münster International Airport	775,235	7.4%	4.3%
Paderborn Airport	731,681	9.7%	4.1%
Zurich Airport	691,228	19.5%	3.8%
London Stansted Airport	689,008	1.9%	3.8%
Malaga International Airport	648,893	16.6%	3.6%
Cologne International Airport	615,656	10.2%	3.4%
Alicante International Airport	557,249	12.1%	3.1%
Leipzig/Halle Airport	442,117	31.1%	2.5%
	18,035,096		100.0%

[1] Berlin Tegel Airport: 1,916,790; Schönefeld International Airport: 155,219.
Air Berlin sold 13.5 million seats in 2005. The table above includes both passenger arrivals, departures, and connecting flights.

Source: *Air Berlin plc Prospectus*, April 19, 2006, p. 72.

5 Air Berlin's IPO

EXHIBIT 7 Air Berlin's fleet

Aircraft model	Number of aircraft	Number of seats	Average age (in years)	Owned/ leased
Boeing 737-400	5	167	9.9	Owned
Boeing B737-700	5	144	4.1	Operating lease
Boeing B737-800	15	186	4.7	Owned
Boeing B737-800	20	186	5.9	Operating lease
Airbus A320 family	5	180	0.3	Owned
Airbus A320 family	3	132	1	Operating lease
Fokker F100	3	100	16.2	Operating lease
Average	56	173	5.6	

Source: *Air Berlin plc Prospectus*, April 19, 2006, p. 73.

Expected delivery schedule	Number of aircraft
2006	9
2007	13
2008	8
2009	9
2010	9
2011	10
Total	**58**

Source: *Air Berlin plc Prospectus*, April 19, 2006, p. 73.

5 Air Berlin's IPO

EXHIBIT 8   Sales and distribution

As a percentage of total ticket sales	2005	2004	2003
Distribution channel			
Single-seat ticket sales	56.0%	52.5%	44.2%
Air Berlin website	21.4%	15.8%	10.0%
Air Berlin service centre	4.8%	5.8%	6.4%
Air Berlin airport ticket counters	2.2%	1.9%	1.5%
Travel agencies	25.3%	27.0%	24.6%
Other	2.3%	2.0%	1.7%
Bulk ticket sales to charter and package and tour operators	44.0%	47.5%	55.8%
Total ticket sales	**100.0%**	**100.0%**	**100.0%**

Source: *Air Berlin plc Prospectus*, April 19, 2006, p. 74.

EXHIBIT 9   Shares prior to the offer

Prior to completion of the offer	Shares owned (number)	Shares owned (%)
Ringerike GmbH & Co. Luftahrbeteiligungs KG	2,600,000	26.0%
Hans Joachim Knieps	2,500,000	25.0%
Werner Huehn	1,500,000	15.0%
Severin Schulte	1,250,000	12.5%
Rudolf Schulte	1,250,000	12.5%
Joachim Hunold	500,001	5.0%
Johannes Zurnieden	400,000	4.0%
Free Float	–	0.0%
Total	10,000,001	100.0%

Source: *Air Berlin plc Prospectus*, April 19, 2006, p. 9.

EXHIBIT 10 **WACC and discounted cash flow (DCF) assumptions**

Weighted average cost of capital (WACC)

Cost of debt (%)	6.5%
Cost of equity (%)	12.9%
Beta	1.1
Equity risk premium (%)	4.5%
Risk free rate (%)	6.0%
WACC (%)	8.3%
Terminal growth rate (%)	0.0%

DCF assumptions

	2005–10	2010–15	2015–19
Average annual % change			
Traffic (%)	11.3%	5.0%	5.0%
Average fare per Pax (%)	2.1%	0.5%	0.5%
Unit cost (%)	0.4%	1.0%	0.5%
Average			
EBIT margin (%)	5.9%	7.1%	7.6%
Capex	277	242	198

Source: "Air Berlin: Betting on Business Traffic and a World Cup Boost," Analyst Report, Morgan Stanley, June 21, 2006, p. 10.

PRO-FORMA STATEMENTS

Air Berlin: Pro-forma Statements

€ millions – Year end Dec 31	2004	2005	2006e	2007e	2008e
Scheduled	971.1	1,129.0	1,364.3	1,601.9	1,835.3
Seat-only	505.0	632.2	818.6	1,025.2	1,248.0
Revenue %	*52.0*	*56.0*	*60.0*	*64.0*	*68.0*
Charter	466. 1	496.8	545.7	576.7	587.3
Revenue %	*48.0*	*44,0*	*40,0*	*36,0*	*32,0*
Ancillary	28.8	34.0	53.9	73.8	92.5
Airport taxes	29.1	31.4	33.6	35.9	38.5
Other operating income	18.3	25.6	27.4	29.3	31.4
Total revenues	1,047.3	1,220.0	1,479.2	1,741.0	1,997.7
% change	20.8%	16.5%	21.2%	17.7%	14.7%
Expenses					
Salaries	(100.8)	(116.9)	(140.0)	(161.9)	(181.7)
Fuel	(171.4)	(239.5)	(314.1)	(437.3)	(492.0)
Other maintenance	(23.8)	(27.5)	(32.0)	(37.2)	(43.2)
Catering costs	(52.6)	(58.5)	(53.4)	(54.8)	(63.7)
Operating leases	(75.6)	(96.2)	(85.9)	(67.8)	(54.2)
Navigation charges	(99.2)	(109.0)	(120.6)	(133.3)	(156.5)
Airport & handling charges	(282.6)	(333.4)	(372.5)	(411.9)	(469.5)
Marketing & distribution costs	(53.4)	(66.4)	(71.9)	(77.9)	(91.5)
Other	(113.5)	(115.5)	(125.1)	(135.5)	(157.5)
Depreciation & amortization	(74.9)	(62.6)	(82.9)	(119.7)	(139.9)
Total costs	(1,047.9)	(1,225.5)	(1,398.2)	(1,637.3)	(1,849.9)
Total operating costs	(973.0)	(1,163.0)	(1,315.4)	(1,517.6)	(1,710.0)
Operating income	(0.6)	(5.5)	81.0	103.7	147.8
Financial expenses	(13.3)	(19.0)	(24.9)	(27.4)	(2.4)
Financial income	1.6	2.9	8.9	10.3	9.3
Other non-operating	29.1	(49.2)	–	–	–
Share of associates	0.3	–	–	–	–
Pre-tax income	17.0	(70.9)	64.9	86.6	129.7
Income tax	(19.9)	(45.0)	(10.4)	(17.3)	(29.8)
Net income/(loss)	(2.9)	(115.9)	54.5	69.3	99.9
% change	−107.8%	3918.1%	−147.1%	27.0%	44.2%
Reported EPS	(0.29)	(11.59)	0.92	1.16	1.68

Source: "Air Berlin: Betting on Business Traffic and a World Cup Boost," Analyst Report, Morgan Stanley, June 21, 2006, p. 27.

5 Air Berlin's IPO

EXHIBIT 10 WACC and discounted cash flow (DCF) assumptions (continued)

PRO-FORMA STATEMENTS

Air Berlin: Pro-forma Statements

€ million – Year end Dec 31	2004	2005	2006e	2007e	2008e
Free cash flow					
Net income	(3)	(116)	55	69	100
Depreciation & amortization	75	63	83	120	140
Impairments/other	1	5	–	–	–
Forex gains/losses	(16)	60	–	–	–
Interest expenses	–	1	–	–	–
Income tax expenses	(2)	–	–	–	–
Associates	–	–	–	–	–
Change in derivative fair value	11	(17)	–	–	–
Changes in assets	(17)	(39)	(1)	(1)	(1)
Changes in liabilities	83	109	40	46	53
Operating cash flow	133	66	177	234	292
Capex	(28)	(133)	(281)	(401)	(260)
Sales of assets	31	30	77	49	21
Other	–	–	–	–	–
Free cash flow	136	(37)	(28)	(118)	52
Balance sheet					
Total fixed assets	740	755	876	1,108	1,208
Total non-cash current assets	57	118	119	121	122
Cash	88	189	401	283	336
Total current assets	145	307	520	404	458
Total assets	884	1,062	1,397	1,513	1,666
Total current liabilities	268	387	427	474	527
Long-term debt	380	381	381	381	381
Provisions	53	97	97	97	97
Total liabilities	701	865	905	952	1,005
Total capital	184	197	492	561	661
Total shareholders' funds & liabilities	884	1,062	1,397	1,513	1,666

Source: "Air Berlin: Betting on Business Traffic and a World Cup Boost," Analyst Report, Morgan Stanley, June 21, 2006,

6 The Air France–KLM merger

*We have always been convinced of the necessity of consolidation in the airline indus-
try. Today, we announce a combination with KLM that will create the first European
airline group, which is a milestone in our industry. This will bring significant benefits to customers, shareholders and employees. Capitalizing on the two brands and
on the complementary strengths of both companies, we should, within SkyTeam, be
able to capture enhanced growth opportunities.*

– Jean-Cyril Spinetta, Chairman and CEO of Air France

*KLM has been pointing out the need for consolidation in light of the challenges fac-
ing our industry, and we have not made it a secret we were looking for a strong European partner. Through this innovative partnership with Air France and our
subsequent expected participation in the SkyTeam alliance, we are confident that we
have secured a sustainable future for our company. Our valuable Schiphol hub will
be an integral part of the dual hub strategy of the new airline group, allowing us to
build on what KLM and its staff have achieved over nearly 85 years.*

– Leo van Wijk, President and CEO of KLM

On September 30, 2003, Air France and KLM Royal Dutch Airlines – two European
airlines that provided international passenger and cargo airline services – issued a
press release that announced their planned merger. The merger envisaged the creation of
the leading European airline Air France–LM. In 2003, both airlines were the primary
national ("flag carrying") airlines in their home countries, France and the Netherlands.
However, poor industry conditions put pressure on the airlines' growth and operating margins. In the fiscal year ending on March 31, 2003, Air France, the larger of the two airlines, reported an increase in total sales of slightly more than one percent to €12,687
million and a net profit of €120 million (€0.55 per share). KLM performed worse than Air
France. In the same fiscal year, KLM reported a decrease in total sales of slightly less than
one percent to €6,485 million and a loss (before extraordinary items) of €186 million
(€3.97 per share).

For a number of years, KLM had been searching for a strategic partner, which seemed
to be of essential importance given the deteriorating industry conditions. Initially, KLM
attempted to form an alliance with the Italian flag carrier, Alitalia. However, this alliance
soon appeared to be unsuccessful because of the poor functioning of Milan Malpensa Airport, an unexpected delay in the privatization of Alitalia, and cultural incompatibilities
between the Italians and the Dutch.[1] After breaking with Alitalia, KLM kept on searching
for another partner. In early 2000, talks about joining forces with British Airways
remained unfruitful, as KLM and its main shareholder, the Dutch state, were unwilling to
hand over control to the British flag carrier.[2] In the second half of 2003, Air France came
to the rescue.

Professor Erik Peek prepared this case. The case is intended solely as the basis for class discussion and is not
intended to serve as an endorsement, source of primary data, or illustration of effective or ineffective management.

[1] "KLM Ends Venture With Alitalia, Imperiling US Airline Alliance," *Wall Street Journal,* May 1, 2000"; "Alitalia is Seeking Damages for Breakup with KLM," *Wall Street Journal*, August 2, 2000.

[2] "Europe's Flag Airlines: Going Nowhere," Businessweek, February 26, 2001.

KLM Royal Dutch Airlines[3]

KLM Royal Dutch Airlines was founded in 1919, which, at the time of the merger, made it the oldest continuously operating airline in the world. Landmarks in the company's history were its very first scheduled flight to London in 1920, its first intercontinental flight to Jakarta (formerly Batavia) in 1924, and its operating scheduled flights to New York from 1946.

Over the years, the core activities of KLM remained very much the same. The airline provided worldwide passenger and cargo transport, engineering and maintenance, and, in a later stage, charter and low-cost scheduled flights. KLM operated its charter and low-cost flights primarily through its subsidiaries Buzz and Transavia. In 1994, KLM served 153 cities in 81 countries on six continents and ranked eighth among the largest international airlines based upon ton-kilometer traffic on international flights. Nine years later, KLM served 350 cities in 73 countries on six continents and ranked fifth among the largest international airlines.

In its prospectus from 1994, which accompanied the issuance of 18.5 million additional ordinary shares, the airline summarized its most important operating risks. First, the airline operated in an industry that was cyclical and highly competitive. The cyclical nature could have a strong adverse effect on KLM's profitability because, as every other airline, it had a high degree of operating leverage (high fixed-to-variable cost ratio). Second, the airline's profitability depended strongly on exchange rate fluctuations as well as on fluctuations in aircraft fuel prices. Third, because in many parts of the world airlines and international air traffic were highly regulated, KLM's operations could be affected by foreign governments' actions of protectionism.

Within this uncertain economic environment, KLM's corporate objective was "… to position itself as an airline operating worldwide from a European base that provides quality service for passengers and cargo shippers at competitive cost levels." The strategy that KLM used to attain this objective was to:

- *Increase customer preference.* KLM focused on achieving a high level of customer satisfaction, for example, by closely monitoring customer demand and by expanding its "Flying Dutchman" frequent flyer program.

- *Strengthen its market presence around the world.* KLM strengthened its market presence in the world's major air transportation markets by expanding its hub-and-spoke operations at Schiphol Airport and by creating alliances with other European, American, and Asian airlines. For example, in 1989, KLM had acquired a 20 percent stake in Northwest Airlines, a North American airline having its operations hubs in Boston, Detroit, and Minneapolis. This acquisition helped KLM to gain better access to American destinations. The alliance between KLM and Northwest implied that both airlines operated as a joint venture on transatlantic flights, while KLM did all their marketing in Europe and Northwest in the US.

- *Reduce its costs to at least an internationally competitive level.* During the early 1990s, KLM launched a restructuring program that aimed to reduce its costs and increase its productivity. The program included spinning off noncore business units, network optimization, eliminating the first class section on intercontinental flights, redesigning business processes, and acquiring more efficient aircraft. KLM launched a second restructuring program, Focus 2000, in 1996, and a third one, Baseline, in 2000.

In 2003, KLM's shares were listed on the Amsterdam Euronext Exchange and on the New York Stock Exchange. Since early in KLM's history, the Dutch state had been KLM's primary shareholder. The state's ownership interest in KLM gradually decreased over the years, from 38 percent of the votes in 1994 to 14 percent in 2003. Nonetheless, the state remained able to effectively influence the airline's major (non-operating) decisions through various mechanisms. First, up to the date of the merger, the state had the option to obtain a 50.1 percent voting interest to prevent any undesirable accumulation of share ownership in the hands of others. This option was especially important to prevent a country imposing restrictions on KLM exercising international traffic rights. Because such traffic rights were the result of bilateral treaties between governments and tied to domestically owned airlines, countries could deny these rights to KLM if in their view the airline was no longer in Dutch hands. Second, the articles of association offered the state the right to appoint a majority of the Supervisory Board. Third, the state held the majority of KLM's priority shares, through which it had a veto over important decisions such as the issuance of shares, payments of stock dividends, and changes in the articles of association.

The merger agreement[4]

During 2002, while renewed negotiations between British Airways and KLM reached deadlock, KLM representatives also started to meet with Air France representatives to talk about the possibilities of cooperation. Parallel to these meetings, Air France's North American alliance partners, Continental Airlines and Delta Airlines, discussed possible cooperation with KLM's North American alliance partner, Northwest Airlines. In August 2002, the three North American airlines signed a ten-year agreement to improve schedule connections between the airlines and to share codes, frequent flyer programs, and airport lounges. After the signing of the agreement, the three airlines encouraged Air France and KLM to start similar cooperation in Europe. However, because the French state was planning to privatize Air France (i.e., reduce its shareholdings to a level below 20 percent), Air France and KLM envisaged a closer form of cooperation. Initially, both parties discussed the option of creating a dual listed company structure. Air France and KLM would keep their separate listings but cross-hold 50 percent of the shares of each other's operating subsidiaries. Because Air France had a substantially greater market value than KLM, Air France would also become the direct owner of 52 percent of KLM's shares and certain of its assets would be excluded from the transaction. However, the idea of creating a dual listed company structure appeared too complex and both airlines soon opted for a simpler alternative, which they presented to their shareholders on September 30, 2003.

The alternative proposal implied that the former shareholders of KLM and Air France became shareholders of the publicly listed holding company Air France–KLM, which would hold 100 percent of the shares of two private operating companies, Air France and KLM. Former Air France shareholders would receive one Air France–KLM share for every Air France share that they held. In exchange for ten KLM shares, former KLM shareholders would receive 11 Air France–KLM shares plus ten Air France–KLM warrants. The warrants had a strike price of €20.00, were exercisable after 18 months and had an exercise period of three-and-a-half years. Three warrants gave the warrant holder the right to purchase two Air France–KLM shares.

Based on Air France's closing price on September 29, 2003, the estimated value of one warrant was equal to €1.68 (according to the Air France–KLM merger announcement). This warrant value was based on the following assumptions:

- The September 29 AIR France(–KLM) share price was €13.69.
- The risk-free rate equaled 2.89 percent.
- The estimated future volatility of the AIR France(–KLM) share price was 40 percent.
- Estimated dividends per share were €0.096, €0.144, and €0.188 during the exercise period (based on I/B/E/S estimates).

Based on the AIR France (-KLM) share price of €13.69 and a warrant value of €1.68, the total value of the offer for KLM shareholders equaled €16.74 per share ($11/10 \times €13.69 + €1.68$), which implied a premium of 40 percent over KLM's closing share price on September 29, 2003. After the share exchange, former KLM shareholders would own 19 percent of the ordinary shares (and voting rights) of Air France-KLM. The share exchange offer would commence only after approval from the EU and US competition authorities, and if no third party announced a public offer for either KLM's or Air France's shares.

The transaction between Air France and KLM was not a full-blown merger. The two private operating companies, Air France and KLM, remained separate entities, in particular because it was important to preserve the two established brand names. Further, the Dutch state retained the option to acquire a 50.1 percent voting interest in KLM (the operating company) if necessary to preserve KLM's landing rights.

Motivation for the merger

Airline industry analysts tend to distinguish two phases of evolution in a deregulated airline industry – i.e., the expansion phase and the consolidation phase. To illustrate, in the 1970s, the US government deregulated

[4]Material in this section is drawn from the Air France–KLM merger prospectus (April 5, 2004).

the US airline industry, which led to a serious expansion of supply from 1978 to 1990. In this expansion phase, US airlines responded by cutting their costs, but their operating margins experienced a secular decline. In the early stages of consolidation, from 1986 onwards, mergers resulted in the elimination of several brands, but did not restrict or reallocate capacity. Since the mergers initially raised costs, profit margins remained under pressure. In the later stages of the consolidation phase, US airlines reallocated their capacity from unprofitable (geographical) areas to profitable (geographical) areas. This significantly improved US airlines' profit margins. In the mid-1990s, the European airline industry was in a different stage of development than the US airline industry. At that time, European airlines had just entered into the earlier stages of consolidation by creating alliances. However, alliances made it difficult to reallocate capacity and improve profitability. Furthermore, government interference hindered efficient allocation of capacity.[5]

During the late 1990s and the early 2000s, the profit potential of the European airline industry changed substantially. At the end of the 1990s, Europe had an increasing number of large and small airlines, many airports close together, and most governments supporting loss-making national airlines. Government support resulted in very few unprofitable companies leaving the market. At the same time, many airlines started downgrading their product by offering low levels of service on short-haul flights to compete on costs. All major airports had capacity constraints, which (in combination with their slot trading system that favored current slot-owners) made access to established airports difficult for new entrants. However, new entrants, such as Ryanair and easyJet were moving to smaller, local airports to avoid the capacity constraints of the major airports. These new entrants further intensified the competition (on costs) in the European airline industry. Finally, the use of web booking systems made the market more transparent. Customers were able to easily compare prices, which substantially reduced switching costs.

After 2000, the profit potential of the European airline industry improved slightly. The European Commission had allowed governments to cover insurance risks and costs faced by airlines after the September 11, 2001 terrorist attacks; however, other forms of government support were no longer allowed. Further, after September 2001, many airlines significantly reduced (fixed) capacity, which reduced competition. Finally, more and more countries signed bilateral "open skies" agreements with the US, implying that European airlines could fly to any place in the US, at any fare, at any time (but only from their home countries). In early 2004, a European agreement with the US was being negotiated, implying that, for example, the German national airline Lufthansa would be allowed to fly from Milan to New York. Nonetheless, KLM's return on equity during the fiscal years ending in 2001, 2002, and 2003 was 3.7, −7.8, and −24.1 percent respectively.

Exhibit 1 reports KLM's and Air France's motivation for entering into the merger agreement, as it was set out at the merger presentation on September 30, 2003.

Response of the Dutch Investor Association

In early 2004, the Dutch Investor Association (VEB; Vereniging voor Effectenbezitters) began to oppose the merger proposal. The VEB was of the opinion that during the months following the merger, KLM's value had increased substantially due to changed circumstances, which would justify a higher takeover price. KLM shareholders had to decide before May 5, 2004 (just before KLM's publication of its 2003/2004 financial statements) whether or not they wished to offer their shares to Air France. The VEB claimed that KLM shareholders should be able to take these latest financial results into account when making their decision. Air France and KLM refused this, supported by a Dutch court decision on April 29, 2004. **Exhibit 2** sets out the VEB's objections in detail.

On May 6, 2004, KLM announced that net profit, operating profit, and revenues for the fiscal year 2003/2004 were €24 million, €120 million, and €5,870 million, respectively.

Questions

1 Evaluate the motivating factors behind the Air France–KLM merger. Does the merger effectively address the strategic challenges faced by KLM and Air France?

---

[5]See "Global Airlines: Survival of the Fittest," *Goldman Sachs Global Research*, September 22, 1997.

2 Calculate the present value of the synergies. To what extent is the actual market response to the merger announcement consistent with the estimated value of the expected performance improvements?

3 To what extent can the premium be justified by the expected performance improvements (as presented in **Exhibit 1**)?

4 Critically analyze each of the VEB's (Dutch Investor Association) objections to the proposed takeover price (as presented in **Exhibit 2**). Do you have any evidence that Air France shareholders agree with the VEB?

5 If you were a shareholder of KLM, would you support this merger proposal?

EXHIBIT 1 Appendix to the offer document

Strategic rationale of the transaction

The airline industry is fragmented and its current competitive structure, with national carriers for each individual country, is an inheritance from a former era. This has contributed to low profitability and lack of value creation for shareholders. The need for structural changes and consolidation in Europe is widely accepted, but has not yet commenced as a consequence of regulatory and political constraints.

The single European market and its current enlargement to some 455 million inhabitants reinforce the need for consolidation.

The evolution of the European regulatory framework highlighted by (i) the November 2002 European Court of Justice ruling and (ii) the mandate given in June 2003 to the European Commission to negotiate the open sky agreement with the US now creates an attractive environment for a value creating combination.

If commercial alliances have contributed over the past years to initiate the first steps towards consolidation, deeper cooperation is now needed to generate significant and sustainable synergies.

The proposed transaction between Air France and KLM is the first significant move in this context and will create a leading airline group in Europe with aggregated revenues of EUR 19.2 billion (2002/03 fiscal year).

The combination with KLM is a major step in Air France's strategy. In parallel, KLM's strategy over the years has consistently been built on two pillars: the strengthening of its own organization, as well as the participation in a global alliance, for which it seeks a strong European partner. The combination with Air France is the achievement of this strategy.

The transaction will benefit from the complementarities of the two airlines' operations:

- Two reputable and strong brands that will be further strengthened.

- Two operational hubs (Paris CDG and Amsterdam Schiphol) which are among the most efficient in Europe and provide significant development potential.

- Two complementary networks both in medium and long haul. In medium haul Air France has a strong position in Southern Europe and KLM has developed a strong position in Northern and North Eastern Europe, and both will be able to expand their positions in Central and Eastern Europe. The long haul networks currently consist of 101 destinations

of which only 31 are common (essentially the world's largest cities with high traffic volumes).

- A combined network of 226 destinations with 93 new destinations for KLM passengers and 48 new destinations for Air France passengers.

- A strong presence in cargo where Air France and KLM are the 4th and 11th largest in the world respectively but with complementary capabilities and expertise.

- A strong combination in the field of aircraft maintenance, creating one of the largest MRO providers worldwide.

- SkyTeam will eventually become the second largest global airline alliance and with its partners being able to offer passengers a more truly worldwide network.

Synergies

Potential synergies arising from the proposed transaction have been thoroughly assessed and quantified by a joint working group of Air France and KLM who have reviewed the feasibility and quantum of the synergies and their build-up over time.

Sales and distribution

By coordinating the two sales organizations the new group will have an improved presence around the world and will be able to offer a wider range of products to passengers. Cost savings could be achieved by coordinating the sales structures of the two companies. A joint negotiation position with catering and ground-handling partners could also lead to additional benefits.

Network/revenue management and fleet

By full code sharing, harmonizing the flight schedules and optimizing common management revenue policy the two airlines will be able to offer more destinations, a larger number and more convenient connections for passengers and to improve sales performance.

Cargo

The offering of an improved product through a more extensive network in combination with coordinated freighter planning, should lead to an increase of revenues. Cost savings should also be possible by more efficient hub handling.

Engineering and maintenance

The two airlines will be able to integrate purchasing of stock, to create centres of excellence in engineering and optimize the use of existing E&M platforms.

IT

Converging the IT applications used by both airlines should generate considerable cost savings in the medium term.

Other

Optimizing and harmonizing other activities such as simulator utilization and joint purchasing of goods should deliver further cost savings.

The identified potential synergies are expected to result in an annual improvement of the combined operating income (earnings before interest and tax) of between EUR 385 million and EUR 495 million, following a gradual implementation over a period of five years, with further upward potential thereafter.

Approximately 60 percent of potential synergies are expected to be derived from cost savings.

This does not include additional expected synergies from marketing cooperation with respective partners. Furthermore, any improvement from the common fleet policy and lower capital expenditure requirements have not yet been determined and have not been taken into account in these estimates.

KLM restructuring plan

The KLM restructuring plan, which was announced in April 2003, with targeted annual operating income improvement of EUR 650 million by April 1, 2005, are additional to the synergies mentioned above. The KLM management remains fully committed to achieving this objective.

Estimated value of the synergies

Synergies by activity (Euro amounts in millions)

Activity	Main actions	Year 3 (2006/2007)	Year 5 (2008/2009)
Sales/Distribution	Coordination of sales structures; Sales cost improvements; Handling and catering.	€40	€100
Network, revenue management, fleet	Network/scheduling management; Revenue management harmonization; optimization of fleet utilization; Coordinated management.	€95–130	€30–195
Cargo	Network optimization; Commercial alignments; support services.	€35	€35
Maintenance	Procurement; Insourcing; pooling (stocks etc.).	€25	€60–€65
IT systems	Progressive convergence of IT systems	€20	€50–€70
Other	Procurement synergies	€5–€10	€10–€30
Total cost savings		€220–€260	€385–€495

Total expected synergies per year (Euro amounts in millions)

	2004/2005	2005/2006	2006/2007	2007/2008	2008/2009	Long-term
Total savings	65–75	110–135	220–260	295–370	385–495	>600

6 The Air France–KLM merger

EXHIBIT 2 Press release of the Dutch Investor Association (VEB): "Air France shareholders get it on the cheap", April 19, 2004[a]

After two postponements on 22 March and 31 March, KLM and Air France announced they intend to pursue their merger plans unchanged. This means that Air France will make an offer worth €784 million, whereby each KLM share will be worth 1.1 Air France shares plus a warrant. Far too low an offer.

Half a year has gone by since the merger was announced on 30 September 2003. In the intervening six months a number of circumstances have emerged that would justify a higher bid. The prospectus and the bid offer show that KLM is worth considerably more than was apparent until now. There are other questions that remain unanswered that would provide a clearer view of KLM's value. Here are ten reasons why the Air France bid is far too low.

Net equity per share is €34

KLM net worth (assets after debt) is €1,501 million, or €34.14 per share. At an Air France share price of €15 the offer amounts to €17.80 per KLM share. The bid is thus equivalent to just over its net equity value. Air France shareholders will obtain half KLM for free.

A further point is that KLM owns significant intangible assets that are not valued on the balance sheet. This includes the KLM brand name and the landing rights owned by KLM which have a definite economic value. Since these important intangibles are not valued at all in the balance sheet, a price in excess of net equity value stands to reason.

The bid is worth a mere seven times earnings (2004) and five times earnings (2005)

Analysts forecast a substantial increase of profit for Fiscal 2004/2005 and the following Fiscal. They predict earnings in the €100–€110 million range in 2004. In the following year they could reach the €150–€170 million range. This equates to €2.50 and €3.60 per share. The bid is thus seven times expected earnings for 2004 and five times expected earnings for 2005. Compared with other listed companies, whose average p/e ratio is 14, this is a very low valuation. Prices paid for other airline companies score are 17 times 2004 earnings and 11 times 2005.

Real estate assets include a surplus value of at least €248 million, or €5.60 per share

The bid documentation (p. F-158) prepared by Air France and KLM reveals significant hidden reserves in KLM's stock of real estate. These are valued in KLM's balance sheet at €331 million. Price at purchase was €728 million, 55 percent of which has been written off. According to KLM these assets are now worth €248 million more. Put against 44.2 million shares on the market this corresponds to a surplus value of €5.60 per share. Specialists say the surplus value is closer to the €450–€650 million bracket!

Unlike Air France, KLM has accumulated a pension fund surplus of €2.4 billion

According to French GAAP (Generally Accepted Accounting Principles) KLM equity is worth about €3 billion, roughly double the equity according to Dutch GAAP and four times the value of the bid. Some significant modifications have been made to arrive at these figures. On the one hand the pension fund reserve has been added to shareholder equity. This is worth €2.4 billion. Against that a negative adjustment has to be made for contingent tax liabilities falling upon KLM of €811 million. French GAAP values equity per share at €69.

The exchange ratio is partly the result of operating results in 2002/2003 and 2003/2004: These were seriously depressed by the SARS health scare and the crisis in Iraq

KLM has been looking for years for a partner. There were several previous rounds of negotiation with British Airways. In 2001 a merger attempt with Alitalia failed. Processing the consequences of this failure was unpleasant. KLM was obliged to pay Alitalia €275 million, which was equivalent to €6 per KLM share. The media reported that KLM had refused an out of court settlement worth €50 million. The Alitalia costs appear as a charge in the 2002/2003 accounts. Last year operating results came under pressure as a result of the SARS health scare which significantly reduced passenger traffic to and from Asia. The first quarter of calendar 2003 put heavy pressure on both sales and profit

[a]Reprinted with permission from the Vereniging van Effectenbezitters.

6 The Air France–KLM merger

as a result of the coming war in Iraq and the danger of terrorist attacks directed at aircraft. It is obvious that these factors depressed the price negotiations which clearly took account of current operational results. KLM would have been far better served by sitting it out until it could enter into negotiations from a more comfortable and more profitable situation.

The last two quarters show results significantly above the estimates of analysts

The merger and the price were announced on 30 September. In the intervening period KLM published its quarterly results, first on 23 October 2003 (Q2) and then on 22 January 2004 (Q3). KLM's results exceeded – even significantly – expectations. This has led to KLM anticipating a slightly positive result for 2003/2004 – despite SARS, Iraq, the low dollar and a poor economy. These improvements alone would have justified an adjustment of the price.

The earnings trend on the French side is less attractive. In the last nine months Air France net profit has fallen from €143 million to €80 million.

Air France gets control of KLM without paying a premium

Air France will be the masters in the newly merged company. Previous Air France shareholders will hold onto an 81 percent share in the company. The CEO will be a Frenchman, Jean-Cyrille Spinetta. In both the Executive and the Supervisory Boards the Dutch will be in a minority. Of the eight Executive Board Directors four will be Dutch and four will be French. Although both companies pay lip-service to the mantra of a merger, it is in reality a takeover. Air France pitches a bid priced in its own shares for KLM and gains control. It might be that the changing of the guard will take place in stages to allow landing rights to be preserved, but after three years this formal structure will be dissolved as well. In cases of takeover, a control premium payable in addition to the standard economic valuation is the norm. Air France is not paying it.

KLM has started a cost savings program worth €650 million, but KLM shareholders will get only 19 percent of the benefit

On 8 May 2003 KLM announced a cost cutting programme designed to yield €650 million in savings. The major share of these cost reductions have still to be carried out. On 22 January KLM announced that €125 millions worth of savings had been achieved. Clearly, successful execution of the programme will lead to bet-

ter profitability at KLM. If the cost reduction programme is implemented in full and half of the benefits are given back to the customer in the form of reduced fares, operational results will go up by €325 million. Stripping out 35 percent corporation tax, this leads to a contribution of €211 million to the bottom line. If the transaction goes through, KLM shareholders will own 19 percent of the joint company, as a result of which only 19 percent of these benefits will flow to KLM shareholders. But every single percentage point of the improvement will have come from the business they used to own.

Key factors show that KLM should obtain over 30 percent of the merged airline

On a total passengers carried basis KLM is the world's tenth largest airline and Air France is number three. Taken by sales, Air France with revenues worth €12.7 billion is about twice the size of KLM (revenues of €6.5 billion). A revenue criterion thus leads to a 66:34 ratio: KLM shareholders deserve a one-third share in the merged airline. Other measures of size lead to the same ratio. Based on four criteria – sales, number of aircraft, shareholder equity, and headcount – an average ratio comes out at 69:31. The figure means that the KLM figure should be 63 percent higher than the agreed 19 percent. If there are no signs of structural differences in profitability between Air France and KLM – and nothing has emerged to show this – these yardsticks can be used to make a reliable estimate of what the share swap ratio should be.

Benefits of synergy

The bid prospectus (p. 50) lists significant benefits of synergy the two companies expect to achieve if the merger goes through. Year One factors for €75 million in synergy benefits, rising to €450 million in Year Five. Clearly KLM shareholders should be compensated for these synergies in the form of a proper price offer, or share swap. It is scarcely an adequate response to claim that, because Air France has brought out an offer priced in shares, KLM shareholders will thereby participate in the benefits. For whatever reasons that they may consider relevant – let us say, for issues of control – KLM shareholders may decide to decline the offer to become Air France shareholders. If they accept the merger and do decide to become Air France shareholders they will share in the benefits of synergy to the tune of a mere 19 percent.

Key dates

Above are ten reasons why the offer for KLM is far too low. In terms of procedure there are two important dates. On Monday 19 April an Extraordinary General Meeting of Shareholders will be held. Information about the offer will be given, questions will be answered and a proposal to change the Articles of Association – which will permit the merger – will be put to the vote. At 11 a.m. on 3 May the offer will close. Prior to that KLM shareholders will have to decide whether they want to accept or reject the bid. If less than 70 percent of the shares are tendered the transaction will be a dead letter. If less than 95 percent of shares are tendered, KLM's share listing will be maintained.

We have tried to shed light on the true worth of KLM. It is significantly higher than the current bid offer. This will not dispense KLM shareholders from taking their own decision. That can be based on other decisions such as enthusiasm over the prospects of Air France, a need for cash or whatever.

Peter Paul de Vries
Chairman of Vereniging van Effectenbezitters (Dutch Investor Association)

EXHIBIT 3 **Abridged merger prospectus**

Unaudited condensed *pro forma* consolidated financial information

The following unaudited condensed *pro forma* consolidated financial information is being provided to give you a better understanding of what the results of operations and financial position of Air France-KLM might have looked like had the offer of Air France for KLM common shares occurred on an earlier date. The unaudited condensed *pro forma* financial information is based on the estimates and assumptions set forth in the notes to such information. The unaudited condensed *pro forma* consolidated financial information is preliminary and is being furnished solely for illustrative purposes and, therefore, is not necessarily indicative of the combined results of operations or financial position of Air France–KLM that might have been achieved for the dates or periods indicated, nor is it necessarily indicative of the results of operations or financial position of Air France–KLM that may, or may be expected to, occur in the future. No account has been taken within the unaudited condensed *pro forma* consolidated financial statements of any synergy or efficiency that may, or may be expected to, occur following the offer.

For accounting purposes, the combination will be accounted for as Air France's acquisition of KLM using the purchase method of accounting under both French and US GAAP. Under French GAAP, this determination has been based on the assessment of effective control of KLM by Air France, primarily through the ability of Air France to control the significant decisions of KLM as a result of its deciding vote on the strategic management committee. Under US GAAP, Air France believes that its ability to cast the deciding vote for majority matters of the strategic management committee, combined with its ownership of 49 percent of the voting share capital of KLM, and its ownership of all of the outstanding depositary receipts related to the administered shareholdings which will exist following the completion of the exchange offer, will provide Air France with a controlling financial interest in KLM, and that consolidation of KLM provides the most meaningful presentation of the combined financial position and results of operations of Air France–KLM. We have also concluded that Air France should initially measure all assets, liabilities and non-controlling interests of KLM at their fair values at the date of completion of the exchange offer.

As a result of the above considerations under French GAAP and US GAAP, the accompanying unaudited *pro forma* financial information includes adjustments to reflect the fair values of KLM's net assets as further described in the accompanying footnotes. The final combination will be accounted for based on the final determination of the transaction value and the fair values of KLM's identifiable assets and liabilities at the date of exchange of control. Therefore, the actual goodwill amount, as well as other balance sheet items, could differ from the preliminary unaudited condensed *pro forma* consolidated financial information presented herein, and in turn affect items in the preliminary unaudited condensed *pro forma* consolidated income statements and balance sheet, such as amortization of intangible assets, income of equity affiliates, long-term assets, negative goodwill, pre-paid pension assets, and related income taxes.

The following unaudited *pro forma* consolidated financial information gives *pro forma* effect to the offer, after giving effect to the *pro forma* adjustments described in the notes to the unaudited *pro forma* consolidated financial information. The unaudited condensed *pro forma* consolidated income statements for the financial year ended March 31, 2003 and for the six months ended September 30, 2003 give effect to the offer and the business combination as if they had occurred on April 1, 2002. The unaudited condensed *pro forma* consolidated balance sheet as of September 30, 2003 gives effect to the offer and the business combination as if they had occurred on September 30, 2003. The unaudited condensed *pro forma* consolidated financial information of Air France–KLM is based on the historical consolidated financial statements of Air France, which are included elsewhere in this prospectus, and on the historical consolidated financial statements of KLM, which are included in KLM's Annual Report on Form 20-F for the year ended March 31, 2003, as amended, and in the unaudited interim condensed consolidated financial statements for the six months ended September 30, 2003 filed by KLM on Form 6-K dated December 30, 2003, incorporated by reference in this prospectus. The historical financial statements of Air France and KLM are prepared in accordance with French GAAP and Dutch GAAP, respectively. Dutch GAAP differs in some respects from French GAAP. Accordingly, the historical financial statements of KLM have been adjusted to French GAAP for all periods presented in this unaudited condensed *pro forma* consolidated financial information.

Air France has presented the unaudited condensed *pro forma* consolidated financial information in accordance with both French GAAP and US GAAP for the year ended March 31, 2003 and as of September 30, 2003 and for the six-month period then ended in order to fulfill regulatory requirements in the United States. The combined entity will continue to prepare its consolidated financial statements in accordance with French GAAP until application of IFRS becomes mandatory within the European Union for financial years beginning on or after January 1, 2005. Air France will also provide additional information in accordance with US GAAP in order to fulfill regulatory requirements in the United States.

These unaudited condensed *pro forma* consolidated financial statements are only a summary and should be read in conjunction with the historical consolidated financial statements and related notes of Air France and KLM.

UNAUDITED CONDENSED *PRO FORMA* COMBINED INCOME STATEMENT
FOR THE SIX-MONTH PERIOD ENDED SEPTEMBER 30, 2003

	French GAAP		
(euro amounts in millions)	Air France	KLM	*pro forma* combined
Net sales	€6,193	€3,036	€9,229
Salaries and related costs	(2,025)	(922)	(2,947)
Depreciation and amortization	(618)	(218)	(806)
Aircraft fuel	(657)	(396)	(1,053)
Landing fees and other rents	(654)	(268)	(922)
Aircraft maintenance materials and outside repairs	(186)	(263)	(449)
Aircraft rent	(239)	(133)	(372)
Selling expenses and passenger commissions	(533)	(191)	(724)
Contracted services and passenger revenues	(533)	(286)	(819)
Other operating expenses	(660)	(264)	(924)
Income (loss) from operations	88	95	213
Restructuring costs	(11)	(75)	(86)
Interest expense	(71)	(53)	(124)
Interest income and other financial income, net	65	26	91
Other income (expense), net	0	7	7
Gain on sale of stock subsidiaries	0	12	12
Income of equity affiliates	22	7	32
Income (loss) before taxes and minority interests and goodwill amortization	93	19	145
Income tax	(32)	4	(38)
Minority interest	(1)	0	(1)
Goodwill amortization and impairment	(8)	(2)	115
Income (loss) from continuing operations	€52	€21	€221

The accompanying notes are an integral part of the unaudited condensed *pro forma* consolidated financial statements.

UNAUDITED CONDENSED *PRO FORMA* COMBINED INCOME STATEMENT
FOR THE YEAR ENDED MARCH 30, 2003

| (euro amounts in millions) | French GAAP | | |
	Air France	KLM	*pro forma* combined
Net sales	€12,687	€6,367	€19,054
Salaries and related costs	(3,856)	(1,714)	(5,570)
Depreciation and amortization	(1,310)	(528)	(1,776)
Aircraft fuel	(1,369)	(866)	(2,235)
Landing fees and other rents	(1,362)	(525)	(1,887)
Aircraft maintenance materials and outside repairs	(477)	(642)	(1,119)
Aircraft rent	(521)	(256)	(777)
Selling expenses and passenger commissions	(1,157)	(486)	(1,643)
Contracted services and passenger revenues	(1,086)	(594)	(1,680)
Other operating expenses	(1,357)	(663)	(2,020)
Income (loss) from operations	192	93	347
Restructuring costs	(13)	0	(13)
Interest expense	(161)	(140)	(301)
Interest income and other financial income, net	76	(4)	72
Other income (expense), net	0	(42)	(42)
Gain on sale of stock subsidiaries	4	6	10
Income of equity affiliates	29	(4)	31
Income (loss) before taxes and minority interests and goodwill amortization	127	(91)	104
Income tax	13	30	22
Minority interest	(4)	0	(4)
Goodwill amortization and impairment	(16)	(4)	230
Income (loss) from continuing operations	€120	€ (65)	€352

The accompanying notes are an integral part of the unaudited condensed *pro forma* consolidated financial statements.

UNAUDITED CONDENSED *PRO FORMA* COMBINED BALANCE SHEET, SEPTEMBER 30, 2003

(euro amounts in millions)	French GAAP		
	Air France	**KLM**	*pro forma* combined
Current assets:			
Cash and cash equivalents	€1,202	€55	€1,257
Short-term investments and restricted cash	169	475	644
Accounts receivables	1,574	728	2,302
Inventories	209	145	354
Prepaid expenses and other	559	2,511	1,981
Total current assets	3,713	3,914	6,538
Flight and ground equipment, net	6,353	2,350	8,674
Flight and ground equipment under capital lease, net	1,515	2,592	3,708
Investment in equity affiliates	312	216	484
Investment in securities	103	0	66
Deferred income taxes	76	53	657
Other non-current assets	154	10	164
Intangible assets	159	48	207
Goodwill	103	12	103
Total assets	€12,488	€9,195	€20,705
Current liabilities:			
Current maturities of long-term debt	€223	€16	€239
Short-term obligation (other)	297	148	445
Current obligation under capital leases	113	151	265
Trade payables	1,204	546	1,750
Deferred revenue on ticket sales	807	471	1,278
Taxes payable	4	11	15
Accrued salaries, related benefits and employee-related liabilities	559	236	795
Other current liability	626	329	955
Total current liabilities	3,833	1,908	5,741
Long-term debt	2,349	591	2,940
Non-current obligation under capital leases	1,204	2,453	3,657
Pension liability	601	4	641
Provisions	450	223	1,906
Other non-current liability	0	212	212
Deferred tax liability, non-current	0	747	747
Minority interest	29	0	29
Total stockholders' equity	4,022	3,058	4,833
Total liabilities and stockholders' equity	€12,488	€9,195	€20,705

The accompanying notes are an integral part of the unaudited condensed *pro forma* consolidated financial statements

Excerpts from the notes to the *pro forma* financial statements – significant differences between Dutch GAAP and French GAAP (euro amounts in millions, except per share data)

KLM prepares its consolidated financial statements in accordance with Dutch GAAP, which differ in certain material respects from French GAAP. For purposes of preparing the unaudited condensed *pro forma* consolidated financial information, KLM's historical consolidated financial statements have been adjusted to conform to French GAAP as applied by Air France for each period presented. These adjustments have been made based on estimates of the management of Air France and KLM. These adjustments are unaudited, and may not fully reflect the application of French GAAP for the periods presented as if KLM had prepared its financial statements using French GAAP. Upon completion of the exchange offer, Air France and KLM will perform a detailed review of their accounting policies and financial statement classifications, and additional adjustments may be required to conform the KLM financial statements to Air France-KLM's financial statements as presented under French GAAP.

Although Air France and KLM do not expect that this detailed review will result in material changes to accounting policies or classifications other than noted below, no such assurance can be given at this time. The table below summarizes the net effect of French GAAP adjustments on KLM's stockholders' equity as of September 30, 2003:

Note	Differences	Stockholders' equity at September 30, 2003
1	Pension benefits	€2,355
2	Derivative instruments	11
4	Accounting for treasury stock	23
7	Frequent flyer program	(16)
5	Deferred income taxes	(811)
	Stockholders' equity without tax	€1,562

Note 1 Pension benefits

Under Dutch GAAP, pension costs for KLM's defined benefit pension plans are generally expensed on the basis of the actuarially determined contributions that KLM is required to pay under various worldwide pension schemes. Air France accounts for the costs and obligations of its pension plans in accordance with French GAAP, which does not significantly differ from IAS 19.

This French GAAP adjustment provides for the costs and obligations related to KLM's pension plans as if these amounts had been determined using IAS 19 as applied on a historical basis of accounting. This adjustment, reflected in the "French GAAP adjustment" third column of the condensed *pro forma* income statements resulted in a decrease in Salaries and related costs by €45 million and €170 million for the six months ended September 30, 2003 and for the year ended March 31, 2003, respectively. The KLM balance sheet at September 30, 2003 was adjusted as follows in this respect: an increase in the "Prepaid expenses and other" caption of €2,336 million and a decrease in Provisions by €19 million resulting in an increase in stockholders' equity before tax by €2,355 million.

Note 2 Derivative instruments

Under Dutch GAAP, derivatives are recorded separately on the balance sheet and are accounted for at fair value. Changes in the fair value of derivatives which meet certain criteria for cash flow hedge accounting may be deferred and recognized in other comprehensive income until such time as the hedged transaction is recognized. Ineffective portions of hedges are recognized immediately in earnings. Under French GAAP qualifying hedge instruments are presented on the balance sheet net of the hedged item. For cash flow hedges, changes in values of derivative instruments are deferred, as no separate presentation of other comprehensive income is included under French GAAP.

Certain derivatives do not meet the criteria for hedge accounting under Dutch GAAP, but do meet criteria for hedge accounting under French GAAP. As a result, changes in fair values of certain derivatives have been included in income under Dutch GAAP but would have been deferred under French GAAP. The French GAAP adjustment gives effect to reclassifications to reflect net presentation of qualifying hedges, and reverses the effects of changes in fair values of cash flow hedges that had been included in other comprehensive income under Dutch GAAP. In addition, the impacts on income of some non-qualifying derivatives under Dutch GAAP which meet French GAAP criteria have been reversed. The September 30, 2003 balance sheet impacts are described in the following table (in € millions):

Flight equipment	€(110)
Other non-current assets	(409)
Long-term debt	(291)
Capital lease obligation	(239)
Stockholders' equity before tax	11

6 The Air France–KLM merger

Before tax, the income (loss) statement adjustment amounts to €(13) million and €(11) million for the six months ended September 30, 2003 and the year ended March 31, 2003, respectively.

Note 3 Recognition of restructuring costs

Under Dutch GAAP, €75 million (with a €26 million tax effect) arising from decisions made by KLM's Board of Managing Directors have been classified as extraordinary items in the unaudited condensed *pro forma* consolidated financial information. Under French GAAP, the expense of €49 million relating to the restructuring provision would have been recognized as the actual costs were incurred. The provision balance at March 31, 2003 is reversed in the balance sheet as a Dutch GAAP to French GAAP adjustment. During the six months ended September 30, 2003, the restructuring costs did qualify for French GAAP purposes and consequently were recorded in the Dutch GAAP to French GAAP reconciliation, with an impact of €75 million on restructuring costs with a related tax impact of €26 million.

Note 4 Accounting for treasury stock

Under French GAAP, treasury shares held by Air France to fulfill commitments under employee stock option plans are accounted for as an asset. Provisions are recorded in order to record the shares at the lower of cost or market value, with related gains and losses recognized in the income statement. Under Dutch GAAP, the purchase price of these shares is deducted from stockholders' equity. The French GAAP adjustment reclassifies €23 million of KLM's acquired treasury shares to short-term investments and recognizes a realized income on the sale of those shares for an amount of €13 million for the six month period ended September 30, 2003 and a loss of €(16) million in the income statement for the year ended March 31, 2003.

Note 5 Deferred income taxes

These adjustments reflect the deferred tax impacts of the French GAAP adjustments listed above, except for treasury stock adjustments which are tax exempted in the Netherlands. Income tax effect has been calculated using the KLM current tax rate of 34.5 percent. The net tax effect of French GAAP adjustments is a decrease in stockholders' equity of KLM of €811 million (an increase by €747 million of the deferred tax liabilities and a decrease by €64 million of the deferred tax assets).

For the year ended March 31, 2003, the deferred income taxes caption also reflects the French GAAP

reclassification, from operating income and income tax to extraordinary items, net of tax, of the outcome of the dispute between KLM and Alitalia.

Note 6 Lease deposits

Under Dutch GAAP, lease deposits are either classified as investments in debt securities or other noncurrent assets, or deducted from financial debt, while under French GAAP lease deposits are offset with financial debt (obligation under capital leases). This reclassification leads to the decrease of financial debt and lease deposits by €475 million.

Note 7 Frequent flyer program

Under Dutch GAAP, the liability recorded for the accrued costs related to flight awards earned by members of the frequent flyer program is classified as a long-term liability. Under French GAAP, amounts accrued related to the Fréquence Plus frequent flyer program are included in advance ticket liability in the consolidated balance sheet of Air France and classified as a current liability for purposes of the *pro forma* financial information. The French GAAP adjustment reclassifies €42 million provision recorded by KLM under Dutch GAAP to unearned revenue in accordance with French GAAP as applied by Air France. This reclassification impacts provision for €26 million, stockholders' equity for €10 million and deferred tax assets for €6 million.

Note 8 Inventory

Under Dutch GAAP, certain rotable and exchangeable parts have been classified in inventories. Under French GAAP, these items are classified as flight equipment. The net book value of these rotable parts and exchangeable components is €66 million at September 30, 2003.

Note 9 Other

Under French GAAP, unrealized foreign exchange gain or loss on working capital elements is classified in financial income or expense. This reclassification amounts to €17 million and €22 million for the six months ended September 30, 2003 and the year ended March 31, 2003, respectively. In addition, as required under French GAAP, the Goodwill amortization or impairment caption has been reclassified to a separate line item below operating income. This reclassification amounts to €2 million and €4 million for the six months ended September 30, 2003 and the year ended March 31, 2003, respectively.

Note 10 Discontinued operation and extraordinary Items

Under French GAAP, KLM would have presented the disposal of its business "Buzz" as a discontinued operation in the income statement. This disposal was consummated during the six months ended September 30, 2003.

In addition, the outcome of the dispute between KLM and Alitalia would have been presented as an extraordinary item net of tax under French GAAP. This results in a reclassification of €(276) million and €95 million from operating income and income tax to extraordinary items, respectively, in the KLM *pro forma* French GAAP income statement for the year ended March 31, 2003. Discontinued operation net of tax, extraordinary items net of tax and cumulative effect of change in accounting principles are captions below income (loss) from continuing operations and are not presented in the *pro forma* condensed income statements.

Excerpts from the notes to the *pro forma* financial statements – *pro forma* adjustments (euro amounts in millions, except per share data)

Under French GAAP, Air France is the acquirer of KLM and will account for its acquisition of KLM using the purchase method of accounting. Under the purchase method, Air France will allocate the total purchase price of KLM to the acquired assets and liabilities (including previously unrecognized items) based on their relative fair values as determined on the date of the transaction. This unaudited condensed *pro forma* consolidated financial information has been prepared and presented assuming that Air France will acquire a 100 percent controlling economic interest in KLM following the completion of the combination and the conditional acquisition of the Cumulative Preference Shares A. Under French GAAP, the estimated aggregate purchase price has been calculated as follows (in € millions, except number of shares and per share data):

KLM common shares outstanding	46,810,000
Exchange ratio into Air France's shares	1.10
Equivalent number of Air France's shares	51,491,000
Air France's share price	13.34
Estimated fair value of Air France shares issued	686.9
Estimated fair value of Air France warrants issued	73.5
Estimated fair value of preferred and priority shares	35.5
Estimated transaction-related expenses	15.1
Total estimated purchase price consideration	811.0

The preliminary allocation of its purchase price reflected herein presents preliminary estimates of fair values as determined at September 30, 2003. Such estimates are based on an independent appraisal. The actual allocation of the purchase price will be based on the fair values determined at the date of the transaction, which may differ, in some respects, from those presented below. The estimated excess of purchase price consideration over the approximate value of KLM's net assets, the estimated fair value adjustments and the estimated negative goodwill are as follows (in € millions):

Total estimated purchase price consideration	811
Less: KLM's net assets under French GAAP	(3,058)
Consideration of fair values of acquired assets and liabilities:	
Reduction in fair value of aircraft	(675)
Reduction in reported value of intangible assets	(12)
Incremental fair value of buildings and lands	248
Reduction in fair value of equity investment	(44)
Reduction in fair value in pension and post-retirement plans and increase in pension provision	(1,125)
Deferred tax adjustments	528
Other items, net	66
Excess of the fair value of net assets acquired over purchase consideration	(1,233)

Preliminary estimates of fair values and the final purchase price allocation may materially differ from preliminary amounts and allocations provided in this section. This analysis presents a preliminary allocation of purchase price to the assets and liabilities of KLM, based on independent appraisals conducted at September 30, 2003. The final allocation of purchase price will be completed at the latest at the end of the fiscal year following the acquisition fiscal period, and will be based on valuations and appraisals conducted as of the date of the exchange offer closing date, as specified under French GAAP. We have identified aircraft and pension plans valuations as the most significant areas for potential material discrepancies between *pro forma* and final purchase price allocation.

Aircraft market value references are principally US dollar-based and therefore, the euro-denominated fair value of the KLM fleet may fluctuate significantly based on €/$ exchange rate fluctuations. The exchange rate retained for the purpose of the *pro forma* purchase price allocation was $1.13 per €1.00. Should this exchange rate fluctuate to $1.18 for €1.00 or $1.24 for €1.00, the downward fair value adjustment to the KLM fleet would increase by €140 million or €270 million, respectively. Should the exchange rate fluctuate oppositely to $1.07 for €.00, the downward fair value adjustment to the KLM fleet would decrease by €155 million.

The purchase price allocation may also differ significantly from our preliminary estimates, based on market conditions and assumptions prevailing to the pension plans valuation, mainly based on long term discount rates, anticipated inflation, stock market current valuation, overall economic prospects, and changes in agreements applicable to pensions in the Netherlands and to KLM employees. As further discussed below, the purchase price allocation may also need to be revised in case the overfunded pension plan assets recognition would be limited by the asset ceiling rules introduced by IAS 19.

Under French GAAP, in accordance with the accounting rules governing the purchase method of accounting, Air France is not allowed to recognize intangible assets, such as KLM's trademark or certain take-off and landing slots, when a negative residual goodwill amount results from the purchase price allocation.

KLM sponsors a number of pension benefit plans across the various locations where it operates. As of September 30, 2003, total obligations in respect of these plans amount to €7,055 million, and available pension funds assets have been fair valued at €8,260 million. Benefit plans for employees outside the Netherlands account for less than 5 percent of total obligations. In the Netherlands, pension benefits consist of final or average career salary plans which are funded through separate legal entities to which employees also contribute. Other post-employment benefits consist of sponsored medical coverage for some retirees, resulting in an estimated obligation ("PBO") for these plans of €67 million with no related assets. The adjustment to the carrying value of the KLM pension plans is based on this preliminary assessment of PBO and current values of plan assets. As of September 30, 2003, some plans have assets in excess of the PBO estimated by external actuaries. Under French GAAP, the amount of net asset which can be recognized is limited by the asset ceiling rules introduced by IAS 19. These rules limit the amount of net asset which can be recognized on the employer's balance sheet to the present value of any economic benefits available in the form of refunds from the plans or reductions in future contributions to the plans. Following the proposed transaction, the asset ceiling limitation will also consider amounts of cumulative unrecognized actuarial losses and past service costs in determining the maximum asset to be recorded by the combined companies. As of September 30, 2003, the amount of net asset recognized is €1,247 million.

Following the completion of the transaction Air France will perform a full valuation of the acquired KLM plans, in order to determine the actual amount of pension assets to be included in the allocation of purchase price to the acquired plans of KLM. This valuation will occur as of the closing date for the proposed transaction. It is not possible to predict at this time

what the final value of the pension asset will be or whether the amount of such asset to be recorded by Air France will need to be reduced by a provision as a result of the asset ceiling restrictions. As a result, the final value to be allocated to the acquired plans could be subject to significant change. Furthermore, the amount of net pension asset recorded would be subject to reconsideration of the asset ceiling test, which could result in significant increases or decreases of the provision/non-cash impacts to Air France's results of operations.

For purposes of the presentation of the *pro forma* condensed consolidated income statements, the adjustments listed above have been presented as if the transaction had occurred on the first day of the first period presented. The impacts of the *pro forma* allocation of purchase consideration affect the results of operations for the six-month period ended September 30, 2003 and the year ended March 31, 2003 as follows:

- Note 11 Tangible assets. Reflects adjustments to the reported depreciation of KLM based on the reduction in the fair value of the fixed assets.

- Note 12 Investments in equity affiliates. Reflects adjustments to the carrying value of KLM's investments in affiliates, primarily KLM's 50 percent investment in Martinair. For purposes of the *pro forma* income statements, the decrease in the carrying value of Martinair has been attributed to the fleet assets having an estimated remaining useful life of seven years. The amortization of these adjustments results in an increase to the reported income from this equity investee of €3 million and €6 million for the six months ended September 30, 2003 and the year ended March 31, 2003, respectively.

- Note 13 Goodwill. This adjustment reflects the elimination of the amounts of historical goodwill and goodwill amortization of €2 million for the six-month period ended September 30, 2003 and €4 million for the year ended March 31, 2003.

- Note 14 Negative goodwill. For French GAAP purposes, the excess of the purchase consideration over the fair value of the individual assets and liabilities recognized above results in residual negative goodwill of €1,233 million. Under French GAAP, the residual negative goodwill is allocated to the income statement on a straight line method over a period that reflects assumptions made and management plans as of the acquisition date. On a preliminary basis, Air France's management has estimated that a five-year period would satisfy these criteria. Therefore, for *pro forma* purposes, the negative goodwill amount has been amortized over a five-year period which results in a positive adjustment to net income of €246 million per year ended March 31, 2003 and €123 million for the six months ended September 30, 2003.

The above list is not exhaustive, and there may be other assets and liabilities which may have to be adjusted to fair value when both final valuations and allocations are made following the completion of the exchange offer.

Air France will complete the determination of fair values and the allocation of the purchase price after the completion of the exchange offer. French GAAP allows Air France to complete the purchase price allocation no later than the end of the fiscal year subsequent to the fiscal year in which the exchange offer was completed. The determination of fair values will be based on an independent appraisal.

The exchange ratio agreed between Air France and KLM implicitly valued KLM at less than KLM's net asset value. KLM performs an impairment test whenever there is an indication that the carrying amounts of its assets may not be recoverable. KLM has performed impairment tests on its owned and financially leased aircraft in a manner consistent with Statement of Financial Accounting Standards No. 144 (SFAS 144) under US GAAP as well as in accordance with the Guideline of the Council for Annual Reporting No. 121 (RJ 121) under Netherlands GAAP. SFAS 144 requires the recognition of an impairment loss if the carrying amount of a long-lived asset or group of assets is not recoverable and exceeds its fair value. The carrying amount of an asset or group of assets is generally not recoverable if it exceeds the sum of the undiscounted, pre-tax, future cash flows expected to result from the use and eventual disposition of the asset or group of assets. Assets must be grouped at the lowest level for which identifiable cash flows are largely independent of the cash flows of other assets. Under Netherlands GAAP, KLM compared the carrying amount of each asset group (cash generating unit) to its recoverable amount, which is defined as the higher of the net selling price and its value in use.

In conducting its impairment tests, KLM grouped its fleet assets into four groups:

- KLM's wide body fleet,
- KLM's 737 fleet,
- KLM's regional fleet, and
- Transavia's fleet.

KLM's wide body fleet, which is used for long-haul destinations, consists of a total of five different kinds of aircraft. Impairment tests for KLM's wide body fleet were conducted for each of these kinds of aircraft,

because KLM monitors and optimizes its employment of, and revenues from, each of these kinds of aircraft separately. Therefore, KLM considers this the lowest level for which identifiable cash flows are largely independent of the cash flows of other assets. Impairment tests for KLM's 737 fleet, KLM's regional fleet, and Transavia's fleet were conducted at the fleet level instead of by aircraft type or subtype level because in KLM's operations the aircraft composing those fleets are generally interchangeable and therefore cash flows of types or subtypes are not meaningfully identifiable. In its impairment tests KLM:

- calculated total cash flows during the estimated economic life of each type of asset by multiplying the estimated annual cash flows from that asset type by the remaining average economic life of that asset type,
- estimated future cash flows based on historical cash flows and KLM's business plan for 2004–2005,
- estimated the residual asset value at the end of each aircraft's estimated economic life by reference to KLM's depreciation calculations, the Aircraft Value Reference Guide (published by the Aircraft Value Reference Company), and KLM's historical sales experience,
- considered the estimated residual asset value as a cash inflow at the end of the asset's economic life,
- assumed that KLM would replace each of its aircraft at the end of its economic life, and did not take into account expected changes in yields.

Based on undiscounted cash flows, the asset groups described above passed the recoverability test under SFAS 144 and RJ 121. Although KLM assumed that its aircraft would be replaced at the end of their economic life, KLM also considered the potential scenario involving a gradual decline in operations, under which KLM would be unable to invest in replacement aircraft, and concluded that such a scenario would take decades to transpire and is remote within the time-frame covered by KLM's estimated future cash flows.

KLM's management and supervisory boards agreed to accept Air France's offer at a significant discount to KLM's net asset value after they reviewed all of the strategic options available to KLM, including remaining an independent company, and concluded that at that time there was no superior strategic alternative to the combination. In assessing the offer in light of the fact that the consideration offered by Air France was below KLM's net asset value, the KLM management and supervisory boards considered certain factors, including the benefits that KLM believed may

6 The Air France–KLM merger

arise from combining certain complementary features of Air France's and KLM's businesses, KLM's expectation that cost savings and revenue-increasing synergies could be realized following completion of the offer, and the benefits associated with KLM's expected admission into the SkyTeam alliance (subject to KLM's fulfilling the admission criteria) following completion of the offer. The factors that the KLM management

and supervisory boards considered in arriving at their decisions to approve and recommend the offer to holders of KLM's common shares are described in KLM's Solicitation/ Recommendation Statement on Schedule 14D-9, which has been filed with the Securities and Exchange Commission and which is being mailed to KLM's shareholders together with this prospectus.

6 The Air France–KLM merger

EXHIBIT 4   **KLM–Air France merger announcement, September 30, 2003**

A: KLM share price from June 30, 2003 to May 5, 2004

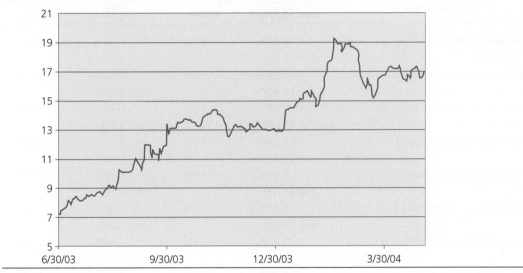

Source: Thomson Datastream.

B: Air France share price from June 30, 2003 to May 5, 2004

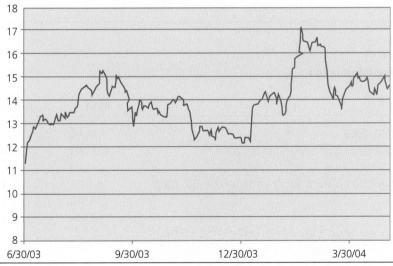

Source: Thomson Datastream.

6 The Air France–KLM merger

C: Stock returns (and prior day's closing share prices) surrounding the merger announcement

	KLM return (previous closing price)	Dutch AEX Index	Air France return (previous closing price)	French CAC40 Index
3 days before accouncement (day −3)	−2.81% (on 11.75)	−1.24%	−1.66% (on 14.45)	−1.02%
2 days before announcement (day −2)	3.85% (on 11.42)	−1.34%	−4.86% (on 14.21)	−0.43%
1 day before announcement (day −1)	0.84% (on 11.86)	−0.46%	1.26% (on 13.52)	−0.87%
Day of the announcement (day 0)	12.54% (on 11.96)	−1.84%	−4.16% (on 13.69)	−1.68%
1 day after announcement (day +1)	−5.69% (on 13.46)	1.56%	−1.75% (on 13.12)	1.79%
2 days after announcement (day +2)	3.47% (on 12.68)	0.93%	4.58% (on 12.89)	0.06%
3 days after announcement (day +3)	−0.30% (on 13.12)	2.87%	−1.48% (on 13.48)	3.24%
From day −10 to day +10	14.78% (on 11.91)	−1.54%	−4.62% (on 14.50)	0.18%
From day −5 to day 5	16.06% (on 11.27)	−2.68%	−5.67% (on 14.64)	−0.35%
From September 30, 2003 to May 5, 2004	45.90% (on 11.96)	10.60%	6.50% (on 13.69)	16.96%

Source: Thomson Datastream.

D: Valuation data and other information

	KLM	Air France
Closing price on September 30, 2003	11.96	13.69
Number of ordinary shares outstanding on September 30, 2003	46,809,699	219,780,887
Beta	1.63	1.36
Yield on government bonds with ten years' maturity on September 30, 2003	4.14%	4.13%
Statutory tax rate in 2003	34.5%	35.43%
Effective tax rate in 2003	32.0%	13.27%

7 Measuring impairment at Dofasco[1]

It was December 15, 2008, when Joanne Bell received an e-mail with the most recent earnings projections for ArcelorMittal Dofasco. Bell had just joined the ArcelorMittal Dofasco financial accounting team after a few years of audit experience at a large Chartered Accountancy (CA) firm. She was perplexed by the challenge before her and knew she had a long night ahead.

ArcelorMittal Dofasco had undergone significant ownership changes in the past few years. When the firm had first been acquired, the market had placed a premium share value on the Dofasco subsidiary. However, in light of the recent economic downturn, the financial accounting group at Dofasco was required to reassess the values assigned to the subsidiary's net assets and determine whether a change in asset fair values existed as a result of the revised economic outlook.

Bell's supervisor, Sean Collins, the director of financial accounting at Dofasco had called a group meeting for the next day to discuss the implications of the economic situation on the value of the intangible assets recognized at Dofasco's acquisition.

The steel industry in Canada

The steel industry was one of Canada's largest manufacturing industries with sales of $14 billion and production of 14.9 million tons. In 2008, the steel industry provided 30,000 direct jobs to the Canadian economy. Although steel manufacturing companies were located across Canada, the majority of the companies were located in Ontario. See **Exhibit 1** for geographic dispersion of steel manufacturers.

Modern steelmaking in Canada consisted of two different methods: the integrated process and the electric arc furnace process. The integrated process was the traditional steelmaking process, which combined iron ore, coke, limestone, and scrap metal in a blast furnace to produce molten iron. The molten iron was then refined in a basic oxygen furnace to produce liquid steel, which was cast into slabs at the customer's request. Integrated steelmakers were highly capital-intensive and produced two million to four million tons of steel annually.[2] The electric arc furnace process relied primarily on recycled scrap steel, which was reheated to produce liquid steel. These steel manufacturers were known as mini-mill steelmakers. Mini-mill steelmakers were typically less

[1]Identities have been disguised. This case has been written on the basis of published sources only. Consequently, the interpretation and perspectives presented in this case are not necessarily those of Dofasco or any of its employees.

[2]Industry Canada, "An Overview of Steel Products and Processes," http://www.ic.gc.ca/eic/site/pm-mp.nsf/eng/mm01289.html, accessed August 12, 2009.

capital-intensive than integrated steel makers and had the capacity to produce 250,000 to one million tons of steel annually.[3]

As a result of the capital-intensive nature of the business, the steel industry was challenged by high fixed costs and, as a result, preferred large batch sizes for production. To secure volume contracts, a steel company relied heavily on strong customer relationships and its ability to effectively match product technology with evolving customer needs. Successful steel companies generated sufficient cash flow to satisfy their financial debt, reinvest in technologies and foster growth and innovation with their customers.

The Canadian steel industry had undergone dynamic changes in recent years as a result of changes in the global industry. During the 1990s, the global steel industry was hugely fragmented, largely state-owned and crippled with debt. Profits were scarce as industry players struggled to manage high fixed costs, labor-intensive operations and stagnant growth. Shortly after the turn of the millennium, the industry experienced a renaissance in terms of profitability and rate of growth. This renaissance was a result of consolidation in the industry, which allowed for greater efficiencies in production and the ability to better access and serve global markets. Furthermore, the trend toward fully integrated business models reduced steelmakers' risk from input price volatilities by spurring greater self-sufficiency in sourcing their raw material supplies. Developing economies such as Brazil, Russia, India, and China experienced consistently above-average gross domestic product (GDP) growth, leading to vast business opportunities, especially for those companies already present in global markets. **Exhibit 2** highlights the financial improvements resulting from the steel industry trend toward greater efficiency.

Dofasco Inc.

Clifton and Frank Sherman founded the Dominion Steel Casting Company in 1912 to manufacture castings for Canadian railways. In 1917, the company merged with its subsidiary, the Hamilton Steel Wheel Company. In 1980, the company, located in Hamilton, Ontario, Canada, adopted the name Dofasco Inc.

Dofasco's product lines include hot-rolled, cold-rolled, galvanized, Extragal™, Galvalume™, and tinplate flat-rolled steels, in addition to tubular products, laser-welded blanks, and Zyplex™, a proprietary laminate[4] Although Dofasco's single largest market was the automotive industry, the company also targeted customers in the construction, energy, manufacturing, pipe and tube, appliance, packaging, and steel distribution industries.

Dofasco had been a pioneer of innovative steelmaking throughout its history. For example, Dofasco introduced the first universal steel plate mill in Canada and was the first company in North America to adopt basic oxygen furnace technology. In 1996, Dofasco led North America in adopting an electric arc furnace and slab caster. By diverging from its traditional integrated steelmaking process and operating a mini-mill, Dofasco moved into a leading position as a North American steel solutions provider.

In addition, since the company's founding, Dofasco had maintained a reputation for commitment to both its employees and the Hamilton community, reflected in its corporate philosophy: "Our product is steel. Our strength is people. Our home is Hamilton."[5] Dofasco was the first Canadian manufacturer to introduce employee profit–sharing, and it maintained a history of positive labor relations. The Dofasco profit–sharing plan had been acknowledged as the core element and reason behind Dofasco's non-unionized workforce at the Hamilton plant. In 1997, Dofasco became the first Canadian company to sign a voluntary Environment Management Agreement with the federal and provincial governments, and the company played a leadership role in the Hamilton Industrial Environmental Association. Dofasco donated millions of dollars to regional charitable campaigns, hospitals and educational institutions and was regarded as an outstanding corporate citizen.

A Hostile Takeover

On November 23, 2005, Arcelor SA (Arcelor), the world's second-largest steelmaker, put forth an unsolicited proposal to Dofasco shareholders, offering $55 per share in attempt to gain control of Dofasco. Arcelor, which was based in Luxembourg, had grown through consolidation focusing on acquisitions in developing

---

[3]*Ibid.*

[4]"Dofasco Inc. 2004 Annual Report," http://www.sedar.com, accessed July 31, 2009.

[5]Meredith Macleod and Naomi Powell, "Unions Not the Dofasco Way," *Hamilton Spectator*, March 20, 2008, http://www.thespec.com/News/Business/article/342323, accessed August 12, 2009.

economies. In alignment with its corporate strategy, Arcelor management hoped to use Dofasco as a springboard into the North American steel market.

Although Arcelor offered a 27.3 percent premium over Dofasco's previous day's stock closing price, the bid was not supported by Dofasco management, and Dofasco's board of directors urged shareholders not to tender the offer. During the same day, Dofasco shares increased 34.2 percent, which suggested that investors would wait for another bid.[6] Analysts believed that through the purchase of Dofasco, a supplier to the Ford Motor Company, Arcelor's share of the North American automotive steel market would increase from 1 percent to 12 percent. In Europe, Arcelor supplied the steel in one out of every two cars.[7]

On November 25, 2005, a white knight entered the bidding when German-based steelmaker ThyssenKrupp AG (ThyssenKrupp), the world's ninth largest steelmaker, announced a friendly offer of $61.50 per common share for control of Dofasco.[8] Dofasco's board of directors unanimously recommended accepting the offer because, unlike Arcelor, ThyssenKrupp would allow Dofasco both to continue operations under its own name and management and to continue some form of the profit-sharing system. ThyssenKrupp planned for the Dofasco plant to become ThyssenKrupp's new North American headquarters.[9]

A bidding war for control of Dofasco continued between Arcelor and ThyssenKrupp into January of 2006. Analysts were not surprised, citing Dofasco's location and several internally generated intangible assets – including raw materials contracts, intellectual capacity through product and operational innovations, and strong customer relations (see **Exhibit 3**) – as attractive and valuable qualities of the company.[10]

Finally, on January 24, 2006, Arcelor outbid ThyssenKrupp by offering $71 per common share or $4.939 billion for control of Dofasco. ThyssenKrupp announced that it would not increase its offer because doing so would downgrade its own credit ratings and go beyond the point of creating economic value. Dofasco's white knight had stepped aside, and Dofasco's board of directors publicly announced their support for the Arcelor offer and agreed to a closing date of March 1, 2006.

Exhibit 4 provides the details of the external valuation at the March 1, 2006 closing date for the acquisition, which was completed by DeJong Evaluation at the request of Dofasco's board of directors. **Exhibits 5 and 6** provide excerpts from Dofasco's balance sheet just prior to the acquisition and the estimated fair values of Dofasco's net assets at the date of acquisition.

A steel giant is born

Days after the Dofasco board of directors announced support for Arcelor's bid for Dofasco, India-based Mittal Steel Company NV (Mittal) announced an unsolicited US$22.8 billion offer for Arcelor. Mittal's bid for Arcelor was an attempt to form a global powerhouse and establish itself as the only steelmaker capable of producing more than 100 million tons of steel annually. An Arcelor–Mittal merger represented a milestone in the global steel industry. As a combined entity, the company would be capable of tripling the capacity of Mittal's nearest rival, Japan's Nippon Steel, and would hold 10 percent of the global market share.[11]

Mittal Steel was the world's largest steel manufacturer with shipments of 49.2 million tons and revenues of more than US$28.1 billion in 2005. The company had 16 steelmaking operations in four continents, customers in more than 150 countries and 224,000 employees. The company was headed by Lakshmi Mittal, one of the world's richest men, who had an estimated fortune of more than £15 billion.[12]

[6]"Arcelor Launches $4B Bid for Dofasco," November 24, 2005, http://www.redorbit.com/news/science/313090/arcelor_launches_4b_bid_for_dofasco/index.html, accessed August 12, 2009.

[7]"Arcelor Raises Offer for Dofasco," *New York Times*, December 23, 2005, http://www.nytimes.com/2005/12/23/business/worldbusiness/23iht-arcelor.html, accessed August 11, 2009.

[8]"ThyssenKrupp Tops Arcelor SA's Bid for Dofasco," November 28, 2005, http://www.streetinsider.com/Mergers+and+Acquisitions/ThyssenKrupp+Tops+Arcelor+SAs+Bid+for+Dofasco/406983.html.

[9]"Dofasco and ThyssenKrupp Announce a Friendly All-Cash Deal," press release, November 28, 2005, http://www.dofasco.ca/bins/content_page.asp?cid=2347-2349-100900, accessed August 11, 2009.

[10]"Arcelor Raises Offer for Dofasco," *New York Times*, December 23, 2005, http://www.nytimes.com/2005/12/23/business/worldbusiness/23iht-arcelor.html, accessed August 11, 2009.

[11]James Kanter et al., "Arcelor Agrees to Mittal Takeover," *New York Times*, http://www.nytimes.com/2006/06/25/business/worldbusiness/25iht-steel.html?pagewanted=1&_r=1, accessed August 11, 2009.

[12]"Mittal Steel Unveils Arcelor Bid," *BBC News*, http://news.bbc.co.uk/2/hi/business/4653516.stm, accessed August 17, 2009.

7 Measuring impairment at Dofasco

Operating both integrated and mini-mill facilities, Mittal Steel had set the pace for consolidation and globalization in the steel industry (see **Exhibit 7** for a list of recent acquisitions). Furthermore, the company produced most of its iron ore and coking coal manufacturing inputs through ownership of mines. Lakshmi Mittal believed that US$1.6 billion in annual savings synergies could be reached before 2008 through the amalgamation of Arcelor's operations with those of Mittal.[13]

Despite attempts by Arcelor's board and management to circumvent the acquisition using both a white knight strategy[14] and a poison pill strategy[15], in June 2006, Arcelor agreed to a US$33.1 billion takeover by Mittal. The takeover price represented more than a 50 percent increase in the Arcelor share price prior to the initial takeover talks in January.[16] Furthermore, Mittal and Arcelor reached an agreement to combine the two companies in a merger of equals, as ArcelorMittal, headquartered in Luxembourg.

ArcelorMittal

Following the merger, ArcelorMittal continued to pursue its growth strategy, by undertaking 35 transactions in 2007 (see **Exhibit 8** for the geographic range of these transactions). The company became known as having proven expertise in acquiring companies and turning around under-performing assets. As a result of several successful acquisitions in 2007, the company boasted earnings before interest taxes, depreciation, and amortization (EBITDA) of US$19.2 billion, making 2007 a record year for the company.[17]

The sudden global recession

ArcelorMittal started out 2008, believing it would be another promising year as a result of rapidly increasing commodity prices and full-capacity utilization fueled by China's rapid growth. However by mid-2008, the subprime mortgage crisis in the United States had contributed to a banking crisis that led to the demise of massive financial institutions and tremendous credit market constraints. A Depression-era plunge in world equity markets wiped out trillions of dollars of wealth and collapsed consumer confidence. The economy rapidly deteriorated, forcing a sudden halt to capital goods projects and durable goods spending, which greatly affected steel operations across the globe. Companies and governments were less inclined to invest in infrastructure improvements. Decreased confidence among consumers limited the purchase of automobiles, and rising unemployment put a strain on the construction market. All markets had limited opportunities to obtain financing, which further decreased incentives for companies, governments and consumers to demand steel products.

Consequently, the market prices for steel plummeted in the fourth quarter of 2008, from record highs experienced in August 2008, thus forcing steel companies to sharply cut back production (see **Exhibit 9**). By the end of 2008, most steel entities were operating at a very low production level of 40 percent.[18]

At Dofasco, production levels averaged 60 percent, as a result of the North American automotive market significantly scaling back projection levels and compounded by the risk that a few of the major North American car manufacturers would be forced into bankruptcy protection. Sales and margins suffered in the last quarter of 2008. As a result of the significantly changed market conditions, the favorable outlook at the time of the Dofasco acquisition in 2006 had changed dramatically, and a much more negative outlook was anticipated until at least the end of 2010 (see **Exhibit 10** for 2008 enterprise value estimates).

[13]"Mittal Shareholders Approve ArcelorMittal Merger," *Reuters*, August 28, 2007, http://in.reuters.com/article/businessNews/idIN India-29195120070828, accessed August 17, 2009.

[14]A "white knight strategy" refers to a situation where a potential acquirer is sought out by a target company's management to take over the company to avoid a hostile takeover.

[15]A "poison pill strategy" is a strategy designed to fend off a hostile takeover attempt.

[16]James Kanter *et al* "Arcelor Agrees to Mittal Takeover," *New York Times*, http://www.nytimes.com/2006/06/25/business/world business/25iht-steel.html?pagewanted=1&_r=1, accessed August 16, 2009.

[17]Lakshmi N. Mittal, "Steel Sans Frontiers: Why Global Is a Good Business Model," speech to the Federation of Industrialists (Luxembourg) (FEDIL), January 22, 2008, http://www.fedil.lu/Uploads/Publications/Documents/71_1_SpeechLakshmiNMittal.pdf, accessed December 3, 2008.

[18]Interview with ArcelorMittal Dofasco Management, August 17, 2009.

Bell's task

Bell pulled out the memo prepared by Collins, the director of financial accounting at Dofasco (see **Exhibit 10**), which summarized his thoughts on the potential future cash flows for Dofasco and the resulting valuation of the division. Bell knew that the dismal forecasted earnings for the operations implied a potential impairment of the operation's assets under International Financial Reporting Standards but she was unsure of what the actual impairment loss might be. She knew that she would also have to review the March 1, 2006, fair value estimates and determine how the original $4.939 billion purchase price had been allocated to the various tangible and intangible assets and liabilities. Her understanding was that despite the large premium paid for the Dofasco shares, no portion of the purchase price discrepancy was allocated to goodwill, though she was unclear as to why this would have been the case. She wondered what the impact of the economic downturn might have been on any goodwill, had it been recorded. Bell also pulled out the DeJong fair value assessments for the various intangibles that were part of the purchase on March 1, 2006 (see **Exhibits 11, 12, 13**, and **14**). She understood that the evaluators had relied on an income approach, by using the projected EBITDA derived from each intangible to determine its value. She wondered how the revised EBITDA projections would change the recoverable value of Dofasco's intangible assets.

Bell knew she had a long night in front of her trying to understand both the original acquisition and the current values of the assets. She didn't want to disappoint her new supervisor by appearing unprepared for the meeting! She pulled out her summary of the impairment rules included in the International Financial Reporting Standards (see **Exhibit 15**), took a sip of her chai latte, put her pen to paper, and got to work.

EXHIBIT 1   **Number of iron and steel mills in Canada by region**

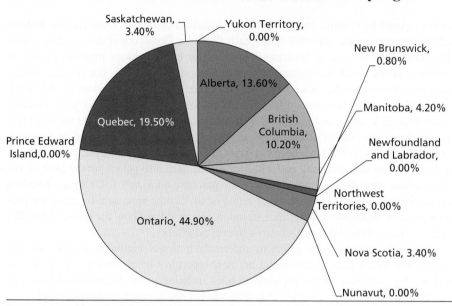

Source: Adapted from Statistics Canada, "Number of Establishments in Canada by Type and Region: December 2008 – Iron and Steel Mills and Ferro-Alloy Manufacturing (NAICS 3311)," Canadian Business Patterns Database, December 2008, http://www.ic.gc.ca/cis-sic/cis-sic.nsf/ILF-/cis3311etbe.html#est1, accessed August 12, 2009.

7 Measuring impairment at Dofasco

EXHIBIT 2 **Steel manufacturing revenues per employee**

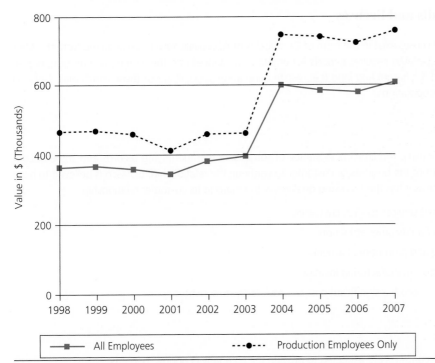

Source: Statistics Canada, "Manufacturing Revenues per Employee: 1998–2007 – All Employees vs. Production Employees: Iron and Steel Mills and Ferro-Alloy Manufacturing (NAICS 3311)," special tabulation, unpublished data, Annual Survey of Manufactures, 1998–2003; Annual Survey of Manufactures and Logging, 2004 to 2007, http://www.ic.gc.ca/cis-sic/cis-sic.nsf/IDE/cis3311-pere.html, accessed August 12, 2009.

EXHIBIT 3   **Dofasco Inc. – internally generated intangible assets, January 2006**

Environmental permits and licenses

Environmental permits and licenses exist in the form of Certificates of Approvals, which are acquired from the Ministry of Environment (MOE). Dofasco requires permits for emitting substances into the air (i.e., air emission, noise), water (i.e., water usage and discharge) and land (i.e., waste generating sites). Without these certificates, Dofasco could not legally run its steel operations.

Customer lists

A significant customer relationship requires the existence of some customer identifying records and some obligation or advantage on the part of the business or customer to continue the relationship. Dofasco is believed to have an identifiable customer base as it has the following qualities with regard to its customer relationship:

1   Offers exclusive products or services to such customers

2   Not dependent on brand for customer attraction

3   Little need for advertising and promotional activities

4   Not contingent on Dofasco's manufacturing location

5   Sells goods and services for which a significant cost is associated with substitution

Supply contracts

Dofasco's natural gas supply contracts are expected to provide the company economic benefits.

Internal research and development

New Product Development (NPD) initiatives were identified during the valuation process and characterized as one of the following:

1   Advanced High Strength Steels – Lightweight, high-strength steel for automotive sector.

2   Other Steel Products – Other grades of hot-rolled and cold-rolled steel products for use in the automotive markets.

3   Coating – New coating applications for use in exposed steel products. Limited use in automotive market.

Source: ArcelorMittal Dofasco Financial Accounting Group.

EXHIBIT 4   **Dofasco Inc. company valuation**

┌─────────────────────────┐
│ *DeJong Evaluation* │
└─────────────────────────┘

MEMO

To:	Sean Collins, Director of Financial Accounting at Dofasco
From:	DeJong Evaluation
Date:	01-Mar-06
Re:	Fair Value Assessment – Enterprise Value

DOFASCO'S STEEL OPERATIONS
ENTERPRISE VALUE – AS OF MARCH 1, 2006

CAD $ millions	2006	2007	2008	2009	2010	2011 -> (Residual)
EBITDA	$400	$550	$600	$650	$700	$700
Synergies from acquisition	50	100	100	150	150	150
Total	450	650	700	800	850	850
Income tax rate of 34.12%	154	222	239	273	290	290
After-tax earnings	296	428	461	527	560	560
Cash flow adjustments						
Capital expenditures	−100	−100	−100	−100	−100	−100
Change in working capital	30	90	50	50	–	–
Net cash flow	226	418	411	477	460	460
Terminal value						5,500
Discount factor (9%)	0.917	0.842	0.772	0.708	0.650	0.596
Present value of net cash flow	**$208**	**$352**	**$317**	**$338**	**$299**	**$3,279**
Total Enterprise value	**$4,794**					

Source: ArcelorMittal Dofasco Financial Accounting Group.

7 Measuring impairment at Dofasco

EXHIBIT 5 **Dofasco Inc. – excerpt from consolidated balance sheet[1] February 28, 2006 (in CDN$ millions)**

Current Assets	
Cash and cash equivalents	$ 50.00
Short-term investments	–
Accounts receivable	655.44
Inventories	1,421.67
Future income taxes	74.70
Other current assets	26.56
Fixed and other assets	
Fixed assets	2,258.71
Future income tax assets	47.02
Accrued pension benefit	90.07
Investments and other assets	30.43
Total Assets	$4,654.61
Current Liabilities	
Short-term borrowings	$ 225.03
Accounts payable and accrued liabilities	607.50
Income and other taxes payable	46.00
Dividends payable	25.95
Current requirements on long-term debt	49.97
Long-term liabilities	
Long-term debt	695.29
Future income tax liabilities	84.78
Employee future benefits	735.33
Other long-term liabilities	57.30
Minority Interest	43.46
Total Liabilities	$2,570.61
Net Carrying Value	$2,084.00

Source: ArcelorMittal Dofasco Financial Accounting Group.
[1]Prepared in accordance with Canadian Generally Accepted Accounting Principles (GAAP).

EXHIBIT 6 **Dofasco Inc. – estimated fair values at acquisition[1] March 1, 2006 (in CDN$ millions)[2]**

Current Assets	
Cash and cash equivalents	$ 50.00
Short-term investments	
Accounts receivable	605.00
Inventories	1,600.00
Future income taxes	74.70
Other current assets	49.89
Fixed and other assets	
Fixed assets	
Land	120.00
Building	964.00
Machinery and equipment	3,960.00
Construction in progress	110.00
Future income tax assets	47.02
Accrued pension benefit	–
Investments and other assets	31.43
Total Assets	$7,612.04
Current Liabilities	
Short-term borrowings	$225.03
Accounts payable and accrued liabilities	651.00
Income and other taxes payable	46.00
Dividends payable	25.95
Current requirements on long-term debt	49.97
Long-term liabilities	
Long-term debt	595.29
Future income tax liabilities	84.78
Employee future benefits	1,055.33
Other long-term liabilities	57.30
Minority Interest	43.46
Total Liabilities	$2,834.11
Net Fair Value	$4,777.93

Source: ArcelorMittal Dofasco Financial Accounting Group.

[1]Fair values provided by DeJong Evaluation.

[2]DeJong Evaluation expected any purchase price discrepancy to be allocated mostly to definite life intangibles rather than to goodwill.

7 Measuring impairment at Dofasco

EXHIBIT 7   **Recent Mittal Steel Company NV acquisitions**

YEAR	COMPANY	COUNTRY
1997	Thyssen Duisberg	Germany
1998	Inland Steel	USA
1999	Unimetal	France
2001	Sidex	Romania
2001	Annaba	Algeria
2003	Nova Hut	Czech Republic
2004	BH Steel	Bosnia
2004	Balkan Steel	Macedonia
2004	PHS	Poland
2004	Iscor	South Africa
2005	ISG	USA
2005	Hunan Valin	China
2005	Kryvorizhstal	Ukraine

Source: ArcelorMittal, "History," http://www.arcelormittal.com/index.php?lang=en&page=15, accessed August 18, 2009.

EXHIBIT 8   **ArcelorMittal 2007 takeover transactions by country**

Argentina	Poland
Austria	Russia
Brazil	Slovakia
Canada	South Africa
China	Turkey
Estonia	United Kingdom
France	United States
Germany	Uruguay
Italy	Venezuela
Mexico	

Source: ArcelorMittal, "History," http://www.arcelormittal.com/index.php?lang=en&page=15, accessed August 18, 2009.

EXHIBIT 9 **Historical steel prices**

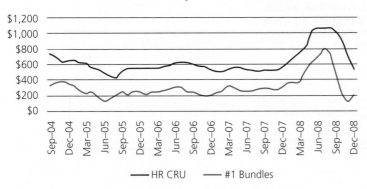

Steel Prices by Product (US$/NT)

Note: NT = Net Tons (2000 lbs); HR CRU = Price of hot roll steel monitored by CRU Steel Price Index; #1 Bundles = Price of scrap bundles in the Chicago area.
Source: ArcelorMittal Dofasco Marketing Group.

EXHIBIT 10 Dofasco enterprise value December 15, 2008

DOFASCO
ENTERPRISE VALUE
DECEMBER 15, 2008

File   Edit   View   Favorites   Tools   Help

DOFASCO™   ArcelorMittal

To:	Dofasco Financial Accounting Group
From:	Sean Collins, Director of Financial Accounting at Dofasco
Date:	15-Dec-08 6:46 PM
Re:	Dofasco Enterprise Value -Year End 2008

Hello Team,

Below you will find the earnings projections for ArcelorMittal Dofasco. You will notice a substantial change from the projections made and enterprise value at Arcelor's acquisition on March 1, 2006. These projections will guide our discussions regarding the impairment of intangible assets tomorrow.

Note that the 9 percent Arcelor Historical Discount Rate was applied for the enterprise valuation by DeJong Evaluation on March 1, 2006. A 13 percent ArcelorMittal Corporate Discount Rate is applied broadly across other ArcelorMittal subsidiaries.

Company sales managers are predicting a 20 percent–30 percent decline in revenues as a result of the current economic situation. As a team I expect us to determine the implication of this decline on the valuation of ArcelorMittal Dofasco's identified intangible assets.

I am looking forward to a productive meeting tomorrow morning.

S.C.

DOFASCO'S STEEL OPERATIONS
ENTERPRISE VALUE – AS OF DECEMBER 31, 2008

CAD $ millions	2009	2010	2011	2012	2013	2014
EBITDA	$250	$400	$500	$500	$500	$500
Less: Tax	85	136	171	171	171	171
After-Tax Earnings	165	264	329	329	329	329
Cash flow adjustments						
Capital expenditures	–80	–90	–90	–90	–90	–90
Change in working capital	90	90	50	50	–	–
Net operating free cash flow	$260	$400	$460	$460	$410	$410
Terminal cash value						$3,000

Valuation Using Arcelor Historical Discount Rate

Discount Factor (9%)	0.917	0.842	0.772	0.708	0.650	0.596
Present Value of Cash Flow	$238.5	$336.7	$355.2	$325.9	$266.5	$1,788.8
Enterprise Value	$3,311.6					

Valuation Using ArcelorMittal Corporate Discount Rate

Discount Factor (13%)	0.885	0.783	0.693	0.613	0.543	0.480
Present Value of Cash Flow	$230.1	$313.3	$318.8	$282.1	$222.5	$1,441.0
Enterprise Value	$2,807.8					

Source: ArcelorMittal Dofasco Financial Accounting Group.

EXHIBIT 11   DeJong evaluation – environmental permit valuation estimates

> *DeJong Evaluation*

MEMO

To:	Sean Collins, Director of Financial Accounting at Dofasco
From:	DeJong Evaluation
Date:	01-Mar-06
Re:	Fair Value Assessment – Dofasco Permits and Licenses

As the employment of environmental permits is vital to Dofasco's operations, the fair value of these permits is determined by the earnings foregone in the absence of the permits on hand. DeJong Evaluation has provided both hi and low estimates for the earnings foregone in the absence of environmental permits. The estimated cost to acquire the necessary environmental permits would be approximately $1.4M, which includes the consulting and application fees along with the necessary site reviews conducted by the Ministry of Environment. This cost is factored into the foregone earnings provided below. The permits expire at the end of 2011.

Net working capital and fixed assets are key supportive assets to this intangible asset. In order to accurately determine the fair value of the permits, a required return on assets directly related to the permit use must be deducted from the after-tax earnings applied in the valuation. Furthermore, a 11 percent discount rate has been adopted as the appropriate rate of return specific to intangible assets. Intangible assets are considered to be the highest risk asset component of an overall business enterprise as may have little, if any, liquidity, and poor versatility for redeployment elsewhere in the business enterprise.

FAIR VALUE DATA

CAD $ millions	2006	2007	2008	2009	2010	2011
Total Earnings Foregone						
HI end value	$350	$375	$400	$425	$440	$450
LO end value	$345	$365	$395	$415	$425	$435
Income Tax Rate	34.12%	**Discount Rate**		11%		
After-tax returns on contributory assets						
	$235	$245	$260	$270	$270	$270
Discount Factor (11%)	0.901	0.812	0.731	0.659	0.593	0.535
High Value	−$3.98	$1.66	$2.57	$6.58	$11.79	$14.15
Present Value	$32.78					
Low Value	−$6.95	−$3.68	$0.17	$2.24	$5.93	$8.86
Present Value	$6.57					

Source: ArcelorMittal Dofasco Financial Accounting Group.

EXHIBIT 12 DeJong evaluation – customer lists valuation estimates

> **DeJong Evaluation**

MEMO

To: Sean Collins, Director of Financial Accounting at Dofasco
From: DeJong Evaluation
Date: 01-Mar-06
Re: Fair Value Assessment – Dofasco Customer Lists

Dofasco's ability to meet customer needs has prompted much of its steel-making and product innovations. Furthermore, Dofasco's specialized product offering has developed long-term relationships in many of its markets. Arcelor citied Dofasco's strong customer relations as value driver for the purchase of Dofasco. Value derived from customer lists is expected to expire after eight years.

The income approach, using an excess earnings method to value the acquired customer relationships has been applied. The excess earnings method estimates the fair value of an asset based on expected future economic benefits discounted to present value. DeJong evaluators have provided both high and low EBITDA margin estimates. Margin estimates are based on a High and Low range of production costs such as market price fluctuations for raw material inputs.

Net working capital, fixed assets, technology and Dofasco's assembled workforce are key supportive assets to this intangible asset. In order to accurately determine the fair value of the Dofasco's customer relationships, a required return on assets directly related to the customer lists use must be deducted from the after-tax earnings applied in the valuation. Furthermore, a 11 percent discount rate has been adopted as the appropriate rate of return specific to intangible assets. Intangible assets are considered to be the highest risk asset component of an overall business enterprise as may have little, if any, liquidity, and poor versatility for redeployment elsewhere in the business enterprise.

FAIR VALUE DATA

CAD $ millions	2006	2007	2008	2009	2010	2011	2012	2013	2014	2015
Revenue										
Automotive	$976	$1,065	$978	$882	$813	$630	$450	$270	$90	$–
Construction	490	538	491	456	425	349	271	194	116	38
Distribution	386	362	284	223	189	114	38	–	–	–
Consumer	296	308	270	237	213	169	21	73	24	–
Total	$2,148	$2,273	$2,023	$1,798	$1,640	$1,262	$880	$537	$230	$38
EBITDA Margin – High	10.8%	18.2%	22.8%	24.6%	24.6%	24.6%	24.5%	24.6%	24.8%	23.7%
EBITDA – High	$232.0	$413.0	$461.0	$442.0	$403.0	$310.0	$216.0	$132.0	$57.0	$9.0
EBITDA Margin – Low	9.9%	16.4%	21.2%	23.4%	23.3%	23.3%	23.3%	23.4%	23.5%	22.5%
EBITDA – Low	$213.4	$371.7	$428.7	$419.9	$382.9	$294.5	$205.2	$125.4	$54.2	$8.6
Earnings After Tax	*Tax Rate*	34.12%								
EBITDA – High	$152.8	$272.1	$303.7	$291.2	$265.5	$204.2	$142.3	$87.0	$37.6	$5.9
EBITDA – Low	$140.6	$244.9	$282.4	$276.6	$252.2	$194.0	$135.2	$82.6	$35.7	$5.6
After-Tax Return on Contributory Assets										
Net working capital	$17.3	$17.7	$15.6	$13.7	$12.6	$9.7	$6.7	$4.1	$1.8	$0.3
Fixed assets	167.0	222.4	203.6	183.3	170.9	131.2	91.5	55.3	24.0	4.0
Technology	15.5	19.8	16.6	16.4	15.2	11.7	8.1	5.0	2.1	0.4
Assembled workforce	9.0	11.9	11.1	9.0	9.1	7.0	4.9	–	1.0	0.2
Total	$208.8	$271.8	$246.9	$222.4	$207.8	$159.6	$111.2	$64.4	$28.9	$4.9
Net Return on Customer Relationship										
High	–$56.0	$0.3	$56.8	$68.8	$57.7	$44.6	$31.1	$22.6	$8.7	$1.0
Low	–$68.2	–$26.9	$35.5	$54.2	$44.4	$34.4	$24.0	$18.2	$6.8	$0.7

Present Value of Net Return on Customer Relationship				**Discount Rate**			11%			
Discount Factor	0.901	0.812	0.731	0.659	0.593	0.535	0.482	0.434	0.391	0.352
Future Returns – High	–$50.4	$0.2	$41.5	$45.3	$34.2	$23.9	$15.0	$9.8	$3.4	$0.4
Present Value – High	$123.3									
Future Returns – Low	–$61.4	–$21.9	$26.0	$35.7	$26.4	$18.4	$11.6	$7.9	$2.6	$0.3
Present Value Low	$45.6									

Source: ArcelorMittal Dofasco Financial Accounting Group.

EXHIBIT 13   DeJong evaluation – Dofasco supply contracts

> *DeJong Evaluation*

MEMO

To: Sean Collins, Director of Financial Accounting at Dofasco
From: DeJong Evaluation
Date: 01-Mar-06
Re: Fair Value Assessment – Dofasco Supply Contracts

After a review of Dofasco's significant supply contracts, it appears that Dofasco's natural gas contract is its sole contract which holds significant value relative to current market terms. DeJong has determined the present value of this contract to be approximately $10 million CAD. These natural gas contracts will be useful over the next two years.

A 11 percent discount rate has been adopted as the appropriate rate of return specific to intangible assets. Intangible assets are considered to be the highest risk asset component of an overall business enterprise as may have little, if any, liquidity, and poor versatility for redeployment elsewhere in the business enterprise.

FAIR VALUE DATA

CAD $ millions	2006	2007
Supply Contract Benefit	**$6.5**	**$5.1**
Discount Factor (11%)	0.901	0.812
Future Benefit	**$5.9**	**$4.1**
Present Value	**$10.0**	

Source: ArcelorMittal Dofasco Financial Accounting Group.

EXHIBIT 14   DeJong evaluation – internal development valuation estimates

DeJong Evaluation

MEMO

To:	Sean Collins, Director of Financial Accounting at Dofasco
From:	DeJong Evaluation
Date:	01-Mar-06
Re:	Fair Value Assessment – New Product Development

Only those new product development (NPD) initiatives, where research and development activities have been substantially completed and near the commercialization stage will be considered for the 'internal research and development' intangible asset valuation. The estimated fair value of these significant NPD initiatives will be determined based on several factors, which include the projected after-tax earnings on the sales of the new products in the market, less costs to develop. Similar to the valuation of other intangibles, this process is known as the earnings approach to asset valuation. Given Dofasco's capacity restraints, after-tax earnings foregone on existing product that would have otherwise been produced (ie., opportunity cost) should also be considered.

The useful life of this intangible asset will range from 10 to 15 years; this assumes these NPDs will be replaced by new NPDs following that period. A discount rate of 15 percent was determined to be the minimal expected return on the NPDs.

In order to assess the reasonability of the earnings approach, the research and development costs incurred to date such as salaries and benefits of those employees involved in the projects, cost of materials, testing, overhead and upfront licensing fees have been determined. These costs are known as the 'costs to replicate.' The costs to replicate must be exceeded by an estimated future economic benefit of the initiative to confirm that the NPD projects have future inherit value. The current after tax cost to replicate is $7.5 million CAD. Currently value exists beyond the 'costs to replicate.'

FAIR VALUE DATA

CAD $ millions	2006	2007	2008	2009	2010	2011	2012	2013	2014	2015
EBITDA from NPD – High Estimates										
Advanced High Strength Steels	$1	$2	$4	$5	$5	$5	$5	$5	$5	$5
Other Steel Products	5	8	9	10	10	10	10	10	10	10
Coating	1	2	4	4	4	4	4	4	4	4
Total	$7	$12	$17	$19	$19	$19	$19	$19	$19	$19
EBITDA from NPD – Low Estimates										
Advanced High Strength Steels	$1	$1	$2	$2	$2	$2	$2	$2	$2	$2
Other Steel Products	4	6	8	8	8	8	8	8	8	8
Coating	1	1	2	2	2	2	2	2	2	2
Total	$6	$8	$12	$12	$12	$12	$12	$12	$12	$12
Costs to complete NPD	$5	$4	$3	$–	$–	$–	$–	$–	$–	$–
Foregone operating margin on products no longer produced	$3	$3	$3	$3	$3	$3	$3	$3	$3	$3
Discount Rate 15.00%	**Tax Rate**		34.12%							
Discount Factor	0.870	0.756	0.658	0.572	0.497	0.432	0.376	0.327	0.284	0.247
Value of NPD – High Estimates	–$0.6	$2.5	$4.8	$6.0	$5.2	$4.6	$4.0	$3.4	$3.0	$2.6
Present Value – High Estimates	$35.5									
Value of NDP – Low Estimates	–$1.1	$0.5	$2.6	$3.4	$2.9	$2.6	$2.2	$1.9	$1.7	$1.5
Present Value – Low Estimates	$18.2									

Source: ArcelorMittal Dofasco Financial Accounting Group.

EXHIBIT 15   Summary of IAS 36 – impairment of assets

Cash-generating units

Under international accounting standards (IAS 36), intangible assets that do not generate independent cash flows on their own are grouped into cash-generating units (CGU). A CGU is the smallest group of assets that generates cash inflows, which are largely independent of the cash flows from other assets or groups of assets.

Goodwill is assigned to a CGU or to a group of CGUs, which are expected to benefit from the synergies of the combination.

Lifespan of intangible assets

Intangible assets are classified as having either indefinite or definite lives. In general, when no legal, regulatory, contractual, competitive, economic, or other factors limit the useful life of an intangible to the enterprise, the useful life of an intangible asset is considered to be **indefinite**. Conversely, **definite** life intangibles have a foreseeable limit to the period which the asset is expected to benefit the entity. Definite life intangible assets are amortized over their useful life or pattern of expected future benefits.

Impairment testing under IAS 36 – assets other than goodwill

	Definite Life Assets	**Indefinite Life Assets**
Impairment Assessment Timing	Assessed for circumstances of impairment at each reporting date. Determine the recoverable amount if impairment seems possible.	Assessed for impairment any time during an annual period, provided it is performed at the same time every year. Determine the recoverable amount for the asset or CGU.
Impairment Test	Compare the carrying amount of the asset to the recoverable amount. When the recoverable amount is less than the carrying amount, an impairment loss exists. The recoverable amount is the higher of: a) the *fair value less costs to sell,* which is the amount that could be obtained from a sale of the asset in an arm's-length transaction less the costs directly attributable to the sale; or b) the *value in use,* which is the present value of future cash flows expected to be derived from the asset or cash-generating unit.	Compare the carrying amount of the asset to the recoverable amount. When the recoverable amount is less than the carrying amount, an impairment loss exists. The recoverable amount is the higher of: a) the *fair value less costs to sell,* which is the amount that could be obtained from a sale of the asset in an arm's-length transaction less the costs directly attributable to the sale; or b) the *value in use,* which is the present value of future cash flows expected to be derived from the asset or cash-generating unit.
Impairment Loss	The impairment loss is equal to the carrying amount of the asset or CGU less the recoverable amount.	The impairment loss is equal to the carrying amount of the asset or CGU less the recoverable amount.

An impairment loss recognized in prior periods for an asset other than goodwill can be reversed if there has been a change in the estimates used to determine the asset's recoverable amount since the last impairment loss was recognized. Under such circumstances, the carrying amount of the asset is increased to its recoverable amount; however, the increased carrying amount cannot exceed the original carrying amount (net of any accumulated amortization).

Impairment testing under IAS 36 – goodwill

A CGU to which goodwill has been allocated must be tested for impairment at least annually, at the same time every year or whenever there is an indication that the unit may be impaired (see examples above). The impairment test involves comparing the carrying amount of the CGU, including the goodwill, with the recoverable amount of the CGU. If the carrying amount of the CGU exceeds the recoverable amount of the CGU, the entity must recognize an impairment loss.

An impairment loss from goodwill should be allocated to reduce the carrying amount of the CGU in the following order:

1 Reduce the carrying amount of any goodwill allocated to the CGU; and then
2 Reduce the carrying amount of each asset in the CGU on a pro rata basis.[1]

Impairment losses for goodwill cannot be reversed as subsequent increases in value of goodwill are believed to be internally generated rather than a reversal of the previous impairment.

---

[1]However, a carrying amount of an asset cannot be reduced below the highest of its fair value less costs to sell (if determinable), its value in use (if determinable) and zero.

8 The initial public offering of PartyGaming Plc

On June 30, 2005, PartyGaming Plc offered 781,629,050 of its ordinary shares for public trading on the London Stock Exchange. The offer price of the shares was 116 pence per ordinary share. The number of shares offered for public trading represented approximately 19.5 percent of PartyGaming's 4 billion shares outstanding.

An investment in PartyGaming's shares was not without risks. In its prospectus, Party-Gaming warned its prospective investors that they

> ... should be aware that an investment in PartyGaming Plc involves a high degree of risk and that, if certain of the risks described in Part 3 occur, they may lose all or a very substantial part of their investment. Accordingly, an investment in the Shares is only suitable for investors who are particularly knowledgeable in investment matters and who are able to bear the complete loss of their investment.

PartyGaming and its industry[1]

PartyGaming was founded in 1997. Between 1997 and 2005 the company had become one of the largest online gaming suppliers in the world. In 2005, the company generated the largest proportion of its revenues from accommodating online poker games, partly by means of its own website PartyPoker.com – the world's leading online poker site. Specifically, online poker produced 92 percent of the company's revenues; the remaining 8 percent came from online casino and bingo games. The company had achieved its leading position in online poker through a timely entry into the online poker market, supported by effective online and offline sales and marketing, a reliable technology, and high-level customer support.

In 1997, Ruth Parasol started PartyGaming with the launch of the Starluck casino site, which was operated and managed from the Caribbean. Three years later, Anurag Dikshit and Vikrant Bhargava – who would later become the company's Operations and Marketing Directors – became investors in PartyGaming and started to develop the company's poker business. The poker site PartyPoker.com was launched in 2001 from Canada. With the help of famous poker player Mike Sexton, PartyGaming was able to attract a lot of publicity for its new website by organizing the "PartyPoker.com Million" tournament, for which the qualification rounds took place online. In 2002 and 2003, PartyGaming launched PartyBingo.com and moved its operations to Hyderabad (India) and its headquarters to Gibraltar.

The online gaming market had experienced rapid growth in the years just prior to 2005. Primary drivers of this growth were the increasing worldwide popularity of the internet as well as the increasing customer awareness of the sector's existence. Increasing customer awareness had resulted from greater television exposure and intensified marketing activities by the major industry players. In addition, online gaming companies had invested in their growth by developing new products and improving payment processing, transaction

Professor Erik Peek prepared this case. The case is intended solely as the basis for class discussion and is not intended to serve as an endorsement, source of primary data, or illustration of effective or ineffective management.

[1]The material in this and the following sections largely draws from PartyGaming's IPO prospectus (June 14, 2005).

services, and customer support. Industry analysts did not expect this growth to stop in the near term. The online sector's share of the global gaming market was expected to increase from 3 to 8 percent between 2004 and 2009.

Industry analysts estimated the size of the global online and offline gaming market to be $243 billion (in revenues) in 2004 and $282 billion in 2009. The online gaming market was estimated to generate revenue of approximately $8.2 billion in 2004 and $22.7 billion in 2009. In 2004, online casino and bingo games accounted for 29 percent of the online gaming revenues, whereas online poker games accounted for 13 percent. Respectively 50 percent, 27 percent, and 15 percent of the global online gaming revenues had been generated from the US, Europe, and Asia. Industry analysts expected the US share of the global online gaming market to decline to 40 percent in 2009 as a result of the above-average market growth in Europe and Asia. The key drivers of such growth would be the increasing number of internet users, the increasing popularity of gaming, increasing marketing investments made by the industry players, and the development of new distribution channels, such as mobile phones.

Poker had become more popular over the years mostly because of the increased television coverage of poker tournaments and the exposure of the game on popular television shows. Because many of the poker players around the world were still playing offline, the online poker market could potentially grow from the migration of offline players to online play. Analysts estimated that this migration, in combination with the attraction of new poker players, could make the online poker market's revenues grow from slightly more than $1 billion in 2004 to close to $6.4 billion in 2009 – representing 28 percent of the global online gaming market. In comparison, analysts estimated that the online casino market would grow from $2,157 million (in revenues) in 2004 to $5,587 million in 2009. According to PartyGaming's management there were a number of barriers to entry to the online poker market, creating a competitive advantage for the company:

- *Player liquidity*. To be able to organize games with a wide range of stakes at all times of players' choosing, online poker providers needed to have a large customer base.

- *Software control*. The leading online poker providers had invested significant amounts in software. Having control over their own software helped them to make the software improvements that were necessary for attracting and retaining customers.

- *Payment processing expertise*. To attract and maintain customers, online poker providers must be able to provide a wide range of payment methods (credit cards, e-checks, online wallets) and must have built a reputation for quick, efficient, and error-free payment processing.

- *Customer support*. Online poker providers must make significant investments in customer service operations.

- *Marketing and global reach*. Online poker providers needed to have significant market resources to penetrate new geographic markets and increase advertising expenditures as competition increased.

Having the mission to be the world's largest gaming company, with the most trusted brands, innovative technology, and high-level customer service, PartyGaming focused its strategy on the following areas: (1) sustain brand value and maintain leadership in its current markets, (2) expand to markets outside the US, first in Europe, later in Asia, (3) continue to provide innovative technology and high-level customer support, (4) stretch the "Party" brand to other games, either acquired or self-developed, and (5) make use of alternative delivery channels, such as mobile phones and interactive television.

In 2004, PartyGaming was the undisputed market leader in the online poker segment. Based on the average ring game rake – the amount of money the provider takes from the pot – the company had a market share of 54 percent. The five next-largest providers of online poker gaming all had market shares between 5 and 8 percent.

The risks

As pointed out, an investment in PartyGaming's ordinary shares involved substantial risks. The following risks were especially high:

- *Regulatory risks*. One apparent risk affecting the online gaming market in 2005 was that in many countries national gaming laws had been developed to govern offline gaming activities and were not particularly suited to govern online gaming activities. Consequently, in some of PartyGaming's geographical segments there was much uncertainty about whether the supply of online gaming was legal or not. In some countries, foreign suppliers of online gaming were not able to obtain a license and it was uncertain whether and how local regulators would bring actions against foreign suppliers who had no license but were not physically present. PartyGaming ran the risk that regulators would change their laws and take actions that would inhibit the company's ability to process payments and advertise in a particular country. The advantage of these regulatory risks was, however, that they prevented many other companies from entering PartyGaming's industry, thereby reducing competition.

■ *Taxation risks.* PartyGaming and most of its group companies had their domicile in Gibraltar, where they were exempt from paying taxes because they offered no services to Gibraltarians or Gibraltar residents. However, in early 2005 the European Commission and the governments of Gibraltar and the UK had agreed to abolish the Gibraltar exempt company tax regime by the end of 2010. PartyGaming would even lose its tax exempt status – and become subject to a 35 percent tax rate – on December 31, 2007, if it had a change in ownership before June 30, 2006, and immediately lose its tax exempt status if it had a change in ownership after June 30, 2006. At the time of the IPO, it was still unclear what regulators would consider a "change in ownership." Party-Gaming expected that the IPO would not be treated as a change in ownership. The company's principal shareholders had agreed not to dispose of their shares within two years of the IPO. Further, the decision to abolish the exempt company tax regime had been appealed to the European Court. Finally, the government of Gibraltar was seeking alternative ways to provide companies with an attractive tax regime.

■ *Technology risks.* PartyGaming ran the risk that hackers would attempt to gain access to its systems and disrupt its services. Further, the growing demand for the company's online gaming services could lead to a situation in which its technological architecture as well as the technological architecture of its third-party providers was not developed enough to ensure the absence of errors, failures, interruptions, or delays in the provision of its services. Finally, PartyGaming needed to make investments in technology that facilitated the delivery of its online gaming services to customers who were not using personal computers but other devices such as mobile phones or television set-top devices.

■ *Competitive risks.* Other companies in PartyGaming's industry offered formidable competition. At the time of the IPO there were more than 2,000 online gaming sites and more than 200 online poker sites competing for the same customers. An increasing proportion of PartyGaming's revenues came from "third-party skins" – third-party brands that used PartyGaming's platform and shared their revenues. Third-party skins were competition to the company's own operations and brought significant risks of disputes and litigation.

■ *Intellectual property rights.* A substantial part of PartyGaming's technology and know-how was proprietary and any misappropriated or unauthorized disclosure of its technology and know-how could harm the company's competitive advantage. Similarly, the use of "Party" domain names or the "Party" brand by third parties without approval could harm the value of the company's brand. In some countries where PartyGaming operated, national laws did not sufficiently protect the company's intellectual property rights, or actions to enforce its intellectual property rights, were costly. PartyGaming also ran the risk that other technology companies would claim that their intellectual property rights were infringed by PartyGaming, which could result in litigation.

■ *Risks of international expansion.* Because of the legal uncertainties in the US, Party-Gaming planned to expand internationally. Competition outside the US was, however, stronger than within the US. Further, international expansion would bring a number of additional risks, such as legal, political, cultural, and currency risks. Operating on an international scale could also increase the company's transaction costs.

■ *Short operating history.* PartyGaming's short operating history made it difficult to assess the company's prospects. In its prospectus, the company reported that it did not expect that its rapid historic growth would persist in the future. In order to grow, Party-Gaming should innovate new products and services, countering the declining growth of the online poker market. The company also expected that, when growth would decline, the cyclicality and seasonality (lower yields per active player day in the second quarter, higher yields in the first and fourth quarters) of its operations would become more pronounced.

■ *Principal shareholders.* After the IPO, the principal shareholders of PartyGaming would hold close to 73 percent of the company's ordinary shares. Consequently, they could have a decisive influence on the company's financial and operating decisions as well as the success of any takeover offer.

8 The initial public offering of PartyGaming Plc

Although PartyGaming had no physical presence in the US, it did not block US customers from signing up to the company's websites. The company generated almost 87 percent of its revenues from the US, where the regulatory risks were significant. It advertised its gaming sites in the US and made use of the services of US payment processors to collect from and pay out funds to its US customers. At the time of the IPO, the US Department of Justice considered the US operations of PartyGaming illegal. Further, at least seven US states had laws that explicitly prohibited online gaming, while many other states prohibited all forms of unlicensed gaming. US federal laws were, however, inconclusive about whether online gaming was indeed illegal and the status of state laws in the matter was unclear. The company had not received an official notification from any US authority that it sought to bring action against the company for its US operations. Any future action by US authorities to issue an injunction, impose fines or imprisonment, or seize gaming proceeds could, however, impose considerable (legal) costs upon the company and reduce the company's revenues and profits.

US law enforcement officials targeted their enforcement activities at US-based companies who provided services such as IT, payment processing, and advertising to PartyGaming. In particular, they alleged the violation of US laws to discourage US banks from processing online gaming transactions and US media from advertising online gaming sites. As a consequence, several banks, such as Citibank, financial service companies, such as PayPal, and media companies, such as Discovery, had decided not to provide any services to PartyGaming. Another threat to PartyGaming's US operations was posed by the proposals of the US Congress to prohibit online gaming or the provision of payment processing services to online gaming companies. Over past years, several proposals were made but did not receive sufficient support to be passed. In 2005, the US Congress would consider the "Kyl Bill," which sought to prohibit the processing of online gaming transactions. At the time of the IPO, this proposal seemed to lack sufficient support from the US Congress.

PartyGaming's governance

In early 2005 PartyGaming's Board of Directors comprised four executive directors and four nonexecutive directors. All nonexecutive directors were denoted as independent. The company's board had established an audit committee, a remuneration committee, a nominations committee, and an ethics committee. The company's CEO was Richard Lawrence Segal, who had joined the company in August 2004, after having been the CEO of cinema operator Odeon Limited for seven years.

Two executive directors were also principal shareholders of PartyGaming. After the IPO, Anurag Dikshit, Operations Director, would own 31.6 percent of the company's shares; Vikrant Bhargava, Marketing Director, would own 16.3 percent. Two other principal shareholders were co-founder Ruth Parasol – owning 16.3 percent – and her husband, Russell DeLeon – owning 9.0 percent. Each of the principal shareholders had agreed not to sell any shares during the 12 months following the IPO. Principal shareholders owning more than 15 percent of the company's shares had the right to nominate one nonexecutive director. However, they also agreed that at any time at least half of the company's board would comprise independent directors.

PartyGaming's performance

At the time of the IPO, PartyGaming's management considered the company's key strengths to be its high-margin business model, its strong marketing program and brand name, its large active player base, its high-quality and innovative technology, its offering of a wide variety of pay-in and withdrawal methods, its high-level 24/7 customer support, its well-developed systems of risk management and fraud detection, and its strong management team.

To sustain brand value and attract active players, PartyGaming made significant investments in marketing. The company made use of a variety of marketing strategies such as television and radio advertising, affiliate marketing (sharing revenues with other sites that market PartyGaming sites), direct mail, sign-up bonuses, and sponsorships. In addition, PartyGaming invested in the retention of customers by organizing the PartyPoker.com Million Tournaments, for which the qualification rounds were held online, introducing player loyalty programs (award schemes), and awarding bonuses to existing players who pay in new funds.

As evidence of PartyGaming's marketing success stands the large increase in the company's registered poker and casino players prior to 2005. **Exhibit 1** shows the number of registered and active poker and casino players by period, as well as the average yield per player day. The number of active players, the average daily active players, active player days (average daily active players times the number of days in a period), and yield per active player day were PartyGaming's key performance indicators. The yield per active player day followed a seasonal pattern. In 2003 (2004), the yield per active poker player day was $21.0 ($19.8), $18.1 ($18.7), $18.8 ($18.9), and $20.0 ($19.1) in the first, second, third, and fourth quarter, respectively. Although PartyGaming had a large player base, the company was reliant on a relatively small number of customers. For example, close to 10 percent of the active poker players contributed 70 percent of the company's revenues from poker games. Similarly, 5 percent of the active casino players contributed 82 percent of the company's revenues from casino games.

Exhibit 2 shows PartyGaming's financial statements for the fiscal years 2003 and 2004, as well as for three fiscal quarters. These figures illustrate PartyGaming's growth in revenues and profits. One apparent development was the strong decline in equity between 2003 and 2004. The reason for this decline was the acquisition of PartyGaming Holdings Limited by PartyGaming Plc in 2004. PartyGaming acquired its interest in PartyGaming Holdings Limited in a transaction under common control. An acquisition under common control occurs when the acquirer and the target firm are both controlled by the same party. As a result of this transaction, PartyGaming Plc became the group's ultimate parent company. International Accounting Standards did not require acquisitions under common control to be accounted for using the purchase method. Consequently, PartyGaming used the pooling method to account for the acquisition, and the deficit in equity reflected the group's cumulative profits as if the new group structure had always been in place.

Questions

1 The initial offer price of PartyGaming's ordinary shares was 116 pence per share. Which sales growth and net operating profit margin assumptions are consistent with an offer price of 116 pence?

2 Using your own assumptions, estimate the value of PartyGaming's ordinary shares at the time of the IPO. How do the risks that PartyGaming faced affect your value estimate?

EXHIBIT 1 **Information about PartyGaming's registered and active players**

	Fiscal year ending December 31, 2002	Fiscal year ending December 31, 2003	Fiscal year ending December 31, 2004	Three months ending March 31, 2005
Total registered poker players	105,000	1,283,000	5,225,000	6,603,000
Total registered casino players	535,000	903,000	1,296,000	1,376,000
Registered real-money poker players	20,000	210,000	806,000	1,020,000
Of which active players (in the last month of the period)	6,000	125,000	324,000	411,000
Registered real-money casino and bingo players	282,000	320,000	374,000	388,000
Of which active players (in the last month of the period)	4,000	9,000	13,000	14,000
Average daily active poker players	1,297	17,043	77,094	121,570
Average yield per active poker player day	$20.8	$19.5	$19.1	$18.6
Average daily active casino and bingo players	580	832	1,797	1,875
Average yield per active casino and bingo player day	$90.7	$96.9	$73.9	$73.1

Source: PartyGaming's IPO prospectus (June 14, 2005). The item "total registered players" includes "play money" players who participate in games for free.

EXHIBIT 2   **PartyGaming's consolidated income statements, balance sheets, cash flow statements, and *pro forma* income statement and segment information for two fiscal years and three fiscal quarters**

CONSOLIDATED INCOME STATEMENTS ($ Millions)

	Three months ending March 31, 2005	Three months ending December 31, 2004	Three months ending March 31, 2004	Fiscal year ending December 31, 2004	Fiscal year ending December 31, 2003
Revenue – net gaming revenue	222.6	194.0	115.4	601.6	153.1
Other operating revenue/(expenses)	−0.3	0.4	0.0	0.1	0.4
Administrative expenses					
– other administrative expenses	−23.3	−21.6	−15.8	−73.1	−29.4
– share-based payments	−4.6	−2.3	0.0	−3.2	0.0
– strategic review costs	−1.5	0.0	0.0	0.0	0.0
Distribution expenses	−64.6	−48.8	−28.7	−142.2	−34.9
Profit from operating activities	128.3	121.7	70.9	383.2	89.2
Finance income	0.6	0.8	0.2	1.4	0.0
Finance costs	−3.0	−4.4	−0.1	−12.9	0.0
Share of losses of associate	−0.3	0.0	0.0	0.0	0.0
Profit before tax	125.6	118.1	71.0	371.7	89.2
Tax	−8.2	−7.4	−3.9	−21.6	−5.6
Profit after tax	117.4	110.7	67.1	350.1	83.6
Minority interest	0.0	0.0	−1.6	−1.6	−6.6
Profit from ordinary activities attributable to equity holders of the parent	117.4	110.7	65.5	348.5	77.0
Net earnings per share ($ cents)	3.11	2.93	1.73	9.23	2.04
Net earnings per share ($ cents) – diluted	3.09	2.91	1.72	9.16	2.02
Weighted average shares outstanding	3,776	3,776	3,776	3,776	3,776
Weighted average shares outstanding, diluted	3,803	3,803	3,803	3,803	3,803

8 The initial public offering of PartyGaming Plc

PRO FORMA INCOME STATEMENT AND SEGMENT INFORMATION ($ Millions)

	Three months ending March 31, 2005	Three months ending December 31, 2004	Three months ending March 31, 2004	Fiscal year Ending December 31, 2004	Fiscal year ending December 31, 2003
Revenues					
– Poker	210.3	183.5	102.9	553.0	123.7
– Casino/Bingo	12.3	10.5	12.5	48.6	29.4
– Other	0.0	0.0	0.0	0.0	0.0
Administrative expenses					
– Transaction fees	−10.1	−8.9	−6.2	−29.3	−9.8
– Staff costs	−10.5	−8.0	−4.3	−21.8	−8.3
– Depreciation and amortization	−1.7	−1.4	−0.8	−4.6	−1.1
– Other overheads	−7.1	−5.6	−4.5	−20.6	−10.2
Distribution expenses					
– Affiliate fees	−23.6	−18.8	—	−53.7	−13.3
– Customer acquisition and retention (primarily advertising)	−24.1	−14.5	—	−37.6	−10.6
– Chargebacks (amounts unrecoverable from customers)	−11.6	−10.2	—	−36.7	−8.2
– Customer bonuses	−3.7	−4.1	—	−10.0	−1.6
– Web-hosting	−1.6	−1.2	—	−4.2	−1.2
Profit before tax					
– Poker	128.0	118.0	64.5	360.1	81.2
– Casino/Bingo	6.2	6.0	6.7	28.4	8.2
– Other	−8.6	−5.9	−0.2	−16.8	−0.2
Impairment losses – trade receivables	−11.7	−10.1	−10.3	42.2	−9.9
Impairment losses – other	0.0	0.0	0.0	0.0	−0.4

CONSOLIDATED BALANCE SHEETS ($ Millions)

	Three months ending March 31, 2005	Three months ending December 31, 2004	Three months ending March 31, 2004	Fiscal year ending December 31, 2004	Fiscal year ending December 31, 2003
Intangible assets	7.7	7.7	8.0	7.7	0.0
property, plant, and equipment	25.4	13.3	9.1	13.3	5.7
Investment in associates	1.5	0.0	0.0	0.0	0.0
Total non-current assets	34.6	21.0	17.1	21.0	5.7
Trade and other receivables	132.9	107.8	76.5	107.8	53.2
Cash and cash equivalents	78.3	133.9	131.7	133.9	74.6
Short-term investments	3.5	0.0	0.0	0.0	0.0
Total current assets	214.7	241.7	208.2	241.7	127.8
Total assets	249.3	262.7	225.3	262.7	133.5
Bank overdraft	2.9	1.8	2.3	1.8	0.0
Trade and other payables	46.4	39.5	18.7	39.5	14.4
Shareholder loans	229.3	223.9	0.0	223.9	0.0
Income taxes	36.2	28.0	10.7	28.0	6.7
Client liabilities and progressive prize pools	124.1	104.6	49.1	104.6	35.4
Provisions	7.9	4.7	3.0	4.7	1.9
Total current liabilities	446.8	402.5	83.8	402.5	58.4
Trade and other payables	5.0	6.1	7.5	6.1	0.0
Shareholder loans	80.2	258.9	0.0	258.9	0.0
Total non-current liabilities	85.2	265.0	7.5	265.0	0.0
Share capital	0.1	0.0	0.0	0.0	0.0
Share premium account	0.4	0.4	0.4	0.4	0.4
Retained earnings	534.4	417.0	134.0	417.0	68.6
Other reserve	−825.4	−825.4	−0.4	−825.4	−0.4
Share option reserve	7.8	3.2	0.0	3.2	0.0
Equity attributable to equity holders of the parent	−282.7	−404.8	134.0	−404.8	68.6
Minority interest	0.0	0.0	0.0	0.0	6.5
Total liabilities and shareholders' equity	249.3	262.7	225.3	262.7	133.5

CONSOLIDATED CASH FLOW STATEMENTS ($ Millions)

	Three months ending March 31, 2005	Three months ending December 31, 2004	Three months ending March 31, 2004	Fiscal year ending December 31, 2004	Fiscal year ending December 31, 2003
Profit before tax	125.6	118.1	71.0	371.7	89.2
Adjustment for:					
Amortization of intangibles	0.0	0.1	0.0	0.3	0.2
Interest expense	3.0	4.4	0.1	12.9	0.0
Interest income	−0.6	−0.8	−0.2	−1.4	0.0
Depreciation of property, plant, and equipment	1.7	1.3	0.8	4.3	0.9
Gains on sale of property, plant, and equipment	0.0	0.0	0.0	0.0	0.1
Increase in share-based payments reserve	4.6	2.3	0.0	3.2	0.0
Loss on investment in associate	0.3	0.0	0.0	0.0	0.0
Operating cash flows before movements in working capital and provisions	134.6	125.4	71.7	391.0	90.4
Increase in trade and other receivables	−24.6	−15.3	−23.3	−54.6	−48.1
Increase in trade and other payables	26.5	31.3	15.2	89.9	43.4
Increase in provisions	3.2	−3.5	1.1	2.8	0.4
Income taxes paid	−0.8	0.0	0.0	0.0	0.0
Cash generated/(used) by working capital	4.3	12.5	−7.0	38.1	−4.3
Net cash from operating activities	138.9	137.9	64.7	429.1	86.1
Purchases of property, plant, and equipment	−13.8	−4.0	−4.1	−11.9	−5.9
Purchases of intangible assets	0.0	0.0	0.0	0.0	−0.2
Purchase of minority interest in subsidiary	0.0	0.0	−5.8	−5.8	0.0
Interest received	0.6	0.5	0.2	1.4	0.0
Purchase and cancelation of own shares	0.0	0.0	−0.1	−2.0	−3.1
Investment in associated undertaking	−1.8	0.0	0.0	0.0	0.0
Increase in short-term investments	−3.5	0.0	0.0	0.0	0.0
Net cash used in investing activities	−18.5	−3.5	−9.8	−18.3	−9.2
Issue of shares	0.0	0.0	0.0	0.9	0.0
Interest paid	−3.8	−4.6	−0.1	−11.0	0.0
Equity dividends paid	0.0	0.0	0.0	0.0	−8.1
Payments to shareholders	−173.3	−113.5	0.0	−343.2	0.0
Net cash used in financing activities	−177.1	−118.1	−0.1	−353.3	−8.1

Source: PartyGaming's IPO Prospectus (June 14, 2005). Note that at the time of the IPO, the total number of shares outstanding was 4,000,000,000.

8 The initial public offering of PartyGaming Plc

9 Two European hotel groups (A): Equity analysis

Accor[1]

In 2005, France-based Accor SA was Europe's largest and the world's fourth largest hotel group (based on the number of rooms). The company employed 168,000 people in 140 countries and operated restaurants, casinos, travel agencies, and 4,065 hotels with 475,433 rooms in 90 countries. Major brand names owned by Accor included Sofitel, Novotel, Mercure, Ibis, Formule 1, Motel 6, and Red Roof Inn. Fifty-two percent of the company's hotel rooms were located in Europe and 29 percent in the US. Accor did not own all of its hotels. About 60 percent of its rooms were owned or leased, 20 percent were operated under management contracts, and 20 percent were franchised. In 2005, Accor's hotel business generated €5.2 billion in revenues, whereas its casino, restaurant, travel, and onboard train business generated €1.8 billion in revenues.

Accor generated a smaller proportion of revenues (approximately €0.6 billion) from selling service vouchers. The voucher system worked as follows. Accor's customers – mostly companies and institutions – purchased various types of vouchers from Accor at face value plus a service premium. These customers' beneficiaries, such as their employees, could use the vouchers to purchase services from affiliated service providers. Because the service providers had to pay a refund commission upon redemption, Accor's revenues consisted of the service premiums, the refund commissions, and the interest earned in the period between the issuance and the redemption of the vouchers. Examples of service vouchers were Accor's "Ticket restaurant" vouchers for meals, "Childcare" vouchers for family assistance services, and "Domiphone" vouchers for elderly home-help services.

In its hotel business, Accor served several segments, ranging from the upscale segment with Sofitel to the budget segment with Motel 6 and Formule 1. The company's preferred operating structure depended on the type of segment. For example, Accor preferred to operate its hotels under management contracts in the upscale segment and franchised in the budget segment. Under a management contract structure, Accor typically signed a 25-year agreement to manage a hotel and retained a 25 percent interest in the company that owned the hotel. Accor planned to open another 200,000 new hotel rooms between 2006 and 2010, primarily in the economy segment. In mature markets, which would account for 33 percent of the new openings, the company preferred to grow through low-capital-intensive property development, such as through management contracts and franchises. In total, Accor expected that it would invest €2.5 billion in the expansion of its hotel business between 2006 and 2010. During the same period, the company planned to invest €500 million in its services business.

Exhibit 2 shows Accor's financial statements for the fiscal years ending December 31, 2004 and 2005. Accor applied International Financial Reporting Standards for the first time in its 2005 financial statements. In 2005, Accor's total revenues grew by close to 8.0 percent. Revenues in the hotel segment increased by 4.8 percent, of which 1.2 percent came from the company's expansion of its capacity and 3.6 percent represented growth on a like-for-like basis (e.g., because of increases in occupancy rates or average room rates).

Professor Erik Peek prepared this case. The case is intended solely as the basis for class discussion and is not intended to serve as an endorsement, source of primary data, or illustration of effective or ineffective management.

[1]Most of the material in this section comes from Accor's 2005 Annual Report.

Revenues from Accor's service operations increased from €518 million to €630 million (21.7 percent) and by 14.1 percent on a like-for-like basis. The revenue growth of 12.9 percent in Accor's other operating segments was primarily driven by the creation of Groupe Lucien Barrièrre in the casino segment, where the reported growth was 47.7 percent but like-for-like growth did not exceed 1 percent. Like-for-like revenue growth in the other segments ranged from 3.3 percent in the travel agencies business to 6.9 percent in the restaurants business.

NH Hoteles[2]

Spain-based NH Hoteles SA competed with Accor primarily in the midscale segment of the European hotel market. In 2005, NH Hoteles ranked seventh among Europe's largest hotel chains, after brands such as Hilton, Holiday Inn, Novotel, and Mercure. The total number of rooms that NH Hoteles operated was 38,054 at the beginning of 2006. About 47 percent of these rooms were leased, 27 percent were owned, 14 percent were managed, and 12 percent were leased with a purchase option. In 2005, the company's hotel business generated close to €910 million in revenues. Next to investing in hotels, NH Hoteles had invested a smaller proportion of its capital in the development and exploitation of real estate properties. The company's revenues in this segment consisted of revenues from the exploitation of a private and exclusive golf club and revenues from the sale of luxury apartments and villas. The real estate activities were managed by an exchange-listed company, Sotogrande SA, in which NH Hoteles had an 80 percent stake. By the end of 2005, NH Hoteles had made a public bid for Sotogrande's remaining shares. Sotogrande's real estate business generated €83.4 million in revenues in 2005, largely stemming from the sale of real estate.

NH Hoteles followed a strategy of international expansion. Whereas in 1999, NH Hoteles had operations only in its domestic market (Spain), five years later, the company had developed clear market presence in especially Germany and the Benelux (Belgium and the Netherlands). In early 2006, 34 percent of the company's rooms were located in Spain, 24 percent in Germany, 18 percent in the Benelux, and 14 percent in Latin America. In 2005, NH Hoteles opened 2,329 new rooms. Management expected that by the end of 2008 the number of leased, owned or managed hotel rooms would have increased to 41,509, of which 36 percent would be located in Spain, 22 percent in Germany, 16 percent in the Benelux, and 16 percent in Latin America. NH Hoteles acquired its first hotel in the UK in 2005 and planned to open its first hotel in France in 2008.

Exhibit 3 shows NH Hoteles' financial statements for the fiscal years ending December 31, 2004 and 2005. NH Hoteles applied International Financial Reporting Standards for the first time in its 2005 financial statements. In 2005, the company's total revenues grew by close to 1.0 percent. Revenues in the hotel segment increased by 4.5 percent, but revenues from NH Hoteles' real estate operations decreased by 26.8 percent. Operating profits and pretax profits in the hotel business were €58.2 million and €34.1 million, respectively, compared with €53.7 million and €54.2 million, respectively, in the real estate business.

Questions

1   Are the financial statements of Accor and NH Hoteles comparable? Which adjustments to the financial statements would you consider necessary before comparing the companies' financial performance?

2   Compare Accor's and NH Hoteles' price-earnings ratios and market-to-book ratios at the end of fiscal year 2005. What may explain the difference in these ratios between Accor and NH Hoteles?

---

[2]Most of the material in this section comes from NH Hoteles' 2005 Annual Report.

EXHIBIT 1 **Key performance indicators for Accor and NH Hoteles in fiscal 2005: Revenue per available room (RevPAR)**

	Segment	Occupancy rate		Average room rate		RevPAR	
		31/12/05 (in %)	Change from last year (in perc. points)	31/12/05	Change from last year (in %)	31/12/05	Change from last year
Accor	Upscale and midscale Europe	63.2%	−0.7	€94	2.60%	€59	1.50%
	Economy Europe	72.5%	−0.3	€50	4.00%	€36	3.50%
	Economy US	65.9%	0.9	$44	4.40%	$29	5.70%
NH Hoteles	Europe	66.6%	4.8	€73	−1.3%	€49	3.5%
	Latin America	66.0%	8.5	€53	4.5%	€35	13.4%

EXHIBIT 2   **Accor's consolidated income statements, balance sheets, and cash flow statements for the fiscal years ending December 31, 2004 and 2005**

CONSOLIDATED INCOME STATEMENTS (€ millions)

	Fiscal year ending December 31, 2005	Fiscal year ending December 31, 2004
Revenue	7,562	7,013
Other operating revenue	60	51
Consolidated revenue	**7,622**	**7,064**
Cost of goods sold	(747)	(676)
Employee benefits expense	(2,915)	(2,710)
Energy, maintenance, and repairs	(372)	(346)
Taxes, insurance, and service charges (co-owned properties)	(299)	(279)
Other operating expenses	(1,303)	(1,228)
EBITDAR	**1,986**	**1,825**
Rental expense	(837)	(790)
EBITDA	**1,149**	**1,035**
Depreciation, amortization, and provision expense	(432)	(423)
EBIT	**717**	**612**
Net financial expense	(135)	(123)
Dividend income from non-consolidated companies	6	5
Exchange gains and losses	6	13
Movement in provisions	1	4
Share of profit of associates after tax	8	2
Operating profit before tax and non-recurring items	**603**	**513**
Restructuring costs	(43)	(22)
Impairment losses	(107)	(52)
Gains and losses on management of hotel properties	72	(8)
Gains and losses on management of other assets	(37)	(23)
Profit before tax	**488**	**408**
Income tax expense	(124)	(152)
Net profit	**364**	**256**
Minority interests	(31)	(23)
Net profit, group share	**333**	**233**
Net earnings per share (€)	1.55	1.08
Net earnings per share (€) – diluted	1.55	1.08
Dividend payout per share (€)	1.15	1.30
Net book value per share (€)	20.02	14.56
Net book value per share (€) – diluted	20.02	14.56
Weighted average shares outstanding	214.783	214.783
Weighted average shares outstanding, diluted	214.783	214.783
End-of-year share price (€)	46.46	32.21

CONSOLIDATED BALANCE SHEETS (€ millions)

	Fiscal year ending December 31, 2005	Fiscal year ending December 31, 2004
Goodwill	1,897	1,667
Intangible assets	437	400
Property, plant, and equipment	3,891	3,717
Financial assets	1,212	1,220
Deferred tax assets	387	279
Non-current assets	**7,824**	**7,283**
Inventories	64	69
Trade receivables	1,508	1,272
Other receivables and accruals	770	628
Service vouchers reserve funds	327	346
Receivables on disposals of assets	23	44
Short-term loans	39	45
Current financial assets	600	77
Cash and cash equivalents	1,763	1,589
Current assets	**5,094**	**4,070**
Non-current assets held for sale	260	0
Total assets	**13,178**	**11,353**
Shareholders' equity, group share	4,301	3,128
Minority interests	95	70
Total shareholders' equity and minority interests	**4,396**	**3,198**
Convertible bonds	1,001	950
Other long-term debt	520	2,258
Long-term finance lease liabilities	352	337
Long-term provisions	171	147
Non-current liabilities	**2,358**	**4,004**
Trade payables	849	760
Other payables and income tax payable	1,460	1,228
Service vouchers in circulation	1,940	1,561
Current provisions	203	148
Short-term debt and finance lease liabilities	1,915	382
Bank overdrafts	57	72
Current liabilities	**6,424**	**4,151**
Liabilities held for sale	0	0
Total liabilities and shareholders' equity	**13,178**	**11,353**

9 Two European hotel groups (A): Equity analysis

CONSOLIDATED CASH FLOW STATEMENTS (€ millions)

	Fiscal year ending December 31, 2005	Fiscal year ending December 31, 2004
EBITDA	1,149	1,035
Net financial expense	(122)	(101)
Income tax expense	(200)	(144)
Noncash revenue and expense included in EBITDA	0	14
Elimination of provision movements included in net financial expense, income tax expense and non-recurring taxes	102	43
Dividends received from associates	6	6
Funds from operations	**935**	**853**
Cash received (paid) on non-recurring transactions (included in restructuring costs and non-recurring taxes)	(124)	(67)
Decrease (increase) in working capital	271	130
Net cash from operating activities	**1,082**	**916**
Renovation and maintenance expenditure	(449)	(314)
Development expenditure	(479)	(680)
Proceeds from disposals of assets	313	429
Net cash used in investments/divestments	**(615)**	**(565)**
Proceeds from issue of share capital	822	312
Reduction in capital	0	0
Dividends paid	(287)	(284)
Repayments of long-term debt	(702)	(49)
Payment of finance lease liabilities	(52)	(33)
New long-term debt	664	128
Increase (decrease) in short-term debt	(178)	131
Net cash from financing activities	**267**	**205**
Effect of changes in exchange rates	(27)	11
Net change in cash and cash equivalents	**707**	**567**
Cash and cash equivalents at beginning of the period	1,594	1,024
Effect of changes in fair value of cash and cash equivalents	5	3
Cash and cash equivalents at end of period	**2,306**	**1,594**

EXHIBIT 3 **NH Hoteles' consolidated income statements, balance sheets, and cash flow statements for the fiscal years ending December 31, 2004 and 2005**

CONSOLIDATED INCOME STATEMENTS (€ thousands)

	Fiscal year ending December 31, 2005	Fiscal year ending December 31, 2004
Net turnover	976,543	965,035
Other operating income	17,466	20,997
Net profit/(loss) on disposals of long-term assets	2,689	(2,455)
Raw materials and consumables	(108,533)	(107,203)
Staff costs	(300,802)	(298,438)
Write-down	(68,101)	(62,019)
Net losses due to asset impairment	(799)	(15,288)
Leases	(169,490)	(164,390)
External services	(235,601)	(216,935)
Other operating charges	(1,422)	(2,941)
Operating profit/(loss)	**111,950**	**116,363**
Profit and loss of companies valued using the equity method	(649)	(550)
Financial income	9,961	11,373
Interest expense	(35,188)	(36,832)
Net differences on exchange (income/(expense))	2,152	1,129
Profit before taxation of ongoing activities	**88,226**	**91,483**
Corporation tax	(17,813)	(25,680)
Minority interests	(8,170)	(10,600)
Profit/(loss) for the year	**62,243**	**55,203**
Net earnings per share (€)	0.52	0.46
Net earnings per share (€) – diluted	0.52	0.46
Dividend payout per share (€)	0.26	0.26
Net book value per share (€)	6.46	5.97
Net book value per share (€) – diluted	6.46	5.97
Weighted average shares outstanding	119,318	118,889
Weighted average shares outstanding, diluted	119,318	118,889
End-of-year share price (€)	13.25	9.76

9 Two European hotel groups (A): Equity analysis

CONSOLIDATED BALANCE SHEETS (€ thousands)

	Fiscal year ending December 31, 2005	Fiscal year ending December 31, 2004
Tangible fixed assets	1,408,314	1,357,574
Goodwill	113,586	96,834
Intangible assets	59,397	61,967
Holdings in associated companies	92,728	36,834
Permanent investments – loans and accounts receivable not available for trading	94,481	50,764
Permanent investments – other	22,436	16,193
Advance taxes	35,868	40,877
Other long-term assets	3,998	6,037
Total long-term assets	**1,830,808**	**1,667,080**
Inventories	96,902	83,519
Trade debtors	130,356	81,425
Taxes refundable	13,527	14,119
Other debtors	14,367	19,916
Current-asset investments – financial asset investments at maturity	26,621	64,142
Current-asset investments – traded financial assets	1,223	500
Own shares	0	257
Cash and banks and other cash equivalents	18,039	23,751
Other current assets	10,947	9,409
Total current assets	**311,982**	**297,038**
Total assets	**2,142,790**	**1,964,118**
Net equity attributable to shareholders of the Controlling Company	770,586	709,935
Minority interests	119,682	137,266
Total net worth	**890,268**	**847,201**
Debenture loans and other traded securities	83	108
Bank loans and overdrafts	592,871	563,857
Creditors for finance leases	316	13,568
Other long-term liabilities	81,335	81,589
Provisions for charges and liabilities	42,999	44,696
Deferred taxes	114,254	128,935
Total long-term liabilities	**831,858**	**832,753**
Debenture loans and other traded securities	25	25
Bank loans and overdrafts	136,829	38,461
Creditors for finance leases	399	615
Trade creditors and other accounts payable	169,394	148,767
Other current financial liabilities	1,130	1,094
Taxes and social security contributions	36,971	26,161
Provisions for charges and liabilities	7,892	40,252
Other current liabilities	68,024	28,789
Total current liabilities	**420,664**	**284,164**
Total liabilities and net equity	**2,142,790**	**1,964,118**

CONSOLIDATED CASH FLOW STATEMENTS (€ thousands)

	Fiscal year ending December 31, 2005	Fiscal year ending December 31, 2004
Consolidated profit/(loss) before taxes	88,226	91,483
Depreciation and amortization of tangible and intangible assets	68,101	62,019
Losses on asset impairment (net)	799	15,288
Provisions (net)	878	392
Profit and loss on sale of tangible and intangible assets	(2,689)	2,455
Profit and loss of companies consolidated using the equity method	649	550
Financial income	(9,961)	(11,373)
Interest expense	35,188	36,832
Adjusted profit/(loss)	**181,191**	**197,646**
(Increase)/decrease in inventories	(13,383)	(3,669)
(Increase)/decrease in trade debtors and other accounts receivable	(42,790)	8,427
(Increase)/decrease in other current assets	(1,538)	1,822
Increase/(decrease) in trade creditors	20,627	(6,920)
Increase/(decrease) in other current liabilities	38,031	(17,379)
Increase/(decrease) in provisions for charges and liabilities	(40,773)	(16,622)
Income taxes paid	(16,573)	(20,680)
Total net cash flows from operating activities	**124,792**	**142,625**
Financial income	9,961	11,373
Group and associated companies and joint ventures	(53,488)	27,922
Tangible and intangible assets and property investments	(128,758)	(90,601)
Permanent investments	(44,979)	(24,403)
Investments and other current financial assets	37,055	(20,935)
Other assets	7,048	(7,779)
Total net cash flows from investing activities	**(173,161)**	**(104,423)**
Dividends paid	(29,882)	(29,882)
Pre-paid interest on debt	(36,388)	(37,564)
Changes in equity instruments – reserves	23,518	(2,304)
Changes in equity instruments – minority interests	(25,754)	(6,401)
Changes in bank loans and overdrafts	128,582	32,244
Changes in leasing	(13,468)	(616)
Changes in debenture loans and other traded securities	(25)	(22)
Other long-term liabilities	(3,926)	(22,603)
Total net cash flow from financing activities	**42,657**	**(67,148)**
Increase/decrease in cash or cash equivalents	**(5,712)**	**(28,946)**
Cash and cash equivalents at the beginning of the year	23,751	52,697
Cash and cash equivalents at the end of the year	**18,039**	**23,751**

9 Two European hotel groups (A): Equity analysis

EXHIBIT 4   Excerpts from the notes to Accor's and NH Hoteles' financial statements for the fiscal year ending December 31, 2005

A. Accor

Note 1. Summary of significant accounting policies

[...] In accordance with the optional exemptions to the retrospective application of IFRSs provided by IFRS 1, the Group has elected:

- Not to restate business combinations that occurred before January 1, 2004.
- To transfer cumulative translation differences at January 1, 2004 to retained earnings.
- To designate, at the date of transition to IFRS, a financial instrument as a financial asset or financial liability at fair value through profit or loss or as available for sale.

The Group has elected not to apply the following optional exemptions:

- Measurement of property, plant and equipment and intangible assets at fair value at the transition date, and use of that fair value as deemed cost.
- Application of IFRS 2 "Share-based Payment" to equity instruments granted on or before November 7, 2002 and to those granted after November 7, 2002 that vested before the date of transition to IFRS.

The other optional exemptions are not applicable to Accor Group.

D.2. Property, plant, and equipment

Property, plant, and equipment are measured at cost less accumulated depreciation and any accumulated impairment losses, in accordance with IAS 16 "Property, Plant, and Equipment". Cost includes borrowing costs directly attributable to the construction of assets. Assets under construction are measured at cost less any accumulated impairment losses. They are depreciated from the date when they are ready for use. Property, plant, and equipment are depreciated on a straight-line basis over their estimated useful lives, determined by the components method, from the date when they are put in service. The main depreciation periods applied are as follows:

	Upscale and Midscale hotels	Economy hotels
Buildings and capitalized construction-related costs	50 years	35 years
Building improvements, fixtures and fittings	7 to 25 years	7 to 25 years
Equipment	5 to 10 years	5 to 10 years

Note 6. Rental expense

Rental expense amounted to €837 million in fiscal 2005 compared with €790 million in fiscal 2004. In accordance with the policy described in note 1.D.4, the expense reported on this line only concerns operating leases. [...]

Rental expense is recognized on a straight-line basis over the lease term, even if payments are not made on that basis. Most leases have been signed for periods exceeding the traditional nine-year term of commercial leases in France, primarily to protect Accor against the absence of commercial property rights in certain countries. None of the leases contain any clauses requiring advance payment of rentals in the case of a ratings downgrade or other adverse event affecting Accor, and there are no cross-default clauses or covenants.

The €837 million in rental expense corresponds to 1,510 hotel leases, including 58 percent with a purchase option. Where applicable, the option price corresponds to either a pre-agreed percentage of the owner's original investment or the property's market value when the option is exercised. The options are generally exercisable after 10 or 12 years. Certain contracts allow for the purchase of the property at the appraised value at the end of the lease.

C. Minimum rental commitments (cash basis)

Minimum future rentals in the following tables only correspond to long-term rental commitments in the Hotels Division. The other divisions' rental commitments are generally for periods of less than three years and are not reflected in the tables below. Undiscounted minimum future rentals in foreign currency have been converted at the closing exchange rate and for the period beyond January 1, 2006, based on latest known rates, are as follows:

Years	€ millions	Years	€ millions
2006	659	2016	542
2007	656	2017	518
2008	656	2018	467
2009	655	2019	436
2010	651	2020	358
2011	643	2021	280
2012	625	2022	240
2013	610	2023	168
2014	594	2024	129
2015	567	>2025	489
		Total	9,943

Note 18.1 Property, plant, and equipment by nature

(in € millions)	2004	2005
Land	522	527
Buildings	2,644	2,544
Fixtures	1,777	1,955
Equipment and furniture	1,525	1,666
Constructions in progress	179	268
Property, plant, and equipment, at cost	6,647	6,960
Buildings	(929)	(817)
Fixtures	(949)	(1,021)
Equipment and furniture	(982)	(1,096)
Constructions in progress	(6)	(5)
Total of depreciation	(2,866)	(2,939)
Land	(7)	(7)
Buildings	(56)	(118)
Constructions in progress	0	(5)
Total of impairment	(63)	(130)
Property, plant and equipment, net	3,717	3,891

Changes in the carrying amount of property, plant, and equipment during the period were as follows:

(in € millions)	2004	2005
Net carrying amount at beginning of period	3,914	3,717
Property, plant, and equipment of newly acquired companies	19	159
Capital expenditure	463	601
Disposals	(205)	(129)
Depreciation for the period	(383)	(392)
Impairment losses for the period	(5)	(86)
Translation adjustment	(72)	198
Reclassifications on non current assets held for sale	0	(260)
Other reclassifications	(14)	83
Net carrying amount at end of period	3,717	3,891

Borrowing costs included in the carrying amount of property, plant and equipment at December 31, 2005 came to €6 million. The capitalization rate used to determine the amount of borrowing costs eligible for capitalization was 4.93 percent (Group average borrowing cost at December 31, 2004).

Note 22.1 Details of trade receivables

(in € millions)	2004	2005
Gross value	1,342	1,575
Provisions	(70)	67
Net	3,717	3,891

Note 22.2 Details of other receivables and accruals

(in € millions)	2004	2005
Recoverable VAT	208	207
Prepaid payroll taxes	7	9
Other prepaid and recoverable taxes	21	97
Other receivables	264	287
Other prepaid expenses	141	194
Other receivables and accruals	641	794
Provisions	(13)	(24)
Other receivables and accruals, net	628	770

B. NH Hoteles

Note 2.3 Main decisions concerning the first application

In accordance with the standard first applied, the Group has applied the IFRS fully, apart from the following exceptions provided for in said standards:

- Business combinations: IFRS 3 shall not apply retrospectively to any business combinations that took place prior to the changeover date (1 January 2004).

- The Group has decided, on the date of the changeover to the IFRS, to state part of its tangible fixed assets at fair value, deeming this value to be the market cost attributed on said date, in accordance with IFRS 1, based on the assessment made by an independent expert.

- The balance of translation differences as at January 1st 2004 has been cancelled. This cancellation has been recorded as a reduction in the value of the reserves of the consolidated companies where said differences originated.

- Financial instruments: the Group has decided to apply IAS 32 and 39 as from January 1st 2005, as allowed by said Standards. Their application essentially involves:

9 Two European hotel groups (A): Equity analysis

a) Classifying own shares held, the balance of which was 259 thousand euros on that date, as a lower value of net worth.

b) Stating derivative contracts at their market value, recording an increase in net worth of 3,492 thousand euros.

Note 5.1 Accounting policies – tangible fixed assets

Tangible fixed assets are stated at cost, less accumulated depreciation and any recognized loss for impairment, except for those dependent companies whose tangible fixed assets were acquired before 31 December 1983 where the cost price was revalued in accordance with various different legal provisions. Later additions have been stated at cost.

At the time of the changeover to IFRS, the Group has restated at fair value certain pieces of land based on assessments made by an independent expert, by a gross total amount of 217 million euros. The revalued cost of this land has been regarded as cost in the changeover to the IFRS. The Group's policy has been not to revalue any of its tangible fixed assets when closing its accounts for subsequent financial years. Set out below is the information concerning said revaluation (€ thousands):

Book value at origin	Fair value	Gain	Tax effect	Effect on reserves	Attributable to minority interests
207,972	424,867	217,075	34,796	170,002	12,277

The costs of extensions, modernizations, or improvements which represent an increase in productivity, capacity, or efficiency, or extend the life of existing assets are recorded as an increase in the cost of the related assets. Expenditure for maintenance and repairs is charged to consolidated expense as incurred.

The Group charges depreciation for its tangible fixed assets on a straight-line basis. The cost of the assets is spread over the years of their useful lives as shown in the following table:

	Estimated useful life in years
Constructions	33–50
Plant and machinery	10–12
Other plant, tools and furniture	5–10
Other investments	4–5

Note 9 Tangible fixed assets

Set out below is an analysis of the movements on the different tangible asset accounts in 2005 (thousand euros):

	Balance as at 31.12.04	Change in the scope of consolidation	Translation differences	Net additions/ disposals	Balance as at 31.12.05
COST					
Land and buildings	1,207,315	755	27,233	4,838	1,240,141
Technical plant and machinery	345,946	(215)	5,027	35,245	386,003
Other plant, tools, and furniture	256,025	(249)	3,985	18,249	278,010
Other investments	20,238	(223)	2,017	11,449	33,481
Fixed assets under construction	25,835	32	239	10,418	36,524
	1,855,359	100	38,501		1,974,159
ACCUMULATED DEPRECIATION					
Constructions	(111,860)	275	(7,817)	(11,308)	(130,710)
Technical plant and machinery	(160,748)	271	(704)	(16,232)	(177,413)
Other plant, tools, and furniture	(145,419)	100	(2,343)	(23,885)	(171,547)
Other investments	(12,083)	219	(1,924)	(3,524)	(17,312)
	(430,110)	865	(12,788)	(54,949)	(496,982)
Provisions	(67,675)		(1,111)	(77)	(68,863)
Net book value	1,357,574				1,408,314

Note 13 Trade debtors

"Trade debtors" record the different debtor accounts relating to the Group's current activities as well as the Controlling Company's earlier industrial activities. Set out below is an analysis of "Trade debtors" as at 31 December (thousand euros):

(in € thousands)	2005	2004
Trade accounts receivable for services provided	96,042	87,496
Trade debtors for sales of property products	45,542	4,971
	141,584	92,467
Less provision for bad debts	(11,228)	(11,042)
Total	130,356	81,425

Movements of the provision for bad debts during the years ended on 31 December 2005 and 2004 are as follows (thousand euros):

(in € thousands)	2005	2004
Balance as at 1 January	11,042	10,168
Translation differences	96	(56)
Charges	90	2,932
Applications	0	(1,902)
Balance as at 31 December	11,228	11,042

Note 19 Creditors for finance leases

[. ..] During the year ended on 31 December 2005, the average effective interest rate for the debt was 6.24 percent (7.20 percent in 2004). The interest rates were set on the date of the contract. The leases are paid on a fixed basis and no agreement has been made for the contingent rent payments.

Note 27.5 Operating leases

As at 31 December 2005 and 2004, the Group had acquired commitments for future minimum lease payments under operating leases that cannot be cancelled, falling due on the following dates:

(in € thousands)	2005	2004
Less than one year	175,557	169,493
Between two and five years	483,035	520,584
More than five years	743,660	848,720
Total	1,402,252	1,538,797

The table above, records present value of lease payments using an interest rate in line with the weighted cost of capital of the NH Hoteles Group. This table also includes, guarantee fees commitments arising from hotels operated under management contracts. The average life of the operating lease agreements signed by the NH Hoteles Group varies between 15 and 25 years.

10 Two European hotel groups (B): Debt analysis

At the end of fiscal year 2005, European hotel group Accor SA had a substantial amount of publicly traded convertible and nonconvertible bonds outstanding. The company had issued three tranches of convertible bonds in 2002, 2003, and 2005. The first tranche of convertible "OCEANE" bonds, which was issued in May 2002, consisted of 3,415,424 (publicly traded) bonds. The bonds had an issue price of €166.89, an annual interest rate of 1 percent, and a gross yield to maturity of 3.125 percent. One May 2002 OCEANE bond was exchangeable for three new or existing Accor shares before January 1, 2005, exchangeable for two Accor shares between January 1, 2005 and January 1, 2006, and exchangeable for one Accor share between January 1, 2006 and January 1, 2007. If bondholders would not exchange their bonds for shares, Accor would redeem €58.86, €60.14, and €61.47 on January 1, 2005, 2006, and 2007, respectively. The second tranche of convertible OCEANE bonds was issued in October 2003. This tranche consisted of 15,304,348 (publicly traded) bonds due January 2008. These bonds had an issue price of €41.25, an annual interest rate of 1.75 percent and were exchangeable for new or existing Accor shares when Accor's share price would exceed €44.27. The third tranche consisted of 116,279 convertible bonds which were due in May 2010. These convertible bonds had an issue price of €4,300, an annual interest rate of 3.25 percent and were exchangeable for 100 Accor shares.

Early in 2006, 6,383,362 bonds from the second tranche and all bonds from the first and third tranche were still outstanding. In addition to these convertible bonds, Accor had issued senior unsecured public debt for an amount of €400 million (due in December 2006). Two of the world's largest rating agencies, Standard and Poor's and Fitch, had rated Accor and its public debt at BBB.

Accor's competitor NH Hoteles S.A. had almost no public debt outstanding at the end of fiscal year 2005. In 1955 the company had issued bonds for an amount of €450,000. These bonds had a coupon rate of 6.75 percent. At the end of 2005, an amount of €83,000 in public bonds was still outstanding. At that time, the bonds had a yield to maturity of slightly more than 9.5 percent. Because of the small size of NH Hoteles' public debt, the company and its debt were not rated by one of the large rating agencies.

Question

Determine a credit rating for NH Hoteles' debt. Compare the rating to Accor's rating. If NH Hoteles' credit rating differs from Accor's rating, what explains the difference?

Professor Erik Peek prepared this case. The case is intended solely as the basis for class discussion and is not intended to serve as an endorsement, source of primary data, or illustration of effective or ineffective management.

EXHIBIT 1 Selected historical financial information

(in € millions)		2005 (IFRS)	2004 (IFRS)	2003 (local GAAP)	2002 (local GAAP)	2001 (local GAAP)
Net income	Accor	364	256	270	430	474
	NH Hoteles	62	55	51	86	82
After-tax net interest expense	Accor	(88)	(80)	(48)	(43)	(60)
	NH Hoteles	(16)	(17)	(21)	(24)	(16)
Sales	Accor	7,562	7,013	6,774	7,071	7,218
	NH Hoteles	977	965	922	886	762
Total assets	Accor	13,178	11,353	10,956	11,275	12,100
	NH Hoteles	2,143	1,964	1,845	1,977	1,934
Market capitalization	Accor	9,604	6,431	7,153	5,749	8,098
	NH Hoteles	1,584	1,167	1,089	1,250	1,335

EXHIBIT 2 **Excerpts from Accor's and NH Hoteles' annual reports for the fiscal year ending December 31, 2005**

A. Accor

Note 29. Debt by currency and maturity

Note 29.A. Long and short-term debt
Long and short-term debt at December 31, 2005 breaks down as follows by currency and interest rate after hedging transactions:

(in € millions)	2004	Effective rate in 2004 (%)	2005	Effective rate in 2005 (%)
EUR	2,583	4.59	2,311	4.50
USD	495	6.10	560	5.07
AUD	114	6.41	116	6.62
Other currencies	114	6.18	137	5.37
Long and short-term borrowings	**3,306**	**4.93**	**3,124**	**4.72**
Long and short term finance lease liabilities	370		388	
Purchase commitments	90		119	
Changes in fair value of financial liabilities	37		12	
Liability derivatives	23		13	
Other short-term financial liabilities and bank overdrafts	173		189	
Long and short-term debt	**3,999**		**3,845**	

Note 29.B. Maturities of debt
At December 31, 2005, maturities of debt were as follows:

	2004	2005
Year Y+1	454	1,972
Year Y+2	1,948	462
Year Y+3	287	929
Year Y+4	703	157
Year Y+5	444	57
Year Y+6	33	68
Beyond	130	200
Total long and short-term debt	**3,999**	**3,845**

At December 31, 2005, Accor had several unused confirmed lines of credit with maturities of more than one year, for a total of €2,395 million, expiring between January 2007 and October 2009. As a result, €77 million in short-term facilities that the Group intends to roll over has been reclassified as long-term debt. After reclassifications, long-term unused confirmed lines of credit total €2,318 million.

Note 29.D. Long and short-term debt by interest rate after hedging

	Fixed rate debt		Variable rate debt		Total debt	
(in € millions)	Amount	Rate	Amount	Rate	Amount	Rate
December 31, 2004	1,793	6.01%	1,513	3.61%	3,306	4.93%
December 31, 2005	1,698	4.97%	1,426	4.41%	3,124	4.72%

At December 31, 2005, fixed rate debt was denominated primarily in EUR (86 percent) and USD (10 percent), while variable rate debt was denominated mainly in EUR (59 percent), USD (27 percent), and AUD (8 percent). The Group's loan agreements do not contain any rating triggers. Acceleration clauses stipulate that the interest cover ratio (ratio of EBITDA to interest expense plus one-third of annual rental expense) may not exceed $3.8\times$. These clauses apply solely to lines of credit that were not used at December 31, 2005.

None of the €3,124 million in debt carried in the balance sheet at December 31, 2005 is subject to any acceleration clauses. None of the Group's loan agreements contain any cross default clauses. Cross acceleration clauses only concern loans for periods of at least three years and they would be triggered only for similar loans representing a significant amount.

B. NH Hoteles

Note 17 Debenture loans and other traded securities

Set out below is an analysis of bonds and debentures outstanding as at 31 December (thousand euros):

	2005 Long-term	2005 Short-term	2004 Long-term	2004 Short-term
Series B debentures	83	23	108	23
Bond and debenture interest		2		2
Total	83	25	108	25

This 1955 series B bond issue pays interest at 6.75 percent a year and is being redeemed in increasing payments and shall be fully redeemed by 2009. This issue is secured by a bank guarantee.

Note 18 Bank loans and overdrafts

Set out below is an analysis of bank loans and overdrafts as at 31 December 2005 (thousand euros):

	Drawn down	2006	2007	2008	2009	Remainder
Mortgage loans						
Fixed interest	49,082	11,513	23,771	1,290	1,313	11,195
Variable interest	80,494	13,915	27,460	4,438	3,349	31,331
Long-term unsecured loans						
Fixed interest	1,402	356	534	344	168	0
Variable interest	419,979	43,990	116,791	83,924	84,426	90,848
Credit lines (variable interest)						
Variable interest	181,599	64,980	81,086	28,495	7,038	
Accrued interest	3,113	3,113				
Debt formalisation expense	(5,969)	(1,038)	(1,039)	(1,039)	(1,039)	(1,814)
Debt situation as at 31.12.05	729,700	136,829	248,603	117,452	95,255	131,561

The line "Long term unsecured loans, variable interest," includes a syndicated loan granted to NH Hoteles, SA by 25 European banks, on 23rd June 2004, for 350 million euros. As at 31st December 2005, this loan had been drawn down in full. This loan expires on 23rd June 2010 and pays annual interest at one-month Euribor plus a spread that varies between 1.1 percent and 0.60 percent depending on the Net financial debt/EBITDA ratio. Repayments are to be made in five instalments. The first will be made in July 2006. This loan requires that certain financial ratios be complied with. As at 31st December 2005, none of these are in a position that is likely to trigger off a declaration of early termination by the lending entities.

Furthermore, the line "Long term unsecured loans, variable interest" includes a syndicated loan through Banco Bilbao Vizcaya Argentaria granted to NH Hoteles, SA for a maximum of 42.07 million euros, to be used to finance the acquisition, via a takeover bid, of shares in Promociones Eurobuilding, SA (a company merged into NH Hoteles, SA in 2002). As at 31st December 2005, 29 million euros were still outstanding. The interest on this loan is charged at a rate equal to Euribor plus a spread and the loan will be repaid gradually starting in 2001 and ending in 2011.

Set out below are the average rates of financing of the Group during 2005 and 2004:

	2005	2004
Mortgage loans		
Fixed interest	5.09%	5.09%
Variable interest	EURIBOR +1.18%	EURIBOR +1.09%
Long-term unsecured loans		
Fixed interest	5.19%	5.19%
Variable interest	EURIBOR +0.74%	EURIBOR +0.80%
Credit lines		
Variable interest	EURIBOR +0.26%	EURIBOR +0.33%

Note 20 Other long-term liabilities

Set out below is an analysis of "Other long-term liabilities" as at 31 December 2005 and 2004 (in thousand euros):

	2005	2004
Preference shares issued by subsidiary companies	28,122	42,307
Right of beneficial use of Hotel Plaza de Armas	11,960	13,455
Residencial Marlin, S.L.	9,000	9,000
Financial instruments	4,089	7,746
Capital grants	3,446	3,645
Purchase minority interests in NH Hoteles Deutschland, GmbH and NH Hoteles Austria, GmbH	15,000	
Other liabilities	9,718	5,436
Total	81,335	81,589

The line "Preference shares issued by subsidiary companies" records the preference shares issued by NH Participaties NV outstanding as at 31 December 2005 and 2004 which have, by their nature, been classified as a financial liability. These preference shares earn interest at a fixed annual rate of 5.55 percent and mature on 1 January 2008. The line "Capital grants" basically records, as at 31 December 2005, a total of 3.45 million euros (3.64 million euros as at 31 December 2004) for the grants received to build the hotels and golf courses of subsidiary company Sotogrande. The amount recorded for "Residencial Marlin, SL" represents 50 percent of the participating loan granted to that company by the minority shareholder of Sotogrande, SA, which has a 50 percent holding in said company. This participating loan expires on July 2007 (see Note 11.1). As mentioned in Note 2.6.6 of these annual accounts, this year the NH Hoteles Group has acquired the remaining 20 percent of NH Hoteles Deutschland, GmbH, and NH Hoteles Austria, GmbH, for 45 million euros. As at 31 December 2005, 30 million euros were still outstanding, 15 million of which are recorded as short-term in the caption "Other current liabilities" (see Note 25), and the last instalment is due to be paid in 2007.

10 Two European hotel groups (B): Debt analysis

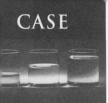

11 Valuation ratios in the airline industry

I n mid-2001, the US airline industry appeared to be headed into its first cyclical downturn in ten years. In May, air travel fell in the United States for the first time in a decade
and ticket prices softened.[1] In addition, profitability in the industry (as measured by return
on equity, "ROE") declined from 25 percent in 1997 to 12 percent in 2000. Analysts forecasted that ROE would decline further to 2.3 percent in 2001.[2]

   The downturn also affected industry valuation ratios. For example, price-to-book ratios
declined from 2.8 in 1997 to 2.0 in 2000,[3] while price-to-earnings ratios, which were 8.3
in 1997, were not meaningful in mid-2001 since aggregate earnings for the industry were
negative.[4] However, these ratios varied widely across firms. For example, in mid-2001,
price-to-book ratios ranged from a low of 0.4 to a high of 3.7, and price-to-earnings ratios
for firms with positive earnings ranged from 8 to 22.

Industry overview

The deregulation of the US domestic market in 1978 was a turning point for domestic air
travel. The 20 years following this event saw real fares decline by 50 percent, and air traffic triple.[5] The period was also marked by turbulence for many firms that had pioneered
air travel in the United States, with Pan Am, Eastern, and TWA being forced into
bankruptcy. By mid-2001, the industry was dominated by a relatively small number of
long-haul national-international carriers, while dozens of regional and commuter carriers
competed for "point-to-point" (or nonstop) short-haul routes.[6]

National carriers

Six national carriers, United Airlines, American Airlines, Delta Air Lines, Northwest Airlines, US Airways, and Continental Airlines provided both long-haul domestic and international service for US-based passengers. Using "hub-and-spoke" networks, long-haul

Professors Paul Healy and Krishna Palepu and Research Associate Jonathan Barnett prepared this case. This case
was developed from published sources. HBS cases are developed solely as the basis for class discussion. Cases
are not intended to serve as endorsements, sources of primary data, or illustrations of effective or ineffective
management.

[1]Airline traffic growth was predicted to increase 3.5 percent in 2001, a marked decline from the 4.7 percent and
5.2 percent increases in 1999 and 2000. Yield (or average revenue per passenger) was forecast to grow 4 percent
in 2001. Stephen Klein and Richard Stice, *Airlines,*Standard & Poor's (S&P) Industry Surveys, March 29, 2001.

[2]Stephen Sanborn, *The Air Transport Industry,*Value Line Investment Survey, June 15, 2001.

[3]S&P Research Insight.

[4]The airline industry's average beta was 0.89. Given the long-term government bond rate in June 2001 of 5.7 percent and the long-term risk premium of 7.6 percent, the average cost of equity for the industry was therefore
12.5 percent. (S&P Research Insight.)

[5]"Air Travel, Air Trouble," *The Economist,*July 7, 2001.

[6]In 2000, the ten largest US airlines accounted for 92.3 percent of total US traffic. (Stephen Klein and Richard
Stice, *Airlines,* S&P Industry Surveys, March 29, 2001.)

carriers or their regional "spoke" affiliates shuttled passengers from lightly traveled markets to central hubs where they could connect to longer flight-legs. In addition to enabling long-haul carriers to take advantage of economies of scale on their long flights, the hub-and-spoke system had increased concentration in many of the smaller "hub" cities, where the hub carrier owned a dominant share of the terminal gates.

Long-haul carriers had little control over the pricing of key inputs, including aircraft and jet fuel. Two suppliers, Boeing and Airbus, controlled the development and production of large-scale jet aircraft, and the price of jet fuel was heavily influenced by the impact of OPEC's oil production policies on global supply. Labor costs, the other major airline operating cost, were typically determined through intense and protracted negotiations between each carrier and the more than one dozen unions that represented distinct groups of airline personnel (e.g., pilots, attendants, mechanics, baggage handlers, etc.).

The economics of the airline business made it difficult for operators to pass on production-cost increases to passengers. Given their high fixed costs and low marginal costs, airline carriers had frequently resorted to fare reductions to boost flight capacity and yield (defined as average revenue per passenger). However, competing airlines were quick to match or undercut rivals' fare reductions, resulting in periodic fare wars. Thus, the continual threat of intense price competition dampened the industry's prospects for revenue growth.

Long-haul carriers developed a number of responses to the challenges of price competition and yield management. In the 1980s, frequent flyer programs were introduced to increase customer loyalty and mitigate the effect of fare wars. In the 1990s, the industry was quick to take advantage of the internet to improve the booking and ticketing process. However, the results were mixed: while online reservation systems helped airlines to improve yield management, the broad dissemination of information on competing flight schedules and fares enabled price-sensitive consumers to search for the lowest possible fares.

In response to growth opportunities in international travel in the mid-1990s, long-haul carriers had used alliances to strengthen their international presence. Alliances took advantage of "open skies" treaties between the United States and other governments that permitted code-sharing and partial ownership between international airlines. In mid-2001, there were four global airline alliances involving US carriers.[7] However, allegiance within the alliances had proven weak, with a number of carriers switching alliance memberships.

Regional carriers

US regional carriers, such as America West, ComAir, Frontier Airlines, Mesa Air, and SkyWest Airlines, typically provided nonstop short-haul service. Many of these airlines were affiliated with long-haul carriers. Affiliations typically permitted regional carriers to schedule flights under a "code-sharing" arrangement, so that each carrier could sell seats for flights on joint routes. To schedule these trips, regional affiliates, operating under the major carrier's designator code, were granted access to that carrier's computer reservation system.

Regional carriers were subject to many of the same economic forces as their long-haul counterparts. They, too, had little control over fuel prices and were forced to negotiate with a small number of aircraft manufacturers.[8] However, some of the newer regional carriers did not have a unionized labor force, making it easier to design flexible work arrangements and to manage labor costs.

Recent technological advances in the design of regional jets had opened up new opportunities for regional carriers in under-served domestic markets. Although jet aircraft were first introduced to US passenger service in 1958, they had proved uneconomical for small markets. However, following the 1995 introduction of new low-cost jet aircraft by Brazil's Embraer and Canada's Bombardier, regional jet operations proliferated as the short-haul markets that were previously abandoned by major airlines became viable destinations.[9] In addition to opening new markets, the seating capacity and travel range of regional jets continued to expand. As a result, regional jets were increasingly used not only to feed passengers to hub airports, but also to

11 Valuation ratios in the airline industry

[7]The four major global airline alliances included the Star Alliance (anchored by United Airlines and Lufthansa), the OneWorld alliance (anchored by American Airlines and British Airways), the SkyTeam alliance (anchored by Delta Air Lines and Air France), and Wings (anchored by KLM and Northwest Airlines). Each alliance also included a number of smaller carriers.

[8]While long-haul and regional carriers could not directly influence the price of jet fuel, both types of carriers frequently hedged their fuel-price risk using futures as part of a comprehensive risk-management strategy.

[9]Breakeven capacity for a regional jet was approximately 50 percent, versus 63 percent for larger jet aircraft. In 2000 there were an estimated 529 regional jets in service in the United States versus 137 in 1997. (Stephen Klein and Richard Stice, Airlines, Standard & Poor's ("S&P") Industry Surveys, March 29, 2001.)

provide point-to-point competition against carriers employing full-sized jets. Having recognized the value of regional carriers, major airlines had recently taken steps to increase their control over such operators, primarily through acquiring equity positions.

Strategy and performance for four airline carriers

The following brief sketches of two long-haul carriers (American Airlines and Delta Air Lines), one regional carrier (SkyWest Airlines), and one hybrid carrier (Southwest Airlines) illustrate the differences in business strategy and performance experienced by firms in the airline industry. See **Exhibits 1** and **2** for a comparison of the recent financial performance of these carriers.

American Airlines

American Airlines ("American"), the principal operating subsidiary of parent AMR Corporation, traced its roots back to the Embry-Riddle Company in the early 1920s. Later renamed the Aviation Corporation (AVCO), American became one of the first US airline giants through the acquisition of 82 smaller airlines.

In 2000, American was the largest US airline based on revenues. It operated hubs in Dallas-Forth Worth, Chicago O'Hare, Miami, and San Juan (Puerto Rico), and provided service to 169 destinations throughout North America, Europe, the Caribbean, Latin America, and the Pacific Rim.[10] The company owned two regional airlines operating as "American Eagle," American Eagle Airlines and Executive Airlines, which provided connecting service from eight of American's high-traffic hubs to smaller markets in the United States, Canada, the Caribbean, and the Bahamas. American was also a member of the global OneWorld alliance, which linked the operations of American, British Airways, Canadian Airlines, Cathay Pacific Airways, Qantas Airways, Finnair, Iberia, and LanChile. In addition to its passenger services, American was one of the largest airfreight carriers in the world, providing a full range of freight and mail services to shippers throughout its system.[11]

On most of its nonstop domestic routes, American faced competition from one or more of the other US long-haul carriers, regional airlines, and other cargo-service firms. As many as nine airlines provided service on American's most competitive routes. Its pricing decisions were affected, in part, by competition from other airlines, some of which had cost structures significantly lower than American's and could therefore operate profitably at lower fare levels. On international routes, American competed with state-owned carriers, foreign investor-owned carriers, international cargo service providers, and US airlines that had been granted authority to provide international passenger service.[12]

American touted several sources of competitive advantage. First, its fleet of aircraft, one of the youngest in the United States, was efficient and quiet. Second, in 2000, the company began aggressively deploying its American Eagle regional jet fleet. Third, by operating a comprehensive domestic and international route network anchored by efficient hubs, the company expected to be able to benefit from whatever traffic growth occurred. The firm's chairman, Donald Carty, reported in his 2000 *Letter to Shareholders* that American would continue to expand its domestic and international network in Boston, New York, Los Angeles, San Jose, Paris, and Taipei. Finally, through its AAdvantage frequent flyer program, the largest in the industry, its More Room Throughout Coach program, and its continuing efforts to provide superior service, American sought to enhance its position in the industry.

During 2000, American's revenues increased by 11 percent. Net income for the year declined by 17 percent, although profits before special items and discontinued operations rose nearly 19 percent.[13] Despite 4 percent revenue growth for the three months ended March 31, 2001, American reported a net loss from continuing operations of $43 million, versus a net gain of $89 million in the same quarter for 2000.[14] These results primarily

---

[10]In its 2000 10-K Report, American reported that domestic and foreign operations comprised 71 percent and 29 percent of total revenues, respectively.

[11]As reported in American's 2000 10-K Report, American's revenue mix consisted of 90 percent passenger service and 10 percent cargo and other.

[12]AMR Corp., December 31, 2000 10-K Report.

[13]AMR Corp., December 31, 2000 10-K Report.

[14]AMR Corp., March 31, 2001 10-Q Report.

reflected an increase in fares, offset by higher fuel costs. To mitigate the financial impact of the downturn in air travel in mid-2001, American retired older aircraft, cancelled options to purchase new jets, imposed a management hiring freeze, and deferred spending on capital projects. Despite these changes, analysts predicted that American would show a loss for 2001.[15] For 2002, analysts expected that American would show revenue growth of 8 percent and return to profitability, with an expected return on equity of 8.5 percent.[16]

Delta Air Lines

Delta Air Lines ("Delta") was founded as the world's first crop-dusting service in 1924 (then named Huff Daland Dusters). In 1928, the company began to diversify by securing airmail contracts, and in 1929 inaugurated passenger service between Dallas and Jackson, Mississippi. Following World War II and throughout the 1950s and 1960s, Delta prospered as a major regional airline. During the 1970s and 1980s, the company expanded its domestic network, largely by acquiring other regional carriers (including Northeast Airlines and Western Airlines). In 1991 it made a major push into international markets.

In 2001, Delta operated four hubs located in Atlanta, Cincinnati, Dallas-Fort Worth, and Salt Lake City. The company was the largest US airline in terms of aircraft departures and number of passengers served, and the third largest US airline in terms of operating revenues.[17] Including its wholly owned regional subsidiaries Atlantic Southeast Airlines, Inc. and ComAir, Inc., Delta serviced 201 US cities in 45 states, the District of Columbia, the US Virgin Islands, and Puerto Rico, as well as 50 cities in 32 countries in Europe, Asia, Latin America, the Caribbean, and Canada.[18] The company also operated a cargo service.[19]

Delta's services included the Delta Shuttle, Delta Express, the Delta Connection Program, and its international alliances. The Delta Shuttle was a high-frequency service providing hourly nonstop service between New York's La Guardia Airport and both Washington, DC's Ronald Reagan National Airport and Boston's Logan International Airport. Delta Express was a low-fare, leisure-oriented service providing flights from select cities in the Northeast and Midwest to five destinations in Florida. The Delta Connection Program was Delta's regional carrier serving passengers in small and medium-sized cities. Finally, the company's international alliance agreements included code-sharing, frequent flyer benefits, shared or reciprocal access to passenger lounges, joint advertising, and other marketing arrangements with Aeromexico, Aeropostal, Air France, Air Jamaica, CSA Czech Airlines, Korean Air, China Southern, Royal Air Maroc, South African Airways, and Transbrasil.

Despite its prominent industry rankings, Delta sustained several years of heavy losses in the early 1990s, and in 1994 announced a drastic cost-cutting plan dubbed the Leadership 7.5 program.[20] The restructuring initiative, which included a 20 percent reduction in the company's workforce, a realignment of its domestic route system, and the discontinuation of less profitable European routes, was designed to eliminate $2 billion in operating expenses over a three-year period, and to reduce the cost of flying to 7.5 cents per mile, per seat. Though the company was successful in engineering a quick financial comeback, posting a profit in the fourth quarter of fiscal 1995, the accompanying reduction in the company's customer service team resulted in a significant increase in passenger complaints, and by 1997, Delta dropped to last place in on-time rankings among the ten leading US airlines.[21]

In 2000, Delta also struggled with a number of labor issues. In May, its pilots' contract expired and was followed by months of unproductive negotiations. When the impasse dragged into December, the pilots retaliated by refusing voluntary overtime during one of the airline's busiest seasons, forcing Delta to cancel 3,500 flights over the course of the month and an additional 1,700 flights during the first ten days of 2001.[22] Although Delta reached an agreement with its mainline pilots in April 2001, granting them substantial pay raises, it continued to be negatively impacted by the ComAir pilots' strike announced on March 26, 2001.

[15]Thompson Financial, FirstCall estimates.

[16]Stephen Sanborn, AMR Corp., *Value Line Investment Survey*, June 15, 2001.

[17]Rankings are based on calendar year-end data. Delta Air Lines, 2000 10-K Report.

[18]Delta acquired Atlantic Southeast Airlines and ComAir in 1999.

[19]In 2000, cargo and other revenues accounted for 6 percent of total revenues; passenger revenues represented the remaining 94 percent.

[20]Delta Air Lines Inc., June 30, 1994 Annual Report.

[21]For additional background information, see Thomas Derdack, *The International Directory of Company Histories*, vol. 39 (St. James Press).

[22]Thomas Derdack, *The International Directory of Company Histories*, vol. 39.

ComAir was the second largest regional airline in the United States, and some analysts believed that the outcome of these negotiations would be an "industry-defining event … likely to affect regional pilot pay scales throughout the industry."[23] By mid-June of 2001, the dispute remained unresolved and was estimated to be costing Delta $3–4 million per day in lost revenues.

During 2000, Delta's revenues increased 12 percent, yet profits fell by 31 percent. Excluding extraordinary items and discontinued operations, profits fell 25 percent.[24] In an effort to improve the bottom line, Delta reduced advertising costs, retired aircraft, released employees, and implemented a new management structure. The company's Chairman and CEO, Leo F. Mullin, also announced the industry's largest regional jet order ever, designed to "cement [Delta's] competitive advantage in this important market."[25]

Analysts predicted that the current difficult economic climate and the accompanying slowing in demand for air transport would result in a net loss for Delta for 2001, followed by a moderate rebound in 2002. Consensus forecasts called for an 8 percent return on equity in 2002, growing to 13 percent between 2004 and 2006.[26]

SkyWest Airlines

In 1972, attorney J. Ralph Atkin founded SkyWest Airlines (then named "Inter American Aviation, Inc.") so that he and four friends could own a plane for fun. That same year, Atkin decided to offer commercial flights. Since then, SkyWest Airlines ("SkyWest"), the principal operating subsidiary of SkyWest Inc., had grown to become one of the larger regional airlines in the United States. The company operated a fleet of 108 aircraft from six hubs located in Los Angeles, Salt Lake City, San Francisco, Portland, and Seattle/Tacoma. It offered passenger and airfreight service with over 1,000 daily departures to 68 destinations in 14 western states and Canada.

Nearly 70 percent of SkyWest flights were jointly coded with Delta Air Lines and United Airlines flights under long-term revenue code-sharing relationships.[27] Under the terms of these relationships, on SkyWest-controlled flights, SkyWest oversaw scheduling, ticketing, pricing, and seat inventories, and received a pro-rated portion of passenger fares. On contract routes, where SkyWest's major airline partner handled these functions, SkyWest received negotiated payments per flight departure and incentives based on passenger volumes and levels of customer satisfaction.[28] SkyWest first became a code-sharing partner with Delta Air Lines in Salt Lake City in 1987, and teamed up with United Airlines in Los Angeles in 1997.

SkyWest management attributed the carrier's success in securing these contracts to its delivery of high-quality customer service and argued that these relationships provided important benefits for SkyWest. First, they enabled the carrier to "reduce reliance on any single major airline [designator] code and to enhance and stabilize operating results through a mixture of SkyWest-controlled flying and contract flying."[29] They also provided SkyWest with opportunities to grow the airline. Based on its existing Delta Connection and United Express code-sharing contracts, which were to be in place until 2008 and 2010, SkyWest had committed to acquire an additional 113 regional jets with options on another 119 aircraft. However, this commitment was not without risk, since both Delta and United could terminate the code-sharing arrangements "for any or no reason" with 180 days advance notice.[30]

SkyWest primarily competed with other regional airlines, some of which were owned by or were operated as code-sharing partners of major airlines. On certain routes, SkyWest also competed with low-fare carriers and other major airlines. While SkyWest's joint affiliation with Delta and United distinguished it from the majority of its competitors, so, too, did the carrier's strong relationship with its wholly non-unionized workforce.

[23]Caglar Somek, Delta Air Lines, Credit Suisse First Boston, May 22, 2001.

[24]Delta Air Lines Inc., June 30, 2000 Annual Report.

[25]Delta Air Lines Inc., June 30, 2000 Annual Report.

[26]Damon Churchwell, Delta Air Lines, *Value Line Investment Survey*, June 15, 2001.

[27]SkyWest operated as the Delta Connection in Salt Lake City and as United Express in Los Angeles, San Francisco, Denver, and the Pacific Northwest. SkyWest's contract business was nearly evenly distributed between United Airlines (55 percent) and Delta Air Lines (45 percent). (Caglar Somek, Delta Air Lines, Credit Suisse First Boston, May 22, 2001.)

[28]SkyWest Inc., March 31, 2001 10-K Report.

[29]SkyWest Inc., March 31, 2001 Annual Report.

[30]SkyWest Inc., March 31, 2000 Annual Report.

11 Valuation ratios in the airline industry

For the year ended March 31, 2001, SkyWest reported that revenues grew 12 percent, versus 22 percent in 2000. Profits were flat due to a nearly 17 percent increase in operating expenses, primarily from increased fuel costs and, to a lesser extent, from increased salaries and wages as the airline continued to add personnel.[31] Despite the slowdown in revenue growth, analysts forecasted that SkyWest's sales would grow at a compound annual growth rate of more than 30 percent between 2002 and 2005, while earnings were forecasted to grow 32 percent in 2002 and 22 percent in 2003. Based on these forecasts, the company was expected to generate a return on equity of nearly 23 percent in 2002 and 2003.[32]

Southwest Airlines

Founded in 1971 with three Boeing 737 aircraft serving just three destinations in Texas, Southwest Airlines ("Southwest") rapidly grew to become a major domestic airline. Based on data for the second quarter of 2001, Southwest operated 344 aircraft, provided scheduled service to 57 destinations in 29 states, and was the largest US airline based on domestic departures and the fourth largest based on number of domestic passengers served.[33]

Southwest had achieved its rapid growth by positioning itself as a cost leader in the industry. To accomplish this position, Southwest offered its customers "no-frills" service at a low price. It had elected not to develop the costly hub-and-spoke networks used by United, American, Delta, and the other major domestic carriers. Instead, the company provided frequent flights to conveniently located, but typically less congested, satellite airports such as Dallas Love Field, Chicago Midway, and T.F. Green in Providence, Rhode Island. In so doing, Southwest was able to develop a record for reliable on-time performance and achieved high asset utilization. High asset utilization and tight control over operating expenses were maintained through the operation of a single type of aircraft, the Boeing 737, which simplified scheduling, maintenance, flight operations, and training activities. As a result of these and other activities, Southwest reduced the amount of time an aircraft sat idle at a gate to approximately 25 minutes (less than half of the industry average), which reduced the number of aircraft and gate facilities that would otherwise be required.

There were other notable differences between Southwest and other major US carriers. For example, Southwest did not enter into code-sharing relationships with other airlines, nor did it maintain any commuter feeder relationships. Southwest also eschewed both a ticket reservation system (to avoid paying fees to travel agents), and the commonly used multi-tier pricing strategy, in favor of a simple fare structure that featured low, unrestricted, unlimited, everyday coach fares. Being majority-owned by its employees, Southwest had enjoyed strong relationships with its predominantly non-unionized work force, yielding further cost savings and labor flexibility. Finally, Southwest's frequent flyer program also differed from those of the other major airlines, with travel awards based on the number of trips taken, rather than on the number of miles accrued. All told, management estimated that the company's strategy resulted in its providing approximately 90 percent of all low-fare airline service in the United States.[34]

Fiscal 2000 was Southwest's twenty-second consecutive year of profitability and ninth consecutive year of increased profits. During 2000, Southwest's revenues and profits increased by 19 percent and 27 percent, respectively, and the company earned a 22 percent return on equity.[35] For the three months ended March 31, 2001, revenues and profits increased 15 percent and 25 percent, respectively, compared to the same quarter one year earlier.[36] 2001 and 2002 consensus forecasts for revenue and earnings growth were 11 percent and 19 percent, and 12 percent and 24 percent, respectively. Based on these estimates, analysts predicted a ROE of 17 percent in 2001 and 17.5 percent in 2002.[37]

[31]SkyWest Inc., March 31, 2001 10-K Report.

[32]Thompson Financial FirstCall and casewriter estimates.

[33]Southwest Airlines Co., December 31, 2000 10-K Report.

[34]Southwest Airlines Co., December 31, 2000 Annual Report.

[35]Southwest Airlines Co., December 31, 2000 Annual Report.

[36]Southwest Airlines Co., March 31, 2001 10-Q Report.

[37]Thorpe, Warren, Southwest Airlines, *Value Line Investment Survey*, June 15, 2001.

11 Valuation ratios in the airline industry

Questions

1 Match the valuation multiples below with each of the four airlines discussed in the case. What is your reasoning for the matches you selected?

VALUATION MULTIPLES[38]

Airline	Price/Earnings	Price/Book Value
A	7.5	0.8
B	6.8	1.2
C	16.8	3.1
D	26.8	4.9

2 What is the general relationship between a company's strategy, its current performance, and price-to-book and price-to-earnings ratios?

[38]The ratios were calculated using fiscal 2000 year-end figures. (Source: Case writer estimates.)

EXHIBIT 1   Comparison of financial performance for American Airlines, Delta Airlines, Skywest Airlines, and Southwest Airlines

American Airlines	2000	1999	1998	1997	1996
Net operating profit margin	0.05	0.07	0.08	0.06	0.07
Net operating asset turnover	1.74	1.96	2.34	2.03	2.16
Operating ROA = product of above	0.09	0.13	0.18	0.13	0.16
Spread	0.05	0.05	0.11	0.08	0.10
Net financial leverage	0.65	0.35	0.32	0.58	1.16
Financial leverage gain	0.03	0.02	0.03	0.05	0.12
ROE = Operating ROA + Financial leverage gain	0.12	0.15	0.21	0.17	0.27
5-year compound annual growth rates (CAGR):					
Revenues	3.1				
Assets	6.0				
Equity	14.6				
Beta	1.16				

Delta Air Lines	2000	1999	1998	1997	1996
Net operating profit margin	0.06	0.09	0.08	0.07	0.02
Net operating asset turnover	2.25	3.33	3.46	4.12	4.30
Operating ROA = product of above	0.13	0.29	0.26	0.29	0.09
Spread	0.07	0.01	0.19	0.15	−0.01
Net financial leverage	0.51	0.07	0.29	0.23	0.59
Financial leverage gain	0.04	0.00	0.06	0.03	−0.01
ROE = Operating ROA + Financial leverage gain	0.17	0.29	0.32	0.32	0.09
5-year compound annual growth rates (CAGR):					
Revenues	6.1				
Assets	12.4				
Equity	18.3				
Beta	0.76				

SkyWest Airlines	2000	1999	1998	1997	1996
Net operating profit margin	0.09	0.11	0.11	0.08	0.04
Net operating asset turnover	2.64	2.88	3.75	2.18	1.87
Operating ROA = product of above	0.24	0.32	0.40	0.18	0.07
Spread	0.16	0.28	0.39	0.17	0.09
Net financial leverage	−0.35	−0.35	−0.51	−0.02	0.14
Financial leverage gain	−0.06	−0.10	−0.20	0.00	0.01
ROE = Operating ROA + Financial leverage gain	0.18	0.22	0.20	0.18	0.08
5-year compound annual growth rates (CAGR):					
Revenues	16.1				
Assets	20.1				
Equity	17.2				
Beta	0.70				

Southwest Airlines	2000	1999	1998	1997	1996
Net operating profit margin	0.11	0.10	0.11	0.09	0.07
Net operating asset turnover	1.71	1.78	1.95	2.21	1.91
Operating ROA = product of above	0.19	0.19	0.21	0.19	0.13
Spread	0.15	0.12	0.09	−0.01	0.07
Net financial leverage	0.16	0.11	0.06	0.05	0.25
Financial leverage gain	0.02	0.01	0.01	0.00	0.02
ROE = Operating ROA + Financial leverage gain	0.21	0.20	0.22	0.19	0.15
5-year growth rates (CAGR):					
Revenues	14.5				
Assets	15.4				
Equity	18.5				
Beta	0.72				

Source: OneSource, Dow Jones Interactive, and case writer estimates, August 1, 2001.

11 Valuation ratios in the airline industry

INDEX